Marriages of Jefferson County [West] Virginia

1801 through 1890

J. Lester Link

HERITAGE BOOKS
2007

HERITAGE BOOKS
AN IMPRINT OF HERITAGE BOOKS, INC.

Books, CDs, and more—Worldwide

For our listing of thousands of titles see our website
at
www.HeritageBooks.com

Published 2007 by
HERITAGE BOOKS, INC.
Publishing Division
65 East Main Street
Westminster, Maryland 21157-5026

Copyright © 1973 J. Lester Link

All rights reserved. No part of this book may be reproduced or transmitted in any form or by any means, electronic or mechanical, including photocopying, recording or by any information storage and retrieval system without written permission from the author, except for the inclusion of brief quotations in a review.

International Standard Book Number: 978-1-58549-670-9

MARRIAGES

JEFFERSON COUNTY

VIRGINIA - WEST VIRGINIA

1801 through 1890

- - - -

TRANSCRIBED

and

COMPILED ALPHABETICALLY

by

J. LESTER LINK

- - - -

UNDER THE SUPERVISION AND KINDNESS OF

JOHN E. OTT, COUNTY COURT CLERK

- - - -

AND WITH THE PARTICULAR ASSISTANCE OF

MRS. SARAH WATSON HUMPSTON

and

OTHER OFFICE PERSONNEL

FOREWORDS

The records in this book contain information concerning more than 10,000 persons. In the transcription, editing has been held to a minimum and most abbreviations have been spelled out.

Where dates are not complete, the most logical approximate from the original record is given in order to facilitate the location of the record in the original. Dates preceeded by (L), indicates the date the license was issued and not necessarily the date of marriage.

Numerals in parentheses, such as (1), following the names of the parties married; indicates the original source of the transcription as follows:

(1) - Source one comprising two volumes: (A) an original volume entitled, "Record of Marriages - No. 1 - 1801-1853" and (B) a volume entitled, "An alphabetical transcript of the marriage records of Jefferson County from 1801 to 1853 arranged by the husbands. The original record is made of the lists of marriages furnished by the ministers who performed the ceremonies and give only the names of the husband and the wife, the date of marriage and the name of the minister. The original marriage bonds have been lost and the list may not contain all of the marriages due to omissions by the ministers. The original spellings have been retained. 1933/34. (Signed) Stanley P. Shugert." The present transcription has followed "the Shugert transcription" primarily and apparent contradictions have been compared and corrected with the original.

(2) - Source two is a volume opening with the title of: "Register of Marriage Licenses issued by the Clerk of the County Court of Jefferson County, Virginia." This volume covers the period of 1850-1865 and contains some of the marriage license records for marriages listed in volume (1) A above.

(3) - Source three is a volume entitled: "Record of Marriages - No. 3 - 1865-1890 - Jefferson County."

May those who use this transcription and compilation find it both useful and satisfying.

GRATIA DEI FINIVI: J. L. L.
September 4 Anno Domini 1973

Abel, James and Margaret Wenis (2) - (L) August 28, 1852

Abell, Joseph F. and Lucy M. Crane (2) - (L) June 17, 1852

Abert, Sophia and John T. Cookus (1) - December 18, 1834

Abriel, Mary Catharine and James M. Johnston (2) - (L) October 25, 1859

Adam, John Jacob and Margaret Spotts (1) - November 3, 1826

Adams, B. L. (cold.) Charlotte Louisa Talbott (3) - August 28, 1879
Place of marriage, Charlestown - Age of husband, 26 - Age of wife, 24 - Both are Single - Both were born in Jefferson County, West Virginia - Both reside in Jefferson County, West Virginia.

Adams, Daniel and S. E. (Eliza) Shugert (2) - (L) December 4, 1851

Adams, David C. and Rosanna White (3) - January 31, 1877
Place of marriage, Shepherdstown - Age of husband, 38 - Age of wife, 18 - Husband is a Widower - Wife is Single - Husband was born in Fairfax County, Virginia - Wife was born in Charles City County, Virginia - Both reside in Jefferson County, West Virginia. (Consent of Bride's guardian in writing.)

Adams, George E. and Alice V. Yontz (3) - January 4, 1866
Place of marriage, Shepherdstown, West Virginia - Age of husband, 22 - Age of wife, 20 - Both are Single - Both were born in Jefferson County, West Virginia - Both reside in Jefferson County, West Virginia - Husband's parents are James A. and Sarah Adams - Wife's parents are Cornelius and Mary Yontz - Occupation of husband is Confectioner.

Adams, Hatty (cold.) Enos Wilson (3) - December 16, 1875
For further information see - Wilson, Enos.

Adams, James and Helen Blue (3) - December 3, 1868
Place of marriage, Jefferson County - Age of husband, 21 - Age of wife, 22 - Husband is Single - Wife is a Widow - Husband was born in Jefferson County - Wife was born in Jefferson, Virginia - Both reside in Jefferson County - Occupation of husband is Laborer.

Adams, Jose P. and Eliza Hamilton (1) - 1813

Adams, Mary Ann and James B. Wilkins (1) - May 7, 1829

Adams, Noah F. (cold.) Eliza Ann Smith (3) - June 15, 1876
Place of marriage, near Duffields - Age of husband, 26 - Age of wife, 21 - Both are Single - Both were born in Jefferson County, West Virginia - Both reside in Jefferson County, West Virginia.

Adams, Sallie and Charles Agustus Kerns (3) - April 18, 1871
For further information see - Kerns, Charles Agustus.

Adams, Seaton (cold.) Bettie Thornton (3) - February 12, 1880
Place of marriage, Charlestown - Age of husband, 24 - Age of wife, 21 - Both are Single - Both were born in Jefferson County, West Virginia - Both reside in Jefferson County, West Virginia.

Adams, William A. and Ellen V. Snyder (3) -   September 14, 1865
   Place of marriage, Shepherdstown - Age of husband, 26 years - Age of
   wife, 21 years - Both are Single - Both were born at Shepherdstown,
   Jefferson County - Both reside at Shepherdstown - Husband's parents
   are James and Sarah Adams - Wife's parents are John Snyder -
   Occupation of husband is Confectioner.

Addy, John and Nancy Malone (1) -   June 8, 1815

Adelsberger, Mary E. and John Piper, Jr. (3) -   May 16, 1874
   For further information see - Piper, John, Jr.

Agner, Susana and William Haylock (1) -   November 21, 1811

Ahalt, Ezra and Virginia M. Griggs (2) -   (L) December 18, 1854

Ainsworth, Catharine Lucinda and Singleton Trenary (2) -   (L) May 28, 1860

Ainsworth, Eliza and Thomas Longerbeam (2) -   (L) January 8, 1856

Ainsworth, Florence Rosella and Joseph B. Fletcher (3) -   February 25, 1886
   For further information see - Fletcher, Joseph B.

Ainsworth, M. E. and Abram Bell (3) -   October 1, 1878
   For further information see - Bell, Abram.

Ainsworth, Rose E. and George Forber (3) -   December 19, 1867
   For further information see - Forber, George

Aisquith, Archie H. and Mary Rutherford (3) -   July 13, 1868
   Place of marriage, Jefferson County - Age of husband, 23 - Age of
   wife, 20 - Both are Single - Both were born at Charlestown - Both
   reside at Charlestown - Husband's parents are Charles and Margaret -
   Wife's parents are Thomas and Mary - Occupation of husband is
   Druggist.   (Issued at 6:30 A. M. July 13, 1868 - Father gives
   consent.)

Aisquith, C. M. and M. S. Baylor (bride) (3) -   December 3, 1867
   Place of marriage, Jefferson County - Age of husband, 26 - Age of
   wife, 23 - Both are Single - Both were born in Jefferson - Both
   reside in Jefferson - Husband's parents are C. W. and M. S. - Wife's
   parents are Robert W. and Mary - Occupation of husband is Druggist.

Aisquith, E. W. and James Ed. Wyatt (3) -   November 22, 1881
   For further information see - Wyatt, James Ed.

Aisquith, Edward and Mrs. R. R. Baylor (3) -   May 2, 1866
   Place of marriage, Capt. Robert Baylor's, Jefferson County - Age of
   husband, 23 - Age of wife, 20 - Husband is Single - Wife is a
   Widow - Husband was born at Charlestown, Jefferson County,
   Virginia - Wife was born in Mississippi - Both reside in Jefferson
   County, West Virginia - Husband's parents are Charles W. and
   Margaret S. Aisquith - Wife's parents are Thomas Likens - Occupation
   of husband is Merchant.

Aisquith, Edward M. and Ann A. Briscoe (2) -   (L) December 8, 1856

Aisquith, Mary V. and Andrew J. Mark (3) -   February 17, 1869
   For further information see - Mark, Andrew J.

Aisquith, Mary Virginia and M. B. Allen (3) -   June 5, 1877
     For further information see - Allen, M. B.

Alban, Annie E. and Charles W. Barrett (3) -   March 13, 1889
     For further information see - Barrett, Charles W.

Albin, Alice O. and H. W. Hoffmaster (3) -   September 5, 1882
     For further information see - Hoffmaster, H. W.

Albin, Mary E. and Joseph A. Jackson (3) -   October 26, 1880
     For further information see - Jackson, Joseph A.

Alder, W. B. and Mary Alice Whitmore (3) -   June 30, 1886
     Place of marriage, Harpers Ferry - Age of husband, 22 - Age of wife, 23 - Both are Single - Both were born in Loudoun County, Virginia - Husband resides in Jefferson County - Wife resides in Jefferson County, West Virginia.

Aldridge, Harriet West and Dennis M. Matthews (3) -   June 1, 1875
     For further information see - Matthews, Dennis M.

Alexander, Alice (colored) Carter Roman (3) -   January 13, 1870
     For further information see - Roman, Carter.

Alexander, Charlotte and John A. Straith (2) -   (L) August 25, 1864
     For further information see - Straith, John A.

Alexander, Emily (malattoes) Daniel Draper (2) -   (L) September 15, 1855

Alexander, Emily Jane and John Shewbridge (1) -   October 26, 1848

Alexander, George and Sarah Henderson (3) -   September 6, 1866
     Place of marriage, Parsonage M. E. Church, Harpers Ferry - Age of husband, 26 - Age of wife, 17 - Both are Single - Husband was born in Albemarle County, Virginia - Wife was born in Rockingham County, Virginia - Both reside at Harpers Ferry, Jefferson County, West Virginia - Husband's parents are Henry and Winey Alexander - Wife's parents are Henry and Julia Henderson - Occupation of husband is Laborer.

Alexander, Jennie and John Wesley Webster (3) -   January 24, 1884
     For further information see - Webster, John Wesley.

Alexander, Margaret (free negroes) Tom Goings (2) -   (L) March 29, 1852

Alexander, Mary E. and Jacob Rose (3) -   November 14, 1866
     For further information see - Rose, Jacob.

Alexander, Mary F. and Thomas D. Ranson (3) -   April 12, 1871
     For further information see - Ranson, Thomas D.

Alexander, Peter and Annie Mary Elizabeth House (3) -   December 21, 1882
     Place of marriage, Bride's residence near Harpers Ferry - Age of husband, 22 - Age of wife, 20 - Both are Single - Wife was born in State of Maryland - Both reside in Jefferson County, West Virginia. (Consent of bride's father in writing vouched for by her brother.)

Alexander, Richard A. and Julia L. Butler (3) - September 15, 1874
   Place of marriage, near Shepherdstown - Age of husband, 25 - Age of
   wife, 25 - Both are Single - Both were born in Jefferson County,
   West Virginia - Husband resides in Maryland - Wife resides in
   Jefferson County, West Virginia.

Alexander, William F. and A. C. Henkle (3) - April 9, 1868
   Place of marriage, Jefferson County - Age of husband, 28 - Age of
   wife, 22 - Both are Single - Both were born in Jefferson County -
   Both reside in Jefferson - Husband's parents are W. P. and Hannah
   L. - Wife's parents are John T. and Mary - Occupation of husband is
   Physician.

Allemong, Anne and Bazel Claspill (1) - 1821

Allemong, Catherine and James P. Hughes (1) - January 14, 1830

Allemong, Christian and Frances Kercheville (1) - August 11, 1825

Allemong, Samuel H. and Margaret K. Woods (1) - September 17, 1829

Allen, Ann and George Hoffmaster (2) - (L) November 17, 1860

Allen, Carry (cold.) Brown Weaver (3) - December 30, 1884
   For further information see - Weaver, Brown.

Allen, Charles A. and Sarah I. Walters (3) - December 17, 1866
   Place of marriage, Shepherdstown, West Virginia - Age of husband,
   21 - Age of wife, 16 - Both are Single - Husband was born at Bengall
   State of Maine - Wife was born in Berkeley County, West Virginia -
   Both reside in Jefferson County, West Virginia - Husband's parents
   are Laban and Martha A. Allen - Wife's parents are James W. and
   Sarah Walters - Occupation of husband is Carpenter.

Allen, Edward (cold.) Lucinda Burns (3) - March 3, 1881
   Place of marriage, near Ripon - Age of husband, 27 - Age of wife,
   21 - Both are Single - Husband was born in Botetourt County,
   Virginia - Wife was born in Clarke County, Virginia - Both reside
   in Jefferson County, West Virginia.

Allen, Emory C. and Johana O'Brien (3) - December 24, 1876
   Place of marriage, Harpers Ferry - Age of husband, 25 - Age of wife,
   25 - Both are Single - Husband was born in Clarke County, Virginia -
   Wife was born in Ireland - Both reside in Jefferson County, West
   Virginia.

Allen, Henry and Mary Furl (3) -. December 10, 1874
   Place of marriage, Charles Town - Age of husband, 21 last March -
   Age of wife, 27 - Both are Single - Husband was born in Jefferson
   County, West Virginia - Wife was born in Shenandoah County,
   Virginia - Both reside in Jefferson County, West Virginia.

Allen, Hugh P. and Fanny Shepherd (3) - January 26, 1888
   Place of marriage, Shepherdstown - Age of husband, 29 - Age of wife,
   28 - Both are Single - Both were born in Jefferson County, West
   Virginia - Both reside in Jefferson County, West Virginia.

Allen, Jack and Fanny L. Roberts (3) - November 18, 1873
   Place of marriage, Middleway - Age of husband, 34 - Age of wife,
   24 - Both are Single - Husband was born in Loudoun County,
   Virginia - Wife was born in Jefferson County, West Virginia -
   Husband resides in Fauquier County, Virginia - Wife resides in
   Jefferson County, West Virginia.

Allen, James and Susannah Workman (1) - October 5, 1818

Allen, James and Elizabeth Hall (3) - April 18, 1878
   Place of marriage, Summit Point - Age of husband, 44 - Age of wife,
   32 - Husband is a Widower - Wife is a Widow - Husband was born in
   Clarke County, Virginia - Wife was born in Jefferson County, West
   Virginia - Both reside in Jefferson County, West Virginia.

Allen, James W. and Susan Pierce (1) - February 5, 1852

Allen, James W. and Julia N. Pendleton (2) - (L) February 13, 1856

Allen, James William and Susan Pierce (2) - (L) February 5, 1852

Allen, Jesse and Martha M. C. Allison (2) - (L) October 15, 1850

Allen, Jesse and Martha E. Allison (1) - October 31, 1850

Allen, John and Fanny Frances Fisher (2) - (L) November 3, 1856

Allen, John F. and Helen Brantner (3) - February 23, 1882
   Place of marriage, Charlestown - Age of husband, 26 - Age of wife,
   23 - Both are Single - Both were born in Jefferson County, West
   Virginia - Both reside in Jefferson County, West Virginia.

Allen, John W. and Virginia C. Osburn (3) - November 25, 1868
   Place of marriage, Jefferson County - Age of husband, 31 - Age of
   wife, 24 - Both are Single - Husband was born in Loudoun County -
   Wife was born in Jefferson, Virginia - Both reside in Jefferson
   County - Husband's parents are Edmund and Margaret - Wife's parents
   are William and Margaret - Occupation of husband is Farmer.

Allen, Joseph and Jane Craig (1) - November 25, 1804

Allen, Joseph T. and Elvira C. Painter (3) - November 29, 1882
   Place of marriage, near Halltown - Age of husband, 22 - Age of wife,
   22 - Both are Single - Both were born in Jefferson County, West
   Virginia - Both reside in Jefferson County, West Virginia.

Allen, Lawrence and Lena Hedges (3) - May 30, 1889
   Place of marriage, Charlestown - Age of husband, 22 - Age of wife,
   23 - Both are Single - Both were born in Jefferson County, West
   Virginia - Both reside in Jefferson County, West Virginia.

Allen, M. B. and Mary Virginia Aisquith (3) - June 5, 1877
   Place of marriage, Charlestown - Age of husband, 32 - Age of wife,
   29 - Both are Single - Husband was born in Giles County, Virginia -
   Wife was born in Jefferson County, West Virginia - Husband resides
   in Bland County, Virginia - Wife resides in Jefferson County, West
   Virginia.

Allen, M. C. (bride) and E. C. Watson (3) - February 12, 1868
   For further information see - Watson, E. C.

Allen, Maggie and H. W. Kearney (3) - March 28, 1867
   For further information see - Kearney, H. W.

Allen, Mrs. Martha and John H. Reed (3) - June 24, 1873
   For further information see - Reed, John H.

Allen, Martha (cold.) Benjamin Brown (3) - August 20, 1878
   For further information see - Brown, Benjamin.

Allen, Milicent and R. O. Allen (3) - April 3, 1884
   For further information see - Allen, R. O.

Allen, R. O. and Milicent Allen (3) - April 3, 1884
   Place of marriage, near Ripon - Age of husband, 50 - Age of wife,
   28 - Husband is a Widower - Wife is Single - Husband was born in
   Clarke County, Virginia - Wife was born in Jefferson County, West
   Virginia - Both reside in Jefferson County, West Virginia.

Allingsworth, Lucy and James H. Manuel (3) - August 23, 1880
   For further information see - Manuel, James H.

Allison, Ann H. and Sidney Murphy (2) - (L) September 4, 1858

Allison, Christy Ann and James J. Jones (1) - June 1, 1817

Allison, Hezekiah B. and Mary Fisher (1) - July 27, 1817

Allison, James and Elizabeth Hartman (1) - March 19, 1822

Allison, John and Elizabeth Cornwell (1) - 1819

Allison, John B. and Sarah Grubb (1) - February 15, 1821

Allison, L. R. (cold.) Mary F. Martin (3) - February 27, 1888
   Place of marriage, Bolivar - Age of husband, 30 - Age of wife, 28 -
   Husband is Single - Wife is a Widow - Husband was born at Richmond -
   Wife was born in Jefferson County, West Virginia - Both reside in
   Jefferson County, West Virginia.

Allison, Martha E. and Jesse Allen (1) - October 31, 1850

Allison, Martha M. C. and Jesse Allen (2) - (L) October 15, 1850

Allison, N. O. and Martha Ann Wigginton (2) - (L) September 18, 1858

Allstadt, Barbary and Stephen Dalgarn (1) - August 4, 1825

Allstadt, Daniel and Susan Garnhart (1) - April 27, 1808

Allstadt, Daniel and Barbary Lansiskes (1) - June 27, 1816

Allstadt, Harriet E. and Joseph L. Russell (1) - November 20, 1832

Allstadt, John Hall and Mary Ann Gardner (1) - February 16, 1837

Allstadt, John Y. and Annie E. Cockrell (3) -   December 18, 1866
    Place of marriage, near Charlestown, Jefferson County - Age of
    husband, 25 - Age of wife, 20 - Both are Single - Both were born in
    Jefferson County, West Virginia - Both reside in Jefferson County,
    West Virginia - Husband's parents are John H. and Mary A. Allstadt -
    Wife's parents are John G. and Elizabeth Cockrell - Occupation of
    husband is Farmer.

Allstadt, Sarah Elizabeth and Henry Clay Cromwell (2) -   (L) January 28, 1856

Allstadt, Sue V. and Jacob T. Henkle (3) -   December 5, 1876
    For further information see - Henkle, Jacob T.

Allwen, Charles and Mary Tolley (3) -   November 11, 1871
    Place of marriage, Charles Town - Age of husband, 45 - Age of wife,
    35 - Husband is a Widower - Wife is Single - Husband was born in
    Germany - Wife was born in Virginia - Both reside in Jefferson
    County - Husband's parents are Mike and Fredericka - Wife's parents
    are John - Occupation of husband is Mason.

Ambler, Charles E. and Susan W. Keyes (2) -   (L) September 4, 1860

Ambler, Jane K. and John A. Washington (3) -   November 26, 1890
    For further information see - Washington, John A.

Ambler, R. J. and Annie M. Willis (2) -   (L) August 12, 1857

Ambrose, Catherine Ann and George W. Hardy (3) -   October 1, 1876
    For further information see - Hardy, George W.

Ambrose, Mary and Benjamin F. Hardy (3) -   December 30, 1877
    For further information see - Hardy, Benjamin F.

Ambrose, Nancy F. and William S. Henrety (3) -   September 5, 1872
    For further information see - Henrety, William S.

Ambrose, W. C. and Isaac N. Smith (3) -   March 3, 1868
    For further information see - Smith, Isaac N.

Ambrose, W. T. and Catherine Henretty (3) -   November 21, 1872
    Place of marriage, Shepherdstown - Age of husband, 25 - Age of wife,
    21 - Both are Single - Husband was born in Page County, Virginia -
    Wife was born in Berkeley, West Virginia - Husband resides in
    Jefferson County, West Virginia - Wife resides in Berkeley, West
    Virginia - Husband's parents are G. and H. Ambrose - Wife's parents
    are Daniel and Susan - Occupation of husband is Farmer.

Amey, Jennie V. and Ed. L. Whittington (3) -   December 16, 1885
    For further information see - Whittington, Ed. L.

Anan, Daniel and Virginia O. Butcher (3) -   October 21, 1869
    Place of marriage, Jefferson County - Age of husband, 23 - Age of
    wife, 23 - Husband was born in Maryland - Wife was born in Jefferson
    County - Husband resides in Maryland - Wife resides in Jefferson
    County.

Anderson, Anna Bettie and A. F. Bentz (3) -   October 26, 1881
    For further information see - Bentz, A. F.

Anderson, Annie E. D. and John T. Trussell (3) -. January 13, 1875
    For further information see - Trussell, John T.

Anderson, Archibald and Anne Jane Stephenson (1) - February 17, 1819

Anderson, Archie B. and Georgiana Foulk (3) - December 17, 1878
    Place of marriage, Middleway - Age of husband, 22 - Age of wife,
    18 - Both are Single - Husband was born in Jefferson County, West
    Virginia - Wife was born in Berkeley County, West Virginia - Both
    reside in Jefferson County, West Virginia.

Anderson, Austin L. and Anna E. Lawson (3) - December 26, 1876
    Place of marriage, near Middleway - Age of husband, 22 - Age of
    wife, 23 - Both are Single - Husband was born in Jefferson County,
    West Virginia - Wife was born in Washington City - Both reside in
    Jefferson County, West Virginia.

Anderson, Daniel T. and Margaret Holmes (1) - May 22, 1833

Anderson, Evelina and William Mills (1) - December 19, 1821

Anderson, George W. and Virginia B. Drish (3) - August 19, 1886
    Place of marriage, Charlestown - Age of husband, 23 - Age of wife,
    26 - Both are Single - Husband was born in Frederick County,
    Virginia - Wife was born in Jefferson County, West Virginia - Both
    reside in Jefferson County, West Virginia.

Anderson, George W. F. and Mary M. Hyatt (3) - December 12, 1871
    Place of marriage, Jefferson County - Age of husband, 28 - Age of
    wife, 18 - Both are Single - Husband was born in Jefferson County -
    Wife was born in Frederick County - Husband resides in Jefferson -
    Wife resides in Jefferson County - Husband's parents are George W.
    and Margaret Elizabeth - Wife's parents are John W. and Rachel A. -
    Occupation of husband is Farmer. (Father's consent.)

Anderson, Ida M. and James H. Burk (3) - December 5, 1883
    For further information see - Burk, James H.

Anderson, Isadore V. and John P. Whalen (3) - August 7, 1873
    For further information see - Whalen, John P.

Anderson, J. (bride) and J. W. Zombro (3) - January 3, 1872
    For further information see - Zombro, J. W.

Anderson, James and Catherine Buckmaster (1) - January 26, 1802

Anderson, James (cold.) Katie Jones (3) - December 26, 1867
    Place of marriage, Jefferson County - Age of husband, 23 - Age of
    wife, 30 - Both are Single - Husband was born in Alleghany County,
    Virginia - Wife was born in Jefferson - Both reside in Jefferson
    County - Husband's parents are William and Harriet - Wife's parents
    are Charity - Occupation of husband is Farmer.

Anderson, James and Mary Jane Merritt (3) - January 5, 1870
    Place of marriage, Jefferson County - Age of husband, 22 - Age of
    wife, 18 - Both were born in Jefferson County - Both reside in
    Jefferson County. (Brother sworen that father is willing.)

Anderson, James (cold.) Jennie Thornton (3) - July 16, 1873
Place of marriage, near Charlestown - Age of husband, 25 - Age of
wife, 21 - Both are Single - Husband was born at Richmond - Wife was
born in Jefferson County, West Virginia - Both reside in Jefferson
County, West Virginia.

Anderson, James (cold.) Amanda Jackson (3) - October 28, 1880
Place of marriage, Charlestown - Age of husband, 40 - Age of wife,
25 - Husband is a Widower - Wife is Single - Husband was born at
Richmond, Virginia - Wife was born in Fairfax County, Virginia -
Both reside in Jefferson County, West Virginia.

Anderson, Jeremiah and Ruth West (1) - March 29, 1835

Anderson, John and Mary Elizabeth Shrodes (1) - December 14, 1849

Anderson, Joseph and Lucinda Taylor (3) - June 7, 1868
Place of marriage, Jefferson County - Age of husband, 45 - Age of
wife, 32 - Husband is Single - Wife is a Widow - Husband was born in
North Carolina - Wife was born in Virginia - Both reside in
Jefferson County - Occupation of husband is Farmer.

Anderson, Joseph E. and Eliza P. Ware (2) - (L) April 6, 1852

Anderson, Joseph E. and Eliza P. Ware (1) - April 8, 1852

Anderson, M. J. (bride) and G. H. Wakeman (3) - March 29, 1882
For further information see - Wakeman, G. H.

Anderson, Maria Ella (cold.) James W. McDaniel (3) - December 27, 1882
For further information see - McDaniel, James W.

Anderson, Maria L. and Thomas E. Woodward (3) - May 1, 1866
For further information see - Woodward, Thomas E.

Anderson, Mary (cold.) John W. Welcome (3) - April 15, 1880
For further information see - Welcome, John W.

Anderson, Mary Ann and William L. Hall (1) - October 14, 1824

Anderson, Mary V. (cold.) Jerry M. Johnson (3) - April 20, 1887
For further information see - Johnson, Jerry M.

Anderson, Philip A. and Ann B. SaintClair (3) - November 2, 1870
Place of marriage, Jefferson County - Age of husband, 44 - Age of
wife, 38 - Husband was born in Frederick County, Virginia - Wife was
born in Jefferson County - Husband resides in Jefferson County -
Wife resides in West Virginia.

Anderson, Randolph C. S. and Sarah E. G. Crim (3) - July 28, 1885
Place of marriage, Middleway - Age of husband, 24 - Age of wife,
23 - Both are Single - Husband was born in Jefferson County, West
Virginia - Wife was born in Frederick County, Virginia - Both reside
in Jefferson County, West Virginia.

Anderson, S. J. (bride) and R. W. Welsh (3) - December 17, 1867
For further information see - Welsh, R. W.

Anderson, Sally (cold.) Newton Stubbs (3) - November 3, 1873
For further information see - Stubbs, Newton.

Anderson, Sidney A. and George W. Feltner (3) -   September 6, 1866
    For further information see - Feltner, George W.

Anderson, Solomon and Susan Rebecca Robinson (3) -   September 18, 1871
    Place of marriage, Jefferson County - Age of husband, 24 - Age of wife, 21 - Both are Single - Both were born in Virginia - Husband resides in Jefferson - Wife resides in West Virginia - Husband's parents are Peter and Rachel - Wife's parents are Walker and Lucinda - Occupation of husband is Railroad.

Anderson, W. E. and Eliza Conrad (3) -   December 7, 1871
    Place of marriage, Jefferson County - Age of husband, 50 - Age of wife, 28 - Husband is a Widower - Wife is Single - Husband was born in Frederick County, Maryland - Wife was born in Warren County, Virginia - Husband resides in Jefferson - Wife resides in Jefferson County - Wife's parents are Joseph and Jane - Occupation of husband is Bee Keeper.

Anderson, William H. and Anna Elizabeth Lucas (3) -   June 15, 1882
    Place of marriage, Charlestown - Age of husband, 25 - Age of wife, 18 - Both are Single - Husband was born in Frederick County, Virginia - Wife was born in Alleghany County, Maryland - Husband resides in Jefferson County, West Virginia. - Wife resides in Jefferson County. (Consent of bride's father in person.)

Anderson, William J. and America Locke (3) -   April 27, 1875
    Place of marriage, Charlestown - Age of husband, 27 - Age of wife, 27 - Both are Single - Both were born in Jefferson County, West Virginia - Both reside in Jefferson County, West Virginia.

Andrew, Richard E. and Mary V. Conner (3) -   December 26, 1878
    Place of marriage, Charlestown - Age of husband, 24 - Age of wife, 34 - Husband is Single - Wife is a Widow - Husband was born at Washington City - Wife was born at Woodstock, Shenandoah County, Virginia - Husband resides in Washington County, Maryland - Wife resides at Charlestown, Jefferson County, West Virginia.

Andrews, Ann R. Page and George Rowan Robinson (2) -   (L) September 15, 1855

Andrews, Charles E. and Sarah Melinda Bell Grove (3) -   May 13, 1884
    Place of marriage, Bride's residence near Pipertown - Age of husband, 28 - Age of wife, 20 - Both are Single - Both were born in Jefferson County, West Virginia - Both reside in Jefferson County, West Virginia. (Consent of bride's father vouched for by her brother William.)

Andrews, Helen Agatha and William Thomas Muck (3) -   March 29, 1875
    For further information see - Muck, William Thomas.

Andrews, James M. and Clarene E. Miller. (3) -   (1870)
    Age of husband, 44 - Age of wife, 31 - Husband was born in Warren County, Virginia - Wife was born in Virginia - Both reside in Jefferson County.

Andrews, John W. and Agatha Ellen Licklider (divorced) (2) -
    (L) February 7, 1860
    (A marked through notation indicates her as "Widow of David Staley.")

Andrews, Lila and Magruder Maury (3) -　　　　　　　October 25, 1865
　　For further information see - Maury, Magruder.

Andrews, M. P. and Anna Robinson (2) -　　　　　　　(L) July 5, 1861
　　Time of marriage; July 6, 1861 - Place of marriage, Shepherdstown -
　　Full names of parties, M. P. Andrews and Anna Robinson - Age of
　　husband, 26 years - Age of wife, 24 years - Both are Single - Place
　　of husband's bitth; Clarke County, Virginia - Place of wife's birth;
　　Jefferson County, Virginia - Place of husband's residence;
　　Moorfield, Hardy County, Virginia - Place of wife's residence;
　　Shepherdstown, Jefferson County, Virginia - Names of husband's
　　parents, Rev. C. W. Andrews and S. N. Andrews - Names of wife's
　　parents, Archibald and Anna K. Robinson - Occupation of husband is
　　Lawyer - Given under my hand this 5th day of July, 1861 - M. P.
　　Andrews.

Andrews, Mary J. and Melvin T. Stephens (3) -　　　　August 4, 1870
　　For further information see - Stephens, Melvin T.

Andrews, Sarah Elizabeth and Joseph L. Eichelberger (3) -　　July 9, 1881
　　For further information see - Eichelberger, Joseph L.

Andson, Anne and George Vestal (1) -　　　　　　　　November 20, 1828

Andsworth, Sarah and Richard Stone (1) -　　　　　　August 15, 1819

Angel, George N. and Anna D. Hobbs (3) -　　　　　　December 18, 1879
　　Place of marriage, near Harpers Ferry - Age of husband, 25 - Age of
　　wife, 21 - Both are Single - Husband was born in Frederick County,
　　Maryland - Wife was born in Jefferson County, West Virginia - Both
　　reside in Jefferson County, West Virginia.

Angell, Daniel and Elizabeth Frances Riley (2) -　　(L) November 28, 1854

Angell, Lewis W. and Emma J. Webb (3) -　　　　　　　December 22, 1886
　　Place of marriage, Harpers Ferry - Age of husband, 34 - Age of wife,
　　27 - Both are Single - Husband was born in Jefferson County, West
　　Virginia - Wife was born in Loudoun County, Virginia - Both reside
　　in Jefferson County, West Virginia.

Angell, Martha S. and Henry D. Middlekauff (2) -　　(L) November 23, 1860

Anthony, William and Frances Keyes (1) -　　　　　　November 18, 1830

Apenzeller, Henry and Mary Lang (1) -　　　　　　　　March 8, 1827

Appell, John and Hannah Staubb (3) -　　　　　　　　December 15, 1889
　　Place of marriage, Saint Andrews Chapel - Age of husband, 24 - Age
　　of wife, 22 - Both are Single - Both were born in Jefferson County,
　　West Virginia - Both reside in Jefferson County, West Virginia.

Apsey, William and Louisa Earnshaw (1) -　　　　　　December 27, 1836

Armentrout, George W. and Sallie E. Haines (3) -　　February 10, 1869
　　Place of marriage, Jefferson County - Age of husband, 36 - Age of
　　wife, 29 - Both are Single - Husband was born in Rockingham County,
　　Virginia - Wife was born in Jefferson County - Husband resides in
　　Page County, Virginia - Wife resides in Jefferson County - Husband's
　　parents are Philip and Peggy - Wife's parents are Jacob and Hannah -
　　Occupation of husband is Bricklayer.

Armentrout, John H. and Elizabeth Sigler (3) -	October 27, 1885
  Place of marriage, Harpers Ferry - Age of husband, 23 - Age of wife,
  22 - Both are Single - Both were born in Jefferson County, West
  Virginia - Both reside in Jefferson County, West Virginia.

Armour, James W. and Catherine C. Saunders (1) -	November 14, 1823

Armstead, Robert (colored) Lydia Johnson (3) -	(1870)
  Age of husband, 34 - Age of wife, 32 - Husband was born in Frederick
  County, Virginia - Wife was born in Jefferson County - Both reside
  in Jefferson County. (This marriage is marked void in the
  original.)

Armstrong, Abram and Lucy Nelson (3) -	February 15, 1872
  Place of marriage, Jefferson County, West Virginia - Age of husband,
  26 - Age of wife, 26 - Both are Single - Husband was born in
  Jefferson County - Wife was born in Jefferson County, Virginia -
  Husband resides in Jefferson County - Wife resides in Jefferson
  County, West Virginia - Husband's parents are Harvey and Pricilla -
  Wife's parents are David and Dolley - Occupation of husband is
  Blacksmith.

Armstrong, David S. and Ellen Hoofmaster (3) -	(1868)
  Age of husband, 50 - Age of wife, 40 - Husband is a Widower - Wife
  is a Widow - Husband was born in Preston - Wife was born in Loudoun,
  Virginia - Both reside in Jefferson - Occupation of husband is
  Mechanic.

Armstrong, Elizabeth and James Gay (3) -	July 27, 1865
  For further information see - Gay, James.

Armstrong, F. E. and Nannie H. VanDoren (2) -	(L) July 21, 1857

Armstrong, James William and Ella Russell (3) -	April 15, 1875
  Place of marriage, Harpers Ferry - Age of husband, 23 - Age of wife,
  18 - Both are Single - Both were born in Jefferson County, West
  Virginia - Husband resides in Berkeley County, West Virginia - Wife
  resides in Jefferson County, West Virginia. (Consent of bride's
  mother in writing.)

Armstrong, Jennie C. and Charles H. Hoffmaster (3) -	August 15, 1882
  For further information see - Hoffmaster, Charles H.

Armstrong, Macellus and Sarah J. Smith (3) -	January 29, 1884
  Place of marriage, Mechanickstown - Age of husband, 21 - Age of
  wife, 16 - Both are Single - Both were born in Jefferson County,
  West Virginia - Both reside in Jefferson County, West Virginia.
  (Consent of bride's mother in writing.)

Armstrong, William and Eliza Breedin (1) -	October 10, 1816

Arnesty, Mary (cold.) Simon P. Walker (3) -	December 23, 1880
  For further information see - Walker, Simon P.

Arnett, Alverta and Isaac F. Santemyers (3) -	November 27, 1889
  For further information see - Santemyers, Isaac F.

Arnett, Daniel W. and Maria Louisa Carter (3) -   October 15, 1873
   Place of marriage, Shepherdstown - Age of husband, 26 - Age of wife,
   23 - Both are Single - Husband was born in Berkeley County, West
   Virginia - Wife was born in Jefferson County, West Virginia - Both
   reside in Jefferson County, West Virginia.

Arter, Jared M. (cold.) Emma Carter (3) -   July 14, 1890
   Place of marriage, Charlestown - Age of husband, 35 - Age of wife,
   27 - Both are Single - Both were born in Jefferson County, West
   Virginia - Both reside in Jefferson County, West Virginia.

Arter, John A. (cold.) Virginia White (3) -   January 13, 1881
   Place of marriage, near Harpers Ferry - Age of husband, 21 - Age of
   wife, 21 - Both are Single - Both were born in Jefferson County,
   West Virginia - Both reside in Jefferson County, West Virginia.

Arter, John A. (cold.) Eliza A. Bacchus (3) -   November 23, 1886
   Place of marriage, Charlestown - Age of husband, 27 - Age of wife,
   22 - Husband is a Widower - Wife is Single - Both were born in
   Jefferson County, West Virginia - Both reside in Jefferson County,
   West Virginia.

Arter, Thomas (cold.) Mabel Clinton (3) -   September 23, 1884
   Place of marriage, Bolivar - Age of husband, 28 - Age of wife, 21 -
   Both are Single - Both were born in Jefferson County, West
   Virginia - Both reside in Jefferson County.

Arter, William A. (cold.) Rosa A. Scott (3) -   April 24, 1878
   Place of marriage, Charlestown - Age of husband, 28 - Age of wife,
   21 - Both are Single - Husband was born in Virginia - Wife was born
   in Jefferson County, West Virginia - Both reside in Jefferson
   County, West Virginia.

Arthur, Annie and Thomas F. Kerfott (3) -   December 11, 1879
   For further information see - Kerfott, Thomas F.

Arthur, Elizabeth (widow) and John Kershaw (2) -   (L) January 14, 1854

Arthur, Margaret and J. Rose (3) -   October 24, 1867
   For further information see - Rose, J.

Arthur, William L. and Mary D. Edwards (3) -   October 31, 1867
   Place of marriage, Jefferson County - Age of husband, 26 - Age of
   wife, 21 - Both are Single - Both were born in Jefferson County -
   Both reside in Jefferson County - Husband's parents are Robert and
   Elizabeth - Wife's parents are Amelia.

Arthur, William L. and Mary J. Burke (3) -   December 9, 1879
   Place of marriage, Shepherdstown - Age of husband, 38 - Age of
   wife, 28 - Husband is a Widower - Wife is a Widow - Husband was born
   in Jefferson County, West Virginia - Wife was born in Washington
   County, Maryland - Both reside in Jefferson County, West Virginia.

Arvin, J. W. and Anna Rebecca Kidwiler (3) -   December 25, 1888
   Place of marriage, Harpers Ferry - Age of husband, 27 - Age of wife,
   22 - Both are Single - Husband was born at Richmond, Virginia - Wife
   was born in Jefferson County, West Virginia - Husband resides in
   Berkeley County, West Virginia - Wife resides in Jefferson County,
   West Virginia.

Arvin, John W. and Caroline E. Wager (2) -　　　　　　(L) April 29, 1856

Arvin, Martha and Hiram Carney (1) -　　　　　　　　September 27, 1832

Arvin, Nancy and Joseph Gore (1). -　　　　　　　　　June 28, 1808

Arvin, Robert and Utica Carney (2) -　　　　　　　　(L) March 23, 1861

Arvin, Robert and Maggie Reed (3) -　　　　　　　　　June 9, 1881
 Place of marriage, Bolivar - Age of husband, 40 - Age of wife, 19 -
 Husband is a Widower - Wife is Single - Husband was born in
 Jefferson County, West Virginia - Wife was born in Loudoun County,
 Virginia - Both reside in Jefferson County, West Virginia.
 (Consent of bride's mother in writing.)

Arvin, Thomas E. and Mary E. Wingate (3) -　　　　　February 9, 1882
 Place of marriage, Harpers Ferry - Age of husband, 43 - Age of wife,
 23 - Both are Single - Both were born in Jefferson County, West
 Virginia - Both reside in Jefferson County, West Virginia.

Ash, Maud May and John W. Fauver (3) -　　　　　　　August 27, 1889
 For further information see - Fauver, John W.

Ashbaugh, C. C. (bride) and L. A. Osbourn (3) -　　March 26, 1879
 For further information see - Osbourn, L. A.

Ashbaugh, Mary Ellen and Henry Dumm (2) -　　　　　(L) December 2, 1863
 For further information see - Dumm, Henry.

Ashby, Amanda and Michael Pilken (2) -　　　　　　　(L) December 30, 1862
 For further information see - Pilken, Michael.

Ashby, Annie and Frank Taylor (3) -　　　　　　　　　May 10, 1879
 For further information see - Taylor, Frank.

Ashby, Frank (cold.) Geraldine Williams (3) -　　　October 2, 1890
 Place of marriage, Charlestown - Age of husband, 23 - Age of wife,
 23 - Both are Single - Husband was born in Frederick County,
 Virginia - Wife was born in Madison County, Virginia - Husband
 resides in Warren County, Virginia - Wife resides in Jefferson
 County, West Virginia.

Ashby, James (cold.) Cornelia Shorts (3) -　　　　　May 30, 1878
 Place of marriage, near Duffields - Age of husband, 22 - Age of
 wife, 22 - Both are Single - Husband was born in Frederick County,
 Virginia - Wife was born in Jefferson County, West Virginia - Both
 reside in Jefferson County, West Virginia.

Ashby, John W. and Margaret Joyce (2) -　　　　　　(L) January 8, 1853

Ashby, Lee (cold.) Magie Clarke (3) -　　　　　　　August 16, 1883
 Place of marriage, Harpers Ferry - Age of husband, 22 - Age of wife,
 21 - Both are Single - Husband was born at Baltimore, Maryland -
 Wife was born in Virginia - Both reside in Jefferson County, West
 Virginia.

Ashby, Lucy and Joseph A. Dixon (2) -　　　　　　　(L) April 3, 1861
 For further information see - Dixon, Joseph A.

Ashby, Mary and George W. Pierce (3) -   August 8, 1872
    For further information see - Pierce, George W.

Ashby, Mary C. and Patrick McNarsey (3) -   October 21, 1867
    For further information see - McNarsey, Patrick

Ashby, Patrick and Sarah Margaret Lloyd (3) -   June 15, 1875
    Place of marriage, Charlestown - Age of husband, 20 - Age of wife, 19 - Both are Single - Husband was born in Jefferson County, West Virginia - Wife was born in Clarke County, Virginia - Both reside in Jefferson County, West Virginia. (Consent of father of each party in person.)

Ashby, Sally McHenry and David F. Wilson (3) -   April 18, 1881
    For further information see - Wilson, David F.

Ashton, Thomas and Julia DeC. Garnett (3) -   December 5, 1876
    Place of marriage, Shepherdstown - Age of husband, 33 - Age of wife, 28 - Husband is a Widower - Wife is a Widow - Husband was born at Philadelphia - Wife was born in Maryland - Both reside in Jefferson County, West Virginia.

Ashwood, Jennie and Joseph B. Griffith (3) -   October 14, 1889
    For further information see - Griffith, Joseph B.

Atar, Sophia and William McCoy (1) -   May 25, 1819

Athey, Elizabeth and Thomas E. Brown (3) -   November 28, 1865
    For further information see - Brown, Thomas E.

Athey, George W. and Citha Jane Triggs (2) -   (L) (1862)
    Time of marriage; October 12, (1862) - Place of marriage, near Leetown - Names, George W. Athey and Citha Jane Triggs - Age of husband, 32 years - Age of wife, 26 years - Both are Single - Both were born in Jefferson - Both reside in Jefferson - Names of husband's parents James W. and Rebecca - Names of wife's parents Jeremiah and Catharine - Occupation of husband is Farmer.

Athey, Harriet A. and Daniel W. Snyder (3) -   March 27, 1877
    For further information see - Snyder, Daniel W.

Athey, James T. and Mrs. Jane Rutherford (3) -   December 19, 1875
    Place of marriage, Middleway - Age of husband, 49 - Age of wife, 33 - Husband is a Widower - Wife is a Widow - Both were born in Jefferson County, West Virginia - Both reside in Jefferson County, West Virginia.

Athey, Lydia and James W. Colbert (3) -   December 29, 1881
    For further information see - Colbert, James W.

Athey, Martha Ann and Thomas J. Flood (1) -   January 24, 1847

Athey, Mary and Robert B. Tharp (3) -   May 22, 1890
    For further information see - Tharp, Robert B.

Athey, Mary E. and Lewis Jolly (2) -   (L) May 8, 1862
    For further information see - Jolly, Lewis.

Athey, Susan C. and John A. McCormick (2) -   (L) November 24, 1862
    For further information see - McCormick, John A.

Athy, Deborah and Charles Clewell (1) -   1824

Athy, Elizabeth and John Sullivan (1) -   October 15, 1815

Athy, Matilda and Thomas Claspy (1) -   March 6, 1822

Atkins, Mary C. and Henry F. Staley (3) -   November 28, 1886
    For further information see - Staley, Henry F.

Atkinson, E. M. (bride) and V. L. Perry (3) -   October 31, 1867
    For further information see - Perry, V. L.

Atkinson, Lydia M. and R. T. B. Garrott (3) -   November 10, 1870
    For further information see - Garrott, R. T. B.

Atkinson, Thomas and Eliza Cornwell (1) -   February 22, 1815

Ator, Solomon and Sarah Wykoff (1) -   1814

Atwell, Charles W. and Lucy B. Jackson (3) -   December 24, 1885
    Place of marriage, Millville - Age of husband, 37 - Age of wife,
    14 - Both are Single - Husband was born in Loudoun County,
    Virginia - Wife was born in Jefferson County, West Virginia - Both
    reside in Jefferson County, West Virginia. (Consent of bride's
    mother in person.)

Atwell, Virginia and William Fields (3) -   February 21, 1889
    For further information see - Fields, William.

Atwell, William and Maria S. Heskett (1) -   November 21, 1825

Atwell, William H. and Bettie J. O'Bannon (3) -   March 26, 1878
    Place of marriage, Charlestown - Age of husband, 24 - Age of wife,
    23 - Both are Single - Husband was born in Loudoun County,
    Virginia - Wife was born in Jefferson County, West Virginia -
    Husband resides at Washington City - Wife resides in Jefferson
    County, West Virginia.

Ault, Jacob and Mary Drew (1) -   September 24, 1809

Ault, William J. and Maggie Cox (3) -   April 20, 1871
    Place of marriage, Jefferson County - Age of husband, 22 - Age of
    wife, 20 - Both are Single - Husband was born in Jefferson County -
    Wife was born in Virginia - Both reside in Jefferson County -
    Husband's parents are Adam and Catherine - Wife's parents are
    William and Sarah - Occupation of husband is Laborer.

Avery, Linda and W. G. Russell, Jr. (3) -   May 23, 1883
    For further information see - Russell, W. G., Jr.

Avey, Alice O. and Charles L. Whittington (3) -   March 7, 1872
    For further information see - Whittington, Charles L.

Avey, Edmund and Mary C. Smith (3) -   November 7, 1886
    Place of marriage, Harpers Ferry - Age of husband, 23 - Age of
    wife, 22 - Both are Single - Husband was born in Jefferson County,
    West Virginia - Wife was born at Baltimore City - Both reside in
    Jefferson County, West Virginia.

Avey, Mary C. and George C. Welty (3) -   July 18, 1876
   For further information see - Welty, George C.

Avey, William and Ann Cecilia Crane (2) -   (L) April 26, 1856

Avis, Ann Catharine and Edward V. Kercheval (1) -   June 9, 1847

Avis, Anna E. and William O. Stickler (3) -   March 4, 1884
   For further information see - Stickler, William O.

Avis, Clara and William G. Earnshaw (3) -   January 7, 1874
   For further information see - Earnshaw, William G.

Avis, Elizabeth and Jonathan T. Hall (1) -   January 9, 1817

Avis, Elizabeth and Joseph Lenox (1) -   April 16, 1829

Avis, Mrs. Elizabeth (widow) and Washington Busey (1) -   June 30, 1836

Avis, J. R. and S. J. Roan (bride) (3) -   January 2, 1871
   Place of marriage, Charles Town - Age of husband, 23 - Age of wife, 22 - Both are Single - Husband was born in Jefferson - Wife was born in Virginia - Both reside in Jefferson County - Husband's parents are J. Avis - Wife's parents are J. W. and Helen - Occupation of husband is Gentleman. (This marriage is crossed out in the original record.)

Avis, Jeannette and Ezekiel D. Young (2) -   (L) October 11, 1856

Avis, John and Nancy Hyatt (1) -   June 15, 1820

Avis, John R. and Sarah J. Roan (3) -   January 2, 1871
   Place of marriage, Charles Town - Age of husband, 23 - Age of wife, 22 - Both are Single - Husband was born in Jefferson County - Wife was born in Frederick County - Both reside in Jefferson County - Husband's parents are John Avis - Wife's parents are J. W. and Helen - Occupation of husband is Gentleman.

Avis, Lettie V. and Charles M. Hough (3) -   January 10, 1867
   For further information see - Hough, Charles M.

Avis, Lucy T. and George A. Mock (3) -   October 15, 1884
   For further information see - Mock, George A.

Avis, Margaret G. and Elmer E. Stoneseifer (3) -   March 26, 1889
   For further information see - Stoneseifer, Elmer E.

Avis, Martha F. and Robert Nicholson (2) -   (L) September 24, 1857

Avis, Mary and Robert Downs (1) -   November 5, 1834

Avis, Mary E. and William W. Cockrill (3) -   April 21, 1880
   For further information see - Cockrill, William W.

Avis, Mary J. and Thomas V. Cockrill (3) -   December 31, 1879
   For further information see - Cockrill, Thomas V.

Avis, Mary L. and Colin P. Light (3) -   December 21, 1871
   For further information see - Light, Colin P.

Avis, Samuel and Ann Moaler (1) -   March 19, 1818

Avis, Sarah Ann and Paul Washburn (1) -   1827

Avis, Sarah J. (nee Rowan, divorced) and Frank L. Beller (3) -   May 7, 1877
   For further information see - Beller, Frank L.

Avis, Virginia S. and A. J. Roderick (2) -   (L) October 23, 1856

Avis, William I. and Mary E. Webb (3) -   January 19, 1882
   Place of marriage, Charlestown - Age of husband, 35 - Age of wife,
   26 - Both are Single - Husband was born in Jefferson County, West
   Virginia - Wife was born in Loudoun County, Virginia - Both reside
   in Jefferson County, West Virginia.

Avis, William R. and Maggie Wood (3) -   January 18, 1872
   Place of marriage, Jefferson County, West Virginia - Age of husband,
   24 - Age of wife, 20 - Both are Single - Husband was born in
   Jefferson County, Virginia - Wife was born in Clarke County,
   Virginia - Husband resides at Charlestown, West Virginia - Wife
   resides in Jefferson County, West Virginia - Husband's parents are
   W. A. - Wife's parents are Bennett and Mary - Occupation of husband
   is Blacksmith.   (David F. Wood.)

Ayer, Catherine and Thomas Wilt (1) -   December 29, 1825

Ayer, Phebe and James Morlat (1) -   January 10, 1832

Bacchus, Eliza A. (cold.) John A. Arter (3) -   November 23, 1886
    For further information see - Arter, John A.

Bacchus, Sarah (cold.) Charles Carter (3) -   March 5, 1881
    For further information see - Carter, Charles.

Backhouse, Anna P. and James Myers (2) -   (L) June 5, 1857

Backhouse, Frances and Newton Moler (3) -   October 30, 1867
    For further information see - Moler, Newton.

Backhouse, George and Catherine M. Ridenour (1) -   1820

Backhouse, Mary Ellen and James W. Milton (2) -   (L) September 20, 1852

Backhouse, Pleasant C. and John W. Walraven (2) -   (L) October 18, 1856

Backhouse, Sarah A. and John T. Harris (2) -   (L) February 19, 1861

Backus, Jefferson (cold.) Tina Lucas (3) -   March 22, 1888
    Place of marriage, Charlestown - Age of husband, 34 - Age of wife,
    36 - Husband is Single - Wife is a Widow - Both were born in
    Jefferson County, West Virginia - Both reside in Jefferson County,
    West Virginia.

Backus, Lillie E. and Hiram A. Carroll (3) -   December 4, 1890
    For further information see - Carroll, Hiram A.

Backus, Lydia and Henry Mitchel (3) -   November 7, 1865
    For further information see - Mitchel, Henry.

Baden, Annie A. and William M. Graham (3) -   November 23, 1887
    For further information see - Graham, William M.

Baden, Mary and Jacob Coons (son of Jacob Coons, Sr.) (1) - October 26, 1823

Baden, Mary C. and W. W. Butts (3) -   November 23, 1870
    For further information see - Butts, W. W.

Badger, Mary and Benjamin Hoffman (2) -   (L) June 23, 1862
    For further information see - Hoffman, Benjamin.

Badger, Samuel J. and Mary Magaha (3) -   April 29, 1874
    Place of marriage, Shepherdstown - Age of husband, 25 - Age of wife,
    23 - Both are Single - Both were born in Jefferson County, West
    Virginia - Both reside in Jefferson County, West Virginia.

Badger, William and Sarah Morrison (3) -   December 26, 1876
    Place of marriage, Charles Town - Age of husband, 26 - Age of wife,
    25 - Both are Single - Husband was born in Jefferson County, West
    Virginia - Wife was born in State of Ohio - Both reside in Jefferson
    County, West Virginia.

Baer, Charles S. and Ruth Ann Fink (3) -   August 11, 1883
    Place of marriage, Kabletown - Age of husband, 25 - Age of wife,
    23 - Both are Single - Both were born in Jefferson County, West
    Virginia - Both reside in Jefferson County, West Virginia.

Bagley, Sarah and Oscar B. Gue (3) -   July 5, 1886
    For further information see - Gue, Oscar B.

Bahl, Alexandrine M. and George D. Cummins (1). -   June 24, 1847

Bailey, Jesse E. and Alice Elizabeth Hunsicker (3) -   June 7, 1881
    Place of marriage, Charlestown - Age of husband, 23 - Age of wife,
    23 - Both are Single - Husband was born in Frederick County, State
    of Maryland - Wife was born in Jefferson County, West Virginia -
    Both reside in Jefferson County, West Virginia.

Bailey, John and F. E. Custer (3) -   November 11, 1868
    Place of marriage, Jefferson County - Age of husband, 32 - Age of
    wife, 18 - Both are Single - Husband was born in Virginia - Wife was
    born in Jefferson County - Husband resides in Jefferson County -
    Wife resides in West Virginia - Husband's parents are Thomas and
    Catherine - Wife's parents are Reuben and Ann E. - Occupation of
    husband is Farmer.

Bailey, Major (cold.) Phebe Brown (3) -   January 7, 1875
    Place of marriage, Charles Town - Age of husband, 74 - Age of wife,
    67 - Husband is a Widower - Wife is a Widow - Both were born in
    Jefferson County, West Virginia - Both reside in Jefferson County,
    West Virginia.

Bailey, Mary (cold.) James Cook (3) -   February 16, 1888
    For further information see - Cook, James.

Bain, Carrie V. and Charles J. Ramsburg (3) -   February 5, 1890
    For further information see - Ramsburg, Charles J.

Bain, Robert M. and Martha Ellen McDaniel (2) -   (L) November 13, 1850
    (Sebastian McDaniel sworn.)

Bain, Robert M. and Martha E. McDaniel (1) -   November 14, 1850

Baker, Aaron F. and Elizabeth A. Hess (2) -   (L) October 11, 1858

Baker, Adelaide T. and Leander Burgess (2) -   (L) July 14, 1858

Baker, Alice L. and W. B. Dunlap (3) -   October 15, 1890
    For further information see - Dunlap, W. B.

Baker, Ann C. and Archibald Shearer (1) -   May 11, 1826

Baker, Ann C. and Thomas W. Gilmore (1) -   May 23, 1826

Baker, Ann Katharine and George Glass (3) -   September 27, 1881
    For further information see - Glass, George.

Baker, Corbin and Mary Ann Davis (1) -   August 4, 1833

Baker, Corbina C. and Lewis Neall (1) -   May 12, 1818

Baker, Daniel and Mary C. M. Ridenour (3) -   October 27, 1885
    Place of marriage, Harpers Ferry - Age of husband, 65 - Age of wife,
    55 - Husband is a Widower - Wife is a Widow - Husband was born at
    Hagerstown, Maryland - Wife was born in Jefferson County, West
    Virginia - Both reside in Washington County, Maryland.

Baker, Eleanor and John Hinkle (1) -   May 2, 1820

Baker, Elizabeth B. and Dennis O. Lauglin (1) -   March 7, 1816

Baker, Ellen Morrow and Baker Tapscott (1) -   January 20, 1824

Baker, Eugene and Anna M. Wiltshire (2) -   (L) April 1, 1859

Baker, Henry C. and Anna Laura Dunlap (3) -   October 19, 1887
    Place of marriage, Charlestown - Age of husband, 24 - Age of wife, 22 - Both are Single - Husband was born in Carroll County, Maryland - Wife was born in Pennsylvania - Both reside in Jefferson County, West Virginia.

Baker, Lewis Jackson and Mary E. Smith (3) -   December 30, 1871
    Place of marriage, Jefferson County, West Virginia - Age of husband, 24 - Age of wife, 23 - Both are Single - Both were born in Virginia - Both reside in Jefferson County - Husband's parents are John and Catherine - Wife's parents are James and Ruth - Occupation of husband is Engineer.

Baker, Lydia (3) -
    For further information see - Mitchell, Lewis.

Baker, Lydia and Edmund Robinson (3) -   December, 1866
    For further information see - Robinson, Edmund.

Baker, Lydia (colored) Horace Robinson (3) -   June 5, 1870
    For further information see - Robinson, Horace.

Baker, Mary and Nathaniel Windel (3) -   September 15, 1875
    For further information see - Windel, Nathaniel.

Baker, Nathaniel C. and Isabella Pennington (1) -   August 30, 1841

Baker, Peter and Mary A. Gruber (2) -   (L) November 14, 1860

Baker, T. M. and Mary Whittington (3) -   October 29, 1890
    Place of marriage, Charlestown - Age of husband, 21 - Age of wife, 22 - Both are Single - Husband was born in Frederick County, Maryland - Wife was born in Jefferson County, West Virginia - Both reside in Jefferson County, West Virginia.

Balch, Emily A. and George W. Oram (3) -   June 23, 1888
    For further information see - Oram, George W.

Balch, George B. and Ann Maria Beall (1) -   February 19, 1829

Baldwin, Jane F. and John J. Hicks (2) -   (L) December 19, 1860

Baldwin, Lutie and Benjamin Hartzell (3) -   January 31, 1878
    For further information see - Hartzell, Benjamin.

Baldwin, Sarah Ann and William J. Cox (2) -   (L) March 25, 1853

Baldwin, Sarah A. and William J. Cox (1) -   March 25, 1853

Bales, Jefferson F. and Ann Maria Rust (2) -   (L) November 17, 1851

Bales, Jefferson and Ann Maria Rust (1) -   November 18, 1851

Ballenger, Benjamin and Mary Catherine Stewart (3) - September 15, 1875
Place of marriage, County - Age of husband, 25 - Age of wife, 18 -
Both are Single - Husband was born in Loudoun County, Virginia -
Wife was born in Jefferson County, West Virginia - Both reside in
Jefferson County, West Virginia. (Consent of bride's father in
person.)

Ballenger, Oscar and Lucy Catherine Stewart (3) - January 14, 1881
Place of marriage, Charlestown - Age of husband, 23 - Age of wife,
21 - Both are Single - Husband was born in Loudoun County,
Virginia - Wife was born in Jefferson County, West Virginia - Both
reside in Jefferson County, West Virginia.

Baltimore, Frank (cold.) Sally Russell (3) - June 11, 1887
Place of marriage, Charlestown - Age of husband, 23 - Age of wife,
24 - Both are Single - Both were born in Jefferson County, West
Virginia - Both reside in Jefferson County, West Virginia.

Baltimore, Lewis (cold.) Sarah Ann Crawford (3) - March 27, 1889
Place of marriage, Charlestown - Age of husband, 29 - Age of wife,
24 - Both are Single - Both were born in Virginia - Husband resides
in Clarke County, Virginia - Wife resides in Jefferson County, West
Virginia.

Bane, Christian and Hannah Coal (1) - January 9, 1828

Bane, Christiana and William Melvin (3) - December 8, 1868
For further information see - Melvin, William.

Bane, Elizabeth J. and Tobias Hendricks (3) - December 8, 1875
For further information see - Hendricks, Tobias.

Bane, Fanny B. and Thomas O. Link (3) - December 7, 1880
For further information see - Link, Thomas O.

Bane, Garrett W. and Sarah Elizabeth Grubb (3) - November 4, 1875
Place of marriage, near Duffields - Age of husband, 46 - Age of
wife, 27 - Husband is a Widower - Wife is Single - Husband was born
in Jefferson County, West Virginia - Wife was born in Loudoun
County, Virginia - Both reside in Jefferson County, West Virginia.

Bane, Georgiana and Charles J. Ramey (3) - October 27, 1881
For further information see - Ramey, Charles J.

Bane, Harry F. and Bessie W. Conklyn (3) - January 8, 1889
Place of marriage, Bride's Residence - Age of husband, 28 - Age of
wife, 20 - Both are Single - Both were born in Jefferson County,
West Virginia - Both reside in Jefferson County, West Virginia.
(Consent of bride's father in person.)

Bane, James W. and Arabella Byers (3) - April 16, 1885
Place of marriage, Shepherdstown - Age of husband, 30 - Age of wife,
25 - Both are Single - Husband was born in Jefferson County - Wife
was born in Jefferson County, West Virginia - Both reside in
Jefferson County, West Virginia.

Bane, Sally H. and James A. Ronemous (3) - April 25, 1878
For further information see - Ronemous, James A.

Bane, Snyder and Bessie P. Conley (3) - May 29, 1890
Place of marriage, Brown's Crossing - Age of husband, 22 - Age of wife, 17 - Both are Single - Husband was born in Jefferson County, West Virginia - Wife was born at Cumberland, Maryland - Both reside in Jefferson County, West Virginia. (Consent of bride's father in writing.)

Bane, Susan E. and John W. Marshall (3) - November 21, 1866
For further information see - Marshall, John W.

Bane, Virginia B. and James M. Gordon (3) - June 1, 1882
For further information see - Gordon, James M.

Bane, William H. and Sally C. Mattox (3) - March 30, 1871
Place of marriage, Jefferson County - Age of husband, 22 - Age of wife, 21 - Both are Single - Husband was born in Jefferson County - Wife was born in Virginia - Husband resides in Jefferson County - Wife resides in Missouri - Husband's parents are James and Maria - Wife's parents are Lizzie - Occupation of husband is Farmer.

Bane, Zephaniah and Marietta Sheetz (2) - (L) December 18, 1854

Bane, Zephaniah and Lena Belle Watson (3) - December 20, 1888
Place of marriage, Leetown - Age of husband, 24 - Age of wife, 22 - Both are Single - Both were born in Jefferson County, West Virginia - Both reside in Jefferson County, West Virginia.

Baney, J. A. (bride) and L. F. Slifer (3) - December 9, 1867
For further information see - Slifer, L. F.

Baney, J. J. and _____ Feagans (bride) (3) - September 26, 1871
Place of marriage, Jefferson County - Age of husband, 22 - Age of wife, 25 - Both are Single - Both were born in Virginia - Husband resides in Jefferson - Wife resides in West Virginia - Husband's parents are Thadus and Susan - Wife's parents are Cylas and Sarah - Occupation of husband is Miller.

Banick, Mary A. and Samuel H. Griffith (2) - (L) February 21, 1852

Banks, George W. and Mary I. Tanner (3) - August 26, 1889
Place of marriage, Shepherdstown - Age of husband, 34 - Age of wife, 30 - Both are Single - Both were born in Jefferson County, West Virginia - Both reside in Jefferson County, West Virginia.

Banks, Robert T. and Annie L. Bowers (3) - March 9, 1887
Place of marriage, Shepherdstown - Age of husband, 27 - Age of wife, 25 - Both are Single - Both were born in Jefferson County, West Virginia - Both reside in Jefferson County, West Virginia.

Banks, Susanna and Daniel M. Koontz (3) - March 4, 1890
For further information see - Koontz, Daniel M.

Banks, Victoria and William Davis (3) - April 27, 1869
For further information see - Davis, William.

Banks, Washington and Martha James (2) - (L) June 19, 1854
(D. W. Cook says her father agrees to the match.)

Banton, William and Sary Lindsay (1) - February 29, 1816

Barber, Edmond and Cressey Webb (1) - February 4, 1819

Barbour, Alfred M. and Kate A. Daniel (2) - (L) January 4, 1858

Barbre, Martha C. and C. C. Baughman (3) - January 23, 1884
   For further information see - Baughman, C. C.

Barey, George and Catherine Hyser (1) - April 7, 1825

Bargason, William Henry (cold.) Fanny Williams (3) - May 20, 1886
   Place of marriage, Summit Point - Age of husband, 30 - Age of wife,
   19 - Both are Single - Both were born in Jefferson County, West
   Virginia - Both reside in Jefferson County, West Virginia.
   (Bride has neither father nor mother.)

Baringer, Charles F. and Ann Elizabeth Chisohm (2) - (L) April 14, 1856

Baringer, Charles F. and Mary Louisa Glasford (2) - (L) April 16, 1860

Barlow, Anne and Robert Orr (1) - July 17, 1843

Barnard, C. R. and Henry N. Gittings (2) - (L) May 31, 1861
   For further information see - Gittings, Henry N.

Barnbent, Mary Ann and Henry Buckles (1) - April 18, 1844

Barnes, Adial P. and Lillie B. Glenn (3) - June 6, 1883
   Place of marriage, Charlestown - Age of husband, 32 - Age of wife,
   20 - Both are Single - Husband was born in Worcester County,
   Maryland - Wife was born in Jefferson County, West Virginia -
   Husband resides in Worcester County, Maryland - Wife resides in
   Jefferson County, West Virginia. (Consent of bride's father in
   person.)

Barnes, Elizabeth G. and Joseph A. Raum (2) - (L) September 6, 1860

Barnes, Lucy J. and John V. Shaull (2) - (L) September 21, 1859

Barnes, Mildred S. and Thomas Jarmey (3) - March 23, 1881
   For further information see - Jarmey, Thomas.

Barnes, Nathan Norval and Annie Isler (3) - December 22, 1880
   Place of marriage, Gerardstown, Berkeley County - Age of husband,
   22 - Age of wife, 19 - Both are Single - Both were born in Jefferson
   County, West Virginia - Both reside in Jefferson County, West
   Virginia. (Consent of bride's mother in writing.)

Barnes, Ruth Ann and Jacob Picking (1) - December 15, 1836

Barnett, Martha and Michael Shue (1) - July 30, 1825

Barnhart, Catharine Ann and John D. Bateman (2) - (L) December 18, 1852

Barnhart, Charles L. and Mollie E. Ronemous (3) - December 15, 1874
   Place of marriage, Duffields - Age of husband, 26 - Age of wife,
   23 - Both are Single - Both were born in Jefferson County, West
   Virginia - Both reside in Jefferson County, West Virginia.

Barnhart, James E. and Mary E. Case (3) - February 3, 1881
    Place of marriage, Shepherdstown - Age of husband, 34 - Age of wife,
    30 - Both are Single - Husband was born in Jefferson County, West
    Virginia - Wife was born at Staunton, Virginia - Both reside in
    Jefferson County, West Virginia.

Barnhart, L. A. and M. Roberts (bride) (3) - March 26, 1868
    Place of marriage, Jefferson County - Age of husband, 35 - Age of
    wife, 35 - Husband is Single - Wife is a Widow - Husband was born in
    Frederick County - Wife was born in Georgia - Both reside in
    Jefferson - Occupation of husband is Farmer.

Barnhart, Margaret and Jacob Hout (1) - March 22, 1820

Barnhart, Mary Catharine and John Samuel Feaman (2) - (L) October 11, 1854

Barnhart, Samuel D. and Annie E. Waters (3) - January 19, 1881
    Place of marriage, Shepherdstown - Age of husband, 30 - Age of wife,
    26 - Both are Single - Both were born in Jefferson County, West
    Virginia - Both reside in Jefferson County, West Virginia.

Barns, Alcinda M. and Charles C. Cochran (2) - (L) May 7, 1855

Barns, M. F. and James D. Wigginton (3) - March 31, 1875
    For further information see - Wigginton, James D.

Barns, Nathan and Mary H. Grantham (1) - January 31, 1837

Baroff, R. M. and Alice Winebrenner (3) - December 19, 1872
    Place of marriage, Jefferson County, West Virginia - Age of husband,
    22 - Age of wife, 20 - Both are Single - Both were born in
    Virginia - Both reside in Virginia - Husband's parents are Samuel
    and Hannah - Wife's parents are Lewis W. and Mary - Occupation of
    husband is Farmer. (Father's consent.)

Baron, Alexander and Mary Elizabeth Earnest (2) - (L) February 28, 1852

Barr, Agnes and Bushrod Stewart (3) - December 31, 1884
    For further information see - Stewart, Bushrod.

Barr, Albert D. and Mary S. Spotts (3) - May 23, 1867
    Place of marriage, Charlestown - Age of husband, 22 - Age of wife,
    21 - Both are Single - Husband was born at Hollidaysburg,
    Pennsylvania - Wife was born at Charles Town, Virginia - Both reside
    at Charles Town - Husband's parents are Samuel T. and Charlott S.
    Barr - Wife's parents are George W. and Mary S. Spotts - Occupation
    of husband is Printer.

Barr, Clara A. and James O. B. Fellers (3) - November 7, 1882
    For further information see - Fellers, James O. B.

Barr, Lydia and William Furr (3) - March 20, 1888
    For further information see - Furr, William.

Barrett, Amanda J. and John McGolarick (3) - June 21, 1870
    For further information see - McGolarick, John.

Barrett, Charles and Elizabeth Wimmer (1) - July 4, 1822

Barrett, Charles W. and Annie E. Alban (3) - March 13, 1889
    Place of marriage, Charlestown - Age of husband, 42 - Age of wife,
    18 - Husband is a Widower - Wife is Single - Husband was born in
    Jefferson County, West Virginia - Wife was born in Clarke County,
    Virginia - Both reside in Jefferson County, West Virginia -
    (Consent of bride's father in person.)

Barrett, Daniel S. and Sarah Jane Brittain (2) - (L) December 29, 1856

Barrett, Ella and James Leech (3) - September 25, 1890
    For further information see - Leech, James.

Barrett, George C. and Martha Ellen Bowers (3) - March 20, 1879
    Place of marriage, Shepherdstown - Age of husband, 26 - Age of wife,
    22 - Both are Single - Husband was born in Berkeley County, West
    Virginia - Wife was born in Jefferson County - Both reside in
    Jefferson County, West Virginia.

Barrett, Jane and John H. Wilt (3) - April 19, 1882
    For further information see - Wilt, John H.

Barrett, Joseph W. and Mary M. Bowers (3) - January 19, 1881
    Place of marriage, Harpers Ferry - Age of husband, 23 - Age of wife,
    24 - Both are Single - Both were born in Jefferson County, West
    Virginia - Both reside in Jefferson County, West Virginia.

Barrett, Nora Mason and Edward Jones (3) - August 28, 1879
    For further information see - Jones, Edward.

Barrett, Rebecca Jane and Samuel Dooley (2) - (L) May 21, 1856

Barrett, Samuel W. and Catharine R. Whittington (2) - (L) December 24, 1858

Barringer, James N. and Lucinda Jane Shirley (2) - (L) December 9, 1857

Barron, Alexander and Mary Elizabeth Earnest (1) - March 5, 1852

Barron, Alexander and Mary E. Oden (3) - November 13, 1866
    Place of marriage, Residence of Thomas Oden - Age of husband, 41 -
    Age of wife, 24 - Husband is a Widower - Wife is Single - Husband
    was born in Fauquier County, Virginia - Wife was born in Jefferson
    County, West Virginia - Both reside in Jefferson County, West
    Virginia - Husband's parents are Thomas W. and Ann Barron - Wife's
    parents are Thomas and Matilda Oden - Occupation of husband is
    Farmer.

Barron, Annie M. and John Keller (3) - January 4, 1866
    For further information see - Keller, John.

Barron, Jane Frances and John A. Manuel (2) - (L) December 26, 1859

Barron, Walter and Mary E. Howell (3) - August 24, 1881
    Place of marriage, Charlestown - Age of husband, 22 - Age of wife,
    21 - Both are Single - Both were born in Jefferson County, West
    Virginia - Both reside in Jefferson County, West Virginia.

Barrow, Alice and James Kirby (3) - April 16, 1879
    For further information see - Kirby, James.

Barrow, Charles M. and Mrs. Emma Jones (3) -   October 13, 1885
   Place of marriage, near Leetown - Age of husband, 42 - Age of wife,
   33 - Husband is Single - Wife is a Widow - Both were born in
   Frederick County, Virginia - Both reside in Jefferson County.

Barrow, George and Angeline Pier (3) -   May 29, 1866
   Place of marriage, C. Barrel's in Jefferson County - Age of husband,
   21 - Age of wife, 22 - Both are Single - Wife was born in Shenandoah
   County, Virginia - Husband resides in Clarke County, Virginia -
   Wife resides in Jefferson County, West Virginia - Wife's parents are
   John and Mary Pier - Occupation of husband is Laborer.

Barrow, Roxillanna and Thomas Wamix (3) -   February 1, 1866
   For further information see - Wamix, Thomas.

Bartholomes, Thuiscan and Mary E. Keller (2) -   (L) November 17, 1859

Bartle, Alice V. and J. William Rodrick (3) -   November 22, 1888
   For further information see - Rodrick, J. William

Bartlett, John Perkins and Emma M. Whitfield Swallow (3) -   October 3, 1877
   Place of marriage, Charlestown - Age of husband, 29 - Age of wife,
   23 - Both are Single - Husband was born in New York - Wife was born
   at City of London, England - Husband resides in State of Virginia -
   Wife resides in Jefferson County, West Virginia. (Send
   certificate of marriage to Alexanderia, Arlington County, Virginia.
   50¢ paid.)

Bartlett, Joseph C. and Eleanor A. Worthington (2) -   (L) May 19, 1860

Bascue, James S. and Martha Penwell (3) -   April 26, 1872
   Place of marriage, Jefferson County - Age of husband, 56 - Age of
   wife, 38 - Husband is a Widower - Wife is a Widow - Husband was born
   in Virginia - Wife was born in Pennsylvania - Husband resides in
   Virginia - Wife resides in West Virginia - Husband's parents are
   Charles and Rachel - Wife's parents are John - Occupation of husband
   is Carpenter.

Basem, Charles and Rachel Buckles (1) -   January 16, 1816

Baske, Jemima and John Duke (1) -   October 22, 1805

Bass, Bettie and Henry D. Craddock (3) -   March 19, 1890
   For further information see - Craddock, Henry D.

Bast, Fanny and George W. Spence (3) -   May 3, 1882
   For further information see - Spence, George W.

Bast, Margaret A. and Jacob Underdonk (3) -   December 10, 1883
   For further information see - Underdonk, Jacob.

Bateman, Annie (cold.) George Edward Newman (3) -   September 30, 1876
   For further information see - Newman, George Edward.

Bateman, Benjamin and Elizabeth C. Brady (2) -   (L) August 28, 1857

Bateman, Francis and Hannah Ann Myers (2) -   (L) June 18, 1856

Bateman, James (cold.) Nancy Ann Nourse (2) -   (L) May 5, 1852

Bateman, Jane (cold.) John Pierce (2) - (L) August 15, 1855

Bateman, Jessee and Mary Crawford (1) - January 23, 1825

Bateman, John D. and Catharine Ann Barnhart (2) - (L) December 18, 1852

Bateman, Josiah and Mary Hiett (1) - July 19, 1827

Bateman, Mary (free cold.) Samuel Henry Johnson (2) - (L) March 6, 1858

Bateman, Mary and Heaton Myers (2) - (L) September 28, 1858

Bateman, Mary J. and Michael A. Marquest (2) - (L) December 6, 1860

Bateman, Rachael and Rodney Mahony (3) - August 7, 1870
For further information see - Mahony, Rodney.

Bateman, Sarah Ann and Solomon Flemming (1) - March 14, 1833

Bates, Lucy H. and A. A. Taliaferro (3) - April 22, 1886
For further information see - Taliaferro, A. A.

Bates, Mary and T. M. Macoughtry (3) - May 13, 1874
For further information see - Macoughtry, T. M.

Bates, Solomon O. and Margaret A. Shirley (1) - December 19, 1849

Bates, William G. and Susan R. Smith (3) - December 17, 1885
Place of marriage, Middleway - Age of husband, 26 - Age of wife,
25 - Both are Single - Both were born in Jefferson County, West
Virginia - Both reside in Jefferson County, West Virginia.

Baughman, C. C. and Martha C. Barbre (3) - January 23, 1884
Place of marriage, Charlestown - Age of husband, 25 - Age of wife,
21 - Both are Single - Husband was born in State of Maryland - Wife
was born in State of Illinois - Husband resides in State of
Illinois - Wife resides in Jefferson County, West Virginia.

Baum, Aaron and Jennie Zimmerman (3) - January 6, 1886
Place of marriage, Charlestown - Age of husband, 30 - Age of wife,
21 - Both are Single - Husband was born in State of Pennsylvania -
Wife was born in Berkeley County, West Virginia - Husband resides in
Pennsylvania - Wife resides in Jefferson County, West Virginia.

Baumgardner, Mary C. and James W. Ott (3) - January 25, 1887
For further information see - Ott, James W.

Bauserman, J. M. and Maud E. VanHorn (3) - October 2, 1890
Place of marriage, Shepherdstown - Age of husband, 25 - Age of wife,
23 - Both are Single - Husband was born in Shenandoah County,
Virginia - Husband resides in Shenandoah County, Virginia - Wife
resides in Jefferson County, West Virginia.

Baxley, Almira Virginia and Samuel R. Merchant (3) - April 22, 1873
For further information see - Merchant, Samuel R.

Baxley, Claude and M. Salina Williams (3) - September 5, 1867
    Place of marriage, Jefferson County - Age of husband, 27 - Age of
    wife, 23 - Both are Single - Husband was born at Baltimore - Wife
    was born in Jefferson County, Virginia - Husband resides at
    Baltimore, Maryland - Wife resides in Jefferson County, West
    Virginia - Husband's parents are H. W. and A. - Wife's parents are
    J. J. and Helen - Occupation of husband is Professor and Physician.

Baxter, Rebecca and George Freeman (3) - February 7, 1867
    For further information see - Freeman, George.

Baycroft, Elijah and Catherine Kist (1) - 1825

Bayless, John and Sarah Shadwell (1) - 1827

Baylis, John and Rachael Wortman (1) - 1813

Baylis, John and Sarah Karman (1) - June 16, 1816

Baylis, Lucinda and William Gannon (1) - October 29, 1814

Bayliss, Jane L. and Joseph R. Morrow (2) - (L) November 5, 1857

Bayliss, John H. and Sarah Potts (3) - May 23, 1872
    Place of marriage, Jefferson County - Age of husband, 49 - Age of
    wife, 30 - Husband is a Widower - Wife is a Widow - Husband was born
    in Virginia - Wife was born in Maryland - Both reside in West
    Virginia - Husband's parents are John and Sarah - Occupation of
    husband is Bricklayer.

Bayliss, Sarah J. and John T. Riley (2) - (L) October 8, 1853

Bayliss, Thomas and Mary Margaret Ann Morrow (1) - September 1, 1835

Baylor, Charles E. and Mary N. Simmons (3) - December 17, 1890
    Place of marriage, Charlestown - Age of husband, 34 - Age of wife,
    21 - Both are Single - Both were born in Jefferson County, West
    Virginia - Both reside in Jefferson County, West Virginia.

Baylor, Hattie (cold.) Moton Cole (3) - November 5, 1885
    For further information see - Cole, Moton.

Baylor, Henry B. and Annie Shirley (3) - October 27, 1880
    Place of marriage, Middleway - Age of husband, 29 - Age of wife,
    24 - Both are Single - Both were born in Jefferson County, West
    Virginia - Both reside in Jefferson County, West Virginia.

Baylor, Julia M. and Robert V. Shirley (2) - (L) October 23, 1857

Baylor, M. S. (bride) and C. M. Aisquith (3) - December 3, 1867
    For further information see - Aisquith, C. M.

Baylor, Martha Todd and John McFarlane (1) - December 5, 1820

Baylor, Moses (cold.) Florence Brunswick (3) - December 11, 1877
    Place of marriage, Middleway - Age of husband, 48 - Age of wife,
    21 - Husband is a Widower - Wife is Single - Both were born in
    Jefferson County, West Virginia - Both reside in Jefferson County,
    West Virginia.

Baylor, Nancy (cold.) Frederick Eskard (3) -   June 23, 1874
    For further information see - Eskard, Frederick.

Baylor, Mrs. R. R. and Edward Aisquith (3) -   May 2, 1866
    For further information see - Aisquith, Edward.

Baylor, Richard C. and Kate K. Likens (2) -   (L) July 22, 1863
    Place of marriage, Charlestown - Age of husband, 24 years - Age of
    wife, 18 years - Both are Single - Husband was born in Jefferson
    County, Virginia - Wife was born in Mississippi - Both reside in
    Jefferson County - Names of husband's parents are Robert W. and
    Mary Baylor - Names of wife's parents are Thomas J. and Myra
    Likens - Occupation of husband is Soldier in Confederate Army -
    License issued, July 22, 1863 - Thomas A. Moore, Clerk.

Baylor, T. G. and S. M. Beckwith (bride) (3) -   January 6, 1881
    Place of marriage, near Charlestown - Age of husband, 32 - Age of
    wife, 29 - Both are Single - Both were born in Jefferson County,
    West Virginia - Both reside in Jefferson County, West Virginia.

Beahm, Henry and Julia Ann Lock (1) -   December 18, 1833

Beal, Albert and Mary Snook (1) -   March 28, 1829

Beal, Erasmus and Eliza Frago (1) -   1825

Beale, Clara B. and Henry V. Daniels (2) -   (L) May 14, 1863
    For further information see - Daniels, Henry V.

Beale, M. D. and William S. Cochran (3) -   January 31, 1869
    For further information see - Cochran, William S.

Beall, Ann Maria and George B. Balch (1) -   February 19, 1829

Beall, Bettie and Richard Henderson (3) -   April 26, 1881
    For further information see - Henderson, Richard.

Beall, Elizabeth and Grifin Taylor (1) -   January 16, 1823

Beall, George B. and Janet Yates (1) -   October 1826

Beall, Harriet S. and David Nicholls (1) -   July 30, 1815

Beall, Harriett L. and Robert Burke (1) -   September 17, 1833

Beall, Helen Margaret and Mann R. Page (1) -   October 24, 1825

Beall, Helen V. and Ebenezer Vickers (2) -   (L) November 7, 1857

Beall, Herzzena B. and Thomas M. Laidley (2) -   (L) April 3, 1857

Beall, M. Louisa and J. A. Davenport (3) -   August 18, 1880
    For further information see - Davenport, J. A.

Beall, Matilda B. and Thomas B. Dunn (1) -   October 11, 1827

Beall, Mary E. and W. H. Spangler (3) -   November 15, 1873
    For further information see - Spangler, W. H.

Beall, Mary J. and C. Frank Gallaher (3) -   June 28, 1871
    For further information see - Gallaher, C. Frank.

Beall, Olin and F. V. Glenn (3) -   October 24, 1882
    Place of marriage, Charlestown - Age of husband, 27 - Age of wife,
    21 - Both are Single - Husband was born in Maryland - Wife was born
    in Jefferson County, West Virginia - Both reside in Jefferson
    County, West Virginia.

Beall, Sarah A. and Gideon Leicingring (3) -   April 24, 1866
    For further information see - Leicingring, Gideon.

Beall, Thomas W. and Julia A. Holt (2) -   (L) July 23, 1853

Beall, Thomas W. and Julia A. Holt (1) -   July 28, 1853

Beall, William D. and Jane H. Frame (1) -   August 19, 1834

Beall, Zuriah and Edmund Wagner (1) -   July 8, 1810

Bealle, Annie O. and David E. Henderson (3) -   December 1, 1870
    For further information see - Henderson, David E.

Beard, Rebeca and Arch R. Brown (3) -   January 1, 1889
    For further information see - Brown, Arch R.

Beard, Thomas H. and Henrietta Bingham (2) -   (L) December 17, 1857

Bearley, William and Eliza Rockenbaugh (1) -   March 5, 1818

Bearman, William (cold.) Charlotte McCan (3) -   April 23, 1874
    Place of marriage, Shepherdstown - Age of husband, 27 - Age of wife,
    21 - Both are Single - Both were born in Jefferson County, West
    Virginia - Both reside in Jefferson County, West Virginia.

Beavers, Alexander and Mrs. Phebe Ramsburg (3) -   August 31, 1875
    Place of marriage, near Lee Town - Age of husband, 50 - Age of wife,
    26 - Husband is a Widower - Wife is a Widow - Husband was born in
    Prince William County, Virginia - Wife was born in Jefferson County,
    West Virginia - Both reside in Jefferson County, West Virginia.

Beavers, Ella E. V. and William J. Cook (3) -   December 24, 1890
    For further information see - Cook, William J.

Beavers, Joseph B. and Patsie J. L. Moler (3) -   December 26, 1865
    Place of marriage, near Unionville - Age of husband, 30 - Age of
    wife, 22 - Both are Single - Husband was born in Clarke County,
    Virginia - Wife was born in Jefferson County, West Virginia -
    Husband resides in Clarke County, Virginia - Wife resides in
    Jefferson County, West Virginia - Husband's parents are Abraham and
    Pleasant Beavers - Wife's parents are Charles and Jane Margaret
    Moler - Occupation of husband is, Farmer.

Beck, C. A. and Ella D. Taylor (3) -   January 5, 1881
    Place of marriage, Charlestown - Age of husband, 22 - Age of wife,
    20 - Both are Single - Husband born in State of Ohio - Wife was
    born in Jefferson County, West Virginia - Both reside in Jefferson
    County, West Virginia. (Consent of bride's father in writing.)

Beck, C. L. and Mary B. Custer (3) - June 20, 1883
   Place of marriage, Summit Point - Age of husband, 28 - Age of wife,
   22 - Both are Single - Husband was born in Ohio - Wife was born in
   Jefferson County, West Virginia - Husband resides in Jefferson
   County - Wife resides in Jefferson County, West Virginia.

Beck, David and Mary E. Ruhl (3) - November 25, 1869
   Place of marriage, Jefferson County - Age of husband, 22 - Age of
   wife, 18 - Husband was born at Harpers Ferry - Wife was born in
   Jefferson County - Both reside in Jefferson County. (In writing
   parents consent.)

Beck, Maggie and Shepherd Gatrell (3) - March 4, 1873
   For further information see - Gatrell, Shepherd.

Beckenbaugh, John M. and Nannie C. Douglas (3) - November 19, 1868
   Place of marriage, Jefferson County - Age of husband, 29 - Age of
   wife, 24 - Both are Single - Husband was born in Frederick County,
   Maryland - Wife was born in Washington County, Maryland - Husband
   resides at Sharpsburg, Maryland - Wife resides in Washington County,
   Maryland - Husband's parents are George and Martha - Wife's parents
   are Robert and Helena - Occupation of husband is Physician.

Beckham, Anna Amelia and James L. Hooff (2) - (L) April 11, 1851

Beckham, Ann Amelia and James L. Hooff (1) - April 15, 1851

Beckham, Armstead and Elenor Lyle (1) - October 23, 1814

Beckham, Armsted and Jane Frame (1) - January 22, 1818

Beckham, Camp. and Martha B. Stephenson (1) - February 27, 1823

Beckham, Fountaine and Ann Stephenson (1) - 1825

Beckham, H. C. and Ann A. Wright (3) - October 7, 1868
   Place of marriage, Jefferson County - Age of husband, 27 - Age of
   wife, 26 - Both are Single - Husband was born in Virginia - Wife was
   born in West Virginia - Both reside in Jefferson County - Husband's
   parents are C. C. and Mary C. - Wife's parents are Mary - Occupation
   of husband is Physician.

Beckwith, R. B. and Sally E. Hite (1) - September 23, 1813

Beckwith, S. M. (bride) and T. G. Baylor (3) - January 6, 1881
   For further information see - Baylor, T. G.

Becraft, Nathaniel W. and Eliza Jane Busey (2) - (L) November 24, 1851

Becraft, Nathaniel and Eliza Jane Busy (1) - November 25, 1851

Bedinger, E. W. and Anna M. Billmyer (3) - March 16, 1869
   Place of marriage, Jefferson County - Age of husband, 38 - Age of
   wife, 24 - Husband is a Widower - Wife is Single - Husband was born
   in Kentucky - Wife was born in Jefferson County - Both reside in
   Jefferson County - Husband's parents are B. and S. E. Bedinger -
   Wife's parents are C. and M. F. D. Billmyer - Occupation of husband
   is Minister of the Gospel.

Bedinger, Everett W. and Sally E. Lucas (2) - (L) May 31, 1852

Bedinger, M. R. and Seth B. Foster (1) - December 11, 1808

Bedinger, Solomon S. and Mildred B. Washington (2) - (L) February 8, 1854

Bedinger, Susan Peyton and Frederick Ellsworth (1) - May 1826

Bedinger, Virginia Ann and William Lucas (1) - July 13, 1830

Beebe, Charles and Mary Hughes (2) - (L) December 19, 1850

Beebe, Charles and Mary Hughes (1) - December 19, 1850

Beeler, Adaline and George A. Hayden (1) - April 24, 1828

Beeler, Benjamin and Jane Wood (1) - December 31, 1807

Beeler, Fannie C. and L. M. Smith (2) - (L) April 2, 1855

Beeler, Hannah E. and William C. Byers (3) - September 1, 1881
   For further information see - Byers, William C.

Beeler, Lucretia and Johnathan McComb (1) - 1814

Beeler, Sarah C. and William A. Carter (1) - November 25, 1824

Bell, Abram and M. E. Ainsworth (3) - October 1, 1878
   Place of marriage, near Myers Town - Age of husband, 25 - Age of
   wife, 21 - Both are Single - Husband was born in Clarke County,
   Virginia - Wife was born in Jefferson County, West Virginia -
   Husband resides in Clarke County, Virginia - Wife resides in
   Jefferson County, West Virginia.

Bell, Benjamin and Milly Douglass (1) - 1813

Bell, Corbina E. and Edward Hunt (2) - (L) December 7, 1853

Bell, Eddy F. and Charles W. Brown (3) - December 22, 1881
   For further information see - Brown, Charles W.

Bell, Edward S. and Catherine Virginia Eaty (1) - June 3, 1822

Bell, Ellis M. and Lucy A. Boyer (3) - June 9, 1881
   Place of marriage, Brown's Crossing - Age of husband 22 - Age of
   wife, 18 - Both are Single - Husband was born in Clarke County,
   Virginia - Wife was born in Jefferson County, West Virginia - Both
   reside in Jefferson County, West Virginia. (Consent of bride's
   father in person.)

Bell, Francis Adam and Nancy Virginia Thompson (3) - March 2, 1885
   Place of marriage, Charlestown - Age of husband, 29 - Age of wife,
   24 - Husband is a Widower - Wife is Single - Husband was born in
   Clarke County, Virginia - Wife was born in Berkeley County, West
   Virginia - Husband resides in Clarke County, Virginia - Wife
   resides in Jefferson County, West Virginia.

Bell, Hariett L. and James R. Earnshaw (3) - May 16, 1878
   For further information see - Earnshaw, James R.

Bell, Henderson M. and Mrs. Martha V. Timberlake (3) -   October 19, 1886
   Place of marriage, Charlestown - Age of husband, 60 - Age of wife,
   37 - Husband is a Widower - Wife is a Widow - Husband was born at
   Staunton, Virginia - Wife was born in Jefferson County - Husband
   resides at Staunton, Virginia - Wife resides in Jefferson County,
   West Virginia.

Bell, Jacob Perry and Mary Ellen Lally (2) -   (L) May 18, 1852

Bell, Jacob Perry and Mary Ellen Laly (1) -   May 27, 1852

Bell, James and Rachel Bushman (1) -   July 13, 1831

Bell, John R. and Catherine Chapman (1) -   May 14, 1829

Bell, John R. and Mary V. Brown (3) -   February 29, 1876
   Place of marriage, near Kearneysville - Age of husband, 22 - Age of
   wife, 28 - Both are Single - Husband was born in Clarke County,
   Virginia - Wife was born in Berkeley County, West Virginia - Both
   reside in Jefferson County, West Virginia.

Bell, Lydia C. and John W. Swimley (2) -   (L) November 21, 1861
   For further information see - Swimley, John W.

Bell, Mary Ann and Archibald Ritchie (1) -   October 20, 1818

Bell, Mary E. and Alfred N. Pierce (2) -   (L) November 20, 1857

Bell, Polly and John Hendricks (1) -   November 15, 1804

Bellar, Ephraim S. and Sarah Reed (1) -   May 30, 1816

Bellar, Lidia and Emanuel C. F. Gibboney (1) -   August 1, 1816

Beller, Frank L. and Sarah J. Avis (nee Rowan, divorced) (3) -   May 7, 1877
   Place of marriage, Charlestown - Age of husband, 23 - Age of wife,
   28 - Husband is Single - Wife is a Widow by divorce - Both were born
   in Jefferson County, West Virginia - Both reside in Jefferson
   County, West Virginia.

Beller, Maggie Daniel and Alfred Farra Tanquary (3) -   December 28, 1886
   For further information see - Tanquary, Alfred Farra.

Bellinger, Mary and John L. Bryan (1) -   April 29, 1819

Belsterling, Deborah and Augustus M. Cridler (1) -   December 21, 1848

Belsterling, Elizabeth and Rezin Cross (1) -   May 28, 1833

Belsterling, Mary and William Nunemaker (1) -   January 6, 1825

Belts, Margaret V. and J. M. Robinson (3) -   July 25, 1865
   For further information see - Robinson, J. M.

Beltz, Alice M. and B. W. Pitzer (3) -   March 14, 1882
   For further information see - Pitzer, B. W.

Beltz, Luvena and Michael Wright (3) -   February 10, 1880
   For further information see - Wright, Michael.

Beltz, Mary E. and John P. Trussell (1) -   April 12, 1849

Beltz, Sarah M. and John Milburn (3) -   October 29, 1868
    For further information see - Milburn, John.

Beltz, Susan C. and Lawrence Wright (3) -   May 10, 1888
    For further information see - Wright, Lawrence.

Beltz, William A. and Ella R. Johnson (3) -   February 21, 1878
    Place of marriage, near Shepherdstown - Age of husband, 23 - Age of
    wife, 18 - Both are Single - Husband was born in Jefferson County,
    West Virginia - Wife was born in Preston County, Virginia - Both
    reside in Jefferson County, West Virginia. (Consent of bride's
    father in person.)

Bender, Fannie (cold.) Benjamin Dunmore (3) -   June 30, 1887
    For further information see - Dunmore, Benjamin.

Bender, Fanny H. and James P. Wintermoyer (3) -   November 14, 1878
    For further information see - Wintermoyer, James P.

Bender, John William and Emma E. Lamar (3) -   December 24, 1878
    Place of marriage, Middleway - Age of husband, 25 - Age of wife,
    25 - Both are Single - Both were born in Berkeley County, West
    Virginia - Husband resides in Berkeley County, West Virginia - Wife
    resides in Jefferson County, West Virginia.

Bender, Mary Debie and George Dunlap (3) -   June 18, 1874
    For further information see - Dunlap, George.

Bender, Sally E. and William H. Ury (3) -   May 16, 1878
    For further information see - Ury, William H.

Bener, George William (cold.) Annie Smith (3) -   December 12, 1885
    Place of marriage, Shepherdstown - Age of husband, 34 - Age of wife,
    28 - Both are Single - Both were born in Jefferson County, West
    Virginia - Both reside in Jefferson County, West Virginia.

Bener, Martha (cold.) Aaron W. Smith (3) -   November 27, 1879
    For further information see - Smith, Aaron W.

Benner, Christian and Nancy Strauls (2) -   (L) September 10, 1859

Benner, George W. and Mary Frances Conrad (3) -   December 24, 1885
    Place of marriage, Charlestown - Age of husband, 25 - Age of wife,
    24 - Both are Single - Husband was born in Pennsylvania - Wife was
    born in Jefferson County, West Virginia - Both reside in Jefferson
    County, West Virginia.

Benner, Harriet and John F. Weller (3) -   November 24, 1874
    For further information see - Weller, John F.

Benner, Henry J. and Lucy V. Grantham (3) -   March 28, 1876
    Place of marriage, Charlestown - Age of husband, 27 - Age of wife,
    18 - Both are Single - Husband was born in Frederick County,
    Virginia - Wife was born in Jefferson County, West Virginia - Both
    reside in Jefferson County, West Virginia. (Consent of bride's
    father in writing.)

Benner, James W. and Mary C. Shaull (3) -   January 11, 1870
    Age of husband, 23 - Age of wife, 21 - Husband was born in Frederick
    County, Virginia - Wife was born in Jefferson - Both reside in
    Jefferson County.

Benner, John and E. J. West (3) -   April 4, 1872
    Place of marriage, Jefferson County - Age of husband, 21 - Age of
    wife, 22 - Both are Single - Husband was born in Pennsylvania - Wife
    was born in Jefferson County, Virginia - Both reside in Jefferson
    County, West Virginia - Husband's parents are Washington and
    Catherine C. - Wife's parents are Thomas - Occupation of husband is
    Farmer.

Benner, S. Ann and George R. Ware (3) -   November 29, 1870
    For further information see - Ware, George R.

Benner, S. H. and Mary Alice Engle (3) -   September 28, 1881
    Place of marriage, Charlestown - Age of husband, 22 - Age of wife,
    21 - Both are Single - Husband was born in Pennsylvania - Wife was
    born in Jefferson County, West Virginia - Both reside in Jefferson
    County, West Virginia.

Benner, Sarah C. and Henry Toup (3) -   December 20, 1866
    For further information see - Toup, Henry.

Benner, Sarah Jane and John Cook (2) -   (L) May 1, 1858

Bennett, Alexander and Bertha M. Reynolds (3) -   November 27, 1888
    Place of marriage, Shepherdstown - Age of husband, 23 - Age of wife,
    20 - Both are Single - Husband was born in Jefferson County, West
    Virginia - Wife was born in Washington County, Maryland - Husband
    resides in Washington County, Maryland - Wife resides in Jefferson
    County, West Virginia. (Consent of bride's father in writing.)

Bennett, Betsy and William Stone (1) -   January 20, 1820

Bennett, Bunbury C. and Mary A. Painter (2) -   (L) September 26, 1860

Bennett, Catharine and William R. Jenkins (2) -   (L) (1862)
    For further information see - Jenkins, William R.

Bennett, Edward and Phebe Mendenhall (1) -   September 30, 1828

Bennett, Elizabeth and A. McIntire (1) -   January 19, 1804

Bennett, George and Ellie Cunningham (3) -   September 4, 1871
    Place of marriage, Jefferson County - Age of husband, 22 - Age of
    wife, 25 - Both are Single - Husband was born in Clarke County -
    Wife was born in Jefferson - Husband resides in Jefferson - Wife
    resides in West Virginia - Husband's parents are Peter and Phebe -
    Occupation of husband is Railroad.

Bennett, Harry (cold.) Maggie Robinson (3) -   July 31, 1884
    Place of marriage, Charlestown - Age of husband, 22 - Age of wife,
    21 - Both are Single - Husband was born at Harrisburg,
    Pennsylvania - Wife was born in Jefferson County, West Virginia -
    Both reside in Jefferson County, West Virginia.

Bennett, Hatie V. and Joseph C. Hann (3) -   October 10, 1887
    For further information see - Hann, Joseph C.

Bennett, Levi and Elizabeth Stephen (1) -   August 27, 1818

Bennett, Lucy J. and Thomas T. Chapman (3) -   April 1873
For further information see - Chapman, Thomas T.

Bennett, Mary and Robert Young (1) -   September 20, 1816

Bennett, Mason and Mary Elizabeth Michaels (2) -   (L) October 2, 1850

Bennett, Mason and Mary Elizabeth Michaels (1) -   October 4, 1850

Bennett, Nellie R. and Samuel Humrickhouse, Jr. (3) -   January 31, 1888
For further information see - Humrickhouse, Samuel, Jr.

Bennett, William A. and Bettie Campbell (3) -   October 27, 1880
Place of marriage, Charlestown - Age of husband, 28 - Age of wife,
28 - Both are Single - Husband was born in Maryland - Wife was born
in Jefferson County, West Virginia - Husband resides in Maryland -
Wife resides in Jefferson County, West Virginia.

Benson, Henrietta and John Hough (3) -   October 28, 1885
For further information see - Hough, John.

Benson, L. T. and Fannie Crawford (3) -   November 13, 1877
Place of marriage, Harpers Ferry - Age of husband, 45 - Age of wife,
40 - Husband is a Widower - Wife is Single - Husband was born in
Saint Mary County, Maryland - Wife was born in Ireland - Husband
resides in Washington County, Maryland - Wife resides in Jefferson
County, West Virginia.   (By Thomas Benson.)

Benter, G. A. and Emma L. Rau (3) -   November 11, 1875
Place of marriage, near Halltown - Age of husband, 31 - Age of wife,
18 - Both are Single - Husband was born at Wurttemberg, Germany -
Wife was born in Jefferson County, West Virginia - Husband resides
at Wheeling, West Virginia - Wife resides in Jefferson County, West
Virginia.   (Consent of bride's father in writing.)

Bentz, A. F. and Anna Bettie Anderson (3) -   October 26, 1881
Place of marriage, Bolivar - Age of husband, 30 - Age of wife, 21 -
Both are Single - Husband was born in Berkeley County, West
Virginia - Wife was born in Jefferson County, West Virginia -
Husband resides in Berkeley County, West Virginia - Wife resides in
Jefferson County, West Virginia.

Bentz, William and Ellen Homes (1) -   May 11, 1845

Berger, John and Mary Mader (2) -   (L) July 26, 1850

Berisford, Thomas and Catharine McGraven (3) -   September 29, 1868
Place of marriage, Jefferson County - Age of husband, 31 - Age of
wife, 23 - Both are Single - Husband was born in Ireland - Wife was
born in New York - Both reside in Jefferson County - Occupation of
husband is Silversmith.

Berkeley, Henry (cold.) Sarah Crawford (3) -   July 30, 1885
Place of marriage, Charlestown - Age of husband, 47 - Age of wife,
22 - Husband is a Widower - Wife is Single - Husband was born in
Louisa County, Virginia - Wife was born in Augusta County,
Virginia - Both reside in Jefferson County, West Virginia.

Berlin, Catherine and Peter J. Daylong (1) -   October 3, 1833

Berry, A. Holmes and Lucy E. Manning (3) -   October 13, 1874
    Place of marriage, Charlestown - Age of husband, 22 next December -
    Age of wife, 20 - Both are Single - Husband was born in Berkeley
    County, West Virginia -Wife was born in Jefferson County, West
    Virginia - Both reside in Jefferson County, West Virginia.
    (Consent of bride's father in person.)

Berry, Bell (cold.) Benjamin Brady (3) -   January 9, 1879
    For further information see - Brady, Benjamin.

Berry, Dinah (cold.) Peter Berryman (3) -   March 30, 1873
    For further information see - Berryman, Peter.

Berry, Drucilla and William Miller (1) -   1812

Berry, Frances and Thornton Morrison (3) -   February 2, 1874
    For further information see - Morrison, Thornton.

Berry, Frances (cold.) Thornton Morrison (3) -   February 2, 1874
    For further information see - Morrison, Thornton.

Berry, George (cold.) Rose Stevenson (3) -   December 23, 1880
    Place of marriage, Summit Point - Age of husband, 28 - Age of wife,
    19 - Both are Single - Both were born in Jefferson County, West
    Virginia - Both reside in Jefferson County, West Virginia.
    (Consent of bride's mother in writing.)

Berry, Harriet (cold.) Lewis Cross (3) -   June 18, 1885
    For further information see - Cross, Lewis.

Berry, Helen and John G. Lane (1) -   May 14, 1850

Berry, Henry and Sarah H. V. Swearingen (1) -   July 4, 1822

Berry, Jesse (cold.) Josephine Robinson (3) -   December 31, 1876
    Place of marriage, Mount Pleasant - Age of husband, 28 - Age of
    wife, 22 - Both are Single - Both were born in Jefferson County,
    West Virginia - Both reside in Jefferson County, West Virginia.

Berry, Julia (cold.) Samuel T. Wood (3) -   August 10, 1876
    For further information see - Wood, Samuel T.

Berry, Maria (cold.) Alexander Perry (3) -   February 23, 1882
    For further information see - Perry, Alexander.

Berry, Martha (cold.) Thomas Doleman (3) -   October 28, 1880
    For further information see - Doleman, Thomas.

Berry, Mary (cold.) David Taylor (3) -   June 11, 1874
    For further information see - Taylor, David.

Berry, Matilda W. and Vincent M. Butler (2) -   (L) April 21, 1853

Berry, Matilda W. and Vincent M. Butler (1) -   April 28, 1853

Berry, Mildred and James Clark (1) -   1820

Berry, Robert (colored) Jenine Williams (3) -   September 22, 1870
    Place of marriage, Jefferson County - Age of husband, 25 - Age of
    wife, 19 - Both were born in Jefferson County - Both reside in
    Jefferson County. (Mother consents.)

Berry, Rosalie T. and John C. VanWyck (2) -   (L) April 5, 1858

Berry, William and Charity Johnson (3) -   May 10, 1871
    Place of marriage, Jefferson County - Age of husband, 25 - Age of
    wife, 19 - Both are Single - Husband was born in Virginia - Wife was
    born in Jefferson County - Both reside in Jefferson County -
    Husband's parents are Adrian and Hannah - Wife's parents are Henry -
    Occupation of husband is Farmer. (Consent P.)

Berry, William (cold.) Lucy David (3) -   December 18, 1884
    Place of marriage, near Summit Point - Age of husband, 38 - Age of
    wife, 32 - Husband is a Widower - Wife is Single - Both were born in
    Jefferson County, West Virginia - Both reside in Jefferson County,
    West Virginia.

Berryman, Amelia and George Henderson (3) -   (1869)
    For further information see - Henderson, George.

Berryman, Peter (cold.) Dinah Berry (3) -   March 30, 1873
    Place of marriage, near Duffields - Age of husband, 38 - Age of
    wife, 35 - Both are Single - Both were born in Jefferson County,
    West Virginia - Both reside in Jefferson County, West Virginia -
    Husband's parents are William and Priscilla - Occupation of husband
    is Farm Hand.

Bescue, Emily C. and Jacob Tree (3) -   March 4, 1884
    For further information see. - Tree, Jacob.

Best, Betsey and John Stidman (1) -   1812

Best, Jacob S. and Mary E. Frischer (3) -   February 26, 1885
    Place of marriage, Shepherdstown - Age of husband, 27 - Age of wife,
    22 - Both are Single - Husband was born in State of Maryland - Wife
    was born in Tennessee - Both reside in Jefferson County, West
    Virginia.

Best, Mary Jane and Andrew Brantner (2) -   (L) June 20, 1857

Best, William and Mahala Near (1) -   September 16, 1828

Bestor, Maria L. and Amosa VanCamp (1) -   August 8, 1836

Betts, Margaret and Notley Dearing (1) -   July 9, 1829

Bettz, Margaret and Thomas Lane (2) -   (L) September 12, 1863
    For further information see - Lane, Thomas.

Betz, Mrs. Elizabeth and James Jackson Ritter (3) -   November 16, 1873
    For further information see - Ritter, James Jackson.

Biggs, Daniel and Elenor Cullumber (1) -   March 15, 1807

Biller, Jacob and Henrietta Rodeffer (3) -   January 8, 1873
    Place of marriage, near Summit Point - Age of husband, 23 - Age of
    wife, 22 next June - Both are Single - Both were born in Shenandoah
    County, Virginia - Both reside in Jefferson County, West Virginia -
    Husband's parents are Absolom and Barbara - Wife's parents are
    Jonathan and Mary - Occupation of husband is Farmer.

Billman, John M. and Martha Sloan (2) -   (L) September 19, 1857

Billman, Nelly K. and Frank Mater (3) -   March 27, 1883
    For further information see - Mater, Frank.

Billmyer, Anna M. and E. W. Bedinger (3) -   March 16, 1869
    For further information see - Bedinger, E. W.

Billmyer, Frank L. and Hiberna L. Snyder (3) -   April 29, 1884
    Place of marriage, Charlestown - Age of husband, 25 - Age of wife,
    21 - Both are Single - Both were born in Jefferson County, West
    Virginia - Both reside in Jefferson County, West Virginia.

Billmyer, Jeanetta W. and John C. Bridner (3) -   February 8, 1877
    For further information see - Bridner, John C.

Billmyer, Martin and Mrs. Sarah Ann Orndorff (2) -   (L) September 27, 1856

Billmyer, Robert L. and Emma A. Huyett (3) -   (1870)
    Age of husband, 27 - Age of wife, 20 - Both were born in Virginia -
    Husband resides in Berkeley County - Wife resides in Jefferson
    County.   (Father consents.)

Billmyer, Sallie and M. N. Lemen (3) -   April 24, 1878
    For further information see - Lemen, M. N.

Billmyre, John S. and Rosa Ellen Shreck (3) -   March 17, 1884
    Place of marriage, Harpers Ferry - Age of husband, 24 - Age of wife,
    19 - Both are Single - Both were born in Jefferson County, West
    Virginia - Both reside in Jefferson County, West Virginia.
    (Consent of bride's father in person.)

Billmyre, Margaret and Thomas Newton Lemon (1) -   April 7, 1827

Billups, Joseph R. and Margaret M. Rawn (3) -   October 4, 1870
    Place of marriage, Jefferson County - Age of husband, 40 - Age of
    wife, 28 - Husband was born in Virginia - Wife was born in Indiana -
    Husband resides at Baltimore - Wife resides in Jefferson County.

Bilmire, Susan and James Massey (1) -   December 27, 1832

Bilmyer, Elizabeth and Gotlib Null (1) -   April 4, 1816

Bilson, Emma and John H. Lee (2) -   (L) December 15, 1860

Bilson, Emma and John H. Lee (3) -   November 13, 1878
    For further information see - Lee, John H.

Bilson, Mary Ann and Thomas H. Percival (2) -   (L) January 21, 1852

Bilson, Mary Ann and Thomas H. Percival (1) -   January 21, 1852

41

Bilson, Sophia and G. W. Graham (3) -   June 16, 1870
    For further information see - Graham, G. W.

Bilson, William and Mary Hoffman (1) -   June 11, 1835

Bingham, Henrietta and Thomas H. Beard (2) -   (L) December 17, 1857

Bird, Mrs. Hannah V. and William C. H. French (3) -   November 25, 1875
    For further information see - French, William C. H.

Birdsell, Charles and Ann Morningstar (3) -   September 8, 1887
    Place of marriage, Charlestown - Age of husband, 56 - Age of wife,
    48 - Both are Single - Husband was born in State of Pennsylvania -
    Wife was born in Maryland - Husband resides in Jefferson County at
    present - Wife resides in Jefferson County, West Virginia at
    present.

Birkitt, Sarah Jane and William L. Hedges (2) - (L) December 18, 1862
    For further information see - Hedges, William L.

Bisber, Stetson and Harriet Shields (1) -   December 14, 1823

Bishop, Ann E. and Russell H. Dearing (1) -   July 7, 1835

Bishop, Elizabeth and John Wise (1) -   June 2, 1823

Bishop, Mrs. Hattie A. and Bernard Purcell (3) -   July 10, 1879
    For further information see - Purcell, Bernard.

Bishop, Jane R. and Jacob Shough (1) -   August 13, 1835

Bishop, Julia A. and Charles William Stolle (3) -   December 2, 1880
    For further information see - Stolle, Charles William.

Bishop, Nimrod and Sarah Bishop (2) -   (L) October 7, 1854

Bishop, Sarah and Nimrod Bishop (2) -   (L) October 7, 1854

Bissell, W. W. and Joanna Dillow (3) -   August 31, 1890
    Place of marriage, Harpers Ferry - Age of husband, 32 - Age of wife,
    22 - Both are Single - Husband was born in Pennsylvania - Wife was
    born in Ireland - Husband resides in Pennsylvania - Wife resides in
    Jefferson County, West Virginia.

Bitner, Erwin and Ida Marlatt (3) -   March 31, 1890
    Place of marriage, Shepherdstown - Age of husband, 22 - Age of wife,
    22 - Both are Single - Husband was born in Washington County,
    Maryland - Wife was born in Berkeley County, West Virginia - Both
    reside in Jefferson County, West Virginia.

Black, James and Nancy McMurran (1) -   December 21, 1820

Black, William L. and Estella Koonce (3) -   October 16, 1890
    Place of marriage, Harpers Ferry - Age of husband, 27 - Age of wife,
    21 - Both are Single - Husband was born in Bedford County,
    Pennsylvania - Wife was born in Jefferson County, West Virginia -
    Both reside in Jefferson County, West Virginia.

Blackborn, Elizabeth Strong and William Gidin (1) - January 15, 1818

Blackborne, Thomas and Mary Righly (1) - October 5, 1820

Blackburn, Anna and George Bryan (1) - May 19, 1816

Blackburn, C. and John W. Parker (3) - November 6, 1868
 For further information see - Parker, John W.

Blackburn, Elizabeth S. and Randolph Kownslar (1) - September 6, 1850

Blackburn, Fanny (cold.) James Bradford (3) - January 2, 1874
 For further information see - Bradford, James.

Blackburn, Henry and Abey Burrell (3) - December 28, 1869
 Place of marriage, Jefferson County - Age of husband, 21 - Age of
 wife, 22 - Both were born in Jefferson County - Both reside in
 Jefferson County. (Ages sworn to by Carter Roman.)

Blackburn, Louisa and James Grimes (1) - July 23, 1829

Blackburn, Maria and Charles W. Ferguson (3) - June 3, 1871
 For further information see - Ferguson, Charles W.

Blackburn, Mary Ann and Bayn Smallwood (1) - March 7, 1824

Blackburn, Thomas and Ann Hale (1) - June 10, 1826

Blackford, Eliza P. and Daniel Cockrell (2) - (L) March 12, 1855

Blackford, J. H. and Nannie Harman (3) - November 10, 1887
 Place of marriage, Duffields - Age of husband, 32 - Age of wife,
 24 - Both are Single - Husband was born in Jefferson County, West
 Virginia - Wife was born in Berkeley County, West Virginia - Both
 reside in Jefferson County, West Virginia.

Blackford, John W. and Mary L. Littleton (3) - January 14, 1874
 Place of marriage, near Leetown - Age of husband, 25 - Age of wife,
 21 - Both are Single - Husband was born in Jefferson County, West
 Virginia - Wife was born in Loudoun County, Virginia - Both reside
 in Jefferson County, West Virginia.

Blackford, Oscar J. and Emma J. Ronemous (3) - December 12, 1882
 Place of marriage, near Duffields - Age of husband, 29 - Age of
 wife, 28 - Both are Single - Both were born in Jefferson County,
 West Virginia - Husband resides in Jefferson County, West Virginia.

Blackford, Virginia Helen and Jacob H. Engle (2) - (L) May 15, 1855

Blackley, Mrs. Ann and James Croft (3) - April 1, 1875
 For further information see - Croft, James.

Blackwell, John and Rebecca Davenport (1) - February 9, 1819

Blair, Phillis (cold.) John Purndon (3) - April 2, 1885
 For further information see - Purndon, John.

Blake, Charles and Rebecca A. McCarty (1) - October 6, 1829

Blake, Charles V. and Mary A. Feagan (3) - September 24, 1868
   Place of marriage, Jefferson County - Age of husband, 28 - Age of
   wife, 24 - Both are Single - Husband was born in Jefferson County -
   Wife was born in Berkeley - Husband resides in Clarke County - Wife
   resides in Jefferson.- Husband's parents are Silas and Sarah -
   Wife's parents are Charles and Rebecca - Occupation of husband is
   Wheelwright.

Blake, Hannah T. and George E. L. Phillips (2) - (L) March 21, 1859

Blake, John A. and Margaret Ann Rust (2) - (L) July 17, 1860

Blake, Julia (cold.) James Newman (3) - August 16, 1879
   For further information see - Newman, James.

Blake, Mary and John W. Steele (2) - (L) November 21, 1850

Blake, Mary and John W. Steele (1) - November 21, 1850

Blamer, Cornelia S. and E. L. Fifer (3) - November 8, 1870
   For further information see - Fifer, E. L.

Blanchard, Adeline and James H. Holt (2) - (L) December 25, 1852

Blessing, Ida J. and Willard Morrow (3) - April 15, 1885
   For further information see. - Morrow, Willard.

Blessing, John William W. and Virginia Mason Jones (3) - December 10, 1874
   Place of marriage, Harpers Ferry - Age of husband, 21 last May - Age
   of wife, 23 last June - Both are Single - Both were born in
   Jefferson County, West Virginia - Both reside in Jefferson County,
   West Virginia.   (J. W. Butt informant.)

Blessing, Mary E. and Charles M. Grim (3) - May 13, 1873
   For further information see - Grim, Charles M.

Blinco, John and Nancy Dillow (1) - February 17, 1825

Blincoe, Frances J. and Henry C. Niswaner (2) - (L) May 19, 1860

Blincoe, Harriet Ann and Daniel Dulany (2) - (L) September 9, 1850

Blincoe, Harriet Ann and Daniel Dulany (1) - September 12, 1850

Blincoe, Joseph and Harriet Dillow (1) - August 27, 1835

Blincoe, Juliet and Samuel Kelly (2) - (L) March 16, 1855

Blockley, Anne Maria and James McCasey (2) - (L) January 18, 1865
   For further information see - McCasey, James.

Blockley, May and William Henry Brent (3) - March 28, 1877
   For further information see - Brent, William Henry.

Blue, Belle and Franklin Cartier (3) - March 18, 1869
   For further information see - Cartier, Franklin.

Blue, Elizabeth and Uriah Blue (1) - November 27, 1823

Blue, Elizabeth and Samuel Moore (1) - 1827

Blue, Helen and James Adams (3) -   December 3, 1868
    For further information see - Adams, James.

Blue, Helen and Raleigh Robinson (3) -   December 12, 1872
    For further information see - Robinson, Raleigh.

Blue, Jacob and Margaret Blue (1) -   March 1826

Blue, Jane and David Shall (1) -   March 18, 1819

Blue, John and Virginia Gorrell (3) -   March 12, 1867
    Place of marriage, Cedar Hill - Age of husband, 21 - Age of wife,
    21 - Both are Single - Husband was born in Clarke County, Virginia -
    Wife was born in Jefferson County - Both reside in Jefferson
    County, West Virginia - Husband's parents are John and Margaret
    Blue - Wife's parents are Joseph and Eliza Gorrell - Occupation of
    husband is Farmer.

Blue, Julia (free cold.) John Griffin Washington (2) -   (L) July 1, 1863
    For further information see - Washington, John Griffin.

Blue, Lydia Ann and George Whitmore (3) -   July 30, 1866
    For further information see - Whitmore, George.

Blue, M. A. (bride) and J. H. Stipe (3) -   April 7, 1868
    For further information see - Stipe, J. H.

Blue, Margaret and Edward Cross (1) -   September 12, 1822

Blue, Margaret and Jacob Blue (1) -   March 1826

Blue, Mary and Michael Blue (1) -   March 14, 1822

Blue, Mary (free Cold.) James Williams (2) -   (L) December 25, 1856

Blue, Mary (cold.) Jacob Parker (3) -   March 31, 1881
    For further information see - Parker, Jacob.

Blue, Mary C. and John A. Childs (2) -   (L) March 16, 1860

Blue, Michael and Mary Blue (1) -   March 14, 1822

Blue, Nancy and James Howard (1) -   April 10, 1821

Blue, Rachel and Abraham Roberts (1) -   1820

Blue, Richard and Eveline Lee (3) -   May 21, 1869
    Place of marriage, Jefferson County - Both were born in Jefferson
    County - Both reside in Jefferson County. (Father consents in
    writing.)

Blue, Sarah and John Rutherford (1) -   December 18, 1832

Blue, Sarah (cold.) John Harris (3) -   January 22, 1868
    For further information see - Harris, John.

Blue, Sarah (cold.) Robert Magill (3) -   March 20, 1879
    For further information see - Magill, Robert

Blue, Seaton and Julian McCann (3) - September 1, 1866
    Place of marriage, Shepherdstown - Age of husband, 24 - Age of wife,
    21 - Both are Single - Both were born in Jefferson County, West
    Virginia - Both reside at Shepherdstown, Jefferson County -
    Husband's parents are Henry and Lucie Blue - Wife's parents are
    George and Millie McCann - Occupation of husband is Laborer.

Blue, Susan (cold.) Alec Myers (3) - March 16, 1876
    For further information see - Myers, Alec.

Blue, Uriah and Elizabeth Blue (1) - November 27, 1823

Board, J. M. C. and Sarah M. Kerns (2) - (L) October 27, 1857

Board, Jacob and Elizabeth Powell (1) - August 9, 1821

Board, Mary and Joshua Clip (1) - August 22, 1824

Bobst, I. W. and Mary A. Holmes (3) - November 23, 1880
    Place of marriage, Harpers Ferry - Age of husband, 33 - Age of wife,
    17 - Both are Single - Husband was born in Burkes County,
    Pennsylvania - Wife was born in Jefferson County, West Virginia -
    Both reside in Jefferson County, West Virginia. (Consent of
    bride's father in writing.)

Bocock, Ella F. and Charles D. Price (3) - June 6, 1888
    For further information see - Price, Charles D.

Bodine, William H. and Lydia A. Wilson (3) - November 25, 1880
    Place of marriage, Shepherdstown - Age of husband, 49 - Age of wife,
    30 - Husband is a Widower - Wife is Single - Husband was born in New
    Jersey - Wife was born in Maryland - Husband resides in Clarke
    County, Virginia - Wife resides in Jefferson County, West Virginia.

Boerley, Elizabeth and C. J. Hagan (3) - September 7, 1875
    For further information see - Hagan, C. J.

Bogenson, Richard and Mary B. Johnson (3) - (1869)
    Age of husband, 24 - Age of wife, 18 - Husband was born in Jefferson
    County, West Virginia - Wife was born in Jefferson - Husband resides
    in Jefferson County - Wife resides in Jefferson County, West
    Virginia. (Father in person consents.)

Boggerson, L. (bride) and F. Brockenborro (3) - April 11, 1868
    For further information see - Brockenborro, F.

Boggess, Julia A. and John W. Roberts (2) - (L) October 19, 1860

Boggess, William and Ann West (1) - October 1, 1835

Bohn, Catherine and Lewis Heinschman (1) - August 28, 1834

Boland, Mary L. and Jackson McDonald (2) - (L) October 22, 1857

Bolden, Fanny (cold.) Isaac Murray (3) - January 7, 1879
    For further information see - Murray, Isaac.

Boley, Alexander and Jane Catharine Wilborn (2) - (L) January 28, 1854

Boley, Elizabeth and George Harrison (1) - February 8, 1825

Boley, Jacob and Hannah Chamberlin (1) -   September 11, 1828

Boley, Margaret and Robert Lemon (1) -   January 15, 1818

Boley, Nancy and Jacob Gorrell (1) -   October 14, 1819

Boley, Sarah and Leonard Sadler (1) -   March 2, 1819

Boltz, William M. and Virginia Davis Lloyd (3) -   February 25, 1879
    Place of marriage, near Ripon - Age of husband, 25 - Age of wife,
    16 - Husband is a Widower - Wife is Single - Husband was born in
    Berkeley County, West Virginia - Wife was born in Jefferson County,
    West Virginia - Husband resides in Berkeley County, West Virginia -
    Wife resides in Jefferson County, West Virginia. (Consent of
    bride's father in person.)

Boltz, William M. and Mary Isadore Gruber (3) -   March 3, 1886
    Place of marriage, near Middleway - Age of husband, 32 - Age of
    wife, 23 - Husband is a Widower - Wife is Single - Both were born in
    Berkeley County, West Virginia - Husband resides in Berkeley County,
    West Virginia - Wife resides in Jefferson County, West Virginia.

Bond, George W. and Sarah O. Laughlin (1) -   July 29, 1828

Bond, L. Montgomery, Jr. and Fannie H. Packet (3) -   August 1, 1871
    Place of marriage, Jefferson County - Age of husband, 25 - Age of
    wife, 21 - Both are Single - Husband was born at Philadelphia,
    Pennsylvania - Wife was born in Virginia - Husband resides in
    Pennsylvania - Wife resides in West Virginia - Husband's parents are
    L. M. and G. Bond, Sr. - Wife's parents are John B. and Lucie E. -
    Occupation of husband is Merchant.

Bond, Melia and George Pearl (3) -   February 3, 1867
    For further information see - Pearl, George.

Bond, Sarah and Michael Gompf (1) -   September 2, 1832

Bonham, Fannie and Nicholas Moore (3) -   November 7, 1867
    For further information see - Moore, Nicholas.

Bonham, John L. and Margaret R. Ward (2) -   (L) May 18, 1857

Bonus, Mary Bell and Robert Hopenft (3) -   February 27, 1888
    For further information see - Hopenft, Robert.

Border, Daniel and Susanna Snyder (1) -   January 15, 1845

Border, Daniel M. and Clara C. Getzendanner (3) -   March 24, 1880
    Place of marriage, Kearneysville - Age of husband, 29 - Age of wife,
    22 - Both are Single - Husband was born at Shepherdstown, Jefferson
    County, West Virginia - Wife was born at Frederick City, Frederick
    County, Maryland - Both reside in Jefferson County, West Virginia.

Border, Sarah and Richard D. Lamar (3) -   November 12, 1873
    For further information see - Lamar, Richard D.

47

Boreman, Jacob and Sarah Morris (3) - March 18, 1871
    Place of marriage, Jefferson County - Age of husband, 39 - Age of
    wife, 40 - Husband is Single - Wife is a Widow - Both were born in
    Jefferson County - Both reside in Jefferson County - Husband's
    parents are Robert and Sarah - Wife's parents are Adam and Betzsey -
    Occupation of husband is Farmer.

Boren, David and Margaret Likens (1) - June 23, 1850

Boren, Margaret and Michael Dempsey (3) - (1870)
    For further information see - Dempsey, Michael.

Borggess, Sally Ann (colored) Dallas Carter (3) - February 17, 1870
    For further information see - Carter, Dallas.

Bossell, Mary (cold.) A. L. Carpenter (3) - August 29, 1887
    For further information see - Carpenter, A. L.

Bost, Clara V. and A. James Snyder (3) - December 16, 1890
    For further information see - Snyder, A. James.

Boswell, Amelia and Thomas Crofford (1) - August 31, 1831

Boswell, Courtney and Vincent Dorsey (3) - February 23, 1871
    For further information see - Dorsey, Vincent.

Boswell, Ella and Edward Orndorff (3) - March 9, 1871
    For further information see - Orndorff, Edward.

Boswell, Lizzie and John M. Watts (3) - December 26, 1889
    For further information see - Watts, John M.

Botelar, Mary M. and John G. Mason (3) - March 16, 1870
    For further information see - Mason, John G.

Boteler, Angelica S. and Henry A. Didier (2) - (L) September 7, 1860

Boteler, Elizabeth L. and Rezin D. Shepherd (2) - (L) June 9, 1858

Boteler, H. M. (bride) and D. D. Pendleton (3) - April 25, 1866
    For further information see - Pendleton, D. D.

Boteler, Henry and Ann F. Lane (1) - June 21, 1825

Boteler, Robert H. and Margaret Marshall (2) - (L) December 13, 1860

Bothwell, Charles E. and Katherine P. Faulstick (3) - August 11, 1890
    Place of marriage, Charlestown - Age of husband, 43 - Age of wife,
    32 - Both are Single - Husband was born at Galena, Illinois - Wife
    was born at Wheeling, West Virginia - Husband resides at New York
    City - Wife resides in Jefferson County, West Virginia.

Botts, Benjamin and Eliza Johnson (3) - November 25, 1865
    Place of marriage, Summit Point, Jefferson County - Age of husband,
    25 - Age of wife, 20 - Both are Single - Husband was born in Fairfax
    County, Virginia - Wife was born in Jefferson County - Both reside
    in Jefferson County - Husband's parents are Coman and Sina Botts -
    Wife's parents are Abem and Eliza Johnson - Occupation of husband is
    Laborer.

Botts, James A. (cold.) Gertrude V. Brady (3) -   December 4, 1889
   Place of marriage, Charlestown - Age of husband, 24 - Age of wife,
   21 - Both are Single - Husband was born at Petersburg, Virginia -
   Wife was born in Jefferson County, West Virginia - Husband resides
   in Essex County, New Jersey - Wife resides in Jefferson County, West
   Virginia.

Botts, Jennie (cold.) William H. Tucker (3) -   December 26, 1888
   For further information see - Tucker, William H.

Botts, Lawson and Sarah Elizabeth Ranson (2) -   (L) January 29, 1851

Botts, Lawson and Sarah Elizabeth Ranson (1) -   January 29, 1851

Bountain, Sarah and John Foreman (1) -   August 24, 1820

Bovan, Margaret and George Washington Sargeant (2) -   (L) March 10, 1851

Bowden, Stephen and Rebeca Hutson (1) -   May 16, 1817

Bowen, Mary Ann and William Nelson Ray (1) -   August 19, 1832

Bowen, Rebecca E. and George M. Myers (3) -   April 10, 1879
   For further information see - Myers, George M.

Bowers, Ann Amelia and Abram Stump (3) -   December 7, 1880
   For further information see - Stump, Abram.

Bowers, Annie E. and George W. Winebrenner (3) -   December 23, 1879
   For further information see - Winebrenner, George W.

Bowers, Annie L. and Robert T. Banks (3) -   March 9, 1887
   For further information see - Banks, Robert T.

Bowers, Charles J. and Georgiana Nicely (3) -   January 29, 1880
   Place of marriage, Middleway - Age of husband, 39 - Age of wife,
   24 - Husband is a Widower - Wife is Single - Both were born in
   Jefferson County, West Virginia - Both reside in Jefferson County,
   West Virginia.

Bowers, David William and Lulie Edwards (3) -   July 17, 1889
   Place of marriage, Charlestown - Age of husband, 23 - Age of wife,
   19 - Both are Single - Husband was born in Jefferson County, West
   Virginia - Wife was born in Loudoun County, Virginia - Both reside
   in Jefferson County, West Virginia. (Consent of bride's father in
   writing.)

Bowers, George D. and Alice H. Hoffman (2) -   (L) February 15, 1858

Bowers, George Franklin and Annie C. Taylor (3) -   May 8, 1888
   Place of marriage, Shepherdstown - Age of husband, 25 - Age of wife,
   23 - Both are Single - Both were born in Jefferson County, West
   Virginia - Both reside in Jefferson County, West Virginia.

Bowers, Mrs. Georgianna and R. P. Kline (3) -   June 7, 1887
   For further information see - Kline, R. P.

Bowers, Georgianna and John W. Hefferline (3) -   January 11, 1888
   For further information see - Hefferline, John W.

Bowers, Henry and Ann Legget (1) -   February 21, 1826

Bowers, Henry and Mrs. Catharine O'Brien (2) -   (L) April 5, 1856

Bowers, Henry F. and Margaret Elizabeth Horn (2) -   (L) March 20, 1855

Bowers, Hester A. and John Thomas Entler (3) -   October 15, 1868
    For further information see - Entler, John Thomas.

Bowers, Jacob and Priscilla Kidwell (1) -   March 18, 1823

Bowers, James B. and A. Eliza Roderick (3) -   January 23, 1868
    Place of marriage, Jefferson County - Age of husband, 35 - Age of
    wife, 19 - Both are Single - Husband was born at Shenandoah - Wife
    was born in Jefferson County - Both reside in Jefferson - Husband's
    parents are P. W. and L. - Wife's parents are John and Ann -
    Occupation of husband is Farmer.   (Father consents.)

Bowers, John and Catherine Nase (1) -   September 6, 1808

Bowers, John and Mary Sombro (1) -   February 2, 1826

Bowers, John and Mary Courtney (1) -   March 8, 1832

Bowers, Martha Ellen and George C. Barrett (3) -   March 20, 1879
    For further information see - Barrett, George C.

Bowers, Mary M. and Joseph W. Barrett (3) -   January 19, 1881
    For further information see - Barrett, Joseph W.

Bowers, Mary V. and Isaac Dixon (3) -   October 18, 1887
    For further information see - Dixon, Isaac.

Bowers, Octavia R. and Charles L. Thomas (3) -   October 23, 1888
    For further information see - Thomas, Charles L.

Bowers, Raleigh and Mary E. Hornar (1) -   February 14, 1842

Bowers, Sarah and Isaac Davis (1) -   December 3, 1829

Bowler, Maggie and James Welsh (3) -   January 8, 1889
    For further information see - Welsh, James.

Bowler, Mary and Michael Higgins (3) -   January 8, 1889
    For further information see - Higgins, Michael.

Bowling, Martha A. and William Conrad (2) -   (L) August 30, 1858

Bowls, Agnes and Jacob Turner (3) -   (L) October 13, 1866
    For further information see - Turner, Jacob.

Bowman, Adam and Emma J. Easterday (3) -   October 21, 1879
    Place of marriage, Shepherdstown - Age of husband, 44 - Age of wife,
    44 - Both are Single - Husband was born in Jefferson County - Wife
    was born in Jefferson County, West Virginia - Both reside in
    Jefferson County, West Virginia.

Bowman, Georgiana (cold.) George Washington (3) -   December 30, 1879
    For further information see - Washington, George.

Bowman, Lucy (cold.) David Whiting (3) -   May 29, 1878
    For further information see - Whiting, David.

Bowman, Mary and Charles Lewis (3) -   October 31, 1872
    For further information see - Lewis, Charles.

Bowman, Matilda (free Coloured) James Webb (2) -   (L) December 26, 1854

Bowman, Nancy (cold.) John W. Butler (3) -   December 27, 1883
    For further information see - Butler, John W.

Bowman, Rosa (cold.) Jacob Wheeler (3) -   August 15, 1876
    For further information see - Wheeler, Jacob.

Bowsmith, Catherine and Martin Holmes (1) -   June 14, 1814

Boxwell, Mary and Henry Staub (1) -   December 28, 1830

Boxwell, Warner M. and Katie F. Simpson (3) -   December 26, 1889
    Place of marriage, Shepherdstown - Age of husband, 29 - Age of wife, 19 - Both are Single - Husband was born in Frederick County, Virginia - Wife was born in Jefferson County, West Virginia - Both reside in Jefferson County, West Virginia. (Consent of bride's mother in writing.)

Boyd, Ada P. C. and John A. Clipp (3) -   September 25, 1873
    For further information see - Clipp, John A.

Boyd, Charles E. and Mattie E. Hinton (3) -   September 13, 1888
    Place of marriage, near Middleway - Age of husband, 22 - Age of wife, 22 - Both are Single - Husband was born in Berkeley County, West Virginia - Wife was born in Jefferson County, West Virginia - Husband resides in Frederick County, Virginia - Wife resides in Jefferson County, West Virginia.

Boyd, Charles W. L. and Rosa V. L. Mason (3) -   December 23, 1883
    Place of marriage, near Kabletown - Age of husband, 21 - Age of wife, 19 - Both are Single - Husband was born in Jefferson County, West Virginia - Wife was born in Clarke County, Virginia - Both reside in Jefferson County, West Virginia. (Consent of bride's father in writing.)

Boyd, Henry P. and Mary Pitzer (3) -   February 13, 1878
    Place of marriage, Middleway District - Age of husband, 26 - Age of wife, 21 - Both are Single - Husband was born in Maryland - Wife was born in Berkeley County, West Virginia - Both reside in Jefferson County, West Virginia.

Boyd, Israel V. and Nancy J. West (3) -   December 17, 1874
    Place of marriage, near Kabletown - Age of husband, 23 - Age of wife, 17 - Both are Single - Both were born in Jefferson County, West Virginia - Both reside in Jefferson County, West Virginia. (Consent of bride's mother and step-father in writing.)

Boyd, John J. M. and Kate R. Currie (3) - October 9, 1889
  Place of marriage, Bride's Residence - Age of husband, 20 - Age of
  wife, 21 - Both are Single - Husband was born in Rockingham County,
  Virginia - Wife was born in Jefferson County, West Virginia -
  Husband resides in Rockingham County, Virginia - Wife resides in
  Jefferson County, West Virginia. (Consent of groom's father in
  writing.)

Boyd, Mary E. and Edward Rockenbaugh (3) - August 24, 1876
  For further information see - Rockenbaugh, Edward.

Boyd, Sarah E. and G. H. Rhineman (3) - May 18, 1875
  For further information see - Rhineman, G. H.

Boyer, Carrie M. and Jacob T. Smallwood (3) - September 18, 1890
  For further information see - Smallwood, Jacob T.

Boyer, John G. and Sarah V. Gageby (3) - (L) December 27, 1881
  Place of marriage, Charlestown - Age of husband, 26 - Age of wife,
  22 - Both are Single - Both were born in Jefferson County, West
  Virginia - Both reside in Jefferson County, West Virginia.
  (January 10, 1882 is crossed out in the original.)

Boyer, Lilian B. and Henry A. Stewart (3) - December 5, 1878
  For further information see - Stewart, Henry A.

Boyer, Lucy A. and Ellis M. Bell (3) - June 9, 1881
  For further information see - Bell, Ellis M.

Boyer, Samuel and Mahala Ann Homes (1) - October 27, 1848

Boyers, G. W., Jr. and Alice H. Mitchell (3) - November 30, 1876
  Place of marriage, Charles Town - Age of husband, 22 - Age of wife,
  20 - Both are Single - Husband was born in Jefferson County, West
  Virginia - Wife was born in Fauquier County, Virginia - Both reside
  in Jefferson County, West Virginia. (Consent of bride's father in
  person.)

Boyers, George W. and Eliza Maria Young (2) - (L) September 30, 1851

Boyers, George W. and Eliza Maria Young (1) - September 30, 1851

Boyers, James and Sarah Kimes (1) - February 8, 1827

Boyers, Margaret and Daniel Huyett (3) - May 2, 1870
  For further information see - Huyett, Daniel.

Boyers, Sallie E. and Joseph H. Vanvactor (3) - December 30, 1872
  For further information see - Vanvactor, Joseph H.

Boyers, Sarah and William Kimes (1) - April 11, 1812

Boyle, Daniel T. and Mary E. Nunnamaker (3) - June 3, 1869
  Place of marriage, Jefferson County - Age of husband, 24 - Age of
  wife, 20 - Both are Single - Husband was born in Jefferson County,
  West Virginia - Wife was born in Virginia - Both reside in Jefferson
  County. (Mother consents in writing filed.)

Boyle, Edward and Susana Dutch (1) - July 20, 1808

Boyron, Jessee and Annie Ruperrow (1) -   February 23, 1804

Bozworth, William and Nancy Butt (1) -   July 27, 1809

Bracher, Ann (colored) Hamilton Perkins (3) -   June 7, 1870
For further information see - Perkins, Hamilton.

Brackenridge, Margaret and Dr. James Hall (1) -   (circa) 1817

Brackett, L. E. (bride) and S. W. Lightner (3) -   June 1884
For further information see - Lightner, S. W.

Bradfield, W. I. and Mary E. Gageby (3) -   April 6, 1887
Place of marriage, Charlestown - Age of husband, 35 - Age of wife,
30 - Husband is a Widower - Wife is Single - Husband was born in
Loudoun County, Virginia - Wife was born in Jefferson County, West
Virginia - Both reside in Jefferson County, West Virginia.

Bradford, George (cold.) Alice Mason (3) -   April 20, 1887
Place of marriage, Charlestown - Age of husband, 35 - Age of wife,
30 - Both are Single - Husband was born in Green County, Virginia -
Wife was born in Maryland - Husband resides in Jefferson County,
West Virginia - Wife resides in Jefferson County.

Bradford, James (cold.) Fanny Blackburn (3) -   January 2, 1874
Place of marriage, Charlestown - Age of husband, 35 - Age of wife,
25 - Both are Single - Husband was born in Fauquier County,
Virginia - Wife was born in Jefferson County, West Virginia - Both
reside in Jefferson County, West Virginia.

Bradford, Thomas (cold.) Katy Brown (3) -   July 23, 1885
Place of marriage, Charlestown - Age of husband, 23 - Age of wife,
21 - Both are Single - Both were born in Jefferson County, West
Virginia - Both reside in Jefferson County, West Virginia.

Bradshaw, Eliza and William Hamilton (1) -   1813

Bradshaw, Florence and George Jackson (3) -   June 2, 1886
For further information see - Jackson, George.

Bradshaw, Mary Elizabeth and David M. Entler (2) -   (L) (1862)
For further information see - Entler, David M.

Bradshear, Henry A. and Mary Jane Rodrick (3) -   May 24, 1887
Place of marriage, Harpers Ferry - Age of husband, 25 - Age of wife,
15 - Both are Single - Both were born in Jefferson County, West
Virginia - Husband resides in Jefferson County, West Virginia - Wife
resides in Jefferson County. (Consent of bride's father in
person.)

Brady, Benjamin (cold.) Bell Berry (3) -   January 9, 1879
Place of marriage, Summit Point - Age of husband, 22 - Age of wife,
23 - Both are Single - Both were born in Jefferson County, West
Virginia - Both reside in Jefferson County, West Virginia.

Brady, Caroline and James McDaniel (2) -   (L) February 24, 1852

Brady, Elizabeth C. and Benjamin Bateman (2) -   (L) August 28, 1857

53

Brady, George R. and Mary E. Furtney (3) -   July 9, 1881
    Place of marriage, Harpers Ferry - Age of husband, 23 - Age of wife,
    22 - Both are Single - Husband was born in Jefferson County - Wife
    was born in Jefferson County, West Virginia - Both reside in
    Jefferson County, West Virginia.

Brady, Gertrude V. (cold.) James A. Botts (3) -   December 4, 1889
    For further information see - Botts, James A.

Brady, Henry and Hannah Hutchison (3) -   November 18, 1865
    Place of marriage, Charlestown, Jefferson County - Age of husband,
    56 - Age of wife, 45 - Both are Single - Husband was born in Loudoun
    County, Virginia - Wife was born in Jefferson County, West
    Virginia - Both reside in Jefferson County.

Brady, James E. and Phebe Hart (3) -   July 8, 1867
    Place of marriage, Charlestown - Age of husband, 32 - Age of wife,
    22 - Both are Single - Husband was born at Charlestown, West
    Virginia - Wife was born in Jefferson County - Both reside at
    Charlestown, West Virginia - Husband's parents are Helen Thornton -
    Wife's parents are Mary Hart - Occupation of husband is Farmer.

Brady, James W. and Martha Ellen McBee (2) -   (L) November 28, 1853

Brady, Lee (cold.) Anna Helm (3) -   December 25, 1884
    Place of marriage, Charlestown - Age of husband, 22 - Age of wife,
    26 - Both are Single - Husband was born in Page County, Virginia -
    Wife was born in Jefferson County, West Virginia - Both reside in
    Jefferson County, West Virginia.

Brady, Lydia Taylor (cold.) George M. Hart (3) -   June 10, 1867
    For further information see - Hart, George M.

Brady, Malcolm and Martha E. Hart (3) -   April 25, 1871
    Place of marriage, Jefferson County - Age of husband, 25 - Age of
    wife, 21 - Both are Single - Husband was born in Loudoun County -
    Wife was born in Jefferson County - Both reside in Jefferson
    County - Husband's parents are Malcolm and Sallie - Wife's parents
    are Thomas and Ellen - Occupation of husband is Stone Mason.

Brady, Randolph and Emma Hart (3) -   December 21, 1871
    Place of marriage, Jefferson County - Age of husband, 28 - Age of
    wife, 25 - Both are Single - Husband was born in Loudoun County -
    Wife was born in Jefferson County - Both reside in Jefferson
    County - Husband's parents are Malcolm and Sallie - Wife's parents
    are Thomas and Ellen - Occupation of husband is Farmer.

Brady, Sarah (cold.) William H. Jackson (3) -   January 23, 1879
    For further information see - Jackson, William H.

Bragg, Mary F. and Peter Crim (3) -   November 5, 1874
    For further information see - Crim, Peter.

Bragonier, J. S. and Rosalie T. Butler (3) -   October 31, 1888
    Place of marriage, Charlestown - Age of husband, 40 - Age of wife,
    22 - Husband is a Widower - Wife is Single - Both were born in
    Jefferson County, West Virginia - Both reside in Jefferson County,
    West Virginia.

Bramhal, Betsy and Gustavus T. Mitchell (1) -   March 16, 1815

Bramhall, Margaret and Abram Byers (1) -   December 25, 1825

Branch, John (cold.) Massie Branson (3) -   May 22, 1881
    Place of marriage, Middleway - Age of husband, 40 - Age of wife,
    28 - Husband is a Widower - Wife is Single - Husband was born at
    Richmond - Wife was born in Berkeley County - Both reside in
    Jefferson County, West Virginia.

Brannam, T. and Lucy Goings (3) -   April 4, 1872
    Place of marriage, Jefferson County - Age of husband, 42 - Age of
    wife, 28 - Husband is a Widower - Wife is a Widow - Husband was born
    at Fairfax, Virginia - Wife was born in Jefferson County, West
    Virginia - Both reside in Jefferson County, West Virginia -
    Husband's parents are Joseph and Lucy - Wife's parents are Alfred
    and Annie - Occupation of husband is Farmer.

Brannard, Mary and Alexander Murphy (2) -   (L) May 4, 1864
    For further information see - Murphy, Alexander.

Brannon, Margaret and Jeremiah McGraw (3) -   April 12, 1889
    For further information see - McGraw, Jeremiah.

Brannon, Martin and Kate McCave (3) -   August 4, 1867
    Place of marriage, Martinsburg - Age of husband, 40 - Age of wife,
    35 - Both are Single - Both were born in Ireland - Husband resides
    at Duffields - Wife resides at Harpers Ferry - Husband's parents are
    John and Bridget - Wife's parents are Benard - Occupation of husband
    is Laborer.

Bransom, Anna and Harrison Robinson (3) -   June 8, 1867
    For further information see - Robinson, Harrison.

Branson, Ann (cold.) Thomas Lee (3) -   July 5, 1880
    For further information see - Lee, Thomas.

Branson, Benjamin W. (cold.) Rebecca Walker (3) -   October 13, 1890
    Place of marriage, Charlestown - Age of husband, 42 - Age of wife,
    43 - Both are Single - Both were born in Jefferson County, West
    Virginia - Both reside in Jefferson County, West Virginia.

Branson, Harvy (cold.) Nannie Cole (3) -   February 22, 1890
    Place of marriage, Charlestown - Age of husband, 22 - Age of wife,
    17 - Both are Single - Both were born in Jefferson County, West
    Virginia - Both reside in Jefferson County, West Virginia.

Branson, Lucy (3) -
    For further information see - Lomax, Arthur.

Branson, Lucy (cold.) Charles Buckner (3) -   June 7, 1883
    For further information see - Buckner, Charles.

Branson, Mary (cold.) Richard Finister (3) -   January 29, 1878
    For further information see - Finister, Richard.

Branson, Massie (cold.) John Branch (3) -   May 22, 1881
    For further information see - Branch, John.

Branson, Sophia (colored) John McCan (3) -   June 16, 1866
    For further information see - McCan, John.

Branson, Wilson and George Ann Clinton (3) - December 27, 1865
Place of marriage, near Duffields Depot - Age of husband, 23 - Age
of wife, 17 - Both are Single - Both were born in Jefferson County,
West Virginia - Both reside in Jefferson County, West Virginia -
Husband's parents are Nancy Branson - Wife's parents are Lucy
Clinton - Occupation of husband is Laborer.

Brantner, Andrew and Mary Jane Best (2) - (L) June 20, 1857

Brantner, Charles W. and Mary Elizabeth Maddex (3) - December 21, 1876
Place of marriage, near Duffields - Age of husband, 23 next March -
Age of wife, 22 - Both are Single - Husband was born in Jefferson
County, West Virginia - Wife was born in Clarke County, Virginia -
Both reside in Jefferson County, West Virginia.

Brantner, Helen and John F. Allen (3) - February 23, 1882
For further information see - Allen, John F.

Brantner, John and Mary F. Brooks (1) - June 22, 1845

Brantner, Lilly and Harry Hendricks (3) - December 25, 1887
For further information see - Hendricks, Harry.

Brantner, Mary and Henry Miller (3) - February 12, 1867
For further information see - Miller, Henry.

Brantner, Minnie and Harvey H. Hendricks (3) - December 3, 1889
For further information see - Hendricks, Harvey H.

Brantner, Raleigh and Mary Clum (1) - June 17, 1819

Brantner, Raleigh and Elizabeth Wysong (1) - April 1, 1827

Brantner, Samuel and Elizabeth Engle (1) - 1824

Brantner, Thomas L. and Alice Shirley (3) - December 5, 1878
Place of marriage, near Duffields - Age of husband, 27 - Age of
wife, 22 - Both are Single - Both were born in Jefferson County,
West Virginia - Both reside in Jefferson County, West Virginia.

Braxton, Francis C. and Ellenoir M. Lackland (3) - November 22, 1888
Place of marriage, Charlestown - Age of husband, 29 - Age of wife,
28 - Both are Single - Both were born in Virginia - Husband resides
in Alabama - Wife resides in Jefferson County, West Virginia.

Braxton, Lee (cold.) Emma Moton (3) - June 15, 1887
Place of marriage, Bolivar - Age of husband, 24 - Age of wife, 24 -
Both are Single - Both were born in Jefferson County, West
Virginia - Both reside in Jefferson County, West Virginia.

Breckenridge, Samuel T. and Juliet B. Reed (3) - December 20, 1885
Place of marriage, near Kabletown - Age of husband, 23 - Age of
wife, 22 - Both are Single - Husband was born in Loudoun County,
Virginia - Wife was born in Jefferson County, West Virginia -
Husband resides in Loudoun County, Virginia - Wife resides in
Jefferson County, West Virginia.

Bredin, Mary Brent and Joshua Morton (1) - October 29, 1823

Breedin, Eliza and William Armstrong (1) - October 10, 1816

Breedin, Louisa and William W. Frazier (1) -   January 28, 1817

Breedin, Ma. and Marain T. Wickham (1) -   December 19, 1805

Breedin, Narcissa and Philip Hoffman (1) -   December 1, 1811

Breedin, Sarah A. and Henry V. Swearinger (1) -   January 26, 1819

Brendle, John C. and Drusilla Hodges (1) -   March 18, 1827

Breneman, John and Emily E. Griffith (3) -   March 13, 1879
Place of marriage, East of Shenandoah River - Age of husband, 42 -
Age of wife, 20 - Both are Single - Husband was born in Rockingham
County, Virginia - Wife was born in Jefferson County, West
Virginia - Both reside in Jefferson County, West Virginia.
(Consent of bride's father in writing.)

Brent, William Henry and May Blockley (3) -   March 28, 1877
Place of marriage, Charlestown - Age of husband, 31 - Age of wife,
25 - Both are Single - Both were born in Jefferson County, West
Virginia - Both reside in Jefferson County, West Virginia.

Bresnahan, James T. and Ella A. Briggs (3) -   February 5, 1890
Place of marriage, Harpers Ferry - Age of husband, 24 - Age of wife,
22 - Both are Single - Husband was born at Washington, D. C. - Wife,
was born in Jefferson County, West Virginia - Husband resides at
Washington, D. C. - Wife resides in Jefferson County, West Virginia.

Breu, Henry and Mary Kneisel (1) -   May 30, 1835

Brewer, Samuel C. and Angelica Huyett (2) -   (L) February 8, 1864
Time of marriage, February 18, 1864 - Place of marriage, at bride's
father's near Shepherdstown - Names, Samuel C. Brewer and Angelica
Huyett - Age of husband, 21 years last April - Age of wife, 22
years - Both are Single - Husband was born in Washington County,
Maryland - Wife was born in Jefferson County, Virginia - Husband's
residence, Washington County, Maryland - Wife's residence, Jefferson
County, Virginia - Husband's parents are John A. and Leah H.
Brewer - Wife's parents are Charles and Elizabeth Huyett -
Occupation of husband is Farmer - License issued, February 8,
1864 - Thomas A. Moore, Clerk.

Brian, Barbary and Samuel Groomes (1) -   1812

Bridener, Caroline C. and Lewis Upright (3) -   February 10, 1869
For further information see - Upright, Lewis.

Bridner, Elizabeth and Francis M. Eckles (3) -   February 4, 1885
For further information see - Eckles, Francis M.

Bridner, John C. and Jeanetta W. Billmyer (3) -   February 8, 1877
Place of marriage, Bolivar - Age of husband, 24 - Age of wife, 20 -
Both are Single - Both were born in Jefferson County, West
Virginia - Both reside in Jefferson County, West Virginia.
(Consent of bride's mother in writing.)

Briggs, Charles H. and Emma Eugenia Loman (3) - May 20, 1878
   Place of marriage, Bolivar - Age of husband, 32 - Age of wife, 18 -
   Husband is a Widower - Wife is Single - Husband was born in State of
   New York - Wife was born in Jefferson County - Both reside in
   Jefferson County, West Virginia.   (Consent of bride's father in
   person.)

Briggs, Ella A. and James T. Bresnahan (3) - February 5, 1890
   For further information see - Bresnahan, James T.

Brill, Emma S. and Samuel Hausenfluck (3) - August 3, 1889
   For further information see - Hausenfluck, Samuel.

Brillhart, Jesse and Alcinda F. Custer (3) - October 17, 1871
   Place of marriage, Jefferson County - Age of husband, 51 - Age of
   wife, 35 - Husband is a Widower - Wife is Single - Husband was born
   in Pennsylvania - Wife was born in Virginia - Both reside in West
   Virginia - Husband's parents are Samuel and Katie F. - Wife's
   parents are Samuel and Mary - Occupation of husband is Farmer.

Brining, Mary E. and James W. Packett (3) - September 6, 1881
   For further information see - Packett, James W.

Brining, Michael E. and Minnie Emory (3) - August 16, 1890
   Place of marriage, Middleway - Age of husband, 22 - Age of wife,
   23 - Both are Single - Both were born in Jefferson County, West
   Virginia - Both reside in Jefferson County, West Virginia.

Briscoe, Ann A. and Edward M. Aisquith (2) - (L) December 8, 1856

Briscoe, Bacckus and Elizabeth Colston (3) - March 8, 1873
   Place of marriage, at Rippon - Age of husband, 50 - Age of wife,
   35 - Husband is a Widower - Wife is a Widow - Both were born in
   Jefferson County, West Virginia - Both reside in Jefferson County,
   West Virginia - Husband's parents are Lewis and Sally - Wife's
   Parents are Raleigh and Susan - Occupation of husband is Shoemaker.

Briscoe, Courtney Ann and Robert Gates Hite (1) - January 19, 1823

Briscoe, David L. and Ella Straith (3) - December 12, 1872
   Place of marriage, Charlestown, Jefferson, West Virginia - Age of
   husband, 32 - Age of wife, 29 - Husband is a Widower - Wife is
   Single - Husband was born in Saint Marys County, Maryland - Wife was
   Born in Jefferson County, West Virginia - Husband resides at
   Baltimore, Maryland - Wife resides in Jefferson County, West
   Virginia - Husband's parents are Walter H. T. and Emmeline W. -
   Wife's parents are J. A. and Mary - Occupation of husband is Lawyer.

Briscoe, Elizabeth and George Zorge (1) - August 26, 1830

Briscoe, Elizabeth C. and William H. D. Hall (1) - March 7, 1848

Briscoe, Ellen M. and Tighlman Waters (2) - (L) July 31, 1854

Briscoe, Frances Amelia and William R. Gallaher (2) - (L) August 6, 1864
   For further information see - Gallaher, William R.

Briscoe, Fanny Elean and Henry Shepherd (1) - May 7, 1822

Briscoe, H. L. and M. Roberta Mix (3) - November 30, 1882
   Place of marriage, Bride's Residence - Age of husband, 30 - Age of
   wife, 30 - Both are Single - Both were born in Jefferson County,
   West Virginia - Both reside in Jefferson County, West Virginia.

Briscoe, Hannah (colored) Frank Smith (3) - June 11, 1870
   For further information see - Smith, Frank.

Briscoe, J. F. and M. G. Butler (bride) (3) - January 17, 1884
   Place of marriage, Charlestown - Age of husband, 26 - Age of wife,
   22 - Both are Single - Husband was born in Montgomery County,
   Maryland - Wife was born in Jefferson County, West Virginia - Both
   reside in Jefferson County, West Virginia.

Briscoe, J. G. and Maggie Rohr (3) - February 14, 1866
   Place of marriage, Harpers Ferry, West Virginia - Age of husband,
   38 - Age of wife, 38 - Husband is a Widower - Wife is a Widow -
   Husband was born in Kent County, Maryland - Wife was born in
   Franklin County, Pennsylvania - Both reside at Harpers Ferry, West
   Virginia - Husband's parents are James and Emaline Briscoe - Wife's
   parents are Jacob and Ida Julewalder - Occupation of husband is
   Merchant.

Briscoe, Jannie (cold.) Charles Cook (3) - July 15, 1880
   For further information see - Cook, Charles.

Briscoe, Katie (cold.) Elbert Rodgers (3) - March 18, 1880
   For further information see - Rodgers, Elbert.

Briscoe, Nancie and Samuel Brown (3) - September 30, 1866
   For further information see - Brown, Samuel.

Briscoe, Samuel and Eliza Croeson (1) - October 19, 1815

Briscoe, Thomas H. (cold.) Mary Sheffer (3) - June 14, 1883
   Place of marriage, near Halltown - Age of husband, 34 - Age of wife,
   22 - Both are Single - Husband was born in North Carolina - Wife was
   born in Virginia - Both reside in Jefferson County, West Virginia.

Brison, Banjamin and Jane Chapman (1) - December 28, 1831

Britner, Alice D. and Edward H. Hoffman (3) - March 27, 1883
   For further information see - Hoffman, Edward H.

Britner, Dora and Henry C. Martin (3) - September 30, 1875
   For further information see - Martin, Henry C.

Britner, Sally V. and Charles Hiser (3) - May 21, 1867
   For further information see - Hiser, Charles.

Britner, William and Nellie R. Show (3) - April 7, 1885
   Place of marriage, Shepherdstown - Age of husband, 23 - Age of wife,
   18 - Both are Single - Both were born in Jefferson County, West
   Virginia - Both reside in Jefferson County, West Virginia.
   (Consent of bride's father in person.)

Britt, Richard E. and Lizzie J. Leslie (3) -   November 8, 1890
   Place of marriage, Charlestown - Age of husband, 23 - Age of wife,
   21 - Both are Single - Husband was born at Pottsville,
   Pennsylvania - Wife was born in Loudoun County, Virginia - Husband
   resides at Philadelphia, Pennsylvania - Wife resides in Jefferson
   County, West Virginia.

Brittain, Joseph, Jr. and Ellen M. Rieley (2) -   (L) December 7, 1850

Brittain, Joseph, Jr. and Ellen M. Riley (1) -   December 12, 1850

Brittain, Mary and Talbot S. Duke (1) -   June 6, 1845

Brittain, Sarah Jane and Daniel S. Barrett (2) -   (L) December 29, 1856

Britton, Amanda (widow) and Thomas D. Ryan (2) -   (L) July 7, 1860

Brockenborro, F. and L. Boggerson (bride) (3) -   April 11, 1868
   Place of marriage, Jefferson County - Age of husband, 28 - Age of
   wife, 27 - Both are Single - Husband was born in Clarke County,
   Virginia - Wife was born in Jefferson County - Both reside in
   Jefferson - Husband's parents are John and Annie - Wife's parents
   are Arthur and Ellen - Occupation of husband is Mason.
   (Permission by parents.)

Broderick, Michael and Catharine Donovan (1) -   June 18, 1850

Bromwicks, Annie (cold.) William Roman (3) -   January 1, 1868
   For further information see - Roman, William.

Brooke, George W. and Laura B. Shaner (3) -   May 9, 1872
   Place of marriage, Jefferson County - Age of husband, 22 - Age of
   wife, 21 - Both are Single - Husband was born in Pennsylvania -
   Wife was born in Virginia - Both reside in Virginia - Husband's
   parents are John R. and Mary E. - Wife's parents are Ebenezer -
   Occupation of husband is Machinist.

Brooke, St.George T. and Mary H. Brown (3) -   August 15, 1882
   Place of marriage, Charlestown - Age of husband, 38 - Age of wife,
   23 - Both are Single - Husband was born in Albemarle County,
   Virginia - Wife was born in Jefferson County, West Virginia -
   Husband resides at Morgantown, West Virginia - Wife resides in
   Jefferson County, West Virginia.

Brookins, Lizzie (cold.) Edward Howell (3) -   October 20, 1880
   For further information see - Howell, Edward.

Brooks, Abram (cold.) Mollie Coleman (3) -   December 24, 1880
   Place of marriage, Shepherdstown - Age of husband, 25 - Age of wife,
   25 - Both are Single - Husband was born in Montgomery County,
   Maryland - Wife was born in Jefferson County, West Virginia -
   Husband resides in Maryland - Wife resides in Jefferson County, West
   Virginia.

Brooks, Barney and D. A. Jones (3) -   (1869)
   Age of husband, 49 - Age of wife, 30 - Both were born in Jefferson
   County - Both reside in Jefferson County.

Brooks, Beverly (cold.) Milly Turner (3) -　　　　　　　　　July 6, 1882
　　Place of marriage, Charlestown - Age of husband, 27 - Age of wife,
　　22 - Both are Single - Husband was born in Jefferson County, West
　　Virginia - Wife was born in Maryland - Husband resides in Jefferson
　　County, West Virginia - Wife resides in Jefferson County.

Brooks, Charles W. and Virginia Saunders (3) -　　　　　　November 11, 1869
　　Place of marriage, Jefferson County - Age of husband, 40 - Age of
　　wife, 25 - Husband was born in England - Wife was born in Jefferson
　　County - Both reside in Jefferson County.

Brooks, Delia (cold.) Jere Russ (3) -　　　　　　　　　　December 23, 1882
　　For further information see - Russ, Jere.

Brooks, Elizabeth Jane and William J. Bryant (2) -　　(L) November 22, 1863
　　For further information see - Bryant, William J.

Brooks, George and Emma Jackson (3) -　　　　　　　　　　　　　　　(1868)
　　Place of marriage, Jefferson County - Age of husband, 21 - Age of
　　wife, 18 - Both are Single - Both were born in Virginia - Husband
　　resides in Jefferson County - Wife resides in Jefferson County, West
　　Virginia - Wife's parents are Jack and Margaret - Occupation of
　　husband is Laborer.

Brooks, James A. and Margaret O. Fouke (2) -　　　　　　　　　(L) (1862)
　　Time of marriage, February 18, 1862 - Names, James A. Brooks and
　　Margaret O. Fouke - Age of husband, 21 years, 1 month, 21 days - Age
　　of wife, 21 years, May 9, 1861 - Condition of husband, Single -
　　Condition of wife, Single - Place of husband's birth, Brooklyn, New
　　York - Place of wife's birth, near Shepherdstown - Place of
　　Husband's residence, Knoxville, Tennessee - Place of wife's
　　residence, Shepherdstown - Names of husband's parents, James and
　　_____ Brooks - Names of wife's parents, Marquis and Elizabeth -
　　Occupation of husband is Soldier in Southern Army - James A. Brooks.

Brooks, John A. and Susan Ann Nisswaner (2) -　　(L) December 18, 1852

Brooks, Madison and Louisa Jackson (3) -　　　　　　　　　　　　(1868)
　　Age of husband, 50 - Age of wife, 60 - Husband is a Widower - Wife
　　is Single - Both were born in Virginia - Both reside in Jefferson
　　County - Occupation of husband is Farmer.

Brooks, Mary F. and John Brantner (1) -　　　　　　　　　　June 22, 1845

Brooks, Peter (cold.) Louisa Willis (3) -　　　　　　　　　May 16, 1883
　　Place of marriage, Charlestown - Age of husband, 24 - Age of wife,
　　22 - Both are Single - Both were born in Jefferson County, West
　　Virginia - Both reside in Jefferson County, West Virginia.

Brooks, William and Abigal Verner (1) -　　　　　　　　　March 28, 1820

Brooks, William (cold.) Harriet Ranson (3) -　　　　　　January 6, 1883
　　Place of marriage, Harpers Ferry - Age of husband, 31 - Age of wife,
　　30 - Both are Single - Husband was born at Savannah, Georgia - Wife
　　was born in Jefferson County, West Virginia - Both reside in
　　Jefferson County, West Virginia.

Brotherton, Anna and J. Butler Kearfoot (3) -　　　　　February 23, 1875
　　For further information see - Kearfoot, J. Butler.

Brotherton, John W. and Maria S. Dorsey (1) -   December 14, 1848

Brotherton, Lee Griggs and Laura T. Licklider (2) -   (L) January 24, 1863
Time of marriage, January 27, 1863 - Place of marriage, Shepherdstown - Names, Lee Griggs Brotherton and Laura T. Licklider - Age of husband, 26 years - Age of wife, 27 years - Both are Single - Both were born in Jefferson County - Both reside in Jefferson County - Husband's parents are Thomas and Elizabeth Brotherton - Wife's parents are Adam and Elizabeth Licklider - Occupation of husband is Carpenter - Liscense issued, January 24, 1863 - Thomas A. Moore, Clerk.

Brotherton, Lydia and Winfield L. Huffmaster (3) -   December 21, 1875
For further information see - Huffmaster, Winfield L.

Brotherton, Mary Ellen and Burr H. Strother (2) -   (L) September 1, 1857

Brotherton, Robert R. and Lucinda Stewart (2) -   (L) August 29, 1857

Brotherton, Thomas and Elizabeth Griggs (1) -   December 15, 1825

Brotherton, Thomas and Mary Jane Spotts (2) -   (L) December 23, 1851

Brotherton, Thomas and Mary Jane Spotts (1) -   December 23, 1851

Brown, Alonz B. and Sarah E. Vaughn (3) -   March 16, 1871
Place of marriage, Jefferson County - Age of husband, 29 - Age of wife, 21 - Both are Single - Husband was born at New York - Wife was born in Virginia - Both reside in Loudoun County, Virginia - Husband's parents are Emory and Elizabeth - Wife's parents are Thomas W. and Thersa J. - Occupation of husband is Gentleman. (Sworn brother Jacob Vaughn.)

Brown, Amanda and Oliver Hall (3) -   (1868)
For further information see - Hall, Oliver.

Brown, Ann Catharine and Columbus C. Mitchell (2) -   (L) November 21, 1855

Brown, Anna E. and William F. Gageby (2) -   (L) March 22, 1860

Brown, Annie (cold.) John William Shorts (3) -   January 16, 1890
For further information see - Shorts, John William.

Brown, Annie Virginia and Arthur Lee Derry (3) -   March 25, 1885
For further information see - Derry, Arthur Lee.

Brown, Arch R. and Rebeca Beard (3) -   January 1, 1889
Place of marriage, Martinsburg - Age of husband, 28 - Age of wife, 24 - Both are Single - Both were born in Jefferson County, West Virginia - Husband resides in Berkeley County, West Virginia - Wife resides in Jefferson County, West Virginia.

Brown, Arthur and Elizabeth E. Willis (1) -   June 1, 1826

Brown, Arthur (cold.) Rosa Hall (3) -   November 6, 1883
Place of marriage, Bride's Residence - Age of husband, 22 - Age of wife, 19 - Both are Single - Husband was born in Jefferson County, West Virginia - Wife was born in Jefferson County - Both reside in Jefferson County, West Virginia. (Father and mother of bride both dead.)

Brown, Benjamin (cold.) Martha Allen (3) -   .   August 20, 1878
    Place of marriage, Charlestown - Age of husband, 32 - Age of wife,
    21 - Both are Single - Husband was born at Washington City - Wife
    was born in Frederick County, Virginia - Both reside in Jefferson
    County, West Virginia.

Brown, Bettie (cold.) Webb McKinney (3) -   December 29, 1879
    For further information see - McKinney, Webb.

Brown, Bing and Nettie J. Roberts (3) -   November 22, 1888
    Place of marriage, Charlestown - Age of husband, 22 - Age of wife,
    23 - Both are Single - Husband was born in Maryland - Wife was born
    in Jefferson County, West Virginia - Both reside in Jefferson
    County, West Virginia.

Brown, Burgess W. and Eveline Gregory (1) - .   December 13, 1834

Brown, Carver W. and Sarah E. Skinner (2) -   (L) September 3, 1852

Brown, Carver W. and Sarah E. Skinner (1) -   September 8, 1852

Brown, Cassins Z. and Katy Fowler (3) -   February 16, 1888
    Place of marriage, Middleway - Age of husband, 25 - Age of wife,
    19 - Both are Single - Husband was born in State of Ohio - Wife was
    born in Jefferson County, West Virginia - Husband resides in
    Berkeley County, West Virginia - Wife resides in Jefferson County,
    West Virginia. (Consent of bride's father in person.)

Brown, Charles W. and Eddy F. Bell (3) -   December 22, 1881
    Place of marriage, near Kearneysville - Age of husband, 24 - Age of
    wife, 21 - Both are Single - Husband was born in Jefferson County,
    West Virginia - Wife was born in Clarke County, Virginia - Both
    reside in Jefferson County, West Virginia.

Brown, Delphy (cold.) William H. Payne (3) -   February 8, 1886
    For further information see - Payne, William H.

Brown, Edgenier (cold.) Lucy Wilson (3) -   September 4, 1886
    Place of marriage, Mount Pleasant - Age of husband, 26 - Age of
    Wife, 22 - Both are Single - Husband was born in Jefferson County -
    Wife was born in Jefferson County, West Virginia - Both reside in
    Jefferson County, West Virginia.

Brown, Edward and Fanny Roman (3) -   (1869)
    Age of husband, 23 - Age of wife, 16 - Both were born in Jefferson
    County - Both reside in Jefferson County. (Parents consent by
    son.)

Brown, Elijah (cold.) Louisa Gray (3) -   November 5, 1881
    Place of marriage, near Charlestown - Age of husband, 51 - Age of
    wife, 51 - Husband is a Widower - Wife is a Widow - Husband was born
    in Cumberland County, Virginia - Wife was born in Jefferson County,
    West Virginia - Both reside in Jefferson County, West Virginia.

Brown, Elijah (cold.) Lucinda Parker (3) -   April 19, 1888
    Place of marriage, near Kabletown - Age of husband, 56 - Age of
    wife, 40 - Husband is a Widower - Wife is a Widow - Husband was
    born at Richmond, Virginia - Wife was born in Jefferson County,
    West Virginia - Both reside in Jefferson County, West Virginia.

Brown, Elizabeth and Robert Stevens (1) -　　　　August 14, 1806

Brown, Ellen and Edmun Merrida (3) -　　　　　　July 25, 1871
　　For further information see - Merrida, Edmun.

Brown, Ellen (cold.) Alfred Ranson (3) -　　　　May 30, 1882
　　For further information see - Ranson, Alfred.

Brown, Esther G. and John Buckmaster (1) -　　　March 3, 1827

Brown, Fannie V. and E. Hunter Swann (3) -　　　December 26, 1889
　　For further information see - Swann, E. Hunter.

Brown, Fanny (cold.) James Albert Thomas (3) -　December 28, 1882
　　For further information see - Thomas, James Albert.

Brown, Fanny (cold.) Richard Jackson (3) -　　　January 1, 1885
　　For further information see - Jackson, Richard.

Brown, Florence E. and Joseph A. Carlisle (3) -　December 6, 1889
　　For further information see - Carlisle, Joseph A.

Brown, Forrest W. and Emily Beverly Tucker (3) -　June 11, 1885
　　Place of marriage, Charlestown - Age of husband, 29 - Age of wife,
　　22 - Both are Single - Husband was born in Jefferson County, West
　　Virginia - Wife was born at Richmond City, Virginia - Both reside in
　　Jefferson County, West Virginia.

Brown, Francis M. and Catharine B. Rutherford (2) -　(L) September 25, 1856

Brown, Frank (cold.) Teresa Thomas (3) -　　　　　August 3, 1887
　　Place of marriage, Charlestown - Age of husband, 21 - Age of wife,
　　20 - Both are Single - Husband was born in Jefferson County, West
　　Virginia - Wife was born in Maryland - Both reside in Jefferson
　　County, West Virginia. (Bride has neither father nor mother.)

Brown, George A. and Emma Jane Pendleton (3) -　May 25, 1871
　　Place of marriage, Jefferson County - Age of husband, 31 - Age of
　　wife, 18 - Both are Single - Husband was born in Virginia - Wife was
　　born in Jefferson County - Both reside in Jefferson County -
　　Husband's parents are Richard and Mary - Wife's parents are John and
　　Harriet - Occupation of husband is Farmer. (Consent P.)

Brown, George Nathan and Lizzie Turner (3) -　　May 9, 1872
　　Place of marriage, Jefferson County - Age of husband, 22 - Age of
　　wife, 21 - Both are Single - Both were born in Virginia - Both
　　reside in Virginia - Husband's parents are Alexander and Caroline -
　　Wife's parents are Benjamin and Millie - Occupation of husband is
　　Farmer.

Brown, George Thomas (cold.) Susan Brown (3) -　December 2, 1880
　　Place of marriage, Bolivar - Age of husband, 23 - Age of wife, 18 -
　　Both are Single - Husband was born in Maryland - Wife was born in
　　Jefferson County, West Virginia - Husband resides in Maryland -
　　Wife resides in Jefferson County, West Virginia.

Brown, Hannah (cold.) Albert Smith (3) -　　　　December 28, 1882
　　For further information see - Smith, Albert.

Brown, Henry (cold.) Jane Patterson (3) -   September 22, 1881
    Place of marriage, Charlestown - Age of husband, 31 - Age of wife,
    22 - Both are Single - Husband was born in Maryland - Wife was born
    in Jefferson County, West Virginia - Both reside in Jefferson
    County, West Virginia.

Brown, Jacob B. and Emily Entler (2) -   (L) November 12, 1858

Brown, James and Mary Showmann (1) -   June 11, 1803

Brown, Jane and W. S. Merchant (3) -   March 18, 1873
    For further information see - Merchant, W. S.

Brown, Jane (cold.) Thornton Nelson (3) -   December 13, 1877
    For further information see - Nelson, Thornton.

Brown, John (cold.) Eliza Thornton (3) -   March 1, 1888
    Place of marriage, Middleway - Age of husband, 28 - Age of wife,
    29 - Both are Single - Husband was born at Washington, D. C. - Wife
    was born in Jefferson County, West Virginia - Both reside in
    Jefferson County, West Virginia.

Brown, John H. and Mary B. Smallwood (3) -   February 4, 1880
    Place of marriage, Bolivar - Age of husband, 33 - Age of wife, 22 -
    Both are Single - Husband was born at Baltimore, Maryland - Wife was
    born in Jefferson County, West Virginia - Both reside in Jefferson
    County, West Virginia.

Brown, John W. (cold.) Mary V. Stribling (3) -   May 10, 1877
    Place of marriage, Summit Point - Age of husband, 26 - Age of wife,
    24 - Both are Single - Both were born in Jefferson County, West
    Virginia - Both reside in Jefferson County, West Virginia.

Brown, Joseph and Mary Ann Mitchell (1) -   April 7, 1825

Brown, Joseph (cold.) Eliza Hunter (3) -   July 19, 1886
    Place of marriage, Summit Point - Age of husband, 21 - Age of wife,
    21 - Both are Single - Both were born in Jefferson County, West
    Virginia - Husband resides in Jefferson County - Wife resides in
    Jefferson County, West Virginia.

Brown, Josephine (cold.) Alexander Devinger (3) -   November 8, 1887
    For further information see - Devinger, Alexander.

Brown, Kate (cold.) Thomas Coleman (3) -   December 22, 1885
    For further information see - Coleman, Thomas.

Brown, Katy (cold.) Thomas Bradford (3) -   July 23, 1885
    For further information see - Bradford, Thomas.

Brown, Laura and Thomas Parker (3) -   May 28, 1874
    For further information see - Parker, Thomas.

Brown, Laura (cold.) Lewis Morgan (3) -   November 8, 1876
    For further information see - Morgan, Lewis.

Brown, Lewis (cold.) Ellen McDaniel (3) -   December 23, 1875
    Place of marriage, near Bloomery - Age of husband, 26 - Age of wife,
    19 - Both are Single - Husband was born in Frederick County,
    Virginia - Wife was born in Jefferson County, West Virginia - Both
    reside in Jefferson County, West Virginia. (Consent of bride's
    father in person.)

Brown, Lucy (cold.) Holmes Norris (3) -   April 19, 1882
    For further information see - Norris, Holmes.

Brown, Lucy Ann and John A. Finnell (3) -   December 14, 1875
    For further information see - Finnell, John A.

Brown, M. S. and Annie E. Gallaher (3) -   November 26, 1867
    Place of marriage, Jefferson County - Age of husband, 28 - Age of
    wife, 23 - Both are Single - Husband was born at Winchester,
    Virginia - Wife was born in Jefferson County - Both reside in
    Jefferson County - Husband's parents are John and Mary - Wife's
    parents are John - Occupation of husband is Tobaconist.

Brown, Margaret C. and George H. Willingham (3) -   June 21, 1866
    For further information see - Willingham, George H.

Brown, Margaret T. and Robert Fulton (1) -   October 27, 1807

Brown, Margaretta T. and Robert T. Brown (1) -   December 1827

Brown, Maria and Theophilus W. Buckmaster (1) -   January 1, 1818

Brown, Maria J. and William C. Johnson (3) -   June 21, 1877
    For further information see - Johnson, William C.

Brown, Martha (cold.) Thomas G. Washington (3) -   May 2, 1889
    For further information see - Washington, Thomas G.

Brown, Martin S. and Elizabeth Smith (1) -   May 3, 1827

Brown, Mary (free cold.) James William Steen (2) -   (L) October 13, 1852

Brown, Mary and Samuel Jones (3) -   September 24, 1868
    For further information see - Jones, Samuel.

Brown, Mary E. (cold.) George F. Creamer (3) -   December 2, 1883
    For further information see - Creamer, George F.

Brown, Mary H. and St.George T. Brooke (3) -   August 15, 1882
    For further information see - Brooke, St.George T.

Brown, Mary M. and Samuel T. Taylor (3) -   June 17, 1885
    For further information see - Taylor, Samuel T.

Brown, Mary R. and John W. Gardner (1) -   May 14, 1850

Brown, Mary V. and John R. Bell (3) -   February 29, 1876
    For further information see - Bell, John R.

Brown, Mary V. (cold.) Henry Luckett (3) -   June 7, 1888
    For further information see - Luckett, Henry.

Brown, Milford (cold.) Phebe Dickinson (3) - May 29, 1879
   Place of marriage, near Charlestown - Age of husband, 23 - Age of
   wife, 24 - Both are Single - Husband was born in Rockingham County,
   Virginia - Wife was born in Augusta County, Virginia - Both reside
   in Jefferson County, West Virginia. (No return of minister.
   License returned June 18, 1884.)

Brown, Milly (cold.) Hamilton Robinson (3) - February 23, 1878
   For further information see - Robinson, Hamilton.

Brown, Phebe (cold.) Major Bailey (3) - January 7, 1875
   For further information see - Bailey, Major.

Brown, Rachael and John Molar (1) - April 10, 1817

Brown, Rebeca and Isaac Foussett (1) - 1812

Brown, Robert and Mary Johnson (3) - January 6, 1872
   Place of marriage, Jefferson County, West Virginia - Age of husband,
   31 - Age of wife, 21 - Both are Single - Husband was born in Warren
   County, Virginia - Wife was born in Page County, Virginia - Husband
   resides in Jefferson County, West Virginia - Wife resides in
   Jefferson County - Husband's parents are Alexander and Caroline -
   Wife's parents are Ewell and Phoebe - Occupation of husband is
   Farmer.

Brown, Robert and Lucy Simmons (3) - May 2, 1872
   Place of marriage, Jefferson County - Age of husband, 23 - Age of
   wife, 21 - Both are Single - Both were born in Virginia - Both
   reside in Virginia - Husband's parents are Henry and Rachael -
   Wife's parents are David and Lettes - Occupation of husband is
   Manufacturer.

Brown, Robert (cold.) Lucy Devonshire (3) - October 11, 1888
   Place of marriage, Shepherdstown - Age of husband, 24 - Age of wife,
   22 - Both are Single - Both were born in Jefferson County, West
   Virginia - Both reside in Jefferson County, West Virginia.

Brown, Robert T. and Margaretta T. Brown (1) - December 1827

Brown, Samuel and Nancie Briscoe (3) - September 30, 1866
   Place of marriage, near Leetown, Jefferson County - Age of husband,
   35 - Age of wife, 25 - Both are Single - Both were born in Jefferson
   County, West Virginia - Both reside in Jefferson County, West
   Virginia - Husband's parents are Margaret Brown - Wife's parents are
   Louis and Sallie Briscoe - Occupation of husband is Farmer.

Brown, Samuel (cold.) Ella Mason (3) - September 30, 1886
   Place of marriage, Kearneysville - Age of husband, 23 - Age of wife,
   18 - Both are Single - Both were born in Jefferson County, West
   Virginia - Both reside in Jefferson County, West Virginia.
   (Consent of bride's mother vouched for by William Goens.)

Brown, Sarah and Washington Busey (1) - December 16, 1831

Brown, Solomon (free colored) Susan Matilda Harvey (2) - (L) September 3, 1856

Brown, Susan (cold.) George Thomas Brown (3) - December 2, 1880
   For further information see - Brown, George Thomas.

Brown, Tanzon Margaret and Levi Moler (1) -   October 22, 1829

Brown, Thomas (cold.) Sely Carey (3) -   April 12, 1888
Place of marriag, Charlestown - Age of husband, 27 - Age of wife,
23 - Husband is Single - Wife is a Widow - Husband was born in
Rockingham County, Virginia - Wife was born in Jefferson County,
West Virginia - Both reside in Jefferson County, West Virginia.

Brown, Thomas E. and Elizabeth Athey (3) -   November 28, 1865
Place of marriage, near Zion Church, Jefferson County - Age of
husband, 26 - Age of wife, 22 - Both are Single - Husband was born
in Rockingham County, Virginia - Wife was born in Clarke County,
Virginia - Both reside in Jefferson County, West Virginia -
Husband's parents are Thomas E. and Annie Brown - Wife's parents are
Levi and Agnes Athey - Occupation of husband is Sadler.

Brown, W. W. and Mary J. Engle (3) -   February 6, 1878
Place of marriage, near Unionville - Age of husband, 28 - Age of
wife, 23 - Both are Single. - Both were born in Jefferson County,
West Virginia - Both reside in Jefferson County, West Virginia.

Brown, William and Elizabeth Cook (1) -   February 19, 1822

Brown, William H. (cold.) Emma G. H. Jackson (3) -   March 18, 1880
Place of marriage, Harpers Ferry - Age of husband, 23 - Age of wife,
18 - Both are Single - Husband was born in Fauquier County,
Virginia - Wife was born in Essex County, Virginia - Husband resides
at Washington, D. C. - Wife resides in Jefferson County, West
Virginia. (Consent of bride's mother in writing.)

Brown, William H. and Julia F. Hannah (3) -   February 17, 1885
Place of marriage, near Leetown - Age of husband, 31 - Age of wife,
16 - Both are Single - Husband was born in Warren County, Virginia -
Wife was born in Jefferson County, West Virginia - Both reside in
Jefferson County, West Virginia. (Consent of bride's father in
person.)

Brua, Mary E. and Adam Young (1) -   April 25, 1833

Brua, R. H. and Jane E. Kirby (2) -   (L) November 27, 1858

Bruce, Anthony and Ann Wren (2) -   (L) November 18, 1854

Bruce, Mary and John Camine (1) -   April 5, 1828

Bruce, Mary and William Sifert (2) -   (L) December 23, 1854

Brue, Ann Caroline and Philip Coonts (1) -   1827

Bruer, George B. and Mary E. Little (1) -   January 5, 1832

Brumbaugh, G. S. and S. A. Thompson (bride) (3) -   March 13, 1868
Place of marriage, Jefferson County - Age of husband, 23 - Age of
wife, 16 - Both are Single - Husband was born at Shenandoah - Wife
was born in Berkeley County - Both reside in Jefferson - Husband's
parents are Joseph and Elizabeth - Wife's parents are Joseph -
Occupation of husband is Farmer. (Father willing.)

Bruner, Daniel H. and Lydia Byers (1) -   September 4, 1817

Brunswick, Florence (cold.) Moses Baylor (3) -   December 11, 1877
    For further information see - Baylor, Moses.

Brunswick, Frances (cold.) Daniel Hall (3) -   March 26, 1874
    For further information see - Hall, Daniel.

Brunswick, James L. (cold.) Betty Howard (3) -   November 2, 1876
    Place of marriage, Shepherdstown - Age of husband, 23 - Age of wife, 22 - Both are Single - Both were born in Jefferson County, West Virginia - Both reside in Jefferson County, West Virginia.

Brunswick, James L. (cold.) Maggie Smith (3) -   January 18, 1883
    Place of marriage, Harpers Ferry - Age of husband, 26 - Age of wife, 27 - Husband is a Widower - Wife is Single - Husband was born in Jefferson County, West Virginia - Wife was born at Frederick, Maryland - Both reside in Jefferson County, West Virginia.

Brunswick, Lizzie (cold.) Daniel Hall (3) -   August 11, 1887
    For further information see - Hall, Daniel.

Brunswick, Martha (cold.) C. M. Turner (3) -   December 24, 1888
    For further information see - Turner, C. M.

Brunswick, Sarah L. (cold.) James L. Weaver (3) -   September 4, 1888
    For further information see - Weaver, James L.

Brunswick, Virginia and Thomas Reeves (3) -   February 1, 1876
    For further information see - Reeves, Thomas.

Brunz, Anthony and Catharine Laport (2) -   (L) March 30, 1852

Bryan, Charles and Phoebe A. McCormack (1) -   March 28, 1831

Bryan, George and Anna Blackburn (1) -   May 19, 1816

Bryan, John L. and Mary Bellinger (1) -   April 29, 1819

Bryan, Samuel and Catherine Grove (1) -   April 22, 1817

Bryant, William J. and Elizabeth Jane Brooks (2) -   (L) November 22, 1863
    Time of marriage, November 23, 1863 - Place of marriage, Charlestown - Names, William J. Bryant and Elizabeth Jane Brooks - Age of husband, 21 years, May 25, 1863 - Age of wife, 22 years, August 15, 1863 - Both are Single - Husband was born in Lee County, Virginia - Wife was born in England - Husband's residence in Lee County, Virginia - Wife's residence at Charlestown, Jefferson County, Virginia - Names of husband's parents are John and Rachel Bryant - Wife's parents are Unknown - Occupation of husband is Soldier in Federal Army - License issued, November 22, 1863 - Thomas A. Moore, Clerk.

Bryant, William R. and Maggie B. Snapp (3) -   March 12, 1883
    Place of marriage, Charlestown - Age of husband, 38 - Age of wife, 28 - Both are Single - Husband was born in State of Virginia - Wife, was born in Frederick County, Virginia - Husband resides at Pittsburg, Pennsylvania - Wife resides in Jefferson County, West Virginia.

Bryarly, Thomas M. and Nannie T. Staley (3) -   February 24, 1881
   Place of marriage, Shepherdstown - Age of husband, 30 - Age of wife,
   23 - Both are Single - Husband was born in Berkeley County, West
   Virginia - Wife was born in Jefferson County, West Virginia -
   Husband resides in Berkeley County, West Virginia - Wife resides in
   Jefferson County, West Virginia.

Bryson, Mary and George Leiper (1) -   November 4, 1804

Buchanan, James A. and Rosa M. Parran (2) -   (L) September 15, 1857

Buck, Henry and Hannah Fizer (1) -   November 21, 1816

Buck, Thomas E. and E. M. Snyder (3) -   May 29, 1865
   Place of marriage, Jefferson County - Age of husband, 29 years - Age
   of wife, 19 years - Both are Single - Husband was born in Vermont -
   Wife was born in Jefferson County, West Virginia - Husband resides
   in Connecticut - Wife resides in Jefferson County - Husband's
   parents are Thomas M. Buck and (nee) Mary Brown - Wife's parents are
   Jeremiah Snyder - Husband's occupation is Physician.

Buckey, Ann Elizabeth and Jacob Crowl (2) -   (L) May 24, 1851

Buckey, Ann Elizabeth and Jacob Crowl (1) -   May 29, 1851

Buckey, Thomas W. and Louisa C. Packett (3) -   October 27, 1870
   Place of marriage, Jefferson County - Age of husband, 24 - Age of
   wife, 22 - Husband was born in Pennsylvania - Wife was born in
   Jefferson County - Husband resides in Pennsylvania - Wife resides in
   Jefferson County.

Buckles, Catherine E. and Robert J. Waggoner (1) -   March 31, 1841

Buckles, David H. and Mary L. Moler (3) -   June 10, 1868
   Age of husband, 31 - Age of wife, 26 - Both are Single - Husband was
   born in Loudoun County - Wife was born in Jefferson County - Both
   reside in Jefferson County - Husband's parents are George and
   Catharine - Wife's parents are Henry and Harriet - Occupation of
   husband is Farmer.

Buckles, Eliza and Charles Harper (1) -   April 6, 1830

Buckles, Elvina and Thomas Stipes (1) -   1820

Buckles, Elvina and Thomas Stypes (1) -   1822

Buckles, Henry and Mary Ann Barnbent (1) -   April 18, 1844

Buckles, John and Winifred Kerchival (1) -   January 17, 1828

Buckles, M. A. (bride) and T. G. Rust (3) -   December 27, 1871
   For further information see - Rust, T. G.

Buckles, Mary and John H. Rogers (1) -   March 31, 1812

Buckles, Mary Ann Abigail and Corban West (1) -   March 31, 1825

Buckles, Mollie A. and Thomas B. Vanmeter (3) -   March 16, 1869
   For further information see - Vanmeter, Thomas B.

Buckles, P. P. (bride) and A. L. Moore (3) - April 3, 1872
For further information see - Moore, A. L.

Buckles, Pheby and Henry Stipes (1) - 1819

Buckles, Rachel and Charles Basem (1) - January 16, 1816

Buckles, Sally and John B. Showman (1) - December 29, 1807

Buckles, Sarah Bell and John Marshall (1) - May 25, 1820

Buckles, Solomon and Sarah Gannon (1) - 1819

Buckly, Daniel and Caroline M. Hite (1) - July 26, 1836

Buckly, John W. and Susanna Wentzell (1) - July 5, 1851

Buckmaster, Catherine and James Anderson (1) - January 26, 1802

Buckmaster, John and Nancy Davis (1) - January 15, 1816

Buckmaster, John and Esther G. Brown (1) - March 3, 1827

Buckmaster, Theophilus W. and Maria Brown (1) - January 1, 1818

Buckner, Charles (cold.) Lucy Branson (3) - June 7, 1883
Place of marriage, Duffields - Age of husband, 26 - Age of wife,
18 - Both are Single - Husband was born in Madison County,
Virginia - Wife was born in Jefferson County, West Virginia - Both
reside in Jefferson County, West Virginia. (Consent of bride's
father in writing.)

Buffington, Griffin Taylor and Ellen Dora Sanbower (3) - August 18, 1878
Place of marriage, Shepherdstown - Age of husband, 28 - Age of wife,
18 - Both are Single - Both were born in Loudoun County, Virginia -
Husband resides in Loudoun County, Virginia - Wife resides in
Jefferson County, West Virginia. (Consent of bride's stepfather,
Jacob Cookus, in person.)

Bull, Mary and Samuel Webb (1) - January 5, 1806

Bunkins, William (cold.) Sarah Dorsey (3) - December 13, 1873
Place of marriage, Shepherdstown - Age of husband, 38 - Age of wife,
21 - Husband is a Widower - Wife is Single - Husband was born in
Jefferson County, West Virginia - Wife was born in Washington
County, Maryland - Both reside in Jefferson County, West Virginia.

Buracker, William S. and Carrie L. Gaehle (3) - August 25, 1889
Place of marriage, Charlestown - Age of husband, 25 - Age of wife,
21 - Both are Single - Husband was born in Page County, Virginia -
Wife was born at Baltimore, Maryland - Husband resides at Baltimore,
Maryland - Wife resides in Jefferson County, West Virginia.

Burges, John (cold.) Maranda Curtis (3) - December 18, 1866
    Place of marriage, Halltown, Jefferson County, West Virginia - Age
    of husband, 25 - Age of wife, 18 - Both are Single - Husband was
    born at Richmond, Virginia - Wife was born in Jefferson County,
    West Virginia - Both reside in Jefferson County, West Virginia -
    Husband's parents are Peter and Mollie Burges - Wife parents are
    John and Catharine Curtis - Occupation of husband is Laborer.

Burgess, Leander and Adelaide T. Baker (2) - (L) July 14, 1858

Burk, James H. and Ida M. Anderson (3) - December 5, 1883
    Place of marriage, near Summit Point - Age of husband, 27 - Age of
    wife, 25 - Both are Single - Husband was born in Wood County, West
    Virginia - Wife was born in Jefferson County, West Virginia -
    Husband resides at Parkersburg, West Virginia - Wife resides in
    Jefferson County, West Virginia.

Burk, John W. (cold.) Lucy Ann Wilson (3) - October 24, 1888
    Place of marriage, Charlestown - Age of husband, 22 - Age of wife,
    18 - Both are Single - Both were born in Jefferson County, West
    Virginia - Both reside in Jefferson County, West Virginia.
    (Consent of bride's mother in writing.)

Burk, Mary and Daniel Cremer (1) - 1822

Burke, George F. and Mary A. Kerfott (3) - November 20, 1872
    Place of marriage, Charlestown - Age of husband, 27 - Age of wife,
    24 - Both are Single - Husband was born at Shepherdstown, Virginia -
    Wife was born in Washington County, Maryland - Both reside in
    Jefferson County.

Burke, Mary J. and William L. Arthur (3) - December 9, 1879
    For further information see - Arthur, William L.

Burke, Richard (cold.) Julia Winston (3) - December 25, 1890
    Place of marriage, Halltown - Age of husband, 21 - Age of wife, 21 -
    Both are Single - Husband was born in Jefferson County, West
    Virginia - Wife was born in Nelson County, Virginia - Both reside in
    Jefferson County, West Virginia.

Burke, Robert and Harriett L. Beall (1) - September 17, 1833

Burket, Daniel and Mary Elizabeth Gabriel (3) - December 25, 1873
    Place of marriage, near Kearneysville - Age of husband, 23 - Age of
    wife, 18 - Both are Single - Both were born in Washington County,
    Maryland - Husband resides in Washington County, Maryland - Wife
    resides in Jefferson County, West Virginia. (Consent of bride's
    mother in writing.)

Burket, J. P. and F. A. Crane (bride) (3) - July 13, 1865
    Place of marriage, Shepherdstown, Jefferson County - Age of husband,
    47 years - Age of wife, 29 years - Husband is a Widower - Wife is
    Single - Husband was born at Martinsburg, Berkeley County - Wife was
    born at Charlestown, Jefferson County - Both residents of
    Charlestown - Husband's parents are John and Mary Burket - Wife's
    parents are Abraham and Ann C. Crane - Occupation of husband is
    Tailor.

Burkins, Essie (cold.) Peter Hall (3) - January 7, 1886
    For further information see - Hall, Peter.

Burleigh, Thomas J. and Mattie E. Moore (3) - July 15, 1878
    Place of marriage, Harpers Ferry - Age of husband, 26 - Age of wife,
    20 - Both are Single - Husband was born in Jefferson County, West
    Virginia - Wife was born in Fauquier County, Virginia - Both reside
    in Jefferson County, West Virginia. (Consent of bride's mother in
    writing.)

Burnet, Eliza and John E. West (2) - (L) January 2, 1864
    For further information see - West, John E.

Burnett, Adam (cold.) Emily Taylor (3) - February 16, 1888
    Place of marriage, Charlestown - Age of husband, 35 - Age of wife,
    28 - Both are Single - Both wre born in Jefferson County, West
    Virginia - Both reside in Jefferson County, West Virginia.

Burnett, Hannah T. and Sylvanus G. Moler (1) - May 17, 1831

Burnett, Helen and John Clouser (3) - November 24, 1870
    For further information see - Clouser, John

Burnett, Lottie C. and George W. Whittington (3) - August 26, 1890
    For further information see - Whittington, George W.

Burnett, Sarah and Revd. James Hanson (1) - February 3, 1825

Burnett, William A. and Julia M. Holmes (3) - February 5, 1889
    Place of marriage, Harpers Ferry - Age of husband, 24 - Age of wife,
    20 - Both are Single - Husband was born in Maryland - Wife was born
    in Jefferson County, West Virginia - Husband resides in Maryland -
    Wife resides in Jefferson County, West Virginia. (Consent of
    bride's father in writing.)

Burns, Allen (cold.) Annie Jones (3) - October 2, 1888
    Place of marriage, Leetown - Age of husband, 25 - Age of wife, 35 -
    Both are Single - Both were born in Jefferson County, West
    Virginia - Both reside in Jefferson County, West Virginia.

Burns, Ann C. and Alfred H. Roberts (2) - (L) June 9, 1856

Burns, Betty (cold.) Harrison Lewis (3) - July 31, 1884
    For further information see - Lewis, Harrison.

Burns, Caleb and Jane Amanda Lock (2) - (L) February 6, 1856

Burns, Elizabeth and John Wintermoyer (2) - (L) July 28, 1851

Burns, Eugene E. and Martha Hobbs (3) - (L) January 18, 1880
    Place of marriage, Harpers Ferry - Age of husband, 30 - Age of wife,
    36 - Husband is Single - Wife is a Widow - Husband was born in New
    York State - Wife was born in Jefferson County, West Virginia - Both
    reside in Jefferson County, West Virginia. (Parties married April
    18, 1880.)

Burns, Fannie E. and Luther R. Huyett (3) - January 18, 1882
    For further information see - Huyett, Luther R.

Burns, Hanrete L. and Valentine Jacobs (1) - August 25, 1829

73

Burns, J. E. and Maie A. Daniels (3) - October 23, 1888
    Place of marriage, near Harpers Ferry - Age of husband, 28 - Age of wife, 23 - Both are Single - Husband was born in Howard County, Maryland - Wife was born in Jefferson County, West Virginia - Both reside in Jefferson County, West Virginia.

Burns, J. Ed. and Bettie H. Shugert (3) - April 6, 1880
    Place of marriage, Charlestown - Age of husband, 24 - Age of wife, 23 - Both are Single - Both were born in Jefferson County, West Virginia - Both reside in Jefferson County, West Virginia.

Burns, Jane C. W. and John F. Sullivan (2) - (L) March 11, 1854

Burns, John and Martha E. Lock (2) - (L) March 29, 1852

Burns, John and Martha E. Lock (1) - March 31, 1852

Burns, John and Mary S. Stump (3) - September 13, 1866
    Place of marriage, Shepherdstown, Jefferson County - Age of husband, 21 - Age of wife, 21 - Both are Single - Both were born in Berkeley County, West Virginia - Both reside in Berkeley County, West Virginia - Husband's parents are John and Eliza Burns - Wife's parents are John and Susan Stump - Occupation of husband is Farmer.

Burns, Joseph J. and Eveline E. Lloyd (1) - August 29, 1829

Burns, Lucinda (cold.) Edward Allen (3) - March 3, 1881
    For further information see - Allen, Edward.

Burns, Maria D. and John Dennis (1) - August 26, 1818

Burns, Mary (cold.) James Franklin (3) - December 26, 1876
    For further information see - Franklin, James.

Burns, Mary E. and Thomas Frasier (3) - December 16, 1874
    For further information see - Frasier, Thomas.

Burns, Nancy A. (cold.) W. H. Butcher (3) - December 25, 1872
    For further information see - Butcher, W. H.

Burns, Robert (cold.) Annie Taylor (3) - August 6, 1884
    Place of marriage, Charlestown - Age of husband, 22 - Age of wife, 23 - Both are Single - Husband was born in Jefferson County, West Virginia - Wife was born in Jefferson County - Husband resides in Jefferson County - Wife resides in Jefferson County, West Virginia.

Burns, Samuel and Eliza Fulk (1) - December 30, 1830

Burns, Susan E. and C. H. B. Sullivan (1) - June 18, 1850

Burns, William (cold.) Edmonia Fletcher (3) - November 4, 1890
    Place of marriage, Charlestown - Age of husband, 23 - Age of wife, 22 - Both are Single - Husband was born in Jefferson County, West Virginia - Wife was born in Frederick County, Virginia - Both reside in Jefferson County, West Virginia.

Burns, William G. and Ann Downey (1) - February 24, 1834

Burns, William M. and Laura A. Rohrer (3) - December 23, 1879
    Place of marriage, at Ripon - Age of husband, 21 - Age of wife, 22 -
    Both are Single - Husband was born in Jefferson County, West
    Virginia - Wife was born in State of Pennsylvania - Both reside in
    Jefferson County, West Virginia.

Burr, Edmund and Mary McKnight (1) - December 30, 1824

Burr, Emma and John D. McGarry (3) - May 30, 1877
    For further information see - McGarry, John D.

Burr, James and Jane Leah Slemons (1) - February 1, 1827

Burr, James William and Alice M. Roberts (3) - September 13, 1882
    Place of marriage, Kearneysville - Age of husband, 26 - Age of wife,
    22 - Both are Single - Both were born in Jefferson County, West
    Virginia - Both reside in Jefferson County, West Virginia.

Burr, John William and Willie E. Wiltshire (2) - (L) February 22, 1855

Burr, Margaret Ann and Wendell S. Small (3) - January 22, 1874
    For further information see - Small, Wendell S.

Burr, Sarah Jane and Davenport Wiltshire (2) - (L) March 19, 1855

Burr, William and Margaret Young (1) - May 18, 1809

Burrell, Abey and Henry Blackburn (3) - December 28, 1869
    For further information see - Blackburn, Henry.

Burton, Hattie and D. A. Stewart (3) - April 7, 1887
    For further information see - Stewart, D. A.

Burton, Henry A. and M. Vandalia Reed (3) - March 21, 1877
    Place of marriage, Bolivar - Age of husband, 26 - Age of wife, 21 -
    Both are Single - Husband was born in Rhode Island - Wife was born
    in Jefferson County, West Virginia - Husband resides at Charles
    Town - Wife resides at Bolivar, Jefferson County, West Virginia.

Burton, James H. and Elizabeth C. Keller (2) - (L) October 1, 1851

Burton, James H. and Eugenia Harper Mauzy (2) - (L) June 4, 1859

Burton, M. E. and Clarence Lee Hilleary (3) - July 14, 1888
    For further information see - Hilleary, Clarence Lee.

Burton, Warner W. and Annie A. Nunnymaker (3) - November 21, 1865
    Place of marriage, Bolivar, Jefferson County - Age of husband, 32 -
    Age of wife, 22 - Husband is a Widower - Wife is Single - Husband
    was born in Rhode Island - Wife was born in Jefferson County -
    Husband resides at Charlestown, Jefferson County - Wife resides at
    Bolivar, Jefferson County - Husband's parents are William and Annie
    Burton - Wife's parents are Henry and Henrietta Nunnymaker -
    Occupation of husband is Silversmith.

Burton, Warren W. and Sarah J. Hopkins (2) - (L) October 7, 1856

Burwell, Edwin B. and Cecelia P. Washington (1) - March 15, 1822

Burwell, Eliza (cold.) Richard Walker (3) -   December 29, 1881
    For further information see - Walker, Richard.

Busey, Ann T. and Charles Stidman (1) -   May 31, 1834

Busey, Catharine T. and Samuel Hill (1) -   August 22, 1833

Busey, Eliza Jane and Nathaniel W. Becraft (2) -   (L) November 24, 1851

Busey, Milton J. (cold.) Jennie Price (3) -   January 27, 1876
    Place of marriage, Leetown - Age of husband, 27 -Age of wife, 26 -
    Both are Single - Husband was born in Frederick County, Maryland -
    Wife was born in Rockbridge County, Virginia - Both reside in
    Jefferson County, West Virginia.

Busey, Nannie (cold.) William Allan Ross (3) -   January 31, 1886
    For further information see - Ross, William Allan.

Busey, Sarah D. and Henry Coalman (2) -   (L) August 21, 1852

Busey, Virginia (cold.) Alexander Rhodes (3) -   August 11, 1885
    For further information see - Rhodes, Alexander.

Busey, Washington and Sarah Brown (1) -   December 16, 1831

Busey, Washington and Mrs. Elizabeth Avis (widow) (1) -   June 30, 1836

Bushman, Lydia and John W. Clendening (1) -   February 14, 1850

Bushman, Lydia Ann and James H. Clendening (2) -   (L) March 24, 1851

Bushman, Lydia Ann and James Clendening (1) -   March 27, 1851

Bushman, Rachel and James Bell (1) -   July 13, 1831

Buskirk, William V. and Orra Moore Dixon (1) -   March 20, 1832

Bussard, William and Sarah E. Ott (3) -   February 15, 1866
    Place of marriage, Harpers Ferry, West Virginia - Age of husband,
    21 - Age of wife, 17 - Both are Single - Both were born in
    Jefferson County, West Virginia - Both reside in Jefferson County,
    West Virginia - Husband's parents are George and Elizabeth Bussard -
    Wife's parents are Israel Ott - Occupation of husband is Laborer.

Busse, Antone and Mary Zoll (2) -   (L) April 30, 1852

Busy, Eliza Jane and Nathaniel Becraft (1) -   November 25, 1851

Busy, Luly (cold.) John L. Woods (3) -   November 8, 1887
    For further information see - Woods, John L.

Butcher, R. Hume and Virginia Opie (1) -   September 26, 1844

Butcher, Virginia O. and Daniel Anan (3) -   October 21, 1869
    For further information see - Anan, Daniel.

Butcher, W. H. (cold.) Nancy A. Burns (3) -   December 25, 1872
   Place of marriage, Jefferson County, West Virginia - Age of husband,
   23 - Age of wife, 20 - Both are Single - Husband was born in
   Maryland - Wife was born in Jefferson County, West Virginia - Both
   reside in Jefferson County, West Virginia - Husband's parents are
   Peter and Ellen - Wife's parents are Charles and Fanny - Occupation
   of husband is Farmer.   (Charles Burns.)

Butler, Ann Margaret and Jacob Frederick Sponder (2) -   (L) April 8, 1853
   (W. H. Turk witness as to age of parties.)

Butler, Elizabeth and Adam Link, Jr. (1) -   May 4, 1821

Butler, Elmira and James H. Claspy (2) -   (L) August 26, 1861
   For further information see - Claspy, James H.

Butler, Ferdinand R. and Sarah Ann Janney (2) -   (L) July 16, 1852

Butler, Hannah Frances and Charles Richard Clowe (2) -   (L) (1861)
   For further information see - Clowe, Charles Richard.

Butler, James and Virginia Dillow (3) -   September 17, 1868
   Place of marriag, Jefferson County - Age of husband, 27 - Age of
   wife, 23 - Husband is Single - Wife is a Widow - Husband was born in
   Maryland - Wife was born in Virginia - Both reside in Jefferson
   County - Occupation of husband is Blacksmith.

Butler, John W. (cold.) Nancy Bowman (3) -   December 27, 1883
   Place of marriage, near Duffields - Age of husband, 28 - Age of
   wife, 28 - Both are Single - Husband was born in Berkeley County,
   West Virginia - Wife was born in Jefferson County, West Virginia -
   Both reside in Jefferson County, West Virginia.

Butler, Julia L. and Richard A. Alexander (3) -   September 15, 1874
   For further information see - Alexander, Richard A.

Butler, Lucy and Samuel Ogleton (1) -   1813

Butler, Lucy and R. M. Marshall (3) -   November 6, 1872
   For further information see - Marshall, R. M.

Butler, M. G. (bride) and J. F. Briscoe (3) -   January 17, 1884
   For further information see - Briscoe, J. F.

Butler, Mary and Samuel Ruckle (1) -   October 21, 1830

Butler, Mary A. and Thomas A. Dillow (2) -   (L) May 27, 1858

Butler, Mary V. and Milton H. Moore (3) -   August 31, 1887
   For further information see - Moore, Milton H.

Butler, Matilda V. and George W. Moore, Jr. (3) -   October 21, 1885
   For further information see - Moore, George W., Jr.

Butler, Nannie and John W. Taylor (3) -   April 20, 1869
   For further information see - Taylor, John W.

Butler, Nannie M. and A. Compton Moore (3) -   November 12, 1879
   For further information see - Moore, A. Compton.

Butler, Rosalie T. and J. S. Bragonier (3) -　　　　　October 31, 1888
　　For further information see - Bragonier, J. S.

Butler, Sallie E. (cold.) Wilson Dunmore, Jr. (3) -　　December 15, 1887
　　For further information see - Dunmore, Wilson, Jr.

Butler, Sally and Garland Moore (1) -　　　　　　　　　March 1832

Butler, Samuel and Eliza Jones (1) -　　　　　　　　　October 19, 1815

Butler, Thomas and Catherine Catlett (1) -　　　　　　October 3, 1810

Butler, Vincent M. and Matilda W. Berry (2) -　　　(L) April 21, 1853

Butler, Vincent M. and Matilda W. Berry (1) -　　　　April 28, 1853

Butler, William and Kate H. Lucas (3) -　　　　　　　April 23, 1873
　　Place of marriage, near Shepherdstown - Age of husband, 25 - Age of
　　wife, 22 - Both are Single - Both were born in Jefferson County,
　　West Virginia - Both reside in Jefferson County, West Virginia -
　　Husband's parents are C. T. and Virginia - Wife's parents are
　　Robert A. and Kate - Occupation of husband is Farmer.

Butt, Artridge and John Redrick (1) -　　　　　　　　November 16, 1814

Butt, Asey and Joshua Roderick (1) -　　　　　　　　　1812

Butt, David and Rachael Kirby (1) -　　　　　　　　　July 4, 1816

Butt, Elizabeth and Edward G. Hardesty (3) -　　　　December 16, 1879
　　For further information see - Hardesty, Edward G.

Butt, Elizabeth Ellen and John A. Lashorn (2) -　　(L) May 24, 1855

Butt, James W. and Ella Rose Harrell (3) -　　　　　February 5, 1880
　　Place of marriage, Harpers Ferry - Age of husband, 33 - Age of wife,
　　20 - Both are Single - Both were born in Jefferson County, West
　　Virginia - Both reside in Jefferson County, West Virginia.
　　(Consent of bride's father in writing.)

Butt, Letticia and Thomas Hall (1) -　　　　　　　　June 28, 1810

Butt, Levina and John T. Ringer (3) -　　　　　　　December 28, 1871
　　For further information see - Ringer, John T.

Butt, Mary E. and George D. Creamer (3) -　　　　　December 19, 1867
　　For further information see - Creamer, George D.

Butt, Nancy and William Bozworth (1) -　　　　　　　July 27, 1809

Butt, Nancy and Abraham Eversole (1) -　　　　　　　1812

Butt, Nanie and William A. McIntire (3) -　　　　　(1869)
　　For further information see - McIntire, William A.

Butt, Samuel and Ann Rebecca Frazer (1) -　　　　　May 26, 1831

Butt, Samuel and Mary Ann Fiser (2) -　　　　　　　(L) March 6, 1855

Butt, Sarah (widow) and Milton Cloud (2) -　　　　(L) August 1, 1854

Butt, W. H. H. and Martha Holmes (3) - (1879)
   Place of marriage, Harpers Ferry - Age of husband, 35 - Age of wife,
   25 - Both are Single - Both were born in Jefferson County, West
   Virginia - Both reside in Jefferson County, West Virginia.

Button, Charles and Jane Read (1) - 1820

Butts, Eliza Virginia and G. W. Hill (3) - January 1, 1889
   For further information see - Hill, G. W.

Butts, Emma and H. P. Jackson (3) - (1868)
   For further information see - Jackson, H. P.

Butts, Emma and Dennis Buzzard (3) - November 29, 1885
   For further information see - Buzzard, Dennis.

Butts, John and Susanah Wright (1) - March 2, 1823

Butts, John and Sarah Wright (1) - March 24, 1831

Butts, Jonathan and Mattie Sisler (3) - April 27, 1886
   Place of marriage, near Shepherdstown - Age of husband, 24 - Age of
   wife, 21 - Both are Single - Both were born in Maryland - Both
   reside in Jefferson County, West Virginia.

Butts, Jonathan and Mattie Sisler (3) - April 9, 1887
   Place of marriage, near Shepherdstown - Age of husband, 24 - Age of
   wife, 21 - Both are Single - Both were born in Maryland - Both
   reside in Jefferson County.

Butts, Linda A. and William L. Keyser (3) - August 26, 1890
   For further information see - Keyser, William L.

Butts, Lucy E. and Curtis McGoldrick (2) - (L) January 27, 1859

Butts, W. W. and Mary C. Baden (3) - November 23, 1870
   Place of marriage, Jefferson County - Age of husband, 25 - Age of
   wife, 20 - Both were born in Virginia - Husband resides in Jefferson
   County, West Virginia - Wife resides in Jefferson County. (Consent
   of father in writing as to lady.)

Butts, William E. and Jennie Kaufman (3) - December 12, 1884
   Place of marriage, Harpers Ferry - Age of husband, 25 - Age of wife,
   22 - Both are Single - Husband was born in Loudoun County - Wife was
   born in Jefferson County - Husband resides in Loudoun County - Wife
   resides in Jefferson County, West Virginia.

Buzzard, Albert and Ann Catharine Pifer (2) - (L) August 15, 1863
   Time of marriage, August 16, 1863 - Place of marriage, Harpers
   Ferry - Names, Albert Buzzard and Ann Catharine Pifer - Age of
   Husband, 23 years - Age of wife, 21 years and 13 days - Both are
   Single - Both were born in Jefferson County - Both reside in
   Jefferson County - Names of husband's parents, George and Elizabeth
   Buzzard - Names of wife's parents, John and Lucinda Pifer -
   Occupation of husband is Farmer - License issued, August 15, 1863 -
   T. A. Moore, Clerk.

Buzzard, Christena and George W. Piper (3) - (1870)
   For further information see - Piper, George W.

Buzzard, Dennis and Eve Ann Kephart (3) - February 17, 1871
   Place of marriage, Jefferson County - Age of husband, 22 - Age of
   wife, 24 - Both are Single - Both were born in Jefferson County -
   Both reside in Jefferson County - Husband's parents are George and
   Elizabeth - Wife's parents are Levi - Occupation of husband is
   Laborer.

Buzzard, Dennis and Emma Butts (3) - November 29, 1885
   Place of marriage, near Harpers Ferry - Age of husband, 29 - Age of
   wife, 28 - Husband is a Widower - Wife is a Widow - Both were born
   in Jefferson County, West Virginia - Both reside in Jefferson
   County, West Virginia.

Buzzard, Eliza and William Stull (2) - (L) September 1, 1854

Buzzard, Jane and John Nick (3) - May 25, 1879
   For further information see - Nick, John.

Buzzard, John and Ellen Virginia Schmitt (3) - December 16, 1873
   Place of marriage, near Duffields - Age of husband, 19 - Age of
   wife, 16 - Both are Single - Both were born in Jefferson County,
   West Virginia - Both reside in Jefferson County, West Virginia.
   (Consent of groom's father in person and Bride's father in writing.)

Buzzard, Joseph and Molly Jamison (3) - July 4, 1878
   Place of marriage, Harpers Ferry - Age of husband, 22 - Age of wife,
   21 - Both are Single - Husband was born in Jefferson County, West
   Virginia - Wife was born in Maryland - Both reside in Jefferson
   County, West Virginia.

Buzzard, Joseph and Molly Mars (3) - August 24, 1886
   Place of marriage, Harpers Ferry - Age of husband, 28 - Age of wife,
   21 - Husband is a Widower - Wife is Single - Both were born in
   Jefferson County, West Virginia - Both reside in Jefferson County,
   West Virginia.

Buzzard, Mary and Levi Wilt (3) - November 17, 1881
   For further information see - Wilt, Levi.

Buzzard, Mary Melinda and John W. Dodge (3) - August 26, 1886
   For further information see - Dodge, John W.

Buzzard, Virginia and P. L. Purcell (3) - October 14, 1890
   For further information see - Purcell, P. L.

Buzzard, William S. and Katie Painter (3) - August 18, 1889
   Age of husband, 23 - Age of wife, 17 - Both are Single - Both were
   born in Jefferson County, West Virginia - Both reside in Jefferson
   County, West Virginia. (Consent of bride's father in writing.)

Byers, Abram and Margaret Bramhall (1) - December 25, 1825

Byers, Alexander and Rachael Levick (1) - October 26, 1813

Byers, Arabella and James W. Bane (3) - April 16, 1885
   For further information see - Bane, James W.

Byers, Barbara and Thomas Thornburg (1) - December 5, 1813

Byers, Daniel (colored) Hannah Short (3) -   February 17, 1870
    Place of marriage, Jefferson County - Age of husband, 21 - Age of
    wife, 22 - Husband was born in Jefferson - Wife was born in
    Jefferson County - Both reside in Jefferson County.

Byers, Ella S. and W. E. Phelps (3) -   March 22, 1882
    For further information see - Phelps, W. E.

Byers, Ellen and A. J. Horetz (3) -   December 21, 1876
    For further information see - Horetz, A. J.

Byers, George N. and E. B. Rentch (3) -   June 6, 1871
    Place of marriage, Jefferson County - Age of husband, 36 - Age of
    wife, 24 - Both are Single - Husband was born in Virginia - Wife was
    born in Jefferson County - Husband resides in Tennessee - Wife
    resides in Jefferson County - Husband's parents are George and
    Margaret - Wife's parents are Daniel and Savilla - Occupation of
    husband is Druggist.

Byers, Lydia and Daniel H. Bruner (1) -   September 4, 1817

Byers, Mary Elizabeth and John P. Hill (2) -   (L) July 22, 1850

Byers, Mary Elizabeth and John P. Hill (1) -   July 23, 1850

Byers, Robert C. and Eliza Jane Crider (2) -   (L) February 22, 1861

Byers, Susan and George Folch (1) -   April 11, 1809

Byers, William C. and Hannah E. Beeler (3) -   September 1, 1881
    Place of marriage, Charlestown - Age of husband, 21 - Age of wife,
    22 - Both are Single - Husband was born in State of Maryland - Wife
    was born in State of Virginia - Both reside in Jefferson County,
    West Virginia.

Byers, William C. and Nora Jones (3) -   December 28, 1885
    Place of marriage, Charlestown - Age of husband, 26 - Age of wife,
    25 - Husband is a Widower - Wife is a Widow - Husband was born in
    State of Maryland - Wife was born in Jefferson County, West
    Virginia - Both reside in Jefferson County, West Virginia.

Byington, F. and Sarah C. Hurst (2) -   (L) January 8, 1861

Byrd, Charles C. and Jane C. Turner (1) -   October 3, 1823

Byrd, Courtney B. and Joseph R. Jones (2) -   (L) September 19, 1860

Byrd, Henry and Mary McKenney (1) -   June 29, 1833

Byrd, Richard E. and E. Bolling Flood (3) -   September 15, 1886
    Place of marriage, Martinsburg, Berkeley County - Age of husband,
    26 - Age of wife, 22 - Both are Single - Husband was born in
    Frederick County, Virginia - Wife was born at Richmond - That both
    reside in Jefferson County, West Virginia is crossed out in the
    original.

Byrne, John and Kate Walsh (3) -   January 19, 1874
    Place of marriage, Harpers Ferry - Age of husband, 30 - Age of wife,
    26 - Both are Single - Both were born in Ireland - Husband resides
    in Rockingham County, Virginia - Wife resides in Jefferson County,
    West Virginia.

Cage, Mary and Samuel Lancaster (1) -   April 7, 1831

Cain, John and Eliza Crim (3) -   October 7, 1873
   Place of marriage, near Summit Point - Age of husband, 23 - Age of
   wife, 18 - Both are Single - Husband was born in Frederick County,
   Virginia - Wife was born in Berkeley County, West Virginia - Both
   reside in Jefferson County, West Virginia. (Father's consent in
   writing.)

Cain, Mary Susan (cold.) William Franklin Poindexter (3) -   October 19, 1879
   For further information see - Poindexter, William Franklin.

Calahan, Thomas and Margaret Fitch (1) -   September 30, 1845

Caldwell, Joseph and Mary Wright (1) -   March 24, 1831

Caldwell, T. M. and Jennie T. Kearsley (3) -   September 4, 1878
   Place of marriage, Charlestown - Age of husband, 34 - Age of wife,
   22 - Both are Single - Husband was born in State of Tennessee -
   Wife was born in Jefferson County, West Virginia - Husband resides
   in Tennessee - Wife resides in Jefferson County, West Virginia.

Caldwell, William S. and Sarah McDonald (1) -   October 24, 1818

Calhoun, William and Rachael Pierce (1) -   July 21, 1827

Calla, Dennis M. and Eliza Jane Holmes (1) -   August 25, 1849

Callahan, Eliza M. and William A. Carr (3) -   March 21, 1882
   For further information see - Carr, William A.

Callahan, George and Katie Gerling (3) -   February 9, 1888
   Place of marriage, Martinsburg - Age of husband, 27 - Age of wife,
   24 - Both are Single - Husband was born in Jefferson County, West
   Virginia - Wife was born in Berkeley County - Both reside in
   Jefferson County.

Callar, W. T. and Addie Cross (3) -   July 15, 1885
   Place of marriage, Harpers Ferry - Age of husband, 43 - Age of wife,
   31 - Husband is a Widower - Wife is Single - Husband was born in
   State of Pennsylvania - Wife was born in Jefferson County, West
   Virginia - Both reside in Jefferson County, West Virginia.

Callison, Elizabeth and Abraham Roderick (1) -   July 1, 1828

Calvert, Ellen Virginia and James D. Fulk (2) -   (L) March 16, 1858

Cameron, Ann C. and Zachariah Shugert (2) -   (L) February 18, 1856

Cameron, Annie M. and James H. Elgin (3) -   October 25, 1871
   For further information see - Elgin, James H.

Cameron, Bettie (cold.) Thornton Nelson (3) -   December 26, 1876
   For further information see - Nelson, Thornton.

Cameron, Catherine and John Snively (1) -   April 6, 1820

Cameron, Katherine and William Culumber (1) -   December 21, 1820

Cameron, Mary E. and David Humphreys (2) -   (L) October 27, 1858

Cameron, Mary E. and R. S. M. Hoffman (3) - September 14, 1869
For further information see - Hoffman, R. S. M.

Cameron, Sarah and James Underwood (2) - (L) January 1, 1859

Cameron, William and Elizabeth Myers (1) - May 19, 1835

Camine, Eden and Nancy Lay (1) - April 8, 1821

Camine, John and Mary Bruce (1) - April 5, 1828

Cammeron, Nancy and Stephen Roots (1) - 1827

Campbell, Ann Eliza and Andrew J. West (2) - (L) January 9, 1856

Campbell, Bettie and William A. Bennett (3) - October 27, 1880
For further information see - Bennett, William A.

Campbell, Caleb and Ellen Wintermoyer (3) - July 9, 1883
Place of marriage, Charlestown - Age of husband, 34 - Age of wife, 23 - Husband is a Widower - Wife is Single - Husband was born in Page County, Virginia - Wife was born in Jefferson County, West Virginia - Husband resides in Jefferson County - Wife resides in Jefferson County, West Virginia.

Campbell, Catharine H. and Allen C. Hammond (2) - (L) January 29, 1855

Campbell, Edmund A. and Hannah D. Grant (3) - August 15, 1887
Place of marriage, Harpers Ferry - Age of husband, 21 - Age of wife, 22 - Both are Single - Both were born in Jefferson County, West Virginia - Both reside in Jefferson County, West Virginia.

Campbell, Harvey (cold.) Ida Fields (3) - July 8, 1883
Place of marriage, Charlestown - Age of husband, 23 - Age of wife, 21 - Both are Single - Husband was born in Page County, Virginia - Wife was born in Culpeper County, Virginia - Husband resides in Jefferson County - Wife resides in Jefferson County, West Virginia.

Campbell, J. W. and S. E. Hooff (bride)(3) - March 11, 1868
Place of marriage, Jefferson County - Age of husband, 21 - Age of wife, 21 - Both are Single - Husband was born in Loudoun County - Wife was born in Clarke County - Both reside in Clarke County - Husband's parents are Henry and Amelia - Wife's parents are Armstead and Harriet - Occupation of husband is Farmer.

Campbell, Jacob A. and Elizabeth Davis (2) - (L) August 17, 1857

Campbell, James W. and Jane C. Moore (2) - (L) September 12, 1854

Campbell, James W. and Mary B. Garrett (3) - February 15, 1877
Place of marriage, near Lee Town - Age of husband, 38 - Age of wife, 30 - Husband is a Widower - Wife is Single - Husband was born in Berkeley County, West Virginia - Wife was born in Caroline County, Virginia - Husband resides in Berkeley County, West Virginia - Wife resides in Jefferson County, West Virginia.

Campbell, Jere (cold.) Belle Mason (3) -   May 16, 1880
   Place of marriage, Kearneysville - Age of husband, 23 - Age of wife,
   22 - Both are Single - Husband was born at Great Capon, West
   Virginia - Wife was born in Jefferson County, West Virginia - Both
   reside in Jefferson County, West Virginia.

Campbell, John S. and Maggie A. Wooddy (3) -   June 29, 1887
   Place of marriage, Charlestown - Age of husband, 28 - Age of wife,
   19 - Both are Single - Husband was born in Fulton County,
   Pennsylvania - Wife was born in Jefferson County, West Virginia -
   Husband resides at Roanoke, Virginia - Wife resides in Jefferson
   County, West Virginia. (Consent of bride's father in person.)

Campbell, Julia A. (free colored) Benjamin Hart (1) -   December 13, 1849

Campbell, Lee (cold.) Rachael Hopewell (3) -   December 26, 1889
   Place of marriage, Shepherdstown - Age of husband, 23 - Age of wife,
   27 - Both are Single - Husband was born in Loudoun County,
   Virginia - Wife was born in Jefferson County, West Virginia - Both
   reside in Jefferson County, West Virginia.

Campbell, Lucie S. and James Wysong (2) -   (L) October 14, 1856

Campbell, Margaret A. and Joseph J. Whittington (2) -   (L) July 10, 1852

Campbell, Mary Eliza and Thomas J. West (3) -   January 2, 1879
   For further information see - West, Thomas J.

Campbell, Octavia Jane and James H. Thompson (2) -   (L) March 20, 1860

Campbell, Randolph and Margaret Elizabeth Whittington (3) -   February 20, 1884
   Place of marriage, Charlestown - Age of husband, 34 - Age of wife,
   17 - Husband is a Widower - Wife is Single - Husband was born in
   Clarke County, Virginia - Wife was born in Jefferson County, West
   Virginia - Both reside in Jefferson County, West Virginia. (Consent
   of bride's father proved by the oath of William P. Whittington,
   brother of bride.)

Campbell, Robert (cold.) Betty Jackson (3) -   December 11, 1873
   Place of marriage, Charlestown - Age of husband, 29 - Age of wife,
   28 - Both are Single - Husband was born in Rockingham County,
   Virginia - Wife was born in Loudoun County, Virginia - Both reside
   in Jefferson County, West Virginia.

Campbell, Susan and Benjamin Hunter (3) -   June 6, 1867
   For further information see - Hunter, Benjamin.

Campbell, W. C. and Anna G. Child (3) -   June 7, 1882
   Place of marriage, Harpers Ferry - Age of husband, 31 - Age of wife,
   25 - Both are Single - Husband was born in Berkeley County, West
   Virginia - Wife was born in State of Ohio - Husband resides in
   Roanoke County, Virginia - Wife resides in Jefferson County.

Campbell, William P. and Mary W. Duke (3) -   June 13, 1883
   Place of marriage, Charlestown - Age of husband, 25 - Age of wife,
   21 - Both are Single - Husband was born in Jefferson County, West
   Virginia - Wife was born at Staunton, Augusta County, Virginia -
   Husband resides at Cumberland, Maryland - Wife resides in Jefferson
   County, West Virginia.

Canada, Mary (cold.) Fielding Hill (3) -   September 16, 1884
   For further information see - Hill, Fielding.

Canann, Eliza and Jacob R. Keller (3) -   February 17, 1887
   For further information see - Keller, Jacob R.

Cane, Elizabeth and John Roderick (1) -   January 5, 1836

Caniford, Sarah E. and John D. Hart (3) -   March 15, 1887
   For further information see - Hart, John D.

Canniford, James W. and Lucy E. Conrad (3) -   April 12, 1887
   Place of marriage, Charlestown - Age of husband, 25 - Age of wife,
   21 - Both are Single - Husband was born in Clarke County, Virginia -
   Wife was born in Jefferson County, West Virginia - Husband resides
   in Clarke County, Virginia - Wife resides in Jefferson County, West
   Virginia.

Canpher, George W. and Abigail Watson (3) -   October 5, 1886
   Place of marriage, Charlestown - Age of husband, 32 - Age of wife,
   25 - Both are Single - Husband was born in Loudoun County,
   Virginia - Wife was born in Jefferson County - Husband resides in
   Loudoun County, Virginia - Wife resides in Jefferson County, West
   Virginia.

Cantwell, Elizabeth and James Halpen (2) -   (L) December 12, 1851

Canvoisie, Anne and Harry Sadler (3) -   August 5, 1878
   For further information see - Sadler, Harry.

Capehart, Stephen P. and Susan S. Woods (2) -   (L) November 6, 1855

Cardoga, John D. M. and Lizzie B. Packett (3) -   September 10, 1878
   Place of marriage, near Charlestown - Age of husband, 30 - Age of
   wife, 23 - Both are Single - Husband was born in State of Delaware -
   Wife was born in Jefferson County, West Virginia - Husband resides
   in State of Delaware - Wife resides in Jefferson County, West
   Virginia.

Carell, Ann W. and Henry Kimes (1) -   September 26, 1839

Carer, William and M. J. Hooff (3) -   November 28, 1867
   Place of marriage, Jefferson County - Age of husband, 22 - Age of
   wife, 19 - Both are Single - Husband was born in Pennsylvania -
   Wife was born in Jefferson - Both reside in Jefferson. (Mother
   consents.)

Carey, E. and Rebecca Tracey (3) -   September 5, 1869
   Place of marriage, Jefferson County - Age of husband, 21 - Age of
   wife, 21 - Husband was born in Maryland - Wife was born in
   Illinois - Husband resides in Maryland - Wife resides in West
   Virginia. (Father in writing consents.)

Carey, Sabina (cold.) Aron Warner (3) -   September 20, 1880
   For further information see - Warner, Aron.

Carey, Sely (cold.) Thomas Brown (3) -   April 12, 1888
   For further information see - Brown, Thomas.

Carlan, Mary Ellen and John W. Roulett (3) -   March 20, 1884
   For further information see - Roulett, John W.

Carlisle, Joseph A. and Florence E. Brown (3) -   December 6, 1889
   Place of marriage, Charlestown - Age of husband, 21 - Age of wife,
   21 - Both are Single - Husband was born in Knox County, Ohio - Wife
   was born in Loudoun County, Virginia - Husband resides in Loudoun
   County, Virginia - Wife resides in Jefferson County, West Virginia.

Carlisle, Leander and Dorcas C. Reed (2) -   (L) June 18, 1851

Carman, George W. and E. A. S. Faulkner (2) -   (L) November 19, 1851

Carman, George W. and E. A. S. Faulkner (1) -   November 20, 1851

Carney, Hiram and Martha Arvin (1) -   September 27, 1832

Carney, Hyram and Margaret Harding (1) -   April 28, 1814

Carney, Utica and Robert Arvin (2) -   (L) March 23, 1861

Carothers, William Weston and Elizabeth A. Roberts (3) -   January 24, 1871
   Place of marriage, Smithfield - Age of husband, 23 - Age of wife,
   21 - Both are Single - Husband was born in Cumberland County,
   Pennsylvania - Wife was born in Jefferson County - Both reside in
   Jefferson County - Husband's parents are William Weston and
   Catherine Elizabeth - Wife's parents are Joel and Sarah Roberts -
   Occupation of husband is Farmer.

Carpenter, A. L. (cold.) Mary Bossell (3) -   August 29, 1887
   Place of marriage, Charlestown - Age of husband, 27 - Age of wife,
   23 - Both are Single - Husband was born in Madison County,
   Virginia - Wife was born in Page County, Virginia - Both reside in
   Jefferson County, West Virginia.

Carper, Eliza J. and William F. Weis (3) -   December 5, 1882
   For further information see - Weis, William F.

Carper, James N. and Eliza Triggs (3) -   March 25, 1886
   Place of marriage, Middleway - Age of husband, 30 - Age of wife,
   19 - Both are Single - Husband was born in State of Virginia - Wife
   was born in Berkeley County, West Virginia - Husband resides in
   Berkeley County, West Virginia - Wife resides in Jefferson County,
   West Virginia. (Consent of bride's father in person.)

Carper, John P. and Annie B. Potts (3) -   July 3, 1888
   Place of marriage, Charlestown - Age of husband, 28 - Age of wife,
   15 - Both are Single - Husband was born at Winchester, Virginia -
   Wife was born in Jefferson County, West Virginia - Both reside in
   Jefferson County, West Virginia. (Consent of bride's father in
   person.)

Carper, Mary E. and John Shackfort (3) -   August 1, 1878
   For further information see - Shackfort, John.

Carr, Joshua (colored) Millie Dorsey (3) -   April 14, 1870
   Place of marriage, Jefferson County - Age of husband, 25 - Age of
   wife, 21 - Both were born in Virginia - Both reside in Jefferson
   County. (Age sworn to by Lucas Werrick.)

Carr, William and Sarah Hoffman (1) - April 11, 1815

Carr, William A. and Eliza M. Callahan (3) - March 21, 1882
Place of marriage, Shepherdstown - Age of husband, 26 - Age of wife, 23 - Both are Single - Both were born in Washington County, Maryland - Husband resides in Washington County, Maryland - Wife resides in Jefferson County, West Virginia.

Carrell, Eli H. and Margaret Gibson (1) - July 30, 1834

Carrell, William H. and Eliza J. Clipp (1) - August 29, 1848

Carrol, William C. and Susan R. Lock (3) - February 22, 1866
Place of marriage, Charlestown, Jefferson County - Age of husband, 34 - Age of wife, 30 - Both are Single - Both were born at Charlestown, Jefferson County - Husband resides in Florida - Wife resides at Charlestown, Jefferson County - Husband's parents are G. W. and Senceline Carrol - Wife parents are William S. and Rachel Lock - Occupation of husband is Merchant.

Carroll, George B. and Sensalina Shirley (1) - February 21, 1828

Carroll, Hiram A. and Lillie E. Backus (3) - December 4, 1890
Place of marriage, Ripon - Age of husband, 30 - Age of wife, 32 - Husband is Single - Wife is a Widow - Both were born in Jefferson County, West Virginia - Both reside in Jefferson County, West Virginia.

Carroll, John W. and Amelia Ann Hough (3) - November 11, 1874
Place of marriage, County - Age of husband, 22 - Age of wife, 21 - Both are Single - Husband was born in Loudoun County, Virginia - Wife was born in Clarke County, Virginia - Husband resides in Loudoun County, Virginia - Wife resides in Jefferson County, West Virginia.

Carroll, Lewis and M. Ann Huff (3) - April 11, 1867
Place of marriage, Jefferson County, West Virginia - Age of husband, 45 - Age of wife, 23 - Husband is a Widower - Wife is Single - Both were born in Clarke County, Virginia - Husband resides in Clarke County, Virginia - Wife resides in Jefferson County, West Virginia - Husband's parents are John and D. Carroll - Wife's parents are B. and Virginia Huff - Occupation of husband is Farmer.

Carroll, Patrick and Mary Jane Smith (2) - (L) September 4, 1858

Carson, Hanah and Thomas Turner (1) - May 7, 1818

Carson, James B. and Ann Daugherty (1) - June 26, 1806

Carson, Mary and John Nichols (1) - November 19, 1818

Carter, Attie E. and William J. Coulter (3) - March 15, 1890
For further information see - Coulter, William J.

Carter, Benjamin and Maria Mason (3) - April 11, 1868
Place of marriage, Jefferson County - Age of husband, 29 - Age of wife, 15 - Both are Single - Both were born in Jefferson County - Both reside in Jefferson -Wife's parents are Lucinda - Occupation of husband is Farmer. (Mother consents.)

87

Carter, Charles (cold.) Sarah Bacchus (3) - March 5, 1881
　Place of marriage, Charlestown - Age of husband, 23 - Age of wife,
　20 - Both are Single - Husband was born in State of Virginia - Wife
　was born in Jefferson County, West Virginia - Both reside in
　Jefferson County, West Virginia. (Consent of bride's mother in
　writing and the father in person.)

Carter, Dallas (colored) Sally Ann Borggess (3) - February 17, 1870
　Place of marriage, Jefferson County - Age of husband, 22 - Age of
　wife, 22 - Husband was born in Jefferson - Wife was born in
　Jefferson County - Both reside in Jefferson County.

Carter, Edward and Sarah Timberlake (1) - 1825

Carter, Eliza (colored) Robert White (3) - October 12, 1870
　For further information see - White, Robert.

Carter, Emily (cold.) Richard Stevenson (3) - December 26, 1867
　For further information see - Stevenson, Richard.

Carter, Emma (cold.) Jared M. Arter (3) - July 14, 1890
　For further information see - Arter, Jared M.

Carter, George (cold.) Anna Mason (3) - July 21, 1883
　Place of marriage, Kearneysville - Age of husband, 29 - Age of wife,
　25 - Both are Single - Both were born in Jefferson County, West
　Virginia - Both reside in Jefferson County, West Virginia.

Carter, Henrietta (cold.) Carter Robinson (3) - April 24, 1889
　For further information see - Robinson, Carter.

Carter, Horace (cold.) Charlotte Parker (3) - April 5, 1888
　Place of marriage, Charlestown - Age of husband, 25 - Age of wife,
　35 - Husband is Single - Wife is a Widow - Husband was born in
　Henrico County, Virginia - Wife was born in Jefferson County, West
　Virginia - Both reside in Jefferson County, West Virginia.

Carter, Isaac N. and Ann Margaret Kearsley (1) - May 9, 1826

Carter, Isabel (cold.) Thomas Williams (3) - July 3, 1878
　For further information see - Williams, Thomas.

Carter, Jackson (cold.) Alleatha E. Hart (3) - May 12, 1886
　Place of marriage, Charlestown - Age of husband, 23 - Age of wife,
　21 - Both are Single - Both were born in Jefferson County, West
　Virginia - Both reside in Jefferson County, West Virginia.

Carter, Jacob (cold.) Ann Fellman (3) - December 25, 1882
　Place of marriage, near Leetown - Age of husband, 25 - Age of wife,
　17 - Both are Single - Both were born in Jefferson County, West
　Virginia - Both reside in Jefferson County, West Virginia.

Carter, James (cold.) Lyddy Weaver (3) - February 22, 1890
　Place of marriage, Charlestown - Age of husband, 30 - Age of wife,
　25 - Husband is a Widower - Wife is Single - Husband was born in
　King George County, Virginia - Wife was born in Jefferson County,
　West Virginia - Both reside in Jefferson County, West Virginia.

Carter, James R. (cold.) Maria Drew (3) -   January 11, 1877
    Place of marriage, Duffields - Age of husband, 22 - Age of wife,
    21 - Both are Single - Both were born in Jefferson County, West
    Virginia - Both reside in Jefferson County, West Virginia.

Carter, Joseph K. and Jane C. Roberts (3) -   October 23, 1878
    Place of marriage, Middleway - Age of husband, 30 - Age of wife,
    23 - Both are Single - Husband was born in Clarke County, Virginia -
    Wife was born in Jefferson County, West Virginia - Husband resides
    in Clarke County, Virginia - Wife resides in Jefferson County, West
    Virginia.

Carter, Josephine (cold.) Charles Weaver (3) -   December 30, 1879
    For further information see - Weaver, Charles.

Carter, Louisa and Alex Jefries (3) -   April 16, 1871
    For further information see - Jefries, Alex.

Carter, Lucinda (cold.) David Washington, Jr. (3) -   July 26, 1883
    For further information see - Washington, David, Jr.

Carter, Luther and Martha Jane Morgan (2) -   (L) July 29, 1851

Carter, Luther and Martha Jane Morgan (1) -   July 31, 1851

Carter, Maria (cold.) Thomas McDaniel (3) -   October 21, 1880
    For further information see - McDaniel, Thomas.

Carter, Maria Louisa and Daniel W. Arnett (3) -   October 15, 1873
    For further information see - Arnett, Daniel W.

Carter, Mary (cold.) Andrew Reeler (3) -   January 1, 1868
    For further information see - Reeler, Andrew.

Carter, Patsy P. and Bushrod W. Stewart (2) -   (L) December 10, 1857

Carter, Robert (cold.) Matilda King (3) -   February 10, 1876
    Place of marriage, near Charlestown - Age of husband, 23 - Age of
    wife, 22 - Husband is a Widower - Wife is Single - Husband was born
    in Rappahannock County, Virginia - Wife was born in Clarke County,
    Virginia - Both reside in Jefferson County, West Virginia.

Carter, Robert (cold.) Lizzie Hill (3) -   July 30, 1883
    Place of marriage, Harpers Ferry - Age of husband, 24 - Age of wife,
    21 - Both are Single - Both were born in Jefferson County, West
    Virginia - Both reside in Jefferson County, West Virginia.

Carter, Sarah N. and Edward A. Gallaher (2) -   (L) December 16, 1856

Carter, Thomas H. and Lydia Ross (3) -   (1868)
    Age of husband, 19 - Age of wife, 22 - Both are Single - Both were
    born in Jefferson County - Both reside in Jefferson - Wife's parents
    are Lucy Wheeler - Occupation of husband is Farmer. (Mother
    consents.)

Carter, William A. and Sarah C. Beeler (1) -   November 25, 1824

Cartier, Franklin and Belle Blue (3) -   March 18, 1869
    Place of marriage, Jefferson County - Age of husband, 22 - Age of
    wife, 21 - Both are Single - Both were born in Jefferson County -
    Husband resides in Clarke County, Virginia - Wife resides in
    Jefferson County - Husband's parents are William and Catherine -
    Wife's parents are John and Margaret - Occupation of husband is
    Farmer.

Cary, John B. and Fannie E. Daniels (3) -   November 7, 1867
    Place of marriage, Jefferson County - Age of husband, 28 - Age of
    wife, 24 - Both are Single - Husband was born in Maryland - Wife was
    born in Jefferson County - Husband resides in Virginia - Wife
    resides in Jefferson County - Wife's parents are Catherine E.
    Daniels - Occupation of husband is Merchant.

Case, Mary E. and James E. Barnhart (3) -   February 3, 1881
    For further information see - Barnhart, James E.

Casey, Thomas and Mary Cunningham (2) -   (L) July 3, 1852

Cash, Samuel and Sarah B. Wallace (3) -   January 3, 1870
    Place of marriage, Jefferson County - Age of husband, 22 - Age of
    wife, 21 - Both were born in Virginia - Both reside in Jefferson
    County.

Cassady, Peter and Rebecca Smithy (1) -   June 2, 1825

Cassell, James F. and Peach Isabelle Smith (3) -   July 31, 1889
    Place of marriage, Harpers Ferry - Age of husband, 22 - Age of wife,
    16 - Both are Single - Husband was born in York County,
    Pennsylvania - Wife was born in Loudoun County, Virginia - Both
    reside in Jefferson County, West Virginia. (Consent of bride's
    father in person.)

Cassidy, Susan (cold.) John Johnson (3) -   July 9, 1887
    For further information see - Johnson, John.

Castle, Jane and Thomas Roach (3) -   (1869)
    For further information see - Roach, Thomas.

Castleman, Emily C. and H. B. Littlepage (3) -   November 18, 1869
    For further information see - Littlepage, H. B.

Castleman, Estelle S. and Jaqueline S. Powers(3) -   February 16, 1881
    For further information see - Powers, Jaqueline S.

Castleman, Mary E. and Logan Osburn, Jr. (3) -.   August 27, 1874
    For further information see - Osburn, Logan, Jr.

Castleman, Sarah Catherine and Henry Licklider (2) -   (L) June 2, 1862
    For further information see - Licklider, Henry.

Caswell, Henry (colored) Susan Johnson (3) -   (1870)
    Age of husband, 26 - Age of wife, 25 - Husband was born in Georgia -
    Wife was born in Virginia - Both reside in Jefferson County.

Caten, George and Margaret Hunter (2) -   (L) July 24, 1850

Caten, George and Margaret Hunter (1) -   July 25, 1850

Caten, James and Ann Lindsey (1) -   February 5, 1835

Caten, James and Martha Taylor (2) -   (L) September 30, 1850

Caten, James and Martha Taylor (widow) (1) -   October 1, 1850

Catlett, Catherine and Thomas Butler (1) -   October 3, 1810

Catlett, Eveline and Ed. Mason (1) -   October 30, 1813

Caton, Ida L. and Arthur L. Moler (3) -   March 22, 1882
     For further information see - Moler, Arthur L.

Caton, John W. and Emma G. Moler (3) -   January 3, 1882
     Place of marriage, Shepherdstown - Age of husband, 26 - Age of wife, 23 - Both are Single - Both were born in Jefferson County, West Virginia - Both reside in Jefferson County, West Virginia.

Caton, Mary Ellen and James Flanagin (3) -   September 7, 1869
     For further information see - Flanagin, James.

Catrow, Charles and Kitty McKinney (1) -   1822

Cavalier, Charles J. and Mamie Kemp (3) -   December 27, 1887
     Place of marriage, Bolivar - Age of husband, 22 - Age of wife, 20 - Both are Single - Both were born in Jefferson County, West Virginia - Both reside in Jefferson County. (Consent of bride's father in writing.)

Cavalier, Daisey P. and William H. Daggett (3) -   June 5, 1889
     For further information see - Daggett, William H.

Cavalier, Mary F. and Joseph P. Schilling (3) -   (1870)
     For further information see - Schilling, Joseph P.

Cavalier, Nannie E. and J. William Rider (3) -   January 2, 1884
     For further information see - Rider, J. William.

Cave, Ann Catherine and Levi Steadman (1) -   June 11, 1835

Cave, Elizabeth and John Daniel Ott (3) -   December 15, 1873
     For further information see - Ott, John Daniel.

Caven, James (colored) Fanas Lane (3) -   September 6, 1870
     Place of marriage, Jefferson.

Cavilier, Eugene G. and Daniel G. Henkle (3) -   November 15, 1877
     For further information see - Henkle, Daniel G.

Ceanon, Dennis W. and Ann Welsh (2) -   (L) February 11, 1854

Chamberlain, Alice V. and William Outcalt (3) -   November 14, 1865
     For further information see - Outcalt, William.

Chamberlain, Nancy and Abraham Ott (1) -   March 17, 1831

Chamberlin, Hannah and Jacob Boley (1) -   September 11, 1828

Chamberlin, Mary E. and Thomas Johnson (2) -   (L) October 28, 1850

Chamberlin, Mary E. and Thomas Johnson (1) -   October 31, 1850

Chambers, Annie C. and William A. Moore (3) -   May 29, 1886
For further information see - Moore, William A.

Chambers, E. J. (bride) and W. W. Wentsell (3) -   December 12, 1871
For further information see - Wentsell, W. W.

Chambers, Elizabeth and Charles E. Young (1) -   April 25, 1848

Chambers, Emma R. and W. H. Rokenbaugh (3) -   November 4, 1885
For further information see - Rokenbaugh, W. H.

Chambers, Helen J. and William H. H. Miller (3) -   March 28, 1866
For further information see - Miller, William H. H.

Chambers, Julia D. and C. W. Littlejohn (3) -   March 24, 1877
For further information see - Littlejohn, C. W.

Chambers, Meta H. and George E. Lane (3) -   December 20, 1877
For further information see - Lane, George E.

Chambers, Tillie E. and J. W. Colby (3) -   March 18, 1885
For further information see - Colby, J. W.

Chamblin, Anna V. and George W. Clipp (3) -   February 18, 1873
For further information see - Clipp, George W.

Chamblin, James E. and Hannah E. Shrodes (2) -   (L) March 19, 1853

Chamblin, Josephine and James H. Starr (3) -   December 17, 1879
For further information see - Starr, James H.

Chandler, William F. and Mary N. Harper (2) -   (L) June 8, 1857

Chaplain, Annie E. (Chapline, cousins) and Joseph Augustus
   Chaplain (ine) (2) -   (L) September 3, 1855

Chaplain (ine), Joseph Augustus and Annie E. Chaplain
   (Chapline, cousins) (2) -   (L) September 3, 1855

Chapline, Ida V. and James H. Rogers (3) -   April 27, 1882
For further information see - Rogers, James H.

Chapline, Isaac W. and Fanny Manning O'Connell (3) -   April 22, 1879
Place of marriage, near Shepherdstown - Age of husband, 60 - Age of wife, 32 - Husband is a Widower - Wife is Single - Both were born in Jefferson County, West Virginia - Both reside in Jefferson County, West Virginia.

Chapline, Virginia and Richard Williams (1) -   June 1849

Chapman, Catherine and John R. Bell (1) -   May 14, 1829

Chapman, Daniel and Eveline Wallingsford (1) -   April 11, 1822

Chapman, Elizabeth and Isaac McCartney (1) -   January 24, 1842

Chapman, Henry and Hannah Hyatt (1) -   September 26, 1832

Chapman, James and Clema Manuel (3) - July 22, 1875
Place of marriage, Charlestown - Age of husband, 22 - Age of wife,
18 - Both are Single - Husband was born in Jefferson County, West
Virginia - Wife was born in Rappahannock County, Virginia - Both
reside in Jefferson County, West Virginia. (Consent of father in
person at this office.)

Chapman, James W. and Catherine N. Wageley (2) - (L) April 1, 1856

Chapman, Jane and Benjamin Brison (1) - December 28, 1831

Chapman, Lydia Ann and James M. Hosier (2) - (L) November 26, 1859

Chapman, Mary Elizabeth and Joseph Gardner (2) - (L) December 13, 1855

Chapman, Sarah and Jacob Gruber (1) - January 15, 1842

Chapman, Strother and Mary Whittington (1) - November 15, 1832

Chapman, Susan and William Mullenix (1) - February 21, 1814

Chapman, Thomas T. and Lucy J. Bennett (3) - April 1873
Place of marriage, Shepherdstown - Age of husband, 30 - Age of wife,
19 - Both are Single - Husband was born in Berkeley County, West
Virginia - Wife was born in Maryland - Both reside at
Shepherdstown - Husband's parents are Joseph and Phebe A. - Wife's
parents are Washington A. - Occupation of husband is Tanner.
(Consent of bride's father in writing.)

Chappell, Abner Merican and Catharine S. Lloyd (3) - July 29, 1869
Place of marriage, Jefferson County - Age of husband, 22 - Age of
wife, 17 - Husband was born in Loudoun County - Wife was born in
West Virginia - Husband resides in Clarke County, Virginia - Wife
resides in West Virginia. (Harrison Lloyd's son swearing that
father gives his consent.)

Chargs, Daniel (cold.) Sarah Jackson (3) - March 23, 1874
Place of marriage, Charles Town - Age of husband, 39 - Age of wife,
33 - Husband is Single - Wife is a Widow - Both were born in
Jefferson County, West Virginia - Husband resides at New Orleans,
Louisiana - Wife resides in Jefferson County, West Virginia.

Chase, Daniel (cold.) Harriet Rust (3) - April 7, 1887
Place of marriage, Summit Point - Age of husband, 52 - Age of wife,
42 - Husband is a Widower - Wife is a Widow - Both were born in
Jefferson County, West Virginia - Husband resides in Berkeley
County, West Virginia - Wife resides in Jefferson County, West
Virginia.

Chase, George W. and Elizabeth J. Ridenour (2) - (L) December 5, 1855

Chase, Mary Belle and Albert C. Rowzee (3) - February 21, 1883
For further information see - Rowzee, Albert C.

Chase, Phil. Andrew (cold.) Ainsey Gaul (3) - October 19, 1889
Place of marriage, Charlestown - Age of husband, 37 - Age of wife,
35 - Husband is Single - Wife is a Widow - Both were born in
Jefferson County, West Virginia - Both reside in Jefferson County,
West Virginia.

Chelf, Ann Weadon and George Nunnamaker (2) -   (L) September 9, 1853

Chelf, Ann Weadon and George Nunnamaker (1) -   September 11, 1853

Cherry, Mary and James Harris (1) -   December 12, 1805

Chew, H. V. and Robert Earl (3) -   June 13, 1876
    For further information see - Earl, Robert.

Chew, M. B. (bride) and W. O. Norris (3) -   November 5, 1872
    For further information see - Norris, W. O.

Chew, Roger Preston and Louisa Fontaine Washington (3) -   August 15, 1871
    Place of marriage, Jefferson County - Age of husband, 28 - Age of
    wife, 27 - Both are Single - Husband was born in Loudoun County -
    Wife was born at Mount Vernon - Both reside in Jefferson County -
    Husband's parents are Roger Augustine - Wife's parents are Elenor
    Love - Occupation of husband is Farmer.

Child, Anna G. and W. C. Campbell (3) -   June 7, 1882
    For further information see - Campbell, W. C.

Childs, J. William and Anna Fry Smith (3) -   April 7, 1886
    Place of marriage, Middleway - Age of husband, 25 - Age of wife,
    21 - Both are Single - Husband was born in Clarke County, Virginia -
    Wife was born in Jefferson County, West Virginia - Husband resides
    in Clarke County, Virginia - Wife resides in Jefferson County, West
    Virginia.

Childs, John A. and Mary C. Blue (2) -   (L) March 16, 1860

Chipley, James and Ann M. Dixon (1) -   November 10, 1834

Chipley, Sarah Priscilla and Jeremiah Gittings (1) -   December 24, 1816

Chisohm, Ann Elizabeth and Charles F. Baringer (2) -   (L) April 14, 1856

Chiswell, Laura L. and Joshua N. Rawlins (3) -   September 14, 1869
    For further information see - Rawlins, Joshua N.

Christ, Newman and Matilda McCard (3) -   November 7, 1872
    Place of marriage, Jefferson County, West Virginia - Age of husband,
    26 - Age of wife, 21 - Husband is a Widower - Wife is Single -
    Husband was born in Shenandoah County - Wife was born in Clarke -
    Both reside in Jefferson County - Husband's parents are Orage and
    Sarah - Wife's parents are William and Maria - Occupation of husband
    is Dining Servant.

Claig, Daniel and Mrs. Melvina Kenny (3) -   May 4, 1887
    Place of marriage, Charlestown - Age of husband, 32 - Age of wife,
    30 - Husband is Single - Wife is a Widow - Husband was born in
    Warren County, Virginia - Wife was born in Shenandoah County,
    Virginia - Husband resides in Jefferson County, West Virginia -
    Wife resides in Jefferson County.

Clanly, Henry and Eliza Wintermoyer (2) - (L) January 22, 1863
Time of marriage, January 25, 1863 - Place of marriage,
Shepherdstown - Names, Henry Clanly and Eliza Wintermoyer - Age of
husband, 39 years - Age of wife, 35 years - Both are Single -
Husband was born in Frederick County, Maryland - Wife was born in
Jefferson County, Virginia - Both live in Shepherdstown - Names of
husband's parents, Unknown - Wife's parents are Philip and __?__
Wintermoyer - Occupation of husband is Shoemaker - Liscense issued,
January 22, 1863.

Clapham, Thomas J. and Emma W. Reynolds (3) - February 24, 1887
Place of marriage, Shepherdstown - Age of husband, 28 - Age of wife,
28 - Both are Single - Husband was born in Loudoun County,
Virginia - Wife was born in Jefferson County, West Virginia - Both
reside in Jefferson County, West Virginia.

Clappen, J. O. (cold.) H. A. Jones (bride) (3) - May 31, 1886
Place of marriage, Harpers Ferry - Age of husband, 21 - Age of wife,
21 - Both are Single - Both were born in Loudoun County, Virginia -
Both reside in Jefferson County, West Virginia.

Clappy, John and Mary Cutshaw (1) - August 27, 1829

Clark, Charles (cold.) Ellen Devonshire (3) - August 31, 1876
Place of marriage, Shepherdstown - Age of husband, 23 - Age of wife,
22 - Both are Single - Both were born in Jefferson County, West
Virginia - Both reside in Jefferson County, West Virginia.

Clark, Elizabeth and Samuel Sheetz (1) - July 28, 1818

Clark, Emma A. and James B. Newlin (3) - September 4, 1877
For further information see - Newlin, James B.

Clark, George (cold.) Margaret Wood (3) - December 16, 1880
Place of marriage, Shepherdstown - Age of husband, 24 - Age of wife,
21 - Both are Single - Both were born in Jefferson County, West
Virginia - Both reside in Jefferson County, West Virginia.

Clark, James and Mildred Berry (1) - 1820

Clark, John William and Nettie Lee Finnell (3) - August 3, 1880
Place of marriage, Charlestown - Age of husband, 25 - Age of wife,
19 - Both are Single - Husband was born in Rappahannock County,
Virginia - Wife was born in Clarke County, Virginia - Both reside in
Jefferson County, West Virginia. (Consent of bride's mother in
writing.)

Clark, Mary and Henry Rockenbough (1) - September 22, 1816

Clark, Nick and Bettie Smith (3) - December 31, 1868
Place of marriage, Harpers Ferry - Age of husband, 23 - Age of wife,
21 - Both are Single - Husband was born in Maryland - Wife was born
in Virginia - Both reside at Harpers Ferry - Husband's parents are
George and Annie - Wife's parents are Wima - Occupation of husband
is Laborer.

Clarke, Charles and M. Johnson (3) -   March 12, 1868
    Place of marriage, Jefferson County - Age of husband, 22 - Age of
    wife, 18 - Both are Single - Husband was born in North Carolina -
    Wife was born in Jefferson - Both reside in Jefferson - Husband's
    parents are John and Sophia - Wife's parents are William and Posey -
    Occupation of husband is Farmer.

Clarke, Charles H. and Julia Lyder (3) -   December 27, 1866
    Place of marriage, Shepherdstown, Jefferson County - Age of husband,
    25 - Age of wife, 22 - Both are Single - Both were born in Frederick
    County, Virginia - Both reside in Frederick County, Virginia -
    Husband's parents are Nancy F. Clarke - Wife's parents are Jacob and
    Lucinda Lyder - Occupation of husband is Farmer.

Clarke, Fenton and Nancy Trimer (3) -   February 16, 1867
    Place of marriage, Shepherdstown, West Virginia - Age of husband,
    23 - Age of wife, 26 - Both are Single - Husband was born at
    Harrisonburg, Virginia - Wife was born in Jefferson County, West
    Virginia - Husband resides in Jefferson County, West Virginia -
    Wife resides at Kearneysville, Virginia - Husband's parents are
    Samuel and Jane Clarke - Wife's parents are Reuben and Nancy
    Trimer - Occupation of husband is Farmer.

Clarke, Magie (cold.) Lee Ashby (3) -   August 16, 1883
    For further information see - Ashby, Lee.

Clarke, Mary and William Fitzpatrick (3) -   September 28, 1870
    For further information see - Fitzpatrick, William.

Clarkson, Catherine B. and Edmund B. Stephen (1) -   October 11, 1849

Claspill, Bazel and Anne Allemong (1) -   1821

Claspy, James H. and Elmira Butler (2) -   (L) August 26, 1861
    Time of marriage, August 27, 1861 - Place of marriage, Middleway -
    Age of husband, 26 years, 5 months - Age of wife, 21 years,
    2 months - Both are Single - Place of husband's birth, Harpers
    Ferry - Place of wife's birth, Harpers Ferry - Place of husband's
    residence, Fayetteville, North Carolina - Place of wife's residence,
    Middleway, Jefferson County - Names of husband's parents, John and
    Mary Claspy - Names of wife's parents, George and Tamar Butler -
    Occupation of husband is Armorer - James H. Claspy.

Claspy, Mary Virginia and James A. Merrick, Jr. (2) -   (L) November 8, 1851

Claspy, Mary Virginia and James A. Merrick (1) -   November 8, 1851

Claspy, Thomas and Matilda Athy (1) -   March 6, 1822

Clayburn, Norman and Julia L. Kidwell (3) -   June 9, 1887
    Place of marriage, Shepherdstown - Age of husband, 23 - Age of wife,
    21 - Both are Single - Husband was born in Washington County,
    Maryland - Wife was born in Jefferson County, West Virginia -
    Husband resides in Washington County, Maryland - Wife resides in
    Jefferson County, West Virginia.

Clayton, D. G. and Rebecca Fenton (1) -   October 18, 1849

Clayton, Jane and Mathew Megarry (1) -   February 20, 1807

Clege, Margaret and Joseph T. Mathews (2) -   (L) August 24, 1850

Clegg, Margaret and J. Thomas Mathews (1) -   September 6, 1850

Clegget, Thomas and Fannie Traynor (3) -   October 3, 1871
   Place of marriage, Jefferson County - Age of husband, 28 - Age of wife, 22 - Both are Single - Husband was born in Maryland - Wife was born in Virginia - Both reside in Jefferson - Wife's parents are John.

Clemmer, W. B. and E. G. Way (bride) (3) -   November 10, 1868
   Place of marriage, Jefferson County - Age of wife, 24 - Both are Single - Husband was born in New York - Wife was born in Jefferson County - Both reside in Jefferson County, West Virginia - Husband's parents are A. and Margaret - Wife's parents are G. and Mary A. - Occupation of husband is U. S. Assessor.

Clemmons, Mary and Isaac Williams (1) -   December 24, 1818

Clendening, James H. and Lydia Ann Bushman (2) -   (L) March 24, 1851

Clendening, James and Lydia Ann Bushman (1) -   March 27, 1851

Clendening, John W. and Lydia Bushman (1) -   February 14, 1850

Clendening, Sarah A. and John H. Ramey (3) -   December 9, 1879
   For further information see - Ramey, John H.

Clendenning, D. W. and Maggie J. Shoemaker (3) -   December 28, 1876
   Place of marriage, near Middleway - Age of husband, 26 - Age of wife, 27 - Both are Single - Husband was born in Frederick County, Virginia - Wife was born in Pennsylvania - Both reside in Jefferson County, West Virginia.

Cleveland, James P. and Ida Imes (3) -   September 16, 1884
   Place of marriage, Harpers Ferry - Age of husband, 29 - Age of wife, 22 - Both are Single - Husband was born in Jefferson County, West Virginia - Wife was born in State of Maryland - Both reside in Jefferson County.

Cleveland, Katherine and Magnus L. Cockrell (3) -   May 22, 1879
   For further information see - Cockrell, Magnus L.

Cleveland, Katie and Magnus L. Cockrell (3) -.   November 18, 1879
   For further information see - Cockrell, Magnus L.

Cleveland, Malissa and Charles Thomas Hightman (3) -   December 25, 1879
   For further information see - Hightman, Charles Thomas.

Clewell, Charles and Deborah Athy (1) -   1824

Clifford, J. R. (cold.) M. E. C. Franklin (bride) (3) -   December 28, 1876
   Place of marriage, Harpers Ferry - Age of husband, 26 - Age of wife, 18 in March - Both are Single - Husband was born in Hardy now Grant County, West Virginia - Wife was born in Rockbridge County, Virginia - Husband resides in Berkeley County, West Virginia - Wife resides in Jefferson County, West Virginia. (Consent of bride's father in writing.)

Climer, Isaac and Nancy Duke (1) -   January 29, 1818

Cline, John H. and Hannah F. Cox (3) -   November 1, 1869
    Place of marriage, Jefferson County - Age of husband, 21 - Age of
    wife, 18 - Husband was born in Maryland - Wife was born in West
    Virginia - Both reside in Jefferson County. (Father consents in
    writing.)

Cline, Joseph and Rebecca Jackson (1) -   April 14, 1833

Clineferburgh, Cornelius and Sally Southers (1) -   February 24, 1820

Clinton, Amelia and Richard W. Kearns (3) -   May 5, 1873
    For further information see - Kearns, Richard W.

Clinton, Annie (cold.) James Twyman (3) -   December 30, 1875
    For further information see - Twyman, James.

Clinton, Basil (cold.) Georgia Gibson (3) -   December 25, 1884
    Place of marriage, Bolivar - Age of husband, 29 - Age of wife, 26 -
    Both are Single - Both were born in Jefferson County, West
    Virginia - Both reside in Jefferson County, West Virginia.

Clinton, George Ann and Wilson Branson (3) -   December 27, 1865
    For further information see - Branson, Wilson.

Clinton, James (cold.) Sarah Thomas (3) -   February 3, 1887
    Place of marriage, Harpers Ferry - Age of husband, 21 - Age of wife,
    21 - Both are Single - Both were born in Jefferson County, West
    Virginia - Both reside in Jefferson County.

Clinton, Laura (cold.) John Edwards (3) -   December 30, 1875
    For further information see - Edwards, John.

Clinton, Lucy and James Wheeler (3) -   October 22, 1871
    For further information see - Wheeler, James.

Clinton, Mabel (cold.) Thomas Arter (3) -   September 23, 1884
    For further information see - Arter, Thomas.

Clip, David W. and Hannah M. Clip (2) -   (L) January 31, 1851

Clip, David W. and Hannah M. Clip (1) -   February 2, 1851

Clip, Eliza and William B. Grubb (2) -   (L) May 12, 1851

Clip, Hannah M. and David W. Clip (2) -   (L) January 31, 1851

Clip, Hannah M. and David W. Clip (1) -   February 2, 1851

Clip, John and Elizabeth Huffmaster (2) -   (L) January 31, 1865
    Time of marriage, February 2, 1865 - Place of marriage, Shannon Dale
    Furnace - Names, John Clip and Elizabeth Huffmaster - Age of
    husband, 23 years - Age of wife, 26 years - Both are Single - Both
    reside in Jefferson County - Both were born in Jefferson County -
    Husband's parents are William and Elizabeth - Wife's parents are
    Samuel and Elizabeth - Occupation of husband is Farmer - License
    issued January 31, 1865 - Thomas A. Moore, Clerk.

Clip, John T. and Sarah C. Dillow (3) -   January 27, 1889
  Place of marriage, near Kabletown - Age of husband, 67 - Age of
  wife, 68 - Husband is a Widower - Wife is a Widow - Husband was born
  in Jefferson County, West Virginia - Wife was born in Berkeley
  County - Both reside in Jefferson County, West Virginia.

Clip, John William and Mary Hoffmaster (2) -   (L) November 20, 1856

Clip, Joshua and Mary Board (1) -   August 22, 1824

Clip, Louisa J. and Charles Langdon (2) -   (L) October 23, 1851

Clip, Louisa Jane and Charles Langdon (2) -   (L) June 28, 1852

Clip, Louisa Jane and Charles Langdon (1) -   June 28, 1852

Clip, Martha E. and Samuel M. Clip (2) -   (L) February 1, 1851

Clip, Martha E. and Samuel M. Clip (1) -   February 1, 1851

Clip, Mary A. and Silas Clip (3) -   April 22, 1868
  For further information see - Clip, Silas.

Clip, Samuel M. and Martha E. Clip (2) -   (L) February 1, 1851

Clip, Samuel M. and Martha E. Clip (1) -   February 1, 1851

Clip, Silas and Mary A. Clip (3) -   April 22, 1868
  Age of husband, 23 - Age of wife, 23 - Both are Single - Both were
  born in Jefferson County - Both reside in Jefferson - Husband's
  parents are Jacob and Polly - Wife's parents are Joshua - Occupation
  of husband is Farmer.

Clipp, Charles W. and M. S. A. Clipp (3) -   February 18, 1869
  Place of marriage, Jefferson County - Age of husband, 24 - Age of
  wife, 18 - Both are Single - Both were born in Jefferson County -
  Both reside in Jefferson County - Husband's parents are James W. and
  Elizabeth - Wife's parents are David W. and H. Maria - Occupation of
  husband is Farmer.   (Father consents in writing.)

Clipp, Eliza J. and William H. Carrell (1) -   August 29, 1848

Clipp, Fanny and George W. West (3) -   January 27, 1886
  For further information see - West, George W.

Clipp, George W. and Anna V. Chamblin (3) -   February 18, 1873
  Place of marriage, Charles Town - Age of husband, 28 - Age of wife,
  30 - Both are Single - Husband was born in Jefferson County, West
  Virginia - Wife was born in Loudoun County, Virginia - Both reside
  in Jefferson County, West Virginia - Husband's parents are John T.
  and Tamson C. - Wife's parents are Unknown - Occupation of husband
  is Manufacturer.

Clipp, Jere O. and Martha J. Wilt (3) -   March 7, 1882
  Place of marriage, Charlestown - Age of husband, 26 - Age of wife,
  24 - Both are Single - Both were born in Jefferson County, West
  Virginia - Both reside in Jefferson County, West Virginia.

Clipp, John A. and Ada P. C. Boyd (3) -　　　　　　　　September 25, 1873
　　Place of marriage, near Kabletown - Age of husband, 23 - Age of
　　wife, 17 - Both are Single - Both were born in Jefferson County,
　　West Virginia - Both reside in Jefferson County, West Virginia -
　　Wife's parents are Robert M. E. Boyd. (Father's consent in
　　writing. James B. Clipp, sworn.)

Clipp, John W. and Laura R. Johnston (3) - .　　　　　December 12, 1888
　　Place of marriage, Halltown - Age of husband, 26 - Age of wife, 24 -
　　Both are Single - Husband was born in Jefferson County, West
　　Virginia - Wife was born in Frederick County, Virginia - Both
　　reside in Jefferson County, West Virginia.

Clipp, Laura B. and Albert Gray (3) - .　　　　　　　　March 1, 1888
　　For further information see - Gray, Albert.

Clipp, Lillie and Douglas Staubb (3) -　　　　　　　　December 15, 1889
　　For further information see - Staubb, Douglas.

Clipp, M. S. A. and Charles W. Clipp (3) -　　　　　　February 18, 1869
　　For further information see - Clipp, Charles W.

Clipp, Maggie and Joseph F. Willingham (3) -　　　　　September 17, 1885
　　For further information see - Willingham, Joseph F.

Clipp, Martha P. and Milton Smith (3) - .　　　　　　April 12, 1870
　　For further information see - Smith, Milton.

Clipp, Mary E. E. and William W. Everhart (3) -　　　February 4, 1880
　　For further information see - Everhart, William W.

Clipp, Molly B. and William J. Gore (3) -　　　　　　November 22, 1883
　　For further information see - Gore, William J.

Clipp, Nellie and William H. Moler (3) -　　　　　　 December 5, 1889
　　For further information see - Moler, William H.

Clipp, Rosa J. and Thomas J. Creamer (3) -　　　　　 March 13, 1884
　　For further information see - Creamer, Thomas J.

Clipp, Sarah J. and William W. Myers (3) -　　　　　 December 9, 1869
　　For further information see - Myers, William W.

Clipp, Thomas and Elizabeth Hoffmaster (3) -　　　　 September 10, 1872
　　Place of marriage, Jefferson County - Age of husband, 24 - Age of
　　wife, 24 - Both are Single - Husband was born in Jefferson County -
　　Wife was born in Maryland - Both reside in Jefferson County, West
　　Virginia - Husband's parents are William and Elizabeth - Wife's
　　parents are John and Eliza - Occupation of husband is Farmer.
　　(Brother sworn.)

Clothier, James and Elizabeth Redman (1) -　　　　　 November 21, 1830

Clothier, Julia Ann and William D. Lemon (1) -　　　 January 10, 1831

Cloud, Lydia Ann and A. L. Kanode (3) -　　　　　　　 January 28, 1875
　　For further information see - Kanode, A. L.

Cloud, Milton and Sarah Butt (widow) (2) -　　　　　 (L) August 1, 1854

Cloud, Milton and Harriet Jane Harvin (2)   (L) (1862)
    Time of marriage, September 21, 1862 - Place of marriage,
    Shepherdstown - Names, Milton Cloud and Harriet Jane Harvin - Age of
    husband, 47 years - Age of wife, 35 years - Condition of husband is
    Single - Condition of wife is Single - Place of husband's birth was
    in Loudoun County, Virginia - Place of wife's birth was in Jefferson
    County, Virginia - Both live in Jefferson County - Occupation of
    husband is Shoemaker - Jacob W. Staley.

Clouser, John and Helen Burnett (3) -   November 24, 1870
    Place of marriage, Jefferson County - Age of husband, 36 - Age of
    wife, 19 - Both were born in Virginia - Husband resides in
    Jefferson County, West Virginia - Wife resides in Jefferson County.
    (Mother by her son William consents.)

Clowe, Charles Richard and Hannah Frances Butler (2) -   (L) (1861)
    Time of marriage, October 1, 1861 - Place of marriage, Middleway -
    Names, Charles Richard Clowe and Hannah Frances Butler - Age of
    husband, 27 years - Age of wife, 23 years - Condition of husband is
    Single - Condition of wife is Single - Place of husband's birth was
    in Loudon County - Place of wife's birth was in Jefferson County -
    Place of husband's residence is at Fayettsville, North Carolina -
    Place of wife's residence is at Middleway, Virginia - Names of
    husband's parents are Charles B. and Hanah Clowe - Names of wife's
    parents are George H. and Tamar Jane Butler - Occupation of husband
    is Millwright - Charles R. Clowe.

Cloy, Elizabeth M. and John Elliott (1) -   December 28, 1833

Clum, Lydia and Henry Hout (1) -   February 5, 1832

Clum, Mary and Raleigh Brantner (1) -   June 17, 1819

Clymer, Eliza Jane and Samuel M. Knott (2) -   (L) January 16, 1854

Clymer, Ella L. and Edgar F. Ronemous (3) -   July 9, 1889
    For further information see - Ronemous, Edgar F.

Coal, Hannah and Christian Bane (1) -   January 9, 1828

Coale, C. and Grace Wilkenson (3) -   (1869)
    Age of husband, 30 - Age of wife, 20 - Both were born in Virginia -
    Both reside in Jefferson County. (Parents dead. No guardian.)

Coalman, Bettie (cold.) Moses Hunter (3) -   May 29, 1882
    For further information see - Hunter, Moses.

Coalman, Henry and Sarah D. Busey (2) -   (L) August 21, 1852

Coalman, Maggie and Rufus Middlekauff (3) -   (1870)
    For further information see - Middlekauff, Rufus.

Coates, Hannah Frances and John Jenkins (2) -   (L) January 29, 1853

Coates, Mary J. and John Griffiths (1) -   August 6, 1835

Coats, Erma Jane and Loraine McKlain Kemp (3) -   January 26, 1871
    For further information see - Kemp, Loraine McKlain.

Cobler, Susan and Martin Entler (1) -   November 26, 1808

Cochran, Charles C. and Alcinda M. Barns (2) - (L) May 7, 1855

Cochran, William S. and M. D. Beale (3) - January 31, 1869
    Place of marriage, Jefferson County - Age of husband, 37 - Age of
    wife, 24 - Both are Single - Husband was born in Scotland - Wife was
    born in Jefferson County, Virginia - Husband resides at Hagerstown,
    Maryland - Wife resides in Jefferson County - Husband's parents are
    John and Margaret - Wife's parents are Albert and Mary - Occupation
    of husband is Mechanical Engineer.

Cochrane, Grace M. and J. Harry Parr (3) - July 30, 1889
    For further information see - Parr, J. Harry.

Cochrane, Mary D. and Theodore M. Conner (3) - November 14, 1889
    For further information see - Conner, Theodore M.

Cocke, John H. and Ruth A. Howell (3) - November 22, 1882
    Place of marriage, Charlestown - Age of husband, 35 - Age of wife,
    39 - Both are Single - Husband was born in Fluvanna County,
    Virginia - Wife was born in Jefferson County, West Virginia -
    Husband resides in Fluvanna County, Virginia - Wife resides in
    Jefferson County, West Virginia.

Cockeral, Susan and John McTillan (1) - January 3, 1820

Cockerll, Kate E. and Andrew E. Marsteller (3) - March 6, 1872
    For further information see - Marsteller, Andrew E.

Cockrell, A. E. and Emily L. Nunnamaker (3) - December 14, 1880
    Place of marriage, Bolivar - Age of husband, 32 - Age of wife, 28 -
    Both are Single - Both were born in Jefferson County, West
    Virginia - Both reside in Jefferson County, West Virginia.

Cockrell, Adam and Eliza Ann Merritt (2) - (L) November 2, 1858

Cockrell, Ann R. and Jacob Meritt (3) - December 20, 1866
    For further information see - Meritt, Jacob.

Cockrell, Annie E. and John Y. Allstadt (3) - December 18, 1866
    For further information see - Allstadt, John Y.

Cockrell, Daniel and Eliza P. Blackford (2) - (L) March 12, 1855

Cockrell, Fannie H. and Henry H. Hoke (3) - October 15, 1889
    For further information see - Hoke, Henry H.

Cockrell, Fanny and John William Onderdonk (3) - May 13, 1884
    For further information see - Onderdonk, John William.

Cockrell, Hannah and Isaac Hiedwohl (2) - (L) February 21, 1855

Cockrell, Joseph and Nancy Wood (1) - January 4, 1816

Cockrell, Joseph H. and Wied. Young (3) - November 25, 1868
    Age of husband, 24 - Age of wife, 19 - Both are Single - Husband was
    born in Jefferson County - Wife was born in Jefferson, Virginia -
    Both reside in Jefferson County - Husband's parents are David and
    C. C. - Wife's parents are Samuel and Sarah - Occupation of husband
    is Carpenter. (Parents dead and no guardian.)

Cockrell, L. G. and Ella Ott (3) - June 6, 1877
Place of marriage, Bolivar - Age of husband, 24 - Age of wife, 21 -
Both are Single - Both were born in Jefferson County, West
Virginia - Both reside in Jefferson County, West Virginia.

Cockrell, Lucy A. and G. B. Rodeffer (3) - January 31, 1882
For further information see - Rodeffer, G. B.

Cockrell, Magnus L. and Katherine Cleveland (3) - May 22, 1879
Place of marriage, Harpers Ferry - Age of husband, 31 - Age of wife,
21 - Both are Single - Both were born in Jefferson County, West
Virginia - Both reside in Jefferson County, West Virginia. (Not
executed. License returned July 15, 1879. Renewed number 78.)

Cockrell, Magnus L. and Katie Cleveland (3) - November 18, 1879
Place of marriage, Harpers Ferry - Age of husband, 31 - Age of wife,
21 - Both are Single - Both were born in Jefferson County, West
Virginia - Both reside in Jefferson County, West Virginia.

Cockrell, Nannie D. and J. Fletcher Melvin (3) - October 17, 1883
For further information see - Melvin, J. Fletcher.

Cockrell, Peter P. and Margaret A. Ruckle (1) - June 28, 1847

Cockrell, Sally C. and S. H. Redman (3) - December 14, 1882
For further information see - Redman, S. H.

Cockrill, David S. and Almira R. E. Hilbert (3) - March 17, 1884
Place of marriage, Charlestown - Age of husband, 33 - Age of wife,
26 - Both are Single - Both were born in Jefferson County, West
Virginia - Husband resides in Shannon County, South Dakota - Wife
resides in Jefferson County, West Virginia.

Cockrill, Larkin and Christiana Warner (1) - May 27, 1806

Cockrill, Thomas V. and Mary J. Avis (3) - December 31, 1879
Place of marriage, Charlestown - Age of husband, 26 - Age of wife,
26 - Both are Single - Both were born in Jefferson County - Both
reside in Jefferson County, West Virginia.

Cockrill, William W. and Mary E. Avis (3) - April 21, 1880
Place of marriage, Charlestown - Age of husband, 21 - Age of wife,
21 - Both are Single - Both were born in Jefferson County, West
Virginia - Both reside in Jefferson County, West Virginia.

Cocks (Cox), John and Wealthy Ann Evans (1) - December 27, 1825

Coe, William W. and Sallie R. Travers (3) - January 7, 1880
Place of marriage, Charlestown - Age of husband, 33 - Age of wife,
25 - Both are Single - Husband was born in Litchfield County,
Connecticut - Both reside in Jefferson County, West Virginia.
(This record is crossed out in the original.)

Coe, William W. and Sallie R. Travers (3) - January 7, 1880
Place of marriage, Charlestown - Age of husband, 33 - Age of wife,
25 - Both are Single - Husband was born in State of Connecticut -
Wife was born at Baltimore - Both reside in Jefferson County, West
Virginia.

Coffenbarger, Sarah M. and Tobias Hendricks (2) - (L) May 15, 1858

Coffin, Virginia and Townsend Hough (3) - December 26, 1872
    For further information see - Hough, Townsend.

Coffinbarger, Ann A. and Joseph M. Painter (2) - (L) March 26, 1855

Coffinbarger, Ella B. and Luther Demory (3) - October 11, 1888
    For further information see - Demory, Luther.

Coffinbarger, George B. and Rose Fleming (3) - (1884)
    Place of marriage, Shepherdstown - Age of husband, 25 - Age of wife, 22 - Both are Single - Both were born in Jefferson County, West Virginia - Both reside in Jefferson County, West Virginia.

Coffinberger, James W. and Susan Eugenia Fleming (3) - January 27, 1881
    Place of marriage, Shepherdstown - Age of husband, 27 - Age of wife, 26 - Both are Single - Husband was born in Berkeley County - Wife was born in Jefferson County, West Virginia - Both reside in Jefferson County, West Virginia.

Coffman, Sallie and William G. Miller (3) - November 19, 1890
    For further information see - Miller, William G.

Cogal, John and Jane Ann Piper (3) - July 14, 1878
    Place of marriage, Pipertown - Age of husband, 25 - Age of wife, 23 - Both are Single - Husband was born in Loudoun County, Virginia - Wife was born in Jefferson County, West Virginia - Both reside in Jefferson County, West Virginia.

Cogel, Julia Ann and Thomas H. Harder (3) - May 29, 1881
    For further information see - Harder, Thomas H.

Cogle, Catherine and Charles Potts (3) - April 3, 1879
    For further information see - Potts, Charles.

Cogle, Elizabeth and James W. Hawk (3) - July 22, 1883
    For further information see - Hawk, James W.

Cogle, Ella and George W. Hawk (3) - March 4, 1890
    For further information see - Hawk, George W.

Cogle, John and Catherine Piper (1) - August 26, 1824

Cogle, Jonathan and Mary Piper (2) - (L) August 2, 1854

Cogle, Samuel Turner and Martha Jane Lay (3) - November 2, 1879
    Place of marriage, Bolivar - Age of husband, 28 - Age of wife, 29 - Both are Single - Both were born in Jefferson County, West Virginia - Both reside in Jefferson County, West Virginia.

Cogle, Sarah Elizabeth and Thomas William Piper (3) - August 12, 1886
    For further information see - Piper, Thomas William.

Cogle, Sarah L. and James H. Staub (3) - December 25, 1887
    For further information see - Staub, James H.

Colbert, Anthony and Rebecca Harris (1) - September 29, 1827

Colbert, Benjamin C. and Annie M. Gray (3) -   April 6, 1886
    Place of marriage, Bolivar - Age of husband, 21 - Age of wife, 21 -
    Both are Single - Both were born in Maryland - Both reside in
    Jefferson County, West Virginia.

Colbert, Edy M. and Wilbert H. Derry (3) -   May 20, 1885
    For further information see - Derry, Wilbert H.

Colbert, Elizabeth (cold.) Charles Wood (3) -   November 3, 1886
    For further information see - Wood, Charles.

Colbert, Fanny and David Taylor (1) -   October 8, 1815

Colbert, Harriet B. and Thomas L. Hess (3) -   March 11, 1880
    For further information see - Hess, Thomas L.

Colbert, James W. and Lydia Athey (3) -   December 29, 1881
    Place of marriage, Charlestown - Age of husband, 61 - Age of wife,
    35 - Husband is a Widower - Wife is Single - Husband was born in
    Maryland - Wife was born in Clarke County, Virginia - Both reside in
    Jefferson County, West Virginia.

Colbert, John and Mary Nuce (1) -   April 4, 1816

Colbert, Joseph W. and Sallie V. Kimes (3) -   January 11, 1872
    Place of marriage, Jefferson County, West Virginia - Age of husband,
    26 - Age of wife, 22 - Both are Single - Both were born in Jefferson
    County - Both reside in Jefferson County - Husband's parents are
    J. W. and Margaret - Wife's parents are Henry and Nancy - Occupation
    of husband is Engineer.

Colbert, Mary V. and Shaulter V. Yantis (3) -   January 23, 1883
    For further information see - Yantis, Shaulter V.

Colbert, Mattie M. and John N. Trussell (3) -   February 28, 1877
    For further information see - Trussell, John N.

Colbert, Sallie Ann and Daniel Nathan Oden (3) -   December 14, 1871
    For further information see - Oden, Daniel Nathan.

Colbert, William and Hannah Jac(k)son (1) -   October 1, 1829

Colby, J. W. and Tillie E. Chambers (3) -   March 18, 1885
    Place of marriage, Harpers Ferry - Age of husband, 21 - Age of wife,
    24 - Both are Single - Husband was born in Frederick County,
    Maryland - Wife was born in Jefferson County, West Virginia - Both
    reside in Jefferson County, West Virginia.

Cole, Cesar (cold.) Belle Plate (3) -   December 31, 1874
    Place of marriage, Shepherdstown - Age of husband, 35 - Age of wife,
    25 - Husband is a Widower - Wife is Single - Husband was born in
    Rappahannock County, Virginia - Wife was born in Jefferson County,
    West Virginia - Both reside in Jefferson County, West Virginia.

Cole, Elizabeth (cold.) Arthur Waters (3) -   September 18, 1884
    For further information see - Waters, Arthur.

Cole, Jane (cold.) Henry Jackson (3) -   December 25, 1878
    For further information see - Jackson, Henry.

Cole, Moton (cold.) Hattie Baylor (3) -   November 5, 1885
    Place of marriage, Mount Pleasant - Age of husband, 40 - Age of
    wife, 19 - Both are Single - Husband was born in Rappahannock - Wife
    was born in Jefferson County, West Virginia - Both reside in
    Jefferson County, West Virginia.

Cole, Nannie (cold.) Harvy Branson (3) -   February 22, 1890
    For further information see - Branson, Harvy.

Colegate, Edward D. and Clara Mary Lenox (3) -   June 16, 1881
    Place of marriage, Harpers Ferry - Age of husband, 28 - Age of wife,
    21 - Both are Single - Husband was born at Baltimore, Maryland -
    Wife was born in Jefferson County, West Virginia - Both reside in
    Jefferson County, West Virginia.

Coleman, ___?___ (blks) Mary Ann Wood (1) -   1821

Coleman, Catharine and Benjamin A. May (2) -   (L) August 18, 1862
    For further information see - May, Benjamin A.

Coleman, Josephine and Benjamin F. Ware (3) -   February 25, 1886
    For further information see - Ware, Benjamin F.

Coleman, Margaret and L. D. Maddex (3) -   December 20, 1876
    For further information see - Maddex, L. D.

Coleman, Mary E. and John H. Lenox (2) -   (L) December 23, 1858

Coleman, Mollie (cold.) Abram Brooks (3) -   December 24, 1880
    For further information see - Brooks, Abram.

Coleman, Rose and Abraham Doleman (3) -   January 9, 1873
    For further information see - Doleman, Abraham.

Coleman, Sallie and William Mason (3) -   June 18, 1873
    For further information see - Mason, William.

Coleman, Samuel (cold.) Mrs. Nellie Devinger (3) -   October 2, 1887
    Place of marriage, Ripon - Age of husband, 30 - Age of wife, 37 -
    Husband is Single - Wife is a Widow - Husband was born in Caroline
    County, Virginia - Wife was born in Jefferson County, West
    Virginia - Both reside in Jefferson County, West Virginia.

Coleman, Sophia and George P. Zombro (1) -   May 15, 1832

Coleman, Thomas (cold.) Kate Brown (3) -   December 22, 1885
    Place of marriage, Charlestown - Age of husband, 36 - Age of wife,
    36 - Husband is Single - Wife is a Widow - Both were born in
    Jefferson County, West Virginia - Both reside in Jefferson County,
    West Virginia.

Coles, Henry (cold.) Martha Gaiter (3) -   July 30, 1885
    Place of marriage, Duffields - Age of husband, 25 - Age of wife,
    30 - Both are Single - Husband was born in Rappahannock County,
    Virginia - Wife was born in Jefferson County, West Virginia - Both
    reside in Jefferson County, West Virginia.

Coleston, Solomon and Millie Washington (3) - October 13, 1866
Place of marriage, near Kearneysville, Jefferson County - Age of husband, 22 - Age of wife, 17 - Both are Single - Both were born in Jefferson County, West Virginia - Both reside in Jefferson County, West Virginia - Husband's parents are Elizabeth Coleston - Wife's parents are David and Nellie Washington - Occupation of husband is Laborer.

Colgan, Andrew and Catherine Fitzpatrick (2) - (L) July 5, 1856

Colgen, John and Mary McGuire (2) - (L) July 10, 1857

Collins, Alfred and Lucie Ann Hall (3) - June 3, 1875
Place of marriage, Middleway District - Age of husband, 34 - Age of wife, 29 - Both are Single - Husband was born in Frederick County, Virginia - Wife was born in Augusta County, Virginia - Both reside in Jefferson County, West Virginia.

Collins, Angelina and Lewis Richards (1) - January 19, 1803

Collins, Ann A. and Thomas Hammond (1) - June 18, 1807

Collins, Elizabeth Ann and Levi Kephart (3) - December 12, 1872
For further information see - Kephart, Levi.

Collins, Frances and Jabez Larue (1) - 1816

Collins, James Henry (cold.) Eliza Doyle (3) - February 23, 1888
Place of marriage, Charlestown - Age of husband, 27 - Age of wife, 21 - Both are Single - Husband was born in Halifax County, Virginia - Wife was born in Madison County, Virginia - Both reside in Jefferson County, West Virginia.

Collins, James W. and Martha Ann Whittington (2) - (L) December 26, 1856

Collins, Juliet C. and Samuel Larue (1) - August 31, 1825

Collins, Samuel and Mary McCullough (widow) (2) - (L) February 18, 1864
Time of marriage, February 19, 1864 - Place of marriage, Charlestown - Names, Samuel Collins and Mary McCullough (widow) - Age of husband, 28 years last July - Age of wife, 28 years - Husband is Single - Wife is a Widow - Place of husband's birth was at Belfast, Ireland - Place of wife's birth was at Baltimore, Maryland - Place of husband's residence is at New York City - Place of wife's residence is in Jefferson County, Virginia - Names of husband's parents are David and Jane Collins - Names of wife's parents (not given) - Occupation of husband is Soldier in Federal Army - License issued, February 18, 1864 - T. A. Moore, Clerk.

Collis, Mary E. and Thomas M. Ott (2) - (L) (1863)
For further information see - Ott, Thomas M.

Collis, Susan J. and James H. Propst (2) - (L) June 22, 1860

Colly, Mary C. and John W. Laurence (3) - December 20, 1870
For further information see - Laurence, John W.

Colston, Charles (cold.) Cora Washington (3) - September 22, 1885
   Place of marriage, near Charlestown - Age of husband, 27 - Age of
   wife, 26 - Both are Single - Both were born in Jefferson County -
   Both reside in Jefferson County.

Colston, Elizabeth and Bacckus Briscoe (3) - March 8, 1873
   For further information see - Briscoe, Bacckus.

Colston, Emily (cold.) George William Roper (3) - January 24, 1884
   For further information see - Roper, George William.

Colston, George (cold.) Matilda Galloway (3) - December 11, 1884
   Place of marriage, Charlestown - Age of husband, 59 - Age of wife,
   35 - Husband is a Widower - Wife is Single - Husband was born in
   Berkeley County, West Virginia - Wife was born in Jefferson County -
   Both reside in Jefferson County, West Virginia.

Colston, James (cold.) Rachel Swan (3) - July 30, 1874
   Place of marriage, Charlestown - Age of husband, 21 - Age of wife,
   22 - Both are Single - Both were born in Jefferson County, West
   Virginia - Both reside in Jefferson County, West Virginia.

Colston, Lucy W. and John N. Kitchen (2) - (L) September 9, 1858

Colston, Matilda (cold.) Thomas Jackson (3) - January 4, 1877
   For further information see - Jackson, Thomas.

Colston, Millie and Daniel Ford (3) - October 26, 1871
   For further information see - Ford, Daniel.

Colston, Soloman (cold.) Eliza Newman (3) - March 7, 1889
   Place of marriage, Charlestown - Age of husband, 42 - Age of wife,
   42 - Husband is a Widower - Wife is a Widow - Both were born in
   Jefferson County, West Virginia - Both reside in Jefferson County,
   West Virginia.

Combs, Catherine and Levi Stidman (1) - March 2, 1823

Comer, George and Catharine Ware (3) - February 22, 1877
   Place of marriage, Charles Town - Age of husband, 30 - Age of wife,
   18 - Husband is a Widower - Wife is Single - Husband was born in
   Rockingham County, Virginia - Wife was born in Jefferson County,
   West Virginia - Both reside in Jefferson County, West Virginia.
   (Consent of bride's mother in writing.)

Compton, Elizabeth and Henry Varner (1) - July 31, 1827

Compton, Emily and Isaac Fleming (1) - March 21, 1831

Compton, John and Mary Kensell (1) - September 21, 1827

Con, Emily (cold.) Henry McCan (3) - May 6, 1874
   For further information see - McCan, Henry.

Con, Thomas (cold.) Sarah Cooper (3) - January 11, 1882
   Place of marriage, Bolivar - Age of husband, 21 - Age of wife, 22 -
   Both are Single - Husband was born in Maryland - Wife was born in
   Clarke County, Virginia - Both reside in Jefferson County, West
   Virginia.

Coner, Bertie (cold.) George McDaniel (3) - March 31, 1887
    For further information see - McDaniel, George.

Conklin, Nancy and George Murphy (1) - January 24, 1822

Conklyn, Bessie W. and Harry F. Bane (3) - January 8, 1889
    For further information see - Bane, Harry F.

Conklyn, Catherine and William McGarry (1) - January 18, 1827

Conklyn, Charles C. and Margaret Catherine Welsh (2) - (L) December 17, 1860

Conklyn, James H. and Susan C. Heflebower (2) - (L) November 23, 1857

Conklyn, Margaret and Joseph Croft (1) - May 7, 1830

Conklyn, Mary E. and Charles Drew (2) - (L) February 24, 1857

Conklyn, Sarah and Seth Shoafstall (1) - 1828

Conklyn, William H. and Nancy Jenkins (1) - March 17, 1831

Conland, James and Catharine Ellitt (2) - (L) April 5, 1852

Conley, Bessie P. and Snyder Bane (3) - May 29, 1890
    For further information see - Bane, Snyder.

Conley, Ely and Catherine Yontz (1) - February 22, 1827

Conley, Nettie J. and Bayliss Trussell (3) - March 30, 1875
    For further information see - Trussell, Bayliss.

Conn, Airy (free blacks) Philip Hawkins (1) - August 11, 1831

Conn, Priscilla and Peter D. Cramer (1) - June 4, 1822

Conner, Catherine and John L. Thompson (3) - May 2, 1877
    For further information see - Thompson, John L.

Conner, Hannah F. and John N. Willingham (3) - September 14, 1869
    For further information see - Willingham, John N.

Conner, Margaret Ann and W. T. Gore (3) - May 18, 1875
    For further information see - Gore, W. T.

Conner, Mary E. V. and John C. Taylor (3) - March 21, 1866
    For further Information see - Taylor, John C.

Conner, Mary V. and Richard E. Andrew (3) - December 26, 1878
    For further information see - Andrew, Richard E.

Conner, Rosanna and Daniel Kimes (1) - February 1821

Conner, Sarah and George Everson (1) - February 27, 1817

Conner, Theodore M. and Mary D. Cochrane (3) - November 14, 1889
    Place of marriage, Charlestown - Age of husband, 38 - Age of wife,
    40 - Husband is Single - Wife is a Widow - Husband was born in
    Frederick County, Virginia - Wife was born in Jefferson County, West
    Virginia - Both reside in Jefferson County, West Virginia.

Conrad, Charles W. and Mary E. Woodward (3) - December 11, 1889
Place of marriage, Bride's Residence - Age of husband, 23 - Age of wife, 24 - Both are Single - Both were born in Jefferson County, West Virginia - Both reside in Jefferson County, West Virginia.

Conrad, Eliza and W. E. Anderson (3) - December 7, 1871
For further information see - Anderson, W. E.

Conrad, F. J. and Elizabeth H. Fossett (2) - (L) November 15, 1851

Conrad, Fayette J. and Elizabeth H. Fossett (1) - November 18, 1851

Conrad, Lucy E. and James W. Canniford (3) - April 12, 1887
For further information see - Canniford, James W.

Conrad, Lucy G. and S. J. Strain (3) - October 1, 1867
For further information see - Strain, S. J.

Conrad, Mary Frances and George W. Benner (3) - December 24, 1885
For further information see - Benner, George W.

Conrad, Morris and Catharine Whittington (2) - (L) December 5, 1854

Conrad, Robert T. and Martha J. Leslie (3) - April 14, 1881
Place of marriage, Bride's Residence - Age of husband, 31 - Age of wife, 27 - Both are Single - Husband was born in Warren County, Virginia - Wife was born in Jefferson County, West Virginia - Both reside in Jefferson County, West Virginia.

Conrad, William and Martha A. Bowling (2) - (L) August 30, 1858

Conrad, William B. and Jane E. Shepherd (3) - November 20, 1866
Place of marriage, Amos Shepherd's Residence, Jefferson County - Age of husband, 26 - Age of wife, 22 - Both are Single - Husband was born in Warren County, Virginia - Wife was born in Jefferson County, West Virginia - Both reside in Jefferson County, West Virginia - Husband's parents are James and Lydia Conrad - Wife's parents are Amos and Elizabeth Shepherd - Occupation of husband is Farmer.

Conway, James and Mary Martin (3) - January 16, 1866
Place of marriage, Harpers Ferry - Age of husband, 27 - Age of wife, 27 - Both are Single - Both were born in Ireland - Both reside at Harpers Ferry, West Virginia - Husband's parents are John and Mary Conway - Wife's parents are John and Bridget Martin - Occupation of husband is Clerk.

Conway, Nancy and William Martin (1) - November 21, 1816

Conway, Samuel and Anne Martin (1) - August 17, 1826

Cook, A. A. and Ann Shugart (3) - February 21, 1869
Place of marriage, Jefferson County - Age of husband, 50 - Age of wife, 41 - Husband is a Widower - Wife is a Widow - Husband was born in Maryland - Wife was born in Virginia - Both reside in Jefferson County - Husband's parents are John and Catherine - Wife's parents are Daniel and Mary Cameron - Occupation of husband is Manufacturer.

Cook, Alice (cold.) Joseph Roman (3) - September 28, 1876
For further information see - Roman, Joseph.

Cook, Charles (cold.) Jannie Briscoe (3) - July 15, 1880
    Place of marriage, Charlestown - Age of husband, 22 - Age of wife,
    21 - Both are Single - Both were born in Jefferson County, West
    Virginia - Both reside in Jefferson County, West Virginia.

Cook, Elizabeth and William Brown (1) - February 19, 1822

Cook, Emma (colored) Charles Myers (3) - August 18, 1870
    For further information see - Myers, Charles.

Cook, George and Cementy Harrison (3) - (1865)
    (License not returned.)

Cook, James (cold.) Mary Bailey (3) - February 16, 1888
    Place of marriage, Charlestown - Age of husband, 35 - Age of wife,
    24 - Both are Single - Husband was born in State of Ohio - Wife was
    born in Jefferson County, West Virginia - Both reside in Jefferson
    County, West Virginia.

Cook, James P. and Emma Merret (3) - December 19, 1871
    Place of marriage, Jefferson County - Age of husband, 25 - Age of
    wife, 18 - Both are Single - Both were born in Jefferson County -
    Husband resides in Jefferson - Wife resides in Jefferson County -
    Husband's parents are John and Phebe - Wife's parents are Thomas and
    Margaret - Occupation of husband is Farmer.

Cook, James William and Ellen Crem Mobley (3) - February 1, 1877
    Place of marriage, Harpers Ferry - Age of husband, 29 - Age of wife,
    21 - Both are Single - Both were born in Jefferson County, West
    Virginia - Both reside in Jefferson County, West Virginia.

Cook, John and Sarah Jane Benner (2) - (L) May 1, 1858

Cook, John E. and Mary Virginia Kennedy (2) - (L) April 15, 1859

Cook, John L. and Matilda Potter (2) - (L) June 5, 1858

Cook, Mary and Edward Patterson (3) - August 1, 1867
    For further information see - Patterson, Edward.

Cook, Sallie E. and Lester VanAlstyne (3) - November 12, 1884
    For further information see - VanAlstyne, Lester.

Cook, Samuel and Elizabeth V. Hamill (2) - (L) May 12, 1852

Cook, Sarah Ann and John W. Stidman (1) - November 16, 1834

Cook, Sinah and John Quigley (1) - May 21, 1822

Cook, William J. and Ella E. V. Beavers (3) - December 24, 1890
    Place of marriage, Charlestown - Age of husband, 25 - Age of wife,
    24 - Both are Single - Husband was born in England - Wife was born
    in Clarke County, Virginia - Husband resides in Frederick County,
    Virginia - Wife resides in Jefferson County, West Virginia.

Cooke, Fannie and Thomas Langford (3) - April 20, 1872
    For further information see - Langford, Thomas.

Cooke, H. H. and Elizabeth Morton Porterfield (3) -   October 6, 1877
    Place of marriage, Charlestown - Age of husband, 30 - Age of wife,
    24 - Both are Single - Husband was born in Jefferson County, West
    Virginia - Wife was born at Washington City - Both reside in
    Jefferson County, West Virginia.

Cooke, Henry Pendleton and Mary E. Kennedy (2) -   (L) January 1, 1855

Cooke, Maria Catharine and Henry Spears (2) -   (L) August 3, 1859

Cooke, Mary and James Hamble (1) -   January 9, 1816

Cooksey, Simpson and Sarah A. D. Johns (1) -   November 7, 1848

Cookus, Anna Maria and John Heflebower (2) -   (L) December 11, 1860

Cookus, Eliza Florence and James L. Mathews (3) -   December 29, 1875
    For further information see - Mathews, James L.

Cookus, Elizabeth and Jacob Wysong, Jr. (1) -   March 14, 1813

Cookus, Elizabeth and David Hefflebower (2) -   (L) March 1, 1858

Cookus, Elizabeth Catherine and John H. Show (2) -   (L) (1862)
    For further information see - Show, John H.

Cookus, Elizabeth H. and Joseph H. Kanode (3) -   February 11, 1873
    For further information see - Kanode, Joseph H.

Cookus, J. H. and A. E. Sanbower (bride) (3) -   September 9, 1872
    Age of husband, 36 - Age of wife, 34 - Husband is a Widower - Wife
    is a Widow.

Cookus, John Henry and Ann M. Tylman (2) -   (L) September 21, 1853

Cookus, John Henry and Ann M. Tylman (1) -   Septmeber 28, 1853

Cookus, John T. and Susana Morrow (1) -   April 13, 1813

Cookus, John T. and Sophia Abert (1) -   December 18, 1834

Cookus, John W. and Mary C. Myers (3) -   March 24, 1880
    Place of marriage, Shepherdstown - Age of husband, 25 - Age of wife,
    25 - Both are Single - Both were born in Jefferson County, West
    Virginia - Both reside in Jefferson County, West Virginia.

Cookus, Joseph L. and Luly Snyder (3) -   February 19, 1874
    Place of marriage, Shepherdstown -. Age of husband, 25 - Age of wife,
    25 - Both are Single - Both were born in Jefferson County, West
    Virginia - Both reside in Jefferson County, West Virginia.

Cookus, Maggie A. and Johnson Orrick (2) -   (L) November 5, 1856

Cookus, Margaret Elizabeth and George A. Schoppert (3) -   November 27, 1873
    For further information see - Schoppert, George A.

Cookus, Mary Catharine and John H. Keesecker (2) -   (L) November 30, 1854

Cookus, Michael and Eliza Crow (widow) (1) -   May 7, 1850

Cookus, Sophia and John Kensell (1) - March 22, 1827

Cooley, Peter and Elizabeth Davis Steele (2) - (L) July 7, 1853

Cooley, Peter and Elizabeth Davis Steele (1) - July 11, 1853

Coons, Harriet and Jonathan Irvin (1) - October 26, 1823

Coons, Jacob and Eliza Durst (1) - February 20, 1807

Coons, Jacob (son of Jacob Coons, Sr.) and Mary Baden (1) - October 26, 1823

Coons, John and Elizabeth Ronemus (1) - December 17, 1805

Coonse, Jacob (the third) and Maria Lathan (1) - July 28, 1825

Coonts, Philip and Ann Caroline Brue (1) - . 1827

Cooper, C. W. H. and America V. Vanmetre (3) - October 22, 1866
    Place of marriage, Charlestown, Jefferson County, West Virginia - Age of husband, 24 - Age of wife, 26 - Husband is Single - Wife is a Widow - Husband was born in Loudoun County, Virginia - Wife was born in Jefferson County, West Virginia - Both reside in Jefferson County, West Virginia - Husband's parents are Samuel and Mary Cooper - Wife's parents are James and Elizabeth Roper - Occupation of husband is Miller.

Cooper, Elizabeth T. and Adam Weltzheimer (1) - November 15, 1825

Cooper, Fanny (cold.) Cary Harris (3) - December 28, 1882
    For further information see - Harris, Cary.

Cooper, George and Margaret Daugherty (1) - October 5, 1813

Cooper, Jacob and Mary Dillow (1) - December 31, 1826

Cooper, Martha and Samuel Steadman (1) - September 26, 1815

Cooper, Mary and Thomas Jenkens (1) - April 28, 1825

Cooper, Sally (cold.) Jerry Dohman (3) - October 4, 1875
    For further information see - Dohman, Jerry.

Cooper, Samuel C. and Ida Monday (3) - September 16, 1889
    Place of marriage, Harpers Ferry - Age of husband, 22 - Age of wife, 20 - Both are Single - Husband was born in Jefferson County, West Virginia - Wife was born in Loudoun County, Virginia - Both reside in Jefferson County, West Virginia. (Consent of bride's father in writing.)

Cooper, Sarah (cold.) Thomas Con (3) - January 11, 1882
    For further information see - Con, Thomas.

Cooper, Thomas and Ellen Graham (1) - . June 2, 1832

Cope, James and Mersey McBee (1) - November 29, 1829

Copeland, Nathan H. and Sarah Catharine Duncan (2) - (L) August 27, 1860

Copeland, Phillip D. and Elizabeth Waddell (3) -   January 24, 1867
    Place of marriage, Charlestown - Age of husband, 27 - Age of wife,
    25 - Both are Single - Husband was born in Loudoun County,
    Virginia - Wife was born in Maryland - Husband resides at Baltimore,
    Maryland - Wife resides at Charlestown, Virginia - Husband's parents
    are John and Delia Copeland - Wife's parents are Isaac and Rebecca
    Waddell - Occupation of husband is Carpenter.

Copeland, Thomas and Amanda Jenkins (3) -   April 1, 1879
    Place of marriage, Harpers Ferry - Age of husband, 23 - Age of wife,
    30 - Both are Single - Both were born in Loudoun County, Virginia -
    Husband resides in Loudoun County, Virginia - Wife resides in
    Jefferson County, West Virginia at the time of marriage.

Copenhaver, Lourette and John R. Keller (3) -   December 11, 1890
    For further information see - Keller, John R.

Corbin, James H. (cold.) Adeline Johnson (3) -   December 20, 1888
    Place of marriage, Duffields - Age of husband, 36 - Age of wife,
    21 - Both are Single - Husband was born in Fauquier County,
    Virginia - Wife was born in Jefferson County, West Virginia - Both
    reside in Jefferson County, West Virginia.

Cordell, Asa B. and Lucinda L. Dixon (1) -   December 9, 1830

Cordell, Enos B. and Sarah Ann Humphreys (1) -   January 1, 1829

Cordell, Lucinda L. and James Evans (1) -   December 21, 1848

Cordell, Martha and Arthur S. Wingate (1) -   February 16, 1836

Corder, Bailous and Fannie Rohrer (3) -   June 25, 1885
    Place of marriage, Charlestown - Age of husband, 24 - Age of wife,
    21 - Both are Single - Husband was born in Warren County, Virginia -
    Wife was born in Frederick County, Maryland - Both reside in
    Jefferson County, West Virginia.

Corder, Dora J. and Leonard D. House (3) -   September 15, 1880
    For further information see House, Leonard D.

Corear, Lizzie and H. S. Smallwood (3) -   (1870)
    For further information see - Smallwood, H. S.

Corn, Thomas and Delsa Newman (3) -   (1868)
    Age of husband, 40 - Age of wife, 31 - Husband is a Widower - Wife
    is Single - Husband was born in Maryland - Wife was born in
    Jefferson County - Husband resides in Jefferson County - Wife
    resides in Jefferson County, West Virginia - Occupation of husband
    is Laborer.

Cornell, Charles and Margaret Shrout (3) -   May 14, 1874
    Place of marriage, County - Age of husband, 22 - Age of wife, 17 -
    Both are Single - Husband was born in Loudoun County, Virginia -
    Wife was born in Jefferson County, West Virginia - Both reside in
    Jefferson County, West Virginia. (Consent of bride's father in
    person.)

Cornell, Richdetta and Thomas W. Stickles (3) -   May 1, 1872
    For further information see - Stickles, Thomas W.

Cornwell, Eliza and Thomas Atkinson (1) - February 22, 1815

Cornwell, Elizabeth and John Allison (1) - 1819

Corson, Louis and Margaret Gomph (1) - October 5, 1833

Coss, William and Ann Wade (1) - April 16, 1803

Cost, Laura and Jake S. Osburn (3) - January 25, 1872
    For further information see - Osburn, Jake S.

Cost, Martha and Charles Flora (3) - June 11, 1868
    For further information see - Flora, Charles.

Coulan, Patrick and Mary Dameron (2) - (L) April 22, 1858

Coulter, William J. and Attie E. Carter (3) - March 15, 1890
    Place of marriage, Charlestown - Age of husband, 23 - Age of wife,
    21 - Both are Single - Husband was born in Washington County,
    Maryland - Wife was born in Frederick County, Maryland - Both reside
    in Jefferson County, West Virginia.

Courtney, Mary and John Bowers (1) - March 8, 1832

Courtney, Silas H. and Eliza F. Willson (1) - December 28, 1826

Covert, Fannie A. and Thomas Welch (3) - February 10, 1887
    For further information see - Welch, Thomas.

Covert, Joseph William and Ida Faulk (3) - December 29, 1887
    Place of marriage, Charlestown - Age of husband, 22 - Age of wife,
    18 - Both are Single - Husband was born in Warren County, Virginia -
    Wife was born in Jefferson County, West Virginia - Husband resides
    in Jefferson County, West Virginia - Wife resides in Jefferson
    County. (Consent of bride's father in person.)

Cowan, James (cold.) Lucy Travers (3) - August 2, 1883
    Place of marriage, Charlestown - Age of husband, 40 - Age of wife,
    21 - Both are Single - Husband was born in Rockingham County,
    Virginia - Wife was born in Jefferson County, West Virginia - Both
    reside in Jefferson County, West Virginia.

Cowley, Ida and Clinton Garrett (3) - August 10, 1875
    For further information see - Garrett, Clinton.

Cowley, John T. and Eliza Ferrel (3) - December 20, 1871
    Place of marriage, Jefferson County - Age of husband, 23 - Age of
    wife, 22 - Both are Single - Husband was born in Jefferson County -
    Wife was born in Shenandoah County - Both reside in Jefferson
    County - Husband's parents are John T. and Annie - Occupation of
    husband is Shoemaker.

Cowper, Elizabeth and John Crowl (1) - November 4, 1827

Cox, Hannah F. and John H. Cline (3) - November 1, 1869
    For further information see - Cline, John H.

Cox, Joshua and Elizabeth Stipes (1) - January 14, 1824

Cox, Joshua and Elizabeth Engle (1) - April 5, 1832

Cox, Joshua H. and Annie E. Reed (3) - October 22, 1884
   Place of marriage, Bolivar - Age of husband, 26 - Age of wife, 25 -
   Both are Single - Both were born in Jefferson County, West
   Virginia - Husband resides in Jefferson County, West Virginia - Wife
   resides in Jefferson County.

Cox, Maggie and William J. Ault (3) - April 20, 1871
   For further information see - Ault, William J.

Cox, Minnie Estel and Larrence C. Sagle (3) - December, 1884
   For further information see - Sagle, Larrence C.

Cox, Samuel H. and Mattie J. Roderick (3) - November 6, 1872
   Place of marriage, Jefferson County, West Virginia - Age of husband,
   23 - Age of wife, 17 - Both are Single - Both were born in Jefferson
   County, West Virginia - Both reside in Jefferson County - Husband's
   parents are George W. and Sarah A. - Wife's parents are Hezekiah and
   Mary E. - Occupation of husband is Carpenter. (Consent in
   writing.)

Cox, William and Mary Eversole (1) - May 20, 1807

Cox, William and Mary Lee Lock (3) - October 29, 1882
   Place of marriage, Charlestown - Age of husband, 21 - Age of wife,
   21 - Both are Single - Husband was born in Hampshire County, West
   Virginia - Wife was born in Jefferson County, West Virginia - Both
   reside in Jefferson County, West Virginia.

Cox, William J. and Sarah Ann Baldwin (2) - (L) March 25, 1853

Cox, William J. and Sarah A. Baldwin (1) - March 25, 1853

Coxen, William (cold.) Delia Robinson (3) - December 27, 1888
   Place of marriage, near Myerstown - Age of husband, 21 - Age of
   wife, 21 - Both are Single - Both were born in Jefferson County,
   West Virginia - Both reside in Jefferson County, West Virginia.

Coyle, Almira B. and Eli W. Payne (3) - October 30, 1877
   For further information see - Payne, Eli W.

Coyle, Frances and William Daws (1) - April 9, 1822

Coyle, John M. and Albina S. Crow (2) - (L) August 4, 1856

Coyle, Joseph O. and Courtney H. Smith (1) - January 28, 1835

Coyle, Julius M. and Nettie Feagans (3) - November 25, 1875
   Place of marriage, On Bullskin - Age of husband, 28 - Age of wife,
   22 - Both are Single - Husband was born in Berkeley County, West
   Virginia - Wife was born in Jefferson County, West Virginia - Both
   reside in Jefferson County, West Virginia.

Craddock, Henry D. and Bettie Bass (3) - March 19, 1890
   Place of marriage, Harpers Ferry - Age of husband, 34 - Age of wife,
   28 - Both are Single - Wife resides in Jefferson County, West
   Virginia.

Craig, Jane and Joseph Allen (1) - November 25, 1804

Craig, John and Elizabeth Hall (1) - October 2, 1821

Craighill, Agelta. and Francis Lowndes (1) - November 6, 1817

Craighill, Elizabeth R. and Hunter Davidson (3) - July 17, 1890
For further information see - Davidson, Hunter.

Craighill, Frances T. and Charles C. Lucas (3) - February 28, 1889
For further information see - Lucas, Charles C.

Craighill, Joseph A. and Mary Emeline Lucas (2) - (L) November 22, 1852

Craighill, Joseph A. and Mary E. Lucas (1) - November 22, 1852

Craighill, Mary and W. F. Lippitt, Jr. (3) - August 3, 1887
For further information see - Lippitt, W. F., Jr.

Cramer, Ambrose M. C. and Emily Rowan (1) - May 25, 1820

Cramer, Ambrose W. and Margaret T. Davenport (2) - (L) November 26, 1851

Cramer, Ambrose W. and Margaret T. Davenport (1) - November 27, 1851

Cramer, Caspar and Eliza Davis (1) - March 7, 1809

Cramer, Eliza J. and George W. Sappington (1) - January 8, 1834

Cramer, Elizabeth D. and Joseph L. Shenard (3) - June 18, 1884
For further information see - Shenard, Joseph L.

Cramer, Jane Saunderson and Thomas A. Moore (1) - June 29, 1825

Cramer, Peter D. and Priscilla Conn (1) - June 4, 1822

Cramer, Samuel I. and Eleanor Kearsley (1) - May 26, 1803

Crampton, Mary and Michael Echart (1) - September 14, 1809

Crane, Abraham and Ann Dean (1) - May 4, 1826

Crane, Ann Cecilia and William Avey (2) - (L) April 26, 1856

Crane, F. A. (bride) and J. P. Burket (3) - July 13, 1865
For further information see - Burket, J. P.

Crane, Henry (free cold.) Mary Ellen Winters (2) - (L) July 13, 1860

Crane, Kate S. and Oscar M. Lucas (3) - December 1, 1869
For further information see - Lucas, Oscar M.

Crane, Lucy M. and Joseph F. Abell (2) - (L) June 17, 1852

Crane, Martha V. and James H. Timberlake (3) - June 14, 1876
For further information see - Timberlake, James H.

Crantz, Lottie C. and William B. Osbourn (3) - February 12, 1879
For further information see - Osbourn, William B.

Craul, Maggie N. and John A. Pettigrew (3) - July 10, 1889
For further information see - Pettigrew, John A.

Crawford, Charles Reynolds and Liza Rebecca Flood (3) -   January 14, 1869
    Place of marriage, Charles Town, West Virginia - Age of husband,
    21 - Age of wife, 21 - Both are Single - Husband was born in
    Scotland - Wife was born in Virginia - Both reside at Charlestown -
    Husband's parents are Robert and Sarah - Wife's parents are Thomas
    and Martha - Occupation of husband is Mason. (James T. Athey
    qualified at. as to age.).

Crawford, Daniel and Margaret Smith (1) -   1827

Crawford, Daniel T. and Eliza Ferrells (1) -   March 10, 1825

Crawford, Eliza (cold.) Abram Minor (3) -   June 14, 1890
    For further information see - Minor, Abram.

Crawford, Emily and Robert Skidmore (1) -   April 3, 1834

Crawford, Emily (cold.) James White (3) -   August 23, 1876
    For further information see - White, James.

Crawford, Fannie and L. T. Benson (3) -   November 13, 1877
    For further information see - Benson, L. T.

Crawford, Hester (cold.) Isaac Wilson (3) - .   February 2, 1878
    For further information see - Wilson, Isaac.

Crawford, J. M. and Teresa Ann Madison (2) -   (L) January 19, 1861

Crawford, James and Mary Ellen Lindsey (1) -   February 2, 1826

Crawford, Lydia (cold.) Lewis Florence (3) -   October 24, 1882
    For further information see - Florence, Lewis.

Crawford, Martha E. and John W. Rohr (2) -   (L) July 3, 1854

Crawford, Mary and Jessee Bateman (1) -   January 23, 1825

Crawford, Sarah and Michael Doran (2) -   (L) December 30, 1852

Crawford, Sarah (cold.) Henry Berkeley (3) -   July 30, 1885
    For further information see - Berkeley, Henry.

Crawford, Sarah Ann (cold.) Lewis Baltimore (3) -   March 27, 1889
    For further information see - Baltimore, Lewis.

Crawford, Susan and Abraham Flemings (1) -   1826

Crawford, Washington and Emma Shaull (3) -   February 27, 1877
    Place of marriage, near Summit Point - Age of husband, 25 - Age of
    wife, 21 - Both are Single - Husband was born in Berkeley County,
    West Virginia - Wife was born in Jefferson County, West Virginia -
    Both reside in Jefferson County, West Virginia.

Crawford, William (cold.) Mary E. Moore (3) - .   February 7, 1889
    Place of marriage, Shepherdstown - Age of husband, 23 - Age of wife,
    19 - Both are Single - Both were born in Jefferson County, West
    Virginia - Both reside in Jefferson County, West Virginia.
    (Consent of bride's father in person.)

Creamer, Bettie (cold.) Charles Green (3) -　　　　　　　　March 20, 1890
　　For further information see - Green, Charles.

Creamer, Charles (cold.) Mary E. Williams (3) -　　　　　September 25, 1884
　　Place of marriage, Shepherdstown - Age of husband, 23 - Age of wife,
　　25 - Both are Single - Both were born in Jefferson County, West
　　Virginia - Both reside in Jefferson County.

Creamer, E. B. and Ebenezer P. Miller (3) -　　　　　　　November 17, 1868
　　For further information see - Miller, Ebenezer P.

Creamer, Fannie (cold.) Royal M. Davis (3) -　　　　　　　January 11, 1888
　　For further information see - Davis, Royal M.

Creamer, George A. and Lucy Ann Morgan (2) -　　　　　(L) January 4, 1855

Creamer, George D. and Mary E. Butt (3) -　　　　　　　December 19, 1867
　　Place of marriage, Jefferson County - Age of husband, 26 - Age of
　　wife, 25 - Both are Single - Both were born in Jefferson - Both
　　reside in Jefferson - Husband's parents are Philip and Matilda -
　　Wife's parents are A. and Elizabeth - Occupation of husband is
　　Miller.

Creamer, George F. (cold.) Mary E. Brown (3) -　　　　　December 2, 1883
　　Place of marriage, Shepherdstown - Age of husband, 22 - Age of wife,
　　21 - Both are Single - Husband was born in Berkeley County - Wife
　　was born in Jefferson County, West Virginia - Husband resides in
　　Jefferson County - Wife resides in Jefferson County, West Virginia.

Creamer, Hance (colored persons) Mary Jackson (3) -　　　May 13, 1865
　　Place of marriage, Shepherdstown.

Creamer, Harriet Ann and Thomas J. Fritz (2) -　　　　(L) April 30, 1860

Creamer, John Lewis and Sarah Catherine Thomas (3) -　　November 19, 1874
　　Place of marriage, County near Duffields - Age of husband, 21 - Age
　　of wife, 23 - Both are Single - Husband was born in Maryland - Wife
　　was born in Loudoun County, Virginia - Both reside in Jefferson
　　County, West Virginia.

Creamer, Lewis B. and Susan M. Morgan (2) -　　　　　(L) November 23, 1853

Creamer, Nannie (cold.) John Sly (3) -　　　　　　　　October 12, 1876
　　For further information see - Sly, John.

Creamer, Philip M. and Annie E. Ramsburg (3) -　　　　October 21, 1880
　　Place of marriage, Leetown, West Virginia - Age of husband, 22 - Age
　　of wife, 21 - Both are Single - Both were born in Jefferson County,
　　West Virginia - Both reside in Jefferson County, West Virginia.

Creamer, S. C. (bride) and N. W. Gore (3) -　　　　　　January 2, 1868
　　For further information see - Gore, N. W.

Creamer, Thomas J. and Rosa J. Clipp (3) -　　　　　　March 13, 1884
　　Place of marriage, Charlestown - Age of husband, 24 - Age of wife,
　　21 - Both are Single - Both were born in Jefferson County, West
　　Virginia - Both reside in Jefferson County, West Virginia.

119

Creamer, William (cold.) Hester Staley (3) -   September 11, 1888
   Place of marriage, Shepherdstown - Age of husband, 29 - Age of wife,
   28 - Both are Single - Both were born in Jefferson County, West
   Virginia - Both reside in Jefferson County, West Virginia.

Creighton, Martha and Charles Hobbs (2) -   (L) January 2, 1858

Cremer, Daniel and Mary Burk (1) -   1822

Creps, Eliza and John Taylor (1) -   1827

Creswell, Lizzie Ann and James Augustus Hammond (3) -   September 10, 1872
   For further information see - Hammond, James Augustus.

Cretan, Mary Elizabeth and James Tierney (2) -   (L) December 20, 1851

Crider, Barbara Ann and John W. Taylor (2) -   (L) February 9, 1856

Crider, Eliza Jane and Robert C. Byers (2) -   (L) February 22, 1861

Crider, Martha E. and William H. Myers (3) -   December 5, 1865
   For further information see - Myers, William H.

Crider, Mary C. and David C. Horn (2) -   (L) November 12, 1855

Cridler, Augustus M. and Deborah Belsterling (1) -   December 21, 1848

Crim, A. S. and Eugenia W. Ware (3) -   December 20, 1876
   Place of marriage, near Middleway - Age of husband, 28 - Age of
   wife, 24 - Both are Single - Husband was born in Shenandoah County,
   Virginia - Wife was born in Jefferson County, West Virginia - Both
   reside in Jefferson County, West Virginia.

Crim, Abraham and Ellen Virginia Felton (2) -   (L) April 18, 1864
   Time of marriage, April 26, 1864 - Place of marriage at Porter's
   Factory - Names, Abraham Crim and Ellen Virginia Felton - Age of
   husband, 29 years - Age of wife, 18 years - Husband is a Widower -
   Wife is Single - Husband was born in Hampshire County - Wife was
   born at Wheeling, Ohio County, Virginia - Husband's residence is in
   Berkeley County, Virginia - Wife's residence is in Jefferson County,
   Virginia - Husband's parents are Abraham and Maria Crim - Wife's
   parents are George and Jane - Occupation of husband is, Farmer -
   License issued, April 18, 1864 - T. A. Moore, Clerk. (Consent of
   bride's mother for issuing license given to me in person.) -
   Frederick Fulk.

Crim, Ann E. and Ashby Williams (3) -   June 5, 1888
   For further information see - Williams, Ashby.

Crim, Cora V. and George F. Willingham (3) -   September 14, 1885
   For further information see - Willingham, George F.

Crim, Edward B. and Mary Ann Frith (2) -   (L) December 11, 1856

Crim, Eliza and John Cain (3) -   October 7, 1873
   For further information see - Cain, John.

Crim, Jacob and S. E. Stewart (3) - August 30, 1866
   Place of marriage, Middleway, Jefferson County, West Virginia - Age
   of husband, 25 - Age of wife, 19 - Both are Single - Husband was
   born in Berkeley County, West Virginia - Wife was born in Jefferson
   County, West Virginia - Both reside in Jefferson County, West
   Virginia - Husband's parents are Abraham and Maria Crim - Wife's
   parents are John and S. E. Stewart - Occupation of husband is
   Farmer.

Crim, Jane and George Robinson (1) - November 9, 1818

Crim, Jennie M. and James A. Edwards (3) - November 25, 1875
   For further information see - Edwards, James A.

Crim, Kate L. and Samuel T. Markle (3) - December 28, 1882
   For further information see - Markle, Samuel T.

Crim, Milly C. and Charles S. Watson (3) - November 18, 1874
   For further information see - Watson, Charles S.

Crim, Peter and Mary F. Bragg (3) - November 5, 1874
   Place of marriage, Charles Town - Age of husband, 24 - Age of wife,
   17 - Both are Single - Husband was born in SHenandoah County,
   Virginia - Wife was born in Jefferson County, West Virginia - Both
   reside in Jefferson County, West Virginia. (Consent of bride's
   father in writing.)

Crim, Sarah E. G. and Randolph C. S. Anderson (3) - July 28, 1885
   For further information see - Anderson, Randolph C. S.

Crisfield, Margaret R. and Edward Healey (1) - November 25, 1827

Crisfield, William and Catherine Karman (1) - December 17, 1814

Crisman, William H. and Fanny B. Stein (3) - April 7, 1880
   Place of marriage, Middleway - Age of husband, 27 - Age of wife,
   18 - Both are Single - Husband was born in Frederick County,
   Virginia - Wife was born in Jefferson County, West Virginia - Both
   reside in Jefferson County, West Virginia. (Consent of bride's
   grandmother in writing.)

Crissinger, George N. (cold.) Mary Devonshire (3) - April 4, 1889
   Place of marriage, Charlestown - Age of husband, 22 - Age of wife,
   19 - Both are Single - Husband was born in Berkeley County, West
   Virginia - Wife was born in Jefferson County, West Virginia -
   Husband resides in Berkeley County, West Virginia - Wife resides in
   Jefferson County, West Virginia. (Consent of bride's parents in
   writing.)

Criswell, John and Sarah Wisenall (1) - April 7, 1850

Criswell, John and Mary C. Ecton (3) - November 17, 1880
   Place of marriage, Charlestown - Age of husband, 60 - Age of wife,
   25 - Husband is a Widower - Wife is Single - Husband was born in
   Jefferson County, West Virginia - Wife was born in Maryland - Both
   reside in Jefferson County, West Virginia.

Criswell, Sagnes Roberts and Levi M. Porter (3) - November 15, 1871
   For further information see - Porter, Levi M.

Critzer, Elizabeth and Joseph Myers (1) - January 11, 1821

Croesen, Levi and Phoebe Jenkins (1) - June 20, 1816

Croeson, Eliza and Samuel Briscoe (1) - October 19, 1815

Crofford, Ann and John Keller (1) - December 26, 1830

Crofford, Thomas and Amelia Boswell (1) - August 31, 1831

Croft, James and Mrs. Ann Blackley (3) - April 1, 1875
    Place of marriage, Charlestown - Age of husband, 45 - Age of wife, 30 - Husband is a Widower - Wife is a Widow - Husband was born in Maryland - Wife was born in Jefferson County, West Virginia - Both reside in Jefferson County, West Virginia.

Croft, Joseph and Margaret Conklyn (1) - May 7, 1830

Croft, Mary and John Shepherd (1) - November 17, 1807

Cromwell, Fannie and George B. Lynch (3) - November 29, 1882
    For further information see - Lynch, George B.

Cromwell, Frances (cold.) Miles Smith (3) - December 22, 1881
    For further information see - Smith, Miles.

Cromwell, Frank A. and Emma J. Marlatt (3) - April 24, 1889
    Place of marriage, Charlestown - Age of husband, 31 - Age of wife, 21 - Both are Single - Both were born in Jefferson County, West Virginia - Both reside in Jefferson County, West Virginia.

Cromwell, Granville (cold.) Ailsy Fisher (3) - November 30, 1876
    Place of marriage, near Ripon - Age of husband, 26 - Age of wife, 18 - Both are Single - Husband was born in Goochland County - Wife was born in Jefferson County, West Virginia - Both reside in Jefferson County, West Virginia.

Cromwell, Henry Clay and Sarah Elizabeth Allstadt (2) - (L) January 28, 1856

Cromwell, John William and Annie E. Osbourn (3) - January 26, 1886
    Place of marriage, near Millville - Age of husband, 27 - Age of wife, 25 - Both are Single - Husband was born in Jefferson County, West Virginia - Wife was born in Jefferson County - Both reside in Jefferson County, West Virginia.

Cromwell, Oliver and Jane McPherson (1) - December 14, 1822

Cromwell, Stephen and Eliza Y. Davis (1) - January 23, 1823

Crone, Adam and Matilda Roberts (2) - (L) July 2, 1858

Crookson, A. A. and Emma Brent Cross (2) - (L) December 11, 1863
    Time of marriage - Place of marriage, Harpers Ferry - Names, A. A.
    Crookson and Emma Brent Cross - Age of husband, 24 years - Age of
    wife, 17 years - Both are Single - Husband was born in State of New
    York - Wife was born at Harpers Ferry - Husband's residence is at
    Peekskill, New York - Wife's residence is at Harpers Ferry - Names
    of husband's parents - Names of wife's parents are Rezin and
    Elizabeth Cross - Occupation of husband is Housebuilder - License
    issues, December 11, 1863 at the request of bride's father - Thomas
    A. Moore, Clerk.

Cross, A. M. (cold.) Isaac Slater (3) - December 14, 1867
    For further information see - Slater, Isaac.

Cross, Addie and W. T. Callar (3) - July 15, 1885
    For further information see - Callar, W. T.

Cross, Edward and Margaret Blue (1) - September 12, 1822

Cross, Emma Brent and A. A. Crookson (2) - (L) December 11, 1863
    For further information see - Crookson, A. A.

Cross, Harriet and Robert Melton (1) - January 30, 1820

Cross, Josephine and Thomas Jefferson (3) - November 1866
    For further information see - Jefferson, Thomas.

Cross, Lewis (colored) Rebecca Jackson (3) - January 27, 1870
    Place of marriage, Jefferson County - Age of husband, 24 - Age of
    wife, 19 - Both were born in Jefferson County - Both reside in
    Jefferson County. (Consent of parents.)

Cross, Lewis (cold.) Harriet Berry (3) - June 18, 1885
    Place of marriage, Summit Point - Age of husband, 39 - Age of wife,
    27 - Husband is a Widower - Wife is Single - Both were born in
    Jefferson County, West Virginia - Both reside in Jefferson County,
    West Virginia.

Cross, Mary (cold.) Samuel Early (3) - January 4, 1868
    For further information see - Early, Samuel.

Cross, Mary F. and Michael Keller (3) - August 2, 1877
    For further information see - Keller, Michael.

Cross, Rezin and Elizabeth Belsterling (1) - May 28, 1833

Cross, William and Fannie Hatter (3) - September 28, 1871
    Place of marriage, Jefferson County - Age of husband, 23 - Age of
    wife, 22 - Both are Single - Husband was born in Clarke County -
    Wife was born in Jefferson - Both reside in Jefferson - Husband's
    parents are Charles and Cuita - Wife's parents are Frank and Becca -
    Occupation of husband is Farmer.

Crouch, John D. and Maria Murkwood (1) - April 2, 1826

Crow, A. D. and Mollie J. Poffenberger (3) - December 11, 1878
    Place of marriage, Shepherdstown - Age of husband, 25 - Age of wife,
    20 - Both are Single - Both were born in Maryland - Both reside in
    Jefferson County, West Virginia.

Crow, Albina S. and John M. Coyle (2) -   (L) August 4, 1856

Crow, Eliza (widow) and Michael Cookus (1) -   May 7, 1850

Crow, Elizabeth H. and John F. Langley (1) -   May 13, 1826

Crow, Fannie V. and Henry E. Grosh (3) -   April 11, 1889
    For further information see - Grosh, Henry E.

Crow, Fanny and Joseph C. Show (3) -   November 18, 1869
    For further information see - Show, Joseph C.

Crow, Jacob B. and Ellen E. Yontz (2) -   (L) December 18, 1854

Crow, John William and Elizabeth Traynor (3) -   March 31, 1869
    Place of marriage, Jefferson County - Age of husband, 34 - Age of wife, 26 - Both are Single - Husband was born in Jefferson County - Wife was born in Pennsylvania - Both reside in Jefferson County - Husband's parents are John and Matilda - Wife's parents are John and Eliza - Occupation of husband is Farmer.

Crow, Margaret and David High (1) -   March 24, 1831

Crow, Richard and Ann Perry (1) -   January 1, 1826

Crow, Sally and John Miller (1) -   December 25, 1806

Crowell, Elias L. and Rebecca Link (1) -   September 8, 1820

Crowl, Charles William and A. Clyde McClellan (3) -   January 11, 1888
    Place of marriage, Charlestown - Age of husband, 25 - Age of wife, 23 - Both are Single - Husband was born in Jefferson County, West Virginia - Wife was born in Maryland - Husband resides at Hagerstown, Maryland - Wife resides in Jefferson County, West Virginia at present.

Crowl, Deborah and Thomas Russell (2) -   (L) December 30, 1854

Crowl, E. J. (bride) and G. W. Fossett (3) -   (1872)
    For further information see - Fossett, G. W.

Crowl, Elizabeth and Andrew Rieger (1) -   December 10, 1818

Crowl, Jacob and Ann Elizabeth Buckey (2) -   (L) May 24, 1851

Crowl, Jacob and Ann Elizabeth Buckey (1) -   May 29, 1851

Crowl, Jacob, Jr. and Sarah Gummert (1) -   October 15, 1812

Crowl, John and Elizabeth Cowper (1) -   November 4, 1827

Crowl, Michael P. and Sarah Elizabeth Maddox (3) -   December 14, 1875
    Place of marriage, near Scrabble - Age of husband, 22 - Age of wife, 20 - Both are Single - Husband was born in Berkeley County, West Virginia - Wife was born in Jefferson County, West Virginia - Both reside in Jefferson County, West Virginia. (Consent of bride's father in person.)

Crowl, Peter and Mary Sharp (1) -   October 24, 1816

Crowl, Samuel, Jr. and Mary Link (1) -　　　　　　　　　　June 16, 1814

Crowl, W. Hoke and May Alperetta Wintermoyer (3) -　　January 21, 1886
　　Place of marriage, Shepherdstown - Age of husband, 30 - Age of wife,
　　26 - Both are Single - Husband was born in Berkeley - Wife was born
　　in Jefferson County - Husband resides in Maryland - Wife resides in
　　Jefferson County, West Virginia.

Crusen, Ann and Benjamin Sheeley (1) -　　　　　　　　　August 7, 1806

Crutcher, Ernest and Katie V. Morrow (3) -　　　　　　　April 13, 1882
　　Place of marriage, Summit Point - Age of husband, 26 - Age of wife,
　　23 - Both are Single - Husband was born in Nashville, Tennessee -
　　Wife was born in Jefferson County, West Virginia - Husband resides
　　at Louisiana, Missouri - Wife resides in Jefferson County, West
　　Virginia.

Crutchley, Fanny Estella and Eugene L. Harrison (3) -　　April 29, 1886
　　For further information see - Harrison, Eugene L.

Crutchley, Lydia and Robert B. Dicky (3) -　　　　　　　November 2, 1871
　　For further information see - Dicky, Robert B.

Crutchley, M. F. and Jonathan Jackson (1) -　　　　　　　1819

Crutchley, Will F. and Laura E. Russell (3) -　　　　　　October 19, 1871
　　Place of marriage, Jefferson County - Age of husband, 29 - Age of
　　wife, 22 - Both are Single - Both were born in Virginia - Both
　　reside at Washington, D. C. - Husband's parents are John W. and
　　Jane W. - Wife's parents are John and Mary A. - Occupation of
　　husband is Physician.

Cruzen, Mary Ann and Frederick F. Merrick (2) -　　　(L) December 7, 1850

Cruzen, Mary Ann and Shadrack F. Merrick (1) -　　　　December 12, 1850

Cullman, James and Annie C. Weber (3) -　　　　　　　　January 10, 1889
　　Place of marriage, Harpers Ferry - Age of husband, 27 - Age of wife,
　　21 - Both are Single - Husband was born at Philadelphia,
　　Pennsylvania - Wife was born in Jefferson County, West Virginia -
　　Husband resides at Washington, D. C. - Wife resides in Jefferson
　　County, West Virginia.

Cullumber, Elenor and Daniel Biggs (1) -　　　　　　　　March 15, 1807

Culumber, William and Katherine Cameron (1) -　　　　　December 21, 1820

Cummings, Edward and Louisa Jane Nunburger (2) -　　(L) October 4, 1864
　　Time of marriage - Place of marriage, Harpers Ferry - Names, Edward
　　Cummings and Louisa Jane Nunburger - Age of husband, 21 years - Age
　　of wife, 18 years, October 15, 1864 - Both are Single - Husband was
　　born at New York City - Wife was born in Lancaster County,
　　Pennsylvania - Both reside at Harpers Ferry, Virginia - Names of
　　husband's parents - Names of wife's parents - Occupation of
　　husband - License issued, October 4, 1864 - Consent of bride's
　　mother (widow Smith) certified by applicant for license - T. A.
　　Moore, Clerk.

Cummings, Ellen M. and William H. Slough (3) -　　　　February 8, 1888
　　For further information see - Slough, William H.

125

Cummins, George D. and Alexandrine M. Bahl (1) -   June 24, 1847

Cummins, Levi G. and Sadie Wightman (3) -   October 23, 1889
    Place of marriage, Harpers Ferry - Age of husband, 23 - Age of wife, 24 - Both are Single - Both were born in Loudoun County, Virginia - Husband resides in Loudoun County, Virginia - Wife resides in Jefferson County, West Virginia.

Cunningham, Ellie and George Bennett (3) -   September 4, 1871
    For further information see - Bennett, George

Cunningham, Mary and Thomas Casey (2) -   (L) July 3, 1852

Cunningham, Mary A. and Jesse M. Scofield (1) -   April 13, 1829

Cunningham, Thomas and Maria Sprint (1) -   September 24, 1822

Currie, Charles W. and Emma Virginia Menefee (3) -   April 2, 1872
    Place of marriage, Jefferson County - Age of husband, 34 - Age of wife, 20 - Both are Single - Husband was born in Washington County, Maryland - Both reside in Jefferson County, West Virginia - Husband's parents are John and Sarah - Wife's parents are Joseph and Adelein - Occupation of husband is Farmer. (Vouched for by J. H. Stride.)

Currie, George E. and Sarah Foley (3) -   November 21, 1865
    Place of marriage, Jefferson County - Age of husband, 33 - Age of wife, 28 - Both are Single - Husband was born at Hagerstown, Washington County, Maryland - Wife was born in Jefferson County, West Virginia - Both reside in Jefferson County - Husband's parents are John and Sarah Currie - Wife's parents are Michael and Ann Foley - Occupation of husband is Farmer.

Currie, John and Mary Shirley (1) -   February 13, 1806

Currie, Kate R. and John J. M. Boyd (3) -   October 9, 1889
    For further information see - Boyd, John J. M.

Curry, B. F. and Mollie L. Higgins (3) -   November 27, 1889
    Place of marriage, Harpers Ferry - Age of husband, 27 - Age of wife, 25 - Both are Single - Husband was born in Augusta County, Virginia - Wife was born in Washington County, Maryland - Husband resides in Washington County, Maryland - Wife resides in Jefferson County, West Virginia.

Curry, D. J. and Geneva Gore (3) -   June 15, 1865
    Place of marriage, Bolivar - Age of husband, 24 years - Age of wife, 21 years - Both are Single - Husband was born in Green County, Pennsylvania - Wife was born in Loudoun County, Virginia - Husband resides in Green County, Pennsylvania - Wife resides at Bolivar, Jefferson County, Virginia - Husband's parents are John and Margaret Curry - Wife's parents are William A. and Sarah A. Gore - Occupation of husband is, Sadler.

Curry, Lafayette (cold.) Mary Johnson (3) -   March 3, 1887
    Place of marriage, Middleway.- Age of husband, 23 - Age of wife, 23 - Husband is Single - Wife is a Widow - Both were born in Jefferson County, West Virginia - Both reside in Jefferson County, West Virginia.

Curry, Mary and David McClellan (1) - . January 25, 1806

Curtis, J. B. and M. E. Helferstay (bride) (3) - December 22, 1881
   Place of marriage, Shepherdstown - Age of husband, 28 - Age of wife,
   19 - Both are Single - Husband was born in Pennsylvania - Wife was
   born in Maryland - Husband resides at Philadelphia - Wife resides in
   Jefferson County, West Virginia. (Consent of bride's father in
   person.)

Curtis, Maranda (cold.) John Burges (3) - December 18, 1866
   For further information see - Burges, John.

Custard, Cora L. and William M. Roland (3) - January 18, 1888
   For further information see - Roland, William M.

Custard, Ephraim J. and Ann Elizabeth McIntyre (2) - (L) February 8, 1854

Custard, Mary and Joseph Thompson (1) - May 17, 1835

Custer, Alcinda F. and Jesse Brillhart (3) - October 17, 1871
   For further information see - Brillhart, Jesse.

Custer, Ann Rebecca Virginia and Alexander ST.Clair (2) -(L) December 28, 1852

Custer, Annie S. and Philip T. Lindsay (3) - October 15, 1890
   For further information see - Lindsay, Philip T.

Custer, Charles J. and Annie E. Vorous (3) - October 25, 1881
   Place of marriage, Charlestown - Age of husband, 25 - Age of wife,
   26 - Both are Single - Husband was born in Berkeley County, West
   Virginia - Wife was born in Jefferson County, West Virginia - Both
   reside in Jefferson County, West Virginia.

Custer, Charles Man and Ida V. Fowler (3) - October 21, 1880
   Place of marriage, Leetown, West Virginia - Age of husband, 27 - Age
   of wife, 22 - Both are Single - Husband was born in Berkeley County,
   West Virginia - Wife was born in Jefferson County, West Virginia -
   Husband resides in Berkeley County, West Virginia - Wife resides in
   Jefferson County, West Virginia.

Custer, F. E. and John Bailey (3) - November 11, 1868
   For further information see - Bailey, John.

Custer, Harriet Ellen J. Cecilia and Philip Henry (3) - April 8, 1873
   For further information see - Henry, Philip.

Custer, Lucy B. and Charles B. Payne (3) - June 21, 1881
   For further information see - Payne, Charles B.

Custer, Margaret and John Foreman (1) - December 2, 1830

Custer, Mary Elizabeth and Benjamin F. Wageley (3) - December 3, 1878
   For further information see - Wageley, Benjamin F.

Custer, Mary B. and C. L. Beck (3) - June 20, 1883
   For further information see - Beck, C. L.

Custer, Sarah Catherine and Joseph M. Racey (3) - November 4, 1886
    For further information see - Racey, Joseph M.

Custer, Virginia L. and Christopher C. Henry (3) - August 30, 1881
    For further information see - Henry, Christopher C.

Cutshaw, B. G. and Isaac Stock (3) - December 15, 1868
    For further information see - Stock, Isaac.

Cutshaw, Mary and John Clappy (1) - August 27, 1829

Daggett, William H. and Daisey P. Cavalier (3) - June 5, 1889
    Place of marriage, Harpers Ferry - Age of husband, 30 - Age of wife,
    19 - Both are Single - Husband was born at Springfield,
    Massachusetts - Wife was born in Jefferson County, West Virginia -
    Husband resides at Springfield, Massachusetts - Wife resides in
    Jefferson County, West Virginia.

Dailey, Ann E. and John McCormick, Jr. (2) - (L) July 30, 1859

Dailey, Christiana and Adam L. Demory (2) - (L) June 17, 1858

Dailey, Ettie and Charles D. Kline (3) - June 8, 1884
    For further information see - Kline, Charles D.

Dailey, Florence and Joseph W. Marlow (3) - February 27, 1884
    For further information see - Marlow, Joseph W.

Dailey, John W. and Katie Jackson (3) - October 27, 1890
    Place of marriage, Charlestown - Age of husband, 22 - Age of wife,
    21 - Both are Single - Both were born in Jefferson County, West
    Virginia - Both reside in Jefferson County, West Virginia.

Dailey, Rezin W. and Charlotte Elizabeth Everhart (2) - (L) October 16, 1858

Dailey, Robert L. R. and Ruth A. Earle (3) - September 24, 1890
    Place of marriage, Charlestown - Age of husband, 25 - Age of wife,
    21 - Both are Single - Both were born in Jefferson County, West
    Virginia - Both reside in Jefferson County, West Virginia.

Dailey, Thomas and Margaret N. Griffith (3) - October 1871
    Place of marriage, Jefferson County - Age of husband, 23 - Age of
    wife, 21 - Both are Single - Both were born in Virginia - Both
    reside in West Virginia - Wife's parents are Abraham and Lucretia -
    Occupation of husband is Laborer. (Father.)

Dailey, Thomas and Mary C. Shamblin (3) - October 2, 1890
    Place of marriage, Charlestown - Age of husband, 42 - Age of wife,
    20 - Husband is Divorced - Wife is Single - Husband was born in
    Ohio - Wife was born in Jefferson County, West Virginia - Both
    reside in Jefferson County, West Virginia. (Consent of bride's
    mother in writing.)

Daily, John W. and Mary M. Everhart (3) - November 2, 1865
    Age of husband, 30 - Age of wife, 22 - Both are Single - Husband was
    born in Jefferson County - Wife was born in Loudoun County - Both
    reside in Jefferson County - Husband's parents are Rezin R. and
    Mary E. Daily - Wife's parents are Solomon and Sarah A. Everhart -
    Occupation of husband is Carpenter.

Daily, Margaret Ann and James H. Milton (3) - May 9, 1890
    For further information see - Milton, James H.

Dainer, Eliza and William Holmes (1) - October 19, 1815

Dalamuple, John and Elizabeth Miller (1) - August 31, 1813

Dalgarn, S. S. and Eliza J. Shugert (3) - February 28, 1884
    Place of marriage, Charlestown - Age of husband, 39 - Age of wife,
    30 - Both are Single - Both were born in Jefferson County, West
    Virginia - Both reside in Jefferson County, West Virginia.

Dalgarn, Stephen and Barbary Allstadt (1) - .   August 4, 1825

Dalgarn, William L. and Sallie V. O'Bannon (3) -   April 26, 1877
  Place of marriage, Charlestown - Age of husband, 29 - Age of wife,
  25 - Both are Single - Both were born in Jefferson County, West
  Virginia - Both reside in Jefferson County, West Virginia.

Dameron, Mary and Patrick Coulan (2) - .   (L) April 22, 1858

Dandridge, Sarah P. and Blackburn Hughes (3) - .   September 3, 1873
  For further information see - Hughes, Blackburn.

Dangerfield, Edmund (cold.) Mary Washington (3) -   February 4, 1886
  Place of marriage, Charlestown - Age of husband, 25 - Age of wife,
  35 -Husband is Single - Wife is a Widow - Husband was born in
  Frederick County, Virginia - Wife was born in Jefferson County -
  Both reside in Jefferson County, West Virginia.

Daniel, Allen Preston (cold.) Margaretta Lovett (3) -   June 16, 1886
  Place of marriage, Harpers Ferry - Age of husband, 31 - Age of wife,
  22 - Both are Single - Husband was born in West Virginia - Wife was
  born in Pennsylvania - Husband resides in State of New York - Wife
  resides in Jefferson County, West Virginia.

Daniel, John M. and Anne E. Leavell (3) -   October 29, 1874
  Place of marriage, near Charlestown - Age of husband, 29 - Age of
  wife, 23 - Both are Single - Husband was born in Prince Edward
  County, Virginia - Wife was born in Jefferson County, West Virginia-
  Husband resides at Louisville, Kentucky - Wife resides in Jefferson
  County, West Virginia.

Daniel, Kate A. and Alfred M. Barbour (2) -   (L) January 4, 1858

Daniel, Mary E. A. and John William Hurst (2) -   (L) November 6, 1854

Daniel, William S. and Catherine E. D. Hurst (1) -   August 14, 1834

Daniels, Annie L. and Charles B. Wentzell (3) -   January 5, 1873
  For further information see - Wentzell, Charles B.

Daniels, Benjamin F. and Fannie M. Hessey (2) -   (L) March 29, 1855

Daniels, Cora V. and Adam C. Moler (3) -   February 27, 1872
  For further information see - Moler, Adam C.

Daniels, Dennis M. and Mary Anna Sperry (2) -   (L) May 23, 1864
  Time of marriage, May 26 - **Place of marriage, near Duffields Depot -
  Names, Dennis M. Daniels and Mary Anna Sperry - Age** of husband, 35
  years - Age of wife, 21 years - Husband is a Widower - Wife is
  Single - Husband was born in Jefferson County - Wife was born in
  Frederick County - Both reside in Jefferson County - Names of
  husband's parents, John and Nancy Daniels - Names of wife's parents
  are John and ___?___ - Occupation of husband is - License issued,
  May 23, 1864.

Daniels, Fannie E. and John B. Cary (3) -   November 7, 1867
  For further information see - Cary, John B.

Daniels, Henry V. and Clara B. Beale (2) -   (L) May 14, 1863
    Time of marriage, May 19, 1863 - Place of marriage, Harpers Ferry -
    Age of husband, 24 years - Age of wife, 20 years, May 12, 1863 -
    Both are Single - Husband was born at Philadelphia - Wife was born
    at Harpers Ferry - Both reside in Jefferson County, Virginia - Names
    of husband's parents are Antoine and Jane Daniels - Names of wife's
    parents are Albert and Mary Beale - Occupation of husband is
    Machinist - Father of bride is dead - License issued by consent of
    her mother, May 14, 1863 - Thomas W. Beale.

Daniels, John W. and Mary E. Staley (3) -   March 24, 1880
    Place of marriage, Shepherdstown - Age of husband, 24 - Age of wife,
    22 - Both are Single - Both were born in Jefferson County, West
    Virginia - Both reside in Jefferson County, West Virginia.

Daniels, Lydia H. and Jacob Miller (1) - .   December 8, 1831

Daniels, Maie A. and J. E. Burns (3) -   October 23, 1888
    For further information see - Burns, J. E.

Daniels, Martha M. and William H. Link (3) -   February 21, 1878
    For further information see - Link, William H.

Daniels, Mary A. and John Kearsley Kenedy (2) -   (L) February 23, 1857

Daniels, Rose and Isaac C. Haas (3) -   November 29, 1870
    For further information see - Haas, Isaac C.

Danner, Mary C. and Edward Fatisal (3) -   October 27, 1885
    For further information see - Fatisal, Edward.

Darlington, John W. and Flora B. Shoemaker (3) -   January 10, 1883
    Place of marriage, Charlestown - Age of husband, 30 - Age of wife,
    30 - Both are Single - Husband was born at Winchester, Virginia -
    Wife was born in Franklin County, Pennsylvania - Husband resides at
    Winchester, Virginia - Wife resides in Jefferson County, West
    Virginia.

Daugherty, Ann and James B. Carson (1) -   June 26, 1806

Daugherty, Ann S. and William Yates (1) -   January 10, 1832

Daugherty, Benjamin (cold.) Isabelle James (3) -   November 14, 1887
    Place of marriage, Charlestown - Age of husband, 22 - Age of wife,
    21 - Both are Single - Both were born in Jefferson County, West
    Virginia - Both reside in Jefferson County, West Virginia.

Daugherty, Joseph T. and Mary Ann Tate (1) -   May 12, 1825

Daugherty, Lucy (cold.) Harry Williams (3) -   July 13, 1876
    For further information see - Williams, Harry.

Daugherty, Margaret and George Cooper (1) -   October 5, 1813

Davenport, Amelia and Joseph Strother (1) - .   June 5, 1808

Davenport, Amelia C. and Catesby Woodford (3) -   May 28, 1890
    For further information see - Woodford, Catesby.

Davenport, Ann Simms and John Ransdell (1) -   October 1, 1829

Davenport, Eleanor and Alfred Gaskins (1) - June 7, 1827

Davenport, Fannie and John Thomas Gibson (2) - (L) May 9, 1855

Davenport, J. A. and M. Louisa Beall (3) - August 18, 1880
Place of marriage, Charlestown - Age of husband, 25 - Age of wife, 24 - Both are Single - Husband was born in New York - Wife was born in Jefferson County, West Virginia - Both reside in Jefferson County, West Virginia.

Davenport, Katie (cold.) Jacob Robinson (3) - December 29, 1887
For further information see - Robinson, Jacob.

Davenport, Margaret T. and Ambrose W. Cramer (2) - (L) November 26, 1851

Davenport, Margaret T. and Ambrose W. Cramer (1) - November 27, 1851

Davenport, Mary T. and Daniel D. Forrest (1) - March 21, 1820

Davenport, Rebecca and John Blackwell (1) - February 9, 1819

Davenport, Samuel and Ruth (Alder) H. Hay (1) - May 16, 1818

Davenport, Samuel and Mary Hay (1) - November 23, 1826

Davidson, Hunter and Elizabeth R. Craighill (3) - July 17, 1890
Place of marriage, Charlestown - Age of husband, 28 - Age of wife, 31 - Both are Single - Husband was born at Portsmouth, Virginia - Wife was born at Georgetown, D. C. - Husband resides at Port Deposit, Maryland - Wife resides in Jefferson County, West Virginia.

Davine, Mary and Daniel Ragan (2) - (L) January 8, 1853
(Stephen Burke witness.)

Davis, Miss and Christian Gummert (1) - June 1843

Davis, Ann and Samuel Johnson (1) - December 15, 1825

Davis, Ann E. and James Henry Hooe (3) - August 27, 1889
For further information see - Hooe, James Henry.

Davis, Aquila and Hester Wysong (1) - December 4, 1816

Davis, Cecelia and David Higgins (1) - July 16, 1815

Davis, Clement R. and Sarah Hall Gibbon (1) - April 4. 1820

Davis, Dorcus Johnson and Samuel Forgerson (1) - December 10, 1823

Davis, Eliza and Caspar Cramer (1) - March 7, 1809

Davis, Eliza and Joseph S. Whittington (3) - January 14, 1868
For further information see - Whittington, Joseph S.

Davis, Eliza Catherine and James G. Davis (3) - September 21, 1884
For further information see - Davis, James G.

Davis, Eliza D. and I. R. Franklin (3) - October 29, 1867
For further information see - Franklin, I. R.

Davis, Eliza Y. and Stephen Cromwell (1) - January 23, 1823

Davis, Elizabeth and Jacob A. Campbell (2) - (L) August 17, 1857

Davis, Garland Moore and Martha Newton Strother (1) - February 22, 1825

Davis, Harry and Jane Foreman (3) - February 20, 1886
    Place of marriage, Harpers Ferry - Age of husband, 34 - Age of wife, 40 - Husband is Single - Wife is a Widow - Husband was born at Philadelphia, Pennsylvania - Wife was born in Jefferson County, West Virginia - Husband resides in Washington County, Maryland - Wife redides in Jefferson County, West Virginia.

Davis, Ida May and Thomas Alexander Hoole (3) - September 6, 1888
    For further information see - Hoole, Thomas Alexander.

Davis, Isaac and Sarah Bowers (1) - December 3, 1829

Davis, James and Elenor Morgan (1) - June 27, 1822

Davis, James (cold.) Annie Vester (3) - June 13, 1886
    Place of marriage, near Charlestown - Age of husband, 38 - Age of wife, 30 - Husband is Single - Wife is a Widow - Husband was born in Jefferson County, West Virginia - Wife was born at Charlottesville, Virginia - Both reside in Jefferson County, West Virginia.

Davis, James G. and Eliza Catherine Davis (3) - September 21, 1884
    Place of marriage, Charlestown - Age of husband, 21 - Age of wife, 22 - Both are Single - Both were born in Berkeley County, West Virginia - Both reside in Jefferson County.

Davis, John (colored) Harriet Pendleton (3) - November 10, 1870
    Place of marriage, Jefferson County - Age of husband, 31 - Age of wife, 44 - Both were born in Virginia - Both reside in Jefferson County.

Davis, Lucy (cold.) William Berry (3) - December 18, 1884
    For further information see - Berry, William.

Davis, M. E. (bride) and S. P. Latane (3) - September 10, 1878
    For further information see - Latane, S. P.

Davis, Malinda and Jacob S. Wilt (3) - December 27, 1869
    For further information see - Wilt, Jacob S.

Davis, Maria L. (cold.) William Henry Staley (3) - November 4, 1886
    For further information see - Staley, William Henry.

Davis, Martha (cold.) John Dodson (3) - August 9, 1877
    For further information see - Dodson, John.

Davis, Martha N. and John B. Page (3) - November 17, 1868
    For further information see - Page, John B.

Davis, Mary Ann and John Humphreys (1) - February 11, 1823

Davis, Mary Ann and Corbin Baker (1) - August 4, 1833

Davis, Mary E. and J. O. Johnson (3) - October 10, 1883
    For further information see - Johnson, J. O.

134

Davis, Nancy and John Buckmaster (1) -   January 15, 1816

Davis, Royal M. (cold.) Fannie Creamer (3) -   January 11, 1888
Place of marriage, Shepherdstown - Age of husband, 31 - Age of wife,
27 - Both are Single - Husband was born in Halifax County,
Virginia - Wife was born in Jefferson County, West Virginia - Both
reside in Jefferson County, West Virginia.

Davis, Ruth and Van Goldsbary (1) -   July 28, 1825

Davis, S. H. and S. M. Welshans (bride) (3) -   January 20, 1869
Place of marriage, Jefferson County - Age of husband, 28 - Age of
wife, 23 - Both are Single - Husband was born in Washington County,
Maryland - Wife was born in Jefferson County, Virginia - Husband
resides in Washington County, Maryland - Wife resides in Jefferson
County - Husband's parents are Josiah and Eliza - Wife's parents are
Joseph and Margaret - Occupation of husband is Farmer.

Davis, Mrs. Sally and William Reed (3) -   April 23, 1867
For further information see - Reed, William.

Davis, Samuel and Lucinda Jett (1) -   1812

Davis, Sarah E. and Minor Hurst (1) -   December 22, 1831

Davis, Spencer (cold.) Angeline Johnson (3) -   May 25, 1874
Place of marriage, near Kabletown - Age of husband, 24 - Age of
wife, 23 - Husband is Single - Wife is a Widow - Both were born in
Jefferson County, West Virginia - Both reside in Jefferson County,
West Virginia.

Davis, Thomas and Annie West (3) -   December 23, 1868
Place of marriage, Jefferson County - Age of husband, 35 - Age of
wife, 35 - Husband is Single - Wife is a Widow - Husband was born in
Clarke County, Virginia - Wife was born in Loudoun - Both reside in
Jefferson County - Wife's parents are John and Mary - Occupation of
husband is Laborer.

Davis, William and Victoria Banks (3) -   April 27, 1869
Place of marriage, Jefferson County - Age of husband, 21 - Age of
wife, 21 - Both were born in Virginia - Both reside in Jefferson
County.

Davis, William B. and Nannie K. Starry (3) -   October 18, 1888
Place of marriage, Charlestown - Age of husband, 37 - Age of wife,
35 - Both are Single - Both were born in Jefferson County, West
Virginia - Both reside in Jefferson County, West Virginia.

Davisson, R. Despard and Nellie D. Fleming (3) -   October 19, 1876
Place of marriage, Summit Point - Age of husband, 28 - Age of wife,
26 - Both are Single - Husband was born at Clarksburg, West
Virginia - Wife was born in Jefferson County, West Virginia -
Husband resides in Braxton County, West Virginia - Wife resides in
Jefferson County, West Virginia.

Davy, Molly and James Howard (3) -   August 22, 1867
For further information see - Howard, James.

Daws, William and Frances Coyle (1) -   April 9, 1822

Day, Lucy (cold.) John Henry Robinson (3) -   February 10, 1887
    For further information see - Robinson, John Henry.

Day, William and Lucinda Thompson Mull (2) -   (L) February 18, 1854

Daylong, Peter J. and Catherine Berlin (1) -   October 3, 1833

Deakins, Lydia M. and Hamilton Lay (1) -   August 19, 1834

Dean, Ann and Abraham Crane (1) -   May 4, 1826

Dean, Charity and William P. Easterday (1) -   April 27, 1825

Dean, Mary E. and Richard H. Langley (1) -   November 10, 1848

Dearing, George W. and Keziah Hook (1) -   June 5, 1828

Dearing, Notley and Margaret Betts (1) -   July 9, 1829

Dearing, Notley W. and Mrs. Sarah Ann Washburn (widow of P. B.
    Washburn) -   October 4, 1835

Dearing, Russell H. and Ann E. Bishop (1) -   July 7, 1835

Dearing, Susan and Henry Reed (2) -   (L) December 14, 1852

Dechert, Daniel and Laura Parran Miller (2) -   (L) September 17, 1855

Deck, David M. and Mrs. Fanny C. Seibert (3) -   December 11, 1879
    Place of marriage, near Kearneysville - Age of husband, 38 - Age of
    wife, 42 - Husband is Single - Wife is a Widow - Both were born in
    Berkeley County, West Virginia - Both reside in Jefferson County,
    West Virginia.

Deck, John T. A. and Laura B. Padgett (3) -   April 17, 1884
    Place of marriage, Harpers Ferry - Age of husband, 21 - Age of wife,
    17 - Both are Single - Husband was born in State of Maryland - Wife
    was born in Jefferson County, West Virginia - Husband resides in
    Maryland - Wife resides in Jefferson County, West Virginia.

Deck, Joseph and Mrs. Mary Grall (2) -   (L) October 25, 1852

Deck, Margaret and William T. Hoffman (3) -   April 18, 1867
    For further information see - Hoffman, William T.

Deck, Mary F. and John William Ecton (3) -   May 20, 1880
    For further information see - Ecton, John William.

Deck, Mary M. and Isaac Nelson (2) -   (L) November 1, 1854

Deck, Virginia B. and Dennis M. Schoppert (3) -   May 10, 1881
    For further information see - Schoppert, Dennis M.

Deck, William R. and Margaret Virginia Keyes (2) -   (L) September 30, 1857

Deen, Margaret and Lewis F. Young (1) -   December 4, 1817

Deen, Mary and John Kealhover (1) -   March 24, 1808

Deen, Susan and Samuel Thompson (1) -   June 3, 1810

Deener, John H. and Charlotte Rebecca Marlatt (2) -   (L) May 12, 1853
    (Witness, James H. House.)

Deetz, J. Henry and Susan E. Foreman (3) -   September 24, 1879
    Place of marriage, Bolivar - Age of husband, 26 - Age of wife, 19 -
    Both are Single - Husband was born in Maryland - Wife was born in
    Ohio - Both reside in Jefferson County, West Virginia. (Consent of
    bride's father in writing. Witness, F. Cockrell.)

Deevers, Nancy and Joseph Seaman (1) -   March 13, 1817

Dehoney, Bridget and John McMara (3) -   (1870)
    For further information see - McMara, John.

Dejarnett, Henry W. and Lucretia M. Hill (3) -   December 3, 1873
    Place of marriage, near Duffields - Age of husband, 28 - Age of
    wife, 26 - Both are Single - Husband was born in Pittsylvania
    County, Virginia - Wife was born in Jefferson County, West
    Virginia - Both reside in Jefferson County, West Virginia.

Delaney, Nancie and John Sampson (3) -   December 7, 1865
    For further information see - Sampson, John.

DeLany, Ellen and James K. Polk Pear (3) -   July 24, 1873
    For further information see - Pear, James K. Polk

Delaplane, Joseph and Julia Hinkle (1) -   1814

Delauder, William A. and Mollie E. Kern (3) -   September 25, 1884
    Place of marriage, Harpers Ferry - Age of husband, 24 - Age of wife,
    22 - Both are Single - Husband was born in State of Maryland - Wife
    was born in Jefferson County, West Virginia - Both reside in
    Jefferson County.

Delo, Herman E. and Emma F. Hipsley (3) -   September 17, 1879
    Place of marriage, Charlestown - Age of husband, 23 - Age of wife,
    21 - Both are Single - Both were born in State of Pennsylvania -
    Husband resides in State of Pennsylvania - Wife resides in Jefferson
    County, West Virginia.

Demend, Conrad and Agness West (1) -   September 21, 1815

Deminie, Phobe and Hiram McKinney (1) -   1812

Demory, Adam L. and Christiana Dailey (2) -   (L) June 17, 1858

Demory, Luther and Ella B. Coffinbarger (3) -   October 11, 1888
    Place of marriage, near Unionville, Jefferson County, West
    Virginia - Age of husband, 22 - Age of wife, 22 - Both are Single -
    Husband was born in Loudoun County, Virginia - Wife was born in
    Jefferson County, West Virginia - Husband resides in Anne Arundle
    County, Maryland - Wife resides in Jefferson County, West Virginia.

Demory, Mrs. Sarah C. and Thomas J. Ingram (3) -   March 24, 1875
    For further information see - Ingram, Thomas J.

Dempsey, Michael and Margaret Boren (3) -   (1870)
    Age of husband, 26 - Age of wife, 25 - Both were born in Ireland -
    Both reside in Jefferson County. (Sworn to by David Dohoney as to
    ages.)

Dennis, John and Maria D. Burns (1) - August 26, 1818

Dent, Benjamin B. and Kate E. Shipe (3) - September 12, 1876
    Place of marriage, Bolivar - Age of husband, 32 - Age of wife, 29 -
    Both are Single - Husband was born in Charles County, Maryland -
    Wife was born at Winchester, Virginia - Both reside at Harpers
    Ferry.

Dent, Mathew and Ann Catharine Roper (2) - (L) May 24, 1853

Deppen, Cecelia (cold.) Benjamin Galloway (3) - January 23, 1890
    For further information see - Galloway, Benjamin.

Derow, Catharine and James Foreman (2) - (L) July 29, 1857

Derr, Clara A. and Melvin L. Ronemous (3) - March 12, 1890
    For further information see - Ronemous, Melvin L.

Derr, Henry A. and Mary V. Jones (3) - December 17, 1878
    Place of marriage, Shepherdstown - Age of husband, 23 - Age of wife,
    22 - Both are Single - Both were born in Jefferson County, West
    Virginia - Both reside in Jefferson County, West Virginia.

Derrow, George M. and Augusta E. Shelly (3) - October 25, 1886
    Place of marriage, Harpers Ferry - Age of husband, 23 - Age of wife,
    25 - Both are Single - Husband was born on Rockingham County,
    Virginia - Wife was born in Jefferson County, West Virginia -
    Husband resides in Rockingham County, Virginia - Wife resides in
    Jefferson County, West Virginia.

Derry, Arthur Lee and Annie Virginia Brown (3) - March 25, 1885
    Place of marriage, near Halltown - Age of husband, 22 - Age of wife,
    22 - Both are Single - Husband was born in Loudoun County,
    Virginia - Wife was born in Jefferson County, West Virginia - Both
    reside in Jefferson County, West Virginia.

Derry, Elizabeth E. and Joseph E. B. Peyton (3) - December 24, 1874
    For further information see - Peyton, Joseph E. B.

Derry, James W. and Ellen Jane Oden (3) - January 1, 1882
    Place of marriage, near Zoar Church - Age of husband, 21 - Age of
    wife, 17 - Both are Single - Both were born in Jefferson County,
    West Virginia - Both reside in Jefferson County, West Virginia.
    (License issued, December 31, 1881. Consent of bride's grandfather
    in person. She has neither father nor mother. Thomas Oden, name
    of grandfarher.)

Derry, Laura B. and George W. Oden (3) - October 11, 1875
    For further information see - Oden, George W.

Derry, Laura Bell and George W. Oden (3) - December 30, 1875
    For further information see - Oden, George W.

Derry, Philip H. and Florence E. Hobbs (3) - March 18, 1877
   Place of marriage, Harpers Ferry - Age of husband, 22 - Age of wife,
   19 - Both are Single - Husband was born in Loudoun County,
   Virginia - Wife was born in Jefferson County, West Virginia -
   Husband resides in Loudoun County, Virginia - Wife resides in
   Jefferson County, West Virginia. (Consent of bride's mother
   certified by aunt of bride and also a letter from mother to bride.)

Derry, Solomon and Sophia Shuck (1) - February 26, 1829

Derry, Virginia and Mahlon Lancaster (3) - May 13, 1874
   For further information see - Lancaster, Mahlon.

Derry, Wilbert H. and Edy M. Colbert (3) - May 20, 1885
   Place of marriage, Charlestown - Age of husband, 21 - Age of wife,
   17 - Both are Single - Both were born in Jefferson County, West
   Virginia - Both reside in Jefferson County, West Virginia.
   (Consent of bride's father in person.)

Derry, William W. and Mary E. Hobbs (3) - March 10, 1880
   Place of marriage, Harpers Ferry - Age of husband, 28 - Age of wife,
   25 - Both are Single - Husband was born in Loudoun County,
   Virginia - Wife was born in Jefferson County, West Virginia -
   Husband resides in Loudoun County, Virginia - Wife resides in
   Jefferson County, West Virginia.

Detterman, Viola Virginia and George McCauly (3) - March 15, 1874
   For further information see - McCauly, George.

Devinger, Alexander (cold.) Josephine Brown (3) - November 8, 1887
   Place of marriage, Shepherdstown - Age of husband, 23 - Age of wife,
   22 - Both are Single - Both were born in Jefferson County, West
   Virginia - Both reside in Jefferson County, West Virginia.

Devinger, Mrs. Nellie (cold.) Samuel Coleman (3) - October 2, 1887
   For further information see - Coleman, Samuel.

Devlin, Catherine and Oliver Peacher (3) - October 25, 1886
   For further information see - Peacher, Oliver.

Devlin, Patrick and Mrs. Margaret Mahony (2) - (L) July 26, 1851

Devonshire, Bell (cold.) Wilber Domer (3) - February 10, 1881
   For further information see - Domer, Wilber.

Devonshire, Ellen (cold.) Charles Clark (3) - August 31, 1876
   For further information see - Clark, Charles.

Devonshire, George (cold.) Isabella Lee (3) - September 14, 1884
   Place of marriage, Charlestown - Age of husband, 26 - Age of wife,
   25 - Both are Single - Both were born in Jefferson County, West
   Virginia - Both reside in Jefferson County.

Devonshire, Jennie (cold.) George William Johnson (3) - January 15, 1879
   For further information see - Johnson, George William.

Devonshire, Lucy and Thomas Devonshire (3) - December 27, 1865
   For further information see - Devonshire, Thomas.

Devonshire, Lucy (cold.) Robert Brown (3) -　　　　　October 11, 1888
　　For further information see - Brown, Robert.

Devonshire, Mary (cold.) George N. Crissinger (3) -　　　April 4, 1889
　　For further information see - Crissinger, George N.

Devonshire, Thomas and Lucy Devonshire (3) -　　　December 27, 1865
　　Place of marriage, near Duffields Depot - Age of husband, 28 - Age
　　of wife, 17 - Husband is a Widower - Wife is Single - Husband was
　　born at Shepherdstown, Jefferson County - Wife was born near
　　Shepherdstown - Both reside in Jefferson County, West Virginia -
　　Husband's parents are James and Mariah Devonshire - Wife's parents
　　are George and Jeacy Devonshire - Occupation of husband is Laborer.

Dewar, Maggie F. and Harrison S. Harrell (3) -　　　　　July 20, 1887
　　For further information see - Harrell, Harrison S.

Dhiel, Nelson and Laura V. Getzendanner (3) -　　　　February 1, 1870
　　Place of marriage, Jefferson County - Age of husband, 28 - Age of
　　wife, 19 - Both were born in Maryland - Husband resides in
　　Maryland - Wife resides in Jefferson County. (Father in person
　　consents.)

Dick, Edward H. and Lillie M. Rau (3) -　　　　　　February 16, 1882
　　Place of marriage, near Bolivar - Age of husband, 28 - Age of wife,
　　18 - Both are Single - Husband was born at Zanesville, Ohio - Wife
　　was born at Springfield, Massachusetts - Husband resides at
　　Wheeling, West Virginia - Wife resides in Jefferson County, West
　　Virginia. (Consent of bride's father in person.)

Dickinson, Phebe (cold.) Milford Brown (3) -　　　　　　May 29, 1879
　　For further information see - Brown, Milford.

Dickinson, Susan E. (cold.) Albert S. Hill (3) -　　　January 13, 1890
　　For further information see - Hill, Albert S.

Dicky, Robert B. and Lydia Crutchley (3) -　　　　　November 2, 1871
　　Place of marriage, Harpers Ferry - Age of husband, 22 - Age of wife,
　　23 - Both are Single - Husband was born in Maryland - Wife was born
　　in Virginia - Husband resides in Maryland - Wife resides at
　　Washington, D. C. - Husband's parents are John and Lucretia - Wife's
　　parents are John W. and Jane - Occupation of husband is Watchman.

Didier, Henry A. and Angelica S. Boteler (2) -　　(L) September 7, 1860

Diehl, Hannah L. and Ed. W. Phillips (3) -　　　　　　March 30, 1886
　　For further information see - Phillips, Ed. W.

Dietz, William H. and Marie Reed (2) -　　　　　(L) October 12, 1857

Diggs, Andrew (cold.) Lizzy Smoke (3) -　　　　　　　January 1, 1878
　　Place of marriage, Bolivar - Age of husband, 30 - Age of wife, 21 -
　　Both are Single - Husband was born in Bath County, Virginia - Wife
　　was born in Frederick County, Virginia - Both reside in Jefferson
　　County, West Virginia.

Diggs, Elizabeth (cold.) John Harris (3) -　　　　　December 31, 1885
　　For further information see - Harris, John.

Dillard, T. T. and Lizzie S. Moler (3) -   March 13, 1873
   Place of marriage, near Harpers Ferry - Age of husband, 37 - Age of
   wife, 25 - Both are Single - Husband was born in Spottsylvania
   County, Virginia - Wife was born in Jefferson County, West
   Virginia - Husband resides in Spottsylvania County, Virginia - Wife
   resides in Jefferson County, West Virginia - Husband's parents are
   James D. and Gurdy T. - Wife's parents are George W. and Sarah -
   Occupation of husband is Farmer.

   Dillon, Laura V. and John Y. Mullinax (3) -   December 5, 1865
      For further information see - Mullinax, John Y.

   Dillon, Mary C. and Martin L. Payne (3) -   October 23, 1866
      For further information see - Payne, Martin L.

   Dillow, Ann and Christian Piper (1) -   March 16, 1820

   Dillow, Anna and Thomas Matheny (1) -   February 11, 1819

   Dillow, Caroline and Benjamin Larew (3) -   May 10, 1869
      For further information see - Larew, Benjamin.

   Dillow, David and Nancy Whitehouse (1) -   November 22, 1827

   Dillow, David and Julia Ann Shackleford (2) -   (L) August 10, 1857

   Dillow, Elizabeth and Thomas Dillow (1) -   May 30, 1810

   Dillow, Elizabeth and James Roads (1) -   January 30, 1820

   Dillow, Elizabeth and John Washington Rannels (2) -   (L) February 10, 1852

   Dillow, Elizabeth Jane and Lee H. Dillow (3) -   January 25, 1880
      For further information see - Dillow, Lee H.

   Dillow, Emanuel Washington and Mary Elizabeth Hostler (3) - September 16, 1886
      Place of marriage, Blue Ridge Mountain - Age of husband, 20 - Age of
      wife, 25 - Both are Single - Both were born in Jefferson County,
      West Virginia - Both reside in Jefferson County, West Virginia -
      (Consent of groom's father in person.)

   Dillow, Emma Ann and Levi Kephart (3) -   August 18, 1881
      For further information see - Kephart, Levi.

   Dillow, Harriet and Joseph Blincoe (1) -   August 27, 1835

   Dillow, Hester and William Dillow (1) -   March 17, 1825

   Dillow, Jane Ellen Adoria and Thomas F. Dulany (3) -   September 30, 1875
      For further information see - Dulany, Thomas F.

   Dillow, Joanna and W. W. Bissell (3) -   August 31, 1890
      For further information see - Bissell, W. W.

   Dillow, John and Sally Farr (1) -   September 23, 1847

141

Dillow, John H. and Sarah E. Wiley (3) - December 15, 1881
  Place of marriage, Charlestown - Age of husband, 20 - Age of wife,
  23 - Both are Single - Husband was born in Jefferson County, West
  Virginia - Wife was born in Clarke County, Virginia - Both reside in
  Jefferson County, West Virginia. (Consent of groom's father in
  person.)

Dillow, Joseph and Emma Ann Dulany (2) - (L) May 26, 1851

Dillow, Josiah and Temperence Dillow (1) - September 19, 1822

Dillow, Julia and John Longerbeam (3) - February 8, 1885
  For further information see - Longerbeam, John.

Dillow, Lee H. and Mrs. Ann Wilt (widow of George W. Wilt) (2) -
                                                        (L) May 22, 1852

Dillow, Lee H. and Mrs. Ann Wilt (widow) (1) - May 24, 1852

Dillow, Lee H. and Elizabeth Jane Dillow (3) - January 25, 1880
  Place of marriage, Mountain - Age of husband, 23 - Age of wife, 21 -
  Both are Single - Both were born in Jefferson County, West
  Virginia - Both reside in Jefferson County, West Virginia.
  (Bride's father.)

Dillow, Lucy Virginia and John Foreman (2) - (L) June 20, 1861
  For further information see - Foreman, John.

Dillow, Margaret and William Dillow (1) - November 4, 1820

Dillow, Mary and Jacob Cooper (1) - December 31, 1826

Dillow, Mary Elizabeth and Thomas Penwell, Jr. (2) - (L) May 15, 1858

Dillow, Mary Elizabeth and Charles William Pearl (3) - December 24, 1872

Dillow, Nancy and John Blinco (1) - February 17, 1825

Dillow, Peter and Pheby Wykoff (1) - March 23, 1820

Dillow, Polly and George Ott (1) - October 1, 1818

Dillow, Rose A. and John Wiley (3) - July 13, 1882
  For further information see - Wiley, John.

Dillow, Sally and Charles Painter (3) - February 8, 1885
  For further information see - Painter, Charles.

Dillow, Sarah and Lawrence Stedman (1) - November 22, 1827

Dillow, Sarah and George W. Tacey (2) - (L) November 5, 1858

Dillow, Sarah Ann and William Harr (3) - December 24, 1872

Dillow, Sarah Ann and Frank Jackson (3) - July 5, 1880
  For further information see - Jackson, Frank.

Dillow, Sarah C. and John T. Clip (3) - January 27, 1889
  For further information see - Clip, John T.

Dillow, Sarah Jane and Charles P. Seifert (3) -   September 23, 1886
    For further information see - Seifert, Charles P.

Dillow, Temperence and Josiah Dillow (1) -   September 19, 1822

Dillow, Thomas and Elizabeth Dillow (1) -   May 30, 1810

Dillow, Thomas and Mary Jane Medler (2) -   (L) April 7, 1857

Dillow, Thomas and Hart Painter (3) -   December 23, 1871
    Place of marriage, Jefferson County - Age of husband, 28 - Age of
    wife, 19 - Both are Single - Both were born in Jefferson County -
    Both reside in Jefferson County - Husband's parents are L. H. and
    Nancy - Wife's parents are William and Margaret - Occupation of
    husband is Farmer. (Parents consent.)

Dillow, Thomas A. and Mary A. Butler (2) -   (L) May 27, 1858

Dillow, Thomas J. and Malinda Roby (3) -   September 2, 1885
    Place of marriage, Harpers Ferry - Age of husband, 42 - Age of wife,
    50 - Husband is a Widower by divorce - Wife is the widow of Jacob
    Roby - Both were born in Jefferson County, West Virginia - Both
    reside in Jefferson County, West Virginia.

Dillow, Thomas W. and Cassalina Hodge (2) -   (L) March 11, 1857

Dillow, Thomas W. and Cresy Griffith (3) -   **November 10, 1882**
    Place of marriage, Mountain - Age of husband, 37 - Age of wife, 45 -
    Husband is Single - Wife is a Widow - Both were born in Jefferson
    County, West Virginia - Both reside in Jefferson County, West
    Virginia.

Dillow, Virginia and James Butler (3) -   September 17, 1868
    For further information see - Butler, James.

Dillow, William and Margaret Dillow (1) -   November 4, 1820

Dillow, William and Hester Dillow (1) -   March 17, 1825

Dinkle, Lewis and Maggie A. Kelley (2) -   (L) March 21, 1860

Ditmyer, John and Mary Strobel (3) -   January 23, 1866
    Place of marriage, Harpers Ferry - Age of husband, 24 - Age of wife,
    24 - Both are Single - Husband was born at Bolivar, Jefferson
    County, West Virginia - Wife was born at Hancock, Maryland - Both
    reside at Bolivar, Jefferson County, West Virginia - Husband's
    parents are George and Barbary Ditmyer - Occupation of husband is
    Wagoner.

Dittinger, Eveline and Frank Utart (2) -   (L) January 31, 1860

Dittmyer, George and Mary J. Springer (3) -   (1869)
    Age of husband, 25 - Age of wife, 19 - Both are Single - Husband was
    born in Virginia - Wife was born in Germany - Both reside in
    Jefferson County.   (R. Roman uncle consents.)

Dittmyer, Mary and Leonard Weber (3) -   February 21, 1867
    For further information see - Weber, Leonard.

Divine, Alice A. and B. F. Lewis (3) -   May 16, 1872
    For further information see - Lewis, B. F.

Dixon, Amelia Ann and John Proctor (3) -   May 9, 1872
    For further information see - Proctor, John.

Dixon, Ann (colored) Daniel Hicks (3) -   (1870)
    For further information see - Hicks, Daniel.

Dixon, Ann M. and James Chipley (1) -   November 10, 1834

Dixon, Florence M. (cold.) George W. Jenkins (3) -   March 13, 1876
    For further information see - Jenkins, George W.

Dixon, George (cold.) Nellie Robinson (3) -   July 11, 1888
    Place of marriage, Charlestown - Age of husband, 25 - Age of wife,
    24 - Both are Single - Both were born in Jefferson County, West
    Virginia - Both reside in Jefferson County, West Virginia.

Dixon, George W. and Elizabeth O'Brien (3) -   April 6, 1875
    Place of marriage, Harpers Ferry - Age of husband, 29 - Age of wife,
    25 - Both are Single - Both were born in Washington County,
    Maryland - Both reside in Jefferson County, West Virginia.

Dixon, Harrison (cold.) Virginia Pendleton (3) -   October 30, 1890
    Place of marriage, Charlestown - Age of husband, 25 - Age of wife,
    21 - Both are Single - Husband was born in Fauquier County,
    Virginia - Wife was born in Jefferson County, West Virginia - Both
    reside in Jefferson County, West Virginia.

Dixon, Isaac and Mary V. Bowers (3) -   October 18, 1887
    Place of marriage, Charlestown - Age of husband, 31 - Age of wife,
    28 - Both are Single - Both were born in Jefferson County, West
    Virginia - Both reside in Jefferson County, West Virginia.

Dixon, Jemima (cold.) Alfred Fox (3) -   November 12, 1881
    For further information see - Fox, Alfred.

Dixon, Joseph A. and Lucy Ashby (2) -   (L) April 3, 1861
    Time of marriage, April 4, 1861 - Place of marriage, Halltown -
    Names, Joseph A. Dixon and Lucy Ashby - Age of husband, 24 years -
    Age of wife, 17 years - Both are Single - Place of husband's birth
    was Frederick County, Maryland - Place of wife's birth was Jefferson
    County, Virginia - Both reside in Jefferson County - Names of
    husband's parents are James M. and Sophia Elizabeth Dixon - Names
    of wife's parents are Unknown - Occupation of husband is Miller -
    The bride's father is dead and her mother has given her consent to
    me to obtain this liscense - Given under my hand this 3rd day of
    April, 1861 - William H. Dixon.

Dixon, Lucinda L. and Asa B. Cordell (1) -   December 9, 1830

Dixon, Margaret (cold.) George Washington (3) -   December 10, 1874
    For further information see - Washington, George.

Dixon, Mary and William Hoffman (3) -   October 17, 1878
    For further information see - Hoffman, William.

Dixon, Orra Moore and William V. Buskirk (1) -   March 20, 1832

Dobbins, ? and Thomas Lookout (3) - (1867)
For further information see - Lookout, Thomas.

Dobins, Margaret A. and John H. Shewbridge (3) - December 20, 1866
For further information see - Shewbridge, John H.

Dobsin, William and Susanah Wilson (1) - August 5, 1819

Dobson, Emma and Robert Pease (3) - June 27, 1877
For further information see - Pease, Robert.

Dobson, Florence Rebecca and Silas Benjamin Sisk (3) - February 25, 1880
For further information see - Sisk, Silas Benjamin.

Dobson, John W. and Hester Ann McBride (2) - (L) November 27, 1856

Dobson, Mary V. and M. S. B. Robertson (3) - September 12, 1878
For further information see - Robertson, M. S. B.

Dobson, Nancy and John Meehan (2) - (L) December 21, 1854

Dobson, Susanna and Ramsey Likens (1) - May 21, 1827

Dodd, Mary (cold.) Jacob Walker (3) - October 10, 1876
For further information see - Walker, Jacob.

Dodge, John W. and Mary Melinda Buzzard (3) - August 26, 1886
Place of marriage, Charlestown - Age of husband, 19 - Age of wife,
16 - Both are Single - Both were born in Jefferson County, West
Virginia - Both reside in Jefferson County, West Virginia.
(Consent of groom's mother in writing and of bride's father in
person.)

Dodge, Mary and Cornelius Mobley (3) - October 30, 1881
For further information see - Mobley, Cornelius.

Dodson, John (cold.) Martha Davis (3) - August 9, 1877
Place of marriage, near Charlestown - Age of husband, 31 - Age of
wife, 29 - Both are Single - Husband was born in Berkeley County -
Wife was born in Jefferson County, West Virginia - Both reside in
Jefferson County, West Virginia.

Doggett, Nelly and Daniel Johnson (1) - July 29, 1808

Dohman, Jerry (cold.) Sally Cooper (3) - October 4, 1875
Place of marriage, near Wickliffe - Age of husband, 22 - Age of
wife, 22 - Both are Single - Husband was born in Clarke County,
Virginia - Wife was born in Jefferson County, West Virginia - Both
reside in Jefferson County, West Virginia.

Doleman, Abraham and Rose Coleman (3) - January 9, 1873
Place of marriage, near Summit Point - Age of husband, 23 - Age of
wife, 21 - Both are Single - Husband was born in Clarke County,
Virginia - Wife was born in Jefferson County, West Virginia - Both
reside in Jefferson County, West Virginia - Husband's parents are
James and Lucy - Wife's parents are Nelson and Lucy - Occupation of
husband is Farmer.

Doleman, Delilah and Paul Washburn (1) - 1825

145

Doleman, James (cold.) Mary Johnson (3) - September 21, 1882
   Place of marriage, Mount Pleasant - Age of husband, 22 - Age of
   wife, 21 - Both are Single - Both were born in Jefferson County,
   West Virginia - Both reside in Jefferson County, West Virginia.

Doleman, Jerry (cold.) Martha Moss (3) - March 17, 1880
   Place of marriage, near Wickliffe, Charlestown - Age of husband,
   25 - Age of wife, 20 - Husband is a Widower - Wife is Single - Both
   reside in Jefferson County, West Virginia. (Consent of bride's
   mother certified by W. H. T. Lewis.)

Doleman, Louisa (cold.) Thomas Jackson (3) - November 10, 1881
   For further information see - Jackson, Thomas.

Doleman, Thomas (cold.) Martha Berry (3) - October 28, 1880
   Place of marriage, near Summit Point - Age of husband, 23 - Age of
   wife, 21 - Both are Single - Husband was born in Clarke County,
   Virginia - Wife was born in Jefferson County, West Virginia - Both
   reside in Jefferson County, West Virginia.

Domer, Wilber (cold.) Bell Devonshire (3) - February 10, 1881
   Place of marriage, Shepherdstown - Age of husband, 30 - Age of wife,
   23 - Both are Single - Husband was born in Clarke County, Virginia -
   Wife was born in Jefferson County, West Virginia - Both reside in
   Jefferson County, West Virginia.

Donavan, John and Mrs. Nellie Hayes (3) - April 5, 1874
   Place of marriage, Harpers Ferry - Husband is a Widower - Wife is a
   Widow - Both were born in Cork County, Ireland - Husband resides in
   Clarke County, Virginia - Wife resides in Jefferson County, West
   Virginia at present - Occupation of husband is Farmer.

Donnelly, Dorotha Ann and Alfred L. Hoffman (2) - (L) February 18, 1854

Donnelly, Margaret and David P. Hoffman (2) - (L) November 21, 1860

Donnelly, Rollin S. and Julia O. Johnson (3) - November 2, 1881
   Place of marriage, Charlestown - Age of husband, 34 - Age of wife,
   23 - Both are Single - Both were born in Jefferson County, West
   Virginia - Both reside in Jefferson County, West Virginia.

Donner, Kaby and Michael Myers (1) - June 11, 1803

Donnison, Thomas and Margaret Miller (1) - October 2, 1807

Donovan, Catharine and Michael Broderick (1) - June 18, 1850

Donovan, Julia and John J. McAbee (1) - January 10, 1850

Doody, Mary and John Faherty (3) - November 9, 1874
   For further information see - Faherty, John.

Dooley, B. F. and Lucy Henson (3) - August 26, 1880
   Place of marriage, Charlestown - Age of husband, 28 - Age of wife,
   21 - Both are Single - Both were born in Jefferson County, West
   Virginia - Both reside in Jefferson County, West Virginia.

Dooley, Georgia and W. A. Young (3) - December 19, 1867
   For further information see - Young, W. A.

Dooley, Harry G. and Ida E. Franklin (3) -   December 22, 1890
    Place of marriage, Charlestown - Age of husband, 25 - Age of wife,
    21 - Both are Single - Husband was born in Jefferson County, West
    Virginia - Wife was born in Loudoun County, Virginia - Both reside
    in Jefferson County, West Virginia.

Dooley, Ida Mercy and E. V. Kercheval, Jr. (3) -   June 2, 1881
    For further information see - Kercheval, E. V., Jr.

Dooley, Maggie M. and T. C. Earnshaw (3) -   April 3, 1878
    For further information see - Earnshaw, T. C.

Dooley, Samuel and Rebecca Jane Barrett (2) -   (L) May 21, 1856

Doran, Michael and Sarah Crawford (2) -   (L) December 30, 1852

Dorrough, E. B. and S. E. Strode (bride) (3) -   (1868)
    Age of husband, 22 - Age of wife, 21 - Both are Single - Both were
    born in Page County, Virginia - Both reside in Page County,
    Virginia - Husband's parents are William M. and Sarah - Wife's
    parents are Nonah and Mary T. - Occupation of husband is Boatman.

Dorsey, Caroline and James Sexton (2) -   (L) February 21, 1857

Dorsey, Henry (cold.) Nannie Hopewell (3) -   October 25, 1873
    Place of marriage, Shepherdstown - Age of husband, 22 - Age of wife,
    19 - Both are Single - Both were born in Jefferson County, West
    Virginia - Both reside in Jefferson County, West Virginia.
    (Mother's consent in writing.)

Dorsey, James W. and Louisa T. Heskitt (1) -   May 15, 1828

Dorsey, John T. and Ida Virginia Ramsburg (3) -   October 11, 1883
    Place of marriage, Martinsburg - Age of husband, 26 - Age of wife,
    21 - Both are Single - Both were born in Jefferson County, West
    Virginia - Both reside in Jefferson County, West Virginia.

Dorsey, Maria S. and John W. Brotherton (1) -   December 14, 1848

Dorsey, Millie (colored) Joshua Carr (3) -   April 14, 1870
    For further information see - Carr, Joshua

Dorsey, P. B. and Minnie Fidinger (3) -   May 3, 1888
    Place of marriage, Charlestown - Age of husband, 24 - Age of wife,
    21 - Both are Single - Both were born in Jefferson County - Both
    reside in Jefferson County, West Virginia.

Dorsey, Phebe and Barney Ott (1) -   January 29, 1824

Dorsey, Phebe Ann and John William Frith (2) -   (L) March 14, 1859

Dorsey, Samuel (cold.) Eliza McCann (3) -   December 30, 1885
    Place of marriage, Shepherdstown - Age of husband, 39 - Age of wife,
    28 - Both are Single.

Dorsey, Sarah (cold.) William Bunkins (3) -   December 13, 1873
    For further information see - Bunkins, William.

Dorsey, Vincent and Courtney Boswell (3) - February 23, 1871
    Place of marriage, Jefferson County - Age of husband, 27 - Age of
    wife, 27 - Both are Single - Husband was born in Berkeley County -
    Wife was born in Jefferson County - Husband resides in Berkeley -
    Wife resides in Jefferson County - Husband's parents are John and
    Lucy - Wife's parents are Isaac and Kitty - Occupation of husband is
    Farmer.

Dotts, Elizabeth and Christian Ronemus (1) - December 17, 1812

Douglas, Charles (cold.) Annie Lee (3) - June 24, 1875
    Place of marriage, Shepherdstown - Age of husband, 28 - Age of wife,
    29 - Both are Single - Husband was born in Loudoun County,
    Virginia - Wife was born in Jefferson County, West Virginia - Both
    reside in Jefferson County, West Virginia.

Douglas, James (free colored) Fanny Goins (2) - (L) June 13, 1860

Douglas, Nannie C. and John M. Beckenbaugh (3) - November 19, 1868
    For further information see - Beckenbaugh, John M.

Douglas, William Clay (cold.) Eliza Walker (3) - October 30, 1884
    Place of marriage, Charlestown - Age of husband, 28 - Age of wife,
    22 - Both are Single - Both were born in Warren County, Virginia -
    Husband resides in Jefferson County, West Virginia - Wife resides in
    Jefferson County.

Douglass, George L. and Drusilla A. Rutherford (1) - May 1832

Douglass, Georgia and John Harris (3) - May 16, 1872
    For further information see - Harris, John.

Douglass, Jane S. and John M. Macfarland (2) - (L) May 27, 1853

Douglass, Milly and Benjamin Bell (1) - 1813

Douglass, William and Nancy M. Rutherford (1) - September 9, 1827

Douglass, William A. and Ellen Sappington (2) - (L) June 9, 1852

Douglass, William A. and Ellen Sappington (1) - June 9, 1852

Dove, Mrs. Elizabeth (widow) and William Kemp (2) - (L) October 26, 1850

Dove, Elizabeth (widow) and William Kemp (1) - October 27, 1850

Dovenbarger, William and Mary S. Ullum (2) - (L) January 1, 1861

Dovenberger, Daniel and Catharine Heflebower (2) - (L) January 20, 1852

Dovenberger, Mollie E. and Joseph W. Trussell (3) - January 27, 1875
    For further information see - Trussell, Joseph W.

Dowden, Polly and Henry Endrews (1) - November 13, 1808

Dowdon, R. C. and Mrs. Mary C. Smith (nee Moore) (3) - December 26, 1883
   Place of marriage, Mechanicktown - Age of husband, 46 - Age of wife,
   42 - Husband is Single - Wife is a Widow - Husband was born in
   Prince George County, Maryland - Wife was born in Jefferson County,
   West Virginia - Husband resides in Loudoun County, Virginia - Wife
   resides in Jefferson County, West Virginia.

Downey, Ann and William G. Burns (1) - February 24, 1834

Downey, Susanna L. and James C. Ford (1) - July 28, 1834

Downing, George and Mary E. Krombling (3) - February 25, 1877
   Place of marriage, Charles Town - Age of husband, 25 - Age of wife,
   22 - Husband is a Widower - Wife is Single - Husband was born in
   Berkeley County, West Virginia - Wife was born in Clarke County,
   Virginia - Both reside in Jefferson County, West Virginia.

Downing, Mary and Virgil Eachus (1) - October 21, 1817

Downing, Rachel Rebecca and John D. Hobbs (2) - (L) March 29, 1851
   (Witness to age of parties, Andrew J. Hobbs.)

Downing, Rachel Rebecca and John D. Hobbs (1) - March 29, 1851

Downs, Margaret Emily and John Reed (1) - October 16, 1828

Downs, Mary Ann and Joseph Morrow (2) - (L) April 1, 1852

Downs, Mary Ann and Joseph Morrow (1) - April 1, 1852

Downs, Robert and Mary Avis (1) - November 5, 1834

Doyle, Eliza (cold.) James Henry Collins (3) - February 23, 1888
   For further information see - Collins, James Henry.

Doyle, Luke (cold.) Sarah Queen (3) - August 4, 1881
   Place of marriage, Charlestown - Age of husband, 23 - Age of wife,
   21 - Both are Single - Husband was born in Madison County,
   Virginia - Wife was born in Jefferson County, West Virginia - Both
   reside in Jefferson County, West Virginia.

Draper, Daniel (malattoes) Emily Alexander (2) - (L) September 15, 1855

Draper, Ellen and Nathaniel Rippon (2) - (L) October 4, 1854

Drawbaugh, A. C. and Emma S. Roberts (3) - June 14, 1870
   Place of marriage, Jefferson County - Age of husband, 36 - Age of
   wife, 22 - Husband was born in Pennsylvania - Wife was born in West
   Virginia - Both reside in Jefferson County.

Drenner, Elizabeth and Michael Wolf (2) - (L) February 19, 1851

Drenner, John and Mary Ketro (1) - June 16, 1816

Drew, Benjamin (cold.) Annie Washington (3) - December 18, 1873
   Place of marriage, Jefferson County - Age of husband, 23 - Age of
   wife, 22 - Both are Single - Both were born in Jefferson County,
   West Virginia - Both reside in Jefferson County, West Virginia.

Drew, Bettie (cold.) Daniel Lee (3) -   May 10, 1874
    For further information see - Lee, Daniel.

Drew, Charles and Mary E. Conklyn (2) -   (L) February 24, 1857

Drew, Elizabeth An. and Jared Rice (1) -   1827

Drew, F. W. and Martha C. Rawlins (2) -   (L) October 6, 1852

Drew, Francis W. and Margaret Rawlins (1) -   May 25, 1841

Drew, Lucy (cold.) Alfred Martin (3) -   March 19, 1868
    For further information see - Martin, Alfred.

Drew, Lucy (cold.) Alexander McKinney (3) -   April 12, 1877
    For further information see - McKinney, Alexander.

Drew, Maria (cold.) James R. Carter (3) -   January 11, 1877
    For further information see - Carter, James R.

Drew, Mary and Jacob Ault (1) -   September 24, 1809

Drew, Mary (cold.) W. Washington (3) -   March 26, 1868
    For further information see - Washington, W.

Drew, Sidney (cold.) James Lee (3) -   December 11, 1873
    For further information see - Lee, James.

Drisch, Maggie and Benjamin F. Lester (3) -   November 14, 1872
    For further information see - Lester, Benjamin F.

Drish, James and Jennie Schoppert (3) -   September 26, 1871
    Place of marriage, Jefferson County - Age of husband, 24 - Age of
    wife, 27 - Both are Single - Husband was born in Clarke County -
    Wife was born in Berkeley - Both reside in Jefferson - Husband's
    parents are John W. and Margaret - Wife's parents are Fuller -
    Occupation of husband is Carpenter.

Drish, Mary and Peter Hiram (1) -   September 15, 1807

Drish, Verdie and Richard A. Manuel (3) -   September 25, 1889
    For further information see - Manuel, Richard A.

Drish, Virginia B. and George W. Anderson (3) -   August 19, 1886
    For further information see - Anderson, George W.

Ducker, John and Ann Pyles (1) -   August 3, 1830

Duckett, Thomas B. and Johana Murphy (3) -   December 23, 1869
    Place of marriage, Jefferson County - Age of husband, 34 - Age of
    wife, 40 - Husband was born in Maryland - Wife was born in
    Virginia - Both reside in Jefferson County.

Dudrear, David H. and Mary Frances Johnson (2) -   (L) November 19, 1856

Dudrow, Charles E. and Mary P. Heafer (3) -   November 25, 1875
    Place of marriage, Bolivar - Age of husband, 30 - Age of wife, 23 -
    Both are Single - Husband was born in State of Maryland - Wife was
    born in Jefferson County, West Virginia - Both reside in Jefferson
    County, West Virginia.

Duff, Catharine and Washington McDaniel (1) - October 6, 1831

Duffield, Mary E. and Thomas Rutherford (1) - December 9, 1835

Duffield, Richard and Mary Strother (1) - June 7, 1814

Duffield, Sarah and John M. Jewett (2) - (L) June 1, 1853

Dugan, Mary H. and William N. Fryer (2) - (L) May 26, 1860

Duke, Ann F. and Joseph T. White (3) - November 27, 1877
    For further information see - White, Joseph T.

Duke, Ann Margaret and James W. Engle (2) - (L) May 27, 1851

Duke, Ann M. and James W. Engle (1) - May 28, 1851

Duke, Catherine and Amos Hilliard (1) - October 2, 1834

Duke, Francis and Elizabeth Kenrick (1) - August 19, 1820

Duke, George W. and Emeline Jones (2) - (L) August 15, 1859

Duke, J. E. and Elizabeth Jane Kensey (2) - (L) February 25, 1860

Duke, John and Jemima Baske (1) - October 22, 1805

Duke, M. A. (bride) and A. F. Smith (2) - (L) July 14, 1857

Duke, Mary W. and William P. Campbell (3) - June 13, 1883
    For further information see - Campbell, William P.

Duke, Nancy and Isaac Climer (1) - January 29, 1818

Duke, Robert and Ann N. Moore (1) - 1816

Duke, Robert M. and Mary H. McGarry (3) - February 9, 1875
    Place of marriage, County - Age of husband, 25 - Age of wife, 22 -
    Both are Single - Both were born in Jefferson County, West
    Virginia - Both reside in Jefferson County, West Virginia.

Duke, Sally J. and John H. Engle (3) - February 17, 1880
    For further information see - Engle, John H.

Duke, Talbot S. and Mary Brittain (1) - June 6, 1845

Dulaney, Joseph and Mary Ann Lloyd (1) - May 6, 1834

Dulany, Daniel and Harriet Ann Blincoe (2) - (L) September 9, 1850

Dulany, Daniel and Harriet Ann Blincoe (1) - September 12, 1850

Dulany, Emma Ann and Joseph Dillow (2) - (L) May 26, 1851

Dulany, James and Elizabeth Ingram (2) - (L) March 29, 1859

Dulany, Jane E. and John W. McGraw (3) - July 31, 1879
    For further information see - McGraw, John W.

151

Dulany, Thomas F. and Jane Ellen Adoria Dillow (3) -   September 30, 1875
   Place of marriage, Charlestown - Age of husband, 23 - Age of wife,
   18 - Both are Single - Husband was born in Jefferson County, West
   Virginia - Wife was born in State of Ohio - Both reside in Jefferson
   County, West Virginia.

Dum, Annie E. and John N. Robey (3) -   January 15, 1867
   For further information see - Robey, John N.

Dumm, Henry and Mary Ellen Ashbaugh (2) -   (L) December 2, 1863
   Time of marriage, December 3, 1863 - Place of marriage,
   Charlestown - Names, Henry Dumm and Mary Ellen Ashbaugh - Age of
   husband, 22 years last July - Age of wife, 20 years last May - Both
   are Single - Husband was born at Hesse Cassell, Germany - Wife was
   born at Baltimore - Both reside at Charlestown - Husband's parents
   are John and Mary Catherine - Wife's parents are John and Mary -
   Occupation of husband is Baker and Confectioner - License issued,
   December 2, 1863 - T. A. Moore, Clerk.

Dunaway, E. E. and Lucy D. Wiltshire (3) -   December 18, 1883
   Place of marriage, Leetown - Age of husband, 24 - Age of wife, 26 -
   Both are Single - Husband was born in Lancaster County, Virginia -
   Wife was born in Jefferson County, West Virginia - Both reside in
   Jefferson County, West Virginia.

Duncan, Ella and E. Overlander (3) -   March 14, 1888
   For further information see - Overlander, E.

Duncan, James A. and Elizabeth A. D. Wade (3) -   July 3, 1873
   Place of marriage, Charlestown - Age of husband, 43 - Age of wife,
   22 - Husband is a Widower - Wife is Single - Husband was born at
   Norfolk, Virginia - Wife was born in Montgomery County, Virginia -
   Husband resides at Ashland, Virginia - Wife resides in Jefferson
   County, West Virginia.

Duncan, Joseph and Mary Elizabeth Fritts (2) -   (L) May 26, 1860

Duncan, Sarah Catharine and Nathan H. Copeland (2) -   (L) August 27, 1860

Dunham, John and Polly Holliday (1) -   April 10, 1806

Dunham, Thornton C. and Louisa C. Worley (1) -   January 25, 1830

Dunlap, Anna Laura and Henry C. Baker (3) -   October 19, 1887
   For further information see - Baker, Henry C.

Dunlap, George and Mary Debie Bender (3) -   June 18, 1874
   Place of marriage, Bolivar - Age of husband, 22 - Age of wife, 20 -
   Both are Single - Husband was born at Mechanicsburg, Pennsylvania -
   Wife was born in Jefferson County - Both reside in Jefferson
   County.   (Bride's father consents in writing.)

Dunlap, John M. and Mary I. Stouffer (3) -   March 5, 1890
   Place of marriage, Ripon - Age of husband, 23 - Age of wife, 19 -
   Both are Single - Husband was born at Mechanicsburg, Pennsylvania -
   Wife was born in Cumberland County, Pennsylvania - Both reside in
   Jefferson County, West Virginia.

Dunlap, W. B. and Alice L. Baker (3) - October 15, 1890
   Place of marriage, Charlestown - Age of husband, 24 - Age of wife,
   24 - Both are Single - Husband was born in Lancaster County,
   Pennsylvania - Wife was born in Frederick County, Maryland - Both
   reside in Jefferson County, West Virginia.

Dunlop, Thomas and Cassa Molar (1) - June 12, 1805

Dunmore, Benjamin (cold.) Fannie Bender (3) - June 30, 1887
   Place of marriage, Charlestown - Age of husband, 22 - Age of wife,
   23 - Both are Single - Both were born in Jefferson County, West
   Virginia - Both reside in Jefferson County, West Virginia.

Dunmore, Fanny and Morgan Hook (3) - April 29, 1874
   For further information see - Hook, Morgan.

Dunmore, Fanny (cold.) Richard P. Lawson (3) - October 1, 1890
   For further information see - Lawson, Richard P.

Dunmore, John (cold.) Fannie Staley (3) - December 22, 1881
   Place of marriage, Shepherdstown - Age of husband, 23 - Age of wife,
   20 - Both are Single - Husband was born in Berkeley County, West
   Virginia - Wife was born in Jefferson County, West Virginia - Both
   reside in Jefferson County, West Virginia.

Dunmore, Wilson (cold.) Rebecca Simms (3) - June 9, 1881
   Place of marriage, Shepherdstown - Age of husband, 53 - Age of wife,
   45 - Husband is a Widower - Wife is a Widow - Husband was born in
   Berkeley County - Wife was born in Jefferson County, West Virginia -
   Both reside in Jefferson County, West Virginia.

Dunmore, Wilson, Jr. (cold.) Sallie E. Butler (3) - December 15, 1887
   Place of marriage, Shepherdstown - Age of husband, 24 - Age of wife,
   20 - Both are Single - Husband was born in Virginia - Wife was born
   in Pennsylvania - Husband resides in Jefferson County, West
   Virginia - Wife resides in Jefferson County. (Consent of bride's
   mother in writing.)

Dunn, Annie L. and Samuel H. Plotner (3) - September 20, 1877
   For further information see - Plotner, Samuel H.

Dunn, George and Jennie Lloyd (3) - February 22, 1882
   Place of marriage, Charlestown - Age of husband, 23 - Age of wife,
   22 - Both are Single - Husband was born in Frederick County,
   Virginia - Wife was born in Clarke County, Virginia - Both reside in
   Jefferson County, West Virginia.

Dunn, James and Mary E. Stewart (3) - October 15, 1868
   Place of marriage, Jefferson County - Age of husband, 33 - Age of
   wife, 16 - Husband is a Widower - Wife is Single - Husband was born
   in Virginia - Wife was born in West Virginia - Both reside in West
   Virginia - Husband's parents are George and Sarah - Wife's parents
   are John J. and S. E. - Occupation of husband is Farmer.

Dunn, Jennie and Marshall Fiddler (3) - September 19, 1888
   For further information see - Fiddler, Marshall.

Dunn, Robert A. and Angeline Kindle (3) -   January 24, 1877
    Place of marriage, near Charlestown - Age of husband, 25 - Age of
    wife, 24 - Both are Single - Husband was born in Frederick County,
    Virginia - Wife was born in Berkeley County, West Virginia - Both
    reside in Jefferson County, West Virginia.

Dunn, Thomas B. and Matilda B. Beall (1) -   October 11, 1827

Dunn, William A. and Ida Pope (3) -   October 18, 1887
    Place of marriage, near Charlestown - Age of husband, 23 - Age of
    wife, 22 - Both are Single - Both were born in Clarke County,
    Virginia - Both reside in Jefferson County, West Virginia.

Durst, Eliza and Jacob Coons (1) -   February 20, 1807

Dusinger, Elmer and Laura Muck (3) -   September 24, 1890
    Place of marriage, Charlestown - Age of husband, 23 - Age of wife,
    21 - Both are Single - Both were born in Jefferson County, West
    Virginia - Both reside in Jefferson County, West Virginia.

Dusinger, Ester May and James Grace (3) -   October 1, 1890
    For further information see - Grace, James.

Dust, Barbara and Caspar Jacobs (1) -   September 10, 1807

Dust, Catharine and Aaron H. Snyder (1) -   January 3, 1832

Dust, E. Catharine and Joseph L. Eichelberger (2) -   (L) February 23, 1865
    For further information see - Eichelberger, Joseph L.

Dust, Margaret and Jacob W. Staley (1) -   October 22, 1846

Dust, Nancy and Alexander Link (1) -   June 6, 1816

Dust, Polly and John Laneiskes (1) -   January 2, 1807

Dust, Rebecca and James W. Engle (3) -   June 1, 1876
    For further information see - Engle, James W.

Dust, Susana and Jacob Lickliter (1) -   December 14, 1809

Dutch, Susana and Edward Boyle (1) -   July 20, 1808

Duval, Washington and Ann Maddox (1) -   December 5, 1833

Dyche, Alexander B. and Mary Ann Reiley (2) -   (L) November 6, 1854

Dye, Nancy and John Fraley (1) -   November 24, 1816

Dyott, Rev. Luther R. and Maggie Yantis (3) -   June 7, 1888
    Place of marriage, Harpers Ferry - Age of husband, 25 - Age of wife,
    23 - Both are Single - Husband was born in Maryland - Wife was born
    in West Virginia - Husband resides at Alexandria, Virginia - Wife
    resides in Jefferson County, West Virginia.

Eachus, Virgil and Mary Downing (1) -   October 21, 1817

Eackles, Joseph and Josephine Leavy (3) -   April 28, 1886
Place of marriage, Harpers Ferry - Age of husband, 28 - Age of wife, 25 - Both are Single - Both were born in Jefferson County, West Virginia - Both reside in Jefferson County, West Virginia.

Eades, Mary and Franklin Hoffmaster (2) -   (L) December 15, 1854

Eakle, Catharine V. and Joshua J. Hudson (2) -   (L) October 28, 1859

Eakle, Daniel and Catherine Scarlett (1) -   June 4, 1835

Eakle, George C. and Mary E. Vansant (2) -   (L) September 24, 1851

Eakle, George C. and Mary E. Vansany (1) -   September 25, 1851

Earhart, Joanah and David Johnson (1) -   March 10, 1829

Earhart, Philip, Jr. and Ann McEndree (1) -   November 17, 1821

Earl, George and Ritha Ann Scarlett (3) -   April 19, 1876
Place of marriage, near Keyes Smith - Age of husband, 33 - Age of wife, 21 - Husband is a Widower - Wife is Single - Husband was born in Rhode Island - Wife was born in Jefferson County, West Virginia - Both reside in Jefferson County, West Virginia.

Earl, Robert and H. V. Chew (3) -   June 13, 1876
Place of marriage, near Charlestown - Age of husband, 38 - Age of wife, 31 - Both are Single - Husband was born at Washington City, D. C. - Wife was born in Jefferson County, West Virginia - Both reside in Jefferson County, West Virginia.

Earle, Ruth A. and Robert L. R. Dailey (3) -   September 24, 1890
For further information see - Dailey, Robert L. R.

Earle, Sarah A. and J. M. Ward (3) -   April 5, 1875
For further information see - Ward, J. M.

Early, Robert and Eliza Read (1) -   1820

Early, Samuel (cold.) Mary Cross (3) -   January 4, 1868
Place of marriage, Jefferson County - Age of husband, 23 - Age of wife, 20 - Both are Single - Both were born in Jefferson County, West Virginia - Both reside in Jefferson County - Occupation of husband is Farmer.

Earnest, Mary Elizabeth and Alexander Baron (2) -   (L) February 28, 1852

Earnest, Mary Elizabeth and Alexander Barron (1) -   March 5, 1852

Earnshaw, D. S. and Clara A. Sheets (3) -   December 23, 1885
Place of marriage, Charlestown - Age of husband, 28 - Age of wife, 24 - Both are Single - Both were born in Jefferson County, West Virginia - Both reside in Jefferson County, West Virginia.

Earnshaw, James N. and Mary Isabella Keller (2) -   (L) December 7, 1850

Earnshaw, James R. and Hariett L. Bell (3) - May 16, 1878
   Place of marriage, Harpers Ferry - Age of husband, 26 - Age of wife,
   20 - Both are Single - Both were born in Jefferson County, West
   Virginia - Both reside in Jefferson County, West Virginia.
   (Consent of bride's father in writing.)

Earnshaw, Louisa and William Apsey (1) - December 27, 1836

Earnshaw, Mary Ellen and George W. Stover (1) - November 7, 1848

Earnshaw, T. C. and Maggie M. Dooley (3) - April 3, 1878
   Place of marriage, Charlestown - Age of husband, 28 - Age of wife,
   22 - Both are Single - Both were born in Jefferson County, West
   Virginia - Both reside in Jefferson County, West Virginia.

Earnshaw, Thomas T. and Rebecca J. Harrell (2) - (L) January 28, 1857

Earnshaw, William G. and Clara Avis (3) - January 7, 1874
   Place of marriage, Charlestown - Age of husband, 22 - Age of wife,
   17 - Both are Single - Both were born in Jefferson County, West
   Virginia - Both reside in Jefferson County, West Virginia.
   (Consent of bride's father in person.)

Easterday, Cora E. and Robert S. Leisenring (3) - October 16, 1888
   For further information see - Leisenring, Robert S.

Easterday, Emma J. and Adam Bowman (3) - October 21, 1879
   For further information see - Bowman, Adam.

Easterday, J. H. and Virginia Weddell (2) - (L) November 3, 1856

Easterday, John S. and Jane H. Johnson (3) - November 2, 1887
   Place of marriage, Charlestown - Age of husband, 48 - Age of wife,
   40 - Husband is a Widower - Wife is Single - Both were born in
   Jefferson County, West Virginia - Both reside in Jefferson County,
   West Virginia.

Easterday, Joseph H. and Kate A. Roberts (3) - July 1, 1878
   Place of marriage, Charlestown - Age of husband, 44 - Age of wife,
   42 - Husband is a Widower - Wife is a Widow - Both were born in
   Jefferson County, West Birginia - Both reside in Jefferson County,
   West Virginia.

Easterday, S. Gertrude and Charles F. Wall (3) - December 23, 1884
   For further information see - Wall, Charles F.

Easterday, Sarah B. and F. B. Souders (3) - June 22, 1870
   For further information see - Souders, F. B.

Easterday, William P. and Charity Dean (1) - April 27, 1825

Easterday, William P. and Minnie Roberts (3) - April 17, 1884
   Place of marriage, Charlestown - Age of husband, 25 - Age of wife,
   24 - Both are Single - Husband was born in State of Mississippi -
   Wife was born in State of Ohio - Both reside in Jefferson County,
   West Virginia.

Easton, Eliza J. and Frank Powers (3) - July 4, 1876
   For further information see - Powers, Frank.

Easton, Elmina and William J. Hall (1) -   April 21, 1825

Easton, Tilghman and Barbara C. Rucker (3) -   April 25, 1878
    Place of marriage, Harpers Ferry - Age of husband, 32 - Age of wife,
    33 - Both are Single - Husband was born in Maryland - Wife was born
    in Virginia - Husband resides in Maryland - Wife resides in
    Jefferson County, West Virginia.

Eaty, Catherine Virginia and Edward S. Bell (1) -   June 3, 1822

Eaty, Elizabeth and James Meredith (1) -   June 21, 1819

Ebert, Eliza and Major Swann (1) -   August 18, 1806

Eby, Henry J. and Ella G. Lock (3) -   April 29, 1879
    Place of marriage, Charlestown - Age of husband, 27 - Age of wife,
    28 - Both are Single - Both were born in Jefferson County, West
    Virginia - Both reside in Jefferson County, West Virginia.

Eby, Laura A. and James H. March (2) -   (L) March 2, 1851

Eby, Rachel Alice and Robert B. Mitchell (3) -   April 21, 1881
    For further information see - Mitchell, Robert B.

Eby, Warren and Virginia Lock (1) -   December 4, 1849

Eby, William and Jane Grubb (1) -   April 15, 1824

Echart, Michael and Mary Crampton (1) -   September 14, 1809

Echart, Polly and William Miller (1) -   December 24, 1812

Eckhart, Barbary and George Robb (1) -   June 2, 1808

Eckhart, Hester Ann and John R. Potts (3) -   November 12, 1874
    For further information see - Potts, John R.

Eckhart, Michael and Elizabeth Show (1) -   November 28, 1816

Eckles, Benony and Margaret Scarlet (2) -   (L) August 4, 1855

Eckles, Elizabeth and George Hufmaster, Jr. (2) -   (L) November 2, 1855

Eckles, Francis M. and Elizabeth Bridner (3) -   February 4, 1885
    Place of marriage, Bolivar - Age of husband, 23 - Age of wife, 22 -
    Both are Single - Both were born in Jefferson County, West
    Virginia - Both reside in Jefferson County, West Virginia.

Eckles, John W. and Rachel Hawk (3) -   December 8, 1881
    Place of marriage, Harpers Ferry - Age of husband, 26 - Age of wife,
    22 - Both are Single - Both were born in Jefferson County, West
    Virginia - Both reside in Jefferson County, West Virginia.

Ecton, John William and Mary F. Deck (3) -   May 20, 1880
    Place of marriage, Shepherdstown - Age of husband, 25 - Age of wife,
    19 - Both are Single - Husband was born in Washington County,
    Maryland - Wife was born in Jefferson County, West Virginia -
    Husband resides in Washington County, Maryland - Wife resides in
    Jefferson County, West Virginia. (Consent of bride's father in
    writing.)

Ecton, Mary C. and John Criswell (3) — November 17, 1880
For further information see – Criswell, John.

Eddleman, Elizabeth and John B. Gruber (2) — (L) November 28, 1854

Edeny, Georgiana (cold.) William B. Hill (3) — August 18, 1880
For further information see – Hill, William B.

Edmonds, Elias and Courtney Ann Hite (1) — April 1827

Edmonds, Erom and Priscilla Hyatt (1) — June 3, 1819

Edwards, Alfred and Annie Rust (3) — December 10, 1868
Age of husband, 55 – Age of wife, 30 – Husband is a Widower – Wife is Single – Husband was born in Jefferson County – Wife was born in Jefferson, Virginia – Both reside in Jefferson County – Occupation of husband is Farmer.

Edwards, Alfred (cold.) Susan Stribling (3) — November 13, 1884
Place of marriage, Charlestown – Age of husband, 21 – Age of wife, 20 – Both are Single – Husband was born in Jefferson County, West Virginia – Wife was born in Jefferson County – Both reside in Jefferson County, West Virginia. (Consent of bride's father in writing.)

Edwards, Annie (cold.) Allen Hale (3) — August 27, 1884
For further information see – Hale, Allen.

Edwards, Catherine and William McCasling (1) — 1822

Edwards, David (cold.) Martha Jackson (3) — January 4, 1877
Place of marriage, near Duffields – Age of husband, 22 – Age of wife, 21 – Both are Single – Both were born in Jefferson County, West Virginia – Both reside in Jefferson County, West Virginia.

Edwards, Ellen and John Manuel (3) — January 25, 1872
For further information see – Manuel, John.

Edwards, Emily and Flavous Lucas (3) — November 23. 1865
For further information see – Lucas, Flavous.

Edwards, Ida (cold.) Peter Jackson (3) — December 27, 1888
For further information see – Jackson, Peter.

Edwards, J. W. and Ann Zombro (3) — February 3, 1874
Place of marriage, Summit Point – Age of husband, 30 – Age of wife, 34 – Both are Single – Both were born in Jefferson County, West Virginia – Both reside in Jefferson County, West Virginia.

Edwards, Jacob (cold.) Mollie Frame (3) — April 7, 1874
Place of marriage, Shepherdstown – Age of husband, 23 – Age of wife, 22 – Both are Single – Both were born in Jefferson County, West Virginia – Both reside in Jefferson County, West Virginia.

Edwards, James and Maggie Jenkins (3) -   September 12, 1872
   Place of marriage, Jefferson County - Age of husband, 34 - Age of
   wife, 30 - Husband is Single - Wife is a Widow - Both were born in
   Jefferson County - Husband resides in Jefferson County - Wife
   resides in Jefferson County, West Virginia - Husband's parents are
   Robert and Charity - Wife's parents are Esau and Katty - Occupation
   of husband is Farmer.

Edwards, James A. and Jennie M. Crim (3) -   November 25, 1875
   Place of marriage, near Middleway - Age of husband, 27 - Age of
   wife, 18 - Both are Single - Both were born in Berkeley County, West
   Virginia - Both reside in Jefferson County, West Virginia.
   (Consent of bride's mother in writing, father being dead.)

Edwards, John and J. Streams (3) -   October 14, 1868
   Place of marriage, Jefferson County - Age of husband, ?3 - Age of
   wife, 26 - Both are Single - Husband was born in Virginia - Wife was
   born in Jefferson County - Husband resides in Jefferson County -
   Wife resides in West Virginia - Husband's parents are Maria
   Devonshire - Occupation of husband is Farmer.

Edwards, John (cold.) Laura Clinton (3) -   December 30, 1875
   Place of marriage, Bolivar - Age of husband, 21 - Age of wife, 19 -
   Both are Single - Both were born in Jefferson County, West
   Virginia - Both reside in Jefferson County, West Virginia.
   (Consent of bride's mother certified to by Joseph Page, brother-in-
   law of bride.)

Edwards, Lulie and David William Bowers (3) -   July 17, 1889
   For further information see - Bowers, David William.

Edwards, Lydia F. and Stephen Thompson (3) -   February 28, 1867
   For further information see - Thompson, Stephen.

Edwards, Margaret and John Shell (1) -   December 24, 1845

Edwards, Mary Ann and George W. Willingham (2) -   (L) December 13, 1858

Edwards, Mary D. and William L. Arthur (3) -   October 31, 1867
   For further information see - Arthur, William L.

Edwards, Mollie and Frank Marshall (3) -   December 25, 1886
   For further information see - Marshall, Frank.

Edwards, Molly (cold.) Wesley Gordon (3) -   November 17, 1881
   For further information see - Gordon, Wesley.

Edwards, Nancy and George Sharff (1) -   January 2, 1838

Edwards, Nelson (cold.) Mary Ranson (3) -   April 14, 1873
   Place of marriage, at William Tenill's - Age of husband, 24 - Age of
   wife, 23 - Husband is Single - Wife is a Widow - Both were born in
   Jefferson County, West Virginia - Both reside in Jefferson County,
   West Virginia - Husband's parents are Alfa and Hannah - Wife's
   parents are George and Maria - Occupation of husband is Farm Hand.

Edwards, Nelson (cold.) Anna Harris (3) -   September 11, 1884
   Place of marriage, Duffields - Age of husband, 38 - Age of wife,
   39 - Husband is a Widower - Wife is a Widow - Both were born in
   Jefferson County, West Virginia - Both reside in Jefferson County.

Edwards, Rachel Jane and Benjamin Lee Zombro (3) - November 20, 1878
For further information see - Zombro, Benjamin Lee.

Edwards, Sallie (cold.) George W. Helms (3) - May 30, 1885
For further information see - Helms, George W.

Edwards, Thomas (cold.) Luck Smokes (3) - October 11, 1877
Place of marriage, Halltown - Age of husband, 26 - Age of wife, 23 - Husband is a Widower - Wife is Single - Husband was born in North Carolina - Wife was born in Frederick County, Virginia - Both reside in Jefferson County, West Virginia.

Edwards, William and Frances Huff (3) - January 11, 1866
Place of marriage, Charlestown, Jefferson County - Age of husband, 22 - Age of wife, 19 - Both are Single - Husband was born in Washington County, Maryland - Wife was born in Clarke County, Virginia - Both reside in Jefferson County, West Virginia - Husband's parents are Amelia Edwards - Wife's parents are Harrison and Martha Huff - Occupation of husband is Farmer.

Egan, Thomas and Margaret O'Mara (1) - September 11, 1849

Eichelberger, Ann Eliza and Josiah P. Smeltzer (2) - (L) June 13, 1851

Eichelberger, Blanche and Samuel Y. Smeltzer (3) - January 17, 1877
For further information see - Smeltzer, Samuel Y.

Eichelberger, George W. and Louisa Eichelberger (2) - (L) June 4, 1856

Eichelberger, Joseph L. and Deborah E. Schaeffer (2) - (L) September 30, 1854

Eichelberger, Joseph L. and E. Catharine Dust (2) - (L) February 23, 1865
Time of marriage, March 2, 1865 - Place of marriage, Bride's Father's near Unionville - Names, Joseph L. Eichelberger and E. Catharine Dust - Age of husband, 37 years, October 2, 1864 - Age of wife, 34 years - Husband is a Widower - Wife is Single - Husband was born in Frederick County, Maryland - Wife was born in Jefferson County, Virginia - Both reside in Jefferson County, Virginia - Husband's parents are Martin and Maria C. Eichelberger - Wife's parents are Isaac and __?__ Dust - Occupation of husband is Farmer - License issued, February 23, 1865 - Thomas A. Moore, Clerk.

Eichelberger, Joseph L. and Sarah Elizabeth Andrews (3) - July 9, 1881
Place of marriage, Shepherdstown - Age of husband, 53 - Age of wife, 32 - Husband is a Widower - Wife is Single - Husband was born in Frederick County, Maryland - Wife was born in Rockingham County, Virginia - Both reside in Jefferson County, West Virginia.

Eichelberger, Louisa and George W. Eichelberger (2) - (L) June 4, 1856

Eleyet, Jane and Samuel McCormick (1) - December 30, 1832

Elgin, James H. and Annie M. Cameron (3) - October 25, 1871
Place of marriage, Jefferson County - Age of husband, 51 - Age of wife, 35 - Husband is a Widower - Wife is Single - Husband was born in Loudoun County, Virginia - Wife was born in Jefferson - Husband resides in Maryland - Wife resides in Jefferson - Husband's parents are William and Mary - Wife's parents are John and E. J. - Occupation of husband is Farmer.

Elgin, Laura K. and William Isaac Henkle (3) -   February 16, 1887
    For further information see - Henkle, William Isaac.

Eliot, William and Hannah Foreman (1) -   November 28, 1832

Elliott, George W. and Mary Elizabeth Hammon (3) -   February 7, 1878
    Place of marriage, Summit Point - Age of husband, 28 - Age of wife,
    22 - Both are Single - Husband was born in Fauquier County,
    Virginia - Wife was born in State of Pennsylvania - Both reside in
    Jefferson County, West Virginia.

Elliott, John and Elizabeth M. Cloy (1) -   December 28, 1833

Elliott, John and Margaret Zombro (3) -   July 9, 1889
    Place of marriage, Charlestown - Age of husband, 36 - Age of wife,
    35 - Both are Single - Husband was born in Clarke County, Virginia -
    Wife was born in Jefferson County, West Virginia - Husband resides
    in Clarke County, Virginia - Wife resides in Jefferson County, West
    Virginia.

Elliott, John C. and Harriet C. Grim (2) -   (L) October 13, 1856

Elliott, Martha A. and P. H. Orndorff (3) -   December 26, 1889
    For further information see - Orndorff, P. H.

Ellitt, Catharine and James Conland (2) -   (L) April 5, 1852

Ellsberry, Mary (cold.) Jacob Rideout (3) -   May 20, 1875
    For further information see - Rideout, Jacob.

Ellsworth, Frederick and Susan Peyton Bedinger (1) -   May 1826

Emmert, Jacob V. and Agusta V. Tennant (3) -   November 17, 1887
    Place of marriage, Shepherdstown - Age of husband, 26 - Age of wife,
    23 - Both are Single - Husband was born in Washington County,
    Maryland - Wife was born in Jefferson County, West Virginia -
    Husband resides in Washington County, Maryland - Wife resides in
    Jefferson County, West Virginia.

Emory, John James and Mary Hester Thompson (2) -   (L) October 7, 1857

Emory, Mary Ann and Richard F. McFillan (2) -   (L) August 9, 1859

Emory, Minnie and Michael E. Brining (3) -   August 16, 1890
    For further information see - Brining, Michael E.

Emory, Samuel R. and Sarah Jane Frith (2) -   (L) July 27, 1858

Endrews, Henry and Polly Dowden (1) -   November 13, 1808

Endsley, Thomas and Mary McCloy (1) -   January 21, 1806

Engle, Alice J. and Raleigh L. Moler (3) -   January 22, 1878
    For further information see - Moler, Raleigh L.

Engle, Amanda and James M. Marshall (3) -   December 19, 1865
    For further information see - Marshall, James M.

Engle, Ann and John Engle (2) -   (L) October 18, 1851

Engle, Benjamin and Mary Ann Whiston (1) - November 14, 1833

Engle, Charles and Rebecca Elizabeth Longerbeam (3) - July 16, 1885
  Place of marriage, Blue Ridge Mountain - Age of husband, 30 - Age of
  wife, 19 - Both are Single - Both were born in Jefferson County,
  West Virginia - Both reside in Jefferson County, West Virginia.
  (Consent of bride's father vouched for by Barney Painter, son-in-law
  of bride's father.)

Engle, Charles J. and Margaret Merritt (2) - (L) June 3, 1858

Engle, Charles W. and Kate A. Rick (3) - September 9, 1886
  Place of marriage, Duffields - Age of husband, 24 - Age of wife,
  22 - Both are Single - Both were born in Jefferson County - Both
  reside in Jefferson County, West Virginia.

Engle, Cornelia S. and John T. Ruhlman (3) - (1869)
  For further information see - Ruhlman, John T.

Engle, Elizabeth and Samuel Brantner (1) - 1824

Engle, Elizabeth and Joshua Cox (1) - April 5, 1832

Engle, Emma A. and David H. Rodefer (3) - December 24, 1882
  For further information see - Rodefer, David H.

Engle, G. Frank and Annie E. Knott (3) - July 11, 1883
  Place of marriage, Shepherdstown - Age of husband, 24 - Age of wife,
  22 - Both are Single - Both were born in Jefferson County, West
  Virginia - Husband resides in Jefferson County - Wife resides in
  Jefferson County, West Virginia.

Engle, Hannah Ellen and John W. Holt (1) - January 1, 1832

Engle, Henry C. and Sarah M. Osbourn (2) - (L) October 13, 1855

Engle, Humphrey W. and Isabella Engle (1) - July 26, 1833

Engle, Isabella and Humphrey W. Engle (1) - July 26, 1833

Engle, Jacob H. and Virginia Helen Blackford (2) - (L) May 15, 1855

Engle, James A. and Elizabeth J. Vanmetre (3) - October 31, 1876
  Place of marriage, near Charlestown - Age of husband, 26 - Age of
  wife, 17 - Both are Single - Both were born in Jefferson County,
  West Virginia - Both reside in Jefferson County, West Virginia.
  (Consent of bride's guardian in person.)

Engle, James W. and Ann Margaret Duke (2) - (L) May 27, 1851

Engle, James W. and Ann M. Duke (1) - May 28, 1851

Engle, James W. and Rebecca Dust (3) - June 1, 1876
  Place of marriage, near Duffields - Age of husband, 48 - Age of
  wife, 47 - Husband is a Widower - Wife is Single - Both were born in
  Jefferson County, West Virginia - Both reside in Jefferson County,
  West Virginia.

Engle, Jesse A. and Mary Elizabeth Moler (3) -   May 2, 1882
    Place of marriage, Harpers Ferry - Age of husband, 26 - Age of wife,
    26 - Both are Single - Husband was born in Jefferson County, West
    Virginia - Wife was born in Jefferson County - Husband resides in
    Jefferson County, West Virginia - Wife resides in Jefferson County.

Engle, Jesse M. and Lulah E. Moler (3) -   October 13, 1880
    Place of marriage, near Duffields - Age of husband, 24 - Age of
    wife, 22 - Both are Single - Both were born in Jefferson County,
    West Virginia - Both reside in Jefferson County, West Virginia.

Engle, Jessee and Mary Melvin (1) -   March 21, 1822

Engle, Jessee E. (bride) and C. G. Johnson (3) -   December 20, 1870
    In the date, 17 is marked out. For further information see
    Johnson, C. G.

Engle, John and Catherine Melvin (1) -   November 7, 1823

Engle, John and Ann Engle (2) -   (L) October 18, 1851

Engle, John H. and Sally J. Duke (3) -   February 17, 1880
    Place of marriage, near Harpers Ferry - Age of husband, 41 - Age of
    wife, 26 - Both are Single - Both were born in Jefferson County,
    West Virginia - Both reside in Jefferson County, West Virginia.

Engle, John H. and Alice M. Reel (3) -   December 8, 1881
    Place of marriage, Shepherdstown - Age of husband, 43 - Age of wife,
    28 - Husband is a Widower - Wife is Single - Husband was born in
    Jefferson County, West Virginia - Wife was born in Maryland - Both
    reside in Jefferson County, West Virginia.

Engle, John M. and Mary Ellen Melvin (2) -   (L) October 28, 1852

Engle, Lydia and Charles Moler (1) -   1819

Engle, Lydia E. and Raleigh V. Moler (3) -   January 5, 1869
    For further information see - Moler, Raleigh V.

Engle, Margaret and William A. McCormick (3) -   September 16, 1890
    For further information see - McCormick, William A.

Engle, Mary and Thomas Melvin (1) -   September 11, 1828

Engle, Mary A. and Robert T. Matthews (3) -   August 24, 1878
    For further information see - Matthews, Robert T.

Engle, Mary Alice and S. H. Benner (3) -   September 28, 1881
    For further information see - Benner, S. H.

Engle, Mary Frances and John S. Strider (2) -   (L) August 25, 1856

Engle, Mary J. and W. W. Brown (3) -   February 6, 1878
    For further information see - Brown, W. W.

Engle, Mary M. and John Moler (3) -   March 3, 1868
    For further information see - Moler, John.

Engle, Sally C. and S. G. M. Rissler (3) -   October 21, 1885
    For further information see - Rissler, S. G. M.

Engle, Samuel and Betsey Wiltshire (1) -   April 13, 1805

Engle, Samuel and Susanna Lechliter (1) -   November 26, 1818

Engle, Samuel D. and Sally North (1) -   September 5, 1815

Engle, Sarah A. and W. S. Kelch (3) -   December 24, 1873
For further information see - Kelch, W. S.

Engle, Sarah E. and Solomon Snyder (3) -   April 12, 1881
For further information see - Snyder, Solomon.

Engle, Susan Frances Rebecca and George W. Miller (2) -   (L) October 5, 1863
For further information see - Miller, George W.

Engle, William and Phebe Melvin (1) -   April 6, 1820

Engle, William, Jr. and M. E. Staley (3) -   November 17, 1868
Place of marriage, Jefferson County - Age of husband, 24 - Age of wife, 21 - Both are Single - Both were born in Jefferson County, Both reside in Jefferson County - Husband's parents are William - Wife's parents are J. W. and M. - Occupation of husband is Farmer.

Engles, Emanuel and Mary McCormick (1) -   August 31, 1815

Engles, Jacob and Elizabeth Smith (1) -   1820

English, Mrs. Ann M. (widow) and Thomas Rawlins (2) -   (L) July 18, 1854

Engram, Eliza V. and John Wiggington (2) -   (L) August 2, 1855

Ensworth, Henry Turner and Hannah Wilson (2) -   (L) September 17, 1863
Time of marriage, September 24, 1863 - Place of marriage, On Shenandoah River, near Willis Mill - Names, Henry Turner Ensworth and Hannah Wilson - Age of husband, 22 years July 7, 1863 - Age of wife, 21 years - Both are Single - Both were born in Jefferson County - Both reside in Jefferson County - Names of husband's parents, Robert and Elizabeth Ensworth - Names of wife's parents, ___?___ and Patsy Wilson - Occupation of husband is Farmer - License issued, September 17, 1863 - Thomas A. Moore, Clerk.

Entler, Ann Rebecca and Milton S. Stephens (2) -   (L) November 15, 1853

Entler, Daniel and Margaret Welshimer (1) -   January 20, 1809

Entler, David M. and Mary Elizabeth Bradshaw (2) -   (L) (1862)
Time of marriage, February 25, 1862 - Place of marriage, Shepherdstown - Names, David M. Entler and Mary Elizabeth Bradshaw - Age of husband, 26 years and 6 months - Age of wife, 21 years - Condition of husband, Single - Condition of wife, Single - Place of husband's birth, Shepherdstown - Place of wife's birth, Shepherdstown - Place of husband's residence, Shepherdstown - Place of wife's residence, Shepherdstown - Names of husband's parents, Daniel and Margaret Entler - Names of wife's parents, William and Sarah Ann Bradshaw - Occupation of husband, Carpenter - D. M. Entler.

Entler, Ellen Virginia and Edward T. Licklider (3) -   October 25, 1876
For further information see - Licklider, Edward T.

Entler, Emily and Jacob B. Brown (2) -   (L) November 12, 1858

Entler, G. W. and Antonetta Tennant (3) -   December 31, 1872
Place of marriage, Jefferson County, West Virginia - Age of husband, 23 - Age of wife, 17 - Both are Single - Husband was born in Jefferson County, West Virginia - Wife was born in Maryland - Both reside in Jefferson County, West Virginia - Husband's parents are Phillip and Sarah - Wife's parents are William and Elizabeth - Occupation of husband is Farmer. (William Tennant.)

Entler, George B. and Carry L. Foutz (3) -   April 2, 1889
Place of marriage, Shepherdstown - Age of husband, 21 - Age of wife, 19 - Both are Single - Both were born in Jefferson County, West Virginia - Both reside in Jefferson County, West Virginia. (Consent of bride's father in writing.)

Entler, George William and Ann Rebecca Staley (1) -   February 1832

Entler, John P. and Alice V. Griffith (3) -   December 27, 1888
Place of marriage, Terrapin Nick - Age of husband, 22 - Age of wife, 21 - Both are Single - Husband was born in Jefferson County, West Virginia - Wife was born in Washington County, Maryland - Both reside in Jefferson County, West Virginia.

Entler, John Philip and Amelia Lucretia Walters (2) -   (L) May 23, 1861
Time of marriage, May 23, 1861 - Place of marriage, Shepherdstown - Age of husband, 23 years and 9 months - Age of wife, 22 years - Both are Single - Place of husband's birth, Jefferson County, Virginia - Place of wife's birth, Berkeley County, Virginia - Both reside in Jefferson County - Names of husband's parents, Philip and Elizabeth Ann - Names of wife's parents, James W. and Sarah Walters - Occupation of husband is Carpenter - James W. Walters.

Entler, John Thomas and Hester A. Bowers (3) -   October 15, 1868
Place of marriage, Jefferson County - Age of husband, 23 - Age of wife, 17 - Both are Single - Both were born in Jefferson County - Husband resides in Jefferson County - Wife resides in West Virginia - Husband's parents are Philip - Wife's parents are John W. and Milley - Occupation of husband is Farmer. (Grandmother consents.)

Entler, Lillie W. and William B. Tennant (3) -   September 28, 1886
For further information see - Tennant, William B.

Entler, Martin and Susan Cobler (1) -   November 26, 1808

Entler, Mary E. and John W. Freeze (3) -   November 20, 1866
For further information see - Freeze, John W.

Entler, Mary E. and William A. Fulk (3) -   May 31, 1887
For further information see - Fulk, William A.

Entler, Rosa P. and Henry W. Myers (3) -   October 12, 1880
For further information see - Myers, Henry W.

Entler, S. A. and Joseph W. Waters (3) -   May 5, 1868
For further information see - Waters, Joseph W.

Entler, Sarah and Jacob Ernst (1) -   January 9, 1814

Entsminger, Charles and Sarah F. Nick (3) - February 11, 1890
Place of marriage, Harpers Ferry - Age of husband, 24 - Age of wife, 22 - Both are Single - Both were born in Jefferson County, West Virginia - Both reside in Jefferson County, West Virginia.

Erb, Margaret and Thomas Sylvester Props (3) - December 26, 1871
For further information see - Props, Thomas Sylvester.

Ernshaw, Thomas and Mary Mallory (1) - 1814

Ernst, Jacob and Sarah Entler (1) - January 9, 1814

Ernst, Margaret E. and Samuel H. Ray (3) - February 8, 1866
For further information see - Ray, Samuel H.

Ernst, Susana and James Fleming (1) - July 8, 1816

Ervin, Mary and Samuel Harding (1) - June 22, 1817

Erwin, Emily and John H. Hutsler (2) - (L) February 1, 1861

Erwin, John E. and Dorsey H. Kirby (2) - (L) January 21, 1861

Erwin, Robert E. and Catherine Thompson (3) - September 25, 1884
Place of marriage, Harpers Ferry - Age of husband, 42 - Age of wife, 24 - Husband is a Widower - Wife is a Widow - Husband was born in Jefferson County, West Virginia - Wife was born in Shenandoah County, Virginia - Both reside in Jefferson County.

Erwin, S. Bulow and Ellen S. Kehler (2) - (L) September 12, 1853

Erwin, S. Bulow and Ellen Sarah Kehler (1) - September 13, 1853

Esbridge, Charles J. and Isabella Kennedy (1) - July 1825

Eskard, Frederick (cold.) Nancy Baylor (3) - June 23, 1874
Place of marriage, near Middleway - Age of husband, 24 - Age of wife, 24 - Both are Single - Husband was born in Frederick County, Virginia - Wife was born in Jefferson County, West Virginia - Both reside in Jefferson County, West Virginia.

Essex, Isaac and Anne Smock (1) - October 5, 1807

Esterlin, John and Sarah Jane Faulkner (2) - (L) November 19, 1851

Esterlin, John and Sarah Jane Faulkner (1) - November 20, 1851

Etchison, Frances E. and James T. Hopper (3) - December 16, 1872
For further information see - Hopper, James T.

Etchison, Frances E. and James T. Hopper (3) - December 18, 1872
For further information see - Hopper, James T.

Etchison, Mollie E. and Moses Wood (3) - November 9, 1869
For further information see - Wood, Moses.

Evans, A. Mason and Harriet L. Scollay (3) - November 27, 1867
Place of marriage, Jefferson County - Age of husband, 25 - Age of wife, 24 - Both are Single - Both were born in Jefferson County - Both reside in Jefferson County - Husband's parents are Samuel and Emeline - Wife's parents are Samuel and Sally - Occupation of husband is, Farmer.

Evans, George and Christena Singe (1) - November 7, 1823

Evans, Harriet B. and Henry Wintermoyer (1) - October 19, 1848

Evans, Isabella M. and James H. Small (3) - August 22, 1866
For further information see - Small, James H.

Evans, James and Lucinda L. Cordell (1) - December 21, 1848

Evans, Mary and William Hall (1) - June 28, 1808

Evans, Mary E. and Samuel H. Fowler (2) - (L) November 4, 1852

Evans, Mary S. and Casper E. Johnson (3) - February 9, 1887
For further information see - Johnson, Casper E.

Evans, Robert B. and Elizabeth J. Hendricks (2) - (L) December 9, 1850

Evans, Samuel and Emeline A. Mason (1) - May 19, 1842

Evans, Wealthy Ann and John Cocks (Cox) (1) - December 27, 1825

Evans, William B. (cold.) Maria E. Lovett (3) - December 27, 1876
Place of marriage, Harpers Ferry - Age of husband, 23 - Age of wife, 24 - Both are Single - Husband was born in Albemarle County, Virginia - Wife was born in Frederick County, Virginia - Husband resides in Albemarle County, Virginia - Wife resides in Jefferson County, West Virginia.

Everhart, Ann Virginia and John W. Grove (2) - (L) January 15, 1856

Everhart, Charlotte Elizabeth and Rezin W. Dailey (2) - (L) October 16, 1858

Everhart, Mary Ann and Barton Scarff (1) - March 10, 1822

Everhart, Mary M. and John W. Daily (3) - November 2, 1865
For further information see - Daily, John W.

Everhart, William W. and Mary E. E. Clipp (3) - February 4, 1880
Place of marriage, near Kabletown - Age of husband, 28 - Age of wife, 23 - Both are Single - Husband was born in Loudoun County, Virginia - Wife was born in Jefferson County, West Virginia - Both reside in Jefferson County, West Virginia.

Eversole, Abraham and Nancy Butt (1) - 1812

Eversole, Elizabeth and William Wiltsher (1) - November 5, 1845

Eversole, Isaac and Sarah Wolverton (1) - January 13, 1811

Eversole, Jacob and Mary McDaniel (1) - 1816

Eversole, James L. and Sarah E. Trivitt (1) - September 28, 1848

Eversole, Mary and William Cox (1) -　　　　　　　　　　　　　　May 20, 1807

Eversole, Peter and Elizabeth Jordan (1) -　　　　　　　　September 22, 1810

Everson, George and Sarah Conner (1) -　　　　　　　　　　February 27, 1817

Ewing, J. W. and Miss Mary Harris (2) -　　　　　　(L) December 27, 1851

Ewing, Moses and Betty C. Thompson (3) -　　　　　　　　　August 18, 1875
　　Place of marriage, Charlestown - Age of husband, 33 - Age of wife,
　　21 - Both are Single - Husband was born in Frederick County,
　　Virginia - Wife was born in Clarke County, Virginia - Husband
　　resides in Clarke County, Virginia - Wife resides in Jefferson
　　County, West Virginia.

Exner, William and Louisa Keller (3) -　　　　　　　　　　　　　　(1868)
　　Age of husband, 21 - Age of wife, 19 - Both are Single - Husband was
　　born in Germany - Wife was born in Jefferson County - Husband
　　resides in Maryland - Wife resides in West Virginia - Husband's
　　parents are William - Wife's parents are Henry and Mary - Occupation
　　of husband is Tinner.

Eyster, Bettie B. and Frank C. McCown (3) -　　　　　　　　June 12, 1879
　　For further information see - McCown, Frank C.

Fadley, Daniel and Sally T. Lemon (3) -   April 8, 1869
   Place of marriage, Jefferson County - Age of husband, 22 - Age of
   wife, 22 - Both are Single - Husband was born in Shenandoah County -
   Wife was born in Berkeley County - Both reside in Jefferson County -
   Occupation of husband is Farmer.

Faherty, John and Mary Doody (3) -   November 9, 1874
   Place of marriage, Harpers Ferry - Age of husband, 25 - Age of wife,
   22 - Both are Single - Husband was born in Ireland - Wife was born
   at Washington City - Husband resides at Ellicott City, Maryland -
   Wife resides at Harpers Ferry.

Fairfax, Ann (cold.) George Lee (3) -   September 4, 1882
   For further information see - Lee, George.

Fairfax, Eliza Christien and Thomas Ragland (1) -   January 22, 1822

Fairfax, Farinda and Perrin Washington (1) -   February 5, 1822

Fairfax, Wilson M. C. and Lucy A. Griffith (1) -   March 2, 1824

Fairman, D. and Jane Kirby (1) -   1819

Fall, John M. and Mrs. Susan Unseld (1) -   January 29, 1850

Fantom, Frances E. and Harold Scarboro (3) -   October 6, 1887
   For further information see - Scarboro, Harold.

Faringsworth, Samuel and Mary Isler (1) -   May 16, 1811

Farnsworth, Elizabeth and Jefferson Johns (2) -   (L) September 4, 1850

Farnsworth, Elizabeth and Jefferson Johns (1) -   September 5, 1850

Farnsworth, Henry S. and Frances Smith (1) -   November 1, 1832

Farnsworth, Margaret and Jefferson Swimley (1) -   April 20, 1848

Farnsworth, Mary E. and David H. Underdonk (3) -   February 7, 1877
   For further information see - Underdonk, David H.

Farr, Elizabeth and Conway Sloan (1) -   June 1827

Farr, Sally and John Dillow (1) -   September 23, 1847

Farr, William H. and Harriet Vanvacter (1) -   January 31, 1833

Farrell, Mrs. (widow) and ? Lockman (1) -   1841

Fatisal, Edward and Mary C. Danner (3) -   October 27, 1885
   Place of marriage, Harpers Ferry - Age of husband, 60 - Age of wife,
   27 - Husband is a Widower - Wife is Single - Husband was born at
   Liverpool, England - Wife was born in Jefferson County, West
   Virginia - Both reside in Jefferson County, West Virginia.

Fauber, Bertie and Joseph Hamilton (3) -   October 24, 1890
   For further information see - Hamilton, Joseph.

Fauble, Eliza and William House (3) -   November 10, 1882
   For further information see - House, William.

Faulk, Ida and Joseph William Covert (3) -　　　　　　　　December 29, 1887
　　For further information see - **Covert, Joseph William.**

Faulkner, E. A. S. and George W. Carman (2) -　　(L) November 19, 1851

Faulkner, E. A. S. and George W. Carman (1) -　　　　November 20, 1851

Faulkner, Hannah and William H. Frier (1) -　　　　　December 20, 1849

Faulkner, Sarah Jane and John Esterlin (2) -　　(L) November 19, 1851

Faulkner, Sarah Jane and John Esterlin (1) -　　　　November 20, 1851

Faulstick, Katherine P. and Charles E. Bothwell (3) -　　August 11, 1890
　　For further information see - **Bothwell, Charles E.**

Fauver, John W. and Maud May Ash (3) -　　　　　　　　August 27, 1889
　　Place of marriage, Charlestown - Age of husband, 23 - Age of wife,
　　22 - Both are Single - Husband was born in Jefferson County, West
　　Virginia - Wife was born in Frederick County, Virginia - Husband
　　resides in Frederick County, Virginia - Wife resides in Jefferson
　　County, West Virginia.

Fauver, Sallie and Will W. Moon (3) -　　　　　　　　　December 25, 1890
　　For further information see - **Moon, Will W.**

Fayman, Ella and Louis W. Kogelschatz (3) -　　　　　March 21, 1883
　　For further information see - **Kogelschatz, Louis W.**

Fayman, Emma K. and D. H. Young (3) -　　　　　　　　September 7, 1881
　　For further information see - **Young, D. H.**

Fayman, Fanny T. and Isaac J. Muck (3) -　　　　　　October 28, 1874
　　For further information see - **Muck, Isaac J.**

Fayman, Joseph P. and Martha E. Spangler (3) -　　　December 19, 1866
　　Place of marriage, John Spangler's, Jefferson County, West
　　Virginia - Age of husband, 27 - Age of wife, 21 - Both are Single -
　　Both were born in Jefferson County, West Virginia - Both reside in
　　Jefferson County, West Virginia - Husband's parents are George and
　　Frances Fayman - Wife's parents are John and M. A. Spangler -
　　Occupation of husband is Assistant Assessor.

Fayman, Margaret V. and Norman Fisher (3) -　　　　　September 7, 1876
　　For further information see - **Fisher, Norman.**

Feagan, Mary A. and Charles V. Blake (3) -　　　　　September 24, 1868
　　For further information see - **Blake, Charles V.**

Feagans, __?__ (bride) and J. J. Baney (3) -　　　　September 26, 1871
　　For further information see - **Baney, J. J.**

Feagans, Edward and Mollie McDonald (3) -　　　　　　March 14, 1889
　　Place of marriage, Charlestown - Age of husband, 30 - Age of wife,
　　27 - Both are Single - Both were born in Jefferson County, West
　　Virginia - Both reside in Jefferson County, West Virginia.

Feagans, Jennie and Otho Selby (3) -　　　　　　　　　November 26, 1872
　　For further information see - **Selby, Otho.**

Feagans, Nettie and Julius M. Coyle (3) -   November 25, 1875
   For further information see - Coyle, Julius M.

Feagans, Wilder and Minnie C. Renner (3) -   February 5, 1879
   Place of marriage, near Ripon - Age of husband, 21 - Age of wife, 19 - Both are Single - Both were born in Jefferson County, West Virginia - Both reside in Jefferson County, West Virginia. (Consent of bride's father in person.)

Feaman, George, Jr. and Elizabeth Wisenall (1) -   April 2, 1815

Feaman, Jacob and Sarah Staley (1) -   September 16, 1824

Feaman, John Samuel and Mary Catharine Barnhart (2) -   (L) October 11, 1854

Feaman, Margaret and Benjamin Wiltshire (1) -   November 9, 1826

Feaman, Mary and John Jackson (1) -   November 11, 1810

Feeley, Thomas and Margaret Spotts (3) -   October 7, 1867
   Place of marriage, Jefferson - Age of husband, 35 - Age of wife, 22 - Husband is a Widower - Wife is a Widow - Husband was born in Ireland - Wife was born in Germany - Both reside in Jefferson County - Husband's parents are Mathew - Wife's parents are Jane - Occupation of husband is Laborer. (Party sworn as to age.)

Fellers, James O. B. and Clara A. Barr (3) -   November 7, 1882
   Place of marriage, near Ripon - Age of husband, 21 - Age of wife, 18 - Both are Single - Husband was born in Clarke County, Virginia - Wife was born in Cumberland County, Pennsylvania - Both reside in Jefferson County, West Virginia. (Consent of bride's father in person.)

Fellers, Mary Ellen and Bennet B. Kisner (3) -   September 27, 1888
   For further information see - Kisner, Bennet B.

Fellman, Ann (cold.) Jacob Carter (3) -   December 25, 1882
   For further information see - Carter, Jacob.

Feltman, Margaret and Corna Smith (2) -   (L) February 11, 1863
   For further information see - Smith, Corna.

Feltman, Mary C. and Eli L. Fiser (2) -   (L) June 1, 1857

Feltner, George W. and Sidney A. Anderson (3) -   September 6, 1866
   Place of marriage, near Smithfield - Age of husband, 22 - Age of wife, 21 - Both are Single - Husband was born in Clarke County, Virginia - Wife was born in Frederick County, Virginia - Husband resides at Smithfield, Jefferson County, West Virginia - Wife resides near Smithfield, Jefferson County - Husband's parents are Deskel and Jane Feltner - Wife's parents are William C. and Maria Gruber - Occupation of husband is Blacksmith.

Feltner, George W. and Sarah B. Mauck (3) -   September 24, 1888
   Place of marriage, Charlestown - Age of husband, 45 - Age of wife, 23 - Husband is a Widower - Wife is Single - Husband was born in Jefferson County, West Virginia - Wife was born in Warren County, Virginia - Husband resides in Warren County, Virginia - Wife resides in Jefferson County, West Virginia.

Feltner, Mrs. Jane E. and John L. Stewart (2) -   (L) November 30, 1852

Feltner, Jane E. (widow) and John L. Stewart (1) -   December 2, 1852

Feltner, Sarah M. and Henry Walter (3) -   September 19, 1865
For further information see - Walter, Henry.

Felton, Ellen Virginia and Abraham Crim (2) -   (L) April 18, 1864
For further information see - Crim, Abraham.

Fenton, Rebecca and D. G. Clayton (1) -   October 18, 1849

Fenton, Thomas G. and Kate Kain (3) -   November 27, 1884
Place of marriage, Charlestown - Age of husband, 28 - Age of wife, 27 - Both are Single - Husband was born in Clarke County, Virginia - Wife was born in Jefferson County - Husband resides in Clarke County, Virginia - Wife resides in Jefferson County, West Virginia.

Ferguson, Charles (cold.) Ann Perkins (3) -   September 14, 1884
Place of marriage, Kearneysville - Age of husband, 47 - Age of wife, 40 - Husband is a Widower - Wife is a Widow - Both were born in Jefferson County, West Virginia - Both reside in Jefferson County.

Ferguson, Charles W. and Maria Blackburn (3) -   June 3, 1871
Place of marriage, Jefferson County - Age of husband, 35 - Age of wife, 30 - Both are Single - Husband was born in Virginia - Wife was born in Jefferson County - Both reside in Jefferson County - Husband's parents are William and Mary - Wife's parents are George and Matilda - Occupation of husband is Farmer.

Ferrel, Eliza and John T. Cowley (3) -   December 20, 1871
For further information see - Cowley, John T.

Ferrell, Charles F. and Ann E. Yontz (3) -   October 9, 1866
Place of marriage, Shepherdstown, Jefferson County - Age of husband, 23 - Age of wife, 21 - Both are Single - Both were born in Jefferson County, West Virginia - Both reside at Shepherdstown, Jefferson County - Husband's parents are Jacob and Susan C. Ferrell - Wife's parents are Cornelius and Mary Yontz - Occupation of husband is Painter.

Ferrell, Lorenza and Emily Hatter (3) -   May 9, 1872
Place of marriage, Jefferson County - Age of husband, 33 - Age of wife, 24 - Both are Single - Both were born in Virginia - Both reside in Virginia - Husband's parents are Samuel and Anna - Wife's parents are Frank and Rebecca - Occupation of husband is Blasting.

Ferrells, Eliza and Daniel T. Crawford (1) -   March 10, 1825

Ferris, William A. and Mary F. Smurr (3) -   May 2, 1866
Place of marriage, John Smurr's, Shepherdstown - Age of husband, 25 - Age of wife, 24 - Both are Single - Husband was born in Schoharie County, New York - Wife was born in Jefferson County, Virginia - Husband resides in Livingston County, New York - Wife resides in Jefferson County, West Virginia - Husband's parents are Peter and Sarah Ferris - Wife's parents are John and Ellin Smurr - Occupation of husband is Clerk.

Feyman, Catherine and Robert Vinconhall (1) -   July 15, 1823

Fiddler, L. L. and Rosa C. Shreck (3) - March 28, 1867
 Place of marriage, Shepherdstown - Age of husband, 21 - Age of wife,
 25 - Both are Single - Husband was born in Clarke County, Virginia -
 Wife was born in Frederick County, Virginia - Husband resides in
 Berkeley County, West Virginia - Wife resides in Frederick County,
 Virginia - Husband's parents are J. and N. M. Fiddler - Wife's
 parents are Jacob and Mary Shreck - Occupation of husband is Farmer.

Fiddler, Marshall and Jennie Dunn (3) - September 19, 1888
 Place of marriage, Charlestown - Age of husband, 30 - Age of wife,
 28 - Both are Single - Both were born in Clarke County, Virginia -
 Husband resides in Clarke County, Virginia - Wife resides in
 Jefferson County, West Virginia.

Fidinger, Joseph N. and Nellie J. Rohr (3) - June 12, 1883
 Place of marriage, Charlestown - Age of husband, 20 - Age of wife,
 22 - Both are Single - Husband was born at Brownville, Maryland -
 Wife was born in Jefferson County, West Virginia - Both reside in
 Jefferson County, West Virginia. (Consent of groom's father in
 person.)

Fidinger, Minnie and P. B. Dorsey (3) - May 3, 1888
 For further information see - Dorsey, P. B.

Fidler, Ella and Charles H. Schreck (3) - August 22, 1887
 For further information see - Schreck, Charles H.

Fidler, Israel and Ann Mercer (1) - October 18, 1832

Fidler, William and Emma Johnson (3) - May 17, 1888
 Place of marriage, Middleway - Age of husband, 23 - Age of wife,
 23 - Both are Single - Both were born in Jefferson County, West
 Virginia - Both reside in Jefferson County, West Virginia.

Field, James C. (cold.) Amelia Mason (3) - April 10, 1884
 Place of marriage, Charlestown - Age of husband, 24 - Age of wife,
 24 - Both are Single - Both were born in Jefferson County, West
 Virginia - Both reside in Jefferson County, West Virginia.

Field, Omer (cold.) John William Rutherford (3) - April 14, 1884
 For further information see - Rutherford, John William.

Fields, Gabriel and Rosanna Hall (3) - July 28, 1866
 Place of marriage, Hillsborough, Loudoun County, Virginia - Age of
 husband, 27 - Age of wife, 15 - Both are Single - Husband was born
 in Loudoun County, Virginia - Wife was born in Jefferson County,
 West Virginia - Both reside in Jefferson County, West Virginia -
 Occupation of husband is Laborer.

Fields, Girtie (cold.) Benjamin Payne (3) - June 16, 1881
 For further information see - Payne, Benjamin.

Fields, Ida (cold.) Harvey Campbell (3) - July 8, 1883
 For further information see - Campbell, Harvey.

Fields, William and Virginia Atwell (3) - February 21, 1889
 Place of marriage, Charlestown - Age of husband, 23 - Age of wife,
 27 - Husband is a Widower - Wife is Single - Both were born in
 Loudoun County, Virginia - Husband resides in Loudoun County,
 Virginia - Wife resides in Jefferson County, West Virginia.

Fifer, E. L. and Cornelia S. Blamer (3) --   November 8, 1870
    Age of husband, 35 - Age of wife, 23 - Husband was born in Jefferson
    County, Virginia - Wife was born in Jefferson County - Husband
    resides in Jefferson County - Wife resides in West Virginia.

Filbert, Nancy and John Lay (1) -   November 30, 1815

Finegan, Michael and Ann Harper (2) -   (L) November 12, 1853

Finister, Richard (cold.) Mary Branson (3) -   January 29, 1878
    Place of marriage, Duffields - Age of husband, 47 - Age of wife,
    22 - Husband is a Widower - Wife is Single - Husband was born at New
    Orleans - Wife was born in Jefferson County, West Virginia - Both
    reside in Jefferson County, West Virginia.

Fink, Ruth Ann and Charles S. Baer (3) -   August 11, 1883
    For further information see - Baer, Charles S.

Finley, James and Henrietta A. Shepherd (2) -   (L) March 28, 1853

Finley, James and Henrietta A. Shepherd (1) -   March 29, 1853

Finnell, John A. and Lucy Ann Brown (3) -   December 14, 1875
    Place of marriage, near Charlestown - Age of husband, 24 - Age of
    wife, 18 - Both are Single - Both were born in Clarke County,
    Virginia - Both reside in Jefferson County, West Virginia.
    (Consent of bride's father in person.)

Finnell, John B. and A. M. Milton (3) -   November 19, 1872
    Place of marriage, Kabletown - Age of husband, 26 - Age of wife,
    17 - Both are Single - Both were born in Virginia - Both reside in
    West Virginia - Husband's parents are Jessee and Adelina - Wife's
    parents are James and Mary E. - Occupation of husband is Clerk.
    (This record is crossed out in the original.)

Finnell, John B. and Annie M. Milton (3)   November 15, 1872
    Place of marriage, Kabletown - Age of husband, 26 - Age of wife,
    17 - Both are Single - Husband was born in Rappahannock County,
    Virginia - Wife was born in Jefferson County - Husband resides in
    Jefferson County - Wife resides in Jefferson County, West Virginia -
    Husband's parents are Jesse and Adelina - Wife's parents are James
    and Mary E. - Occupation of husband is Clerk. (James Milton.)

Finnell, Nettie Lee and John William Clark (3) -   August 3, 1880
    For further information see - Clark, John William.

Fiser, Eli L. and Mary C. Feltman (2) -   (L) June 1, 1857

Fiser, Maggie E. and William M. Rice (3) -   March 9, 1876
    For further information see - Rice, William M.

Fiser, Mary Ann and Samuel Butt (2) -   (L) March 6, 1855

Fisher, Ailsy (cold.) Granville Cromwell (3) -   November 30, 1876
    For further information see - Cromwell, Granville.

Fisher, Catherine and Robert McGlosslim (1) -   October 14, 1821

Fisher, Elizabeth and William Kenear (1) -   August 29, 1815

Fisher, Elizabeth and Joseph Smith (1) - October 8, 1831

Fisher, Fanny Frances and John Allen (2) - (L) November 3, 1856

Fisher, Jacob and Eliza Staley (1) - April 24, 1809

Fisher, James and Ann Hall (widow) (2) - (L) January 6, 1860

Fisher, James W. R. and Clara Smurr (3) - June 6, 1877
 Place of marriage, Shepherdstown - Age of husband, 28 - Age of wife,
 23 - Both are Single - Husband was born in Berkeley County - Wife
 was born in Jefferson County, West Virginia - Husband resides in
 Berkeley County - Wife resides in Jefferson County.

Fisher, John and Caroline M. S. Galihar (1) - 1822

Fisher, Mary and Hezekiah B. Allison (1) - July 27, 1817

Fisher, Mary (cold.) William Robinson (3) - December 18, 1884
 For further information see - Robinson, William.

Fisher, Mary V. and Thomas G. Rawlins (2) - (L) April 7, 1852

Fisher, Norman and Margaret V. Fayman (3) - September 7, 1876
 Place of marriage, Shepherdstown - Age of husband, 21 - Age of wife,
 18 - Both are Single - Husband was born at Hagerstown, Maryland -
 Wife was born in Jefferson County, West Virginia - Both reside in
 Jefferson County, West Virginia. (Consent of bride's father in
 writing.)

Fitch, Margaret and Thomas Calahan (1) - September 30, 1845

Fitchart, Larkin (cold.) Mary Hawkins (3) - August 27, 1866
 Place of marriage, Keys Switch, Jefferson County - Age of husband,
 65 - Age of wife, 50 - Husband is a Widower - Wife is a Widow -
 Husband was born in Clarke County, Virginia - Wife was born at
 Eastern Shore, Maryland - Both reside in Jefferson County, West
 Virginia - Husband's parents are Humphrey and Rose Fitchart -
 Occupation of husband is Gardener.

Fitzgerald, Thomas and Florence Staley (3) - December 13, 1882
 Place of marriage, Shepherdstown - Age of husband, 28 - Age of wife,
 23 - Both are Single - Husband was born in Berkeley County, West
 Virginia - Wife was born in Jefferson County, West Virginia - Both
 reside in Jefferson County, West Virginia.

Fitzpatrick, Catherine and Andrew Colgan (2) - (L) July 5, 1856

Fitzpatrick, William and Mary Clarke (3) - September 28, 1870
 Place of marriage, Jefferson County - Age of husband, 28 - Age of
 wife, 22 - Husband was born in Ireland - Wife was born in Virginia -
 Husband resides in Jefferson County - Wife resides at Winchester.
 (Age of lady sworn to by John D. Wire.)

Fizer, Hannah and Henry Buck (1) - November 21, 1816

Fizer, Sallie C. and John J. Hoffmaster (3) - August 9, 1881
 For further information see - Hoffmaster, John J.

Flagg, George H. and E. C. Washington (3) -   January 23, 1868
    Place of marriage, Jefferson County - Age of husband, 35 - Age of
    wife, 22 - Husband is a Widower - Wife is Single - Both were born in
    Jefferson County - Both reside in Jefferson - Husband's parents are
    J. R. and Susan - Wife's parents are R. B. and C.

Flagg, John R. and Susan Rutherford Hite (1) -   January 6, 1818

Flagg, Sarah Ann and John J. Hammond (2) -   (L) July 18, 1850

Flagg, Sally A. and John J. Hammond (1) -   July 18, 1850

Flagg, Thomas G. and Margaret B. Slemmons (1) -   November 4, 1828

Flanagan, Alice L. and John E. Rentch (3) -   February 12, 1874
    For further information see - Rentch, John E.

Flanagan, Alice L. and Asbury M. Hopper (3) -   October 21, 1875
    For further information see - Hopper, Asbury M.

Flanagan, James and Frances M. Griggs (1) -   November 19, 1835

Flanagan, John G. and Eliza Jane Tomson Krepps (3) -   October 26, 1876
    Place of marriage, Bolivar - Age of husband, 27 - Age of wife, 19 -
    Both are Single - Both were born in Jefferson County, West Virginia-
    Both reside in Jefferson County, West Virginia. (Consent of bride's
    father in writing.)

Flanagan, Kate and William Hunter (3) -   January 14, 1875
    For further information see - Hunter, William.

Flanagan, Mary C. and John C. Licklider (3) -   December 18, 1866
    For further information see - Licklider, John C.

Flanagin, James and Mary Ellen Caton (3) -   September 7, 1869
    Place of marriage, Jefferson County - Both were born in Jefferson
    County - Both reside in Jefferson County. (Father in person
    consents.)

Flanagin, Laura F. and George William Moler (2) -   (L) December 20, 1854

Fleming, Emily and William McElny (2) -   (L) May 14, 1854

Fleming, Georgia and Lewis Wilt (3) -   September 2, 1873
    For further information see - Wilt, Lewis.

Fleming, Ida M. and Eugene H. Gerstell (3) -   March 3, 1885
    For further information see - Gerstell, Eugene H.

Fleming, Isaac and Emily Compton (1) -   March 21, 1831

Fleming, Isaac and Ann Taylor (1) -   July 4, 1833

Fleming, James and Susana Ernst (1) -   July 8, 1816

Fleming, John Q. and Helen W. Frazier (3) -   January 31, 1878
    Place of marriage, Charlestown - Age of husband, 32 - Age of wife,
    20 - Both are Single - Husband was born in Loudoun County,
    Virginia - Wife was born in Jefferson County, West Virginia - Both
    reside in Jefferson County, West Virginia.

Fleming, John Q. and Fannie R. Smith (3) -   October 25, 1883
　　Place of marriage, Charlestown - Age of husband, 31 - Age of wife,
　　22 - Both are Single - Husband was born in Jefferson County, West
　　Virginia - Wife was born in Alleghany County, Maryland - Both reside
　　in Jefferson County, West Virginia.

Fleming, Joseph and Catharine A. Hawn (1) -   April 11, 1850

Fleming, Mary A. and Charles A. Trussell (3) -   January 10, 1877
　　For further information see - Trussell, Charles A.

Fleming, Mary J. and Archibald McCarroll, Jr. (2) -   (L) April 6, 1861
　　For further information see - McCarroll, Archibald, Jr.

Fleming, Nellie D. and R. Despard Davisson (3) -   October 19, 1876
　　For further information see - Davisson, R. Despard.

Fleming, Rose and George B. Coffinbarger (3) -   (1884)
　　For further information see - Coffinbarger, George B.

Fleming, Sarah E. and Rezin Piper (3) -   June 1, 1886
　　For further information see - Piper, Rezin.

Fleming, Susan Eugenia and James W. Coffinberger (3) -   January 27, 1881
　　For further information see - Coffinberger, James W.

Fleming, Virginia and John W. Smallwood (3) -   March 3, 1875
　　For further information see - Smallwood, John W.

Fleming, Zach T. and Amanda Isabella Wilt (3) -   December 19, 1876
　　Place of marriage, Porter's Factory - Age of husband, 28 - Age of
　　wife, 19 - Both are Single - Husband was born in Clarke County,
　　Virginia - Wife was born in Jefferson County, West Virginia - Both
　　reside in Jefferson County, West Virginia.

Flemings, Abraham and Susan Crawford (1) -   1826

Flemings, L. Jennie and Jacob R. Miller (3) -   December 20, 1871
　　For further information see - Miller, Jacob R.

Flemming, Solomon and Sarah Ann Bateman (1) -   March 14, 1833

Fletcher, Carrie Lee and R. W. Williams (3) -   December 14, 1886
　　For further information see - Williams, R. W.

Fletcher, Edmonia (cold.) William Burns (3) -   November 4, 1890
　　For further information see - Burns, William.

Fletcher, Emma Jane and J. B. Whittington (3) -   December 27, 1881
　　For further information see - Whittington, J. B.

Fletcher, Joseph B. and Florence Rosella Ainsworth (3) -   February 25, 1886
　　Place of marriage, near Kabletown - Age of husband, 23 - Age of
　　wife, 20 - Both are Single - Husband was born in Frederick County,
　　Virginia - Wife was born in Jefferson County, West Virginia - Both
　　reside in Jefferson County, West Virginia. (Consent of bride's
　　father in person.)

Flinn, William B. and Minnie E. Stephens (3) -   August 25, 1886
Place of marriage, Charlestown - Age of husband, 26 - Age of wife,
20 - Both are Single - Husband was born in State of Virginia - Wife
was born in Jefferson County, West Virginia - Husband resides in
State of Virginia - Wife resides in Jefferson County, West Virginia
at present. (Consent of bride's father in writing.)

Flint, Fanny (cold.) Daniel Shaw (3) -   December 16, 1880
For further information see - Shaw, Daniel.

Flint, John (cold.) Jennie Seibert (3) -   May 13, 1873
Place of marriage, Shepherdstown - Age of husband, 22 - Age of wife,
22 - Both are Single - Both were born in Jefferson County, West
Virginia - Both reside in Jefferson County, West Virginia -
Husband's parents are John and Sarah - Wife's parents are Jacob and
Susanna - Occupation of husband is Laborer.

Flint, Lucy (cold.) Robert Jackson (3) -   January 28, 1884
For further information see - Jackson, Robert.

Flood, E. Bolling and Richard E. Byrd (3) -   September 15, 1886
For further information see - Byrd, Richard E.

Flood, Liza Rebecca and Charles Reynolds Crawford (3) -   January 14, 1869
For further information see - Crawford, Charles Reynolds.

Flood, Thomas J. and Martha Ann Athey (1) -   January 24, 1847

Flora, Charles and Martha Cost (3) -   June 11, 1868
Place of marriage, Jefferson County - Age of husband, 25 - Age of
wife, 22 - Both are Single - Both were born in Maryland - Husband
resides in Maryland - Wife resides in Jefferson County - Husband's
parents are Thomas and Martha - Wife's parents are John - Occupation
of husband is Carriage.

Flore, James and Frances Eleanor McCormick (1) -   May 26, 1831

Florence, Lewis (cold.) Lydia Crawford (3) -   October 24, 1882
Place of marriage, Shepherdstown - Age of husband, 22 - Age of wife,
21 - Both are Single - Husband was born in Loudoun County,
Virginia - Wife was born in Jefferson County, West Virginia - Both
reside in Jefferson County, West Virginia.

Florence, Robert and Nancy Wilson (1) -   January 1, 1818

Fluke, Fanny and Solomon Sagle (3) -   August 31, 1871
For further information see - Sagle, Solomon.

Fogal, Charles L. and Annie V. Kern (3) -   May 29, 1890
Place of marriage, Charlestown - Age of husband, 27 - Age of wife,
21 - Both are Single - Husband was born in Shenandoah County,
Virginia - Wife was born in Jefferson County, West Virginia -
Husband resides in Shenandoah County, Virginia - Wife resides in
Jefferson County, West Virginia.

Fogle, Elizabeth and George W. Hoff (3) -   December 23, 1875
For further information see - Hoff, George W.

Folch, George and Susan Byers (1) -   April 11, 1809

Foley, Ann and Maurice Lynch (1) -   June 5, 1850

Foley, Sarah and George E. Currie (3) -   November 21, 1865
    For further information see - Currie, George E.

Folk, Daniel and Rebecca Gaunters (1) -   1826

Folk, Daniel H. and Hettie Lemen (3) -   January 29, 1890
    Place of marriage, Shepherdstown - Age of husband, 28 - Age of wife,
    28 - Both are Single - Husband was born in Berkeley County, West
    Virginia - Wife was born in Jefferson County, West Virginia -
    Husband resides in Berkeley County, West Virginia - Wife resides in
    Jefferson County, West Virginia.

Folk, Daniel J. and Jennie Hilton (3) -   August 30, 1889
    Place of marriage, Shepherdstown - Age of husband, 30 - Age of wife,
    23 - Husband is Single - Wife is a Widow - Husband was born in
    Jefferson County, West Virginia - Wife was born in Washington
    County, Maryland - Both reside in Jefferson County, West Virginia.

Folk, Franciscus and Martin Yantz (1) -   June 10, 1832

Forber, George and Rose E. Ainsworth (3) -   December 19, 1867
    Place of marriage, Jefferson County - Age of husband, 25 - Age of
    wife, 17 - Both are Single - Both were born in Jefferson - Both
    reside in Jefferson - Wife's parents are Robert - Occupation of
    husband is Farmer.

Ford, Bettie (cold.) George W. Johnson (3) -   March 25, 1886
    For further information see - Johnson, George W.

Ford, Daniel and Millie Colston (3) -   October 26, 1871
    Place of marriage, Jefferson County - Age of husband, 22 - Age of
    wife, 25 - Husband is Single - Wife is a Widow - Both were born in
    Virginia - Both reside in West Virginia - Husband's parents are
    Daniel and Matilda - Wife's parents are David and Nellie -
    Occupation of husband is Farmer.

Ford, Eliza (cold.) Fortune McClean (3) -   September 14, 1876
    For further information see - McClean, Fortune.

Ford, Eliza (cold.) George Mason (3) -   September 27, 1877
    For further information see - Mason, George.

Ford, Ella (cold.) Thomas Simmons (3) -   March 15, 1886
    For further information see - Simmons, Thomas.

Ford, Henry and Eliza Hill (3) -   January 4, 1869
    Place of marriage, Jefferson County - Age of husband, 40 - Age of
    wife, 25 - Both are Single - Both were born in Virginia - Husband
    resides in Jefferson County - Wife resides in Jefferson County, West
    Virginia - Occupation of husband is Farmer.

Ford, James C. and Susanna L. Downey (1) -   July 28, 1834

Ford, Jennie (cold.) William Hanion (3) -   June 27, 1878
    For further information see - Hanion, William.

Ford, Mary Cornelia and William Pane (3) -   July 13, 1871
    For further information see - Pane, William.

Ford, **Rachel** (cold.) Charles Reed (3) -   June 6, 1878
    For further information see - **Reed, Charles.**

Ford, Robert E. (cold.) Ida Mason (3) -   December 31, 1878
    Place of marriage, Charlestown - **Age of husband, 36** - Age of wife,
    24 - Both are Single - Both were born in Jefferson County, West
    Virginia - Husband resides in Pennsylvania - Wife resides in
    Jefferson County, West Virginia.

Ford, William and Mary Ann Jefferson (3) -   January 6, 1874
    Place of marriage, Smithfield - **Age of husband, 22** - Age of wife,
    21 - Both are Single - Husband was born in Berkeley County, West
    Virginia - Wife was born in Jefferson County, West Virginia - Both
    reside in Jefferson County, West Virginia.

Foreman, Arrabella and R. S. Hensell (3) -   September 10, 1867
    For further information see - **Hensell, R. S.**

Foreman, Daniel and Sarah Zombro (1) -   May 28, 1822

Foreman, Eliza and Daniel Zombro (1) -   July 31, 1828

Foreman, George and Elizabeth M. White (2) -   (L) December 1, 1853
    (Consent of Miss White's mother proved by the oath of Alexander
    White, the brother of the intended bride.)

Foreman, George B. H. and Rebecca A. E. Morrow (2) -   (L) May 13, 1853
    (Witness, F. J. Harley.)

Foreman, Hannah and William Eliot (1) -   November 28, 1832

Foreman, Harriet and Alexander White (2) -   (L) December 10, 1853

Foreman, Jacob J. and Mary Ellen Jane Wilson (2) -   (L) February 16, 1855

Foreman, James and Catharine Derow (2) -   (L) July 29, 1857

Foreman, James and Mollie Piper (3) -   January 7, 1888
    Place of marriage, Harpers Ferry - **Age of husband, 48** - Age of wife,
    28 - Husband is a Widower - **Wife is Single** - Both were born in
    Jefferson County, West Virginia - Both reside in Jefferson County,
    West Virginia. (Issued, December 30, 1887.)

Foreman, Jane and Henry Waters (3) -   February 24, 1870
    For further information see - **Waters, Henry.**

Foreman, Jane and Harry Davis (3) -   February 20, 1886
    For further information see - **Davis, Harry.**

Foreman, John and Mary Smith (1) -   1812

Foreman, John and Sarah Bountain (1) -   August 24, 1820

Foreman, John and Margaret Custer (1) -   December 2, 1830

Foreman, John and Lucy Virginia Dillow (2) - (L) June 20, 1861
Time of marriage, June 20, 1861 - Place of marriage, Jefferson
County - Full names, John Foreman and Lucy Virginia Dillow - Age of
husband, 21 years - Age of wife, 18 years - Both are Single - Both
were born in Jefferson County - Both live in Jefferson County -
Names of husband's parents are mother, Matilda Foreman - Names of
wife's parents are David and Sarah Ann Dillow - Occupation of
husband is Laborer - David (X) Dillow.

Foreman, John and Elizabeth Rebecca Ward (3) - March 18, 1877
Place of marriage, Harpers Ferry - Age of husband, 35 - Age of wife,
33 - Both are Single - Both were born in Jefferson County, West
Virginia - Both reside in Jefferson County, West Virginia.

Foreman, Julia Frances and Martin H. Miller (2) - (L) December 6, 1852

Foreman, Lewis F. and Fannie M. Schmitt (3) - March 11, 1890
Place of marriage, Harpers Ferry - Age of husband, 24 - Age of wife,
23 - Both are Single - Both were born in Jefferson County, West
Virginia - Both reside in Jefferson County, West Virginia.

Foreman, Mrs. Lizzie and Craton Sealock (3) - January 6, 1878
For further information see - Sealock, Craton.

Foreman, Mary and Samuel Piles (1) - July 30, 1806

Foreman, Susan E. and J. Henry Deetz (3) - September 24, 1879
For further information see - Deetz, J. Henry.

Forgerson, Samuel and Dorcus Johnson Davis (1) - December 10, 1823

Forrest, Agnes L. and John M. Macfarland (3) - December 10, 1878
For further information see - Macfarland, John M.

Forrest, Daniel D. and Mary T. Davenport (1) - March 21, 1820

Forrest, Elizabeth D. and Richard D. Rutherford (3) - February 10, 1876
For further information see - Rutherford, Richard D.

Forrest, N. T. (bride) and B. B. Ranson (3) - December 28, 1870
For further information see - Ranson, B. B.

Forsha, Elizabeth and Henry Kachney (1) - August 26, 1845

Fortney, I. H. and Mary C. Spangler (3) - May 21, 1868
Place of marriage, Jefferson County - Age of husband, 22 - Age of
wife, 19 - Both are Single - Husband was born at Washington, D. C. -
Wife was born in Jefferson County - Both reside in Jefferson
County - Wife's parents are Washington - Occupation of husband is
Telegraph Operator.

Fossett, Alexander and Elizabeth Little (1) - April 1825

Fossett, Alexander and Susan Penn (1) - March 24, 1832

Fossett, Elizabeth H. and F. J. Conrad (2) - (L) November 15, 1851

Fossett, Elizabeth H. and Fayette J. Conrad (1) - November 18, 1851

Fossett, G. W. and E. J. Crowl (bride) (3) - (1872)
Age of husband, 22 - Age of wife, 19 - Both are Single - Both were born in Jefferson County - Both reside in Jefferson County - Husband's parents are Alex and Susan - Wife's parents are G. W. and Ruth - Occupation of husband is Postmaster.

Fossett, George W. and Narcissa O'Laughlin (3) - November 18, 1890
Place of marriage, Bolivar - Age of husband, 41 - Age of wife, 36 - Husband is a Widower - Wife is Single - Husband was born in Jefferson County, West Virginia - Wife was born in Jefferson County - Both reside in Jefferson County, West Virginia.

Fossett, Martha and John M. Phillips (3) - November 11, 1869
For further information see - Phillips, John M.

Fossett, Sarah A. K. and Simeon H. Vanhorn (2) - (L) February 3, 1859

Fossett, Thomas and Sarah Ann McMullen (2) - (L) December 12, 1850

Foster, Seth B. and M. R. Bedinger (1) - December 11, 1808

Fouk, Margaret and Jacob Friend (1) - December 30, 1828

Fouke, Frederick and Harriet Guy (1) - April 6, 1813

Fouke, Margaret O. and James A. Brooks (2) - (L) (1862)
For further information see - Brooks, James A.

Fouke, Mary A. and Stephen Roberts (2) - (L) January 2, 1852

Foulk, Georgiana and Archie B. Anderson (3) - December 17, 1878
For further information see - Anderson, Archie B.

Foulke, E. V. (cold.) Henry C. Grayson (3) - April 2, 1874
For further information see - Grayson, Henry C.

Foulke, M. E. and Franklin Newberry (3) - September 11, 1867
For further information see - Newberry, Franklin.

Fountain, Bettie E. (cold.) Simon Walker (3) - May 25, 1866
For further information see - Walker, Simon.

Foussett, Isaac and Rebeca Brown (1) - 1812

Foutz, Carry L. and George B. Entler (3) - April 2, 1889
For further information see - Entler, George B.

Foutz, Eliza Jane and John J. Fraley (2) - (L) February 18, 1861

Foutz, Jackson and Margaret Ellen Snyder (2) - (L) May 14, 1860

Foutz, William J. and Mary Q. Hawn (3) - March 7, 1889
Place of marriage, near Shepherdstown - Age of husband, 26 - Age of wife, 26 - Both are Single - Both were born in Jefferson County, West Virginia - Both reside in Jefferson County, West Virginia.

Fowler, Charles H. and Mary Virginia Horn (3) - March 7, 1878
    Place of marriage, Brown's Crossing - Age of husband, 22 - Age of
    wife, 23 - Both are Single - Husband was born in Berkeley County,
    West Virginia - Wife was born in Jefferson County, West Virginia -
    Both reside in Jefferson County, West Virginia.

Fowler, Ida V. and Charles Man Custer (3) - October 21, 1880
    For further information see - Custer, Charles Man.

Fowler, Katy and Cassins Z. Brown (3) - February 16, 1888
    For further information see - Brown, Cassins Z.

Fowler, Mary Jane and John J. Ramsburg (2) - (L) April 20, 1857

Fowler, Samuel H. and Mary E. Evans (2) - (L) November 4, 1852

Fox, Alfred (cold.) Jemima Dixon (3) - November 12, 1881
    Place of marriage, Charlestown - Age of husband, 26 - Age of wife,
    20 - Both are Single - Husband was born in Loudoun County,
    Virginia - Wife was born in Jefferson County, West Virginia -
    Husband resides at Harrisburg, Pennsylvania - Wife resides in
    Jefferson County, West Virginia. (Consent of bride's father in
    person.)

Fox, Barbara and Branson Tharp (3) - January 18, 1888
    For further information see - Tharp, Branson.

Fox, Benjamin F. (cold.) Eliza Diah Pullett (3) - August 24, 1882
    Place of marriage, Shepherdstown - Age of husband, 34 - Age of wife,
    33 - Husband is Single - Wife is a Widow - Both were born in
    Jefferson County, West Virginia - Both reside in Jefferson County,
    West Virginia.

Fox, Ellen and John F. Tise (3) - January 21, 1880
    For further information see - Tise, John F.

Fox, Emma V. and Jacob L. Hoffman (3) - February 24, 1874
    For further information see - Hoffman, Jacob L.

Fox, George and Elizabeth Link (1) - August 9, 1807

Fox, Hannah (cold.) Cornelius Ridout (3) - October 10, 1890
    For further information see - Ridout, Cornelius.

Fox, Humphrey (cold.) Sarah Perry (3) - January 12, 1878
    Place of marriage, Middleway - Age of husband, 23 - Age of wife,
    18 - Both are Single - Husband was born in Jefferson County, West
    Virginia - Wife was born in Rockbridge County, Virginia - Both
    reside in Jefferson County, West Virginia.

Fox, Jacob and Gracy Jackson (3) - October 18, 1866
    Place of marriage, Dr. Mix, Jefferson County, West Virginia - Age of
    husband, 40 - Age of wife, 40 - Husband is Single - Wife is a
    Widow - Both were born in Jefferson County, West Virginia - Both
    reside in Jefferson County, West Virginia - Husband's parents are
    Jacob and Bettie Fox - Occupation of husband is Laborer.

Fox, Jemima and Jonathan J. Gladden (3) - August 1, 1866
    For further information see - Gladden, Jonathan J.

Fox, Jemima and H. Johnson Myers (3) - October 3, 1871
For further information see - Myers, H. Johnson.

Fox, John H. and Hannah Washington (3) - November 1866
Age of husband, 21 - Age of wife, 19.- Both are Single - Both were
born in Jefferson County, West Virginia - Both reside in Jefferson
County, West Virginia - Husband's parents are John and Elizabeth
Fox - Wife's parents are David and Nellie Washington - Occupation of
husband is Laborer.

Fox, John H. (cold.) Lucy Washington (3) - January 7, 1877
Place of marriage, Charles Town - Age of husband, 31 - Age of wife,
23 - Husband is a Widower - Wife is Single - Both were born in
Jefferson County, West Virginia - Both reside in Jefferson County,
West Virginia.

Fox, John W. (cold.) Ella Morton (3) - October 1, 1885
Place of marriage, Bolivar - Age of husband, 23 - Age of wife, 22 -
Both are Single - Husband was born in Jefferson County, West
Virginia - Wife was born in Jefferson County - Both reside in
Jefferson County.

Fox, Josiah (cold.) Mary Nourse (3) - January 19, 1888
Place of marriage, Bride's Residence - Age of husband, 32 - Age of
wife, 29 - Both are Single - Husband was born in Clarke County,
Virginia - Wife was born in Jefferson County, West Virginia - Both
reside in Jefferson County, West Virginia.

Fox, Larkin M. and Emma Rodefer (3) - October 28, 1886
Place of marriage, Charlestown - Age of husband, 33 - Age of wife,
27 - Both are Single - Husband was born in Warren County, Virginia -
Wife was born in Hardy County, Virginia - Husband resides in Clarke
County, Virginia - Wife resides in Jefferson County, West Virginia.

Fox, Lucinda (cold.) Charles Edward Roper (3) - May 11, 1886
For further information see - Roper, Charles Edward.

Fox, Mary and Samuel Taylor (3) - September 7, 1876
For further information see - Taylor, Samuel.

Fox, Nancy and David N. Huff (3) - June 9, 1889
For further information see - Huff, David N.

Fox, Susan (cold.) Philip Rust (3) - February 8, 1879
For further information see - Rust, Philip.

Frago, Eliza and Erasmus Beal (1) - 1825

Frait, George and Mary Shepherd (1) - June 4, 1804

Fraley, John and Nancy Dye (1) - November 24, 1816

Fraley, John J. and Eliza Jane Foutz (2) - (L) February 18, 1861

Fraley, Lettie and Mordecai H. Walker (2) - (L) November 24, 1855

Frame, Frances E. B. and Ambrose R. H. Ranson (2) - (L) October 12, 1854

Frame, Jane and Armsted Beckham (1) - January 22, 1818

Frame, Jane H. and William D. Beall (1) -   August 19, 1834

Frame, John (cold.) Amanda Washington (3) -   October 3, 1867
Place of marriage, Jefferson - Age of husband, 40 - Age of wife, 35 - Both are Single - Both were born in Jefferson County - Both reside in Jefferson County - Husband's parents are Susan - Occupation of husband is Barber. (cold.)

Frame, Mollie (cold.) Jacob Edwards (3) -   April 7, 1874
For further information see - Edwards, Jacob.

Frame, Rebeca Ann and Nathaniel Sergins (1) -   July 15, 1828

Francis, Susan and Thomas Turflinger (1) -   October 9, 1806

Frank, Henry and Hannah Young (1) -   April 21, 1824

Franklin, I. R. and Eliza D. Davis (3) -   October 29, 1867
Place of marriage, Jefferson County - Age of husband, 27 - Age of wife, 24 - Both are Single - Husband was born in Loudoun County - Wife was born in Jefferson County, Virginia - Husband resides in Loudoun County - Wife resides in Jefferson County - Husband's parents are B. Y. and M. - Wife's parents are M. N. - Occupation of husband is Gunteman.

Franklin, Ida E. and Harry G. Dooley (3) -   December 22, 1890
For further information see - Dooley, Harry G.

Franklin James (cold.) Mary Burns (3) -   December 26, 1876
Place of marriage, Ripon - Age of husband, 25 - Age of wife, 18 - Both are Single - Both were born in Clarke County, Virginia - Both reside in Jefferson County, West Virginia. (Consent of bride's father in person.)

Franklin, M. E. C. (bride) (cold.) J. R. Clifford (3) -   December 28, 1876
For further information see - Clifford, J. R.

Franklin, Philip (cold.) Emma Jane Johnson (3) -   January 1, 1880
Place of marriage, near Clarke Line at H. W. Cattleman's - Age of husband, 24 - Age of wife, 18 - Both are Single - Husband was born in Clarke County, Virginia - Wife was born in Jefferson County - Both reside in Jefferson County, West Virginia. (Consent of bride's mother certified by bride's brother.)

Franks, Henry Thornton and Elizabeth Stewart (2) -   (L) December 13, 1854

Frarey, Eliza and Joseph Hoffmaster (2) -   (L) October 14, 1858

Frasier, Thomas and Mary E. Burns (3) -   December 16, 1874
Place of marriage, County - Age of husband, 23 - Age of wife, 21 - Both are Single - Husband was born in Loudoun County, Virginia - Wife was born in Jefferson County, West Virginia - Husband resides in Loudoun County, Virginia - Wife resides in Jefferson County, West Virginia.

Frazer, Ann Rebecca and Samuel Butt (1) -   May 26, 1831

Frazier, Annie A. and William F. Sechrist (3) -   April 30, 1890
For further information see - Sechrist, William F.

Frazier, Elizabeth and William Sargent (1) - December 27, 1821

Frazier, Helen W. and John Q. Fleming (3) - January 31, 1878
For further information see - Fleming, John Q.

Frazier, James W. B. and Elizabeth R. Righstine (3) - March 22, 1866
Place of marriage, Shepherdstown, Jefferson County - Age of husband,
26 - Age of wife, 21 - Both are Single - Husband was born in
Berkeley County, Virginia - Wife was born in Jefferson County,
Virginia - Husband resides in Berkeley County, West Virginia - Wife
resides in Jefferson County, West Virginia - Husband's parents are
Thomas and Eliza Frazier - Wife's parents are Adam and Mary
Righstine - Occupation of husband is Fireman.

Frazier, Jonathan and Elizabeth Gruber (2) - (L) February 15, 1853

Frazier, Jonathan and Elizabeth Gruber (widow) (1) - February 15, 1853

Frazier, Mollie E. E. and William D. Payne (3) - September 7, 1875
For further information see - Payne, William D.

Frazier, Nancy (cold.) John Snyder (3) - February 16, 1882
For further information see - Snyder, John.

Frazier, William W. and Louisa Breedin (1) - January 28, 1817

Frederick, Susan and Christian Homer (2) - (L) April 12, 1852

Freeman, Alex (cold.) Julia V. Lovett (3) - June 3, 1889
Place of marriage, Harpers Ferry - Age of husband, 33 - Age of wife,
28 - Both are Single - Husband was born at Baltimore, Maryland -
Wife was born at Winchester, Virginia - Husband resides in New
York - Wife resides in Jefferson County, West Virginia.

Freeman, Fontaine (cold.) Elizabeth Moore (3) - March 8, 1877
Place of marriage, Bloomery - Age of husband, 24 - Age of wife, 22 -
Husband is a Widower - Wife is Single - Husband was born in
Jefferson County, West Virginia - Wife was born in Berkeley County,
West Virginia - Both reside in Jefferson County, West Virginia.

Freeman, George and Rebecca Baxter (3) - February 7, 1867
Place of marriage, Shepherdstown, Jefferson County - Age of husband,
25 - Age of wife, 35 - Both are Single - Husband was born in New
York - Wife was born in Maryland - Both reside in Maryland -
Husband's parents are George and Sarah Freeman - Wife's parents are
William and Catharine Baxter - Occupation of husband is Boatsman.

Freeman, Lula T. and Philip Vornes (3) - May 7, 1885
For further information see - Vornes, Philip.

Freeman, Martha (cold.) Horace Streams (3) - January 6, 1876
For further information see - Streams, Horace.

Freeman, Rachel and Oliver Timbers (3) - December 23, 1871
For further information see - Timbers, Oliver.

Freeman, William F. (cold.) Sally Washington (3) - December 25, 1873
Place of marriage, Charles Town - Age of husband, 25 - Age of wife,
22 - Both are Single - Both were born in Jefferson County, West
Virginia - Both reside in Jefferson County, West Virginia.

Freeze, Benjamin and Elizabeth Grant (1) -   December 28, 1833

Freeze, John W. and Mary E. Entler (3) -   November 20, 1866
Place of marriage, Shepherdstown, Jefferson County, West Virginia -
Age of husband, 22 - Age of wife, 19 - Both are Single - Husband was
born in Berkeley County, West Virginia - Wife was born in Jefferson
County, West Virginia - Both reside in Jefferson County, West
Virginia - Husband's parents are Benjamin F. and Mary E. Freeze -
Wife's parents are Philip A. and Sarah Entler - Occupation of
husband is Farmer.

Freeze, Margaret Ellen and Charles O. Lambert (2) -   (L) June 2, 1860

French, James H. and Mary E. House (2) -   (L) July 5, 1853

French, William C. H. and Mrs. Hannah V. Bird (3) -   November 25, 1875
Place of marriage, Harpers Ferry - Age of husband, 35 - Age of wife,
38 - Husband is Single - Wife is a Widow - Both were born in
Maryland - Both reside in Jefferson County, West Virginia.

Frese, Catharine and John T. Miller (2) -   (L) August 13, 1851

Frieland, Juliana and William McCarty (2) -   (L) May 16, 1859

Friend, Jacob and Margaret Fouk (1) -   December 30, 1828

Frier, Margaret and George W. Merchant (1) -   October 24, 1831

Frier, William H. and Hannah Faulkner (1) -   December 20, 1849

Friland, William and Sarah Metheny (1) -   April 8, 1819

Frischer, Mary E. and Jacob S. Best (3) -   February 26, 1885
For further information see - Best, Jacob S.

Frith, John William and Phebe Ann Dorsey (2) -   (L) March 14, 1859

Frith, Lewis and Alice M. Sagel (3) -   March 6, 1877
Place of marriage, Harpers Ferry - Age of husband, 28 - Age of wife,
21 - Both are Single - Husband was born in Maryland - Wife was born
in Jefferson County, West Virginia - Husband resides in State of
Illinois - Wife resides in Jefferson County, West Virginia.

Frith, Mary Ann and Edward B. Crim (2) -   (L) December 11, 1856

Frith, Sarah Jane and Samuel R. Emory (2) -   (L) July 27, 1858

Fritts, Franklin T. and Geneva Reed (3) -   June 12, 1881
Place of marriage, Harpers Ferry - Age of husband, 27 - Age of wife,
23 - Both are Single - Husband was born in Loudoun County,
Virginia - Wife was born in Jefferson County, West Virginia - Both
reside in Jefferson County, West Virginia.

Fritts, Mary Elizabeth and Joseph Duncan (2) -   (L) May 26, 1860

Fritts, William H. and Sarah E. Russell (3) -   March 23, 1875
Place of marriage, Charles Town - Age of husband, 34 - Age of wife,
22 - Both are Single - Husband was born in Loudoun County,
Virginia - Wife was born in Jefferson County, West Virginia - Both
reside in Jefferson County, West Virginia.

Fritz, Thomas J. and Harriet Ann Creamer (2) - (L) April 30, 1860

Froggatt, Mary and John Hoffer (2) - (L) October 11, 1853

Froggett, Mary and John Hofer (1) - October 13, 1853

Fry, Helen M. and John W. Miller (3) - March 9, 1871
    For further information see - Miller, John W.

Fry, Jessey and Jennie Hatfield (3) - March 5, 1873
    Place of marriage, Middleway - Age of husband, 28 - Age of wife,
    24 - Both are Single - Husband was born in Shenandoah County,
    Virginia - Wife was born in Rockingham - Both reside in Jefferson
    County, West Virginia - Husband's parents are Joseph and Elizabeth -
    Occupation of husband is Farmer.

Fry, Katy V. and Joseph T. Grantham (3) - March 8, 1876
    For further information see - Grantham, Joseph T.

Fry, L. E. (bride) and A. H. Tanquary (3) - April 2, 1867
    For further information see - Tanquary, A. H..

Fry, Lydia Ann and LaFayette Smith (2) - (L) September 6, 1858

Frye, Elizabeth and Lewis Fyser (1) - August 2, 1832

Fryer, John and Elizabeth Gaines (1) - February 14, 1805

Fryer, William N. and Mary H. Dugan (2) - (L) May 26, 1860

Fulk, Aaron and Eleanor Smurr (2) - (L) December 7, 1852

Fulk, Aaron and Eleanor Smurr (1) - December 7, 1852

Fulk, Benjamin F. and Gertrude V. Johnson (3) - February 12, 1885
    Place of marriage, Charlestown - Age of husband, 26 - Age of wife,
    25 - Both are Single - Husband was born in Jefferson County, West
    Virginia - Wife was born in Preston County, West Virginia - Husband
    resides in Berkeley County, West Virginia - Wife resides in
    Jefferson County, West Virginia.

Fulk, Eliza and Samuel Burns (1) - December 30, 1830

Fulk, Frederick A. and Hester Ann Thompson (2) - (L) December 19, 1854

Fulk, Henry Clay and Ann Elizabeth Martin (2) - (L) October 1, 1856

Fulk, James D. and Ellen Virginia Calvert (2) - (L) March 16, 1858

Fulk, William A. and Mary E. Entler (3) - May 31, 1887
    Place of marriage, Charlestown - Age of husband, 23 - Age of wife,
    23 - Both are Single - Both were born in Jefferson County, West
    Virginia - Both reside in Jefferson County, West Virginia.

Fuller, William McP. and Jane S. Macfarland (2) - (L) March 24, 1859

Fulton, Robert and Margaret T. Brown (1) - October 27, 1807

Furey, Martin L. and Mary C. Henry (3) - March 28, 1871
  Place of marriage, Jefferson County - Age of husband, 28 - Age of wife, 27 - Both are Single - Both were born in Jefferson County - Both reside in Jefferson County - Husband's parents are Henry and Rebecca - Wife's parents are Philip and Mary Ann - Occupation of husband is Farmer.

Furl, Mary and Henry Allen (3) - December 10, 1874
  For further information see - Allen, Henry.

Furlong, Elisa and Abraham Whiting (3) - November 19, 1868
  For further information see - Whiting, Abraham

Furman, David and Matilda Smith (1) - January 17, 1819

Furr, Charles C. and May P. VanLear (3) - July 4, 1889
  Place of marriage, Harpers Ferry - Age of husband, 28 - Age of wife, 23 - Both are Single - Husband was born in Augusta County, Virginia - Wife was born in Jefferson County, West Virginia - Husband resides in Augusta County, Virginia - Wife resides in Jefferson County, West Virginia.

Furr, James Henry (cold.) Tiny Williams (3) - April 29, 1886
  Place of marriage, Shepherdstown - Age of husband, 23 - Age of wife, 25 - Both are Single - Husband was born in Page County, Virginia - Wife was born in Jefferson County, West Virginia - Both reside in Jefferson County, West Virginia.

Furr, Mary E. and Samuel Riley (3) - November 9, 1880
  For further information see - Riley, Samuel.

Furr, W. L. and R. V. Grant (bride) (3) - December 23, 1874
  Place of marriage, Shepherdstown - Age of husband, 27 - Age of wife, 21 - Both are Single - Husband was born in Clarke County, Virginia - Wife was born in Jefferson County, West Virginia - Both reside in Jefferson County, West Virginia.

Furr, William and Lydia Barr (3) - March 20, 1888
  Place of marriage, Charlestown - Age of husband, 29 - Age of wife, 21 - Husband is Single - Wife is a Widow - Both were born in Clarke County, Virginia - Both reside in Jefferson County, West Virginia.

Furtney, C. E. (bride) and S. W. Geary (3) - February 27, 1889
  For further information see - Geary, S. W.

Furtney, Mary E. and George R. Brady (3) - July 9, 1881
  For further information see - Brady, George R.

Fydinger, Alberta and John J. Wooddy (3) - January 24, 1883
  For further information see - Wooddy, John J.

Fyser, Lewis and Elizabeth Frye (1) - August 2, 1832

Ga, Nathan (cold.) Charity McDanel (3) - October 27, 1881
    Place of marriage, Charlestown - Age of husband, 21 - Age of wife,
    20 - Both are Single - Husband was born in White Hill County, South
    Carolina - Wife was born in Jefferson County, West Virginia - Both
    reside in Jefferson County, West Virginia. (Consent of bride's
    mother in person.)

Gabriel, Mary Elizabeth and Daniel Burket (3) - December 25, 1873
    For further information see - Burket, Daniel.

Gaehle, Carrie L. and William S. Buracker (3) - August 25, 1889
    For further information see - Buracker, William S.

Gageby, Maggie and Charles W. Hill (3) - January 25, 1888
    For further information see - Hill, Charles W.

Gageby, Mary E. and W. I. Bradfield (3) - April 6, 1887
    For further information see - Bradfield, W. I.

Gageby, Sarah V. and John G. Boyer (3) - (L) December 27, 1881
    For further information see - Boyer, John G.

Gageby, William F. and Anna E. Brown (2) - (L) March 22, 1860

Gain, E. C. and S. C. Ogden (bride) (3) - April 7, 1868
    Place of marriage, Jefferson County - Age of husband, 19 - Age of
    wife, 20 - Both are Single - Husband was born in Berkeley - Wife was
    born in Jefferson - Both reside in Jefferson County - Husband's
    parents are Christ and Lydia - Wife's parents are Ann - Occupation
    of husband is Farmer. (Permission given by parents.)

Gaines, Absolom and Elonor Ridgeway (1) - March 30, 1806

Gaines, Benjamin and Sarah Smithey (1) - August 16, 1818

Gaines, Clarianna and Zachariah Riley (1) - September 13, 1827

Gaines, Elizabeth and John Fryer (1) - February 14, 1805

Gains, Virginia and John Price (2) - (L) December 23, 1863
    For further information see - Price, John.

Gaiter, Lucy (nee Brandon)(cold.) Arthur Lomax (3) - January 11, 1883
    For further information see - Lomax, Arthur.

Gaiter, Martha (cold.) Henry Coles (3) - July 30, 1885
    For further information see - Coles, Henry.

Galihar, Caroline M. S. and John Fisher (1) - 1822

Gallagher, Mary and Joseph Kelly (3) - August 10, 1868
    For further information see - Kelly, Joseph.

Gallaher, Annie and Thomas Winston (3) - September 28, 1887
    For further information see - Winston, Thomas.

Gallaher, Annie E. and M. S. Brown (3) - November 26, 1867
    For further information see - Brown, M. S.

Gallaher, C. Frank and Mary J. Beall (3) -   June 28, 1871
   Place of marriage, Jefferson County - Age of husband, 28 - Age of
   wife, 28.- Both are Single - Husband was born in Virginia - Wife was
   born in Jefferson County - Both reside in Jefferson County -
   Husband's parents are John.W. and Mary - Wife's parents are Thomas
   and Louisa - Occupation of husband is Plasterer.

Gallaher, C. Horace and Fannie Shep Sappington (3) -   October 23, 1872
   Place of marriage, Jefferson County - Age of husband, 33 - Age of
   wife, 27 - Both are Single - Husband was born in Jefferson County -
   Husband resides in Jefferson County - Husband's parents are Horatio
   N. and Adeline - Occupation of husband is Express Agent.

Gallaher, Celestine and John N. Whitington (3) -   November 27, 1867
   For further information see - Whitington, John N.

Gallaher, Edward A. and Sarah N. Carter (2) -   (L) December 16, 1856

Gallaher, Horatio N. and Adaline B. Hayden (1) -   September 2, 1830

Gallaher, Mary J. C. and William C. Lipscomb (1) -   February 21, 1850

Gallaher, Mary W. and Michael S. Weller (3) -   December 24, 1868
   For further information see - Weller, Michael S.

Gallaher, Mattie and Ed. Haas (3) -   January 28, 1875
   For further information see - Haas, Ed.

Gallaher, Nannie E. and Thomas K. Starry (2) -   (L) March 11, 1852

Gallaher, Nannie E. and Thomas K. Starry (1) -   March 11, 1852

Gallaher, William R. and Frances Amelia Briscoe (2) -   (L) August 6, 1864
   Time of marriage, August 8, 1864 - Place of marriage, Woodbury,
   Jefferson County, Virginia - Names, William R. Gallaher and Frances
   Amelia Briscoe - Age of husband, - Age of wife, - Both are Single -
   Place of husband's birth, - Place of wife's birth, Jefferson County,
   Virginia - Place of husband's residence is Waynesborough, Augusta
   County, Virginia - Place of wife's residence is Jefferson County,
   Virginia - Names of husband's parents are Hugh L. and   ?
   Gallaher - Names of wife's parents are Thomas and Juliet W.
   Briscoe - Occupation of husband is   - License issued, August 6, 1864.

Galloway, Benjamin (cold.) Cecelia Deppen (3) -   January 23, 1890
   Place of marriage, Charlestown - Age of husband, 60 - Age of wife,
   40 - Husband is a Widower - Wife is a Widow - Husband was born in
   Jefferson County, West Virginia - Wife was born in Maryland - Both
   reside in Jefferson County, West Virginia.

Galloway, John (cold.) Julia Green (3) -   August 29, 1878
   Place of marriage, Charlestown - Age of husband, 25 - Age of wife,
   36 - Both are Single - Both were born in Jefferson County, West
   Virginia - Both reside in Jefferson County, West Virginia.

Galloway, Lucy and Edward Washington (3) -   March 23, 1871
   For further information see - Washington, Edward.

Galloway, Mary (cold.) Frank Mitchell (3) -   April 1, 1884
   For further information see - Mitchell, Frank.

Galloway, Matilda (cold.) George Colston (3) -   December 11, 1884
    For further information see - Colston, George.

Galloway, Samuel (cold.) Lizzy Reed (3) -   October 5, 1876
    Place of marriage, Charlestown - Age of husband, 27 - Age of wife,
    22 - Both are Single - Both were born in Jefferson County, West
    Virginia - Both reside in Jefferson County, West Virginia.

Galton, Ann and Samuel Greenwalt (2) -   (L) August 27, 1860

Gamil, Belle and Crast Swain (3) -   January 28, 1885
    For further information see - Swain, Crast.

Gannon, Emma and Gabriel L. Myers (3) -   February 15, 1872
    For further information see - Myers, Gabriel L.

Gannon, Molly and B. F. Rodeffer (3) -   February 17, 1881
    For further information see - Rodeffer, B. F.

Gannon, Sarah and Solomon Buckles (1) -   1819

Gannon, William and Lucinda Baylis (1) -   October 29, 1814

Gannt, Mary Jane and William W. Palmer (2) -   (L) April 4, 1851

Gano, John M. and Sarah E. Lancaster (2) -   (L) August 4, 1859

Gant, Charles R. and Annie Kelley (3) -   April 27, 1872
    Place of marriage, Jefferson County - Age of husband, 24 - Age of
    wife, 22 - Both are Single - Husband was born in Maryland - Wife was
    born in Pennsylvania - Both reside in Jefferson County, West
    Virginia - Husband's parents are William and Ann M. - Occupation of
    husband is Farmer.

Garber, Jacob A. and Nannie C. Roof (3) -   January 25, 1888
    Place of marriage, Harpers Ferry - Age of husband, 24 - Age of wife,
    22 - Both are Single - Husband was born in Berkeley County - Wife
    was born in Jefferson County - Both reside in Jefferson County, West
    Virginia.

Gardener, Garvis S. and Margaret Hains (1) -   May 31, 1832

Gardener, Violet P. and John Mayers (1) -   August 3, 1824

Gardner, Ann Rebecca and John C. Hunter (2) -   (L) August 24, 1854

Gardner, Barbara and Frederick Reek (2) -   (L) September 15, 1857

Gardner, C. H. and Frances Reeler (3) -   January 9, 1869
    Place of marriage, Jefferson County - Age of husband, 30 - Age of
    wife, 20 - Both are Single - Husband was born in Massachusetts -
    Wife was born in Jefferson County - Both reside in Jefferson
    County - Husband's parents are Charles and Elizabeth - Wife's
    parents are James and Catherine - Occupation of husband is Teacher.
    (Father consents in writing.)

Gardner, Fanny and Jacob Waters (3) -   September 24, 1877
    For further information see - Waters, Jacob.

Gardner, Frances M. and Thomas C. Trussell (2) -   (L) January 26, 1857

Gardner, Frank H. and Nannie E. Hess (3) - February 24, 1874
  Place of marriage, near Harpers Ferry - Age of husband, 26 - Age of
  wife, 24 - Both are Single - Both were born in Jefferson County,
  West Virginia - Both reside in Jefferson County, West Virginia.

Gardner, J. P. and Joanna Hammer (3) - August 25, 1874
  Place of marriage, Bolivar - Age of husband, 28 - Age of wife, 18 -
  Both are Single - Husband was born in Frederick County, Maryland -
  Wife was born in Jefferson County, West Virginia - Both reside in
  Jefferson County, West Virginia. (Consent of bride's father in
  writing.)

Gardner, James and Anna M. House (3) - February 20, 1886
  Place of marriage, Harpers Ferry - Age of husband, 34 - Age of wife,
  27 - Both are Single - Both were born in Jefferson County, West
  Virginia - Husband resides in Washington County, Maryland - Wife
  resides in Jefferson County, West Virginia.

Gardner, John W. and Mary R. Brown (1) - May 14, 1850

Gardner, John W. and Sarah Jane Ott (3) - May 24, 1880
  Place of marriage, Charlestown - Age of husband, 55 - Age of wife,
  20 - Husband is a Widower - Wife is Single - Both were born in
  Jefferson County, West Virginia - Both reside in Jefferson County,
  West Virginia. (Consent of bride's father in person.)

Gardner, Joseph and Mary Elizabeth Chapman (2) - (L) December 13, 1855

Gardner, Mary Ann and John Hall Allstadt (1) - February 16, 1837

Gardner, Mary G. and Thomas K. Laley (2) - (L) December 19, 1853
  (Consent of Miss Gardner's mother proved by the oath of John S.
  Hunter and Mrs. Gardner's handwriting.)

Gardner, Sarah Ann and Samuel Young (1) - June 25, 1829

Gardner, William and Nancy Murphy (1) - February 3, 1819

Garnett, Julia DeC. and Thomas Ashton (3) - December 5, 1876
  For further information see - Ashton, Thomas.

Garney, James William and Mary M. Wooddy (3) - September 7, 1876
  Place of marriage, Charlestown - Age of husband, 27 - Age of wife,
  23 - Both are Single - Husband was born in Jefferson County, West
  Virginia - Wife was born in Loudoun County, Virginia - Both reside
  in Jefferson County, West Virginia.

Garney, Mary B. and Charles W. Smith (3) - January 12, 1882
  For further information see - Smith, Charles W.

Garnhart, Henry and Sarah Showman (1) - March 10, 1825

Garnhart, Mary Ann and Robert Ridenhour (1) - February 27, 1817

Garnhart, Susan and Daniel Allstadt (1) - April 27, 1808

Garrett, Clinton and Ida Cowley (3) - August 10, 1875
    Place of marriage, Charles Town - Age of husband, 22 - Age of wife,
    22 - Both are Single - Husband was born in Warren County, Virginia -
    Wife was born in Jefferson County, West Virginia - Both reside in
    Jefferson County, West Virginia.

Garrett, Mary B. and James W. Campbell (3) - February 15, 1877
    For further information see - Campbell, James W.

Garrett, Oliver J. and Catharine Ward (2) - (L) February 9, 1853

Garrison, Edward and Catharine Kelly (2) - (L) June 19, 1858

Garrison, Lewis S. and Catharine Snyder (1) - April 25, 1850

Garrison, Lewis J. and Margaret Winebrenner (2) - (L) June 24, 1858

Garrison, Louisa and Rev. Thomas Littleton (1) - December 17, 1818

Garrison, T. M. and Virginia G. Hessey (3) - December 30, 1874
    Place of marriage, Charles Town - Age of husband, 28 - Age of wife,
    21 - Both are Single - Husband was born in New Jersey - Wife was
    born in Jefferson County, West Virginia - Husband resides in State
    of Ohio - Wife resides in Jefferson County, West Virginia.

Garrison, Thomas J. and Viola Monegan (3) - December 15, 1885
    Place of marriage, Charlestown - Age of husband 23 - Age of wife,
    21 - Both are Single - Both were born in Jefferson County, West
    Virginia - Both reside in Jefferson County, West Virginia.

Garrott, A. F. and Mary Virginia Henkle (3) - December 9, 1880
    Place of marriage, near Unionville - Age of husband, 36 - Age of
    wife, 30 - Both are Single - Husband was born in Maryland - Wife was
    born in Jefferson County, West Virginia - Husband resides in
    Maryland - Wife resides in Jefferson County, West Virginia.

Garrott, R. T. B. and Lydia M. Atkinson (3) - November 10, 1870
    Place of marriage, Jefferson County - Age of husband, 30 - Age of
    wife, 22 - Husband was born in Maryland - Wife was born in Jefferson
    County - Husband resides in Maryland - Wife resides in West Virginia.

Garthier, Jerry (col.) Lucy Lucklet (3) - January 4, 1868
    Age of husband, 38 - Age of wife, 36 - Husband is Single - Wife is a
    Widow - Husband was born in Maryland - Wife was born in Jefferson
    County, West Virginia - Both reside in Jefferson County - Occupation
    of husband is Blacksmith.

Gartrell, Richard and Maria V. Kearney (1) - September 9, 1819

Gary, Leroy and Elizabeth Wiltsher (1) - January 11, 1846

Gary, Patrick M. and Sarah Elizabeth Johnson (2) - (L) October 26, 1852

Gaskins, Alfred and Eleanor Davenport (1) - June 7, 1827

Gaster, John Shafer and Margaret Eliza Schoppertt (3) - February 12, 1880
    Place of marriage, Shepherdstown - Age of husband, 36 - Age of wife,
    28 - Husband is Single - Wife is a Widow - Husband was born at
    Hagerstown, Maryland - Wife was born in Jefferson County, West
    Virginia - Husband resides at Alexahdria, Virginia - Wife resides in
    Jefferson County, West Virginia.

Gates, Ambrose (cold.) Emily Herbert (3) - December 28, 1875
Place of marriage, near Charlestown - Age of husband, 21 - Age of wife, 22 - Both are Single - Both were born in Jefferson County, West Virginia - Both reside in Jefferson County, West Virginia.

Gatrell, Harriet E. and William H. Helferstay (2) - (L) January 24, 1863
For further information see - Helferstay, William H.

Gatrell, Mary Ellen and Donly Turner (2) - (L) April 17, 1858

Gatrell, Shepherd and Maggie Beck (3) - March 4, 1873
Place of marriage, Charles Town - Age of husband, 22 - Age of wife, 19 - Both are Single - Both were born in Jefferson County, West Virginia - Husband resides in Berkeley County, West Virginia - Wife resides in Jefferson County, West Virginia - Wife's parents are John and Elizabeth - Occupation of husband is Miller. (Father's consent in writing.)

Gaul, Ainsey (cold.) Phil. Andrew Chase (3) - October 19, 1889
For further information see - Chase, Phil. Andrew.

Gaul, David (cold.) Ailsie Thomas (3) - January 18, 1882
Place of marriage, Summit Point - Age of husband, 28 - Age of wife, 25 - Both are Single - Both were born in Jefferson County, West Virginia - Both reside in Jefferson County, West Virginia.

Gaunters, Rebecca and Daniel Folk (1) - 1826

Gay, James and Elizabeth Armstrong (3) - July 27, 1865
Place of marriage, Jefferson County - Age of husband, 40 years - Age of wife, 40 years - Husband is Single - Wife is a Widow - Husband was born in Washington County, Maryland - Wife was born in Jefferson County, West Virginia - Both reside in Jefferson County - Husband's parents are John and Elizabeth Gay - Wife's parents are John and Nancie Fraley - Occupation of husband is Farmer.

Gay, Maria Jane (cold.) Charles A. Ross (3) - September 8, 1886
For further information see - Ross, Charles A.

Gay, Nathan (cold.) Fanny Hays (3) - July 8, 1886
Place of marriage, Charlestown - Age of husband, 26 - Age of wife, 21 - Husband is a Widower by divorce - Wife is Single - Husband was born in North Carolina - Wife was born in Jefferson County, West Virginia - Husband resides in Jefferson County - Wife resides in Jefferson County, West Virginia.

Gaynor, Patrick and Ann E. McCarty (nee Jenkins) (3) - April 27, 1873
Place of marriage, Harpers Ferry - Age of husband, 30 - Age of wife, 37 - Husband is Single - Wife is a Widow - Husband was born at Tipperary, Ireland - Wife was born in Loudoun County, Virginia - Both reside in Loudoun County, Virginia - Husband's parents are James and Alice - Wife's parents are Reuben and Ella J. Jenkins - Occupation of husband is Stone Mason.

Geary, S. W. and C. E. Furtney (bride) (3) - February 27, 1889
Place of marriage, Harpers Ferry - Age of husband, 28 - Age of wife, 24 - Both are Single - Husband was born at. Martinsburg, West Virginia - Wife was born in Loudoun County, Virginia - Both reside in Jefferson County, West Virginia.

Geasland, Harrison and Emily Hoffmaster (2) -   (L) November 17, 1860

Geaslen, Sarah Ellen and James Henry Griffith (3) -   October 27, 1887
   For further information see - Griffith, James Henry.

George, John S. and Eliza A. Merrick (2) -   (L) November 12, 1859

Gerling, Katie and George Callahan (3) -   February 9, 1888
   For further information see - Callahan, George.

Gerstell, Eugene H. and Ida M. Fleming (3) -   March 3, 1885
   Place of marriage, Shepherdstown - Age of husband, 27 - Age of wife,
   25 - Both are Single - Husband was born in Mineral County, West
   Virginia - Wife was born in Jefferson County, West Virginia -
   Husband resides in Mineral County, West Virginia - Wife resides in
   Jefferson County, West Virginia.

Getzendanner, Clara C. and Daniel M. Border (3) -   March 24, 1880
   For further information see - Border, Daniel M.

Getzendanner, Harrison and Fannie E. Myers (3) -   February 14, 1878
   Place of marriage, near Middleway - Age of husband, 37 - Age of
   wife, 28 - Both are Single - Husband was born in Maryland - Wife was
   born in Jefferson County, West Virginia - Husband resides in
   Missouri - Wife resides in Jefferson County, West Virginia.

Getzendanner, Harry C. and Anna J. Morgan (3) -   November 28, 1882
   Place of marriage, near Shepherdstown - Age of husband, 21 - Age of
   wife, 21 - Both are Single - Husband was born at Frederick City,
   Maryland - Wife was born in Jefferson County, West Virginia - Both
   reside in Jefferson County, West Virginia.

Getzendanner, Laura V. and Nelson Dhiel (3) -   February 1, 1870
   For further information see - Dhiel, Nelson.

Gibbon, Sarah Hall and Clement R. Davis (1) -   April 4, 1820

Gibboney, Emanuel C. F. and Lidia Bellar (1) -   August 1, 1816

Gibbons, A. H. and James H. Kerney (1) -   January 21, 1813

Gibbons, Elizabeth Emma and Benjamin Tomlinson (1) -   March 1, 1832

Gibbons, Gilbert and Sarah H. Offutt (1) -   July 26, 1805

Gibbs, William and Francis Ranson (1) -   June 18, 1807

Gibson, Eliza (free cold.) Rodney Warwick (2) -   (L) April 6, 1863
   For further information see - Warwick, Rodney.

Gibson, Georgia (cold.) Basil Clinton (3) -   December 25, 1884
   For further information see. - Clinton, Basil.

Gibson, John T., Jr. and Bettie T. Moore (3) -   December 13, 1877
   Place of marriage, near Charlestown - Age of husband, 29 - Age of
   wife, 27 - Both are Single - Both were born in Jefferson County,
   West Virginia - Both reside in Jefferson County, West Virginia.

Gibson, John Thomas and Fannie Davenport (2) -   (L) May 9, 1855

Gibson, John W. and Mary Elizabeth Trussell (2) - (L) January 11, 1865
Time of marriage, January 17, 1865 - Place of marriage, Bride's Father's Residence - Names, John W. Gibson and Mary Elizabeth Trussell - Age of husband, 24 years - Age of wife, 26 years - Both are Single - Husband was born in Loudoun County, Virginia - Wife was born in Jefferson County, Virginia - Both reside in Jefferson County, Virginia - Husband's parents are Phineas and Harriet Gibson - Wife's parents are Bayliss and Angelina Trussell - Occupation of husband is Farmer - License issued, January 11, 1865 - T. A. Moore, Clerk.

Gibson, Margaret and Eli H. Carrell (1) -   July 30, 1834

Gibson, Samuel (colored) Frances Thornton (3) -   February 9, 1867
Place of marriage, Benjamin Timberlake's - Age of husband, 25 - Age of wife, 16 - Both are Single - Both were born in Madison County, Virginia - Both reside in Jefferson County - Husband's parents are Allen and Rachel Gibson - Wife's parents are Squire and Nancy Thornton - Occupation of husband is Farmer. (Brother's permission.)

Gibson, Solomon (cold.) Ann Redman (3) -   August 20, 1874
Place of marriage, at or near Charles Town - Age of husband, 23 - Age of wife, 21 - Both are Single - Husband was born in Clarke County, Virginia - Wife was born in Warren County, Virginia - Both reside in Jefferson County, West Virginia.

Gibson, Sue H. and Charles H. Kemper (3) -   December 13, 1876
For further information see - Kemper, Charles H.

Giddy, John H. and Lucy M. Potts (3) -   January 25, 1888
Place of marriage, Harpers Ferry - Age of husband, 44 - Age of wife, 25 - Husband is a Widower by divorce - Wife is Single - Husband was born in Jefferson County, West Virginia - Wife was born in Allegheny County, Maryland - Both reside in Jefferson County, West Virginia.

Gidin, William and Elizabeth Strong Blackborn (1) -   January 15, 1818

Gilbert, Berdie L. and T. A. Milton (3) -   March 13, 1889
For further information see - Milton, T. A.

Gilbert, Catharine and David Ogden (1) -   April 19, 1831

Gilbert, Elizabeth and Charles H. Isler (3) -   September 15, 1886
For further information see - Isler, Charles H.

Gilbert Helen and John Lewis (3) -   December 24, 1866
For further information see - Lewis, John.

Gilbert, John J. and Rose Grantham (3) -   June 2, 1875
Place of marriage, Middleway - Age of husband, 30 - Age of wife, 25 - Both are Single - Husband was born in Berkeley County, West Virginia - Wife was born in Jefferson County, West Virginia - Both reside in Jefferson County, West Virginia.

Gilbert, Mary Ann and Francis Joseph Harley (1) -   August 18, 1825

Gilbert, Mollie and Charles J. Seibert (3) -   July 7, 1885
For further information see - Seibert, Charles J.

Gilbert, W. H. and Lillie Grantham (3) -   December 10, 1885
    Place of marriage, Middleway - Age of husband, 28 - Age of wife,
    26 - Both are Single - Both were born in Jefferson County, West
    Virginia - Husband resides at Baltimore City - Wife resides in
    Jefferson County, West Virginia.

Gill, Andrew J. and Sarah D. A. Young (3) -   November 16, 1869
    Place of marriage, Jefferson County - Age of husband, 24 - Age of
    wife, 29 - Husband was born in Virginia - Wife was born in Jefferson
    County - Both reside in Jefferson County.

Gill, Sarah and John Turner (1) -   February 19, 1818

Gillaspie, Thomas C. and Elizabeth Lambaugh (1) -   September 10, 1848

Gillispie, Martha and Lewis Herring (1) -   April 7, 1818

Gilmore, Thomas W. and Ann C. Baker (1) -   May 23, 1826

Ginter, Adam and Bettie Vint (3) -   February 5, 1878
    Place of marriage, Charlestown - Age of husband, 48 - Age of wife,
    36 - Husband is Single - Wife is a Widow - Both were born in York
    County, Pennsylvania - Husband resides in York County,
    Pennsylvania - Wife resides in Jefferson County, West Virginia.

Gittings, Henry N. and C. R. Godfrey (nee Barnard) (2) -   (L) May 31, 1861
    Time of marriage, May 31, 1861 - Place of marriage, Charlestown,
    Jefferson County, Virginia - Age of husband, 35 years - Age of wife,
    38 years - Husband is a Widower - Wife is a Widow - Husband was born
    in Baltimore County, Maryland - Wife was born at Schenectady, New
    York - Both now living in Jefferson County, Virginia - Names of
    husband's parents are James C. and Rebecca N. Giddings - Names of
    wife's parents are John and   ?   - Occupation of husband is
    Soldier in Confederate Army - Henry N. Gittings.

Gittings, Jeremiah and Sarah Priscilla Chipley (1) -   December 24, 1816

Gladden, Jonathan J. and Jemima Fox (3) -   August 1, 1866
    Place of marriage, Harpers Ferry, Jefferson County, West Virginia -
    Age of husband, 22 - Age of wife, 30 - Both are Single - Husband was
    born in Rockingham County, Virginia - Wife was born in Loudoun
    County, Virginia - Husband resides in Rockingham County, Virginia -
    Wife resides at Bolivar, Jefferson County, West Virginia - Husband's
    parents are William and Hannah Gladden - Wife's parents are James
    Fox and Sallie Brady - Occupation of husband is Farmer.

Glaize, E. D. and Albina Robertson (3) -   March 27, 1873
    Place of marriage, Charlestown - Age of husband, 21 - Age of wife,
    21 - Both are Single - Husband was born in Frederick County,
    Virginia - Wife was born in Jefferson County, West Virginia - Both
    reside in Jefferson County, West Virginia - Husband's parents are
    George and S. A. Glaize - Wife's parents are M. S. B. and A. C.
    Robertson - Occupation of husband is Laborer.

Glasford, Elizabeth and James McClure (1) -   November 22, 1832

Glasford, H. and S. A. Moler (bride) (3) -   December 21, 1871
    Place of marriage, Jefferson County - Age of husband, 25 - Age of
    wife, 20 - Both are Single - Occupation of husband is Farmer.

Glasford, Mary Louisa and Charles F. Baringer (2) -   (L) April 16, 1860

Glass, George and Ann Katharine Baker (3) -   September 27, 1881
Place of marriage, Martinsburg, Berkeley County, West Virginia - Age of husband, 37 - Age of wife, 38 - Husband is a Widower - Wife is Single - Husband was born in Clarke County, Virginia - Wife was born in Washington County, Maryland - Husband resides in Clarke County, Virginia - Wife resides in Jefferson County, West Virginia - Husband's parents are Lewis F. and Mary M. Glass - Wife's parents are Elias and Mary Baker - Occupation of husband is Deputy Clerk of County and Circut Courts, Clarke County, Virginia.

Glass, Samuel and Elizabeth Johnson (1) -   April 13, 1809

Glasscock, Benjamin P. and Lucinda McEndree (1) -   April 10, 1832

Glassford, William A. and Margaret E. Keyes (3) -   October 19, 1865
Place of marriage, Charlestown, Jefferson County, West Virginia - Age of husband, 26 years - Age of wife, 22 years - Both are Single - Husband was born at Smithfield, Jefferson County, West Virginia - Wife was born near Rippon, Jefferson County, West Virginia - Both reside near Rippon, Jefferson County - Husband's parents are James Glassford and Jane Glassford - Wife's parents are Joseph and Mary J. Keyes - Occupation of husband is Farmer.

Glasson, Mary and Sezel Morris (3) -   June 11, 1867
For further information see - Morris, Sezel.

Glenn, F. V. and Olin Beall (3) -   October 24, 1882
For further information see - Beall, Olin.

Glenn, Lillie B. and Adial P. Barnes (3) -   June 6, 1883
For further information see - Barnes, Adial P.

Glessner, John Z. and Henrietta M. Young (1) -   May 1, 1832

Glogen, H. B. and Rachael Hobbs (3) -   October 22, 1867
Place of marriage, Jefferson County - Age of husband, 26 - Age of wife, 28 - Husband is Single - Wife is a Widow - Husband was born in Michigan - Wife was born in Maryland - Both reside at Harpers Ferry - Husband's parents are Michael and May - Wife's parents are Rachael - Occupation of husband is Machinist.

Glow, John (cold.) Annie Henderson (3) -   March 9, 1889
Place of marriage, Charlestown - Age of husband, 23 - Age of wife, 22 - Both are Single - Husband was born in Madison County, Virginia - Wife was born in Loudoun County, Virginia - Both reside in Jefferson County, West Virginia.

Godfrey, C. R. (nee Barnard) and Henry N. Gittings (2) -   (L) May 31, 1861
For further information see - Gittings, Henry N.

Goens, C. H. and L. V. Roper (bride) (3) -   November 19, 1868
Place of marriage, Jefferson County - Age of husband, 24 - Age of wife, 19 - Both are Single - Both were born in Jefferson County - Both reside in Jefferson County - Husband's parents are L. and Sarah - Wife's parents are Osburn and Louise - Occupation of husband is Farmer.   (Parent consents.)

Goens, William (cold.) Hatty Washington (3) -   May 26, 1886
    Place of marriage, Kearneysville - Age of husband, 24 - Age of wife,
    21 - Both are Single - Both were born in Jefferson County, West
    Virginia - Both reside in Jefferson County, West Virginia.

Goings, Harriet and Joseph Hill (1) -   January 30, 1806

Goings, Henry (free mixtures) Elizabeth Hart (1) -   November 26, 1826

Goings, John H. (cold.) Edmonia McCard (3) -   December 15, 1885
    Place of marriage, Ripon - Age of husband, 45 - Age of wife, 26 -
    Husband is a Widower - Wife is Single - Both were born in Jefferson
    County, West Virginia - Both reside in Jefferson County, West
    Virginia.

Goings, Lucy and T. Brannam (3) -   April 4, 1872
    For further information see - Brannam, T.

Goings, Tom (free negroes) Margaret Alexander (2) -   (L) March 29, 1852

Goins, Fanny (free colored) James Douglas (2) -   (L) June 13, 1860

Goins, John and Sarah McDaniel (3) -   December 28, 1871
    Place of marriage, Jefferson County - Age of husband, 34 - Age of
    wife, 27 - Both are Single - Both were born in Jefferson County -
    Husband resides in Jefferson - Wife resides in Jefferson County -
    Husband's parents are Thomas and Theresa - Wife's parents are George
    and Ellen - Occupation of husband is Farmer.

Goins, Joseph (cold.) Lucy Sims (3) -   January 23, 1873
    Place of marriage, near Kabletown - Age of husband is 27 next
    August - Age of wife, 24 - Both are Single - Both were born in
    Jefferson County, West Virginia - Both reside in Jefferson County,
    West Virginia - Husband's parents are Lawson and Sarah - Wife's
    parents are, mother Eliza - Occupation of husband is Farmer.

Goins, Sarah and William H. Roper (3) -   July 14, 1873
    For further information see - Roper, William H.

Goins, William (free colored) Martha Johnson (2) -   (L) February 23, 1863
    Time of marriage, Thursday, February 26, 1863 - Place of marriage,
    Charlestown - Names, William Goins and Martha Johnson (free
    colored) - Age of husband, 29 years the 4th of next March - Age of
    wife, 35 years - Both are Single - Both were born in this County -
    Both live in this County- Names of husband's parents, Lawson and
    Sally Goins - Names of wife's mother, Kitty - Occupation of husband
    is Farm Hand - License issued, February 23, 1863 - Thomas A. Moore,
    Clerk.

Golden, Joseph and Sarah Scarlet (3) -   November 15, 1865
    Place of marriage, Harpers Ferry, West Virginia - Age of husband,
    27 - Age of wife, 21 - Both are Single - Husband was born at
    Philadelphia, Pennsylvania - Wife was born in Loudoun County,
    Virginia - Both reside at Harpers Ferry, West Virginia - Husband's
    parents are Joseph and Ellen Golden - Wife's parents are Eliza
    Scarlet - Occupation of husband is Farmer.

Goldsbary, Van and Ruth Davis (1) -   July 28, 1825

Goldsboro, Mary and Thomas H. Jackson (3) - November 10, 1890
    For further information see - Jackson, Thomas H.

Goldsborough, Charles W. and Henrietta E. Lee (3) - November 7, 1865
    Place of marriage, Shepherdstown - Age of husband, 24 - Age of wife,
    22 - Both are Single - Husband was born in Frederick County,
    Maryland - Wife was born in Jefferson County, West Virginia -
    Husband resides in Frederick County, Maryland - Wife resides at
    Shepherdstown, Jefferson County - Husband's parents are Charles H.
    and Amelia Goldsborough - Wife's parents are Edmund I. and Henrietta
    Lee - Occupation of husband is Physician.

Goldsborough, George W. and Susanna Margaret Pearl (3) - January 9, 1873
    Place of marriage, Harpers Ferry - Age of husband, 22 - Age of wife,
    21 - Both are Single - Both were born in Jefferson County, West
    Virginia - Both reside in Jefferson County, West Virginia -
    Husband's parents are William and Elizabeth Goldsborough - Wife's
    parents are David and Julia Ann Pearl - Occupation of husband is
    Farmer.

Goldsborough, Susan and George Jackson (1) - May 18, 1809

Goldsborough, W. and Martha Penaral (3) - October 17, 1867
    Place of marriage, Jefferson - Age of husband, 40 - Husband is a
    Widower - Wife is a Widow - Both were born in Jefferson County -
    Both reside in Jefferson County - Husband's parents are Cornelius
    and E. R. - Occupation of husband is Laborer.

Goldsbury, Susanna and John Neslop (1) - September 5, 1833

Golliday, Matilda C. and John W. Whittington (3) - June 12, 1877
    For further information see - Whittington, John W.

Golliday, Thomas L. and Sarah E. Kipps (3) - November 7, 1889
    Place of marriage, Harpers Ferry - Age of husband, 23 - Age of wife,
    22 - Both are Single - Husband was born in Shenandoah County,
    Virginia - Wife was born in Jefferson County, West Virginia -
    Husband resides in Shenandoah County, Virginia - Wife resides in
    Jefferson County, West Virginia.

Golsbary, James and Elizabeth Wycoff (1) - June 15, 1820

Gompf, Jacob and Celia Ann Roderick (1) - May 26, 1836

Gompf, Jacob and Sythia Oliver (2) - (L) April 26, 1855

Gompf, Mary Virginia and Oscar S. Gompf (2) - (L) March 25, 1861

Gompf, Michael and Sarah Bond (1) - September 2, 1832

Gompf, Oscar S. and Mary Virginia Gompf (2) - (L) March 25, 1861

Gomph, Jane M. and Charles W. Melton (1) - May 29, 1828

Gomph, Margaret and Louis Corson (1) - October 5, 1833

Good, Catharine and Benjamin Landrist (1) - December 11, 1827

Goodlow, Caroline and William H. Hays (1) - July 7, 1848

Gordon, Frank and Virginia Gordon (3) -   October 24, 1888
   Place of marriage, Middleway - Age of husband, 27 - Age of wife,
   29 - Husband is Single - Wife is a Widow - Both were born in
   Jefferson County, West Virginia - Both reside in Jefferson County,
   West Virginia.

Gordon, James M. and Virginia B. Bane (3) -   June 1, 1882
   Place of marriage, Mag Willie (farm) - Age of husband, 23 - Age of
   wife, 22 - Both are Single - Husband was born in Clarke County,
   Virginia - Wife was born in Jefferson County, West Virginia -
   Husband resides in Jefferson County, West Virginia - Wife resides in
   Jefferson County.

Gordon, John and Sarah Spotts (1) -   February 6, 1817

Gordon, Peter (colored persons) Bettie Tolbert (3) -   August 3, 1865
   Place of marriage, Charlestown - Age of husband, 25 years - Age of
   wife, 21 years - Both are Single - Husband was born at York Town,
   Virginia - Wife was born near Charlestown - Both reside at
   Charlestown - Husband's parents are mother's name Rosie Smith -
   Wife's parents are John and Rosettie Tolbert - Occupation of
   husband is Laborer.

Gordon, Simon (cold.) Rachel Smith (3) -   June 17, 1878
   Place of marriage, Charlestown - Age of husband, 22 - Age of wife,
   19 - Both are Single - Husband was born in Albemarle County,
   Virginia - Wife was born in Jefferson County, West Virginia - Both
   reside in Jefferson County, West Virginia.

Gordon, Virginia and Frank Gordon (3) -   October 24, 1888
   For further information see - Gordon, Frank.

Gordon, Wesley (cold.) Molly Edwards (3) -   November 17, 1881
   Place of marriage, Bolivar - Age of husband, 39 - Age of wife, 30 -
   Husband is Single - Wife is a Widow - Husband was born in
   Rappahannock County, Virginia - Wife was born in Jefferson County,
   West Virginia - Both reside in Jefferson County, West Virginia.

Gore, Dennis (cold.) Mary Thornton (3) -   September 21, 1890
   Place of marriage, Charlestown - Age of husband, 22 - Age of wife,
   18 - Both are Single - Both were born in Jefferson County, West
   Virginia - Both reside in Jefferson County, West Virginia.
   (Consent of bride's mother in writing.)

Gore, Geneva and D. J. Curry (3) -   June 15, 1865
   For further information see - Curry, D. J.

Gore, James W. and Fanny Whittington (3) -   January 26, 1876
   Place of marriage, Charlestown - Age of husband, 26 - Age of wife,
   19 - Both are Single - Wife was born in Jefferson County, West
   Virginia - Husband resides in Jefferson County, West Virginia - Wife
   resides in Jefferson, West Virginia.   (Written consent of father.)

Gore, Joseph and Nancy Arvin (1) -   June 28, 1808

Gore, Margaret E. and Peter Jacobs (2) -   (L) April 3, 1852

Gore, Margaret E. and Peter Jacobs (1) -   April 15, 1852

Gore, N. W. and S. C. Creamer (bride) (3) -　　　　　　　　January 2, 1868
　　Place of marriage, Jefferson County - Age of husband, 23 - Age of
　　wife, 17 - Both are Single - Husband was born in Loudoun County -
　　Wife was born in Jefferson County - Both reside in Jefferson
　　County - Husband's parents are Thomas and Mary Ann - Wife's parents
　　are Philip and Matilda - Occupation of husband is Farmer.
　　(Parents willing.)

Gore, W. T. and Margaret Ann Conner (3) -　　　　　　　　　May 18, 1875
　　Place of marriage, Charlestown - Age of husband, 25 - Age of wife,
　　22 - Both are Single - Husband was born in Loudoun County, Virginia -
　　Wife was born in Jefferson County, West Virginia - Both reside in
　　Jefferson County, West Virginia.

Gore, William J. and Catherine E. Lee (3) -　　　　　　　　January 1, 1878
　　Place of marriage, Watson's Factory - Age of husband, 29 - Age of
　　wife, 17 - Both are Single - Both reside in Jefferson County, West
　　Virginia.　(Consent of bride's father in writing.)

Gore, William J. and Molly B. Clipp (3) -　　　　　　　　November 22, 1883
　　Place of marriage, near Charlestown - Age of husband, 35 - Age of
　　wife, 23 - Husband is a Widower - Wife is Single - Husband was born
　　in Loudoun County, Virginia - Wife was born in Jefferson County,
　　West Virginia - Both reside in Jefferson County, West Virginia.

Gorman, M. A. (bride) and G. W. Henson (3) -　　　　　　　February 7, 1872
　　For further information see - Henson, G. W.

Gorrel, Bonfield and Sarah R. Small (3) -　　　　　　　　November 21, 1865
　　Place of marriage, Jefferson County - Age of husband, 22 - Age of
　　wife, 19 - Both are Single - Husband was born in Harford County,
　　Maryland - Wife was born in Berkeley County, West Virginia -
　　Husband resides in Harford County, Maryland - Wife resides in
　　Jefferson County - Husband's parents are S. C. and Priscilla
　　Gorrel - Wife's parents are William and Margaret Small - Occupation
　　of husband is Farmer.

Gorrell, Frances R. and Alexander Newcomer (1) -　　　　　　May 18, 1847

Gorrell, George W. and Mary C. Moore (2) -　　　　　(L) December 31, 1853

Gorrell, Jacob and Nancy Boley (1) -　　　　　　　　　　　October 14, 1819

Gorrell, Louisa and J. Walker Snyder (3) -　　　　　　　　August 26, 1869
　　For further information see - Snyder, J. Walker.

Gorrell, Virginia and John Blue (3) -　　　　　　　　　　　March 12, 1867
　　For further information see - Blue, John.

Gorster, Sarah Rebecca and William Thomas Hoffman (2) - (L) September 10, 1855

Gossling, Harry J. and Ella L. Haines (3) -　　　　　　　　April 10, 1890
　　Place of marriage, Ripon - Age of husband, 29 - Age of wife, 30 -
　　Both are Single - Husband was born at Manchester, England - Wife was
　　born in Jefferson County, West Virginia - Husband resides at
　　Philadelphia, Pennsylvania - Wife resides in Jefferson County, West
　　Virginia.

Gould, A. Lawrence and Annie S. H. Lambaugh (2) -　　(L) January 2, 1858

Goulding, Mary and Lloyd Norris (1) -   November 12, 1834

Gower, Clara C. and Lee Myers (3) -   October 20, 1885
  For further information see - Myers, Lee.

Goyins, Nancy E. (cold.) Emanuel Johnson (3) -   September 19, 1867
  For further information see - Johnson, Emanuel.

Grace, James and Ester May Dusinger (3) -   October 1, 1890
  Place of marriage, Shepherdstown - Age of husband, 21 - Age of wife,
  21 - Both are Single - Husband was born in South Wales, England -
  Wife was born in Washington County, Maryland - Both reside in
  Jefferson County, West Virginia.

Graham, Eliza Ann and Richard Russell (1) -   November 26, 1835

Graham, Ellen and Thomas Cooper (1) -   June 2, 1832

Graham, G. W. and Sophia Bilson (3) -   June 16, 1870
  Place of marriage, Jefferson County - Age of husband, 24 - Age of
  wife, 21 - Husband was born in New York - Wife was born in Jefferson
  County - Husband resides in Virginia - Wife resides in Jefferson
  County.

Graham, Mathew and Jane More (1) -   June 12, 1804

Graham, William and Harriet Piles (1) -   September 1, 1834

Graham, William and Josephine Manuel (3) -   June 12, 1879
  Place of marriage, Shepherdstown - Age of husband, 30 - Age of wife,
  20 - Both are Single - Both were born in Jefferson County, West
  Virginia - Both reside in Jefferson County, West Virginia. (No
  return.)

Graham, William and Florence B. Humrickhouse (3) -   January 20, 1881
  Place of marriage, Shepherdstown - Age of husband, 32 - Age of wife,
  22 - Both are Single - Both were born in Jefferson County, West
  Virginia - Both reside in Jefferson County, West Virginia.

Graham, William M. and Annie A. Baden (3) -   November 23, 1887
  Place of marriage, Harpers Ferry - Age of husband, 42 - Age of wife,
  40 - Both are Single - Both were born in Jefferson County - Husband
  resides in State of Connecticut - Wife resides at Harpers Ferry.

Grall, Mrs. Mary and Joseph Deck (2) -   (L) October 25, 1852

Grandstaff, Lemuel B. and Harriet A. Williams (3) -   February 8, 1887
  Place of marriage, Shepherdstown - Age of husband, 20 - Age of wife,
  24 - Both are Single - Both were born in Hardy County, West
  Virginia - Both reside in Jefferson County. (Consent of groom's
  father in writing.)

Granen, Owen and Julia Holmes (2) -   (L) June 8, 1860

Grant, Elizabeth and Benjamin Freeze (1) -   December 28, 1833

Grant, Fanny and William H. Wilhelm (3) -   December 30, 1878
  For further information see - Wilhelm, William H.

Grant, Hannah D. and Edmund A. Campbell (3) -   August 15, 1887
For further information see - Campbell, Edmund A.

Grant, John W. and Julia B. Smoots (3) -   February 26, 1873
Place of marriage, Shepherdstown - Age of husband, 23 - Age of wife, 18 - Both are Single - Both were born in Jefferson County, West Virginia - Both reside in Jefferson County, West Virginia - Husband's parents are John W. and Margaret S. - Wife's parents are Jacob A. and Susan J. - Occupation of husband in Clerk. (Consent of bride's father in person.)

Grant, Jonathan, Jr. and Mary Jane Smith (1) -   August 9, 1836

Grant, R. V. (bride) and W. L. Furr (3) -   December 23, 1874
For further information see - Furr, W. L.

Grantham, Ann Louisa and John W. Luke (2) -   (L) November 17, 1852

Grantham, Anna L. and James F. Wageley (3) -   January 22, 1878
For further information see - Wageley, James F.

Grantham, Caroline C. and George W. Shirley (2) -   (L) February 3, 1852

Grantham, Edith M. and James Amon Shirley (3) -   April 29, 1880
For further information see - Shirley, James Amon.

Grantham, Eliza Cornelia and William A. Larue (2) -   (L) April 25, 1863
For further information see - Larue, William A.

Grantham, H. M. A. and John W. Smith (3) -   April 16, 1867
For further information see - Smith, John W.

Grantham, James and Lucy Reed (3) -   April 12, 1866

Grantham, John and Phebe Grantham (1) -   November 28, 1826

Grantham, John S. and Lucy E. Sharff (1) -   May 9, 1850

Grantham, Joseph T. and Katy V. Fry (3) -   March 8, 1876
Place of marriage, near Middleway - Age of husband, 24 - Age of wife, 21 - Both are Single - Both were born in Jefferson County, West Virginia - Both reside in Jefferson County, West Virginia.

Grantham, Lillie and W. H. Gilbert (3) -   December 10, 1885
For further information see - Gilbert, W. H.

Grantham, Lucy V. and Henry J. Benner (3) -   March 28, 1876
For further information see - Benner, Henry J.

Grantham, Mary and James Shirley, Jr. (1) -   January 13, 1824

Grantham, Mary H. and Nathan Barns (1) -   January 31, 1837

Grantham, Phebe and John Grantham (1) -   November 28, 1826

Grantham, Rose and John J. Gilbert (3) -   June 2, 1875
For further information see - Gilbert, John J.

Grantham, William and Henrietta Maria Waugh (1) -   January 15, 1824

Graves, George B. and Minnie E. Harlow (3) -   April 10, 1890
    Place of marriage, Harpers Ferry - Age of husband, 32 - Age of wife,
    22 - Both are Single - Husband was born in Albemarle County,
    Virginia - Wife was born in Jefferson County, West Virginia -
    Husband resides in Albemarle County, Virginia - Wife resides in
    Jefferson County, West Virginia.

Graves, Mary and Lewis Piper (1) -   October 10, 1816

Gray, Albert and Laura B. Clipp (3) -   March 1, 1888
    Place of marriage, Mountain Top - Age of husband, 21 - Age of wife,
    21 - Both are Single - Husband was born in Warren County, Virginia -
    Wife was born in Jefferson County, West Virginia - Both reside in
    Jefferson County, West Virginia.

Gray, Andrew (free colored) Maria Wood (1) -   July 27, 1821

Gray, Ann Eliza and Amos Ridenour (3) -   December 22, 1881
    For further information see - Ridenour, Amos.

Gray, Annie M. and Benjamin C. Colbert (3) -   April 6, 1886
    For further information see - Colbert, Benjamin C.

Gray, Frances A. and William H. Mason (3) -   October 5, 1886
    For further information see - Mason, William H.

Gray, Frances Ellen and George W. Viands (3) -   May 2, 1876
    For further information see - Viands, George W.

Gray, Fannie and Samuel Walen (3) -   December 1866
    For further information see - Walen, Samuel.

Gray, Hannah M. and Wilson H. Magaha (3) -   November 16, 1869
    For further information see - Magaha, Wilson H.

Gray, Harmon and Mary E. Roderick (3) -   October 8, 1868
    Place of marriage, Jefferson County - Age of husband, 23 - Age of
    wife, 22 - Both are Single - Husband was born in Jefferson - Wife
    was born in West Virginia - Both reside in Jefferson County -
    Husband's parents are Absolom and Frances - Wife's parents are John
    and Elsa - Occupation of husband is Farmer.

Gray, Jane Elizabeth and Daniel Rodrick (3) -   October 16, 1878
    For further information see - Rodrick, Daniel.

Gray, John and Rosa Rodrick (3) -   June 7, 1883
    Place of marriage, Charlestown - Age of husband, 23 - Age of wife,
    21 - Both are Single - Both were born in Jefferson County, West
    Virginia - Both reside in Jefferson County, West Virginia. (Bride's
    mother and father both dead.)

Gray, Louisa (cold.) Elijah Brown (3) -   November 5, 1881
    For further information see - Brown, Elijah.

Gray, Thomas Jefferson and Mary Hannah Penwell (3) -   September 20, 1887
    Place of marriage, Charlestown - Age of husband, 23 - Age of wife,
    21 - Both are Single - Both were born in Jefferson County, West
    Virginia - Both reside in Jefferson County, West Virginia.

Gray, William Benjamin and Emma Jane Piper (3) -   April 20, 1879
    Place of marriage, Mountain - Age of husband, 27 - Age of wife, 19 -
    Both are Single - Both were born in Jefferson County, West
    Virginia - Both reside in Jefferson County, West Virginia.
    (Consent of bride's father in person.)

Grayson, Henry C. (cold.) E. V. Foulke (3) -   April 2, 1874
    Place of marriage, Kearneysville - Age of husband, 26 - Age of wife,
    19 - Both are Single - Husband was born in Jefferson County, West
    Virginia - Wife was born in Berkeley County, West Virginia - Both
    reside in Jefferson County, West Virginia. (Consent of bride's
    father in person.)

Green, Albert (cold.) Rebecca Robinson (3) -   March 13, 1879
    Place of marriage, Charlestown - Age of husband, 25 - Age of wife,
    22 - Both are Single - Husband was born in Clarke County, Virginia -
    Wife was born in Jefferson County, West Virginia - Both reside in
    Jefferson County, West Virginia.

Green, Annie L. and John Porterfield (3) -   August 9, 1876
    For further information see - Porterfield, John.

Green, Arthur (cold.) Mary Catherine Williams (3) -   May 16, 1878
    Place of marriage, Charlestown - Age of husband, 22 - Age of wife,
    19 - Both are Single - Husband was born in Fauquier County,
    Virginia - Wife was born in Jefferson County, West Virginia - Both
    reside in Jefferson County, West Virginia. (Consent of bride's
    father in writing.)

Green, Benjamin D. and Elizabeth Walker (1) -   June 16, 1834

Green, Bertha C. and C. L. Knick (3) -   December 14, 1887
    For further information see - Knick, C. L.

Green, Charles (cold.) Bettie Creamer (3) -   March 20, 1890
    Place of marriage, Charlestown - Age of husband, 28 - Age of wife,
    27 - Both are Single - Husband was born in Rappahannock County,
    Virginia - Wife was born in Jefferson County, West Virginia -
    Husband resides in Rappahannock County, Virginia - Wife resides in
    Jefferson County, West Virginia.

Green, Edward and Hetty Nichols (3) -   March 22, 1873
    Place of marriage, near Leetown - Age of husband, 23 - Age of wife,
    21 - Both are Single - Husband was born in Rockingham County,
    Virginia - Wife was born in Jefferson County, West Virginia - Both
    reside in Jefferson County, West Virginia - Husband's parents are
    Adam and Emma - Occupation of husband is Farm Hand.

Green, Estelle S. P. and Charles H. Lewis (2) -   (L) October 30, 1855

Green, Flora McDonald and Cruger Womley Smith (3) -   January 11, 1887
    For further information see - Smith, Cruger Womley.

Green, George (cold.) Mary Ranson (3) -   April 11, 1889
    Place of marriage, Charlestown - Age of husband, 73 - Age of wife,
    65 - Husband is a Widower - Wife is a Widow - Both were born in
    Jefferson County, West Virginia - Both reside in Jefferson County,
    West Virginia.

Green, George W. and Emma O. Nicholas (3) -　　　　　　March 4, 1886
　　Place of marriage, Harpers Ferry - Age of husband, 39 - Age of wife,
　　21 - Both are Single - Both were born in Maryland - Both reside in
　　Jefferson County, West Virginia.

Green, James (cold.) Emma J. Wilson (3) -　　　　　　　　March 26, 1883
　　Place of marriage, Charlestown - Age of husband, 21 - Age of wife,
　　18 - Both are Single - Husband was born in Tennessee - Wife was born
　　in Jefferson County, West Virginia - Both reside in Jefferson
　　County, West Virginia. (Consent of bride's mother in writing.)

Green, James F. and Maria Kelly (2) -　　　　　　　(L) August 20, 1858

Green, John (cold.) Fanny Myers (3) -　　　　　　　　　August 30, 1876
　　Place of marriage, Duffields - Age of husband, 33 - Age of wife,
　　18 - Both are Single - Both were born in Loudoun County, Virginia -
　　Both reside in Jefferson County, West Virginia. (Bride has neither
　　father nor mother.)

Green, John Henry (cold.) Mary Parker (3) -　　　　　December 11, 1879
　　Place of marriage, Charlestown - Age of husband, 40 - Age of wife,
　　23 - Husband is a Widower - Wife is Single - Husband was born in
　　Wythe County, Virginia - Wife was born in Fauquier County,
　　Virginia - Both reside in Jefferson County, West Virginia.

Green, John W. and Mollie V. Hannah (3) -　　　　　　December 2, 1885
　　Place of marriage, near Leetown - Age of husband, 32 - Age of wife,
　　19 - Both are Single - Husband was born in Rockbridge County,
　　Virginia - Wife was born in Jefferson County, West Virginia - Both
　　reside in Jefferson County, West Virginia. (Consent of bride's
　　father in person.)

Green, Julia (cold.) John Galloway (3) -　　　　　　　August 29, 1878
　　For further information see - Galloway, John.

Green, Lucy and Mason Pendleton (3) -　　　　　　　　　　April 11, 1872
　　For further information see - Pendleton, Mason.

Green, Lucy (cold.) Charles Reeler (3) -　　　　　　November 30, 1876
　　For further information see - Reeler, Charles.

Green, Nancy (cold.) Captain Thomas (3) -　　　　　September 28, 1876
　　For further information see - Thomas, Captain.

Green, Rachel (cold.) John Owings (3) -　　　　　　　　August 30, 1877
　　For further information see - Owings, John.

Green, Rebeca Ann (cold.) John W. Phillips (3) -　　　October 1, 1888
　　For further information see - Phillips, John W.

Green, Richard A. and Martha Ellen Light (2) -　　(L) November 21, 1854

Green, Robert (cold.) Caroline Washington (3) -　　December 26, 1883
　　Place of marriage, Bride's Residence - Age of husband, 23 - Age of
　　wife, 21 - Both are Single - Husband was born in Shenandoah County,
　　Virginia - Wife was born in Berkeley County - Both reside in
　　Jefferson County, West Virginia.

Green, Sarah (cold.) John Newman (3) -　　　　　　　　October 5, 1882
　　For further information see - Newman, John.

Green, William and Ann Strider (1) - February 28, 1822

Green, William A. (cold.) Bettie Jones (3) - February 15, 1888
Place of marriage, Charlestown - Age of husband, 35 - Age of wife, 35 - Both are Single - Husband was born in Prince William County, Virginia - Wife was born in Jefferson County, West Virginia - Both reside in Jefferson County, West Virginia.

Greenfellow, Joshua and S. A. Turner (3) - January 30, 1868
Place of marriage, Jefferson County - Age of husband, 22 - Age of wife, 19 - Both are Single - Husband was born in Berkeley County - Wife was born in Jefferson County - Husband resides in Maryland - Wife resides in Jefferson - Occupation of husband is Farmer.

Greenwalt, Samuel and Ann Galton (2) - (L) August 27, 1860

Greenwalt, Sarah and James Snipe (3) - December 26, 1870
For further information see - Snipe, James.

Greenwood, B. E. and Rosa V. Lambert (3) - December 23, 1889
Place of marriage, Shepherdstown - Age of husband, 25 - Age of wife, 22 - Both are Single - Both were born in Jefferson County, West Virginia - Husband resides at Roanoke, Virginia - Wife resides in Jefferson County, West Virginia.

Greenwood, Maggie and Thomas B. Miller (3) - September 28, 1881
For further information see - Miller, Thomas B.

Greenwood, Thomas C. and Laura C. Waters (3) - September 3, 1884
Place of marriage, Shepherdstown - Age of husband, 21 - Age of wife, 22 - Both are Single - Both were born in Jefferson County - Both reside in Jefferson County.

Greer, Isabella and Dennis Moriarty (2) - (L) January 2, 1854

Greer, Mary and John H. King (1) - May 1, 1828

Greer, Sarah C. and David McKiney (3) - August 5, 1869
For further information see - McKiney, David.

Greggs, Fanie J. and Thomas W. Timberlake (3) - (September 1865)

Gregory, Eveline and Burgess W. Brown (1) - December 13, 1834

Gregory, Mary A. and John Matheny (1) - December 5, 1833

Grey, George and Agnus Johnson (3) - August 24, 1872
Place of marriage, Jefferson County - Age of husband, 21 - Age of wife, 16 - Both are Single - Husband was born in Warren County, Virginia - Wife was born at Frederick, Maryland - Husband resides in Jefferson County - Wife resides in Jefferson County, West Virginia - Husband's parents are Lewis and Maria - Wife's parents are Samuel and Louisa - Occupation of husband is Farmer. (Mother's consent.)

Grey, Sallie and G. W. Holmes (3) - May 28, 1868
For further information see - Holmes, G. W.

Grey, William F. and Emma Jackson (3) -   January 3, 1877
    Place of marriage, near Halltown - Age of husband, 26 - Age of wife,
    17 - Both are Single - Husband was born in Page County, Virginia -
    Wife was born in Clarke County, Virginia - Both reside in Jefferson
    County, West Virginia. (Consent of bride's father in writing.)

Griffee, John and Nancy Partridge (1) -   October 20, 1818

Griffin, S. G. (cold.) Anna M. Washington (3) -   September 3, 1873
    Place of marriage, Shepherdstown - Age of husband, 23 - Age of wife,
    21 - Both are Single - Husband was born at Baltimore City - Wife was
    born in Jefferson County, West Virginia - Husband resides in
    Kentucky - Wife resides in Jefferson County, West Virginia.

Griffith, Alice V. and John P. Entler (3) -   December 27, 1888
    For further information see - Entler, John P.

Griffith, Ann and James J. McFillin (1) -   March 24, 1831

Griffith, Bettie E. and Wilmer L. Shell (3) -   March 6, 1888
    For further information see - Shell, Wilmer L.

Griffith, Cresy and Thomas W. Dillow (3) -   November 10, 1882
    For further information see - Dillow, Thomas W.

Griffith, Emily E. and John Breneman (3) -   March 13, 1879
    For further information see - Breneman, John.

Griffith, James H., Jr. and Ann Maria McDonald (2) -   (L) November 13, 1852

Griffith, James H., Jr. and Ann Maria McDonald (1) -   November 23, 1852

Griffith, James Henry and Sarah Ellen Geaslen (3) -   October 27, 1887
    Place of marriage, Charlestown - Age of husband, 21 - Age of wife,
    23 - Both are Single - Husband was born in Clarke County, Virginia -
    Wife was born in Baltimore County, Maryland - Both reside in
    Jefferson County, West Virginia.

Griffith, Joseph B. and Jennie Ashwood (3) -   October 14, 1889
    Place of marriage, Charlestown - Age of husband, 25 - Age of wife,
    21 - Both are Single - Husband was born in Clarke County, Virginia -
    Wife was born in Frederick County, Virginia - Both reside in
    Jefferson County, West Virginia.

Griffith, Lucy A. and Wilson M. C. Fairfax (1) -   March 2, 1824

Griffith, M. J. and William Painter (3) -   November 27, 1867
    For further information see - Painter, William.

Griffith, Margaret N. and Thomas Dailey (3) -   October 1871
    For further information see - Dailey, Thomas.

Griffith, Martha Rosanna and Charles Hodgkinson (3) -   September 1, 1886
    For further information see - Hodgkinson, Charles.

Griffith, Martin L. and Susan Malatt (3) -   November 30, 1879
   Place of marriage, Residence of Bride's Father near Billmyer's
   Mill - Age of husband, 21 - Age of wife, 21 in February - Both are
   Single - Both were born in Maryland - Both reside in Jefferson
   County, West Virginia. (Consent of bride's father in person.)

Griffith, Mary and Andrew Scheidaunt (1) -   1825

Griffith, Samuel H. and Mary A. Banick (2) -   (L) February 21, 1852

Griffith, Sarah and William Smith (1) -   July 24, 1836

Griffith, Silas E. and Ella J. Warfield (3) -   December 24, 1889
   Place of marriage, Shepherdstown - Age of husband, 23 - Age of wife,
   18 - Both are Single - Husband was born in Washington County,
   Maryland - Wife was born in Jefferson County, West Virginia - Both
   reside in Jefferson County, West Virginia. (Consent of bride's
   parents in writing.)

Griffith, William H. and Martha C. Whittington (3) -   March 6, 1878
   Place of marriage, Charlestown - Age of husband, 37 - Age of wife,
   18 - Husband is a Widower - Wife is Single - Husband was born in
   Loudoun County, Virginia - Wife was born in Jefferson County, West
   Virginia - Both reside in Jefferson County, West Virginia.
   (Consent of bride's father in person.)

Griffiths, Charles and Ann Rebecca Wentzell (1) -   December 25, 1836

Griffiths, John and Mary J. Coates (1) -   August 6, 1835

Griggs, Eliza Lee and Ambrose C. Timberlake (2) -   (L) October 5, 1858

Griggs, Elizabeth and Thomas Brotherton (1) -   December 15, 1825

Griggs, Elizabeth B. and Samuel Watkins Lackland (1) -   January 29, 1823

Griggs, Frances M. and James Flanagan (1) -   November 19, 1835

Griggs, Mary Ann (Widow of Thomas Griggs) and William Long (2) -
   (L) January 7, 1854

Griggs, Virginia M. and Ezra Ahalt (2) -   (L) December 18, 1854

Griggs, William H. and Rachel Vanvacter (1) -   May 26, 1831

Grim, Charles M. and Mary E. Blessing (3) -   May 13, 1873
   Place of marriage, Charlestown - Age of husband, 29 - Age of wife,
   23 - Both are Single - Husband was born in Frederick County,
   Virginia - Wife was born in Jefferson County, West Virginia -
   Husband resides at Cumberland, Maryland - Wife resides in Jefferson
   County, West Virginia - Husband's parents are John W. and Ann E. -
   Wife's parents are Frederick and Emily - Occupation of husband is
   Carpenter.

Grim, Eliza A. and John Lake (3) -   December 24, 1871
   For further information see - Lake, John.

Grim, F. T. (bride) and G. A. Seal (3) -   September 30, 1872
   For further information see - Seal, G. A.

213

Grim, Harriet C. and John C. Elliott (2) -   (L) October 13, 1856

Grimes, James and Louisa Blackburn (1) -   July 23, 1829

Grist, Alfred H. and Elizabeth Lemen (1) -   July 25, 1833

Groff, James and Delila King (2) -   (L) July 16, 1855

Groomes, Margaret and David Moore (1) -   1812

Groomes, Samuel and Barbary Brian (1) -   1812

Groover, Elizabeth and Daniel Hewett (1) -   December 6, 1818

Groover, Mary and Adam Moler (1) -   September 1822

Grosh, Henry E. and Fannie V. Crow (3) -   April 11, 1889
    Place of marriage, Shepherdstown - Age of husband, 27 - Age of wife, 23 - Both are Single - Husband was born at Williamsport, Maryland - Wife was born in Jefferson County, West Virginia - Husband resides at Williamsport, Maryland - Wife resides in Jefferson County, West Virginia.

Grove, Ann M. R. and B. F. Rodeffer (3) -   October 12, 1876
    For further information see - Rodeffer, B. F.

Grove, Catherine and Samuel Bryan (1) -   April 22, 1817

Grove, Davis R. and Elizabeth J. Hendricks (3) -   October 19, 1882
    Place of marriage, near Charlestown - Age of husband, 29 - Age of wife, 28 - Husband is Single - Wife is a Widow - Both were born in Jefferson County, West Virginia - Both reside in Jefferson County, West Virginia.

Grove, Elias E. and Martha Jane White (3) -   August 10, 1882
    Place of marriage, near Summit Point - Age of husband, 27 - Age of wife, 18 - Both are Single - Husband was born in Frederick County, Maryland - Wife was born in Clarke County, Virginia - Husband resides in Jefferson County, West Virginia - Wife resides in Jefferson County. (Consent of bride's mother certified by James R. Carrell her brother-in-law.)

Grove, Elizabeth and Adam Wilson (2) -   (L) August 2, 1851

Grove, Jane E. and M. A. Keesecker (3) -   June 18, 1884
    For further information see - Keesecker, M. A.

Grove, John W. and Ann Virginia Everhart (2) -   (L) January 15, 1856

Grove, Louis H. and Mary E. Hawk (3) -   December 18, 1871
    Place of marriage, Jefferson County - Age of husband, 26 - Age of wife, 24 - Both are Single - Husband was born in Jefferson County - Wife was born in Loudoun - Both reside in Jefferson County - Husband's parents are Thomas and Mary Ann - Wife's parents are Elijah and Eliza - Occupation of husband is Laborer.

Grove, Malachi and Hannah Kasaker (1) -   July 17, 1808

Grove, Margaret A. and Edward B. Hooper (3) -   February 2, 1871
    For further information see - Hooper, Edward B.

Grove, Mary E. and George Wilt (3) - December 23, 1877
For further information see - Wilt, George

Grove, Maurice and Mary Elizabeth Matheny (3) - April 7, 1878
Place of marriage, near Manning's Ferry - Age of husband, 25 - Age
of wife, 22 - Husband is Single - Wife is a Widow by divorce - Both
were born in Jefferson County, West Virginia - Both reside in
Jefferson County, West Virginia.

Grove, Rezin F. and Mary Elizabeth Piper (3) - June 5, 1879
Place of marriage, Bolivar - Age of husband, 23 - Age of wife, 19 -
Both are Single - Both were born in Jefferson County, West Virginia-
Both reside in Jefferson County, West Virginia. (Consent of bride's
father in person, Va. 43.)

Grove, Robert C. and Nannie M. Mason (3) - January 21, 1875
Place of marriage, Scrabble - Age of husband, 25 - Age of wife, 22 -
Both are Single - Husband was born in Maryland - Wife was born in
Jefferson County, West Virginia - Both reside in Jefferson County,
West Virginia.

Grove, Sarah and Adam Snyder (1) - December 26, 1848

Grove, Sarah Malinda Bell and Charles E. Andrews (3) - May 13, 1884
For further information see - Andrews, Charles E.

Grove, Thomas and Mary Piper (2) - (L) March 5, 1852

Grove, Thomas and Mary Piper (1) - March 9, 1852

Grove, Thomas T. and Drusilla Newitt (1) - February 3, 1834

Grove, William R. and Annie E. Winebrenner (3) - April 14, 1872
Place of marriage, Jefferson County, West Virginia - Age of husband,
23 - Age of wife, 19 - Both are Single - Both were born in Jefferson
County, West Virginia - Both reside in Jefferson County, West
Virginia - Husband's parents are Henry and Mary - Wife's parents are
Thomas and Susan - Occupation of husband is Farmer. (Henry
Winebrenner.)

Grubb, Annie and John Henry Rose (3) - March 23, 1884
For further information see - Rose, John Henry.

Grubb, Bulah J. and W. A. McCauley (3) - September 23, 1890
For further information see - McCauley, W. A.

Grubb, Helen V. and Samuel W. Lakin (3) - June 6, 1889
For further information see - Lakin, Samuel W.

Grubb, Jane and William Eby (1) - April 15, 1824

Grubb, Nancy and Abraham Hains (1) - December 31, 1818

Grubb, Ruth and Samuel Haines (1) - December 1, 1831

Grubb, Sarah and John B. Allison (1) - February 15, 1821

Grubb, Sarah Elizabeth and Garrett W. Bane (3) - November 4, 1875
For further information see - Bane, Garrett W.

Grubb, William B. and Eliza Clip (2) - (L) May 12, 1851

Grubbs, Clarence E. and Rosie B. Oyerly (3) - December 10, 1890
    Place of marriage, Bride's Residence - Age of husband, 29 - Age of wife, 26 - Both are Single - Husband was born in Loudoun County, Virginia - Wife was born in Jefferson County, West Virginia - Both reside in Jefferson County, West Virginia.

Gruber, Anne Maria and David B. Rosenberger (3) - January 30, 1878
    For further information see - Rosenberger, David B.

Gruber, Bettie B. and W. H. Suthard (3) - November 7, 1875
    For further information see - Suthard, W. H.

Gruber, Charles W. and Mary Ellen Rosenberger (3) - November 3, 1875
    Place of marriage, near Middleway - Age of husband, 22 - Age of wife, 28 - Both are Single - Both were born in Jefferson County, West Virginia - Both reside in Jefferson County, West Virginia.

Gruber, Elizabeth and Jonathan Frazier (2) - (L) February 15, 1853

Gruber, Elizabeth (widow) and Jonathan Frazier (1) - February 15, 1853

Gruber, Jacob and Sarah Chapman (1) - January 15, 1842

Gruber, Jacob A. and Mary Jane Light (2) - (L) October 3, 1853

Gruber, Jacob A. and Mary Jane Light (widow) (1) - October 4, 1853

Gruber, John B. and Susan B. Woodward (1) - June 23, 1850

Gruber, John B. and Elizabeth Eddleman (2) - (L) November 28, 1854

Gruber, Joseph M. and Olive C. Ware (3) - February 3, 1887
    Place of marriage, Charlestown - Age of husband, 30 - Age of wife, 30 - Both are Single - Both were born in Jefferson County, West Virginia - Both reside in Jefferson County.

Gruber, Martha Jane and R. H. Ryon (2) - (L) September 20, 1859

Gruber, Mary A. and Peter Baker (2) - (L) November 14, 1860

Gruber, Mary Isadore and William M. Boltz (3) - March 3, 1886
    For further information see - Boltz, William M.

Gruber, Solomon and Mary E. Ogden (2) - (L) October 19, 1855

Gruber, Susanna and Uriah Hetterly (2) - (L) December 23, 1851

Gruber, Susanna and Uriah Hetterly (1) - December 23, 1851

Gue, Oscar B. and Sarah Bagley (3) - July 5, 1886
    Place of marriage, Harpers Ferry - Age of husband, 21 - Age of wife, 18 - Both are Single - Husband was born in West Virginia - Wife was born in Maryland - Husband resides in West Virginia - Wife resides in Jefferson County, West Virginia. (Bride has neither father nor mother nor guardian.)

Guilford, E. W. and Berta A. Wood (3) -   October 21, 1890
Place of marriage, Charlestown - **Age of husband, 25** - Age of wife,
21 - Both are Single - Husband **was born at Washington, D. C.** - Wife
was born at Westerville, Ohio - **Husband resides** in Prince George
County, Maryland - Wife resides in **Jefferson County,** West Virginia.

Guillam, Rezin and Rachael Undernunk (1) -   December 27, 1806

Gummert, Christian and Miss Davis (1) -   June 1843

Gummert, Sarah and Jacob Crowl, Jr. (1) -   October 15, 1812

Gummert, Susannah and Hugh McNamee (1) -   March 18, 1819

Guy, Harriet and Frederick Fouke (1) -   April 6, 1813

Guy, John H. and Mary E. Ranson (3) -   October 12, 1871
Place of marriage, Jefferson County - **Age of husband, 40** - Age of
wife, 22 - Both are Single - Both **were born in Virginia** - Husband
resides in Virginia - Wife resides in **West Virginia** - Husband's
parents are Samuel A. and Annie H. - **Wife's parents are James M.** and
Mary E. - Occupation of husband is **Lawyer.**

Guy, Louisa (cold.) James Williams (3) -   March 20, 1888
For further information see - **Williams, James.**

Haas, Ed. and Mattie Gallaher (3) -   January 28, 1875
    Place of marriage, Charlestown - Age of husband, 21 - Age of wife,
    21 - Both are Single - Both were born in Loudoun County, Virginia -
    Both reside in Jefferson County, West Virginia.

Haas, Isaac C. and Rose Daniels (3) -   November 29, 1870
    Place of marriage, Jefferson County - Age of husband, 26 - Age of
    wife, 22 - Both were born in Virginia - Husband resides in New
    York - Wife resides in Jefferson County.

Hack, Henry and Barbara Mettar (2) -   (L) April 6, 1861
    Time of marriage, April 7, 1861 - Place of marriage, Harpers Ferry,
    Jefferson County, Virginia - Names, Henry Hack and Barbara Mettar -
    Age of husband, Forty Four (44) years - Age of wife, Thirty Nine
    (39) - Husband's condition, Single - Wife's condition, Widow - Both
    reside in Jefferson County, Virginia - Names of husband's parents,
    Not Known - Names of wife's parents, Michael and Barbara Mettar -
    Occupation of husband is Workman on Rail Road - Given under my hand
    this 6th of April, 1861 -   ?   Zoll.

Hackley, Millard F. and Annie Riley (3) -   April 18, 1881
    Place of marriage, Harpers Ferry - Age of husband, 24 - Age of wife,
    22 - Both are Single - Both were born in Jefferson County, West
    Virginia - Both Reside in Jefferson County, West Virginia.

Hackley, Sarah Catherine and Charles E. Ross (2) -   (L) March 15, 1864
    For further information see - Ross, Charles E.

Hafer, Emma J. and John H. Powers (3) -   September 22, 1870
    For further information see - Powers, John H.

Hafner, William and Caroline Sexton (3) -   December 20, 1877
    Place of marriage, Harpers Ferry - Age of husband, 29 - Age of wife,
    27 - Both are Single - Husband was born at Philadelphia,
    Pennsylvania - Wife was born in Jefferson County, West Virginia -
    Both reside in Jefferson County, West Virginia.

Hagan, C. J. and Elizabeth Boerley (3) -   September 7, 1875
    Place of marriage, Harpers Ferry - Age of husband, 36 - Age of wife,
    24 - Both are Single - Husband was born at Baltimore City,
    Maryland - Wife was born in Jefferson County, West Virginia - Both
    reside in Jefferson County, West Virginia.

Hagan, Charles and Bridget Powers (2) -   (L) October 3, 1857

Hagan, Lizzie and Hugh Hickman (3) -   April 28, 1889
    For further information see - Hickman, Hugh.

Hagan, Mary and David Huff (3) -   August 5, 1879
    For further information see - Huff, David.

Hagan, Mary and R. B. Kline (3) -   August 18, 1889
    For further information see - Kline, R. B.

Hagan, Rachel (cold.) William Sandy Jones (3) -   July 15, 1880
    For further information see - Jones, William Sandy.

Hageley, George H. and Kate Thurman (3) - December 15, 1870
  Place of marriag, Jefferson County - Age of husband, 24 - Age of
  wife, 25 - Husband was born in Virginia - Wife was born in
  Kentucky - Both reside in Jefferson County.

Hagley, George H. and Martha A. Trussell (3) - November 19, 1874
  Place of marriage, Shepherdstown - Age of husband, 28 - Age of wife,
  31 - Husband is a Widower - Wife is Single - Both were born in
  Jefferson County, West Virginia - Both reside in Jefferson County,
  West Virginia.

Hagley, Jacob T. and Laura M. Shirley (3) - November 8, 1876
  Place of marriage, Unionville - Age of husband, 27 - Age of wife,
  22 - Both are Single - Both were born in Jefferson County, West
  Virginia - Both reside in Jefferson County, West Virginia.

Hagley, Molly E. and B. W. Petty (3) - October 8, 1874
  For further information see - Petty, B. W.

Haine, Catherine and George Hansecker (1) - December 16, 1819

Haines, C. (cold.) M. Hardy (bride) (3) - December 26, 1867
  Place of marriage, Jefferson County - Age of husband, 21 - Age of
  wife, 27 - Husband is Single - Wife is a Widow - Both were born in
  Augusta County, Virginia - Both reside in Jefferson County -
  Occupation of husband is Laborer.

Haines, Elizabeth and John Haines (1) - March 3, 1821

Haines, Ella L. and Harry J. Gossling (3) - April 10, 1890
  For further information see - Gossling, Harry J.

Haines, Jacob and Mary Ann Reed (1) - August 8, 1816

Haines, Jeremiah and Victoria Howard (3) - February 10, 1877
  Place of marriage, Bolivar - Age of husband, 30 - Age of wife, 22 -
  Both are Single - Husband was born in Washington County, Maryland -
  Wife was born in Jefferson County, West Virginia - Both reside in
  Jefferson County, West Virginia.

Haines, John and Elizabeth Haines (1) - March 3, 1821

Haines, Mary Ann and Rollins Jett (2) - (L) May 24, 1858

Haines, Nancy and James Jones (1) - March 27, 1827

Haines, Rebecca C. and David Heller (1) - September 13, 1831

Haines, Sallie E. and George W. Armentrout (3) - February 10, 1869
  For further information see - Armentrout, George W.

Haines, Samuel and Ruth Grubb (1) - December 1, 1831

Hains, Abraham and Nancy Grubb (1) - December 31, 1818

Hains, Margaret and Garvis S. Gardener (1) - May 31, 1832

Hains, Philip and Nancy Reed (1) - October 1, 1812

Hale, Allen (cold.) Annie Edwards (3) -   August 27, 1884
    Place of marriage, Bolivar - Age of husband, 70 - Age of wife, 40 -
    Husband is a Widower - Wife is a Widow - Husband was born in North
    Carolina - Wife was born in Jefferson County - Husband resides in
    Jefferson County - Wife resides in Jefferson County, West Virginia.

Hale, Ann and Thomas Blackburn (1) -   June 10, 1826

Haley, Bettie and Marcellus Kercheval (3) -   June 1, 1882
    For further information see - Kercheval, Marcellus.

Haley, M. G. (bride) and G. J. Moreland (3) -   August 29, 1867
    For further information see - Moreland, G. J.

Hall, Ann (widow) and James Fisher (2) -   (L) January 6, 1860

Hall, Baden (cold.) Clara McDaniel (3) -   December 27, 1883
    Place of marriage, near Bloomery Mill - Age of husband, 22 - Age of
    wife, 18 - Both are Single - Both were born in Jefferson County,
    West Virginia - Both reside in Jefferson County, West Virginia.
    (Consent of bride's father in person.)

Hall, Charles and Lelia Williams (3) -   December 26, 1871
    Place of marriage, Jefferson County - Age of husband, 22 - Age of
    wife, 19 - Both are Single - Both were born in Jefferson County,
    West Virginia - Husband resides at Chambersburg, Pennsylvania - Wife
    resides in Jefferson County, West Virginia - Husband's parents are
    Daniel and Dapthea - Wife's parents are Charles and Patsy -
    Occupation of husband is Farmer.   (Simon Walker.)

Hall, Daniel (cold.) Frances Brunswick (3) -   March 26, 1874
    Place of marriage, Middleway - Age of husband, 26 - Age of wife,
    19 - Both are Single - Both were born in Jefferson County, West
    Virginia - Both reside in Jefferson County, West Virginia.
    (Consent of bride's father in person.)

Hall, Daniel (cold.) Lizzie Brunswick (3) -   August 11, 1887
    Place of marriage, Middleway - Age of husband, 35 - Age of wife,
    21 - Husband is a Widower - Wife is Single - Both were born in
    Jefferson County, West Virginia - Both reside in Jefferson County,
    West Virginia.

Hall, Eliza (cold.) Lee Thomas (3) -   February 8, 1883
    For further information see - Thomas, Lee.

Hall, Elizabeth and John Craig (1) -   October 2, 1821

Hall, Elizabeth and James Allen (3) -   April 18, 1878
    For further information see - Allen, James.

Hall, George W. and Augusta Morgan (1) -   December 18, 1849

Hall, J. W. (cold.) A. E. McDonald (bride) (3) -   January 1, 1868
    Place of marriage, Jefferson County - Age of husband, 23 - Age of
    wife, 22 - Both are Single - Both were born in Jefferson County -
    Both reside in Jefferson County - Occupation of husband is Farmer.

Hall, Dr. James and Margaret Brackenridge (1) -   (circa) 1817

Hall, Jonathan T. and Elizabeth Avis (1) -   January 9, 1817

Hall, Joseph and Charlotte Strider (1) -   June 1, 1809

Hall, Joseph and Helen Taylor (3) -   April 9, 1871
    Place of marriage, Jefferson County - Age of husband, 21 - Age of
    wife, 22 - Both are Single - Husband was born in Jefferson County -
    Wife was born in Virginia - Both reside in Jefferson County -
    Husband's parents are Jeff and Katie - Wife's parents are John and
    Caroline - Occupation of husband is Farmer.

Hall, Lucie Ann and Alfred Collins (3) -   June 3, 1875
    For further information see - Collins, Alfred.

Hall, Lucinda (cold.) Thomas Newman (3) -   May 7, 1885
    For further information see - Newman, Thomas.

Hall, Minnie J. and R. L. Magruder (3) -   December 19, 1883
    For further information see - Magruder, R. L.

Hall, Oliver and Amanda Brown (3) -   (1868)
    Age of husband, 27 - Age of wife, 21 - Both are Single - Husband was
    born in Jefferson County, Virginia - Wife was born in Jefferson
    County - Husband resides in Jefferson County - Wife resides in
    Jefferson County, West Virginia - Occupation of husband is Laborer.

Hall, Peter (cold.) Essie Burkins (3) -   January 7, 1886
    Place of marriage, On Shenandoah River in this County - Age of
    husband, 21 - Age of wife, 21 - Both are Single - Both were born in
    Jefferson County, West Virginia - Both reside in Jefferson County,
    West Virginia.

Hall, Rosa (cold.) James William Mackey (3) -   December 24, 1873
    For further information see - Mackey, James William.

Hall, Rosa (cold.) Arthur Brown (3) -   November 6, 1883
    For further information see - Brown, Arthur.

Hall, Rosanna and Gabriel Fields (3) -   July 28, 1866
    For further information see - Fields, Gabriel.

Hall, Sarah and Jesse Prichard (1) -   October 15, 1805

Hall, Sarah Ann and Joshua Roberts (1) -   March 18, 1823

Hall, Sarah E. (cold.) Charles Ed. Mitchell (3) -   June 16, 1889
    For further information see - Mitchell, Charles Ed.

Hall, Susan and Hezekiah Thomas (1) -   March 20, 1823

Hall, Thomas and Letticia Butt (1) -   June 28, 1810

Hall, Thomas H. and Martha Worthington (1) -   May 15, 1817

Hall, William and Mary Evans (1) -   June 28, 1808

Hall, William H. D. and Elizabeth S. Hite (1) -   February 18, 1840

Hall, William H. D. and Elizabeth C. Briscoe (1) -   March 7, 1848

Hall, William J. and Elmina Easton (1) -   April 21, 1825

Hall, William L. and Mary Ann Anderson (1) -   October 14, 1824

Halpen, James and Elizabeth Cantwell (2) -   (L) December 12, 1851

Halpin, Ann and Thomas Walsh (2) -   (L) May 6, 1858
   (T. Boesley says they are both 21.)

Halpin, Catharine and James Murray (2) -   (L) August 22, 1851

Halpin, Katherine and Marcus B. Stewart (3) -   June 8, 1881
   For further information see - Stewart, Marcus B.

Hamble, James and Mary Cooke (1) -   January 9, 1816

Hamill, Elizabeth V. and Samuel Cook (2) -   (L) May 12, 1852

Hamilton, Eliza and Jose P. Adams (1) -   1813

Hamilton, Eliza Grove and Stephen B. Wolford (1) -   July 26, 1853

Hamilton, H. A. and John M. Pope (3) -   August 8, 1867
   For further information see - Pope, John M.

Hamilton, James and Amanda Jones (3) -   September 7, 1874
   Place of marriage, County - Age of husband, 50 - Age of wife, 34 -
   Husband is a Widower - Wife is Single - Husband was born in
   Frederick County, Virginia now Clarke - Wife was born in Loudoun
   County, Virginia - Both reside in Jefferson County, West Virginia.
   (Information of Robert Ainsworth.)

Hamilton, James (cold.) Nannie E. Veney (3) -   May 6, 1885
   Place of marriage, Harpers Ferry - Age of husband, 22 - Age of wife,
   21 - Both are Single - Both were born in Jefferson County, West
   Virginia - Both reside in Jefferson County, West Virginia.

Hamilton, John (cold.) Virginia Johnson (3) -   November 11, 1886
   Place of marriage, Harpers Ferry - Age of husband, 43 - Age of wife,
   42 - Husband is a Widower - Wife is a Widow - Husband was born in
   King and Queen County, Virginia - Wife was born in Loudoun County,
   Virginia - Both reside in Jefferson County, West Virginia.

Hamilton, Joseph and Bertie Fauber (3) -   October 24, 1890
   Place of marriage, Charlestown - Age of husband, 20 - Age of wife,
   21 - Both are Single - Both were born in Jefferson County, West
   Virginia - Both reside in Jefferson County, West Virginia.
   (Consent of groom's father in person.)

Hamilton, Joseph (cold.) Nellie Strother (3) -   December 18, 1890
   Place of marriage, Harpers Ferry - Age of husband, 21 - Age of wife,
   21 - Both are Single - Both were born in Jefferson County, West
   Virginia - Both reside in Jefferson County, West Virginia.

Hamilton, William and Eliza Bradshaw (1) -   1813

Hammer, Joanna and J. P. Gardner (3) -   August 25, 1874
   For further information see - Gardner, J. P.

Hammer, John C. and Annie D. Manuel (3) - May 17, 1881
   Place of marriage, Bolivar - Age of husband, 28 - Age of wife, 19 -
   Both are Single - Both were born in Jefferson County, West Virginia -
   Husband resides at Washington, D. C. - Wife resides in Jefferson
   County, West Virginia. (Consent of bride's guardian, father and
   mother both dead.)

Hammon, Elizabeth and Michael Wilt (1) - August 2, 1827

Hammon, Mary Elizabeth and George W. Elliott (3) - February 7, 1878
   For further information see - Elliott, George W.

Hammond, Allen C. and Catharine H. Campbell (2) - (L) January 29, 1855

Hammond, Fanny R. and John Packett (1) - March 14, 1816

Hammond, James Augustus and Lizzie Ann Creswell (3) - September 10, 1872
   Place of marriage, Jefferson County - Age of husband, 25 - Age of
   wife, 30 - Both are Single - Husband was born in Washington County,
   Maryland - Wife was born in Berkeley County, Virginia - Husband
   resides in Illinois - Wife resides in Jefferson County, West
   Virginia - Wife's parents are Andrew and Mary Jane - Occupation of
   husband is Farmer.

Hammond, Jane B. and George H. Pierce (2) - (L) September 22, 1856

Hammond, Jane Baxter and Philip Henry Hooff (1) - June 24, 1823

Hammond, John J. and Sarah Ann Flagg (2) - (L) July 18, 1850

Hammond, John J. and Sally A. Flagg (1) - July 18, 1850

Hammond, Mary E. and Joseph Vanvacter (1) - May 24, 1832

Hammond, Mary P. and G. Frank Lloyd (2) - (L) October 20, 1856

Hammond, Thomas and Ann A. Collins (1) - June 18, 1807

Hamtramick, John F. and Eliza C. Selby (1) - December 1825

Hamtrauck, Eliza and L. F. Williamson (3) - January 1869
   For further information see - Williamson, L. F.

Hanbey, Penelope Jacqueline and John Thompson (3) - September 25, 1873
   For further information see - Thompson, John.

Hanby, George W. and Alice Virginia Thompson (3) - March 25, 1885
   Place of marriage, Shepherdstown - Age of husband, 48 - Age of wife,
   18 - Both are Single - Husband was born in Shenandoah County,
   Virginia - Wife was born in Jefferson County, West Virginia - Both
   reside in Jefferson County, West Virginia. (Consent of bride's
   father in person.)

Hanby, Jennie and John Price (3) - May 14, 1878
   For further information see - Price, John.

Hancock, Eben T. and Kizziah J. Smith (widow) (2) - (L) December 6, 1851

Haneys, Betsy and Samuel Smallwood (1) - December 28, 1815

Hanion, William (cold.) Jennie Ford (3) - June 27, 1878
Place of marriage, Charlestown - Age of husband, 28 - Age of wife, 27 - Both are Single - Husband was born at Baltimore, Maryland - Wife was born in Jefferson County, West Virginia - Both reside in Jefferson County, West Virginia.

Hankey, John C. and Ellen Jane Lancaster (3) - January 28, 1877
Place of marriage, Harpers Ferry - Age of husband, 37 - Age of wife, 26 - Husband is a Widower - Wife is Single - Husband was born in Frederick County, Maryland - Wife was born in Loudoun County, Virginia - Husband resides in Frederick County, Maryland - Wife resides in Jefferson County, West Virginia.

Hann, Joseph C. and Hatie V. Bennett (3) - October 10, 1887
Place of marriage, Shepherdstown - Age of husband, 23 - Age of wife, 19 - Both are Single - Husband was born in Pennsylvania - Wife was born in Jefferson County, West Virginia - Husband resides in Pennsylvania - Wife resides in Jefferson County, West Virginia. (Consent of bride's mother in writing.)

Hanna, Isaac N. and Mary V. Hoffman (2) - (L) January 23, 1860

Hannah, Daniel W. and Sarah E. Underdonk (3) - March 29, 1866
Place of marriage, Henry Underdonk's, Jefferson County - Age of husband, 26 - Age of wife, 21 - Both are Single - Both were born in Jefferson County, Virginia - Both reside in Jefferson County, West Virginia - Husband's parents are James W. and Mary O. Hannah - Wife's parents are Henry and Julia Underdonk - Occupation of husband is Farmer.

Hannah, David W. and Sue Schoppert (3) - March 1, 1871
Place of marriage, Jefferson County - Age of husband, 26 - Age of wife, 22 - Both are Single - Husband was born in Virginia - Wife was born in Jefferson County - Husband resides in West Virginia - Wife resides in Jefferson County - Husband's parents are James and Mary - Wife's parents are Jacob and Nancy - Occupation of husband is Farmer.

Hannah, James and Mary Wade (1) - April 27, 1836

Hannah, Julia F. and William H. Brown (3) - February 17, 1885
For further information see - Brown, William H.

Hannah, Mollie V. and John W. Green (3) - December 2, 1885
For further information see - Green, John W.

Hansecker, George and Catherine Haine (1) - December 16, 1819

Hansher, Mary and Vincent G. Moore (3) - November 19, 1888
For further information see - Moore, Vincent G.

Hanson, Revd. James and Sarah Burnett (1) - February 3, 1825

Harbin, Elizabeth and John Smith (1) - July 14, 1834

Hardee, George William and Margaret Catherine Taylor (3).-   March 4, 1883
    Place of marriage, Middleway - Age of husband, 28 - Age of wife,
    21 - Both are Single - Both were born in Frederick County, Virginia -
    Both reside in Jefferson County, West Virginia.

Harden, Sarah and John Wiggington (1) -   1816

Harden, Sarah and James White (3) -   April 6, 1871
    For further information see - White, James.

Harder, Annie M. and Fonrose Penwell (3) -   August 13, 1884
    For further information see - Penwell, Fonrose.

Harder, Fanny Elizabeth and Francis Medler (3) -   April 30, 1877
    For further information see - Medler, Francis.

Harder, Thomas H. and Eliza Painter (3) -   October 12, 1876
    Place of marriage, Harpers Ferry - Age of husband, 24 - Age of wife,
    25 - Both are Single - Both were born in Jefferson County, West
    Virginia - Both reside in Jefferson County, West Virginia.

Harder, Thomas H. and Julia Ann Cogel (3) -   May 29, 1881
    Place of marriage, Bolivar - Age of husband, 26 - Age of wife, 21 -
    Husband is a Widower - Wife is Single - Husband was born in
    Jefferson County, West Virginia - Both reside in Jefferson County,
    West Virginia.

Hardesty, Edward G. and Elizabeth Butt (3) -   December 16, 1879
    Place of marriage, Middleway - Age of husband, 25 - Age of wife,
    23 - Both are Single - Both were born in Jefferson County, West
    Virginia - Both reside in Jefferson County, West Virginia.

Hardesty, George and Mary Morris (1) -   August 9, 1805

Hardesty, Kirk and Clara Shaull (3) -   April 15, 1869
    Place of marriage, Jefferson County - Age of husband, 24 - Age of
    wife, 24 - Both are Single - Husband was born in Clarke County,
    Virginia - Wife was born in Pennsylvania - Husband resides in Clarke
    County, Virginia - Wife resides in Jefferson County - Occupation of
    husband is Farmer.

Hardesty, Otho J. and Mary V. Swimley (3) -   September 2, 1873
    Place of marriage, near Smithfield - Age of husband, 23 - Age of
    wife, 23 - Both are Single - Husband was born in Clarke County,
    Virginia - Wife was born in Jefferson County, West Virginia - Both
    reside in Jefferson County, West Virginia.

Hardesty, Priscilla and Alexander Riley (1) -   November 14, 1826

Harding, Ann and John Luckey (1) -   July 22, 1824

Harding, Annie C. and J. G. Sullivan (3) -   October 18, 1883
    For further information see - Sullivan, J. G.

Harding, Elizabeth and Levi R. Show (1) -   September 26, 1833

Harding, Margaret and Hyram Carney (1) -   April 28, 1814

Harding, Samuel and Mary Ervin (1) -   June 22, 1817

Hardy, Benjamin F. and Mary Ambrose (3) - ....December 30, 1877
   Place of marriage, Bolivar - Age of husband, 20 - Age of wife, 20 -
   Both are Single - Husband was born in State of Maryland - Wife was
   born in Jefferson County, West Virginia - Husband resides in
   Maryland - Wife resides in Jefferson County, West Virginia.

Hardy, George W. and Catherine Ann Ambrose (3) - October 1, 1876
   Place of marriage, Harpers Ferry - Age of husband, 50 - Age of wife,
   48 - Husband is a Widower - Wife is a Widow - Husband was born in
   Maryland - Wife was born in Jefferson County, West Virginia -
   Husband resides in Maryland - Wife resides in Jefferson County, West
   Virginia.

Hardy, M. (bride) (cold.) C. Haines (3) - December 26, 1867
   For further information see - Haines, C.

Harious, Eliza (cold.) James Whiting (3) - December 25, 1877
   For further information see - Whiting, James.

Harlan, G. Boyd and Margaretta Kesel (3) - June 24, 1867
   Place of marriage, Charlestown - Age of husband, 38 - Age of wife,
   28 - Both are Single - Husband was born in Berkeley County, West
   Virginia - Wife was born in Jefferson County - Husband resides in
   Berkeley County, West Virginia - Wife resides in Jefferson County -
   Husband's parents are John and Nancy - Wife's parents are William
   and Ellen - Occupation of husband is Farmer.

Harley, Francis Joseph and Mary Ann Gilbert (1) - August 18, 1825

Harley, Maria W. and George W. Welsh (2) - (L) April 8, 1859

Harlow, Hattie A. and John L. Obaugh (3) - July 6, 1887
   For further information see - Obaugh, John L.

Harlow, Minnie E. and George B. Graves (3) - April 10, 1890
   For further information see - Graves, George B.

Harman, Jacob H. (colored) Ann R. Kidwilder (3) - (1870)
   Age of husband, 22 - Age of wife, 22 - Husband was born in
   Maryland - Wife was born in Jefferson County - Both reside in
   Jefferson County. (Endorsed by John R. Ray.) (This record is
   marked through in the original.)

Harman, Jacob H. and Ann K. Kidwiler (3) - September 29, 1870
   Place of marriage, Jefferson County - Age of husband, 22 - Age of
   wife, 22 - Husband was born in Maryland - Wife was born in Jefferson
   County - Both reside in Jefferson County. (Endorsed by J. R. Ray.)

Harman, John W. and Ann R. Link (2) - (L) June 2, 1856

Harman, Nannie and J. H. Blackford (3) - November 10, 1887
   For further information see - Blackford, J. H.

Harman, Walter and Maggie A. Ronemous (3) - November 17, 1886
   Place of marriage, Duffields - Age of husband, 26 - Age of wife,
   24 - Both are Single - Husband was born in Berkeley County - Wife
   was born in Jefferson County - Both reside in Jefferson County, West
   Virginia.

Harman, William F. and Matilda C. Myers (3) - February 28, 1871
   Place of marriage, Jefferson County - Age of husband, 22 - Age of
   wife, 22 - Both are Single - Husband was born at Funkstown,
   Pennsylvania - Wife was born in Jefferson County - Husband resides
   at Funkstown, Pennsylvania - Wife resides in Jefferson County -
   Husband's parents are Peter and Sarah - Wife's parents are James W.
   and Maria - Occupation of husband is Blacksmith.

Harmer, William H. and Mahala A. Krepps (3) - October 16, 1873
   Place of marriage, Harpers Ferry - Age of husband, 30 - Age of wife,
   23 - Both are Single - Wife was born in Jefferson County, West
   Virginia - Husband resides at Washington City - Wife resides in
   Jefferson County, West Virginia.

Harp, Ada and Charles D. Keplinger (3) - April 24, 1884
   For further information see - Keplinger, Charles D.

Harp, Bettie and M. E. Spohn (3) - April 12, 1883
   For further information see - Spohn, M. E.

Harp, Florence and Charles A. Licklider (3) - October 29, 1873
   For further information see - Licklider, Charles A.

Harper, Ann and Michael Finegan (2) - (L) November 12, 1853

Harper, Charles and Eliza Buckles (1) - April 6, 1830

Harper, Mary N. and William F. Chandler (2) - (L) June 8, 1857

Harpin, Robert and Mary A. Higgens (3) - (1868)
   Age of husband, 22 - Age of wife, 21 - Both are Single - Husband was
   born in Jefferson County - Wife was born in Ireland - Husband resides
   in Jefferson County - Wife resides in West Virginia - Husband's
   parents are James and Elizabeth - Wife's parents are Caroline -
   Occupation of husband is Railroad Agency. (Brother swearing as to
   age of sister.)

Harr, William and Sarah Ann Dillow (3) - December 24, 1872

Harrell, Ella Rose and James W. Butt (3) - February 5, 1880
   For further information see - Butt, James W.

Harrell, Harrison S. and Maggie F. Dewar (3) - July 20, 1887
   Place of marriage, Charlestown - Age of husband, 35 - Age of wife,
   33 - Husband is a Widower - Wife is Single - Husband was born in
   Hamilton County, Ohio - Wife was born in Minnesota - Husband resides
   at Detroit, Michigan - Wife resides at Richwood, Minnesota.

Harrell, Mary E. and Thomas W. Spink (3) - (1868)
   For further information see - Spink, Thomas W.

Harrell, Mollie R. and Marshall J. Rohr (3) - July 22, 1880
   For further information see - Rohr, Marshall J.

Harrell, Rebecca J. and Thomas T. Earnshaw (2) - (L) January 28, 1857

Harris, Albert (colored) Mary S. Travers (3) - January 1, 1870
   Place of marriage, Harpers Ferry - Age of husband, 23 - Age of wife,
   21 - Husband was born at Winchester, Virginia - Wife was born in
   Augusta County, Virginia - Both reside in Jefferson County.

Harris, Anna (cold.) Nelson Edwards (3) -　　　　September 11, 1884
　　For further information see - Edwards, Nelson.

Harris, Annie R. and Samuel A. Washington (3) -　　　May 29, 1890
　　For further information see - Washington, Samuel A.

Harris, Cary (cold.) Fanny Cooper (3) -　　　　　December 28, 1882
　　Place of marriage, Duffields - Age of husband, 22 - Age of wife,
　　19 - Both are Single - Both were born in Jefferson County, West
　　Virginia - Both reside in Jefferson County, West Virginia.
　　(Consent of bride's father in writing.)

Harris, Cary (cold.) Lucy Morris (3) -　　　　　November 17, 1887
　　Place of marriage, near Halltown - Age of husband, 27 - Age of wife,
　　39 - Husband is a Widower - Wife is a Widow - Both were born in
　　Jefferson County, West Virginia - Both reside in Jefferson County,
　　West Virginia.

Harris, Eliza and J. E. Walters (2) -　　　　　(L) April 22, 1863
　　For further information see - Walters, J. E.

Harris, Eliza and John H. Schoppert (3) -　　　　October 23, 1866
　　For further information see - Schoppert, John H.

Harris, Fairfax (cold.) Sarah Wilson (3) -　　　　October 25, 1879
　　Place of marriage, Charlestown - Age of husband, 39 - Age of wife,
　　32 - Husband is a Widower - Wife is a Widow - Husband was born in
　　Warren County, Virginia - Wife was born in Jefferson County, West
　　Virginia - Both reside in Jefferson County, West Virginia.

Harris, George and Drusilla Wintermoyer (1) -　　　February 11, 1847

Harris, George and Harriet A. Shauck (2) -　　　　(L) June 14, 1854

Harris, George (cold.) Mary Jane Twyman (3) -　　　July 3, 1890
　　Place of marriage, Charlestown - Age of husband, 25 - Age of wife,
　　18 - Both are Single - Husband was born in Augusta County,
　　Virginia - Wife was born in Jefferson County, West Virginia - Both
　　reside in Jefferson County, West Virginia.

Harris, George L. and Louisa Young (1) -　　　　　May 16, 1816

Harris, Hannah and John Miller (1) -　　　　　　May 23, 1812

Harris, Henry (cold.) Julia McCann (3) -　　　　August 30, 1888
　　Place of marriage, Shepherdstown - Age of husband, 21 - Age of wife,
　　18 - Both are Single - Husband was born in Page County, Virginia -
　　Wife was born in Jefferson County, West Virginia - Both reside in
　　Jefferson County, West Virginia. (Consent of bride's father in
　　person.)

Harris, James and Mary Cherry (1) -　　　　　　December 12, 1805

Harris, John (cold.) Sarah Blue (3) -　　　　　January 22, 1868
　　Age of husband, 28 - Age of wife, 21 - Both are Single - Husband
　　was born in Augusta, Virginia - Wife was born in Jefferson County -
　　Both reside in Jefferson - Occupation of husband is Laborer.

Harris, John and Georgia Douglass (3) - May 16, 1872
    Place of marriage, Jefferson County - Age of husband, 36 - Age of
    wife, 27 - Husband is Single - Wife is a Widow - Husband's parents
    are Samuel and Millie - Occupation of husband is Farmer.

Harris, John (cold.) Elizabeth Diggs (3) - December 31, 1885
    Place of marriage, Halltown - Age of husband, 24 - Age of wife, 23 -
    Both are Single - Husband was born in State of Maryland - Wife was
    born in Jefferson County, West Virginia - Both reside in Jefferson
    County, West Virginia.

Harris, John T. and Sarah A. Backhouse (2) - (L) February 19, 1861

Harris, Laura (cold.) James Jackson (3) - December 26, 1887
    For further information see - Jackson, James.

Harris, Lulie (cold.) Ashby Mitchell (3) - January 16, 1889
    For further information see - Mitchell, Ashby.

Harris, Martha (cold.) John Hester (3) - July 19, 1883
    For further information see - Hester, John.

Harris, Mary and John Riley (1) - March 3, 1825
Harris, Miss Mary and J. W. Ewing (2) - (L) December 27, 1851
Harris, Molly and Jacob Hiedwohl (3) - February 24, 1885
    For further information see - Hiedwohl, Jacob.

Harris, Rebecca and Anthony Colbert (1) - September 29, 1827

Harris, Sarah (cold.) B. F. Veney (3) - July 29, 1887
    For further information see - Veney, B. F.

Harris, Stephen (cold.) Rebecca Shorts (3) - April 19, 1883
    Place of marriage, Duffields - Age of husband, 22 - Age of wife,
    27 - Both are Single - Both were born in Jefferson County, West
    Virginia - Both reside in Jefferson County, West Virginia.

Harris, Susanna (cold.) John W. Rutherford (3) - May 26, 1881
    For further information see - Rutherford, John W.

Harris, W. J. and L. H. Spicer (bride) (3) - July 25, 1871
    Place of marriage, Jefferson County - Age of husband, 26 - Age of
    wife, 21 - Both are Single - Both were born in Virginia - Both
    reside in West Virginia - Husband's parents are W. J. and Sarah E. -
    Wife's parents are John E. and Margaret E. - Occupation of husband
    is Blacksmith.

Harris, William J. and Ruth McGoldrick (2) - (L) April 11, 1861
    Time of marriage, April 25, 1861 - Place of marriage, Harpers
    Ferry - Names of parties, William J. Harris and Ruth McGoldrick -
    Age of husband, 39 years - Age of wife, 27 years - Both are Single -
    Place of husband's birth is Frederick County (near Clarke) - Place
    of wife's birth is Pennsylvania - Place of husband's residence is
    Clarke County - Wife resides in Jefferson County - Husband's parents
    are George L. and Lacy T. Harris - Wife's parents are John and Susan
    McGoldrick - Occupation of husband is Farmer - Given under my hand
    this 11th day of April, 1861 - William J. Harris.

Harrison, Anna and Phil Weskell (3) - (1872)
    For further information see - Weskell, Phil.

Harrison, Annie S. and Clarence Summers Hunter (3) -   June 23, 1887
    For further information see - Hunter, Clarence Summers.

Harrison, Bud and Anna Simmons (3) -   April 18, 1867
    Place of marriage, Charles Town - Age of husband, 23 - Age of wife,
    23 - Both are Single - Husband was born at Richmond City - Wife was
    born in Clarke County, Virginia - Both reside in Jefferson County,
    West Virginia - Husband's parents are William and Matilda
    Harrison - Wife's parents are David and Lettie Simmons - Occupation
    of husband is Farming.

Harrison, Cementy and George Cook (3) -   (1865)
    (License not returned.)

Harrison, Eugene L. and Fanny Estella Crutchley (3) -   April 29, 1886
    Place of marriage, Harpers Ferry - Age of husband, 20 - Age of wife,
    21 - Both are Single - Husband was born in Maryland - Wife was born
    at Washington City - Husband resides in Maryland - Wife resides in
    Jefferson County, West Virginia. (Consent of groom's mother in
    writing.)

Harrison, George and Elizabeth Boley (1) -   February 8, 1825

Harrison, Ida Virginia and Towner Schley (3) -   October 22, 1873
    For further information see - Schley, Towner.

Harrison, Lewis (cold.) Lizzy Taylor (3) -   March 10, 1877
    Place of marriage, Summit Point - Age of husband, 30 - Age of wife,
    18 - Both are Single - Husband was born in Brunswick County,
    Virginia - Wife was born in Clarke County, Virginia - Both reside
    in Jefferson County, West Virginia. (Consent of bride's father in
    person.)

Harrison, Mary and Samuel B. Harrison (3) -   January 8, 1867
    For further information see - Harrison, Samuel B.

Harrison, Samuel B. and Mary Harrison (3) -   January 8, 1867
    Place of marriage, Shepherdstown - Age of husband, 48 - Age of wife,
    40 - Husband is a Widower - Wife is a Widow - Both were born in
    Berkeley County, West Virginia - Husband resides at Duffields Depot,
    West Virginia - Wife resides at Hedgesville, West Virginia -
    Husband's parents are John B. and Teresa Harrison - Wife's parents
    are William and Sarah Mason - Occupation of husband is Merchant.

Hart, Alice (cold.) Philip Lucas (3) -   December 3, 1882
    For further information see - Lucas, Philip.

Hart, Alleatha E. (cold.) Jackson Carter (3) -   May 12, 1886
    For further information see - Carter, Jackson.

Hart, Benjamin (free colored).Julia A. Campbell (1) -   December 13, 1849

Hart, Benjamin and Octavia Roper (3) -   July 10, 1873
    Place of marriage, near Charlestown - Age of husband, 22 - Age of
    wife, 26 - Both are Single - Both were born in Jefferson County,
    West Virginia - Both reside in Jefferson County, West Virginia.

Hart, Daniel (cold.) Alice Murray (3) -   March 27, 1884
   Place of marriage, Charlestown - Age of husband, 24 - Age of wife,
   21 - Both are Single - Both were born in Jefferson County, West
   Virginia - Both reside in Jefferson County, West Virginia.

Hart, Elizabeth (free mixtures) Henry Goings (1) -   November 26, 1826

Hart, Emma and Randolph Brady (3) -   December 21, 1871
   For further information see - Brady, Randolph.

Hart, Frances E. and Edward Morrison (2) -   (L) November 17, 1851

Hart, Frances E. and Edward Morrison (1) -   November 18, 1851

Hart, George M. (cold.) Lydia Taylor Brady (3) -   June 10, 1867
   Place of marriage, Jefferson County - Age of husband, 23 - Age of
   wife, 27 - Both are Single - Husband was born in Jefferson County,
   West Virginia - Wife was born in Loudoun County, Virginia - Both
   reside in Jefferson County, West Virginia - Husband's parents are
   Thomas and Mary Ellen Hart - Wife's parents are A. and Sarah Brady -
   Occupation of husband is Laborer.

Hart, George M. (cold.) Laura M. Taylor (3) -   May 15, 1888
   Place of marriage, Charlestown - Age of husband, 44 - Age of wife,
   41 - Husband is a Widower - Wife is Single - Both were born in
   Jefferson County, West Virginia - Both reside in Jefferson County,
   West Virginia,

Hart, Harriet B. and Thomas W. Hiskett (2) -   (L) April 20, 1854

Hart, James E. and Phoebe V. W. Hiskett (2) -   (L) July 14, 1854

Hart, Jane M. and Joseph R. Moore (2) -   (L) April 5, 1853

Hart, John D. and Sarah E. Caniford (3) -   March 15, 1887
   Place of marriage, Charlestown - Age of husband, 23 - Age of wife,
   22 - Both are Single - Both were born in Clarke County, Virginia -
   Husband resides in Clarke County, Virginia - Wife resides in
   Jefferson County, West Virginia.

Hart, L. T. and Mrs. Dora Spotts (3) -   December 9, 1884
   Place of marriage, Shepherdstown - Age of husband, 26 - Age of wife,
   25 - Husband is a Widower - Wife is a Widow - Husband was born in
   Jefferson County, West Virginia - Wife was born in Jefferson
   County - Both reside in Jefferson County, West Virginia.

Hart, Louisa (cold.) Thomas Mitchell (3) -   August 6, 1881
   For further information see - Mitchell, Thomas.

Hart, Martha E. and Malcolm Brady (3) -   April 25, 1871
   For further information see - Brady, Malcolm.

Hart, Mary A. and William H. Levi (2) -   (L) January 10, 1852

Hart, Phebe and James E. Brady (3) -   July 8, 1867
   For further information see - Brady, James E.

Hartman, Elizabeth and James Allison (1) -   March 19, 1822

Hartness, Conrad and Mary Vores (1) -   November 22, 1825

Hartness, Elizabeth and Elisha Webb (1) -   November 6, 1817

Hartness, George and Ellen Moler (1) -   1825

Hartness, Mahala and David B. Wire (1) -   March 29, 1829

Hartzell, Benjamin and Lutie Baldwin (3) -   January 31, 1878
    Place of marriage, Shepherdstown - Age of husband, 22 - Age of wife,
    25 - Both are Single - Husband was born in Pennsylvania - Wife was
    born in Jefferson County, West Virginia - Both reside in Jefferson
    County, West Virginia.

Harvey, Julia Ann and Franklin Lane (3) -   November 2, 1873
    For further information see - Lane, Franklin.

Harvey, Leonora and Adam Kidwiler, Jr. (3) -   April 9, 1880
    For further information see - Kidwiler, Adam, Jr.

Harvey, Susan Matilda (free colored) Solomon Brown (2) - (L) September 3, 1856

Harvin, Harriet Jane and Milton Cloud (2) -   (L) (1862)
    For further information see - Cloud, Milton.

Hass, Annie T. and William Lee Kerfott (3) -   October 14, 1880
    For further information see - Kerfott, William Lee.

Hasson, James and Susan Johnson (3) -   January 10, 1867
    Place of marriage, Leetown, West Virginia - Age of husband, 23 - Age
    of wife, 18 - Both are Single - Husband was born in Warren County,
    Virginia - Wife was born in Jefferson County, Virginia - Both reside
    in Jefferson County, West Virginia - Husband's parents are George
    and W. Hasson - Wife's parents are W. and M. Johnson - Occupation of
    husband is Farmer.   (Father's permission,)

Hatfield, Jennie and Jessey Fry (3) -   March 5, 1873
    For further information see - Fry, Jessey.

Hatter, Emily and Lorenza Ferrell (3) -   May 9, 1872
    For further information see - Ferrell, Lorenza.

Hatter, Fannie and William Cross (3) -   September 28, 1871
    For further information see - Cross, William.

Haugh, C. A. V. (bride) and C. J. F. B. Price (3) -   April 29, 1879
    For further information see - Price, C. J. F. B.

Hausenfluck, Samuel and Emma S. Brill (3) -   August 3, 1889
    Place of marriage, Charlestown - Age of husband, 48 - Age of wife,
    22 - Husband is a Widower - Wife is Single - Husband was born in
    Sheandoah County, Virginia - Wife was born in Frederick County,
    Virginia - Husband resides in Frederick County, Virginia - Wife
    resides in Jefferson County, West Virginia.

Hawk, George W. and Ella Cogle (3) -   March 4, 1890
    Place of marriage, Harpers Ferry - Age of husband, 22 - Age of wife,
    21 - Both are Single - Husband was born in Jefferson County, West
    Virginia - Wife was born in Loudoun County, Virginia - Both reside
    in Jefferson County, West Virginia.

Hawk, James Henry and Mary Ellen Wilt (3) - December 25, 1884
    Place of marriage, Blue Ridge Mountain - Age of husband, 24 - Age of
    wife, 23 - Both are Single - Both were born in Jefferson County,
    West Virginia - Both reside in Jefferson County, West Virginia.

Hawk, James W. and Elizabeth Cogle (3) - July 22, 1883
    Place of marriage, near Harpers Ferry - Age of husband, 23 - Age of
    wife, 18 - Both are Single - Husband was born in West Virginia -
    Wife was born in Virginia - Both reside in Jefferson County, West
    Virginia. (Consent of bride's parents sworn by Rezin Piper.)

Hawk, James W. and Annie Hunt (3) - September 15, 1888
    Place of marriage, Harpers Ferry - Age of husband, 36 - Age of wife,
    24 - Husband is a Widower - Wife is Single - Both were born in
    Loudoun County, Virginia - Both reside in Jefferson County, West
    Virginia.

Hawk, John W. and Molly Staubs (3) - August 7, 1887
    Place of marriage, Harpers Ferry - Age of husband, 28 - Age of wife,
    22 - Both are Single - Both were born in Jefferson County, West
    Virginia - Both reside in Jefferson County, West Virginia.

Hawk, Mary E. and Louis H. Grove (3) - December 18, 1871
    For further information see - Grove, Louis H.

Hawk, Rachel and John W. Eckles (3) - December 8, 1881
    For further information see - Eckles, John W.

Hawk, Wells J. and Sarah B. Worthington (2) - (L) August 11, 1856

Hawkens, Francis M. and Louisa Willson (1) - 1825

Hawkens, Jeremiah and Margaret Lafferty (1) - December 28, 1825

Hawkins, Mary (cold.) Larkin Fitchart (3) - August 27, 1866
    For further information see - Fitchart, Larkin.

Hawkins, Philip (free blacks) Airy Conn (1) - August 11, 1831

Hawn, Ann Rebecca and Isaac N. Walters (2) - (L) April 17, 1856

Hawn, Catharine A. and Joseph Fleming (1) - April 11, 1850

Hawn, George and Mary Hoffman (widow) (1) - October 19, 1835

Hawn, John R. and Rosa A. Miller (2) - (L) January 2, 1861

Hawn, Martha and John H. Hill (3) - August 2, 1866
    For further information see - Hill, John H.

Hawn, Mary Q. and William J. Foutz (3) - March 7, 1889
    For further information see - Foutz, William J.

Hay, Mary and Samuel Davenport (1) - November 23, 1826

Hay, Ruth (Alder) H. and Samuel Davenport (1) - May 16, 1818

Hayden, Adaline B. and Horatio N. Gallaher (1) - September 2, 1830

Hayden, George A. and Adaline Beeler (1) - April 24, 1828

Hayden, Martina and John T. Linthiam (2) -   (L) July 31, 1850

Hayes, Mrs. Nellie and John Donavan (3) -   April 5, 1874
    For further information see - Donavan, John.

Haylock, William and Susana Agner (1) -   November 21, 1811

Haymaker, Emily and Thomas Reed (1) -   June 6, 1816

Hayne, G. W. and Bettie B. McDonald (3) -   January 11, 1876
    Place of marriage, near Leetown - Age of husband, 27 - Age of wife,
    22 - Both are Single - Husband was born in Berkeley County, West
    Virginia - Wife was born in Jefferson County, West Virginia - Both
    reside in Jefferson County, West Virginia.

Hays, Andrew and Euphemia Williams (1) -   January 8, 1834

Hays, Drusy (cold.) Arthur Parker (3) -   July 5, 1883
    For further information see - Parker, Arthur.

Hays, Fanny (cold.) Nathan Gay (3) -   July 8, 1886
    For further information see - Gay, Nathan.

Hays, William H. and Caroline Goodlow (1) -   July 7, 1848

Hays, William H. B. and Lydia A. Peacher (2) -   (L) January 24, 1859

Hayslett, John H. and Kate Hunter (3) -   December 9, 1880
    Place of marriage, Bride's Residence - Age of husband, 46 - Age of
    wife, 43 - Both are Single - Both were born in Jefferson County,
    West Virginia - Both reside in Jefferson County, West Virginia.

Hayslett, William D. and Georgietta M. Hunter (3) -   March 30, 1875
    Place of marriage, County - Age of husband, 35 - Age of wife, 31 -
    Both are Single - Husband was born in Jefferson County, West
    Virginia - Wife was born in Berkeley County, West Virginia - Both
    reside in Jefferson County, West Virginia.

Heafer, George R. and Clara Belle Keller (3) -   November 26, 1884
    Place of marriage, Harpers Ferry - Age of husband, 30 - Age of wife,
    18 - Both are Single - Husband was born in Jefferson County, West
    Virginia - Wife was born in Jefferson County - Both reside in
    Jefferson County, West Virginia. (Consent of bride's mother in
    writing.)

Heafer, Jesse B. and Lizzie Stewart (3) -   December 24, 1888
    Place of marriage, Harpers Ferry - Age of husband, 22 - Age of wife,
    21 - Both are Single - Husband was born in Jefferson County, West
    Virginia - Wife was born in Pennsylvania - Both reside in Jefferson
    County, West Virginia.

Heafer, Louisa R. and Joseph E. Webb (3) -   April 1889
    For further information see - Webb, Joseph E.

Heafer, Mary P. and Charles E. Dudrow (3) -   November 25, 1875
    For further information see - Dudrow, Charles E.

Healey, Edward and Margaret R. Crisfield (1) -   November 25, 1827

Heath, Jonas and Matilda Jinkins (1) -   June 26, 1823

Heck, Barbara C. and John A. Phalen (3) - February 20, 1889
    For further information see - Phalen, John A.

Heck, Carry and John J. Kane (3) - December 27, 1888
    For further information see - Kane, John J.

Heck, Catherine and John Edward Quick (3) - July 15, 1871
    For further information see - Quick, John Edward.

Heck, Sallie and F. R. Langston (3) - December 26, 1889
    For further information see - Langston, F. R.

Hedges, Baley and Sarah Lemon (1) - February 11, 1813

Hedges, Lena and Lawrence Allen (3) - May 30, 1889
    For further information see - Allen, Lawrence.

Hedges, Lucy G. and J. W. Reed (3) - November 6, 1872
    For further information see - Reed, J. W.

Hedges, Millissa M. and Harrison Hoff (3) - October 24, 1888
    For further information see - Hoff, Harrison.

Hedges, S. A. and Bettie Hill (3) - (1868)
    Age of husband, 35 - Age of wife, 26 - Both are Single - Husband was born in Maryland - Wife was born in Jefferson County - Husband resides in Maryland - Wife resides in Jefferson - Wife's parents are David and Bettie - Occupation of husband is Minister.

Hedges, William L. and Sarah Jane Birkitt (2) - (L) December 18, 1862
    Time of marriage, December 18, 1862 - Place of marriage, Charlestown, Jefferson County, Virginia - Names of parties, William L. Hedges and Sarah Jane Birkitt - Age of husband, 46 years - Age of wife, 23 years - Condition of husband is Widower - Condition of wife is Single - Place of husband's birth is Jefferson County, Virginia - Place of wife's birth is Loudoun County, Virginia - Both reside at Charles Town - Names of husband's parents are Baily T. and Sarah Hedges - Names of wife's parents are John T. and Sarah Birkitt - Occupation of husband is Merchant - Liscense issued, December 18, 1862.

Hedrick, Joseph M. and Mary D. Murphy (3) - October 20, 1868
    Place of marriage, Jefferson County - Age of husband, 23 - Age of wife, 24 - Both are Single - Husband was born at Georgetown, D. C. - Wife was born in Jefferson County - Husband resides in Jefferson County - Wife resides in West Virginia - Husband's parents are David and B. A. - Wife's parents are George and Catharine - Occupation of husband is Farmer.

Hefelstray, Harriet and David Hess (3) - February 11, 1869
    For further information see - Hess, David.

Hefferline, John W. and Georgianna Bowers (3) - January 11, 1888
    Place of marriage, Leetown - Age of husband, 40 - Age of wife, 32 - Husband is a Widower - Wife is a Widow - Husband was born in Frederick County, Virginia - Wife was born in Jefferson County, West Virginia - Husband resides in Frederick County, Virginia - Wife resides in Jefferson County, West Virginia.

Hefflebower, David and Elizabeth Cookus (2) - (L) March 1, 1858

Heflebower, Catharine and Daniel Dovenberger (2) -   (L) January 20, 1852

Heflebower, Daniel and Sarah M. Morrow (2) -   (L) November 12, 1855

Heflebower, Daniel and Frances Schaeffer (3) -   November 4, 1873
　　Place of marriage, Charlestown - Age of husband, 28 - Age of wife,
　　22 - Both are Single - Both were born in Jefferson County, West
　　Virginia - Both reside in Jefferson County, West Virginia.

Heflebower, Jane and Henry Stouffer (3) -   January 8, 1873
　　For further information see - Stouffer, Henry.

Heflebower, John and Anna Maria Cookus (2) -   (L) December 11, 1860

Heflebower, Rebecca F. and P. Gould Parker (2) -   (L) August 25, 1855

Heflebower, Sarah and George W. Marshall (2) -   (L) December 5, 1853

Heflebower, Susan C. and James H. Conklyn (2) -   (L) November 23, 1857

Heidwhol, James M. and Martha E. Littleton (3) -   January 28, 1875
　　Place of marriage, Charlestown - Age of husband, 24 - Age of wife,
　　20 - Both are Single - Husband was born in Jefferson County, West
　　Virginia - Wife was born in Loudoun County, Virginia - Husband
　　resides in Jefferson County, West Virginia - Wife resides in Loudoun
　　County, Virginia.

Heidwohl, Mary and Uriah Lock (1) -   April 6, 1831

Heinschman, Lewis and Catherine Bohn (1) -   August 28, 1834

Helferstay, Jennie and C. M. Swain (3) -   February 25, 1890
　　For further information see - Swain, C. M.

Helferstay, M. E. (bride) and J. B. Curtis (3) -   December 22, 1881
　　For further information see - Curtis, J. B.

Helferstay, William H. and Harriet E. Gatrell (2) -   (L) January 24, 1863
　　Time of marriage, January 27, 1863 - Place of marriage,
　　Shepherdstown - Names, William H. Helferstay and Harriet E.
　　Gatrell - Age of husband, 23 years - Age of wife, 19 years last
　　September - Both are Single - Both were born in Berkeley County -
　　Husband resides at Martinsburg, Berkeley County - Wife resides at
　　Shepherdstown, Jefferson County - Husband's parents are Henry and
　　Sarah Helferstay - Wife's parents are Charles and Ellen R.
　　Gatrell - Occupation of husband is Machinist - License issued,
　　January 24, 1863 - Thomas A. Moore, Clerk.

Heller, David and Rebecca C. Haines (1) -   September 13, 1831

Heller, H. C. and Emma Louise King (3) -   June 15, 1887
　　Place of marriage, Harpers Ferry - Age of husband, 29 - Age of wife,
　　26 - Both are Single - Husband was born in Virginia - Wife was born
　　in Maryland - Husband resides in Virginia - Wife resides in
　　Jefferson County, West Virginia at present.

Heller, Henry and Rebecca A. Smallwood (1) -   April 17, 1829

Heller, Susanna and Jacob Hiedwhol, Jr. (1) -   December 18, 1827

Helm, Anna (cold.) Lee Brady (3) - December 25, 1884
    For further information see - Brady, Lee.

Helm, John William (cold.) Mary Howard (3) - September 26, 1886
    Place of marriage, Charlestown - Age of husband, 50 - Age of wife,
    25 - Husband is a Widower - Wife is Single - Husband was born in
    Rappahannock County, Virginia - Wife was born in Jefferson County,
    West Virginia - Both reside in Jefferson County, West Virginia.

Helm, Laura (cold.) Isaac Ross (3) - June 17, 1877
    For further information see - Ross, Isaac.

Helm, Laura (cold.) Richard Johnson (3) - June 3, 1885
    For further information see - Johnson, Richard.

Helms, George W. (cold.) Sallie Edwards (3) - May 30, 1885
    Place of marriage, Charlestown - Age of husband, 22 - Age of wife,
    21 - Both are Single - Husband was born in Culpeper County,
    Virginia - Wife was born in Maryland - Both reside in Jefferson
    County, West Virginia.

Helms, Mary and Charles Taylor (3) - November 28, 1872
    For further information see - Taylor, Charles.

Henderschurch, Eleanor and Christian Hommer (2) - (L) April 20, 1857

Henderson, Annie (cold.) John Glow (3) - March 9, 1889
    For further information see - Glow, John.

Henderson, David E. and Annie O. Bealle (3) - December 1, 1870
    Place of marriage, Jefferson County - Age of husband, 38 - Age of
    wife, 31 - Both were born in Virginia - Both reside in Jefferson
    County.

Henderson, Elizabeth L. and J. W. Hilleary (3) - December 18, 1867
    For further information see - Hilleary, J. W.

Henderson, George and Amelia Berryman (3) - (1869)
    Age of husband, 22 - Age of wife, 17 - Husband was born in
    Virginia - Wife was born in Jefferson County - Both reside in
    Jefferson County. (Parents in writing give consent.)

Henderson, Janet L. and John Hilleary (2) - (L) September 11, 1860

Henderson, Levi and Louisa Rust (3) - September 5, 1871
    Place of marriage, Jefferson County - Age of husband, 22 - Age of
    wife, 19 - Both are Single - Husband was born in Virginia - Wife was
    born in Jefferson - Husband resides in Virginia - Wife resides in
    West Virginia - Husband's parents are Mary E. - Wife's parents are
    Sarah - Occupation of husband is Shoemaker.

Henderson, Richard and Bettie Beall (3) - April 26, 1881
    Place of marriage, Bride's Residence - Age of husband, 37 - Age of
    wife, 39 - Both are Single - Both were born in Jefferson County,
    West Virginia - Both reside in Jefferson County, West Virginia.

Henderson, Sarah and George Alexander (3) - September 6, 1866
    For further information see - Alexander, George.

Hendon, Benjamin (colored) J. Ann Wheeler (3) -   March 10, 1870
   Place of marriage, Residence of Bride's Father, Charlestown,
   Jefferson County, West Virginia - Age of husband, 24 - Age of wife,
   21 - Husband was born in Virginia - Wife was born in Jefferson
   County, Virginia - Both reside in Jefferson County, West Virginia.

Hendricks, A. C. and Sarah E. Ronemous (3) -   February 18, 1873
   Place of marriage, near Duffields - Age of husband, 26 - Age of
   wife, 24 - Both are Single - Both were born in Jefferson County,
   West Virginia - Both reside in Jefferson County, West Virginia -
   Husband's parents are William and Ruhama - Wife's parents are Henry
   and Sarah Jane - Occupation of husband is Mechanic.

Hendricks, Ambrose and Maggie S. Ronemous (3) -   September 29, 1880
   Place of marriage, Unionville - Age of husband, 26 - Age of wife,
   24 - Both are Single - Both were born in Jefferson County, West
   Virginia - Both reside in Jefferson County, West Virginia.

Hendricks, Daniel, Jr. and Mary Osborn (1) -   March 8, 1821

Hendricks, Daniel W. and Sarah M. Link (2) -   (L) November 3, 1858

Hendricks, Elizabeth J. and Robert B. Evans (2) -   (L) December 9, 1850

Hendricks, Elizabeth J. and Davis R. Grove (3) -   October 19, 1882
   For further information see - Grove, Davis R.

Hendricks, Harry and Lilly Brantner (3) -   December 25, 1887
   Place of marriage, Harpers Ferry - Age of husband, 22 - Age of wife,
   22 - Both are Single - Both were born in Jefferson County, West
   Virginia - Husband resides in Jefferson County, West Virginia - Wife
   resides in Jefferson County.

Hendricks, Harvey H. and Minnie Brantner (3) -   December 3, 1889
   Place of marriage, Charlestown - Age of husband, 22 - Age of wife,
   23 - Both are Single - Both were born in Jefferson County, West
   Virginia - Both reside in Jefferson County, West Virginia.

Hendricks, James and Elizabeth Osburn (1) -   March 23, 1820

Hendricks, James M. and Sarah E. Knott (3) -   February 12, 1867
   Place of marriage, Unionville, West Virginia - Age of husband, 23 -
   Age of wife, 24 - Both are Single - Both were born in Jefferson
   County, West Virginia - Both reside in Jefferson County, West
   Virginia - Husband's parents are James and Sophia Hendricks - Wife's
   Parents are Samuel and Margaret Knott - Occupation of husband is
   Farmer.   (Brother's permission; Samuel M. Knott.)

Hendricks, John and Polly Bell (1) -   November 15, 1804

Hendricks, John and Sarah Roderick (1) -   August 10, 1809

Hendricks, John B. and Catharine Melvin (3) -   December 20, 1883
   Place of marriage, near Duffields - Age of husband, 50 - Age of
   wife, 25 - Husband is a Widower - Wife is Single - Both were born in
   Jefferson County, West Virginia - Both reside in Jefferson County,
   West Virginia.

Hendricks, John W. and Catharine Snyder (2) -   (L) May 29, 1854

Hendricks, Kate Lee and George C. Link (3) - August 17, 1880
For further information see - Link, George C.

Hendricks, Margaret A. and John C. Sencenny (2) - (L) October 10, 1860

Hendricks, Mary and William Marshall (1) - December 30, 1825

Hendricks, Milton B. and Ida W. Herr (3) - November 3, 1881
Place of marriage, Bride's Residence - Age of husband, 23 - Age of wife, 22 - Both are Single - Both were born in Jefferson County, West Virginia - Both reside in Jefferson County, West Virginia.

Hendricks, Minnie Lee and Charles G. Moler (3) - June 11, 1885
For further information see - Moler, Charles G.

Hendricks, Morris K. and Anna B. Osbourn (3) - February 5, 1885
Place of marriage, Shepherdstown - Age of husband, 25 - Age of wife, 25 - Both are Single - Husband was born in Jefferson County, West Virginia - Wife was born in Cooper County, Missouri - Both reside in Jefferson County, West Virginia.

Hendricks, N. M. (M.D.) and Katherine S. Moler (3) - December 3, 1885
Place of marriage, Shepherdstown - Age of husband, 24 - Age of wife, 22 - Both are Single - Both were born in Jefferson County, West Virginia - Both reside in Jefferson County, West Virginia.

Hendricks, Tobias and Sarah M. Coffenbarger (2) - (L) May 15, 1858

Hendricks, Tobias and Elizabeth J. Bane (3) - December 8, 1875
Place of marriage, near Duffields - Age of husband, 23 - Age of wife, 22 - Both are Single - Both were born in Jefferson County, West Virginia - Both reside in Jefferson County, West Virginia.

Hendricks, Virginia C. and James W. Snyder (2) - (L) February 11, 1861

Henkle, A. C. and William F. Alexander (3) - April 9, 1868
For further information see - Alexander, William F.

Henkle, Daniel G. and Eliza J. Kerney (1) - April 8, 1845

Henkle, Daniel G. and Eugene G. Cavilier (3) - November 15, 1877
Place of marriage, Bolivar - Age of husband, 34 - Age of wife, 26 - Both are Single - Both were born in West Virginia - Both reside in Jefferson County, West Virginia. (Written permission of her father.)

Henkle, Jacob T. and Sue V. Allstadt (3) - December 5, 1876
Place of marriage, At Residence of Bride's Father - Age of husband, 27 - Age of wife, 21 - Both are Single - Both were born in Jefferson County, West Virginia - Both reside in Jefferson County, West Virginia.

Henkle, Mary Virginia and A. F. Garrott (3) - December 9, 1880
For further information see - Garrott, A. F.

Henkle, William Isaac and Laura K. Elgin (3) - February 16, 1887
Place of marriage, Harpers Ferry - Age of husband, 31 - Age of wife, 25 - Both are Single - Husband was born in Jefferson County, West Virginia - Wife was born in State of Maryland - Both reside in Jefferson County.

Henretty, Catherine and W. T. Ambrose (3) -   November 21, 1872
    For further information see - Ambrose, W. T.

Henrety, William S. and Nancy F. Ambrose (3) -   September 5, 1872
    Place of marriage, Jefferson County - Age of husband, 24 - Age of
    wife, 23 - Both are Single - Husband was born in Shenandoah County,
    Virginia - Wife was born in Page County, Virginia - Both reside in
    Jefferson County, West Virginia - Husband's parents are James and
    Susan - Wife's parents are George and Harriet - Occupation of
    husband is Farmer.

Henrick, Frank and Margaret E. Kelly (3) -   (1869)
    Age of husband, 26 - Age of wife, 21 - Husband was born in Ireland -
    Wife was born in Jefferson County - Both reside in Jefferson
    County. (Mother in writing gives consent.)

Henry, A. E. and George D. Johnson (3) -   October 17, 1867
    For further information see - Johnson, George D.

Henry, Christopher C. and Ida Lock (3) -   October 31, 1877
    Place of marriage, near Leetown - Age of husband, 23 - Age of wife,
    19 - Both are Single - Both were born in Jefferson County, West
    Virginia - Both reside in Jefferson County, West Virginia.
    (Consent of bride's father in writing.)

Henry, Christopher C. and Virginia L. Custer (3) -   August 30, 1881
    Place of marriage, Martinsburg - Age of husband, 27 - Age of wife,
    23 - Husband is a Widower - Wife is Single - Husband was born in
    Berkeley County, West Virginia - Wife was born in Jefferson County,
    West Virginia - Both reside in Jefferson County, West Virginia.

Henry, Kate (cold.) Frank Robinson (3) -   April 30, 1884
    For further information see - Robinson, Frank.

Henry, Mary C. and Martin L. Furey (3) -   March 28, 1871
    For further information see - Furey, Martin L.

Henry, Philip and Harriet Ellen J. Cecilia Custer (3) - April 8, 1873
    Place of marriage, near Leetown - Age of husband, 22 - Age of wife,
    19 - Both are Single - Husband was born in Berkeley County, West
    Virginia - Wife was born in Jefferson County, West Virginia - Both
    reside in Jefferson County, West Virginia - Husband's parents are
    Philip and Mary - Wife's parents are Ephraim and Ann Elizabeth -
    Occupation of husband is Farmer. (Consent of bride's father in
    person.)

Henry, Roberta B. and George W. Lloyd (3) -   January 3, 1889
    For further information see - Lloyd, George W.

Henry, Rozier (cold.) Julia Smith (3) -   December 28, 1889
    Place of marriage, Harpers Ferry - Age of husband, 24 - Age of wife,
    21 - Both are Single - Husband was born in Shenandoah County,
    Virginia - Wife was born in Warren County, Virginia - Both reside in
    Jefferson County, West Virginia.

Hensel, Edward L. and Mary F. Hensel (3) - December 31, 1868
   Place of marriage, Jefferson County - Age of husband, 24 - Age of
   wife, 22 - Both are Single - Both were born in Virginia - Both
   reside in Berkeley County - Husband's parents are David L. and Mary
   A. - Wife's parents are William J. and Catharine - Occupation of
   husband is Farmer.

Hensel, Mary F. and Edward L. Hensel (3) - December 31, 1868
   For further information see - Hensel, Edward L.

Hensell, R. S. and Arrabella Foreman (3) - September 10, 1867
   Place of marriage, Jefferson - Age of husband, 26 - Age of wife,
   20 - Both are Single - Husband was born in Berkeley County,
   Virginia - Wife was born in Jefferson County, West Virginia - Both
   reside in Jefferson County, West Virginia - Wife's parents are Jacob
   Foreman - Occupation of husband is Farmer. (Father in writing
   gives consent.)

Henson, G. W. and M. A. Gorman (bride) (3) - February 7, 1872
   Place of marriage, Jefferson County, West Virginia - Age of husband,
   29 - Age of wife, 25 - Both are Single - Husband was born in
   Jefferson County - Wife was born in Jefferson County, Virginia -
   Husband resides in Allegany County, Maryland - Wife resides in
   Jefferson County, West Virginia - Husband's parents are William P.
   and M. O. H. - Wife's parents are John P. and M. - Occupation of
   husband is Carpenter.

Henson, James L. and Marietta King (2) - (L) March 30, 1857

Henson, Lucy and B. F. Dooley (3) - August 26, 1880
   For further information see - Dooley, B. F.

Henson, Margaret Ann and James K. Lee (1) - November 1, 1832

Henson, Sally A. and George Hilbert (3) - February 18, 1869
   For further information see - Hilbert, George.

Herbert, Ann (cold.) Sidney Wilson (3) - December 18, 1889
   For further information see - Wilson, Sidney.

Herbert, Charles (cold.) Hannah Sims (3) - July 4, 1881
   Place of marriage, Charlestown - Age of husband, 34 - Age of wife,
   40 - Husband is a Widower - Wife is a Widow - Husband was born in
   Frederick County, Maryland - Wife was born in Jefferson County, West
   Virginia - Both reside in Jefferson County, West Virginia.

Herbert, Charles W. (cold.) Mary Evelyn Jackson (3) - September 9, 1874
   Place of marriage, Charles Town - Age of husband, 27 - Age of wife,
   21 - Both are Single - Husband was born in Frederick County,
   Maryland - Wife was born in Jefferson County, West Virginia - Both
   reside in Jefferson County, West Virginia.

Herbert, Emily (cold.) Ambrose Gates (3) - December 28, 1875
   For further information see - Gates, Ambrose.

Herbert, Evelyn (cold.) James D. Jackson, Jr. (3) - November 17, 1890
   For further information see - Jackson, James D., Jr.

Herbert, John (cold.) Martha Ellen Walker (3) -   August 23, 1877
   Place of marriage, Charlestown - Age of husband, 22 - Age of wife,
   21 - Both are Single - Both were born in Jefferson County, West
   Virginia - Both reside in Jefferson County, West Virginia.

Herbert, John (cold.) Emily Willis (3) -   October 23, 1884
   Place of marriage, Charlestown - Age of husband, 24 - Age of wife,
   21 - Both are Single - Both were born in Jefferson County, West
   Virginia - Husband resides in Jefferson County, West Virginia - Wife
   resides in Jefferson County.

Herbert, Mary and John Ripple (1) -   1813

Herbert, Rezin (cold.) Sarah Jackson (3) -   December 11, 1873
   Place of marriage, Charlestown - Age of husband, 34 - Age of wife,
   30 - Both are Single - Husband was born in Jefferson County, West
   Virginia - Wife was born in Clarke County, Virginia - Both reside in
   Jefferson County, West Virginia.

Herbert, William H. and Mary A. Wolf (3) -   December 13, 1877
   Place of marriage, Harpers Ferry - Age of husband, 35 - Age of wife,
   29 - Husband is Single - Wife is a Widow - Wife was born in
   Maryland - Husband resides in Loudoun County, Virginia - Wife resides
   in Jefferson County, West Virginia.

Herbs, Edmund and Nellie Timberlake (3) -   November 29, 1866
   Place of marriage, William A. Morgan's near Shepherdstown - Age of
   husband, 63 - Age of wife, 60 - Husband is a Widower - Wife is a
   Widow - Husband was born in Jefferson County, West Virginia - Wife
   was born in Frederick County, Virginia - Both reside in Jefferson
   County, West Virginia - Husband's parents are Anthony and Fannie
   Herbs - Occupation of husband is Laborer.

Herbst, Henry and M. A. Shewbridge (3) -   November 28, 1882
   Place of marriage, Bolivar - Age of husband, 37 - Age of Wife, 17 -
   Both are Single - Husband was born at Madgeburg, Germany - Wife was
   born at Georgetown, D. C. - Both reside in Jefferson County, West
   Virginia.   (Consent of bride's father in person.)

Herod, Eliza (cold.) Daniel Turner (3) -   November 3, 1874
   For further information see - Turner, Daniel.

Herr, A. H. and Narcissa Hoffman (1) -   February 23, 1850

Herr, Belle and Thomas W. Norris (3) -   November 21, 1877
   For further information see - Norris, Thomas W.

Herr, Edward G. W. and Mary Ann Osbourn (2) -   (L) May 5, 1855

Herr, Ida W. and Milton B. Hendricks (3) -   November 3, 1881
   For further information see - Hendricks, Milton B.

Herr, Nannie B. and William H. Kearfott (3) -   December 5, 1888
   For further information see - Kearfott, William H.

Herrin, Frank (cold.) Jane Johnson (3) -   May 27, 1884
   Place of marriage, Charlestown - Age of husband, 30 - Age of wife,
   22 - Both are Single - Husband was born in Augusta County,
   Virginia - Wife was born in Jefferson County, West Virginia - Both
   reside in Jefferson County, West Virginia.

Herring, Lewis and Martha Gillispie (1) -   April 7, 1818

Herrington, Augusta F. and Benjamin Moore (1) -   November 12, 1833

Herrington, Molly and William Starky (3) -   October 15, 1884
    For further information see - Starky, William.

Hertshue, Annie M. and Henry T. Mitchell (3) -   December 6, 1866
    For further information see - Mitchell, Henry T.

Heskett, Landon and Maria Lay (1) -   November 16, 1832

Heskett, Maria S. and William Atwell (1) -   November 21, 1825

Heskett, Sophia and Henry F. McEndree (1) -   February 22, 1836

Heskitt, Louisa T. and James W. Dorsey (1) -   May 15, 1828

Hess, David and Harriet Hefelstray (3) -   February 11, 1869
    Place of marriage, Jefferson County - Age of husband, 57 - Age of
    wife, 34 - Husband is a Widower - Wife is a Widow - Husband was born
    in Berkeley County, Virginia - Wife was born in Berkeley County -
    Both reside in Berkeley County - Wife's parents are Lashorer -
    Occupation of husband is Farmer.

Hess, Elizabeth A. and Aaron F. Baker (2) -   (L) October 11, 1858

Hess, John P. and Florence E. Strider (3) -   April 9, 1879
    Place of marriage, near Halltown - Age of husband, 29 - Age of wife,
    25 - Both are Single - Both were born in Jefferson County, West
    Virginia - Both reside in Jefferson County, West Virginia.

Hess, Joseph Franklin and Catharine Elizabeth Swimley (2) -
                                                              (L) February 15, 1861

Hess, Lorenzo D. and Mary Moler (2) -   (L) March 29, 1855

Hess, Nannie E. and Frank H. Gardner (3) -   February 24, 1874
    For further information see - Gardner, Frank H.

Hess, R. C. and Sue V. Koontz (3) -   February 5, 1879
    Place of marriage, near Shepherdstown - Age of husband, 25 - Age of
    wife, 24 - Both are Single - Husband was born in Jefferson County,
    West Virginia - Wife was born in Berkeley County, West Virginia -
    Both reside in Jefferson County, West Virginia.

Hess, Thomas L. and Harriet B. Colbert (3) -   March 11, 1880
    Place of marriage, Charlestown - Age of husband, 28 - Age of wife,
    26 - Both are Single - Both were born in Jefferson County, West
    Virginia - Both reside in Jefferson County, West Virginia.

Hessey, Elizabeth C. and William Hessey (2) -   (L) July 20, 1858

Hessey, Fannie M. and Benjamin F. Daniels (2) -   (L) March 29, 1855

Hessey, Virginia G. and T. M. Garrison (3) -   December 30, 1874
    For further information see - Garrison, T. M.

Hessey, William and Elizabeth C. Hessey (2) -   (L) July 20, 1858

243

Hester, John (cold.) Martha Harris (3) - July 19, 1883
 Place of marriage, near Charlestown - Age of husband, 21 - Age of wife, 19 - Both are Single - Husband was born in Virginia - Wife was born in Jefferson County, West Virginia - Both reside in Jefferson County, West Virginia. (Consent of bride's mother in writing; father not living.)

Hetterly, Uriah and Susanna Gruber (2) - (L) December 23, 1851

Hetterly, Uriah and Susanna Gruber (1) - December 23, 1851

Hewett, Daniel and Elizabeth Groover (1) - December 6, 1818

Hiatt, Simeon and Mary Mowser (1) - July 1822

Hibbard, John A. and Amelia Elizabeth Stickels (3) - November 14, 1878
 Place of marriage, Rock's Ferry - Age of husband, 23 - Age of wife, 25 - Both are Single - Both were born in Clarke County, Virginia - Husband resides in Clarke County, Virginia - Wife resides in Jefferson County, West Virginia.

Hibbens, Cyrus and Elizabeth Shirley (1) - December 22, 1805

Hickey, Camelia and Austin McCan (2) - (L) November 21, 1857

Hickman, Hugh and Lizzie Hagan (3) - April 28, 1889
 Place of marriage, Harpers Ferry - Age of husband, 32 - Age of wife, 30 - Husband is Single - Wife is a Widow - Husband was born in Montgomery County, Maryland - Wife was born in Jefferson County, West Virginia - Husband resides in Montgomery County, Maryland - Wife resides in Jefferson County, West Virginia.

Hickman, Mary and William S. Taylor (1) - March 4, 1829

Hicks, Adaline A. and Benjamin F. Ramey (3) - November 23, 1869
 For further information see - Ramey, Benjamin F.

Hicks, Daniel (colored) Ann Dixon (3) - (1870)
 Age of husband, 23 - Age of wife, 21 - Both were born in Virginia - Both reside in Jefferson County.

Hicks, John J. and Jane F. Baldwin (2) - (L) December 19, 1860

Hicks, Sarah (cold.) Charles Williams (3) - December 20, 1885
 For further information see - Williams, Charles

Hicks, Susan F. and George W. Howell (3) - September 5, 1867
 For further information see - Howell, George W.

Hicks, Thomas and Emily VonBlucher (3) - November 12, 1885
 Place of marriage, Charlestown - Age of husband, 35 - Age of wife, 19 - Husband is a Widower - Wife is Single - Husband was born in England - Wife was born in Jefferson County, West Virginia - Husband resides at Troy, New York - Wife resides in Jefferson County, West Virginia. (Consent of bride's mother in person.)

Hiedwhol, Jacob, Jr. and Susanna Heller (1) - December 18, 1827

Hiedwohl, George W. and Eliza Morgan (3) -   Jxanuary 1, 1874
    Place of marriage, Charlestown - Age of husband, 27 - Age of wife,
    30 - Both are Single - Both were born in Jefferson County, West
    Virginia - Both reside in Jefferson County, West Virginia.

Hiedwohl, Isaac and Hannah Cockrell (2) -   (L) February 21, 1855

Hiedwohl, Jacob and Molly Harris (3) -   February 24, 1885
    Place of marriage, Martinsburg - Age of husband, 36 - Age of wife,
    30 - Both are Single - Both were born in Jefferson County, West
    Virginia - Both reside in Jefferson County, West Virginia.

Hiett, Ann and William Rankins (1) -   July 23, 1834

Hiett, Catharine and John Marshall (1) -   January 19, 1837

Hiett, Mary and Josiah Bateman (1) -   July 19, 1827

Hiett, Sarah and Lewis McCloy (1) -   September 7, 1826

Higgens, Edward I. and Kate Line (3) -   (1869)
    Age of husband, 31 - Age of wife, 27 - Both are Single - Both were
    born in Ireland - Both reside in Jefferson County.

Higgens, Mary A. and Robert Harpin (3) -   (1868)
    For further information see - Harpin, Robert.

Higgins, Andrew and Sarah Jane Slavin (3) -   January 23, 1866
    Place of marriage, Harpers Ferry - Age of husband, 25 - Age of wife,
    21 - Both are Single - Husband was born in Ireland - Wife was born
    in Jefferson County, West Virginia - Both reside in Jefferson
    County, West Virginia - Husband's parents are Patrick and Mary
    Higgins - Wife's parents are Lawrence and Mary Slavin - Occupation
    of husband is Laborer.

Higgins, David and Cecelia Davis (1) -   July 16, 1815

Higgins, Michael and Mary Bowler (3) -   January 8, 1889
    Place of marriage, Harpers Ferry - Age of husband, 35 - Age of wife,
    30 - Both are Single - Husband was born in Ireland - Wife was born
    in Jefferson County, West Virginia - Both reside in Jefferson
    County, West Virginia.

Higgins, Mollie L. and B. F. Curry (3) -   November 27, 1889
    For further information see - Curry, B. F.

Higgins, Patrick and Mary Ann Slavan (2) -   (L) April 13, 1858

Higgins, Sarah Jane and William Hopcraft (3) -   October 28, 1879
    For further information see - Hopcraft, William.

Higgs, Alice V. and Alonzo M. Ring (3) -   December 11, 1889
    For further information see - Ring, Alonzo M.

Higgs, Dora Virginia and A. W. Showalter (3) -   October 10, 1888
    For further information see - Showalter, A. W.

High, David and Margaret Crow (1) -   March 24, 1831

Hightman, Charles Thomas and Malissa Cleveland (3). — December 25, 1879
   Place of marriage, Harpers Ferry - Age of husband, 23 - Age of wife,
   23 - Both are Single - Husband was born in Frederick County,
   Maryland - Wife was born in Jefferson County, West Virginia -
   Husband resides in Frederick County, Maryland - Wife resides in
   Jefferson County, West Virginia.

Hilbert, Almira R. E. and David S. Cockrill (3) - March 17, 1884
   For further information see - Cockrill, David S.

Hilbert, George and Sally A. Henson (3) - February 18, 1869
   Place of marriage, Jefferson County - Age of husband, 25 - Age of
   wife, 22 - Both are Single - Husband was born at Baltimore - Wife
   was born in Jefferson County - Husband resides at Baltimore - Wife
   resides in Jefferson County - Husband's parents are John and
   Elizabeth - Wife's parents are William P. and M. A. - Occupation of
   husband is Express.

Hilbert, Sallie D. and John C. Myers (3) - May 30, 1889
   For further information see - Myers, John C.

Hill, Albert S. (cold.) Susan E. Dickinson (3) - January 13, 1890
   Place of marriage, Harpers Ferry - Age of husband, 30 - Age of wife,
   25 - Both are Single - Both were born in Augusta County, Virginia -
   Both reside in Jefferson County, West Virginia.

Hill, Ann Elizabeth and Joseph M. Stonebraker (2) - (L) October 23, 1855

Hill, Barbara J. and Jacob Williams (3) - September 15, 1870
   For further information see - Williams, Jacob.

Hill, Bettie and S. A. Hedges (3) - (1868)
   For further information see - Hedges, S. A.

Hill, Charles W. and Maggie Gageby (3) - January 25, 1888
   Place of marriage, Browns Crossing - Age of husband, 21 - Age of
   wife, 24 - Both are Single - Husband was born in Berkeley County -
   Wife was born in Jefferson County - Both reside in Jefferson County,
   West Virginia.

Hill, Eliza and Henry Ford (3) - January 4, 1869
   For further information see - Ford, Henry.

Hill, Fielding (cold.) Mary Canada (3) - September 16, 1884
   Place of marriage, Charlestown - Age of husband, 28 - Age of wife,
   22 - Both are Single - Husband was born in State of Virginia - Wife
   was born in State of Maryland - Both reside in Jefferson County.

Hill, Franklin P. and Virginia Voorhees (3) - January 22, 1889
   Place of marriage, Charlestown - Age of husband, 27 - Age of wife,
   25 - Both are Single - Husband was born at Winchester, Virginia -
   Wife was born in Berkeley County, West Virginia - Both reside in
   Jefferson County, West Virginia.

Hill G. W. and Eliza Virginia Butts (3) - January 1, 1889
   Place of marriage, Martinsburg, Berkeley County - Age of husband,
   22 - Age of wife, 17 next May - Both are Single - Husband was born
   in Tennessee - Wife was born in Jefferson County, West Virginia -
   Both reside in Jefferson County, West Virginia. (Consent of
   bride's father in writing.)

Hill, George J. and Fannie D. Trussell (3) - November 28, 1888
    Place of marriage, Harpers Ferry - Age of husband, 27 - Age of wife, 24 - Both are Single - Both were born in Jefferson County, West Virginia - Both reside in Jefferson County, West Virginia.

Hill, Ida M. and Samuel B. Neill (3) - February 1, 1881
    For further information see - Neill, Samuel B.

Hill, Isaac R. and Hattie B. Keplinger (3) - January 20, 1880
    Place of marriage, Shepherdstown - Age of husband, 26 - Age of wife, 27 - Both are Single - Husband was born in Berkeley County, West Virginia - Wife was born in Jefferson County, West Virginia - Both reside in Jefferson County, West Virginia.

Hill, J. Taylor and Sarah Ellen Moler (3) - October 20, 1874
    Place of marriage, County - Age of husband, 27 - Age of wife, 25 - Both are Single - Husband was born in Berkeley County, West Virginia - Wife was born in Jefferson County, West Virginia - Both reside in Jefferson County, West Virginia.

Hill, Jacob and Alsey Whitehouse (1) - 1824

Hill, Jane (cold.) James Whiting (3) - July 24, 1873
    For further information see - Whiting, James.

Hill, Jennie (cold.) Benjamin Jackson (3) - December 2, 1880
    For further information see - Jackson, Benjamin.

Hill, John H. and Martha Hawn (3) - August 2, 1866
    Place of marriage, Lutheran Parsonage, Shepherdstown - Age of husband, 23 - Age of wife, 21 - Both are Single - Husband was born in Jefferson County, West Virginia - Wife was born in Berkeley County, West Virginia - Husband resides in Jefferson County, West Virginia - Wife resides in Berkeley County, West Virginia - Husband's parents are William and Ellen Hill - Wife's parents are George and Mary V. Hawn - Occupation of husband is Farmer.

Hill, John H. (cold.) Etta Lovett (3) - January 1, 1889
    Place of marriage, Harpers Ferry - Age of husband, 22 - Age of wife, 28 - Both are Single - Husband was born in Jefferson County, West Virginia - Wife was born at Winchester, Virginia - Both reside in Jefferson County, West Virginia.

Hill, John H. and Laura V. Hynes (3) - January 28, 1890
    Place of marriage, Shepherdstown - Age of husband, 45 - Age of wife, 35 - Husband is a Widower - Wife is Single - Husband was born in Jefferson County, West Virginia - Wife was born in Washington County, Maryland - Both reside in Jefferson County, West Virginia.

Hill, John P. and Mary Elizabeth Byers (2) - (L) July 22, 1850

Hill, John P. and Mary Elizabeth Byers (1) - July 23, 1850

Hill, Joseph and Harriet Goings (1) - January 30, 1806

Hill, Lizzie (cold.) Robert Carter (3) - July 30, 1883
    For further information see - Carter, Robert.

Hill, Lucretia M. and Henry W. Dejarnett (3) - December 3, 1873
    For further information see - Dejarnett, Henry W.

Hill, M. F. (bride) and R. O. Vanvactor (3) - August 3, 1884
    For further information see - Vanvactor, R. O.

Hill, Mary E. and James K. P. Leslie (3) - February 2, 1875
    For further information see - Leslie, James K. P.

Hill, Mary Ellen and E. O. McKee (3) - March 28, 1882
    For further information see - McKee, E. O.

Hill, Nancy and John Thornton (3) - July 27, 1867
    For further information see - Thornton, John.

Hill, Nathan (cold.) Laura Powell (3) - July 6, 1876
    Place of marriage, Charlestown - Age of husband, 34 - Age of wife, 22 - Husband is a Widower - Wife is Single - Both were born in Jefferson County, West Virginia - Both reside in Jefferson County, West Virginia.

Hill, R. W. and Virginia Milton (3)- September 20, 1877
    Place of marriage, near Shannondale - Age of husband, 28 - Age of wife, 21 - Both are Single - Husband was born in Jefferson County, West Virginia - Wife was born in Missouri - Both reside in Jefferson County, West Virginia.

Hill, Samuel and Catharine T. Busey (1) - August 22, 1833

Hill, Sarah V. and George R. Staley (2) - (L) December 2, 1856

Hill, Thomas N. and Maggie A. Oyerley (3) - March 21, 1876
    Place of marriage, Charles Town - Age of husband, 29 - Age of wife, 23 - Both are Single - Both were born in Jefferson County, West Virginia - Both reside in Jefferson County, West Virginia.

Hill, Volney P. and Julia Ann Trussell (3) - June 4, 1873
    Place of marriage, Unionville - Age of husband, 31 - Age of wife, 29 - Both are Single - Husband was born in Frederick County, Virginia - Wife was born in Jefferson County, West Virginia - Husband resides in Loudoun County, Virginia - Wife resides in Jefferson County, West Virginia.

Hill, W. G. and Delpha Powell (3) - February 12, 1872
    Place of marriage, Jefferson County, West Virginia - Age of husband, 23 - Age of wife, 22 - Both are Single - Husband was born in Jefferson County - Wife was born in Jefferson County, Virginia - Husband resides in Jefferson County - Wife resides in Jefferson County, West Virginia - Husband's parents are William and Rebecca - Wife's parents are Joseph and Lucy - Occupation of husband is Mechanic.

Hill, William B. (cold.) Georgiana Edeny (3) - August 18, 1880
    Place of marriage, Harpers Ferry - Age of husband, 30 - Age of wife, 16 - Both are Single - Husband was born in Jefferson County, West Virginia - Wife was born in Maryland - Both reside in Jefferson County, West Virginia. (Consent of bride's father in writing.)

Hillary, William and Augusta Washington (3) -   May 7, 1867
   Place of marriage, Charlestown - Age of husband, 44 - Age of wife,
   19 - Both are Single - Husband was born in Jefferson County, West
   Virginia - Wife was born in Clarke County, Virginia - Both reside at
   Charlestown - Husband's parents are Sissem and Dolley Hillary -
   Wife's parents are Henry and Lucy Washington - Occupation of husband
   is Farmer.

Hilleary, Clarence Lee and M. E. Burton (3) -   July 14, 1888
   Place of marriage, Charlestown - Age of husband, 25 - Age of wife,
   25 - Both are Single - Husband was born in Frederick County,
   Maryland - Wife was born at Richmond, Virginia - Husband resides at
   Springfield, Ohio - Wife resides in Jefferson County, West Virginia.

Hilleary, Edith E. and William A. Holmes (3) -   February 5, 1880
   For further information see - Holmes, William A.

Hilleary, J. W. and Elizabeth L. Henderson (3) -   December 18, 1867
   Place of marriage, Jefferson County - Age of husband, 37 - Age of
   wife, 26 - Both are Single - Husband was born in Maryland - Wife was
   born in Jefferson County - Husband resides in Maryland - Wife
   resides in Jefferson - Wife's parents are Richard and Eliza B. -
   Occupation of husband is Physician.

Hilleary, John and Janet L. Henderson (2) -   (L) September 11, 1860

Hilleary, Thomas and Mary Elizabeth Marshall (2) -   (L) (May 1861)
   Time of marriage, May 30 - Place of marriage, near Shepherdstown -
   Age of husband, 33 years - Age of wife, 25 years - Condition of
   husband is a Widower - Condition of wife is Single - Place of
   husband's birth was State of Maryland - Place of wife's birth was
   Jefferson County - Names of husband's parents are John Henry and
   Cornelia Hilleary - Names of wife's parents are John and Ruhama
   Marshall - Place of husband's residence is Frederick County,
   Maryland - Place of wife's residence is Jefferson County,
   Virginia - Occupation of husband is Farmer.   John W. Marshall.

Hilliard, Amos and Catherine Duke (1) -   October 2, 1834

Hills, Elizabeth (cold.) Gideon Johnson (3) -   June 14, 1875
   For further information see - Johnson, Gideon.

Hilton, Jennie and Daniel J. Folk (3) -   August 30, 1889
   For further information see - Folk, Daniel J.

Hime, David Jackson and Sarah C. Strother (3) -   September 13, 1867
   Place of marriage, Jefferson - Age of husband, 24 - Age of wife,
   22 - Both are Single - Both were born in Fauquier County, Virginia -
   Both reside in Fauquier County, Virginia - Husband's parents are
   John - Wife's parents are Ann - Occupation of husband is Farmer.

Hinderkrich, Sarah and Elihue H. Hughes (3) -   May 26, 1870
   For further information see - Hughes, Elihue H.

Hines, Mary E. and Jesse D. Price (3) -   September 28, 1870
   For further information see - Price, Jesse D.

Hinkle, Harriot and Joshua Motter (1) -   March 7, 1826

Hinkle, John and Eleanor Baker (1) -   May 2, 1820

Hinkle, Julia and Joseph Delaplane (1) -	1814
Hinkle, Matilda and William Moore (1) -	December 20, 1816
Hinton, Mattie E. and Charles E. Boyd (3) -	September 13, 1888

For further information see - Boyd, Charles E.

Hipkin, Hannah (cold.) Samuel Mason (3) -   January 24, 1887
   For further information see - Mason, Samuel.

Hipsley, Emma F. and Herman E. Delo (3) -   September 17, 1879
   For further information see - Delo, Herman E.

Hiram, Peter and Mary Drish (1) -   September 15, 1807

Hiser, Charles and Sally V. Britner (3) -   May 21, 1867
   Place of marriage, Shepherdstown - Age of husband, 22 - Age of wife, 19 - Both are Single - Husband was born in Frederick County, Maryland - Wife was born in Jefferson County, Virginia - Husband resides at Martinsburg, West Virginia - Wife resides at Shepherdstown - Husband's parents are Lewis and Ann Hiser - Wife's parents are Gregerory and Catherine Britner - Occupation of husband is Baker. (Father's permission; present.)

Hiskett, Phoebe V. W. and James E. Hart (2) -   (L) July 14, 1854

Hiskett, Sarah J. and George J. Ridgway (2) -   (L) June 1, 1854

Hiskett, Thomas W. and Harriet B. Hart (2) -   (L) April 20, 1854

Hitaffer, David and Martha J. Wingate (widow) (2) -   (L) December 27, 1852

Hitaffer, Mary C. and Charles T. Roderick (3) -   August 22, 1871
   For further information see - Roderick, Charles T.

Hite, Caroline M. and Daniel Buckly (1) -   July 26, 1836

Hite, Courtney Ann and Elias Edmonds (1) -   April 1827

Hite, Elizabeth S. and William H. D. Hall (1) -   February 18, 1840

Hite, Frances C. and William Waters (1) -   December 22, 1825

Hite, Frances Madison and James Lackland Ranson (1) -   May 16, 1820

Hite, Joseph and Elizabeth Smith (1) -   November 23, 1817

Hite, Primus and Annie Louis (3) -   July 21, 1866
   Place of marriage, Harpers Ferry, Jefferson County, West Virginia - Age of husband, 36 - Age of wife, 23 - Husband is a Widower - Wife is Single - Husband was born in Jefferson County, West Virginia - Wife was born in Alleghaney County, Maryland - Both reside in Jefferson County, West Virginia - Husband's parents are Samuel and Esther Hite - Wife's parents are Ann M. Louis - Occupation of husband is Laborer.

Hite, Robert Gates and Courtney Ann Briscoe (1) -   January 19, 1823

Hite, Sally E. and R. B. Beckwith (1) -   September 23, 1813

Hite, Susan (colored) Reubin Twinman (3) -   June 4, 1870
    For further information see - Twinman, Reubin.

Hite, Susan Rutherford and John R. Flagg (1) -   January 6, 1818

Hoagins, Jane and Jessee Lovett (3) -   January 2, 1871
    For further information see - Lovett, Jessee.

Hoagins, Jane (cold.) Jessee Lovett (3) -   January 2, 1871
    For further information see - Lovett, Jessee.

Hobbs, Andrew J. and Martha A. Kelison (3) -   January 7, 1869
    Place of marriage, Jefferson County - Age of husband, 38 - Age of
    wife, 27 - Husband is a Widower - Wife is Single - Both were born in
    Jefferson County - Both reside in Jefferson County - Husband's
    parents are Samuel and Sarah - Wife's parents are George and
    Martha - Occupation of husband is Merchant.

Hobbs, Anna D. and George N. Angel (3) -   December 18, 1879
    For further information see - Angel, George N.

Hobbs, Charles and Martha Creighton (2) -   (L) January 2, 1858

Hobbs, Florence E. and Philip H. Derry (3) -   March 18, 1877
    For further information see - Derry, Philip H.

Hobbs, Frances and James Pane (3) -   June 23, 1866
    For further information see - Pane, James.

Hobbs, John D. and Rachel Rebecca Downing (2) -   (L) March 29, 1851
    (Witness to age of parties, Andrew J. Hobbs.)

Hobbs, John D. and Rachel Rebecca Downing (1) -   March 29, 1851

Hobbs, Martha and Eugene E. Burns (3) -   (L) January 18, 1880
    For further information see - Burns, Eugene E.

Hobbs, Mary E. and William W. Derry (3) -   March 10, 1880
    For further information see - Derry, William W.

Hobbs, Rachael and H. B. Glogen (3) -   October 22, 1867
    For further information see - Glogen, H. B.

Hobbs, Samuel and Sarah Krout (1) -   April 22, 1819

Hockenberry, James H. and Ann E. Stoliper (3) -   August 9, 1883
    Place of marriage, Charlestown - Age of husband, 60 - Age of wife,
    37 - Husband is a Widower - Wife is a Widow - Husband was born in
    Franklin County, Pennsylvania - Wife was born in Maryland - Husband
    resides at Martinsburg - Wife resides in Jefferson County West
    Virginia.

Hodge, Ann C. and Vance R. Whitington (3) -   April 23, 1867
    For further information see - Whitington, Vance R.

Hodge, Cassalina and Thomas W. Dillow (2) -   (L) March 11, 1857

Hodge, Isaac N. and Susan V. Russell (2) -   (L) April 18, 1854
    (William Mader says the lady is of age.)

Hodges, Drusilla and John C. Brendle (1) -   March 18, 1827

Hodges, Ellen and Corleccus Whitington (3) -   February 18, 1868
For further information see - Whitington, Corleccus.

Hodges, Euphemia and Jacob Kimes (1) -   December 18, 1827

Hodges, Mary Ann and James W. Smith (2) -   (L) September 27, 1860

Hodgkinson, Charles and Martha Rosanna Griffith (3) -   September 1, 1886
Place of marriage, near Duffields - Age of husband, 22 - Age of wife, 24 - Both are Single - Husband was born in England - Wife was born in Clarke County, Virginia - Both reside in Jefferson County, West Virginia.

Hofer, John and Mary Froggett (1) -   October 13, 1853

Hoff, Ann Elizabeth and William F. Sisk (3) -   August 24, 1882
For further information see - Sisk, William F.

Hoff, Annie Elizabeth and James W. Hough (3) -   May 5, 1886
For further information see - Hough, James W.

Hoff, George W. and Elizabeth Fogle (3) -   December 23, 1875
Place of marriage, near Harpers Ferry - Age of husband, 42 - Age of wife, 22 - Husband is a Widower - Wife is Single - Husband was born in Clarke County, Virginia - Wife was born in Frederick County, Maryland - Both reside in Jefferson County, West Virginia.

Hoff, Harrison and Millissa M. Hedges (3) -   October 24, 1888
Place of marriage, Charlestown - Age of husband, 21 - Age of wife, 21 - Both are Single - Husband was born in Caledonia County, Pennsylvania - Wife was born in Jefferson County, West Virginia - Both reside in Jefferson County, West Virginia.

Hoffer, John and Mary Froggatt (2) -   (L) October 11, 1853

Hoffman, Abby E. and John N. Tabler (3) -   November 27, 1873
For further information see - Tabler, John N.

Hoffman, Alfred L. and Dorotha Ann Donnelly (2) -   (L) February 18, 1854

Hoffman, Alice H. and George D. Bowers (2) -   (L) February 15, 1858

Hoffman, Anne and Levi Moler (1) -   June 4, 1827

Hoffman, Benjamin and Mary Badger (2) -   (L) June 23, 1862
Time of marriage, June 24, 1862 - Place of marriage, near Shepherdstown - Names, Benjamin Hoffman and Mary Badger - Age of husband, 44 years - Age of wife, 19 years - Condition of husband is a Widower - Condition of wife is Single - Place of birth, both born in Jefferson County - Both live in Jefferson County - Names of husband's parents are David and Margaret Hoffman - Names of wife's parents are Daniel and Elizabeth Badger - Occupation of husband is Miller - Mother's consent given in writing - Liscense issued, June 23, 1862.

Hoffman, David P. and Margaret Donnelly (2) -   (L) November 21, 1860

Hoffman, Edna E. and Daniel E. Louden (3) -   June 3, 1890
For further information see - Louden, Daniel E.

Hoffman, Edward H. and Alice D. Britner (3) -   March 27, 1883
Place of marriage, Shepherdstown - Age of husband, 24 - Age of wife, 22 - Both are Single - Both were born in Jefferson County, West Virginia - Both reside in Jefferson County, West Virginia.

Hoffman, Elizabeth and Jacob Mathaas (2) -   (L) August 21, 1851

Hoffman, Elizabeth and Jacob Mathews (1) -   August 24, 1851

Hoffman, Dr. George H. C. and Vinie C. Kessler (3) -   December 27, 1871
Place of marriage, Jefferson County - Age of husband, 26 - Age of wife, 26 - Both are Single - Both were born in Frederick County, Maryland - Both reside in Jefferson County - Husband's parents are Fran A. and Rebecca A. - Wife's parents are A. C. and C. M. - Occupation of husband is Physician.

Hoffman, George L. and Mary E. Osborn (3) -   November 20, 1866
Place of marriage, Reformed Church, Shepherdstown - Age of husband, 23 - Age of wife, 17 - Both are Single - Both were born in Jefferson County, West Virginia - Both reside in Jefferson County, West Virginia - Husband's parents are David and Mary Hoffman - Wife's parents are James and Margaret Osborn - Occupation of husband is Farmer.

Hoffman, H. Kate and James P. Staley (3) -   November 6, 1883
For further information see - Staley, James P.

Hoffman, Jacob L. and Emma V. Fox (3) -   February 24, 1874
Place of marriage, Shepherdstown - Age of husband, 24 - Age of wife, 17 - Both are Single - Both were born in Jefferson County, West Virginia - Both reside in Jefferson County, West Virginia. (Father's consent in writing.)

Hoffman, James W. and Eliza J. Loudan (3) -   February 5, 1884
Place of marriage, Molers Cross Roads - Age of husband, 30 - Age of wife, 18 - Both are Single - Both were born in Jefferson County, West Virginia - Both reside in Jefferson County, West Virginia. (Consent of bride's parents in writing.)

Hoffman, John and Mary Miller (1) -   October 1, 1818

Hoffman, John and Mary Martin (1) -   June 9, 1824

Hoffman, Julia and Fillmore Reynolds (3) -   December 24, 1878
For further information see - Reynolds, Fillmore.

Hoffman, L. Jane and Louis E. Lambert (3) -   November 7, 1871
For further information see - Lambert, Louis E.

Hoffman, Laura J. and C. J. Merritt (3) -   November 4, 1889
For further information see - Merritt, C. J.

Hoffman, Margaret and George Osborne (1) -   October 7, 1809

Hoffman, Margaret Elizabeth and John L. Lewis (3) -   December 2, 1882
For further information see - Lewis, John L.

Hoffman, Mary and William Bilson (1) - June 11, 1835

Hoffman, Mary (widow) and George Hawn (1) - October 19, 1835

Hoffman, Mary V. and Isaac N. Hanna (2) - (L) January 23, 1860

Hoffman, Mollie V. and Charles J. Knott (3) - October 16, 1884
For further information see - Knott, Charles J.

Hoffman, Narcissa and A. H. Herr (1) - February 23, 1850

Hoffman, Philip and Narcissa Breedin (1) - December 1, 1811

Hoffman, R. S. M. and Mary E. Cameron (3) - September 14, 1869
Place of marriage, Jefferson County - Age of husband, 22 - Age of wife, 21 - Husband was born in Pennsylvania - Wife was born in Jefferson County - Both reside in Jefferson County.

Hoffman, Robert N. and Ellen L. Humrickhouse (2) - (L) May 16, 1861
Time of marriage, May 16 - Place of marriage, Shepherdstown - Age of husband, 21 years and 7 days - Age of wife, 22 last January - Both are Single - Place of husband's birth was Pennsylvania - Place of wife's birth was Shepherdstown - Both reside at Shepherdstown - Names of husband's parents are Charles W. and Sarah A. Hoffman - Names of wife's parents are Samuel and Eliza Humrickhouse - Occupation of husband is Teacher - Given under my hand May 16, 1861, I. F. Hoffman.

Hoffman, Sallie and William Marshall (3) - February 21, 1888
For further information see - Marshall, William.

Hoffman, Sally A. and Samuel J. Loudoun (3) - June 15, 1882
For further information see - Loudoun, Samuel J.

Hoffman, Sarah and William Carr (1) - April 11, 1815

Hoffman, William and Mary Dixon (3) - October 17, 1878
Place of marriage, Shepherdstown - Age of husband, 24 - Age of wife, 25 - Both are Single - Both were born in Jefferson County, West Virginia - Both reside in Jefferson County, West Virginia.

Hoffman, William T. and Margaret Deck (3) - April 18, 1867
Place of marriage, Shepherdstown - Age of husband, 36 - Age of wife, 24 - Husband is a Widower - Wife is Single - Husband was born in Jefferson County, West Virginia - Wife was born in Berkeley County, West Virginia - Husband resides in Jefferson County, West Virginia - Wife resides in Berkeley County, West Virginia - Husband's parents are David and Mary Hoffman - Wife's parents are David and Leathey Deck - Occupation of husband is Farmer.

Hoffman, William Thomas and Sarah Rebecca Gorster (2) - (L) September 10, 1855

Hoffmaster, Annie Beall and Joseph Edward Wright (3) - February 18, 1887
For further information see - Wright, Joseph Edward.

Hoffmaster, Charles H. and Jennie C. Armstrong (3) - August 15, 1882
Place of marriage, Charlestown - Age of husband, 23 - Age of wife, 22 - Both are Single - Husband was born in Jefferson County, West Virginia - Wife was born in Clarke County, Virginia - Both reside in Jefferson County, West Virginia.

Hoffmaster, Elizabeth and Thomas Clipp (3) -   September 10, 1872
    For further information see - Clipp, Thomas.

Hoffmaster, Emily and Harrison Geasland (2) -   (L) November 17, 1860

Hoffmaster, Florence and George H. Whitmore (3) -   November 16, 1876
    For further information see - Whitmore, George H.

Hoffmaster, Franklin and Mary Eades (2) -   (L) December 15, 1854

Hoffmaster, George and Ann Allen (2) -   (L) November 17, 1860

Hoffmaster, H. W. and Alice O. Albin (3) -   September 5, 1882
    Place of marriage, Kabletown - Age of husband, 29 - Age of wife, 24 - Both are Single - Husband was born in Jefferson County, West Virginia - Wife was born in Clarke County, Virginia - Husband resides in York County, Nebraske - Wife resides in Jefferson County, West Virginia.

Hoffmaster, John J. and Sallie C. Fizer (3) -   August 9, 1881
    Place of marriage, Shepherdstown - Age of husband, 21 - Age of wife, 22 - Both are Single - Both were born in Jefferson County, West Virginia - Both reside in Jefferson County, West Virginia.

Hoffmaster, Joseph and Eliza Frarey (2) -   (L) October 14, 1858

Hoffmaster, Louisa and W. H. Miller (3) -   March 29, 1885
    For further information see - Miller, W. H.

Hoffmaster, Malinda E. and John William Lewis (2) -   (L) October 23, 1857

Hoffmaster, Mary and John William Clip (2) -   (L) November 20, 1856

Hoffmaster, Mary and David Myers (3) -   December 11, 1883
    For further information see - Myers, David.

Hoffmaster, Samuel and Ellen Harriet Swann (2) -   (L) June 3, 1856

Hogan, Anne and Patrick Winn (2) -   (L) April 24, 1851

Hogan, Christopher and Margaret C. Neely (2) -   (L) October 21, 1854

Hoke, Henry H. and Fannie H. Cockrell (3) -   October 15, 1889
    Place of marriage, near Bolivar - Age of husband, 23 - Age of wife, 22 - Both are Single - Husband was born in Frederick County, Maryland - Wife was born in Jefferson County, West Virginia - Husband resides in Frederick County, Maryland - Wife resides in Jefferson County, West Virginia.

Holden, George and Sarah Elizabeth O'Bannon (2) -   (L) January 11, 1859

Holliday, Fanny (cold.) Charles W. Lee (3) -   August 16, 1877
    For further information see - Lee, Charles W.

Holliday, John W. and Catherine Staley (1) -   May 23, 1822

Holliday, Polly and John Dunham (1) -   April 10, 1806

Hollingsworth, C. C. and Mary J. Mozier (3) - March 30, 1873
    Place of marriage, Harpers Ferry - Age of husband, 25 - Age of wife,
    25 - Both are Single - Husband was born in Frederick County,
    Virginia - Wife was born in Pennsylvania - Both reside in Jefferson
    County, West Virginia - Occupation of husband is Miller.

Holmes, Charles William (cold.) Clara Wade (3) - February 17, 1881
    Place of marriage, Shepherdstown - Age of husband, 26 - Age of wife,
    22 - Both are Single - Husband was born in Jefferson County, West
    Virginia - Wife was born in Montgomery County, Maryland - Both
    reside in Jefferson County, West Virginia.

Holmes, Eliza Jane and Dennis M. Calla (1) - August 25, 1849

Holmes, G. W. and Sallie Grey (3) - May 28, 1868
    Place of marriage, Jefferson County - Age of husband, 38 - Age of
    wife, 30 - Husband is a Widower - Wife is a Widow - Husband was born
    in Clarke County - Both reside in Jefferson County - Husband's
    parents are Briscoe and May - Wife's parents are Solomon -
    Occupation of husband is Laborer.

Holmes, Joseph and Scotia W. Parmer (2) - (L) August 11, 1851

Holmes, Joseph and Scotia Parmer (1) - August 11, 1851

Holmes, Julia and Owen Granen (2) - (L) June 8, 1860

Holmes, Julia M. and William A. Burnett (3) - February 5, 1889
    For further information see - Burnett, William A.

Holmes, Julius C. and Annie A. O'Bannon (3) - July 5, 1866
    Place of marriage, Charlestown, Jefferson County, West Virginia -
    Age of husband, 25 - Age of wife, 23 - Both are Single - Husband was
    born in Baltimore County, Maryland - Wife was born at Charlestown,
    Jefferson County, West Virginia - Husband resides at Baltimore City,
    Maryland - Wife resides at Charlestown, Jefferson County, West
    Virginia - Husband's parents are John E. Holmes and Amelia Holmes -
    Wife's parents are Hiram O'Bannon and Mary O'Bannon - Occupation of
    husband is Carpenter.

Holmes, Louisa (cold.) Daniel Johnson (3) - September 22, 1880
    For further information see - Johnson, Daniel.

Holmes, M. E. (cold.) William Morgan (3) - January 5, 1868
    For further information see - Morgan, William.

Holmes, Margaret and Daniel T. Anderson (1) - May 22, 1833

Holmes, Martha and W. H. H. Butt (3) - (1879)
    For further information see - Butt, W. H. H.

Holmes, Martin and Catherine Bowsmith (1) - June 14, 1814

Holmes, Mary A. and I. W. Bobst (3) - November 23, 1880
    For further information see - Bobst, I. W.

Holmes, William and Eliza Dainer (1) - October 19, 1815

Holmes, William A. and Edith E. Hilleary (3) - February 5, 1880
　Place of marriage, near Ripon - Age of husband, 25 - Age of wife,
　23 - Both are Single - Husband was born in Clarke County, Ohio -
　Wife was born in Morgan County, West Virginia - Husband resides at
　Philadelphia, Pennsylvania - Wife resides in Jefferson County, West
　Virginia.

Holt, Elizabeth and Joseph W. Miller (1) - May 1, 1845

Holt, Emily and Lewis Keyser (1) - July 24, 1834

Holt, James H. and Adeline Blanchard (2) - (L) December 25, 1852

Holt, John and Delily Spranks (1) - November 15, 1807

Holt, John W. and Hannah Ellen Engle (1) - January 1, 1832

Holt, Julia A. and Thomas W. Beall (2) - (L) July 23, 1853

Holt, Julia A. and Thomas W. Beall (1) - July 28, 1853

Homar, Charles D. and Mary P. A. Moore (3) - July 24, 1877
　Place of marriage, Middleway - Age of husband, 27 - Age of wife,
　29 - Both are Single - Husband was born in Jefferson County, West
　Virginia - Wife was born at Cumberland, Maryland - Both reside in
　Jefferson County, West Virginia.

Homar, Sarah A. and Collin A. McClure (2) - (L) May 15, 1854

Homer, Ann C. and Snowden H. Watson (3) - November 23, 1875
　For further information see - Watson, Snowden H.

Homer, B. D. and M. C. Leagree (bride) (3) - February 22, 1870
　Place of marriage, Jefferson County - Age of husband, 36 - Age of
　wife, 30 - Both were born in Jefferson - Husband resides in
　Jefferson - Wife resides in Jefferson County.

Homer, Christian and Susan Frederick (2) - (L) April 12, 1852

Homer, Emma B. and George W. Moore (3) - December 2, 1875
　For further information see - Moore, George W.

Homer, Henry S. and Mrs. Margaret Shafer (3) - January 13, 1886
　Place of marriage, Age of husband, 34 - Age of wife,
　35 - Husband is Single - Wife is a Widow - Both were born in
　Jefferson County - Husband resides in Jefferson County - Wife
　resides in Jefferson County, West Virginia.

Homer, Mrs. Mary A. and Lawrence R. McClellan (3) - July 27, 1876
　For further information see - McClellan, Lawrence R.

Homes, Ellen and William Bentz (1) - May 11, 1845

Homes, Mahala Ann and Samuel Boyer (1) - October 27, 1848

Homes, Thomas (cold.) Sally Stribling (3) - December 27, 1882
　Place of marriage, Shepherdstown - Age of husband, 23 - Age of wife,
　21 - Both are Single - Husband was born in Rappahannock County,
　Virginia - Wife was born in Jefferson County, West Virginia - Both
　reside in Jefferson County, West Virginia.

Hommer, Christian and Eleanor Henderschurch (2) - (L) April 20, 1857

Hoock, James H. and Alzier T. Manuel (2) - (L) February 13, 1854

Hood, Barbara and John Prichet (1) - October 30, 1808

Hood, Mary E. and James L. Shewbridge (3) - October 24, 1871
    For further information see - Shewbridge, James L.

Hooe, James Henry and Ann E. Davis (3) - August 27, 1889
    Place of marriage, Charlestown - Age of husband, 66 - Age of wife, 59 - Husband is a Widower - Wife is a Widow - Husband was born in Fairfax County, Virginia - Wife was born in Loudoun County, Virginia - Both reside in Jefferson County, West Virginia.

Hooe, John H. and Sarah R. Robertson (3) - May 8, 1876
    Place of marriage, Charles Town - Age of husband, 22 - Age of wife, 21 - Both are Single - Both were born in Jefferson County, West Virginia - Both reside in Jefferson County, West Virginia.

Hoof, George W. and Sarah Victoria Milton (2) - (L) August 4, 1855

Hooff, J. B. and D. E. Lisk (bride) (3) - January 23, 1872
    Place of marriage, Jefferson County, West Virginia - Age of husband, 23 - Age of wife, 15 - Both are Single - Both were born in Jefferson County, Virginia - Both reside in Jefferson County, West Virginia - Husband's parents are Joseph and Joanna - Wife's parents are Henry and Rebecca - Occupation of husband is Cooper. (Fontain Jenkins.)

Hooff, James L. and Anna Amelia Beckham (2) - (L) April 11, 1851

Hooff, James L. and Ann Amelia Beckham (1) - April 15, 1851

Hooff, M. J. and William Carer (3). - November 28, 1867
    For further information see - Carer, William.

Hooff, Philip Henry and Jane Baxter Hammond (1) - June 24, 1823

Hooff, S. E. (bride) and J. W. Campbell (3) - March 11, 1868
    For further information see - Campbell, J. W.

Hooff, William and Frances R. Packett (1) - March 4, 1822

Hooffman, Joseph and Elizabeth Wager (1) -. June 27, 1812

Hoofmaster, Ellen and David S. Armstrong (3) - (1868)
    For further information see - Armstrong, David S.

Hook, James (cold.) Susan Mills (3) - January 17, 1875
    Place of marriage, Kearneysville - Age of husband, 22 - Age of wife, 21 - Both are Single - Both were born in Jefferson County, West Virginia - Both reside in Jefferson County, West Virginia.

Hook, Josephine (cold.) Wesley Seibert (3) - January 15, 1879
    For further information see - Seibert, Wesley.

Hook, Keziah and George W. Dearing (1) - June 5, 1828

Hook, Morgan and Fanny Dunmore (3) - April 29, 1874
   Place of marriage, Shepherdstown - Age of husband, 26 - Age of wife,
   24 - Both are Single - Both were born in Jefferson County, West
   Virginia - Both reside in Jefferson County, West Virginia.

Hook, Sarah B. (cold.) John H. Turley (3) - March 24, 1875
   For further information see - Turley, John H.

Hoole, Thomas Alexander and Ida May Davis (3) - September 6, 1888
   Place of marriage, Charlestown - Age of husband, 20 - Age of wife,
   18 - Both are Single - Both were born in Jefferson County, West
   Virginia - Both reside in Jefferson County, West Virginia.
   (Consent of parents in person and writing.)

Hooper, Edward B. and Margaret A. Grove (3) - February 2, 1871
   Place of marriage, Shepherdstown - Age of husband, 51 - Age of wife,
   42 - Husband is a Widower - Wife is a Widow - Husband was born in
   Berkeley County - Wife was born in Berkeley - Both reside in
   Berkeley - Husband's parents are Abram and Catherine - Wife's
   parents are George and Margaret - Occupation of husband is Butcher.

Hooper, Maria E. and James W. Jones (1) - July 13, 1847

Hooser, Mary and Henry Nichols (1) - February 16, 1815

Hootte, Mary Ann and Daniel Lashhorn (1) - June 15, 1824

Hoover, A. J. and Annie C. Hoover (3) - July 21, 1890
   Place of marriage, Harpers Ferry - Age of husband, 23 - Age of wife,
   22 - Both are Single - Both were born in Virginia - Husband resides
   in Virginia - Wife resides in Jefferson County, West Virginia.

Hoover, Annie C. and A. J. Hoover (3) - July 21, 1890
   For further information see - Hoover, A. J.

Hoover, Sophia L. and S. F. Roadefer (3) - September 27, 1886
   For further information see - Roadefer, S. F.

Hopcraft, William and Sarah Jane Higgins (3) - October 28, 1879
   Place of marriage, Harpers Ferry - Age of husband, 27 - Age of wife,
   33 - Husband is Single - Wife is a Widow - Husband was born in
   Oxfordshire, England - Wife was born in Jefferson County, West
   Virginia - Husband resides at Cumberland, Maryland - Wife resides in
   Jefferson County, West Virginia. (Returned January 1883.)

Hopenft, Robert and Mary Bell Bonus (3) - February 27, 1888
   Place of marriage, Harpers Ferry - Age of husband, 24 - Age of wife,
   21 - Both are Single - Wife was born in Jefferson County, West
   Virginia - Wife resides in Jefferson County, West Virginia.

Hopewell, Catherine (cold.) John Stevens (3) - April 15, 1874
   For further information see - Stevens, John.

Hopewell, Ellen R. and Laurence Washington (3) - August 14, 1867
   For further information see - Washington, Laurence.

Hopewell, Henry (cold.) Sallie Wilkinson (3) - July 21, 1877
Place of marriage, Shepherdstown - Age of husband, 22 - Age of wife, 22 - Both are Single - Both were born in Jefferson County, West Virginia - Both reside in Jefferson County, West Virginia. (Parents consent per note from D. S. Rentch.)

Hopewell, Nannie (cold.) Henry Dorsey (3) - October 25, 1873
For further information see - Dorsey, Henry.

Hopewell, Rachael (cold.) Lee Campbell (3) - December 26, 1889
For further information see - Campbell, Lee.

Hopewell, Thomas J. (cold.) Mary Smith (3) - February 5, 1885
Place of marriage, near Shepherdstown - Age of husband, 23 - Age of wife, 21 - Both are Single - Husband was born in Jefferson County, West Virginia - Wife was born in Culpeper County, Virginia - Both reside in Jefferson County, West Virginia.

Hopkins, Patrick and Bridget Kelly (2) - (L) August 14, 1852

Hopkins, Sarah J. and Warren W. Burton (2) - (L) October 7, 1856

Hopper, Asbury M. and Alice L. Flanagan (3) - October 21, 1875
Place of marriage, near Old Furnace - Age of husband, 36 - Age of wife, 23 - Both are Single - Husband was born in Rappahannock County, Virginia - Wife was born in Jefferson County, West Virginia - Both reside in Jefferson County, West Virginia.

Hopper, James T. and Frances E. Etchison (3) - December 16, 1872
Place of marriage, Jefferson County - Age of husband, 25 - Age of wife, 25 - Both are Single - Husband was born in Rappahannock County, Virginia - Wife was born in Virginia - Husband resides in Rappahannock County, Virginia - Wife resides in Virginia - Husband's parents are John and Elizabeth B. - Wife's parents are Lorenza and Elizabeth - Occupation of husband is Agent. (This record is crossed out in the original.)

Hopper, James T. and Frances E. Etchison (3) - December 18, 1872
Place of marriage, Shepherdstown - Age of husband, 25 - Age of wife, 25 - Both are Single - Both were born in Virginia - Husband resides in Virginia - Wife resides in West Virginia - Husband's parents are John and Elizabeth B. - Wife's parents are Lorenza and Elizabeth - Occupation of husband is Agent.

Horetz, A. J. and Ellen Byers (3) - December 21, 1876
Place of marriage, near Shepherdstown - Age of husband, 21 - Age of wife, 22 - Both are Single - Husband was born in Pennsylvania - Wife was born in Jefferson County, West Virginia - Husband resides in Berkeley County, West Virginia - Wife resides in Jefferson County, West Virginia.

Horkinson, George and Elizabeth Myers (1) - December 30, 1813

Horman, Samuel and Lucinda Smart (1) - November 23, 1845

Horn, Cornelia Ann and Isaac Thompson (3) - March 12, 1873
For further information see - Thompson, Isaac.

Horn, David C. and Mary C. Crider (2) - (L) November 12, 1855

Horn, Katie and James William Ringer (3) - September 10, 1879
    For further information see - Ringer, James William.

Horn, Margaret Elizabeth and Henry F. Bowers (2) - (L) March 20, 1855

Horn, Mary Virginia and Charles H. Fowler (3) - March 7, 1878
    For further information see - Fowler, Charles H.

Horn, Michael and Esther Jones (1) - October 3, 1809

Hornar, Mary E. and Raleigh Bowers (1) - February 14, 1842

Horner, Sady O. and S. W. Swayne (3) - July 3, 1883
    For further information see - Swayne, S. W.

Hornsby, Elizabeth and David Sheeley (1) - February 27, 1806

Hosier, Ann E. and John J. Shirley (2) - (L) July 13, 1853

Hosier, James M. and Lydia Ann Chapman (2) - (L) November 26, 1859

Hospital, Andrew and Mary Spoont (1) - June 9, 1807

Hostler, Howanna and S. G. Johnson (3) - December 25, 1888
    For further information see - Johnson, S. G.

Hostler, John H. and Mary Ann Penwell (2) - (L) June 1, 1852

Hostler, John H. and Mary Ann Penwell (1) - June 10, 1852

Hostler, Mary Elizabeth and Emanuel Washington Dillow (3) - September 16, 1886
    For further information see - Dillow, Emanuel Washington.

Hostler, Nannie C. and Thomas W. Ott (3) - December 11, 1883
    For further information see - Ott, Thomas W.

Hough, Amelia Ann and John W. Carroll (3) - November 11, 1874
    For further information see - Carroll, John W.

Hough, Charles M. and Lettie V. Avis (3) - January 10, 1867
    Place of marriage, Charlestown, West Virginia - Age of husband, 23 - Age of wife, 19 - Both are Single - Husband was born in Loudoun County, Virginia - Wife was born in Jefferson County, West Virginia - Husband resides in Clarke County, Virginia - Wife resides at Charlestown, West Virginia - Husband's parents are A. T. M. and Harriet Hough - Wife's parents are John and S. A. Avis - Occupation of husband is Blacksmith.

Hough, Derizo C. and Martha Mathias (2) - (L) October 31, 1855

Hough, George and Phoebe Howell (3) - December 14, 1886
    Place of marriage, Hillsboro, Virginia - Age of husband, 21 - Age of wife, 21 - Both are Single - Husband was born in Loudoun County, Virginia - Wife was born in Jefferson County, West Virginia - Husband resides in Loudoun County, Virginia - Wife resides in Jefferson County, West Virginia.

Hough, James H. and Eliza Matson (3) -   April 12, 1877
   Place of marriage, near Charlestown - Age of husband, 22 - Age of
   wife, 22 - Both are Single - Husband was born in Jefferson County,
   West Virginia - Wife was born in Frederick County, Maryland - Both
   reside in Jefferson County, West Virginia.

Hough, James W. and Annie Elizabeth Hoff (3) -   May 5, 1886
   Place of marriage, Charlestown - Age of husband, 22 - Age of wife,
   18 - Both are Single - Husband was born in Loudoun County,
   Virginia - Wife was born in Jefferson County, West Virginia - Both
   reside in Jefferson County, West Virginia. (Consent of bride's
   father in person.)

Hough, John and Henrietta Benson (3) -   October 28, 1885
   Place of marriage, Charlestown - Age of husband, 26 - Age of wife,
   24 - Both are Single - Both were born in Jefferson County, West
   Virginia - Both reside in Jefferson County, West Virginia.

Hough, John Elliott and Rebecca Wooddy (3) -   July 28, 1880
   Place of marriage, Charlestown - Age of husband, 27 - Age of wife,
   18 - Both are Single - Husband was born in Clarke County, Virginia -
   Wife was born in Jefferson County, West Virginia - Both reside in
   Jefferson County, West Virginia. (Consent of bride's father in
   person.)

Hough, Townsend and Virginia Coffin (3) -   December 26, 1872
   Place of marriage, Jefferson County, West Virginia - Age of husband,
   25 - Age of wife, 22 - Both are Single - Husband was born in Loudoun
   County, Virginia - Wife was born in Jefferson County, West
   Virginia - Husband resides in Loudoun County, Virginia - Wife
   resides in Jefferson County, West Virginia - Husband's parents are
   Bushrod and Jane W. - Wife's parents are Lewis and Garard -
   Occupation of husband is Farmer.

Houke, Lucy J. and Alfred B. Wilson (3) -   December 7, 1871
   For further information see - Wilson, Alfred B.

House, Anna M. and James Gardner (3) -   February 20, 1886
   For further information see - Gardner, James.

House, Annie E. and John W. Ingram (3) -   July 22, 1869
   For further information see - Ingram, John W.

House, Annie Mary Elizabeth and Peter Alexander (3) -   December 21, 1882
   For further information see - Alexander, Peter.

House, Lafayette V. and Louisa G. Staley (3) -   November 24, 1886
   Place of marriage, Shepherdstown - Age of husband, 23 - Age of wife,
   18 - Both are Single - Husband was born in State of Maryland - Wife
   was born in Jefferson County, West Virginia - Husband resides in
   State of Maryland - Wife resides in Jefferson County, West Virginia.
   (Consent of bride's father in person.)

House, Leonard D. and Dora J. Corder (3) -   September 15, 1880
   Place of marriage, Harpers Ferry - Age of husband, 28 - Age of wife,
   22 - Both are Single - Husband was born in Jefferson County, West
   Virginia - Wife was born in Loudoun County, Virginia - Both reside
   in Jefferson County, West Virginia.

House, Mary E. and James H. French (2) -   (L) July 5, 1853

House, Mary E. and William McSherry (3) -   January 24, 1867
   For further information see - McSherry, William.

House, Samuel and Annie Travis (3) -   August 28, 1881
   Place of marriage, Harpers Ferry - Age of husband, 28 - Age of wife,
   21 - Both are Single - Both were born in Jefferson County, West
   Virginia - Both reside in Jefferson County, West Virginia.

House, William and Eliza Fauble (3) -   November 10, 1882
   Place of marriage, Harpers Ferry - Age of husband, 21 - Age of wife,
   21 - Both are Single - Both were born in Maryland - Both reside in
   Jefferson County, West Virginia.

Houser, Ann R. and Emanuel Kidwiler (3) -   October 18, 1866
   For further information see - Kidwiler, Emanuel.

Houston, Sallie and Jackson Powers (3) -   April 27, 1871
   For further information see - Powers, Jackson.

Hout, Harry Lee and Sally Lemen (3) -   June 30, 1885
   Place of marriage, Shepherdstown - Age of husband, 23 - Age of wife,
   23 - Both are Single - Husband was born in Jefferson County, West
   Virginia - Wife was born in Berkeley County, West Virginia - Both
   reside in Jefferson County, West Virginia.

Hout, Henry and Lydia Clum (1) -   February 5, 1832

Hout, Jacob and Margaret Barnhart (1) -   March 22, 1820

Hout, Selma A. and James H. Wolff (3) -   February 20, 1873
   For further information see - Wolff, James H.

Houtt, George and Mary M. Long (1) -   March 9, 1815

Howard, Alfred and Nancy M. Lemon (1) -   December 14, 1826

Howard, Ann Rebecca Darkus and Samuel J. Strider (1) -   October 21, 1828

Howard, Betty (cold.) James L. Brunswick (3) -   November 2, 1876
   For further information see - Brunswick, James L.

Howard, James and Nancy Blue (1) -   April 10, 1821

Howard, James and Molly Davy (3) -   August 22, 1867
   Place of marriage, Shepherdstown - Age of husband, 23 - Age of wife,
   24 - Both are Single - Husband was born in Kentucky - Wife was born
   in Loudoun County, Virginia - Both reside in Jefferson County, West
   Virginia - Husband's parents are Thomas and Mary - Wife's parents
   are Eli and Elizabeth - Occupation of husband is Farmer.

Howard, John (cold.) Mary Ellen Payne (3) -   December 27, 1882
   Place of marriage, Duffields - Age of husband, 28 - Age of wife,
   20 - Both are Single - Husband was born in Shenandoah County,
   Virginia - Wife was born in Jefferson County, West Virginia - Both
   reside in Jefferson County, West Virginia.   (Consent of bride's
   mother in writing.)

Howard, Joseph (colored) Harriet Reed (3) -   June 8, 1870
   Place of marriage, Jefferson County - Age of husband, 43 - Age of
   wife, 25 - Both were born in Virginia - Both reside in Jefferson
   County.

Howard, Julian and Eleanor L. Washington (3) - May 5, 1880
   Place of marriage, Charlestown - Age of husband, 26 - Age of wife,
   24 - Both are Single - Husband was born at Richmond, Virginia - Wife
   was born at Mount Vernon, Virginia - Husband resides at Richmond,
   Virginia - Wife resides in Jefferson County, West Virginia.

Howard, M. (bride) and J. F. Voorhees (3) - (1867)
   For further information see - Voorhees, J. F.

Howard, Mary (cold.) John William Helm (3) - September 26, 1886
   For further information see - Helm, John William.

Howard, Mollie and Michael Welsh (3) - March 3, 1870
   For further information see - Welsh, Michael.

Howard, Patience and George Myers (1) - November 28, 1833

Howard, Peter and Sarah Hyser (1) - September 8, 1825

Howard, Victoria and Jeremiah Haines (3) - February 10, 1877
   For further information see - Haines, Jeremiah.

Howard, William A. and Annie Sloan (2) - (L) November 17, 1863
   Time - Place - Names, William A. Howard and Annie Sloan - Age of
   husband, 22 years - Age of wife, 24 years - Both are Single - Place
   of husband's birth at Louisville, Kentucky - Place of wife's birth
   in Jefferson County, Virginia - Place of husband's residence at
   Louisville, Kentucky - Place of wife's residence at Harpers Ferry,
   Virginia - Names of husband's parents - Names of wife's parents -
   Occupation of husband is Soldier in Federal Army - License issued,
   November 17, 1863 - T. A. Moore, Clerk.

Howell, Caroline and Thomas West (2) - (L) April 5, 1852

Howell, Caroline and Thomas West (1) - April 6, 1852

Howell, Edward (cold.) Lizzie Brookins (3) - October 20, 1880
   Place of marriage, Charlestown - Age of husband, 32 - Age of wife,
   18 - Both are Single - Husband was born in Jefferson County, West
   Virginia - Wife was born in Loudoun County, Virginia - Both reside
   in Jefferson County, West Virginia. (Consent of bride's mother in
   writing.)

Howell, Fanny (cold.) William Reid (3) - September 3, 1878
   For further information see - Reid, William.

Howell, George W. and Susan F. Hicks (3) - September 5, 1867
   Place of marriage, Jefferson - Age of husband, 27 - Age of wife,
   25 - Both are Single - Husband was born in Loudoun County,
   Virginia - Wife was born in Jefferson County, West Virginia - Both
   reside in Jefferson County, West Virginia - Husband's parents are
   Craver and Amy Howell - Wife's parents are Levi Hicks - Occupation
   of husband is Farmer.

Howell, John M. and Emily R. Taylor (3) - April 14, 1871
   Place of marriage, Jefferson County - Age of husband, 30 - Age of
   wife, 27 - Both are Single - Husband was born in Jefferson County -
   Wife was born in Virginia - Husband's parents are David and Hannah -
   Occupation of husband is Farmer. (Issued at Charlestown.)

Howell, John M. and Emma R. Taylor (3) -   April 19, 1871
    Place of marriage, Jefferson County - **Age of husband, 30** - Age of
    wife, 27 - Both are Single - **Husband was born in Jefferson County** -
    Wife was born in Virginia - **Both reside in Jefferson County** -
    Husband's parents are David and Hannah - **Wife's parents are S. James
    and Emily G.** - Occupation of husband is Farmer. (This record is
    crossed out in the original.)

Howell, John M. and Fannie S. Lafitte (3) -   March 24, 1874
    Place of marriage, Charlestown - **Age of husband, 33** - Age of wife,
    30 - Husband is a Widower - **Wife is Single** - Husband was born in
    Jefferson County, West Virginia - Wife was born in Maryland - Both
    reside in Jefferson County, West Virginia.

Howell, Joseph R. and Susan Miller (3) -   December 13, 1868
    Place of marriage, Jefferson County - **Age of husband, 35** - Age of
    wife, 25 - Both are Single - Husband was born in Jefferson - Wife
    was born in Clarke, Virginia - **Both reside in Jefferson County** -
    Husband's parents are James and Maria - **Wife's parents are Susan** -
    Occupation of husband is Farmer.

Howell, Mary E. and Walter Barron (3) -   August 24, 1881
    For further information see - Barron, Walter.

Howell, Phoebe and George Hough (3) -   December 14, 1886
    For further information see - Hough, George.

Howell, Ruth and John Moler (1) -   June 19, 1832

Howell, Ruth A. and John H. Cocke (3) -   November 22, 1882
    For further information see - Cocke, John H.

Howell, Torsend B. and Mary Frances Moore (3) -   December 19, 1876
    Place of marriage, near Ripon - Age of husband, 29 - Age of wife,
    23 - Both are Single - Husband was born in Loudoun County,
    Virginia - Wife was born in Berkeley County, West Virginia - Both
    reside in Jefferson County, West Virginia.

Hoxton, S. and Fanny Robinson (3) -   October 14, 1868
    Place of marriage, Jefferson County - Both are Single - Husband was
    born in Alexandria County, Virginia - **Wife was born in Jefferson
    County** - Husband resides in Maryland - Wife resides in West
    Virginia - Husband's parents are J. and Sarah - Occupation of
    husband is Teacher. (I **have** no evidence that said preacher has
    been duly licensed by this state.)

Hudson, Eliza A. and William F. Weirick (2) -   (L) November 26, 1851

Hudson, John J. and Mrs. Ann Kennedy (widow) (2) -   (L) December 17, 1853

Hudson, Joshua J. and Catharine V. Eakle (2) -   (L) October 28, 1859

Hue, Levi and Sarah Elizabeth McCoy (1) -   February 19, 1830

Huff, David and Mary Hagan (3) -   August 5, 1879
    Place of marriage, Charlestown - Age of husband, 20 last December -
    Age of wife, 21 last April - Both are Single - Husband was born in
    Clarke County, Virginia - Wife was born in Washington County,
    Maryland - Both reside in Jefferson County, West Virginia.
    (Consent of groom's father in person (52).)

Huff, David N. and Nancy Fox (3) -   June 9, 1889
    Place of marriage, Leetown - Age of husband, 31 - Age of wife, 28 -
    Husband is Divorced - Wife is Single - Husband was born in Clarke
    County, Virginia - Wife was born in Page County, Virginia - Both
    reside in Jefferson County, West Virginia.

Huff, Frances and William Edwards (3) -   January 11, 1866
    For further information see - Edwards, William.

Huff, M. Ann and Lewis Carroll (3) -   April 11, 1867
    For further information see - Carroll, Lewis.

Huff, Noah W. and Ella M. Price (3) -   June 3, 1875
    Place of marriage, Shepherdstown - Age of husband, 20 - Age of wife,
    21 - Both are Single - Husband was born in Clarke County, Virginia -
    Wife was born in Jefferson County, West Virginia - Both reside in
    Jefferson County, West Virginia - Wife's parents are mother C.
    Price. (Consent of grandfather in person; consent of mother in
    writing.)

Huffman, Anna and John Y. Myers (3) -   March 6, 1867
    For further information see - Myers, John Y.

Huffman, Polly and John Shugart (1) -   March 10, 1814

Huffmaster, Barbara Ann and Thomas E. Orem (2) -   (L) October 12, 1855

Huffmaster, Elizabeth and John Clip (2) -   (L) January 31, 1865
    For further information see - Clip, John.

Huffmaster, Winfield L. and Lydia Brotherton (3) -   December 21, 1875
    Place of marriage, near Hopewell - Age of husband, 28 - Age of wife,
    17 - Both are Single - Both were born in Jefferson County, West
    Virginia - Both reside in Jefferson County, West Virginia.
    (Consent of bride's father in writing.)

Hufman, Jane and Henry V. Onderdunk (2) -   (L) May 20, 1851

Hufman, John and Hanah Roach (1) -   March 12, 1818

Hufmaster, George, Jr. and Elizabeth Eckles (2) -   (L) November 2, 1855

Hufmaster, John William and Rebecca Kirk (2) -   (L) December 21, 1852

Hufmaster, John W. and Rebecca Kirk (1) -   December 22, 1852

Hufmaster, Mary and George W. Morris (2) -   (L) November 26, 1853

Hughes, Blackburn and Sarah P. Dandridge (3) -　　　　　September 3, 1873
　　Place of marriage, near Leetown - Age of husband, 39 - Age of wife,
　　34 - Both are Single - Husband was born in Cumberland County,
　　Virginia - Wife was born in Jefferson County, West Virginia -
　　Husband resides at Martinsburg, Berkeley County, West Virginia -
　　Wife resides in Jefferson County, West Virginia.

Hughes, Daniel T. and A. E. McCarrell (3) -　　　　　June 15, 1881
　　Place of marriage, near Middletown, Virginia - Age of husband, 29 -
　　Age of wife, 33 - Husband is Single - Wife is a Widow - Husband was
　　born in Berkeley County, West Virginia - Wife was born in Frederick
　　County, Virginia - Both reside in Jefferson County, West Virginia.

Hughes, Elihue H. and Sarah Hinderkrich (3) -　　　　　May 26, 1870
　　Place of marriage, Jefferson County - Age of husband, 33 - Age of
　　wife, 25 - Husband was born in Maryland - Wife was born in Germany -
　　Both reside in Jefferson County.

Hughes, Elizabeth and Washington Piper (2) -　　　　(L) July 9, 1851

Hughes, Harriet and Samuel W. Patterson (2) -　　　　(L) January 15, 1855

Hughes, James and Mary Piper (1) -　　　　　October 19, 1815

Hughes, James H. and Mary F. Lock (3) -　　　　　October 28, 1880
　　Place of marriage, near Ripon - Age of husband, 24 - Age of wife,
　　20 - Both are Single - Husband was born in Clarke County, Virginia -
　　Wife was born in Jefferson County, West Virginia - Husband resides
　　in Clarke County, Virginia - Wife resides in Jefferson County, West
　　Virginia.　(Consent of bride's mother in writing.)

Hughes, James P. and Catherine Allemong (1) -　　　　　January 14, 1830

Hughes, Laura and W. W. McKaig (3) -　　　　　October 25, 1865
　　For further information see - McKaig, W. W.

Hughes, Mary and Charles Beebe (2) -　　　　(L) December 19, 1850

Hughes, Mary and Charles Beebe (1) -　　　　　December 19, 1850

Hughs, James and Laura A. Spangler (3) -　　　　　October 18, 1866
　　Place of marriage, Bolivar M. E. Church - Age of husband, 22 - Age
　　of wife, 21 - Both are Single - Husband was born at Philadelphia,
　　Pennsylvania - Wife was born at Harpers Ferry, West Virginia -
　　Husband resides at Philadelphia, Pennsylvania - Wife resides at
　　Harpers Ferry, West Virginia - Husband's parents are James and
　　Louisa Hughs - Wife's parents are Washington and Hannah Spangler -
　　Occupation of husband is Clerk.

Hulver, John J. W. and Nannie Schoppert (3) -　　　　　September 13, 1874
　　Place of marriage, Summit Point - Age of husband, 23 - Age of wife,
　　21 - Both are Single - Husband was born in Hardy County, West
　　Virginia - Wife was born in Jefferson County, West Virginia - Both
　　reside in Jefferson County, West Virginia.

Hummer, E. F. and Janie E. Ripon (3) -   September 15, 1887
   Place of marriage, County - Age of husband, 30 - Age of wife, 21 -
   Both are Single - Husband was born in Clarke County, Virginia - Wife
   was born in Jefferson County, West Virginia - Husband resides in
   Clarke County, Virginia - Wife resides in Jefferson County, West
   Virginia.

Humphreys, Bettie R. and William B. Sutton (2) -   (L) April 10, 1852

Humphreys, David and Mary E. Cameron (2) -   (L) October 27, 1858

Humphreys, John and Mary Ann Davis (1) -   February 11, 1823

Humphreys, Roger and Hannah Wager (1) -   June 25, 1807

Humphreys, Sarah Ann and Enos B. Cordell (1) -   January 1, 1829

Humrickhouse, Ada and Thomas H. Miller (3) -   July 30, 1873
   For further information see - Miller, Thomas H.

Humrickhouse, Ellen L. and Robert N. Hoffman (2) -   (L) May 16, 1861
   For further information see - Hoffman, Robert N.

Humrickhouse, Eugene and Boyd H. Keller (3) -   December 27, 1887
   For further information see - Keller, Boyd H.

Humrickhouse, Florence B. and William Graham (3) -   January 20, 1881
   For further information see - Graham, William.

Humrickhouse, George W. and Mary Lee Spohn (3) -   May 25, 1880
   Place of marriage, Shepherdstown - Age of husband, 24 - Age of wife,
   18 - Both are Single - Husband was born in Jefferson County, West
   Virginia - Wife was born in State of Maryland - Both reside in
   Jefferson County, West Virginia. (Consent of bride's mother in
   writing.)

Humrickhouse, Maria and C. R. Roush (3) -   October 23, 1872
   For further information see - Roush, C. R.

Humrickhouse, S. P. and Wilmena T. Warner (3) -   February 17, 1870
   Place of marriage, Jefferson County - Age of husband, 38 - Age of
   wife, 31 - Both were born in Jefferson - Husband resides in
   Jefferson - Wife resides in Jefferson County.

Humrickhouse, Samuel, Jr. and Nellie R. Bennett (3) -   January 31, 1888
   Place of marriage, Shepherdstown - Age of husband, 36 - Age of wife,
   17 - Both are Single - Husband was born in Jefferson County, West
   Virginia - Wife was born in Jefferson County - Both reside in
   Jefferson County, West Virginia. (Consent of bride's mother in
   writing.)

Hunsicker, Alice Elizabeth and Jesse E. Bailey (3) -   June 7, 1881
   For further information see - Bailey, Jesse E.

Hunsicker, Maggie and S. E. McCarty (3) -   May 15, 1877
   For further information see - McCarty, S. E.

Hunt, Annie and James W. Hawk (3) -   September 15, 1888
   For further information see - Hawk, James W.

Hunt, Edward and Corbina E. Bell (2) -　　　　　　　(L) December 7, 1853

Hunt, I. G. and Elizabeth A. Tearney (3) -　　　　　　May 19, 1874
　　Place of marriage, Charlestown - Age of husband, 27 - Age of wife,
　　21 - Both are Single - Both were born in Jefferson County, West
　　Virginia - Both reside in Jefferson County, West Virginia.

Hunt, James and Elizabeth Welsh (2) -　　　　　　(L) November 15, 1852

Hunter, Andrew (cold.) Hetty J. Schley (3) -　　　　September 2, 1875
　　Place of marriage, Charlestown - Age of husband, 35 - Age of wife,
　　22 - Husband is a Widower - Wife is Single - Husband was born in
　　Jefferson County, West Virginia - Wife was born in Berkeley County,
　　West Virginia - Both reside in Jefferson County, West Virginia.

Hunter, Anthony (cold.) Sarah Smith (3) -　　　　　December 24, 1867
　　Place of marriage, Jefferson County - Age of husband, 37 - Age of
　　wife, 32 - Husband is Single - Wife is a Widow - Both were born in
　　Jefferson County - Both reside in Jefferson County - Occupation of
　　husband is Laborer.

Hunter, Benjamin and Susan Campbell (3) -　　　　　June 6, 1867
　　Place of marriage, Charles Town - Age of husband, 35 - Age of wife,
　　22 - Husband is a Widower - Wife is Single - Both were born in
　　Jefferson County, West Virginia - Husband resides in Jefferson
　　County, West Virginia - Wife resides at Charlestown - Husband's
　　parents are William Hunter - Wife's parents are William and Phillis
　　Campbell - Occupation of husband is Farmer.

Hunter, Clarence Summers and Annie S. Harrison (3) -　　June 23, 1887
　　Place of marriage, Shepherdstown - Age of husband, 26 - Age of wife,
　　26 - Both are Single - Husband was born in Berkeley County, West
　　Virginia - Wife was born in Berkeley County - Husband resides at
　　Baltimore, Maryland - Wife resides in Jefferson County, West Virginia.

Hunter, David and Rebecca S. E. Huston (1) -　　　　June 15, 1830

Hunter, Eliza (cold.) Joseph Brown (3) -　　　　　　July 19, 1886
　　For further information see - Brown, Joseph.

Hunter, Elizabeth and John Y. Watson (3) -　　　　September 6, 1870
　　For further information see - Watson, John Y.

Hunter, Elizabeth P. and William H. Travers (2) -　　(L) August 16, 1853

Hunter, Emma (cold.) Albert Johnson (3) -　　　　　April 15, 1880
　　For further information see - Johnson, Albert.

Hunter, Emma (cold.) Richard Morris (3) -　　　　　December 1883
　　For further information see - Morris, Richard.

Hunter, George and Susan Sowers (3) -　　　　　　December 1, 1868
　　Age of husband, 21 - Age of wife, 21 - Both are Single - Husband was
　　born in Jefferson County - Wife was born in Jefferson, Virginia -
　　Both reside in Jefferson County - Occupation of husband is Laborer.

Hunter, Georgietta M. and William D. Hayslett (3) -　　March 30, 1875
　　For further information see - Hayslett, William D.

Hunter, Israel (cold.) Laura Ransel (3) -   January 11, 1883
    Place of marriage, Summit Point - Age of husband, 23 - Age of wife,
    21 - Both are Single - Husband was born in Loudoun County,
    Virginia - Wife was born in Jefferson County, West Virginia - Both
    reside in Jefferson County, West Virginia.

Hunter, James (cold.) Virginia Hunter (3) -   September 15, 1881
    Place of marriage, Summit Point - Age of husband, 29 - Age of wife,
    25 - Husband is Single - Wife is a Widow - Husband was born in
    Loudoun County, Virginia - Wife was born in Berkeley County, West
    Virginia - Both reside in Jefferson County, West Virginia.

Hunter, James H. L. and Mary E. Wright (2) -   (L) May 16, 1855

Hunter, John C. and Ann Rebecca Gardner (2) -   (L) August 24, 1854

Hunter, John H. (cold.) Lucy Washington (3) -   February 25, 1880
    Place of marriage, Harpers Ferry - Age of husband, 23 - Age of wife,
    26 - Husband is Single - Wife is a Widow - Husband was born in
    Jefferson County, West Virginia - Wife was born at Lexington,
    Virginia - Both reside in Jefferson County, West Virginia.

Hunter, Kate and John H. Hayslett (3) -   December 9, 1880
    For further information see - Hayslett, John H.

Hunter, Lee Anna (cold.) Daniel Payne (3) -   November 11, 1883
    For further information see - Payne, Daniel.

Hunter, Margaret and George Caten (2) -   (L) July 24, 1850

Hunter, Margaret and George Caten (1) -   July 25, 1850

Hunter, Mary E. and Thomas H. Kent (of Jur.) (2) -   (L) September 21, 1852

Hunter, Mary J. E. and David H. Strother (2) -   (L) May 4, 1861
    For further information see - Strother, David H.

Hunter, Mary V. and Charles O. Lambert (3) -   May 16, 1876
    For further information see - Lambert, Charles O.

Hunter, Milly (cold.) Thomas Wood (3) -   September 25, 1873
    For further information see - Wood, Thomas.

Hunter, Moses (cold.) Bettie Coalman (3) -   May 29, 1882
    Place of marriage, Summit Point - Age of husband, 25 - Age of wife,
    22 - Both are Single - Husband was born in Jefferson County, West
    Virginia - Wife was born in Jefferson County - Husband resides in
    Jefferson County, West Virginia - Wife resides in Jefferson County.

Hunter, Sarah Elizabeth and Austin Thompson (2) -   (L) January 31, 1860

Hunter, Virginia (cold.) James Hunter (3) -   September 15, 1881
    For further information see - Hunter, James.

Hunter, William and Kate Flanagan (3) -   January 14, 1875
    Place of marriage, Charles Town - Age of husband, 32 - Age of wife,
    30 - Husband is Single - Wife is a Widow - Husband was born in
    Jefferson County, West Virginia - Wife was born in State of
    Missouri - Both reside in Jefferson County, West Virginia.

Huntsberry, Annie E. and A. McCarrol (3) -   February 25, 1869
   For further information see - McCarrol, A.

Huntsberry, Elizabeth H. and Adam Young (3) -   May 21, 1866
   For further information see - Young, Adam.

Hurst, Anne E. and Edward L. Wager (2) -   (L) July 5, 1851

Hurst, Anne E. and Edward L. Wager (1) -   July 7, 1851

Hurst, Catherine E. D. and William S. Daniel (1) -   August 14, 1834

Hurst, Fanny and William Stanhope (1) -   December 20, 1804

Hurst, Jennie A. and William Wallace (2) -   (L) October 11, 1859

Hurst, John William and Mary E. A. Daniel (2) -   (L) November 6, 1854

Hurst, K. D. (bride) and J. G. Wyatt (2) -   (L) January 10, 1860

Hurst, Minor and Sarah E. Davis (1) -   December 22, 1831

Hurst, Sarah C. and F. Byington (2) -   (L) January 8, 1861

Hurst, William and Mary Shirley (1) -   February 3, 1820

Huston, Rebecca S. E. and David Hunter (1) -   June 15, 1830

Huston, Sarah R. and Horatio R. Riddle (2) -   (L) January 27, 1851

Huston, Sarah R. and Horatio R. Riddle (1) -   January 27, 1851

Hutchison, Lucy A. (cold.) William Lucas (3) -   October 20, 1886
   For further information see - Lucas, William.

Hutchison, Mary and George Jackson (3) -   March 12, 1868
   For further information see - Jackson, George.

Hutchison, Hannah and Henry Brady (3) -   November 18, 1865
   For further information see - Brady, Henry.

Hutsler, John H. and Emily Erwin (2) -   (L) February 1, 1861

Hutson, Rebeca and Stephen Bowden (1) -   May 16, 1817

Huyett, Angelica and Samuel C. Brewer (2) -   (L) February 8, 1864
   For further information see - Brewer, Samuel C.

Huyett, Charles and Jane E. Turner (3) -   October 28, 1868
   Place of marriage, Jefferson County - Age of husband, 55 - Age of wife, 40 - Husband is a Widower - Wife is Single - Husband was born in Berks County, Pennsylvania - Wife was born in Jefferson County - Husband resides in Jefferson County - Wife resides in West Virginia - Husband's parents are Abraham and Eve - Wife's parents are Robert and Jane - Occupation of husband is Farmer. (No evidence that he is legally authorized.)

Huyett, Daniel and Margaret Boyers (3) -   May 2, 1870
    Place of marriage, Jefferson County - Age of husband, 26 - Age of
    wife, 22 - Both were born in Maryland - Husband resides in
    Maryland - Wife resides in Jefferson County. (Ages sworn to by
    F. D. Boyers, brother to lady.)

Huyett, Emma A. and Robert L. Billmyer (3) -   (1870)
    For further information see - Billmyer, Robert L.

Huyett, Luther R. and Fannie E. Burns (3) -   January 18, 1882
    Place of marriage - Residence of Bride's Parents - Age of husband,
    30 - Age of wife, 22 - Both are Single - Husband was born in Clarke
    County, Virginia - Wife was born in Jefferson County, West
    Virginia - Both reside in Jefferson County, West Virginia.

Huyett, Samuel M. and Ida M. Osbourn (3) -   December 19, 1889
    Place of marriage, Shepherdstown - Age of husband, 36 - Age of wife,
    26 - Both are Single - Both were born in Jefferson County, West
    Virginia - Husband resides in Berkeley County, West Virginia - Wife
    resides in Jefferson County, West Virginia.

Hyatt, Catherine Beatrice Baker and C. J. Snapp (3) -   January 26, 1887
    For further information see - Snapp, C. J.

Hyatt, Hannah and Henry Chapman (1) -   September 26, 1832

Hyatt, Lydia E. and Lloyd Watson (3) -   November 12, 1879
    For further information see - Watson, Lloyd.

Hyatt, Mary M. and George W. F. Anderson (3) -   December 12, 1871
    For further information see - Anderson, George W. F.

Hyatt, Nancy and John Avis (1) -   June 15, 1820

Hyatt, Priscilla and Erom Edmonds (1) -   June 3, 1819

Hyland, Joanna and Auguste Koetzner (2) -   (L) October 15, 1853

Hylton, Nancy and John Shaner (1) -   April 24, 1810

Hynes, Laura V. and John H. Hill (3) -   January 28, 1890
    For further information see - Hill, John H.

Hyser, Catherine and George Barey (1) -   April 7, 1825

Hyser, Sarah and Peter Howard (1) -   September 8, 1825

Iler, Israel Henry and Mary Elizabeth Stultz (2) - (L) July 14, 1853

Imes, Ida and James P. Cleveland (3) - September 16, 1884
    For further information see - Cleveland, James P.

Ingram, Elizabeth and Samuel Linton (2) - (L) September 15, 1853

Ingram, Elizabeth and James Dulany (2) - (L) March 29, 1859

Ingram, Elizabeth and John Knoble (3) - May 8, 1870
    For further information see - Knoble, John.

Ingram, John and Mary Ann C. Kline (3) - March 28, 1866
    Place of marriage, Smithfield, Jefferson County - Age of husband, 21 - Age of wife, 20 - Both are Single - Husband was born at Jacksonville, Illinois - Wife was born at Shepherdstown, Jefferson County - Both reside at Smithfield, West Virginia - Husband's parents are Daniel and Mary E. Ingram - Wife's parents are Henry and Ann C. Kline - Occupation of husband is Farmer.

Ingram, John W. and Annie E. House (3) - July 22, 1869
    Place of marriage, Jefferson County - Age of husband, 20 - Age of wife, 24 - Husband was born in Jefferson County - Wife was born in West Virginia - Husband resides in Jefferson County - Wife resides in West Virginia. (Step Father consents in person.)

Ingram, Jonathan and Margaret Ann Linton (2) - (L) August 22, 1857

Ingram, Lettie Ann and Andrew Wright (2) - (L) October 15, 1855

Ingram, Louisa V. and Michael E. Thompson (2) - (L) January 24, 1859

Ingram, Sarah and Charles C. Sherman (3) - November 20, 1875
    For further information see - Sherman, Charles C.

Ingram, Thomas J. and Mrs. Sarah C. Demory (3) - March 24, 1875
    Place of marriage, Bolivar - Age of husband, 25 - Age of wife, 29 - Husband is Single - Wife is a Widow - Both were born in Jefferson County, West Virginia - Husband resides at Springfield, Illinois - Wife resides in Jefferson County, West Virginia.

Irvig, Mary L. and John W. Strother (3) - July 15, 1869
    For further information see - Strother, John W.

Irvin, Alfred (cold.) Rachel Parker (3) - December 4, 1873
    Place of marriage, near Charlestown - Age of husband, 35 - Age of wife, 25 - Both are Single - Both were born in Jefferson County, West Virginia - Both reside in Jefferson County, West Virginia.

Irvin, Alfred (cold.) Frances Whalen (3) - October 4, 1876
    Place of marriage, Charles Town - Age of husband, 66 - Age of wife, 50 - Husband is a Widower - Wife is a Widow - Husband was born in Frederick County, Virginia - Wife was born in Jefferson County, West Virginia - Both reside in Jefferson County, West Virginia.

Irvin, Dolly and Jasper Thompson (3) - October 28, 1869
    For further information see - Thompson, Jasper.

Irvin, Harriet (free coloured) Joseph Pippin (2) - (L) February 15, 1860

Irvin, Jonathan and Harriet Coons (1) -   October 26, 1823

Irvin, Mary C. and George Price (2) -   (L) February 3, 1852

Isbell, Ada and Armistead S. Lippitt (3) -   April 24, 1883
     For further information see - Lippitt, Armistead S.

Isler, Annie and Nathan Norval Barnes (3) -   December 22, 1880
     For further information see - Barnes, Nathan Norval.

Isler, Catherine and Jeremiah Richards (1) -   February 16, 1818

Isler, Charles H. and Elizabeth Gilbert (3) -   September 15, 1886
     Place of marriage, Middleway - Age of husband, 22 - Age of wife,
     22 - Both are Single - Husband was born in State of Mississippi -
     Wife was born in Jefferson County, West Virginia - Both reside in
     Jefferson County, West Virginia.

Isler, Edith Lee and Charles H. Johnson (3) -   December 23, 1885
     For further information see - Johnson, Charles H.

Isler, Mary and Samuel Faringsworth (1) -   May 16, 1811

Jackson, Amanda (cold.) James Anderson (3) -   October 28, 1880
    For further information see - Anderson, James.

Jackson, Annie E. and John J. Ridgway (3) -   November 28, 1883
    For further information see - Ridgway, John J.

Jackson, Benjamin (cold.) Jennie Hill (3) -   December 2, 1880
    Place of marriage, Charlestown - Age of husband, 22 - Age of wife,
    21 - Both are Single - Both were born in Jefferson County, West
    Virginia - Both reside in Jefferson County, West Virginia.

Jackson, Benjamin (cold.) Charlotte Wells (3) -   September 13, 1888
    Place of marriage, Summit Point - Age of husband, 35 - Age of wife,
    40 - Both are Single - Both were born in Jefferson County, West
    Virginia - Both reside in Jefferson County, West Virginia.

Jackson, Betty (cold.) Robert Campbell (3) -   December 11, 1873
    For further information see - Campbell, Robert.

Jackson, Carrie P. and George W. Staub (3) -   June 2, 1878
    For further information see - Staub, George W.

Jackson, Catha and Warner Peters (1) -   March 16, 1820

Jackson, Charity A. (cold.) Charles Robinson (3) -   April 6, 1882
    For further information see - Robinson, Charles.

Jackson, Charles and Georgia Nelson (3) -   March 31, 1869
    Place of marriage, Jefferson County - Age of husband, 25 - Age of
    wife, 21 - Both are Single - Husband was born in Jefferson County -
    Both reside in Jefferson County - Occupation of husband is Laborer.

Jackson, Charles and Lucy Rankins (3) -   December 29, 1887
    Place of marriage, Harpers Ferry - Age of husband, 21 - Age of wife,
    21 - Both are Single - Both reside in Jefferson County, West
    Virginia.

Jackson, David (cold.) Emily Williams (3) -   November 20, 1882
    Place of marriage, Charlestown - Age of husband, 27 - Age of wife,
    36 - Husband is Single - Wife is a Widow - Husband was born in
    Augusta County, Virginia - Wife was born in Jefferson County, West
    Virginia - Both reside in Jefferson County, West Virginia.

Jackson, Ellen (colored persons) Aaron Matin (3) -   September 23, 1865
    For further information see - Matin, Aaron.

Jackson, Elvira Eliza and Joel Peregoy (1) -   November 12, 1830

Jackson, Emma and George Brooks (3) -   (1868)
    For further information see - Brooks, George.

Jackson, Emma and William F. Grey (3) -   January 3, 1877
    For further information see - Grey, William F.

Jackson, Emma G. H. (cold.) William H. Brown (3) -   March 18, 1880
    For further information see - Brown, William H.

Jackson, Frank and Sarah Ann Dillow (3) - July 5, 1880
Place of marriage, Charlestown - Age of husband, 21 - Age of wife, 17 - Both are Single - Husband was born in Warren County, Virginia - Wife was born in Jefferson County, West Virginia - Both reside in Jefferson County, West Virginia. (Consent of bride's father in person.)

Jackson, George and Susan Goldsborough (1) - May 18, 1809

Jackson, George and Mary Hutchison (3) - March 12, 1868
Place of marriage, Jefferson County - Age of husband, 29 - Age of wife, 19 - Both are Single - Husband was born in Loudoun County - Wife was born in Jefferson - Both reside in Jefferson - Occupation of husband is Farmer. (Father willing.)

Jackson, George and Florence Bradshaw (3) - June 2, 1886
Place of marriage, Charlestown - Age of husband, 26 - Age of wife, 24 - Both are Single - Husband was born in Clarke County, Virginia - Wife was born in Maryland - Both reside in Jefferson County, West Virginia.

Jackson, George W. (cold.) Joanna Jackson (3) - August 23, 1884
Place of marriage, Harpers Ferry - Age of husband, 31 - Age of wife, 25 - Both are Single - Both were born in Loudoun County, Virginia - Husband resides in Maryland - Wife resides in Jefferson County, West Virginia.

Jackson, Gracy and Jacob Fox (3) - October 18, 1866
For further information see - Fox, Jacob.

Jackson, H. P. and Emma Butts (3) - (1868)
Age of husband, 28 - Age of wife, 18 - Both are Single - Husband was born in Georgia - Wife was born in Jefferson County - Both reside in Jefferson County - Occupation of husband is Carpenter. (Parents dead.)

Jac(k)son, Hannah and William Colbert (1) - October 1, 1829

Jackson, Hannah (cold.) Thomas Roberts (3) - March 31, 1886
For further information see - Roberts, Thomas.

Jackson, Henrietta and George William Tabb (3) - October 26, 1871
For further information see - Tabb, George William.

Jackson, Henry (cold.) Julia King (3) - (L) September 21, 1866
Age of husband, 23 - Age of wife, 18 - Both are Single - Both were born in Clarke County, Virginia - Both reside in Jefferson County, West Virginia - Husband's parents are Bettie Turner - Wife's parents are King - Occupation of husband is Farmer.

Jackson, Henry (cold.) Jane Cole (3) - December 25, 1878
Place of marriage, Charlestown - Age of husband, 38 - Age of wife, 32 - Husband is a Widower - Wife is a Widow - Husband was born in Clarke County, Virginia - Wife was born in Jefferson County, West Virginia - Husband resides in Clarke County, Virginia - Wife resides in Jefferson County, West Virginia.

Jackson, Herbert (cold.) Annie Martin (3) - October 14, 1887
   Place of marriage, Charlestown - Age of husband, 22 - Age of wife,
   21 - Both are Single - Both were born in Jefferson County, West
   Virginia - Both reside in Jefferson County, West Virginia.

Jackson, James (cold.) Laura Harris (3) - December 26, 1887
   Place of marriage, Charlestown - Age of husband, 22 - Age of wife,
   21 - Both are Single - Both were born in Jefferson County, West
   Virginia - Husband resides in Jefferson County, West Virginia - Wife
   resides in Jefferson County.

Jackson, James D., Jr. (cold.) Evelyn Herbert (3) - November 17, 1890
   Place of marriage, Charlestown - Age of husband, 25 - Age of wife,
   23 - Both are Single - Husband was born in Jefferson County, West
   Virginia - Wife was born in Frederick County, Virginia - Both reside
   in Jefferson County, West Virginia.

Jackson, Joanna (cold.) George W. Jackson (3) - August 23, 1884
   For further information see - Jackson, George W.

Jackson, John and Mary Feaman (1) - November 11, 1810

Jackson, John, Jr. and Catherine Ruid (1) - September 28, 1809

Jackson, Jonathan and M. F. Crutchley (1) - 1819

Jackson, Joseph and Catherine Nelson (1) - April 11, 1822

Jackson, Joseph (cold.) Louisa Lee (3) - September 2, 1880
   Place of marriage, Charlestown - Age of husband, 27 - Age of wife,
   21 - Both are Single - Husband was born in Clarke County, Virginia -
   Wife was born in Culpeper County, Virginia - Both reside in
   Jefferson County, West Virginia.

Jackson, Joseph A. and Mary E. Albin (3) - October 26, 1880
   Place of marriage, near Kabletown - Age of husband, 22 - Age of
   wife, 21 - Both are Single - Both were born in Clarke County,
   Virginia - Both reside in Jefferson County, West Virginia.

Jackson, Katie and John W. Dailey (3) - October 27, 1890
   For further information see - Dailey, John W.

Jackson, L. M. (bride) and W. A. Thomas (3) - December 19, 1872
   For further information see - Thomas, W. A.

Jackson, Lina (cold.) William Fleming Minor (3) - October 7, 1874
   For further information see - Minor, William Fleming.

Jackson, Louisa and Madison Brooks (3) - (1868)
   For further information see - Brooks, Madison.

Jackson, Louisa and John H. Washington (3) - July 29, 1869
   For further information see - Washington, John H.

Jackson, Lucy B. and Charles W. Atwell (3) - December 24, 1885
   For further information see - Atwell, Charles W.

Jackson, Lucy L. A. (cold.) John B. Jordan (3) - November 13, 1889
   For further information see - Jordan, John B.

Jackson, Martha (cold.) David Edwards (3) -   January 4, 1877
    For further information see - Edwards, David.

Jackson, Mary and John McKinney (1) -   1825

Jackson, Mary (colored persons) Hance Creamer (3) -   May 13, 1865
    For further information see - Creamer, Hance.

Jackson, Mary and John Pendleton (3) -   September 24, 1868
    For further information see - Pendleton, John.

Jackson, Mary Evelyn (cold.) Charles W. Herbert (3) -   September 9, 1874
    For further information see - Herbert, Charles W.

Jackson, Millie and I. Johnson (3) -   February 15, 1868
    For further information see - Johnson, I.

Jackson, Nancy and Grafton Todd (3) -   November 26, 1872
    For further information see - Todd, Grafton.

Jackson, Peter (cold.) Ida Edwards (3) -   December 27, 1888
    Place of marriage, Charlestown - Age of husband, 27 - Age of wife,
    30 - Both are Single - Husband was born in Culpeper County,
    Virginia - Wife was born in Clarke County, Virginia - Both reside in
    Jefferson County, West Virginia.

Jackson, Rebecca and Joseph Cline (1) -   April 14, 1833

Jackson, Rebecca (colored) Lewis Cross (3) -   January 27, 1870
    For further information see - Cross, Lewis.

Jackson, Richard (cold.) Fanny Brown (3) -   January 1, 1885
    Place of marriage, Harpers Ferry - Age of husband, 35 - Age of wife,
    26 - Husband is a Widower - Wife is a Widow - Both were born in
    Jefferson County, West Virginia - Both reside in Jefferson County,
    West Virginia.

Jackson, Robert (cold.) Lucy Flint (3) -   January 28, 1884
    Place of marriage, Shepherdstown - Age of husband, 39 - Age of wife,
    26 - Husband is a Widower - Wife is a Widow - Husband was born in
    Culpeper County, Virginia - Wife was born in Jefferson County, West
    Virginia - Both reside in Jefferson County, West Virginia.

Jackson, Samuel (colored) Harriet Mason (3) -   December 1, 1870
    Place of marriage, Jefferson County - Age of husband, 24 - Age of
    wife, 21 - Both were born in Virginia - Both reside in Jefferson
    County.

Jackson, Sarah (cold.) Rezin Herbert (3) -   December 11, 1873
    For further information see - Herbert, Rezin.

Jackson, Sarah (cold.) Daniel Chargs (3) -   March 23. 1874
    For further information see - Chargs, Daniel.

Jackson, Sarah J. and Edward Trent (3) -   October 23, 1872
    For further information see - Trent, Edward.

Jackson, Thomas (cold.) Matilda Colston (3) -   January 4, 1877
    Age of husband, 22 - Age of wife, 22 - Both are Single - Husband was
    born in Jefferson County, West Virginia - Wife was born in Clarke
    County, Virginia - Both reside in Jefferson County, West Virginia.

Jackson, Thomas (cold.) Louisa Doleman (3) -   November 10, 1881
    Place of marriage, Summit Point - Age of husband, 23 - Age of wife,
    21 - Both are Single - Both were born in Jefferson County, West
    Virginia - Both reside in Jefferson County, West Virginia.

Jackson, Thomas H. and Mary Goldsboro (3) -   November 10, 1890
    Place of marriage, Mrs. Painter's - Age of husband, 23 - Age of
    wife, 20 - Both are Single - Both were born in Jefferson County,
    West Virginia - Both reside in Jefferson County, West Virginia.
    (Levi Wilt assures me of bride's father's consent.)

Jackson, W. G. and Julia M. Langdon (3) -   September 21, 1881
    Place of marriage, Kabletown - Age of husband, 26 - Age of wife,
    22 - Both are Single - Husband was born in Clarke County, Virginia -
    Wife was born in Jefferson County, West Virginia - Husband resides
    in Clarke County, Virginia - Wife resides in Jefferson County, West
    Virginia.

Jackson, Walter C. (cold.) Mary Newman (3) -   November 12, 1888
    Place of marriage, Charlestown - Age of husband, 25 - Age of wife,
    28 - Both are Single - Both were born in Jefferson County, West
    Virginia - Both reside in Jefferson County, West Virginia.

Jackson, William and Mary Ellen Skinner (2) -   (L) September 24, 1854

Jackson, William A. and Lucinda Myers (3) -   December 25, 1877
    Place of marriage, Harpers Ferry - Age of husband, 23 - Age of wife,
    35 - Husband is Single - Wife is a Widow - Husband was born in
    Warren County, Virginia - Wife was born in Loudoun County, Virginia -
    Both reside in Jefferson County, West Virginia.

Jackson, William H. (cold.) Sarah Brady (3) -   January 23, 1879
    Place of marriage, Jefferson County - Age of husband, 23 - Age of
    wife, 25 - Husband is Single - Wife is a Widow - Husband was born in
    Culpeper County, Virginia - Wife was born in Loudoun County,
    Virginia - Both reside in Jefferson County, West Virginia.

Jacobs, Casper and Barbara Dust (1) -   September 10, 1807

Jacobs, George and Elizabeth Mandell (1) -   May 27, 1823

Jacobs, John and Priscilla Rion (1) -   October 1, 1814

Jacobs, Peter and Margaret E. Gore (2) -   (L) April 3, 1852

Jacobs, Peter and Margaret E. Gore (1) -   April 15, 1852

Jacobs, Susan V. and W. M. Monroe (3) -   (1868)
    For further information see - Monroe, W. M.

Jacobs, Valentine and Hanrete L. Burns (1) -   August 25, 1829

Jagielle, Miss Apollonia and Major Gaspar Tochman (2) - (L) August 4, 1851

James, Charles (cold.) Sally Johnson (3) - November 21, 1886
Place of marriage, Ripon - Age of husband, 26 - Age of wife, 23 -
Both are Single - Husband was born in Warren County, Virginia - Wife
was born in Clarke County, Virginia - Both reside in Jefferson
County, West Virginia.

James, Isabelle (cold.) Benjamin Daugherty (3) - November 14, 1887
For further information see - Daugherty, Benjamin.

James, John W. and Annie J. Ardella Niswarner (3) - January 1, 1879
Place of marriage, Mountain - Age of husband, 23 - Age of wife, 18 -
Both are Single - Husband was born in Loudoun County, Virginia -
Wife was born in Jefferson County, West Virginia - Husband resides
in Loudoun County, Virginia - Wife resides in Jefferson County, West
Virginia. (Consent of bride's father in person.)

James, Martha and Washington Banks (2) - (L) June 19, 1854
(D. W. Cook says her father agrees to the match.)

James, Thomas and Elizabeth Welshimer (1) - March 22, 1810

Jamison, Molly and Joseph Buzzard (3) - July 4, 1878
For further information see - Buzzard, Joseph.

Janney, Amos and Ann Rowles (1) - January 12, 1826

Janney, Josephine M. and Warner A. Thomson (2) - (L) December 8, 1851

Janney, Katie and Gerard D. Moore (3) - July 30, 1889
For further information see - Moore, Gerard D.

Janney, Sarah Ann and Ferdinand R. Butler (2) - (L) July 16, 1852

Jarboe, J. W. M. and Margaret L. Keller (2) - (L) September 17, 1855

Jarmey, Thomas and Mildred S. Barnes (3) - March 23, 1881
Place of marriage, Charlestown - Age of husband, 29 - Age of wife,
26 - Both are Single - Husband was born in Clarke County, Virginia -
Wife was born in Jefferson County, West Virginia - Both reside in
Jefferson County, West Virginia.

Jarvis, David and Annie Nora Manuel (3) - June 12, 1884
Place of marriage, Halltown - Age of husband, 27 - Age of wife, 17 -
Both are Single - Husband was born in Franklin County, New York -
Wife was born in Jefferson County, West Virginia - Both reside in
Jefferson County, West Virginia. (Consent of bride's father in
person.)

Jasper, Robert T. and Elizabeth Gray Selden (3) - October 18, 1876
Place of marriage, Charlestown - Age of husband, 30 in December
next - Age of wife, 25 - Both are Single - Husband was born at New
York City - Wife was born in Jefferson County, West Virginia -
Husband resides in State of New Jersey - Wife resides in Jefferson
County, West Virginia.

Jefferson, Frances and Eli Smith (1) - February 26, 1828

281

Jefferson, John (cold.) Lizzie Jones (3) - August 28, 1884
    Place of marriage, Middleway - Age of husband, 24 - Age of wife, 19 - Both are Single - Both were born in Jefferson County - Both reside in Jefferson County. (Bride's mother dead and father does not live here.)

Jefferson, Mary Ann and William Ford (3) - January 6, 1874
    For further information see - Ford, William.

Jefferson, Sally (cold.) Simon Walker (3) - January 22, 1874
    For further information see - Walker, Simon.

Jefferson, Thomas and Josephine Cross (3) - November 1866
    Age of husband, 28 - Age of wife, 18 - Husband is a Widower - Wife is Single - Husband was born in South Carolina - Wife was born in Berkeley County, West Virginia - Both reside in Jefferson County, West Virginia - Husband's parents are Richard and Philis Jefferson - Wife's parents are Joseph and Caroline Cross - Occupation of husband is Laborer.

Jefferson, Thomas (cold.) Harriet Smith (3) - February 1, 1875
    Place of marriage, Harpers Ferry - Age of husband, 40 - Age of wife, 27 - Husband is a Widower - Wife is Single - Husband was born in South Carolina - Wife was born in Jefferson County, West Virginia - Both reside in Jefferson County, West Virginia.

Jefferson, Thomas (cold.) Evelina Lewis (3) - January 23, 1889
    Place of marriage, Charlestown - Age of husband, 46 - Age of wife, 24 - Husband is a Widower - Wife is Single - Husband was born in Jefferson County, West Virginia - Wife was born in Clarke County, Virginia - Both reside in Jefferson County, West Virginia.

Jefries, Alex and Louisa Carter (3) - April 16, 1871
    Place of marriage, Jefferson County - Age of husband, 21 - Age of wife, 18 - Both are Single - Husband was born in Jefferson County - Wife was born in Virginia - Both reside in Jefferson County - Husband's parents are Alex and Lydia M. - Wife's parents are Isaac and Jane - Occupation of husband is Farmer.

Jemckings, Katie (cold.) James Wood (3) - June 26, 1879
    For further information see - Wood, James.

Jenkens, Catharine and William Sagle (1) - June 15, 1826

Jenkens, Thomas and Mary Cooper (1) - April 28, 1825

Jenkins, Alice (cold.) Joseph Walker (3) - September 4, 1884
    For further information see - Walker, Joseph.

Jenkins, Amanda and Thomas Copeland (3) - April 1, 1879
    For further information see - Copeland, Thomas.

Jenkins, Catherine C. and Samuel Myers (1) - March 3, 1836

Jenkins, Elizabeth A. and Daniel McKnight (3) - May 13, 1866
    For further information see - McKnight, Daniel.

Jenkins, George W. (cold.) Florence M. Dixon (3) -   March 13, 1876
   Place of marriage, Charles Town - Age of husband, 21 - Age of wife,
   19 - Both are Single - Husband was born in Frederick County,
   Maryland - Wife was born in Jefferson County, West Virginia - Both
   reside in Jefferson County, West Virginia. (Consent of bride's
   father in person.)

Jenkins, John and Hannah Frances Coates (2) -   (L) January 29, 1853

Jenkins, Kate and John W. Turner (3) -   November 15, 1888
   For further information see - Turner, John W.

Jenkins, Keziah and Isaac Smith (1) -   October 29, 1835

Jenkins, Leander and Deborah Shambling (1) -   December 14, 1826

Jenkins, Maggie and James Edwards (3) -   September 12, 1872
   For further information see - Edwards, James.

Jenkins, Mary (cold.) Samuel Whiting (3) -   December 1, 1881
   For further information see - Whiting, Samuel.

Jenkins, Milly (cold.) Thomas Wilson (3) -   April 20, 1876
   For further information see - Wilson, Thomas.

Jenkins, Nancy and William H. Conklyn (1) -   March 17, 1831

Jenkins, Phoebe and Levi Croesen (1) -   June 20, 1816

Jenkins, Rebecca and John Potts (3) -   March 2, 1870
   For further information see - Potts, John.

Jenkins, Robert (cold.) Alice Robinson (3) -   December 28, 1875
   Place of marriage, Duffields - Age of husband, 21 - Age of wife,
   24 - Husband is Single - Wife is a Widow - Both were born in
   Jefferson County, West Virginia - Both reside in Jefferson County,
   West Virginia.

Jenkins, Sally (cold.) Anthony Williams (3) -   December 21, 1876
   For further information see - Williams, Anthony.

Jenkins, William R. and Catharine Bennett (2) -   (L) (1862)
   Time of marriage, February 1, 1862 - Place of marriage, near
   Duffields - Names, William R. Jenkins and Catharine Bennett - Age of
   husband, 27 years - Age of wife, 30 years - Condition of husband is
   Single - Condition of wife is Single - Place of husband's birth in
   Rappahannock County, Virginia - Place of wife's birth in Jefferson
   County, Virginia - Husband's residence is in Jefferson County,
   Virginia - Wife's residence is in Jefferson County, Virginia - Names
   of husband's parents are William and Milly Jenkins - Names of wife's
   parents are Thomas and Malinda Bennett - Occupation of husband is
   Soldier in Southern Army - William R. Jenkins.

Jenkins, William R. and Virginia Zombro (3) -   June 18, 1885
   Place of marriage, Charlestown - Age of husband, 50 - Age of wife,
   43 - Husband is a Widower - Wife is a Widow - Husband was born in
   Rappahannock County, Virginia - Wife was born in Jefferson County,
   West Virginia - Both reside in Jefferson County, West Virginia.

Jenkins, Zachariah and Elizabeth Sagle (1) -   March 18, 1819

Jennings, J. Henry and Anna V. Roberts (3) -   February 26, 1874
    Place of marriage, Middleway - Age of husband, 33 - Age of wife,
    23 - Both are Single - Husband was born in Shenandoah County,
    Virginia - Wife was born in Berkeley County, West Virginia - Husband
    resides in Frederick County, Virginia - Wife resides in Jefferson
    County, West Virginia.

Jett, Ann and George Lathan (1) -   October 24, 1819

Jett, Lucinda and Samuel Davis (1) -   1812

Jett, Polly and Aaron Rawlins (1) -   July 6, 1817

Jett, Polly and John Write (1) -   June 2, 1825

Jett, Rawleigh and Sarah Ann Notingham (1) -   May 25, 1820

Jett, Rollins and Mary Ann Haines (2) -   (L) May 24, 1858

Jewett, Ellen M. and John K. White (1) -   November 19, 1839

Jewett, John M. and Sarah Duffield (2) -   (L) June 1, 1853

Jinkens, Delilah and Henry Sagle (1) -   September 16, 1817

Jinkins, Matilda and Jonas Heath (1) -   June 26, 1823

Johns, Charlie H. and Emma K. Sites (3) -   February 28, 1883
    Place of marriage, Bride's Residence - Age of husband, 31 - Age of
    wife, 22 - Both are Single - Husband was born in Jefferson County,
    West Virginia - Wife was born in Washington County, Maryland -
    Husband resides in Clarke County, Virginia - Wife resides in
    Jefferson County, West Virginia.

Johns, Jefferson and Elizabeth Farnsworth (2) -   (L) September 4, 1850

Johns, Jefferson and Elizabeth Farnsworth (1) -   September 5, 1850

Johns, Kate and F. B. Myers (3) -   August 4, 1870
    For further information see - Myers, F. B.

Johns, Mary E. and G. R. Marquette (3) -   June 22, 1875
    For further information see - Marquette, G. R.

Johns, Sarah A. D. and Simpson Cooksey (1).-   November 7, 1848

Johnson, A. A. (bride) and W. S. Turner (3) -   October 31, 1872
    For further information see - Turner, W. S.

Johnson, Adeline (cold.) James H. Corbin (3) -   December 20, 1888
    For further information see - Corbin, James H.

Johnson, Agnus and George Grey (3) -   August 24, 1872
    For further information see - Grey, George.

Johnson, Albert (cold.) Emma Hunter (3) -   April 15, 1880
    Place of marriage, near Middleway.- Age of husband, 26 - Age of
    wife, 21 - Both are Single - Husband was born in Berkeley County,
    West Virginia - Wife was born in Jefferson County, West Virginia -
    Both reside in Jefferson County, West Virginia.

Johnson, Alfred and Anne Luckett (3) -   December 28, 1871
    Place of marriage, Jefferson County - Age of husband, 26 - Age of
    wife, 21 - Both are Single - Husband was born in Page County,
    Virginia - Wife was born in Jefferson County, West Virginia -
    Husband resides in Jefferson County - Wife resides in Jefferson
    County, West Virginia - Husband's parents are Tom and Jane - Wife's
    parents are Wash and Bettie - Occupation of husband is Farmer.

Johnson, Alice and Frank Robinson (3) -   December 23, 1869
    For further information see - Robinson, Frank.

Johnson, Alice (cold.) Edward Williams (3) -   October 4, 1883
    For further information see - Williams, Edward.

Johnson, Angeline (cold.) Spencer Davis (3) -   May 25, 1874
    For further information see - Davis, Spencer.

Johnson, Annie (cold.) Charles Wilkinson (3) -   March 5, 1874
    For further information see - Wilkinson, Charles.

Johnson, Mrs. Annie D. and James W. Milton (3) -   January 22, 1884
    For further information see - Milton, James W.

Johnson, Barger (cold.) Girtie Wells (3) -   December 23, 1880
    Place of marriage, Summit Point - Age of husband, 23 - Age of wife,
    24 - Both are Single - Both were born in Jefferson County, West
    Virginia - Both reside in Jefferson County, West Virginia.

Johnson, Barger (cold.) Nancey Robinson (3) -   October 26, 1890
    Place of marriage, Summit Point - Age of husband, 29 - Age of wife,
    21 - Husband is a Widower - Wife is Single - Both were born in
    Jefferson County, West Virginia - Both reside in Jefferson County,
    West Virginia.

Johnson, Belle (cold.) George W. Lee (3) -   February 23, 1888
    For further information see - Lee, George W.

Johnson, C. G. and Jessee E. Engle (bride) (3) -   December 20, 1870
                              (In the date, 17 is marked out.)
    Place of marriage, Harpers Ferry - Age of husband, 24 - Age of wife,
    20 - Both are Single - Husband was born at Charlestown - Wife was
    born at Harpers Ferry - Husband resides at Charlestown - Wife
    resides at Harpers Ferry - Husband's parents are Thomas and Sarah
    J. - Wife's parents are Philip and L. E. - Occupation of husband is
    Butcher.   (By father's consent.)

Johnson, Casper E. and Mary S. Evans (3) -   February 9, 1887
    Place of marriage, Charlestown - Age of husband, 43 - Age of wife,
    37 - Husband is a Widower - Wife is Single - Husband was born in
    Jefferson County - Wife was born in Berkeley County - Husband
    resides in Berkeley County - Wife resides in Jefferson County.

Johnson, Catharine and Benjamin F. Ramsburg (3) -   October 19, 1865
    For further information see - Ramsburg, Benjamin F.

Johnson, Charity and William Berry (3) -   May 10, 1871
    For further information see - Berry, William.

Johnson, Charles H. and Edith Lee Isler (3) - December 23, 1885
　Place of marriage, Middleway - Age of husband, 24 - Age of wife,
　19 - Both are Single - Both were born in Jefferson County, West
　Virginia - Both reside in Jefferson County, West Virginia.
　(Consent of bride's mother in writing.)

Johnson, Conrad A. and Mary E. Wageley (3) - August 31, 1871
　Place of marriage, Jefferson County - Age of husband, 22 - Age of
　wife, 22 - Both are Single - Husband was born in Berkeley County -
　Wife was born in Jefferson - Both reside in Jefferson County -
　Husband's parents are Samuel and Milley - Wife's parents are James
　W. and Annie - Occupation of husband is Shoemaker.

Johnson, D. R. and Mrs. L. V. Stalfort (3) - September 19, 1888
　Place of marriage, Harpers Ferry - Age of husband, 33 - Age of wife,
　31 - Husband is Single - Wife is a Widow - Husband was born in
　Pennsylvania - Wife was born in Maryland - Both reside in Jefferson
　County, West Virginia at this time.

Johnson, Daniel and Nelly Doggett (1) - July 29, 1808

Johnson, Daniel (cold.) Louisa Holmes (3) - September 22, 1880
　Place of marriage, Ripon - Age of husband, 53 - Age of wife, 30 -
　Husband is a Widower - Wife is Single - Husband was born in Fairfax
　County, Virginia - Wife was born in Clarke County, Virginia - Both
　reside in Jefferson County, West Virginia.

Johnson, David and Joanah Earhart (1) - March 10, 1829

Johnson, David and Mary Washington (3) - June 8, 1867
　Place of marriage, Duffields - Age of husband, 20 - Age of wife,
　21 - Both are Single - Both were born at Duffields, Jefferson
　County - Both reside at Duffields, Jefferson County - Husband's
　parents are Griff and Ann Johnson - Occupation of husband is
　Laborer. (Father's consent in writing.)

Johnson, E. B. and Annie E. Mobley (3) - August 17, 1878
　Place of marriage, Charlestown - Age of husband, 41 - Age of wife,
　24 - Husband is a Widower - Wife is Single - Husband was born in
　Pennsylvania - Wife was born in Jefferson County, West Virginia -
　Both reside in Jefferson County, West Virginia.

Johnson, Ed. (cold.) Rachael Twyman (3) - March 15, 1888
　Place of marriage, Charlestown - Age of husband, 26 - Age of wife,
　21 - Both are Single - Both were born in Jefferson County, West
　Virginia - Both reside in Jefferson County.

Johnson, Eliza and Benjamin Botts (3) - November 25, 1865
　For further information see - Botts, Benjamin.

Johnson, Elizabeth and Samuel Glass (1) - April 13, 1809

Johnson, Elizabeth (cold.) Thomas Jones (3) - June 6, 1888
　For further information see - Jones, Thomas.

Johnson, Ella R. and William A. Beltz (3) - February 21, 1878
　For further information see - Beltz, William A.

Johnson, Emanuel (cold.) Nancy E. Goyins (3) -   September 19, 1867
    Place of marriage, Jefferson - Age of husband, 24 - Age of wife,
    19 - Both are Single - Husband was born in Page County, Virginia -
    Wife was born in Jefferson County - Both reside in Jefferson
    County - Husband's parents are John - Wife's parents are Lawson -
    Occupation of husband is Farmer. (Father in person gives his
    consent.)

Johnson, Emily (cold.) Lewis Summers (3) -   June 1, 1881
    For further information see - Summers, Lewis.

Johnson, Emma and William Fidler (3) -   May 17, 1888
    For further information see - Fidler, William.

Johnson, Emma Jane (cold.) Philip Franklin (3) -   January 1, 1880
    For further information see - Franklin, Philip.

Johnson, Emmit Henry (cold.) Annie Robinson (3) -   October 15, 1885
    Place of marriage, Middleway - Age of husband, 23 - Age of wife,
    21 - Both are Single - Both were born in Jefferson County, West
    Virginia - Both reside in Jefferson County.

Johnson, George and Martha Seibert (3) -   October 2, 1872
    Place of marriage, Jefferson County - Age of husband, 22 - Age of
    wife, 21 - Both are Single - Both were born in Virginia - Both
    reside in West Virginia - Husband's parents are William and Ellen -
    Wife's parents are Jacob and Susana - Occupation of husband is
    Farmer.

Johnson, George (cold.) Louisa Robinson (3) -   September 5, 1882
    Place of marriage, Charlestown - Age of husband, 29 - Age of wife,
    26 - Husband is Single - Wife is a Widow - Husband was born in
    Prince George County, Maryland - Wife was born in Jefferson County,
    West Virginia - Both reside in Jefferson County, West Virginia.

Johnson, George D. and A. E. Henry (3) -   October 17, 1867
    Place of marriage, Jefferson - Age of husband, 22 - Age of wife,
    21 - Both are Single - Both were born in Berkeley County - Both
    reside in Jefferson County - Husband's parents are A. J. and B. E. -
    Wife's parents are Philip and M. E. - Occupation of husband is
    Blacksmith.

Johnson, George W. (cold.) Bettie Ford (3) -   March 25, 1886
    Place of marriage, Charlestown - Age of husband, 26 - Age of wife,
    27 - Both are Single - Both were born in Jefferson County, West
    Virginia - Both reside in Jefferson County, West Virginia.

Johnson, George William (cold.) Jennie Devonshire (3) -   January 15, 1879
    Place of marriage, Shepherdstown - Age of husband, 29 - Age of wife,
    22 - Both are Single - Both were born in Jefferson County, West
    Virginia - Both reside in Jefferson County, West Virginia.

Johnson, Gertrude V. and Benjamin F. Fulk (3) -   February 12, 1885
    For further information see - Fulk, Benjamin F.

Johnson, Gideon (cold.) Elizabeth Hills (3) -   June 14, 1875
    Place of marriage, Charlestown - Age of husband, 45 - Age of wife,
    23 - Husband is a Widower - Wife is Single - Husband was born in
    Page County, Virginia - Wife was born in King William County,
    Virginia - Both reside in Jefferson County, West Virginia.

Johnson, Harriet (cold.) Budd Taylor (3) -   October 25, 1883
For further information see - Taylor, Budd.

Johnson, Harry (cold.) Mary Robinson (3) -   September 24, 1890
Place of marriage, Harpers Ferry - Age of husband, 22 - Age of wife, 21 - Both are Single - Both were born in Jefferson County, West Virginia - Both reside in Jefferson County, West Virginia.

Johnson, Huey (cold.) Maggie Johnson (3) -   February 7, 1884
Place of marriage, Charlestown - Age of husband, 22 - Age of wife, 22 - Both are Single - Husband was born in Page County, Virginia - Wife was born in Augusta County, Virginia - Both reside in Jefferson County, West Virginia.

Johnson, I. and Millie Jackson (3) -   February 15, 1868
Place of marriage, Jefferson County - Age of husband, 22 - Age of wife, 25 - Husband is Single - Wife is a Widow - Husband was born in Augusta, Virginia - Wife was born in Jefferson - Both reside in Jefferson - Husband's parents are Nelson and Rachel - Wife's parents are Samuel and Sarah - Occupation of husband is Farmer.

Johnson, J. O. and Mary E. Davis (3) -   October 10, 1883
Place of marriage, Charlestown - Age of husband, 28 - Age of wife, 25 - Both are Single - Both were born in Jefferson County, West Virginia - Both reside in Jefferson County, West Virginia.

Johnson, Jane (cold.) Frank Herrin (3) -   May 27, 1884
For further information see - Herrin, Frank.

Johnson, Jane H. and John S. Easterday (3) -   November 2, 1887
For further information see - Easterday, John S.

Johnson, Jerry M. (cold.) Mary V. Anderson (3) -   April 20, 1887
Place of marriage, Charlestown - Age of husband, 25 - Age of wife, 24 - Both are Single - Husband was born in Jefferson County, West Virginia - Wife was born in Maryland - Both reside in Jefferson County.

Johnson, John (cold.) Susan Cassidy (3) -   July 9, 1887
Place of marriage, At Home - Age of husband, 44 - Age of wife, 35 - Husband is a Widower - Wife is Single - Both were born in Jefferson County, West Virginia - Both reside in Jefferson County, West Virginia.

Johnson, John H. (cold.) Anna Maria Virginia Stribling (3) - September 6, 1881
Place of marriage, Ripon - Age of husband, 26 - Age of wife, 21 - Both are Single - Husband was born in Pennsylvania - Wife was born in Virginia - Both reside in Jefferson County, West Virginia.

Johnson, John M. and Mary Smith (1) -   March 8, 1827

Johnson, John William and Jennie Rutherford (3) -   October 24, 1875
Place of marriage, near Kearneysville - Age of husband, 22 - Age of wife, 24 - Both are Single - Both were born in Jefferson County, West Virginia - Both reside in Jefferson County, West Virginia.

Johnson, Jonathan (J. W.) and Christana Ware (2) -   (L) May 14, 1855

Johnson, Julia O. and Rollin S. Donnelly (3) -   November 2, 1881
For further information see - Donnelly, Rollin S.

Johnson, Kennedy (colored) Hanney Thompson (3) - January 13, 1870
  Place of marriage, Jefferson County - Age of husband, 23 - Age of
  wife, 20 - Both were born in Jefferson County - Both reside in
  Jefferson County. (Mother consents.)

Johnson, Lewis (cold.) Eliza Thompson (3) - January 19, 1882
  Place of marriage, near Charlestown - Age of husband, 22 - Age of
  wife, 21 - Both are Single - Both were born in Jefferson County,
  West Virginia - Both reside in Jefferson County, West Virginia.

Johnson, Lizzie and Joseph Walker (3) - October 24, 1872
  For further information see - Walker, Joseph.

Johnson, Lizzie (cold.) Charles Taylor (3) - June 7, 1883
  For further information see - Taylor, Charles.

Johnson, Lizzie (cold.) Samuel Thornton (3) - February 1, 1888
  For further information see - Thornton, Samuel.

Johnson, Louisa (cold.) John Thomas William Franklin Price (3) -
                                                February 22, 1883
  For further information see - Price, John Thomas William Franklin.

Johnson, Lucinda (cold.) Cornelius Powell (3) - September 15, 1887
  For further information see - Powell, Cornelius.

Johnson, Lydia (colored) Robert Armstead (3) - (1870)
  For further information see - Armstead, Robert.

Johnson, M. and Charles Clarke (3) - March 12, 1868
  For further information see - Clarke, Charles.

Johnson, Maggie (cold.) Huey Johnson (3) - February 7, 1884
  For further information see - Johnson, Huey.

Johnson, Mahala (cold.) Thomas Jones (3) - September 25, 1879
  For further information see - Jones, Thomas.

Johnson, Margaret (cold.) Charles Ed. Murphy (3) - September 17, 1876
  For further information see - Murphy, Charles Ed.

Johnson, Martha (free colored) William Goins (2) - (L) February 23, 1863
  For further information see - Goins, William.

Johnson, Mary and Samuel Rockenbough (1) - September 26, 1816

Johnson, Mary and Robert Brown (3) - January 6, 1872
  For further information see - Brown, Robert.

Johnson, Mary (cold.) James Doleman (3) - September 21, 1882
  For further information see - Doleman, James.

Johnson, Mary (cold.) Charles Thornhill (3) - May 29, 1884
  For further information see - Thornhill, Charles.

Johnson, Mary (cold.) Lafayette Curry (3) - March 3, 1887
  For further information see - Curry, Lafayette.

Johnson, Mary A. and William Rust (3) - December 1866
  For further information see - Rust, William.

Johnson, Mary Ann and Henry W. McAnley (2) -   (L) April 12, 1852

Johnson, Mary B. and Richard Bogenson (3) -   (1869)
    For further information see - Bogenson, Richard.

Johnson, Mary F. (cold.) Richard Posey (3) -   July 9, 1881
    For further information see - Posey, Richard.

Johnson, Mary Frances and David H. Dudrear (2) -   (L) November 19, 1856

Johnson, Mary Jane Virginia and John W. Whittington (2) -(L) February 16, 1854

Johnson, Mary L. and William Kimes (3) -   August 2, 1877
    For further information see - Kimes, William.

Johnson, Meredith (cold.) Mary Richardson (3) -   January 16, 1874
    Place of marriage, Middleway - Age of husband, 23 - Age of wife,
    21 - Both are Single - Both were born in Jefferson County, West
    Virginia - Both reside in Jefferson County, West Virginia.

Johnson, Nathan (free colored.) Martha Osburn (2) -   (L) November 1, 1853

Johnson, Peter John and Elizabeth Medler (1) -   May 17, 1827

Johnson, Peyton (cold.) Annie Parker (3) -   June 1, 1885
    Place of marriage, Charlestown - Age of husband, 28 - Age of wife,
    16 - Both are Single - Both were born in Jefferson County, West
    Virginia - Both reside in Jefferson County, West Virginia.
    (Consent of bride's mother in person; father dead.)

Johnson, Richard (cold.) Laura Melon (3) -   November 30, 1876
    Place of marriage, near Charlestown - Age of husband, 47 - Age of
    wife, 35 - Both are Single - Husband was born in Halifax County,
    Virginia - Wife was born in Jefferson County, West Virginia - Both
    reside in Jefferson County, West Virginia.

Johnson, Richard (cold.) Laura Helm (3) -   June 3, 1885
    Place of marriage, Charlestown - Age of husband, 23 - Age of wife,
    24 - Both are Single - Husband was born in Clarke County, Virginia -
    Wife was born in Jefferson County, Virginia - Both reside in
    Jefferson County, West Virginia.

Johnson, Richard C. and Mary F. Woodward (3) -   August 10, 1865
    Place of marriage, Jefferson County - Age of husband, 22 years - Age
    of wife, 20 years - Both are Single - Husband was born at Kabletown,
    Jefferson County, Virginia - Wife was born in Clarke County,
    Virginia - Both reside in Orsborn Township - Husband's parents are
    David and Annie Johnson - Wife's parents are Thomas E. and Mary A.
    Woodward - Occupation of husband is Manufacturer.

Johnson, S. G. and Howanna Hostler (3) -   December 25, 1888
    Place of marriage, Bride's Residence - Age of husband, 23 - Age of
    wife, 22 - Both are Single - Husband was born in Fayette County,
    Pennsylvania - Wife was born in Jefferson County, West Virginia -
    Both reside in Jefferson County, West Virginia.

Johnson, Sally and James Rice (1) -   December 26, 1816

Johnson, Sally (cold.) Charles James (3) -   November 21, 1886
    For further information see - James, Charles.

Johnson, Samuel and Ann Davis (1) -   December 15, 1825

Johnson, Samuel and Elizabeth Palmer (3) -   August 22, 1865
    Place of marriage, Shepherdstown - Age of husband, 30 years - Age of
    wife, 20 years - Husband is a Widower - Wife is Single - Husband was
    born at Greenville, West Virginia - Wife was born in Rappahannock
    County, Virginia - Both reside in Jefferson County - Husband's
    parents are William H. Johnson and (nee) Sarah Smurr - Wife's parents
    are Josiah and Frances Palmer - Occupation of husband is Farmer.

Johnson, Samuel Henry (free Cold.) Mary Bateman (2) -   (L) March 6, 1858

Johnson, Sarah and James McClean (1) -   March 17, 1818

Johnson, Sarah Elizabeth and Patrick M. Gary (2) -   (L) October 26, 1852

Johnson, Susan and James Hasson (3) -   January 10, 1867
    For further information see - Hasson, James.

Johnson, Susan (colored) Henry Caswell (3) -   (1870)
    For further information see - Caswell, Henry.

Johnson, Thomas and Sarah Stephen (1) -   October 30, 1817

Johnson, Thomas and Mary E. Chamberlin (2) -   (L) October 28, 1850

Johnson, Thomas and Mary E. Chamberlin (1) -   October 31, 1850

Johnson, Thomas (cold.) Jane E. Moore (3) -   April 7, 1881
    Place of marriage, Harpers Ferry - Age of husband, 45 - Age of wife,
    28 - Husband is a Widower - Wife is Single - Both were born in
    Jefferson County, West Virginia - Both reside in Jefferson County,
    West Virginia.

Johnson, Thomas Warner (cold.) Maria Prince (3) -   April 10, 1880
    Place of marriage, Charlestown - Age of husband, 39 - Age of wife,
    33 - Husband is a Widower - Wife is Single - Both were born in
    Jefferson County, West Virginia - Both reside in Jefferson County,
    West Virginia.

Johnson, Thompson and Fanny Rickard (1) -   December 6, 1826

Johnson, Virginia (cold.) John Hamilton (3) -   November 11, 1886
    For further information see - Hamilton, John.

Johnson, Washington (cold.) Nettie Young (3) -   January 4, 1877
    Place of marriage, near Duffields - Age of husband, 22 - Age of
    wife, 21 - Both are Single - Both were born in Jefferson County,
    West Virginia - Both reside in Jefferson County, West Virginia.

Johnson, William C. and Maria J. Brown (3) -   June 21, 1877
    Place of marriage, Charlestown - Age of husband, 23 - Age of wife,
    23 - Both are Single - Both were born in Jefferson County, West
    Virginia - Both reside in Jefferson County, West Virginia.

Johnson, William M. and Caroline B. Vanmetre (3) -   November 26, 1878
    Place of marriage, near Leetown - Age of husband, 23 - Age of wife,
    23 - Both are Single - Husband was born in Jefferson County, West
    Virginia - Wife was born in Berkeley County, West Virginia - Both
    reside in Jefferson County, West Virginia.

Johnson, William R. and Mary A. Leavell (3) - October 28, 1885
   Place of marriage, Charlestown - Age of husband, 40 - Age of wife,
   30 - Both are Single - Husband was born in Chesterfield County,
   Virginia - Wife was born in Jefferson County, West Virginia -
   Husband resides in Fayette County, West Virginia - Wife resides in
   Jefferson County, West Virginia.

Johnson, Winnie (cold.) George Shelton (3) - August 22, 1881
   For further information see - Shelton, George.

Johnston, Baldwin and Mary Elizabeth Marlatt (2) - (L) February 11, 1854

Johnston, David and Anna D. Myers (2) - (L) (1861)
   Time of marriage, December 12, 1861 - Place of marriage, near
   Kabletown - Age of husband, 54 years, 1 month, 24 days - Age of
   wife, about 30 years - Condition of husband is a Widower - Condition
   of wife is Single - Place of husband's birth was in Jefferson
   County, Virginia - Place of wife's birth was in Jefferson County,
   Virginia - Place of husband's residence is Jefferson County,
   Virginia - Place of wife's residence is Jefferson County, Virginia -
   Names of husband's parents are David and Amy Johnston - Names of
   wife's parents are Jacob and Mary Myers - Occupation of husband is
   Manufacturer - William Oyerly.

Johnston, Helen T. and John B. Turner (2) - (L) April 25, 1857

Johnston, J. D. and Hannah F. Ott (3) - July 23, 1890
   Place of marriage, Halltown - Age of husband, 29 - Age of wife, 24 -
   Both are Single - Both were born in Jefferson County, West
   Virginia - Both reside in Jefferson County, West Virginia.

Johnston, James M. and Mary Catharine Abriel (2) - (L) October 25, 1859

Johnston, Laura R. and John W. Clipp (3) - December 12, 1888
   For further information see - Clipp, John W.

Jolley, Hannah and George W. Swartz (3) - December 31, 1889
   For further information see - Swartz, George W.

Jolley, Joseph L. and Lillie L. Ring (3) - January 2, 1889
   Place of marriage, Middleway - Age of husband, 25 - Age of wife,
   26 - Both are Single - Both were born in Jefferson County, West
   Virginia - Both reside in Jefferson County, West Virginia.

Jolly, Lewis and Mary E. Athey (2) - (L) May 8, 1862
   Time of marriage, May 8, 1862 - Place of marriage, Middleway -
   Names, Lewis Jolly and Mary E. Athey - Age of husband, 35 years -
   Age of wife, 25 years - Both are Single - Place of husband's birth
   was in Frederick County, Virginia - Place of wife's birth was in
   Jefferson County, Virginia - Both reside in Jefferson County,
   Virginia - Names of husband's parents are Landon and Letty Jolly -
   Names of wife's parents are James W. Athey, father - Occupation of
   husband is Blacksmith - Liscense issued, May 8, 1862.

Jones, Adrain and Mary Lemen (1) - February 5, 1839

Jones, Amanda and James Hamilton (3) - September 7, 1874
   For further information see - Hamilton, James.

Jones, Ann and George Washington (3) - September 28, 1871
    For further information see - Washington, George.

Jones, Anna and Moses Matheny (1) - January 26, 1826

Jones, Anna (cold.) William Smith (3) - January 27, 1876
    For further information see - Smith, William.

Jones, Annie (cold.) Allen Burns (3) - October 2, 1888
    For further information see - Burns, Allen.

Jones, Annie M. and Frank C. Thomas (3) - May 14, 1872
    For further information see - Thomas, Frank C.

Jones, Benjamin and Susana Martin (1) - 1814

Jones, Bettie (cold.) William A. Green (3) - February 15, 1888
    For further information see - Green, William A.

Jones, Bettie C. and William H. Moler (3) - January 27, 1886
    For further information see - Moler, William H.

Jones, Burniss (cold.) Frank Willis (3) - April 19, 1883
    For further information see - Willis, Frank.

Jones, Burrell (cold.) Belle Riley (3) - April 28, 1887
    Place of marriage, Charlestown - Age of husband, 30 - Age of wife, 24 - Both are Single - Husband was born in Clarke County, Virginia - Wife was born in Pennsylvania - Husband resides in Jefferson County, West Virginia - Wife resides in Jefferson County.

Jones, Cora (cold.) John Moton (3) - August 21, 1890
    For further information see - Moton, John.

Jones, Courtney H. and Samuel Stone (1) - June 22, 1817

Jones, D. A. and Barney Brooks (3) - (1869)
    For further information see - Brooks, Barney.

Jones, Dinah (cold.) Daniel Strother (3) - April 5, 1888
    For further information see - Strother, Daniel.

Jones, Drusilla and Joseph McKee (1) - December 27, 1831

Jones, Easter (cold.) Charles Franklin Webb (3) - September 13, 1883
    For further information see - Webb, Charles Franklin.

Jones, Edward and Nora Mason Barrett (3) - August 28, 1879
    Place of marriage, Harpers Ferry - Age of husband, 21 - Age of wife, 19 - Both are Single - Husband was born in Loudoun County, Virginia - Wife was born in Jefferson County, West Virginia - Both reside in Jefferson County, West Virginia. (Consent of bride's father in person.)

Jones, Eliza and Samuel Butler (1) - October 19, 1815

Jones, Emeline and George W. Duke (2) - (L) August 15, 1859

Jones, Mrs. Emma and Charles M. Barrow (3) - October 13, 1885
    For further information see - Barrow, Charles M.

Jones, Emma F. and I. Keyes Strider (3) - February 4, 1880
   For further information see - Strider, I. Keyes.

Jones, Esther and Michael Horn (1) - October 3, 1809

Jones, Fannie and Jacob H. Lashhorn (3) - November 19, 1882
   For further information see - Lashhorn, Jacob H.

Jones, Francis and M. A. Link (3) - March 10, 1868
   Place of marriage, Jefferson County - Age of husband, 26 - Age of
   wife, 19 - Both are Single - Both were born in Jefferson County -
   Both reside in Jefferson - Husband's parents are Joseph B. and
   Eliza - Wife's parents are Adam and Mana - Occupation of husband is
   Farmer. (Parents willing.)

Jones, George (cold.) Lucy Thornton (3) - (1867)
   Age of husband, 34 - Age of wife, 27 - Husband is a Widower - Wife
   is a Widow - Husband was born in Warren County, Virginia - Wife was
   born in Jefferson - Both reside in Jefferson - Occupation of husband
   is Laborer.

Jones, George W. and A. C. Nichols (3) - February 27, 1868
   Place of marriage, Jefferson County - Age of husband, 22 - Age of
   wife, 19 - Both are Single - Both were born in Jefferson County -
   Both reside in Jefferson - Husband's parents are Joseph B. and
   Elizabeth - Wife's parents are D. B. and Margaret - Occupation of
   husband is Farmer. (Father gives consent.)

Jones, George W. and Mary C. Kidwiler (3) - October 31, 1878
   Place of marriage, Harpers Ferry - Age of husband, 31 - Age of wife,
   27 - Both are Single - Both were born in Jefferson County, West
   Virginia - Both reside in Jefferson County, West Virginia.

Jones, George W. (cold.) Eliza Turner (3) - October 17, 1885
   Place of marriage, Harpers Ferry - Age of husband, 24 - Age of wife,
   24 - Husband is Single - Wife is a Widow - Husband was born in
   Rappahannock County, Virginia - Wife was born in Culpeper County,
   Virginia - Both reside in Jefferson County.

Jones, H. A. (bride) (cold.) J. O. Clappen (3) - May 31, 1886
   For further information see - Clappen, J. O.

Jones, Isaac and Maggie E. Lucas (3) - December 14, 1871
   Place of marriage, Jefferson County - Age of husband, 28 - Age of
   wife, 24 - Both are Single - Both were born in Jefferson - Both
   reside in Jefferson County - Husband's parents are Joseph and E. -
   Wife's parents are Edward and Eliza - Occupation of husband is
   Farmer.

Jones, James and Nancy Offutt (1) - August 11, 1814

Jones, James and Nancy Haines (1) - March 27, 1827

Jones, James and Elizabeth Yontz (1) - May 26, 1853

Jones, James (cold.) Kate Morgan (3) - November 15, 1880
   Place of marriage, Charlestown - Age of husband, 22 - Age of wife,
   21 - Both are Single - Husband was born in Maryland - Wife was born
   in Jefferson County, West Virginia - Both reside in Jefferson
   County, West Virginia.

Jones, James F. and H. R. Robinson (3) - November 12, 1867
    Place of marriage, Jefferson County - Age of husband, 26 - Age of
    wife, 18 - Both are Single - Husband was born in Berkeley County -
    Wife was born in Jefferson County - Husband resides in Berkeley
    County - Wife resides in Jefferson County.- Occupation of husband is
    Farmer.

Jones, James J. and Christy Ann Allison (1) - June 1, 1817

Jones, James W. and Maria E. Hooper (1) - July 13, 1847

Jones, James W. and Lydia A. Mock (2) - (L) February 10, 1858

Jones, John (colored) Ann Smith (3) - May 11, 1870
    Place of marriage, Jefferson County - Age of husband, 27 - Age of
    wife, 24 - Husband was born in Virginia - Wife was born in Jefferson
    County - Both reside in Jefferson County.

Jones, Joseph R. and Courtney B. Byrd (2) - (L) September 19, 1860

Jones, Katie (cold.) James Anderson (3) - December 26, 1867
    For further information see - Anderson, James.

Jones, Leonard and Mary Ann Myers (2) - (L) April 28, 1860

Jones, Leonard R. and Mary C. Rice (3) - December 21, 1871
    Place of marriage, Jefferson County - Age of husband, 25 - Age of
    wife, 22 - Both are Single - Husband was born in Berkeley County -
    Wife was born in Berkeley - Husband resides in Berkeley - Wife
    resides in Jefferson County - Husband's parents are John and Betty -
    Wife's parents are John and Rebecca R. - Occupation of husband is
    Farmer.

Jones, Lillie Lee and George W. Sandbower (3) - June 5, 1884
    For further information see - Sandbower, George W.

Jones, Lizzie (cold.) John Jefferson (3) - August 28, 1884
    For further information see - Jefferson, John.

Jones, Louisa (cold.) Daniel Kelley (3) - December 29, 1887
    For further information see - Kelley, Daniel.

Jones, Lucy (cold.) Richard Webster (3) - December 27, 1881
    For further information see - Webster, Richard.

Jones, Mary and John William Thomas (3) - August 1, 1872
    For further information see - Thomas, John William.

Jones, Mary (cold.) Jacob Turner (3) - April 26, 1883
    For further information see - Turner, Jacob.

Jones, Mary V. and Henry A. Derr (3) - December 17, 1878
    For further information see - Derr, Henry A.

Jones, Mary Virginia and Charles Weaver (3) - July 8, 1871
    For further information see - Weaver, Charles.

Jones, Nancy (cold.) Thomas McKinney (3) - December 29, 1874
    For further information see - McKinney, Thomas.

295

Jones, Nannie C. and Daniel H. Nichols (3) -   June 9, 1880
   For further information see - Nichols, Daniel H.

Jones, Nora and William C. Byers (3) -   December 28, 1885
   For further information see - Byers, William C.

Jones, O. A. and Mary J. Walker (3) -   November 26, 1867
   Place of marriage, Jefferson County - Age of husband, 27 - Age of
   wife, 31 - Both are Single - Husband was born in Clarke County,
   Virginia - Wife was born in Jefferson County - Husband resides in
   Clarke County, Virginia - Wife resides in Jefferson County -
   Occupation of husband is Farmer.

Jones, Paul L. and Lucie A. Thompson (3) -   August 13, 1866
   Place of marriage, Residence of J. A. Thompson - Age of husband,
   27 - Age of wife, 24 - Both are Single - Husband was born in
   Limestone County, Alabama - Wife was born in Clarke County,
   Virginia - Husband resides in Limestone County, Alabama - Wife
   resides in Jefferson County, West Virginia - Husband's parents are
   J. N. S. and Eliza Jones - Wife's parents are John A. and Mary E.
   Thompson - Occupation of husband is Farmer.

Jones, Rachael and Harrison Smith (3) -   May 16, 1869
   For further information see - Smith, Harrison.

Jones, Richard and Catherine Miller (1) -   October 7, 1824

Jones, Sallie (cold.) John William Mundy (3) -   May 1, 1883
   For further information see - Mundy, John William.

Jones, Sam (cold.) Evelina Turner (3) -   November 10, 1881
   Place of marriage, Duffields - Age of husband, 40 - Age of wife,
   40 - Husband is Single - Wife is a Widow - Husband was born in
   Prince Edward County, Virginia - Wife was born in Jefferson County,
   West Virginia - Both reside in Jefferson County, West Virginia.

Jones, Samuel and Mary Brown (3) -   September 24, 1868
   Place of marriage, Jefferson County - Age of husband, 26 - Age of
   wife, 17 - Both are Single - Both were born in Jefferson County -
   Both reside in Jefferson County - Occupation of husband is Farmer.
   (Grandfather consents.)

Jones, Samuel and Mary Ellen Wintermoyer (3) -   May 12, 1869
   Place of marriage, Jefferson County - Age of husband, 28 - Age of
   wife, 21 - Both are Single - Husband was born in Maryland - Wife was
   born in Jefferson County - Both reside in Jefferson County.
   (Mother gives her consent in person.).

Jones, Samuel (cold.) Lucy Strother (3) -   January 23, 1890
   Place of marriage, Bolivar - Age of husband, 23 - Age of wife, 19 -
   Both are Single - Both were born in Jefferson County, West
   Virginia - Both reside in Jefferson County, West Virginia.
   (Consent of bride's father in writing.)

Jones, Samuel T. and Anna M. Stephens (3) -   October 23, 1878
   Place of marriage, Bolivar - Age of husband, 38 - Age of wife, 24 -
   Both are Single - Husband was born in Washington County, Maryland -
   Wife was born in Frederick County, Maryland - Both reside in
   Jefferson County, West Virginia.

Jones, Sarah A. and Frank H. Morell (3) -   September 23, 1872
   For further information see - Morell, Frank H.

Jones, Stephen (cold.) Flora Washington (3) -   February 23, 1888
   Place of marriage, Charlestown - Age of husband, 54 - Age of wife,
   48 - Husband is Single - Wife is a Widow - Husband was born in
   Madison County, Virginia - Wife was born in Jefferson County, West
   Virginia - Both reside in Jefferson County, West Virginia.

Jones, Susan R. and Daniel T. Morrison (3) -   January 29, 1873
   For further information see - Morrison, Daniel T.

Jones, Thomas (cold.) Virginia Walker (3) -   May 10, 1877
   Place of marriage, Middleway - Age of husband, 21 - Age of wife,
   21 - Both are Single - Both were born in Jefferson County, West
   Virginia - Both reside in Jefferson County, West Virginia.

Jones, Thomas (cold.) Mahala Johnson (3) -   September 25, 1879
   Place of marriage, Summit Point - Age of husband, 25 - Age of wife,
   21 - Both are Single - Husband was born in Clarke County, Virginia -
   Wife was born in Jefferson County, West Virginia - Both reside in
   Jefferson County, West Virginia.

Jones, Thomas (cold.) Elizabeth Johnson (3) -   June 6, 1888
   Place of marriage, Middleway - Age of husband, 33 - Age of wife,
   28 - Husband is a Widower - Wife is Single - Both were born in
   Jefferson County, West Virginia - Both reside in Jefferson County,
   West Virginia.

Jones, Thomas H. and Frances Rockenbaugh (3) -   March 26, 1873
   Place of marriage, Near Shepherdstown - Age of husband, 22 March 5 -
   Age of wife, 18 - Both are Single - Both were born in Jefferson
   County, West Virginia - Both reside in Jefferson County, West
   Virginia - Husband's parents are Joseph B. and Elizabeth - Wife's
   parents are Thomas S. and Mary - Occupation of husband is Farmer.
   (Consent of bride's father in writing.)

Jones, Virginia Mason and John William W. Blessing (3) -   December 10, 1874
   For further information see - Blessing, John William W.

Jones, William and Elizabeth Swan (1) -   August 1, 1816

Jones, William Sandy (cold.) Rachel Hagan (3) -   July 15, 1880
   Place of marriage, Charlestown - Age of husband, 21 - Age of wife,
   21 - Both are Single - Husband was born in Augusta County, Virginia -
   Wife was born in Jefferson County, West Virginia - Both reside in
   Jefferson County, West Virginia.

Jordan, Elizabeth and Peter Eversole (1) -   September 22, 1810

Jordan, John B. (cold.) Lucy L. A. Jackson (3) -   November 13, 1889
   Place of marriage, Summit Point - Age of husband, 30 - Age of wife,
   23 - Both are Single - Both were born in Jefferson County, West
   Virginia - Husband resides at Washington, D. C. - Wife resides in
   Jefferson County, West Virginia.

Jordan, Philip (cold.) Charity Lucas (3) -　　　　　　　January 10, 1878
　　Place of marriage, Charlestown - Age of husband, 23 - Age of wife,
　　21 - Both are Single - Both were born in Jefferson County, West
　　Virginia - Both reside in Jefferson County, West Virginia.

Jordan, Susan (cold.) George Wells (3) -　　　　　　　September 29, 1880
　　For further information see - Wells, George.

Joyce, Margaret and John W. Ashby (2) -　　　　　　　(L) January 8, 1853

Julius, Moten and Amanda Smith (3) -　　　　　　　　　January 1, 1867
　　Place of marriage, Shepherdstown, West Virginia - Age of husband,
　　23 - Age of wife, 24 - Both are Single - Husband was born in
　　Fauquier County, Virginia - Wife was born in Jefferson County, West
　　Virginia - Both reside in Jefferson County, West Virginia -
　　Husband's parents are Benton and Elizabeth Julius - Wife's parents
　　are Darcus Smith - Occupation of husband is Laborer.

Kable, Charles H. and Annie E. Reinhart (3) - April 27, 1870
  Place of marriage, Jefferson County - Age of husband, 35 - Age of
  wife, 22 - Husband was born in Virginia - Wife was born in
  Maryland - Both reside in Jefferson County.

Kable, Clarence and Ida Miller (3) - December 19, 1888
  Place of marriage, Shenandoah Junction - Age of husband, 21 - Age of
  wife, 21 - Both are Single - Both were born in Jefferson County,
  West Virginia - Both reside in Jefferson County, West Virginia.

Kachney, Henry and Elizabeth Forsha (1) - August 26, 1845

Kahler, John and Ann Towner (1) - September 16, 1819

Kain, Kate and Thomas G. Fenton (3) - November 27, 1884
  For further information see - Fenton, Thomas G.

Kane, John J. and Carry Heck (3) - December 27, 1888
  Place of marriage, Harpers Ferry - Age of husband, 24 - Age of wife,
  21 - Both are Single - Both were born in Jefferson County, West
  Virginia - Both reside in Jefferson County, West Virginia.

Kane, Julia Ann and William McCoy (1) - November 3, 1836

Kane, Mary C. and Edward Walters (3) - April 19, 1882
  For further information see - Walters, Edward.

Kane, Maurice J. and Mollie O'Connell (3) - January 13, 1886
  Place of marriage, Harpers Ferry - Age of husband, 27 - Age of wife,
  22 - Both are Single - Both were born in Jefferson County - Husband
  resides in Jefferson County - Wife resides in Jefferson County, West
  Virginia.

Kane, Michael and Anna Lee Painter (3) - November 9, 1880
  Place of marriage, Harpers Ferry - Age of husband, 24 - Age of wife,
  17 - Both are Single - Both were born in Jefferson County, West
  Virginia - Both reside in Jefferson County, West Virginia.
  (Consent of bride's guardian in person.)

Kaney, Elizabeth Ann and William F. Kaney (2) - (L) August 2, 1859

Kaney, William F. and Elizabeth Ann Kaney (2) - (L) August 2, 1859

Kanode, A. L. and Lydia Ann Cloud (3) - January 28, 1875
  Place of marriage, County - Age of husband, 22 - Age of wife, 20 -
  Both are Single - Husband was born in Washington County, Maryland -
  Wife was born in Jefferson County, West Virginia - Husband resides
  in Maryland - Wife resides in Jefferson County, West Virginia.

Kanode, Joseph H. and Elizabeth H. Cookus (3) - February 11, 1873
  Place of marriage, Shepherdstown - Age of husband, 64 - Age of wife,
  45 - Husband is a Widower - Wife is a Widow - Both were born in
  Washington County, Maryland - Both reside in Jefferson County, West
  Virginia - Husband's parents are John and Mary - Wife's parents are
  (nee) Baer - Occupation of husband is Farmer.

Karman, Catherine and William Crisfield (1) - December 17, 1814

Karman, Sarah and John Baylis (1) - June 16, 1816

Karmar, Pinkie and John Smallwood (3) - February 6, 1884
    For further information see - Smallwood, John.

Kasaker, Hannah and Malachi Grove (1) - July 17, 1808

Kaufman, Jennie and William E. Butts (3) - December 12, 1884
    For further information see - Butts, William E.

Keadle, John H. and Susan Weisinger (1) - December 25, 1832

Keaidler, William and M. E. Myers (3) - January 2, 1868
    Place of marriage, Jefferson County - Age of husband, 28 - Age of
wife, 21 - Both are Single - Husband was born in Berkeley County,
West Virginia - Wife was born in Jefferson County, West Virginia -
Husband resides in Berkeley County - Wife resides in Jefferson
County - Husband's parents are David and Rhumaer - Wife's parents
are James W. and Maria - Occupation of husband is Farmer.

Kealhover, John and Mary Deen (1) - March 24, 1808

Kearfoot, J. Butler and Anna Brotherton (3) - February 23, 1875
    Place of marriage, Shepherdstown - Age of husband, 44 - Age of wife,
46 - Husband is a Widower - Wife is Single - Husband was born in
Berkeley County, West Virginia - Wife was born in Jefferson County,
West Virginia - Husband resides in Berkeley County, West Virginia -
Wife resides in Jefferson County, West Virginia.

Kearfoot, John P. and Hester Lemon (1) - August 23, 1827

Kearfoot, William H. and Nannie B. Herr (3) - December 5, 1888
    Place of marriage, Shepherdstown - Age of husband, 20 - Age of wife,
18 - Both are Single - Husband was born in Berkeley County, West
Virginia - Wife was born in Jefferson County, West Virginia - Both
reside in Jefferson County, West Virginia. (Consent of groom's
father and bride's father in person.)

Kearney, H. W. and Maggie Allen (3) - March 28, 1867
    Place of marriage, near Leetown, West Virginia - Age of husband,
29 - Age of wife, 23 - Both are Single - Husband was born in
Jefferson County, West Virginia - Wife was born in Loudoun County,
Virginia - Both reside in Jefferson County, West Virginia -
Husband's parents are I. T. and Elizabeth Kearney - Wife's parents
are Edward and Margaret Allen - Occupation of husband is Farmer.
(William McQuilkin.)

Kearney, Maria V. and Richard Gartrell (1) - September 9, 1819

Kearns, Richard W. and Amelia Clinton (3) - May 5, 1873
    Place of marriage, Middleway - Age of husband, 25 - Age of wife,
21 - Both are Single - Husband was born in Jefferson County, West
Virginia - Wife was born in Frederick County, Virginia - Both reside
in Jefferson County, West Virginia - Husband's parents are William
and Matilda - Occupation of husband is Shoemaker.

Kearns, T. W. and A. E. Pultz (bride) (3) - March 25, 1868
    Age of husband, 22 - Age of wife, 30 - Husband is Single - Wife is a
Widow - Husband was born in Jefferson County - Wife was born in
Berkeley - Both reside in Jefferson County - Husband's parents are
William and Matilda - Wife's parents are John L. Rusler - Occupation
of husband is Shoemaker.

Kearsley, Anna H. and George W. Lambright (3) -   March 26, 1874
For further information see - Lambright, George W.

Kearsley, Ann Margaret and Isaac N. Carter (1) -   May 9, 1826

Kearsley, Eleanor and Samuel I. Cramer (1) -   May 26, 1803

Kearsley, Elizabeth F. and John J. Wysong (3) -   March 26, 1879
For further information see - Wysong, John J.

Kearsley, Jennie T. and T. M. Caldwell (3) -   September 4, 1878
For further information see - Caldwell, T. M.

Kearsley, Meta B. and Andrew K. Selden (3) -   November 5, 1879
For further information see - Selden, Andrew K.

Kearsley, Rebecca A. and Herbert H. Reese (3) -   January 30, 1889
For further information see - Reese, Herbert H.

Keats, Samuel and Sarah Ellen Ross (3) -   April 13, 1882
Place of marriage, Charlestown - Age of husband, 21 - Age of wife, 18 - Both are Single - Husband was born in Washington County, Maryland - Wife was born in Jefferson County, West Virginia - Husband resides in Jefferson County - Wife resides in Jefferson County, West Virginia. (Consent of bride's father in writing.)

Keesecker, Emma K. and William C. Link (3) -   December 22, 1886
For further information see - Link, William C.

Keesecker, John H. and Mary Catharine Cookus (2) -   (L) November 30, 1854

Keesecker, M. A. and Jane E. Grove (3) -   June 18, 1884
Place of marriage, Harpers Ferry - Age of husband, 25 - Age of wife, 20 - Both are Single - Both were born in Maryland - Husband resides in Maryland - Wife resides in Jefferson County, West Virginia. (Consent of bride's father in writing.)

Kehler, Ellen S. and S. Bulow Erwin (2) -   (L) September 12, 1853

Kehler, Ellen Sarah and S. Bulow Erwin (1) -   September 13, 1853

Kelch, W. S. and Sarah A. Engle (3) -   December 24, 1873
Place of marriage, Harpers Ferry - Age of husband, 22 - Age of wife, 18 - Both are Single - Husband was born in State of Ohio - Wife was born in Jefferson County, West Virginia - Husband resides in State of Ohio - Wife resides in Jefferson County, West Virginia. (Consent of bride's father in writing.)

Kelison, Martha A. and Andrew J. Hobbs (3) -   January 7, 1869
For further information see - Hobbs, Andrew J.

Keller, Boyd H. and Eugene Humrickhouse (3) -   December 27, 1887
Place of marriage, Shepherdstown - Age of husband, 21 - Age of wife, 21 - Both are Single - Husband was born at Chambersburg, Pennsylvania - Wife was born in Jefferson County, West Virginia - Husband resides in Berkeley County, West Virginia - Wife resides in Jefferson County.

Keller, Clara Belle and George R. Heafer (3) -   November 26, 1884
For further information see - Heafer, George R.

Keller, Elizabeth C. and James H. Burton (2) - . (L). October 1, 1851

Keller, Emily and George F. Shreck (2) - (L) September 29, 1856

Keller, Harry J. and Fannie A. Smith (3) - July 18, 1888
Place of marriage, Harpers Ferry - Age of husband, 22 - Age of wife,
23 - Both are Single - Husband was born at Winchester, Virginia -
Wife was born at Luray, Virginia - Husband resides at Luray,
Virginia - Wife resides in Jefferson County, West Virginia.

Keller, Jacob R. and Eliza Canann (3) - February 17, 1887
Place of marriage, Shepherdstown - Age of husband, 30 - Age of wife,
38 - Husband is a Widower - Wife is Single - Husband was born in
Warren County, Virginia - Wife was born in Jefferson County - Both
reside in Jefferson County.

Keller, John and Sarah Stypes (1) - 1822

Keller, John and Ann Crofford (1) - December 26, 1830

Keller, John and Annie M. Barron (3) - January 4, 1866
Place of marriage, Harpers Ferry, West Virginia - Age of husband,
26 - Age of wife, 25 - Both are Single - Husband was born in
Frederick County, Virginia - Wife was born in Fauquier County,
Virginia - Both reside at Harpers Ferry, West Virginia - Husband's
parents are Peter and Elizabeth Keller - Wife's parents are John and
Catherine Barron - Occupation of husband is Shoemaker.

Keller, John, Jr. and Mary S. Lee (2) - (L) April 26, 1851

Keller, John, Jr. and Mary S. Lee (1) - April 27, 1851

Keller, John R. and Lourette Copenhaver (3) - December 11, 1890
Place of marriage, Harpers Ferry - Age of husband, 25 - Age of wife,
23 - Both are Single - Both were born in Shenandoah County,
Virginia - Husband resides in Shenandoah County, Virginia - Wife
resides in Jefferson County, West Virginia.

Keller, Louisa and William Exner (3) - (1868)
For further information see - Exner, William.

Keller, Margaret L. and J. W. M. Jarboe (2) - (L) September 17, 1855

Keller, Mary E. and Thuiscan Bartholomes (2) - (L) November 17, 1859

Keller, Mary Isabella and James N. Earnshaw (2) - (L) December 7, 1850

Keller, Michael and Mary F. Cross (3) - August 2, 1877
Place of marriage, Bolivar - Age of husband, 24 - Age of wife, 25 -
Both are Single - Both were born in Jefferson County, West
Virginia - Both reside in Jefferson County, West Virginia.

Kelley, Annie and Charles R. Gant (3) - April 27, 1872
For further information see - Gant, Charles R.

Kelley, Daniel (cold.) Louisa Jones (3) - December 29, 1887
Place of marriage, Charlestown - Age of husband, 49 - Age of wife,
50 - Both are Single - Husband was born in Madison County,
Virginia - Wife was born in Jefferson County, West Virginia - Both
reside in Jefferson County, West Virginia.

Kelley, Maggie A. and Lewis Dinkle (2) -   (L) March 21, 1860

Kellison, Annie and John Roope (3) -   May 13, 1880
   For further information see - Roope, John.

Kellison, George and Catherine Kirk (2) -   (L) July 25, 1860

Kelly, Bridget and Patrick Hopkins (2) -   (L) August 14, 1852

Kelly, Catharine and Edward Garrison (2) -   (L) June 19, 1858

Kelly, Ellen and George H. Stobbs (3) -   October 25, 1875
   For further information see - Stobbs, George H.

Kelly, Fanny A. W. and James Orem (3) -   December 25, 1879
   For further information see - Orem, James.

Kelly, J. Harrison and Elizabeth A. McCurdy (2) -   (L) December 15, 1851

Kelly, J. Harrison and Elizabeth A. McCurdy (1) -   December 18, 1851

Kelly, James W. and Ellie May Wingate (3) -   February 19, 1882
   Place of marriage, Harpers Ferry - Age of husband, 23 - Age of wife,
   16 - Both are Single - Husband was born in Jefferson County, West
   Virginia - Wife was born in Loudoun County, Virginia - Both reside
   in Jefferson County, West Virginia. (Consent of bride's mother in
   writing.)

Kelly, Joseph and Mary Gallagher (3) -   August 10, 1868
   Place of marriage, Jefferson County - Age of husband, 21 - Age of
   wife, 22 - Both are Single - Husband was born at Harpers Ferry -
   Wife was born at Martinsburg - Husband resides in Jefferson
   County - Wife resides at Martinsburg - Husband's parents are
   Alexander and Margaret - Occupation of husband is Merchant.

Kelly, Margaret E. and Frank Henrick (3) -   (1869)
   For further information see - Henrick, Frank.

Kelly, Maria and Adam Nicholls (1) -   August 24, 1815

Kelly, Maria and James F. Green (2) -   (L) August 20, 1858

Kelly, Nancy Ellen and Lockland J. Sloan (3) -   (1869)
   For further information see - Sloan, Lockland J.

Kelly, Samuel and Juliet Blincoe (2) -   (L) March 16, 1855

Kelsey, David and Henrietta Young (2) -   (L) December 27, 1850

Kelsey, George H. and Georgie E. Starry (3) -   September 22, 1886
   Place of marriage, Charlestown - Age of husband, 29 - Age of wife,
   29 - Both are Single - Husband was born at Chicago, Illinois - Wife
   was born in Jefferson County, West Virginia - Both reside in
   Jefferson County, West Virginia.

Kemp, Addie V. and F. H. Mauzy (3) -   October 22, 1890
   For further information see - Mauzy, F. H.

Kemp, John Henry Orndorff and Virginia Washington Lewis (3) - October 28, 1880
  Place of marriage, Residence of Bride's Mother - Age of husband,
  34 - Age of wife, 34 - Both are Single - Husband was born in State
  of Maryland - Wife was born in Jefferson County, West Virginia -
  Husband resides in State of Maryland - Wife reside in Jefferson
  County, West Virginia.

Kemp, Loraine McKlain and Erma Jane Coats (3) -   January 26, 1871
  Place of marriage, Harpers Ferry - Age of husband, 26 - Age of wife,
  19 - Both are Single - Husband was born in Frederick County,
  Maryland - Wife was born in Jefferson County - Husband resides at
  Knoxville, Maryland - Wife resides in Jefferson County, Virginia -
  Husband's parents are Bernard and Kemp - Wife's parents are Daset
  L. and Isabella - Occupation of husband is Carpenter. (Oath of
  J. D. Porterfield.)

Kemp, Mamie and Charles J. Cavalier (3) -   December 27, 1887
  For further information see - Cavalier, Charles J.

Kemp, Sarah Ann and James W. Steadman (2) -   (L) April 16, 1860

Kemp, William and Mrs. Elizabeth Dove (widow) (2) -   (L) October 26, 1850

Kemp, William and Elizabeth Dove (widow) (1) -   October 27, 1850

Kemper, Charles H. and Sue H. Gibson (3) -   December 13, 1876
  Place of marriage, near Charlestown - Age of husband, 31 - Age of
  wife, 32 - Both are Single - Husband was born in Fauquier County,
  Virginia - Wife was born in Jefferson County, West Virginia -
  Husband resides in Fauquier County, Virginia - Wife resides in
  Jefferson County, West Virginia.

Kendall, Amos B. and Rebecca E. Lantsbaugh (3) -   September 12, 1878
  Place of marriage, Middleway - Age of husband, 25 - Age of wife,
  25 - Both are Single - Husband was born in Hampshire County, West
  Virginia - Wife was born in State of Pennsylvania - Both reside in
  Jefferson County, West Virginia.

Kendrick, George W. and Lydia M. Musgrove (3) -   August 5, 1890
  Place of marriage, Leetown, West Virginia - Age of husband, 21 - Age
  of wife, 20 - Both are Single - Husband was born at Martinsburg,
  West Virginia - Wife was born in Jefferson County, West Virginia -
  Both reside in Jefferson County, West Virginia. (Consent of bride's
  father.)

Kenear, William and Elizabeth Fisher (1) -   August 29, 1815

Kenedy, John Kearsley and Mary A. Daniels (2) -   (L) February 23, 1857

Kennedy, Andrew and Mary Ann Riddle Lane (1) -   January 2, 1822

Kennedy, Mrs. Ann (widow) and John J. Hudson (2) -   (L) December 17, 1853

Kennedy, George S. and Rebecca Swearingen (1) -   September 21, 1831

Kennedy, Isabella and Charles J. Esbridge (1) -   July 1825

Kennedy, John W. and Sarah M. Rutherford (2) -   (L) April 25, 1857

Kennedy, Mary E. and Henry Pendleton Cooke (2) -   (L) January 1, 1855

305

Kennedy, Mary E. and Daniel S. Mumma (3) - December 18, 1884
    For further information see - Mumma, Daniel S.

Kennedy, Mary Virginia and John E. Cook (2) - (L) April 15, 1859

Kennedy, S. D. and Mary Salaen (3) - June 22, 1869
    Place of marriage, Jefferson County - Age of husband, 36 - Age of wife, 22 - Husband was born in Virginia - Wife was born in West Virginia - Husband resides in New York - Wife resides in West Virginia.

Kennedy, Sarah D. and John Selden (2) - (L) January 4, 1858

Kennedy, Thomas and Mary Wysong (1) - . February 23, 1813

Kenney, Annie Lee and Frank Williams (3) - . December 11, 1889
    For further information see - Williams, Frank.

Kenny, Mrs. Melvina and Daniel Claig (3) - May 4, 1887
    For further information see - Claig, Daniel.

Kenrick, Elizabeth and Francis Duke (1) - August 19, 1820

Kensell, John and Sophia Cookus (1) - March 22, 1827

Kensell, Mary and John Compton (1) - September 21, 1827

Kensey, Elizabeth Jane and J. E. Duke (2) - . (L) February 25, 1860

Kent, Thomas H. (of Jur.) and Mary E. Hunter (2) - (L) September 21, 1852

Kephart, C. E. and S. J. Lee (bride) (3) - December 23, 1872
    Place of marriage, Jefferson County - Age of husband, 23 - Age of wife, 18 - Both are Single - Husband was born in Maryland - Wife was born in Virginia - Husband's parents are Harman and Malinda - Wife's parents are John B. and Julia A. - Occupation of husband is Manufacturer.

Kephart, Elizabeth E. and James E. Moler (2) - (L) December 7, 1857

Kephart, Eve Ann and Dennis Buzzard (3) - February 17, 1871
    For further information see - Buzzard, Dennis.

Kephart, Irene J. and L. S. McNamara (3) - March 5, 1890
    For further information see - McNamara, L. S.

Kephart, Jacob M. and Susan E. Rider (3) - October 10, 1866
    Place of marriage, near Halltown, Jefferson County - Age of husband, 29 - Age of wife, 24 - Both are Single - Husband was born in Frederick County, Maryland - Wife was born in Jefferson County, West Virginia - Both reside in Jefferson County, West Virginia - Husband's parents are John and Ellen Kephart - Wife's parents are William and Elizabeth Rider - Occupation of husband is Farmer.

Kephart, John and Ellen Moler (1) - 1825

Kephart, John Lewis and Emily Virginia Moler (2) - (L) November 6, 1860

Kephart, Levi and Elizabeth Ann Collins (3) -   December 12, 1872
    Place of marriage, Jefferson County, West Virginia - Age of husband,
    59 - Age of wife, 35 - Husband is a Widower - Wife is Single -
    Husband was born in Frederick County, Maryland - Wife was born in
    Chester County, Pennsylvania - Husband resides in Jefferson County,
    West Virginia - Wife resides in Jefferson County - Husband's parents
    are John and Eve - Wife's parents are Collins - Occupation of
    husband is Mechanic.

Kephart, Levi and Emma Ann Dillow (3) -   August 18, 1881
    Place of marriage, Pipertown - Age of husband, 69 - Age of wife,
    50 - Husband is a Widower - Wife is a Widow - Husband was born in
    Maryland - Wife was born in Loudoun County, Virginia - Both reside
    in Jefferson County, West Virginia.

Kephart, Margaret U. and Samuel M. Knott (2) -   (L) February 8, 1858

Kephart, Mary J. and Henry C. Moler (2) -   (L) February 25, 1851

Keplinger, Annie M. and Mayberry McBee (3) -   February 13, 1868
    For further information see - McBee, Mayberry.

Keplinger, Charles D. and Ada Harp (3) -   April 24, 1884
    Place of marriage, Shepherdstown - Age of husband, 31 - Age of wife,
    27 - Both are Single - Both were born in Jefferson County - Both
    reside in Jefferson County, West Virginia.

Keplinger, Hattie B. and Isaac R. Hill (3) -   January 20, 1880
    For further information see - Hill, Isaac R.

Keplinger, Kate M. and David S. Orndorff (3) -   June 15, 1869
    For further information see - Orndorff, David S.

Kercheval, E. V., Jr. and Ida Mercy Dooley (3) -   June 2, 1881
    Place of marriage, Charlestown - Age of husband, 25 - Age of wife,
    22 - Both are Single - Husband was born in Clarke County, Virginia -
    Wife was born in Jefferson County, West Virginia - Husband resides
    in Clarke County, Virginia - Wife resides in Jefferson County, West
    Virginia.

Kercheval, Edward V. and Ann Catharine Avis (1) -   June 9, 1847

Kercheval, Marcellus and Bettie Haley (3) -   June 1, 1882
    Place of marriage, Charlestown - Age of husband, 27 - Age of wife,
    28 - Both are Single - Husband was born in Clarke County, Virginia -
    Wife was born in Jefferson County, West Virginia - Husband resides
    in Jefferson County, West Virginia - Wife resides in Jefferson County.

Kercheville, Frances and Christian Allemong (1) -   August 11, 1825

Kerchival, Nancy and James F. King (1) -   February 10, 1820

Kerchival, Winifred and John Buckles (1) -   January 17, 1828

Kerfott, Mary A. and George F. Burke (3) -   November 20, 1872
    For further information see - Burke, George F.

Kerfott, Thomas F. and Annie Arthur (3) -   December 11, 1879
   Place of marriage, Shepherdstown - Age of husband, 22 - Age of wife,
   21 - Both are Single - Husband was born in Berkeley County, West
   Virginia - Wife was born in Jefferson County, West Virginia - Both
   reside in Jefferson County, West Virginia.

Kerfott, William Lee and Annie T. Hass (3) -   October 14, 1880
   Place of marriage, Charlestown - Age of husband, 22 - Age of wife,
   16 - Both are Single - Husband was born in Maryland - Wife was born
   in Pennsylvania - Both reside in Jefferson County, West Virginia.
   (Consent of bride's father in writing.)

Kerman, Elizabeth and Josiah Miller (1) -   June 10, 1810

Kern, Annie V. and Charles L. Fogal (3) -   May 29, 1890
   For further information see - Fogal, Charles L.

Kern, Michael and Mary Ann Taylor (3) -   May 9, 1867
   Place of marriage, Harpers Ferry, West Virginia - Age of husband,
   47 - Age of wife, 25 - Both are Single - Husband was born in
   Ireland - Wife was born in Clarke County, Virginia - Husband resides
   at Charlestown - Wife resides in Jefferson County, West Virginia -
   Husband's parents are Michael and Catharine Kern - Wife's parents
   are Griffton Taylor - Occupation of husband is Foreman Baltimore and
   Ohio Railroad.

Kern, Mollie E. and William A. Delauder (3) -   September 25, 1884
   For further information see - Delauder, William A.

Kerney, Eliza J. and Daniel G. Henkle (1) -   April 8, 1845

Kerney, James H. and A. H. Gibbons (1) -   January 21, 1813

Kerney, Josiah T. and Elizabeth Walper (1) -   February 3, 1825

Kerney, Mary C. and William Y. McQuilkin (3) -   November 2, 1865
   For further information see - McQuilkin, William Y.

Kerney, Peter W. and Margaret Strother (1) -   December 5, 1820

Kerney, Sally M. and W. Manning Lemen (3) -   October 17, 1877
   For further information see - Lemen, W. Manning.

Kerney, Uriah B. and Elizabeth C. Woods (1) -   November 17, 1836

Kerney, William F. and Mary A. Lemen (1) -   September 17, 1850

Kerns, Charles Agustus and Sallie Adams (3) -   April 18, 1871
   Place of marriage, Jefferson County - Age of husband, 22 - Age of
   wife, 18 - Both are Single - Husband was born in Culpepper County,
   Virginia - Wife was born in Virginia - Husband resides in Culpeper
   County, Virginia - Wife resides in Jefferson County - Husband's
   parents are Leo and Anna - Wife's parents are Lewis J. - Occupation
   of husband is Baker.

Kerns, John William and Mary F. McKernan (3) -   June 16, 1885
    Place of marriage, Harpers Ferry - Age of husband, 29 - Age of wife,
    19 - Husband is a Widower - Wife is Single - Husband was born in
    Alleghany County, Maryland - Wife was born in Washington County,
    Maryland - Husband resides in Alleghany County, Maryland - Wife
    resides in Washington County, Maryland. (Consent of bride's father
    in person.)

Kerns, Sarah M. and J. M. C. Board (2) -   (L) October 27, 1857

Kershaw, John and Elizabeth Arthur (widow) (2) -   (L) January 14, 1854

Kesel, Margaretta and G. Boyd Harlan (3) -   June 24, 1867
    For further information see - Harlan, G. Boyd.

Kesler, Elizabeth and William Williams (2) -   (L) July 22, 1852

Kessler, A. M. and Alice R. Koonce (3) -   February 22, 1872
    Age of husband, 26 - Age of wife, 21 - Both are Single - Husband was
    born at Frederick, Maryland - Wife was born in Jefferson County,
    Virginia - Wife resides in Jefferson County, West Virginia -
    Husband's parents are A. P. - Wife's parents are George and Bettie -
    Occupation of husband is Physician.

Kessler, Elizabeth and William Williams (1) -   July 29, 1852

Kessler, Vinie C. and Dr. George H. C. Hoffman (3) -   December 27, 1871
    For further information see - Hoffman, Dr. George H. C.

Ketro, Mary and John Drenner (1) -   June 16, 1816

Key, George (cold.) Fanny Tucker (3) -   May 23, 1883
    Place of marriage, near Charlestown - Age of husband, 21 - Age of
    wife, 18 - Both are Single - Husband was born in State of Maryland -
    Wife was born in Jefferson County, West Virginia - Both reside in
    Jefferson County, West Virginia. (Consent of bride's father in
    person.)

Keyes, Frances and William Anthony (1) -   November 18, 1830

Keyes, Humphrey and Mary Yates (1) -   September 1826

Keyes, Isabella and Thomas P. Williams (1) -   March 13, 1821

Keyes, Jacob and Cecilia Wilson (2) -   (L) January 26, 1855

Keyes, Lucretia and Jesse H. Moore (1) -   1827

Keyes, Margaret E. and William A. Glassford (3) -   October 19, 1865
    For further information see - Glassford, William A.

Keyes, Margaret Virginia and William R. Deck (2) -   (L) September 30, 1857

Keyes, Mary Jane and H. N. Zombro (2) -   (L) September 7, 1863
    For further information see - Zombro, H. N.

Keyes, Mary V. and George Spaulding (3) -   April 1872
    For further information see - Spaulding, George.

Keyes, Rebecca and Jacob Sharff (1) -   April 17, 1832

Keyes, Susan W. and Charles E. Ambler (2) -   (L) September 4, 1860

Keyes, Thomas, Jr. and Maria Smith (1) -   August 30, 1828

Keyser, Deliah J. and Josiah P. Weller (2) -   (L) December 6, 1858

Keyser, Emma A. and Charles W. Spangler (3) -   February 16, 1880
For further information see - Spangler, Charles W.

Keyser, James H. and Elizabeth Hannah Steadman (2) -   (L) May 22, 1861
Time of marriage, May 26, 1861 - Place of marriage, Bolivar - Age of husband, 23 years - Age of wife, 21 years - Both are Single - Both live in Bolivar - Both were born in Jefferson County - Names of husband's parents are Lewis L. Keyser - Names of wife's parents are Levi L. Steadman - Occupation of husband is Butcher - Charles Johnson.

Keyser, Lewis and Emily Holt (1) -   July 24, 1834

Keyser, Rev. M. E. and Martha E. Krepps (3) -   March 7, 1872
Place of marriage, Jefferson County, West Virginia - Age of husband, 34 - Age of wife, 26 - Both are Single - Husband was born in Baltimore County, Maryland - Wife was born at Harpers Ferry, Virginia - Husband resides at Baltimore, Maryland - Wife resides in Jefferson County, West Virginia.

Keyser, William L. and Linda A. Butts (3) -   August 26, 1890
Place of marriage, Harpers Ferry - Age of husband, 37 - Age of wife, 31 - Both are Single - Husband was born in Howard County, Maryland - Wife was born in Loudoun County, Virginia - Both reside in Jefferson County, West Virginia.

Kidd, Joseph F. and Elizabeth Pool (2) -   (L) April 23, 1860

Kidwell, Charles W. and Elizabeth Warfield (1) -   December 28, 1848

Kidwell, John Henry and Sarah Ann Lay (2) -   (L) December 17, 1851

Kidwell, John W. and Mary E. Saylor (2) -   (L) August 2, 1855

Kidwell, Julia L. and Norman Clayburn (3) -   June 9, 1887
For further information see - Clayburn, Norman.

Kidwell, Pink B. and Thomas J. Pierce (3) -   April 6, 1880
For further information see - Pierce, Thomas J.

Kidwell, Priscilla and Jacob Bowers (1) -   March 18, 1823

Kidwilder, Ann R. (colored) Jacob H. Harman (3) -   (1870)
For further information see - Harman, Jacob H.

Kidwiler, Adam, Jr. and Leonora Harvey (3) -   April 9, 1880
Place of marriage, Harpers Ferry - Age of husband, 28 - Age of wife, 25 - Both are Single - Husband was born in Jefferson County, West Virginia - Wife was born in Loudoun County, Virginia - Both reside in Jefferson County, West Virginia.

Kidwiler, Ann K. and Jacob H. Harman (3) -   September 29, 1870
For further information see - Harman, Jacob H.

Kidwiler, Anna Rebecca and J. W. Arvin (3) -   December 25, 1888
    For further information see - Arvin, J. W.

Kidwiler, Emanuel and Ann R. Houser (3) -   October 18, 1866
    Place of marriage, Harpers Ferry M. E. Church - Age of husband, 27 -
    Age of wife, 27 - Husband is Single - Wife is a Widow - Husband was
    born in Jefferson County, West Virginia - Wife was born in Washington
    County, Maryland - Both reside in Jefferson County, West Virginia -
    Husband's parents are Susana Dixon - Wife's parents are Peter and
    Margaret Houser - Occupation of husband is Laborer.

Kidwiler, John R. and Eva E. Nuse (3) -   February 6, 1890
    Place of marriage, Shepherdstown - Age of husband, 23 - Age of wife,
    21 - Both are Single - Husband was born in Jefferson County, West
    Virginia - Wife was born at Kansas City, Maryland - Both reside in
    Jefferson County, West Virginia.

Kidwiler, Mary C. and George W. Jones (3) -   October 31, 1878
    For further information see - Jones, George W.

Kidwiler, Susan and Reed T. Thompson (3) -   September 18, 1878
    For further information see - Thompson, Reed T.

Kien, William and Margaret Mouser (1) -   February 28, 1820

Kigle, John W. and Isabella Pitchers (3) -   November 22, 1870
    Place of marriage, Jefferson County - Age of husband, 27 - Age of
    wife, 22 - Both were born in Virginia - Husband resides in Jefferson
    County, West Virginia - Wife resides in Jefferson County.

Killmer, David and Rebecca Smith (1) -   April 11, 1833

Kilmer, Dennis M. and Ida M. Smurr (3) -   December 6, 1882
    Place of marriage, Shepherdstown - Age of husband, 33 - Age of wife,
    25 - Both are Single - Husband was born in Berkeley County, West
    Virginia - Wife was born in Jefferson County, West Virginia -
    Husband resides in Berkeley County, West Virginia - Wife resides in
    Jefferson County, West Virginia.

Kimble, Sarah E. and John T. Willis (3) -   January 19, 1871
    For further information see - Willis, John T.

Kime, Eliza and James Stephenson (1) -   May 29, 1804

Kime, Elizabeth and David Schall (1) -   October 13, 1816

Kime, John and Margaret Shall (1) -   October 3, 1816

Kime, Sally and John Shall (1) -   March 11, 1813

Kimes, Allen M. and Sarah Ann Miller (3) -   November 17, 1880
    Place of marriage, Shepherdstown - Age of husband, 24 - Age of wife,
    27 - Both are Single - Both were born in Jefferson County, West
    Virginia - Both reside in Jefferson County, West Virginia.

Kimes, Annie E. and Samuel W. Pitzer (3) -   April 24, 1884
    For further information see - Pitzer, Samuel W.

Kimes, Daniel and Rosanna Conner (1) -   February 1821

311

Kimes, Henry and Ann W. Carell (1) - September 26, 1839

Kimes, Jacob and Euphemia Hodges (1) - December 18, 1827

Kimes, Mollie E. and I. F. Poisal (3) - October 22, 1868
    For further information see - Poisal, I. F.

Kimes, Sallie V. and Joseph W. Colbert (3) - January 11, 1872
    For further information see - Colbert, Joseph W.

Kimes, Sarah and James Boyers (1) - February 8, 1827

Kimes, William and Sarah Boyers (1) - April 11, 1812

Kimes, William and Mary L. Johnson (3) - August 2, 1877
    Place of marriage, Harpers Ferry - Age of husband, 56 - Age of wife, 35 - Husband is a Widower - Wife is Single - Both were born in Jefferson County, West Virginia - Both reside in Jefferson County, West Virginia.

Kindle, Angeline and Robert A. Dunn (3) - January 24, 1877
    For further information see - Dunn, Robert A.

Kindle, Martha and B. F. Martin (3) - July 3, 1879
    For further information see - Martin, B. F.

King, Caroline and Thomas Tredrea (3) - September 29, 1875
    For further information see - Tredrea, Thomas.

King, Delila and James Groff (2) - (L) July 16, 1855

King, Emma Louise and H. C. Heller (3) - June 15, 1887
    For further information see - Heller, H. C.

King, James and Susan Koonce (1) - October 8, 1833

King, James (cold.) Nancy Lucas (3) - December 19, 1878
    Place of marriage, Charlestown - Age of husband, 24 - Age of wife, 25 - Both are Single - Husband was born in Clarke County, Virginia - Wife was born in Jefferson County, West Virginia - Both reside in Jefferson County, West Virginia.

King, James F. and Nancy Kerchival (1) - February 10, 1820

King, John and Emma N. Thompson (3) - January 11, 1888
    Place of marriage, Charlestown - Age of husband, 27 - Age of wife, 22 - Both are Single - Both were born in Jefferson County, West Virginia - Both reside in Jefferson County, West Virginia.

King, John H. and Mary Greer (1) - May 1, 1828

King, Julia (cold.) Henry Jackson (3) - (L) September 21, 1866
    For further information see - Jackson, Henry.

King, Laura A. and Thomas D. Rian (1) - December 23, 1849

King, Marietta and James L. Henson (2) - (L) March 30, 1857

King, Matilda (cold.) Robert Carter (3) - February 10, 1876
    For further information see - Carter, Robert.

King, Susanna and Shaderick Penn (1) -   November 4, 1824

King, Thomas M. and Ellen C. Robinson (3) -   October 25, 1865
    Place of marriage, Shepherdstown - Age of husband, 26 years - Age of
    wife, 26 years - Both are Single - Husband was born at Washington
    City, D. C. - Wife was born in Jefferson County, West Virginia -
    Husband resides in Fairfax County, Virginia - Wife resides in
    Jefferson County, West Virginia - Wife's parents are Archibald and
    Ann R. Robinson - Occupation of husband is Farmer.

King, Willis and Stephanna Pearl (3) -   July 28, 1887
    Place of marriage, Charlestown - Age of husband, 35 - Age of wife,
    17 - Both are Single - Both were born in Jefferson County, West
    Virginia - Both reside in Jefferson County, West Virginia.
    (Consent of bride's mother in writing.)

Kipps, Sarah E. and Thomas L. Golliday (3) -   November 7, 1889
    For further information see - Golliday, Thomas L.

Kirby, Dorsey H. and John E. Erwin (2) -   (L) January 21, 1861

Kirby, E. F. and M. E. Wilson (bride) (3) -   (1872)
    Age of husband, 35 - Age of wife, 22 - Husband is a Widower - Wife
    is Single - Husband was born in England - Wife was born in Jefferson
    County, West Virginia - Husband's parents are Edward and Margaret -
    Wife's parents are James and Maria - Occupation of husband is
    Machinist.

Kirby, Emma Frances and Anthony Nunamaker (2) -   (L) November 20, 1854

Kirby, James and Alice Barrow (3) -   April 16, 1879
    Place of marriage, Charlestown - Age of husband, 22 - Age of wife,
    17 - Both are Single - Husband was born in Hardy County, West
    Virginia - Wife was born in Frederick County, Virginia - Both reside
    in Jefferson County, West Virginia. (Consent of bride's father in
    person.)

Kirby, Jane and D. Fairman (1) -   1819

Kirby, Jane E. and R. H. Brua (2) -   (L) November 27, 1858

Kirby, Rachael and David Butt (1) -   July 4, 1816

Kirk, Catherine and George Kellison (2) -   (L) July 25, 1860

Kirk, Charles and Mrs. Catharine Tally (widow) (2) -   (L) November 14, 1853

Kirk, Rebecca and John William Hufmaster (2) -   (L) December 21, 1852

Kirk, Rebecca and John W. Hufmaster (1) -   December 22, 1852

Kirwan, Kate C. and John S. Staunton (3) -   January 9, 1882
    For further information see - Staunton, John S.

Kirwan, Lawrence L. and Emma J. F. Turk (2) -   (L) September 4, 1860

313

Kisner, Bennet B. and Mary Ellen Fellers (3) - September 27, 1888
   Place of marriage, Charlestown - Age of husband, 26 - Age of wife,
   21 - Both are Single - Husband was born in Berkeley County - Wife
   was born in Jefferson County, West Virginia - Both reside in
   Jefferson County, West Virginia.

Kist, Catherine and Elijah Baycroft (1) - 1825

Kitchen, John N. and Lucy W. Colston (2) - (L) September 9, 1858

Kitchen, Mary Ann and John J. Monroe (1) - October 27, 1831

Kline, Ann C. and William Page (3) - June 9, 1865
   For further information see - Page, William.

Kline, Charles D. and Ettie Dailey (3) - June 8, 1884
   Place of marriage, Bloomery - Age of husband, 32 - Age of wife, 22 -
   Both are Single - Husband was born in Frederick County, Virginia -
   Wife was born in Jefferson County, West Virginia - Both reside in
   Jefferson County, West Virginia.

Kline, Henry and Catharine Tompkins (1) - September 7, 1832

Kline, Iona E. and James W. Moore (3) - May 14, 1878
   For further information see - Moore, James W.

Kline, Jesse Gillmore and Mary Ott (3) - September 8, 1871
   Place of marriage, Jefferson County - Age of husband, 23 - Age of
   wife, 21 - Both are Single - Both were born in Jefferson - Husband
   resides in Jefferson - Wife resides in West Virginia - Occupation of
   husband is Farmer. (This record is crossed out in the original.)

Kline, Mary Ann C. and John Ingram (3) - March 28, 1866
   For further information see - Ingram, John.

Kline, Milard Fillmore and Annie C. Ott (3) - May 22, 1871
   Place of marriage, Jefferson County - Age of husband, 22 - Age of
   wife, 22 - Both are Single - Husband was born in Virginia - Wife was
   born in Jefferson County - Both reside in Jefferson County -
   Husband's parents are Henry and Ann C. - Wife's parents are Israel
   and Margaret - Occupation of husband is Farmer.

Kline, R. B. and Mary Hagan (3) - August 18, 1889
   Place of marriage, Leetown - Age of husband, 49 - Age of wife, 29 -
   Husband is a Widower - Wife is a Widow - Husband was born in
   Jefferson County, West Virginia - Wife was born in Frederick County,
   Maryland - Both reside in Jefferson County, West Virginia.

Kline, R. P. and Mrs. Georgianna Bowers (3) - June 7, 1887
   Place of marriage, Middleway - Age of husband, 46 - Age of wife,
   31 - Husband is a Widower - Wife is a Widow - Both were born in
   Jefferson County, West Virginia - Both reside in Jefferson County,
   West Virginia.

Kline, William H. and Hebernia Mask (3) -					July 6, 1865
    Place of marriage, Shepherdstown - Age of husband, 28 years - Age of wife, 22 years - Both are Single - Husband was born in Baltimore County, Maryland - Wife was born at Moorefield, Virginia - Husband resides at Baltimore City - Wife resides at Baltimore City - Husband's parents are John and Elizabeth Kline - Wife's parents are Isaac and Mary Mask - Occupation of husband is Butcher.

Klise, Sarah and Presley Marmaduke (1) -					September 26, 1810

Knadler, M. M. and Sophrana Rice (3) -					December 20, 1876
    Place of marriage, near Shepherdstown - Age of husband, 24 - Age of wife, 22 - Both are Single - Husband was born in Berkeley County, West Virginia - Wife was born in Jefferson County, West Virginia - Husband resides in Berkeley County, West Virginia - Wife resides in Jefferson County, West Virginia.

Knadler, Samuel J. and Annie B. Shewbridge (3) -					April 6, 1886
    Place of marriage, Summit Point - Age of husband, 26 - Age of wife, 29 - Both are Single - Husband was born in Washington County, Maryland - Wife was born in Jefferson County, West Virginia - Husband resides in Washington County, Maryland - Wife resides in Jefferson County, West Virginia.

Kneisel, Mary and Henry Breu (1) -					May 30, 1835

Knick, C. L. and Bertha C. Green (3) -					December 14, 1887
    Place of marriage, Harpers Ferry - Age of husband, 23 - Age of wife, 21 - Both are Single - Both were born in State of Virginia - Husband resides in State of Virginia - Wife resides in Jefferson County.

Knight, Jacob and Mary McGuth (1) -					1813

Knoble, John and Elizabeth Ingram (3) -					May 8, 1870
    Place of marriage, Jefferson County - Age of husband, 50 - Age of wife, 31 - Both were born in Virginia - Both reside in Jefferson County. (Ages sworn to by John Pridgcole.)

Knot, Armistead T. M. and Eliza Lee (2) -					(L) September 18, 1860

Knott, Anna C. and Isaac M. Ramsbottom (3) -					May 3, 1888
    For further information see - Ramsbottom, Isaac M.

Knott, Annie E. and G. Frank Engle (3) -					July 11, 1883
    For further information see - Engle, G. Frank.

Knott, C. H. and Susan G. Reinhart (3) -					February 23, 1869
    Place of marriage, Jefferson County - Age of husband, 27 - Age of wife, 19 - Both are Single - Husband was born in Jefferson County - Wife was born in Virginia - Both reside in Jefferson County - Husband's parents are Samuel and Margaret - Wife's parents are C. and Ann M. - Occupation of husband is Farmer. (Parents dead; No guardian; Brother gives consent.)

Knott, Charles J. and Mollie V. Hoffman (3) -					October 16, 1884
    Place of marriage, Bethesda - Age of husband, 23 - Age of wife, 22 - Both are Single - Both were born in Jefferson County, West Virginia - Both reside in Jefferson County.

Knott, George M. and Fannie E. Thomas (3) -   March 26, 1884
    Place of marriage, Bethesda Church - Age of husband, 28 - Age of
    wife, 19 - Both are Single - Husband was born in Jefferson County,
    West Virginia - Wife was born in Frederick County, Maryland - Both
    reside in Jefferson County, West Virginia. (Consent of guardian
    in person.)

Knott, Jennie H. and D. F. Koontz (3) -   March 13, 1889
    For further information see - Koontz, D. F.

Knott, John L. and Mary Virginia Reinhart (2) - (L) January 20, 1860

Knott, Mary V. and Lee H. Moler (3) -   June 9, 1868
    For further information see - Moler, Lee H.

Knott, Rosa L. and J. S. Renner (3) -   August 20, 1889
    For further information see - Renner, J. S.

Knott, S. T. and Lilly A. Reinhart (3) -   February 14, 1883
    Place of marriage, Bethesda Church - Age of husband, 23 - Age of
    wife, 22 - Both are Single - Both were born in Jefferson County,
    West Virginia - Both reside in Jefferson County, West Virginia.

Knott, Samuel M. and Eliza Jane Clymer (2) -   (L) January 16, 1854

Knott, Samuel M. and Margaret U. Kephart (2) -   (L) February 8, 1858

Knott, Sarah E. and James M. Hendricks (3) -   February 12, 1867
    For further information see - Hendricks, James M.

Knott, William J. and Margaret Ann Moler (2) -   (L) January 14, 1853
    (Ages of parties and residence of same proved by the oath of Jacob
    Reinhart.)

Knouff, Elizabeth and Jacob Staley (1) -   September 5, 1810

Knox, Christopher and Catharine Wilt (2) -   (L) December 25, 1850

Knox, John and Ann Piper (1) -   July 8, 1824

Knupp, Valentine and Christina Rosenberger (1) - July 28, 1833

Koch, Margaret and John Pester (2) -   (L) July 26, 1850

Koetzner, Auguste and Joanna Hyland (2) -   (L) October 15, 1853

Kogelschatz, Louis W. and Ella Fayman (3) -   March 21, 1883
    Place of marriage, Shepherdstown - Age of husband, 25 - Age of wife,
    21 - Both are Single - Husband was born at City of Baltimore - Wife
    was born in Jefferson County, West Virginia - Husband resides in
    Berkeley County, West Virginia - Wife resides in Jefferson County,
    West Virginia.

Kohlhousen, T. F. and J. V. McClure (bride) (3) -   October 2, 1872
  Place of marriage, Jefferson County - Age of husband, 23 - Age of
  wife, 24 - Both are Single - Husband was born at Winchester,
  Virginia - Wife was born in Frederick, Virginia - Husband resides at
  Grafton, West Virginia - Wife resides in Jefferson, West Virginia -
  Husband's parents are F. W. and E. Kohlhousen - Wife's parents are
  J. C. and C. B. McClure - Occupation of husband is Farmer. (J. C.
  McClure.)

Kohlhousen, William A. and Sarah E. McClure (2) -   (L) April 5, 1859

Kolsch, Margaret and John Posler (1) -   June 18, 1850

Koonce, Alice R. and A. M. Kessler (3) -   February 22, 1872
  For further information see - Kessler, A. M.

Koonce, Charles and Hattie R. Moler (3) -   December 30, 1883
  Place of marriage, Charlestown - Age of husband, 23 - Age of wife,
  21 - Both are Single - Both were born in Jefferson County, West
  Virginia - Both reside in Jefferson County, West Virginia.

Koonce, Estella and William L. Black (3) -   October 16, 1890
  For further information see - Black, William L.

Koonce, Imogene F. and Charles Edward Young (3) -   July 6, 1875
  For further information see - Young, Charles Edward.

Koonce, Mary E. and Laban Sparks (3) -   September 1, 1869
  For further information see - Sparks, Laban.

Koonce, Susan and James King (1) -   October 8, 1833

Koontz, Charles R. and Lucy G. Taylor (3) -   December 17, 1889
  Place of marriage, Bride's Residence - Age of husband, 21 - Age of
  wife, 19 - Both are Single - Both were born in Jefferson County,
  West Virginia - Both reside in Jefferson County, West Virginia.
  (Consent of bride's father in person.)

Koontz, D. F. and Jennie H. Knott (3) -   March 13, 1889
  Place of marriage, near Shepherdstown - Age of husband, 31 - Age of
  wife, 24 - Both are Single - Both were born in Jefferson County,
  West Virginia - Both reside in Jefferson County, West Virginia.

Koontz, Daniel M. and Susanna Banks (3) -   March 4, 1890
  Place of marriage, Shepherdstown - Age of husband, 26 - Age of wife,
  23 - Both are Single - Both were born in Jefferson County, West
  Virginia - Both reside in Jefferson County, West Virginia.

Koontz, Sue V. and R. C. Hess (3) -   February 5, 1879
  For further information see - Hess, R. C.

Koontz, Victor and Lutie Snader (3) -   October 4, 1888
  Place of marriage, Kellers - Age of husband, 27 - Age of wife, 21 -
  Both are Single - Husband was born in Franklin County,
  Pennsylvania - Wife was born in Carroll County, Maryland - Husband
  resides in Franklin County, Pennsylvania - Wife resides in Jefferson
  County, West Virginia.

Kopp, Amos and Eliza Scott (3) -   July 7, 1871
   Place of marriage, Jefferson County - Age of husband, 49 - Age of
   wife, 41 - Both are Single - Both were born in Shenandoah County -
   Husband resides in Shenandoah County - Wife resides in Jefferson
   County - Husband's parents are Jacob and Rosanna - Wife's parents
   are John and Elizabeth - Occupation of husband in Farmer.

Kownslar, Randolph and Elizabeth S. Blackburn (1) -   September 6, 1850

Kraps, Kitty and George Ware (1) -   December 4, 1817

Kremer, Rev. Leighton G. and Nannie L. Reynolds (3) -   December 9, 1886
   Place of marriage, Duffields - Age of husband, 34 - Age of wife,
   24 - Both are Single - Husband was born in Pennsylvania - Wife was
   born in Jefferson County, West Virginia - Husband resides in
   Maryland - Wife resides in Jefferson County, West Virginia.

Krepps, Eliza Jane Tomson and John G. Flanagan (3) -   October 26, 1876
   For further information see - Flanagan, John G.

Krepps, John and Ann Pilcher (2) -   (L) July 19, 1861
   Time of marriage, (blank) - Place of marriage, Bolivar - Names of
   parties, John Krepps and Ann Pilcher - Age of husband, About Forty
   Years - Age of wife, Twenty Five Years - Condition of husband is a
   Widower - Condition of wife is Single - Place of birth, Both at
   Harpers Ferry - Both live at Bolivar - Names of husband's parents
   are Unknown - Names of wife's parents are Sidney A. and Susan
   Pilcher - Occupation of husband is Armorer - Given under my hand
   this 19th day of July, 1861 - S. A. Pilcher.

Krepps, Mahala A. and William H. Harmer (3) -   October 16, 1873
   For further information see - Harmer, William H.

Krepps, Martha E. and Rev. M. E. Keyser (3) -   March 7, 1872
   For further information see - Keyser, Rev. M. E.

Kreps, Christiana and Peter Staley (1) -   February 27, 1816

Kreps, John and Mary Adeline Melhorn (1) -   October 25, 1836

Kreps, Mary Ann and Rawleigh Selser (1) -   July 28, 1825

Kretzer, David and Rosanna Poffinberger (1) -   May 25, 1826

Krombling, Mary E. and George Downing (3) -   February 25, 1877
   For further information see - Downing, George.

Krout, Catherine and James Shoebridge (1) -   September 5, 1826

Krout, Mary and John Stedman (1) -   April 29, 1832

Krout, Sarah and Samuel Hobbs (1) -   April 22, 1819

Krout, Sarah Jane and John Newton Whittington (2) -   (L) February 9, 1853

Krout, Sarah Jane and John N. Whittington (1) -   February 10, 1853

Kuhl, Frederick and Julia A. Roeder (3) -   February 19, 1879
   Place of marriage, Harpers Ferry - Age of husband, 24 - Age of wife,
   20 - Both are Single - Husband was born at Baltimore, Maryland -
   Wife was born in Jefferson County, West Virginia - Husband resides
   in Maryland - Wife resides in Jefferson County, West Virginia.
   (Consent of bride's guardian in person.)

Laboldt, Philip and Catharine Leibig (2) -   (L) May 17, 1860

Lackland, Charlotte H. and Thomas E. Sublett (2) -   (L) April 5, 1859

Lackland, Ellenoir M. and Francis C. Braxton (3) -   November 22, 1888
For further information see - Braxton, Francis C.

Lackland, Fanny and Lawrence Washington (3) -   June 14, 1876
For further information see - Washington, Lawrence.

Lackland, Samuel Watkins and Elizabeth B. Griggs (1) -   January 29, 1823

Lackland, Thomas and Martha Ellen Willis (2) -   (L) August 22, 1851

Lackland, Thomas and Martha Ellen Willis (1) -   August 26, 1851

Lafferty, Elizabeth and William Nicholl (1) -   May 18, 1820

Lafferty, Margaret and Jeremiah Hawkens (1) -   December 28, 1825

Lafitte, Fannie S. and John M. Howell (3) -   March 24, 1874
For further information see - Howell, John M.

Laidley, Thomas M. and Herzzena B. Beall (2) -   (L) April 3, 1857

Laise, Charles F. and Cora A. Roberts (3) -   November 18, 1885
Place of marriage, Charlestown - Age of husband, 28 - Age of wife, 21 - Both are Single - Husband was born in Pennsylvania - Wife was born in Frederick County, Virginia - Husband resides in Berkeley County, West Virginia - Wife resides in Jefferson County, West Virginia at present.

Lake, John and Eliza A. Grim (3) -   December 24, 1871
Place of marriage, Jefferson County - Age of husband, 33 - Age of wife, 35 - Both are Single - Husband was born in New York - Wife was born in Maryland - Both reside in Jefferson County - Husband's parents are John and Mary - Wife's parents are Thomas D. G. and Elizabeth A. - Occupation of husband is Tanner.

Lakin, Samuel W. and Helen V. Grubb (3) -   June 6, 1889
Place of marriage, Bolivar - Age of husband, 25 - Age of wife, 23 - Both are Single - Both were born in Loudoun County, Virginia - Husband resides in Washington County, Maryland - Wife resides in Jefferson County, West Virginia.

Laley, Eliza and John Price (1) -   1825

Laley, Elizabeth and Jacob Reasler (1) -   1825

Laley, Laura N. and Eugien Storm (3) -   April 5, 1869
For further information see - Storm, Eugien.

Laley, Thomas K. and Mary G. Gardner (2) -   (L) December 19, 1853
(Consent of Miss Gardner's mother proved by the oath of John S. Hunter and Mrs. Gardner's hand writing.)

Lally, Mary Ellen and Jacob Perry Bell (2) -   (L) May 18, 1852

Laly, Mary Ellen and Jacob Perry Bell (1) -   May 27, 1852

Lamar, Emma E. and John William Bender (3) - December 24, 1878
For further information see - Bender, John William.

Lamar, Richard D. and Sarah Border (3) - November 12, 1873
Place of marriage, near Shepherdstown - Age of husband, 23 - Age of wife, 21 - Both are Single - Husband was born in Frederick County, Maryland - Wife was born in Jefferson County, West Virginia - Husband resides at Frederick City, Maryland - Wife resides in Jefferson County, West Virginia.

Lamas, Josephine and Anthony L. Pine (2) - (L) May 11, 1857

Lambaugh, Annie S. H. and A. Lawrence Gould (2) - (L) January 2, 1858

Lambaugh, Elizabeth and Thomas C. Gillaspie (1) - September 10, 1848

Lambert, Charles O. and Margaret Ellen Freeze (2) - (L) June 2, 1860

Lambert, Charles O. and Mary V. Hunter (3) - May 16, 1876
Place of marriage, near Middleway - Age of husband, 38 - Age of wife, 34 - Husband is a Widower - Wife is Single - Husband was born at Frederick City, Maryland - Wife was born in Berkeley County, West Virginia - Husband resides in Berkeley County - Wife resides in Jefferson County, West Virginia.

Lambert, Ellen L. and John T. Miller (3) - September 17, 1868
For further information see - Miller, John T.

Lambert, Fannie L. and Robert G. Miller (3) - March 3, 1890
For further information see - Miller, Robert G.

Lambert, James and Mary E. Simpson (2) - (L) November 30, 1853

Lambert, Louis E. and L. Jane Hoffman (3) - November 7, 1871
Place of marriage, Charles Town - Age of husband, 24 - Age of wife, 18 - Both are Single - Husband was born in Maryland - Wife was born in Pennsylvania - Both reside in Jefferson County - Husband's parents are Frederick and Catherine E. - Wife's parents are John P. and Teresa - Occupation of husband is Barber.

Lambert, Rosa V. and B. E. Greenwood (3) - December 23, 1889
For further information see - Greenwood, B. E.

Lambert, Susan Belinda and George W. Sappington (2) - (L) March 20, 1851

Lambright, George W. and Anna H. Kearsley (3) - March 26, 1874
Place of marriage, Charlestown - Age of husband, 26 - Age of wife, 21 - Both are Single - Husband was born in Alleghany County, Maryland - Wife was born in Jefferson County, Virginia - Husband resides at Knoxville, Tennessee - Wife resides in Jefferson County, West Virginia.

Lamon, W. H. and Maggie Wilson (3) - April 26, 1887
Place of marriage, near Middleway - Age of husband, 28 - Age of wife, 22 - Both are Single - Husband was born in Berkeley County, West Virginia - Wife was born in Maryland - Husband resides in Berkeley County, West Virginia - Wife resides in Jefferson County.

Lancaster, Ellen Jane and John C. Hankey (3) - January 28, 1877
For further information see - Hankey, John C.

Lancaster, Mahlon and Virginia Derry (3) -   May 13, 1874
    Place of marriage, Harpers Ferry - Age of husband, 22 - Age of wife, 20 - Both are Single - Husband was born in Jefferson County, West Virginia - Wife was born in Loudoun County, Virginia - Both reside in Jefferson County, West Virginia. (Consent of bride's father in person.)

Lancaster, Samuel and Mary Cage (1) -   April 7, 1831

Lancaster, Sarah A. L. and John H. Miller (2) -   (L) October 1, 1851

Lancaster, Sarah E. and John M. Gano (2) -   (L) August 4, 1859

Lancaster, Sarah E. and George C. Mobberly (3) -   December 9, 1874
    For further information see - Mobberly, George C.

Lance, John and Mary McLaughlin (1) -   1822

Landers, Edward and Maria Dora Storm (3) -   February 27, 1876
    Place of marriage, Bolivar - Age of husband, 49 - Age of wife, 34 - Husband is a Widower - Wife is a Widow - Husband was born in Ireland - Wife was born at Cumberland, Maryland - Both reside in Jefferson County, West Virginia.

Landrist, Benjamin and Catharine Good (1) -   December 11, 1827

Lands, Benjamin F. (cold.) Emily Powell (3) -   August 29, 1878
    Place of marriage, Charlestown - Age of husband, 28 - Age of wife, 22 - Both are Single - Husband was born in Frederick County, Maryland - Wife was born in Jefferson County, West Virginia - Both reside in Jefferson County, West Virginia.

Lane, Ann F. and Henry Boteler (1) -   June 21, 1825

Lane, Fanas (colored) James Caven (3) -   September 6, 1870
    Place of marriage, Jefferson.

Lane, Franklin and Julia Ann Harvey (3) -   November 2, 1873
    Place of marriage, Jefferson County - Age of husband, 44 - Age of wife, 33 - Both are Single - Husband was born in Jefferson County, West Virginia - Wife was born in Clarke County, Virginia - Both reside in Jefferson County, West Virginia.

Lane, George E. and Meta H. Chambers (3) -   December 20, 1877
    Place of marriage, Harpers Ferry - Age of husband, 25 - Age of wife, 18 - Both are Single - Husband was born in Maryland - Wife was born in Jefferson County, West Virginia - Both reside in Jefferson County, West Virginia. (Consent of bride's father in person.)

Lane, John G. and Helen Berry (1) -   May 14, 1850

Lane, Mary Ann Riddle and Andrew Kennedy (1) -   January 2, 1822

Lane, Thomas and Margaret Bettz (2) - (L) September 12, 1863
  Time of marriage, September 15, 1863 - Place of marriage, near
  Kerneysville - Names are Thomas Lane and Margaret Bettz - Both are
  Single - Husband was born in Lycoming County, Pennsylvania - Wife
  was born in Pendleton County, Virginia - Husband's residence is
  Where he was born - Wife's residence is Jefferson County, Virginia -
  Names of husband's parents are James and Mary Lane - Wife's parents
  are Martin and Margaret Jane Bettz - Occupation of husband is
  Soldier in Federal Army - License issued, September 12, 1863 in
  presence of bride's father - Thomas A. Moore, Clerk.

Laneiskes, John and Polly Dust (1) - January 2, 1807

Lang, Marinas and Mrs. Susan Elizabeth Mackenzie (2) - (L) November 26, 1852

Lang, Mary and Henry Apenzeller (1) - March 8, 1827

Langdon, Charles and Louisa J. Clip (2) - (L) October 23, 1851

Langdon, Charles and Louisa Jane Clip (2) - (L) June 28, 1852

Langdon, Charles and Louisa Jane Clip (1) - June 28, 1852

Langdon, Julia M. and W. G. Jackson (3) - September 21, 1881
  For further information see - Jackson, W. G.

Langdon, Mattie J. and J. W. Thomas (3) - March 16, 1886
  For further information see - Thomas, J. W.

Langdon, Rosa E. and H. S. Waple (3) - June 1, 1881
  For further information see - Waple, H. S.

Langdon, William and Margaret M. Rodrick (3) - December 20, 1877
  Place of marriage, Charlestown - Age of husband, 65 - Age of wife,
  43 - Husband is a Widower - Wife is a Widow - Husband was born in
  Pennsylvania - Wife was born in Jefferson County, West Virginia -
  Both reside in Jefferson County, West Virginia.

Langford, Thomas and Fannie Cooke (3) - April 20, 1872
  Place of marriage, Jefferson County, West Virginia - Age of husband,
  28 - Age of wife, 21 - Both are Single - Husband was born in
  Jefferson County, West Virginia - Wife was born in Jefferson
  County - Husband resides in Jefferson County - Wife resides in
  Jefferson County, West Virginia - Husband's parents are Phil and
  Nancy - Occupation of husband is Farmer.

Langley, John F. and Elizabeth H. Crow (1) - May 13, 1826

Langley, Richard H. and Mary E. Dean (1) - November 10, 1848

Langston, F. R. and Sallie Heck (3) - December 26, 1889
  Place of marriage, Charlestown - Age of husband, 33 - Age of wife,
  24 - Both are Single - Both were born in Jefferson County, West
  Virginia - Both reside in Jefferson County, West Virginia.

Lanham, Clara Virginia and John Matthew O'Keef (3) - February 21, 1878
  For further information see - O'Keef, John Matthew.

Lanham, E. F. and Mary E. Pope (3) - September 9, 1882
   Place of marriage, near Summit Point - Age of husband, 27 - Age of wife, 19 - Both are Single - Husband was born in Clarke County, Virginia - Wife was born in Frederick County, Virginia - Husband resides in Clarke County, Virginia - Wife resides in Jefferson County, West Virginia. (Consent of bride's father in person.)

Lansiskes, Barbary and Daniel Allstadt (1) - June 27, 1816

Lantsbaugh, Rebecca E. and Amos B. Kendall (3) - September 12, 1878
   For further information see - Kendall, Amos B.

Lantsbaugh, Sarah A. and Charles E. Rosenberger (3) - December 16, 1879
   For further information see - Rosenberger, Charles E.

Lao, Thomas and Margaret Ann McKennan (2) - (L) May 23, 1855

Lape, Catharine and Augustus Shope (1) - September 25, 1827

Laport, Catharine and Anthony Brunz (2) - (L) March 30, 1852

Larew, Benjamin and Caroline Dillow (3) - May 10, 1869
   Place of marriage, Jefferson County - Age of husband, 24 - Age of wife, 22 - Both are Single - Both were born in Virginia - Both reside in Jefferson County.

Larue, Columbus M. and Mattie Ann Roeder (3) - June 14, 1890
   Place of marriage, Harpers Ferry - Age of husband, 22 - Age of wife, 15 - Both are Single - Both were born in Jefferson County, West Virginia - Both reside in Jefferson County, West Virginia.

Larue, Jabez and Frances Collins (1) - 1816

Larue, Jane Elizabeth and Preston Longerbeam (3) - October 21, 1886
   For further information see - Longerbeam, Preston.

Larue, Samuel and Juliet C. Collins (1) - August 31, 1825

Larue, William A. and Eliza Cornelia Grantham (2) - (L) April 25, 1863
   Time of marriage, April 28, 1863 - Place of marriage, near Middleway - Names, William A. Larue and Eliza Cornelia Grantham - Age of husband, 28 years - Age of wife, 28 years - Both are Single - Place of husband's birth was Clarke County, Virginia - Place of wife's birth was Jefferson County, Virginia - Place of husband's residence is Clarke County, Virginia - Place of wife's residence is Jefferson County, Virginia - Names of husband's parents are John B. and ?___ Larue - Names of wife's parents are James and Phebe F. Grantham - Occupation of husband is Farmer - License issued, April 25, 1863 - Thomas A. Moore, Clerk.

Lashhorn, Daniel and Mary Ann Hootte (1) - June 15, 1824

Lashhorn, Emma and John W. Lock (3) - October 9, 1884
   For further information see - Lock, John W.

Lashhorn, Jacob H. and Fannie Jones (3) -   November 19, 1882
   Place of marriage, Shepherdstown - Age of husband, 22 - Age of wife,
   18 - Both are Single - Husband was born in Berkeley County, West
   Virginia - Wife was born in Jefferson County, West Virginia - Both
   reside in Jefferson County, West Virginia.   (Consent of bride's
   father in writing.)

Lashhorn, John P. and Rosa Lee Morningstar (3) -   January 18, 1888
   Place of marriage, Leetown - Age of husband, 24 - Age of wife, 17 -
   Both are Single - Husband was born in Berkeley County, West
   Virginia - Wife was born in Jefferson County, West Virginia - Both
   reside in Jefferson County, West Virginia. (Consent of bride's
   father in person.)

Lashorn, John A. and Elizabeth Ellen Butt (2) -   (L) May 24, 1855

Latamer, T. W. and Mary J. Quigley (3) -   October 25, 1867
   Place of marriage, Jefferson - Both are Single - Husband was born in
   Charles County, Maryland - Wife was born in Jefferson County - Both
   reside in Jefferson County - Husband's parents are T. W. and
   Emoline - Wife's parents are John and Mary - Occupation of husband
   is Merchant.

Latamer, Thomas F. and V. F. Latamer (3) -   October 16, 1867
   Place of marriage, Jefferson County - Age of husband, 33 - Age of
   wife, 29 - Both are Single - Husband was born in Prince George
   County, Maryland - Wife was born in Charles County, Maryland -
   Husband resides in Maryland - Wife resides at Shepherdstown -
   Husband's parents are R. B. and J. C. - Wife's parents are T. H. and
   Emeline - Occupation of husband is Attorney at Law.

Latamer, V. F. and Thomas F. Latamer (3) -   October 16, 1867
   For further information see - Latamer, Thomas F.

Latane, S. P. and M. E. David (bride) (3) -   September 10, 1878
   Place of marriage, near Charlestown - Age of husband, 42 - Age of
   wife, 38 - Both are Single - Husband was born in Essex County,
   Virginia - Wife was born in King and Queen County, Virginia -
   Husband resides in Essex County, Virginia - Wife resides in
   Jefferson County, West Virginia.

Lathan, George and Ann Jett (1) -   October 24, 1819

Lathan, Maria and Jacob Coonse (the third) (1) -   July 28, 1825

Laughlin, John and Mary E. Shoemaker (3) -   August 24, 1869
   Place of marriage, Jefferson County - Age of husband, 27 - Age of
   wife, 23 - Both were born in Pennsylvania - Husband resides in
   Pennsylvania - Wife resides in Jefferson County, West Virginia.

Laughlin, Sarah O. and George W. Bond (1) -   July 29, 1828

Laughlin, Thomas and Susan Wood (1) -   November 2, 1820

Lauglin, Dennis O. and Elizabeth B. Baker (1) -   March 7, 1816

Laurence, Catherine and George Warner (1) -   November 6, 1813

Laurence, John W. and Mary C. Colly (3) -   December 20, 1870
   Place of marriage, Jefferson County - Age of husband, 52 - Age of
   wife, 31 - Husband was born in Virginia - Wife was born in
   Maryland - Both reside in Jefferson County.

Lawson, Anna E. and Austin L. Anderson (3) -   December 26, 1876
   For further information see - Anderson, Austin L.

Lawson, Richard P. (cold.) Fanny Dunmore (3) -   October 1, 1890
   Place of marriage, Shepherdstown - Age of husband, 47 - Age of wife,
   27 - Husband is a Widower - Wife is a Widow - Husband was born in
   Frederick County, Maryland - Wife was born in Jefferson County, West
   Virginia - Husband resides at Baltimore, Maryland - Wife resides in
   Jefferson County, West Virginia.

Lawson, Thomas (cold.) Ann Reeler (3) -   May 25, 1874
   Place of marriage, near Leetown - Age of husband, 22 - Age of wife,
   24 - Both are Single - Husband was born in Loudoun County,
   Virginia - Wife was born in Jefferson County, West Virginia - Both
   reside in Jefferson County, West Virginia.

Lay, Hamilton and Lydia M. Deakins (1) -   August 19, 1834

Lay, John and Nancy Filbert (1) -   November 30, 1815

Lay, Margaret and John Wilt (1) -   April 15, 1827

Lay, Maria and Landon Heskett (1) -   November 16, 1832

Lay, Maria and Jacob Piper (2) -   (L) June 20, 1853

Lay, Martha Jane and Samuel Turner Cogle (3) -   November 2, 1879
   For further information see - Cogle, Samuel Turner.

Lay, Mary Elizabeth and James M. Virts (3) -   March 20, 1873
   For further information see - Virts, James M.

Lay, Nancy and Eden Camine (1) -   April 8, 1821

Lay, Octavia Elizabeth and Charles E. Whitnall (3) -   December 19, 1885
   For further information see - Whitnall, Charles E.

Lay, S. M. and Elmer Peacher (3) -   April 1, 1889
   For further information see - Peacher, Elmer.

Lay, Sarah Ann and John Henry Kidwell (2) -   (L) December 17, 1851

Leach, Maggie E. and Henry Snowdon (3) -   June 11, 1885
   For further information see - Snowdon, Henry.

Leach, Sallie E. and John Minn (3) -   December 13, 1887
   For further information see - Minn, John.

Leagree, M. C. (bride) and B. D. Homer (3) -   February 22, 1870
   For further information see - Homer, B. D.

League, Henry S. and Ida F. Nicely (3) -   May 2, 1877
   Place of marriage, Middleway - Age of husband, 28 - Age of wife,
   22 - Both are Single - Both were born in Jefferson County, West
   Virginia - Both reside in Jefferson County, West Virginia.

League, James W. and Lizzie Sherman (3) -   November 14, 1871
   Place of marriage, Jefferson County - Age of husband, 27 - Age of
   wife, 25 - Both are Single - Both were born in Jefferson County -
   Both reside in Jefferson County - Husband's parents are Samuel W.
   and Mary E. - Wife's parents are John H. and Rebecca - Occupation of
   husband is Merchant.

Leaning, Annie (nee Shults) and John A. Water (3) -   November 19, 1878
   For further information see - Water, John A.

Learmont, John and Emma Sponceller (3) -   April 12, 1886
   Place of marriage, Charlestown - Age of husband, 65 - Age of wife,
   40 - Both are Single - Husband was born in Scotland - Wife was born
   in Jefferson County, West Virginia - Husband resides in Nebraska -
   Wife resides in Jefferson County, West Virginia.

Leavell, Anne E. and John M. Daniel (3) -   October 29, 1874
   For further information see - Daniel, John M.

Leavell, Mary A. and William R. Johnson (3) -   October 28, 1885
   For further information see - Johnson, William R.

Leavell, William T. and Anne Yates (1) -   November 18, 1847

Leavy, Josephine and Joseph Eackles (3) -   April 28, 1886
   For further information see - Eackles, Joseph.

Leavy, Teresa and William Henry Stuart (3) -   July 19, 1883
   For further information see - Stuart, William Henry.

Lece, Mary C. and John Long (3) -   February 12, 1883
   For further information see - Long, John.

Lechliter, Susanna and Samuel Engle (1) -   November 26, 1818

Leckliter, Margaret and Daniel Moler (1) -   January 1825

Ledwick, Massey and Ninian R. Machbee (1) -   August 25, 1814

Lee, Annie (cold.) Charles Douglas (3) -   June 24, 1875
   For further information see - Douglas, Charles.

Lee, Bettie (cold.) Henry Washington (3) -   April 3, 1884
   For further information see - Washington, Henry.

Lee, Catherine E. and William J. Gore (3) -   January 1, 1878
   For further information see - Gore, William J.

Lee, Charles W. (cold.) Fanny Holliday (3) -   August 16, 1877
   Place of marriage, Charlestown - Age of husband, 25 - Age of wife,
   26 - Both are Single - Both were born in Loudoun County, Virginia -
   Both reside in Jefferson County, West Virginia.

Lee, Daniel and Elizabeth Thompson (2) -   (L) September 12, 1850

Lee, Daniel and Elizabeth Thompson (1) -   September 12, 1850

Lee, Daniel (cold.) Bettie Drew (3) - May 10, 1874
Place of marriage, Jefferson County - Age of husband 21 - Age of wife, 21 - Both are Single - Both were born in Jefferson County, West Virginia - Both reside in Jefferson County, West Virginia.

Lee, Edmund J. and Eliza H. Shepherd (1) - October 1, 1823

Lee, Eliza and Armistead T. M. Knot (2) - (L) September 18, 1860

Lee, Ellen and John Simms Powell (1) - September 19, 1844

Lee, Eveline and Richard Blue (3) - May 21, 1869
For further information see - Blue, Richard.

Lee, Francis and Mary Strider (3) - August 16, 1866
Age of husband, 22 - Age of wife, 26 - Both are Single - Both were born in Jefferson County, West Virginia - Both reside in Jefferson County, West Virginia - Husband's parents are Francis and Vinee Lee - Wife's parents are Thomas and Maria Devonshire - Occupation of husband is Laborer.

Lee, Fanny (cold.) Laurence Williams (3) - September 2, 1875
For further information see - Williams, Laurence.

Lee, George (cold.) Ann Fairfax (3) - September 4, 1882
Place of marriage, Charlestown - Age of husband, 31 - Age of wife, 33 - Husband is Single - Wife is a Widow - Husband was born in Georgia - Wife was born in Warren County, Virginia - Both reside in Jefferson County, West Virginia.

Lee, George W. (cold.) Belle Johnson (3) - February 23, 1888
Place of marriage, Charlestown - Age of husband, 37 - Age of wife, 33 - Both are Single - Husband was born in Jefferson County, West Virginia - Wife was born in Rappahannock County, Virginia - Both reside in Jefferson County, West Virginia.

Lee, Henrietta E. and Charles W. Goldsborough (3) - November 7, 1865
For further information see - Goldsborough, Charles W.

Lee, Henry and Ann Walters (1) - April 12, 1827

Lee, Isabella (cold.) George Devonshire (3) - September 14, 1884
For further information see - Devonshire, George.

Lee, James (cold.) Sidney Drew (3) - December 11, 1873
Place of marriage, near Duffields - Age of husband, 22 - Age of wife, 24 - Both are Single - Both were born in Jefferson County, West Virginia - Both reside in Jefferson County, West Virginia.

Lee, James K. and Margaret Ann Henson (1) - November 1, 1832

Lee, John H. and Emma Bilson (2) - (L) December 15, 1860

Lee, John H. and Emma Bilson (3) - November 13, 1878
Place of marriage, Charlestown - Age of husband 40 - Age of wife, 37 - Husband is a Widower by divorce - Wife is a Widow by divorce - Both were born in Jefferson County, West Virginia - Both reside in Jefferson County, West Virginia.

Lee, John J. and Ellen Morris (3) -   (1869)
    Age of husband, 21 - Age of wife, 19 - Husband was born in Jefferson
    County, West Virginia - Wife was born in Jefferson County - Both
    reside in Jefferson County, West Virginia.   (Consent of parents.)

Lee, Laura M. and W. A. Simpson (3) -   April 14, 1880
    For further information see - Simpson, W. A.

Lee, Louisa (cold.) Joseph Jackson (3) -   September 2, 1880
    For further information see - Jackson, Joseph.

Lee, Margaret (cold.) Robert Walters (3) -   January 13, 1890
    For further information see - Walters, Robert.

Lee, Martha (cold.) Thornton Nelson (3) -   September 19, 1867
    For further information see - Nelson, Thornton.

Lee, Mary (colored) Andrew G. Ross (3) -   (1870)
    For further information see - Ross, Andrew G.

Lee, Mary (cold.) Benjamin Stribling (3) -   May 18, 1880
    For further information see - Stribling, Benjamin.

Lee, Mary Jane and James Henry Whitlock (3) -   May 6, 1871
    For further information see - Whitlock, James Henry.

Lee, Mary S. and John Keller, Jr. (2) -   (L) April 26, 1851

Lee, Mary S. and John Keller, Jr. (1) -   April 27, 1851

Lee, S. J. (bride) and C. E. Kephart (3) -   December 23, 1872
    For further information see - Kephart, C. E.

Lee, Sarah Ann and John W. Rockenbaugh (2) -   (L) June 14, 1853

Lee, Taylor (cold.) Catherine McCan (3) -   May 6, 1874
    Place of marriage, Shepherdstown - Age of husband, 26 - Age of wife,
    25 - Both are Single - Both were born in Jefferson County, West
    Virginia - Both reside in Jefferson County, West Virginia.

Lee, Thomas (cold.) Ann Branson (3) -   July 5, 1880
    Place of marriage, Duffields - Age of husband, 25 - Age of wife,
    22 - Both are Single - Husband was born in Berkeley County, West
    Virginia - Wife was born in Jefferson County, West Virginia - Both
    reside in Jefferson County, West Virginia.

Lee, Victoria and Squire Watson (3) -   August 5, 1877
    For further information see - Watson, Squire.

Lee, Virginia Frances and Adam J. Lenhart (2) -   (L) November 24, 1859

Lee, William F. and Lillie M. Parran (2) -   (L) September 13, 1859

Leech, James and Ella Barrett (3) -   September 25, 1890
    Place of marriage, Harpers Ferry - Age of husband, 37 - Age of wife,
    25 - Husband is a Widower - Wife is Single - Husband was born in
    Rockbridge County, Virginia - Wife was born in Jefferson County,
    West Virginia - Both reside in Jefferson County, West Virginia.

Leever, Rosa and William Sisk (3) - January 21, 1888
For further information see - Sisk, William.

Lefevre, J. S. and Mary Elizabeth Wysong (3) - June 8, 1881
Place of marriage, Charlestown - Age of husband, 32 - Age of wife, 27 - Both are Single - Husband was born in Berkeley County, West Virginia - Wife was born in Jefferson County, West Virginia - Husband resides in Berkeley County, West Virginia - Wife resides in Jefferson County, West Virginia.

Legge, John Francis and Ellen May Reynolds (3) - April 13, 1887
Place of marriage, Shepherdstown - Age of husband, 40 - Age of wife, 28 - Husband is a Widower - Wife is Single - Husband was born in England - Wife was born in Jefferson County, West Virginia - Husband resides at Washington City - Wife resides in Jefferson County, West Virginia.

Legget, Ann and Henry Bowers. (1) - February 21, 1826

Leggett, T. W. and Frances V. Traynor (3) - October 3, 1871
Place of marriage, Jefferson County - Age of husband, 28 - Age of wife, 22 - Both are Single - Husband was born in Maryland - Wife was born in Jefferson - Husband resides in Jefferson - Wife resides in West Virginia - Husband's parents are Robert and Rebecca - Wife's parents are John and Lizzie - Occupation of husband is Pump Contractor. (This record is crossed out in the original.)

Leibig, Catharine and Philip Laboldt (2) - (L) May 17, 1860

Leicingring, Gideon and Sarah A. Beall (3) - April 24, 1866
Place of marriage, Charlestown, Jefferson County - Age of husband, 63 - Age of wife, 48 - Husband is a Widower - Wife is Single - Husband was born in Lehigh County, Pennsylvania - Wife was born in Jefferson County, Virginia - Both reside in Jefferson County, West Virginia - Husband's parents are Peter and Susana Leicingring - Wife's parents are Thomas N. and Louisa A. Beall - Occupation of husband is Merchant.

Leicklider, George and Jane Melvin (1) - November 12, 1827

Leickliter, Conrad, Jr. and Ruhama Molar (1) - March 20, 1817

Leiper, George and Mary Bryson (1) - November 4, 1804

Leiper, Mary and John Reynolds (1) - February 6, 1817

Leisenring, Robert S. and Cora E. Easterday (3) - October 16, 1888
Place of marriage, Charlestown - Age of husband, 29 - Age of wife, 27 - Both are Single - Husband was born in State of Pennsylvania - Wife was born in Jefferson County, West Virginia - Husband resides in State of Kansas - Wife resides in Jefferson County, West Virginia.

Lemen, Adrian W. and Sarah E. Walker (3) - September 21, 1870
Place of marriage, Jefferson County - Age of husband, 27 - Age of wife, 29 - Husband was born in Berkeley - Wife was born in Jefferson County, Virginia - Husband resides in Berkeley - Wife resides in Jefferson County.

Lemen, Elizabeth and Alfred H. Grist (1) - July 25, 1833

Lemen, Hettie and Daniel H. Folk (3) -   January 29, 1890
    For further information see - Folk, Daniel H.

Lemen, Joseph and Mary Catherine Price (2) -   (L) January 24, 1852

Lemen, M. N. and Sallie Billmyer (3) -   April 24, 1878
    Place of marriage, Shepherdstown - Age of husband, 33 - Age of wife,
    25 - Both are Single - Husband was born in Jefferson, West
    Virginia - Wife was born in Jefferson County, West Virginia -
    Husband resides in Jefferson County - Wife resides in Jefferson,
    West Virginia.

Lemen, Mary and Adrian Jones (1) -   February 5, 1839

Lemen, Mary A. and William F. Kerney (1) -   September 17, 1850

Lemen, Sally and Harry Lee Hout (3) -   June 30, 1885
    For further information see - Hout, Harry Lee.

Lemen, W. Manning and Sally M. Kerney (3) -   October 17, 1877
    Place of marriage, near Shepherdstown - Age of husband, 30 - Age of
    wife, 24 - Both are Single - Husband was born in Berkeley County,
    West Virginia - Wife was born in Jefferson County, West Virginia -
    Both reside in Jefferson County, West Virginia.

Lemon, Hester and John P. Kearfoot (1) -   August 23, 1827

Lemon, Martha S. and William H. Turk (2) -   (L) September 12, 1856

Lemon, Nancy M. and Alfred Howard (1) -   December 14, 1826

Lemon, Robert and Margaret Boley (1) -   January 15, 1818

Lemon, Sally T. and Daniel Fadley (3) -   April 8, 1869
    For further information see - Fadley, Daniel.

Lemon, Sarah and Baley Hedges (1) -   February 11, 1813

Lemon, Thomas and Polly Williamson (1) -   1806

Lemon, Thomas Newton and Margaret Billmyre (1) -   April 7, 1827

Lemon, William D. and Julia Ann Clothier (1) -   January 10, 1831

Lenhart, Adam J. and Virginia Frances Lee (2) -   (L) November 24, 1859

Lenhart, Henry and Sarah B. Myers (1) -   August 24, 1834

Lenox, Bettie and G. F. Lewis (2) -   (L) May 24, 1860

Lenox, Clara Mary and Edward D. Colegate (3) -   June 16, 1881
    For further information see - Colegate, Edward D.

Lenox, Jane and Walter Shirley (1) -   June 9, 1825

Lenox, John H. and Mary E. Coleman (2) -   (L) December 23, 1858

Lenox, Joseph and Elizabeth Avis (1) -   April 16, 1829

Lerch, Robert L. and Susie Simmons (3) -   July 17, 1890
    Place of marriage, Harpers Ferry - Age of husband, 29 - Age of wife,
    23 - Both are Single - Husband was born at Washington, D. C. - Wife
    was born in Jefferson County, West Virginia - Husband resides at
    Washington, D. C. - Wife resides in Jefferson County, West Virginia.

Leslie, James K. P. and Mary E. Hill (3) -   February 2, 1875
    Place of marriage, Charlestown - Age of husband, 29 - Age of wife,
    21 - Both are Single - Both were born in Jefferson County, West
    Virginia - Both reside in Jefferson County, West Virginia.

Leslie, Lizzie J. and Richard E. Britt (3) -   November 8, 1890
    For further information see - Britt, Richard E.

Leslie, Martha J. and Robert T. Conrad (3) -   April 14, 1881
    For further information see - Conrad, Robert T.

Lester, Benjamin F. and Maggie Drisch (3) -   November 14, 1872
    Place of marriage, Charlestown - Age of husband, 25 - Age of wife,
    22 - Both are Single - Husband was born in North Carolina - Wife was
    born in Virginia - Husband resides in Frederick County, Virginia -
    Wife resides in Clarke County, Virginia - Husband's parents are
    John and Eliza - Wife's parents are John and Margaret - Occupation
    of husband is Shoemaker.

Levell, Julia Yates and E. S. McDonald (3) -   October 12, 1869
    For further information see - McDonald, E. S.

Levering, Righter and Mary E. Stephenson (1) -   January 15, 1834

Levi, William H. and Mary A. Hart (2) -   (L) January 10, 1852

Levick, Mary and Thomas Morris (1) -   June 30, 1814

Levick, Rachael and Alexander Byers (1) -   October 26, 1813

Levy, Mary C. and Winfield Scott Reed (3) -   August 12, 1875
    For further information see - Reed, Winfield Scott.

Lewelynn, Emma J. and Price W. Vian (3) -   July 23, 1872
    For further information see - Vian, Price W.

Lewis, B. F. and Alice A. Divine (3) -   May 16, 1872
    Place of marriage, Jefferson County - Age of husband, 30 - Age of
    wife, 17 - Both are Single - Both were born in Virginia - Both
    reside in West Virginia - Husband's parents are B. F. and Ann -
    Wife's parents are D. M. - Occupation of husband is Carpenter.
    (Father in writing.)

Lewis, Catharine and Albion L. Miles (2) -   (L) December 23, 1851

Lewis, Catharine M. and Joseph Myers (2) -   (L) (1861)
    For further information see - Myers, Joseph.

Lewis, Charles and Mary Bowman (3) -   October 31, 1872
    Place of marriage, Jefferson County - Age of husband, 26 - Age of
    wife, 22 - Both are Single - Both were born in Virginia - Both
    reside in West Virginia - Husband's parents are John and Betty -
    Wife's parents are Garret - Occupation of husband is Laborer.

Lewis, Charles H. and Estelle S. P. Green (2) - (L) October 30, 1855

Lewis, Charles H. and Elizabeth B. Lewis (3) - August 1889
Place of marriage, Bride's Residence - Age of husband, 32 - Age of wife, 35 - Husband is a Widower - Wife is Single - Both were born in Jefferson County, West Virginia - Both reside in Jefferson County, West Virginia.

Lewis, Charles S. and Ida Wageley (3) - November 17, 1880
Place of marriage, Leetown - Age of husband, 24 - Age of wife, 18 - Both are Single - Both were born in Jefferson County, West Virginia - Both reside in Jefferson County, West Virginia. (Consent of bride's father in writing.)

Lewis, David and Mary B. Yauck (1) - 1825

Lewis, David (cold.) Fannie Ross (3) - April 4, 1878
Place of marriage, Charlestown - Age of husband, 21 - Age of wife, 18 - Both are Single - Both were born in Jefferson County, West Virginia - Both reside in Jefferson County, West Virginia. (Written permission by her father.)

Lewis, Elizabeth B. and Charles H. Lewis (3) - August 1889
For further information see - Lewis, Charles H.

Lewis, Evelina (cold.) Thomas Jefferson (3) - January 23, 1889
For further information see - Jefferson, Thomas.

Lewis, Fanny A. and John L. Lewis (3) - September 20, 1882
For further information see - Lewis, John L.

Lewis, Fanny O. and Gregg Robinson (3) - December 26, 1872
For further information see - Robinson, Gregg.

Lewis, G. F. and Bettie Lenox (2) - (L) May 24, 1860

Lewis, Harrison (cold.) Betty Burns (3) - July 31, 1884
Place of marriage, near Ripon - Age of husband, 26 - Age of wife, 19 - Both are Single - Both were born in Jefferson County, West Virginia - Both reside in Jefferson County, West Virginia. (Consent of bride's father in person.)

Lewis, John and Helen Gilbert (3) - December 24, 1866
Place of marriage, Harpers Ferry, West Virginia - Age of husband, 21 - Age of wife, 17 - Both are Single - Husband was born in King and Queen County, Maryland - Wife was born in Jefferson County, West Virginia - Both reside in Jefferson County, West Virginia - Husband's parents are Zachariah and Mary Lewis - Wife's parents are Isaac and Sarah Gilbert - Occupation of husband is Laborer.

Lewis, John (cold.) Maria Trinafer (3) - September 16, 1875
Place of marriage, near Charlestown - Age of husband, 24 - Age of wife, 19 - Both are Single - Both were born in Jefferson County, West Virginia - Both reside in Jefferson County, West Virginia.

333

Lewis, John L. and Mary J. Thomson (3) - December 4, 1866
Place of marriage, Shepherdstown, Jefferson County, West Virginia -
Age of husband, 26 - Age of wife, 26 - Both are Single - Both were
born in Jefferson County, West Virginia - Both reside in Jefferson
County, West Virginia - Husband's parents are Samuel and Mary A.
Lewis - Wife's parents are James and Mary Thomson - Occupation of
husband is Farmer.

Lewis, John L. and Fanny A. Lewis (3) - September 20, 1882
Place of marriage, Berryville, Clarke County - Age of husband, 40 -
Age of wife, 28 - Husband is a Widower - Wife is Single - Both were
born in Berkeley County, West Virginia - Both reside in Jefferson
County, West Virginia.

Lewis, John L. and Margaret Elizabeth Hoffman (3) - December 2, 1882
Place of marriage, Shepherdstown - Age of husband, 19 - Age of wife,
26 - Both are Single - Both were born in Jefferson County, West
Virginia - Both reside in Jefferson County, West Virginia.
(Consent of groom's parents in writing.)

Lewis, John William and Malinda E. Hoffmaster (2) - (L) October 23, 1857

Lewis, Lydia E. and John J. Shaull (3) - March 30, 1869
For further information see - Shaull, John J.

Lewis, Mary C. and Winfield S. Shaull (3) - April 15, 1874
For further information see - Shaull, Winfield S.

Lewis, Mary C. and John W. Lock (3) - June 1, 1882
For further information see - Lock, John W.

Lewis, Robert B. and Emma J. Manuel (3) - August 30, 1889
Place of marriage, Harpers Ferry - Age of husband, 23 - Age of wife,
18 - Both are Single - Wife was born in Jefferson County, West
Virginia - Both reside in Jefferson County, West Virginia.
(Consent of bride's parents in writing.)

Lewis, Robert Byra and Laura L. Parran (3) - December 16, 1868
Place of marriage, Jefferson County - Age of husband, 27 - Age of
wife, 22 - Both are Single - Husband was born in West Moreland
County, Virginia - Wife was born in Jefferson - Husband resides in
West Moreland County, Virginia - Wife resides in Jefferson County -
Wife's parents are Richard and Laura - Occupation of husband is
Lawyer.

Lewis, Robert H. and Louis E. Middlekauff (3) - December 18, 1868
Place of marriage, Jefferson County - Age of husband, 28 - Age of
wife, 24 - Both are Single - Both were born in Maryland - Husband
resides in Maryland - Wife resides in Jefferson County, West
Virginia - Husband's parents are A. W. and Sarah - Wife's parents
are Samuel D. and C. - Occupation of husband is Farmer.

Lewis, Samuel E. and Mary E. Smith (3) - January 29, 1884
Place of marriage, Mechanickstown - Age of husband, 20 - Age of
wife, 21 - Both are Single - Husband was born in Washington County,
Maryland - Wife was born in Jefferson County, West Virginia - Both
reside in Jefferson County, West Virginia. (Consent of groom's
father in writing.)

Lewis, Virginia Washington and John Henry Orndorff Kemp (3) - October 28, 1880
For further information see - Kemp, John Henry Orndorff.

Licklider, Agatha Ellen (divorced) and John W. Andrews (2) -
(L) February 7, 1860
(A marked through notation indicates her as "Widow of David Staley.")

Licklider, Charles A. and Florence Harp (3) - October 29, 1873
Place of marriage, Shepherdstown - Age of husband, 25 - Age of wife, 21 - Both are Single - Both were born in Jefferson County, West Virginia - Both reside in Jefferson County, West Virginia.

Licklider, Edward T. and Ellen Virginia Entler (3) - October 25, 1876
Place of marriage, Martinsburg - Age of husband, 23 last January - Age of wife, 24 last April - Both are Single - Both were born in Jefferson County, West Virginia - Both reside in Jefferson County, West Virginia.

Licklider, Elizabeth M. and Adam C. Link (2) - (L) September 9, 1854

Licklider, Helen G. and Daniel Staley (2) - (L) January 23, 1855

Licklider, Henry and Sarah Catherine Castleman (2) - (L) June 2, 1862
Time of marriage, June 2, (1862) - Place of marriage, Shepherdstown - Names, Henry Licklider and (Sarah Catherine) Castleman - Age of husband, 57 - Age of wife, 45 - Condition of husband is a Widower - Condition of wife is Single - Place of husband's birth was Maryland - Place of wife's birth was Jefferson County - Place of wife's residence is Berkeley - Place of husband's residence is Jefferson - Names of husband's parents is blank - Names of wife's parents is (George Castleman) - Occupation of husband is Farmer.

Licklider, John C. and Mary C. Flanagan (3) - December 18, 1866
Place of marriage, Mrs. F. Flanagan's, Jefferson County, West Virginia - Age of husband, 31 - Age of wife, 23 - Both are Single - Both were born in Jefferson County, West Virginia - Both reside in Jefferson County, West Virginia - Husband's parents are George and Jane Licklider - Wife's parents are James and Frances Flanagan - Occupation of husband is Farmer.

Licklider, Laura T. and Lee Griggs Brotherton (2) - (L) January 24, 1863
For further information see - Brotherton, Lee Griggs.

Licklider, Sarah Margaret and Daniel W. Staley (3) - May 30, 1871
For further information see - Staley, Daniel W.

Licklider, Thomas and Rhua Marshall (3) - June 6, 1872
Place of marriage, Jefferson County - Age of husband, 45 - Age of wife, 33 - Husband is a Widower - Wife is Single - Both were born in Virginia - Both reside in West Virginia - Husband's parents are Adam and Elizabeth - Wife's parents are John and Rhua - Occupation of husband is Farmer.

Lickliter, Elizabeth and Jacob Staley (1) - March 21, 1816

Lickliter, Jacob and Susana Dust (1) - December 14, 1809

Light, Colin P. and Mary L. Avis (3) -   December 21, 1871
    Place of marriage, Jefferson County - Age of husband, 22 - Age of
    wife, 23 - Both are Single - Both were born in Jefferson County -
    Husband resides in Berkeley - Wife resides in Jefferson County -
    Husband's parents are John C. and Mary J. - Wife's parents are
    David and Ellen - Occupation of husband is Miller.

Light, J. H. and Edith P. Neel (3) -   July 4, 1888
    Place of marriage, Shepherdstown - Age of husband, 29 - Age of wife,
    23 - Both are Single - Husband was born in Frederick County,
    Virginia - Wife was born in Pocahontas County, West Virginia -
    Husband resides in Monroe County, West Virginia - Wife resides at
    Shepherdstown, West Virginia.

Light, Martha Ellen and Richard A. Green (2) -   (L) November 21, 1854

Light, Mary Jane and Jacob A. Gruber (2) -   (L) October 3, 1853

Light, Mary Jane (widow) and Jacob A. Gruber (1) -   October 4, 1853

Lightfoot, Julia (cold.) Daniel W. Peeler (3) -   July 24, 1873
    For further information see - Peeler, Daniel W.

Lightner, S. W. and L. E. Brackett (bride) (3) -   June 1884
    Place of marriage, Harpers Ferry - Age of husband, 36 - Age of wife,
    28 - Both are Single - Husband was born in Pennsylvania - Wife was
    born in State of Maine - Both reside in Jefferson County, West
    Virginia.

Likens, Ann Doyne and Jacob Medtart (1) -   November 21, 1830

Likens, Elizabeth G. and Christian J. Wolff (1) -   April 21, 1825

Likens, Esther L. and Paul Smith (1) -   December 5, 1831

Likens, James and Sarah Mouser (1) -   April 8, 1813

Likens, Kate K. and Richard C. Baylor (2) -   (L) July 22, 1863
    For further information see - Baylor, Richard C.

Likens, Margaret and David Boren (1) -   June 23, 1850

Likens, Maria Jane and Thomas A. Moore (1) -   June 29, 1836

Likens, Ramsey and Susanna Dobson (1) -   May 21, 1827

Lillibridge, George and Rachel Sappington (1) -   March 8, 1827

Lindsay, Elizabeth and James Walton (1) -   November 19, 1812

Lindsay, Philip T. and Annie S. Custer (3) -   October 15, 1890
    Place of marriage, Charlestown - Age of husband, 22 - Age of wife,
    20 - Both are Single - Both were born in Jefferson County, West
    Virginia - Both reside in Jefferson County, West Virginia.

Lindsay, Samuel K. and Rebecca Way (1) -   October 9, 1847

Lindsay, Sary and William Banton (1) -   February 29, 1816

Lindsey, Ann and James Caten (1) -   February 5, 1835

Lindsey, Mary Ellen and James Crawford (1) - February 2, 1826

Line, Jac (son of Henry) and Mary B. Wysong (1) - April 24, 1823

Line, John D. and Mary C. Lock (2) - (L) June 2, 1852

Line, Julia L. and John L. Mayer (2) - (L) December 13, 1858

Line, Kate and Edward I. Higgens (3) - (1869)
    For further information see - Higgens, Edward I.

Link, Adam, Jr. and Elizabeth Butler (1) - May 4, 1821

Link, Adam, Jr. and Sarah Osborn (1) - May 27, 1824

Link, Adam C. and Elizabeth M. Licklider (2) - (L) September 9, 1854

Link, Adam S. and Amanda Snyder (3) - October 19, 1875
    Place of marriage, near Duffields - Age of husband, 23 - Age of wife, 20 - Both are Single - Both were born in Jefferson County, West Virginia - Both reside in Jefferson County, West Virginia. (Consent of bride's father in person.)

Link, Alexander and Nancy Dust (1) - June 6, 1816

Link, Alice N. and James B. Osburn (3) - November 11, 1871
    For further information see - Osburn, James B.

Link, Ann R. and John W. Harman (2) - (L) June 2, 1856

Link, Daniel and Maria B. Osbourn (2) - (L) November 11, 1858

Link, Elizabeth and George Fox (1) - August 9, 1807

Link, George C. and Kate Lee Hendricks (3) - August 17, 1880
    Place of marriage, Duffields - Age of husband, 22 - Age of wife, 19 - Both are Single - Both were born in Jefferson County, West Virginia - Both reside in Jefferson County, West Virginia. (Consent of bride's father in person.)

Link, H. T. and Eve Kate Osbourn (3) - February 28, 1878
    Place of marriage, Shepherdstown - Age of husband, 31 - Age of wife, 22 - Both are Single - Both were born in Jefferson County, West Virginia - Both reside in Jefferson County, West Virginia.

Link, J. Luther and Estellah Snader (3) - March 30, 1880
    Place of marriage, Unionville - Age of husband, 23 - Age of wife, 20 - Both are Single - Husband was born in Jefferson County, West Virginia - Wife was born in Frederick County, Maryland - Both reside in Jefferson County, West Virginia. (Consent of bride's father in person.)

Link, M. A. and Francis Jones (3) - March 10, 1868
    For further information see - Jones, Francis.

Link, M. C. (bride) and A. P. Rineheart (3) - December 5, 1867
    For further information see - Rineheart, A. P.

337

Link, Martha Virginia and Jacob S. Moler (3) - January 16, 1877
For further information see - Moler, Jacob S.

Link, Mary and Samuel Crowl, Jr. (1) - June 16, 1814

Link, Rebecca and Elias L. Crowell (1) - September 8, 1820

Link, Samuel V. and Ellen Lee Towner (2) - (L) December 3, 1859

Link, Sarah and David T. Nichols (3) - October 22, 1879
For further information see - Nichols, David T.

Link, Sarah M. and Daniel W. Hendricks (2) - (L) November 3, 1858

Link, T. J. and Jennie H. Maddox (3) - November 6, 1878
Age of husband, 34 - Age of wife, 22 - Both are Single - Both were
born in Jefferson County, West Virginia - Both reside in Jefferson
County, West Virginia.

Link, Thomas and Elizabeth Melvin (2) - (L) February 25, 1854

Link, Thomas O. and Fanny B. Bane (3) - December 7, 1880
Place of marriage, Duffields - Age of husband, 22 - Age of wife,
22 - Both are Single - Both were born in Jefferson County, West
Virginia - Both reside in Jefferson County, West Virginia.

Link, William C. and Emma K. Keesecker (3) - December 22, 1886
Place of marriage, Shepherdstown - Age of husband, 25 - Age of wife,
27 - Both are Single - Both were born in Jefferson County, West
Virginia - Both reside in Jefferson County, West Virginia.

Link, William H. and Martha M. Daniels (3) - February 21, 1878
Place of marriage, near Unionville - Age of husband, 23 - Age of
wife, 18 - Both are Single - Both were born in Jefferson County,
West Virginia - Both reside in Jefferson County, West Virginia.
(Consent of bride's father in writing.)

Linthiam, John T. and Martina Hayden (2) - (L) July 31, 1850

Linton, John Henry and Mrs. Mary Penwell (3) - December 31, 1874
Place of marriage, County - Age of husband, 30 - Age of wife, 32 -
Husband is a Widower - Wife is a Widow - Husband was born in
Frederick County, Maryland - Wife was born in Jefferson County, West
Virginia - Both reside in Jefferson County, West Virginia.

Linton, Margaret Ann and Jonathan Ingram (2) - (L) August 22, 1857

Linton, Samuel and Elizabeth Ingram (2) - (L) September 15, 1853

Linton, Samuel and Elizabeth Snyder (2) - (L) July 28, 1854

Lippitt, Armistead S. and Ada Isbell (3) - April 24, 1883
Place of marriage, near Ripon - Age of husband, 38 - Age of wife,
32 - Both are Single - Both were born in State of Virginia - Husband
resides in Clarke County, Virginia - Wife resides in Jefferson
County, West Virginia.

Lippitt, W. F., Jr. and Mary Craighill (3) - . August 3, 1887
    Place of marriage, Charlestown - Age of husband, 21 - Age of wife,
    21 - Both are Single - Both were born in Jefferson County, West
    Virginia - Both reside in Jefferson County, West Virginia.

Lipscomb, William C. and Mary J. C. Gallaher (1) - February 21, 1850

Lisk, D. E. (bride) and J. B. Hooff (3) - January 23, 1872
    For further information see - Hooff, J. B.

Little, Andrew J. and Ann Elizabeth Wood (3) - June 6, 1871
    Place of marriage, Jefferson County - Age of husband, 23 - Age of
    wife, 22 - Both are Single - Husband was born in Maryland - Wife was
    born in Virginia - Husband resides in Maryland - Wife resides in
    Jefferson County - Husband's parents are Charles A. and Mary S. -
    Wife's parents are Bennett and Mary - Occupation of husband is
    Butcher. (This record is crossed out in the original.)

Little, Andrew Jackson and Ann Elizabeth Wood (3) - July 5, 1871
    Place of marriage, Jefferson County - Age of husband, 23 - Age of
    wife, 22 - Both are Single - Husband was born at Baltimore,
    Maryland - Wife was born in Clarke, Virginia - Husband resides at
    Baltimore, Maryland - Wife resides in Jefferson County - Husband's
    parents are Charles A. and Mary S. - Wife's parents are Bennett and
    Mary - Occupation of husband is Butcher.

Little, Elizabeth and Alexander Fossett (1) - April 1825

Little, George and Mary Young (1) - April 19, 1810

Little, Mary E. and George B. Bruer (1) - January 5, 1832

Littlejohn, C. W. and Julia D. Chambers (3) - March 24, 1877
    Place of marriage, Harpers Ferry - Age of husband, 29 - Age of wife,
    27 - Both are Single - Both were born in Jefferson County, West
    Virginia - Both reside in Jefferson County, West Virginia.

Littlejohn, Rudolph S. and Julia A. Wernway (1) - October 21, 1845

Littlepage, H. B. and Emily C. Castleman (3) - November 18, 1869
    Place of marriage, Jefferson County - Age of husband, 28 - Age of
    wife, 19 - Husband was born in Virginia - Wife was born in Jefferson
    County - Husband resides in Virginia - Wife resides in Jefferson
    County. (Father consents in person of lady.)

Littleton, Addie and Howard Travener (3) - December 23, 1870
    For further information see - Travener, Howard.

Littleton, James T. and Laura B. Tavener (3) - January 28, 1875
    Place of marriage, Charlestown - Age of husband, 29 - Age of wife,
    23 - Both are Single - Husband was born in Clarke County, Virginia -
    Wife was born in Loudoun County, Virginia - Husband resides in
    Jefferson County, West Virginia - Wife resides in Clarke County,
    Virginia.

Littleton, Kate and Turner Marcus (3) - August 2, 1887
    For further information see - Marcus, Turner.

Littleton, Martha E. and James M. Heidwhol (3) - January 28, 1875
    For further information see - Heidwhol, James M.

Littleton, Mary L. and John W. Blackford (3) - January 14, 1874
    For further information see - Blackford, John W.

Littleton, Nannie F. and Thomas M. Shaull (3) - October 24, 1871
    For further information see - Shaull, Thomas M.

Littleton, Richard K. and Sarah K. O'Bannon (1) - January 4, 1831

Littleton, Rev. Thomas and Louisa Garrison (1) - December 17, 1818

Lloyd, Andrew J. and Mary A. Stewart (3) - December 1866
    Age of husband, 28 - Age of wife, 20 - Husband is a Widower - Wife is Single - Husband was born in Clarke County, Virginia - Wife was born in Jefferson County, West Virginia - Both reside in Jefferson County, West Virginia - Husband's parents are Henry and Sarah Lloyd - Wife's parents are B. W. and Patsie Stewart - Occupation of husband is Farmer.

Lloyd, Catharine S. and Abner Merican Chappell (3) - July 29, 1869
    For further information see - Chappell, Abner Merican.

Lloyd, Eveline E. and Joseph J. Burns (1) - August 29, 1829

Lloyd, Fanny T. and French M. Thompson (3) - September 6, 1881
    For further information see - Thompson, French M.

Lloyd, G. Frank and Mary P. Hammond (2) - (L) October 20, 1856

Lloyd, George W. and Roberta B. Henry (3) - January 3, 1889
    Place of marriage, Summit Point - Age of husband, 35 - Age of wife, 17 - Both are Single - Husband was born in Clarke County, Virginia - Wife was born in Frederick County, Virginia - Both reside in Jefferson County, West Virginia. (Consent of bride's father in writing.)

Lloyd, Hattie and T. A. Nicely (3) - January 22, 1889
    For further information see - Nicely, T. A.

Lloyd, J. H. and Lizzie Pitsnogle (3) - April 11, 1889
    Place of marriage, near Leetown - Age of husband, 27 - Age of wife, 27 - Both are Single - Husband was born in Clarke County, Virginia - Wife was born in Berkeley County, West Virginia - Both reside in Jefferson County, West Virginia.

Lloyd, James W. and Ada V. Show (3) - October 30, 1890
    Place of marriage, Charlestown - Age of husband, 33 - Age of wife, 22 - Both are Single - Husband was born in Clarke County, Virginia - Wife was born in Jefferson County, West Virginia - Both reside in Jefferson County, West Virginia.

Lloyd, Jennie and George Dunn (3) - February 22, 1882
    For further information see - Dunn, George.

Lloyd, John T. and Mary Nistrolson (3) - March 4, 1874
    Place of marriage, Harpers Ferry - Age of husband, 23. (This record is crossed out in the original.)

Lloyd, Lucinda and G. W. Smallwood (3) - December 16, 1871
    For further information see - Smallwood, G. W.

Lloyd, Mary Ann and Joseph Dulaney (1) -   May 6, 1834

Lloyd, Sarah Margaret and Patrick Ashby (3) -   June 15, 1875
    For further information see - Ashby, Patrick.

Lloyd, Virginia Davis and William M. Boltz (3) -   February 25, 1879
    For further information see - Boltz, William M.

Lock, Ben and Maria Welsh (1) -   February 3, 1842

Lock, Elisha and Sarah Ann Yost (1) -   June 10, 1844

Lock, Ella G. and Henry J. Eby (3) -   April 29, 1879
    For further information see - Eby, Henry J.

Lock, Ida and Christopher C. Henry (3) -   October 31, 1877
    For further information see - Henry, Christopher C.

Lock, Jane Amanda and Caleb Burns (2) -   (L) February 6, 1856

Lock, Jeanie D. and John M. Stickler (3) -   December 17, 1867
    For further information see - Stickler, John M.

Lock, John W. and Mary C. Lewis (3) -   June 1, 1882
    Place of marriage, Charlestown - Age of husband, 30 - Age of wife, 21 - Both are Single - Husband was born in Jefferson County, West Virginia - Wife was born in Berkeley County, West Virginia - Husband resides in Jefferson County, West Virginia - Wife resides in Jefferson County.

Lock, John W. and Emma Lashhorn (3) -   October 9, 1884
    Place of marriage, Charlestown - Age of husband, 52 - Age of wife, 29 - Husband is a Widower - Wife is Single - Husband was born in Jefferson County, West Virginia - Wife was born in Berkeley County - Both reside in Jefferson County.

Lock, Julia Ann and Henry Beahm (1) -   December 18, 1833

Lock, Kate and James William Manuel (3) -   July 4, 1878
    For further information see - Manuel, James William.

Lock, Lucie M. and Charles G. Skinner (3) -   January 14, 1874
    For further information see - Skinner, Charles G.

Lock, Maria and Walter Shirley (1) -   July 22, 1827

Lock, Martha E. and John Burns (2) -   (L) March 29, 1852

Lock, Martha E. and John Burns (1) -   March 31, 1852

Lock, Mary C. and John D. Line (2) -   (L) June 2, 1852

Lock, Mary F. and James H. Hughes (3) -   October 28, 1880
    For further information see - Hughes, James H.

Lock, Mary Lee and William Cox (3) -   October 29, 1882
    For further information see - Cox, William.

Lock, Remington S. and Rebecca Ann Shaull (2) -   (L) December 19, 1853

341

Lock, Sarah C. and Washington P. Young (1) -   December 30, 1849

Lock, Sarah Ellen and Joseph Morrow (1) -   November 15, 1832

Lock, Susan R. and William C. Carrol (3) -   February 22, 1866
    For further information see - Carrol, William C.

Lock, Uriah and Mary Heidwohl (1) -   April 6, 1831

Lock, Virginia and Warren Eby (1) -   December 4, 1849

Lock, Virginia M. and Edwin H. Miller (3) -   October 9, 1883
    For further information see - Miller, Edwin H.

Lock, Virginia R. and John Ogden Murray (3) -   June 11, 1872
    For further information see - Murray, John Ogden.

Lock, Zachariah and Margaret Ellen McDaniel (1) -   April 10, 1848

Locke, America and William J. Anderson (3) -   April 27, 1875
    For further information see - Anderson, William J.

Locke, Oregon and William Schonkee (3) -   June 14, 1865

Locke, Sally R. and Jacob M. Stickle (3) -   April 1, 1880
    For further information see - Stickle, Jacob M.

Lockman, __?__ and Mrs. Farrell (widow) (1) -   1841

Logan, Joseph and Elizabeth Murray (3) -   October 11, 1869
    Place of marriage, Jefferson County - Age of husband, 38 - Age of
    wife, 30 - Both were born in Virginia - Both reside in Jefferson
    County.

Logie, John C. and Anne A. Sloan (2) -   (L) November 18, 1851

Logie, John C. and Anne A. Sloan (1) -   November 19, 1851

Loman, Benjamin and Ellen A. Peacher (2) -   (L) July 21, 1852

Loman, Benjamin and Ellen A. Peacher (1) -   July 22, 1852

Loman, Ellen V. and James A. Mitchell (3) -   August 31, 1875
    For further information see - Mitchell, James A.

Loman, Emma Eugenia and Charles H. Briggs (3) -   May 20, 1878
    For further information see - Briggs, Charles H.

Loman, Thomas Hessey and Clara Belle Peacher (3) -   December 14, 1880
    Place of marriage, Harpers Ferry - Age of husband, 29 - Age of wife,
    23 - Both are Single - Husband was born in Jefferson County, West
    Virginia - Wife was born at Muscatine, Iowa - Both reside in
    Jefferson County, West Virginia.

Loman, Virginia I. and Elijah R. Wachter (3) -   February 19, 1867
    For further information see - Wachter, Elijah R.

Lomax, Arthur (cold.) Lucy Gaiter (nee Branson). (3) - January 11, 1883
    Place of marriage, Charlestown - Age of husband, 32 - Age of wife,
    29 - Husband is Single - Wife is a Widow - Husband was born in
    Fauquier County, Virginia - Wife was born in Jefferson County, West
    Virginia - Both reside in Jefferson County, West Virginia.

Long, Benjamin F. and Nannie R. Needy (3) - March 13, 1879
    Place of marriage, near Kearneysville - Age of husband, 26 - Age of
    wife, 20 - Both are Single - Husband was born in Loudoun County,
    Virginia - Wife was born in Jefferson County, West Virginia -
    Husband resides in Frederick County, Maryland - Wife resides in
    Jefferson County, West Virginia. (Consent of bride's parents
    certified by G. A. Stewart.)

Long, Hester and Thomas Wilders (1) - December 19, 1824

Long, John and Mary C. Lece (3) - February 12, 1883
    Place of marriage, Shenandoah Junction - Age of husband, 32 - Age of
    wife, 23 - Both are Single - Husband was born in Maryland - Wife was
    born in Virginia - Both reside in Jefferson County, West Virginia.

Long, Lararaina and John H. Swope (3) - (1870)
    For further information see - Swope, John H.

Long, Mary M. and George Houtt (1) - March 9, 1815

Long, Sally and George Payne (1) - June 12, 1827

Long, William and Mary Ann Griggs (widow of Thomas Griggs) (2) -
    (L) January 7, 1854

Longbrake, John H. and Sophia D. Miller (3) - May 27, 1869
    Place of marriage, Jefferson County - Age of husband, 25 - Age of
    wife, 22 - Husband was born in Ohio - Wife was born in West
    Virginia - Husband resides in Jefferson County - Wife resides in
    West Virginia.

Longerbeam, Elizabeth and Barney Painter (3) - March 29, 1876
    For further information see - Painter, Barney.

Longerbeam, Elizabeth (cold.) John Strother (3) - September 14, 1878
    For further information see - Strother, John.

Longerbeam, John and Julia Dillow (3) - February 8, 1885
    Place of marriage, Blue Ridge Mountain - Age of husband, 40 - Age of
    wife, 26 - Husband is a Widower - Wife is Single - Husband was born
    in Clarke County, Virginia - Wife was born in Jefferson County, West
    Virginia - Both reside in Jefferson County, West Virginia.

Longerbeam, Preston and Jane Elizabeth Larue (3) - October 21, 1886
    Place of marriage, Blue Ridge Mountain - Age of husband, 21 - Age of
    wife, 16 - Both are Single - Both were born in Jefferson County,
    West Virginia - Both reside in Jefferson County, West Virginia.
    (Consent of bride's father in person.)

Longerbeam, Rebecca Elizabeth and Charles Engle (3) - July 16, 1885
    For further information see - Engle, Charles.

Longerbeam, Sarah Birdie and Samuel H. Penwell (3) - October 21, 1886
    For further information see - Penwell, Samuel H.

Longerbeam, Thomas and Eliza Ainsworth (2) -   (L) January 8, 1856

Lookout, Thomas and __?__ Dobbins (3) -   (1867)
Age of husband, 32 - Age of wife, 21 - Both are Single - Husband was born in Russell County, Virginia - Wife was born in Clarke County, Virginia - Husband resides in Rockbridge County, Virginia - Wife resides in Jefferson County, West Virginia - Husband's parents are Thomas and Julia - Wife's parents are Samuel - Occupation of husband is Farmer. (Father gives his consent in person.)

Lot, Francis and John Small (1) -   May 17, 1832

Lott, Mary and John Young (1) -   September 8, 1808

Loudan, Eliza J. and James W. Hoffman (3) -   February 5, 1884
For further information see - Hoffman, James W.

Louden, Daniel E. and Edna E. Hoffman (3) -   June 3, 1890
Place of marriage, Shepherdstown - Age of husband, 26 - Age of wife, 21 - Both are Single - Both were born in Jefferson County, West Virginia - Both reside in Jefferson County, West Virginia.

Louden, Mary Ellen and Jacob Potts (3) -   January 23, 1873
For further information see - Potts, Jacob.

Loudon, Daniel and Eliza Smith (3) -   August 20, 1865
Place of marriage, near Rineheart's S. House - Age of husband, 19 years - Age of wife, 31 years - Both are Single - Both were born in Jefferson County - Both reside in Jefferson County - Husband's parents are William and Mary Loudon - Wife's parents are Henry and (nee) Ruth Wright - Occupation of husband is Laborer.

Loudon, Thomas and Mary Walman (1) -   September 14, 1815

Loudoun, Samuel J. and Sally A. Hoffman (3) -   June 15, 1882
Place of marriage, Martinsburg - Age of husband, 23 - Age of wife, 25 - Both are Single - Both were born in Jefferson County, West Virginia - Husband resides in Jefferson County, West Virginia - Wife resides in Jefferson County.

Louis, Annie and Primus Hite (3) -   July 21, 1866
For further information see - Hite, Primus.

Lovett, Etta (cold.) John H. Hill (3) -   January 1, 1889
For further information see - Hill, John H.

Lovett, Jeremiah (colored) Nancy Lucas (3) -   (1870)
Age of husband, 25 - Age of wife, 21 - Both were born in Virginia - Both reside in Jefferson County.

Lovett, Jessee (cold.) Jane Hoagins (3) -   January 2, 1871
Place of marriage, Smithfield - Age of husband, 50 - Age of wife, 40 - Husband is a Widower - Wife is Single - Husband was born in Jefferson County - Wife was born in Frederick County - Both reside in Jefferson County - Husband's parents are Robert and Juda Lovett - Occupation of husband is Farmer.

Lovett, Jessee and Jane Hoagins (3) - January 2, 1871
  Place of marriage, Smithfield - Age of husband, 50 - Age of wife,
  40 - Husband is a Widower - Wife is Single - Husband was born in
  Jefferson - Wife was born in Virginia - Both reside in Jefferson
  County - Husband's parents are Robert and Juda - Occupation of
  husband is Farmer. (This record is crossed out in the original.)

Lovett, Julia V. (cold.) Alex Freeman (3) - June 3, 1889
  For further information see - Freeman, Alex.

Lovett, Margaretta (cold.) Allen Preston Daniel (3) - June 16, 1886
  For further information see - Daniel, Allen Preston.

Lovett, Maria E. (cold.) William B. Evans (3) - December 27, 1876
  For further information see - Evans, William B.

Lowndes, Francis and Agelta. Craighill (1) - November 6, 1817

Lowndes, Harriet and Samuel Scollay (1) - January 21, 1823

Lowry, Horace (cold.) Martha Whiting (3) - September 9, 1874
  Place of marriage, Charlestown - Age of husband, 28 - Age of wife,
  24 - Both are Single - Both were born in Jefferson County, West
  Virginia - Both reside in Jefferson County, West Virginia.

Lowry, Margaret (cold.) Gabriel Mitchell (3) - April 19, 1888
  For further information see - Mitchell, Gabriel.

Lowry, Mary W. and Daniel Morgan (1) - October 22, 1806

Lowry, Newton and Levina Rust (3) - March 17, 1875
  Place of marriage, Kearneysville - Age of husband, 24 - Age of wife,
  23 - Both are Single - Both were born in Jefferson County, West
  Virginia - Both reside in Jefferson County, West Virginia.

Loyd, Sarah Margaret and A. D. Myers (3) - August 18, 1885
  For further information see - Myers, A. D.

Lucas, Anna Elizabeth and William H. Anderson (3) - June 15, 1882
  For further information see - Anderson, William H.

Lucas, Archie (cold.) Mary Ross (3) - May 15, 1886
  Place of marriage, Charlestown - Age of husband, 25 - Age of wife,
  21 - Both are Single - Husband was born in Jefferson County, West
  Virginia - Wife was born in Clarke County, Virginia - Both reside in
  Jefferson County, West Virginia.

Lucas, Bearsheba (free mixtures) John Welcome (1) - November 23, 1826

Lucas, Bettie P. and Robert R. Lucas (3) - October 31, 1866
  For further information see - Lucas, Robert R.

Lucas, Charity (cold.) Philip Jordan (3) - January 10, 1878
  For further information see - Jordan, Philip.

345

Lucas, Charles (cold.) Katy T. Washington (3) -   March 4, 1884
    Place of marriage, Charlestown - Age of husband, 23 - Age of wife,
    18 - Both are Single - Husband was born in Jefferson County, West
    Virginia - Wife was born at Washington City - Both reside in
    Jefferson County, West Virginia. (Consent of bride's father in
    person.)

Lucas, Charles C. and Frances T. Craighill (3) -   February 28, 1889
    Place of marriage, Charlestown - Age of husband, 28 - Age of wife,
    28 - Both are Single - Husband was born at Muscatine, Iowa - Wife
    was born in Jefferson County, West Virginia - Both reside in
    Jefferson County, West Virginia.

Lucas, Elizabeth and William McMurran (1) -   February 1832

Lucas, Fannie V. and Robert M. Lucas (3) -   March 23, 1876
    For further information see - Lucas, Robert M.

Lucas, Flavous and Emily Edwards (3) -   November 23, 1865
    Place of marriage, near Bolivar, Jefferson County - Age of husband,
    23 - Age of wife, 23 - Both are Single - Husband was born in Loudoun
    County, Virginia - Wife was born in Jefferson County - Both reside
    in Jefferson County, West Virginia - Husband's parents are Louis and
    Jemina Lucas - Wife's parents are Edmund and Elizabeth Lucas -
    Occupation of husband is Blacksmith.

Lucas, John A. and Martha Ann Porter (3) -   April 11, 1877
    Place of marriage, Shepherdstown - Age of husband, 25 - Age of wife,
    23 - Both are Single - Husband was born in Jefferson County, West
    Virginia - Wife was born in Washington County, Maryland - Both
    reside in Jefferson County, West Virginia.

Lucas, Kate H. and William Butler (3) -   April 23, 1873
    For further information see - Butler, William.

Lucas, Lewis C. and Mary M. Lucas (3) -   October 29, 1874
    Place of marriage, Charlestown - Age of husband, 28 - Age of wife,
    28 - Both are Single - Both were born in Jefferson County, West
    Virginia - Both reside in Jefferson County, West Virginia.

Lucas, Louisa (cold.) Logan Robinson (3) -   December 27, 1876
    For further information see - Robinson, Logan.

Lucas, Lulie and William R. Miller (3) -   January 4, 1877
    For further information see - Miller, William R.

Lucas, Maggie E. and Isaac Jones (3) -   December 14, 1871
    For further information see - Jones, Isaac.

Lucas, Manuel (cold.) Eviline Thomas (3) -   March 29, 1879
    Place of marriage, Charlestown - Age of husband, 45 - Age of wife,
    30 - Husband is a Widower - Wife is Single - Both were born in
    Jefferson County, West Virginia - Both reside in Jefferson County,
    West Virginia.

Lucas, Mary (cold.) John W. Shorts (3) -   September 15, 1887
    For further information see - Shorts, John W.

Lucas, Mary E. and Joseph A. Craighill (1) -   November 22, 1852

Lucas, Mary E. and Parker H. Strode (3) - January 23, 1866
    For further information see - Strode, Parker H.

Lucas, Mary Emeline and Joseph A. Craighill (2) - (L) November 22, 1852

Lucas, Mary M. and Lewis C. Lucas (3) - October 29, 1874
    For further information see - Lucas, Lewis C.

Lucas, Nancy (colored) Jeremiah Lovett (3) - (1870)
    For further information see - Lovett, Jeremiah.

Lucas, Nancy (cold.) James King (3) - December 19, 1878
    For further information see - King, James.

Lucas, Oscar M. and Kate S. Crane (3) - December 1, 1869
    Place of marriage, Jefferson County - Age of husband, 27 - Age of wife, 25 - Both were born in Jefferson County - Both reside in Jefferson County.

Lucas, Philip (cold.) Alice Hart (3) - December 3, 1882
    Place of marriage, Shepherdstown - Age of husband, 27 - Age of wife, 21 - Both are Single - Husband was born in Frederick County, Virginia - Wife was born in Jefferson County, West Virginia - Both reside in Jefferson County, West Virginia.

Lucas, Robert M. and Fannie V. Lucas (3) - March 23, 1876
    Place of marriage, Martinsburg - Age of husband, 22 - Age of wife, 22 - Both are Single - Both were born in Jefferson County, West Virginia - Both reside in Jefferson County, West Virginia.

Lucas, Robert R. and Bettie P. Lucas (3) - October 31, 1866
    Place of marriage, Dr. R. A. Lucas', Jefferson County - Age of husband, 24 - Age of wife, 23 - Both are Single - Both were born in Jefferson County, West Virginia - Both reside in Jefferson County, West Virginia - Husband's parents are Edward and Mary E. Lucas - Wife's parents are R. A. and Catharine A. Lucas. - Occupation of husband is Farmer.

Lucas, Sally E. and Everett W. Bedinger (2) - (L) May 31, 1852

Lucas, Tina (cold.) Jefferson Backus (3) - March 22, 1888
    For further information see - Backus, Jefferson.

Lucas, William and Virginia Ann Bedinger (1) - July 13, 1830

Lucas, William (cold.) Lucy A. Hutchinson (3) - October 20, 1886
    Place of marriage, near Charlestown - Age of husband, 25 - Age of wife, 23 - Both are Single. - Husband was born in Jefferson County - Wife was born in Amherst County, Virginia - Both reside in Jefferson County.

Luck, Daniel H. and Georigna Wilson (3) - December 28, 1869
    Place of marriage, Jefferson County - Age of husband, 23 - Age of wife, 18 - Husband was born in Loudoun County - Wife was born in Jefferson County - Both reside in Jefferson County. (Consent of mother in writing.)

Luckett, Anne and Alfred Johnson (3) - December 28, 1871
    For further information see - Johnson, Alfred.

Luckett, Benjamin (cold.) Betty Murray (3) -   July 26, 1887
    Place of marriage, near Charlestown - Age of husband, 29 - Age of wife, 23 - Both are Single - Both were born in Jefferson County, West Virginia - Both reside in Jefferson County, West Virginia.

Luckett, Eugene (cold.) Lizzie Newman (3) -   June 11, 1889
    Place of marriage, Charlestown - Age of husband, 25 - Age of wife, 21 - Both are Single - Both were born in Jefferson County, West Virginia - Both reside in Jefferson County, West Virginia.

Luckett, Fanny (cold.) Samuel McDaniel (3) -   November 10, 1875
    For further information see - McDaniel, Samuel.

Luckett, Henry (cold.) Mary V. Brown (3) -   June 7, 1888
    Place of marriage, Halltown - Age of husband, 28 - Age of wife, 26 - Husband is Single - Wife is Divorced - Both were born in Jefferson County, West Virginia - Both reside in Jefferson County, West Virginia.

Luckett, Robert (cold.) Delphry Reeler (3) -   January 6, 1881
    Place of marriage, Charlestown - Age of husband, 22 - Age of wife, 18 - Both are Single - Both were born in Jefferson County, West Virginia - Both reside in Jefferson County, West Virginia. (Consent of bride's father in person.)

Luckey, John and Ann Harding (1) -   July 22, 1824

Lucklet, Lucy (col.) Jerry Garthier (3) -   January 4, 1868
    For further information see - Garthier, Jerry.

Ludwick, George F. and Phebe F. Smith (1) -   December 10, 1829

Luke, John W. and Ann Louisa Grantham (2) -   (L) November 17, 1852

Lunn, William and Annie F. Morrell (3) -   January 21, 1890
    Place of marriage, Harpers Ferry - Age of husband, 41 - Age of wife, 30 - Both are Single - Husband was born in Spottsylvania County, Virginia - Wife was born in Jefferson County, West Virginia - Both reside in Jefferson County, West Virginia.

Lupton, Elizabeth A. and William H. Miller (3) -   August 22, 1869
    For further information see - Miller, William H.

Lupton, Mary E. and James H. Stickley (3) -   July 19, 1889
    For further information see - Stickley, James H.

Lupton, Sarah and Josiah Yerkes (1) -   December 12, 1805

Lyder, Julia and Charles H. Clarke (3) -   December 27, 1866
    For further information see - Clarke, Charles H.

Lyle, Elenor and Armstead Beckham (1) -   October 23, 1814

Lyle, John and Margaret Mark (1) -   September 21, 1802

Lynch, George B. and Fannie Cromwell (3) -   November 29, 1882
    Place of marriage, Harpers Ferry - Age of husband, 26 - Age of wife, 23 - Both are Single - Both were born in Jefferson County, West Virginia - Both reside in Jefferson County, West Virginia.

Lynch, Maurice and Ann Foley (1) - June 5, 1850
Lynn, Nehemiah C. and Mary E. Norris (2) - (L) January 6, 1854

Macbee, Allen and Rebecca Riley (1) -   February 4, 1819

Macfarland, Jane S. and William McP. Fuller (2) -   (L) March 24, 1859

Macfarland, John M. and Jane S. Douglass (2) -   (L) May 27, 1853

Macfarland, John M. and Agnes L. Forrest (3) -   December 10, 1878
    Place of marriage, Charlestown - Age of husband, 22 - Age of wife,
    19 - Both are Single - Husband was born in Jefferson County, West
    Virginia - Wife was born at Staunton, Virginia - Both reside in
    Jefferson County, West Virginia.

Macgill, Charles G. W. and Louisa T. McEndree (2) -   (L) September 19, 1859

Machbee, Ninian R. and Massey Ledwick (1) -   August 25, 1814

Mack, William and Mary Ellen Winkoop (2) -   (L) July 18, 1853

Mack, William and Mary Ellen Wynkoop (1) -   July 18, 1853

Mackenzie, Mrs. Susan Elizabeth and Marinas Lang (2) -   (L) November 26, 1852

Mackey, James William (cold.) Rosa Hall (3) -   December 24, 1873
    Place of marriage, near Harpers Ferry - Age of husband, 22 - Age of
    wife, 21 - Both are Single - Husband was born in Berkeley County,
    West Virginia - Wife was born in Jefferson County, West Virginia -
    Both reside in Jefferson County, West Virginia.

Mackey, Robert and Sarah Washington (3) -   February 2, 1871
    Place of marriage, Shepherdstown - Age of husband, 27 - Age of wife,
    21 - Both are Single - Both were born in Jefferson County - Both
    reside in Jefferson County - Husband's parents are David and Maria -
    Wife's parents are James - Occupation of husband is Paper Manufactor.

Mackey, Rosa (cold.) Nelson Twyman (3) -   December 27, 1876
    For further information see - Twyman, Nelson.

Macoughtry, F. S. (bride) and S. F. White (3) -   June 25, 1867
    For further information see - White, S. F.

Macoughtry, T. M. and Mary Bates (3) -   May 13, 1874
    Place of marriage, Jefferson County - Age of husband, 26 - Age of
    wife, 23 - Both are Single - Both were born in Jefferson County,
    West Virginia - Both reside in Jefferson County, West Virginia.

Maddex, L. D. and Margaret Coleman (3) -   December 20, 1876
    Place of marriage, Duffields - Age of husband, 25 - Age of wife,
    21 - Both are Single - Husband was born in Clarke County, Virginia -
    Wife was born in Jefferson County, West Virginia - Both reside in
    Jefferson County, West Virginia.

Maddex, Mary Elizabeth and Charles W. Brantner (3) -   December 21, 1876
    For further information see - Brantner, Charles W.

Maddex, Turner Wysong and Ellanora Shaner (3) -   September 7, 1886
    Place of marriage, Charlestown - Age of husband, 25 - Age of wife,
    18 - Both are Single - Both were born in Jefferson County - Both
    reside in Jefferson County, West Virginia.

Maddox, Ann and Washington Duval (1) -   December 5, 1833

Maddox, Catharine and Joseph Mullen (1) -   May 23, 1833

Maddox, Jennie H. and T. J. Link (3) -   November 6, 1878
   For further information see - Link, T. J.

Maddox, Mary F. and Francis A. Simpson (3) -   September 18, 1866
   For further information see - Simpson, Francis A.

Maddox, Sarah Elizabeth and Michael P. Crowl (3) -   December 14, 1875
   For further information see - Crowl, Michael P.

Mader, Mary and John Berger (2) -   (L) July 26, 1850

Madison, Bettie (cold.) Thomas Queen (3) -   October 15, 1890
   For further information see - Queen, Thomas.

Madison, John and Emily Nelson (1) -   July 5, 1826

Madison, Mary Ellen (cold.) James H. Young (3) -   November 15, 1890
   For further information see - Young, James H.

Madison, Teresa Ann and J. M. Crawford (2) -   (L) January 19, 1861

Magaeh, David and Louisa Mash (3) -   April 15, 1880
   Place of marriage, Shepherdstown - Age of husband, 28 - Age of wife,
   24 - Both are Single - Husband was born in Jefferson County, West
   Virginia - Wife was born in Louisiana - Both reside in Jefferson
   County, West Virginia.

Magaha, Mary and Samuel J. Badger (3) -   April 29, 1874
   For further information see - Badger, Samuel J.

Magaha, Wilson H. and Hannah M. Gray (3) -   November 16, 1869
   Place of marriage, Jefferson County - Age of husband, 32 - Age of
   wife, 22 - Husband was born in Virginia - Wife was born in Jefferson
   County - Both reside in Jefferson County. (Age of lady sworn to by
   her brother W. Gray.)

Magill, Robert (cold.) Sarah Blue (3) -   March 20, 1879
   Place of marriage, Charlestown - Age of husband, 30 - Age of wife,
   24 - Both are Single - Husband was born in Clarke County, Virginia -
   Wife was born in Jefferson County - Both reside in Jefferson County,
   West Virginia.

Magowan, William and Catharine Ann Ott (1) -   December 31, 1832

Magruder, R. L. and Minnie J. Hall (3) -   December 19, 1883
   Place of marriage, near or at Shepherdstown - Age of husband, 34 -
   Age of wife, 28 - Both are Single - Wife was born in Jefferson
   County, West Virginia - Husband resides at Washington, D. C. -Wife
   resides in Jefferson County, West Virginia.

Magruder, W. S. and Mary B. Warfield (3) -   October 2, 1877
   Place of marriage, near Shepherdstown - Age of husband, 38 - Age of
   wife, 24 - Husband is a Widower - Wife is Single - Husband was born
   in Jefferson County, West Virginia - Wife was born in Maryland -
   Both reside in Jefferson County, West Virginia.

Mahaffy, Nancy Jane and Joseph Henry Rutherford (2) -   (L) November 2, 1857

351

Mahoney, Sarah and Jacob Piper (1) - October 6, 1848

Mahony, James and Mary Jane Roby (2) - (L) February 2, 1856

Mahony, Mrs. Margaret and Patrick Devlin (2) - (L) July 26, 1851

Mahony, Mary and Jonah Watson (1) - August 30, 1832

Mahony, Rodney and Rachael Bateman (3) - August 7, 1870
    Age of husband, 22 - Age of wife, 18 - Husband was born in Loudoun
    County, Virginia - Wife was born in Jefferson County, Virginia -
    Husband resides in Virginia - Wife resides in Jefferson County.

Mahorney, Rachael (cold.) Ross Nelson (3) - May 9, 1888
    For further information see - Nelson, Ross.

Mainefield, Samuel (cold.) Hanna Newman (3) - August 11, 1888
    Place of marriage, Harpers Ferry - Age of husband, 53 - Age of wife,
    47 - Both are Single - Both were born in Jefferson County, West
    Virginia - Both reside in Jefferson County, West Virginia.

Malatt, Isaac and Emily Jane Stanley (3) - April 19, 1883
    Place of marriage, Charlestown - Age of husband, 50 - Age of wife,
    33 - Husband is a Widower - Wife is Single - Husband was born in
    Washington County, Maryland - Wife was born in State of Virginia -
    Both reside in Jefferson County, West Virginia.

Malatt, Susan and Martin L. Griffith (3) - November 30, 1879
    For further information see - Griffith, Martin L.

Malleory, Eliza D. and Matthias Spangler (1) - May 6, 1824

Malleory, Thomas and Mary Taylor (1) - June 28, 1834

Mallory, Mary and Thomas Ernshaw (1) - 1814

Malone, Nancy and John Addy (1) - June 8, 1815

Malony, Ellen and William Malony (2) - (L) January 20, 1852

Malony, William and Ellen Malony (2) - (L) January 20, 1852

Mandell, Elizabeth and George Jacobs (1) - May 27, 1823

Manier, Daniel and Sarah McCormick (1) - May 10, 1832

Manning, Annie J. (nee Matthews) and Thomas E. Rodrick (3) - September 7, 1889
    For further information see - Rodrick, Thomas E.

Manning, Lucy E. and A Holmes Berry (3) - October 13, 1874
    For further information see - Berry, A. Holmes.

Manning, Mary Monroe and William Beale Willis (2) - (L) October 25, 1864
    For further information see - Willis, William Beale.

Manning, Thomas J. and M. Virginia McCormick (2) - (L) May 12, 1856

Manning, Virginia and Taylor Smith (3) - August 26, 1869
    For further information see - Smith, Taylor.

Mansfield, Jane and William Rafferty (3) -- April 24, 1883
    For further information see - Rafferty, William.

Manuel, Alzier T. and James H. Hoock (2) - (L) February 13, 1854

Manuel, Annie D. and John C. Hammer (3) - May 17, 1881
    For further information see - Hammer, John C.

Manuel, Annie Nora and David Jarvis (3) - June 12, 1884
    For further information see - Jarvis, David.

Manuel, C. C. and Georgiana Walters (3) - January 4, 1873
    Place of marriage, Shepherdstown, Jefferson County, West Virginia - Age of husband, 28 - Age of wife, 24 - Both are Single - Husband was born in Prince William County, Virginia - Wife was born in Berkeley County, West Virginia - Both reside in Jefferson County, West Virginia - Husband's parents are John and Elizabeth - Wife's parents are James and Sarah Walters - Occupation of husband is Farmer.

Manuel, Caroline Virginia and David L. Whittington (3) - December 28, 1875
    For further information see - Whittington, David L.

Manuel, Clema and James Chapman (3) - July 22, 1875
    For further information see - Chapman, James.

Manuel, Edward T. and Mary Ellen Underdonk (3) - March 28, 1871
    Place of marriage, Jefferson County - Age of husband, 23 - Age of wife, 19 - Both are Single - Both were born in Jefferson County - Both reside in Jefferson County - Husband's parents are W. E. and Mary F. - Wife's parents are Henry and May J. - Occupation of husband is Paper Manufacturer. (Mother's consent by uncle, J. H. Hill.)

Manuel, Elizabeth and James G. Russell (3) - October 5, 1871
    For further information see - Russell, James G.

Manuel, Emma J. and Robert B. Lewis (3) -- August 30, 1889
    For further information see - Lewis, Robert B.

Manuel, Fannie L. and W. H. Peacher (3) - June 26, 1889
    For further information see - Peacher, W. H.

Manuel, George W. and Annie Jane Mathews (3) - May 24, 1877
    Place of marriage, Harpers Ferry - Age of husband, 26 - Age of wife, 21 - Both are Single - Both were born in Jefferson County, West Virginia - Both reside in Jefferson County, West Virginia.

Manuel, Ida and Walter J. Potts (3) - October 21, 1890
    For further information see - Potts, Walter J.

Manuel, James H. and Lucy Allingsworth (3) - August 23, 1880
    Place of marriage, Charlestown - Age of husband, 21 - Age of wife, 21 - Both are Single - Both were born in Jefferson County, West Virginia - Both reside in Jefferson County, West Virginia.

Manuel, James T. and Julia Ann Wealth (3) - July 11, 1869
    Place of marriage, Jefferson County - Age of husband, 39 - Age of wife, 22 - Husband was born in Virginia - Wife was born in West Virginia - Husband resides in Jefferson County - Wife resides in West Virginia.

353

Manuel, James William and Kate Lock (3) - July 4, 1878
  Place of marriage, Charlestown - Age of husband, 23 - Age of wife,
  21 - Both are Single - Husband was born in Rappahannock County,
  Virginia - Wife was born in Jefferson County, West Virginia - Both
  reside in Jefferson County, West Virginia.

Manuel, John and Ellen Edwards (3) - January 25, 1872
  Place of marriage, Jefferson County, West Virginia - Age of husband,
  22 - Age of wife, 21 - Both are Single - Both were born in Jefferson
  County, Virginia - Both reside in Jefferson County, West Virginia -
  Husband's parents are John and Mary - Wife's parents are Thomas and
  Ellen - Occupation of husband is Farmer.

Manuel, John A. and Jane Frances Barron (2) - (L) December 26, 1859

Manuel, Josephine and William Graham (3) - June 12, 1879
  For further information see - Graham, William.

Manuel, Josephine and Robert L. Ridgeway (3) - September 24, 1883
  For further information see - Ridgeway, Robert L.

Manuel, M. E. and Thomas Shipway (3) - April 25, 1872
  For further information see - Shipway, Thomas.

Manuel, Mary E. and J. M. Winkler (3) - December 30, 1873
  For further information see - Winkler, J. M.

Manuel, Richard A. and Verdie Drish (3) - September 25, 1889
  Place of marriage, Charlestown - Age of husband, 23 - Age of wife,
  23 - Both are Single - Both were born in Jefferson County, West
  Virginia - Both reside in Jefferson County, West Virginia.

Manuel, Sarah Catherine and John W. Rannels (3) - August 26, 1879
  For further information see - Rannels, John W.

Manuel, William E. and Alice Webb (3) - July 24, 1883
  Place of marriage, Harpers Ferry or Bolivar - Age of husband, 25 -
  Age of wife, 22 - Both are Single - Both were born in Jefferson
  County, West Virginia - Both reside in Jefferson County, West
  Virginia.

Manuel, William F. and Anna P. Whitson (2) - (L) December 13, 1855

March, James H. and Laura A. Eby (2) - (L) March 2, 1851

Marcus, J. C. and Bertie Trenary (3) - January 27, 1885
  Place of marriage, Charlestown - Age of husband, 24 - Age of wife,
  22 - Both are Single - Both were born in Loudoun County - Husband
  resides in Loudoun County - Wife resides in Jefferson County, West
  Virginia.

Marcus, Turner and Kate Littleton (3) - August 2, 1887
  Place of marriage, Jefferson County - Age of husband, 21 - Age of
  wife, 21 - Both are Single - Husband was born in Virginia - Wife was
  born in Jefferson County, West Virginia - Husband resides in Loudoun
  County, Virginia - Wife resides in Jefferson County, West Virginia.

Mark, Andrew J. and Mary V. Aisquith (3) -　　　　　　　　February 17, 1869
　　Place of marriage, Jefferson County - Age of husband, 26 - Age of
　　wife, 25 - Both are Single - Husband was born in Alabama - Wife was
　　born in Jefferson County - Husband resides in Louisiana - Wife
　　resides in Jefferson County - Husband's parents are Andrew - Wife's
　　parents are S. William and May - Occupation of husband is Planter.

Mark, John and Elizabeth Menser (1) -　　　　　　　　　　　　April 1824

Mark, Margaret and John Lyle (1) -　　　　　　　　　　September 21, 1802

Mark, Samuel and Ann S. North (1) -　　　　　　　　　　　　March 3, 1808

Markell, James T. and Elmira Swearingen (1) -　　　　　November 7, 1839

Markell, John S. and Emma Walling (1) -　　　　　　　November 19, 1844

Markle, Samuel T. and Kate L. Crim (3) -　　　　　　December 28, 1882
　　Place of marriage, Bride's Residence - Age of husband, 42 - Age of
　　wife, 24 - Husband is a Widower - Wife is Single - Husband was born
　　in Berkeley County, West Virginia - Wife was born in Berkeley
　　County - Both reside in Jefferson County, West Virginia.

Markwood, Catherine and Samuel Rust (1) -　　　　　　December 28, 1823

Marlatt, Charlotte Rebecca and John H. Deener (2) -　(L) May 12, 1853
　　(Witness, James H. House.)

Marlatt, Cora E. and T. A. Pritchard (3) -　　　　　　December 21, 1887
　　For further information see - Pritchard, T. A.

Marlatt, Emma J. and Frank A. Cromwell (3) -　　　　　　April 24, 1889
　　For further information see - Cromwell, Frank A.

Marlatt, Hannah Frances and Jonathan C. Miller (2) - (L) November 28, 1857

Marlatt, Ida and Erwin Bitner (3) -　　　　　　　　　　　March 31, 1890
　　For further information see - Bitner, Erwin.

Marlatt, Mary Elizabeth and Baldwin Johnston (2) -　(L) February 11, 1854

Marlett, James W. and Ann M. Stop (3) -　　　　　　　　　　　　　(1869)
　　Age of husband, 35 - Age of wife, 22 - Husband was born in Jefferson
　　County, West Virginia - Wife was born in Maryland - Both reside in
　　Jefferson County, West Virginia.

Marlow, George W. and Mary Catherine Urton (3) -　　　　June 24, 1875
　　Place of marriage, Charlestown - Age of husband, 34 - Age of wife,
　　27 - Both are Single - Both were born in Loudoun County, Virginia -
　　Both reside in Jefferson County, West Virginia.

Marlow, Joseph W. and Florence Dailey (3) -　　　　　February 27, 1884
　　Place of marriage, Harpers Ferry - Age of husband, 23 - Age of wife,
　　21 - Both are Single - Both were born in Jefferson County, West
　　Virginia - Both reside in Jefferson County, West Virginia.

Marmaduke, Kate V. and Presley Marmaduke (2) -　　(L) December 14, 1861
　　For further information see - Marmaduke, Presley.

Marmaduke, Presley and Sarah Klise (1) -　　　　　　September 26, 1810

Marmaduke, Presley and Kate V. Marmaduke (2) -   (L) December 14, 1861
  Time of marriage, December 15, 1861 - Place of marriage, Berryville,
  Clarke County, Virginia - Full names of parties married, Presley
  Marmaduke and Kate V. Marmaduke - Age of husband, 34 years - Age of
  wife, 24 years - Condition of husband is Single - Condition of wife
  is Single - Place of husband's birth is Loudoun County, Virginia -
  Place of wife's birth is Loudoun County, Virginia - Place of
  husband's residence is Jefferson County, Virginia - Place of Wife's
  residence is Jefferson County, Virginia - Names of husband's
  parents are John A. and Catharine Marmaduke - Names of wife's
  parents are Silas and Catharine Marmaduke - Occupation of husband
  is Tanner - Given under my hand this 14th day of December, 1861 -
  John Reed, Jr.

Marmaduke, Silas and Catharine McEndree (1) -   July 20, 1832

Marmaduke, William H. and Miranda W. Noland (2) -   (L) April 12, 1856

Marquest, Michael A. and Mary J. Bateman (2) -   (L) December 6, 1860

Marquette, G. R. and Mary E. Johns (3) -   June 22, 1875
  Place of marriage, Harpers Ferry - Age of husband, 24 - Age of wife,
  22 - Both are Single - Both were born in Jefferson County, West
  Virginia - Both reside in Jefferson County, West Virginia.

Mars, Amasa W. and Ann Snyder (1) -   1822

Mars, Molly and Joseph Buzzard (3) -   August 24, 1886
  For further information see - Buzzard, Joseph.

Marsh, Emma (cold.) John Israel Yates (3) -   October 8, 1885
  For further information see - Yates, John Israel.

Marshall, Elizabeth V. and Jacob S. Trammel (3) -   May 28, 1866
  For further information see - Trammel, Jacob S.

Marshall, Frank and Mollie Edwards (3) -   December 25, 1886
  Place of marriage, Wickliffe - Age of husband, 21 - Age of wife,
  21 - Both are Single - Both were born in Clarke County, Virginia -
  Both reside in Jefferson County, West Virginia.

Marshall, George W. and Sarah Heflebower (2) -   (L) December 5, 1853

Marshall, J. D. (cold.) Lula Robinson (3) -   April 23, 1885
  Place of marriage, Charlestown - Age of husband, 30 - Age of wife,
  22 - Both are Single - Husband was born in Rappahannock County -
  Wife was born in Jefferson County, West Virginia - Both reside in
  Jefferson County, West Virginia.

Marshall, James and Elonor McMakin (1) -   November 5, 1805

Marshall, James and Margaret Stipp (1) -   December 21, 1819

Marshall, James M. and Amanda Engle (3) -   December 19, 1865
  Place of marriage, William Engle's, Jefferson County - Age of
  husband, 24 - Age of wife, 21 - Both are Single - Both were born in
  Jefferson County, West Virginia - Both reside in Jefferson County -
  Husband's parents are John and Rhuhana Marshall - Wife's parents are
  William and Phoeby Engle - Occupation of husband is Farmer.

Marshall, John and Sarah Bell Buckles (1) -   May 25, 1820

Marshall, John and Ruhanny Melvin (1) -   January 18, 1827

Marshall, John and Catharine Hiett (1) -   January 19, 1837

Marshall, John W. and Susan E. Bane (3) -   November 21, 1866
    Place of marriage, Elk Branch Church, Jefferson County - Age of
    husband, 36 - Age of wife, 28 - Both are Single - Both were born in
    Jefferson County, West Virginia - Both reside in Jefferson County,
    West Virginia - Husband's parents are John and Rhuhama Marshall -
    Wife's parents are William and Sarah Bane - Occupation of husband is
    Farmer.

Marshall, Margaret and Robert H. Boteler (2) -   (L) December 13, 1860

Marshall, Mary Elizabeth and Thomas Hilleary (2) -   (L) (May 1861)
    For further information see - Hilleary, Thomas.

Marshall, Mildred and Marshall B. Perry (1) -   February 9, 1832

Marshall, R. M. and Lucy Butler (3) -   November 6, 1872
    Place of marriage, Jefferson County, West Virginia - Age of husband,
    28 - Age of wife, 23 - Both are Single - Both were born in Jefferson
    County, West Virginia - Husband resides in Berkeley County, West
    Virginia - Wife resides in Jefferson County, West Virginia -
    Husband's parents are J. M. and R. N. Marshall - Wife's parents are
    W. G. and L. Butler - Occupation of husband is Physician.

Marshall, Rhua and Thomas Licklider (3) -   June 6, 1872
    For further information see - Licklider, Thomas.

Marshall, Rose and Jacob Rush (3) -   November 30, 1865
    For further information see - Rush, Jacob.

Marshall, W. K. and Minnie Lee Strider (3) -   October 19, 1887
    Place of marriage, Charlestown - Age of husband, 33 - Age of wife,
    24 - Both are Single - Husband was born at Romney, Hampshire County,
    West Virginia - Wife was born in Jefferson County, West Virginia -
    Husband resides in Hampshire County, West Virginia - Wife resides in
    Jefferson County, West Virginia.

Marshall, William and Mary Hendricks (1) -   December 30, 1825

Marshall, William and Sallie Hoffman (3) -   February 21, 1888
    Place of marriage, Shepherdstown - Age of husband, 21 - Age of wife,
    23 - Both are Single - Husband was born in Washington County,
    Maryland - Wife was born in Jefferson County, West Virginia -
    Husband resides in Maryland - Wife resides in Jefferson County, West
    Virginia.

Marsteller, Andrew E. and Kate E. Cockerll (3) -   March 6, 1872
    Place of marriage, Jefferson County, West Virginia - Age of husband,
    25 - Age of wife, 18 - Both are Single - Husband was born at Harpers
    Ferry, Virginia - Wife was born in Jefferson County, Virginia - Both
    reside in Jefferson County, West Virginia - Husband's parents are
    Asa C. and Sarah Ann - Wife's parents are George W. and Ellen -
    Occupation of husband is Wagon Maker.

Martin, A. H. and Fannie Poffenberger (3) -   December 30, 1887
    Place of marriage, Charlestown - Age of husband, 26 - Age of wife,
    18 - Both are Single - Husband was born in Pennsylvania - Wife was
    born in Jefferson County, West Virginia - Husband resides at
    Brooklyn, New York - Wife resides in Jefferson County, West
    Virginia. (Consent of bride's father in writing.)

Martin, Albert (cold.) Mary Frances Payne (3) -   November 12, 1878
    Place of marriage, Bolivar - Age of husband, 24 - Age of wife, 18 -
    Both are Single - Husband was born in Clarke County, Virginia - Wife
    was born in Jefferson County, West Virginia - Both reside in
    Jefferson County, West Virginia. (Consent of father certified by
    James Johnson (cold.).)

Martin, Alfred (cold.) Lucy Drew (3) -   March 19, 1868
    Place of marriage, Jefferson County - Age of husband, 21 - Age of
    wife, 17 - Both are Single - Both were born in Jefferson County -
    Both reside in Jefferson County - Occupation of husband is Farmer.

Martin, Ann Elizabeth and Henry Clay Fulk (2) -   (L) October 1, 1856

Martin, Anne and Samuel Conway (1) -   August 17, 1826

Martin, Annie (cold.) Herbert Jackson (3) -   October 14, 1887
    For further information see - Jackson, Herbert.

Martin, B. F. and Martha Kindle (3) -   July 3, 1879
    Place of marriage, near Charlestown - Age of husband, 27 - Age of
    wife, 22 - Both are Single - Husband was born in Warren County,
    Virginia - Wife was born in Jefferson County, West Virginia - Both
    reside in Jefferson County, West Virginia.

Martin, Benijah and Eliza Niseley (1) -   October 25, 1827

Martin, Eliza and Christopher Moser (1) -   October 14, 1802

Martin, Henry C. and Dora Britner (3) -   September 30, 1875
    Place of marriage, Shepherdstown - Age of husband, 25 - Age of wife,
    18 - Both are Single - Husband was born at Cumberland, Maryland -
    Wife was born in Jefferson County, West Virginia - Both reside in
    Jefferson County, West Virginia. (Consent of bride's father in
    person.)

Martin, Isaac and Annie Williams (3) -   October 22, 1885
    Place of marriage, Kearneysville - Age of husband, 21 - Age of wife,
    18 - Both are Single - Husband was born in Warren County, Virginia -
    Wife was born in Loudoun County, Virginia - Both reside in Jefferson
    County, West Virginia. (Consent of bride's mother vouched for by
    James Tillett.)

Martin, James A. and Catharine Salvin (3) -   (1869)
    Age of husband, 23 - Age of wife, 21 - Both are Single - Husband was
    born in Ireland - Wife was born in Jefferson County - Husband
    resides in Berkeley - Wife resides in Jefferson County - Husband's
    parents are Thomas and Margaret - Wife's parents are C. and Julia -
    Occupation of husband is Railroad.

Martin, Mary and Silas Melvin (1) -   November 5, 1818

Martin, Mary and John Hoffman (1) -   June 9, 1824

Martin, Mary and James Conway (3) - For further information see - Conway, James. — January 16, 1866

Martin, Mary F. (cold.) L. R. Allison (3) - For further information see - Allison, L. R. — February 27, 1888

Martin, Ruhanna and George D. McGlincy (1) - — February 9, 1832

Martin, Sadie and Henry Norris (3) - For further information see - Norris, Henry. — June 8, 1887

Martin, Susana and Benjamin Jones (1) - — 1814

Martin, Victoria and J. D. Miller (3) - For further information see - Miller, J. D. — February 28, 1887

Martin, William and Nancy Conway (1) - — November 21, 1816

Mash, Julia (cold.) William Roy (3) - For further information see - Roy, William. — December 29, 1874

Mash, Louisa and David Magaeh (3) - For further information see - Magaeh, David. — April 15, 1880

Mask, Hebernia and William H. Kline (3) - For further information see - Kline, William H. — July 6, 1865

Maslin, Thomas, Jr. and Elizabeth L. Timberlake (3) - — December 15, 1875
Place of marriage, Charles Town - Age of husband, 24 - Age of wife, 24 - Both are Single - Husband was born in Hardy County, West Virginia - Wife was born in Jefferson County, West Virginia - Husband resides in Hardy County, West Virginia - Wife resides in Jefferson County, West Virginia.

Mason, Alexander and Elizabeth Strode (1) - — February 17, 1807

Mason, Alice (cold.) George Bradford (3) - For further information see - Bradford, George. — April 20, 1887

Mason, Amelia (cold.) James C. Field (3) - For further information see - Field, James C. — April 10, 1884

Mason, Anna (cold.) George Carter (3) - For further information see - Carter, George. — July 21, 1883

Mason, Belle (cold.) Jere Campbell (3) - For further information see - Campbell, Jere. — May 16, 1880

Mason, Ed. and Eveline Catlett (1) - — October 30, 1813

Mason, Elizabeth and Andrew J. Painter (3) - For further information see - Painter, Andrew J. — July 16, 1882

Mason, Ella (cold.) Samuel Brown (3) - For further information see - Brown, Samuel. — September 30, 1886

Mason, Emeline A. and Samuel Evans (1) - — May 19, 1842

Mason, Frances (cold.) Lee May (3) - For further information see - May, Lee. — March 21, 1888

Mason, George (cold.) Eliza Ford (3) - September 27, 1877
  Place of marriage, Shepherdstown - Age of husband, 25 - Age of wife,
  26 - Both are Single - Husband was born in Jefferson County, West
  Virginia - Wife was born in Berkeley County, West Virginia - Both
  reside in Jefferson County, West Virginia.

Mason, Harriet (colored) Samuel Jackson (3) - December 1, 1870
  For further information see - Jackson, Samuel.

Mason, Ida (cold.) Robert E. Ford (3) - December 31, 1878
  For further information see - Ford, Robert E.

Mason, John G. and Mary M. Botelar (3) - March 16, 1870
  Place of marriage, Jefferson County - Age of husband, 31 - Age of
  wife, 24 - Husband was born in Virginia - Wife was born in Jefferson
  County - Husband resides in Virginia - Wife resides in Jefferson
  County.

Mason, Maria and Benjamin Carter (3) - April 11, 1868
  For further information see - Carter, Benjamin.

Mason, Nannie M. and Robert C. Grove (3) - January 21, 1875
  For further information see - Grove, Robert C.

Mason, Paint. (cold.) Ben Stripling (3) - July 24, 1883
  For further information see - Stripling, Ben.

Mason, Rosa C. and C. L. Sheets (3) - December 29, 1888
  For further information see - Sheets, C. L.

Mason, Rosa V. L. and Charles W. L. Boyd (3) - December 23, 1883
  For further information see - Boyd, Charles W. L.

Mason, Samuel (cold.) Hannah Hipkin (3) - January 24, 1887
  Place of marriage, Shepherdstown - Age of husband, 34 - Age of wife,
  27 - Both are Single - Husband was born in Warren County, Virginia -
  Wife was born in Jefferson County, West Virginia - Husband resides
  in Jefferson County, West Virginia - Wife resides in Jefferson
  County.

Mason, Thompson B. and Sarah C. Taylor (2) - (L) October 23, 1855

Mason, W. S. and O. L. Yates (bride) (3) - October 29, 1868
  Place of marriage, Jefferson County - Age of husband, 23 - Age of
  wife, 21 - Both are Single - Husband was born in Frederick County,
  Virginia - Wife was born in Jefferson County - Husband resides in
  Jefferson County - Wife resides in West Virginia - Husband's parents
  are G. F. Mason - Wife's parents are Francis - Occupation of husband
  is Druggist.

Mason, William and Sallie Coleman (3) - June 18, 1873
  Place of marriage, Summit Point - Age of husband, 22 - Age of wife,
  21 - Both are Single - Husband was born in Clarke County, Virginia -
  Wife was born in Berkeley County, West Virginia - Both reside in
  Jefferson County, West Virginia - Wife's parents are Nelson and L.
  Coleman - Occupation of husband is Laborer.

Mason, William H. and Frances A. Gray (3) -   October 5, 1886
    Place of marriage, Loudoun County, Virginia - Age of husband, 27 -
    Age of wife, 22 - Both are Single - Husband was born in Clarke
    County, Virginia - Wife was born in Jefferson County - Both reside
    in Jefferson County, West Virginia.

Massey, Emily (cold.) Robert Williams (3) -   May 14, 1888
    For further information see - **Williams, Robert.**

Massey, James and Susan Bilmire (1) -   December 27, 1832

Massey, Joseph G. and Ann Pollock (1) -   November 25, 1822

Massey, Nancy and Robert W. Riley (1) -   August 11, 1816

Massey, Samuel and Sarah Suffrons (1) -   October 27, 1808

Mater, Frank and Nelly K. Billman (3) -   March 27, 1883
    Place of marriage, Harpers Ferry - Age of husband, 27 - Age of wife,
    17 - Both are Single - Both were born in Jefferson County, West
    Virginia - Both reside in Jefferson County, West Virginia.
    (Consent of bride's father in person.)

Mathaas, Jacob and Elizabeth Hoffman (2) -   (L) August 21, 1851

Matheny, Elizabeth and Samuel Wells (1) -   February 4, 1821

Matheny, Hannah and Jefferson Stidman (1) -   March 30, 1826

Matheny, J. A. R. and Mary C. Turner (3) -   February 28, 1878
    Place of marriage, Charlestown - Age of husband, 28 - Age of wife,
    23 - Husband is a Widower - Wife is Single - Husband was born in
    Jefferson County, West Virginia - Wife was born in Rockingham
    County, Virginia - Both reside in Jefferson County, West Virginia.

Matheny, Jacob A. R. and Mary Elizabeth Ott (3) -   February 9, 1873
    Place of marriage, at Adam Snyder's - Age of husband, 22 - Age of
    wife, 16 - Both are Single - Both were born in Jefferson County -
    Both reside in Jefferson County, West Virginia - Husband's parents
    are Jonah - Wife's parents are Addison and Sarah Catherine -
    Occupation of husband in Shoemaker. (Father's consnet in person.)

Matheny, James and Mary Shrodes (1) -   July 25, 1834

Matheny, John and Mary A. Gregory (1) -   December 5, 1833

Matheny, Mary Elizabeth and Maurice Grove (3) -   April 7, 1878
    For further information see - **Grove, Maurice.**

Matheny, Moses and Anna Jones (1) -   January 26, 1826

Matheny, Patsy and Jacob Roby (1) -   June 13, 1834

Matheny, Thomas and Anna Dillow (1) -   February 11, 1819

Mathews, Annie Jane and George W. Manuel (3) -   May 24, 1877
    For further information see - **Manuel, George W.**

Mathews, Rev. H. and Hannah VanSwearingen (2) -   (L) June 18, 1855

Mathews, J. Thomas and Margaret Clegg (1) - September 6, 1850

Mathews, Jacob and Elizabeth Hoffman (1) - August 24, 1851

Mathews, James L. and Eliza Florence Cookus (3) - December 29, 1875
　　Place of marriage, Shepherdstown - Age of husband, 44 - Age of wife,
　　20 - Husband is a Widower - Wife is Single - Husband was born at
　　Ellicott City, Maryland - Wife was born in Jefferson County, West
　　Virginia - Husband resides at Cumberland, Maryland - Wife resides in
　　Jefferson County, West Virginia.

Mathews, John (cold.) Violet Ross (3) - July 13, 1887
　　Place of marriage, Ripon - Age of husband, 30 - Age of wife, 30 -
　　Both are Single - Both were born in Jefferson County, West Virginia -
　　Both reside in Jefferson County, West Virginia.

Mathews, Joseph T. and Margaret Clege (2) - (L) August 24, 1850

Mathews, Mary and Samuel Myers (3) - March 29, 1870
　　For further information see - Myers, Samuel.

Mathias, J. P. T. and Elizabeth Agnes McCurdy (3) - July 2, 1879
　　Place of marriage, Charlestown - Age of husband, 30 - Age of wife,
　　21 - Both are Single - Husband was born in Frederick County,
　　Maryland - Wife was born in Jefferson County, West Virginia -
　　Husband resides at Baltimore City - Wife resides in Jefferson
　　County, West Virginia.

Mathias, Martha and Derizo C. Hough (2) - (L) October 31, 1855

Mathias, Mary and John Roberts (1) - August 13, 1815

Mathias, Park G. and Gertie Shoemaker (3) - November 26, 1890
　　Place of marriage, Charlestown - Age of husband, 29 - Age of wife,
　　25 - Both are Single - Husband was born in Frederick County,
　　Maryland - Wife was born in Pennsylvania - Both reside in Jefferson
　　County, West Virginia.

Matin, Aaron (colored persons) Ellen Jackson (3) - September 23, 1865
　　Place of marriage, Shepherdstown - Age of husband, 38 years - Age of
　　wife, 17 years - Both are Single - Husband was born in Maryland -
　　Wife was born in Berkeley County - Both reside in Jefferson County -
　　Husband's parents are John and Aley Matin - Wife's parents are John
　　and Margaret Jackson - Occupation of husband is Laborer.

Matson, Eliza and James H. Hough (3) - April 12, 1877
　　For further information see - Hough, James H.

Mattheny, Maggie J. and Tillason T. Thomas (3) - April 29, 1884
　　For further information see - Thomas, Tillason T.

Matthews, Annie J.
　　For further information see - Rodrick, Thomas E.

Matthews, Dennis M. and Harriet West Aldridge (3) - June 1, 1875
　　Place of marriage, near Charlestown - Age of husband, 37 - Age of
　　wife, 23 - Both are Single - Husband was born in Baltimore County,
　　Maryland - Wife was born in Jefferson County, West Virginia -
　　Husband resides in Baltimore County, Maryland - Wife resides in
　　Jefferson County, West Virginia.

Matthews, Eliza Morton and Robert Sherrard (1) -   July 18, 1826

Matthews, Elizabeth and William Matthews (3) -   July 14, 1868
For further information see - Matthews, William.

Matthews, Hester A. and James Orndorff (3) -   March 10, 1870
For further information see - Orndorff, James.

Matthews, Isaac and Mary Ann Richardson (2) -   (L) March 2, 1854

Matthews, Joseph and Sarah Myers (1) -   December 30, 1824

Matthews, Robert T. and Mary A. Engle (3) -   August 24, 1878
Place of marriage, Harpers Ferry - Age of husband, 23 - Age of wife, 21 - Both are Single - Both were born in Jefferson County, West Virginia - Both reside in Jefferson County, West Virginia.

Matthews, William and Elizabeth Matthews (3) -   July 14, 1868
Place of marriage, Jefferson County - Both are Single - Husband was born in Maryland - Wife was born in Berkeley County - Both reside at Charlestown - Husband's parents are William and Sarah - Wife's parents are C. H. and Elizabeth - Occupation of husband is Engineer.

Mattox, Sally C. and William H. Bane (3) -   March 30, 1871
For further information see - Bane, William H.

Mauck, Sarah B. and George W. Feltner (3) -   September 24, 1888
For further information see - Feltner, George W.

Maury, Magruder and Lila Andrews (3) -   October 25, 1865
Place of marriage, Shepherdstown - Age of husband, 29 years - Age of wife, 24 years - Husband was born at Fredericksburg, Virginia - Wife was born at Pittsburg, Pennsylvania - Husband resides at Fredericksburg, Virginia - Wife resides at Shepherdstown, West Virginia - Husband's parents are Richard B. and Ellen Maury - Wife's parents are Charles W. and Sallie P. Andrews - Occupation of husband is Minister of the Gospel.

Mauzy, Eugenia Harper and James H. Burton (2) -   (L) June 4, 1859

Mauzy, F. H. and Addie V. Kemp (3) -   October 22, 1890
Place of marriage, Bolivar - Age of husband, 29 - Age of wife, 21 - Both are Single - Both were born in Jefferson County, West Virginia - Husband resides at Canton, Ohio - Wife resides in Jefferson County, West Virginia.

Mauzy, Franklin P. and Mary F. Smallwood (2) -   (L) October 6, 1851

Mauzy, Lizzie E. and George W. Smith (3) -   June 13, 1881
For further information see - Smith, George W.

363

May, Benjamin A. and Catharine Coleman (2) - (L) August 18, 1862
Time of marriage, August 19, 1862 - Place of marriage, Middleway -
Names, Benjamin A. May and Catharine Coleman - Age of husband, 27
years old - Age of wife, 22 years - Condition of husband is Single -
Condition of wife is Single - Place of husband's birth was
Rockingham County, Virginia - Place of wife's birth was Jefferson
County, Virginia - Place of husband's residence is Jefferson County,
Virginia - Place of wife's residence is Jefferson County, Virginia -
Names of husband's parents are Adam A. and Ann May - Names of wife's
parents are Michael and Mary Coleman - Occupation of husband is
Carpenter - Given under my hand this 18th day of August 1862 -
Benjamin A. May.

May, Hester (cold.) William Spellman (3) - March 31, 1875
For further information see - Spellman, William.

May, James (cold.) Matilda Slaughter (3) - May 29, 1883
Place of marriage, Charlestown - Age of husband, 25 - Age of wife,
19 - Both are Single - Husband was born in Jefferson County, West
Virginia - Wife was born in Madison County, Virginia - Both reside
in Jefferson County, West Virginia. (Consent of bride's mother in
person.)

May, Lee (cold.) Frances Mason (3) - March 21, 1888
Place of marriage, Charlestown - Age of husband, 23 - Age of wife,
25 - Both are Single - Husband was born in Augusta County, Virginia -
Wife was born in Clarke County, Virginia - Both reside in Jefferson
County.

Mayer, Jacob and Sally Walpert (1) - November 22, 1811

Mayer, John L. and Julia L. Line (2) - (L) December 13, 1858

Mayers, John and Violet P. Gardener (1) - August 3, 1824

McAbee, John J. and Julia Donovan (1) - January 10, 1850

McAlister, James and Mary Ellen Wintermoyer (2) - (L) June 21, 1851

McAnley, Henry W. and Mary Ann Johnson (2) - (L) April 12, 1852

McAnly, Florence and Theodore Rogers (3) - November 13, 1879
For further information see - Rogers, Theodore.

McBee, Fanny Kate and John Wesley Shaner (3) - (1884)
For further information see - Shaner, John Wesley.

McBee, George and Mary E. Needy (2) - (L) December 8, 1856

McBee, Harriet and Hiram McBride (1) - December 31, 1829

McBee, Martha Ellen and James W. Brady (2) - (L) November 28, 1853

McBee, Mayberry and Annie M. Keplinger (3) - February 13, 1868
Place of marriage, Jefferson County - Age of husband, 25 - Age of wife, 23 - Both are Single - Both were born in Berkeley County - Husband resides in Berkeley - Wife resides in Jefferson - Husband's parents are Hugh and Catharine - Wife's parents are John and Catherine - Occupation of husband is Farmer.

McBee, Mersey and James Cope (1) - November 29, 1829

McBee, Susan and J. Wintermoyer (3) - (1868)
For further information see - Wintermoyer, J.

McBride, Elizabeth Frances and Lance L. Wilson (2) - (L) December 23, 1858

McBride, Hester Ann and John W. Dobson (2) - (L) November 27, 1856

McBride, Hiram and Harriet McBee (1) - December 31, 1829

McBride, Mary and Kiger Wilson (2) - (L) October 14, 1857

McCall, Emma and George W. Mispelhored (3) - December 7, 1869
For further information see - Mispelhored, George W.

McCan, Austin and Camelia Hickey (2) - (L) November 21, 1857

McCan, Catherine (cold.) Taylor Lee (3) - May 6, 1874
For further information see - Lee, Taylor.

McCan, Charlotte (cold.) William Bearman (3) - April 23, 1874
For further information see - Bearman, William.

McCan, George and Bettie C. Unseld (3) - January 4, 1870
Place of marriage, Jefferson County - Age of husband, 24 - Age of wife, 23 - Husband was born in Maryland - Wife was born in Virginia - Both reside in Jefferson County.

McCan, George W. (cold.) Mary Jane Stubbs (3) - May 11, 1886
Place of marriage, Shepherdstown - Age of husband, 52 - Age of wife, 27 - Husband is a Widower - Wife is Single - Husband was born in Jefferson County, West Virginia - Wife was born in Clarke County, Virginia - Both reside in Jefferson County, West Virginia.

McCan, Henry (cold.) Emily Con (3) -   May 6, 1874
    Place of marriage, Shepherdstown - Age of husband, 23 - Age of wife,
    21 - Both are Single - Both were born in Jefferson County, West
    Virginia - Both reside in Jefferson County, West Virginia.

McCan, John (colored) Sophia Branson (3) -   June 16, 1866
    Place of marriage, Shepherdstown - Age of husband, 24 - Age of wife,
    25 - Husband is Single - Wife is a Widow - Both were born in
    Jefferson County, Virginia - Both reside in Jefferson County, West
    Virginia - Occupation of husband is Laborer.

McCann, Eliza (cold.) Samuel Dorsey (3) -   December 30, 1885
    For further information see - Dorsey, Samuel.

McCann, Henry, Jr. (cold.) Maria Sorrell (3) -   June 30, 1881
    Place of marriage, Shepherdstown - Age of husband, 24 - Age of wife,
    23 - Both are Single - Both were born in Jefferson County, West
    Virginia - Both reside in Jefferson County, West Virginia.

McCann, Julia (cold.) Henry Harris (3) -   August 30, 1888
    For further information see - Harris, Henry.

McCann, Julian and Seaton Blue (3) -   September 1, 1866
    For further information see - Blue, Seaton.

McCard, Charles H. (cold.) Maria E. Thornton (3) -   October 23, 1879
    Place of marriage, Charles Town - Age of husband, 21 - Age of wife,
    19 - Both are Single - Both were born in Jefferson County, West
    Virginia - Both reside in Jefferson County, West Virginia.
    (Neither father nor mother - License issued at brother's request.)

McCard, Edmonia (cold.) John H. Goings (3) -   December 15, 1885
    For further information see - Goings, John H.

McCard, Lettie (cold.) Robert Williams (3) -   May 6, 1880
    For further information see - Williams, Robert.

McCard, Matilda and Newman Christ (3) -   November 7, 1872
    For further information see - Christ, Newman.

McCarrell, A. E. and Daniel T. Hughes (3) -   June 15, 1881
    For further information see - Hughes, Daniel T.

McCarrol, A. and Annie E. Huntsberry (3) -   February 25, 1869
    Place of marriage, Jefferson County - Age of husband, 33 - Age of
    wife, 24 - Husband is a Widower - Wife is Single - Husband was born
    in Pennsylvania - Wife was born in Virginia - Both reside in
    Jefferson County - Husband's parents are Archibald and Mary - Wife's
    parents are Henry P. and Lucy G. - Occupation of husband is
    Manufacturer.

McCarroll, Archibald, Jr. and Mary J. Fleming (2) -   (L) April 6, 1861
  Time of marriage, April 30, 1861 - Place of marriage, Jefferson
  County - Names, Archibald McCarroll, Jr. and Mary J. Fleming - Age
  of husband, 25 years - Age of wife, Twenty One (21) - Both are
  Single - Place of husband's birth was at Philadelphia, Pennsylvania -
  Place of wife's birth was in Jefferson County, Virginia - Husband's
  residence is in Frederick County, Virginia - Wife's residence is in
  Jefferson County, Virginia - Husband's parents are Archibald and
  Mary McCarroll - Wife's parents are Solomon and Sarah Fleming -
  Occupation of husband is Manufacturer - Given under my hand this
  6th day of April, 1861 - Solomon Fleming.

McCarroll, Margaret and James W. Ware (1) -   April 1850

McCartney, Isaac and Elizabeth Chapman (1) -   January 24, 1842

McCarty, Ann E. (nee Jenkins) and Patrick Gaynor (3) -   April 27, 1873
  For further information see - Gaynor, Patrick.

McCarty, George and Elizabeth L. Watson (1) -   September 10, 1834

McCarty, Rebecca A. and Charles Blake (1) -   October 6, 1829

McCarty, S. E. and Maggie Hunsicker (3) -   May 15, 1877
  Place of marriage, Charlestown - Age of husband, 24 - Age of wife,
  21 - Both are Single - Husband was born at Winchester - Wife was
  born in Shenandoah County, Virginia - Husband resides at Winchester -
  Wife resides in Jefferson County, West Virginia.

McCarty, Sally and Alexander Watson (1) -   July 5, 1821

McCarty, William and Juliana Frieland (2) -   (L) May 16, 1859

McCarty, William and Martha A. Roderick (2) -   (L) December 13, 1859

McCasey, James and Anne Maria Blockley (2) -   (L) January 18, 1865
  Time of marriage, January 19, 1865 - Place of marriage, Charlestown,
  Jefferson County, Virginia - Names, James McCasey and Anne Maria
  Blockley - Age of husband, 28 years - Age of wife, 22 years - Both
  are Single - Husband was born in Queens County, Ireland - Wife was
  born in - Husband's residence is Washington City - Wife's residence
  is Jefferson County, Virginia - Husband's parents are Martin and
  Anne McCasey - Wife's parents are - Occupation of husband is -
  License issued, January 18, 1865 - T. A. Moore, Clerk.

McCasling, William and Catherine Edwards (1) -   1822

McCauley, W. A. and Bulah J. Grubb (3) -   September 23, 1890
  Place of marriage, Harpers Ferry - Age of husband, 26 - Age of wife,
  20 - Both are Single - Husband was born at Baltimore, Maryland -
  Wife was born in Jefferson County, West Virginia - Both reside in
  Jefferson County, West Virginia. (Consent of bride's father in
  writing.)

McCauly, George and Viola Virginia Detterman (3) -   March 15, 1874
  Place of marriage, near Kearneysville - Age of husband, 29 - Age of
  wife, 24 - Both are Single - Both were born in Rockingham County,
  Virginia - Both reside in Jefferson County, West Virginia.

McCauly, James and Lidia Morgan (1) -   April 30, 1812

McCave, Kate and Martin Brannon (3) -   August 4, 1867
　For further information see - Brannon, Martin.

McCeary, J. W. and Ella Snyder (3) -   February 11, 1869
　Place of marriage, Jefferson County - Age of husband, 26 - Age of
　wife, 23 - Both are Single - Husband was born in Berkeley County,
　Virginia - Wife was born in Maryland - Husband resides at Baltimore,
　Maryland - Wife resides in Jefferson County - Husband's parents are
　John and Marinda - Wife's parents are Rachael - Occupation of
　husband is Merchant.

McChan, Louisa (cold.) James Snyder (3) -   November 24, 1881
　For further information see - Snyder, James.

McChan, Sarah Allen (cold.) John Wesley Thompson (3) -   October 3, 1880
　For further information see - Thompson, John Wesley.

McChann, Hannah (cold.) William Wells (3) -   June 2, 1879
　For further information see - Wells, William.

McClanahan, William T. and Nannie Virginia Rightstine (3) -   June 10, 1880
　Place of marriage, Shepherdstown - Age of husband, 40 - Age of wife,
　30 - Both are Single - Husband was born in Botetourt County,
　Virginia - Wife was born in Jefferson County, Virginia - Husband
　resides at Salem, Virginia - Wife resides in Jefferson County, West
　Virginia.

McClean, Fortune (cold.) Eliza Ford (3) -   September 14, 1876
　Place of marriage, Charles Town - Age of husband, 23 - Age of wife,
　22 - Both are Single - Both were born in Jefferson County, West
　Virginia - Both reside in Jefferson County, West Virginia.

McClean, James and Sarah Johnson (1) -   March 17, 1818

McCleary, Miranda and John Ronemous (2) -   (L) January 2, 1858

McClellan, A. Clyde and Charles William Crowl (3) -   January 11, 1888
　For further information see - Crowl, Charles William.

McClellan, David and Mary Curry (1) -   January 25, 1806

McClellan, Lawrence R. and Mrs. Mary A. Homer (3) -   July 27, 1876
　Place of marriage, Middleway - Age of husband, 28 - Age of wife,
　38 - Husband is Single - Wife is a Widow - Husband was born in
　Jefferson County, West Virginia - Wife was born in Jefferson - Both
　reside in Jefferson County, West Virginia.

McClellan, William and Ann Way (1) -   October 4, 1834

McCloy, Lewis and Sarah Hiett (1) -   September 7, 1826

McCloy, Mary and Thomas Endsley (1) -   January 21, 1806

McClure, Collin A. and Sarah A. Homar (2) -   (L) May 15, 1854

McClure, Daniel and Jane McKee (1) -   April 27, 1824

McClure, Ella H. and Judson J. Shultz (3) -   July 5, 1881
　For further information see - Shultz, Judson J.

McClure, George H. and Mary Rosenberger (1) - September 30, 1832

McClure, J. V. (bride) and T. F. Kohlhousen (3) - October 2, 1872
For further information see - Kohlhousen, T. F.

McClure, James and Elizabeth Glasford (1) - November 22, 1832

McClure, Sarah E. and William A. Kohlhousen (2) - (L) April 5, 1859

McClure, William and Margaret Williams (1) - 1819

McComb, Johnathan and Lucretia Beeler (1) - 1814

McCormack, Phoebe A. and Charles Bryan (1) - March 28, 1831

McCormick, Annie L. and Joseph McLane (3) - October 30, 1889
For further information see - McLane, Joseph.

McCormick, Brockenbrough and Ann Timberlake (1) - April 8, 1830

McCormick, Frances Eleanor and James Flore (1) - May 26, 1831

McCormick, George and ? Merchant (1) - September 23, 1820

McCormick, John, Jr. and Ann E. Dailey (2) - (L) July 30, 1859

McCormick, John A. and Susan C. Athey (2) - (L) November 24, 1862
Time of marriage, November 25, 1862 - Place of marriage, near Summit Point - Names, John A. McCormick and Susan C. Athey - Age of husband, 29 years - Age of wife, 24 years - Both are Single - Husband was born in Clarke County, Virginia - Wife was born in Jefferson County, Virginia - Husband's residence is in Clarke County, Virginia - Wife's residence is in Jefferson County, Virginia - Husband's parents are John and Jane McCormick - Wife's parents are Levi and ? Athey - Occupation of husband is Soldier in Confederate Army - Liscense issued by R. T. Brown in my absence from home, November 24, 1862.

McCormick, M. Virginia and Thomas J. Manning (2) - (L) May 12, 1856

McCormick, Mary and Emanuel Engles (1) - August 31, 1815

McCormick, Samuel and Jane Eleyet (1) - December 30, 1832

McCormick, Sarah and Daniel Manier (1) - May 10, 1832

McCormick, William A. and Margaret Engle (3) - September 16, 1890
Place of marriage, Halltown - Age of husband, 27 - Age of wife, 19 - Both are Single - Both were born in Jefferson County, West Virginia - Both reside in Jefferson County, West Virginia. (Consent of bride's father in person.)

McCoughtry, Susan and John G. Myers (1) - November 15, 1832

McCoughtry, William and Sarah Richardson (1) - September 27, 1808

McCown, Frank C. and Bettie B. Eyster (3) -　　　　　　　　　　June 12, 1879
　　Place of marriage, Halltown - Age of husband, 28 - Age of wife, 24 -
　　Both are Single - Husband was born in Hancock County, West
　　Virginia - Wife was born at Chambersburg, Pennsylvania - Husband
　　resides at Philadelphia - Wife resides in Jefferson County, West
　　Virginia.

McCoy, Sarah Elizabeth and Levi Hue (1) -　　　　　　February 19, 1830

McCoy, William and Sophia Atar (1) -　　　　　　　　　　May 25, 1819

McCoy, William and Julia Ann Kane (1) -　　　　　　　November 3, 1836

McCroy, Zipporah and William H. Mock (3) -　　　　　　August 13, 1884
　　For further information see - Mock, William H.

McCullough, Mary (widow) and Samuel Collins (2) -　　(L) February 18, 1864
　　For further information see - Collins, Samuel.

McCurdy, Charles H. and Amanda Wysong (2) -　　　　(L) October 31, 1853

McCurdy, Elizabeth A. and J. Harrison Kelly (2) -　(L) December 15, 1851

McCurdy, Elizabeth A. and J. Harrison Kelly (1) -　　December 18, 1851

McCurdy, Elizabeth Agnes and J. P. T. Mathias (3) -　　July 2, 1879
　　For further information see - Mathias, J. P. T.

McDade, Margaret and Jonathan Murphy (1) -　　　　　　March 17, 1806

McDanel, Charity (cold.) Nathan Ga (3) -　　　　　　　October 27, 1881
　　For further information see - Ga, Nathan.

McDaniel, Charity (cold.) Robert Henry Morris (3) -　　January 5, 1888
　　For further information see - Morris, Robert Henry.

McDaniel, Clara (cold.) Baden Hall (3) -　　　　　　December 27, 1883
　　For further information see - Hall, Baden.

McDaniel, Ellen (cold.) Lewis Brown (3) -　　　　　December 23, 1875
　　For further information see - Brown, Lewis.

McDaniel, Emily (cold.) Frank Smith (3) -　　　　　August 11, 1882
　　For further information see - Smith, Frank.

McDaniel, Fannie and Andrew Ross (3) -　　　　　　　November 30, 1865
　　For further information see - Ross, Andrew.

McDaniel, Frederick (cold.) Emma Tucker (3) -　　　　May 28, 1885
　　Place of marriage, Charlestown - Age of husband, 21 - Age of wife,
　　22 - Both are Single - Both were born in Jefferson County, West
　　Virginia - Both reside in Jefferson County, West Virginia.

McDaniel, George (cold.) Bertie Coner (3) -　　　　　March 31, 1887
　　Place of marriage, Charlestown - Age of husband, 22 - Age of wife,
　　18 - Both are Single - Both were born in Jefferson County, West
　　Virginia - Both reside in Jefferson County, West Virginia.
　　(Consent of bride's father in writing.)

McDaniel, Harriet and Samuel Roland (1) -　　　　　November 1, 1832

McDaniel, Harrison and Martha Williams (3) -   May 21, 1866
   Place of marriage, Jefferson - Age of husband, 24 - Age of wife,
   20 - Both are Single - Husband was born in Loudoun County,
   Virginia - Wife was born in Jefferson County, Virginia - Both reside
   in Jefferson County, West Virginia - Husband's parents are George
   and Ellen McDaniel - Wife's parents are George W. and Maria
   Williams - Occupation of husband is Laborer.

McDaniel, Howard and Elizabeth Robinson (3) -   May 18, 1890
   Place of marriage, Mechanickstown - Age of husband, 23 - Age of
   Wife, 21 - Both are Single - Husband was born in Jefferson County,
   West Virginia - Wife was born in Clarke County, Virginia - Both
   reside in Jefferson County, West Virginia.

McDaniel, Jackson and Esther Ann Milton (1) -   November 28, 1847

McDaniel, James and Harriet Murphy (1) -   February 14, 1826

McDaniel, James and Caroline Brady (2) -   (L) February 24, 1852

McDaniel, James W. (cold.) Maria Ella Anderson (3) -   December 27, 1882
   Place of marriage, near Kearneysville - Age of husband, 21 - Age of
   wife, 22 - Both are Single - Both were born in Jefferson County,
   West Virginia - Both reside in Jefferson County, West Virginia.

McDaniel, Lydia Jane (cold.) Richard Wilson (3) -   August 1, 1878
   For further information see - Wilson, Richard.

McDaniel, Margaret Ellen and Zachariah Lock (1) -   April 10, 1848

McDaniel, Martha Ellen and Robert M. Bain (2) -   (L) November 13, 1850
   (Sebastian McDaniel sworn.)

McDaniel, Martha E. and Robert M. Bain (1) -   November 14, 1850

McDaniel, Mary and Jacob Eversole (1) -   1816

McDaniel, Mary (cold.) Henry Times (3) -   November 22, 1882
   For further information see - Times, Henry.

McDaniel, Patsy Louisa (cold.) Jackson Roberson (3) -   December 24, 1884
   For further information see - Roberson, Jackson.

McDaniel, Robert R. (cold.) Margaret Ellen Williams (3) -   September 15, 1886
   Place of marriage, Charlestown - Age of husband, 49 - Age of wife,
   44 - Husband is a Widower - Wife is Single - Husband was born in
   Loudoun County, Virginia - Wife was born in Frederick County,
   Virginia - Both reside in Jefferson County, West Virginia.

McDaniel, Samuel (cold.) Fanny Luckett (3) -   November 10, 1875
   Place of marriage, near Bloomery Mill - Age of husband, 28 - Age of
   wife, 17 - Both are Single - Both were born in Jefferson County,
   West Virginia - Both reside in Jefferson County, West Virginia.
   (Consent of bride's mother in writing.)

McDaniel, Sarah and John Goins (3) -   December 28, 1871
   For further information see - Goins, John.

McDaniel, Thomas (cold.) Maria Carter (3) - October 21, 1880
    Place of marriage, Duffields - Age of husband, 22 - Age of wife,
    23 - Husband is Single - Wife is a Widow - Both were born in
    Jefferson County, West Virginia - Both reside in Jefferson County,
    West Virginia.

McDaniel, Virginia and John Richcreek (2) - (L) December 14, 1854

McDaniel, Washington and Catharine Duff (1) - October 6, 1831

McDaniels, Gennet C. and Benjamin M. Seckman (3) - November 24, 1868
    For further information see - Seckman, Benjamin M.

McDonald, A. and Ida M. Propps (3) - June 26, 1889
    Place of marriage, Harpers Ferry - Age of husband, 28 - Age of wife,
    21 - Both are Single - Husband was born at Winchester, Virginia -
    Wife was born in Jefferson County, West Virginia - Husband resides
    at Winchester, Virginia - Wife resides in Jefferson County, West
    Virginia.

McDonald, A. E. (bride) (cold.) J. W. Hall (3) - January 1, 1868
    For further information see - Hall, J. W.

McDonald, Ann Maria and James H. Griffith, Jr. (2) - (L) November 13, 1852

McDonald, Ann Maria and James H. Griffith, Jr. (1) - November 23, 1852

McDonald, Bettie B. and G. W. Hayne (3) - January 11, 1876
    For further information see - Hayne, G. W.

McDonald, Charles B. and Amelia M. Small (3) - April 28, 1881
    Place of marriage, Leetown - Age of husband, 23 - Age of wife, 22 -
    Both are Single - Husband was born in Clarke County, Virginia - Wife
    was born in Jefferson County, West Virginia - Both reside in
    Jefferson County, West Virginia.

McDonald, E. S. and Julia Yates Levell (3) - October 12, 1869
    Place of marriage, Jefferson County - Age of husband, 36 - Age of
    wife, 20 - Husband was born in Hampshire County, West Virginia -
    Wife was born in Jefferson County - Husband resides in Kentucky -
    Wife resides in Jefferson County. (Father in person consents.)

McDonald, Elizabeth V. and William H. VanDevinter (3) - August 27, 1866
    For further information see - VanDevinter, William H.

McDonald, Jackson and Mary L. Boland (2) - (L) October 22, 1857

McDonald, James and Susana Young (1) - January 23, 1806

McDonald, Maggie M. and John A. Ritter (3) - July 24, 1886
    For further information see - Ritter, John A.

McDonald, Mary Ann and Arthur J. Suddith (2) - (L) August 11, 1852

McDonald, Mary Ann and Arthur J. Suddith (1) - August 12, 1852

McDonald, Mollie and Edward Feagans (3) - March 14, 1889
    For further information see - Feagans, Edward.

McDonald, R. V. and Ann M. West (3) -   November 24, 1881
  Place of marriage, Bride's Residence - Age of husband, 27 - Age of
  wife, 23 - Both are Single - Both were born in Jefferson County,
  West Virginia - Both reside in Jefferson County, West Virginia.

McDonald, Sarah and William S. Caldwell (1) -   October 24, 1818

McDonald, Sarah Jane and Charles B. Stinger (2) -   (L) June 21, 1860

McDowell, Rosa (cold.) Albert Royston (3) -   September 10, 1890
  For further information see - Royston, Albert.

McElny, William and Emily Fleming (2) -   (L) May 14, 1854

McEndree, Ann and Philip Earhart, Jr. (1) -   November 17, 1821

McEndree, Catharine and Silas Marmaduke (1) -   July 20, 1832

McEndree, Henry F. and Sophia Heskett (1) -   February 22, 1836

McEndree, Louisa T. and Charles G. W. Macgill (2) -   (L) September 19, 1859

McEndree, Lucinda and Benjamin P. Glasscock (1) -.   April 10, 1832

McEndrie, Elizabeth and John W. Ware (1) -   December 26, 1816

McFall, Thomas and Mary J. Scott (3) -   October 16, 1871
  Place of marriage, Jefferson County - Age of husband, 23 - Age of
  wife, 25 - Both are Single - Husband was born in Virginia - Wife was
  born in Ireland - Husband resides in Indiana - Wife resides in
  Maryland - Husband's parents are William and Susan - Wife's parents
  are William and Bridget - Occupation of husband is Merchant.

McFarlane, John and Martha Todd Baylor (1) -   December 5, 1820

McFillan, Richard F. and Mary Ann Emory (2) -   (L) August 9, 1859

McFillin, James J. and Ann Griffith (1) -   March 24, 1831

McGaha, Elizabeth and John Wintermoyer (3) -   June 20, 1870
  For further information see - Wintermoyer, John.

McGarry, Annie E. and John W. Schaeffer (3) -   January 31, 1871
  For further information see - Schaeffer, John W.

McGarry, Emma R. and Nelson T. Snyder (3) -   September 13, 1877
  For further information see - Snyder, Nelson T.

McGarry, John D. and Emma Burr (3) -   May 30, 1877
  Place of marriage, Shepherdstown - Age of husband, 29 - Age of wife,
  24 - Both are Single - Both were born in Jefferson County, West
  Virginia - Both reside in Jefferson County, West Virginia.

McGarry, Laura A. and Joseph T. White (3) -   December 3, 1889
  For further information see - White, Joseph T.

McGarry, Mary H. and Robert M. Duke (3) -   February 9, 1875
  For further information see - Duke, Robert M.

McGarry, Robert and Mary Shope (1) -   November 16, 1823

McGarry, William and Catherine Conklyn (1) - January 18, 1827

McGee, Ann and William Reed (1) - January 25, 1831

McGill, Emma (cold.) Charles Ross (3) - February 10, 1886
For further information see - Ross, Charles.

McGill, Eveline and Osborn Quinn (3) - July 25, 1868
For further information see - Quinn, Osborn.

McGinnis, Elizabeth Virginia and Jacob C. Tutwiler (2) - (L) August 5, 1858

McGinnis, J. W. and Rosanna E. Shaull (2) - (L) February 5, 1861

McGinnis, Sarah Jane and Jonathan Pettit (2) - (L) December 2, 1857

McGlincy, George D. and Ruhanna Martin (1) - February 9, 1832

McGlincy, Sarah and Jacob Mitchell (1) - May 26, 1833

McGlosslim, Robert and Catherine Fisher (1) - October 14, 1821

McGolarick, John and Amanda J. Barrett (3) - June 21, 1870
Place of marriage, Jefferson County - Age of husband, 23 - Age of wife, 20 - Both were born in Jefferson County - Both reside in Jefferson County. (Consent of father in person.)

McGoldrick, Curtis and Lucy E. Butts (2) - (L) January 27, 1859

McGoldrick, Martha and Thomas Penwell, Sr. (2) - (L) April 7, 1860

McGolrick, Rachel Ann and Jacob Wolf, Jr. (2) - (L) October 24, 1856

McGoldrick, Ruth and William J. Harris (2) - (L) April 11, 1861
For further information see - Harris, William J.

McGraven, Catharine and Thomas Berisford (3) - September 29, 1868
For further information see - Berisford, Thomas.

McGraw, James and Sarah McMullen (1) - 1822

McGraw, Jeremiah and Margaret Brannon (3) - April 12, 1889
Place of marriage, Harpers Ferry - Age of husband, 40 - Age of wife, 40 - Both are Single - Both were born in Jefferson County, West Virginia - Both reside in Jefferson County, West Virginia.

McGraw, John W. and Jane E. Dulany (3) - July 31, 1879
Place of marriage, Harpers Ferry - Age of husband, 25 - Age of wife, 22 - Husband is Single - Wife is a Widow - Husband was born in Jefferson County, West Virginia - Wife was born in Ohio - Both reside in Jefferson County, West Virginia.

McGuire, Margaret Emily and John Evelyn Page (1) - February 18, 1823

McGuire, Mary and John Colgen (2) - (L) July 10, 1857

McGuth, Mary and Jacob Knight (1) - 1813

McIntire, A. and Elizabeth Bennett (1) - January 19, 1804

McIntire, Prudence and Cornelius Middaugh (1) -   June 26, 1811

McIntire, William A. and Nanie Butt (3) -   (1869)
Age of husband, 24 - Age of wife, 18 - Both are Single - Husband was born in Jefferson County - Wife was born in Berkeley - Both reside in Jefferson County - Occupation of husband is Farmer. (Father consents in person.)

McIntyre, Ann Elizabeth and Ephraim J. Custard (2) -   (L) February 8, 1854

McKaig, W. W. and Laura Hughes (3) -   October 25, 1865
Place of marriage, Jefferson County - Age of husband, 23 years - Age of wife, 22 years - Both are Single - Husband was born at Cumberland, Maryland - Wife was born at Baltimore, Maryland - Husband resides at Cumberland, Maryland - Wife resides in Jefferson County, West Virginia - Husband's parents are W. W. McKaig and Priscilla McKaig - Wife's parents are George and Sarah Hughes - Occupation of husband is Iron Founderor.

McKeannan, Elizabeth Virginia and Francis Quinn (3) -   July 26, 1886
For further information see - Quinn, Francis.

McKee, E. O. and Mary Ellen Hill (3) -   March 28, 1882
Place of marriage, Shepherdstown - Age of husband, 28 - Age of wife, 23 - Both are Single - Husband was born in Berkeley County, West Virginia - Wife was born in Jefferson County, West Virginia - Husband resides in Berkeley County, West Virginia - Wife resides in Jefferson County, West Virginia.

McKee, Jane and Daniel McClure (1) -   April 27, 1824

McKee, Joseph and Drusilla Jones (1) -   December 27, 1831

McKee, Joseph and Hannah Shoemaker (1) -   June 9, 1836

McKennan, Margaret Ann and Thomas Lao (2) -   (L) May 23, 1855

McKennan, Thomas J. and Mary Elizabeth Wigginton (2) -   (L) May 23, 1855

McKenney, Mary and Henry Byrd (1) -   June 29, 1833

McKenney, Mary Catharine and Adam P. S. Poisal (2) -   (L) May 18, 1863
For further information see - Poisal, Adam P. S.

McKernan, Mary F. and John William Kerns (3) -   June 16, 1885
For further information see - Kerns, John William.

McKiney, David and Sarah C. Greer (3) -   August 5, 1869
Place of marriage, Jefferson County - Age of husband, 21 - Age of wife, 21 - Husband was born in Jefferson County, West Virginia - Wife was born in Warren County, Virginia - Husband resides in Jefferson County, West Virginia - Wife resides in West Virginia.

McKinney, Alexander (cold.) Lucy Drew (3) -   April 12, 1877
Place of marriage, Duffields - Age of husband, 22 - Age of wife, 21 - Both are Single - Both were born in Jefferson County, West Virginia - Both reside in Jefferson County, West Virginia.

McKinney, Annie (cold.) Samuel Ranson (3) -   November 27, 1879
For further information see - Ranson, Samuel.

McKinney, Francis and Elizabeth Stall (1) - November 11, 1816

McKinney, Hiram and Phobe Deminie (1) - 1812

McKinney, James and Jane Vestal (1) - November 18, 1823

McKinney, Jane and Samuel Sullivan (1) - December 30, 1829

McKinney, John and Mary Jackson (1) - 1825

McKinney, Kitty and Charles Catrow (1) - 1822

McKinney, Thomas (cold.) Nancy Jones (3) - December 29, 1874
 Place of marriage, Middleway - Age of husband, 66 - Age of wife, 57 - Husband is a Widower - Wife is a Widow - Both were born in Jefferson County, West Virginia - Both reside in Jefferson County, West Virginia.

McKinney, Webb (cold.) Bettie Brown (3) - December 29, 1879
 Place of marriage, Harpers Ferry - Age of husband, 22 - Age of wife, 22 - Both are Single - Both were born in Jefferson County - Both reside in Jefferson County, West Virginia.

McKnight, Caroline and David Shirley (1) - February 21, 1828

McKnight, Daniel and Elizabeth A. Jenkins (3) - May 13, 1866
 Place of marriage, Westcliff Parish, Jefferson County, West Virginia - Age of husband, 21 - Age of wife, 21 - Both are Single - Husband was born in Loudoun County, Virginia - Wife was born in Clarke County, Virginia - Both reside in Clarke County, Virginia - Husband's parents are George and Mary McKnight - Wife's parents are Thomas and Ellen Jenkins - Occupation of husband is Carpenter.

McKnight, Mary and Edmund Burr (1) - December 30, 1824

McKnight, Savilla and John Shrode (1) - February 27, 1829

McKown, William E. and Fannie E. Wageley (3) - January 15, 1872
 Place of marriage, Jefferson County, West Virginia - Age of husband, 25 - Age of wife, 28 - Both are Single - Husband was born in Berkeley County, Virginia - Wife was born in Berkeley County - Husband resides in Illinois - Wife resides in Jefferson County - Husband's parents are Joseph and Mary R. - Wife's parents are David and Mary - Occupation of husband is Farmer.

McKune, Pamelia and John Musgrove (2) - (L) June 8, 1858

McLane, Joseph and Annie L. McCormick (3) - October 30, 1889
 Place of marriage, Harpers Ferry - Age of husband, 28 - Age of wife, 25 - Both are Single - Husband was born in Washington County, Maryland - Wife was born in Washington - Both reside in Washington County, Maryland.

McLane, Mary S. and Albert T. Roeder (3) - October 22, 1879
 For further information see - Roeder, Albert T.

McLaughlin, Mary and John Lance (1) - 1822

McMahon, Dennis and Mary Peacher (3) -   August 31, 1876
    Place of marriage, Old Furnace or Bolivar - Age of husband, 21 - Age
    of wife, 21 - Both are Single - Husband was born at Woodstock,
    Shenandoah County, Virginia - Wife was born in Jefferson County,
    West Virginia - Both reside in Jefferson County, West Virginia.

McMaken, Helen and John Rose (3) -   September 30, 1884
    For further information see - Rose, John.

McMakin, Elonor and James Marshall (1) -   November 5, 1805

McMara, John and Bridget Dehoney (3) -   (1870)
    Age of husband, 27 - Age of wife, 22 - Both were born in Ireland -
    Both reside in Jefferson County. (Age sworn to by her brother.)

McMechen, William M. and Virginia Rutherford (3) -   December 8, 1868
    Place of marriage, Jefferson County - Age of husband, 26 - Age of
    wife, 23 - Both are Single - Husband was born in Harrison County,
    Virginia - Wife was born in Jefferson, Virginia - Husband resides at
    New York City - Wife resides in Jefferson County - Husband's parents
    are James H. and E. Ann - Wife's parents are Thomas and Mary -
    Occupation of husband is Merchant. (No evidence that he has been
    licensed.)

McMiltin, Robert and Mary Rockenbourg (1) -   April 15, 1824

McMullen, Sarah and James McGraw (1) -   1822

McMullen, Sarah Ann and Thomas Fossett (2) -   (L) December 12, 1850

McMullin, John and Elizabeth Seller (1) -   October 14, 1827

McMurran, Margaret and Francis R. Shepherd (2) - (L) November 21, 1855

McMurran, Nancy and James Black (1) -   December 21, 1820

McMurran, William and Elizabeth Lucas (1) -   February 1832

McNamara, L. S. and Irene J. Kephart (3) -   March 5, 1890
    Place of marriage, Uvilla - Age of husband, 46 - Age of wife, 22 -
    Husband is a Widower - Wife is Single - Husband was born in
    Dorchester County, Maryland - Wife was born in Jefferson County,
    West Virginia - Husband resides in Dorchester County, Maryland -
    Wife resides in Jefferson County, West Virginia.

McNamee, Hugh and Susannah Gummert (1) -   March 18, 1819

McNanly, L. Winie and William A. H. Turner (3) -   April 26, 1890
    For further information see - Turner, William A. H.

McNarsey, Patrick and Mary C. Ashby (3) -   October 21, 1867
    Place of marriage, Jefferson - Age of husband, 22 - Age of wife,
    21 - Both are Single - Husband was born in Jefferson County - Wife
    was born in Berkeley County - Husband resides in Jefferson County -
    Wife resides at Baltimore - Wife's parents are George and L.
    Ashby - Occupation of husband is Laborer.

McNealy, Walter L. and Julia E. Renoe (3) -   November 19, 1890
    Place of marriage, Charlestown - Age of husband, 26 - Age of wife,
    30 - Both are Single - Husband was born in Loudoun County,
    Virginia - Wife was born in Fauquier County, Virginia - Husband
    resides in Page County, Virginia - Wife resides in Jefferson County,
    West Virginia.

McPherson, Jane and Oliver Cromwell (1) -   December 14, 1822

McPherson, M. A. and John Nichols (1) -   January 21, 1835

McQuilkin, A. R. and Ellen G. Rush (2) -   (L) April 7, 1854
    (Got by William A. Marshall who says both are of age.)

McQuilkin, William Y. and Mary C. Kerney (3) -   November 2, 1865
    Place of marriage, Shepherdstown - Age of husband, 42 - Age of wife,
    23 - Husband is a Widower - Wife is Single - Both were born in
    Jefferson County, West Virginia - Both reside in Jefferson County,
    West Virginia - Husband's parents are Thomas and Sarah McQuilkin -
    Wife's parents are Josiah T. and Elizabeth Kerney - Occupation of
    husband is Farmer.

McSherry, Elizabeth and Thomas Wilt (3) -   March 25, 1875
    For further information see - Wilt, Thomas.

McSherry, Margaret A. and George W. Wilt (3) -   January 23, 1868
    For further information see - Wilt, George W.

McSherry, Richard and Anna Bell Watkins (3) -   February 27, 1878
    Place of marriage, near Cameron's - Age of husband, 23 - Age of
    wife, 21 - Both are Single - Both were born in Jefferson County,
    West Virginia - Both reside in Jefferson County, West Virginia.

McSherry, William and Mary E. House (3) -   January 24, 1867
    Place of marriage, Charlestown - Age of husband, 27 - Age of wife,
    24 - Both are Single - Both were born in Jefferson County, West
    Virginia - Both reside in Jefferson County, West Virginia -
    Husband's parents are William McSherry and Nancy Scarlett - Wife's
    parents are William and Catharine House - Occupation of husband is
    Farmer.

McTillan, John and Susan Cockeral (1) -   January 3, 1820

McVeave, Joseph and Louise Agnes Ruff (3) -   May 8, 1889
    Place of marriage, near Shepherdstown - Age of husband, 23 - Age of
    wife, 18 - Both are Single - Husband was born at Baltimore - Wife
    was born in Baltimore County - Both reside in Jefferson County, West
    Virginia.

Medder, John and Barbara Zoll (2) - (L) November 16, 1850

Medder, John and Barbara Zoll (1) - November 18, 1850

Medler, Ann Catharine and David Seigel (2) - (L) September 7, 1857

Medler, Elizabeth and Peter John Johnson (1) - May 17, 1827

Medler, Eveline and John Rohrer (1) - March 16, 1824

Medler, Francis and Fanny Elizabeth Harder (3) - April 30, 1877
Place of marriage, Mountain - Age of husband, 25 - Age of wife, 19 -
Both are Single - Both were born in Jefferson County, West
Virginia - Both reside in Jefferson County, West Virginia.
(Consent of bride's father in person.)

Medler, Mary Jane and Thomas Dillow (2) - (L) April 7, 1857

Medtart, Jacob and Ann Doyne Likens (1) - November 21, 1830

Meehan, John and Nancy Dobson (2) - (L) December 21, 1854

Megarry, Mathew and Jane Clayton (1) - February 20, 1807

Melhorn, Henrietta H. and John W. Stahl (2) - (L) November 26, 1858

Melhorn, Mary Adeline and John Kreps (1) - October 25, 1836

Melon, Laura (cold.) Richard Johnson (3) - November 30, 1876
For further information see - Johnson, Richard.

Melton, Charles W. and Jane M. Gomph (1) - May 29, 1828

Melton, Robert and Harriot Cross (1) - January 30, 1820

Melvin, Catharine and John B. Hendricks (3) - December 20, 1883
For further information see - Hendricks, John B.

Melvin, Catherine and John Engle (1) - November 7, 1823

Melvin, Elizabeth and Thomas Link (2) - (L) February 25, 1854

Melvin, J. Fletcher and Nannie D. Cockrell (3) - October 17, 1883
Place of marriage, near Charlestown - Age of husband, 25 - Age of
wife, 23 - Both are Single - Both were born in Jefferson County,
West Virginia - Both reside in Jefferson County, West Virginia.

Melvin, Jacob S. and Susan Hester Snyder (2) - (L) February 15, 1855

Melvin, James A. and Mary V. Trussell (3) - December 12, 1871
Place of marriage, Jefferson County - Age of husband, 24 - Age of
wife, 23 - Both are Single - Both were born in Jefferson County -
Husband resides in Jefferson - Wife resides in Jefferson County -
Husband's parents are John and Catherine - Wife's parents are
Craven and Eliza - Occupation of husband is Farmer.

Melvin, Jane and George Leicklider (1) - November 12, 1827

Melvin, John and Nancy Snyder (1) - October 25, 1827

Melvin, Mary and Jessee Engle (1) -   March 21, 1822

Melvin, Mary Ellen and John M. Engle (2) -   (L) October 28, 1852

Melvin, Mary S. (widow) and Lawrence Troy (2) -   (L) March 15, 1858

Melvin, Phebe and William Engle (1) -   April 6, 1820

Melvin, Ruhanny and John Marshall (1) -   January 18, 1827

Melvin, Samuel and Blanchy Osburn (1) -   February 18, 1819

Melvin, Silas and Elizabeth Osborne (1) -   October 22, 1805

Melvin, Silas and Mary Martin (1) -   November 5, 1818

Melvin, Thomas and Mary Engle (1) -   September 11, 1828

Melvin, William and Christiana Bane (3) -   December 8, 1868
    Place of marriage, Jefferson County - Age of husband, 28 - Age of wife, 28 - Both are Single - Husband was born in Jefferson County - Wife was born in Jefferson, Virginia - Both reside in Jefferson County - Husband's parents are John and Kitty - Wife's parents are William and Sarah - Occupation of husband is Farmer.

Mendenhall, Han. and Hugh Reed (1) -   January 2, 1823

Mendenhall, Phebe and Edward Bennett (1) -   September 30, 1828

Menefee, Emma Virginia and Charles W. Currie (3) -   April 2, 1872
    For further information see - Currie, Charles W.

Menser, Elizabeth and John Mark (1) -   April 1824

Mercer, Ann and Israel Fidler (1) -   October 18, 1832

Mercer, Elizabeth and Adam Verdier (1) -   September 2, 1802

Mercer, Mary E. and George W. Ramsburg (2) -   (L) April 8, 1861
    For further information see - Ramsburg, George W.

Merchant, ? and George McCormick (1) -   September 23, 1820

Merchant, Alfred K. and Nancy R. Belle Ramey (3) -   April 6, 1876
    Place of marriage, Charlestown - Age of husband, 24 - Age of wife, 21 - Both are Single - Both were born in Warren County, Virginia - Husband resides in Warren County, Virginia - Wife resides in Jefferson County, West Virginia.

Merchant, George R. and Elmira J. Vorous (3) -   October 22, 1889
    Place of marriage, Middleway - Age of husband, 31 - Age of wife, 23 - Both are Single - Husband was born in Montgomery County, Maryland - Wife was born in Clarke County, Virginia - Husband resides at Frederick, Maryland - Wife resides in Jefferson County, West Virginia.

Merchant, George W. and Margaret Frier (1) -   October 24, 1831

Merchant, Mattie V. and George C. Rumberger (3) -   September 2, 1872
    For further information see - Rumberger, George C.

Merchant, Samuel R. and Almira Virginia Baxley (3) -.　　　April 22, 1873
    Place of marriage, near Kearneysville - Age of husband, 22 - Age of
    wife, 19 - Both are Single - Both were born in Morgan County - Both
    reside in Jefferson County, West Virginia - Husband's parents are
    John and Catherine - Wife's parents are Samuel and Mary - Occupation
    of husband is Farmer.　(Consent of bride's father in person.)

Merchant, W. S. and Jane Brown (3) -　　　　　　　　　　　March 18, 1873
    Place of marriage, Charles Town - Age of husband, 29 - Age of wife,
    29 - Husband is a Widower - Wife is Single - Husband was born in
    Berkeley County, West Virginia - Wife was born in Jefferson County,
    West Virginia - Both reside in Jefferson County, West Virginia -
    Husband's parents are Hiram and Rachel - Wife's parents are Joseph
    M. and Mary - Occupation of husband is Butcher.

Merchant, W. S. and Mary E. O'Bannon (3) -　　　　　　　　March 3, 1885
    Place of marriage, Charlestown - Age of husband, 41 - Age of wife,
    30 - Husband is a Widower - Wife is Single - Husband was born in
    Berkeley County, West Virginia - Wife was born in Jefferson County,
    West Virginia - Both reside in Jefferson County, West Virginia.

Meredith, James and Elizabeth Eaty (1) -　　　　　　　　　June 21, 1819

Meritt, Jacob and Ann R. Cockrell (3) -　　　　　　　　December 20, 1866
    Place of marriage, Duffields Depot, Jefferson County - Age of
    husband, 22 - Age of wife, 18 - Both are Single - Both were born in
    Jefferson County, West Virginia - Both reside in Jefferson County,
    West Virginia - Husband's parents are Jacob and Margaret Meritt -
    Wife's parents are Adam and Eliza Cockrell - Occupation of husband
    is Farmer.

Merret, Emma and James P. Cook (3) -　　　　　　　　　December 19, 1871
    For further information see - Cook, James P.

Merrick, Eliza A. and John S. George (2) -　　　　(L) November 12, 1859

Merrick, Frederick F. and Mary Ann Cruzen (2) -　　(L) December 7, 1850

Merrick, James A., Jr. and Mary Virginia Claspy (2) -　(L) November 8, 1851

Merrick, James A. and Mary Virginia Claspy (1) -　　November 8, 1851

Merrick, Shadrack F. and Mary Ann Cruzen (1) -　　　December 12, 1850

Merrida, Edmun and Ellen Brown (3) -　　　　　　　　　　July 25, 1871
    Place of marriage, Jefferson County - Age of husband, 26 - Age of
    wife, 21 - Both are Single - Both were born in Virginia - Both
    reside in West Virginia.- Husband's parents are Robert and Mary
    Jane - Wife's parents are Jacob and Millie - Occupation of husband
    is Stone Quarryman.

Merritt, Agatha R. and Charles F. Unseld (3) -　　　　October 11, 1881
    For further information see - Unseld, Charles F.

Merritt, Anna and John Rickamore (3) -　　　　　　　　October 25, 1887
    For further information see - Rickamore, John.

Merritt, C. J. and Laura J. Hoffman (3) -   November 4, 1889
    Place of marriage, Charlestown - Age of husband, 23 - Age of wife,
    23 - Both are Single - Both were born in Washington County,
    Maryland - Husband resides at Pittsburg, Pennsylvania - Wife resides
    in Jefferson County, West Virginia.

Merritt, Eliza Ann and Adam Cockrell (2) -   (L) November 2, 1858

Merritt, Margaret and Charles J. Engle (2) -   (L) June 3, 1858

Merritt, Mary Jane and James Anderson (3) -   January 5, 1870
    For further information see - Anderson, James.

Mesener, William H. and Lillie Seibert (3) -   December 27, 1887
    Place of marriage, Middleway - Age of husband, 29 - Age of wife,
    29 - Both are Single - Both were born in Frederick County, Virginia -
    Husband resides in Clarke County, Virginia - Wife resides in Jefferson
    County.

Metcalf, Maria E. and John L. Weller (2) -   (L) December 22, 1852

Metheny, Sarah and William Friland (1) -   April 8, 1819

Mettar, Barbara and Henry Hack (2) -   (L) April 6, 1861
    For further information see - Hack, Henry.

Mhler, A. G. and M. H. Moulder (bride) (3) -   November 3, 1870
    Place of marriage, Jefferson County - Age of husband, 25 - Age of
    wife, 21 - Husband was born at Alexander - Wife was born in
    Jefferson County - Husband resides at Alexander - Wife resides in
    West Virginia.

Michaels, Mary Elizabeth and Mason Bennett (2) -   (L) October 2, 1850

Michaels, Mary Elizabeth and Mason Bennett (1) -   October 4, 1850

Middaugh, Cornelius and Prudence McIntire (1) -   June 26, 1811

Middlekauff, Harry B. and Martha E. Whitmore (3) -   January 8, 1890
    Place of marriage, Charlestown - Age of husband, 25 - Age of wife,
    24 - Both are Single - Husband was born in Jefferson County, West
    Virginia - Wife was born in Loudoun County, Virginia - Both reside
    in Jefferson County, West Virginia.

Middlekauff, Henry D. and Martha S. Angell (2) -   (L) November 23, 1860

Middlekauff, Louis E. and Robert H. Lewis (3) -   December 18, 1868
    For further information see - Lewis, Robert H.

Middlekauff, Rufus and Maggie Coalman (3) -   (1870)
    Age of husband, 27 - Age of wife, 24 - Husband was born in
    Maryland - Wife was born in Jefferson County, Virginia - Husband
    resides in Jefferson County, West Virginia - Wife resides in
    Jefferson County.

Middleton, Ann P. W. and Hiram Baldwin Seaman (1) -   March 24, 1829

Milburn, John and Sarah M. Beltz (3) -   October 29, 1868
   Place of marriage, Jefferson County - Age of husband, 24 - Age of
   wife, 19 - Both are Single - Husband was born at New Oreleans - Wife
   was born in Jefferson County - Husband resides in Jefferson County -
   Wife resides in West Virginia - Husband's parents are John and
   Elizabeth - Wife's parents are Daniel J. and Sarah - Occupation of
   husband is Farmer.   (Henry C. Fulk her uncle and trustee gives
   consent.)

Miles, Albion L. and Catharine Lewis (2) -   (L) December 23, 1851

Miles, Thomas (cold.) Maria Thompson (3) -   September 11, 1873
   Place of marriage, Charlestown - Age of husband, 24 - Age of wife,
   21 - Both are Single - Both were born in Jefferson County, West
   Virginia - Both reside in Jefferson County, West Virginia.

Miles, William Braxton (cold.) Mary Nourse (3) -   February 4, 1880
   Place of marriage, Charlestown - Age of husband, 20 - Age of wife,
   21 - Both are Single - Both were born in Jefferson County, West
   Virginia - Both reside in Jefferson County, West Virginia.
   (Consent of groom's father in person.).

Millar, Eleanor and Benedict Padget (1) -   October 16, 1823

Miller, Abraham and Mary L. Turner (3) -   July 29, 1874
   Place of marriage, Kearneysville - Age of husband, 26 - Age of wife,
   19 - Both are Single - Husband was born in Jefferson County, West
   Virginia - Wife was born in Berkeley County, West Virginia - Both
   reside in Jefferson County, West Virginia.   (Consent of bride's
   father in person.)

Miller, Alberta and Robert W. Supinger (3) -   December 21, 1874
   For further information see - Supinger, Robert W.

Miller, Annie E. and John E. Rentch (3) -   August 17, 1876
   For further information see - Rentch, John E.

Miller, Brice and Susanah Purnell (1) -   August 21, 1806

Miller, Catharine and Joseph Smith (1) -   July 8, 1819

Miller, Catherine and Richard Jones (1) -   October 7, 1824

Miller, Clarene E. and James M. Andrews (3) -   (1870)
   For further information see - Andrews, James M.

Miller, E. J. (bride) and W. G. Smith (3) -   May 5, 1868
   For further information see - Smith, W. G.

Miller, Ebenezer P. and E. B. Creamer (3) -   November 17, 1868
   Place of marriage, Jefferson County - Age of husband, 51 - Age of
   wife, 40 - Husband is a Widower - Wife is Single - Husband was born
   in Virginia - Wife was born in Jefferson County - Husband resides in
   District of Columbia - Wife resides in West Virginia - Husband's
   parents are Samuel and Hannah - Wife's parents are S. J. and E. M. -
   Occupation of husband is Clerk War Department.

Miller, Edwin H. and Virginia M. Lock (3) - October 9, 1883
   Place of marriage, Charlestown - Age of husband, 40 - Age of wife,
   40 - Husband is Single - Wife is a Widow - Husband was born in State
   of Mississippi - Wife was born in State of Pennsylvania - Husband
   resides in State of Mississippi - Wife resides in Jefferson County,
   West Virginia.

Miller, Elizabeth and Jacob Sheetz (1) - May 30, 1809

Miller, Elizabeth and John Dalamuple (1) - August 31, 1813

Miller, Fannie Mary and John James Woodward (3) - January 17, 1871
   For further information see - Woodward, John James.

Miller, George W. and Susan Frances Rebecca Engle (2) - (L) October 5, 1863
   Time of marriage, October 8, 1863 - Place of marriage, at Edwin C.
   Engle's near Duffields Depot - Names, George W. Miller and Susan
   Frances Rebecca Engle - Age of husband, 25 years last April - Age of
   wife, 18 years October 18, 1863 - Both are Single - Both were born
   in Jefferson County - Both reside in Jefferson County - Names of
   husband's parents are Jacob J. and Catharine Miller - Names of wife's
   parents are Edwin C. and Nancy A. Engle - Occupation of husband is
   Farmer - License issued in presence of bride's father - Given under
   my hand this 5th day of October, 1863 - Thomas A. Moore, Clerk.

Miller, Henry and Elizabeth Young (1) - January 22, 1807

Miller, Henry and Mary Brantner (3) - February 12, 1867
   Place of marriage, Shepherdstown, West Virginia - Age of husband,
   25 - Age of wife, 40 - Husband is Single - Wife is a Widow - Husband
   was born at Toronto, Canada - Wife was born at Shepherdstown, West
   Virginia - Both reside at Shepherdstown, West Virginia - Husband's
   parents are John and Catharine Miller - Wife's parents are Daniel
   Brooks - Occupation of husband is Miller.

Miller, Ida and Clarence Kable (3) - December 19, 1888
   For further information see - Kable, Clarence.

Miller, Isaac and Lucretia Werrick (3) - June 15, 1869
   Place of marriage, Jefferson County - Age of husband, 22 - Age of
   wife, 17 - Husband was born in Pennsylvania - Wife was born in West
   Virginia - Husband resides in Jefferson County - Wife resides in
   West Virginia.

Miller, J. D. and Victoria Martin (3) - February 28, 1887
   Place of marriage, Harpers Ferry - Age of husband, 26 - Age of wife,
   23 - Both are Single - Both were born in Jefferson County, West
   Virginia - Both reside in Jefferson County, West Virginia.

Miller, Jacob and Lydia H. Daniels (1) - December 8, 1831

Miller, Jacob G. and Margaret E. V. Sigler (2) - (L) December 11, 1858

Miller, Jacob J. and Catharine Ronemous (2) -   (L) November 19, 1862
   Time of marriage, November 25, 1862 - Place of marriage, Parsonage,
   Elk Branch - Names of parties, Jacob J. Miller and Catharine
   Ronemous - Age of husband, 45 years - Age of wife, 45 years -
   Husband is a Widower - Wife is Single - Both were born in Jefferson
   County - Both reside in Jefferson County - Husband's parents are
   Jacob and Susan Miller - Wife's parents are, Christian names
   unknown - Occupation of husband is Farmer - Jacob J. Miller.

Miller, Jacob R. and L. Jennie Flemings (3) -   December 20, 1871
   Age of husband, 22 - Age of wife, 20 - Both are Single - Both were
   born in Jefferson County - Both reside in Jefferson County -
   Husband's parents are Jacob J. and Catharine - Wife's parents are
   Isaac Flemings - Occupation of husband is Farmer. (Vouched for
   Elisha S. Snyder.)

Miller, James H. and Cora Shirley (3) -   December 10, 1879
   Place of marriage, Unionville - Age of husband, 24 - Age of wife,
   22 - Both are Single - Both were born in Jefferson County, West
   Virginia - Both reside in Jefferson County, West Virginia.

Miller, John and Sally Crow (1) -   December 25, 1806

Miller, John and Hannah Harris (1) -   May 23, 1812

Miller, John and Harriet Welshans (2) -   (L) February 14, 1855

Miller, John H. and Sarah A. L. Lancaster (2) -   (L) October 1, 1851

Miller, John J. W. and Margaret Ann Wright (3) -   September 16, 1869
   Place of marriage, Jefferson County - Age of husband, 21 - Age of
   wife, 19 - Husband was born in West Virginia - Wife was born in
   Maryland - Both reside in Jefferson County. (Parents dead, no
   guardian.)

Miller, John T. and Catharine Frese (2) -   (L) August 13, 1851

Miller, John T. and Ellen L. Lambert (3) -   September 17, 1868
   Place of marriage, Jefferson County - Age of husband, 38 - Age of
   wife, 23 - Husband is a Widower - Wife is Single - Husband was born
   in Berkeley County - Wife was born in Jefferson County - Both reside
   in Jefferson County - Wife's parents are Joseph and Barbara -
   Occupation of husband is Blacksmith.

Miller, John W. and Helen M. Fry (3) -   March 9, 1871
   Place of marriage, Jefferson County - Age of husband, 26 - Age of
   wife, 21 - Both are Single - Husband was born in Page County,
   Virginia - Wife was born in Shenandoah County, Virginia - Both
   reside in Jefferson - Husband's parents are Benjamin F. and
   Angeline - Wife's parents are Joseph and Elizabeth - Occupation of
   husband is Farmer.

Miller, Jonathan C. and Hannah Frances Marlatt (2) -   (L) November 28, 1857

Miller, Joseph W. and Elizabeth Holt (1) -   May 1, 1845

Miller, Josiah and Elizabeth Kerman (1) -   June 10, 1810

Miller, Kate B. and Thomas W. Smith (3) -   February 2, 1881
   For further information see - Smith, Thomas W.

Miller, Laura Parran and Daniel Dechert (2) -   (L) September 17, 1855

Miller, Lillie M. and Charles M. Weaver (3) -   March 20, 1884
For further information see - Weaver, Charles M.

Miller, Maggie L. and Robert Myers (3) -   September 19, 1879
For further information see - Myers, Robert.

Miller, Margaret and Thomas Donnison (1) -   October 2, 1807

Miller, Margaret and Raleigh Moler (1) -   December 19, 1833

Miller, Margaret C. and Samuel Walton (3) -.   February 27, 1879
For further information see - Walton, Samuel.

Miller, Martin H. and Julia Frances Foreman (2) -   (L) December 6, 1852

Miller, Martin H. and Maria Louisa Wilson (2) -   (L) January 9, 1865
Time of marriage, January 10, 1865 - Place of marriage, Kabletown - Names, Martin H. Miller and Maria Louisa Wilson - Age of husband, 30 years - Age of wife, 24 years - Husband is a Widower - Wife is Single - Both were born in Jefferson County, Virginia - Both reside in Jefferson County, Virginia - Names of husband parents are - Names of wife's parents are Asaph and Nancy Wilson - Occupation of husband is Farmer - License issued January 9, 1865.

Miller, Mary and Harrison Waite (1) -   September 2, 1817

Miller, Mary and John Hoffman (1) -   October 1, 1818

Miller, Mary and John Snyder (1) -   1827

Miller, Mary and Samuel Ridenour (1) -   December 21, 1830

Miller, Mary Catharine and William Ronemous (2) -   (L) October 29, 1851

Miller, Milton B. and Edna Jane Trussell (2) -   (L) November 15, 1864
Time of marriage, November 17, 1864 - Place of marriage, Residence of Bride's Mother - Names, Milton B. Miller and Edna Jane Trussell - Age of husband, 37 years August 18, 1864 - Age of wife, 31 years September 27, 1864 - Both are Single - Both were born in Jefferson County - Both reside in Jefferson County - Names of husband's parents are Solomon and Margaret Miller - Names of wife's parents are ___?___ and ___?___ Trussell - Occupation of husband is Shoemaker - License issued November 15, 1864 - T. A. Moore, Clerk.

Miller, Robert G. and Fannie L. Lambert (3) -   March 3, 1890
Place of marriage, Shepherdstown - Age of husband, 25 - Age of wife, 24 - Both are Single - Both were born in Jefferson County, West Virginia - Both reside in Jefferson County, West Virginia.

Miller, Rosa A. and John R. Hawn (2) -   (L) January 2, 1861

Miller, Sarah and Caleb Woodly (1) -   September 16, 1819

Miller, Sarah Ann and Allen M. Kimes (3) -   November 17, 1880
For further information see - Kimes, Allen M.

Miller, Sarah F. and Thomas B. Moore (2) -   (L) June 6, 1857

Miller, Sophia D. and John H. Longbrake (3) -   May 27, 1869
  For further information see - Longbrake, John H.

Miller, Susan and Joseph R. Howell (3) -   December 13, 1868
  For further information see - Howell, Joseph R.

Miller, Thomas B. and Maggie Greenwood (3) -   September 28, 1881
  Place of marriage, Shepherdstown - Age of husband, 28 - Age of wife,
  21 - Both are Single - Husband was born at Harpers Ferry - Wife was
  born at Shepherdstown - Husband resides at Washington, D. C. - Wife
  resides in Jefferson County, West Virginia.

Miller, Thomas H. and Ada Humrickhouse (3). -   July 30, 1873
  Place of marriage, Shepherdstown - Age of husband, 28 - Age of wife,
  20 March 10 - Both are Single - Both were born in Jefferson County,
  West Virginia - Both reside in Jefferson County, West Virginia -
  Wife's parents are G. W. Humrickhouse. (Father's consent in
  writing.)

Miller, Thomas H. and Gertrude Milton (3) -   December 12, 1878
  Place of marriage, Middleway - Age of husband, 31 - Age of wife,
  21 - Husband is a Widower - Wife is Single - Both were born in
  Jefferson County, West Virginia - Both reside in Jefferson County,
  West Virginia.

Miller, Uriah and Elizabeth Thornburg (1) -   January 20, 1824

Miller, W. H. and Louisa Hoffmaster (3) -   March 29, 1885
  Place of marriage, Charlestown - Age of husband, 48 - Age of wife,
  27 - Husband is a Widower - Wife is Single - Both were born in
  Jefferson County, West Virginia - Both reside in Jefferson County,
  West Virginia.

Miller, William and Polly Echart (1) -   December 24, 1812

Miller, William and Drucilla Berry (1) -   1812

Miller, William G. and Sallie Coffman (3) -   November 19, 1890
  Place of marriage, Charlestown - Age of husband, 24 - Age of wife,
  19 - Both are Single - Husband was born in Morgan County, West
  Virginia - Wife was born in Jefferson County, West Virginia -
  Husband resides at Baltimore, Maryland - Wife resides in Jefferson
  County, West Virginia.

Miller, William H. and Elizabeth A. Lupton (3) -   August 22, 1869
  Place of marriage, Jefferson County - Age of husband, 33 - Age of
  wife, 38 - Husband was born in Maryland - Wife was born in
  Virginia - Husband resides in Jefferson County - Wife resides in
  Jefferson County, West Virginia.

Miller, William H. H. and Helen J. Chambers (3) -   March 28, 1866
  Place of marriage, Jacob Miller's, Jefferson County - Age of
  husband, 25 - Age of wife, 18 - Both are Single - Husband was born
  in Jefferson County, Virginia - Wife was born in Tuscarawas County,
  Ohio - Both reside in Jefferson County, West Virginia - Husband's
  parents are Jacob J. and Catherine Miller - Wife's parents are
  Joseph D. and Elizabeth Chambers - Occupation of husband is Farmer.

Miller, William R. and Lulie Lucas (3) - January 4, 1877
    Place of marriage, Shepherdstown - Age of husband, 24 - Age of wife,
    22 - Both are Single - Both were born in Jefferson County, West
    Virginia - Both reside in Jefferson County, West Virginia.

Mills, John and Catharine Waters (3) - (1867)
    Age of husband, 40 - Age of wife, 33 - Husband is a Widower - Wife is
    a Widow - Husband was born in England - Wife was born in Jefferson
    County - Both reside in Jefferson County.

Mills, Joseph (colored) Maria Thompson (3) - (1870)
    Age of husband, 30 - Age of wife, 18 - Both were born in Virginia -
    Both reside in Jefferson County. (Consent of parents.)

Mills, Julia and William W. Mills (3) - May 28, 1885
    For further information see - Mills, William W.

Mills, Lucy (cold.) William Robinson (3) - March 27, 1879
    For further information see - Robinson, William.

Mills, Nathaniel and Mary S. Niceley (3) - September 29, 1870
    Place of marriage, Jefferson County - Age of husband, 21 - Age of
    wife, 19 - Both were born in Virginia - Both reside in Jefferson
    County. (No parents or guardian. Consent of brother of lady.)

Mills, Susan (cold.) James Hook (3) - January 17, 1875
    For further information see - Hook, James.

Mills, William and Evelina Anderson (1) - December 19, 1821

Mills, William W. and Julia Mills (3) - May 28, 1885
    Place of marriage, Charlestown - Age of husband, 22 - Age of wife,
    20 - Both are Single - Both were born in Fauquier County, Virginia -
    Both reside in Jefferson County, West Virginia. (Consent of bride's
    father in writing.)

Milstead, Sarah Elizabeth and James W. Thomas (3) - June 25, 1874
    For further information see - Thomas, James W.

Milton, A. M. and John B. Finnell (3) - November 19, 1872
    For further information see - Finnell, John B.

Milton, Annie M. and John B. Finnell (3) - November 15, 1872
    For further information see - Finnell, John B.

Milton, Esther Ann and Jackson McDaniel (1) - November 28, 1847

Milton, Gertrude and Thomas H. Miller (3) - December 12, 1878
    For further information see - Miller, Thomas H.

Milton, James H. and Margaret Ann Daily (3) - May 9, 1890
    Place of marriage, Charlestown - Age of husband, 31 - Age of wife,
    34 - Husband is Divorced - Wife is Single - Both were born in
    Jefferson County, West Virginia - Both reside in Jefferson County,
    West Virginia.

Milton, James W. and Mary Ellen Backhouse (2) - (L) September 20, 1852

Milton, James W. and Mrs. Annie D. Johnson (3) - January 22, 1884
　　Place of marriage, Johnsons Factory - Age of husband, 55 - Age of
　　wife, 55 - Husband is a Widower - Wife is a Widow - Both were born
　　in Jefferson County, West Virginia - Both reside in Jefferson
　　County, West Virginia.

Milton, R. F. and Lizzie Myers (3) - February 26, 1884
　　Place of marriage, Charlestown - Age of husband, 24 - Age of wife,
　　26 - Both are Single - Husband was born in State of Missouri - Wife
　　was born in Jefferson County, West Virginia - Husband resides in
　　Missouri - Wife resides in Jefferson County, West Virginia.

Milton, Sarah Victoria and George W. Hoof (2) - (L) August 4, 1855

Milton, T. A. and Berdie L. Gilbert (3) - March 13, 1889
　　Place of marriage, Charlestown - Age of husband, 27 - Age of wife,
　　22 - Both are Single - Husband was born in Berkeley County, West
　　Virginia - Wife was born in Jefferson County, West Virginia -
　　Husband resides in Berkeley County, West Virginia - Wife resides in
　　Jefferson County, West Virginia.

Milton, Virginia and R. W. Hill (3) - September 20, 1877
　　For further information see - Hill, R. W.

Minchen, Mary E. and John L. Richards (2) - (L) October 21, 1852

Minchen, Mary E. and John L. Richards (1) - October 25, 1852

Minchin, Lewis and Sarah Proust (1) - November 13, 1833

Mines, Ann K. and Archibald Robinson (1) - March 31, 1831

Minn, John and Sallie E. Leach (3) - December 13, 1887
　　Place of marriage, Engles Switch - Age of husband, 28 - Age of wife,
　　22 - Both are Single - Both were born in Jefferson County, West
　　Virginia - Both reside in Jefferson County.

Minor, Abram (cold.) Eliza Crawford (3) - June 14, 1890
　　Place of marriage, Shepherdstown - Age of husband, 24 - Age of wife,
　　21 - Both are Single - Husband was born in Rappahannock County,
　　Virginia - Wife was born in Jefferson County, West Virginia - Both
　　reside in Jefferson County, West Virginia.

Minor, John (cold.) Dinah Russell (3) - May 27, 1882
　　Place of marriage, near Middleway - Age of husband, 51 - Age of
　　wife, 50 - Husband is a Widower - Wife is a Widow - Husband was born
　　in Caroline County, Virginia - Wife was born in Jefferson County -
　　Husband resides in Jefferson County, West Virginia - Wife resides in
　　Jefferson County.

Minor, William Fleming (cold.) Lina Jackson (3) - October 7, 1874
　　Place of marriage, County - Age of husband, 22 - Age of wife, 21 -
　　Both are Single - Both were born in Virginia - Both reside in
　　Jefferson County, West Virginia.

Mispelhored, George W. and Emma McCall (3) - December 7, 1869
　　Place of marriage, Jefferson County - Age of husband, 24 - Age of
　　wife, 19 - Husband was born at Baltimore - Wife was born in
　　Jefferson County - Husband resides at Grafton - Wife resides in
　　Jefferson County.　(Mother consents in writing.)

390

Mitchel, Henry and Lydia Backus (3) - November 7, 1865
Place of marriage, Charlestown, Jefferson County - Age of husband,
21 - Age of wife, 18 - Both are Single - Husband was born at
Charlestown, Jefferson County - Wife was born at New Orleans,
Louisianna - Both reside at Charlestown, Jefferson County - Husband's
parents are Mitchel - Wife's parents are Charles and Nancy Backus -
Occupation of husband is Farmer.

Mitchell, Alice H. and G. W. Boyers, Jr. (3) - November 30, 1876
For further information see - Boyers, G. W., Jr.

Mitchell, Ashby (cold.) Lulie Harris (3) - January 16, 1889
Place of marriage, Shepherdstown - Age of husband, 22 - Age of wife,
21 - Both are Single - Husband was born in Rappahannock County,
Virginia - Wife was born in Clarke County, Virginia - Husband
resides in Warren County, Virginia - Wife resides in Jefferson
County, West Virginia.

Mitchell, Charles Ed. (cold.) Sarah E. Hall (3) - June 16, 1889
Place of marriage, Summit Point - Age of husband, 31 - Age of wife,
22 - Husband is Single - Wife is a Widow - Husband was born in
Prince William County, Virginia - Wife was born in Jefferson County,
West Virginia - Both reside in Jefferson County, West Virginia.

Mitchell, Columbus C. and Ann Catharine Brown (2) - (L) November 21, 1855

Mitchell, Frank (cold.) Mary Galloway (3) - April 1, 1884
Place of marriage, Charlestown - Age of husband, 29 - Age of wife,
22 - Both are Single - Both were born in Jefferson County, West
Virginia - Both reside in Jefferson County, West Virginia.

Mitchell, Gabriel (cold.) Margaret Lowry (3) - April 19, 1888
Place of marriage, Charlestown - Age of husband, 65 - Age of wife,
50 - Husband is Single - Wife is a Widow - Both were born in
Jefferson County, West Virginia - Both reside in Jefferson County,
West Virginia.

Mitchell, Gustavus T. and Betsy Bramhal (1) - March 16, 1815

Mitchell, Henry T. and Annie M. Hertshue (3) - December 6, 1866
Place of marriage, Bolivar, Jefferson County, West Virginia - Age of
husband, 25 - Age of wife, 20 - Both are Single - Both were born in
Washington County, Maryland - Husband resides at Burketsville,
Washington County, Maryland - Wife resides at Harpers Ferry,
Jefferson County, West Virginia - Husband's parents are William H.
and S. Mitchell - Occupation of husband is Carpenter.

Mitchell, Jacob and Sarah McGlincy (1) - May 26, 1833

Mitchell, James A. and Ellen V. Loman (3) - August 31, 1875
Place of marriage, Harpers Ferry - Age of husband, 27 - Age of wife,
17 - Both are Single - Both were born in Jefferson County, West
Virginia - Both reside in Jefferson County, West Virginia.
(Consent of Randolff Wood, stepfather of bride, in person.)

Mitchell, Joseph (cold.) Caroline Washington (3) - May 12, 1887
Place of marriage, Charlestown - Age of husband, 21 - Age of wife,
21 - Both are Single - Both were born in Jefferson County, West
Virginia - Husband resides in Jefferson County, West Virginia - Wife
resides in Jefferson County.

Mitchell, Lewis (cold.) Lydia Robinson (nee Baker) (3) -   December 28, 1882
    Place of marriage, Shepherdstown - Age of husband, 46 - Age of wife,
    46 - Husband is a Widower - Wife is a Widow - Husband was born in
    Berkeley County, West Virginia - Wife was born in Jefferson County,
    West Virginia - Both reside in Jefferson County, West Virginia.

Mitchell, Mary Ann and Joseph Brown (1) -   April 7, 1825

Mitchell, Mary Margaret Ellen and Nathaniel Warfield (3) -   October 28, 1875
    For further information see - Warfield, Nathaniel.

Mitchell, Milly (cold.) Lewis Porter (3) -   November 6, 1873
    For further information see - Porter, Lewis.

Mitchell, Robert B. and Rachel Alice Eby (3) -   April 21, 1881
    Place of marriage, Charlestown - Age of husband, 24 - Age of wife,
    24 - Both are Single - Husband was born in State of Maryland - Wife
    was born in Jefferson County, West Virginia - Both reside in
    Jefferson County, West Virginia.

Mitchell, Samuel (cold.) Rose Washington (3) -   November 25, 1889
    Place of marriage, Shepherdstown - Age of husband, 21 - Age of wife,
    19 - Both are Single - Husband was born in Rappahannock County,
    Virginia - Wife was born in Jefferson County, West Virginia -
    Husband resides in Warren County, Virginia - Wife resides in
    Jefferson County, West Virginia. (Consent of bride's parents in
    writing.)

Mitchell, Thomas (cold.) Louisa Hart (3) -   August 6, 1881
    Place of marriage, Shepherdstown - Age of husband, 28 - Age of wife,
    19 - Both are Single - Husband was born in Warren County, Virginia -
    Wife was born in Alleghany County, Maryland - Both reside in
    Jefferson County, West Virginia. (Bride has neither father nor
    mother.)

Mix, M. Roberta and H. L. Briscoe (3) -   November 30, 1882
    For further information see - Briscoe, H. L.

Moaler, Ann and Samuel Avis (1) -   March 19, 1818

Mobberly, George C. and Sarah E. Lancaster (3) -   December 9, 1874
    Place of marriage, Harpers Ferry - Age of husband, 23 - Age of wife,
    18 - Both are Single - Both were born in Jefferson County, West
    Virginia - Both reside in Jefferson County, West Virginia.
    (Consent of bride's mother in writing.)

Mobley, Amanda and James William Wiley (3) -   October 28, 1875
    For further information see - Wiley, James William.

Mobley, Annie E. and E. B. Johnson (3) -   August 17, 1878
    For further information see - Johnson, E. B.

Mobley, Cornelius and Mary Dodge (3) -   October 30, 1881
    Place of marriage, Pipertown - Age of husband, 23 - Age of wife,
    30 - Both are Single - Both were born in Jefferson County, West
    Virginia - Both reside in Jefferson County, West Virginia.

Mobley, Ellen Crem and James William Cook (3) -   February 1, 1877
    For further information see - Cook, James William.

Mobley, Liza Ann and John T. Pearl (3) - August 23, 1872
    For further information see - Pearl, John T.

Mock, George A. and Lucy T. Avis (3) - October 15, 1884
    Place of marriage, Charlestown - Age of husband, 28 - Age of wife,
    24 - Both are Single - Both were born in Jefferson County, West
    Virginia - Both reside in Jefferson County.

Mock, Lydia A. and James W. Jones (2) - (L) February 10, 1858

Mock, William H. and Zipporah McCory (3) - August 13, 1884
    Place of marriage, Charlestown - Age of husband, 22 - Age of wife,
    17 - Both are Single - Husband was born in Maryland - Wife was born
    in Jefferson County - Husband resides in Jefferson County - Wife
    resides in Jefferson County, West Virginia. (Consent of bride's
    mother in writing.)

Molar, Cassa and Thomas Dunlop (1) - June 12, 1805

Molar, John and Rachael Brown (1) - April 10, 1817

Molar, Ruhama and Conrad Leickliter, Jr. (1) - March 20, 1817

Moler, Adam and Mary Groover (1) - September 1822

Moler, Adam B. and Elizabeth Ann Moore (3). - January 4, 1877
    Place of marriage, Ripon - Age of husband, 26 - Age of wife, 23 -
    Both are Single - Husband was born in Jefferson County, West
    Virginia - Wife was born in Berkeley County, West Virginia - Both
    reside in Jefferson County, West Virginia.

Moler, Adam C. and Cora V. Daniels (3) - February 27, 1872
    Place of marriage, Jefferson County, West Virginia - Age of husband,
    27 - Age of wife, 19 - Both are Single - Husband was born in
    Jefferson County - Wife was born in Jefferson County, Virginia -
    Husband resides in Jefferson County - Wife resides in Jefferson
    County, West Virginia - Husband's parents are Rawleigh and Margaret -
    Wife's parents are Dennis M. and Ann R. - Occupation of husband is
    Farmer.

Moler, Adella and George E. Nicewarner (3) - April 4, 1889
    For further information see - Nicewarner, George E.

Moler, Ann and Jacob Swagler (1) - May 14, 1818

Moler, Ann and Jacob Moler (1) - 1819

Moler, Annie E. and August Shutts (3) - November 12, 1872
    For further information see - Shutts, August.

Moler, Annie T. and Arthur E. Wilson (2) - (L) December 15, 1856

Moler, Arthur L. and Ida L. Caton (3) - March 22, 1882
    Place of marriage, near Shepherdstown - Age of husband, 21 - Age of
    wife, 21 - Both are Single - Both were born in Jefferson County,
    West Virginia - Both reside in Jefferson County, West Virginia.

Moler, Charles and Lydia Engle (1) - 1819

Moler, Charles G. and Minnie Lee Hendricks (3) -   June 11, 1885
    Place of marriage, near Unionville - Age of husband, 29 - Age of
    wife, 28 - Both are Single - Both were born in Jefferson County,
    West Virginia - Both reside in Jefferson County, West Virginia.

Moler, D. H. and Annie Virginia Staley (3) -   July 14, 1880
    Place of marriage, Charlestown - Age of husband, 21 - Age of wife,
    25 - Both are Single - Both were born in Jefferson County, West
    Virginia - Both reside in Jefferson County, West Virginia.

Moler, Daniel and Margaret Leckliter (1) -   January 1825

Moler, Daniel G. and Helen C. Ronemous (3) -   March 20, 1866
    Place of marriage, near Unionville, Jefferson County - Age of
    husband, 22 - Age of wife, 20 - Both are Single - Both were born in
    Jefferson County - Both reside in Jefferson County, West Virginia -
    Husband's parents are Daniel and Margaret Moler - Wife's parents are
    John and Barbara Ronemous - Occupation of husband is Farmer.

Moler, Daniel J. and Ann Virginia Morrison (2) -   (L) November 6, 1860

Moler, Ellen and George Hartness (1) -   1825

Moler, Ellen and John Kephart (1) -   1825

Moler, Emily Virginia and John Lewis Kephart (2) -   (L) November 6, 1860

Moler, Emma G. and John W. Caton (3) -   January 3, 1882
    For further information see - Caton, John W.

Moler, Francis M. and Rosa B. Moler (3) -   November 27, 1889
    Place of marriage, Charlestown - Age of husband, 36 - Age of wife,
    26 - Both are Single - Both were born in Jefferson County, West
    Virginia - Both reside in Jefferson County, West Virginia.

Moler, George and Sally C. Moore (1) -   1825

Moler, George A. and Martha E. Morrison (2) -   (L) May 7, 1862
    Time of marriage, May 8, 1862 - Place of marriage, William B.
    Morrison's, bride's father - Names, George A. Moler and Martha E.
    Morrison - Age of husband, 29 years - Age of wife, 22 years -
    Condition of both is Single - Place of birth, both were born in
    Jefferson County - Residence is Jefferson County - Names of husband's
    parents are Henry and Harriet Moler - Names of wife's parents are
    William B. and Mary Morrison - Occupation of husband is Farmer.
    Liscense issued, May 7, 1862.

Moler, George Adam and Thersey Moore (1) -   1822

Moler, George Newton and Angelina Shell (3) -   January 25, 1883
    Place of marriage, Molers Cross Roads - Age of husband, 22 - Age of
    wife, 24 - Both are Single - Both were born in Jefferson County,
    West Virginia - Both reside in Jefferson County, West Virginia.

Moler, George W. and Lucy Thompson (3) -   April 16, 1889
    Place of marriage, Shepherdstown - Age of husband, 21 - Age of wife,
    21 - Both are Single - Both were born in Jefferson County, West
    Virginia - Both reside in Jefferson County, West Virginia.

Moler, George William and Laura F. Flanagin (2) -   (L) December 20, 1854

Moler, Georgia A. L. and George T. Trundle (3) -　　　　　　May 28, 1872
　　For further information see - Trundle, George T.

Moler, Hannah E. and R. G. Moler (2) -　　　　　　　　　(L) April 11, 1857

Moler, Hattie R. and Charles Koonce (3) -　　　　　　　December 30, 1883
　　For further information see - Koonce, Charles.

Moler, Henry C. and Mary J. Kephart (2) -　　　　　　　(L) February 25, 1851

Moler, Jacob and Ann Moler (1) -　　　　　　　　　　　　　　　　　　1819

Moler, Jacob S. and Martha Virginia Link (3) -　　　　January 16, 1877
　　Place of marriage, near Unionville - Age of husband, 30 - Age of
　　wife, 21 - Both are Single - Both were born in Jefferson County,
　　West Virginia - Both reside in Jefferson County, West Virginia.

Moler, James E. and Ann Louisa Rohr (1) -　　　　　　　January 6, 1848

Moler, James E. and Elizabeth E. Kephart (2) -　　　　(L) December 7, 1857

Moler, John and Ruth Howell (1) -　　　　　　　　　　　　June 19, 1832

Moler, John and Mary M. Engle (3) -　　　　　　　　　　March 3, 1868
　　Place of marriage, Jefferson County - Age of husband, 30 - Age of
　　wife, 25 - Both are Single - Both were born in Jefferson County -
　　Both reside in Jefferson - Husband's parents are George W. and
　　Sarah - Wife's parents are John and Catherine B. - Occupation of
　　husband is Farmer.

Moler, John G. and Margaret Helen Moler (2) -　　　　(L) November 10, 1855

Moler, Katherine S. and N. M. Hendricks, M. D. (3) -　December 3, 1885
　　For further information see - Hendricks, N. M., (M. D.)

Moler, Lee H. and Mary V. Knott (3) -　　　　　　　　　June 9, 1868
　　Place of marriage, Jefferson County - Age of husband, 31 - Age of
　　wife, 26 - Husband is Single - Wife is a Widow - Both were born in
　　Jefferson County - Both reside in Jefferson County - Husband's
　　parents are Levi and Hester - Wife's parents are Christian -
　　Occupation of husband is Farmer.

Moler, Levi and Anne Hoffman (1) -　　　　　　　　　　　June 4, 1827

Moler, Levi and Tanzon Margaret Brown (1) -　　　　　　October 22, 1829

Moler, Levi and Hester L. Taylor (1) -　　　　　　　　October 25, 1831

Moler, Lizzie S. and T. T. Dillard (3) -　　　　　　　March 13, 1873
　　For further information see - Dillard, T. T.

Moler, Lucy J. and William A. Moler (3) -　　　　　　November 13, 1879
　　For further information see - Moler, William A.

Moler, Lulah E. and Jesse M. Engle (3) -　　　　　　October 13, 1880
　　For further information see - Engle, Jesse M.

Moler, Lydia E. and Samuel C. Noland (3) -　　　　　January 10, 1867
　　For further information see - Noland, Samuel C.

Moler, Margaret Ann and William J. Knott (2) -   (L) January 14, 1853
   (Ages of parties and residence of same proved by the oath of Jacob
   Reinhart.)

Moler, Margaret Helen and John G. Moler (2) -   (L) November 10, 1855

Moler, Mary and Lorenzo D. Hess (2) -   (L) March 29, 1855

Moler, Mary Elizabeth and Jesse A. Engle (3) -   May 2, 1882
   For further information see - Engle, Jesse A.

Moler, Mary Ellen and George B. Stephenson (1) -   May 6, 1849

Moler, Mary L. and David H. Buckles (3) -   June 10, 1868
   For further information see - Buckles, David H.

Moler, Mary V. and Henry M. Snyder (2) -   (L) April 2, 1863
   For further information see - Snyder, Henry M.

Moler, Milton and __?__ (3) -   (L) August 17, 1874
   Place of marriage, near Halltown. (This record in crossed out in
   the original.)

Moler, Nettie B. and William H. Vanmetre (3) -   October 22, 1885
   For further information see - Vanmetre, William H.

Moler, Newton and Frances Backhouse (3) -   October 30, 1867
   Place of marriage, Jefferson County - Age of husband, 23 - Both are
   Single - Husband was born in Jefferson County, Virginia - Wife was
   born in Loudoun County - Both reside in Jefferson County - Husband's
   parents are Henry and Harriet - Wife's parents are George and
   Catharine - Occupation of husband is Farmer.

Moler, Patsie J. L. and Joseph B. Beavers (3) -   December 26, 1865
   For further information see - Beavers, Joseph B.

Moler, Philip R. and Sarah Ann Moler (1) -   July 27, 1848

Moler, R. G. and Hannah E. Moler (2) -   (L) April 11, 1857

Moler, Raleigh and Margaret Miller (1) -   December 19, 1833

Moler, Raleigh L. and Alice J. Engle (3) -   January 22, 1878
   Place of marriage, near Old Furnace - Age of husband, 27 - Age of
   wife, 21 - Both are Single - Both were born in Jefferson County,
   West Virginia - Both reside in Jefferson County, West Virginia.

Moler, Raleigh V. and Lydia E. Engle (3) -   January 5, 1869
   Place of marriage, Jefferson County - Age of husband, 28 - Age of
   wife, 24 - Both are Single - Both were born in Virginia - Husband
   resides in Jefferson County - Wife resides in Jefferson County, West
   Virginia - Husband's parents are Raleigh and Margaret - Wife's
   parents are John and Catherine B. - Occupation of husband is Farmer.

Moler, Robert W. and Theresa M. Strider (1) -   January 25, 1849

Moler, Rosa B. and Francis M. Moler (3) -   November 27, 1889
   For further information see - Moler, Francis M.

Moler, S. A. (bride) and H. Glasford (3) -   December 21, 1871
   For further information see - Glasford, H.

Moler, Sarah Ann and Philip R. Moler (1) -   July 27, 1848

Moler, Sarah Ellen and J. Taylor Hill (3) -   October 20, 1874
   For further information see - Hill, J. Taylor.

Moler, Sarah F. and Emanuel R. Schaeffer (3) -   October 24, 1865
   For further information see - Schaeffer, Emanuel R.

Moler, Sylvanus G. and Hannah T. Burnett (1) -   May 17, 1831

Moler, William A. and Lucy J. Moler (3) -   November 13, 1879
   Place of marriage, near Duffields - Age of husband, 23 - Age of wife,
   18 - Both are Single - Both were born in Jefferson County, West
   Virginia - Both reside in Jefferson County, West Virginia -
   (Consent of bride's mother in writing, father being dead.)

Moler, William H. and Bettie C. Jones (3) -   January 27, 1886
   Place of marriage, Charlestown - Age of husband, 29 - Age of wife,
   32 - Both are Single - Husband was born in Jefferson County, West
   Virginia - Wife was born in Jefferson County -Both reside in
   Jefferson County, West Virginia.

Moler, William H. and Nellie Clipp (3) -   December 5, 1889
   Place of marriage, Charlestown - Age of husband, 21 - Age of wife,
   21 - Both are Single - Both were born in Jefferson County, West
   Virginia - Both reside in Jefferson County, West Virginia.

Moler, William J. and Sarah E. Strider (2) -   (L) April 2, 1863
   Time of marriage, April 14, 1863 - Place of marriage, Residence of
   Bride's Father - Names, William J. Moler are Sarah E. Strider - Age
   of husband, 24 years February 18, 1863 - Age of wife, 22 years
   November 21, 1862 - Both are Single - Both were born in Jefferson
   County - Both reside in Jefferson County - Husband's parents are
   Raleigh and Margaret Moler - Wife's parents are Jacob and Sarah Ann
   Strider - Occupation of husband is Farmer - License issued April 2,
   1863 - Thomas A. Moore, Clerk.

Monday, Ida and Samuel C. Cooper (3) -   September 16, 1889
   For further information see - Cooper, Samuel C.

Monegan, Viola and Thomas J. Garrison (3) -   December 15, 1885
   For further information see - Garrison, Thomas J.

Monroe, John J. and Mary Ann Kitchen (1) -   October 27, 1831

Monroe, W. M. and Susan V. Jacobs (3) -   (1868)
   Age of husband, 24 - Age of wife, 20 - Both are Single - Both were
   born in Loudoun County, Virginia - Both reside in Loudoun County -
   Husband's parents are J. W. and Caroline D. - Wife's parents are
   R. P. and Susan - Occupation of husband is Farmer.

Montgomery, Rhenbecker and James L. Webb (3) -   August 1889
   For further information see - Webb, James L.

Moon, Will W. and Sallie Fauver (3) - December 25, 1890
    Place of marriage, Charlestown - Age of husband, 24 - Age of wife,
    23 - Both are Single - Husband was born in Page County, Virginia -
    Wife was born in Warren County, Virginia - Both reside in Jefferson
    County, West Virginia.

Moor, Clarissa and T. J. W. Sullivan (1) - January 4, 1849

Moor, Sarah A. and James H. Moore (2) - (L) February 21, 1853

Moore, A. Compton and Nannie M. Butler (3) - November 12, 1879
    Place of marriage, Shepherdstown - Age of husband, 24 - Age of wife,
    25 - Both are Single - Both were born in Jefferson County, West
    Virginia - Both reside in Jefferson County, West Virginia.

Moore, A. L. and P. P. Buckles (bride) (3) - April 3, 1872
    Place of marriage, Jefferson County, West Virginia - Age of husband,
    27 - Age of wife, 18 - Both are Single - Both were born in Jefferson
    County, West Virginia - Both reside in Jefferson County, West
    Virginia - Husband's parents are William H. and Virginia - Wife's
    parents are William and Nancy - Occupation of husband is Farmer.
    (William Buckles.)

Moore, Ann N. and Robert Duke (1) - 1816

Moore, Benjamin and Augusta F. Herrington (1) - November 12, 1833

Moore, Bettie and J. G. Wyet (3) - April 22, 1868
    For further information see - Wyet, J. G.

Moore, Bettie M. and John O. Tackett (3) - June 4, 1890
    For further information see - Tackett, John O.

Moore, Bettie T. and John T. Gibson, Jr. (3) - December 13, 1877
    For further information see - Gibson, John T., Jr.

Moore, Cato and Margaret Strother (1) - April 26, 1814

Moore, Cleon and Ellen D. Rutherford (3) - November 13, 1867
    Place of marriage, Charlestown - Age of husband, 26 - Age of wife,
    26 - Both are Single - Husband was born in Jefferson County,
    Virginia - Wife was born in Jefferson County - Both reside in
    Jefferson County - Husband's parents are Thomas A. and M. J. -
    Wife's parents are Thomas and Mary - Occupation of husband is
    Teacher.

Moore, David and Margaret Groomes (1) - 1812

Moore, Eliza A. and Robert S. Thompson (2) - (L) May 1, 1860

Moore, Elizabeth and John Stewart (1) - April 27, 1820

Moore, Elizabeth and P. P. W. Stephenson (1) - December 12, 1842

Moore, Elizabeth (cold.) Fontaine Freeman (3) - March 8, 1877
    For further information see - Freeman, Fontaine.

Moore, Elizabeth Ann and Adam B. Moler (3) - January 4, 1877
    For further information see - Moler, Adam B.

Moore, Ella Virginia and William H. Peters (3) - September 26, 1888
For further information see - Peters, William H.

Moore, Ellen (cold.) Andrew Reeler (3) - December 31, 1882
For futher information see - Reeler, Andrew.

Moore, Fanny and Valentine Shaull (2) - (L) January 2, 1851

Moore, Fanny and Valentine Shaull (1) - January 2, 1851

Moore, Garland and Sally Butler (1) - March 1832

Moore, George W. and Emma B. Homer (3) - December 2, 1875
Place of marriage, Middleway - Age of husband, 51 - Age of wife, 19 - Both are Single - Both were born in Jefferson County, West Virginia - Both reside in Jefferson County, West Virginia. (Consent of mother of bride certified by bride's brother.)

Moore, George W.,Jr. and Matilda V. Butler (3) - October 21, 1885
Place of marriage, Shepherdstown - Age of husband, 25 - Age of wife, 21 - Both are Single - Both were born in Jefferson County, West Virginia - Both reside in Jefferson County, West Virginia.

Moore, Gerard D. and Mollie G. Thomson (3) - February 17, 1885
Place of marriage, At Home of Bride - Age of husband, 27 - Age of wife, 27 - Both are Single - Both were born in Jefferson County, West Virginia - Both reside in Jefferson County, West Virginia.

Moore, Gerard D. and Katie Janney (3) - July 30, 1889
Place of marriage, Charlestown - Age of husband, 32 - Age of wife, 29 - Husband is a Widower - Wife is Single - Husband was born in Jefferson County, West Virginia - Wife was born in Clarke County, Virginia - Both reside in Jefferson County, West Virginia.

Moore, Hannah B. and Charles C. Ring (3) - July 24, 1877
For further information see - Ring, Charles C.

Moore, Henry (cold.) Mary A. Turner (3) - August 8, 1883
Place of marriage, Charlestown - Age of husband, 27 - Age of wife, 21 - Both are Single - Husband was born in King George County, Virginia - Wife was born in Jefferson County, West Virginia - Both reside in Jefferson County, West Virginia.

Moore, Henry H. and Ellen R. Welsh (2) - (L) December 12, 1856

Moore, James H. and Sarah A. Moor (2) - (L) February 21, 1853

Moore, James W. and Iona E. Kline (3) - May 14, 1878
Place of marriage, Middleway - Age of husband, 25 - Age of wife, 32 - Husband is Single - Wife is a Widow - Both were born in Jefferson County, West Virginia - Both reside in Jefferson County, West Virginia.

Moore, Jane C. and James W. Campbell (2) - (L) September 12, 1854

Moore, Jane E. (cold.) Thomas Johnson (3) - April 7, 1881
For further information see - Johnson, Thomas.

Moore, Jarrett and Elizabeth Strother (1) - September 19, 1820

Moore, Jesse H. and Lucretia Keyes (1) -   1827

Moore, John S. and Mary M. Riely (2) -   (L) November 5, 1853

Moore, Joseph R. and Jane M. Hart (2) -   (L) April 5, 1853

Moore, Kitty and John Wilson (1) -   October 14, 1813

Moore, Lidia F. and William Strider (1) -   1816

Moore, Lydia and John C. Rockenbaugh (2) -   (L) November 7, 1851

Moore, Lydia (colored) Moses Young (3) -   1867
   For further information see - Young, Moses.

Moore, Margaret E. and David Stewart (3) -   June 8, 1875
   For further information see - Stewart, David.

Moore, Mary C. and George W. Gorrell (2) -   (L) December 31, 1853

Moore, Mary C.
   For further information see - Dowdon, R. C.

Moore, Mary E. (cold.) William Crawford (3) -   February 7, 1889
   For further information see - Crawford, William.

Moore, Mary Frances and Torsend B. Howell (3) -   December 19, 1876
   For further information see - Howell, Torsend B.

Moore, Mary P. A. and Charles D. Homar (3) -   July 24, 1877
   For further information see - Homar, Charles D.

Moore, Mattie E. and Thomas J. Burleigh (3) -   July 15, 1878
   For further information see - Burleigh, Thomas J.

Moore, Milton H. and Mary V. Butler (3) -   August 31, 1887
   Place of marriage, near Kearneysville - Age of husband, 68 - Age of
   wife, 44 - Husband is a Widower - Wife is Single - Both were born in
   Jefferson County, West Virginia - Husband resides in State of
   Missouri - Wife resides in Jefferson County, West Virginia.

Moore, Nicholas and Fannie Bonham (3) -   November 7, 1867
   Place of marriage, Jefferson County - Age of husband, 26 - Age of
   wife, 21 - Both are Single - Husband was born in Maryland - Wife was
   born in Jefferson County - Husband resides in Clarke County,
   Virginia - Wife resides in Jefferson County - Husband's parents are
   A. M. and Mary - Wife's parents are A. and Eliza - Occupation of
   husband is Farmer.

Moore, Richard H. and Annie Murphy (3) -   September 27, 1866
   Place of marriage, Shepherdstown, Jefferson County - Age of husband,
   28 - Age of wife, 29 - Both are Single - Both were born in Jefferson
   County, West Virginia - Both reside in Jefferson County, West
   Virginia - Husband's parents are Samuel and Rachel Moore -
   Occupation of husband is Laborer.

Moore, Richard Henry (cold.) Sarah Pendleton (3) -   December 31, 1873
   Place of marriage, near Charlestown - Age of husband, 34 - Age of
   wife, 24 - Both are Single - Both were born in Jefferson County,
   West Virginia - Both reside in Jefferson County, West Virginia.

400

Moore, Robert Milton and Mary Louisa Wiltshire (3) - April 26, 1883
Place of marriage, Charlestown - Age of husband, 26 - Age of wife,
25 - Both are Single - Both were born in Jefferson County, West
Virginia - Both reside in Jefferson County, West Virginia.

Moore, Sally C. and George Moler (1) - 1825

Moore, Samuel and Elizabeth Blue (1) - 1827

Moore, Samuel and Mary Sefras (3) - December 16, 1868
Place of marriage, Jefferson County - Age of husband, 33 - Age of
wife, 30 - Both are Single - Husband was born in Jefferson County -
Wife was born in Jefferson - Husband resides in Jefferson County,
Virginia - Wife resides in Jefferson County - Occupation of husband
is Farmer.

Moore, Samuel J. C. and Eleanor G. Scollay (2) - (L) December 12, 1850

Moore, Samuel J. C. and Eleanor G. Scollay (1) - December 12, 1850

Moore, Thersey and George Adam Moler (1) - 1822

Moore, Thomas A. and Jane Saunderson Cramer (1) - June 29, 1825

Moore, Thomas A. and Maria Jane Likens (1) - June 29, 1836

Moore, Thomas B. and Sarah F. Miller (2) - (L) June 6, 1857

Moore, Vincent G. and Mary Hansher (3) - November 19, 1888
Place of marriage, Kearneysville - Age of husband, 43 - Age of wife,
27 - Both are Single - Husband was born in Jefferson County, West
Virginia - Wife was born in Pennsylvania - Both reside in Jefferson
County, West Virginia.

Moore, William and Matilda Hinkle (1) - December 20, 1816

Moore, William A. and Annie C. Chambers (3) - May 29, 1886
Place of marriage, Harpers Ferry - Age of husband, 35 - Age of wife,
35 - Husband is Single - Wife is a Widow - Husband was born in
Loudoun County, Virginia - Wife was born in Frederick County,
Virginia - Both reside in Jefferson County, West Virginia.

More, Jane and Mathew Graham (1) - June 12, 1804

Moreland, G. J. and M. G. Haley (bride) (3) - August 29, 1867
Place of marriage, Jefferson - Age of husband, 30 - Age of wife,
20 - Husband is a Widower - Wife is Single - Husband was born in
Loudoun County, Virginia - Wife was born in Jefferson County, West
Virginia - Both reside in Jefferson County, West Virginia -
Husband's parents are Samuel and Sarah - Wife's parents are Franklin
and Sarah E. - Occupation of husband is Farmer. (Father gives
consent in person.)

Morell, Frank H. and Sarah A. Jones (3) - September 23, 1872
Place of marriage, Jefferson County - Age of husband, 26 - Age of
wife, 22 - Both are Single - Both were born in Maine - Husband
resides in Illinois - Wife resides in Maine - Husband's parents are
A. S. A. and E. Morell - Wife's parents are J. B. and J. M. Jones -
Occupation of husband is Accountant.

Morgan, Ann A. and R. L. Morgan (3) - October 31, 1872
    For further information see - Morgan, R. L.

Morgan, Anna J. and Harry C. Getzendanner (3) - November 28, 1882
    For further information see - Getzendanner, Harry C.

Morgan, Augusta and George W. Hall (1) - December 18, 1849

Morgan, Daniel and Mary W. Lowry (1) - October 22, 1806

Morgan, Elenor and James Davis (1) - June 27, 1822

Morgan, Eliza and George W. Hiedwohl (3) - January 1, 1874
    For further information see - Hiedwohl, George W.

Morgan, Elizabeth and Mathew Ranson (1) - May 4, 1807

Morgan, Elizabeth and Van Swearingen (1) - January 26, 1809

Morgan, Elizabeth B. and Augustine J. Smith (2) - (L) December 3, 1855

Morgan, Harrison (col.) Mary Nicholas (3) - November 11, 1867
    Place of marriage, Jefferson County - Age of husband, 25 - Age of
    wife, 23 - Both are Single - Husband was born in Berkeley County -
    Wife was born in Jefferson - Husband resides in Berkeley - Wife
    resides in Jefferson County - Occupation of husband is Farmer.

Morgan, Jane E. and W. S. Morgan (3) - September 21, 1869
    For further information see - Morgan, W. S.

Morgan, Jeptha and Elanor Thornburg (1) - January 22, 1818

Morgan, Kate (cold.) James Jones (3) - November 15, 1880
    For further information see - Jones, James.

Morgan, Lewis (cold.) Laura Brown (3) - November 8, 1876
    Place of marriage, near Charlestown - Age of husband, 26 - Age of
    wife, 21 - Both are Single - Husband was born in Jefferson County,
    West Virginia - Wife was born in Augusta County, Virginia - Both
    reside in Jefferson County, West Virginia. (Returned December 1882.)

Morgan, Lidia and James McCauly (1) - April 30, 1812

Morgan, Lucy Ann and George A. Creamer (2) - (L) January 4, 1855

Morgan, Margaret and Thomas Powell (1) - October 10, 1833

Morgan, Margaret and Dorsey Tyson (3) - October 16, 1878
    For further information see - Tyson, Dorsey.

Morgan, Martha Jane and Luther Carter (2) - (L) July 29, 1851

Morgan, Martha Jane and Luther Carter (1) - July 31, 1851

Morgan, Nellie and Benjamin Nelson (3) - January 5, 1871
    For further information see - Nelson, Benjamin.

Morgan, R. L. and Ann A. Morgan (3) -   October 31, 1872
    Place of marriage, Jefferson County - Age of husband, 31 - Age of
    wife, 26 - Both are Single - Both were born in Virginia - Husband's
    parents are William and Jane - Wife's parents are Richard and
    Susan - Occupation of husband is Paper Man.

Morgan, Ruhanna and Edward Southwood (1) -   .   July 2, 1818

Morgan, Susan M. and Lewis B. Creamer (2) -   (L) November 23, 1853

Morgan, Thomas and Polly Robinson (1) -   May 3, 1804

Morgan, W. S. and Jane E. Morgan (3) -   .   September 21, 1869
    Place of marriage, Jefferson County - Age of husband, 22 - Age of
    wife, 17, Both were born in Jefferson County - Both reside in
    Jefferson County.   (Father in person consents.)

Morgan, William (cold.) M. E. Holmes (3) -   January 5, 1868
    Place of marriage, Jefferson County - Age of husband, 22 - Age of
    wife, 20 - Husband is a Widower - Wife is Single - Husband was born
    in Jefferson County - Wife was born in Clarke County, Virginia -
    Both reside in Jefferson County - Occupation of husband is Farmer.
    (Mother gives consent.)

Moriarty, Dennis and Isabella Greer (2) -   (L) January 2, 1854

Morlat, James and Phebe Ayer (1) -   January 10, 1832

Morningstar, Andrew Jackson and Sallie A. Seay (3) -   January 9, 1868
    Place of marriage, Jefferson County - Age of husband, 31 - Age of
    wife, 21 - Husband is a Widower - Wife is Single - Husband was born
    in Jefferson County - Wife was born in Nelson County - Both reside
    in Jefferson County - Husband's parents are Jacob and Sarah - Wife's
    parents are Samuel C. and Georgiana - Occupation of husband is Farmer.

Morningstar, Ann and Charles Birdsell (3) -   . September 8, 1887
    For further information see - Birdsell, Charles.

Morningstar, Mary and James B. Turner (3) -   May 14, 1871
    For further information see - Turner, James B.

Morningstar, Rosa Lee and John P. Lashhorn (3) -   January 18, 1888
    For further information see - Lashhorn, John P.

Morningstar, Ruth Anna Jane and James C. Whittington (2) -(L) December 6, 1856

Morrell, Annie F. and William Lunn (3) -   January 21, 1890
    For further information see - Lunn, William.

Morris, Ann Elizabeth and James E. Whittington (3) -   December 20, 1888
    For further information see - Whittington, James E.

Morris, Annie (cold.) James H. Toles (3) -   December 6, 1887
    For further information see - Toles, James H.

Morris, Charlotte (cold.) Morton Shelton (3) -   July 10, 1877
    For further information see - Shelton, Morton.

Morris, E. (cold.) Isaiah Wheeler (3) -   November 17, 1867
    For further information see - Wheeler, Isaiah.

Morris, Ella C. and Charles T. Nichols (3) -   June 18, 1890
    For further information see - Nichols, Charles T.

Morris, Ella Zeon (cold.) John Walker (3) -   July 15, 1880
    For further information see. - Walker, John.

Morris, Ellen and John J. Lee (3) -   (1869)
    For further information see - Lee, John J.

Morris, George W. and Mary Hufmaster (2) -   (L) November 26, 1853

Morris, Katie and Ira Walters (3) -   September 29, 1889
    For further information see - Walters, Ira.

Morris, Lucy (cold.) Cary Harris (3) -   November 17, 1887
    For further information see - Harris, Cary.

Morris, Marcus and Lucy Short (3) -   December 22, 1866
    Place of marriage, near Duffields Depot, Jefferson County - Age of
    husband, 22 - Age of wife, 22 - Both are Single - Both were born in
    Jefferson County, West Virginia - Both reside in Jefferson County,
    West Virginia - Husband's parents are Marcus and Sarah J. Morris -
    Wife's parents are Thomas and Elizabeth Short - Occupation of
    husband is Laborer.

Morris, Mary and George Hardesty (1) -   August 9, 1805

Morris, Mary Selina and W. T. Whittington (3) -   December 2, 1885
    For further information see - Whittington, W. T.

Morris, Richard (cold.) Emma Hunter (3) -   December 1883
    Place of marriage, Charlestown - Age of husband, 35 - Age of wife,
    26 - Both are Single - Husband was born in Louisa County, Virginia -
    Wife was born in Loudoun County, Virginia - Both reside in Jefferson
    County, West Virginia.

Morris, Robert Henry (cold.) Charity McDaniel (3) -   January 5, 1888
    Place of marriage, Charlestown - Age of husband, 29 - Age of wife,
    23 - Husband is a Widower by divorce - Wife is a Widow by divorce -
    Husband was born in Fauquier County, Virginia - Wife was born in
    Jefferson County, West Virginia - Both reside in Jefferson County,
    West Virginia.   (License issued December 31, 1887.)

Morris, Sarah and Jacob Boreman (3) -   March 18, 1871
    For further information see - Boreman, Jacob.

Morris, Sarah E. (cold.) J. W. Throckmorton (3) -   May 15, 1888
    For further information see - Throckmorton, J. W.

Morris, Sezel and Mary Glasson (3) -   June 11, 1867
    Age of husband, 25 - Age of wife, 22 - Both are Single - Husband was
    born at Richmond, Virginia - Wife was born in Jefferson County, West
    Virginia - Husband resides at Hainesville, Berkeley County - Wife
    resides in Jefferson County, West Virginia - Wife's parents are
    Thomas and Cassa Glasson - Occupation of husband is Blacksmith.

Morris, Spencer and Margaret Smith (3) -   November 15, 1867
    Place of marriage, Jefferson County - Age of husband, 23 - Age of
    wife, 27 - Husband is Single - Wife is a Widow - Husband was born in
    Virginia - Wife was born in Jefferson - Both reside in Jefferson
    County - Occupation of husband is Laborer.

Morris, Thomas and Mary Levick (1) -   June 30, 1814

Morris, William T. and Annie F. Shaner (3) -   September 21, 1879
    Place of marriage, Charlestown - Age of husband, 33 - Age of wife,
    21 - Both are Single - Both were born in Jefferson County, West
    Virginia - Both reside in Jefferson County, West Virginia.

Morrison, Ann Virginia and Daniel J. Moler (2) -   (L) November 6, 1860

Morrison, Barthelomew and Mary Jane Whittington (2) -   (L) August 3, 1859

Morrison, Daniel T. and Susan R. Jones (3) -   January 29, 1873
    Place of marriage, Harpers Ferry - Age of husband, 27 - Age of wife,
    20 - Both are Single - Both were born in Jefferson County - Both
    reside in Jefferson County, West Virginia - Husband's parents are
    William and Mary - Wife's parents are Joseph B. and Elizabeth -
    Occupation of husband is Farmer. (Mother's consent in writing,
    sworn.)

Morrison, Edward and Frances E. Hart (2) -   (L) November 17, 1851

Morrison, Edward and Frances E. Hart (1) -   November 18, 1851

Morrison, Elizabeth and William Snyder (1) -   March 1821

Morrison, Emily F. and W. M. Morrison (3) -   (1868)
    For further information see - Morrison, W. M.

Morrison, Martha E. and George A. Moler (2) -   (L) May 7, 1862
    For further information see - Moler, George A.

Morrison, Mary A. and Daniel T. Reynolds (2) -   (L) February 22, 1858

Morrison, Sarah and William Badger (3) -   December 26, 1876
    For further information see - Badger, William.

Morrison, Thornton and Frances Berry (3) -   February 2, 1874
    Place of marriage, near Shepherdstown - Age of husband, 50 - Age of
    wife, 45. (This record is crossed out in the original.)

Morrison, Thornton (cold.) Frances Berry (3) -   February 2, 1874
    Place of marriage, near Shepherdstown - Age of husband, 50 - Age of
    wife, 45 - Husband is Single - Wife is a Widow - Husband was born in
    Jefferson County, West Virginia - Wife was born in Loudoun County,
    Virginia - Both reside in Jefferson County, West Virginia.

Morrison, W. M. and Emily F. Morrison (3) -   (1868)
    Age of husband, 34 - Age of wife, 24 - Both are Single - Husband was
    born in Berkeley County - Wife was born in Jefferson County - Both
    reside in Jefferson County - Husband's parents are D. B. and M. B. -
    Wife's parents are William B. and Mary.

Morrow, F. B. S. and Mary Catharine Rissler (1) -   May 23, 1848

Morrow, Joseph and Sarah Ellen Lock (1) - November 15, 1832

Morrow, Joseph and Mary Ann Downs (2) - (L) April 1, 1852

Morrow, Joseph and Mary Ann Downs (1) - April 1, 1852

Morrow, Joseph R. and Jane L. Bayliss (2) - (L) November 5, 1857

Morrow, Katie V. and Ernest Crutcher (3) - April 13, 1882
 For further information see - Crutcher, Ernest.

Morrow, Mary Margaret Ann and Thomas Bayliss (1) - September 1, 1835

Morrow, R. W. and Lillie M. Walton (3) - January 27, 1886
 Place of marriage, Charlestown - Age of husband, 32 - Age of wife,
 23 - Both are Single - Husband was born in Jefferson County, West
 Virginia - Wife was born in Jefferson County - Both reside in
 Jefferson County, West Virginia.

Morrow, Rebecca A. E. and George B. H. Foreman (2) - (L) May 13, 1853
 (Witness F. J. Harley.)

Morrow, Sarah B. and Ro. Worthington (1) - October 24, 1805

Morrow, Sarah M. and Daniel Heflebower (2) - (L) November 12, 1855

Morrow, Susana and John T. Cookus (1) - April 13, 1813

Morrow, Willard and Ida J. Blessing (3) - April 15, 1885
 Place of marriage, Charlestown - Age of husband, 23 - Age of wife,
 22 - Both are Single - Husband was born in Berkeley County, West
 Virginia - Wife was born in Jefferson County, West Virginia - Both
 reside in Jefferson County, West Virginia.

Morter, Francis and Helen V. Turner (3) - July 10, 1884
 Place of marriage, Snyder's Mill - Age of husband, 25 - Age of wife,
 23 - Both are Single - Husband was born in Cumberland County,
 Pennsylvania - Wife was born in Jefferson County, West Virginia -
 Husband resides in Berkeley County, West Virginia - Wife resides in
 Jefferson County, West Virginia.

Morton, Bertha and F. Redman (3) - November 12, 1868
 For further information see - Redman, F.

Morton, Ella (cold.) John W. Fox (3) - October 1, 1885
 For further information see - Fox, John W.

Morton, Joshua and Mary Brent Bredin (1) - October 29, 1823

Mosby, Eliza (cold.) Frank Nichols (3) - September 15, 1885
 For further information see - Nichols, Frank.

Moser, Christopher and Eliza Martin (1) - October 14, 1802

Moser, Dunham and Evilina Shrodes (1) - July 12, 1825

Moss, Foster and Lucy M. Packett (3) -   June 9, 1880
    Place of marriage, Charlestown - Age of husband, 34 - Age of wife,
    20 - Both are Single - Husband was born in State of New York - Wife
    was born in Jefferson County, West Virginia - Both reside in
    Jefferson County, West Virginia. (Consent of bride's mother in
    writing.)

Moss, Martha (cold.) Jerry Doleman (3) -   March 17, 1880
    For further information see - Doleman, Jerry.

Moton, Emma (cold.) Lee Braxton (3) -   June 15, 1887
    For further information see - Braxton, Lee.

Moton, John (cold.) Cora Jones (3) -   August 21, 1890
    Place of marriage, Bolivar - Age of husband, 21 - Age of wife, 21 -
    Both are Single - Both were born in Jefferson County, West Virginia -
    Both reside in Jefferson County, West Virginia.

Motter, Joshua and Harriot Hinkle (1) -   March 7, 1826

Motter, Louisa and Abraham Reck (1) -   May 15, 1820

Moulder, M. H. (bride) and A. G. Mhler (3) -   November 3, 1870
    For further information see - Mhler, A. G.

Mouser, Margaret and William Kien (1) -   February 28, 1820

Mouser, Sarah and James Likens (1) -   April 8, 1813

Mowser, Mary and Simeon Hiatt (1) -   July 1822

Moyer, David and Elizabeth Schell (1) -   March 1822

Mozier, Mary J. and C. C. Hollingsworth (3) -   March 30, 1873
    For further information see - Hollingsworth, C. C.

Muck, Isaac J. and Fanny T. Fayman (3) -   October 28, 1874
    Place of marriage, Shepherdstown - Age of husband, 21 - Age of wife,
    20 - Both are Single - Husband was born at Wheeling, West Virginia -
    Wife was born in Jefferson County, West Virginia - Husband resides
    at Plymouth, Pennsylvania - Wife resides at Shepherdstown, Jefferson
    County, West Virginia. (Consent of bride's father in writing.)

Muck, Katie and Charles Spong (3) -   October 13, 1889
    For further information see - Spong, Charles.

Muck, Laura and Elmer Dusinger (3) -   September 24, 1890
    For further information see - Dusinger, Elmer.

Muck, William Thomas and Helen Agatha Andrews (3) -   March 29, 1875
    Place of marriage, Shepherdstown - Age of husband, 47 - Age of wife,
    46 - Husband is a Widower - Wife is a Widow - Husband was born in
    Frederick County, Maryland - Wife was born in Jefferson County, West
    Virginia - Both reside in Jefferson County, West Virginia.

Mull, Lucinda Thompson and William Day (2) -   (L) February 18, 1854

Mullen, Joseph and Catharine Maddox (1) -   May 23, 1833

Mullenix, Joshua and Hannah Roach (1) -   May 27, 1821

Mullenix, William and Susana Chapman (1) -　　　　　　February 21, 1814

Mullinax, John Y. and Laura V. Dillon (3) -　　　　　December 5, 1865
    Place of marriage, Jefferson County - Age of husband, 24 - Age of
    wife, 21 - Both are Single - Husband was born in Howard County,
    Maryland - Wife was born at Baltimore, Maryland - Husband resides in
    Howard County, Maryland - Wife resides in Jefferson County, West
    Virginia - Husband's parents are Jonathan and Susan Mullinax - Wife's
    parents are David and Elizabeth Dillon - Occupation of husband is
    Farmer.

Mullinix, Lydia and John Rowland (1) -　　　　　　　September 6, 1829

Mumma, Daniel S. and Mary E. Kennedy (3) -　　　　　December 18, 1884
    Place of marriage, Charlestown - Age of husband, 48 - Age of wife,
    38 - Husband is a Widower - Wife is Single - Both were born in
    Washington County, Maryland - Both reside in Washington County,
    Maryland.

Mundy, John William (cold.) Sallie Jones (3) -　　　May 1, 1883
    Place of marriage, Charlestown - Age of husband, 26 - Age of wife,
    23 - Both are Single - Husband was born in Page County, Virginia -
    Wife was born in Jefferson County, West Virginia - Both reside in
    Jefferson County, West Virginia.

Murkwood, Maria and John D. Crouch (1) -　　　　　　April 2, 1826

Murphy, Alexander and Mary Brannard (2) -　　　　　(L) May 4, 1864
    Time of marriage - Place of marriage, Harpers Ferry - Names,
    Alexander Murphy and Mary Brannard - Age of husband, 24 years - Age
    of wife, 30 years - Both are Single - Place of husband's birth was
    Baltimore, Maryland - Place of wife's birth was Ireland - Both
    reside at Harpers Ferry - Names of husband's parents are James and
    Mary - Names of wife's parents are James and Susan - Occupation of
    husband is Butcher - License issued May 4, 1864 - Thomas A. Moore,
    Clerk.

Murphy, Annie and Richard H. Moore (3) -　　　　　　September 27, 1866
    For further information see - Moore, Richard H.

Murphy, Charles Ed. (cold.) Margaret Johnson (3) -　September 17, 1876
    Place of marriage, near Rippon - Age of husband, 42 - Age of wife,
    22 - Husband is a Widower - Wife is Single - Husband was born in
    Prince William County, Virginia - Wife was born in Clarke County,
    Virginia - Both reside in Jefferson County, West Virginia.

Murphy, George and Nancy Conklin (1) -　　　　　　　January 24, 1822

Murphy, George and Catharine Smith (1) -　　　　　　March 15, 1827

Murphy, Harriet and James McDaniel (1) -　　　　　　February 14, 1826

Murphy, Johana and Thomas B. Duckett (3) -　　　　　December 23, 1869
    For further information see - Duckett, Thomas B.

Murphy, Jonathan and Margaret McDade (1) -　　　　　March 17, 1806

Murphy, Katy F. and George B. Shaull (3) -　　　　　January 5, 1882
    For further information see - Shaull, George B.

Murphy, Mary D. and Joseph M. Hedrick (3) - October 20, 1868
    For further information see - Hedrick, Joseph M.

Murphy, Nancy and William Gardner (1) - February 3, 1819

Murphy, Sidney and Ann H. Allison (2) - (L) September 4, 1858

Murray, Alice (cold.) Philip Williams (3) - July 19, 1877
    For further information see - Williams, Philip.

Murray, Alice (cold.) Daniel Hart (3) - March 27, 1884
    For further information see - Hart, Daniel.

Murray, Betty (cold.) Benjamin Luckett (3) - July 26, 1887
    For further information see - Luckett, Benjamin.

Murray, Charles (cold.) Ginnie Taylor (3) - December 20, 1883
    Place of marriage, Ripon - Age of husband, 23 - Age of wife, 22 - Both are Single - Husband was born in Page County, Virginia - Wife was born in Jefferson County, West Virginia - Husband resides in Clarke County, Virginia - Wife resides in Jefferson County, West Virginia.

Murray, Elizabeth and Joseph Logan (3) - October 11, 1869
    For further information see - Logan, Joseph.

Murray, Isaac (cold.) Fanny Bolden (3) - January 7, 1879
    Place of marriage, Harpers Ferry - Age of husband, 52 - Age of wife, 40 - Both are Single - Husband was born in Rockingham County, Virginia - Both reside in Jefferson County, West Virginia.

Murray, Jacob Franklin (cold.) Ellen Spencer (3) - July 31, 1884
    Place of marriage, Charlestown - Age of husband, 23 - Age of wife, 18 - Both are Single - Husband was born in Page County, Virginia - Wife was born in Jefferson County, West Virginia - Both reside in Jefferson County, West Virginia. (Consent of bride's father in person.)

Murray, James and Catharine Halpin (2) - (L) August 22, 1851

Murray, John Ogden and Virginia R. Lock (3) - June 11, 1872
    Place of marriage, Jefferson County - Age of husband, 30 - Age of wife, 28 - Both are Single.

Murray, Joseph (cold.) Fanny Thompson (3) - December 29, 1875
    Place of marriage, near Ripon - Age of husband, 42 - Age of wife, 32 - Husband is a Widower - Wife is a Widow - Husband was born in Page County, Virginia - Wife was born in Rappahannock County, Virginia - Both reside in Jefferson County, West Virginia.

Murray, Sarah (colored) William H. Taylor (3) - November 28, 1870
    For further information see - Taylor, William H.

Murray, Stephen J. and Charlotte M. Schilling (3) - (1870)
    Age of husband, 27 - Age of wife, 26 - Husband was born at Washington - Wife was born in Jefferson - Husband resides in Berkeley - Wife resides in Jefferson County.

Musgrove, John and Pamelia McKune (2) - (L) June 8, 1858

Musgrove, John H. and Mary Ellen Strippy (3) - . September 23, 1869
   Place of marriage, Jefferson County - Age of husband, 40 - Age of
   wife, 31 - Both were born in Jefferson County - Both reside in
   Jefferson County.

Musgrove, Lydia M. and George W. Kendrick (3) - August 5, 1890
   For further information see - Kendrick, George W.

Muzzy, F. W. and Mary V. Schley (3) - April 11, 1882
   Place of marriage, near Shepherdstown - Age of husband, 30 - Age of
   wife, 23 - Both are Single - Husband was born in Pennsylvania - Wife
   was born in Jefferson County, West Virginia - Husband resides at
   Philadelphia - Wife resides in Jefferson County, West Virginia.

Myers, A. D. and Sarah Margaret Loyd (3) - . August 18, 1885
   Place of marriage, near Ripon - Age of husband, 28 - Age of wife,
   21 - Both are Single - Husband born in Pennsylvania - Wife was
   born in Jefferson County, West Virginia - Husband resides in Clarke
   County, Virginia - Wife resides in Jefferson County, West Virginia.

Myers, A. J. and Geneva Ruhl (3) - November 20, 1883
   Place of marriage, Bolivar - Age of husband, 20 - Age of wife, 22 -
   Both are Single - Husband was born in Berkeley County, West
   Virginia - Wife was born in Jefferson County, West Virginia -
   Husband resides in Berkeley County, West Virginia - Wife resides in
   Jefferson County, West Virginia. (Consent of groom's mother in
   writing.)

Myers, Alec (cold.) Susan Blue (3) - March 16, 1876
   Place of marriage, near Charlestown - Age of husband, 24 - Age of
   wife, 19 - Both are Single - Both were born in Jefferson County,
   West Virginia - Both reside in Jefferson County, West Virginia.

Myers, Anna D. and David Johnston (2) - (L) (1861)
   For further information see - Johnston, David.

Myers, Annie F. and George W. Welsh (3) - June 26, 1867
   For further information see - Welsh, George W.

Myers, Benjamin F. and Maggie E. Stouffer (3) - August 31, 1869
   Place of marriage, Jefferson County - Age of husband, 23 - Age of
   wife, 24 - Both were born in Pennsylvania - Husband resides in
   Pennsylvania - Wife resides in Jefferson County, West Virginia.

Myers, Charlotte and A. Robinson (3) - September 30, 1869
   For further information see - Robinson, A.

Myers, Charles (colored) Emma Cook (3) - August 18, 1870
   Place of marriage, Jefferson County - Age of husband, 22 - Age of
   wife, 19 - Husband was born in Virginia - Wife was born in Jefferson
   County - Both reside in Jefferson County. (Father consents in
   writing.)

Myers, David and Mary Hoffmaster (3) - December 11, 1883
   Place of marriage, Charlestown - Age of husband, 21 - Age of wife,
   25 - Both are Single - Both were born in Jefferson County, West
   Virginia - Both reside in Jefferson County, West Virginia.

Myers, Elizabeth and George Horkinson (1) - December 30, 1813

Myers, Elizabeth and John E. Thompson (1) - December 9, 1824

Myers, Elizabeth and William Cameron (1) - May 19, 1835

Myers, Emanuel and Maria Wilson (3) - August 11, 1869
Place of marriage, Jefferson County - Age of husband, 22 - Age of wife, 21 - Husband was born in Jefferson County, West Virginia - Wife was born in Jefferson County - Both reside in Jefferson County, West Virginia.

Myers, F. B. and Kate Johns (3) - August 4, 1870
Place of marriage, Jefferson County - Age of husband, 23 - Age of wife, 22 - Husband was born in New Jersey - Wife was born in Jefferson County, Virginia - Husband resides in New Jersey - Wife resides in Jefferson County.

Myers, Fannie E. and Harrison Getzendanner (3) - February 14, 1878
For further information see - Getzendanner, Harrison.

Myers, Fanny (cold.) John Green (3) - August 30, 1876
For further information see - Green, John.

Myers, Gabriel L. and Emma Gannon (3) - February 15, 1872
Place of marriage, Jefferson County, West Virginia - Age of husband, 21 - Age of wife, 18 - Both are Single - Husband was born in Germany - Wife was born in Jefferson County, Virginia - Husband resides in Jefferson County - Wife resides in Jefferson County, West Virginia - Husband's parents are Hirsch and Jeanem - Wife's parents are Henry and Annie C. - Occupation of husband is Merchant.

Myers, George and Patience Howard (1) - November 28, 1833

Myers, George M. and Rebecca E. Bowen (3) - April 10, 1879
Place of marriage, near Middleway - Age of husband, 24 - Age of wife, 22 - Both are Single - Husband was born in Jefferson County, West Virginia - Wife was born in Frederick County, Virginia - Both reside in Jefferson County, West Virginia.

Myers, H. Johnson and Jemima Fox (3) - October 3, 1871
Place of marriage, Jefferson County - Age of husband, 28 - Age of wife, 35 - Husband is Single - Wife is a Widow - Both were born in Loudoun - Both reside in Jefferson - Husband's parents are Philip and Carey - Wife's parents are Malcolm and Salley Brady - Occupation of husband is Laborer.

Myers, Hannah Ann and Francis Bateman (2) - (L) June 18, 1856

Myers, Heaton and Mary Bateman (2) - (L) September 28, 1858

Myers, Henry W. and Rosa P. Entler (3) - October 12, 1880
Place of marriage, Shepherdstown - Age of husband, 23 - Age of wife, 20 - Both are Single - Both were born in Jefferson County, West Virginia - Both reside in Jefferson County, West Virginia. (Consent of bride's mother in writing.)

Myers, Isaac D. and Katie E. Stickles (3) - November 25, 1890
  Place of marriage, Charlestown - Age of husband, 21 - Age of wife,
  19 - Both are Single - Both were born in Clarke County, Virginia -
  Husband resides in Clarke County, Virginia - Wife resides in
  Jefferson County, West Virginia. (Consent of bride's father in
  writing.)

Myers, James and Anna P. Backhouse (2) - (L) June 5, 1857

Myers, James W. and Ann Elizabeth Welsh (1) - October 25, 1847

Myers, John and Mary Ann Elizabeth Pultz (2) - (L) February 20, 1858

Myers, John C. and Sallie D. Hilbert (3) - May 30, 1889
  Place of marriage, Harpers Ferry - Age of husband, 25 - Age of wife,
  22 - Both are Single - Husband was born in Rockingham County,
  Virginia - Wife was born in Jefferson County, West Virginia -
  Husband resides in Rockingham County, Virginia - Wife resides in
  Jefferson County, West Virginia.

Myers, John G. and Susan McCoughtry (1) - November 15, 1832

Myers, John Y. and Anna Huffman (3) - March 6, 1867
  Place of marriage, Residence of I. Huffman - Age of husband, 30 -
  Age of wife, 26 - Both are Single - Both were born in Jefferson
  County - Both reside in Jefferson County - Husband's parents are
  Jacob and Mary A. Myers - Wife's parents are John and Rebecca
  Huffman - Occupation of husband is Farmer.

Myers, Joseph and Elizabeth Critzer (1) - January 11, 1821

Myers, Joseph and Catharine M. Lewis (2) - (L) (1861)
  Time of marriage, December 24, 1861 - Place of marriage, Jacob
  Custer's, Jefferson County - Names, Joseph Myers and Catharine M.
  Lewis - Age of husband, 22 years - Age of wife, 21 years - Condition
  of husband is Single - Condition of wife is Single - Place of
  husband's birth was Jefferson County, Virginia - Place of wife's
  birth was Berkeley County, Virginia - Place of husband's residence
  is Jefferson County, Virginia - Place of wife's residence is
  Jefferson County, Virginia - Names of husband's parents are Joseph
  and Elizabeth Myers - Names of wife's parents are B. Franklin and
  Mary Lewis - Occupation of husband is Farmer - Jacob Custer.

Myers, Kate and Robert F. Reynolds (3) - October 7, 1875
  For further information see - Reynolds, Robert F.

Myers, Lee and Clara C. Gower (3) - October 20, 1885
  Place of marriage, Shepherdstown - Age of husband, 23 - Age of wife,
  25 - Both are Single - Husband was born in Jefferson County, West
  Virginia - Wife was born in Washington County, Maryland - Both
  reside in Jefferson County, West Virginia.

Myers, Lizzie and R. F. Milton (3) - February 26, 1884
  For further information see - Milton, R. F.

Myers, Lucinda and William A. Jackson (3) - December 25, 1877
  For further information see - Jackson, William A.

Myers, M. E. and William Keaidler (3) - January 2, 1868
  For further information see - Keaidler, William.

Myers, Mary and Samuel Poland (1) -   April 13, 1832

Myers, Mary A. E. and John J. H. Straith (1) -   November 27, 1833

Myers, Mary Ann and Leonard Jones (2) -   (L) April 28, 1860

Myers, Mary B. and Mayberry C. Small (3) -   March 4, 1880
    For further information see - **Small, Mayberry C.**

Myers, Mary C. and John W. Cookus (3) -   March 24, 1880
    For further information see - **Cookus, John W.**

Myers, Mary Elizabeth and Thomas M. Thompson (2) -   (L) March 31, 1856

Myers, Mary S. and James W. Shepherd (3) -   December 11, 1866
    For further information see - **Shepherd, James W.**

Myers, Matilda C. and William F. Harman (3) -   February 28, 1871
    For further information see - **Harman, William F.**

Myers, Michael and Kaby Donner (1) -   June 11, 1803

Myers, Robert and Maggie L. Miller (3) -   September 19, 1879
    Place of marriage, near Kearneysville, **Age of husband, 30** - Age of
    wife, 22 - Both are Single - Husband was born in Berkeley County,
    West Virginia - Wife was born in **Jefferson County, West Virginia** -
    Both reside in **Jefferson County, West Virginia.**

Myers, Samuel and Mary Mathews (3) -   March 29, 1870
    Age of husband, 21 - Age of wife, 21 - **Husband resides in Virginia** -
    Wife resides in Jefferson County.

Myers, Sarah and Joseph Matthews (1) -   December 30, 1824

Myers, Sarah B. and Henry Lenhart (1) -   August 24, 1834

Myers, Sarah Ellen and William Oyerly (1) -   May 2, 1848

Myers, Samuel and Catherine C. Jenkins (1) -   March 3, 1836

Myers, Susan C. (cold.) David Washington Short (3) -   December 11, 1879
    For further information see - **Short, David Washington.**

Myers, William H. and Martha E. Crider (3) -   December 5, 1865
    Place of marriage, near Scrabble, Jefferson County - Age of husband,
    26 - Age of wife, 24 - Both are Single - Husband was born near
    Bedington, Berkeley County - Wife was born in Washington County,
    Maryland - Husband resides near Bedington, Berkeley County - Wife
    resides in Jefferson County, West Virginia - Husband's parents are
    David and Elizabeth Myers - **Wife's parents are John and Eliza
    Crider** - Occupation of husband is Farmer.

Myers, William Henry and Hester Ann Roberts (2) -   (L) October 27, 1856

Myers, William M. and Harriet S. Vanvactor (2) - (L) June 15, 1864
    Time of marriage, June 16, 1864 - Place of marriage, at Bride's
    Mother, Jefferson County - Names, William M. Myers and Harriet S.
    Vanvactor - Age of husband, 22 years March 7, 1864 - Age of wife,
    18 years last September - Both are Single - Both were born in
    Jefferson County - Both reside in Jefferson County - Names of
    husband's parents are Jacob and Mary Ann Myers - Names of wife's
    parents are Joseph and Mary Vanvactor - Occupation of husband is
    Farmer - License issued June 15, 1864 - T. A. Moore, Clerk.
    (Consent of bride's mother given for the marriage of the above
    names parties - Witness: John F. Myers.)

Myers, William W. and Sarah J. Clipp (3) - December 9, 1869
    Place of marriage, Jefferson County - Age of husband, 21 - Age of
    wife, 21 - Both were born in Jefferson County - Both reside in
    Jefferson County. (Ages sworn to by George W. Clipp.)

Myers, William W. and Virginia L. Shell (3) - February 6, 1877
    Place of marriage, near Shepherdstown - Age of husband, 27 - Age of
    wife, 24 - Both are Single - Husband was born in Jefferson County,
    West Virginia - Wife was born in Berkeley County, West Virginia -
    Both reside in Jefferson County, West Virginia.

Myles, Elizabeth and Thomas Riley (1) - April 8, 1806

Mylins, Amalia and Rudolph Rau (3) - July 26, 1870
    For further information see - Rau, Rudolph.

Nachman, Juliet and A. J. Robinson (3) - July 26, 1890
  For further information see - Robinson, A. J.

Nase, Catherine and John Bowers (1) - September 6, 1808

Nathanbush, M. A. C. and Garvis Shirley (1) - May 27, 1819

Neall, Lewis and Corbina C. Baker (1) - May 12, 1818

Near, Ann C. and George W. Strailman (1) - October 23, 1851

Near, Eliza and Thomas Sturdy (1) - July 29, 1832

Near, Mahala and William Best (1) - September 16, 1828

Near, Nancy and John Scarlet (1) - June 4, 1835

Near, Susan and George Piper (1) - July 8, 1824

Near, Susannah and Benjamin Torner (1) - October 11, 1821

Needy, Ann Catharine and Joseph Stephen Staley (2) - (L) December 1, 1852

Needy, George R. and Elizabeth H. Orndorff (2) - (L) December 12, 1857

Needy, Henry F. and Mary E. Traynor (2) - (L) November 23, 1857

Needy, Mary E. and George McBee (2) - (L) December 8, 1856

Needy, Mary E. and George A. Stewart (3) - April 26, 1882
  For further information see - Stewart, George A.

Needy, Nannie R. and Benjamin F. Long (3) - March 13, 1879
  For further information see - Long, Benjamin F.

Neel, Edith P. and J. H. Light (3) - July 4, 1888
  For further information see - Light, J. H.

Neely, Margaret C. and Christopher Hogan (2) - (L) October 21, 1854

Neer, Ann C. and George W. Strailman (2) - (L) October 22, 1851

Neer, George and Malinda Catherine Shover (3) - May 21, 1873
  Place of marriage, Harpers Ferry - Age of husband, 66 - Age of wife,
  45 - Husband is a Widower - Wife is Single - Both were born in
  Loudoun County, Virginia - Husband resides in Loudoun County,
  Virginia - Wife resides in Jefferson County, West Virginia -
  Occupation of husband is Farmer.

Neff, James A. and Charlotte Anna Wilborn (2) - (L) February 15, 1859

Neill, George W. and E. W. Shepard (2) - (L) February 11, 1861

Neill, Samuel B. and Ida M. Hill (3) - February 1, 1881
  Place of marriage, Charlestown - Age of husband, 41 - Age of wife,
  21 - Both are Single - Both were born in Jefferson County, West
  Virginia - Both reside in Jefferson County, West Virginia.

Nelson, Benjamin and Nellie Morgan (3) -　　　　　　　　　　January 5, 1871
　　Place of marriage, Jefferson County - Age of husband, 22 - Age of
　　wife, 23 - Both are Single - Husband was born in Jefferson County -
　　Wife was born in Frederick County - Both reside in Jefferson County -
　　Husband's parents are David and Dolly - Wife's parents are Julia -
　　Occupation of husband is Farmer.

Nelson, Catherine and Joseph Jackson (1) -　　　　　　　April 11, 1822

Nelson, Emily and John Madison (1) -　　　　　　　　　　July 5, 1826

Nelson, George W. and Mary M. Scollay (3) -　　　　　　October 17, 1865
　　Place of marriage, Middleway, Jefferson County - Age of husband,
　　25 years - Age of wife, 21 years - Both are Single - Husband was
　　born in Westmoreland County, Virginia - Wife was born in Jefferson
　　County - Husband resides in Hanover County, Virginia - Wife resides
　　in Jefferson County, West Virginia - Husband's parents are George W.
　　and Jane Nelson - Wife's parents are Dr. S. Scollay and Sarah
　　Scollay - Occupation of husband is Teacher and Farmer.

Nelson, Georgia and Charles Jackson (3) -　　　　　　　March 31, 1869
　　For further information see - Jackson, Charles.

Nelson, Isaac and Mary M. Deck (2) -　　　　　　(L) November 1, 1854

Nelson, J. W. (cold.) Cora Bell Williams (3) -　　　　November 20, 1888
　　Place of marriage, Harpers Ferry - Age of husband, 29 - Age of wife,
　　25 - Both are Single - Both were born in Jefferson County, West
　　Virginia - Both reside in Jefferson County, West Virginia.

Nelson, Lucy and Abram Armstrong (3) -　　　　　　　　February 15, 1872
　　For further information see - Armstrong, Abram.

Nelson, Rachael and Alfred Ranson (3) -　　　　　　　　July 16, 1890
　　For further information see - Ranson, Alfred.

Nelson, Ross (cold.) Rachael Mahorney (3) -　　　　　　May 9, 1888
　　Place of marriage, Harpers Ferry - Age of husband, 25 - Age of wife,
　　30 - Husband is Single - Wife is a Widow - Husband was born in
　　Loudoun County, Virginia - Wife was born in Jefferson County, West
　　Virginia - Both reside in Jefferson County, West Virginia.

Nelson, Thomas H. (cold.) Cora L. Warner (3) -　　　　December 26, 1888
　　Place of marriage, Charlestown - Age of husband, 29 - Age of wife,
　　25 - Both are Single - Husband was born in Jefferson County, West
　　Virginia - Wife was born in Rappahannock County, Virginia - Both
　　reside in Jefferson County, West Virginia.

Nelson, Thornton (cold.) Martha Lee (3) -　　　　　　　September 19, 1867
　　Place of marriage, Jefferson - Age of husband, 24 - Age of wife,
　　17 - Both are Single - Husband was born in Warren County, Virginia -
　　Wife was born in Jefferson County - Both reside in Jefferson County -
　　Husband's parents are Benjamin and Lydia - Wife's parents are Thomas
　　and Hannah - Occupation of husband is Farmer. (Father in person
　　gives consent.)

Nelson, Thornton (cold.) Bettie Cameron (3) -   December 26, 1876
    Place of marriage, Shepherdstown - Age of husband, 34 - Age of wife,
    30 - Husband is a Widower - Wife is a Widow - Husband was born in
    Warren County, Virginia - Wife was born in Clarke County, Virginia -
    Both reside in Jefferson County, West Virginia.

Nelson, Thornton (cold.) Jane Brown (3) -   December 13, 1877
    Place of marriage, Shepherdstown - Age of husband, 36 - Age of wife,
    42 - Husband is a Widower - Wife is a Widow - Husband was born in
    Warren County, Virginia - Wife was born in Jefferson County, West
    Virginia - Both reside in Jefferson County, West Virginia.

Nelson, Virginia (cold.) Miles R. Ranson (3) -   December 8, 1881
    For further information see - Ranson, Miles R.

Nelson, W. M. and Mrs. J. S. Risque (3) -   March 30, 1887
    Place of marriage, Shepherdstown - Age of husband, 30 - Age of wife,
    29 - Husband is Single - Wife is a Widow - Husband was born in
    Clarke County, Virginia - Wife was born in Missouri - Husband resides
    in Clarke County, Virginia - Wife resides in Jefferson County, West
    Virginia.

Neslop, John and Susanna Goldsbury (1) -   September 5, 1833

Nesselrodt, Charles and Mary J. Sine (3) -   February 28, 1888
    Place of marriage, Harpers Ferry - Age of husband, 28 - Age of wife,
    21 - Both are Single - Husband was born in Martinsburg, West
    Virginia - Wife was born in Jefferson County, West Virginia - Both
    reside in Jefferson County, West Virginia.

Neumann, Elizabeth and Joseph Stephens (1) -   February 2, 1832

Newberry, Franklin and M. E. Foulke (3) -   September 11, 1867
    Place of marriage, Jefferson County - Age of husband, 25 - Age of
    wife, 23 - Both are Single - Husband was born in Morgan County,
    Virginia - Wife was born in Jefferson County, West Virginia - Both
    reside in Jefferson County, West Virginia - Husband's parents are
    Oscar and Charlotte - Wife's parents are Jackson - Occupation of
    husband is Farmer.   (Age of lady sworn to by party.)

Newcomer, Alexander and Frances R. Gorrell (1) -   May 18, 1847

Newcomer, Laura E. and John W. Snyder (3) -   October 17, 1867
    For further information see - Snyder, John W.

Newitt, Drusilla and Thomas T. Grove (1) -   February 3, 1834

Newlin, James B. and Emma A. Clark (3) -   September 4, 1877
    Place of marriage, Charlestown - Age of husband, 36 - Age of wife,
    26 - Both are Single - Husband was born at Boston, Massachusetts -
    Wife was born at Harrisburg, Pennsylvania - Both reside in Jefferson
    County, West Virginia.

Newman, Delsa and Thomas Corn (3) -   (1868)
    For further information see - Corn, Thomas.

Newman, Eliza (cold.) Soloman Colston (3) -   March 7, 1889
    For further information see - Colston, Soloman.

Newman, George Edward (cold.) Annie Bateman (3) -   September 30, 1876
    Place of marriage, near Shanan Dale - Age of husband, 24 - Age of
    wife, 21 - Both are Single - Both were born in Jefferson County,
    West Virginia - Both reside in Jefferson County, West Virginia.

Newman, Hanna (cold.) Samuel Mainefield (3) -   August 11, 1888
    For further information see - Mainefield, Samuel.

Newman, Harriet (cold.) Jack Taylor (3) -   August 3, 1881
    For further information see - Taylor, Jack.

Newman, James (cold.) Julia Blake (3) -   August 16, 1879
    Place of marriage, near Charlestown - Age of husband, 24 - Age of
    wife, 22 - Both are Single - Both were born in Jefferson County,
    West Virginia - Both reside in Jefferson County, West Virginia.

Newman, John (cold.) Sarah Green (3) -   October 5, 1882
    Place of marriage, near Shannon Dale - Age of husband, 21 - Age of
    wife, 17 - Both are Single - Both were born in Jefferson County,
    West Virginia - Both reside in Jefferson County, West Virginia.
    (Consent of bride's mother in person.)

Newman, Lizzie (cold.) Eugene Luckett (3) -   June 11, 1889
    For further information see - Luckett, Eugene.

Newman, Mary (cold.) Walter C. Jackson (3) -   November 12, 1888
    For further information see - Jackson, Walter C.

Newman, Nancy (cold.) Charles Taylor (3) -   July 22, 1886
    For further information see - Taylor, Charles.

Newman, Thomas (cold.) Lucinda Hall (3) -   May 7, 1885
    Place of marriage, Charlestown - Age of husband, 24 - Age of wife,
    19 - Both are Single - Both were born in Jefferson County, West
    Virginia - Both reside in Jefferson County, West Virginia.
    (Consent of bride's father certified by Horace Ball, cold.)

Niceley, Mary S. and Nathaniel Mills (3) -   September 29, 1870
    For further information see - Mills, Nathaniel.

Nicely, Ed. D. and Emma E. Watson (3) -   September 19, 1889
    Place of marriage, Charlestown - Age of husband, 24 - Age of wife,
    23 - Both are Single - Both were born in Jefferson County, West
    Virginia - Both reside in Jefferson County, West Virginia.

Nicely, George W. and Mary Catharine Triggs (2) -   (L) April 5, 1856

Nicely, Georgiana and Charles J. Bowers (3) -   January 29, 1880
    For further information see - Bowers, Charles J.

Nicely, Harry S. and Mary M. Watson (3) -   September 10, 1874
    Place of marriage, near Leetown - Age of husband, 25 - Age of wife,
    21 - Both are Single - Both were born in Jefferson County, West
    Virginia - Both reside in Jefferson County, West Virginia.

Nicely, Ida F. and Henry S. League (3) -   May 2, 1877
    For further information see - League, Henry S.

Nicely, Mollie L. and R. W. Riley (3) -   March 21, 1883
    For further information see - Riley, R. W.

Nicely, T. A. and Hattie Lloyd (3) -   January 22, 1889
    Place of marriage, Leetown - Age of husband, 25 - Age of wife, 24 -
    Both are Single - Both were born in Jefferson County, West
    Virginia - Both reside in Jefferson County, West Virginia.

Nicewarner, George E. and Adella Moler (3) -   April 4, 1889
    Place of marriage, Charlestown - Age of husband, 24 - Age of wife,
    21 - Both are Single - Both were born in Jefferson County, West
    Virginia - Both reside in Jefferson County, West Virginia.

Nicewarner, James and Malinda Ott (3) -   April 27, 1887
    Place of marriage, Charlestown - Age of husband, 22 - Age of wife,
    18 - Both are Single - Husband was born in Jefferson County, West
    Virginia - Wife was born in Maryland - Husband resides in Jefferson
    County, West Virginia - Wife resides in Jefferson County.
    (Consent of bride's father in writing.)

Nicewarner, Monroe and Molly Welsh (3) -   October 3, 1877
    Place of marriage, Harpers Ferry - Age of husband, 23 - Age of wife,
    22 - Both are Single - Husband was born in Jefferson County, West
    Virginia - Wife was born in Warren County, Virginia - Both reside in
    Jefferson County, West Virginia.

Nicholas, Emma O. and George W. Green (3) -   March 4, 1886
    For further information see - Green, George W.

Nicholas, Mary (cold.) Harrison Morgan (3) -   November 11, 1867
    For further information see - Morgan, Harrison.

Nicholds, Casandry and Samuel Throp (1) -   1822

Nicholl, William and Elizabeth Lafferty (1) -   May 18, 1820

Nicholls, Adam and Maria Kelly (1) -   August 24, 1815

Nicholls, David and Harriet S. Beall (1) -   July 30, 1815

Nicholls, Jacob and Rebecca Utt (1) -   January 5, 1821

Nichols, A. C. and George W. Jones (3) -   February 27, 1868
    For further information see - Jones, George W.

Nichols, Charles T. and Ella C. Morris (3) -   June 18, 1890
    Place of marriage, Charlestown - Age of husband, 29 - Age of wife,
    22 - Both are Single - Husband was born in Jefferson County, West
    Virginia - Wife was born in Loudoun County, Virginia - Both reside
    in Jefferson County, West Virginia.

Nichols, Daniel H. and Nannie C. Jones (3) -   June 9, 1880
    Place of marriage, Unionville - Age of husband, 29 - Age of wife,
    23 - Both are Single - Both were born in Jefferson County, West
    Virginia - Both reside in Jefferson County, West Virginia.

Nichols, David T. and Sarah Link (3) -   October 22, 1879
    Place of marriage, Unionville - Age of husband, 23 - Age of wife,
    19 - Both are Single - Husband was born in Jefferson County - Wife
    was born in Jefferson County, West Virginia - Both reside in
    Jefferson County, West Virginia. (Consent of bride's father in
    person.)

Nichols, Frank (cold.) Eliza Mosby (3) -   September 15, 1885
    Place of marriage, Ripon - Age of husband, 21 - Age of wife, 20 -
    Both are Single - Husband was born in Frederick County, Virginia -
    Wife was born in Culpeper County, Virginia - Both reside in
    Jefferson County, West Virginia. (Consent of bride's father in
    writing.)

Nichols, Henry and Mary Hooser (1) -   February 16, 1815

Nichols, Hetty and Edward Green (3) -   March 22, 1873
    For further information see - Green, Edward.

Nichols, Jerome T. and Martha E. Rielly (2) -   (L) July 15, 1856

Nichols, John and Mary Carson (1) -   November 19, 1818

Nichols, John and M. A. McPherson (1) -   January 21, 1835

Nichols, Margaret Jane and James W. Triplett (2) -   (L) March 18, 1858

Nichols, Michael T. and Susan P. Stover (2) -   (L) May 14, 1859

Nichols, Patsy (cold.) Henry Powell (3) -   December 22, 1881
    For further information see - Powell, Henry.

Nichols, Sarah E. and A. M. Tinsinan (2) -   (L) December 16, 1854

Nicholson, Isaac F. and Rosa Robinson (3) -   October 3, 1871
    Place of marriage, Jefferson County - Age of husband, 34 - Age of
    wife, 27 - Both are Single - Husband was born at Baltimore,
    Maryland - Wife was born in Jefferson County - Husband resides at
    Baltimore, Maryland - Wife resides in Jefferson County.

Nicholson, Robert and Martha F. Avis (2) -   (L) September 24, 1857

Nicholson, Thomas A. and Catharine M. Wager (2) -   (L) November 28, 1860

Nick, John and Jane Buzzard (3) -   May 25, 1879
    Place of marriage, Harpers Ferry - Age of husband, 22 - Age of wife,
    22 - Both are Single - Both were born in Jefferson County, West
    Virginia - Both reside in Jefferson County, West Virginia.

Nick, Sarah F. and Charles Entsminger (3) -   February 11, 1890
    For further information see - Entsminger, Charles.

Nicolas, Taylor (cold.) Harriet Payne (3) -   April 22, 1875
    Place of marriage, Halltown - Age of husband, 26 - Age of wife, 21 -
    Both are Single - Husband was born in Augusta County, Virginia -
    Wife was born in Jefferson County, West Virginia - Both reside in
    Jefferson County, West Virginia.

Nicolds, Mary Magdalen and Zebede Tribut (1) -   October 21, 1819

Nininger, Thomas E. and Maggie C. Scott (3) -   October 18, 1888
    Place of marriage, Duffields - Age of husband, 27 - Age of wife,
    27 - Both are Single - Husband was born in Botetourt County,
    Virginia - Wife was born at Lexington, Virginia - Husband resides in
    Botetourt County, Virginia - Wife resides in Jefferson County, West
    Virginia.

Niseley, Eliza and Benijah Martin (1) -   October 25, 1827

Nisswaner, Susan Ann and John A. Brooks (2) -   (L) December 18, 1852

Nistrolson, Mary and John T. Lloyd (3) -   March 4, 1874
    For further information see - Lloyd, John T.

Niswarner, Annie J. Ardella and John W. James (3) -   January 1, 1879
    For further information see - James, John W.

Niswaner, Henry C. and Frances J. Blincoe (2) -   (L) May 19, 1860

Noland, George W. and Cornelia A. Riley (3) -   January 10, 1867
    Place of marriage, Charlestown - Age of husband, 29 - Age of wife,
    27 - Both are Single - Husband was born at Baltimore, Maryland -
    Wife was born at Charlestown - West Virginia - Husband resides at
    Baltimore, Maryland - Wife resides at Charlestown, West Virginia -
    Husband's parents are Charles and Elizabeth E. Noland - Wife's
    parents are Joshua and Elizabeth Riley - Occupation of husband is
    House Painter.

Noland, Miranda W. and William H. Marmaduke (2) -   (L) April 12, 1856

Noland, Robert S. and Nettie F. Roberts (3) -   July 23, 1884
    Place of marriage, Charlestown - Age of husband, 24 - Age of wife,
    21 - Both are Single - Husband was born in Berkeley County - Wife
    was born in Muskingum County, Ohio - Husband resides in Frederick
    County, Virginia - Wife resides in Jefferson County, West Virginia.

Noland, Samuel C. and Lydia E. Moler (3) -   January 10, 1867
    Place of marriage, Flowing Spring - Age of husband, 25 - Age of
    wife, 17 - Both are Single - Both were born in Jefferson County,
    West Virginia - Both reside in Jefferson County, West Virginia -
    Husband's parents are Charles and Elizabeth E. Noland - Wife's
    parents are Jacob H. and Virginia Moler - Occupation of husband is
    Farmer.

Noodispaw, Samuel R. and Jinnie Pleasant (3) -   April 9, 1889
    Place of marriage, Harpers Ferry - Age of husband, 30 - Age of wife,
    23 - Both are Single - Husband was born at Williamsport, Maryland -
    Wife was born in Jefferson County, West Virginia - Husband resides
    in Rockingham County, Virginia - Wife resides in Jefferson County,
    West Virginia.

Norman, George and Barbara Workman (1) -   1813

Norris, Harry E. and Anna M. Owens (3) -   August 4, 1884
    Place of marriage, Harpers Ferry - Age of husband, 21 - Age of wife,
    21 - Both are Single - Both were born in Maryland - Husband resides
    at Washington City - Wife resides in Jefferson County, West Virginia.

Norris, Henry and Sadie Martin (3) -   June 8, 1887
    Place of marriage, Bolivar - Age of husband, 21 - Age of wife, 21 -
    Both are Single - Husband was born in Maryland - Wife was born in
    Jefferson County, West Virginia - Husband resides in Maryland - Wife
    resides in Jefferson County, West Virginia.

Norris, Holmes (cold.) Lucy Brown (3) -   April 19, 1882
   Place of marriage, Shepherdstown - Age of husband, 65 - Age of wife,
   38 - Husband is a Widower - Wife is a Widow - Both were born in
   Jefferson County - Husband resides at Carlisle, Pennsylvania - Wife
   resides in Jefferson County.

Norris, John W. and Bettie Wilkeson (3) -   December 24, 1868
   Place of marriage, Jefferson County - Age of husband, 25 - Age of
   wife, 20 - Both are Single - Husband was born in Jefferson County,
   Virginia - Wife was born in Jefferson County - Husband resides in
   Pennsylvania - Wife resides in Jefferson County, West Virginia -
   Husband's parents are Homer and Mary - Wife's parents are Harry and
   Elvenia - Occupation of husband is Laborer.

Norris, Lloyd and Mary Goulding (1) -   November 12, 1834

Norris, Mary E. and Nehemiah C. Lynn (2) -   (L) January 6, 1854

Norris, Thomas W. and Belle Herr (3) -   November 21, 1877
   Place of marriage, Shepherdstown - Age of husband, 55 - Age of wife,
   30 - Husband is a Widower - Wife is Single - Husband was born in
   Culpeper County, Virginia - Wife was born in Maryland - Both reside
   in Jefferson County, West Virginia.

Norris, W. O. and M. B. Chew (bride) (3) -   November 5, 1872
   Place of marriage, Jefferson, West Virginia - Age of husband, 23 -
   Age of wife, 23 - Both are Single - Husband was born in Jefferson
   County, West Virginia - Wife was born in Loudoun, Virginia - Husband
   resides in Jefferson County, West Virginia - Wife resides in
   Jefferson, West Virginia - Husband's parents are W. H. and M.
   Norris - Wife's parents are R. and S. W. Chew - Occupation of husband
   is Farmer.

Norris, William H. and Mary Opie (1) -   October 3, 1843

North, Ann S. and Samuel Mark (1) -   March 3, 1808

North, Nathaniel G. and Mary M. Worthington (1) -   April 30, 1834

North, Sally and Samuel D. Engle (1) -   September 5, 1815

Notingham, Sarah Ann and Rawleigh Jett (1) -   May 25, 1820

Nourse, Mary (cold.) William Braxton Miles (3) -   February 4, 1880
   For further information see - Miles, William Braxton.

Nourse, Mary (cold.) Josiah Fox (3) -   January 19, 1888
   For further information see - Fox, Josiah.

Nourse, Nancy Ann (cold.) James Bateman (2) -   (L) May 5, 1852

Nuce, Mary and John Colbert (1) -   April 4, 1816

Null, Gotlib and Elizabeth Bilmyer (1) -   April 4, 1816

Nunamaker, Anthony and Emma Frances Kirby (2) -   (L) November 20, 1854

Nunberger, Susan and John Sullivan (2) -   (L) November 3, 1864
   For further information see - Sullivan, John.

Nunburger, G. B. and Amanda Warner (3) -   August 1, 1882
    Place of marriage, Charlestown - Age of husband, 22 - Age of wife, 23 - Both are Single - Both were born in Jefferson County, West Virginia - Husband resides in Frederick County, Maryland - Wife resides in Jefferson County.

Nunburger, Louisa Jane and Edward Cummings (2) -   (L) October 4, 1864
    For further information see - Cummings, Edward.

Nunemaker, William and Mary Belsterling (1) -   January 6, 1825

Nunmaker, Anthony and Laura J. Reinhart (3) -   October 28, 1869
    Place of marriage, Jefferson County - Age of husband, 40 - Age of wife, 26 - Husband was born in Jefferson County - Wife was born in Frederick County, Maryland - Both reside in Jefferson County.

Nunnamaker, Emily L. and A. E. Cockrell (3) -   December 14, 1880
    For further information see - Cockrell, A. E.

Nunnamaker, George and Ann Weadon Chelf (2) -   (L) September 9, 1853

Nunnamaker, George and Ann Weadon Chelf (1) -   September 11, 1853

Nunnamaker, Mary E. and Daniel T. Boyle (3) -   June 3, 1869
    For further information see - Boyle, Daniel T.

Nunnymaker, Annie A. and Warner W. Burton (3) -   November 21, 1865
    For further information see - Burton, Warner W.

Nuse, Eva E. and John R. Kidwiler (3) -   February 6, 1890
    For further information see - Kidwiler, John R.

425

O'Bannon, Annie A. and Julius C. Holmes (3) - July 5, 1866
    For further information see - Holmes, Julius C.

O'Bannon, Bettie J. and William H. Atwell (3) - March 26, 1878
    For further information see - Atwell, William H.

O'Bannon, Briant and Harriot M. Saunders (1) - February 4, 1828

O'Bannon, Luranna and George T. Sheetz (3) - June 17, 1875
    For further information see - Sheetz, George T.

O'Bannon, Mary E. and W. S. Merchant (3) - March 3, 1885
    For further information see - Merchant, W. S.

O'Bannon, Mary F. and John C. Stephens (2) - (L) November 27, 1850

O'Bannon, Sallie V. and William L. Dalgarn (3) - April 26, 1877
    For further information see - Dalgarn, William L.

O'Bannon, Sarah Elizabeth and George Holden (2) - (L) January 11, 1859

O'Bannon, Sarah K. and Richard K. Littleton (1) - January 4, 1831

Obaugh, John L. and Hattie A. Harlow (3) - July 6, 1887
    Place of marriage, Charlestown - Age of husband, 28 - Age of wife, 25 - Both are Single - Husband was born in Augusta County, Virginia - Wife was born in Rockbridge County, Virginia - Husband resides in Augusta County, Virginia - Wife resides in Jefferson County, West Virginia at present.

O'Brien, Mrs. Catharine and Henry Bowers (2) - (L) April 5, 1856

O'Brien, Elizabeth and George W. Dixon (3) - April 6, 1875
    For further information see - Dixon, George W.

O'Brien, Johana and Emory C. Allen (3) - December 24, 1876
    For further information see - Allen, Emory C.

O'Brien, Mary and Patrick Walch (2) - (L) February 27, 1854

Ochershausen, George P. and Lillie V. Stonebraker (3) - September 7, 1887
    Place of marriage, Shepherdstown - Age of husband, 50 - Age of wife, 25 - Both are Single - Husband was born at New York City - Wife was born in Jefferson County - Husband resides at New York City - Wife resides in Jefferson County, West Virginia.

O'Connell, Fanny Manning and Isaac W. Chapline (3) - April 22, 1879
    For further information see - Chapline, Isaac W.

O'Connell, Mollie and Maurice J. Kane (3) - January 13, 1886
    For further information see - Kane, Maurice J.

O'Connell, Sally and William H. Rodrick (3) - November 3, 1880
    For further information see - Rodrick, William H.

Oden, Annie C. and Benjamin Oden (3) - February 28, 1871
    For further information see - Oden, Benjamin.

Oden, Benjamin and Annie C. Oden (3) -   February 28, 1871
    Place of marriage, Jefferson County - Age of husband, 26 - Age of
    wife, 27 - Husband is a Widower - Wife is Single - Husband was born
    in Montgomery County, Maryland - Wife was born in Jefferson County -
    Husband resides in Montgomery County, Maryland - Wife resides in
    Jefferson County - Husband's parents are Alfred and Rachel - Wife's
    parents are Thomas and Matilda - Occupation of husband is Farmer.

Oden, Daniel Nathan and Sallie Ann Colbert (3) -.   December 14, 1871
    Place of marriage, Jefferson County - Age of husband, 21 - Age of
    wife, 21 - Both are Single - Both were born in Jefferson County -
    Both reside in Jefferson County - Husband's parents are Thomas and
    Matilda Ann - Wife's parents are Washington and Margaret Ann -
    Occupation of husband is Farmer.

Oden, Ellen Jane and James W. Derry (3) -   January 1, 1882
    For further information see - Derry, James W.

Oden, George W. and Laura B. Derry (3) -   October 11, 1875
    Place of marriage, Harpers Ferry - Age of husband, 24 - Age of wife,
    19 - Both are Single - Husband was born in Jefferson County, West
    Virginia - Wife was born in Loudoun County, Virginia - Both reside
    in Jefferson County, West Virginia. (This record is crossed out in
    the original.)

Oden, George W. and Laura Bell Derry (3) -   December 30, 1875
    Place of marriage, near Harpers Ferry - Age of husband, 24 - Age of
    wife, 19 - Both are Single - Both were born in Jefferson County,
    West Virginia - Both reside in Jefferson County, West Virginia.
    (Consent of bride's father in writing.)

Oden, John P. and Sally A. Sappington (3) -   December 17, 1868
    Place of marriage, Jefferson County - Age of husband, 21 - Age of
    wife, 17 - Both are Single - Husband was born in Jefferson County,
    Virginia - Wife was born in Jefferson - Husband resides in Jefferson
    County, Virginia - Wife resides in Jefferson County - Husband's
    parents are Thomas and Matilda - Wife's parents are George and Susan
    B. - Occupation of husband is Farmer.

Oden, Mary E. and Alexander Barron (3) -   November 13, 1866
    For further information see - Barron, Alexander.

O'Farrell, Margaret A. and John R. Whittington (3) -   September 10, 1874
    For further information see - Whittington, John R.

Offutt, Nancy and James Jones (1) -   August 11, 1814

Offutt, Sarah H. and Gilbert Gibbons (1) -   July 26, 1805

Ogden, Betsy and William Ragan (1) -   1822

Ogden, Charles D. and L. Elizabeth Watson (3) -   January 22, 1874
    Place of marriage, Leetown - Age of husband, 24 - Age of wife, 20 -
    Both are Single - Husband was born in Wood County, West Virginia -
    Wife was born in Jefferson County, West Virginia - Husband resides
    in Wood County, West Virginia - Wife resides in Jefferson County,
    West Virginia. (Consent of bride's father in writing.)

Ogden, David and Catharine Gilbert (1) -   April 19, 1831

Ogden, J. J. and T. E. Watson (bride) (3) -   November 7, 1872
    Place of marriage, Jefferson County, West Virginia - Age of husband,
    27 - Age of wife, 26 - Both are Single - Both were born in Jefferson
    County, West Virginia - Husband resides in Wood County, West
    Virginia - Wife resides in Jefferson County - Husband's parents are
    David and Catharine - Wife's parents are Thomas and Fanny -
    Occupation of husband is Car Builder.

Ogden, Mary E. and Solomon Gruber (2) -   (L) October 19, 1855

Ogden, R. K. and Hattie Roderick (3) -   March 24, 1869
    Age of husband, 25 - Age of wife, 23 - Both are Single - Both were
    born in Jefferson County - Husband resides in Clarke County - Wife
    resides in Jefferson County - Husband's parents are David and
    Catherine - Wife's parents are Benjamin and Mary Ann - Occupation
    of husband is Carpenter.

Ogden, S. C. (bride) and E. C. Gain (3) -   April 7, 1868
    For further information see - Gain, E. C.

Ogden, Verlina and Ezekiel Stipes (1) -   1816

Ogleton, Samuel and Lucy Butler (1) -   1813

O'Keef, John Matthew and Clara Virginia Lanham (3) -   February 21, 1878
    Place of marriage, Bolivar - Age of husband, 26 - Age of wife, 22 -
    Both are Single - Husband was born in Ireland - Wife was born in
    Jefferson County, West Virginia - Both reside in Jefferson County,
    West Virginia.

O'Kelly, Elizabeth and Richard A. Waters (1) -   November 7, 1821

O'Larry, Mary M. and John R. Reiley (3) -   April 6, 1871
    For further information see - Reiley, John R.

O'Laughlin, Narcissa and George W. Fossett (3) -   November 18, 1890
    For further information see - Fossett, George W.

Oliver, Sythia and Jacob Gompf (2) -   (L) April 26, 1855

O'Mara, Margaret and Thomas Egan (1) -   September 11, 1849

Onderdonk, John William and Fanny Cockrell (3) -   May 13, 1884
    Place of marriage, Harpers Ferry - Age of husband, 33 - Age of wife,
    29 - Both are Single - Husband was born in Berkeley County, West
    Virginia - Wife was born in Jefferson County, West Virginia -
    Husband resides in Berkeley County, West Virginia - Wife resides in
    Jefferson County, West Virginia.

Onderdunk, Henry V. and Jane Hufman (2) -   (L) May 20, 1851

O'Neal, John and Susan Wilson (1) -   May 28, 1812

Opie, Margaret S. and George R. Riddle (1) -   January 14, 1846

Opie, Mary and William H. Norris (1) -   October 3, 1843

Opie, Virginia and R. Hume Butcher (1) -   September 26, 1844

Oram, George W. and Emily A. Balch (3) -   June 23, 1888
    Place of marriage, Leetown - Age of husband, 35 - Age of wife, 23 -
    Both are Single - Husband was born at New York City - Wife was born
    in Jefferson County, West Virginia - Husband resides at Philadelphia,
    Pennsylvania - Wife resides in Jefferson County, West Virginia.

Orem, Cornelia A. and Samuel Watson (3) -   December 19, 1867
    For further information see - Watson, Samuel.

Orem, James and Fanny A. W. Kelly (3) -   December 25, 1879
    Place of marriage, near Harpers Ferry - Age of husband, 22 - Age of
    wife, 18 - Both are Single - Both were born in Jefferson County,
    West Virginia - Both reside in Jefferson County, West Virginia.
    (Consent of bride's father and mother in writing - License returned
    June 1881 - No return of minister.)

Orem, Mary Jane and William Watson (2) -   (L) September 13, 1864
    For further information see - Watson, William.

Orem, Thomas E. and Barbara Ann Huffmaster (2) -   (L) October 12, 1855

Orndoff, William and Harriet Smutz (1) -   January 22, 1833

Orndorff, David S. and Kate M. Keplinger (3) -   June 15, 1869
    Place of marriage, Jefferson County - Age of husband, 21 - Age of
    wife, 21 - Husband was born in Jefferson County - Wife was born in
    West Virginia - Husband resides in Jefferson County - Wife resides
    in West Virginia.

Orndorff, Edward and Ella Boswell (3) -   March 9, 1871
    Place of marriage, Jefferson County - Age of husband, 22 - Age of
    wife, 17 - Both are Single - Both were born in Jefferson County -
    Both reside in Jefferson - Husband's parents are Samuel and
    Rebecca - Wife's parents are James and Elizabeth - Occupation of
    husband is Farmer. (In writing consent.)

Orndorff, Elizabeth H. and George R. Needy (2) -   (L) December 12, 1857

Orndorff, H. V. H. and George W. Show (3) -   May 4, 1865
    For further information see - Show, George W.

Orndorff, J. (bride) and J. W. Sigler (3) -   April 14, 1872
    For further information see - Sigler, J. W.

Orndorff, James and Hester A. Matthews (3) -   March 10, 1870
    Place of marriage, Jefferson County - Age of husband, 27 - Age of
    wife, 20 - Husband was born in Jefferson - Wife was born in
    Maryland - Both reside in Jefferson County. (Consent of father in
    writing.)

Orndorff, John and Elizabeth Pear (3) -   February 5, 1868
    Place of marriage, Jefferson County - Age of husband, 27 - Age of
    wife, 21 - Both are Single - Both were born in Shenandoah County,
    Virginia - Husband resides in Shenandoah County, Virginia - Wife
    resides in Jefferson - Occupation of husband is Stone Mason.

Orndorff, P. H. and Martha A. Elliott (3) -   December 26, 1889
    Place of marriage, Harpers Ferry - Age of husband, 35 - Age of wife,
    23 - Both are Single - Husband was born in Virginia - Wife was born
    in Jefferson County, West Virginia - Husband resides in Virginia -
    Wife resides in Jefferson County, West Virginia.

Orndorff, Mrs. Sarah Ann and Martin Billmyer (2) -   (L) September 27, 1856

Ornet, Sallie (colored) Guy Paten (3) -   October 28, 1865
    For further information see - Paten, Guy.

Orr, Robert and Anne Barlow (1) -   July 17, 1843

Orrick, Johnson and Maggie A. Cookus (2) -   (L) November 5, 1856

Osborn, Mary and Daniel Hendricks, Jr. (1) -   March 8, 1821

Osborn, Mary E. and George L. Hoffman (3) -   November 20, 1866
    For further information see - Hoffman, George L.

Osborn, Sarah and Adam Link, Jr. (1) -   May 27, 1824

Osborne, Elizabeth and Silas Melvin (1) -   October 22, 1805

Osborne, George and Margaret Hoffman (1) -   October 7, 1809

Osborne, Virginia and George W. Shutt (3) -   October 16, 1867
    For further information see - Shutt, George W.

Osbourn, Anna B. and Morris K. Hendricks (3) -   February 5, 1885
    For further information see - Hendricks, Morris K.

Osbourn, Annie E. and John William Cromwell (3) -   January 26, 1886
    For further information see - Cromwell, John William.

Osbourn, Emma A. and Thomas W. Osbourn (3) -   March 23, 1876
    For further information see - Osbourn, Thomas W.

Osbourn, Eve Kate and H. T. Link (3) -   February 28, 1878
    For further information see - Link, H. T.

Osbourn, Henry and Emma Rhodes (3) -   March 5, 1872
    Place of marriage, Jefferson County, West Virginia - Age of husband,
    26 - Age of wife, 23 - Both are Single - Husband was born in
    Jefferson County - Wife was born in Jefferson County, Virginia -
    Husband resides in Jefferson County - Wife resides in Jefferson
    County, West Virginia - Husband's parents are William and Kitty -
    Wife's parents are William and Mary A. - Occupation of husband is
    Farmer.   (M. A. Rhodes.)

Osbourn, Ida M. and Samuel M. Huyett (3) -   December 19, 1889
    For further information see - Huyett, Samuel M.

Osbourn, John A. and Willie Thompson (3) -   November 7, 1878
    Place of marriage, Brown's Crossing - Age of husband, 30 - Age of
    wife, 20 - Both are Single - Both were born in Jefferson County,
    West Virginia - Both reside in Jefferson County, West Virginia.
    (Consent of bride's father in writing.)

Osbourn, L. A. and C. C. Ashbaugh (bride) (3) -   March 26, 1879
    Place of marriage, Charlestown - Age of husband, 25 - Age of wife,
    22 - Both are Single - Both were born in Jefferson County, West
    Virginia - Both reside in Jefferson County, West Virginia.

Osbourn, Maria B. and Daniel Link (2) -   (L) November 11, 1858

Osbourn, Mary Ann and Edward G. W. Herr (2) -   (L) May 5, 1855

Osbourn, Sarah M. and Henry C. Engle (2) -   (L) October 13, 1855

Osbourn, Thomas W. and Emma A. Osbourn (3) -   March 23, 1876
    Place of marriage, Duffields - Age of husband, 28 - Age of wife,
    25 - Both are Single - Both were born in Jefferson County, West
    Virginia - Both reside in Jefferson County, West Virginia.

Osbourn, William B. and Lottie C. Crantz (3) -   February 12, 1879
    Place of marriage, Kearneysville - Age of husband, 30 - Age of wife,
    30 - Husband is a Widower - Wife is Single - Husband was born in
    Jefferson County, West Virginia - Wife was born in Maryland - Both
    reside in Jefferson County, West Virginia.

Osburn, Abner and Elizabeth Osburn (2) -   (L) February 17, 1853

Osburn, Abner and Elizabeth Osburn (1) -   February 17, 1853

Osburn, Adaline and John J. Palmer (3) -   March 9, 1869
    For further information see - Palmer, John J.

Osburn, Blanchy and Samuel Melvin (1) -   February 18, 1819

Osburn, Elizabeth and James Hendricks (1) -   March 23, 1820

Osburn, Elizabeth and Abner Osburn (2) -   (L) February 17, 1853

Osburn, Elizabeth and Abner Osburn (1) -   February 17, 1853

Osburn, Jake S. and Laura Cost (3) -   January 25, 1872
    Place of marriage, Jefferson County, West Virginia - Age of husband,
    24 - Age of wife, 21 - Both are Single - Wife was born in Jefferson
    County, Virginia - Husband resides in Jefferson County - Wife
    resides in Jefferson County, West Virginia - Husband's parents are
    James and Margaret - Wife's parents are John and Sarah - Occupation
    of husband is Farmer.

Osburn, James B. and Alice N. Link (3) -   November 11, 1871
    Place of marriage, Jefferson County - Age of husband, 27 - Age of
    wife, 21 - Both are Single - Both were born in Jefferson County -
    Both reside in Jefferson County - Husband's parents are James A. and
    Jane - Wife's parents are John A. and Ann C. - Occupation of husband
    is Farmer.

Osburn, John, Jr. and Ann Catharine VanVactor (1) -   November 6, 1827

Osburn, Logan, Jr. and Mary E. Castleman (3) -   August 27, 1874
    Place of marriage, County - Age of husband, 25 - Age of wife, 21 -
    Both are Single - Husband was born in Jefferson County, West
    Virginia - Wife was born in Clarke County, Virginia - Both reside in
    Jefferson County, West Virginia.

Osburn, Martha (free colored) Nathan Johnson (2) -   (L) November 1, 1853

Osburn, Mary and George W. Shutt (2) -   (L) April 8, 1857

Osburn, Mary C. and Milton Rouse (3) -   August 28, 1873
   For further information see - Rouse, Milton.

Osburn, R. L. and Annie L..Ronemus (3) -   November 3, 1868
   Place of marriage, Jefferson County - Age of husband, 31 - Age of
   wife, 21 - Both are Single - Both were born in Jefferson County -
   Husband resides in Jefferson County - Wife resides in West Virginia -
   Husband's parents are W. F. and Elizabeth - Wife's parents are John
   and Susanna - Occupation of husband is Farmer. (Minister gives
   consent.)

Osburn, Virginia C. and John W. Allen (3) -   November 25, 1868
   For further information see - Allen, John W.

Ott, Abraham and Nancy Chamberlain (1) -   March 17, 1831

Ott, Addison and Sarah Catharine Snyder (2) -   (L) December 1, 1857

Ott, Annie C. and Milard Fillmore Kline (3) -   May 22, 1871
   For further information see - Kline, Milard Fillmore.

Ott, Barney and Phebe Dorsey (1) -   January 29, 1824

Ott, Catharine Ann and William Magowan (1) -   December 31, 1832

Ott, Elizabeth and William Warters (1) -   May 16, 1822

Ott, Ella and L. G. Cockrell (3) -   June 6, 1877
   For further information see - Cockrell, L. G.

Ott, George and Polly Dillow (1) -   October 1, 1818

Ott, George William and Julia Wiltshire (3) -   November 4, 1886
   Place of marriage, Charlestown - Age of husband, 21 - Age of wife,
   19 - Both are Single - Both were born in Jefferson County, West
   Virginia - Both reside in Jefferson County, West Virginia.

Ott, Hannah F. and J. D. Johnston (3) -   July 23, 1890
   For further information see - Johnston, J. D.

Ott, J. K. P. and M. J. Rhinaman (bride) (3) -   February 1882
   Place of marriage, Charlestown - Age of husband, 36 - Age of wife,
   37 - Both are Single - Husband was born in Jefferson County, West
   Virginia - Wife was born in Clarke County, Virginia - Both reside in
   Jefferson County, West Virginia.

Ott, James W. and Mary C. Baumgardner (3) -   January 25, 1887
   Place of marriage, Halltown - Age of husband, 40 - Age of wife, 27 -
   Both are Single - Husband was born in Jefferson County, West
   Virginia - Wife was born in Pennsylvania - Both reside in Jefferson
   County.

Ott, John Daniel and Elizabeth Cave (3) - December 15, 1873
Place of marriage, Jefferson County - Age of husband, 20 - Age of wife, 20 - Both are Single - Both were born in Jefferson County, West Virginia - Both reside in Jefferson County, West Virginia. (Consent of groom's father in person and Bride's mother in writing.)

Ott, Kate E. and George G. Pedrick (2) - (L) (1862)
For further information see - Pedrick, George G..

Ott, Malinda and James Nicewarner (3) - April 27, 1887
For further information see - Nicewarner, James.

Ott, Mary and John Piper (1) - July 26, 1821

Ott, Mary and Jesse Gillmore Kline (3) - September 8, 1871
For further information see - Kline, Jesse Gillmore.

Ott, Mary Elizabeth and Jacob A. R. Matheny (3) - February 9, 1873
For further information see - Matheny, Jacob A. R.

Ott, Sarah E. and William Bussard (3) - February 15, 1866
For further information see - Bussard, William.

Ott, Sarah Jane and John W. Gardner (3) - May 24, 1880
For further information see - Gardner, John W.

Ott, Thomas M. and Mary E. Collis (2) - (L) (1863)
Time of marriage, May 24, 1863 - Place of marriage, near Halltown - Names, Thomas M. Ott and Mary E. Collis - Age of husband, 24 years - Age of wife, 18 years - Both are Single - Place of husband's birth was Jefferson County, Virginia - Place of wife's birth was Prince William County, Virginia - Both reside in Jefferson County - Names of husband's parents are John W. and Mary E. Ott - Names of wife's parents are - Occupation of husband is Merchant. (The father and mother of Miss Collis are both dead and her brother who is her nearest living relative has given his consent for this her marriage. Witts: W. Ott; Gepton (X) Smallwood. Witness: William F. King.)

Ott, Thomas W. and Nannie C. Hostler (3) - December 11, 1883
Place of marriage, Harpers Ferry - Age of husband, 23 - Age of wife, 27 - Both are Single - Both were born in Jefferson County, West Virginia - Husband resides in Jefferson County - Wife resides in Jefferson County, West Virginia.

Outcalt, William and Alice V. Chamberlain (3) - November 14, 1865
Place of marriage, Hopewell Mills - Age of husband, 23 - Age of wife, 16 - Both are Single - Husband was born in Middlesex County, New Jersey - Wife was born in Jefferson County, West Virginia - Husband resides in Berkeley County, West Virginia - Wife resides in Jefferson County, West Virginia - Husband's parents are Jacob and Mary Outcalt - Wife's parents are John and Catharine Chamberlain - Occupation of husband is Clerk.

Overlander, E. and Ella Duncan (3) - March 14, 1888
Place of marriage, Charlestown - Age of husband, 23 - Age of wife, 23 - Both are Single - Husband was born in Jefferson County, West Virginia - Both reside in Jefferson County, West Virginia.

Overton, Catharine and John William Walters (2) - (L) December 23, 1851

Overton, James and Sarah Thropp (1) - December 27, 1831

Owens, Anna M. and Harry E. Norris (3) - August 4, 1884
    For further information see - Norris, Harry E.

Owens, Mildred Marshall and D. W. Willingham (3) - February 24, 1876
    For further information see - Willingham, D. W.

Owings, John (cold.) Rachel Green (3) - August 30, 1877
    Place of marriage, Charlestown - Age of husband, 22 - Age of wife, 22 - Both are Single - Husband was born at Petersburg - Wife was born in Jefferson County, West Virginia - Both reside in Jefferson County, West Virginia.

Oyerley, Maggie A. and Thomas N. Hill (3) - March 21, 1876
    For further information see - Hill, Thomas N.

Oyerly, Rosie B. and Clarence E. Grubbs (3) - December 10, 1890
    For further information see - Grubbs, Clarence E.

Oyerly, William and Sarah Ellen Myers (1) - May 2, 1848

Pack, Harriet and Seth Smith (1) -   1821

Packet, Fannie H. and L. Montgomery Bond, Jr. (3) -   August 1, 1871
    For further information see - Bond, L. Montgomery, Jr.

Packett, Frances R. and William Hooff (1) -   March 4, 1822

Packett, George W. and Cora Wageley (3) -   November 27, 1884
    Place of marriage, near Summit Point - Age of husband, 23 - Age of wife, 19 - Both are Single - Husband was born in Jefferson County, West Virginia - Wife was born in Jefferson County - Both reside in Jefferson County, West Virginia. (Consent of bride's father in person.)

Packett, J. B. and Virginia Tennessee Ring (3) -   November 25, 1884
    Place of marriage, Middleway - Age of husband, 36 - Age of wife, 20 last February - Both are Single - Husband was born in Jefferson County, West Virginia - Wife was born in Jefferson County - Both reside in Jefferson County, West Virginia. (Consent of bride's father in writing.)

Packett, James W. and Mary E. Brining (3) -   September 6, 1881
    Place of marriage, Middleway - Age of husband, 26 - Age of wife, 18 - Both are Single - Husband was born in Jefferson County, West Virginia - Wife was born in Washington County, Maryland - Both reside in Jefferson County, West Virginia. (Consent of bride's father in Writing.)

Packett, John and Fanny R. Hammond (1) -   March 14, 1816

Packett, Lizzie B. and John D. M. Cardoga (3) -   September 10, 1878
    For further information see - Cardoga, John D. M.

Packett, Louisa C. and Thomas W. Buckey (3) -   October 27, 1870
    For further information see - Buckey, Thomas W.

Packett, Lucy M. and Foster Moss (3) -   June 9, 1880
    For further information see - Moss, Foster.

Packett, William B. and Drusilla D. Rutherford (3) -   October 28, 1885
    Place of marriage, Charlestown - Age of husband, 31 - Age of wife, 30 - Both are Single - Both were born in Jefferson County, West Virginia - Both reside in Jefferson County, West Virginia.

Padget, Benedict and Eleanor Millar (1) -   October 16, 1823

Padgett, Laura B. and John T. A. Deck (3) -   April 17, 1884
    For further information see - Deck, John T. A.

Page, Annie (cold.) Charles S. Robinson (3) -   January 23, 1886
    For further information see - Robinson, Charles S.

Page, Handy (cold.) John H. Ross (3) -   December 2, 1888
    For further information see - Ross, John H.

Page, Henry C. and Lizzie D. Timberlake (3) - September 5, 1883
    Place of marriage, Charlestown - Age of husband, 24 - Age of wife,
    24 - Both are Single - Husband was born in Clarke County, Virginia -
    Wife was born in Jefferson County, West Virginia - Husband resides
    in Warren County, Virginia - Wife resides in Jefferson County, West
    Virginia.

Page, John B. and Martha N. Davis (3) - November 17, 1868
    Place of marriage, Jefferson County - Age of husband, 30 - Both are
    Single - Husband was born in Virginia - Wife was born in Jefferson
    County - Husband resides in Virginia - Wife resides in West
    Virginia - Wife's parents are (mother) M. N. - Occupation of husband
    is Merchant.

Page, John Evelyn and Margaret Emily McGuire (1) - February 18, 1823

Page, L. L. (cold.) Georgiana Smith (3) - August 13, 1879
    Place of marriage, Charlestown - Age of husband, 30 - Age of wife,
    22 - Both are Single - Husband was born in New Kent County,
    Virginia - Wife was born in Jefferson County, West Virginia - Both
    reside in Jefferson County, West Virginia.

Page, Mann R. and Helen Margaret Beall (1) - October 24, 1825

Page, Powhatan R. and Elizabeth Scollay (2) - (L) November 10, 1856

Page, William and Ann C. Kline (3) - June 9, 1865
    Place of marriage, Smithfield - Age of husband, 66 years - Age of
    wife, 59 years - Husband is a Widower - Wife is a Widow - Husband
    was born in Albemarle County, Virginia - Wife was born at Smithfield,
    Jefferson County - Both reside at Smithfield - Husband's parents are
    William Page and (nee) Retta Dudley - Wife's parents are William
    Jackson and (nee) Mary A. Walker - Occupation of husband is Shoemaker.

Painter, Andrew J. and Elizabeth Mason (3) - July 16, 1882
    Place of marriage, Loudoun County, Virginia - Age of husband, 21 -
    Age of wife, 21 - Both are Single - Husband was born in Jefferson
    County, West Virginia - Wife was born in Clarke County, Virginia -
    Husband resides in Jefferson County, West Virginia - Wife resides in
    Jefferson County.

Painter, Anna Lee and Michael Kane (3) - November 9, 1880
    For further information see - Kane, Michael.

Painter, Barney and Elizabeth Longerbeam (3) - March 29, 1876
    Place of marriage, near Shanan Dale Furnace - Age of husband, 24 -
    Age of wife, 20 - Both are Single - Both were born in Jefferson
    County, West Virginia - Both reside in Jefferson County, West
    Virginia. (Consent of bride's father in person.)

Painter, Charles and Sally Dillow (3) - February 8, 1885
    Place of marriage, Blue Ridge Mountain - Age of husband, 23 - Age of
    wife, 21 - Both are Single - Both were born in Jefferson County,
    West Virginia - Both reside in Jefferson County, West Virginia.

Painter, Eliza and Thomas H. Harder (3) - October 12, 1876
    For further information see - Harder, Thomas H.

Painter, Elvira C. and Joseph T. Allen (3) - November 29, 1882
    For further information see - Allen, Joseph T.

437

Painter, Harriet and John Wiley (3) - September 3, 1885
    For further information see - Wiley, John.

Painter, Hart and Thomas Dillow (3) - December 23, 1871
    For further information see - Dillow, Thomas.

Painter, James W. and Drusilla Pearl (3) - October 10, 1875
    Place of marriage, Mountain - Age of husband, 26 - Age of wife, 25 - Both are Single - Both were born in Jefferson County, West Virginia - Husband resides in Loudoun County, Virginia - Wife resides in Jefferson County, West Virginia.

Painter, Jonathan and Lucinda Rodrick (2) - (L) November 28, 1856

Painter, Joseph M. and Ann A. Coffinbarger (2) - (L) March 26, 1855

Painter, Julia and Thomas B. Young (3) - December 20, 1877
    For further information see - Young, Thomas B.

Painter, Katie and William S. Buzzard (3) - August 18, 1889
    For further information see - Buzzard, William S.

Painter, Lewis W. and Lizzie Shumbaugh (3) - September 2, 1875
    Place of marriage, Charlestown - Age of husband, 22 - Age of wife, 21 - Both are Single - Husband was born in Jefferson County, West Virginia - Wife was born in Shenandoah County, Virginia - Both reside in Jefferson County, West Virginia.

Painter, Lewis W. and Lillie Lee Painter (3) - November 13, 1883
    Place of marriage, Harpers Ferry - Age of husband, 27 - Age of wife, 21 - Husband is a Widower - Wife is Single - Husband was born in Jefferson County, West Virginia - Wife was born in Loudoun County, Virginia - Both reside in Jefferson County, West Virginia.

Painter, Lillie Lee and Lewis W. Painter (3) - November 13, 1883
    For further information see - Painter, Lewis W.

Painter, Mary A. and Bunbury C. Bennett (2) - (L) September 26, 1860

Painter, Robert and Mary Jane Shambaugh (3) - October 31, 1871
    Place of marriage, Jefferson County - Age of husband, 22 - Age of wife, 25 - Both are Single - Both were born in Virginia - Both reside in West Virginia - Husband's parents are Thomas and Mary Jane - Wife's parents are Daniel C. and Mary Ann - Occupation of husband is Farmer.

Painter, William and M. J. Griffith (3) - November 27, 1867
    Place of marriage, Jefferson County - Age of wife, 21 - Husband is a Widower - Wife is Single - Husband was born in Virginia - Wife was born in Loudoun County, Virginia - Both reside in Jefferson.

Palmer, Elizabeth and Samuel Johnson (3) - August 22, 1865
    For further information see - Johnson, Samuel.

Palmer, John J. and Adaline Osburn (3) -　　　　　　　　　　March 9, 1869
　　Place of marriage, Jefferson County - Age of husband, 62 - Age of
　　wife, 50 - Husband is a Widower - Wife is Single - Husband was born
　　in Loudoun County, Virginia - Wife was born in Jefferson County -
　　Both reside in Jefferson County - Husband's parents are David and
　　Mary - Wife's parents are Balam and Ruth - Occupation of husband is
　　Printer.

Palmer, William W. and Mary Jane Gannt (2) -　　　　　(L) April 4, 1851

Pane, James and Frances Hobbs (3) -　　　　　　　　　　　　June 23, 1866
　　Place of marriage, Jefferson County - Age of husband, 28 - Age of
　　wife, 20 - Husband is a Widower - Wife is Single - Both were born in
　　Jefferson County, West Virginia - Both reside in Jefferson County,
　　West Virginia - Husband's parents are Richard Pane and Elizabeth
　　Pane - Occupation of husband is Laborer.

Pane, William and Mary Cornelia Ford (3) -　　　　　　　　July 13, 1871
　　Place of marriage, Jefferson County - Age of husband, 22 - Age of
　　wife, 22 - Both are Single - Both were born in Virginia - Both
　　reside in West Virginia - Husband's parents are Henry and Kate -
　　Wife's parents are Robert and Eveline - Occupation of husband is
　　Farmer.

Panel, William F. and Rebeca A. Smith (3) -　　　　　　November 10, 1887
　　Place of marriage, Harpers Ferry - Age of husband, 27 - Age of wife,
　　23 - Both are Single - Husband was born in Virginia - Wife was born
　　in West Virginia - Both reside in Jefferson County, West Virginia.

Panitt, Elizabeth (cold.) John Henry Wood (3) -　　　　December 19, 1883
　　For further information see - Wood, John Henry.

Parker, Annie (cold.) Peyton Johnson (3) -　　　　　　　　　June 1, 1885
　　For further information see - Johnson, Peyton.

Parker, Arthur (cold.) Drusy Hays (3) -　　　　　　　　　　　July 5, 1883
　　Place of marriage, Charlestown - Age of husband, 21 - Age of wife,
　　19 - Both are Single - Husband was born in Fauquier County,
　　Virginia - Wife was born in Jefferson County, West Virginia -
　　Husband resides in Jefferson County - Wife resides in Jefferson
　　County, West Virginia.　(Consent of bride's mother certified by
　　Charles Parker.)

Parker, Charles (cold.) Susan Swan (3) -　　　　　　　　　　July 28, 1887
　　Place of marriage, near Charlestown - Age of husband, 43 - Age of
　　wife, 41 - Husband is Single - Wife is a Widow - Both were born in
　　Jefferson County, West Virginia - Both reside in Jefferson County,
　　West Virginia.

Parker, Charles Edward (cold.) Lucy Ranson (3) -　　　　　July 25, 1878
　　Place of marriage, Charlestown - Age of husband, 25 - Age of wife,
　　22 - Both are Single - Both were born in Jefferson County, West
　　Virginia - Both reside in Jefferson County, West Virginia.

Parker, Charlotte (cold.) Horace Carter (3) -　　　　　　　April 5, 1888
　　For further information see - Carter, Horace.

439

Parker, Jacob (cold.) Mary Blue (3) -   March 31, 1881
    Place of marriage, near Charlestown - Age of husband, 21 - Age of
    wife, 16 - Both are Single - Husband was born in Fauquier County,
    Virginia - Wife was born in Jefferson County, West Virginia - Both
    reside in Jefferson County, West Virginia. (Consent of bride's
    father and mother in writing.)

Parker, John W. and C. Blackburn (3) -   November 6, 1868
    Place of marriage, Jefferson County - Age of husband, 21 - Age of
    wife, 22 - Both are Single - Husband was born in Jefferson County,
    Virginia - Wife was born in Jefferson County - Husband resides in
    Jefferson County, West Virginia - Wife resides in West Virginia -
    Occupation of husband is Laborer.

Parker, Lawrence (cold.) Betsy Willis (3) -   September 4, 1890
    Place of marriage, Charlestown - Age of husband, 60 - Age of wife,
    45 - Husband is a Widower - Wife is Single - Both were born in
    Jefferson County, West Virginia - Both reside in Jefferson County,
    West Virginia.

Parker, Lucinda (cold.) Elijah Brown (3) -   April 19, 1888
    For further information see - Brown, Elijah.

Parker, Maria and Albert Rhodes (3) -   December 31, 1868
    For further information see - Rhodes, Albert.

Parker, Mary (cold.) John Henry Green (3) -   December 11, 1879
    For further information see - Green, John Henry.

Parker, P. Gould and Rebecca F. Heflebower (2) -   (L) August 25, 1855

Parker, Rachel (cold.) Alfred Irvin (3) -   December 4, 1873
    For further information see - Irvin, Alfred.

Parker, Thomas and Laura Brown (3) -   May 28, 1874
    Place of marriage, near Kearneysville - Age of husband, 24 - Age of
    wife, 23 - Both are Single - Husband was born in Jefferson County,
    West Virginia - Wife was born in Virginia - Both reside in Jefferson
    County, West Virginia.

Parmer, Scotia W. and Joseph Holmes (2) -   (L) August 11, 1851

Parmer, Scotia and Joseph Holmes (1) -   August 11, 1851

Parr, J. Harry and Grace M. Cochrane (3) -   July 30, 1889
    Place of marriage, Harpers Ferry - Age of husband, 23 - Age of wife,
    19 - Both are Single - Husband was born in Kent County, Maryland -
    Wife was born in Jefferson County, West Virginia - Both reside in
    Jefferson County, West Virginia.

Parran, Laura E. and Thomas H. Towner (2) -   (L) April 26, 1859

Parran, Laura L. and Robert Byra Lewis (3) -   December 16, 1868
    For further information see - Lewis, Robert Byra.

Parran, Lillie M. and William F. Lee (2) -   (L) September 13, 1859

Parran, Rosa M. and James A. Buchanan (2) -   (L) September 15, 1857

Parter, Lydia A. (cold.) David D. Washington (3) -   May 22, 1884
   For further information see - Washington, David D.

Partridge, Nancy and John Griffee (1) -   October 20, 1818

Paten, Guy (colored) Sallie Ornet (3) -   October 28, 1865
   Place of marriage, Charlestown, Jefferson County - Age of husband,
   22 - Age of wife, 17 - Both are Single - Husband was born in
   Jefferson County - Wife was born at Smithfield, Jefferson County -
   Both reside in Jefferson County - Husband's parents are Edmond and
   Charity Paten - Wife's parents are Jossey Ornet - Occupation of
   husband is Laborer.

Paterson, Mary (cold.) John W. Stanton (3) -   June 19, 1889
   For further information see - Stanton, John W.

Patience, John and Lidia Thompson (1) -   January 30, 1814

Patterson, Edward and Mary Cook (3) -   August 1, 1867
   Place of marriage, Jefferson County - Age of husband, 47 - Age of
   wife, 42 - Husband is Single - Wife is a Widow - Wife was born in
   Loudoun County, Virginia - Both reside in Jefferson County, West
   Virginia - Wife's parents are David and Matilda Foreman - Occupation
   of husband is Laborer.

Patterson, Emily and Henry Williams (3) -   December 25, 1866
   For further information see - Williams, Henry.

Patterson, George C. and Emilia J. Steinbracker (3) -   March 1, 1887
   Place of marriage, Charlestown - Age of husband, 43 - Age of wife,
   33 - Husband is a Widower - Wife is Single - Husband was born at
   Philadelphia - Wife was born at New York - Husband resides at
   Baltimore, Maryland - Wife resides in Jefferson County, West Virginia.

Patterson, James F. (cold.) Rebecca Thornton (3) -   March 15, 1888
   Place of marriage, Charlestown - Age of husband, 26 - Age of wife,
   20 - Both are Single - Both were born in Jefferson County, West
   Virginia - Both reside in Jefferson County.

Patterson, Jane (cold.) Henry Brown (3) -   September 22, 1881
   For further information see - Brown, Henry.

Patterson, John (cold.) Nancy Thomas (3) -   September 6, 1883
   Place of marriage, Charlestown - Age of husband, 25 - Age of wife,
   24 - Both are Single - Both were born in Jefferson County, West
   Virginia - Both reside in Jefferson County, West Virginia.

Patterson, Kate (cold.) George W. Washington (3) -   December 13, 1883
   For further information see - Washington, George W.

Patterson, Margaret (colored) Thomas Stripling (3) -   January 25, 1870
   For further information see - Stripling, Thomas.

Patterson, Samuel W. and Harriet Hughes (2) -   (L) January 15, 1855

Patton, Elizabeth and Joseph Wysong (1) -   May 24, 1810

Payne, Benjamin (cold.) Girtie Fields (3) -   June 16, 1881
    Place of marriage, Duffields - Age of husband, 27 - Age of wife,
    17 - Both are Single - Both were born in Jefferson County, West
    Virginia - Both reside in Jefferson County, West Virginia.
    (Consent of bride's father certified by Benjamin Branson, cold.)

Payne, Charles B. and Lucy B. Custer (3) -   June 21, 1881
    Place of marriage, Bride's Residence near Summit Point - Age of
    husband, 27 - Age of wife, 20 - Both are Single - Husband was born
    in State of Maryland - Wife was born in Jefferson County, West
    Virginia - Husband resides in Maryland - Wife resides in Jefferson
    County, West Virginia. (Consent of bride's father in writing.)

Payne, Daniel (cold.) Lee Anna Hunter (3) -   November 11, 1883
    Place of marriage, Summit Point - Age of husband, 25 - Age of wife,
    23 - Both are Single - Both were born in Jefferson County, West
    Virginia - Both reside in Jefferson County, West Virginia.

Payne, Eli W. and Almira B. Coyle (3) -   October 30, 1877
    Place of marriage, Middleway - Age of husband, 58 - Age of wife,
    35 - Both are Single - Husband was born in Berkeley County, West
    Virginia - Wife was born in Maryland - Both reside in Jefferson
    County, West Virginia.

Payne, George and Sally Long (1) -   June 12, 1827

Payne, Harriet (cold.) Taylor Nicolas (3) -   April 22, 1875
    For further information see - Nicolas, Taylor.

Payne, Louisa (colored) Augustian Sanders (3) -   November 17, 1870
    For further information see - Sanders, Augustian.

Payne, Martha (cold.) Willis Strother (3) -   June 21, 1884
    For further information see - Strother, Willis.

Payne, Martin L. and Mary C. Dillon (3) -   October 23, 1866
    Place of marriage, Jefferson County at David Dillon's - Age of
    husband, 26 - Age of wife, 22 - Both are Single - Husband was born
    in Berkeley County, West Virginia - Wife was born at Baltimore City,
    Maryland - Husband resides in Berkeley County, West Virginia -
    Wife resides in Jefferson County, West Virginia - Husband's parents
    are John M. and Mary D. Payne - Wife's parents are David and
    Elizabeth Dillon - Occupation of husband is Farmer.

Payne, Mary Ellen (cold.) John Howard (3) -   December 27, 1882
    For further information see - Howard, John.

Payne, Mary Frances (cold.) Albert Martin (3) -   November 12, 1878
    For further information see - Martin, Albert.

Payne, William D. and Mollie E. E. Frazier (3) -   September 7, 1875
    Place of marriage, Middleway - Age of husband, 29 - Age of wife,
    20 - Both are Single - Husband was born in Berkeley County, West
    Virginia - Wife was born in Jefferson County, West Virginia -
    Husband resides in Berkeley County, West Virginia - Wife resides in
    Jefferson County, West Virginia. (By written consent of W. Hayslett
    her grandfather; her parents being dead.)

Payne, William F. (cold.) Nannie Turner (3) -   December 27, 1888
    Place of marriage, Bolivar - Age of husband, 24 - Age of wife, 22 -
    Both are Single - Both were born in Jefferson County, West Virginia -
    Both reside in Jefferson County, West Virginia.

Payne, William H. (cold.) Delphy Brown (3) -   February 8, 1886
    Place of marriage, Charlestown - Age of husband, 32 - Age of wife,
    23 - Husband is a Widower - Wife is Single - Husband was born in
    Loudoun County, Virginia - Wife was born in Jefferson County, West
    Virginia - Both reside in Jefferson County, West Virginia.

Peacher, Clara Belle and Thomas Hessey Loman (3) -   December 14, 1880
    For further information see - Loman, Thomas Hessey.

Peacher, Ellen A. and Benjamin Loman (2) -   (L) July 21, 1852

Peacher, Ellen A. and Benjamin Loman (1) -   July 22, 1852

Peacher, Elmer and S. M. Lay (3) -   April 1, 1889
    Place of marriage, Harpers Ferry - Age of husband, 24 - Age of wife,
    18 - Both are Single - Husband was born at Baltimore City - Wife was
    born in Clarke County - Both reside in Jefferson County, West Virginia.
    (Consent of bride's father in person.)

Peacher, Emma E. and George N. Wilson (3) -   September 24, 1885
    For further information see - Wilson, George N.

Peacher, Ida M. and John T. Potts (3) -   April 28, 1889
    For further information see - Potts, John T.

Peacher, Lydia A. and William H. B. Hays (2) -   (L) January 24, 1859

Peacher, Mary and Dennis McMahon (3) -   August 31, 1876
    For further information see - McMahon, Dennis.

Peacher, Oliver and Catherine Devlin (3) -   October 25, 1886
    Place of marriage, Harpers Ferry - Age of husband, 46 - Age of wife,
    33 - Husband is a Widower - Wife is Single - Husband was born in
    Washington County, Maryland - Wife was born in Jefferson County,
    West Virginia - Both reside in Washington County, Maryland.

Peacher, W. H. and Fannie L. Manuel (3) -   June 26, 1889
    Place of marriage, Harpers Ferry - Age of husband, 21 - Age of wife,
    21 - Both are Single - Husband was born at Baltimore, Maryland -
    Wife was born in Jefferson County, West Virginia - Both reside in
    Jefferson County, West Virginia.

Pear, Elizabeth and John Orndorff (3) -   February 5, 1868
    For further information see - Orndorff, John.

Pear, James K. Polk and Ellen DeLany (3) -   July 24, 1873
    Place of marriage, near Charlestown - Age of husband, 27 - Age of
    wife, 29 - Both are Single - Husband was born in Berkeley County,
    West Virginia - Wife was born in Jefferson County, West Virginia -
    Both reside in Jefferson County, West Virginia.

Pearce, Sallie (cold.) James Shamblain (3) -   April 24, 1884
    For further information see - Shamblain, James.

Pearl, Charles William and Mary Elizabeth Dillow (3) -   December 24, 1872

Pearl, Daniel B. and Aletha Zimerman (3) -   October 7, 1869
    Place of marriage, Jefferson County - Age of husband, 23 - Age of
    wife, 22 - Husband was born in Jefferson County, West Virginia -
    Wife was born in Maryland - Both reside in Jefferson County.
    (Granted upon endorsement of Joseph W. Glenn.)

Pearl, Drusilla and James W. Painter (3) -   October 10, 1875
    For further information see - Painter, James W.

Pearl, George and Melia Bond (3) -   February 3, 1867
    Place of marriage, Residence of Adam Snyder - Age of husband, 52 -
    Age of wife, 46 - Husband is Single - Wife is a Widow - Husband was
    born in Jefferson County, West Virginia - Wife was born in
    Rockingham County, Virginia - Both reside in Jefferson County, West
    Virginia - Husband's parents are Nathan and Susannah Pearl -
    Occupation of husband is Blacksmith.

Pearl, John T. and Liza Ann Mobley (3) -   August 23, 1872
    Place of marriage, Jefferson County - Age of husband, 21 - Age of
    wife, 22 - Both are Single - Husband was born in Jefferson County -
    Wife was born in Jefferson County, Virginia - Husband resides in
    Jefferson County - Wife resides in Jefferson County, West Virginia -
    Husband's parents are David and Julia A. - Wife's parents are
    Washington and Mary G. - Occupation of husband is Farmer.

Pearl, Nance Sophrania and John Henry Wilt (3) -   July 23, 1885
    For further information see - Wilt, John Henry.

Pearl, Sarah Jane and John W. Wiltshire (2) -   (L) June 13, 1860

Pearl, Stephanna and Willis King (3) -   July 28, 1887
    For further information see - King, Willis.

Pearl, Susanna Margaret and George W. Goldsborough (3) -   January 9, 1873
    For further information see - Goldsborough, George W.

Pearrell, Irene and V. R. Roberts (3) -   February 23, 1887
    For further information see - Roberts, V. R.

Pease, Robert and Emma Dobson (3) -   June 27, 1877
    Place of marriage, Charlestown - Age of husband, 23 - Age of wife,
    18 - Both are Single - Husband was born at Staunton, Virginia -
    Wife was born in Jefferson County, West Virginia - Husband resides
    at Staunton, Virginia - Wife resides in Jefferson County, West
    Virginia.

Pedrick, George G. and Kate E. Ott (2) -   (L) (1862)
    Time of marriage, (between February 25, 1862 and May 7, 1862) -
    Place of marriage, Charlestown - Names of parties, George G. Pedrick
    and Kate E. Ott - Age of husband, 24 years - Age of wife, 18 years -
    Both are Single - Place of husband's birth was Haddonfield, New
    Jersey - Place of wife's birth was Jefferson County, Virginia -
    Place of husband's residence is Baltimore, Maryland - Place of
    wife's residence is Rippon, Jefferson County, Virginia - Names of
    husband's parents are John R. and Sarah A. Pedrick - Names of wife's
    parents are Barney and Margaret Ott - Occupation of husband is
    Carpenter - Barney Ott - George G. Pedrick.

Peeler, Daniel W. (cold.) Julia Lightfoot (3) -   July 24, 1873
    Place of marriage, Charles Town - Age of husband, 21 - Age of wife,
    23 - Both are Single - Both were born in Jefferson County, West
    Virginia - Husband resides at Pittsburg, Pennsylvania - Wife resides
    in Jefferson County, West Virginia.

Penaral, Martha and W. Goldsborough (3) -   October 17, 1867
    For further information see - Goldsborough, W.

Pendleton, Benjamin and Eliza Strother (1) -   October 31, 1805

Pendleton, Benjamin S. and Julia E. Rickard (3) -   October 15, 1884
    Place of marriage, Shepherdstown - Age of husband, 41 - Age of wife,
    31 - Husband is a Widower - Wife is Single - Husband was born in
    Arkansas - Wife was born in Jefferson County, West Virginia -
    Husband resides in Jefferson County, West Virginia - Wife resides in
    Jefferson County.

Pendleton, D. D. and H. M. Boteler (bride) (3) -   April 25, 1866
    Place of marriage, Shepherdstown, Jefferson County - Age of husband,
    26 - Age of wife, 25 - Both are Single - Husband was born in Louisa
    County, Virginia - Wife was born in Jefferson County, Virginia -
    Both reside in Jefferson County, West Virginia - Husband's parents
    are Hugh and Elizabeth Pendleton - Wife's parents are A. R. and
    H. M. Boteler - Occupation of husband is Farmer.

Pendleton, Emma Jane and George A. Brown (3) -   May 25, 1871
    For further information see - Brown, George A.

Pendleton, Harriet (colored) John Davis (3) -   November 10, 1870
    For further information see - Davis, John.

Pendleton, John and Mary Jackson (3) -   September 24, 1868
    Place of marriage, Jefferson County - Age of husband, 21 - Age of
    wife, 21 - Both are Single - Husband was born in Jefferson County -
    Wife was born in Loudoun County, Virginia - Both reside in Jefferson
    County - Occupation of husband is Farmer.

Pendleton, Julia N. and James W. Allen (2) -   (L) February 13, 1856

Pendleton, Lucy (cold.) Frank Spencer (3) -   October 30, 1890
    For further information see - Spencer, Frank.

Pendleton, Mason and Lucy Green (3) -   April 11, 1872
    Place of marriage, Jefferson County - Age of husband, 23 - Age of
    wife, 22 - Both are Single - Both were born in Jefferson County,
    West Virginia - Husband resides in Jefferson County, West Virginia -
    Wife resides in Jefferson, West Virginia - Husband's parents are
    James and Charity - Wife's parents are William and Lucy - Occupation
    of husband is Farming.

Pendleton, Sarah (cold.) Richard Henry Moore (3) -   December 31, 1873
    For further information see - Moore, Richard Henry.

Pendleton, Virginia (cold.) Harrison Dixon (3) -   October 30, 1890
    For further information see - Dixon, Harrison.

Penn, Shaderick and Susanna King (1) -   November 4, 1824

Penn, Susan and Alexander Fossett (1) -   March 24, 1832

Pennington, Isabella and Nathaniel C. Baker (1) - August 30, 1841

Penwell, Fonrose and Annie M. Harder (3) - August 13, 1884
    Place of marriage, Harpers Ferry - Age of husband, 21 - Age of wife, 21 - Both are Single - Husband was born in Jefferson County, West Virginia - Wife was born in Jefferson County - Husband resides in Jefferson County - Wife resides in Jefferson County, West Virginia.

Penwell, Martha and James S. Bascue (3) - April 26, 1872
    For further information see - Bascue, James S.

Penwell, Mrs. Mary and John Henry Linton (3) - December 31, 1874
    For further information see - Linton, John Henry.

Penwell, Mary Ann and John H. Hostler (2) - (L) June 1, 1852

Penwell, Mary Ann and John H. Hostler (1) - June 10, 1852

Penwell, Mary Hannah and Thomas Jefferson Gray (3) - September 20, 1887
    For further information see - Gray, Thomas Jefferson.

Penwell, Samuel H. and Sarah Birdie Longerbeam (3) - October 21, 1886
    Place of marriage, Blue Ridge Mountain - Age of husband, 21 - Age of wife, 16 - Both are Single - Both were born in Jefferson County, West Virginia - Both reside in Jefferson County, West Virginia. (Consent of bride's father in writing.)

Penwell, Thomas, Sr. and Martha McGoldrick (2) - (L) April 7, 1860

Penwell, Thomas, Jr. and Mary Elizabeth Dillow (2) - (L) May 15, 1858

Percival, Thomas H. and Mary Ann Bilson (2) - (L) January 21, 1852

Percival, Thomas H. and Mary Ann Bilson (1) - January 21, 1852

Peregoy, Joel and Elvira Eliza Jackson (1) - November 12, 1830

Perkins, Ann (cold.) Charles Ferguson (3) - September 14, 1884
    For further information see - Ferguson, Charles.

Perkins, Hamilton (colored) Ann Bracher (3) - June 7, 1870
    Place of marriage, Jefferson County - Age of husband, 25 - Age of wife, 32 - Husband was born in North Carolina - Wife was born in Jefferson County - Both reside in Jefferson County.

Perrell, Ignatius and Susan Utt (1) - 1812

Perrell, John and Elizabeth Turner (1) - December 26, 1805

Perry, Alexander (cold.) Maria Berry (3) - February 23, 1882
    Place of marriage, Charlestown - Age of husband, 23 - Age of wife, 21 - Both are Single - Husband was born in Rockbridge County, Virginia - Wife was born in Jefferson County, West Virginia - Both reside in Jefferson County, West Virginia.

Perry, Ann and Richard Crow (1) - January 1, 1826

Perry, Frances S. (cold.) William C. Smith (3) - July 15, 1890
    For further information see - Smith, William C.

Perry, George and Jane Richardson (1) -   February 7, 1807

Perry, Marshall B. and Mildred Marshall (1) -   February 9, 1832

Perry, Mary E. and Benjamin Stipes (2) -   (L) March 23, 1853

Perry, Mary A. and Benjamin Stipes (1) -   March 23, 1853

Perry, Sarah (cold.) Humphrey Fox (3) -   January 12, 1878
    For further information see - Fox, Humphrey.

Perry, V. L. and E. M. Atkinson (bride) (3) -   October 31, 1867
    Place of marriage, Jefferson County - Age of husband, 30 - Age of
    wife, 26 - Husband is a Widower - Wife is Single - Husband was born
    in Maryland - Wife was born in Virginia - Husband resides in
    Maryland - Wife resides in Jefferson County - Husband's parents are
    Thomas - Wife's parents are W. M. and R. B. - Occupation of husband
    is Physician.

Pester, John and Margaret Koch (2) -   (L) July 26, 1850

Peterman, Susan M. and George T. Watson (2) -   (L) October 1, 1857

Peters, Abraham (free mixtures) Everline Peters (1) -   August 6, 1826

Peters, Everline (free mixtures) Abraham Peters (1) -   August 6, 1826

Peters, John and Matilda Ripple (1) -   October 9, 1825

Peters, Warner and Catha Jackson (1) -   March 16, 1820

Peters, William H. and Ella Virginia Moore (3) -   September 26, 1888
    Place of marriage, Charlestown - Age of husband, 20 - Age of wife,
    18 - Both are Single - Husband was born in Maryland - Wife was born
    in Jefferson County, West Virginia - Husband resides at Roanoke,
    Virginia - Wife resides in Jefferson County, West Virginia.
    (Consent of groom's father in writing and her father in person.)

Peterson, Jesse (cold.) Adeline Turner (3) -   March 9, 1873
    Place of marriage, near Leetown at Isaac Strider's - Age of husband,
    28 - Age of wife, 18 - Both are Single - Husband was born in Jefferson
    County, West Virginia - Both reside in Jefferson County, West
    Virginia - Husband's parents are Eveline Peterson, mother - Wife's
    parents are Peter and Erecksine - Occupation of husband is Farm
    Hand.   (Mother's consent in person.)

Petterson, S. C. (cold.) Kate Washington (3) -   November 21, 1867
    Place of marriage, Jefferson County - Age of husband, 29 - Age of
    wife, 23 - Husband is a Widower - Wife is Single - Both were born in
    Jefferson County - Both reside in Jefferson County - Husband's
    parents are R: and H. - Wife's parents are P. and Rebecca -
    Occupation of husband is Barber.

Pettigrew, John A. and Maggie N. Craul (3) -   July 10, 1889
    Place of marriage, Charlestown - Age of husband, 37 - Age of wife,
    30 - Both are Single - Husband was born in Botetourt County,
    Virginia - Wife was born in Jefferson County, West Virginia -
    Husband resides in Botetourt County, Virginia - Wife resides in
    Jefferson County, West Virginia.

Pettit, Jonathan and Sarah Jane McGinnis (2) -   (L) December 2, 1857

Petty, B. W. and Molly E. Hagley (3) -   October 8, 1874
Place of marriage, Charlestown - Age of husband, 30 - Age of wife, 24 - Husband is a Widower - Wife is Single - Husband was born in Warren County, Virginia - Wife was born in Jefferson County, West Virginia - Husband resides in Page County, Virginia - Wife resides in Jefferson County, West Virginia.

Peyton, Joseph E. B. and Elizabeth E. Derry (3) -   December 24, 1874
Place of marriage, Harpers Ferry - Age of husband, 30 - Age of wife, 22 - Both are Single - Both were born in Loudoun County, Virginia - Husband resides in Loudoun County, Virginia - Wife resides in Jefferson County, West Virginia.

Pfister, Louisa and Michael Leopold Werthime (2) -   (L) August 5, 1857

Phalen, John A. and Barbara C. Heck (3) -   February 20, 1889
Place of marriage, Harpers Ferry - Age of husband, 23 - Age of wife, 21 - Both are Single - Husband was born in Washington County, Maryland - Wife was born in Jefferson County, West Virginia - Husband resides in Washington County, Maryland - Wife resides in Jefferson County, West Virginia.

Phalen, Martin William and Sarah Anna Riley (3) -   January 20, 1881
Place of marriage, Harpers Ferry.- Age of husband, 22 - Age of wife, 26 - Both are Single - Husband was born in Maryland - Wife was born in Loudoun County, Virginia - Husband resides in Maryland - Wife resides in Jefferson County, West Virginia. (Returned May 1883.)

Phelan, William and Mary Roderick (1) -   April 13, 1820

Phelps, W. E. and Ella S. Byers (3) -   March 22, 1882
Place of marriage, Shepherdstown - Age of husband, 25 - Age of wife, 23 - Both are Single - Husband was born in Massachusetts - Wife was born in Jefferson County, West Virginia - Both reside in Jefferson County, West Virginia.

Philapy, John W. and Fanny Elizabeth Shaull (2) -   (L) May 27, 1859

Philips, D. Arthur and S. Kate Walters (3) -   June 7, 1876
Place of marriage, Charlestown - Age of husband, 24 - Age of wife, 25 - Both are Single - Husband was born in Page County, Virginia - Wife was born in Jefferson County, West Virginia - Both reside in Jefferson County, West Virginia.

Philips, Henry and Susana Roman (3) -   January 19, 1871
Place of marriage, Smithfield - Age of husband, 22 - Age of wife, 22 - Both are Single - Husband was born in Hanover County, Virginia - Wife was born in Jefferson County - Both reside in Jefferson County - Husband's parents are Cesar and Charlot - Wife's parents are Elizah and Milly - Occupation of husband is Farmer.

Philips, Sallie Ann and John Yates (3) -   November 10, 1866
For further information see - Yates, John.

Phillips, Ed. W. and Hannah L. Diehl (3) -   March 30, 1886
     Place of marriage, Charlestown - Age of husband, 23 - Age of wife,
     19 - Both are Single - Husband was born in Jefferson County, West
     Virginia - Wife was born in Berkeley County - Both reside in
     Jefferson County, West Virginia. (Consent of bride's father in
     person.)

Phillips, George E. L. and Hannah T. Blake (2) -   (L) March 21, 1859

Phillips, John M. and Martha Fossett (3) -.   November 11, 1869
     Place of marriage, Jefferson County - Age of husband, 25 - Age of
     wife, 21 - Husband was born in Pennsylvania - Wife was born in
     Virginia - Husband resides at Kansas City - Wife resides in
     Jefferson County.

Phillips, John W. (cold.) Rebeca Ann Green (3) -   October 1, 1888
     Place of marriage, Charlestown - Age of husband, 23 - Age of wife,
     21 - Both are Single - Husband was born in Clarke County, Virginia -
     Wife was born in Jefferson County, West Virginia - Both reside in
     Jefferson County, West Virginia.

Phillips, Oscar M. and Bessie W. Starry (3) -   February 25, 1885
     Place of marriage, Charlestown - Age of husband, 27 - Age of wife,
     19 - Both are Single - Both were born in Jefferson County, West
     Virginia - Both reside in Jefferson County, West Virginia.
     (Consent of bride's father in person.)

Phillips, S. Lee and Maggie Rissler (3) -   December 5, 1882
     Place of marriage, Charlestown - Age of husband, 26 - Age of wife,
     23 - Both are Single - Both were born in Jefferson County, West
     Virginia - Both reside in Jefferson County, West Virginia.

Picking, Jacob and Ruth Ann Barnes (1) -   December 15, 1836

Pier, Angeline and George Barrow (3) -   May 29, 1866
     For further information see - Barrow, George.

Pierce, Alfred N. and Mary E. Bell (2) -   (L) November 20, 1857

Pierce, George H. and Jane B. Hammond (2) -   (L) September 22, 1856

Pierce, George W. and Mary Ashby (3) -   August 8, 1872
     Place of marriage, Bolivar - Age of husband, 21 - Age of wife, 18 -
     Both are Single - Husband was born in Frederick County, Maryland -
     Wife was born in Jefferson County, Virginia - Husband resides in
     Maryland - Wife resides in Jefferson County, West Virginia -
     Husband's parents are John M. and Ellen - Wife's parents are John W.
     and Peggy - Occupation of husband is Rail Road. (Father consents.)

Pierce, Jerome M. and Annie E. Watt (3) -   August 25, 1878
     Place of marriage, Harpers Ferry - Age of husband, 21 - Age of wife,
     21 - Both are Single - Both were born in Maryland - Husband resides
     in Maryland - Wife resides in Jefferson County, West Virginia.

Pierce, John (cold.) Jane Bateman (2) -   (L) August 15, 1855

Pierce, John T. and Margaret Workman (1) -   1813

Pierce, John T. and Susanna Steward (2) -   (L) March 29, 1856

449

Pierce, Rachael and William Calhoun (1) - July 21, 1827

Pierce, Ruah and Andrew Wright (2) - (L) April 12, 1852

Pierce, Susan and James William Allen (2) - (L) February 5, 1852

Pierce, Susan and James W. Allen (1) - February 5, 1852

Pierce, Thomas J. and Pink B. Kidwell (3) - April 6, 1880
    Place of marriage, Shepherdstown - Age of husband, 23 - Age of wife, 18 - Both are Single - Both were born in Jefferson County, West Virginia - Both reside in Jefferson County, West Virginia. (Consent of bride's parents in writing.)

Pierce, William (cold.) Clarissa Taylor (3) - December 24, 1874
    Place of marriage, near Leetown - Age of husband, 24 - Age of wife, 26 - Both are Single - Husband was born in Berkeley County, West Virginia - Wife was born in Jefferson County, West Virginia - Both reside in Jefferson County, West Virginia.

Pifer, Ann Catharine and Albert Buzzard (2) - (L) August 15, 1863
    For further information see - Buzzard, Albert.

Pilcher, Ann and John Krepps (2) - (L) July 19, 1861
    For further information see - Krepps, John.

Piles, Harriet and William Graham (1) - September 1, 1834

Piles, Lucinda and John Stahl (1) - April 9, 1835

Piles, Samuel and Mary Foreman (1) - July 30, 1806

Pilken, Michael and Amanda Ashby (2) - (L) December 30, 1862
    Time of marriage, January 4, 1863 - Place of marriage, Halltown - Names, Michael Pilken and Amanda Ashby - Age of husband, 23 years - Age of wife, 21 years, January 25, 1863 - Both are Single - Husband was born at Baltimore, Maryland - Wife was born in Clarke County, Virginia - Both live in Jefferson County, Virginia - Husband's parents are William and Elizabeth Pilken - Wife's parents are Martin and Elzabeth Ashby (father dead) - Occupation of husband is Railroad Maker - Liscense issued, December 30, 1862 - Mother's consent given in writing.

Pine, Anthony L. and Josephine Lamas (2) - (L) May 11, 1857

Pinkerton, John and Catharine Shouk (1) - December 5, 1824

Piper, Ann and John Knox (1) - July 8, 1824

Piper, Catherine and John Cogle (1) - August 26, 1824

Piper, Christian and Ann Dillow (1) - March 16, 1820

Piper, Christiana and William Scarlet (1) - June 25, 1807

Piper, Emma Jane and William Benjamin Gray (3) - April 20, 1879
    For further information see - Gray, William Benjamin.

Piper, George and Susan Near (1) - July 8, 1824

Piper, George W. and Christena Buzzard (3) -   (1870)
   Age of husband, 20 - Age of wife, 17 - Both were born in Jefferson
   County, Virginia - Both reside in Jefferson County. (Consent of
   parents in writing and oath of witness Albert Buzzard.)

Piper, Jacob and Sarah Mahoney (1) -   October 6, 1848

Piper, Jacob and Maria Lay (2) -   (L) June 20, 1853

Piper, Jane Ann and John Cogal (3) -   July 14, 1878
   For further information see - Cogal, John.

Piper, John and Mary Ott (1) -   July 26, 1821

Piper, John, Jr. and Mary E. Adelsberger (3) -   May 16, 1874
   Place of marriage, Mountain - Age of husband, 21 in 13 days - Age of
   wife, 23 - Both are Single - Both were born in Jefferson County,
   West Virginia - Both reside in Jefferson County, West Virginia.
   (Consent of groom's father in writing witnessed by John W. Bond.)

Piper, Lewis and Mary Graves (1) -   October 10, 1816

Piper, Margaret and John Thomas (1) -   August 26, 1818

Piper, Mary and James Hughes (1) -   October 19, 1815

Piper, Mary and Thomas Grove (2) -   (L) March 5, 1852

Piper, Mary and Thomas Grove (1) -   March 9, 1852

Piper, Mary and Jonathan Cogle (2) -   (L) August 2, 1854

Piper, Mary Elizabeth and Rezin F. Grove (3) -   June 5, 1879
   For further information see - Grove, Rezin F.

Piper, Mollie and James Foreman (3) -   January 7, 1888
   For further information see - Foreman, James.

Piper, Rezin and Sarah E. Fleming (3) -   June 1, 1886
   Place of marriage, Harpers Ferry - Age of husband, 27 - Age of wife,
   29 - Husband is Single - Wife is a Widow - Husband was born in
   Jefferson County, West Virginia - Wife was born in Maryland - Both
   reside in Jefferson County, West Virginia.

Piper, Thomas William and Sarah Elizabeth Cogle (3) -   August 12, 1886
   Place of marriage, Harpers Ferry - Age of husband, 31 - Age of wife,
   27 - Both are Single - Both were born in Jefferson County, West
   Virginia - Both reside in Jefferson County, West Virginia.

Piper, Washington and Elizabeth Hughes (2) -   (L) July 9, 1851

Pippin, Joseph (free coloured) Harriet Irvin (2) -   (L) February 15, 1860

Pitcher, Sidney and Susana Robinson (1) -   May 27, 1819

Pitchers, Isabella and John W. Kigle (3) -   November 22, 1870
   For further information see - Kigle, John W.

Pitsnogle, Lizzie and J. H. Lloyd (3) -   April 11, 1889
   For further information see - Lloyd, J. H.

451

Pitzer, B. W. and Alice M. Beltz (3) - March 14, 1882
    Place of marriage, Shepherdstown - Age of husband, 23 - Age of wife, 23 - Both are Single - Both were born in Jefferson County, West Virginia - Husband resides in Berkeley County - Wife resides in Jefferson County, West Virginia.

Pitzer, Mary and Henry P. Boyd (3) - . February 13, 1878
    For further information see - Boyd, Henry P.

Pitzer, Samuel W. and Annie E. Kimes (3) - April 24, 1884
    Place of marriage, Shepherdstown - Age of husband, 29 - Age of wife, 31 - Both are Single - Husband was born in Berkeley County - Wife was born in Jefferson County - Husband resides in Berkeley County - Wife resides in Jefferson County, West Virginia.

Plate, Belle (cold.) Cesar Cole (3) - December 31, 1874
    For further information see - Cole, Cesar.

Pleasant, Jinnie and Samuel R. Noodispaw (3) - April 9, 1889
    For further information see - Noodispaw, Samuel R.

Plotner, Samuel H. and Annie L. Dunn (3) - September 20, 1877
    Place of marriage, near Charlestown - Age of husband, 22 - Age of wife, 21 - Both are Single - Husband was born in Berkeley County, West Virginia - Wife was born in Clarke County, Virginia - Both reside in Jefferson County, West Virginia.

Plummer, Thomas G. and Mary A. Strider (2) - (L) June 13, 1859

Poffenberger, Estella J. and William M. Staley (3) - February 23, 1887
    For further information see - Staley, William M.

Poffenberger, Fannie and A. H. Martin (3) - December 30, 1887
    For further information see - Martin, A. H.

Poffenberger, Mollie J. and A. D. Crow (3) - December 11, 1878
    For further information see - Crow, A. D.

Poffinberger, Rosanna and David Kretzer (1) - May 25, 1826

Poindexter, William Franklin (cold.) Mary Susan Cain (3) - October 19, 1879
    Place of marriage, Charlestown - Age of husband, 24 - Age of wife, 22 - Both are Single - Husband was born in Augusta County, Virginia - Wife was born in Clarke County, Virginia - Both reside in Jefferson County, West Virginia.

Poisal, Adam P. S. and Mary Catharine McKenney (2) - (L) May 18, 1863
    Time of marriage, May 18, 1863 - Place of marriage, Harpers Ferry, Virginia - Names, Adam P. S. Poisal and Mary Catharine McKenney - Age of husband, 23 years May 8, 1863 - Age of wife, 22 years - Both are Single - Both were born in Berkeley County, Virginia - Husband resides in Washington County, Maryland - Wife resides in Jefferson County, Virginia - Names of husband's parents are Jacob and Mary Poisal - Names of wife's parents are George and Mary McKenney - Occupation of husband is Soldier in Federal Army - License issued, May 18, 1863.

Poisal, I. F. and Mollie E. Kimes (3) - October 22, 1868
Place of marriage, Jefferson County - Age of husband, 25 - Age of wife, 26 - Both are Single - Husband was born in Berkeley County, Virginia - Wife was born in Jefferson County - Husband resides in Berkeley County - Wife resides in West Virginia - Husband's parents are Sebastian and Eleiln - Wife's parents are Henry and Hannah - Occupation of husband is Carpenter.

Poland, Samuel and Mary Myers (1) - April 13, 1832

Pollock, Ann and Joseph G. Massey (1) - November 25, 1822

Poltz, Eve and Peter Zumbro (1) - June 25, 1809

Pool, Elizabeth and Joseph F. Kidd (2) - (L) April 23, 1860

Pool, Katy and William S. Watson (3) - July 4, 1884
For further information see - Watson, William S.

Pope, Bettie C. and George White (3) - August 16, 1882
For further information see - White, George.

Pope, Ida and William A. Dunn (3) - October 18, 1887
For further information see - Dunn, William A.

Pope, John and Mary E. Watkins (3) - February 3, 1874
Place of marriage, Halltown - Age of husband, 23 in March - Age of wife, 27 - Both are Single - Husband was born in Clarke County, Virginia - Wife was born in Jefferson County, West Virginia - Both reside in Jefferson County, West Virginia.

Pope, John M. and H. A. Hamilton (3) - August 8, 1867
Place of marriage, Jefferson County - Age of husband, 32 - Age of wife, 19 - Both are Single - Husband was born in Germany - Wife was born in Virginia - Husband resides at Berryville, Virginia - Wife resides in Jefferson County, West Virginia - Husband's parents are Michael and Barbara - Wife's parents are J. T. and R. J. - Occupation of husband is Tailor. (Father present and gives consent.)

Pope, Mary E. and E. F. Lanham (3) - September 9, 1882
For further information see - Lanham, E. F.

Port, George W. and Emma M. Welshans (3) - January 1, 1879
Place of marriage, Shepherdstown - Age of husband, 36 - Age of wife, 28 - Husband is a Widower - Wife is Single - Husband was born in England - Wife was born in Jefferson County, West Virginia - Husband resides in New Mexico - Wife resides in Jefferson County, West Virginia.

Porter, James William (cold.) Rachel Wilson (3) - October 7, 1875
Place of marriage, Shepherdstown - Age of husband, 21 - Age of wife, 20 - Both are Single - Both were born in Jefferson County, West Virginia - Both reside in Jefferson County, West Virginia. (Consent of bride's father in writing.)

Porter, Levi M. and Sagnes Roberts Criswell (3) - November 15, 1871
Place of marriage, Jefferson County - Age of husband, 24 - Age of wife, 21 - Both are Single - Husband was born in Clarke County, Ohio - Wife was born in Berkeley County - Both reside in Jefferson County - Husband's parents are Benjamin and Elizabeth - Wife's parents are Andrew and Mary J. - Occupation of husband is Farmer.

Porter, Lewis (cold.) Milly Mitchell (3) - November 6, 1873
    Place of marriage, Shepherdstown - Age of husband, 39 - Age of wife,
    22 - Husband is a Widower - Wife is Single - Both were born in
    Jefferson County, West Virginia - Both reside in Jefferson County,
    West Virginia.

Porter, Martha Ann and John A. Lucas (3) - April 11, 1877
    For further information see - Lucas, John A.

Porter, Susan C. and Christopher Thomas (3) - June 3, 1873
    For further information see - Thomas, Christopher.

Porterfield, Elizabeth Morton and H. H. Cooke (3) - October 6, 1877
    For further information see - Cooke, H. H.

Porterfield, Emma Serena and George Washington (3) - February 16, 1886
    For further information see - Washington, George.

Porterfield, George and Susan Elizabeth Simmons (3) - January 21, 1885
    Place of marriage, Charlestown - Age of husband, 27 - Age of wife,
    25 - Both are Single - Husband was born in Jefferson County, West
    Virginia - Wife was born at Frederick City, Maryland - Both reside
    in Jefferson County, West Virginia.

Porterfield, John and Annie L. Green (3) - August 9, 1876
    Place of marriage, Charles Town - Age of husband, 21 - Age of wife,
    22 - Both are Single - Both were born in Jefferson County, West
    Virginia - Both reside in Jefferson County, West Virginia.

Posey, Richard (cold.) Mary F. Johnson (3) - July 9, 1881
    Place of marriage, Charlestown - Age of husband, 21 - Age of wife,
    21 - Both are Single - Husband was born in Warren County, Virginia -
    Wife was born in Clarke County, Virginia - Both reside in Jefferson
    County, West Virginia.

Posler, John and Margaret Kolsch (1) - June 18, 1850

Potter, Matilda and John L. Cook (2) - (L) June 5, 1858

Potts, Ann and Jonas Shuck (1) - July 3, 1831

Potts, Annie B. and John P. Carper (3) - July 3, 1888
    For further information see - Carper, John P.

Potts, Charles and Catherine Cogle (3) - April 3, 1879
    Place of marriage, Harpers Ferry - Age of husband, 24 - Age of wife,
    22 - Both are Single - Husband was born in Loudoun County,
    Virginia - Wife was born in Jefferson County, West Virginia - Both
    reside in Jefferson County, West Virginia.

Potts, E. F. and Virginia F. Wingas (2) - (L) February 18, 1861

Potts, Henry W. and Eleanor Strode Powell (3) - September 27, 1881
    Place of marriage, Shepherdstown - Age of husband, 34 - Age of wife,
    24 - Both are Single - Husband was born in State of Pennsylvania -
    Wife was born in State of Virginia - Husband resides in
    Pennsylvania - Wife resides in Jefferson County, West Virginia.

Potts, Jacob and Mary Ellen Louden (3) -   January 23, 1873
Place of marriage, Jefferson County - Age of husband, 24 next
April - Age of wife, 21 in April - Both are Single - Husband was
born in Pennsylvania - Wife was born in Jefferson County, West
Virginia - Both reside in Jefferson County, West Virginia -
Husband's parents are John and Mary - Wife's parents are William and
Mary - Occupation of husband is Laborer. (Consent of mother in
writing. Witness sworn.)

Potts, Jane and James W. Smith (3) -   April 11, 1869
For further information see - Smith, James W.

Potts, John and Rebecca Jenkins (3) -   March 2, 1870
Place of marriage, Jefferson County - Age of husband, 23 - Age of
wife, 25 - Husband was born in Pennsylvania - Wife was born in
Virginia - Both reside in Jefferson County. (Ages sworn to by
Welsh T. Hackley.)

Potts, John R. and Hester Ann Eckhart (3) -   November 12, 1874
Place of marriage, Shepherdstown - Age of husband, 21 - Age of wife,
21 - Both are Single - Husband was born in Pennsylvania - Wife was
born in Maryland - Both reside in Jefferson County, West Virginia.

Potts, John T. and Ida M. Peacher (3) -   April 28, 1889
Place of marriage, Charlestown - Age of husband, 23 - Age of wife,
21 - Both are Single - Husband was born in Loudoun County, Virginia -
Wife was born in Jefferson County, West Virginia - Both reside in
Jefferson County, West Virginia.

Potts, Lucy M. and John H. Giddy (3) -   January 25, 1888
For further information see - Giddy, John H.

Potts, Mary and John Henry Wright (3) -   March 5, 1872
For further information see - Wright, John Henry.

Potts, Sarah and John H. Bayliss (3) -   May 23, 1872
For further information see - Bayliss, John H.

Potts, Thomas and Sarah Elizabeth Walraven (2) -   (L) February 18, 1856

Potts, Walter J. and Ida Manuel (3) -   October 21, 1890
Place of marriage, Harpers Ferry - Age of husband, 26 - Age of wife,
26 - Both are Single - Husband was born in Madison County, Ohio -
Wife was born in Jefferson County, West Virginia - Husband resides
in Clarke County, Ohio - Wife resides in Jefferson County, West
Virginia.

Powell, Cornelius (cold.) Lucinda Johnson (3) -   September 15, 1887
Place of marriage, near Charlestown - Age of husband, 34 - Age of
wife, 26 - Both are Single - Both were born in Jefferson County,
West Virginia - Both reside in Jefferson County, West Virginia.

Powell, Delpha and W. G. Hill (3) -   February 12, 1872
For further information see - Hill, W. G.

Powell, Eleanor Strode and Henry W. Potts (3) -   September 27, 1881
For further information see - Potts, Henry W.

Powell, Elizabeth and Jacob Board (1) -   August 9, 1821

Powell, Emily (cold.) Benjamin F. Lands (3) -   August 29, 1878
   For further information see - Lands, Benjamin F.

Powell, George (cold.) Jennie Walker (3) -   November 20, 1884
   Place of marriage, Charlestown - Age of husband, 24 - Age of wife,
   21 - Both are Single - Husband was born in Jefferson County, West
   Virginia - Wife was born in Jefferson County - Both reside in
   Jefferson County, West Virginia.

Powell, Harry (cold.) Alice Williams (3) -   July 21, 1877
   Place of marriage, Charlestown - Age of husband, 25 - Age of wife,
   19 - Husband is a Widower - Wife is Single - Husband was born in
   Jefferson County, West Virginia - Wife was born in Rappahannock
   County, Virginia - Both reside in Jefferson County, West Virginia.
   (Consent of bride's father in Writing.)

Powell, Henry (cold.) Patsy Nichols (3) -   December 22, 1881
   Place of marriage, near Charlestown - Age of husband, 48 - Age of
   wife, 30 - Husband is a Widower - Wife is Single - Both were born in
   Jefferson County, West Virginia - Both reside in Jefferson County,
   West Virginia.

Powell, Jennie (cold.) James Whiting (3) -   June 1, 1882
   For further information see - Whiting, James.

Powell, John Simms and Ellen Lee (1) -   September 19, 1844

Powell, Laura (cold.) Nathan Hill (3) -   July 6, 1876
   For further information see - Hill, Nathan.

Powell, Laura Stewart and William Thomas Roberts (3) -   May 4, 1886
   For further information see - Roberts, William Thomas.

Powell, Mary (cold.) Daniel Stribling (3) -   August 23, 1875
   For further information see - Stribling, Daniel.

Powell, Thomas and Margaret Morgan (1) -   October 10, 1833

Power, Sarah C. and Joseph L. Russell (2) -   (L) November 7, 1860

Powers, Bridget and Charles Hagan (2) -   (L) October 3, 1857

Powers, Elizabeth N. and William C. Shurer (3) -   October 16, 1866
   For further information see - Shurer, William C.

Powers, Frank and Eliza J. Easton (3) -   July 4, 1876
   Place of marriage, Bolivar - Age of husband, 22 - Age of wife, 21 -
   Both are Single - Both were born in Washington County, Maryland -
   Husband resides in Washington County, Maryland - Wife resides in
   Jefferson County, West Virginia.

Powers, Jackson and Sallie Houston (3) -   April 27, 1871
   Place of marriage, Jefferson County - Age of husband, 24 - Age of
   wife, 22 - Both are Single - Husband was born in Jefferson County -
   Wife was born in Page County, Virginia - Both reside in Jefferson
   County - Husband's parents are Joseph and Lucy - Occupation of
   husband is Farmer.

Powers, Jaqueline S. and Estelle S. Castleman (3) - February 16, 1881
   Place of marriage, at H. W. Castleman's - Age of husband, 23 - Age
   of wife, 25 - Both are Single - Both were born in State of Virginia -
   Husband resides in State of Virginia - Wife resides in Jefferson
   County, West Virginia.

Powers, John H. and Emma J. Hafer (3) - September 22, 1870
   Place of marriage, Jefferson County - Age of husband, 24 - Age of
   wife, 20 - Husband was born in Maryland - Wife was born in Jefferson
   County - Husband resides in Maryland - Wife resides in Jefferson
   County.

Price, C. J. F. B. and C. A. V. Haugh (bride) (3) - April 29, 1879
   Place of marriage, Harpers Ferry - Age of husband, 22 - Age of wife,
   23 in June - Both are Single - Husband was born at Harpers Ferry -
   Wife was born at Baltimore City - Husband resides in Garrett County,
   Maryland - Wife resides in Jefferson County, West Virginia.

Price, Charles D. and Ella F. Bocock (3) - June 6, 1888
   Place of marriage, Martinsburg - Age of husband, 26 - Age of wife,
   24 - Both are Single - Husband was born at Richmond, Virginia - Wife
   was born in Appomattox County - Husband resides at Richmond, Virginia -
   Wife resides in Jefferson County, West Virginia.

Price, Ella M. and Noah W. Huff (3) - June 3, 1875
   For further information see - Huff, Noah W.

Price, Ellen Ann and John Thompson (3) - December 21, 1865
   For further information see - Thompson, John.

Price, Emma and D. R. Wells (3) - May 15, 1885
   For further information see - Wells, D. R.

Price, George and Mary C. Irvin (2) - (L) February 3, 1852

Price, Jennie (cold.) Milton J. Busey (3) - January 27, 1876
   For further information see - Busey, Milton J.

Price, Jesse D. and Mary E. Hines (3) - September 28, 1870
   Place of marriage, Jefferson County - Age of husband, 25 - Age of
   wife, 24 - Both were born in Maryland - Both reside in Maryland.
   (Ages sworn to by George Caswell.)

Price, John and Eliza Laley (1) - 1825

Price, John and Virginia Gains (2) - (L) December 23, 1863
   Time of marriage, December 24, 1863 - Place of marriage, near
   Leetown - Names, John Price and Virginia Gains - Age of husband, 24
   year 2nd of last March - Age of wife, 18 the 8th of last August -
   Both are Single - Husband was born in Jefferson County - Wife was
   born in Berkeley County - Both reside in Jefferson County - Husband's
   parents are Henry and Sarah - Wife's parents are Christopher and
   Lydee - Occupation of husband is Miller - License issued December
   23, 1863 - Thomas A. Moore, Clerk.

Price, John and Jennie Hanby (3) - May 14, 1878
   Place of marriage, Charlestown - Age of husband, 46 - Age of wife,
   27 - Husband is a Widower - Wife is Single - Both were born in
   Jefferson County, West Virginia - Both reside in Jefferson County,
   West Virginia.

Price, John F. and Ann Thompson (1) -   September 28, 1821

Price, John Thomas William Franklin (cold.) Louisa Johnson (3) -
                                                February 22, 1883
　　Place of marriage, near Charlestown - Age of husband, 27 - Age of
　　wife, 22 - Both are Single - Husband was born in Montgomery County,
　　Maryland - Wife was born in Clarke County, Virginia - Both reside in
　　Jefferson County, West Virginia.

Price, Mary Catherine and Joseph Lemen (2) -   (L) January 24, 1852

Prichard, Jesse and Sarah Hall (1) -   October 15, 1805

Prichet, John and Barbara Hood (1) -   October 30, 1808

Prince, D. J. and Susan Sowers (3) -   July 26, 1885
　　Place of marriage, Charlestown - Age of husband, 25 - Age of wife,
　　22 - Both are Single - Both were born in Jefferson County, West
　　Virginia - Both reside in Jefferson County, West Virginia.

Prince, Maria (cold.) Thomas Warner Johnson (3) -   April 10, 1880
　　For further information see - Johnson, Thomas Warner.

Pritchard, Frances and John W. Riggle (3) -   January 20, 1874
　　For further information see - Riggle, John W.

Pritchard, Martha and Joseph A. Turner (3) -   October 12, 1875
　　For further information see - Turner, Joseph A.

Pritchard, T. A. and Cora E. Marlatt (3) -   December 21, 1887
　　Place of marriage, Harpers Ferry - Age of husband, 33 - Age of wife,
　　20 - Both are Single - Husband was born in Maryland - Wife was born
　　in Jefferson County, West Virginia - Husband resides in Maryland -
　　Wife resides in Jefferson County. (Consent of bride's father
　　vouched for by her brother.)

Proby, Mary E. and J. H. Walters (3) -   February 22, 1890
　　For further information see - Walters, J. H.

Proctor, John and Amelia Ann Dixon (3) -   May 9, 1872
　　Place of marriage, Jefferson County - Age of husband, 25 - Age of
　　wife, 18 - Both are Single - Both were born in Virginia - Both
　　reside in Virginia - Husband's parents are John and Maria - Wife's
　　parents are Abram and Lucy - Occupation of husband is Farmer.
　　(Sworn to by Robert Dixon, brother.)

Propps, Ida M. and A. McDonald (3) -   June 26, 1889
　　For further information see - McDonald, A.

Props, Thomas Sylvester and Margaret Erb (3) -   December 26, 1871
　　Place of marriage, Jefferson County - Age of husband, 23 - Age of
　　wife, 22 - Both are Single - Husband was born in Clarke County,
　　Virginia - Wife was born in Maryland - Both reside in Clarke County -
　　Husband's parents are Conrad and Mary - Wife's parents are Christian
　　and Mary E. - Occupation of husband is Farmer. (George Zombro.)

Propst, James H. and Susan J. Collis (2) -   (L) June 22, 1860

Proust, Sarah and Lewis Minchin (1) -   November 13, 1833

Pullett, Eliza Diah (cold.) Benjamin F. Fox (3) -   August 24, 1882
   For further information see - Fox, Benjamin F.

Pultz, A. E. (bride) and T. W. Kearns (3) -   March 25, 1868
   For further information see - Kearns, T. W.

Pultz, Lydia and Jones Ridgway (1) -   1821

Pultz, Mary Ann Elizabeth and John Myers (2) -   (L) February 20, 1858

Purcell, Bernard and Mrs. Hattie A. Bishop (3) -   July 10, 1879
   Place of marriage, Charlestown - Age of husband, 25 - Age of wife,
   27 - Husband is Single - Wife is a Widow - Husband was born in
   Loudoun County, Virginia - Wife was born at Bridgeport, Connecticut -
   Both reside in Jefferson County, West Virginia.

Purcell, James and A. E. Walters (3) -   April 5, 1874
   Place of marriage, Harpers Ferry - Age of husband, 23 - Age of wife,
   23 - Both are Single - Husband was born in Ireland - Wife was born
   in Page County, Virginia - Husband resides in Clarke County, Virginia -
   Wife resides in Jefferson County, West Virginia at present.

Purcell, P. L. and Virginia Buzzard (3) -   October 14, 1890
   Place of marriage, Harpers Ferry - Age of husband, 21 - Age of wife,
   19 - Both are Single - Husband was born in Pennsylvania - Wife was
   born in Jefferson County, West Virginia - Both reside in Jefferson
   County, West Virginia.

Purndon, John (cold.) Phillis Blair (3) -   April 2, 1885
   Place of marriage, Flowing Spring - Age of husband, 22 - Age of
   wife, 21 - Both are Single - Husband was born in Louisa County,
   Virginia - Wife was born in Culpeper County, Virginia - Both reside
   in Jefferson County, West Virginia.

Purndon, Julia (cold.) Baily Robinson (3) -   December 28, 1882
   For further information see - Robinson, Baily.

Purnell, Susan and Michael Zimmerman (1) -   May 18, 1809

Purnell, Susanah and Brice Miller (1) -   August 21, 1806

Pyle, John and Sarah Tracey (1) -   May 19, 1822

Pyles, Ann and John Ducker (1) -   August 3, 1830

Queen, Mary (cold.) Charles Moses Taylor (3) -   February 20, 1888
    For further information see - Taylor, Charles Moses.

Queen, Sarah (cold.) Luke Doyle (3) -   August 4, 1881
    For further information see - Doyle, Luke.

Queen, Thomas (cold.) Bettie Madison (3) -   October 15, 1890
    Place of marriage, Charlestown - Age of husband, 26 - Age of wife,
    24 - Both are Single - Both were born in Jefferson County, West
    Virginia - Both reside in Jefferson County, West Virginia.

Quick, John Edward and Catherine Heck (3) -   July 15, 1871
    Place of marriage, Jefferson County - Age of husband, 24 - Age of
    wife, 17 - Both are Single - Husband was born in Virginia - Wife was
    born in Maryland - Both reside in West Virginia - Husband's parents
    are Armstead A. and Margaret Ann - Wife's parents are Robert and
    Mary Catherine - Occupation of husband is Rail Roadman.
    (Mother's consent by Red.)

Quigley, John and Sinah Cook (1) -   May 21, 1822

Quigley, John and Mary Elvira VanSwearingen (1) -   October 20, 1827

Quigley, Lucy B. and Edward H. Reinhart (3) -   January 29, 1873
    For further information see - Reinhart, Edward H.

Quigley, Mary J. and T. W. Latamer (3) -   October 25, 1867
    For further information see - Latamer, T. W.

Quinn, Francis and Elizabeth Virginia McKeannan (3) -   July 26, 1886
    Place of marriage, Harpers Ferry - Age of husband, 34 - Age of wife,
    25 - Husband is a Widower - Wife is Single - Both were born in
    Maryland - Husband resides in Maryland - Wife resides in Jefferson
    County, West Virginia.

Quinn, Osborn and Eveline McGill (3) -   July 25, 1868
    Place of marriage, Jefferson County - Age of husband, 36 - Age of
    wife, 27 - Husband is a Widower - Wife is a Widow - Both were born
    in Jefferson County - Both reside in Jefferson County - Occupation
    of husband is Farmer.

Racey, Joseph M. and Sarah Catherine Custer (3) - November 4, 1886
 Place of marriage, Shepherdstown - Age of husband, 31 - Age of wife,
 22 - Both are Single - Husband was born in Berkeley County now West
 Virginia - Wife was born in Berkeley County, West Virginia - Husband
 resides in Berkeley County, West Virginia - Wife resides in
 Jefferson County, West Virginia.

Rafferty, William and Jane Mansfield (3) - April 24, 1883
 Place of marriage, near Harpers Ferry - Age of husband, 23 - Age of
 wife, 18 - Both are Single - Both were born in Madison County,
 Ohio - Husband resides in Madison County, Ohio - Wife resides in
 Jefferson County, West Virginia. (Consent of bride's father in
 person.)

Ragan, Daniel and Mary Davine (2) - (L) January 8, 1853
 (Stephen Burke, Witness.)

Ragan, William and Betsy Ogden (1) - 1822

Ragland, Thomas and Eliza Christien Fairfax (1) - January 22, 1822

Ramey, Benjamin F. and Adaline A. Hicks (3) - November 23, 1869
 Place of marriage, Jefferson County - Age of husband, 25 - Age of
 wife, 23 - Husband was born in Virginia - Wife was born in
 Jefferson County - Both reside in Jefferson County.

Ramey, Charles J. and Georgiana Bane (3) - October 27, 1881
 Place of marriage, County - Age of husband, 23 - Age of wife, 22 -
 Both are Single - Husband was born in Clarke County, Virginia - Wife
 was born in Jefferson County, West Virginia - Both reside in
 Jefferson County, West Virginia.

Ramey, John H. and Sarah A. Clendening (3) - December 9, 1879
 Place of marriage, Charlestown - Age of husband, 25 - Age of wife,
 22 - Both are Single - Husband was born in Fauquier County,
 Virginia - Wife was born in Frederick County, Virginia - Both reside
 in Jefferson County, West Virginia.

Ramey, Nancy R. Belle and Alfred K. Merchant (3) - April 6, 1876
 For further information see - Merchant, Alfred K.

Ramsbottom, Isaac M. and Anna C. Knott (3) - May 3, 1888
 Place of marriage, Harpers Ferry - Age of husband, 27 - Age of wife,
 23 - Both are Single - Husband was born in State of Virginia - Wife
 was born in Jefferson County, West Virginia - Both reside in
 Jefferson County, West Virginia.

Ramsburg, Annie E. and Philip M. Creamer (3) - October 21, 1880
 For further information see - Creamer, Philip M.

Ramsburg, Benjamin F. and Catharine Johnson (3) - October 19, 1865
 Place of marriage, near Leetown, Jefferson County - Age of husband,
 35 years - Age of wife, 18 years - Both are Single - Both were born
 in Jefferson County, West Virginia - Both reside in Jefferson
 County - Husband's parents are Henry Ramsburg and Elizabeth
 Ramsburg - Wife's parents are Samuel and Mary Johnson - Occupation
 of husband is Shoemaker.

Ramsburg, Charles J. and Carrie V. Bain (3) -   February 5, 1890
    Place of marriage, Charlestown - Age of husband, 23 - Age of wife,
    21 - Both are Single - Both were born in Jefferson County, West
    Virginia - Both reside in Jefferson County, West Virginia.

Ramsburg, George W. and Mary E. Mercer (2) -   (L) April 8, 1861
    Time of marriage, April 9, 1861 - Place of marriage, near Leetown -
    Full names of parties, George W. Ramsburg and Mary E. Mercer - Age
    of husband, 25 years - Age of wife, 17 years - Both are Single -
    Both were born in Jefferson County - Both reside in Jefferson
    County - Names of husband's parents are Henry and Elizabeth Ramsburg -
    Names of wife's parents are Father __?__, Mother Lucinda Mercer -
    Occupation of husband is **Shoemaker** - Given under my hand this 8th day
    of April, 1861 - George W. Ramsburg.

Ramsburg, Ida Virginia and John T. Dorsey (3) -   October 11, 1883
    For further information see - Dorsey, John T.

Ramsburg, John J. and Mary Jane Fowler (2) -   (L) April 20, 1857

Ramsburg, Mrs. Phebe and Alexander Beavers (3) -   August 31, 1875
    For further information see - Beavers, Alexander.

Randal, James F. and Ann M. Underdunk (2) -   (L) January 17, 1859

Randall, Eliza and Jacob Smurr (1) -   March 6, 1831

Randall, Mary E. and Joseph A. Weller (2) -   (L) November 12, 1855

Rankins, Lucy and Charles Jackson (3) -   December 29, 1887
    For further information see - Jackson, Charles.

Rankins, William and Ann Hiett (1) -   July 23, 1834

Rannels, John W. and Sarah Catherine Manuel (3) -   August 26, 1879
    Place of marriage, near Charlestown - Age of husband, 24 - Age of
    wife, 25 - Both are Single - Both were born in Jefferson County,
    West Virginia - Both reside in Jefferson County, West Virginia.

Rannels, John Washington and Elizabeth Dillow (2) -   (L) February 10, 1852

Ransdell, John and Ann Simms Davenport (1) -   October 1, 1829

Ransel, Laura (cold.) Israel Hunter (3) -   January 11, 1883
    For further information see - Hunter, Israel.

Ranson, Alfred (cold.) Ellen Brown (3) -   May 30, 1882
    Place of marriage, Harpers Ferry - Age of husband, 29 - Age of wife,
    23 - Husband is Single - Wife is a Widow - Husband was born in
    Jefferson County, West Virginia - Wife was born in Jefferson County -
    Husband resides in Jefferson County, West Virginia - Wife resides in
    Jefferson County.

Ranson, Alfred and Rachael Nelson (3) -   July 16, 1890
    Place of marriage, Mount Hammond - Age of husband, 37 - Age of wife,
    30 - Husband is a Widower - Wife is a Widow - Both were born in
    Jefferson County, West Virginia - Both reside in Jefferson County,
    West Virginia.

Ranson, Ambrose R. H. and Frances E. B. Frame (2) -   (L) October 12, 1854

Ranson, B. B. and N. T. Forrest (bride) (3) -   December 28, 1870
   Place of marriage, Jefferson County - Age of husband, 26 - Age of
   wife, 23 - Both were born in Virginia - Both reside in Jefferson
   County.

Ranson, Eliza (colored) Jenkin Sanderson (3) -   August 4, 1870
   For further information see - Sanderson, Jenkin.

Ranson, Francis and William Gibbs (1) -   June 18, 1807

Ranson, Harriet (cold.) William Brooks (3) -   January 6, 1883
   For further information see - Brooks, William.

Ranson, James Lackland and Frances Madison Hite (1) -   May 16, 1820

Ranson, Lucy (cold.) Charles Edward Parker (3) -   July 25, 1878
   For further information see - Parker, Charles Edward.

Ranson, Mary (cold.) Nelson Edwards (3) -   April 14, 1873
   For further information see - Edwards, Nelson.

Ranson, Mary (cold.) George Green (3) -   April 11, 1889
   For further information see - Green, George.

Ranson, Mary E. and John H. Guy (3) -   October 12, 1871
   For further information see - Guy, John H.

Ranson, Mathew and Elizabeth Morgan (1) -   May 4, 1807

Ranson, Miles R. (cold.) Virginia Nelson (3) -   December 8, 1881
   Place of marriage, Charlestown - Age of husband, 35 - Age of wife,
   26 - Both are Single - Both were born in Jefferson County, West
   Virginia - Both reside in Jefferson County, West Virginia.

Ranson, Sally (cold.) Newton Williams (3) -   September 28, 1867
   For further information see - Williams, Newton.

Ranson, Samuel (cold.) Annie McKinney (3) -   November 27, 1879
   Place of marriage, Shepherdstown - Age of husband, 21 - Age of wife,
   21 - Both are Single - Both were born in Jefferson County, West
   Virginia - Both reside in Jefferson County, West Virginia.

Ranson, Sarah Elizabeth and Lawson Botts (2) -   (L) January 29, 1851

Ranson, Sarah Elizabeth and Lawson Botts (1) -   January 29, 1851

Ranson, Thomas D. and Mary F. Alexander (3) -   April 12, 1871
   Place of marriage, Jefferson County - Age of husband, 27 - Age of
   wife, 25 - Both are Single - Husband was born in Jefferson County -
   Wife was born in Virginia - Both reside in Jefferson County -
   Husband's parents are James M. and Mary E. - Wife's parents are
   William F. and Maria Ann T. - Occupation of husband is Lawyer.
   (April 10/71 issued at Shepherdstown.)

Ranson, Thomas D. and Mary F. Alexander (3) - April 12, 1871
Place of marriage, Jefferson County - Age of husband, 27 - Age of
wife, 25 - Both are Single - Husband was born in Jefferson County -
Wife was born in Virginia - Both reside in Jefferson County -
Husband's parents are James M. and Mary E. - Wife's parents are
William F. and Maria Ann T. - Occupation of husband is Lawyer.
(April 11/71 issued at Charlestown.) (This record is crossed out
in the original.)

Rau, Clara V. and J. B. Wentzell (3) - November 28, 1878
For further information see - Wentzell, J. B.

Rau, Emma L. and G. A. Benter (3) - November 11, 1875
For further information see - Benter, G. A.

Rau, Lillie M. and Edward H. Dick (3) - February 16, 1882
For further information see - Dick, Edward H.

Rau, Rudolph and Amalia Mylins (3) - July 26, 1870
Place of marriage, Jefferson County - Age of husband, 36 - Age of
wife, 25 - Both were born in Germany - Both reside in Jefferson
County.

Raum, Joseph A. and Elizabeth G. Barnes (2) - (L) September 6, 1860

Rawlins, Aaron and Polly Jett (1) - July 6, 1817

Rawlins, Joseph C. and Ann E. Tutwiler (1) - September 16, 1841

Rawlins, Joshua N. and Laura L. Chiswell (3) - September 14, 1869
Place of marriage, Jefferson County - Age of husband, 22 - Age of
wife, 20 - Both were born in Maryland - Husband resides in Maryland -
Wife resides in Jefferson County. (Father in person consents.)

Rawlins, Margaret and Francis W. Drew (1) - May 25, 1841

Rawlins, Martha C. and F. W. Drew (2) - (L) October 6, 1852

Rawlins, Thomas and Mrs. Ann M. English (widow) (2) - (L) July 18, 1854

Rawlins, Thomas G. and Mary V. Fisher (2) - (L) April 7, 1852

Rawn, Margaret M. and Joseph R. Billups (3) - October 4, 1870
For further information see - Billups, Joseph R.

Ray, Anna L. and H. C. Shull (3) - November 22, 1883
For further information see - Shull, H. C.

Ray, Minnie S. and James F. Thompson (3) - February 28, 1888
For further information see - Thompson, James F.

Ray, Samuel H. and Margaret E. Ernst (3) - February 8, 1866
Place of marriage, Entler Hotel, Shepherdstown - Age of husband,
24 - Age of wife, 23 - Both are Single - Both were born in Jefferson
County, West Virginia - Both reside in Jefferson County, West
Virginia - Husband's parents are Drusilla Ray - Wife's parents are
John and Catharine Ernst - Occupation of husband is Carpenter.

Ray, T. F. and H. E. Warner (bride) (3) - September 28, 1867
  Place of marriage, Shepherdstown - Age of husband, 30 - Age of wife,
  26 - Both are Single - Both were born in Jefferson County, West
  Virginia - Husband resides at New York City - Wife resides in
  Jefferson County, West Virginia - Occupation of husband is Banker.

Ray, William Nelson and Mary Ann Bowen (1) - August 19, 1832

Read, Eliza and Robert Early (1) - 1820

Read, Jane and Charles Button (1) - 1820

Reasler, Jacob and Elizabeth Laley (1) - 1825

Reck, Abraham and Louisa Motter (1) - May 15, 1820

Redferor, E. and Helen V. Taylor (3) - November 28, 1867
  Place of marriage, Jefferson County - Age of husband, 28 - Age of
  wife, 20 - Both are Single - Husband was born in Shenandoah - Wife
  was born in Jefferson - Both reside in Jefferson - Husband's parents
  are William and Sarah - Wife's parents are John W. and Mary C. -
  Occupation of husband is Farmer. (Father consents.)

Redman, Ann (cold.) Solomon Gibson (3) - August 20, 1874
  For further information see - Gibson, Solomon.

Redman, Elizabeth and James Clothier (1) - November 21, 1830

Redman, F. and Bertha Morton (3) - November 12, 1868
  Place of marriage, Jefferson County - Age of husband, 22 - Age of
  wife, 21 - Both are Single - Husband was born in Virginia - Wife was
  born in Jefferson County - Husband resides in Jefferson County -
  Wife resides in West Virginia - Occupation of husband is Laborer.

Redman, Martha (cold.) Robert Trent (3) - December 25, 1873
  For further information see - Trent, Robert.

Redman, S. H. and Sally C. Cockrell (3) - December 14, 1882
  Place of marriage, near Harpers Ferry - Age of husband, 28 - Age of
  wife, 22 - Husband is a Widower - Wife is Single - Husband was born
  in State of Missouri - Wife was born in Jefferson County, West
  Virginia - Husband resides in State of Missouri - Wife resides in
  Jefferson County, West Virginia.

Redmon, James E. and Mary E. Summers (3) - November 16, 1887
  Place of marriage, Charlestown - Age of husband, 28 - Age of wife,
  21 - Husband is a Widower - Wife is Single - Husband was born in
  State of Virginia - Wife was born in Maryland - Husband resides in
  Maryland - Wife resides in Jefferson County, West Virginia at present.

Redrick, John and Artridge Butt (1) - November 16, 1814

Reed, Annie E. and Joshua H. Cox (3) - October 22, 1884
  For further information see - Cox, Joshua H.

Reed, Charles (cold.) Rachel Ford (3) - June 6, 1878
  Place of marriage, Charlestown - Age of husband, 22 - Age of wife,
  26 - Both are Single - Both were born in Jefferson County, West
  Virginia - Both reside in Jefferson County, West Virginia.

Reed, Dorcas C. and Leander Carlisle (2) -   (L) June 18, 1851

Reed, Geneva and Franklin T. Fritts (3) -   June 12, 1881
    For further information see - Fritts, Franklin T.

Reed, Harriet (colored) Joseph Howard (3) -   June 8, 1870
    For further information see - Howard, Joseph.

Reed, Henry and Susan Dearing (2) -   (L) December 14, 1852

Reed, Hugh and Han. Mendenhall (1) -   January 2, 1823

Reed, J. W. and Lucy G. Hedges (3) -   November 6, 1872
    Place of marriage, Jefferson County, West Virginia - Age of husband, 25 - Age of wife, 22 - Both are Single - Both were born in Jefferson County, West Virginia - Husband resides in Loudoun County, Virginia - Wife resides in Jefferson County, West Virginia - Husband's parents are H. and L. Reed - Wife's parents are W. S. and M. M. Hedges - Occupation of husband is Farmer.

Reed, John and Margaret Emily Downs (1) -   October 16, 1828

Reed, John H. and Mrs. Martha Allen (3) -   June 24, 1873
    Place of marriage, Charlestown - Age of husband, 59 - Age of wife, 40 - Husband is a Widower - Wife is a Widow - Both were born in Jefferson County, West Virginia - Husband resides in Washington County, Maryland - Wife resides in Jefferson County, West Virginia.

Reed, John T. and H. Etty Stuart (3) -   February 23, 1887
    Place of marriage, Harpers Ferry - Age of husband, 29 - Age of wife, 22 - Both are Single - Husband was born in Jefferson County - Wife was born in Michigan - Both reside in Jefferson County.

Reed, Juliet B. and Samuel T. Breckenridge (3) -   December 20, 1885
    For further information see - Breckenridge, Samuel T.

Reed, Lizzy (cold.) Samuel Galloway (3) -   October 5, 1876
    For further information see - Galloway, Samuel.

Reed, Lucy and James Grantham (3) -   April 12, 1866

Reed, M. Vandalia and Henry A. Burton (3) -   March 21, 1877
    For further information see - Burton, Henry A.

Reed, Maggie and Robert Arvin (3) -   June 9, 1881
    For further information see - Arvin, Robert.

Reed, Marie and William H. Dietz (2) -   (L) October 12, 1857

Reed, Mary (cold.) George Henry Williams (3) -   July 15, 1874
    For further information see - Williams, George Henry.

Reed, Mary Ann and Jacob Haines (1) -   August 8, 1816

Reed, Mary V. and William A. Reed (3) -   September 11, 1884
    For further information see - Reed, William A.

Reed, Matilda and Adam Whip (1) -   February 28, 1832

Reed, Nancy and Philip Hains (1) -   October 1, 1812

Reed, Sarah and Ephraim S. Bellar (1) - May 30, 1816

Reed, Thomas and Emily Haymaker (1) - June 6, 1816

Reed, Thornton and Mary Shanton (3) - January 11, 1872
Place of marriage, Jefferson County, West Virginia - Age of husband, 26 - Age of wife, 31 - Husband is Single - Wife is a Widow - Both were born in Jefferson County - Both reside in Jefferson County - Husband's parents are John and Delphi - Wife's parents are William and Mary - Occupation of husband is Farmer.

Reed, Thornton (cold.) Mary Shanton (3) - September 15, 1874
Place of marriage, Cameron's - Age of husband, 25 - Age of wife, 30 - Husband is Single - Wife is a Widow - Husband was born in Clarke County, Virginia - Wife was born in Jefferson County, West Virginia - Both reside in Jefferson County, West Virginia.

Reed, William and Ann McGee (1) - January 25, 1831

Reed, William and Mrs. Sally Davis (3) - April 23, 1867
Place of marriage, Duffields - Age of husband, 25 - Age of wife, 28 - Husband is Single - Wife is a Widow - Husband was born in Jefferson County, West Virginia - Wife was born at Harpers Ferry - Both reside in Jefferson County, West Virginia - Husband's parents are George W. and Henrietta Reed - Wife's parents are Jacob and Margaret Decker - Occupation of husband is Farmer.

Reed, William A. and Susan S. Smith (3) - March 28, 1875
Place of marriage, Harpers Ferry - Age of husband, 30 - Age of wife, 28 - Both are Single - Both were born in Loudoun County, Virginia - Both reside in Jefferson County, West Virginia.

Reed, William A. and Mary V. Reed (3) - September 11, 1884
Place of marriage, Harpers Ferry - Age of husband, 40 - Age of wife, 31 - Husband is a Widower - Wife is Single - Both were born in Jefferson County, West Virginia - Both reside in Jefferson County.

Reed, Winfield Scott and Mary C. Levy (3) - August 12, 1875
Place of marriage, Bolivar - Age of husband, 23 - Age of wife, 17 - Both are Single - Husband was born in Washington County, Maryland - Wife was born in Jefferson County, West Virginia - Husband resides in Washington County, Maryland - Wife resides at Bolivar, Jefferson County, West Virginia. (Consent of bride's father in Person.)

Reek, Frederick and Barbara Gardner (2) - (L) September 15, 1857

Reel, Alice M. and John H. Engle (3) - December 8, 1881
For further information see - Engle, John H.

Reeler, Andrew (cold.) Mary Carter (3) - January 1, 1868
Place of marriage, Jefferson County - Age of husband, 42 - Age of wife, 39 - Husband is a Widower - Wife is a Widow - Both were born in Jefferson County - Both reside in Jefferson County - Occupation of husband is Farmer.

Reeler, Andrew (cold.) Ellen Moore (3) - December 31, 1882
Place of marriage, Charlestown - Age of husband, 52 - Age of wife, 40 - Husband is a Widower - Wife is Single - Husband was born in Clarke County, Virginia - Wife was born in Jefferson County, West Virginia - Both reside in Jefferson County, West Virginia.

Reeler, Ann (cold.) Thomas Lawson (3) - May 25, 1874
   For further information see - Lawson, Thomas.

Reeler, Charles (cold.) Lucy Green (3) - November 30, 1876
   Place of marriage, Charles Town - Age of husband, 50 - Age of wife,
   40 - Husband is Single - Wife is a Widow - Both were born in
   Jefferson County, West Virginia - Both reside in Jefferson County,
   West Virginia.

Reeler, Charles H. (cold.) Alice White (3) - March 5, 1884
   Place of marriage, Harpers Ferry - Age of husband, 30 - Age of wife,
   22 - Husband is a Widower - Wife is Single - Both were born in
   Jefferson County, West Virginia - Both reside in Jefferson County,
   West Virginia.

Reeler, Delphry (cold.) Robert Luckett (3) - January 6, 1881
   For further information see - Luckett, Robert.

Reeler, Frances and C. H. Gardner (3) - January 9, 1869
   For further information see - Gardner, C. H.

Reese, Herbert H. and Rebecca A. Kearsley (3) - January 30, 1889
   Place of marriage, Charlestown - Age of husband, 32 - Age of wife,
   24 - Both are Single - Husband was born in Virginia - Wife was born
   in Jefferson County, West Virginia - Husband resides in Georgia -
   Wife resides in Jefferson County, West Virginia.

Reeves, Thomas and Virginia Brunswick (3) - February 1, 1876
   Place of marriage, Harpers Ferry - Age of husband, 26 - Age of wife,
   22 - Both are Single - Husband was born in Albemarle County,
   Virginia - Wife was born in Jefferson County, West Virginia - Both
   reside in Jefferson County, West Virginia.

Reid, William (cold.) Fanny Howell (3) - September 3, 1878
   Place of marriage, Charlestown - Age of husband, 22 - Age of wife,
   22 - Both are Single - Both were born in Jefferson County, West
   Virginia - Both reside in Jefferson County, West Virginia.

Reiley, Fanny and Thomas R. Rutherford (3) - April 3, 1871
   For further information see - Rutherford, Thomas R.

Reiley, Helen M. and Oliver P. Thomas (2) - (L) December 19, 1854

Reiley, John R. and Mary M. O'Larry (3) - April 6, 1871
   Place of marriage, Jefferson County - Age of husband, 22 - Age of
   wife, 21 - Both are Single - Husband was born in Clarke County,
   Virginia - Wife was born in Virginia - Both reside in Jefferson
   County - Husband's parents are Lustre W. and Sidney H. - Wife's
   parents are Dennis and Ellen - Occupation of husband is Stone Mason.

Reiley, Julia and Denis Sheehan (3) - August 8, 1871
   For further information see - Sheehan, Denis.

Reiley, Mary Ann and Alexander B. Dyche (2) - (L) November 6, 1854

Reinhart, Annie E. and Charles H. Kable (3) - April 27, 1870
   For further information see - Kable, Charles H.

Rhineman, G. H. and Sarah E. Boyd (3) - May 18, 1875
    Place of marriage, Charlestown - Age of husband, 26 - Age of wife, 22 - Both are Single - Husband was born in Clarke County, Virginia - Wife was born in Jefferson County, West Virginia - Both reside in Jefferson County, West Virginia.

Rhineman, T. W. and Virginia A. Whitmore (3) - December 21, 1886
    Place of marriage, Charlestown - Age of husband, 34 - Age of wife, 27 - Husband is a Widower - Wife is Single - Husband was born in Clarke County, Virginia - Wife was born in Loudoun County, Virginia - Husband resides in Berkeley County, West Virginia - Wife resides in Jefferson County, West Virginia.

Rhodes, Albert and Maria Parker (3) - December 31, 1868
    Place of marriage, Jefferson County - Age of husband, 33 - Age of wife, 30 - Husband is Single - Wife is a Widow - Both were born in Virginia - Husband resides in Jefferson County - Wife resides in Jefferson County, West Virginia - Occupation of husband is Laborer.

Rhodes, Alexander (cold.) Virginia Busey (3) - August 11, 1885
    Place of marriage, near Leetown - Age of husband, 36 - Age of wife, 35 - Husband is a Widower - Wife is a Widow - Husband was born in North Carolina - Wife was born in Jefferson County, West Virginia - Both reside in Jefferson County, West Virginia.

Rhodes, Emma and Henry Osbourn (3) - March 5, 1872
    For further information see - Osbourn, Henry.

Rhulman, Caroline V. and Samuel V. Strider (2) - (L) November 6, 1852

Rian, Thomas D. and Laura A. King (1) - December 23, 1849

Rice, Adella G. and George D. Thompson (3) - December 24, 1890
    For further information see - Thompson, George D.

Rice, Bettie F. and Roger R. Smith (2) - (L) October 24, 1859

Rice, George W. and Bettie E. Russell (3) - October 18, 1866
    Place of marriage, Thomas Russell's at Harpers Ferry - Age of husband, 26 - Age of wife, 23 - Both are Single - Husband was born in Frederick County, Maryland - Wife was born in Jefferson County, West Virginia - Husband resides at Frederick City, Maryland - Wife resides at Harpers Ferry, Jefferson County, West Virginia - Wife's parents are Thomas and Charity Russell - Occupation of husband is Carpenter.

Rice, James and Sally Johnson (1) - December 26, 1816

Rice, Jared and Elizabeth An. Drew (1) - September 1827

Rice, Mary C. and Leonard R. Jones (3) - December 21, 1871
    For further information see - Jones, Leonard R.

Rice, Sophrana and M. M. Knadler (3) - December 20, 1876
    For further information see - Knadler, M. M.

Rice, William M. and Maggie E. Fiser (3) - March 9, 1876
    Place of marriage, Shepherdstown - Age of husband, 23 - Age of wife,
    18 - Both are Single - Both were born in Jefferson County, West
    Virginia - Both reside in Jefferson County, West Virginia.
    (Consent of bride's father in writing.)

Richard, John L. and Mary E. Minchen (1) -   October 25, 1852

Richards, John L. and Mary E. Minchen (2) -   (L) October 21, 1852

Richards, Jeremiah and Catherine Isler (1) -   February 16, 1818

Richards, Lewis and Angelina Collins (1) -   January 19, 1803

Richardson, Jane and George Perry (1) -   February 7, 1807

Richardson, John (cold.) Mary J. Walker (3) -   October 17, 1889
    Place of marriage, Charlestown - Age of husband, 24 - Age of wife,
    35 - Husband is Single - Wife is a Widow - Husband was born in
    Warren County, Virginia - Wife was born in Jefferson County, West
    Virginia - Both reside in Jefferson County, West Virginia.

Richardson, Louisa (colored) T. T. D. Wells (3) -   September 29, 1870
    For further information see - Wells, T. T. D.

Richardson, Mary (cold.) Meredith Johnson (3) -   January 16, 1874
    For further information see - Johnson, Meredith.

Richardson, Mary Ann and Isaac Matthews (2) -   (L) March 2, 1854

Richardson, Sarah and William McCoughtry (1) -   September 27, 1808

Richcreek, David M. (free mixtures) Darkey Warson (1) -   June 25, 1826

Richcreek, John and Virginia McDaniel (2) -   (L) December 14, 1854

Rick, Kate A. and Charles W. Engle (3) -   September 9, 1886
    For further information see - Engle, Charles W.

Rick, Lewis H. and Mary Eliza Shreck (3) -   December 16, 1880
    Place of marriage, Harpers Ferry - Age of husband, 22 - Age of wife,
    19 - Both are Single - Both were born in Jefferson County, West
    Virginia - Both reside in Jefferson County, West Virginia.
    (Consent of bride's father and mother in writing.)

Rickamore, John and Anna Merritt (3) -   October 25, 1887
    Place of marriage, Harpers Ferry - Age of husband, 33 - Age of wife,
    24 - Both are Single - Both were born in Jefferson County, West
    Virginia - Both reside in Jefferson County, West Virginia.

Rickard, Fanny and Thompson Johnson (1) -   December 6, 1826

Rickard, Julia E. and Benjamin S. Pendleton (3) -   October 15, 1884
    For further information see - Pendleton, Benjamin S.

Rickard, Sallie H. and Benjamin C. Unseld (3) -   September 6, 1887
    For further information see - Unseld, Benjamin C.

Riddle, George R. and Margaret S. Opie (1) -   January 14, 1846

Riddle, Horatio R. and Sarah R. Huston (2) - (L) January 27, 1851

Riddle, Horatio R. and Sarah R. Huston (1) - January 27, 1851

Ridenhour, Robert and Mary Ann Garnhart (1) - February 27, 1817

Ridenour, Amos and Ann Eliza Gray (3) - December 22, 1881
    Place of marriage, Bolivar - Age of husband, 23 - Age of wife, 15 -
Both are Single - Both were born in Maryland - Both reside in
Jefferson County, West Virginia. (Consent of bride's mother and
stepfather in person.)

Ridenour, Catherine M. and George Backhouse (1) - 1820

Ridenour, Elizabeth J. and George W. Chase (2) - (L) December 5, 1855

Ridenour, Frances R. and James N. Smallwood (1) - May 1848

Ridenour, Maggie E. and Richard F. Trussell (3) - January 31, 1877
    For further information see - Trussell, Richard F.

Ridenour, Mary C. M. and Daniel Baker (3) - October 27, 1885
    For further information see - Baker, Daniel.

Ridenour, Samuel and Mary Miller (1) - December 21, 1830

Rideout, Jacob (cold.) Mary Ellsberry (3) - May 20, 1875
    Place of marriage, Harpers Ferry - Age of husband, 24 - Age of wife,
21 - Both are Single - Husband was born in Maryland - Wife was born
in Arkansas - Husband resides at Harpers Ferry, Jefferson County,
West Virginia - Wife resides in Jefferson County, West Virginia.

Rideout, Peter (cold.) Emma Turner (3) - July 20, 1876
    Place of marriage, Duffields - Age of husband, 23 - Age of wife,
23 - Both are Single - Husband was born in Maryland - Wife was born
in Jefferson - Both reside in Jefferson County, West Virginia.

Rider, J. William and Nannie E. Cavalier (3) - January 2, 1884
    Place of marriage, Bolivar - Age of husband, 42 - Age of wife, 24 -
Both are Single - Both were born in Jefferson County, West
Virginia - Both reside in Jefferson County, West Virginia.
(License issued December 29, 1883.)

Rider, Susan E. and Jacob M. Kephart (3) - October 10, 1866
    For further information see - Kephart, Jacob M.

Ridgeway, Elonor and Absolom Gaines (1) - March 30, 1806

Ridgeway, Robert L. and Josephine Manuel (3) - September 24, 1883
    Place of marriage, Charlestown - Age of husband, 22 - Age of wife,
21 - Both are Single - Husband was born in Clarke County, Virginia -
Wife was born in Jefferson County, West Virginia - Both reside in
Jefferson County, West Virginia.

Ridgway, George J. and Sarah J. Hiskett (2) - (L) June 1, 1854

Ridgway, John J. and Annie E. Jackson (3) - November 28, 1883
   Place of marriage, Charlestown - Age of husband, 27 - Age of wife,
   23 - Both are Single - Husband was born in Jefferson County, West
   Virginia - Wife was born in Clarke County, Virginia - Husband
   resides in Jefferson County - Wife resides in Jefferson County, West
   Virginia.

Ridgway, Jones and Lydia Pultz (1) -   1821

Ridout, Cornelius (cold.) Hannah Fox (3) - October 10, 1890
   Place of marriage, Charlestown - Age of husband, 21 - Age of wife,
   21 - Both are Single - Both were born in Jefferson County, West
   Virginia - Both reside in Jefferson County, West Virginia.

Ridout, Fanny (cold.) George Twyman (3) - July 3, 1888
   For further information see - Twyman, George.

Rieger, Andrew and Elizabeth Crowl (1) - December 10, 1818

Rieley, Ellen M. and Joseph Brittain, Jr. (2) - (L) December 7, 1850

Rielly, Martha E. and Jerome T. Nichols (2) - (L) July 15, 1856

Riely, John J. and Lucy O. Taylor (2) - (L) November 22, 1856

Riely, Mary M. and John S. Moore (2) - (L) November 5, 1853

Riggle, John W. and Frances Pritchard (3) - January 20, 1874
   Place of marriage, near Rippon - Age of husband, 30 - Age of wife,
   23 - Husband is a Widower - Wife is Single - Husband was born in
   Frederick County, Virginia - Wife was born in Clarke County,
   Virginia - Both reside in Jefferson County, West Virginia.

Righly, Mary and Thomas Blackborne (1) - October 5, 1820

Righstine, Elizabeth R. and James W. B. Frazier (3) - March 22, 1866
   For further information see - Frazier, James W. B.

Rightstine, Ann Amelia and Thomas Stonesifer (3) - February 11, 1873
   For further information see - Stonesifer, Thomas.

Rightstine, Nannie Virginia and William T. McClanahan (3) - June 10, 1880
   For further information see - McClanahan, William T.

Riley, Alexander and Priscilla Hardesty (1) - November 14, 1826

Riley, Alfred W. and Annie E. Wyndham (3) - April 20, 1875
   Place of marriage, Charles Town - Age of husband, 28 - Age of wife,
   18 - Both are Single - Husband was born in Frederick County,
   Virginia - Wife was born in Clarke County, Virginia - Both reside in
   Jefferson County, West Virginia. (Consent of bride's mother in
   writing.)

Riley, Annie and Millard F. Hackley (3) - April 18, 1881
   For further information see - Hackley, Millard F.

Riley, Belle (cold.) Burrell Jones (3) - April 28, 1887
   For further information see - Jones, Burrell.

475

Riley, Cornelia A. and George W. Noland (3) -   January 10, 1867
   For further information see - Noland, George W.

Riley, Elizabeth Frances and Daniel Angell (2) -   (L) November 28, 1854

Riley, Ellen M. and Joseph Brittain, Jr. (1) -   December 12, 1850

Riley, Isaac and Adeline Waters (2) -   (L) September 21, 1850

Riley, Isaac and Adeline Waters (1) -   September 30, 1850

Riley, John and Mary Harris (1) -   March 3, 1825

Riley, John T. and Sarah J. Bayliss (2) -   (L) October 8, 1853

Riley, Joshua and Mary Spangler (1) -   1822

Riley, P. W. and E. A. Whalen (bride) (3) -   May 21, 1872
   Place of marriage, Jefferson County - Age of husband, 24 - Age of wife, 16 - Both are Single - Husband was born in Ireland - Wife was born in Maryland - Husband resides in West Virginia - Wife resides in Maryland - Husband's parents are John and Margaret - Wife's parents are D. and Mary.

Riley, R. W. and Mollie L. Nicely (3) -   March 21, 1883
   Place of marriage, Middleway - Age of husband, 27 - Age of wife, 20 - Both are Single - Both were born in Jefferson County, West Virginia - Husband resides in Berkeley County, West Virginia - Wife resides in Jefferson County, West Virginia. (Consent of bride's father in writing.)

Riley, Rachel R. and Daniel Stephenson (1) -   April 3, 1834

Riley, Rebecca and Allen Macbee (1) -   February 4, 1819

Riley, Robert W. and Nancy Massey (1) -   August 11, 1816

Riley, Samuel and Mary E. Furr (3) -   November 9, 1880
   Place of marriage, Charlestown - Age of husband, 24 - Age of wife, 22 - Both are Single - Husband was born in Clarke County, Virginia - Wife was born in Jefferson County, West Virginia - Both reside in Jefferson County, West Virginia.

Riley, Sarah and Joseph Wagely (3) -   November 21, 1872
   For further information see - Wagely, Joseph.

Riley, Sarah Anna and Martin William Phalen (3) -   January 20, 1881
   For further information see - Phalen, Martin William.

Riley, Thomas and Elizabeth Myles (1) -   April 8, 1806

Riley, Zachariah and Clarianna Gaines (1) -   September 13, 1827

Rineheart, A. P. and M. C. Link (bride) (3) -   December 5, 1867
   Place of marriage, Jefferson County - Age of husband, 24 - Age of wife, 20 - Both are Single - Both were born in Jefferson County - Both reside in Jefferson - Husband's parents are Christian - Wife's parents are Adam - Occupation of husband is Farmer. (Brother swearing that parent is willing.)

Ring, Alonzo M. and Alice V. Higgs (3) - December 11, 1889
    Place of marriage, Charlestown - Age of husband, 25 - Age of wife,
    20 - Both are Single - Both were born in Jefferson County, West
    Virginia - Both reside in Jefferson County, West Virginia.
    (Consent of bride's father in person.)

Ring, Charles C. and Hannah B. Moore (3) - July 24, 1877
    Place of marriage, Middleway - Age of husband, 23 - Age of wife,
    19 - Both are Single - Both were born in Jefferson County, West
    Virginia - Both reside in Jefferson County, West Virginia.
    (Consent of bride's mother in writing.)

Ring, Lillie L. and Joseph L. Jolley (3) - January 2, 1889
    For further information see - Jolley, Joseph L.

Ring, Virginia Tennessee and J. B. Packett (3) - November 25, 1884
    For further information see - Packett, J. B.

Ring, William L. and Mrs. Selina Shipe (3) - April 27, 1882
    Place of marriage, Middleway - Age of husband, 23 - Age of wife,
    30 - Husband is Single - Wife is a Widow - Husband was born in
    Jefferson County, West Virginia - Wife was born in Jefferson County -
    Husband resides in Jefferson County, West Virginia - Wife resides in
    Jefferson County.

Ringer, James William and Katie Horn (3) - September 10, 1879
    Place of marriage, near Shepherdstown - Age of husband, 25 - Age of
    wife, 29 - Both are Single - Both were born in Jefferson County -
    West Virginia - Both reside in Jefferson County, West Virginia.

Ringer, John T. and Levina Butt (3) - December 28, 1871
    Place of marriage, Jefferson County - Age of husband, 24 - Age of
    wife, 23 - Both are Single - Husband was born in Jefferson County -
    Wife was born in Berkeley County - Both reside in Jefferson County -
    Husband's parents are P. G. and Ruth E. - Wife's parents are V. W.
    and Elizabeth - Occupation of husband is Tinner. (J. W. Butt.)

Rion, Priscilla and John Jacobs (1) - October 1, 1814

Ripon, Janie E. and E. F. Hummer (3) - September 15, 1887
    For further information see - Hummer, E. F.

Ripple, John and Mary Herbert (1) - 1813

Ripple, Matilda and John Peters (1) - October 9, 1825

Rippon, Nathaniel and Ellen Draper (2) - (L) October 4, 1854

Risner, Henry and Amelia Shadwell (1) - March 22, 1833

Risque, Mrs. J. S. and W. M. Nelson (3) - March 30, 1887
    For further information see - Nelson, W. M.

Rissler, Maggie and S. Lee Phillips (3) - December 5, 1882
    For further information see - Phillips, S. Lee.

Rissler, Mary Catharine and F. B. S. Morrow (1) - May 23, 1848

Rissler, S. G. M. and Sally C. Engle (3) - October 21, 1885
Place of marriage, Unionville - Age of husband, 25 - Age of wife, 25 - Both are Single - Both were born in Jefferson County, West Virginia - Both reside in Jefferson County, West Virginia.

Rissler, Thomas L. and Lucy C. Yates (3) - December 18, 1877
Place of marriage, near Kabletown - Age of husband, 22 - Age of wife, 21 - Both are Single - Husband was born in Jefferson County, West Virginia - Wife was born in Culpeper County, Virginia - Both reside in Jefferson County, West Virginia.

Ritchie, Archibald and Mary Ann Bell (1) - October 20, 1818

Ritter, James Jackson and Mrs. Elizabeth Betz (3) - November 16, 1873
Place of marriage, Harpers Ferry - Age of husband, 44 - Age of wife, 33 - Husband is a Widower - Wife is a Widow - Husband was born in Frederick County, Virginia - Wife was born in Berkeley County, West Virginia - Both reside in Jefferson County, West Virginia.

Ritter, John A. and Maggie M. McDonald (3) - July 24, 1886
Place of marriage, Harpers Ferry - Age of husband, 22 - Age of wife, 21 - Both are Single.- Both were born in State of Virginia - Both reside in Jefferson County, West Virginia.

Rixtine, Mary and Philip Staub (1) - April 12, 1831

Roach, Hanah and John Hufman (1) - March 12, 1818

Roach, Hannah and Joshua Mullenix (1) - May 27, 1821

Roach, Thomas and Jane Castle (3) - (1869)
Age of husband, 30 - Age of wife, 20 - Husband was born in Ireland - Wife was born in Maryland - Husband resides in Jefferson County - Wife resides in Maryland. (No parents or guardian.)

Roadefer, S. F. and Sophia L. Hoover (3) - September 27, 1886
Place of marriage, Harpers Ferry - Age of husband, 22 - Age of wife, 21 - Both are Single -.Both were born in Jefferson County, West Virginia - Both reside in Jefferson County, West Virginia.

Roads, James and Elizabeth Dillow (1) - January 30, 1820

Roan, S. J. (bride) and J. R. Avis (3) - January 2, 1871
For further information see - Avis, J. R.

Roan, Sarah J. and John R. Avis (3) - January 2, 1871
For further information see - Avis, John R.

Rob, Eliza and Arthur Russell (1) - May 29, 1804

Robb, George and Barbary Eckhart (1) - June 2, 1808

Roberson, Jackson (cold.) Patsy Lousia McDaniel (3) - December 24, 1884
Place of marriage, near Charlestown - Age of husband, 23 - Age of wife, 18 - Both are Single - Husband was born in Loudoun County, Virginia - Wife was born in Jefferson County, West Virginia - Both reside in Jefferson County, West Virginia. (Consent of bride's father in writing.)

Roberts, Abraham and Rachel Blue (1) - 1820

Roberts, Alfred H. and Ann C. Burns (2) - (L) June 9, 1856

Roberts, Alice M. and James William Burr (3) - September 13, 1882
    For further information see - Burr, James William.

Roberts, Anna V. and J. Henry Jennings (3) - February 26, 1874
    For further information see - Jennings, J. Henry.

Roberts, Clara and John William Rolls (3) - May 11, 1873
    For further information see - Rolls, John William.

Roberts, Cora A. and Charles F. Laise (3) - November 18, 1885
    For further information see - Laise, Charles F.

Roberts, Elizabeth and James E. Watson (3) - September 14, 1869
    For further information see - Watson, James E.

Roberts, Elizabeth A. and William Weston Carothers (3) - January 24, 1871
    For further information see - Carothers, William Weston.

Roberts, Emma and John W. Shewbridge (3) - December 28, 1887
    For further information see - Shewbridge, John W.

Roberts, Emma S. and A. C. Drawbaugh (3) - June 14, 1870
    For further information see - Drawbaugh, A. C.

Roberts, Fanny L. and Jack Allen (3) - November 18, 1873
    For further information see - Allen, Jack.

Roberts, Georgia and William Sennor (3) - July 12, 1868
    For further information see - Sennor, William.

Roberts, Hester Ann and William Henry Myers (2) - (L) October 27, 1856

Roberts, James W. and Mary S. Roberts (1) - January 23, 1845

Roberts, Jane C. and Joseph K. Carter (3) - October 23, 1878
    For further information see - Carter, Joseph K.

Roberts, John and Mary Mathias (1) - August 13, 1815

Roberts, John W. and Julia A. Boggess (2) - (L) October 19, 1860

Roberts, Joshua and Sarah Ann Hall (1) - March 18, 1823

Roberts, Kate A. and Joseph H. Easterday (3) - July 1, 1878
    For further information see - Easterday, Joseph H.

Roberts, Katie and Thacker VanHorn (3) - March 23, 1880
    For further information see - VanHorn, Thacker.

Roberts, M. (bride) and L. A. Barnhart (3) - March 26, 1868
    For further information see - Barnhart, L. A.

Roberts, Margaret L. and Mayberry G. Smith (3) - November 12, 1872
    For further information see - Smith, Mayberry G.

Roberts, Mary Ellen and James W. Wageley (1) - January 21, 1847

Roberts, Mary S. and James W. Roberts (1) - January 23, 1845

Roberts, Matilda and Adam Crone (2) -   (L) July 2, 1858

Roberts, Minnie and William P. Easterday (3) -   April 17, 1884
    For further information see - Easterday, William P.

Roberts, Nettie F. and Robert S. Noland (3) -   July 23, 1884
    For further information see - Noland, Robert S.

Roberts, Nettie J. and Bing Brown (3) -   November 22, 1888
    For further information see - Brown, Bing.

Roberts, Rebecca J. and Lemuel T. Taylor (2) -   (L) December 3, 1851

Roberts, Sarah Elizabeth and John H. Wageley (3) -   December 22, 1880
    For further information see - Wageley, John H.

Roberts, Stephen and Mary A. Fouke (2) -   (L) January 2, 1852

Roberts, Thomas (cold.) Hannah Jackson (3) -   March 31, 1886
    Place of marriage, Charlestown - Age of husband, 29 - Age of wife, 30 - Both are Single - Both were born in Jefferson County, West Virginia - Both reside in Jefferson County, West Virginia.

Roberts, Tina (cold.) Lee Williams (3) -   June 25, 1888
    For further information see - Williams, Lee.

Roberts, V. R. and Irene Pearrell (3) -   February 23, 1887
    Place of marriage, Berkeley - Age of husband, 27 - Age of wife, 21 - Both are Single - Husband was born in Jefferson County - Wife was born in Berkeley County - Both reside in Jefferson County.

Roberts, William Thomas and Laura Stewart Powell (3) -   May 4, 1886
    Place of marriage, Shepherdstown - Age of husband, 31 - Age of wife, 26 - Both are Single - Husband was born in Mecklenburg, Virginia - Wife was born in Fairfax, Virginia - Husband resides in Culpeper, Virginia - Wife resides in Jefferson County, West Virginia.

Robertson, Albina and E. D. Glaize (3) -   March 27, 1873
    For further information see - Glaize, E. D.

Robertson, M. S. B. and Mary V. Dobson (3) -   September 12, 1878
    Place of marriage, Charlestown - Age of husband, 52 - Age of wife, 28 - Husband is a Widower - Wife is Single - Husband was born in Lancaster County, Virginia - Wife was born in Jefferson County, West Virginia - Both reside in Jefferson County, West Virginia.

Robertson, Sarah R. and John H. Hooe (3) -   May 8, 1876
    For further information see - Hooe, John H.

Robey, John N. and Annie E. Dum (3) -   January 15, 1867
    Place of marriage, Castlemans Ferry - Age of husband, 21 - Age of wife, 21 - Both are Single - Husband was born in Loudoun County, Virginia - Wife was born in Frederick County, Virginia - Both reside in Jefferson County, West Virginia - Husband's parents are W. and Jane Robey - Wife's parents are C. and N. Dum - Occupation of husband is Blacksmith.

Robey, Thomas W. and Louisa Vinds (3) - February 25, 1869
   Place of marriage, Jefferson County - Age of husband, 29 - Age of
   wife, 19 - Both are Single - Both were born in Jefferson County -
   Both reside in Jefferson County - Husband's parents are Jacob and
   Malinda - Wife's parents are John and Margaret - Occupation of
   husband is Farmer. (Brother over 21 swearing that parents of lady
   are willing.)

Robinson, A. and Charlotte Myers (3) - September 30, 1869
   Place of marriage, Jefferson County - Age of husband, 27 - Age of
   wife, 20 - Husband was norn in Bath County, Virginia - Wife was born
   in Jefferson County - Both reside in Jefferson County. (Father in
   person consents.)

Robinson, A. J. and Juliet Nachman (3) - July 26, 1890
   Place of marriage, Charlestown - Age of husband, 29 - Age of wife,
   25 - Both are Single - Husband was born at Washington, D. C. - Wife
   was born at Baltimore, Maryland - Husband resides at Washington,
   D. C. - Wife resides in Jefferson County, West Virginia.

Robinson, Adellbert and A. C. Strider (3) - February 27, 1890
   Place of marriage, Walnut Grove - Age of husband, 35 - Age of wife,
   33 - Both are Single - Husband was born in Union County, Ohio - Wife
   was born in Jefferson County, West Virginia - Husband resides in
   Union County, Ohio - Wife resides in Jefferson County, West Virginia.

Robinson, Alice (cold.) Robert Jenkins (3) - December 28, 1875
   For further information see - Jenkins, Robert.

Robinson, Anna and M. P. Andrews (2) - (L) July 5, 1861
   For further information see - Andrews, M. P.

Robinson, Annie (cold.) Emmit Henry Johnson (3) - October 15, 1885
   For further information see - Johnson, Emmit Henry.

Robinson, Archibald and Ann K. Mines (1) - March 31, 1831

Robinson, Baily (cold.) Julia Purndon (3) - December 28, 1882
   Place of marriage, Flowing Spring - Age of husband, 21 - Age of wife,
   25 - Both are Single - Both were born in Louisa County, Virginia -
   Both reside in Jefferson County, West Virginia.

Robinson, Carter (cold.) Henrietta Carter (3) - April 24, 1889
   Place of marriage, Charlestown - Age of husband, 22 - Age of wife,
   18 - Both are Single - Husband was born in Jefferson County, West
   Virginia - Wife was born in Loudoun County, Virginia - Both reside
   in Jefferson County, West Virginia. (Consent of bride's mother
   certified by Charles Wade.)

Robinson, Charles (cold.) Charity A. Jackson (3) - April 6, 1882
   Place of marriage, near Middleway - Age of husband, 28 - Age of
   wife, 25 - Husband is a Widower - Wife is Single - Both were born in
   Jefferson County, West Virginia - Both reside in Jefferson County,
   West Virginia.

481

Robinson, Charles S. (cold.) Annie Page (3) -   January 23, 1886
   Place of marriage, Bolivar - Age of husband, 30 - Age of wife, 22 -
   Husband is a Widower - Wife is Single - Husband was born in
   Jefferson County, West Virginia - Wife was born in Jefferson
   County - Husband resides in Berkeley County, West Virginia - Wife
   resides in Jefferson County, West Virginia.

Robinson, Delia (cold.) William Coxen (3) -   December 27, 1888
   For further information see - Coxen, William.

Robinson, Diana (cold.) George Mansfield Rust (3) -   October 4, 1877
   For further information see - Rust, George Mansfield.

Robinson, Edmun F. and Maggie V. Shambaugh (3) -   August 11, 1880
   Place of marriage, Bloomery - Age of husband, 27 - Age of wife, 23 -
   Both are Single - Husband was born in Luzerne County, Pennsylvania -
   Wife was born in Shenandoah County, Virginia - Both reside in
   Jefferson County, West Virginia.

Robinson, Edmund and Lydia Baker (3) -   December 1866
   Age of husband, 60 - Age of wife, 40 - Husband is a Widower - Wife
   is a Widow - Both were born in Jefferson County, West Virginia -
   Both reside in Jefferson County, West Virginia - Husband's parents
   are James and Alice Robinson - Occupation of husband is Laborer.

Robinson, Elijah (cold.) Mary Thomas (3) -   December 25, 1874
   Place of marriage, Charles Town - Age of husband, 47 - Age of wife,
   30 - Husband is a Widower - Wife is a Widow - Husband was born in
   Frederick County, Virginia - Wife was born in Page County - Husband
   resides in Jefferson County, West Virginia - Wife resides in West
   Virginia.

Robinson, Elizabeth and Howard McDaniel (3) -   May 18, 1890
   For further information see - McDaniel, Howard.

Robinson, Ellen C. and Thomas M. King (3) -   October 25, 1865
   For further information see - King, Thomas M.

Robinson, Fanny and S. Hoxton (3) -   October 14, 1868
   For further information see.- Hoxton, S.

Robinson, Frank and Alice Johnson (3) -   December 23, 1869
   Place of marriage, Jefferson County - Age of husband, 23 - Age of
   wife, 20 - Husband was born in Missouri - Wife was born in
   Virginia - Both reside in Jefferson County. (Consent in writing
   of parents.)

Robinson, Frank (cold.) Kate Henry (3) -   April 30, 1884
   Place of marriage, Middleway - Age of husband, 23 - Age of wife,
   22 - Both are Single - Husband was born in Jefferson County, West
   Virginia - Wife was born in.Jefferson County - Husband resides in
   Jefferson County - Wife resides in Jefferson County, West Virginia.

Robinson, George and Jane Crim (1) -   November 9, 1818

Robinson, George H. (cold.) Virginia Washington (3) -   December 18, 1873
   Place of marriage, Shepherdstown - Age of husband, 21 - Age of wife,
   21 - Both are Single - Both were born in Jefferson County, West
   Virginia - Both reside in Jefferson County, West Virginia.

Robinson, George Rowan and Ann R. Page Andrews (2) - (L) September 15, 1855

Robinson, George W. (cold.) Sarah M. Whiting (3) - April 24, 1882
Place of marriage, Bolivar - Age of husband, 24 - Age of wife, 21 - Both are Single - Husband was born in Jefferson County, West Virginia - Wife was born in Jefferson County - Husband resides in Jefferson County, West Virginia - Wife resides in Jefferson County.

Robinson, Gregg and Fanny O. Lewis (3) - December 26, 1872
Place of marriage, Jefferson County, West Virginia - Age of husband, 23 - Age of wife, 21 - Both are Single - Both were born in Jefferson County, West Virginia - Both reside in Jefferson County, West Virginia - Husband's parents are Henry and Emily - Wife's parents are Davy and Matilda. (Davy Lewis.)

Robinson, H. R. and James F. Jones (3) - November 12, 1867
For further information see - Jones, James F.

Robinson, Hamilton (cold.) Milly Brown (3) - February 23, 1878
Place of marriage, Middleway District - Age of husband, 42 - Age of wife, 24 - Both are Single - Both were born in Jefferson County, West Virginia - Both reside in Jefferson County, West Virginia.

Robinson, Harrison and Anna Bransom (3) - June 8, 1867
Place of marriage, Shepherdstown - Age of husband, 21 - Age of wife, 17 - Both are Single - Both were born in Jefferson County, West Virginia - Both reside at Shepherdstown - Husband's parents are James and Nancy Robinson - Wife's parents are Solomon and Nancy Bransom - Occupation of husband is Farmer.

Robinson, Henry (colored) Violet Smorthus (3) - August 18, 1870
Place of marriage, Jefferson County - Age of husband, 28 - Age of wife, 30 - Wife is a Widow - Husband was born in Virginia - Wife was born in Jefferson County - Both reside in Jefferson County.

Robinson, Henry (cold.) Nelly Williams (3) - October 15, 1879
Place of marriage, near Wickliff - Age of husband, 45 - Age of wife, 25 - Husband is a Widower - Wife is Single - Husband was born in King George County - Wife was born in Prince William County - Both reside in Jefferson County, West Virginia.

Robinson, Horace (colored) Lydia Baker (3) - June 5, 1870
Place of marriage, Jefferson County - Age of husband, 57 - Age of wife, 49 - Husband was born in Virginia - Wife was born in Jefferson County - Both reside in Jefferson County.

Robinson, J. H. (cold.) Julia Smith (3) - January 20, 1876
Place of marriage, Harpers Ferry - Age of husband, 24 - Age of wife, 26 - Both are Single - Husband was born in Jefferson County, West Virginia - Wife was born in Rockingham County, Virginia - Both reside in Jefferson County, West Virginia.

Robinson, J. M. and Margaret V. Belts (3) - July 25, 1865
Place of marriage, Jefferson County - Age of husband, 23 years - Age of wife, 18 years - Both are Single - Husband was born in Barbour County, West Virginia - Wife was born in Pendleton County, Virginia - Husband resides in Taylor County - Wife resides in Jefferson County - Husband's parents are Mathew M. Robinson and (nee) Sarah J. Reed - Wife's parents are Martin Belts and (nee) Margaret J. Blizard - Occupation of husband is Farmer.

483

Robinson, Jacob (cold.) Katie Davenport (3) -   December 29, 1887
    Place of marriage, Charlestown - Age of husband, 22 - Age of wife,
    23 - Both are Single - Husband was born in Jefferson County, West
    Virginia - Wife was born at Washington City - Husband resides in
    Jefferson County, West Virginia - Wife resides in Jefferson County
    at present.

Robinson, James (cold.) Bettie Smith (3) -   November 27, 1890
    Place of marriage, Shepherdstown - Age of husband, 36 - Age of wife,
    35 - Both are Single - Both were born in Jefferson County, West
    Virginia - Both reside in Jefferson County, West Virginia.

Robinson, Jane (cold.) Samuel Roman (3) -   December 23, 1873
    For further information see - Roman, Samuel.

Robinson, John Edward (cold.) Laura A. Strother (3) -   December 21, 1882
    Place of marriage, Bolivar - Age of husband, 23 - Age of wife, 21 -
    Both are Single - Both were born in Jefferson County, West Virginia -
    Husband resides in Jefferson County, West Virginia.

Robinson, John Henry (cold.) Lucy Day (3) -   February 10, 1887
    Place of marriage, Summit Point - Age of husband, 28 - Age of wife,
    22 - Both are Single - Both were born in Jefferson County - Both
    reside in Jefferson County.

Robinson, Josephine (cold.) Jesse Berry (3) -   December 31, 1876
    For further information see - Berry, Jesse.

Robinson, Laura Virginia (cold.) David Stephenson (3) -   March 2, 1876
    For further information see - Stephenson, David.

Robinson, Logan (cold.) Louisa Lucas (3) -   December 27, 1876
    Place of marriage, near Charlestown - Age of husband, 35 - Age of
    wife, 23 - Both are Single - Both were born in Jefferson County,
    West Virginia - Both reside in Jefferson County, West Virginia.

Robinson, Louisa (cold.) George Johnson (3) -   September 5, 1882
    For further information see - Johnson, George.

Robinson, Lucy and William Smith (3) -   December 26, 1869
    For further information see - Smith, William.

Robinson, Lula (cold.) J. D. Marshall (3) -   April 23, 1885
    For further information see - Marshall, J. D.

Robinson, Lydia (nee Baker) (cold.) Lewis Mitchell (3) -   December 28, 1882
    For further information see - Mitchell, Lewis.

Robinson, M. E. (col.) James Warfield (3) -   November 28, 1867
    For further information see - Warfield, James.

Robinson, Maggie (cold.) Harry Bennett (3) -   July 31, 1884
    For further information see - Bennett, Harry.

Robinson, Mary (cold.) Harry Johnson (3) -   September 24, 1890
    For further information see - Johnson, Harry.

Robinson, Nancey (cold.) Barger Johnson (3) -   October 26, 1890
    For further information see - Johnson, Barger.

Robinson, Nellie (cold.) George Dixon (3) -   July 11, 1888
    For further information see - Dixon, George.

Robinson, Phips (cold.) Jane Roman (3) -   April 12, 1887
    Place of marriage, near Smithfield - Age of husband, 25 - Age of
    wife, 25 - Husband is Single - Wife is a Widow - Both were born in
    Jefferson County, West Virginia - Both reside in Jefferson County,
    West Virginia.

Robinson, Polly and Thomas Morgan (1) -   May 3, 1804

Robinson, Raleigh and Helen Blue (3) -   December 12, 1872
    Place of marriage, Charlestown - Age of husband, 24 - Age of wife,
    19 - Both are Single - Both were born in Jefferson County, West
    Virginia - Both reside in Jefferson County, West Virginia -
    Husband's parents are Raleigh and Matilda - Wife's parents are
    Anthony and Caroline - Occupation of husband is Farmer. (Caroline
    Blue.)

Robinson, Rebecca (cold.) Albert Green (3) -   March 13, 1879
    For further information see - Green, Albert.

Robinson, Rosa and Isaac F. Nicholson (3) -   October 3, 1871
    For further information see - Nicholson, Isaac F.

Robinson, Sarah A. and Jacob V. Underdonk (2) -   (L) February 17, 1855

Robinson, Susan Rebecca and Solomon Anderson (3) -   September 18, 1871
    For further information see - Anderson, Solomon.

Robinson, Susana and Sidney Pitcher (1) -   May 27, 1819

Robinson, William (cold.) Lucy Mills (3) -   March 27, 1879
    Place of marriage, Kearneysville - Age of husband, 22 - Age of wife,
    22 - Both are Single - Both were born in Jefferson County, West
    Virginia - Both reside in Jefferson County, West Virginia.

Robinson, William (cold.) Mary Fisher (3) -   December 18, 1884
    Place of marriage, near Summit Point - Age of husband, 25 - Age of
    wife, 24 - Both are Single - Both were born in Jefferson County,
    West Virginia - Both reside in Jefferson County, West Virginia.

Roby, Jacob and Patsy Matheny (1) -   June 13, 1834

Roby, Malinda and Thomas J. Dillow (3) -   September 2, 1885
    For further information see - Dillow, Thomas J.

Roby, Mary Jane and James Mahony (2) -   (L) February 2, 1856

Rockenbaugh, Edward and Mary E. Boyd (3) -   August 24, 1876
    Place of marriage, near Myerstown - Age of husband, 22 - Age of wife,
    19 - Both are Single - Both were born in Jefferson County, West
    Virginia - Both reside in Jefferson County, West Virginia.

Rockenbaugh, Eliza and William Bearley (1) -   March 5, 1818

Rockenbaugh, Frances and Thomas H. Jones (3) -   March 26, 1873
    For further information see - Jones, Thomas H.

Rockenbaugh, John C. and Lydia Moore (2) -   (L) November 7, 1851

Rockenbaugh, John W. and Sarah Ann Lee (2) - (L) June 14, 1853

Rockenbough, Henry and Mary Clark (1) - September 22, 1816

Rockenbough, Samuel and Mary Johnson (1) - September 26, 1816

Rockenbourg, Mary and Robert McMiltin (1) - April 15, 1824

Rodefer, David H. and Emma A. Engle (3) - December 24, 1882
  Place of marriage, Duffields - Age of husband, 24 - Age of wife,
  23 - Both are Single - Both were born in Jefferson County, West
  Virginia - Both reside in Jefferson County, West Virginia.

Rodefer, Emma and Larkin M. Fox (3) - October 28, 1886
  For further information see - Fox, Larkin M.

Rodeffer, B. F. and Ann M. R. Grove (3) - October 12, 1876
  Place of marriage, near Charlestown - Age of husband, 26 - Age of
  wife, 19 - Both are Single - Husband was born in Shenandoah County,
  Virginia - Wife was born in Jefferson County, West Virginia - Both
  reside in Jefferson County, West Virginia. (Consent of bride's
  father in person.)

Rodeffer, B. F. and Molly Gannon (3) - February 17, 1881
  Place of marriage, Harpers Ferry - Age of husband, 29 - Age of wife,
  21 - Husband is a Widower - Wife is Single - Husband was born in
  Shenandoah County, Virginia - Wife was born in Jefferson County,
  West Virginia - Both reside in Jefferson County, West Virginia.

Rodeffer, G. B. and Lucy A. Cockrell (3) - January 31, 1882
  Place of marriage, Charlestown - Age of husband, 25 - Age of wife,
  24 - Both are Single - Husband was born in Hardy County, West
  Virginia - Wife was born in Jefferson County, West Virginia - Both
  reside in Jefferson County, West Virginia.

Rodeffer, Henrietta and Jacob Biller (3) - January 8, 1873
  For further information see - Biller, Jacob.

Roderick, A. Eliza and James B. Bowers (3) - January 23, 1868
  For further information see - Bowers, James B.

Roderick, A. J. and Virginia S. Avis (2) - (L) October 23, 1856

Roderick, Abraham and Elizabeth Callison (1) - July 1, 1828

Roderick, Belle and William H. Young (3) - November 24, 1874
  For further information see - Young, William H.

Roderick, Bettie and John W. Smallwood (3) - February 3, 1876
  For further information see - Smallwood, John W.

Roderick, Celia Ann and Jacob Gompf (1) - May 26, 1836

Roderick, Charles T. and Mary C. Hitaffer (3) - August 22, 1871
  Place of marriage, Harpers Ferry - Age of husband, 24 - Age of wife,
  18 - Both are Single - Husband was born at Harpers Ferry - Wife was
  born in Clarke County - Both reside in Jefferson County - Husband's
  parents are Abram and Elizabeth - Wife's parents are Martha J. -
  Occupation of husband is Laborer. (Mother consents in writing.)

Roderick, Grandiville and Jane Roderick (3) - August 27, 1872
    Place of marriage, Jefferson County - Age of husband, 27 - Age of
    wife, 21 - Both are Single - Husband was born in Jefferson County,
    Virginia - Wife was born in Jefferson County - Husband resides in
    Jefferson County - Wife resides in Jefferson County, West Virginia -
    Husband's parents are John and Aisley - Wife's parents are William
    amd Maria - Occupation of husband is Cooper.

Roderick, Hattie and R. K. Ogden (3) - March 24, 1869
    For further information see - Ogden, R. K.

Roderick, Jane and Grandiville Roderick (3) - August 27, 1872
    For further information see - Roderick, Grandiville.

Roderick, John and Elizabeth Cane (1) - January 5, 1836

Roderick, Joshua and Asey Butt (1) - 1812

Roderick, Martha A. and William McCarty (2) - (L) December 13, 1859

Roderick, Mary and William Phelan (1) - April 13, 1820

Roderick, Mary E. and Harmon Gray (3) - October 8, 1868
    For further information see - Gray, Harmon.

Roderick, Mattie J. and Samuel H. Cox (3) - November 6, 1872
    For further information see - Cox, Samuel H.

Roderick, Sarah and John Hendricks (1) - August 10, 1809

Rodgers, Elbert (cold.) Katie Briscoe (3) - March 18, 1880
    Place of marriage, near Charlestown - Age of husband, 35 - Age of
    wife, 25 - Both are Single - Husband was born in Nansemond,
    Virginia - Wife was born in Jefferson County, West Virginia - Both
    reside in Jefferson County, West Virginia.

Rodrick, Daniel and Jane Elizabeth Gray (3) - October 16, 1878
    Place of marriage, Charlestown - Age of husband, 28 - Age of wife,
    25 - Both are Single - Both were born in Jefferson County, West
    Virginia - Both reside in Jefferson County, West Virginia.

Rodrick, J. William and Alice V. Bartle (3) - November 22, 1888
    Place of marriage, Charlestown - Age of husband, 29 - Age of wife,
    30 - Husband is Single - Wife is a Widow - Husband was born in
    Virginia - Wife was born in Maryland - Husband resides in Maryland -
    Wife resides in Jefferson County, West Virginia at present.

Rodrick, John A. and Mary L. Tucker (3) - August 3, 1879
    Place of marriage, Harpers Ferry - Age of husband, 38 - Age of wife,
    25 - Both are Single - Husband was born in Jefferson County - Wife
    was born in Howard County, Maryland - Both reside in Jefferson
    County, West Virginia.

Rodrick, John R. and Emily A. Welsh (3) - June 11, 1873
    Place of marriage, Charlestown - Age of husband, 34 - Age of wife,
    30 - Both are Single - Both were born in Jefferson County, West
    Virginia - Both reside in Jefferson County, West Virginia.

Rodrick, Lottie J. and George W. Wright (3) - April 2, 1883
    For further information see - Wright, George W.

Rodrick, Lucinda and Jonathan Painter (2) -   (L) November 28, 1856

Rodrick, Margaret M. and William Langdon (3) -   December 20, 1877
    For further information see - Langdon, William.

Rodrick, Mary E. and William H. Wiltshire (3) -   December 15, 1881
    For further information see - Wiltshire, William H.

Rodrick, Mary Jane and Henry A. Bradshear (3) -   May 24, 1887
    For further information see - Bradshear, Henry A.

Rodrick, Rosa and John Gray (3). -   June 7, 1883
    For further information see - Gray, John.

Rodrick, Thomas E. and Annie J. Manning (nee Matthews) (3) - September 7, 1889
    Place of marriage, Harpers Ferry - Age of husband, 22 - Age of wife,
    30 - Husband is Single - Wife is a Widow - Husband was born in
    Jefferson County, West Virginia - Wife was born at Bloomington,
    Pennsylvania - Both reside in Jefferson County, West Virginia.

Rodrick, William H. and Sally O'Connell (3) -   November 3, 1880
    Place of marriage, Charlestown - Age of husband, 24 - Age of wife,
    18 - Both are Single. - Husband was born in Loudoun County,
    Virginia - Wife was born in Jefferson County, West Virginia - Both
    reside in Jefferson County, West Virginia. (Consent of bride's
    mother in writing.)

Roe, William F. and Annie M. Snyder (2) -   (L) October 22, 1853

Roeder, Albert T. and Mary S. McLane (3) -   October 22, 1879
    Place of marriage, Harpers Ferry - Age of husband, 22 - Age of wife,
    21 - Both are Single - Husband was born in Jefferson County - Wife
    was born in Washington County, Maryland - Both reside in Jefferson
    County, West Virginia.

Roeder, Julia A. and Frederick Kuhl (3) -   February 19, 1879
    For further information see - Kuhl, Frederick.

Roeder, Matilda E. and John C. Sutton (3) -   May 22, 1877
    For further information see - Sutton, John C.

Roeder, Mattie Ann and Columbus M. Larue (3) -   June 14, 1890
    For further information see - Larue, Columbus M.

Rogers, James H. and Ida V. Chapline (3) -   April 27, 1882
    Place of marriage, Shepherdstown - Age of husband, 24 - Age of wife,
    24 - Both are Single - Husband was born in West Virginia now Mineral
    County - Wife was born in Jefferson County - Husband resides in
    Mineral County, West Virginia - Wife resides in Jefferson County.

Rogers, John H. and Mary Buckles (1) -   March 31, 1812

Rogers, Margaret Ann and Oliver P. Ruckle (2) -   (L) August 26, 1863
    For further information see - Ruckle, Oliver P.

Rogers, Mary M. and Edward J. Willis (3) -   March 15, 1876
    For further information see - Willis, Edward J.

Rogers, Theodore and Florence McAnly (3) - November 13, 1879
    Place of marriage, Shepherdstown - Age of husband, 21 - Age of wife,
    20 - Both are Single - Both were born in Jefferson County, West
    Virginia - Both reside in Jefferson County, West Virginia.
    (Consent of bride's mother in writing.)

Rohr, Ann Louisa and James E. Moler (1) - January 6, 1848

Rohr, John W. and Martha E. Crawford (2) - (L) July 3, 1854

Rohr, Katy and C. W. Taylor (3) - July 7, 1884
    For further information see - Taylor, C. W.

Rohr, Maggie and J. G. Briscoe (3) - February 14, 1866
    For further information see - Briscoe, J. G.

Rohr, Marshall J. and Mollie R. Harrell (3) - July 22, 1880
    Place of marriage, Charlestown - Age of husband, 25 - Age of wife,
    25 - Both are Single - Both were born in Jefferson County, West
    Virginia - Both reside in Jefferson County, West Virginia.

Rohr, Nellie J. and Joseph N. Fidinger (3) - June 12, 1883
    For further information see - Fidinger, Joseph N.

Rohrer, Fannie and Bailous Corder (3) - June 25, 1885
    For further information see - Corder, Bailous.

Rohrer, John and Eveline Medler (1) - March 16, 1824

Rohrer, Laura A. and William M. Burns (3) - December 23, 1879
    For further information see - Burns, William M.

Rokenbaugh, W. H. and Emma R. Chambers (3) - November 4, 1885
    Place of marriage, Bolivar - Age of husband, 23 - Age of wife, 20 -
    Both are Single - Both were born in Jefferson County, West Virginia -
    Both reside in Jefferson County, West Virginia. (Consent of bride's
    mother in writing.)

Roland, Samuel and Harriet McDaniel (1) - November 1, 1832

Roland, William M. and Cora L. Custard (3) - January 18, 1888
    Place of marriage, Smithfield - Age of husband, 22 - Age of wife,
    22 - Both are Single - Both were born in Jefferson County, West
    Virginia - Both reside in Jefferson County, West Virginia.

Rollinson, Anna and Reuben Stipes (1) - May 1, 1817

Rolls, John William and Clara Roberts (3) - May 11, 1873
    Place of marriage, Charles Town - Age of husband, 22 - Age of wife,
    28 - Husband is a Widower - Wife is a Widow - Husband was born in
    Culpeper County, Virginia - Both reside in Jefferson County, West
    Virginia - Husband's parents are Daniel Smith and Jane - Wife's
    parents are Alfa and Lavina - Occupation of husband is Tanner.

Roman, Betty (cold.) James William Thornton (3) - January 9, 1877
    For further information see - Thornton, James William.

Roman, Carter (colored) Alice Alexander (3) -   January 13, 1870
    Place of marriage, Jefferson County - Age of husband, 25 - Age of
    wife, 19 - Both were born in Jefferson County - Both reside in
    Jefferson County.

Roman, Fanny and Edward Brown (3) -   (1869)
    For further information see - Brown, Edward.

Roman, Jane (cold.) Phips Robinson (3) -   April 12, 1887
    For further information see - Robinson, Phips.

Roman, Joseph (cold.) Alice Cook (3) -   September 28, 1876
    Place of marriage, Middleway - Age of husband, 24 - Age of wife,
    21 - Both are Single - Both were born in Jefferson County, West
    Virginia - Both reside in Jefferson County, West Virginia.

Roman, Samuel (cold.) Jane Robinson (3) -   December 23, 1873
    Place of marriage, Smithfield - Age of husband, 27 - Age of wife,
    22 - Both are Single - Both were born in Jefferson County, West
    Virginia - Both reside in Jefferson County, West Virginia.

Roman, Susana and Henry Philips (3) -   January 19, 1871
    For further information see - Philips, Henry.

Roman, William (cold.) Annie Bromwicks (3) -   January 1, 1868
    Place of marriage, Jefferson County - Age of husband, 21 - Age of
    wife, 18 - Both are Single - Both were born in Jefferson County -
    Both reside in Jefferson County - Occupation of husband is Farmer.
    (Parents consent.)

Ronemous, Catharine and Jacob J. Miller (2) -   (L) November 19, 1862
    For further information see - Miller, Jacob J.

Ronemous, Charles M. and Alice R. Snader (3) -   January 12, 1882
    Place of marriage, Unionville - Age of husband, 23 - Age of wife,
    20 - Both are Single - Husband was born in Jefferson County, West
    Virginia - Wife was born in Maryland - Both reside in Jefferson
    County, West Virginia. (Consent of bride's mother certified by
    her brother Walter.)

Ronemous, Edgar F. and Ella L. Clymer (3) -   July 9, 1889
    Place of marriage, Charlestown - Age of husband, 25 - Age of wife,
    20 - Both are Single - Both were born in Jefferson County, West
    Virginia - Both reside in Jefferson County, West Virginia.
    (Consent of bride's father in writing.)

Ronemous, Emma J. and John G. Unseld (3) -   February 3, 1881
    For further information see - Unseld, John G.

Ronemous, Emma J. and Oscar J. Blackford (3) -   December 12, 1882
    For further information see - Blackford, Oscar J.

Ronemous, Helen C. and Daniel G. Moler (3) -   March 20, 1866
    For further information see - Moler, Daniel G.

Ronemous, James A. and Sally H. Bane (3) -   April 25, 1878
    Place of marriage, Duffields - Age of husband, 24 - Age of wife,
    26 - Both are Single - Both were born in Jefferson County, West
    Virginia - Both reside in Jefferson County, West Virginia.

Ronemous, John and Miranda McCleary (2) -   (L) January 2, 1858

Ronemous, Maggie A. and Walter Harman (3) -   November 17, 1886
For further information see - Harman, Walter.

Ronemous, Maggie S. and Ambrose Hendricks (3) -   September 29, 1880
For further information see - Hendricks, Ambrose.

Ronemous, Melvin L. and Clara A. Derr (3) -   March 12, 1890
Place of marriage, Shepherdstown - Age of husband, 30 - Age of wife, 19 - Both are Single - Husband was born in Jefferson County, West Virginia - Wife was born in Frederick County, Maryland - Both reside in Jefferson County, West Virginia.

Ronemous, Mollie E. and Charles L. Barnhart (3) -   December 15, 1874
For further information see - Barnhart, Charles L.

Ronemous, Sarah E. and A. C. Hendricks (3) -   February 18, 1873
For further information see - Hendricks, A. C.

Ronemous, William and Mary Catharine Miller (2) -   (L) October 29, 1851

Ronemus, Annie L. and R. L. Osburn (3) -   November 3, 1868
For further information see - Osburn, R. L.

Ronemus, Christian and Elizabeth Dotts (1) -   December 17, 1812

Ronemus, Elizabeth and John Coons (1) -   December 17, 1805

Ronemus, Philip and Jane Thompson (1) -   March 4, 1807

Roof, Nannie C. and Jacob A. Garber (3) -   January 25, 1888
For further information see - Garber, Jacob A.

Rookes, Sydney Virginia and Francis Yates (2) -   (L) June 23, 1863
For further information see - Yates, Francis.

Roope, John and Annie Kellison (3) -   May 13, 1880
Place of marriage, Harpers Ferry - Age of husband, 23 - Age of wife, 18 - Both are Single - Husband was born in Maryland - Wife was born in Jefferson County, West Virginia - Husband resides at Pittsburg, Pennsylvania - Wife resides in Jefferson County, West Virginia. (Consent of bride's father in writing.)

Roots, Stephen and Nancy Cammeron (1) -   1827

Roper, America Virginia and John J. Vanmetre (2) -   (L) September 9, 1858

Roper, Ann Catharine and Mathew Dent (2) -   (L) May 24, 1853

Roper, Ann Catharine and Henry Schulz (2) -   (L) September 29, 1864
For further information see - Schulz, Henry.

Roper, Charles Edward (cold.) Lucinda Fox (3) -   May 11, 1886
Place of marriage, Kearneysville - Age of husband, 21 - Age of wife, 18 - Both are Single - Both were born in Jefferson County, West Virginia - Both reside in Jefferson County, West Virginia. (Consent of bride's father in person.)

Roper, George William (cold.) Emily Colston (3) - January 24, 1884
    Place of marriage, Shepherdstown - Age of husband, 21 - Age of wife,
    17 - Both are Single - Both were born in Jefferson County, West
    Virginia - Both reside in Jefferson County, West Virginia.
    (Consent of bride's father in person.)

Roper, L. V. (bride) and C. H. Goens (3) - November 19, 1868
    For further information see - Goens, C. H.

Roper, Octavia and Benjamin Hart (3) - July 10, 1873
    For further information see - Hart, Benjamin.

Roper, William H. and Sarah Goins (3) - July 14, 1873
    Place of marriage, Charlestown - Age of husband, 25 - Age of wife,
    22 - Both are Single - Both were born in Jefferson County, West
    Virginia - Both reside in Jefferson County, West Virginia.

Rose, J. and Margaret Arthur (3) - October 24, 1867
    Place of marriage, Jefferson County - Age of husband, 27 - Age of
    wife, 27 - Both are Single - Husband was born in Tennessee - Wife
    was born in Jefferson County, Virginia - Husband resides in
    Maryland - Wife resides in Jefferson County - Wife's parents are
    Elizabeth - Occupation of husband is Farmer.

Rose, Jacob and Mary E. Alexander (3) - November 14, 1866
    Age of husband, 24 - Age of wife, 23 - Both are Single - Husband was
    born in Warren County, Virginia - Wife was born in Clarke County,
    Virginia - Both reside in Jefferson County, West Virginia - Husband's
    parents are Levi and Susan A. Rose - Wife's parents are Joseph and
    Catharine Alexander - Occupation of husband is Farmer.

Rose, John and Helen McMaken (3) - September 30, 1884
    Place of marriage, near Shepherdstown - Age of husband, 28 - Age of
    wife, 26 - Both are Single - Husband was born in Warren County,
    Virginia - Wife was born in Jefferson County, West Virginia - Both
    reside in Jefferson County.

Rose, John Henry and Annie Grubb (3) - March 23, 1884
    Place of marriage, Harpers Ferry - Age of husband, 24 - Age of wife,
    22 - Both are Single - Both were born in Loudoun County, Virginia -
    Both reside in Jefferson County, West Virginia.

Rosenberger, Annie R. and J. T. Watson (3) - June 8, 1865
    For further information see - Watson, J. T.

Rosenberger, Charles E. and Sarah A. Lantsbaugh (3) - December 16, 1879
    Place of marriage, near Middleway - Age of husband, 26 - Age of wife,
    27 - Both are Single - Husband was born in Jefferson County, West
    Virginia - Wife was born in Pennsylvania - Both reside in Jefferson
    County, West Virginia.

Rosenberger, Christian Y. and Frances V. Watson (3) - December 21, 1865
    Place of marriage, near Leetown, Jefferson County - Age of husband,
    29 - Age of wife, 22 - Both are Single - Husband was born in
    Shenandoah County, Virginia - Wife was born in Clarke County,
    Virginia - Husband resides in Shenandoah County, Virginia - Wife
    resides in Jefferson County, West Virginia - Husband's parents are
    Jacob and Annie Rosenberger - Wife's parents are Ephraim and Eliza
    Watson - Occupation of husband is Farmer.

Rosenberger, Christina and Valentine Knupp (1) - .   July 28, 1833

Rosenberger, David and Elizabeth Schall (1) -   April 3, 1820

Rosenberger, David B. and Anne Maria Gruber (3) -   January 30, 1878
    Place of marriage, near Middleway - Age of husband, 26 - Age of
    wife, 31 - Both are Single - Both were born in Jefferson County,
    West Virginia - Both reside in Jefferson County, West Virginia.

Rosenberger, Elizabeth and Nicholas Shall (1) -   March 26, 1812

Rosenberger, Henry and Jane Shall (1) -   April 16, 1818

Rosenberger, Mary and George H. McClure (1) -   September 30, 1832

Rosenberger, Mary Ellen and Charles W. Gruber (3) -   November 3, 1875
    For further information see - Gruber, Charles W.

Ross, Andrew and Fannie McDaniel (3) -   November 30, 1865
    Place of marriage, near Bolivar, Jefferson County - Age of husband,
    21 - Age of wife, 17 - Husband is a Widower - Wife is Single -
    Husband was born at Charlestown, Jefferson County - Wife was born in
    Jefferson County - Both reside in Jefferson County - Husband's
    parents are Harry and Matilda Ross - Wife's parents are George W.
    and Ellen McDaniel - Occupation of husband is Farmer.

Ross, Andrew G. (colored) Mary Lee (3) - ..   (1870)
    Age of husband, 35 - Age of wife, 28 - Husband was born in
    Virginia - Wife was born in Jefferson County - Both reside in
    Jefferson County.

Ross, Charles (cold.) Emma McGill (3) -   February 10, 1886
    Place of marriage, Charlestown - Age of husband, 23 - Age of wife,
    23 - Both are Single - Husband was born in Clarke County, Virginia -
    Wife was born in Jefferson County, West Virginia - Both reside in
    Jefferson County, West Virginia.

Ross, Charles A. (cold.) Maria Jane Gay (3) -   September 8, 1886
    Place of marriage, near Charlestown - Age of husband, 22 - Age of
    wife, 20 - Both are Single - Husband was born in Jefferson County -
    Wife was born at Richmond - Both reside in Jefferson County, West
    Virginia. (Consent of bride's mother in writing.)

Ross, Charles E. and Sarah Catherine Hackley (2) -   (L) March 15, 1864
    Time of marriage, March 17, 1864 - Place of marriage, near
    Charlestown - Names, Charles E. Ross and Sarah Catherine Hackley -
    Age of husband, 21 years - Age of wife, 17 years, January 1, 1864 -
    Both are Single - Husband was born at New York City - Wife was born
    in Fauquier County, Virginia - Husband resides at Baltimore,
    Maryland - Wife resides in Jefferson County, Virginia - Husband's
    parents are Peter and Catharine Ross - Wife's parents are William
    and Martha Hackley - Occupation of husband is House and Sign
    Painter - License issued, March 15, 1864 - T. A. Moore, Clerk.

Ross, Fannie (cold.) David Lewis (3) -   April 4, 1878
    For further information see - Lewis, David.

Ross, Hetty (cold.) Madison Toliver (3) -   August 29, 1873
    For further information see - Toliver, Madison.

Ross, Isaac (cold.) Laura Helm (3) -   June 17, 1877
    Place of marriage, near Ripon - Age of husband, 24 - Age of wife,
    16 - Both are Single - Husband was born in Page County, Virginia -
    Wife was born in Clarke County, Virginia - Both reside in Jefferson
    County, West Virginia. (Father's consent certified by bride's
    uncle.)

Ross, John H. (cold.) Handy Page (3) -   December 2, 1888
    Place of marriage, Harpers Ferry - Age of husband, 56 - Age of wife,
    49 - Husband is a Widower - Wife is Single - Husband was born in
    Green County, Tennessee - Wife was born in Jefferson County, West
    Virginia - Both reside in Jefferson County, West Virginia.

Ross, John W. and Jane Taylor (3) -   (1869)
    Age of husband, 21 - Age of wife, 20 - Both were born in Virginia -
    Both reside in Jefferson County. (Father in person consents.)

Ross, Lydia and Thomas H. Carter (3) -   (1868)
    For further information see - Carter, Thomas H.

Ross, Mary and Charles Washington (3) -   June 8, 1867
    For further information see - Washington, Charles.

Ross, Mary (cold.) Archie Lucas (3) -   May 15, 1886
    For further information see - Lucas, Archie.

Ross, Sarah Ellen and Samuel Keats (3) -   April 13, 1882
    For further information see - Keats, Samuel.

Ross, Violet (cold.) John Mathews (3) -   July 13, 1887
    For further information see - Mathews, John.

Ross, William Allan (cold.) Nannie Busey (3) -   January 31, 1886
    Place of marriage, near Leetown - Age of husband, 23 - Age of wife,
    19 - Both are Single - Husband was born in Jefferson County, West
    Virginia - Wife was born in Jefferson County - Both reside in
    Jefferson County, West Virginia. (Consent of bride's father in
    person.)

Roulett, John W. and Mary Ellen Carlan (3) -   March 20, 1884
    Place of marriage, Charlestown - Age of husband, 43 - Age of wife,
    25 - Husband is a Widower - Wife is Single - Husband was born in
    Washington County, Maryland - Wife was born at Washington City -
    Both reside in Jefferson County, West Virginia.

Rouse, Milton and Mary C. Osburn (3) -   August 28, 1873
    Place of marriage, near Kabletown - Age of husband, 32 - Age of wife,
    27 - Both are Single - Husband was born in Frederick County,
    Maryland - Wife was born in Jefferson County, West Virginia - Both
    reside in Jefferson County, West Virginia.

Roush, C. R. and Maria Humrickhouse (3) -   October 23, 1872
    Place of marriage, Jefferson County - Age of husband, 27 - Age of
    wife, 20 - Both are Single - Husband was born in Berkeley County -
    Wife was born in Jefferson County, Virginia - Husband resides in
    Berkeley County - Wife resides in Jefferson County - Husband's
    parents are Hugh and Catherine - Wife's parents are S. P. and
    Virginia - Occupation of husband is Farming. (Consent of father.)

Roush, Nicholas and Mary Walpert (1) -   August 21, 1806

Rowan, Ann C. and William C. Orr Stump (3) - June 26, 1866
    For further information see - Stump, William C. Orr.

Rowan, Emily and Ambrose M. C. Cramer (1) - May 25, 1820

Rowan, Sarah J. (3) -
    For further information see - Beller, Frank L.

Rowe, Caroline and John Snodeal (2) - (L) February 11, 1853

Rowe, Harriet and Daniel Stewart (2) - (L) June 12, 1851

Rowland, John and Lydia Mullinix (1) - September 6, 1829

Rowland, Lucy A. and John Witherow (1) - November 5, 1834

Rowland, Lula B. and Straith Trussell (3) - December 31, 1889
    For further information see - Trussell, Straith.

Rowland, Mary E. and David A. **Wageley** (2) - (L) April 25, 1856

Rowles, Ann and Amos Janney (1) - January 12, 1826

Rowzee, Albert C. and Mary Belle Chase (3) - February 21, 1883
    Place of marriage, Shepherdstown - Age of husband, 23 - Age of wife, 23 - Both are Single - Husband was born in Prince George County, Maryland - Wife was born in Iowa - Husband resides at Washington City, D. C. - Wife resides in Jefferson County, West Virginia.

Roy, William (cold.) Julia Mash (3) - December 29, 1874
    Place of marriage, Rippon - Age of husband, 21 - Age of wife, 18 - Both are Single - Husband was born in Warren County, Virginia - Wife was born in Clarke County, Virginia - Both reside in Jefferson County, West Virginia. (Consent of bride's stepfather in person.)

Royston, Albert (cold.) Rosa McDowell (3) - September 10, 1890
    Place of marriage, Charlestown - Age of husband, 23 - Age of wife, 22 - Both are Single - Husband was born in Loudoun County, Virginia - Wife was born in Jefferson County, West Virginia - Both reside in Jefferson County, West Virginia.

Rucker, Barbara C. and Tilghman Easton (3) - April 25, 1878
    For further information see - Easton, Tilghman.

Ruckle, Margaret A. and Peter P. Cockrell (1) - June 28, 1847

Ruckle, Oliver P. and Margaret Ann Rogers (2) - (L) August 26, 1863
    Time of marriage, August 27, 1863 - Place of marriage, near Kearneysville - Names, Oliver P. Ruckle and Margaret Ann Rogers - Age of husband, 24 years - Age of wife, 20 - Both are Single - Husband was born at Baltimore, Maryland - Wife was born in Jefferson County, Virginia - Husband's residence at Baltimore, Maryland - Wife's residence in Jefferson County, Virginia - Husband's parents are Joseph N. and Louisa Ruckle - Wife's parents are Isaac V. and Drusilla Ann Rogers - Occupation of husband is Merchant - License issued, August 26, 1863 - Bride's father present - Thomas A. Moore, Clerk.

Ruckle, Samuel and Mary Butler (1) - October 21, 1830

Ruff, Louise Agnes and Joseph McVeave (3) -　　　　　　May 8, 1889
　　For further information see - McVeave, Joseph.

Ruhl, Geneva and A. J. Myers (3) -　　　　　　　　　November 20, 1883
　　For further information see - Myers, A. J.

Ruhl, Mary E. and David Beck (3) -　　　　　　　　　November 25, 1869
　　For further information see - Beck, David.

Ruhlman, John T. and Cornelia S. Engle (3) -　　　　　　(1869)
　　Age of husband, 28 - Age of wife, 24 - Husband is a Widower - Wife is
　　Single - Both were born in Jefferson County - Husband resides in
　　Illinois - Wife resides in Jefferson County - Husband's parents are
　　Adam T. - Wife's parents are Philip, Jr. and S. Ann - Occupation of
　　husband is Blacksmith.

Ruid, Catherine and John Jackson, Jr. (1) -　　　　　　September 28, 1809

Rumberger, George C. and Mattie V. Merchant (3) -　　September 2, 1872
　　Place of marriage, Jefferson County - Age of husband, 25 - Age of
　　wife, 22 - Both are Single - Husband was born in Washington County,
　　Maryland - Wife was born in Berkeley County, Virginia - Husband
　　resides at Cumberland, Maryland - Wife resides in Jefferson County,
　　West Virginia - Husband's parents are Pharus and Mary - Wife's
　　parents are Hiram and Racel - Occupation of husband is Tin Smith.

Runell, Ann and Genee Runesell (1) -　　　　　　　　　April 15, 1817

Runesell, Genee and Ann Runell (1) -　　　　　　　　　April 15, 1817

Ruperrow, Annie and Jessee Boyron (1) -　　　　　　　February 23, 1804

Rush, Ellen G. and A. R. McQuilkin (2) -　　　　　　(L) April 7, 1854
　　(Got by William A. Marshall who says both are of age.)

Rush, Jacob and Rose Marshall (3) -　　　　　　　　　November 30, 1865
　　Place of marriage, Presbyterian Church, Shepherdstown - Age of
　　husband, 27 - Age of wife, 22 - Both are Single - Husband was born
　　in Berkeley County, West Virginia - Wife was born in Jefferson
　　County, West Virginia - Husband resides in Berkeley County - Wife
　　resides in Jefferson County - Husband's parents are Jacob and Eliza
　　Rush - Wife's parents are James and Eliza Marshall - Occupation of
　　husband is Farmer.

Russ, Jere (cold.) Delia Brooks (3) -　　　　　　　　December 23, 1882
　　Place of marriage, Charlestown - Age of husband, 70 - Age of wife,
　　62 - Husband is Single - Wife is a Widow - Both were born in
　　Jefferson County, West Virginia - Both reside in Jefferson County,
　　West Virginia.

Russell, Arthur and Eliza Rob (1) -　　　　　　　　　May 29, 1804

Russell, Bettie E. and George W. Rice (3) -　　　　　October 18, 1866
　　For further information see - Rice, George W.

Russell, Dinah (cold.) John Minor (3) -　　　　　　　May 27, 1882
　　For further information see - Minor, John.

Russell, Elizabeth and William Schaeffer (1) -　　　　June 28, 1834

Russell, Ella and James William Armstrong (3) - April 15, 1875
    For further information see - Armstrong, James William.

Russell, James G. and Elizabeth Manuel (3) - October 5, 1871
    Place of marriage, Harpers Ferry - Age of husband, 21 - Age of wife, 22 - Both are Single - Husband was born in Harpers Ferry - Wife was born in Jefferson County - Both reside in Jefferson County - Husband's parents are Richard and Susan - Wife's parents are Joseph and Sidney - Occupation of husband is Rail Roadman.

Russell, Joseph L. and Harriet E. Allstadt (1) - November 20, 1832

Russell, Joseph L. and Sarah C. Power (2) - (L) November 7, 1860

Russell, Laura E. and Will F. Crutchley (3) - October 19, 1871
    For further information see - Crutchley, Will F.

Russell, Richard and Eliza Ann Graham (1) - November 26, 1835

Russell, Sally (cold.) Frank Baltimore (3) - June 11, 1887
    For further information see - Baltimore, Frank.

Russell, Sarah E. and William H. Fritts (3) - March 23, 1875
    For further information see - Fritts, William H.

Russell, Susan V. and Isaac N. Hodge (2) - (L) April 18, 1854
    (William Mader says the Lady is of age.)

Russell, Thomas and Deborah Crowl (2) - (L) December 30, 1854

Russell, Thomas H. and Henrietta Zimerman (1) - November 22, 1846

Russell, W. G., Jr. and Linda Avery (3) - May 23, 1883
    Place of marriage, Charlestown - Age of husband, 40 - Age of wife, 25 - Husband is a Widower - Wife is Single - Husband was born at Winchester, Virginia - Wife was born in State of Ohio - Husband resides at Winchester, Virginia - Wife resides in Jefferson County, West Virginia.

Rust, Ann Maria and Jefferson F. Bales (2) - (L) November 17, 1851

Rust, Ann Maria and Jefferson Bales (1) - November 18, 1851

Rust, Annie and Alfred Edwards (3) - December 10, 1868
    For further information see - Edwards, Alfred.

Rust, George Mansfield (cold.) Diana Robinson (3) - October 4, 1877
    Place of marriage, Jefferson County - Age of husband, 60 - Age of wife, 40 - Husband is a Widower - Wife is a Widow - Both were born in Jefferson County, West Virginia - Both reside in Jefferson County, West Virginia.

Rust, Harriet (cold.) Daniel Chase (3) - April 7, 1887
    For further information see - Chase, Daniel.

Rust, Henry D. and Anna M. Vanvactor (2) - (L) September 20, 1860

497

Rust, Henry D. and Rebecca Walters (3) -   October 23, 1872
   Place of marriage, Jefferson County - Age of husband, 36 - Age of
   wife, 31 - Husband is a Widower - Wife is Single - Husband was born
   in Berkeley - Wife was born in Jefferson County, Virginia - Both
   reside in Jefferson County - Husband's parents are Lemuel and
   Catherine - Wife's parents are Isaac and Mary - Occupation of
   husband is Carpenter.

Rust, Henry Edward and Alice Whalan (3) -   June 14, 1871
   Place of marriage, Jefferson County - Age of husband, 24 - Age of
   wife, 21 - Both are Single - Husband was born in Virginia - Wife was
   born in Jefferson County - Both reside in Jefferson County -
   Husband's parents are Henry and Lucinda - Wife's parents are Jerri
   and Frances - Occupation of husband is Whitewasher. (Consent Mo.)

Rust, Levina and Newton Lowry (3) -   March 17, 1875
   For further information see - Lowry, Newton.

Rust, Louisa and Levi Henderson (3) -   September 5, 1871
   For further information see - Henderson, Levi.

Rust, Margaret Ann and John A. Blake (2) -   (L) July 17, 1860

Rust, Philip (cold.) Susan Fox (3) -   February 8, 1879
   Place of marriage, near Kabletown - Age of husband, 26 - Age of
   wife, 18 - Both are Single - Husband was born in Jefferson County,
   West Virginia - Wife was born in Rockbridge County, Virginia - Both
   reside in Jefferson County, West Virginia. (Consent of bride's
   father in person.)

Rust, Samuel and Catherine Markwood (1) -   December 28, 1823

Rust, T. G. and M. A. Buckles (bride) (3) -   December 27, 1871
   Place of marriage, Jefferson County, West Virginia - Age of husband,
   28 - Age of wife, 21 - Both are Single - Both were born in Berkeley
   County - Husband resides at Frostburg, Maryland - Wife resides in
   Jefferson County, West Virginia - Husband's parents are Lemuel and
   Catharine - Wife's parents are John and Mary - Occupation of husband
   is Carpenter.

Rust, William and Mary A. Johnson (3) -   December 1866
   Age of husband, 58 - Age of wife, 21 - Husband is a Widower - Wife is
   Single - Husband was born at Front Royal, Warren County, Virginia -
   Wife was born at Summit Point, Jefferson County, West Virginia -
   Both reside at Charlestown, Jefferson County, West Virginia -
   Husband's parents are Moses and Judia Rust - Occupation of husband
   is Blacksmith.

Rutherford, Catharine B. and Francis M. Brown (2) -   (L) September 25, 1856

Rutherford, Drusilla A. and George L. Douglass (1) -   May 1832

Rutherford, Drusilla D. and William B. Packett (3) -   October 28, 1885
   For further information see - Packett, William B.

Rutherford, Mrs. E. V. and J. J. Watson (3) -   March 26, 1885
   For further information see - Watson, J. J.

Rutherford, Ellen D. and Cleon Moore (3) -   November 13, 1867
   For further information see - Moore, Cleon.

Rutherford, Gerard D. and Rachel Ann Twiggs (2) -   (L) August 8, 1864
    Time of marriage, August 9, 1864 - Palce of marriage, Jefferson
    County at Bride's Brother's - Names, Gerard D. Rutherford and Rachel
    Ann Twiggs - Age of husband, 22 years February 3, 1864 - Age of wife,
    20 years July, 1864 - Both are Single - Husband was born in Jefferson
    County, Virginia - Wife was born in Berkeley County, Virginia - Both
    reside in Jefferson County, Virginia - Names of husband's parents
    are Uriah and Phebe Rutherford - Names of wife's parents are
    Jeremiah and Catherine Twiggs - Occupation of husband is Soldier in
    Confederate Army - License issued August 8, 1864 - Consent of bride's
    mother given for her marriage; her father is dead - T. A. Moore,
    Clerk - Witness, Josiah (X) Wilson - T. A. Moore.

Rutherford, Mrs. Jane and James T. Athey (3) -   December 19, 1875
    For further information see - Athey, James T.

Rutherford, Jennie and John William Johnson (3) -   October 24, 1875
    For further information see - Johnson, John William.

Rutherford, John and Sarah Blue (1) -   December 18, 1832

Rutherford, John and Eliza Smith (3) -   December 14, 1873
    Place of marriage, near Shepherdstown - Age of husband, 65 - Age of
    wife, 30 - Husband is a Widower - Wife is Single - Husband was born
    in Berkeley County, West Virginia - Wife was born in Jefferson
    County, West Virginia - Both reside in Jefferson County, West
    Virginia.

Rutherford, John W. (cold.) Susanna Harris (3) -   May 26, 1881
    Place of marriage, Charlestown - Age of husband, 27 - Age of wife,
    27 - Both are Single - Husband was born in Berkeley County - Wife
    was born in Clarke County, Virginia - Both reside in Jefferson
    County, West Virginia.

Rutherford, John William (cold.) Omer Field (3) -   April 14, 1884
    Place of marriage, Charlestown - Age of husband, 29 - Age of wife,
    26 - Husband is a Widower - Wife is Single - Husband was born in
    Berkeley County, West Virginia - Wife was born in Kentucky - Both
    reside in Jefferson County, West Virginia.

Rutherford, Joseph Henry and Nancy Jane Mahaffy (2) -   (L) November 2, 1857

Rutherford, Mary and Archie H. Aisquith (3) -   July 13, 1868
    For further information see - Aisquith, Archie H.

Rutherford, Nancy M. and William Douglass (1) -   September 9, 1827

Rutherford, Richard D. and Elizabeth D. Forrest (3) -   February 10, 1876
    Place of marriage, Charlestown - Age of husband, 25 - Age of wife,
    23 - Both are Single - Husband was born in Jefferson County, West
    Virginia - Wife was born at Norfolk City - Both reside in Jefferson
    County, West Virginia.

Rutherford, Sarah M. and John W. Kennedy (2) -   (L) April 25, 1857

Rutherford, Thomas and Mary E. Duffield (1) -   December 9, 1835

499

Rutherford, Thomas R. and Fanny Reiley (3) - April 3, 1871
  Place of marriage, Jefferson County - Age of husband, 27 - Age of
  wife, 25 - Both are Single - Husband was born in Jefferson County -
  Wife was born in Virginia - Husband resides in Jefferson County -
  Wife resides in Missouri.

Rutherford, Virginia and William M. McMechen (3) - December 8, 1868
  For further information see - McMechen, William M.

Rutherford, W. S. and Rachel Jane Thompson (3) - March 21, 1866
  Place of marriage, Shepherdstown, Jefferson County - Age of husband,
  30 - Age of wife, 19 - Both are Single - Both were born in Berkeley
  County, West Virginia - Both reside in Jefferson County, West
  Virginia - Husband's parents are James and Elizabeth Rutherford -
  Wife's parents are Joseph and Mary Thompson - Occupation of husband
  is Shoemaker.

Ryan, A. L. (bride) and J. A. Singleton (3) - May 1, 1872
  For further information see - Singleton, J. A.

Ryan, Thomas D. and Amanda Britton (widow) (2) - (L) July 7, 1860

Ryon, R. H. and Martha Jane Gruber (2) - (L) September 20, 1859

Sadler, Harry and Anne Canvoisie (3) -   August 5, 1878
    Place of marriage, Charlestown - Age of husband, 25 - Age of wife,
    27 - Husband is Single - Wife is a Widow - Husband was born in
    Maryland - Wife was born in Augusta County, Virginia - Husband
    resides at Baltimore - Wife resides in Jefferson County, West
    Virginia.

Sadler, Leonard and Sarah Boley (1) -   March 2, 1819

Sagel, Alice M. and Lewis Frith (3) -   March 6, 1877
    For further information see - Frith, Lewis.

Sagle, Elizabeth and Zachariah Jenkins (1) -   March 18, 1819

Sagle, Henry and Delilah Jinkens (1) -   September 16, 1817

Sagle, Larrence C. and Minnie Estel Cox (3) -   December 1884
    Place of marriage, Harpers Ferry - Age of husband, 21 - Age of wife,
    20 - Both are Single - Both were born in Jefferson County, West
    Virginia - Both reside in Jefferson County, West Virginia.
    (Consent of bride's parents in writing.)

Sagle, Mary and William Wheatly (1) -   September 30, 1821

Sagle, Solomon and Fanny Fluke (3) -   August 31, 1871
    Age of husband, 50 - Age of wife, 27 - Husband is a Widower - Wife
    is Single - Both were born in Maryland - Both reside in Jefferson
    County - Occupation of husband is Farmer.

Sagle, William and Catharine Jenkens (1) -   June 15, 1826

Sagle, William and Mary Wheatley (1) -   July 12, 1832

SaintClair, Ann B. and Philip A. Anderson (3) -   November 2, 1870
    For further information see - Anderson, Philip A.

Sakeman, John and Mrs. Mary Sybole (widow) (2) -   (L) July 13, 1853

Salaen, Mary and S. D. Kennedy (3) -   June 22, 1869
    For further information see - Kennedy, S. D.

Salvin, Catharine and James A. Martin (3) -   (1869)
    For further information see - Martin, James A.

Sampson, John and Nancie Delaney (3) -   December 7, 1865
    Place of marriage, Shepherdstown, Jefferson County - Age of husband,
    49 - Age of wife, 28 - Both are Single - Husband was born in York
    County, Pennsylvania - Wife was born in Page County, Virginia - Both
    reside in Jefferson County - Husband's parents are Jacob and Mary
    Sampson - Occupation of husband is Shoemaker.

Sanbower, A. E. (bride) and J. H. Cookus (3) -   September 9, 1872
    For further information see - Cookus, J. H.

Sanbower, Ellen Dora and Griffin Taylor Buffington (3) -   August 18, 1878
    For further information see - Buffington, Griffin Taylor.

Sanbower, George W. and Lillie Lee Jones (3) -   June 5, 1884
    Place of marriage, Shepherdstown - Age of husband, 23 - Age of wife,
    19 - Both are Single - Husband was born in Loudoun County,
    Virginia - Wife was born in Jefferson County, West Virginia - Both
    reside in Jefferson County, West Virginia. (Consent of bride's
    father and mother in writing.)

Sanders, Augustian (colored) Louisa Payne (3) -   November 17, 1870
    Place of marriage, Jefferson County - Age of husband, 26 - Age of
    wife, 18 - Both were born in Virginia - Both reside in Jefferson
    County. (Mother gives consent.)

Sanders, Joshua (cold.) Charlotte Slaughter (3) -   August 16, 1883
    Place of marriage, Charlestown - Age of husband, 41 - Age of wife,
    21 - Both are Single - Husband was born in Pennsylvania - Wife was
    born in Jefferson County, West Virginia - Both reside in Jefferson
    County, West Virginia.

Sanderson, Jenkin (colored) Eliza Ranson (3) -   August 4, 1870
    Palce of marriage, Jefferson County - Age of husband, 28 - Age of
    wife, 26 - Husband was born in Virginia - Wife was born in Jefferson
    County - Both reside in Jefferson County.

Sanner, William C. and Florence C. Wilson (3) -   August 18, 1885
    Place of marriage, Harpers Ferry - Age of husband, 25 - Age of wife,
    25 - Both are Single - Both were born at Baltimore - Both reside at
    Baltimore, Maryland.

Santemyers, Isaac F. and Alverta Arnett (3) -   November 27, 1889
    Place of marriage, Harpers Ferry - Age of husband, 48 - Age of wife,
    32 - Husband is a Widower - Wife is Single - Husband was born in
    Warren County, Virginia - Wife was born in Loudoun County, Virginia -
    Husband resides in Loudoun County, Virginia - Wife resides in
    Jefferson County, West Virginia.

Sappington, Ellen and William A. Douglas (2) -   (L) June 9, 1852

Sappington, Ellen and William A. Douglass (1) -   June 9, 1852

Sappington, Fannie Shep and C. Horace Gallaher (3) -   October 23, 1872
    For further information see - Gallaher, C. Horace.

Sappington, George W. and Eliza J. Cramer (1) -   January 8, 1834

Sappington, George W. and Susan Belinda Lambert (2) -   (L) March 20, 1851

Sappington, Joseph L. and Mary E. Wooddy (3) -   January 5, 1876
    Place of marriage, Charles Town - Age of husband, 21 - Age of wife,
    21 - Both are Single - Both were born in Jefferson County, West
    Virginia - Both reside in Jefferson County, West Virginia.

Sappington, Mary E. and Thomas M. Vansant (1) -   March 13, 1844

Sappington, Oliver H. B. and Caroline Webster (1) -   March 30, 1848

Sappington, Rachel and George Lillibridge (1) -   March 8, 1827

Sappington, Sally A. and John P. Oden (3) -   December 17, 1868
    For further information see - Oden, John P.

Sappington, Susan R. and Denis Weinbrenner (3) -   (1869)
   For further information see - Weinbrenner, Denis.

Sargeant, George Washington and Margaret Bovan (2) -   (L) March 10, 1851

Sargent, William and Elizabeth Frazier (1) -   December 27, 1821

Saunders, Annie (cold.) Albert Washington (3) -   November 13, 1889
   For further information see - Washington, Albert.

Saunders, Catherine C. and James W. Armour (1) -   November 14, 1823

Saunders, Harriot M. and Briant O'Bannon (1) -   February 4, 1828

Saunders, Virginia and Charles W. Brooks (3) -   November 11, 1869
   For further information see - Brooks, Charles W.

Saylor, Jacob F. and Laura Lavinia Vinsonheller (2) -   (L) October 2, 1850

Saylor, Jacob F. and Laura Lavinia Vinsonheller (1) -   October 2, 1850

Saylor, Mary E. and John W. Kidwell (2) -   (L) August 2, 1855

Scarboro, Harold and Frances E. Fantom (3) -   October 6, 1887
   Place of marriage, near Charlestown - Age of husband, 25 - Age of
   wife, 22 - Both are Single - Both were born in Maryland - Husband
   resides in Maryland - Wife resides in Jefferson County, West
   Virginia.

Scarff, Barton and Mary Ann Everhart (1) -   March 10, 1822

Scarlet, John and Nancy Near (1) -   June 4, 1835

Scarlet, Margaret and Benony Eckles (2) -   (L) August 4, 1855

Scarlet, Richard and Clara F. Shewbridge (3) -   February 10, 1887
   Place of marriage, Harpers Ferry - Age of husband, 25 - Age of wife,
   17 - Both are Single - Both were born in Jefferson County, West
   Virginia - Both reside in Jefferson County. (Consent of bride's
   father in writing.)

Scarlet, Sarah and Joseph Golden (3) -   November 15, 1865
   For further information see - Golden, Joseph.

Scarlet, William and Christiana Piper (1) -   June 25, 1807

Scarlett, Catherine and Daniel Eakle (1) -   June 4, 1835

Scarlett, John William and Stacey Ann Staub (widow) (2) - (L) October 31, 1850
   (Samuel Fine prest.)

Scarlett, John W. and Stacy Ann Staub (widow) (1) -   November 1, 1850

Scarlett, Ritha Ann and George Earl (3) -   April 19, 1876
   For further information see - Earl, George.

Schaeffer, Deborah E. and Joseph L. Eichelberger (2) - (L) September 30, 1854

Schaeffer, Emanuel R. and Sarah F. Moler (3) - October 24, 1865
Place of marriage, Jefferson County - Age of husband, 22 years - Age of wife, 22 years - Both are Single - Both were born in Jefferson County, West Virginia - Both reside in Jefferson County - Husband's parents are William and Elizabeth Schaeffer - Wife's parents are Daniel and Mary Jane Moler - Occupation of husband is Farmer.

Schaeffer, Frances and Daniel Heflebower (3) - November 4, 1873
For further information see - Heflebower, Daniel.

Schaeffer, John W. and Annie E. McGarry (3) - January 31, 1871
Place of marriage, Jefferson County - Age of husband, 25 - Age of wife, 25 - Both are Single - Both were born in Jefferson County - Both reside in Jefferson County - Husband's parents are William and Elizabeth - Wife's parents are John and Sarah - Occupation of husband is Farmer.

Schaeffer, Martha Ann and Isaac N. Renner (2) - (L) April 24, 1858

Schaeffer, William and Elizabeth Russell (1) - June 28, 1834

Schall, David and Elizabeth Kime (1) - October 13, 1816

Schall, Elizabeth and David Rosenberger (1) - April 3, 1820

Scheidaunt, Andrew and Mary Griffith (1) - 1825

Schell, Elizabeth and David Moyer (1) - March 1822

Schilling, Charlotte M. and Stephen J. Murray (3) - (1870)
For further information see - Murray, Stephen J.

Schilling, Joseph P. and Mary F. Cavalier (3) - (1870)
Age of husband, 22 - Age of wife, 21 - Both were born at Harpers Ferry - Both reside at Harpers Ferry.

Schley, Hetty J. (cold.) Andrew Hunter (3) - September 2, 1875
For further information see - Hunter, Andrew.

Schley, John E. and May V. Turner (1) - October 24, 1844

Schley, Mary V. and F. W. Muzzy (3) - April 11, 1882
For further information see - Muzzy, F. W.

Schley, Towner and Ida Virginia Harrison (3) - October 22, 1873
Place of marriage, Shepherdstown - Age of husband, 27 - Age of wife, 19 - Both are Single - Husband was born in Jefferson County, West Virginia - Wife was born in Berkeley County, West Virginia - Both reside in Jefferson County, West Virginia. (Consent of bride's father in writing.)

505

Schmidt, Jacob and Anna Smithoats (2) - (L) April 13, 1861
  Time of marriage, April 15, 1861 - Place of marriage, Bolivar -
  Names of parties, Jacob Schmidt and Anna Smithoats - Age of husband,
  25 years - Age of wife, 19 years - Both are Single - Place of
  husband's birth was Kingdom of Bavaria - Place of wife's birth was
  Same - Husband's residence is Berkeley County - Wife's residence is
  Bolivar - Names of husband's parents are Unknown - Joseph Smithoats
  and Margaret (now Will, nee Hibler) - Occupation of husband is
  Armorer - Given under my hand this 13th day of April - John George
  Will.

Schmitt, Ellen Virginia and John Buzzard (3) - December 16, 1873
  For further information see - Buzzard, John.

Schmitt, Fannie M. and Lewis F. Foreman (3) - March 11, 1890
  For further information see - Foreman, Lewis F.

Schonkee, William and Oregon Locke (3) - June 14, 1865

Schonkel, Orregon and James Lee Shewbridge (3) - January 15, 1880
  For further information see - Shewbridge, James Lee.

Schoppart, Mary and James K. Whittington (2) - (L) February 13, 1865
  For further information see - Whittington, James K.

Schoppert, Dennis M. and Virginia B. Deck (3) - May 10, 1881
  Place of marriage, Shepherdstown - Age of husband, 21 - Age of wife,
  22 - Both are Single - Both were born in Jefferson County, West
  Virginia - Both reside in Jefferson County, West Virginia.

Schoppert, George A. and Margaret Elizabeth Cookus (3) - November 27, 1873
  Place of marriage, Shepherdstown - Age of husband, 27 - Age of wife,
  23 - Both are Single - Husband was born in Berkeley County, West
  Virginia - Wife was born in Jefferson County, West Virginia - Both
  reside in Jefferson County, West Virginia.

Schoppert, Jennie and James Drish (3) - September 26, 1871
  For further information see - Drish, James.

Schoppert, John H. and Eliza Harris (3) - October 23, 1866
  Place of marriage, A. Harris', Shepherdstown - Age of husband, 22 -
  Age of wife, 22 - Both are Single - Husband was born in Berkeley
  County, West Virginia - Wife was born in Jefferson County, West
  Virginia - Husband resides in Jefferson County, West Virginia - Wife
  resides at Shepherdstown, Jefferson County, West Virginia - Husband's
  parents are Joseph and Margaret E. Schoppert - Wife's parents are
  Abraham and Sarah A. Harris - Occupation of husband is Cabinet Maker.

Schoppert, Nannie and John J. W. Hulver (3) - September 13, 1874
  For further information see - Hulver, John J. W.

Schoppert, Sue and David W. Hannah (3) - March 1, 1871
  For further information see - Hannah, David W.

Schoppertt, Margaret Eliza and John Shafer Gaster (3) - February 12. 1880
  For further information see - Gaster, John Shafer.

Schreck, Charles H. and Ella Fidler (3) -　　　　　　　　　August 22, 1887
　　Place of marriage, Harpers Ferry - Age of husband, 22 - Age of wife,
　　21 - Both are Single - Both were born in Jefferson County, West
　　Virginia - Both reside in Jefferson County, West Virginia.

Schulz, Henry and Ann Catharine Roper (2) -　　　　　(L) September 29, 1864
　　Time of marriage, September 29, 1864 - Place of marriage, Harpers
　　Ferry - Names of parties, Henry Schulz and Ann Catharine Roper - Age
　　of husband, 28 years - Age of wife, 28 years - Husband is Single -
　　Wife is divorced from former husband, H. Dent - Place of husband's
　　birth was Kingdom of Prussia - Place of wife's birth was Jefferson
　　County, Virginia - Husband's residence is at City of Philadelphia -
　　Wife's residence is Jefferson County, Virginia - Names of husband's
　　parents are John and Louisa Schulz - Names of wife's parents are
　　James and Elizabeth Roper - Occupation of husband is Hotel and
　　Livery Stable Keeper - License issued September 29, 1864 - T. A.
　　Moore, Clerk.

Schuster, George M. and Sarah E. Turk (3) -　　　　　　　　February 5, 1874
　　Place of marriage, Harpers Ferry - Age of husband, 21 - Age of wife,
　　21 - Both are Single - Both were born in Jefferson County, West
　　Virginia - Husband resides at New York City - Wife resides in
　　Jefferson County, West Virginia.

Scofield, Jesse M. and Mary A. Cunningham (1) -　　　　　　　April 13, 1829

Scollay, Eleanor G. and Samuel J. C. Moore (2) -　　　(L) December 12, 1850

Scollay, Eleanor G. and Samuel J. C. Moore (1) -　　　　　December 12, 1850

Scollay, Elizabeth and Powhatan R. Page (2) -　　　　　(L) November 10, 1856

Scollay, Harriet L. and A. Mason Evans (3) -　　　　　　　November 27, 1867
　　For further information see - Evans, A. Mason.

Scollay, Mary M. and George W. Nelson (3) -　　　　　　　　October 17, 1865
　　For further information see - Nelson, George W.

Scollay, Samuel and Harriet Lowndes (1) -　　　　　　　　　January 21, 1823

Scott, Eliza and Amos Kopp (3) -　　　　　　　　　　　　　　　July 7, 1871
　　For further information see - Kopp, Amos.

Scott, John and Augusta J. Swartzwelder (3) -　　　　　　November 19, 1885
　　Place of marriage, Shepherdstown - Age of husband, 27 - Age of wife,
　　24 - Both are Single - Husband was born at Lynchburg, Virginia -
　　Wife was born at Winchester, Virginia - Husband resides at Waco,
　　Texas - Wife resides in Jefferson County, West Virginia.

Scott, Maggie C. and Thomas E. Nininger (3) -　　　　　　　October 18, 1888
　　For further information see - Nininger, Thomas E.

Scott, Mary J. and Thomas McFall (3) -　　　　　　　　　　　October 16, 1871
　　For further information see - McFall, Thomas.

Scott, Rosa A. (cold.) William A. Arter (3) -　　　　　　　　April 24, 1878
　　For further information see - Arter, William A.

507

Seal, G. A. and F. T. Grim (bride) (3) - September 30, 1872
  Place of marriage, Jefferson County - Age of husband, 22 - Age of wife, 18 - Both are Single - Both were born at Winchester, Virginia - Husband resides at Washington, D. C. - Wife resides at Winchester, Virginia - Husband's parents are G. R. and E. Seal - Wife's parents are Charles and A. V. - Occupation of husband is Plumber and C. (Ann V. Grim.)

Sealock, Craton and Mrs. Lizzie Foreman (3) - January 6, 1878
  Place of marriage, Harpers Ferry - Age of husband, 30 - Age of wife, 36 - Husband is Single - Wife is a Widow - Husband was born in Warren County, Virginia - Both reside in Jefferson County, West Virginia.

Sealy, Jane (cold.) Joseph Staley (3) - June 23, 1881
  For further information see - Staley, Joseph.

Seaman, Hiram Baldwin and Ann P. W. Middleton (1) - March 24, 1829

Seaman, Joseph and Nancy Deevers (1) - March 13, 1817

Seanafer, George and Mary Ann Whip (1) - December 5, 1816

Seay, Sallie A. and Andrew Jackson Morningstar (3) - January 9, 1868
  For further information see - Morningstar, Andrew Jackson.

Sechrist, William F. and Annie A. Frazier (3) - April 30, 1890
  Place of marriage, Shepherdstown - Age of husband, 36 - Age of wife, 37 - Both are Single - Husband was born in Hampshire County, West Virginia - Wife was born in Jefferson County, West Virginia - Both reside in Jefferson County, West Virginia.

Seckman, Benjamin M. and Gennet C. McDaniels (3) - November 24, 1868
  Place of marriage, Jefferson County - Age of husband, 21 - Age of wife, 19 - Both are Single - Husband was born in Berkeley County - Wife was born in Jefferson, Virginia - Husband resides in Berkeley County - Wife resides in Jefferson County - Husband's parents are David and Nannie - Wife's parents are S. and Ellen - Occupation of husband is Farmer.

Sefras, Mary and Samuel Moore (3) - December 16, 1868
  For further information see - Moore, Samuel.

Seglar, Jacob and Sarah Storm (1) - November 29, 1823

Seibert, Charles J. and Mollie Gilbert (3) - July 7, 1885
  Place of marriage, Charlestown - Age of husband, 40 - Age of wife, 28 - Both are Single - Husband was born in Frederick County, Virginia - Wife was born in Pennsylvania - Husband resides in Kansas - Wife resides in Jefferson County.

Seibert, Mrs. Fanny C. and David M. Deck (3) - December 11, 1879
  For further information see - Deck, David M.

Seibert, J. E. and Fannie M. Trump (3) - December 24, 1888
  Place of marriage, near Kearneysville - Age of husband, 28 - Age of wife, 23 - Both are Single - Husband was born in Berkeley County, West Virginia - Wife was born in Jefferson County, West Virginia - Both reside in Jefferson County, West Virginia.

Seibert, Jennie (cold.) John Flint (3) -   May 13, 1873
   For further information see - Flint, John.

Seibert, John and Elizabeth B. Wiggenton (3) -   November 24, 1868
   Place of marriage, Jefferson County - Age of husband, 35 - Age of
   wife, 23 - Both are Single - Husband was born in Berkeley County,
   Virginia - Wife was born in Jefferson County, Virginia - Husband
   resides in Frederick County, Virginia - Wife resides in Jefferson
   County - Husband's parents are Jacob F. and Ruhanah - Wife's parents
   are Benjamin and Rebecca - Occupation of husband is Dentist.

Seibert, Lillie and William H. Mesener (3) -   December 27, 1887
   For further information see - Mesener, William H.

Seibert, Martha and George Johnson (3) -   October 2, 1872
   For further information see - Johnson, George.

Seibert, Wesley (cold.) Josephine Hook (3) -   January 15, 1879
   Place of marriage, Shepherdstown - Age of husband, 33 - Age of wife,
   23 - Both are Single - Both were born in Jefferson County, West
   Virginia - Both reside in Jefferson County, West Virginia.

Seifert, Charles P. and Sarah Jane Dillow (3) -   September 23, 1886
   Place of marriage, Harpers Ferry - Age of husband, 23 - Age of wife,
   20 - Both are Single - Husband was born in Pennsylvania - Wife was
   born in Jefferson County, West Virginia - Both reside in Jefferson
   County, West Virginia. (Consent of bride's father in writing.)

Seigel, David and Ann Catharine Medler (2) -   (L) September 7, 1857

Seins, George (colored) Becky Snyder (3) -   May 10, 1870
   Place of marriage, Jefferson County - Age of husband, 23 - Age of
   wife, 26 - Husband was born in Virginia - Wife was born in Jefferson
   County - Both reside in Jefferson County.

Selby, Eliza C. and John F. Hamtramick (1) -   December 1825

Selby, Otho and Jennie Feagans (3) -   November 26, 1872
   Place of marriage, Jefferson County - Age of husband, 23 - Age of
   wife, 25 - Both are Single - Husband was born in Maryland - Wife was
   born in Virginia - Both reside in West Virginia - Husband's parents
   are Richard and Pricilla - Wife's parents are Silas and Sarah -
   Occupation of husband is Carpenter.

Selden, Andrew K. and Meta B. Kearsley (3) -   November 5, 1879
   Place of marriage, Charlestown - Age of husband, 25 - Age of wife,
   20 - Both are Single - Both were born in Jefferson County, West
   Virginia - Both reside in Jefferson County, West Virginia.
   (Consent of bride's father in writing.)

Selden, Elizabeth Gray and Robert T. Jasper (3) -   October 18, 1876
   For further information see - Jasper, Robert T.

Selden, John and Sarah D. Kennedy (2) -   (L) January 4, 1858

Selig, Frederick and Mary Wager (1) -   January 1, 1807

Seller, Elizabeth and John McMullin (1) -   October 14, 1827

Selser, Rawleigh and Mary Ann Kreps (1) -   July 28, 1825

Sencenny, John C. and Margaret A. Hendricks (2) -   (L) October 10, 1860

Sencindiver, George L. and Ella N. Yantis (3) -   April 26, 1883
   Place of marriage, Harpers Ferry - Age of husband, 39 - Age of wife,
   23 - Both are Single - Husband was born in Berkeley County, West
   Virginia - Wife was born in Jefferson County, West Virginia -
   Husband resides in Berkeley County, West Virginia - Wife resides in
   Jefferson County, West Virginia.

Sennor, William and Georgia Roberts (3) -   July 12, 1868
   Place of marriage, Jefferson County - Age of husband, 21 - Age of
   wife, 19 - Both are Single - Husband was born in England - Wife was
   born in Virginia - Husband resides in England - Wife resides in
   Virginia - Wife's parents are Mary - Occupation of husband is Weaver.

Sephus, Benjamin (cold.) Sally Wood (3) -   January 23, 1875
   Place of marriage, Shepherdstown - Age of husband, 23 - Age of wife,
   19 - Both are Single - Both were born in Jefferson County, West
   Virginia - Both reside in Jefferson County, West Virginia.

Sergins, Nathaniel and Rebeca Ann Frame (1) -   July 15, 1828

Sexton, Caroline and William Hafner (3) -   December 20, 1877
   For further information see - Hafner, William.

Sexton, James and Caroline Dorsey (2) -   (L) February 21, 1857

Shackfort, John and Mary E. Carper (3) -   August 1, 1878
   Place of marriage, Charlestown - Age of husband, 35 - Age of wife,
   25 - Both are Single - Husband was born in Culpeper County,
   Virginia - Wife was born in Frederick County, Virginia - Both reside
   in Jefferson County, West Virginia.

Shackleford, Julia Ann and David Dillow (2) -   (L) August 10, 1857

Shadwell, Amelia and Henry Risner (1) -   March 22, 1833

Shadwell, Sarah and John Bayless (1) -   1827

Shafer, Mrs. Margaret and Henry S. Homer (3) -   January 13, 1886
   For further information see - Homer, Henry S.

Shall, David and Jane Blue (1) -   March 18, 1819

Shall, George and Rebecca Thomas (1) -   February 4, 1819

Shall, Jane and Henry Rosenberger (1) -   April 16, 1818

Shall, John and Sally Kime (1) -   March 11, 1813

Shall, Margaret and John Kime (1) -   October 3, 1816

Shall, Nicholas and Elizabeth Rosenberger (1) -   March 26, 1812

Shambaugh, Maggie V. and Edmun F. Robinson (3) -   August 11, 1880
   For further information see - Robinson, Edmun F.

Shambaugh, Mary Jane and Robert Painter (3) -   October 31, 1871
   For further information see - Painter, Robert.

Shamblain, James (cold.) Sallie Pearce (3) - . April 24, 1884
  Place of marriage, Charlestown - Age of husband, 32 - Age of wife, 20 - Husband is a Widower - Wife is Single - Husband was born in Jefferson County, West Virginia - Wife was born in Jefferson County - Husband resides in Jefferson County - Wife resides in Jefferson County, West Virginia. (Father of bride consents in writing.)

Shamblin, Mary C. and Thomas Dailey (3) - . October 2, 1890
  For further information see - Dailey, Thomas.

Shambling, Deborah and Leander Jenkins (1) - December 14, 1826

Shane, David and Lydia Strawbridge (1) - January 12, 1833

Shaner, Alexander J. and Georgianna Swann (2) - (L) June 9, 1851
  (Wit. S. H. Fowler.)

Shaner, Annie F. and William T. Morris (3) - September 21, 1879
  For further information see - Morris, William T.

Shaner, Ellanora and Turner Wysong Maddex (3) - September 7, 1886
  For further information see - Maddex, Turner Wysong.

Shaner, John and Nancy Hylton (1) - April 24, 1810

Shaner, John Wesley and Fanny Kate McBee (3) - (1884)
  Place of marriage, Shepherdstown - Age of husband, 27 - Age of wife, 24 - Both are Single - Both were born in Jefferson County, West Virginia - Both reside in Jefferson County, West Virginia.

Shaner, Laura B. and George W. Brooke (3) - May 9, 1872
  For further information see - Brooke, George W.

Shanks, John T. and C. Peachy Willis (2) - (L) May 27, 1857

Shannon, L. C. and Henry Wilt (3) - February 26, 1868
  For further information see - Wilt, Henry.

Shanton, Mary and Thornton Reed (3) - January 11, 1872
  For further information see - Reed, Thornton.

Shanton, Mary (cold.) Thornton Reed (3) - September 15, 1874
  For further information see - Reed, Thornton.

Sharff, George and Nancy Edwards (1) - January 2, 1838

Sharff, Jacob and Rebecca Keyes (1) - April 17, 1832

Sharff, Lucy E. and John S. Grantham (1) - May 9, 1850

Sharp, Mary and Peter Crowl (1) - October 24, 1816

Shauck, Harriet A. and George Harris (2) - (L) June 14, 1854

Shaul, Frances and Thomas Watson (1) - May 3, 1832

Shaull, Bartholomew and Sarah Watson (1) 1824/1825

Shaull, Clara and Kirk Hardesty (3) - April 15, 1869
  For further information see - Hardesty, Kirk.

Shaull, Elizabeth and James Watson (1) - August 5, 1834

Shaull, Ellen Jane and J. F. Shaull (1) - September 3, 1844

Shaull, Emma and Washington Crawford (3) - February 27, 1877
For further information see - Crawford, Washington.

Shaull, Fanny Elizabeth and John W. Philapy (2) - (L) May 27, 1859

Shaull, George B. and Katy F. Murphy (3) - January 5, 1882
Place of marriage, Middleway - Age of husband, 32 - Age of wife, 21 - Both are Single - Husband was born in Berkeley County, West Virginia - Wife was born in Shenandoah County, Virginia - Both reside in Jefferson County, West Virginia.

Shaull, J. F. and Ellen Jane Shaull (1) - September 3, 1844

Shaull, John J. and Lydia E. Lewis (3) - March 30, 1869
Place of marriage, Jefferson County - Age of husband, 28 - Age of wife, 22 - Both are Single - Both were born in Jefferson County - Both reside in Jefferson County - Husband's parents are N. S. and Mary - Wife's parents are S. and Mary - Occupation of husband is Farmer.

Shaull, John V. and Lucy J. Barnes (2) - (L) September 21, 1859

Shaull, Joseph M. and Ida M. Watson (3) - November 21, 1888
Place of marriage, near Middleway - Age of husband, 27 - Age of wife, 23 - Both are Single - Both were born in Jefferson County, West Virginia - Both reside in Jefferson County, West Virginia.

Shaull, Mary C. and James W. Benner (3) - January 11, 1870
For further information see - Benner, James W.

Shaull, Rebecca Ann and Remington S. Lock (2) - (L) December 19, 1853

Shaull, Rosanna E. and J. W. McGinnis (2) - (L) February 5, 1861

Shaull, Thomas M. and Nannie F. Littleton (3) - October 24, 1871
Place of marriage, Jefferson County - Age of husband, 27 - Age of wife, 20 - Both are Single - Both were born in Virginia - Both reside in West Virginia - Husband's parents are Nicholas and Mary - Wife's parents are Charles J. and Amanda - Occupation of husband is Farmer.

Shaull, Valentine and Fanny Moore (2) - (L) January 2, 1851

Shaull, Valentine and Fanny Moore (1) - January 2, 1851

Shaull, Winfield S. and Mary C. Lewis (3) - April 15, 1874
Place of marriage, County - Age of husband, 25 - Age of wife, 24 - Both are Single - Both were born in Jefferson County, West Virginia - Both reside in Jefferson County, West Virginia.

Shaw, Daniel (cold.) Fanny Flint (3) - December 16, 1880
Place of marriage, Shepherdstown - Age of husband, 26 - Age of wife, 22 - Both are Single - Husband was born in State of Maryland - Wife was born in Jefferson County, West Virginia - Both reside in Jefferson County, West Virginia.

Shearer, Archibald and Ann C. Baker (1) -   May 11, 1826

Shearer, Eugene and Lucy L. Southards (3) -   December 5, 1889
     Place of marriage, Harpers Ferry - Age of husband, 23 - Age of wife,
     22 - Both are Single - Husband was born at Staunton, Virginia - Wife
     was born in Ohio - Husband resides at Staunton, Virginia - Wife
     resides in Jefferson County, West Virginia.

Sheehan, Denis and Julia Reiley (3) -   August 8, 1871
     Place of marriage, Harpers Ferry - Age of husband, 62 - Age of wife,
     35 - Husband is a Widower - Wife is Single - Both were born in
     Ireland - Husband resides in Virginia - Wife resides in West
     Virginia - Husband's parents are John and Catherine - Wife's parents
     are Thomas and Julia - Occupation of husband is Farmer.

Sheeley, Benjamin and Ann Crusen (1) -   August 7, 1806

Sheeley, David and Elizabeth Hornsby (1) -   February 27, 1806

Sheerer, Margaret and William Story (1) -   January 21, 1833

Sheets, C. L. and Rosa C. Mason (3) -   December 29, 1888
     Place of marriage, Harpers Ferry - Age of husband, 24 - Age of wife,
     21 - Both are Single - Husband resides in Virginia - Wife resides in
     Jefferson County, West Virginia.

Sheets, Clara A. and D. S. Earnshaw (3) -   December 23, 1885
     For further information see - Earnshaw, D. S.

Sheets, Mollie and Mason Young (3) -   August 2, 1870
     For further information see - Young, Mason.

Sheetz, Ann and George W. Vanhorn (1) -   September 23, 1830

Sheetz, D. M. and Annie M. Young (3) -   January 16, 1868
     Place of marriage, Jefferson County - Age of husband, 44 - Age of
     wife, 31 - Husband is a Widower - Wife is Single - Both were born in
     Jefferson County - Both reside in Jefferson.

Sheetz, George T. and Luranna O'Bannon (3) -   June 17, 1875
     Place of marriage, Charlestown - Age of husband, 30 - Age of wife,
     32 - Both are Single - Both were born in Jefferson County, West
     Virginia - Husband resides in State of Maryland - Wife resides in
     Jefferson County, West Virginia.

Sheetz, J. S. and Iola Tanner (3) -   September 19, 1887
     Place of marriage, Shepherdstown - Age of husband, 27 - Age of wife,
     23 - Both are Single - Husband was born in Jefferson County, West
     Virginia - Both reside in Jefferson County, West Virginia.

Sheetz, Jacob and Elizabeth Miller (1) -   May 30, 1809

Sheetz, Jacob S. and Ellen Wisenall (2) -   (L) April 13, 1857

Sheetz, John W. and Pheobe Ann Wade (2) -   (L) March 20, 1854

Sheetz, Marietta and Zephaniah Bane (2) -   (L) December 18, 1854

Sheetz, Samuel and Elizabeth Clark (1) -   July 28, 1818

Sheetz, Samuel and Elizabeth Reynolds (3) - July 22, 1869
   Place of marriage, Jefferson County - Age of husband, 90 - Age of
   wife, 42 - Husband resides in Jefferson County, Wife resides in
   West Virginia.

Sheffer, Mary (cold.) Thomas H. Briscoe (3) - June 14, 1883
   For further information see - Briscoe, Thomas H.

Shell, Angelina and George Newton Moler (3) - January 25, 1883
   For further information see - Moler, George Newton.

Shell, Catherine and Abram Shoe (1) - April 5, 1812

Shell, John and Rebecca Vanmetre (1) - January 31, 1819

Shell, John and Margaret Edwards (1) - December 24, 1845

Shell, John R. and Lina P. Walker (3) - November 3, 1875
   Place of marriage, near Shepherdstown - Age of husband, 27 - Age of
   wife, 23 - Both are Single - Husband was born in Berkeley County,
   West Virginia - Wife was born in Jefferson County, West Virginia -
   Both reside in Jefferson County, West Virginia.

Shell, Rosa and Joseph Waldeck (3) - May 27, 1886
   For further information see - Waldeck, Joseph.

Shell, Virginia L. and William W. Myers (3) - February 6, 1877
   For further information see - Myers, William W.

Shell, Wilmer L. and Bettie E. Griffith (3) - March 6, 1888
   Place of marriage, Terrapin Neck - Age of husband, 21 - Age of wife,
   19 - Both are Single - Husband was born in Jefferson County, West
   Virginia - Wife was born in Maryland - Both reside in Jefferson
   County, West Virginia. (Consent of bride's father and mother in
   writing.)

Shelly, Augusta E. and George M. Derrow (3) - October 25, 1886
   For further information see - Derrow, George M.

Shelton, George (cold.) Winnie Johnson (3) - August 22, 1881
   Place of marriage, Charlestown - Age of husband, 31 - Age of wife,
   22 - Husband is Single - Wife is a Widow - Husband was born in
   Fauquier County, Virginia - Wife was born in Jefferson County, West
   Virginia - Both reside in Jefferson County, West Virginia.

Shelton, Morton (cold.) Charlotte Morris (3) - July 10, 1877
   Place of marriage, Bower - Age of husband, 26 - Age of wife, 21 -
   Both are Single - Husband was born in Caroline County, Virginia -
   Wife was born in Jefferson County, West Virginia - Both reside in
   Jefferson County, West Virginia.

Shenard, Joseph L. and Elizabeth D. Cramer (3) - June 18, 1884
   Place of marriage, Charlestown - Age of husband, 41 - Age of wife,
   30 - Both are Single - Husband was born in Hampshire County, West
   Virginia - Wife was born in Jefferson County, West Virginia -
   Husband resides in Nelson County, Virginia - Wife resides in
   Jefferson County, West Virginia.

Shepard, E. W. and George W. Neill (2) - (L) February 11, 1861

Shepherd, Eliza H. and Edmund J. Lee (1) -   October 1, 1823

Shepherd, Fanny and Hugh P. Allen (3) -   January 26, 1888
     For further information see - Allen, Hugh P.

Shepherd, Francis R. and Margaret McMurran (2) -   (L) November 21, 1855

Shepherd, Henrietta A. and James Finley (2) -   (L) March 28, 1853

Shepherd, Henrietta A. and James Finley (1) -   March 29, 1853

Shepherd, Henry and Fanny Elean. Briscoe (1) -   May 7, 1822

Shepherd, James W. and Mary S. Myers (3) -   December 11, 1866
     Place of marriage, near Kabletown, Jefferson County - Age of husband,
     25 - Age of wife, 21 - Both are Single - Both were born in Jefferson
     County, West Virginia - Both reside in Jefferson County, West
     Virginia - Husband's parents are Amos and Ann Elizabeth Shepherd -
     Wife's parents are Jacob and Mary Ann Myers - Occupation of husband
     is Farmer.

Shepherd, Jane E. and William B. Conrad (3) -   November 20, 1866
     For further information see - Conrad, William B.

Shepherd, John and Mary Croft (1) -   November 17, 1807

Shepherd, Mary and George Frait (1) -   June 4, 1804

Shepherd, Rezin D. and Elizabeth L. Boteler (2) -   (L) June 9, 1858

Shepherd, Sarah and Joseph Wiley (1) -   February 18, 1809

Sherman, Charles C. and Sarah Ingram (3) -   November 20, 1875
     Place of marriage, Bolivar - Age of husband, 25 - Age of wife, 24 -
     Both are Single - Husband was born in State of Ohio - Wife was born
     in State of Maryland - Both reside in Jefferson County, West Virginia.

Sherman, Lizzie and James W. League (3) -   November 14, 1871
     For further information see - League, James W.

Sherrard, Robert and Eliza Morton Matthews (1) -   July 18, 1826

Shewbridge, Annie B. and Samuel J. Knadler (3) -   April 6, 1886
     For further information see - Knadler, Samuel J.

Shewbridge, Clara F. and Richard Scarlet (3) -   February 10, 1887
     For further information see - Scarlet, Richard.

Shewbridge, James L. and Mary E. Hood (3) -   October 24, 1871
     Place of marriage, Jefferson County - Age of husband, 24 - Age of
     wife, 19 - Both are Single - Husband was born in Virginia - Wife was
     born in Maryland - Husband resides in Maryland - Wife resides in
     West Virginia - Husband's parents are James - Wife's parents are
     Daniel - Occupation of husband is Contractor. (Father's consent in
     writing.)

Shewbridge, James Lee and Orregon Schonkel (3) -   January 15, 1880
     Place of marriage, Middleway - Age of husband, 24 - Age of wife,
     30 - Husband is Single - Wife is a Widow - Both were born in
     Jefferson County, West Virginia - Both reside in Jefferson County,
     West Virginia.

Shewbridge, John and Mary Smith (1) -   January 1, 1833

Shewbridge, John and Emily Jane Alexander (1) -   October 26, 1848

Shewbridge, John and Barbara Whittington (2) -   (L) February 9, 1852
    (Thomas Hicks sworn.)

Shewbridge, John H. and Margaret A. Dobins (3) -   December 20, 1866
    Age of husband, 36 - Age of wife, 24 - Both are Single - Husband was
    born at Harpers Ferry, Jefferson County, West Virginia - Wife was
    born in Clarke County, Virginia - Husband resides in Clarke County,
    Virginia - Wife resides in Jefferson County, West Virginia -
    Husband's parents are James and Catharine Shewbridge - Wife's
    parents are Samuel and Mary Dobins - Occupation of husband is
    Blacksmith.

Shewbridge, John W. and Emma Roberts (3) -   December 28, 1887
    Place of marriage, Charlestown - Age of husband, 26 - Age of wife,
    21 - Both are Single - Both were born in Jefferson County, West
    Virginia - Husband resides in Jefferson County, West Virginia - Wife
    resides in Jefferson County.

Shewbridge, M. A. and Henry Herbst (3) -   November 28, 1882
    For further information see - Herbst, Henry.

Shields, Harriet and Stetson Bisber (1) -   December 14, 1823

Shiner, Charles D. and Eliza Taylor (3) -   April 21, 1869
    Age of husband, 28 - Age of wife, 21 - Both are Single - Husband was
    born in Frederick County, Virginia - Wife was born in Frederick
    County - Both reside in Frederick.

Shipe, Annie E. and Thomas J. Silman (3) -   July 19, 1886
    For further information see - Silman, Thomas J.

Shipe, Kate E. and Benjamin B. Dent (3) -   September 12, 1876
    For further information see - Dent, Benjamin B.

Shipe, Mrs. Selina and William L. Ring (3) -   April 27, 1882
    For further information see - Ring, William L.

Shipway, Thomas and M. E. Manuel (3) -   April 25, 1872
    Place of marriage, Jefferson County - Age of husband, 41 - Age of
    wife, 36 - Both are Single - Husband was born in Maryland - Wife was
    born in Virginia - Husband resides in Jefferson County, West
    Virginia - Wife resides in Jefferson, West Virginia - Husband's
    parents are Robert and Sarah A. - Wife's parents are John and
    Elizabeth - Occupation of husband is Farming.

Shirley, Alice and Thomas L. Brantner (3) -   December 5, 1878
    For further information see - Brantner, Thomas L.

Shirley, Ann E. and Thomas M. Wintermoyer (3) -   October 19, 1869
    For further information see - Wintermoyer, Thomas M.

Shirley, Annie and Henry B. Baylor (3) -   October 27, 1880
    For further information see - Baylor, Henry B.

Shirley, Cora and James H. Miller (3) -   December 10, 1879
    For further information see - Miller, James H.

Shirley, David and Caroline McKnight (1) -   February 21, 1828

Shirley, Elizabeth and Cyrus Hibbens (1) -   December 22, 1805

Shirley, Elizabeth and David C. Wilson (1) -   September 15, 1828

Shirley, Ephraim and Margaret Tomblinson (1) -   August 18, 1807

Shirley, Garvis and M. A. C. Nathanbush (1) -   May 27, 1819

Shirley, George W. and Caroline C. Grantham (2) -   (L) February 3, 1852

Shirley, James, Sr. and Matilda Vincent (1) -   December 24, 1821

Shirley, James, Jr. and Mary Grantham (1) -   January 13, 1824

Shirley, James Amon and Edith M. Grantham (3) -   April 29, 1880
    Place of marriage, Middleway - Age of husband, 24 - Age of wife,
    26 - Both are Single - Both were born in Jefferson County, West
    Virginia - Both reside in Jefferson County, West Virginia.

Shirley, John J. and Ann E. Hosier (2) -   (L) July 13, 1853

Shirley, Laura M. and Jacob T. Hagley (3) -   November 8, 1876
    For further information see - Hagley, Jacob T.

Shirley, Lucinda Jane and James N. Barringer (2) -   (L) December 9, 1857

Shirley, Margaret A. and Solomon O. Bates (1) -   December 19, 1849

Shirley, Mary and John Currie (1) -   February 13, 1806

Shirley, Mary and William Hurst (1) -   February 3, 1820

Shirley, Robert V. and Julia M. Baylor (2) -   (L) October 23, 1857

Shirley, Sensalina and George B. Carroll (1) -   February 21, 1828

Shirley, Walter and Jane Lenox (1) -   June 9, 1825

Shirley, Walter and Maria Lock (1) -   July 22, 1827

Shoafstall, Seth and Sarah Conklyn (1) -   1828

Shoe, Abram and Catherine Shell (1) -   April 5, 1812

Shoebridge, James and Catherine Krout (1) -   September 5, 1826

Shoebridge, John and Barbara Whittington (1) -   February 17, 1852

Shoemaker, Flora B. and John W. Darlington (3) -   January 10, 1883
    For further information see - Darlington, John W.

Shoemaker, Gertie and Park G. Mathias (3) -   November 26, 1890
    For further information see - Mathias, Park G.

Shoemaker, Hannah and Joseph McKee (1) -   June 9, 1836

Shoemaker, Maggie J. and D. W. Clendenning (3) -   December 28, 1876
    For further information see - Clendenning, D. W.

517

Shoemaker, Mary E. and John Laughlin (3) -   August 24, 1869
    For further information see - Laughlin, John.

Shope, Augustus and Catharine Lape (1) -   September 25, 1827

Shope, Harriet and James Henry Sliff (2) -   (L) August 1, 1853

Shope, Margaret and Daniel Wright (1) -   November 23, 1819

Shope, Mary and Robert McGarry (1) -   November 16, 1823

Short, David Washington (cold.) Susan C. Myers (3) -   December 11, 1879
    Place of marriage, Charlestown - Age of husband, 30 - Age of wife,
    23 - Both are Single - Both were born in Jefferson County, West
    Virginia - Both reside in Jefferson County, West Virginia.

Short, Hannah (colored) James Washington (3) -   January 24, 1867
    For further information see - Washington, James.

Short, Hannah (colored) Daniel Byers (3) -   February 17, 1870
    For further information see - Byers, Daniel.

Short, Jesse (cold.) N. Smith (3) -   December 5, 1867
    Place of marriage, Jefferson County - Age of husband, 27 - Age of
    wife, 24 - Both are Single - Both were born in Jefferson - Both
    reside in Jefferson - Occupation of husband is Laborer.

Short, Lucy and Marcus Morris (3) -   December 22, 1866
    For further information see - Morris, Marcus.

Shorts, Charles (cold.) Mary Wilkison (3) -   December 26, 1887
    Place of marriage, Shepherdstown - Age of husband, 25 - Age of wife,
    21 - Both are Single - Both were born in Jefferson County, West
    Virginia - Husband resides in Jefferson County, West Virginia - Wife
    resides in Jefferson County.

Shorts, Cornelia (cold.) James Ashby (3) -   May 30, 1878
    For further information see - Ashby, James.

Shorts, John W. (cold.) Mary Lucas (3) -   September 15, 1887
    Place of marriage, Charlestown - Age of husband, 22 - Age of wife,
    21 - Both are Single - Both were born in Jefferson County, West
    Virginia - Both reside in Jefferson County, West Virginia.

Shorts, John William (cold.) Annie Brown (3) -   January 16, 1890
    Place of marriage, Charlestown - Age of husband, 28 - Age of wife,
    22 - Husband is a Widower - Wife is Single - Both were born in
    Jefferson County, West Virginia - Both reside in Jefferson County,
    West Virginia.

Shorts, Rebecca (cold.) Stephen Harris (3) -   April 19, 1883
    For further information see - Harris, Stephen.

Shorts, Samuel (free colored) Annie Winters (2) -   (L) May 11, 1863
    Names, Samuel Shorts and Annie Winters (free colored) - Age of
    husband, 35 years - Age of wife, 30 years - Both are Single - Both
    live in Jefferson County - License issued May 11, 1863 - T. A. Moore.

Shough, Catherine Lentz and William B. Yeamans (1) -   September 22, 1825

Shough, Jacob and Jane R. Bishop (1) -   August 13, 1835

Shouk, Catharine and John Pinkerton (1) -   December 5, 1824

Shover, Malinda Catherine and George Neer (3) -   May 21, 1873
    For further information see - Neer, George.

Show, Ada V. and James W. Lloyd (3) -   October 30, 1890
    For further information see - Lloyd, James W.

Show, Charles W. and Sadie M. Underdonk (3) -   September 3, 1885
    Place of marriage, Charlestown - Age of husband, 22 - Age of wife,
    22 - Both are Single - Both were born in Jefferson County, West
    Virginia - Both reside in Jefferson County, West Virginia.

Show, Elizabeth and Michael Eckhart (1) -   November 28, 1816

Show, George W. and H. V. H. Orndorff (3) -   May 4, 1865
    Place of marriage, Shepherdstown - Age of husband, 22 years - Age of
    wife, 20 years - Both are Single - Husband was born at Shepherdstown -
    Wife was born in Jefferson County - Husband resides at Washington,
    D. C. - Wife resides at Shepherdstown - Husband's parents are George
    Show - Wife's parents are William and Harriet Orndorff - Occupation
    of husband is Confectioner.

Show, John H. and Elizabeth Catherine Cookus (2) -   (L) (1862)
    Time of marriage, November 4, 1862 - Place of marriage,
    Shepherdstown - Names, John H. Show and Elizabeth Catherine Cookus -
    Age of husband, 21 years. March 4, 1862 - Age of wife, 17 years July
    31, 1862 - Both are Single - Both were born at Shepherdstown -
    Husband resides near Shepherdstown - Wife resides at Shepherdstown -
    Names of husband's parents are George and Margaret Ellen - Names of
    wife's parents are George and Hortense - Occupation of husband is
    Blacksmith - Bride's father not living - Consent of her mother given
    in writing - T. A. Moore, Clerk.

Show, Joseph C. and Fanny Crow (3) -   November 18, 1869
    Place of marriage, Jefferson County - Age of husband, 24 - Age of
    wife, 19 - Husband was born in Virginia - Wife was born in Jefferson
    County - Husband resides in Virginia - Wife resides in Jefferson
    County. (Mother gives consent in writing.)

Show, Levi R. and Elizabeth Harding (1) -   September 26, 1833

Show, Margaret and John W. Winebrenner (1) -   February 19, 1846

Show, Nanie and J. W. Wysong (3) -   December 24, 1872
    For further information see - Wysong, J. W.

Show, Nellie R. and William Britner (3) -   April 7, 1885
    For further information see - Britner, William.

Showalter, A. W. and Dora Virginia Higgs (3) -   October 10, 1888
    Place of marriage, Charlestown - Age of husband, 22 - Age of wife,
    21 - Both are Single - Husband was born in Augusta County,
    Virginia - Wife was born in Berkeley County, West Virginia - Husband
    resides in Augusta County, Virginia - Wife resides in Jefferson
    County, West Virginia.

519

Showalter, Hettie E. and James N. Smith (3) -   February 26, 1890
   For further information see - Smith, James N.

Showers, Elizabeth and Thomas Watson (1) -   August 14, 1825

Showman, Elizabeth and John Wagley (1) -   March 18, 1819

Showman, Florence E. S. and Allen A. Staley (3) -   December 22, 1880
   For further information see - Staley, Allen A.

Showman, John B. and Sally Buckles (1) -   December 29, 1807

Showman, Sarah and Henry Garnhart (1) -   March 10, 1825

Showmann, Mary and James Brown (1) -   June 11, 1803

Shreck, George F. and Emily Keller (2) -   (L) September 29, 1856

Shreck, Mary Eliza and Lewis H. Rick (3) -   December 16, 1880
   For further information see - Rick, Lewis H.

Shreck, Rosa C. and L. L. Fiddler (3) -   March 28, 1867
   For further information see - Fiddler, L. L.

Shreck, Rosa Ellen and John S. Billmyre (3) -   March 17, 1884
   For further information see - Billmyre, John S.

Shriner, James V. and Annie Valentine (3) -   December 31, 1878
   Place of marriage, Charlestown - Age of husband, 26 - Age of wife,
   24 - Both are Single - Both were born in Maryland - Both reside in
   Jefferson County, West Virginia.

Shrode, John and Savilla McKnight (1) -   February 27, 1829

Shrodes, Evilina and Dunham Moser (1) -   July 12, 1825

Shrodes, Hannah E. and James E. Chamblin (2) -   (L) March 19, 1853

Shrodes, Mary and James Matheny (1) -   July 25, 1834

Shrodes, Mary Elizabeth and John Anderson (1) -   December 14, 1849

Shrout, Margaret and Charles Cornell (3) -   May 14, 1874
   For further information see - Cornell, Charles.

Shuck, Jonas and Ann Potts (1) -   July 3, 1831

Shuck, Sophia and Solomon Derry (1) -   February 26, 1829

Shue, Michael and Martha Barnett (1) -   July 30, 1825

Shugart, Ann and A. A. Cook (3) -   February 21, 1869
   For further information see - Cook, A. A.

Shugart, John and Polly Huffman (1) -   March 10, 1814

Shugert, Bettie H. and J. Ed. Burns (3) -   April 6, 1880
   For further information see - Burns, J. Ed.

Shugert, C. T. and Bessie F. Tanquary (3) - January 11, 1887
   Place of marriage, Summit Point - Age of husband, 26 - Age of wife,
   19 - Both are Single - Husband was born in Jefferson County, West
   Virginia - Wife was born in Jefferson County - Both reside in
   Jefferson County. (Consent of bride's father in person.)

Shugert, Eliza J. and S. S. Dalgarn (3) - February 28, 1884
   For further information see - Dalgarn, S. S.

Shugert, Katie H. and Nimrod Trussell (3) - October 6, 1880
   For further information see - Trussell, Nimrod.

Shugert, Rezin and Maria Tomlinson (2) - (L) November 12, 1863
   Time of marriage, November 12, 1863 - Place of marriage,
   Charlestown - Names, Rezin Shugert and Maria Tomlinson - Age of
   husband, 45 years - Age of wife, 31 years - Husband is a Widower -
   Wife is Single - Husband was born in Jefferson County, Virginia -
   Wife was born in Bedford County, Pennsylvania - Both reside in
   Jefferson County - Names of husband's parents are John and Mary -
   Names of wife's parents are Joseph and Mary - Occupation of husband
   is Saddle and Harness Maker - License issued November 12, 1863 -
   Thomas A. Moore, Clerk.

Shugert, S. E. (Eliza) and Daniel Adams (2) - (L) December 4, 1851

Shugert, Zachariah and Ann C. Cameron (2) - (L) February 18, 1856

Shull, G. W. and Pleasant R. Wilt (3) - October 5, 1882
   Place of marriage, Charlestown - Age of husband, 28 - Age of wife,
   21 - Husband is a Widower - Wife is Single - Husband was born in
   Loudoun County, Virginia - Wife was born in Jefferson County, West
   Virginia - Both reside in Jefferson County, West Virginia.

Shull, George W. and Alice M. Wilt (3) - May 15, 1879
   Place of marriage, near Ripon - Age of husband, 26 - Age of wife,
   22 - Both are Single - Husband was born in Loudoun County,
   Virginia - Wife was born in Jefferson County, West Virginia - Both
   reside in Jefferson County, West Virginia.

Shull, H. C. and Anna L. Ray (3) - November 22, 1883
   Place of marriage, Shepherdstown - Age of husband, 21 - Age of wife,
   21 - Both are Single - Husband was born at Winchester, Virginia -
   Wife was born in Jefferson County, West Virginia - Husband resides
   at Roanoke, Virginia - Wife resides in Jefferson County, West
   Virginia.

Shults, Annie (3)
   For further information see - Water, John A.

Shultz, Judson J. and Ella H. McClure (3) - July 5, 1881
   Place of marriage, near Leetown - Age of husband, 25 - Age of wife,
   23 - Both are Single - Husband was born in State of Indiana - Wife
   was born in Berkeley County, West Virginia - Husband resides in
   State of Indiana - Wife resides in Jefferson County, West Virginia.

Shumbaugh, Lizzie and Lewis W. Painter (3) - September 2, 1875
   For further information see - Painter, Lewis W.

Shurer, William C. and Elizabeth N. Powers (3) -   October 16, 1866
   Place of marriage, Charlestown, Jefferson County - Age of husband,
   33 - Age of wife, 28 - Both are Single - Husband was born in
   Berkeley County, West Virginia - Both reside at Charlestown,
   Jefferson County, West Virginia - Husband's parents are Archey and
   Mary Shurer - Occupation of husband is Merchant.

Shutt, Elizabeth and John B. Webber (1) -   December 21, 1805

Shutt, George W. and Mary Osburn (2) -   (L) April 8, 1857

Shutt, George W. and Virginia Osborne (3) -   October 16, 1867
   Place of marriage, Jefferson - Age of husband, 35 - Age of wife,
   25 - Husband is a Widower. - Wife is Single - Both were born in
   Loudoun County, Virginia - Husband resides at Springfield,
   Illinois - Wife resides in Jefferson County - Husband's parents
   are Jacob and Caroline - Wife's parents are Logan - Occupation of
   husband is Lawyer.

Shutts, August and Annie E. Moler (3) -   November 12, 1872
   Place of marriage, Harpers Ferry - Age of husband, 22 - Age of wife,
   20 - Both are Single - Husband was born in Germany - Wife was born
   in Jefferson County, West Virginia - Husband resides in Berkeley
   County, West Virginia - Wife resides in Jefferson County, West
   Virginia - Husband's parents are G. F. and J. T. Shuts - Wife's
   Parents are Henry and Barbara - Occupation of husband is Coach
   Painter.   (John Moler.)

Sifert, William and Mary Bruce (2) -   (L) December 23, 1854

Siford, C. J. and Mary Waters (3) -   September 10, 1884
   Place of marriage, Charlestown - Age of husband, 28 - Age of wife,
   22 - Both are Single - Husband was born in Frederick County,
   Virginia - Wife was born in Jefferson County, West Virginia - Both
   reside in Jefferson County.

Sigler, Elizabeth and John H. Armentrout (3) -   October 27, 1885
   For further information see - Armentrout, John H.

Sigler, J. W. and J. Orndorff (bride) (3) -   April 14, 1872
   Place of marriage, Jefferson County, West Virginia - Age of husband,
   21 - Age of wife, 18 - Both are Single - Husband was born in
   Jefferson County, West Virginia - Wife was born in Berkeley County -
   Husband resides in Berkeley County - Wife resides in Jefferson
   County, West Virginia - Husband's parents are George and Ann - Wife's
   parents are William and Elizabeth Ann - Occupation of husband is
   Farmer.   (W. O. Orndorff.)

Sigler, Margaret E. V. and Jacob G. Miller (2) -   (L) December 11, 1858

Sigler, Mary E. and James Walker (2) -   (L) October 9, 1850

Sigler, Mary E. and James Walker (1) -   October 11, 1850

Sigler, Mary E. and Abram Smith (2) -   (L) (1862)
   For further information see - Smith, Abram.

Silman, Thomas J. and Annie E. Shipe (3) - .   July 19, 1886
    Place of marriage, near Old Furnace - Age of husband, 22 - Age of
    wife, 21 - Both are Single - Both were born in Jefferson County,
    West Virginia - Husband resides in Jefferson County - Wife resides
    in Jefferson County, West Virginia.

Simmons, Anna and Bud Harrison (3) -   April 18, 1867
    For further information see - Harrison, Bud.

Simmons, Hannah F. (cold.) Walter Travers (3) -   November 17, 1881
    For further information see - Travers, Walter.

Simmons, Lucy and Robert Brown (3) -   May 2, 1872
    For further information see - Brown, Robert.

Simmons, Mary N. and Charles E. Baylor (3) -   December 17, 1890
    For further information see - Baylor, Charles E.

Simmons, Susan Elizabeth and George Porterfield (3) -   January 21, 1885
    For further information see - Porterfield, George.

Simmons, Susie and Robert L. Lerch (3) -   July 17, 1890
    For further information see - Lerch, Robert L.

Simmons, Thomas (cold.) Ella Ford (3) -   March 15, 1886
    Place of marriage, Charlestown - Age of husband, 25 - Age of wife,
    19 - Both are Single - Both were born in Jefferson County, West
    Virginia - Both reside in Jefferson County, West Virginia.
    (Consent of bride's mother in person.)

Simms, Rebecca (cold.) Wilson Dunmore (3) -   June 9, 1881
    For further information see - Dunmore, Wilson.

Simon, James C. and Stella D. Simon (3) -   July 5, 1890
    Place of marriage, Harpers Ferry - Age of husband, 23 - Age of wife,
    22 - Both are Single - Both were born in Virginia - Husband resides
    in Virginia - Wife resides in Jefferson County, West Virginia.

Simon, Stella D. and James C. Simon (3) -   July 5, 1890
    For further information see - Simon, James C.

Simpson, Camilla and John Wilcher (1) -   January 13, 1825

Simpson, Francis A. and Mary F. Maddox (3) -   September 18, 1866
    Place of marriage, Unionville, Jefferson County - Age of husband,
    26 - Age of wife, 24 - Both are Single - Husband was born in
    Alexandria County, Virginia - Wife was born in Berkeley County, West
    Virginia - Both reside near Shepherdstown, Jefferson County -
    Husband's parents are Henry and Elizabeth Simpson - Wife's parents
    are Lorenzo D. and Maria Maddox - Occupation of husband is Carpenter.

Simpson, Katie F. and Warner M. Boxwell (3) -   December 26, 1889
    For further information see - Boxwell, Warner M.

Simpson, Mary E. and James Lambert (2) -   (L) November 30, 1853

Simpson, Mary E. and James H. Willingham (3) -   May 26, 1887
    For further information see - Willingham, James H.

Simpson, W. A. and Laura M. Lee (3) -   April 14, 1880
    Place of marriage, Shepherdstown - Age of husband, 26 - Age of wife,
    19 - Both are Single - Husband was born at Brooklyn, New York - Wife
    was born at Saint Louis, Missouri - Husband resides in United States
    Army - Wife resides in Jefferson County, West Virginia. (Consent
    of bride's mother in writing, father being dead.)

Sims, Hannah (cold.) Charles Herbert (3) -   July 4, 1881
    For further information see - Herbert, Charles.

Sims, James (cold.) Margaret Wilson (3) -   August 13, 1878
    Place of marriage, Charlestown - Age of husband, 23 - Age of wife,
    21 - Both are Single - Husband was born at Richmond, Virginia - Wife
    was born in Albemarle County, Virginia - Both reside in Jefferson
    County, West Virginia.

Sims, Lucy (cold.) Joseph Goins (3) -   January 23, 1873
    For further information see - Goins, Joseph.

Sinclair, Mary F. and George Wyndham (3) -   December 17, 1878
    For further information see - Wyndham, George.

Sine, Mary J. and Charles Nesselrodt (3) -   February 28, 1888
    For further information see - Nesselrodt, Charles.

Singe, Christena and George Evans (1) -   November 7, 1823

Singleton, J. A. and A. L. Ryan (bride) (3) -   May 1, 1872
    Place of marriage, Jefferson County - Age of husband, 30 - Age of
    wife, 26 - Both are Single - Both were born in Virginia - Both
    reside in Virginia - Husband's parents are A. R. and Ehtlantic -
    Wife's parents are J. A. and Elizabeth - Occupation of husband is
    Farmer.

Sisk, Silas Benjamin and Florence Rebecca Dobson (3) -   February 25, 1880
    Place of marriage, Bolivar - Age of husband, 21 - Age of wife, 20 -
    Both are Single - Husband was born in Madison County, Virginia -
    Wife was born in Jefferson County, West Virginia - Both reside in
    Jefferson County, West Virginia. (Consent of bride's father in
    person.)

Sisk, William and Rosa Leever (3) -   January 21, 1888
    Place of marriage, Charlestown - Age of husband, 21 - Age of wife,
    21 - Both are Single - Both were born in Jefferson County, West
    Virginia - Both reside in Jefferson County, West Virginia.

Sisk, William F. and Ann Elizabeth Hoff (3) -   August 24, 1882
    Place of marriage, Charlestown - Age of husband, 25 - Age of wife,
    24 - Both are Single - Husband was born in Culpeper County,
    Virginia - Wife was born in Jefferson County, West Virginia - Both
    reside in Jefferson County, West Virginia.

Sisler, Mattie and Jonathan Butts (3) -   April 27, 1886
    For further information see - Butts, Jonathan.

Sisler, Mattie and Jonathan Butts (3) -   April 9, 1887
    For further information see - Butts, Jonathan.

Sites, Emma K. and Charlie H. Johns (3) -   February 28, 1883
    For further information see - Johns, Charlie H.

Sites, William A. and Fannie M. Trussell (3) -   August 18, 1874
    Place of marriage, near Leetown - Age of husband, 35 - Age of wife,
    36 - Husband is Single - Wife is a Widow - Husband was born in
    Pennsylvania - Wife was born in Jefferson County, West Virginia -
    Both reside in Jefferson County, West Virginia.

Skidmore, Robert and Emily Crawford (1) -   April 3, 1834

Skinner, Mrs. Ann E. and William A. Suddith (2) -   (L) December 3, 1853

Skinner, Charles G. and Lucie M. Lock (3) -   January 14, 1874
    Place of marriage, Charles Town - Age of husband, 29 - Age of wife,
    33 - Both are Single - Husband was born in Fauquier County,
    Virginia - Wife was born in Jefferson County, West Virginia -
    Husband resides in Fauquier County, Virginia - Wife resides in
    Jefferson County, West Virginia.

Skinner, Mary Ellen and William Jackson (2) -   (L) September 24, 1854

Skinner, Sarah E. and Carver W. Brown (2) -   (L) September 3, 1852

Skinner, Sarah E. and Carver W. Brown (1) -   September 8, 1852

Slater, Isaac (cold.) A. M. Cross (3) -   December 14, 1867
    Place of marriage, Jefferson County - Age of husband, 21 - Age of
    wife, 22 - Both are Single - Husband was born in Page County,
    Virginia - Wife was born in Berkeley County - Both reside in
    Jefferson - Occupation of husband is Farmer.

Slaughter, Ben (cold.) Betty Whalen (3) -   April 1, 1877
    Place of marriage, near Kabletown - Age of husband, 33 - Age of
    wife, 16 - Husband is a Widower - Wife is Single - Husband was born
    in Madison County, Virginia - Wife was born in Jefferson County,
    West Virginia - Both reside in Jefferson County, West Virginia.
    (Consent of bride's father in person.)

Slaughter, Charlotte (cold.) Joshua Sanders (3) -   August 16, 1883
    For further information see - Sanders, Joshua.

Slaughter, Matilda (cold.) James May (3) -   May 29, 1883
    For further information see - May, James.

Slavan, Mary Ann and Patrick Higgins (2) -   (L) April 13, 1858

Slaven, Elizabeth and James Walsh (3) -   May 24, 1873
    For further information see - Walsh, James.

Slavin, Sarah Jane and Andrew Higgins (3) -   January 23, 1866
    For further information see - Higgins, Andrew.

Slemmons, Margaret B. and Thomas G. Flagg (1) -   November 4, 1828

Slemons, Jane Leah and James Burr (1) -   February 1, 1827

Slifer, L. F. and J. A. Baney (bride) (3) -   December 9, 1867
    Place of marriage, Jefferson County - Age of husband, 25 - Age of
    wife, 21 - Both are Single - Both were born in Jefferson County -
    Both reside in Jefferson - Husband's parents are Samuel - Wife's
    parents are Thadeus and Susan - Occupation of husband is Farmer.

Sliff, James Henry and Harriet Shope (2) -   (L) August 1, 1853

Slinkman, Albert and Lillie E. Staley (3) -   December 22, 1881
Place of marriage, Shepherdstown - Age of husband, 25 - Age of wife, 20 - Both are Single - Husband was born at Baltimore - Wife was born in Jefferson County, West Virginia - Husband resides at Baltimore - Wife resides in Jefferson County, West Virginia. (Consent of bride's father certified by William M. Staley.)

Sloan, Anne A. and John C. Logie (2) -   (L) November 18, 1851

Sloan, Anne A. and John C. Logie (1) -   November 19, 1851

Sloan, Annie and William A. Howard (2) -   (L) November 17, 1863
For further information see - Howard, William A.

Sloan, Conway, and Elizabeth Farr (1) -   June 1827

Sloan, Lockland J. and Nancy Ellen Kelly (3) -   (1869)
Age of husband, 32 - Age of wife, 34 - Husband was born at Harpers Ferry - Wife was born in Jefferson County - Both reside in Jefferson County.

Sloan, Martha and John M. Billman (2) -   (L) September 19, 1857

Slough, William H. and Ellen M. Cummings (3) -   February 8, 1888
Place of marriage, Harpers Ferry - Age of husband, 26 - Age of wife, 22 - Both are Single - Both were born in Jefferson County, West Virginia - Husband resides in Jefferson County - Wife resides in Jefferson County, West Virginia.

Sly, John (cold.) Nannie Creamer (3) -   October 12, 1876
Place of marriage, Shepherdstown - Age of husband, 22 - Age of wife, 21 - Both are Single - Husband was born in Morgan County, West Virginia - Wife was born in Jefferson County, West Virginia - Both reside in Jefferson County, West Virginia.

Small, Amelia M. and Charles B. McDonald (3) -   April 28, 1881
For further information see - McDonald, Charles B.

Small, James H. and Isabella M. Evans (3) -   August 22, 1866
Place of marriage, Smithfield, Jefferson County, West Virginia - Age of husband, 22 - Age of wife, 19 - Both are Single - Husband was born in Berkeley County, West Virginia - Wife was born in Jefferson County, West Virginia - Husband resides in Berkeley County, West Virginia - Wife resides in Jefferson County, West Virginia - Husband's parents are Jacob and Nancie Small - Wife's parents are Samuel M. and Emeline Evans - Occupation of husband is Farmer.

Small, John and Francis Lot (1) -   May 17, 1832

Small, Mayberry C. and Mary B. Myers (3) -   March 4, 1880
Place of marriage, near Mechanickstown - Age of husband, 30 - Age of wife, 21 - Both are Single - Husband was born in Berkeley County, West Virginia - Wife was born in Jefferson County, West Virginia - Husband resides in Berkeley County, West Virginia - Wife resides in Jefferson County, West Virginia.

Small, Sarah R. and Bonfield Gorrel (3) -   November 21, 1865
For further information see - Gorrel, Bonfield.

Small, Wendell S. and Margaret Ann Burr (3) -   January 22, 1874
   Place of marriage, Jefferson County - Age of husband, 28 - Age of
   wife, 27 - Both are Single - Husband was born in Berkeley County,
   West Virginia - Wife was born in Jefferson County, West Virginia -
   Husband resides in Berkeley County, West Virginia - Wife resides in
   Jefferson County, West Virginia.

Smallwood, Bayn and Mary Ann Blackburn (1) -   March 7, 1824

Smallwood, Bushrod and Mary Jane Whittington (2) -   (L) April 1, 1859

Smallwood, Elizabeth and Michael Wysong (1) -   March 15, 1826

Smallwood, Elizabeth and Adam Weltzheimer (1) -   April 5, 1827

Smallwood, G. W. and Lucinda Lloyd (3) -   December 16, 1871
   Place of marriage, Jefferson County - Age of husband, 25 - Age of
   wife, 21 - Both are Single - Both were born in Clarke County - Both
   reside in Clarke County - Husband's parents are Burr and Eliza -
   Wife's parents are Lawrence and Bettie - Occupation of husband is
   Farmer. (Vouched for Andrew Kennedy.)

Smallwood, H. S. and Lizzie Corear (3) -   (1870)
   Age of husband, 23 - Age of wife, 23 - Both were born in Virginia -
   Both reside in Jefferson County.

Smallwood, J. W. and Mary E. Thomas (3) -   June 22, 1865
   Place of marriage, Brown's Crossing, Jefferson County - Age of
   husband, 26 years - Age of wife, 18 years - Both are Single -
   Husband was born in Clarke County, Virginia - Wife was born in
   Jefferson County, West Virginia - Husband resides at Brown's
   Crossing, Jefferson County - Wife resides at Hazelfield, Jefferson
   County - Husband's parents are Alfred and Cornelia Smallwood -
   Wife's parents are John A. and Jane A. Thomas - Occupation of
   husband is Cooper.

Smallwood, Jacob T. and Carrie M. Boyer (3) -   September 18, 1890
   Place of marriage, Charlestown - Age of husband, 21 - Age of wife,
   17 - Both are Single - Husband was born in Ohio - Wife was born in
   Jefferson County, West Virginia - Both reside in Jefferson County,
   West Virginia. (Consent of bride's father in writing.)

Smallwood, James H. and Mary Alice Utter (3) -   February 25, 1869
   Place of marriage, Jefferson County - Age of husband, 28 - Age of
   wife, 24 - Both are Single - Husband was born in Clarke County,
   Virginia - Wife was born in Warren County - Both reside in
   Jefferson County - Husband's parents are Barny and T. - Wife's
   parents are John and Margaret - Occupation of husband is Cooper.

Smallwood, James N. and Frances R. Ridenour (1) -   May 1848

Smallwood, John and Pinkie Karmar (3) -   February 6, 1884
   Place of marriage, Charlestown - Age of husband, 21 - Age of wife,
   21 - Both are Single - Both were born in Jefferson County, West
   Virginia - Both reside in Jefferson County, West Virginia.

Smallwood, John W. and Virginia Fleming (3) -   March 3, 1875
Place of marriage, near Charles Town - Age of husband, 25 - Age of wife, 22 - Both are Single - Both were born in Loudoun County, Virginia - Husband resides in Loudoun County, Virginia - Wife resides in Jefferson County, West Virginia.

Smallwood, John W. and Bettie Roderick (3) -   February 3, 1876
Place of marriage, Charles Town - Age of husband, 23 - Age of wife, 22 - Both are Single - Husband was born in Clarke County, Virginia - Wife was born in Jefferson County, West Virginia - Both reside in Jefferson County, West Virginia.

Smallwood, Mary B. and John H. Brown (3) -   February 4, 1880
For further information see - Brown, John H.

Smallwood, Mary F. and Franklin P. Mauzy (2) -   (L) October 6, 1851

Smallwood, Rebecca A. and Henry Heller (1) -   April 17, 1829

Smallwood, Samuel and Betsy Haneys (1) -   December 28, 1815

Smallwood, Shipley Sheerer and Lucy Swartz (3) -   August 15, 1883
Place of marriage, Charlestown - Age of husband, 22 - Age of wife, 21 - Both are Single - Both were born in Jefferson County, West Virginia - Both reside in Jefferson County, West Virginia.

Smart, Lucinda and Samuel Horman (1) -   November 23, 1845

Smeltzer, Josiah P. and Ann Eliza Eichelberger (2) -   (L) June 13, 1851

Smeltzer, Samuel Y. and Blanche Eichelberger (3) -   January 17, 1877
Place of marriage, Charles Town - Age of husband, 27 - Age of wife, 26 - Both are Single - Husband was born in Maryland - Wife was born in Jefferson County, West Virginia - Both reside in Jefferson County, West Virginia.

Smith, A. F. and M. A. Duke (bride) (2) -   (L) July 14, 1857

Smith, Aaron W. (cold.) Martha Bener (3) -   November 27, 1879
Place of marriage, Charlestown - Age of husband, 26 - Age of wife, 23 - Both are Single - Husband was born in South Carolina - Wife was born in Virginia - Both reside in Jefferson County, West Virginia.

Smith, Abram and Mary E. Sigler (2) -   (L) (1862)
Time of marriage, Thursday, January 23, 1862 - Place of marriage, Shepherdstown - Abram Smith and Mary E. Sigler - Age of husband, 30 years 5 months 5 days - Age of wife, 24 years 7 months 16 days - Condition of husband is Single - Condition of wife is Single - Place of husband's birth was Washington County, Maryland - Place of wife's birth was Washington County, Maryland - Place of husband's residence is Shepherdstown - Place of wife's residence is Shepherdstown - Names of husband's parents are Jacob E. and Polly Smith - Names of wife's parents are Jacob and Sarah Sigler - Occupation of husband is Carpenter - Abram Smith.

Smith, Albert (cold.) Hannah Brown (3) -   December 28, 1882
    Place of marriage, Middleway - Age of husband, 22 - Age of wife,
    18 - Both are Single - Both were born in Jefferson County, West
    Virginia - Both reside in Jefferson County, West Virginia. (Bride
    has neither father nor mother. Consent of her brother by her
    guardian.)

Smith, Alfred (cold.) Charlotte Smith (3) -   September 4, 1881
    Place of marriage, Duffields - Age of husband, 23 - Age of wife,
    16 - Both are Single - Both were born in Jefferson County, West
    Virginia - Both reside in Jefferson County, West Virginia.
    (Consent of bride's mother in writing.)

Smith, Amanda and Moten Julius (3) -   January 1, 1867
    For further information see - Julius, Moten.

Smith, Ann (colored) John Jones (3) -   May 11, 1870
    For further information see - Jones, John.

Smith, Anna Fry and J. William Childs (3) -   April 7, 1886
    For further information see - Childs, J. William.

Smith, Annie (cold.) George William Bener (3) -   December 12, 1885
    For further information see - Bener, George William.

Smith, Augustine J. and Elizabeth B. Morgan (2) -   (L) December 3, 1855

Smith, Barbary and Richard Whittington (1) -   1821

Smith, Bettie and Nick Clark (3) -   December 31, 1868
    For further information see - Clark, Nick.

Smith, Bettie (cold.) James Robinson (3) -   November 27, 1890
    For further information see - Robinson, James.

Smith, Catharine and George Murphy (1) -   March 15, 1827

Smith, Charles W. and Mary B. Garney (3) -   January 12, 1882
    Place of marriage, Charlestown - Age of husband, 26 - Age of wife,
    22 - Both are Single - Husband was born in Frederick County,
    Virginia - Wife was born in Jefferson County, West Virginia - Both
    reside in Jefferson County, West Virginia.

Smith, Charlotte (cold.) Alfred Smith (3) -   September 4, 1881
    For further information see - Smith, Alfred.

Smith, Corna and Margaret Feltman (2) -   (L) February 11, 1863
    Time of marriage, February 12, 1863 - Place of marriage,
    Shepherdstown - Names, Corna Smith and Margaret Feltman - Age of
    husband, 43 years - Age of wife, 43 years - Husband is Single - Wife
    is a Widow - Both were born in Germany - Both live at Shepherdstown -
    Husband's parents are William and Helen Smith - Wife's parents are
    Unknown - Occupation of husband is Stonemason - License issued,
    February 11, 1863 - T. A. Moore, Clerk.

Smith, Courtney H. and Joseph O. Coyle (1) -   January 28, 1835

529

Smith, Cruger Womley and Flora McDonald Green (3) -   January 11, 1887
  Place of marriage, Charlestown - Age of husband, 42 - Age of wife,
  22 - Both are Single - Husband was born at Clarksburg, West
  Virginia - Wife was born at Richmond - Husband resides at Clarksburg -
  Wife resides in Jefferson County.

Smith, Eli and Frances Jefferson (1) -   February 26, 1828

Smith, Eliza and Daniel Loudon (3) -   August 20, 1865
  For further information see - Loudon, Daniel.

Smith, Eliza and John Rutherford (3) -   December 14, 1873
  For further information see - Rutherford, John.

Smith, Eliza Ann (cold.) Noah F. Adams (3) -   June 15, 1876
  For further information see - Adams, Noah F.

Smith, Elizabeth and Joseph Hite (1) -   November 23, 1817

Smith, Elizabeth and Jacob Engles (1) -   1820

Smith, Elizabeth and Martin S. Brown (1) -   May 3, 1827

Smith, Emily Frances and John L. Thompson (2) -   (L) January 10, 1852

Smith, Fannie A. and Harry J. Keller (3) -   July 18, 1888
  For further information see - Keller, Harry J.

Smith, Fannie R. and John Q. Fleming (3) -   October 25, 1883
  For further information see - Fleming, John Q.

Smith, Frances and Henry S. Farnsworth (1) -   November 1, 1832

Smith, Frank (colored) Hannah Briscoe (3) -   June 11, 1870
  Place of marriage, Jefferson County - Age of husband, 24 - Age of
  wife, 25 - Husband was born in Loudoun County - Wife was born in
  Jefferson County - Both reside in Jefferson County.

Smith, Frank (cold.) Emily McDaniel (3) -   August 11, 1882
  Place of marriage, Charlestown - Age of husband, 30 - Age of wife,
  22 - Both are Single - Husband was born in Madison County,
  Virginia - Wife was born in Jefferson County, West Virginia -
  Husband resides in Jefferson County, West Virginia - Wife resides in
  Jefferson County.

Smith, George W. and Lizzie E. Mauzy (3) -   June 13, 1881
  Place of marriage, Bolivar - Age of husband, 23 - Age of wife, 20 -
  Both are Single - Both were born in Jefferson County, West
  Virginia - Both reside in Jefferson County, West Virginia.
  (Consent of bride's mother in writing.)

Smith, Georgiana (cold.) L. L. Page (3) -   August 13, 1879
  For further information see - Page, L. L.

Smith, Harriet (cold.) Thomas Jefferson (3) -   February 1, 1875
  For further information see - Jefferson, Thomas.

Smith, Harrison and Rachael Jones (3) -					May 16, 1869
  Place of marriage, Jefferson County - Age of husband, 31 - Age of
  wife, 21 - Both are Single - Both were born in Jefferson County -
  Both reside in Jefferson County.

Smith, Isaac and Keziah Jenkins (1) -					October 29, 1835

Smith, Isaac N. and W. C. Ambrose (3) -					March 3, 1868
  Place of marriage, Jefferson County - Age of husband, 36 - Age of
  wife, 25 - Husband is a Widower - Wife is Single - Husband was born
  in Frederick County - Wife was born in Clarke County - Both reside
  in Jefferson - Husband's parents are Lewis F. and Sarah C. - Wife's
  parents are William and Julia - Occupation of husband is Farmer.

Smith, J. Shirley and Verda W. Starry (3) -				September 24, 1879
  Place of marriage, Charlestown - Age of husband, 29 - Age of wife,
  28 - Both are Single - Both were born in Jefferson County, West
  Virginia - Both reside in Jefferson County, West Virginia.

Smith, James N. and Hettie E. Showalter (3) -				February 26, 1890
  Place of marriage, Harpers Ferry - Age of husband, 27 - Age of wife,
  22 - Both are Single - Both were born in Rockingham County,
  Virginia - Husband resides in Rockingham County, Virginia - Wife
  resides in Jefferson County, West Virginia.

Smith, James S. and A. P. Turner (3) -					May 12, 1868
  Age of husband, 22 - Age of wife, 22 - Both are Single - Both were
  born in Jefferson County - Both reside in Jefferson County -
  Husband's parents are John F. and Susan - Wife's parents are Anthony
  and Harriet - Occupation of husband is Painter.

Smith, James W. and Mary Ann Hodges (2) -			(L) September 27, 1860

Smith, James W. and Jane Potts (3) -					April 11, 1869
  Place of marriage, Jefferson County - Age of husband, 26 - Age of
  wife, 19 - Both are Single - Husband was born in Jefferson County -
  Wife was born in Pennsylvania - Both reside in Jefferson County -
  Occupation of husband is Farmer.   (Parents consents.)

Smith, Jefferson and Lucinda West (1) -					February 18, 1834

Smith, John and Elizabeth Harbin (1) -					July 14, 1834

Smith, John W. and George Anna Washington (2) -			(L) November 18, 1851

Smith, John W. and H. M. A. Grantham (3) -				April 16, 1867
  Place of marriage, Smithfield, Jefferson County - Age of husband,
  26 - Age of wife, 33 - Both are Single - Husband was born in
  Frederick County, Virginia - Wife was born in Jefferson County, West
  Virginia - Husband resides in Frederick County, Virginia - Wife
  resides in Jefferson County, West Virginia - Husband's parents are
  James and A. R. Smith - Wife's parents are William and H. M.
  Grantham - Occupation of husband is Farmer.

Smith, John W. and Lucy L. Williams (3) -				September 25, 1890
  Place of marriage, Charlestown - Age of husband, 24 - Age of wife,
  21 - Both are Single - Husband was born in Augusta County, Virginia -
  Wife was born in Rockingham County, Virginia - Husband resides in
  Rockingham County, Virginia - Wife resides in Jefferson County, West
  Virginia.

Smith, Joseph and Catharine Miller (1) -   July 8, 1819

Smith, Joseph and Elizabeth Fisher (1) -   October 8, 1831

Smith, Joseph Cheston and Maria L. Spangler (2) -   (L) May 14, 1863
Time of marriage, May 19, 1863 - **Place** of marriage, Harpers Ferry -
Names, Joseph Cheston Smith and Maria L. Spangler - Age of husband -
Age of wife - Condition of husband is a Widower - Condition of wife
is Single - Husband was born in Washington County, Maryland - Wife
was born at Harpers Ferry - Husband's residence is Washington
County, Maryland - Wife's residence is at Harpers Ferry - Names of
husband's parents are - Names of wife's parents are Emanuel and
__?__ Spangler - Occupation of husband is Farmer - Consent of
bride's father given in writing - License issued, May 14, 1863 -
Thomas A. Moore, Clerk.

Smith, Julia (cold.) J. H. **Robinson** (3) -   January 20, 1876
    For further information see - Robinson, J. H.

Smith, Julia (cold.) Rozier Henry (3) -   December 28, 1889
    For further information see - Henry, Rozier.

Smith, Kizziah J. (widow) and Eben T. Hancock (2) -   (L) December 6, 1851

Smith, L. M. and Fannie C. Beeler (2) -   (L) April 2, 1855

Smith, LaFayette and Lydia Ann Fry (2) -   (L) September 6, 1858

Smith, Lizzie M. and Maurice N. Whittington (3) -   July 16, 1890
    For further information see - Whittington, Maurice N.

Smith, Maggie (cold.) James L. Brunswick (3) -   January 18, 1883
    For further information see - Brunswick, James L.

Smith, Margaret and Daniel Crawford (1) -   1827

Smith, Margaret and Spencer Morris (3) -   November 15, 1867
    For further information see - Morris, Spencer.

Smith, Maria and Thomas Keyes, Jr. (1) -   August 30, 1828

Smith, Mary and John Foreman (1) -   1812

Smith, Mary and John M. Johnson (1) -   March 8, 1827

Smith, Mary and John Shewbridge (1) -   January 1, 1833

Smith, Mary (cold.) Thomas J. Hopewell (3) -   February 5, 1885
    For further information see - Hopewell, Thomas J.

Smith, Mary C. and John B. Watson (2) -   (L) November 12, 1860

Smith, Mrs. Mary C. (nee Moore) and R. C. Dowdon (3) -   December 26, 1883
    For further information see - Dowdon, R. C.

Smith, Mary C. and Edmund Avey (3) -   November 7, 1886
    For further information see - Avey, Edmund.

Smith, Mary E. and Lewis Jackson Baker (3) -   December 30, 1871
    For further information see - Baker, Lewis Jackson.

Smith, Mary E. and Thomas Henry Taylor (3) - March 10, 1874
    For further information see - Taylor, Thomas Henry.

Smith, Mary E. and Samuel E. Lewis (3) - January 29, 1884
    For further information see - Lewis, Samuel E.

Smith, Mary Jane and Jonathan Grant, Jr. (1) - August 9, 1836

Smith, Mary Jane and Patrick Carroll (2) - (L) September 4, 1858

Smith, Matilda and David Furman (1) - January 17, 1819

Smith, Mayberry G. and Margaret L. Roberts (3) - November 12, 1872
    Place of marriage, Smithfield - Age of husband, 29 - Age of wife, 24 - Both are Single - Husband was born in Jefferson County - Wife was born in Berkeley - Husband resides in Frederick - Wife resides in Jefferson County, West Virginia - Husband's parents are James and Ann - Wife's parents are Joseph L. and Sarah A. - Occupation of husband is Farmer.

Smith, Michael and Margaret Wisenall (1) - June 7, 1818

Smith, Miles (cold.) Frances Cromwell (3) - December 22, 1881
    Place of marriage, near Duffields - Age of husband, 40 - Age of wife, 27 - Both are Single - Husband was born in Virginia - Wife was born in Maryland - Both reside in Jefferson County, West Virginia.

Smith, Milford (cold.) Bettie Woolard (3) - March 13, 1890
    Place of marriage, Harpers Ferry - Age of husband, 21 - Age of wife, 16 - Both are Single - Both were born in Jefferson County, West Virginia - Both reside in Jefferson County, West Virginia.

Smith, Milton and Martha P. Clipp (3) - April 12, 1870
    Age of husband, 21 - Age of wife, 21 - Husband was born in Maryland - Wife was born in Jefferson County - Both reside in Jefferson County. (Granted upon endorsement of Sep. Roderick.)

Smith, N. (cold.) Jesse Short (3) - December 5, 1867
    For further information see - Short, Jesse.

Smith, Paul and Esther L. Likens (1) - December 5, 1831

Smith, Peach Isabelle and James F. Cassell (3) - July 31, 1889
    For further information see - Cassell, James F.

Smith, Phebe F. and George F. Ludwick (1) - December 10, 1829

Smith, Rachel (cold.) Simon Gordon (3) - June 17, 1878
    For further information see - Gordon, Simon.

Smith, Rebecca and David Killmer (1) - April 11, 1833

Smith, Rebeca A. and William F. Panel (3) - November 10, 1887
    For further information see - Panel, William F.

Smith, Roger R. and Bettie F. Rice (2) - (L) October 24, 1859

Smith, Rosa (cold.) James William Walker (3) - December 31, 1890
    For further information see - Walker, James William.

Smith, Sarah (cold.) Anthony Hunter (3) -   December 24, 1867
    For further information see - Hunter, Anthony.

Smith, Sarah J. and Macellus Armstrong (3) -   January 29, 1884
    For further information see - Armstrong, Macellus.

Smith, Seth and Harriet Pack (1) -   1821

Smith, Susan R. and William G. Bates (3) -   December 17, 1885
    For further information see - Bates, William G.

Smith, Susan S. and William A. Reed (3) -   March 28, 1875
    For further information see - Reed, William A.

Smith, Taylor and Virginia Manning (3) -   August 26, 1869
    Place of marriage, Jefferson County - Age of husband, 22 - Age of
    wife, 21 - Both were born in West Virginia - Husband resides in
    West Virginia - Wife resides in Jefferson County, West Virginia.

Smith, Thomas W. and Kate B. Miller (3) -   February 2, 1881
    Place of marriage, Mechanicstown - Age of husband, 41 - Age of wife,
    41 - Husband is a Widower - Wife is Single - Husband was born in
    Maryland - Wife was born in Pennsylvania - Both reside in Jefferson
    County, West Virginia.

Smith, W. G. and E. J. Miller (bride) (3) -   May 5, 1868
    Place of marriage, Jefferson County - Age of husband, 38 - Age of
    wife, 28 - Husband is a Widower - Wife is Single - Husband was born
    in Frederick County - Wife was born in Hampshire - Both reside in
    Jefferson County - Husband's parents are W. G. and Mary - Wife's
    parents are Stephen - Occupation of husband is Tailor.

Smith, William and Sarah Griffith (1) -   July 24, 1836

Smith, William and Lucy Robinson (3) -   December 26, 1869
    Place of marriage, Jefferson County - Age of husband, 22 - Age of
    wife, 22 - Both were born in Jefferson County - Both reside in
    Jefferson County.

Smith, William (cold.) Anna Jones (3) -   January 27, 1876
    Place of marriage, Smithfield - Age of husband, 26 - Age of wife,
    22 - Both are Single - Husband was born in Frederick County,
    Maryland - Wife was born in Jefferson County, West Virginia - Both
    reside in Jefferson County, West Virginia.

Smith, William C. (cold.) Frances S. Perry (3) -   July 15, 1890
    Place of marriage, Harpers Ferry - Age of husband, 23 - Age of wife,
    18 - Both are Single - Husband was born in Clarke County, Virginia -
    Wife was born in Loudoun County, Virginia - Both reside in Jefferson
    County, West Virginia. (Consent of bride's father in person.)

Smithey, Sarah and Benjamin Gaines (1) -   August 16, 1818

Smithoats, Anna and Jacob Schmidt (2) -   (L) April 13, 1861
    For further information see - Schmidt, Jacob.

Smithy, Rebecca and Peter Cassady (1) -   June 2, 1825

Smittotz, Margaret and George Will (1) -   April 22, 1849

Smock, Anne and Isaac Essex (1) -   October 5, 1807

Smoke, Lizzy (cold.) Andrew Diggs (3) -   January 1, 1878
    For further information see - Diggs, Andrew.

Smokes, Lucy (cold.) Thomas Edwards (3) -   October 11, 1877
    For further information see - Edwards, Thomas.

Smoots, Julia B. and John W. Grant (3) -   February 26, 1873
    For further information see - Grant, John W.

Smorthus, Violet (colored) Henry Robinson (3) -   August 18, 1870
    For further information see - Robinson, Henry.

Smurr, Clara and James W. R. Fisher (3) -   June 6, 1877
    For further information see - Fisher, James W. R.

Smurr, Eleanor and Aaron Fulk (2) -   (L) December 7, 1852

Smurr, Eleanor and Aaron Fulk (1) -   December 7, 1852

Smurr, Ida M. and Dennis M. Kilmer (3) -   December 6, 1882
    For further information see - Kilmer, Dennis M.

Smurr, Jacob and Eliza Randall (1) -   March 6, 1831

Smurr, James H. and Badoia Spangler (3) -   December 25, 1868
    Place of marriage, Jefferson County - Age of husband, 31 - Age of wife, 25 - Both are Single - Husband was born in Jefferson County, Virginia - Wife was born in Jefferson County - Husband resides in Jefferson County - Wife resides in Jefferson County, West Virginia - Husband's parents are John and Ellen - Wife's parents are John and Ann - Occupation of husband is Painter.

Smurr, Mary F. and William A. Ferris (3) -   May 2, 1866
    For further information see - Ferris, William A.

Smurr, Virginia and John D. Staley (2) -   (L) February 7, 1853

Smutz, Harriet and William Orndoff (1) -   January 22, 1833

Snader, Alice R. and Charles M. Ronemous (3) -   January 12, 1882
    For further information see - Ronemous, Charles M.

Snader, Estellah and J. Luther Link (3) -   March 30, 1880
    For further information see - Link, J. Luther.

Snader, Lutie and Victor Koontz (3) -   October 4, 1888
    For further information see - Koontz, Victor.

Snapp, C. J. and Catherine Beatrice Baker Hyatt (3) -   January 26, 1887
    Place of marriage, near Middleway - Age of husband, 38 - Age of wife, 27 - Husband is a Widower - Wife is Single - Husband was born at Winchester, Frederick County, Virginia - Wife was born in Frederick County, Virginia - Husband resides at Winchester - Wife resides in Jefferson County.

Snapp, Maggie B. and William R. Bryant (3) -   March 12, 1883
    For further information see - Bryant, William R.

Snider, D. S. and Mattie E. Snider (3) -   November 14, 1868
    Place of marriage, Jefferson County - Age of husband, 27 - Age of
    wife, 28 - Both are Single - Wife was born in Jefferson County -
    Husband resides in Clarke County - Wife resides in Jefferson
    County - Husband's parents are George and Elizabeth J. - Wife's
    parents are Daniel and Cyntha - Occupation of husband is Tanner.

Snider, Margaret Ann and Lewis Michael Staub (2) -   (L) May 6, 1857

Snider, Mattie E. and D. S. Snider (3) -   November 14, 1868
    For further information see - Snider, D. S.

Snipe, James and Sarah Greenwalt (3) -   December 26, 1870
    Place of marriage, Jefferson County - Age of husband, 24 - Age of
    wife, 27 - Husband was born in Virginia - Wife was born in
    Maryland - Both reside in Jefferson County.

Snively, John and Catherine Cameron (1) -   April 6, 1820

Snodeal, John and Caroline Rowe (2) -   (L) February 11, 1853

Snodgrass, William and Margaret Wilson (1) -   March 21, 1822

Snook, I. F. and E. C. Todd (bride) (3) -   November 14, 1887
    Place of marriage, Charlestown - Age of husband, 34 - Age of wife,
    25 - Both are Single - Husband was born in State of Maryland - Wife
    was born in Maryland - Husband resides in Maryland - Wife resides in
    Jefferson County, West Virginia at present.

Snook, Mary and Albert Beal (1) -   March 28, 1829

Snowdon, Henry and Maggie E. Leach (3) -   June 11, 1885
    Place of marriage, Bride's Residence - Age of husband, 29 - Age of
    wife, 22 - Both are Single - Husband was born in Montgomery County,
    Maryland - Wife was born in Jefferson County, Virginia - Both reside
    in Jefferson County, West Virginia.

Snyder, A. James and Clara V. Bost (3) -   December 16, 1890
    Place of marriage, Harpers Ferry - Age of husband, 52 - Age of wife,
    37 - Husband is a Widower - Wife is a Widow - Husband was born in
    Jefferson County, West Virginia - Wife was born in Berkeley County,
    West Virginia - Both reside in Jefferson County, West Virginia.

Snyder, Aaron H. and Catharine Dust (1) -   January 3, 1832

Snyder, Adam and Sarah Grove (1) -   December 26, 1848

Snyder, Amanda and Adam S. Link (3) -   October 19, 1875
    For further information see - Link, Adam S.

Snyder, Ann and Amasa W. Mars (1) -   1822

Snyder, Annie M. and William F. Roe (2) -   (L) October 22, 1853

Snyder, Annie P. and Thomas Turner (3) -   February 27, 1873
    For further information see - Turner, Thomas.

Snyder, Becky (colored) George Seins (3) -   May 10, 1870
    For further information see - Seins, George.

Snyder, Catharine and Lewis S. Garrison (1) -   April 25, 1850

Snyder, Catharine and John W. Hendricks (2) -   (L) May 29, 1854

Snyder, Charles N. and Berta Augustine Willingham (3) -   December 20, 1888
    Place of marriage, Charlestown - Age of husband, 28 - Age of wife,
    19 - Both are Single - Both were born in Jefferson County, West
    Virginia - Both reside in Jefferson County, West Virginia.
    (Consent of bride's father in person.)

Snyder, Daniel W. and Harriet A. Athey (3) -   March 27, 1877
    Place of marriage, near Myerstown - Age of husband, 28 - Age of
    wife, 22 - Both are Single - Both were born in Jefferson County,
    West Virginia - Both reside in Jefferson County, West Virginia.

Snyder, E. M. and Thomas E. Buck (3) -   May 29, 1865
    For further information see - Buck, Thomas E.

Snyder, Elizabeth and John Wright (1) -   October 20, 1818

Snyder, Elizabeth and John Snyder (2) -   (L) November 25, 1850

Snyder, Elizabeth and Samuel Linton (2) -   (L) July 28, 1854

Snyder, Ella and J. W. McCeary (3) -   February 11, 1869
    For further information see - McCeary, J. W.

Snyder, Ellen V. and William A. Adams (3) -   September 14, 1865
    For further information see - Adams, William A.

Snyder, Hannah Frances and Jesse Isaiah Staup (2) -   (L) May 9, 1859

Snyder, Henry M. and Mary V. Moler (2) -   (L) April 2, 1863
    Time of marriage, April 14, 1863 - Place of marriage, Residence of
    Bride's Father - Names, Henry M. Snyder and Mary V. Moler - Age of
    husband, 26 years June 7, 1862 - Age of wife, 29 years January 18,
    1863 - Both are Single - Both were born in Jefferson County - Both
    reside in Jefferson County - Husband's parents are John and Nancy
    Snyder - Wife's parents are George W. and Sarah Moler - Occupation
    of husband is Farmer - License issued April 2, 1863 - Thomas A.
    Moore, Clerk.

Snyder, Hiberna L. and Frank L. Billmyer (3) -   April 29, 1884
    For further information see - Billmyer, Frank L.

Snyder, J. Walker and Louisa Gorrell (3) -   August 26, 1869
    Place of marriage, Jefferson County - Age of husband, 27 - Age of
    wife, 27 - Husband was born in Jefferson County, West Virginia -
    Wife was born in Berkeley - Husband resides in Berkeley - Wife
    resides in Jefferson County, West Virginia.

Snyder, Jacob and Susan Catharine Snyder (2) -   (L) October 27, 1854

Snyder, James (cold.) Louisa McChan (3) -   November 24, 1881
    Place of marriage, Bride's Residence - Age of husband, 24 - Age of
    wife, 19 - Both are Single - Both were born in Jefferson County,
    West Virginia - Both reside in Jefferson County, West Virginia.
    (Consent of bride's father in writing.)

Snyder, James W. and Virginia C. Hendricks (2) -   (L) February 11, 1861

Snyder, John and Mary Miller (1) - 1827

Snyder, John and Elizabeth Snyder (2) - (L) November 25, 1850

Snyder, John (cold.) Nancy Frazier (3) - February 16, 1882
    Place of marriage, Shepherdstown - Age of husband, 38 - Age of wife, 26 - Both are Single - Both were born in Jefferson County, West Virginia - Both reside in Jefferson County, West Virginia.

Snyder, John W. and Laura E. Newcomer (3) - October 17, 1867
    Place of marriage, Jefferson - Age of husband, 25 - Age of wife, 19 - Both are Single - Husband was born in Jefferson County - Wife was born in Berkeley County - Husband resides in Berkeley County - Wife resides in Jefferson County - Husband's parents are __?__ and Jane - Wife's parents are Alex and Fannie R. - Occupation of husband is Miller. (Mother gives consent.)

Snyder, Luly and Joseph L. Cookus (3) - February 19, 1874
    For further information see - Cookus, Joseph L.

Snyder, Margaret Ellen and Jackson Foutz (2) - (L) May 14, 1860

Snyder, (Mary) and Samuel Wright (1) - October 30, 1823

Snyder, Mary E. and Jacob M. Stipp (1) - February 16, 1847

Snyder, Nancy and John Melvin (1) - October 25, 1827

Snyder, Nelson T. and Emma R. McGarry (3) - September 13, 1877
    Place of marriage, near Duffields - Age of husband, 25 - Age of wife, 21 - Both are Single - Both were born in Jefferson County, West Virginia - Both reside in Jefferson County, West Virginia.

Snyder, Rose and Harry M. Turner (3) - November 25, 1880
    For further information see - Turner, Harry M.

Snyder, Sarah Catharine and Addison Ott (2) - (L) December 1, 1857

Snyder, Solomon and Sarah E. Engle (3) - April 12, 1881
    Place of marriage, Shenandoah Junction - Age of husband, 59 - Age of wife, 47 - Husband is a Widower - Wife is Single - Husband was born in Washington County, Maryland - Wife was born in Jefferson County, West Virginia - Husband resides in Washington County, Maryland - Wife resides in Jefferson County, West Virginia.

Snyder, Susan Catharine and Jacob Snyder (2) - (L) October 27, 1854

Snyder, Susan Hester and Jacob S. Melvin (2) - (L) February 15, 1855

Snyder, Susanna and Daniel Border (1) - January 15, 1845

Snyder, William and Elizabeth Morrison (1) - March 1821

Sombro, Mary and John Bowers (1) - February 2, 1826

Somers, Margaret (cold.) Robert Washington (3) - May 5, 1874
    For further information see - Washington, Robert.

Sorrell, Maria (cold.) Henry McCann, Jr. (3) - June 30, 1881
    For further information see - McCann, Henry, Jr.

Souders, Edward S. and Carrie V. Tutwiler (3) -   March 2, 1890
    Place of marriage, Shepherdstown - Age of husband, 25 - Age of wife,
    22 - Both are Single - Both were born in Jefferson County, West
    Virginia - Both reside in Jefferson County, West Virginia.

Souders, F. B. and Sarah B. Easterday (3) -   June 22, 1870
    Place of marriage, Charles Town - Age of husband, 30 - Age of wife,
    21 - Husband was born in Maryland - Wife was born at Charles Town -
    Both reside in Jefferson County. (Age of lady sworn to by David
    of Charlestown.)

Southards, Lucy L. and Eugene Shearer (3) -   December 5, 1889
    For further information see - Shearer, Eugene.

Southers, Sally and Cornelius Clineferburgh (1) -   February 24, 1820

Southwood, Edward and Ruhanna Morgan (1) -   July 2, 1818

Sowders, F. B. and Mary Virginia Zeller (3) -   June 4, 1878
    Place of marriage, Shepherdstown - Age of husband, 39 - Age of wife,
    21 - Husband is a Widower - Wife is Single - Husband was born in
    Jefferson County, West Virginia - Wife was born in Frederick County,
    Maryland - Both reside in Jefferson County, West Virginia.

Sowers, Susan and George Hunter (3) -   December 1, 1868
    For further information see - Hunter, George.

Sowers, Susan and D. J. Prince (3) -   July 26, 1885
    For further information see - Prince, D. J.

Spangler, Badoia and James H. Smurr (3) -   December 25, 1868
    For further information see - Smurr, James H.

Spangler, Charles W. and Emma A. Keyser (3) -   February 16, 1880
    Place of marriage, Bolivar - Age of husband, 25 - Age of wife, 22 -
    Both are Single - Both were born in Jefferson County, West Virginia -
    Both reside in Jefferson County, West Virginia.

Spangler, Laura A. and James Hughs (3) -   October 18, 1866
    For further information see - Hughs, James.

Spangler, Maria L. and Joseph Cheston Smith (2) -   (L) May 14, 1863
    For further information see - Smith, Joseph Cheston.

Spangler, Martha E. and Joseph P. Fayman (3) -   December 19, 1866
    For further information see - Fayman, Joseph P.

Spangler, Mary and Joshua Riley (1) -   1822

Spangler, Mary Ann and Benjamin Stipes (1) -   June 28, 1825

Spangler, Mary C. and I. H. Fortney (3) -   May 21, 1868
    For further information see - Fortney, I. H.

Spangler, Matthias and Eliza D. Malleory (1) -   May 6, 1824

Spangler, Telsamore and Jerome F. Stahl (2) -   (L) December 17, 1860

Spangler, W. H. and Mary E. Beall (3) - November 15, 1873
  Place of marriage, Bolivar - Age of husband, 33 - Age of wife, 21 - Both are Single - Both were born in Jefferson County, West Virginia - Both reside in Jefferson County, West Virginia.

Sparks, Laban and Mary E. Koonce (3) - September 1, 1869
  Place of marriage, Jefferson County - Age of husband, 30 - Age of wife, 25 - Husband was born in Indiana - Wife was born in Illinois - Husband resides in Indiana - Wife resides in Jefferson County, West Virginia.

Spaulding, George and Mary V. Keyes (3) - April 1872
  Place of marriage, Jefferson County - Age of husband, 21 - Age of wife, 21 - Both are Single - Both were born in Virginia - Both reside in Virginia - Husband's parents are George and Catherine - Wife's parents are Edward and Alcinda - Occupation of husband is Farmer. (Sworn to by George.)

Speak, Mary and Phineas Spencer (1) - 1816

Spears, Henry and Maria Catharine. Cooke (2) - (L) August 3, 1859

Spellman, William (cold.) Hester May (3) - March 31, 1875
  Place of marriage, Charlestown - Age of husband, 38 - Age of wife, 36 - Both are Single - Both were born in Jefferson County, West Virginia - Both reside in Jefferson County, West Virginia.

Spence, George W. and Fanny Bast (3) - May 3, 1882
  Place of marriage, Shepherdstown - Age of husband, 27 - Age of wife, 23 - Both are Single - Husband was born in Berkeley County, West Virginia - Wife was born in Jefferson County - Husband resides in Jefferson County, West Virginia - Wife resides in Jefferson County.

Spencer, Ellen (cold.) Jacob Franklin Murray (3) - July 31, 1884
  For further information see - Murray, Jacob Franklin.

Spencer, Frank (cold.) Lucy Pendleton (3) - October 30, 1890
  Place of marriage, Charlestown - Age of husband, 21 - Age of wife, 23 - Both are Single - Husband was born in Page County, Virginia - Wife was born in Jefferson County, West Virginia - Both reside in Jefferson County, West Virginia.

Spencer, Joseph and Ann Catherine Sweny (1) - 1820

Spencer, Phineas and Mary Speak (1) - 1816

Spenser, Rose (cold.) James Williams (3) - December 12, 1878
  For further information see - Williams, James.

Sperry, Mary Anna and Dennis M. Daniels (2) - (L) May 23, 1864
  For further information see - Daniels, Dennis M.

Spicer, L. H. (bride) and W. J. Harris (3) - July 25, 1871
  For further information see - Harris, W. J.

Spink, Thomas W. and Mary E. Harrell (3) - (1868)
    Age of husband, 24 - Age of wife, 30 - Both are Single - Husband was
    born in Virginia - Wife was born in West Virginia - Husband resides
    in Virginia - Wife resides in West Virginia - Husband's parents are
    Henry and Sarah - Wife's parents are S. R. and Elizabeth B. -
    Occupation of husband is Shoemaker.

Spohn, M. E. and Bettie Harp (3) - April 12, 1883
    Place of marriage, Shepherdstown - Age of husband, 35 - Age of wife,
    28 - Both are Single - Husband was born in Montgomery County,
    Maryland - Wife was born in Jefferson County, West Virginia - Both
    reside in Jefferson County, West Virginia.

Spohn, Mary Lee and George W. Humrickhouse (3) - May 25, 1880
    For further information see - Humrickhouse, George W.

Sponceller, Emma and John Learmont (3) - April 12, 1886
    For further information see - Learmont, John.

Sponder, Jacob Frederick and Ann Margaret Butler (2) - (L) April 8, 1853
    (W. H. Turk witness as to age of parties.)

Spong, Charles and Katie Muck (3) - October 13, 1889
    Place of marriage, Shepherdstown - Age of husband, 28 - Age of wife,
    23 - Both are Single - Husband was born at Sharpsburg, Maryland -
    Both reside in Jefferson County, West Virginia.

Sponseller, S. B. and Lucy M. Strider (3) - March 31, 1880
    Place of marriage, Bolivar - Age of husband, 23 - Age of wife, 26 -
    Both are Single - Both were born in Jefferson County, West
    Virginia - Both reside in Jefferson County, West Virginia.

Spoont, Mary and Andrew Hospital (1) - June 9, 1807

Spotts, Mrs. Dora and L. T. Hart (3) - December 9, 1884
    For further information see - Hart, L. T.

Spotts, Jacob and Mary Tumblin (2) - (L) March 21, 1859

Spotts, Jacob and Catharine Yontz (2) - (L) (1862)
    Time of marriage, January 21, 1862 - Place of marriage,
    Shepherdstown - Names of parties, Jacob Spotts and Catharine Yontz -
    Age of husband, 23 years - Age of wife, 19 years - Condition of
    husband is Single - Condition of wife is Single - Place of husband's
    birth was Jefferson County - Place of wife's birth was Jefferson
    County - Place of husband's residence is Shepherdstown - Place of
    wife's residence is Shepherdstown - Names of husband's parents are
    Jacob and ___?___ - Names of wife's parents are Martin and Frances
    Yontz - Occupation of husband is Soldier in Southern Army - Consent
    of bride's father given in writing - W. H. Crowl.

Spotts, Kate and Remington Spotts (3) - October 25, 1867
    For further information see - Spotts, Remington.

Spotts, Margaret and John Jacob Adam (1) - November 3, 1826

Spotts, Margaret and Thomas Feeley (3) - October 7, 1867
    For further information see - Feeley, Thomas.

Spotts, Mary Jane and Thomas Brotherton (2) - (L) December 23, 1851

541

Spotts, Mary Jane and Thomas Brotherton (1) - December 23, 1851

Spotts, Mary S. and Albert D. Barr (3) - May 23, 1867
    For further information see - Barr, Albert D.

Spotts, Remington and Kate Spotts (3) - October 25, 1867
    Place of marriage, Jefferson - Age of husband, 24 - Age of wife,
    22 - Husband is Single - Wife is a Widow - Husband was born in
    Clarke County, Virginia - Wife was born in Jefferson County - Both
    reside in Jefferson County - Husband's parents are Jacob and
    Catharine - Wife's parents are Martin and Mary Zontzs - Occupation
    of husband is Laborer.

Spotts, Sarah and John Gordon (1) - February 6, 1817

Spranks, Delily and John Holt (1) - November 15, 1807

Springer, Mary J. and George Dittmyer (3) - (1869)
    For further information see - Dittmyer, George.

Sprint, Maria and Thomas Cunningham (1) - September 24, 1822

Stahl, Jerome F. and Telsamore Spangler (2) - (L) December 17, 1860

Stahl, John and Lucinda Piles (1) - April 9, 1835

Stahl, John W. and Henrietta H. Melhorn (2) - (L) November 26, 1858

Staley, Allen A. and Florence E. S. Showman (3) - December 22, 1880
    Place of marriage, Shepherdstown - Age of husband, 21 - Age of wife,
    24 - Both are Single - Husband was born in Jefferson County, West
    Virginia - Wife was born in Maryland - Both reside in Jefferson
    County, West Virginia.

Staley, Ann Rebecca and George William Entler (1) - February 1832

Staley, Anne E. and George T. White (3) - November 15, 1888
    For further information see - White, George T.

Staley, Annie Virginia and D. H. Moler (3) - July 14, 1880
    For further information see - Moler, D. H.

Staley, Catherine and John W. Holliday (1) - May 23, 1822

Staley, Daniel and Helen G. Licklider (2) - (L) January 23, 1855

Staley, Daniel W. and Sarah Margaret Licklider (3) - May 30, 1871
    Age of husband, 35 - Age of wife, 25 - Both are Single - Husband was
    born in Virginia - Wife was born in Jefferson County - Both reside
    in Jefferson County - Husband's parents are David and Christena -
    Wife's parents are George and Jane - Occupation of husband is
    Farmer. (Returned February 24, 1874.)

Staley, Eliza and Jacob Fisher (1) - April 24, 1809

Staley, Fannie (cold.) John Dunmore (3) - December 22, 1881
    For further information see - Dunmore, John.

Staley, Florence and Thomas Fitzgerald (3) - December 13, 1882
    For further information see - Fitzgerald, Thomas.

Staley, George R. and Sarah V. Hill (2) - (L) December 2, 1856

Staley, Henry F. and Mary C. Atkins (3) - November 28, 1886
Place of marriage, Leetown - Age of husband, 21 - Age of wife, 18 -
Both are Single - Husband was born in Jefferson County - Wife was
born in Clarke County, Virginia - Husband resides in Jefferson
County - Wife resides in Jefferson County, West Virginia.
(Consent of bride's father in person.)

Staley, Hester (cold.) William Creamer (3) - September 11, 1888
For further information see - Creamer, William.

Staley, Jacob and Elizabeth Knouff (1) - September 5, 1810

Staley, Jacob and Elizabeth Lickliter (1) - March 21, 1816

Staley, Jacob and Elizabeth Welshance (1) - April 8, 1821

Staley, Jacob W. and Margaret Dust (1) - October 22, 1846

Staley, James P. and H. Kate Hoffman (3) - November 6, 1883
Place of marriage, Bride's Residence - Age of husband, 35 - Age of
wife, 26 - Husband is a Widower - Wife is Single - Husband was born
in Jefferson County, West Virginia - Wife was born in Jefferson
County - Both reside in Jefferson County, West Virginia.

Staley, John D. and Virginia Smurr (2) - (L) February 7, 1853

Staley, Joseph (cold.) Jane Sealy (3) - June 23, 1881
Place of marriage, Shepherdstown - Age of husband, 21 - Age of wife,
21 - Both are Single - Both were born in Jefferson County, West
Virginia - Both reside in Jefferson County, West Virginia. (Ages
vouched for by D. T. Rentch.)

Staley, Joseph Stephen and Ann Catharine Needy (2) - (L) December 1, 1852

Staley, Lillie E. and Albert Slinkman (3) - December 22, 1881
For further information see - Slinkman, Albert.

Staley, Louisa G. and Lafayette V. House (3) - November 24, 1886
For further information see - House, Lafayette, V.

Staley, M. E. and William Engle, Jr. (3) - November 17, 1868
For further information see - Engle, William, Jr.

Staley, Mary and Solomon Thornburg (1) - January 13, 1813

Staley, Mary E. and John D. Summers (3) - December 12, 1866
For further information see - Summers, John D.

Staley, Mary E. and John W. Daniels (3) - March 24, 1880
For further information see - Daniels, John W.

Staley, Nannie T. and Thomas M. Bryarly (3) - February 24, 1881
For further information see - Bryarly, Thomas M.

Staley, Peter and Christiana Kreps (1) - February 27, 1816

Staley, Sarah and Jacob Feaman (1) - September 16, 1824

Staley, William Henry (cold.) Maria L. Davis (3) - November 4, 1886
    Place of marriage, Mount Pleasant - Age of husband, 27 - Age of
    wife, 23 - Both are Single - Both were born in Jefferson County,
    West Virginia - Both reside in Jefferson County, West Virginia.

Staley, William M. and Estella J. Poffenberger (3) - February 23, 1887
    Place of marriage, Shepherdstown - Age of husband, 34 - Age of wife,
    21 - Both are Single - Both were born in Jefferson County - Both
    reside in Jefferson County.

Stalfort, Mrs. L. V. and D. R. Johnson (3) - September 19, 1888
    For further information see - Johnson, D. R.

Stall, Elizabeth and Francis McKinney (1) - November 11, 1816

Stanhope, William and Fanny Hurst (1) - December 20, 1804

Stanley, Emily Jane and Isaac Malatt (3) - April 19, 1883
    For further information see - Malatt, Isaac.

Stanton, Henry (cold.) Annie Walker (3) - November 6, 1884
    Place of marriage, Charlestown - Age of husband, 22 - Age of wife,
    17 - Both are Single - Husband was born in Page County, Virginia -
    Wife was born in Warren County, Virginia - Husband resides in
    Jefferson County, West Virginia - Wife resides in Jefferson County.

Stanton, John W. (cold.) Mary Paterson (3) - June 19, 1889
    Place of marriage, Charlestown - Age of husband, 23 - Age of wife,
    20 - Both are Single - Husband was born in Page County, Virginia -
    Wife was born in Jefferson County, West Virginia - Both reside in
    Jefferson County, West Virginia. (Consent of bride's father in
    person.)

Starky, William and Molly Herrington (3) - October 15, 1884
    Place of marriage, Charlestown - Age of husband, 25 - Age of wife,
    23 - Both are Single - Husband was born in Clarke County, Virginia -
    Wife was born in Jefferson County, West Virginia - Husband resides
    in Clarke County - Wife resides in Jefferson County.

Starr, James H. and Josephine Chamblin (3) - December 17, 1879
    Place of marriage, near Wickliff - Age of husband, 21 - Age of wife,
    21 - Both are Single - Husband was born in Wood County, West
    Virginia - Wife was born in Jefferson County, West Virginia - Both
    reside in Jefferson County, West Virginia.

Starry, Bessie W. and Oscar M. Phillips (3) - February 25, 1885
    For further information see - Phillips, Oscar M.

Starry, Betty L. and C. W. Trussell (3) - December 21, 1871
    For further information see - Trussell, C. W.

Starry, Caroline and Thomas D. Webster (3) - October 25, 1877
    For further information see - Webster, Thomas D.

Starry, Georgie E. and George H. Kelsey (3) - September 22, 1886
    For further information see - Kelsey, George H.

Starry, Nannie K. and William B. Davis (3) - October 18, 1888
    For further information see - Davis, William B.

Starry, Nicholas and Elizabeth Wysong (1). - July 17, 1806

Starry, Thomas K. and Nannie E. Gallaher (2) - (L) March 11, 1852

Starry, Thomas K. and Nannie E. Gallaher (1) - March 11, 1852

Starry, Verda W. and J. Shirley Smith (3) - September 24, 1879
For further information see - Smith, J. Shirley.

Staub, Ann Margaret and Thomas D. Williams (2) - (L) August 1, 1863
For further information see - Williams, Thomas D.

Staub, George W. and Carrie P. Jackson (3) - June 2, 1878
Place of marriage, At Bride's Father's Residence - Age of husband, 21 - Age of wife, 16 - Both are Single - Both were born in Jefferson County, West Virginia - Both reside in Jefferson County, West Virginia. (Consent of bride's father certified by Lewis Staub.)

Staub, Henry and Mary Boxwell (1) - December 28, 1830

Staub, James H. and Sarah L. Cogle (3) - December 25, 1887
Place of marriage, near Harpers Ferry - Age of husband, 23 - Age of wife, 17 - Both are Single - Husband was born in Jefferson County - Wife was born in Loudoun County - Both reside in Jefferson County. (Consent of bride's father in person.)

Staub, Lewis Michael and Margaret Ann Snider (2) - (L) May 6, 1857

Staub, Philip and Mary Rixtine (1) - April 12, 1831

Staub, Stacey Ann (widow) and John William Scarlett (2) - (L) October 31, 1850
(Samuel Fine prest.)

Staub, Stacy Ann (widow) and John W. Scarlett (1) - November 1, 1850

Staubb, Douglas and Lillie Clipp (3) - December 15, 1889
Place of marriage, Saint Andrews Chapel - Age of husband, 20 - Age of wife, 23 - Both are Single - Both were born in Jefferson County, West Virginia - Both reside in Jefferson County, West Virginia, (Consent of groom's father in person.)

Staubb, Hannah and John Appell (3) - December 15, 1889
For further information see - Appell, John.

Staubs, Molly and John W. Hawk (3) - August 7, 1887
For further information see - Hawk, John W.

Staunton, John S. and Kate C. Kirwan (3) - January 9, 1882
Place of marriage, Harpers Ferry - Age of husband, 31 - Age of wife, 26 - Both are Single - Husband was born in Maryland - Wife was born in Jefferson County, West Virginia - Husband resides in Maryland - Wife resides in Jefferson County, West Virginia.

Staup, Jesse Isaiah and Hannah Frances Snyder (2) - (L) May 9, 1859

St.Clair, Alexander and Ann Rebecca Virginia Custer (2) -(L) December 28, 1852

Steadman, Elizabeth and Humphrey K. White (1) - September 25, 1822

Steadman, Elizabeth Hannah and James H. Keyser (2) -   (L) May 22, 1861
    For further information see - Keyser, James H.

Steadman, Frances Villora and David Stephens (2) -   (L) February 2, 1854

Steadman, James W. and Sarah Ann Kemp (2) -   (L) April 16, 1860

Steadman, Levi and Ann Catherine Cave (1) -   June 11, 1835

Steadman, Samuel and Martha.Cooper (1) -   September 26, 1815

Steadman, W. P. and Annie R. Webster (3) -   March 24, 1870
    Place of marriage, Jefferson County - Age of husband, 21 - Age of
    wife, 21 - Husband resides in Virginia - Wife resides in Jefferson
    County. (Sworn by Mrs. Cox.)

Stedman, John and Mary Krout (1) -   April 29, 1832

Stedman, Lawrence and Sarah Dillow (1) -   November 22, 1827

Steel, Frances and Joseph Strosnider (3) -   May 9, 1878
    For further information see - Strosnider, Joseph.

Steele, Elizabeth Davis and Peter Cooley (2) -   (L) July 7, 1853

Steele, Elizabeth Davis and Peter Cooley (1) -   July 11, 1853

Steele, John W. and Mary Blake (2) -   (L) November 21, 1850

Steele, John W. and Mary Blake (1) -   November 21, 1850

Steele, Martha Ann and John W. Thompson (1) -   August 10, 1848

Steen, James William (free cold.) Mary Brown (2) -   (L) October 13, 1852

Stein, Fanny B. and William H. Crisman (3) -   April 7, 1880
    For further information see - Crisman, William H.

Steinbracker, Emilia J. and George C. Patterson (3) -   March 1, 1887
    For further information see - Patterson, George C.

Stephen, Edmund B. and Catherine B. Clarkson (1) -   October 11, 1849

Stephen, Elizabeth and Levi Bennett (1) -   August 27, 1818

Stephen, Sarah and Thomas Johnson (1) -   October 30, 1817

Stephens, Ann and Joshua F. Wigginton (2) -   (L) October 16, 1856

Stephens, Anna M. and Samuel T. Jones (3) -   October 23, 1878
    For further information see - Jones, Samuel T.

Stephens, David and Frances Villora Steadman (2) -   (L) February 2, 1854

Stephens, John C. and Mary F. O'Bannon (2) -   (L) November 27, 1850

Stephens, Joseph and Elizabeth Neumann (1) -   February 2, 1832

Stephens, Melvin T. and Mary J. Andrews (3) -   August 4, 1870
    Place of marriage, Jefferson County - Age of husband, 21 - Age of
    wife, 23 - Husband was born in Maryland - Wife was born in Jefferson
    County, Virginia - Both reside in Jefferson County. (Granted upon
    endorsement of H. Z. Roderick as to ages of parties.)

Stephens, Milton S. and Ann Rebecca Entler (2) -   (L) November 15, 1853

Stephens, Minnie E. and William B. Flinn (3) -   August 25, 1886
    For further information see - Flinn, William B.

Stephenson, Ann and Fountaine Beckham (1) -   1825

Stephenson, Anne Jane and Archibald Anderson (1) -   February 17, 1819

Stephenson, Daniel and Rachel R. Riley (1) -   April 3, 1834

Stephenson, David (cold.) Laura Virginia Robinson (3) -   March 2, 1876
    Place of marriage, Shepherdstown - Age of husband, 23 - Age of wife,
    22 - Both are Single - Husband was born in Loudoun County, Virginia -
    Wife was born in Jefferson County, West Virginia - Both reside in
    Jefferson County, West Virginia.

Stephenson, George B. and Mary Ellen Moler (1) -   May 6, 1849

Stephenson, George B. and Margaret C. Welch (2) -   (L) June 4, 1858

Stephenson, James and Eliza Kime (1) -   May 29, 1804

Stephenson, Martha B. and Camp. Beckham (1) -   February 27, 1823

Stephenson, Mary (cold.) Thompson Warick (3) -   August 12, 1880
    For further information see - Warick, Thompson.

Stephenson, Mary E. and Righter Levering (1) -   January 15, 1834

Stephenson, P. P. W. and Elizabeth Moore (1) -   December 12, 1842

Stevens, John (cold.) Catherine Hopewell (3) -   April 15, 1874
    Place of marriage, Shepherdstown - Age of husband, 23 - Age of wife,
    21 - Both are Single - Wife was born in Jefferson County, West
    Virginia - Both reside in Jefferson County, West Virginia.

Stevens, Robert and Elizabeth Brown (1) -   August 14, 1806

Stevenson, Richard (cold.) Emily Carter (3) -   December 26, 1867
    Age of husband, 30 - Age of wife, 21 - Husband is a Widower - Wife
    is Single - Both were born in Jefferson County - Both reside in
    Jefferson County - Occupation of husband is Laborer.

Stevenson, Rose (cold.) George Berry (3) -   December 23, 1880
    For further information see - Berry, George.

Steward, Susanna and John T. Pierce (2) -   (L) March 29, 1856

Stewart, Bushrod and Agnes Barr (3) -   December 31, 1884
    Place of marriage, Charlestown - Age of husband, 30 - Age of wife,
    22 - Husband is a Widower - Wife is Single - Both were born in
    Jefferson County, West Virginia - Husband resides in Clarke County,
    Virginia - Wife resides in Jefferson County, West Virginia.

Stewart, Bushrod W. and Patsy P. Carter (2) -   (L) December 10, 1857

Stewart, D. A. and Hattie Burton (3) -   April 7, 1887
  Place of marriage, Charlestown - Age of husband, 27 - Age of wife,
  22 - Both are Single - Husband was born in Alleghaney County,
  Pennsylvania - Wife was born in Jefferson County, West Virginia -
  Both reside in Jefferson County, West Virginia.

Stewart, Daniel and Harriet Rowe (2) -   (L) June 12, 1851

Stewart, David and Margaret E. Moore (3) -   June 8, 1875
  Place of marriage, near Duffields - Age of husband, 59 - Age of
  wife, 39 - Husband is a Widower - Wife is Single - Husband was born
  in Berkeley County, West Virginia - Wife was born in Jefferson
  County, West Virginia - Husband resides in Berkeley County, West
  Virginia - Wife resides in Jefferson County, West Virginia.

Stewart, Elizabeth and Henry Thornton Franks (2) -   (L) December 13, 1854

Stewart, George A. and Mary E. Needy (3) -   April 26, 1882
  Place of marriage, near Vancleavesville - Age of husband, 27 - Age
  of wife, 21 - Both are Single - Husband was born in Alleghany
  County, Pennsylvania - Wife was born in Jefferson County - Husband
  resides in Jefferson County, West Virginia - Wife resides in
  Jefferson County.

Stewart, Henry A. and Lilian B. Boyer (3) -   December 5, 1878
  Place of marriage, Brown's Crossing - Age of husband, 25 - Age of
  wife, 18 - Both are Single - Husband was born in Pennsylvania - Wife
  was born in Jefferson County, West Virginia - Both reside in
  Jefferson County, West Virginia. (Consent of bride's father in
  person.)

Stewart, Rev. James C. and Josephine V. Winters (3) -   (1869)
  Age of husband, 29 - Age of wife, 21 - Both were born in Maryland -
  Both reside in Jefferson County.

Stewart, John and Elizabeth Moore (1) -   April 27, 1820

Stewart, John L. and Mrs. Jane E. Feltner (2) -   (L) November 30, 1852

Stewart, John L. and Jane E. Feltner (widow) (1) -   December 2, 1852

Stewart, Lizzie and Jesse B. Heafer (3) -   December 24, 1888
  For further information see - Heafer, Jesse B.

Stewart, Lucinda and Robert R. Brotherton (2) -   (L) August 29, 1857

Stewart, Lucy Catherine and Oscar Ballenger (3) -   January 14, 1881
  For further information see - Ballenger, Oscar.

Stewart, Marcus B. and Katherine Halpin (3) -   June 8, 1881
  Place of marriage, near Keyes' Ferry - Age of husband, 28 - Age of
  wife, 25 - Both are Single - Husband was born in Alleghany County,
  Pennsylvania - Wife was born in Berkeley County, West Virginia -
  Both reside in Jefferson County, West Virginia.

Stewart, Mary A. and Andrew J. Lloyd (3) -   December 1866
  For further information see - Lloyd, Andrew J.

Stewart, Mary Catherine and Benjamin Ballenger (3) -   September 15, 1875
    For further information see - Ballenger, Benjamin.

Stewart, Mary E. and James Dunn (3) -   October 15, 1868
    For further information see - Dunn, James.

Stewart, Patsy and Philip Williams (3) -   June 10, 1867
    For further information see - Williams, Philip.

Stewart, Robert and Mary Young (1) -   March 1826

Stewart, S. E. and Jacob Crim (3) -   August 30, 1866
    For further information see - Crim, Jacob.

Stewart, William R. and Isabella J. Vanmetre (1) -   April 5, 1849

Stickels, Amelia Elizabeth and John A. Hibbard (3) -   November 14, 1878
    For further information see - Hibbard, John A.

Stickle, Jacob M. and Sally R. Locke (3) -   April 1, 1880
    Place of marriage, Charlestown - Age of husband, 31 - Age of wife,
    23 - Both are Single - Husband was born in Loudoun County, Virginia -
    Wife was born in Jefferson County, West Virginia - Both reside in
    Jefferson County, West Virginia.

Stickler, John M. and Jeanie D. Lock (3) -   December 17, 1867
    Place of marriage, Jefferson County - Age of husband, 25 - Age of
    wife, 19 - Both are Single - Husband was born in Loudoun County -
    Wife was born in Jefferson County - Both reside in Jefferson
    County - Husband's parents are Z. - Wife's parents are Joseph -
    Occupation of husband is Farmer.

Stickler, William O. and Anna E. Avis (3) -   March 4, 1884
    Place of marriage, near Shepherdstown - Age of husband, 28 - Age of
    wife, 25 - Both are Single - Husband was born in Hillsdale County,
    Michigan - Wife was born in Jefferson County, West Virginia -
    Husband resides in Michigan - Wife resides in Jefferson County, West
    Virginia.

Stickles, Katie E. and Isaac D. Myers (3) -   November 25, 1890
    For further information see - Myers, Isaac D.

Stickles, Thomas W. and Richdetta Cornell (3) -   May 1, 1872
    Place of marriage, Jefferson County - Age of husband, 25 - Age of
    wife, 18 - Both are Single - Both were born in Virginia - Both
    reside in West Virginia - Husband's parents are Henry and Mary E. -
    Wife's parents are Thomas and Harriet - Occupation of husband is
    Farmer. (Sworn to be Charles Cornell, brother.)

Stickley, James H. and Mary E. Lupton (3) -   July 19, 1889
    Place of marriage, Harpers Ferry - Age of husband, 27 - Age of wife,
    22 - Both are Single - Husband was born in Rockingham County,
    Virginia - Wife was born in Jefferson County, West Virginia -
    Husband resides in Rockingham County, Virginia - Wife resides in
    Jefferson County, West Virginia.

Stidman, Charles and Ann T. Busey (1) -   May 31, 1834

Stidman, Jefferson and Hannah Matheny (1) -   March 30, 1826

Stidman, John and Betsey Best (1) -   1812

Stidman, John W. and Sarah Ann Cook (1) -   November 16, 1834

Stidman, Levi and Catherine Combs (1) -   March 2, 1823

Stinger, Charles B. and Sarah Jane McDonald (2) -   (L) June 21, 1860

Stipe, J. H. and M. A. Blue (bride) (3) -   April 7, 1868
    Place of marriage, Jefferson County - Age of husband, 34 - Age of
    wife, 23 - Both are Single - Both were born in Clarke County,
    Virginia - Husband resides in Frederick, Virginia - Wife resides in
    Jefferson - Wife's parents are Margaret - Occupation of husband is
    Miller.

Stipes, Benjamin and Mary Ann Spangler (1) -   June 28, 1825

Stipes, Benjamin and Mary E. Perry (2) -   (L) March 23, 1853

Stipes, Benjamin and Mary A. Perry (1) -   March 23, 1853

Stipes, Elizabeth and Joshua Cox (1) -   January 14, 1824

Stipes, Ezekiel and Verlina Ogden (1) -   1816

Stipes, Henry and Pheby Buckles (1) -   1819

Stipes, Mary and Joseph Wentzell (2) -   (L) January 18, 1855

Stipes, Reuben and Anna Rollinson (1) -   May 1, 1817

Stipes, Thomas and Elvina Buckles (1) -   1820

Stipp, Jacob and Ruth Vanmetre (1) -   April 23, 1835

Stipp, Jacob M. and Mary E. Snyder (1) -   February 16, 1847

Stipp, Margaret and James Marshall (1) -   December 21, 1819

Stobbs, George H. and Ellen Kelly (3) -   October 25, 1875
    Place of marriage, near Harpers Ferry - Age of husband, 20 - Age of
    wife, 19 - Both are Single - Both were born in Jefferson County,
    West Virginia - Both reside in Jefferson County, West Virginia -
    (Consent of groom's father in person and bride's father in writing.)

Stock, Isaac and B. G. Cutshaw (3) -   December 15, 1868
    Place of marriage, Jefferson County - Age of husband, 43 - Age of
    wife, 28 - Both are Single - Husband was born in Loudoun County -
    Wife was born in Jefferson - Husband resides in Loudoun County -
    Wife resides in Jefferson County - Husband's parents are William
    and Elizabeth - Wife's parents are George W. and Martha - Occupation
    of husband is Farmer.

Stoliper, Ann E. and James H. Hockenberry (3) -   August 9, 1883
    For further information see - Hockenberry, James H.

Stolle, Charles William and Julia A. Bishop (3) -   December 2, 1880
    Place of marriage, Charlestown - Age of husband, 25 - Age of wife,
    21 - Both are Single - Husband was born in Jefferson County, West
    Virginia - Wife was born in Loudoun County, Virginia - Husband
    resides in Clarke County, Virginia - Wife resides in Jefferson
    County, West Virginia.

Stone, Helen V. and Thomas K. Wallace (2) -   (L) July 19, 1858

Stone, Richard and Sarah Andsworth (1) -   August 15, 1819

Stone, Samuel and Courtney H. Jones (1) -   June 22, 1817

Stone, William and Betsy Bennett (1) -   January 20, 1820

Stonebraker, Joseph M. and Ann Elizabeth Hill (2) -   (L) October 23, 1855

Stonebraker, Lillie V. and George P. Ochershausen (3) -   September 7, 1887
    For further information see - Ochershausen, George P.

Stoneseifer, Elmer E. and Margaret G. Avis (3) -   March 26, 1889
    Place of marriage, Charlestown - Age of husband, 27 - Age of wife,
    24 - Both are Single - Husband was born in Frederick County,
    Maryland - Wife was born in Jefferson County, West Virginia - Both
    reside in Jefferson County, West Virginia.

Stonesifer, Thomas and Ann Amelia Rightstine (3) -   February 11, 1873
    Place of marriage, Shepherdstown - Age of husband, 21 - Age of wife,
    21 - Both are Single - Husband was born in Maryland - Wife was born
    in Jefferson County - Husband resides at Mechanicsburg,
    Pennsylvania - Wife resides in Jefferson County, West Virginia -
    Husband's parents are Daniel and Isabella - Wife's parents are Adam
    and Mary - Occupation of husband is Paper Maker.

Stop, Ann M. and James W. Marlett (3) -   (1869)
    For further information see - Marlett, James W.

Storm, Eugien and Laura N. Laley (3) -   April 5, 1869
    Place of marriage, Jefferson County - Age of husband, 22 - Age of
    wife, 17 - Both are Single - Both were born in Jefferson County -
    Both reside in Jefferson County - Husband's parents are John C. and
    Frances L. - Wife's parents are M. and Susan - Occupation of husband
    is Clerk.   (Mother gives consent in writing.)

Storm, Maria Dora and Edward Landers (3) -   February 27, 1876
    For further information see - Landers, Edward.

Storm, Sarah and Jacob Seglar (1) -   November 29, 1823

Story, William and Margaret Sheerer (1) -   January 21, 1833

Stouffer, Henry and Jane Heflebower (3) -   January 8, 1873
    Place of marriage, near Rippon - Age of husband, 45 - Age of wife,
    31 - Both are Single - Husband was born in York County, Pennsylvania -
    Wife was born in Jefferson County, West Virginia - Both reside in
    Jefferson County, West Virginia - Husband's parents are Joseph and
    Susanna - Wife's parents are Daniel and Lydia Heflebower -
    Occupation of husband is Farmer.

551

Stouffer, Maggie E. and Benjamin F. Myers (3) -   August 31, 1869
    For further information see - Myers, Benjamin F.

Stouffer, Mary I. and John M. Dunlap (3) -   March 5, 1890
    For further information see - Dunlap, John M.

Stover, George W. and Mary Ellen Earnshaw (1) -   November 7, 1848

Stover, Susan P. and Michael T. Nichols (2) -   (L) May 14, 1859

Strailman, George W. and Ann C. Neer (2) -   (L) October 22, 1851

Strailman, George W. and Ann C. Near (1) -   October 23, 1851

Strain, George and Elizabeth Whittington (1) -   April 19, 1827

Strain, S. J. and Lucy G. Conrad (3) -   October 1, 1867
    Place of marriage, Jefferson - Age of husband, 30 - Age of wife,
    20 - Both are Single - Husband was born in Jefferson County - Wife
    was born in Warren County, Virginia - Both reside in Jefferson
    County - Husband's parents are George and Elizabeth - Wife's
    parents are Joseph and Jane - Occupation of husband is Blacksmith.
    (Parents' consents in writing.)

Straith, Ella and David L. Briscoe (3) -   December 12, 1872
    For further information see - Briscoe, David L.

Straith, John A. and Charlotte Alexander (2) -   (L) August 25, 1864
    Time of marriage, August 25, 1864 - Place of marriage, Mrs. Ann
    Burnett's near Charlestown - Names, John A. Straith and Charlotte
    Alexander - Age of husband, 29 years - Age of wife, 28 years - Both
    are Single - Both were born in Jefferson County - Both reside in
    Jefferson County - Names of husband's parents are John J. H. and
    Mary A. E. Straith - Names of wife's parents are William and ?
    Alexander - Occupation of husband is Surgeon and Physician -
    License issued, August 25, 1864 - T. A. Moore, Clerk.

Straith, John J. H. and Mary A. E. Myers (1) -   November 27, 1833

Strauls, Nancy and Christian Benner (2) -   (L) September 10, 1859

Strawbridge, Lydia and David Shane (1) -   January 12, 1833

Strayer, Margaret S. and James E. Thomas (3) -   July 1, 1869
    For further information see - Thomas, James E.

Streams, Horace (cold.) Martha Freeman (3) -   January 6, 1876
    Place of marriage, Jefferson County - Age of husband, 21 - Age of
    wife, 19 - Both are Single - Husband was born in Maryland - Wife was
    born in Jefferson County, West Virginia - Both reside in Jefferson
    County, West Virginia. (Consent of bride's father in person.)

Streams, J. and John Edwards (3) -   October 14, 1868
    For further information see - Edwards, John.

Stribling, Anna Maria Virginia (cold.) John H. Johnson (3) - September 6, 1881
    For further information see - Johnson, John H.

Stribling, Benjamin (cold.) Mary Lee (3) -   May 18, 1880
    Place of marriage, Shepherdstown - Age of husband, 48 - Age of wife,
    48 - Husband is a Widower - Wife is a Widow - Both were born in
    Jefferson County, West Virginia - Both reside in Jefferson County,
    West Virginia.

Stribling, Daniel (cold.) Mary Powell (3) -   August 23, 1875
    Place of marriage, Shepherdstown - Age of husband, 25 - Age of wife,
    21 - Both are Single - Both were born in Jefferson County, West
    Virginia - Both reside in Jefferson County, West Virginia.

Stribling, Mary V. (cold.) John W. Brown (3) -   May 10, 1877
    For further information see - Brown, John W.

Stribling, Sally (cold.) Thomas Homes (3) -   December 27, 1882
    For further information see - Homes, Thomas.

Stribling, Susan (cold.) Alfred Edwards (3) -   November 13, 1884
    For further information see - Edwards, Alfred.

Strickler, Anna and J. D. Waters (3) -   April 22, 1888
    For further information see - Waters, J. D.

Strider, A. C. and Adellbert Robinson (3) -   February 27, 1890
    For further information see - Robinson, Adellbert.

Strider, Ann and William Green (1) -   February 28, 1822

Strider, Anna M. and James M. Trussell (3) -   February 8, 1876
    For further information see - Trussell, James M.

Strider, Charlotte and Joseph Hall (1) -   June 1, 1809

Strider, Florence E. and John P. Hess (3) -   April 9, 1879
    For further information see - Hess, John P.

Strider, I. Keyes and Emma F. Jones (3) -   February 4, 1880
    Place of marriage, Charlestown - Age of husband, 28 - Age of wife,
    26 - Both are Single - Both were born in Jefferson County, West
    Virginia - Both reside in Jefferson County, West Virginia.

Strider, John S. and Mary Frances Engle (2) -   (L) August 25, 1856

Strider, Lucy M. and S. B. Sponseller (3) -   March 31, 1880
    For further information see - Sponseller, S. B.

Strider, Luke C. and Mary G. Tomlinson (3) -   February 11, 1880
    Place of marriage, Charlestown - Age of husband, 28 - Age of wife,
    27 - Both are Single - Both were born in Jefferson County, West
    Virginia - Husband resides at Washington City, D. C. - Wife resides
    in Jefferson County, West Virginia.   (Returned January 1883.)

Strider, Mary and Francis Lee (3) -   August 16, 1866
    For further information see - Lee, Francis.

Strider, Mary A. and Thomas G. Plummer (2) -   (L) June 13, 1859

Strider, Minnie Lee and W. K. Marshall (3) -   October 19, 1887
    For further information see - Marshall, W. K.

553

Strider, Samuel J. and Ann Rebecca Darkus Howard (1) -   October 21, 1828

Strider, Samuel V. and Caroline V. Rhulman (2) -   (L) November 6, 1852

Strider, Mrs. Sarah (widow) and Watts Watson (2) -   (L) January 6, 1857

Strider, Sarah E. and William J. Moler (2) -   (L) April 2, 1863
For further information see - Moler, William J.

Strider, Theresa M. and Robert W. Moler (1) -   January 25, 1849

Strider, William and Lidia F. Moore (1) -   1816

Stripling, Ben (cold.) Paint. Mason (3) -   July 24, 1883
Place of marriage, Kearneysville - Age of husband, 24 - Age of wife, 18 - Both are Single - Both were born in Jefferson County, West Virginia - Both reside in Jefferson County, West Virginia. (Consent of bride's mother certified by Tucker Ford.)

Stripling, Fanny (cold.) Adam Williams (3) -   December 17, 1879
For further information see - Williams, Adam.

Stripling, Thomas (colored) Margaret Patterson (3) -   January 25, 1870
Place of marriage, Jefferson County - Age of husband, 28 - Age of wife, 23 - Husband was born in Virginia - Wife was born in Jefferson County - Both reside in Jefferson County.

Strippy, Mary Ellen and John H. Musgrove (3) -   September 23, 1869
For further information see - Musgrove, John H.

Strobel, Mary and John Ditmyer (3) -   January 23, 1866
For further information see - Ditmyer, John.

Strode, Elizabeth and Alexander Mason (1) -   February 17, 1807

Strode, Parker H. and Mary E. Lucas (3) -   January 23, 1866
Place of marriage, Charlestown, Jefferson County - Age of husband, 29 - Age of wife, 22 - Both are Single - Husband was born in Berkeley County, West Virginia - Wife was born in Jefferson County, West Virginia - Both reside in Jefferson County, West Virginia - Husband's parents are Joseph and Ellenora P. Strode - Wife's parents are Edward and Mary E. Lucas - Occupation of husband is Merchant.

Strode, S. E. (bride) and E. B. Dorrough (3) -   (1868)
For further information see - Dorrough, E. B.

Strosnider, Joseph and Frances Steel (3) -   May 9, 1878
Place of marriage, Charlestown - Age of husband, 29 - Age of wife, 35 - Both are Single - Husband was born in Hardy County, West Virginia - Wife was born in Jefferson County, West Virginia - Both reside in Jefferson County, West Virginia.

Strother, Burr H. and Mary Ellen Brotherton (2) -   (L) September 1, 1857

Strother, Daniel (cold.) Dinah Jones (3) -   April 5, 1888
Place of marriage, Charlestown - Age of husband, 60 - Age of wife, 30 - Husband is Single - Wife is a Widow - Husband was born in Rappahannock County, Virginia - Wife was born in Clarke County, Virginia - Both reside in Jefferson County, West Virginia.

Strother, David H. and Mary J. E. Hunter (2) -   (L) May 4, 1861
    Date of marriage, May 6, 1861 - Place of marriage, Charlestown - Age
    of husband, 44 years and seven months - Age of wife, 28 years -
    Husband is a Widower - Wife is Single - Place of husband's birth was
    in Berkeley County, Virginia - Place of wife's birth was in Jefferson
    County, Virginia - Husband's residence is in Morgan County, Virginia -
    Wife's residence is in Jefferson County, Virginia - Names of
    husband's parents are John and Elizabeth Strother (nee Hunter) -
    Names of wife's parents are David and Rebecca Hunter (nee Lane) -
    Occupation of husband is Artist - David H. Strother.

Strother, Eliza and Benjamin Pendleton (1) -   October 31, 1805

Strother, Elizabeth and Jarrett Moore (1) -   September 19, 1820

Strother, John (black) Margaret Washington (3) -   (1870)
    Age of husband, 21 - Age of wife, 19 - Both were born in Virginia -
    Both reside in Jefferson County. (Parents willing.)

Strother, John (cold.) Elizabeth Longerbeam (3) -   September 14, 1878
    Place of marriage, Harpers Ferry - Age of husband, 25 - Age of wife,
    24 - Both are Single - Husband was born in Culpeper County,
    Virginia - Wife was born in Loudoun County, Virginia - Both reside
    in Jefferson County, West Virginia.

Strother, John W. and Mary L. Irvig (3) -   July 15, 1869
    Place of marriage, Jefferson County - Age of husband, 25 - Age of
    wife, 22 - Husband was born in Virginia - Wife was born in West
    Virginia - Husband resides in Jefferson County - Wife resides in
    West Virginia.

Strother, Joseph and Amelia Davenport (1) -   June 5, 1808

Strother, Laura A. (cold.) John Edward Robinson (3) -   December 21, 1882
    For further information see - Robinson, John Edward.

Strother, Lucy (cold.) Samuel Jones (3) -   January 23, 1890
    For further information see - Jones, Samuel.

Strother, Margaret and Cato Moore (1) -   April 26, 1814

Strother, Margaret and Peter W. Kerney (1) -   December 5, 1820

Strother, Martha Newton and Garland Moore Davis (1) -   February 22, 1825

Strother, Mary and Richard Duffield (1) -   June 7, 1814

Strother, Nellie (cold.) Joseph Hamilton (3) -   December 18, 1890
    For further information see - Hamilton, Joseph.

Strother, Sarah C. and David Jackson Hime (3) -   September 13, 1867
    For further information see - Hime, David Jackson.

Strother, Willis (cold.) Martha Payne (3) -   June 21, 1884
    Place of marriage, Flowing Spring - Age of husband, 45 - Age of
    wife, 37 - Husband is a Widower - Wife is a Widow - Husband was born
    in Culpeper County, Virginia - Wife was born in Amherst County,
    Virginia - Both reside in Jefferson County, West Virginia.

Strothers, Eveline and Moses Turner (3) -   June 14, 1868
    For further information see - Turner, Moses.

Stuart, H. Etty and John T. Reed (3) -   February 23, 1887
    For further information see - Reed, John T.

Stuart, Lizzie and Robert Watson (3) -   December 8, 1881
    For further information see - Watson, Robert.

Stuart, William Henry and Teresa Leavy (3) -   July 19, 1883
    Place of marriage, Bolivar - Age of husband, 25 - Age of wife, 18 -
    Both are Single - Husband was born in Wisconsin - Wife was born in
    Jefferson County, West Virginia - Both reside in Jefferson County,
    West Virginia. (Consent of bride's mother certified by her brother.)

Stubbs, Mary Jane (cold.) George W. McCan (3) -   May 11, 1886
    For further information see - McCan, George W.

Stubbs, Newton (cold.) Sally Anderson (3) -   November 3, 1873
    Place of marriage, Shepherdstown - Age of husband, 25 - Age of wife,
    22 - Both are Single - Husband was born in Rockingham County,
    Virginia - Both reside in Jefferson County, West Virginia.

Stull, William and Eliza Buzzard (2) -   (L) September 1, 1854

Stultz, Mary Elizabeth and Israel Henry Iler (2) -   (L) July 14, 1853

Stump, Abram and Ann Amelia Bowers (3) -   December 7, 1880
    Place of marriage, near Charlestown - Age of husband, 40 - Age of
    wife, 20 - Husband is a Widower - Wife is Single - Husband was born
    in Pennsylvania - Wife was born in Jefferson County, West Virginia -
    Both reside in Jefferson County, West Virginia. (Consent of bride's
    father in person.)

Stump, Mary S. and John Burns (3) -   September 13, 1866
    For further information see - Burns, John.

Stump, William C. Orr and Ann C. Rowan (3) -   June 26, 1866
    Place of marriage, Harpers Ferry, Jefferson County - Age of husband,
    26 - Age of wife, 24 - Both are Single - Husband was born at
    Abbington, Virginia - Wife was born at Charlestown, Jefferson County,
    West Virginia - Both reside at Charlestown, Jefferson County, West
    Virginia - Occupation of husband is Telegraph Opperator.

Sturdy, Thomas and Eliza Near (1) -   July 29, 1832

Stypes, Sarah and John Keller (1) -   1822

Stypes, Thomas and Elvina Buckles (1) -   1822

Sublett, Thomas E. and Charlotte H. Lackland (2) -   (L) April 5, 1859

Suddith, Arthur J. and Mary Ann McDonald (2) -   (L) August 11, 1852

Suddith, Arthur J. and Mary Ann McDonald (1) -   August 12, 1852

Suddith, William A. and Mrs. Ann E. Skinner (2) -   (L) December 3, 1853

Suffrons, Sarah and Samuel Massey (1) -   October 27, 1808

Sullivan, C. H. B. and Susan E. Burns (1) -   June 18, 1850

Sullivan, J. G. and Annie C. Harding (3) -   October 18, 1883
   Place of marriage, Harpers Ferry - Age of husband, 35 - Age of wife,
   35 - Husband is a Widower - Wife is Single - Husband was born in
   Caroline County, Maryland - Wife was born in Jefferson County, West
   Virginia - Husband resides in Queen Anne County, Maryland - Wife
   resides in Jefferson County, West Virginia.

Sullivan, James O. and Mary Jane Sullivan (2) -   (L) March 26, 1857

Sullivan, John and Elizabeth Athy (1) -   October 15, 1815

Sullivan, John and Susan Nunberger (2) -   (L) November 3, 1864
   Time of marriage - Place of marriage, Bolivar - Names, John
   Sullivan and Susan Nunberger - Age of husband, 24 years - Age of
   wife, 22 years - Both are Single - Place of husband's birth was in
   State of New York - Place of wife's birth was in Jefferson County,
   Virginia - Place of husband's residence is in State of New York -
   Place of wife's residence is in Town of Bolivar - Names of husband's
   parents are - Names of wife's parents are Conrad Nunberger and
   Hannah (now Smith) - Occupation of husband is Soldier in Federal
   Army - License issued, November 3, 1864 - T. A. Moore, Clerk.

Sullivan, John F. and Jane C. W. Burns (2) -   (L) March 11, 1854

Sullivan, Mary Jane and James O. Sullivan (2) -   (L) March 26, 1857

Sullivan, Samuel and Jane McKinney (1) -   December 30, 1829

Sullivan, T. J. W. and Clarissa Moor (1) -   January 4, 1849

Sumers, Andrew and Susan M. Watts (1) -   October 28, 1827

Summers, John D. and Mary E. Staley (3) -   December 12, 1866
   Place of marriage, Shepherdstown, West Virginia - Age of husband,
   30 - Age of wife, 25 - Husband is a Widower - Wife is Single -
   Husband was born in Augusta County, Virginia - Wife was born at
   Shepherdstown, Jefferson County, West Virginia - Husband resides at
   Parkersburg, West Virginia - Wife resides at Shepherdstown, Jefferson
   County, West Virginia - Husband's parents are Daniel and Julia
   Summers - Wife's parents are Jacob and Elizabeth Staley - Occupation
   of husband is Clerk.

Summers, Lewis (cold.) Emily Johnson (3) -   June 1, 1881
   Place of marriage, Charlestown - Age of husband, 33 - Age of wife,
   26 - Both are Single - Both were born in Jefferson County, West
   Virginia - Both reside in Jefferson County, West Virginia.

Summers, Mary E. and James E. Redmon (3) -   November 16, 1887
   For further information see - Redmon, James E.

Supinger, Robert W. and Alberta Miller (3) -   December 21, 1874
   Place of marriage, Charles Town - Age of husband, 25 - Age of wife,
   21 - Both are Single - Both were born in Shenandoah County,
   Virginia - Husband resides in Shenandoah County, Virginia - Wife
   resides in Jefferson County, West Virginia.

Suthard, W. H. and Bettie B. Gruber (3) - November 7, 1875
    Place of marriage, near Summit Point - Age of husband, 24 - Age of wife, 15 - Both are Single - Husband was born in Page County, Virginia - Wife was born in Jefferson County, West Virginia - Both reside in Jefferson County, West Virginia. (Consent of bride's mother in writing.)

Sutherland, Rosa J. and D. W. Reinhart (3) - December 20, 1876
    For further information see - Reinhart, D. W.

Sutton, John C. and Matilda E. Roeder (3) - May 22, 1877
    Place of marriage, Harpers Ferry - Age of husband, 35 - Age of wife, 28 - Both are Single - Husband was born at London, England - Wife was born in Jefferson County, West Virginia - Both reside in Jefferson County, West Virginia.

Sutton, William B. and Bettie R. Humphreys (2) - (L) April 10, 1852

Swagler, Jacob and Ann Moler (1) - May 14, 1818

Swain, C. M. and Jennie Helferstay (3) - February 25, 1890
    Place of marriage, Shepherdstown - Age of husband, 30 - Age of wife, 21 - Both are Single - Both were born in Jefferson County, West Virginia - Both reside in Jefferson County, West Virginia.

Swain, Crast and Belle Gamil (3) - January 28, 1885
    Place of marriage, Harpers Ferry - Age of husband, 23 - Age of wife, 23 - Both are Single - Husband was born in Jefferson County, West Virginia - Wife was born in Rockingham County, Virginia - Husband resides in Loudoun County - Wife resides in Jefferson County, West Virginia.

Swallow, Emma M. Whitfield and John Perkins Bartlett (3) - October 3, 1877
    For further information see - Bartlett, John Perkins.

Swan, Elizabeth and William Jones (1) - August 1, 1816

Swan, Rachel (cold.) James Colston (3) - July 30, 1874
    For further information see - Colston, James.

Swan, Susan (cold.) Charles Parker (3) - July 28, 1887
    For further information see - Parker, Charles.

Swann, E. Hunter and Fannie V. Brown (3) - December 26, 1889
    Place of marriage, Charlestown - Age of husband, 31 - Age of wife, 26 - Both are Single - Husband was born in Frederick County, Virginia - Wife was born in Jefferson County, West Virginia - Both reside in Jefferson County, West Virginia.

Swann, Ellen Harriet and Samuel Hoffmaster (2) - (L) June 3, 1856

Swann, Georgianna and Alexander J. Shaner (2) - (L) June 9, 1851
    (Wit. S. H. Fowler.)

Swann, Major and Eliza Ebert (1) - August 18, 1806

Swann, Susan (cold.) Sidney Wilson (3) - October 30, 1873
    For further information see - Wilson, Sidney.

Swartz, George W. and Hannah Jolley (3) -　　　　　　　　December 31, 1889
　　Place of marriage, Middleway - Age of husband, 23 - Age of wife, 20 -
　　Both are Single - Both were born in Jefferson County, West
　　Virginia - Both reside in Jefferson County, West Virginia.
　　(Consent of bride's mother in writing.)

Swartz, Lucy and Shipley Sheerer Smallwood (3) -　　　　　August 15, 1883
　　For further information see - Smallwood, Shipley Sheerer.

Swartzwelder, Augusta J. and John Scott (3) -　　　　　　November 19, 1885
　　For further information see - Scott, John.

Swartzwelder, Maude and Theodore Clark West (3) -　　　November 19, 1885
　　For further information see - West, Theodore Clark.

Swartzwilder, Mary and William Tidvall (3) -　　　　　　September 25, 1883
　　For further information see - Tidvall, William.

Swayne, N. H. and Sarah Ann St.Clair Wager (1) -　　　　September 5, 1832

Swayne, S. W. and Sady O. Horner (3) -　　　　　　　　　　July 3, 1883
　　Place of marriage, Bolivar - Age of husband, 27 - Age of wife, 21 -
　　Husband is a Widower - Wife is Single - Husband was born in Jefferson
　　County, West Virginia - Wife was born in Rockingham County,
　　Virginia - Husband resides in Jefferson County - Wife resides in
　　Jefferson County, West Virginia.

Swearingen, Elmira and James T. Markell (1) -　　　　　　November 7, 1839

Swearingen, Rebecca and George S. Kennedy (1) -　　　　September 21, 1831

Swearingen, Sarah H. V. and Henry Berry (1) -　　　　　　July 4, 1822

Swearingen, Van and Elizabeth Morgan (1) -　　　　　　　January 26, 1809

Swearinger, Henry V. and Sarah A. Breedin (1) -　　　　January 26, 1819

Sweny, Ann Catherine and Joseph Spencer (1) -　　　　　　　　　　1820

Swigart, Maggie J. and James A. Watson (3) -　　　　　　　　　　(1872)
　　For further information see - Watson, James A.

Swigart, Mary E. and James A. Watson (3) -　　　　　　　September 5, 1875
　　For further information see - Watson, James A.

Swimley, Catharine Elizabeth and Joseph Franklin Hess (2) -
　　　　　　　　　　　　　　　　　　　　　　　　　　　　(L) February 15, 1861

Swimley, Henerita and Thomas Watson (3) -　　　　　　　　October 6, 1870
　　For further information see - Watson, Thomas.

Swimley, Henretta and Thomas Watson (3) -　　　　　　　　October 6, 1870
　　For further information see - Watson, Thomas.

Swimley, Jefferson and Margaret Farnsworth (1) -　　　　April 20, 1848

Swimley, John W. and Lydia C. Bell (2) - (L) November 21, 1861
    Time of marriage, November 26, 1861 - Place of marriage, Father's
Residence - Names, John W. Swimley and Lydia C. Bell - Age of
husband, 26 years - Age of wife, 19 years - Condition of husband is
Single - Condition of wife is Single - Place of husband's birth was
in Berkeley County, Virginia - Place of wife's birth was in Berkeley
County, Virginia - Place of husband's residence is in Jefferson
County, Virginia - Place of wife's residence is in Jefferson
County, Virginia - Names of husband's parents are Henry and Mary
Swimley - Names of wife's parents are Vance and Elizabeth Bell -
Occupation of husband is Salesman - Given under my hand this 21st
day of November 1861 - John W. Swimley - Consent of bride's
father given in person - T. A. Moore.

Swimley, Mary V. and Otho J. Hardesty (3) - September 2, 1873
    For further information see - Hardesty, Otho J.

Swope, Celia Ann and John R. Turner (3) - June 2, 1873
    For further information see - Turner, John R.

Swope, John H. and Lararaina Long (3) - (1870)
    Age of husband, 25 - Age of wife, 27 - Husband was born in
Maryland - Wife was born in Virginia - Husband resides in Jefferson
County, West Virginia - Wife resides in Jefferson County.
(Consent of father of lady in writing consenting. All the facts
sworn to by John H. Swope.)

Sybole, Mrs. Mary (widow) and John Sakeman (2) - (L) July 13, 1853

Tabb, George William and Henrietta Jackson (3) - October 26, 1871
   Place of marriage, Jefferson County - Age of husband, 24 - Age of
   wife, 24 - Both are Single - Both were born in Virginia - Both
   reside in West Virginia - Husband's parents are Henry and Frances -
   Occupation of husband is Farmer.

Tabler, J. Calvin and Gertie W. Yantis (3) - February 15, 1888
   Place of marriage, Harpers Ferry - Age of husband, 40 - Age of wife,
   25 - Husband is a Widower - Wife is Single - Husband was born in
   Berkeley County, West Virginia - Wife was born in Jefferson County,
   West Virginia - Both reside in Jefferson County, West Virginia.

Tabler, John N. and Abby E. Hoffman (3) - November 27, 1873
   Place of marriage, near Kabletown - Age of husband, 43 - Age of
   wife, 25 - Both are Single - Husband was born in Berkeley County,
   West Virginia - Wife was born in Jefferson County, West Virginia -
   Husband resides in Berkeley County, West Virginia - Wife resides in
   Jefferson County, West Virginia.

Tacey, George W. and Sarah Dillow (2) - (L) November 5, 1858

Tackett, John O. and Bettie M. Moore (3) - June 4, 1890
   Place of marriage, Oakland - Age of husband, 41 - Age of wife, 31 -
   Both are Single - Husband was born in Stafford County, Virginia -
   Wife was born in Jefferson County, West Virginia - Husband resides
   in Fauquier County, Virginia - Wife resides in Jefferson County,
   West Virginia.

Taff, H. J. and Ida Jane Tutwiler (2) - (L) July 1, 1858

Talbot, Miss Virginia and M. C. Zombro (3) - August 22, 1875
   For further information see - Zombro, M. C.

Talbott, Annie (cold.) Lawrence Washington (3) - March 12, 1883
   For further information see - Washington, Lawrence.

Talbott, Charlotte Louisa (cold.) B. L. Adams (3) - August 28, 1879
   For further information see - Adams, B. L.

Talbott, Ed. P. (cold.) Helen Whalin (3) - April 6, 1876
   Place of marriage, Charlestown - Age of husband, 30 - Age of wife,
   21 - Husband is a Widower - Wife is Single - Both were born in
   Jefferson County, West Virginia - Both reside in Jefferson County,
   West Virginia.

Taliaferro, A. A. and Lucy H. Bates (3) - April 22, 1886
   Place of marriage, Middleway - Age of husband, 27 - Age of wife,
   23 - Both are Single - Husband was born in Caroline County,
   Virginia - Wife was born in Jefferson County, West Virginia -
   Husband resides in Caroline County, Virginia - Wife resides in
   Jefferson County, West Virginia.

Tally, Mrs. Catharine (widow) and Charles Kirk (2) - (L) November 14, 1853

Tanner, Iola and J. S. Sheetz (3) - September 19, 1887
   For further information see - Sheetz, J. S.

Tanner, Mary I. and George W. Banks (3) - August 26, 1889
   For further information see - Banks, George W.

Tanquary, A. H. and L. E. Fry (bride) (3) - April 2, 1867
    Place of marriage, near Smithfield - Age of husband, 32 - Age of wife, 25 - Both are Single - Husband was born in Frederick County, Virginia - Wife was born in Jefferson County, West Virginia - Husband resides in Frederick County, Virginia - Wife resides in Jefferson County, West Virginia - Husband's parents are James and Maria Tanquary - Wife's parents are D. and Rebecca Fry - Occupation of husband is Farmer.

Tanquary, Alfred Farra and Maggie Daniel Beller (3) - December 28, 1886
    Place of marriage, Charlestown - Age of husband, 22 - Age of wife, 21 - Both are Single - Husband was born in Rockbridge County, Virginia - Wife was born in Jefferson County, West Virginia. - Both reside in Jefferson County, West Virginia.

Tanquary, Bessie F. and C. T. Shugert (3) - January 11, 1887
    For further information see - Shugert, C. T.

Tapp, Selona and William Wilson (3) - November 28, 1867
    For further information see - Wilson, William.

Tapscott, Baker and Ellen Morrow Baker (1) - January 20, 1824

Tate, Mary Ann and Joseph T. Daugherty (1) - May 12, 1825

Tavener, Laura B. and James T. Littleton (3) - January 28, 1875
    For further information see - Littleton, James T.

Taylor, Ann and Isaac Fleming (1) - July 4, 1833

Taylor, Annie (cold.) Robert Burns (3) - August 6, 1884
    For further information see - Burns, Robert.

Taylor, Annie C. and George Franklin Bowers (3) - May 8, 1888
    For further information see - Bowers, George Franklin.

Taylor, Budd (cold.) Harriet Johnson (3) - October 25, 1883
    Place of marriage, Bride's Residence - Age of husband, 23 - Age of wife, 20 - Both are Single - Both were born in Jefferson County, West Virginia - Both reside in Jefferson County, West Virginia. (Consent of bride's father in person.)

Taylor, C. W. and Katy Rohr (3) - July 7, 1884
    Place of marriage, Charlestown - Age of husband, 26 - Age of wife, 26 - Both are Single - Both were born in Jefferson County, West Virginia - Husband resides in Clarke County, Virginia - Wife resides in Jefferson County, West Virginia.

Taylor, Charles and Mary Helms (3) - November 28, 1872
    Place of marriage, Jefferson County, West Virginia - Age of husband, 25 - Age of wife, 21 - Both are Single - Both were born in Virginia - Husband's parents are Reuben and Sophia - Wife's parents are Stephen and Hannah - Occupation of husband is Laborer.

Taylor, Charles (cold.) Lizzie Johnson (3) - June 7, 1883
    Place of marriage, Charlestown - Age of husband, 21 - Age of wife, 20 - Both are Single - Husband was born in Page County, Virginia - Wife was born in Washington County, Maryland - Both reside in Jefferson County, West Virginia.

Taylor, Charles (cold.) Nancy Newman (3) - July 22, 1886
   Place of marriage, near Shannon Dale - Age of husband, 22 - Age of
   wife, 23 - Both are Single - Husband was born in Page County,
   Virginia - Wife was born in Jefferson County, West Virginia -
   Husband resides in Jefferson County - Wife resides in Jefferson
   County, West Virginia.

Taylor, Charles Moses (cold.) Mary Queen (3) - February 20, 1888
   Place of marriage, near Charlestown - Age of husband, 23 - Age of
   wife, 25 - Both are Single - Both were born in Jefferson County,
   West Virginia - Both reside in Jefferson County, West Virginia.

Taylor, Clarissa (cold.) William Pierce (3) - December 24, 1874
   For further information see - Pierce, William.

Taylor, David and Fanny Colbert (1) - October 8, 1815

Taylor, David (cold.) Mary Berry (3) - June 11, 1874
   Place of marriage, Summit Point - Age of husband, 26 - Age of wife,
   21 - Both are Single - Husband was born in Clarke County, Virginia -
   Wife was born in Jefferson County, West Virginia - Husband resides
   in Clarke County, Virginia - Wife resides in Jefferson County, West
   Virginia.

Taylor, Eliza and Charles D. Shiner (3) - April 21, 1869
   For further information see - Shiner, Charles D.

Taylor, Ella D. and C. A. Beck (3) - January 5, 1881
   For further information see - Beck, C. A.

Taylor, Emily (cold.) Adam Burnett (3) - February 16, 1888
   For further information see - Burnett, Adam.

Taylor, Emily R. and John M. Howell (3) - April 14, 1871
   For further information see - Howell, John M.

Taylor, Emma R. and John M. Howell (3) - April 19, 1871
   For further information see - Howell, John M.

Taylor, Frank and Annie Ashby (3) - May 10, 1879
   Place of marriage, Charlestown, West Virginia - Age of husband, 21 -
   Age of wife, 21 - Both are Single - Both were born in Jefferson
   County, West Virginia - Both reside in Jefferson County, West
   Virginia.

Taylor, Georgie (cold.) D. Lee Tolbert (3) - September 11, 1879
   For further information see - Tolbert, D. Lee.

Taylor, Ginnie (cold.) Charles Murray (3) - December 20, 1883
   For further information see - Murray, Charles.

Taylor, Grifin and Elizabeth Beall (1) - January 16, 1823

Taylor, Helen and Joseph Hall (3) - April 9, 1871
   For further information see - Hall, Joseph.

Taylor, Helen V. and E. Redferor (3) - November 28, 1867
   For further information see - Redferor, E.

Taylor, Hester L. and Levi Moler (1) - October 25, 1831

Taylor, Jack (cold.) Harriet Newman (3) -   August 3, 1881
    Place of marriage, Charlestown - Age of husband, 39 - Age of wife,
    35 - Both are Single - Husband was born in Madison County, Virginia -
    Wife was born in Jefferson County, West Virginia - Both reside in
    Jefferson County, West Virginia.

Taylor, Jane and John W. Ross (3) -   (1869)
    For further information see - Ross, John W.

Taylor, John and Eliza Creps (1) -   1827

Taylor, John C. and Mary E. V. Conner (3) -   March 21, 1866
    Place of marriage, Shepherdstown, Jefferson County - Age of husband,
    22 - Age of wife, 24 - Both are Single - Husband was born in
    Hampshire County, West Virginia - Wife was born in Jefferson County,
    West Virginia - Husband resides in Frederick County, Virginia - Wife
    resides in Jefferson County, West Virginia - Wife's parents are
    David and Elizabeth Conner - Occupation of husband is Farmer.

Taylor, John W. and Barbara Ann Crider (2) -   (L) February 9, 1856

Taylor, John W. and Nannie Butler (3) -   April 20, 1869
    Place of marriage, Jefferson County - Age of husband, 28 - Age of
    wife, 21 - Both are Single - Both were born in Jefferson County -
    Both reside in Jefferson County.

Taylor, Julia (cold.) George Wells (3) -   September 5, 1883
    For further information see - Wells, George.

Taylor, Laura M. (cold.) George M. Hart (3) -   May 15, 1888
    For further information see - Hart, George M.

Taylor, Lemuel T. and Rebecca J. Roberts (2) -   (L) December 3, 1851

Taylor, Lizzy (cold.) Lewis Harrison (3) -   March 10, 1877
    For further information see - Harrison, Lewis.

Taylor, Lucinda and Joseph Anderson (3) -   June 7, 1868
    For further information see - Anderson, Joseph.

Taylor, Lucy G. and Charles R. Koontz (3) -   December 17, 1889
    For further information see - Koontz, Charles R.

Taylor, Lucy O. and John J. Riely (2) -   (L) November 22, 1856

Taylor, Margaret Catherine and George William Hardee (3) -   March 4, 1883
    For further information see - Hardee, George William.

Taylor, Martha and James Caten (2) -   (L) September 30, 1850

Taylor, Martha (widow) and James Caten (1) -   October 1, 1850

Taylor, Mary and Thomas Malleory (1) -   June 28, 1834

Taylor, Mary Ann and Michael Kern (3) -   May 9, 1867
    For further information see - Kern, Michael.

Taylor, Mollie E. and Charles H. Wright (3) -   August 18, 1884
    For further information see - Wright, Charles H.

Taylor, Nancy (cold.) Samuel Tucker (3) -   August 5, 1875
    For further information see - Tucker, Samuel.

Taylor, Samuel and Mary Fox (3) -   September 7, 1876
    Place of marriage, near Wickliffe - Age of husband, 23 - Age of wife, 17 - Both are Single - Husband was born in Jefferson County, West Virginia - Wife was born in Augusta County, Virginia - Both reside in Jefferson County, West Virginia. (Consent of bride's father in person.)

Taylor, Samuel T. and Mary M. Brown (3) -   June 17, 1885
    Place of marriage, Charlestown - Age of husband, 31 - Age of wife, 23 - Both are Single - Both were born in Jefferson County, West Virginia - Husband resides at Baltimore, Maryland - Wife resides in Jefferson County, West Virginia.

Taylor, Sarah C. and Thompson B. Mason (2) -   (L) October 23, 1855

Taylor, Thomas Henry and Mary E. Smith (3) -   March 10, 1874
    Place of marriage, Shepherdstown - Age of husband, 24 - Age of wife, 30 - Husband is Single - Wife is a Widow of Abraham Smith - Husband was born in Berkeley County, West Virginia - Wife was born in Jefferson County, West Virginia - Both reside in Jefferson County, West Virginia.

Taylor, Walter and Ellen A. Wager (3) -   July 29, 1868
    Place of marriage, Jefferson County - Both are Single - Husband was born at Washington, D. C. - Wife was born in Jefferson County - Both reside in Jefferson County - Husband's parents are Alfred - Wife's parents are G. B. and Ellen A.

Taylor, William H. (colored) Sarah Murray (3) -   November 28, 1870
    Place of marriage, Jefferson County - Age of husband, 24 - Age of wife, 16 - Both were born in Virginia - Both reside in Jefferson County. (Parents give consent.)

Taylor, William S. and Mary Hickman (1) -   March 4, 1829

Tearney, Elizabeth A. and I. G. Hunt (3) -   May 19, 1874
    For further information see - Hunt, I. G.

Tearney, Kate L. and John Walsh (3) -   February 9, 1871
    For further information see - Walsh, John.

Tennant, Agusta V. and Jacob V. Emmert (3) -   November 17, 1887
    For further information see - Emmert, Jacob V.

Tennant, Antonetta and G. W. Entler (3) -   December 31, 1872
    For further information see - Entler, G. W.

Tennant, Joseph S. and Hallie Wintermoyer (3) -   February 19, 1885
    Place of marriage, Shepherdstown - Age of husband, 24 - Age of wife, 23 - Both are Single - Husband was born in State of Maryland - Wife was born in Jefferson County, West Virginia - Both reside in Jefferson County, West Virginia.

Tennant, William B. and Lillie W. Entler (3) - September 28, 1886
    Place of marriage, Charlestown - Age of husband, 25 - Age of wife,
    25 - Both are Single - Husband was born in Washington County,
    Maryland - Wife was born in Jefferson County, West Virginia - Both
    reside in Jefferson County, West Virginia.

Tharp, Branson and Barbara Fox (3) - January 18, 1888
    Place of marriage, Charlestown - Age of husband, 21 - Age of wife,
    22 - Both are Single - Husband was born in Jefferson County, West
    Virginia - Wife was born in Warren County, Virginia - Husband resides
    in Clarke County, Virginia - Wife resides in Jefferson County, West
    Virginia.

Tharp, Robert B. and Mary Athey (3) - May 22, 1890
    Place of marriage, Middleway - Age of husband, 22 - Age of wife,
    22 - Both are Single - Husband was born in Clarke County, Virginia -
    Wife was born in Jefferson County, West Virginia - Husband resides
    in Frederick County, Virginia - Wife resides in Jefferson County,
    West Virginia.

Thomas, Ailsie (cold.) David Gaul (3) - January 18, 1882
    For further information see - Gaul, David.

Thomas, Captain (cold.) Nancy Green (3) - September 28, 1876
    Place of marriage, Charles Town - Age of husband, 21 - Age of wife,
    21 - Both are Single - Husband was born in Page County, Virginia -
    Wife was born in Jefferson County, West Virginia - Both reside in
    Jefferson County, West Virginia.

Thomas, Charles L. and Octavia R. Bowers (3) - October 23, 1888
    Place of marriage, Charlestown - Age of husband, 33 - Age of wife,
    18 - Both are Single - Both were born in Jefferson County, West
    Virginia - Both reside in Jefferson County, West Virginia.
    (Consent of bride's father in writing.)

Thomas, Christopher and Susan C. Porter (3) - June 3, 1873
    Place of marriage, Porter's Factory - Age of husband, 24 - Age of
    wife, 22 - Both are Single - Husband was born in Albemarle County,
    Virginia - Wife was born in Clarke County, Ohio - Husband resides
    at Mount Jackson, Shenandoah County - Wife resides in Jefferson
    County.

Thomas, Elizabeth and Henry Tilghman (1) - November 17, 1825

Thomas, Emma and James Whittington (3) - October 26, 1876
    For further information see - Whittington, James.

Thomas, Eviline (cold.) Manuel Lucas (3) - March 29, 1879
    For further information see - Lucas, Manuel.

Thomas, Fannie E. and George M. Knott (3) - March 26, 1884
    For further information see - Knott, George M.

Thomas, Frank C. and Annie M. Jones (3) - May 14, 1872
    Place of marriage, Jefferson County - Age of husband, 23 - Age of
    wife, 21 - Both are Single - Both were born in Maryland - Husband
    resides in Maryland - Wife resides in West Virginia - Husband's
    parents are William H. and Mary R. - Wife's parents are D. T. and
    Mary - Occupation of husband is Farmer.

Thomas, Hezekiah and Susan Hall (1) - March 20, 1823

Thomas, J. W. and Mattie J. Langdon (3) - March 16, 1886
Place of marriage, Charlestown - Age of husband, 56 - Age of wife, 38 - Husband is a Widower - Wife is Single - Husband was born in State of Virginia - Wife was born in West Virginia - Both reside in Jefferson County, West Virginia.

Thomas, James (cold.) Dora Washington (3) - October 25, 1888
Place of marriage, Charlestown - Age of husband, 32 - Age of wife, 22 - Both are Single - Husband was born in Loudoun County, Virginia - Wife was born in Jefferson County, West Virginia - Both reside in Jefferson County, West Virginia.

Thomas, James Albert (cold.) Fanny Brown (3) - December 28, 1882
Place of marriage, Summit Point - Age of husband, 23 - Age of wife, 22 - Both are Single - Husband was born in State of Maryland - Wife was born in Jefferson County, West Virginia - Both reside in Jefferson County, West Virginia.

Thomas, James E. and Margaret S. Strayer (3) - July 1, 1869
Place of marriage, Jefferson County - Age of husband, 21 - Age of wife, 21 - Husband was born in Pennsylvania - Wife was born in West Virginia - Husband resides in Jefferson County - Wife resides in West Virginia.

Thomas, James W. and Sarah Elizabeth Milstead (3) - June 25, 1874
Place of marriage, Charles Town - Age of husband, 45 - Age of wife, 35 - Husband is a Widower - Wife is Single - Husband was born in Loudoun County, Virginia - Wife was born in Prince William County, Virginia - Husband resides in Clarke County, Virginia - Wife resides in Jefferson County, West Virginia.

Thomas, John and Margaret Piper (1) - August 26, 1818

Thomas, John William and Mary Jones (3) - August 1, 1872
Place of marriage, Charlestown - Age of husband, 23 - Age of wife, 25 - Both are Single - Both were born in Jefferson County, Virginia - Both reside in Jefferson County, West Virginia - Husband's parents are David and Sarah - Wife's parents are Peter and Annie - Occupation of husband is Farmer.

Thomas, Lee (cold.) Eliza Hall (3) - February 8, 1883
Place of marriage, near Charlestown - Age of husband, 22 - Age of wife, 21 - Both are Single - Husband was born in Page County, Virginia - Wife was born in Warren County, Virginia - Both reside in Jefferson County, West Virginia.

Thomas, Leonard and Elizabeth Tilghman (1) - December 8, 1825

Thomas, Lucy (cold.) Oscar Williams (3) - December 12, 1878
For further information see - Williams, Oscar.

Thomas, Mary (cold.) Elijah Robinson (3) - December 25, 1874
For further information see - Robinson, Elijah.

Thomas, Mary E. and J. W. Smallwood (3) - June 22, 1865
For further information see - Smallwood, J. W.

Thomas, Nancy (cold.) John Patterson (3) -   September 6, 1883
    For further information see - Patterson, John.

Thomas, Oliver P. and Helen M. Reiley (2) -   (L) December 19, 1854

Thomas, Rebecca and George Shall (1) -   February 4, 1819

Thomas, Sarah (cold.) James Clinton (3) -   February 3, 1887
    For further information see - Clinton, James.

Thomas, Sarah Catherine and John Lewis Creamer (3) -   November 19, 1874
    For further information see - Creamer, John Lewis.

Thomas, Teresa (cold.) Frank Brown (3) -   August 3, 1887
    For further information see - Brown, Frank.

Thomas, Tillason T. and Maggie J. Mattheny (3) -   April 29, 1884
    Place of marriage, Harpers Ferry - Age of husband, 27 - Age of wife, 21 - Both are Single - Husband was born in Maryland - Wife was born at Philadelphia - Husband resides in Maryland - Wife resides in Jefferson County, West Virginia.

Thomas, W. A. and L. M. Jackson (bride) (3) -   December 19, 1872
    Place of marriage, Harpers Ferry - Age of husband, 26 - Age of wife, 28 - Both are Single - Both were born in Virginia - Both reside in Virginia - Husband's parents are Thomas and Malinda.

Thompson, Alice Virginia and George W. Hanby (3) -   March 25, 1885
    For further information see - Hanby, George W.

Thompson, Ann and John F. Price (1) -   September 28, 1821

Thompson, Austin and Sarah Elizabeth Hunter (2) -   (L) January 31, 1860

Thompson, Betty C. and Moses Ewing (3) -   August 18, 1875
    For further information see - Ewing, Moses.

Thompson, Cary and Charlotte Zoigar (1) -   July 21, 1822

Thompson, Catherine and Robert E. Erwin (3) -   September 25, 1884
    For further information see - Erwin, Robert E.

Thompson, Eliza (cold.) Lewis Johnson (3) -   January 19, 1882
    For further information see - Johnson, Lewis.

Thompson, Elizabeth and Daniel Lee (2) -   (L) September 12, 1850

Thompson, Elizabeth and Daniel Lee (1) -   September 12, 1850

Thompson, Elizabeth and Joseph R. Webb (2) -   (L) May 24, 1858

Thompson, Emma N. and John King (3) -   January 11, 1888
    For further information see - King, John.

Thompson, Fanny (cold.) Joseph Murray (3) -   December 29, 1875
    For further information see - Murray, Joseph.

Thompson, French M. and Fanny T. Lloyd (3) - September 6, 1881
   Place of marriage, near Ripon - Age of husband, 21 - Age of wife,
   22 - Both are Single - Both were born in Jefferson County, West
   Virginia - Husband resides in Clarke County, Virginia - Wife resides
   in Jefferson County, West Virginia.

Thompson, George D. and Adella G. Rice (3) - December 24, 1890
   Place of marriage, Martinsburg - Age of husband, 24 - Age of wife,
   21 - Both are Single - Husband was born in Berkeley County, West
   Virginia - Wife was born in Jefferson County, West Virginia -
   Husband resides in Berkeley County, West Virginia - Wife resides in
   Jefferson County, West Virginia.

Thompson, Hanney (colored) Kennedy Johnson (3) - January 13, 1870
   For further information see - Johnson, Kennedy.

Thompson, Hester Ann and Frederick A. Fulk (2) - (L) December 19, 1854

Thompson, Isaac and Cornelia Ann Horn (3) - March 12, 1873
   Place of marriage, near Duffields - Age of husband, 28 - Age of
   wife, 28 - Both are Single - Both were born in Jefferson County,
   West Virginia - Both reside in Jefferson County, West Virginia -
   Husband's parents are Joseph and Mary Elizabeth - Wife's parents are
   George and Susan Margaret - Occupation of husband is Farmer.

Thompson, James F. and Minnie S. Ray (3) - February 28, 1888
   Place of marriage, Shepherdstown - Age of husband, 28 - Age of wife,
   20 - Both are Single - Husband was born at Martinsburg, West
   Virginia - Wife was born in Jefferson County, West Virginia -
   Husband resides in Berkeley County, West Virginia - Wife resides in
   Jefferson County, West Virginia. (Consent of bride's father in
   writing.)

Thompson, James H. and Octavia Jane Campbell (2) - (L) March 20, 1860

Thompson, James H. (cold.) Mary W. Williams (3) - August 19, 1890
   Place of marriage, Charlestown - Age of husband, 24 - Age of wife,
   22 - Both are Single - Husband was born in Warren County, Virginia -
   Wife was born in Jefferson County, West Virginia - Husband resides
   in Fauquier County, Virginia - Wife resides in Jefferson County,
   West Virginia.

Thompson, Jane and Philip Ronemus (1) - March 4, 1807

Thompson, Jasper and Dolly Irvin (3) - October 28, 1869
   Age of husband, 24 - Age of wife, 21 - Both were born in Virginia -
   Both reside in Jefferson County.

Thompson, Jerimiah and Susan Wolffe (1) - December 23, 1819

Thompson, John and Ellen Ann Price (3) - December 21, 1865
   Place of marriage, Leetown, Jefferson County - Age of husband, 30 -
   Age of wife, 21 - Both are Single - Both were born in Jefferson
   County, West Virginia - Both reside in Jefferson County, West
   Virginia - Husband's parents are Joseph and Mary Thompson - Wife's
   parents are Henry and Sarah Price - Occupation of husband is Farmer.

Thompson, John and Penelope Jacqueline Hanbey (3) - September 25, 1873
Place of marriage, Smithfield - Age of husband, 37 - Age of wife,
21 - Husband is a Widower - Wife is Single - Both were born in
Jefferson County, West Virginia - Both reside in Jefferson County,
West Virginia.

Thompson, John E. and Elizabeth Myers (1) - December 9, 1824

Thompson, John G. and Mary C. Thompson (2) - (L) June 24, 1861
Time of marriage, June 24, 1861 - Place of marriage, Charlestown -
Names, John G. Thompson and Mary C. Thompson - Age of husband, 28
years - Age of wife, 23 years - Condition of husband is Single -
Condition of wife is Single - Place of husband's birth was
Charlestown, Jefferson County, Virginia - Place of wife's birth was
in Jefferson County, Virginia - Place of husband's residence is in
Jefferson County, Virginia - Place of wife's residence is in
Jefferson County, Virginia - Names of husband's parents are James
and Isabella D. Thompson - Names of wife's parents are Joseph and
Mary Thompson - Occupation of husband is Carpenter - Joseph Thompson.

Thompson, John L. and Emily Frances Smith (2) - (L) January 10, 1852

Thompson, John L. and Catherine Conner (3) - May 2, 1877
Place of marriage, Charlestown - Age of husband, 23 - Age of wife,
22 - Both are Single - Husband was born in Loudoun County, Virginia -
Wife was born in Rockingham County, Virginia - Both reside in
Jefferson County, West Virginia.

Thompson, John W. and Martha Ann Steele (1) - August 10, 1848

Thompson, John Wesley (cold.) Sarah Allen McChan (3) - October 3, 1880
Place of marriage, Shepherdstown - Age of husband, 34 - Age of wife,
19 - Husband is a Widower - Wife is Single - Husband was born in
Maryland - Wife was born in Jefferson County, West Virginia -
Husband resides at Baltimore - Wife resides in Jefferson County,
West Virginia. (Consent of bride's father in person.)

Thompson, Joseph and Mary Custard (1) - May 17, 1835

Thompson, Lidia and John Patience (1) - January 30, 1814

Thompson, Lizzie (colored) Lucas Warrick (3) - (1870)
For further information see - Warrick, Lucas.

Thompson, Lucie A. and Paul L. Jones (3) - August 13, 1866
For further information see - Jones, Paul L.

Thompson, Lucy and George W. Moler (3) - April 16, 1889
For further information see - Moler, George W.

Thompson, Maria (colored) Joseph Mills (3) - (1870)
For further information see - Mills, Joseph.

Thompson, Maria (cold.) Thomas Miles (3) - September 11, 1873
For further information see - Miles, Thomas.

Thompson, Mary C. and John G. Thompson (2) - (L) June 24, 1861
For further information see - Thompson, John G.

Thompson, Mary Hester and John James Emory (2) - (L) October 7, 1857

Thompson, Mary J. and Middleton Thompson (3) - January 4, 1870
    For further information see - Thompson, Middleton.

Thompson, Michael E. and Louisa V. Ingram (2) - (L) January 24, 1859

Thompson, Middleton and Mary J. Thompson (3) - January 4, 1870
    Place of marriage, Jefferson County - Age of husband, 24 - Age of wife, 28 - Husband was born in Maryland - Wife was born in Jefferson County - Both reside in Jefferson County.

Thompson, Nancy Virginia and Francis Adam Bell (3) - March 2, 1885
    For further information see - Bell, Francis Adam.

Thompson, Paliteah and Kitty Willson (1) - 1820

Thompson, Rachel Jane and W. S. Rutherford (3) - March 21, 1866
    For further information see - Rutherford, W. S.

Thompson, Reed T. and Susan Kidwiler (3) - September 18, 1878
    Place of marriage, Shepherdstown - Age of husband, 21 - Age of wife, 21 - Both are Single - Both were born in Jefferson County, West Virginia - Both reside in Jefferson County, West Virginia.

Thompson, Robert S. and Eliza A. Moore (2) - (L) May 1, 1860

Thompson, S. A. (bride) and G. S. Brumbaugh (3) - March 13, 1868
    For further information see - Brumbaugh, G. S.

Thompson, Samuel and Susan Deen (1) - June 3, 1810

Thompson, Stephen and Lydia F. Edwards (3) - February 28, 1867
    Place of marriage, Shepherdstown, West Virginia - Age of husband, 27 - Age of wife, 25 - Both are Single - Both were born in Jefferson County, West Virginia - Husband resides in Berkeley County, West Virginia - Wife resides in Jefferson County, West Virginia - Husband's parents are William and Hannah Thompson - Wife's parents are James and Elizabeth Edwards - Occupation of husband is Farmer. (John Edwards' presence.)

Thompson, Thomas M. and Mary Elizabeth Myers (2) - (L) March 31, 1856

Thompson, William N. and Isabella Vanmetre (1) - January 13, 1830

Thompson, Willie and John A. Osbourn (3) - November 7, 1878
    For further information see - Osbourn, John A.

Thomson, Mary J. and John L. Lewis (3) - December 4, 1866
    For further information see - Lewis, John L.

Thomson, Mollie G. and Gerard D. Moore (3) - February 17, 1885
    For further information see - Moore, Gerard D.

Thomson, Warner A. and Josephine M. Janney (2) - (L) December 8, 1851

Thornburg, Elanor and Jeptha Morgan (1) - January 22, 1818

Thornburg, Elizabeth and Uriah Miller (1) - January 20, 1824

Thornburg, Solomon and Mary Staley (1) - January 13, 1813

Thornburg, Thomas and Barbara Byers (1) -   December 5, 1813

Thornhill, Charles (cold.) Mary Johnson (3) -   May 29, 1884
    Place of marriage, Duffields - Age of husband, 45 - Age of wife,
    40 - Husband is a Widower - Wife is a Widow - Husband was born in
    Rappahannock County, Virginia - Wife was born in Jefferson County,
    West Virginia - Both reside in Jefferson County, West Virginia.

Thornton, Bettie (cold.) Seaton Adams (3) -   February 12, 1880
    For further information see - Adams, Seaton.

Thornton, Eliza (cold.) John Brown (3) -   March 1, 1888
    For further information see - Brown, John.

Thornton, Ellen (colored) John Welcome (3) -   April 28, 1870
    For further information see - Welcome, John.

Thornton, Frances (colored) Samuel Gibson (3) -   February 9, 1867
    For further information see - Gibson, Samuel.

Thornton, James William (cold.) Betty Roman (3) -   January 9, 1877
    Place of marriage, Middleway - Age of husband, 23 - Age of wife,
    21 - Both are Single - Both were born in Jefferson County, West
    Virginia - Both reside in Jefferson County, West Virginia.

Thornton, Jennie (cold.) James Anderson (3) -   July 16, 1873
    For further information see - Anderson, James.

Thornton, John and Nancy Hill (3) -   July 27, 1867
    Place of marriage, Charlestown - Age of husband, 32 - Age of wife,
    30 - Husband is a Widower - Wife is Single -. Both were born in
    Jefferson County, Virginia - Both reside in Jefferson County, West
    Virginia - Husband's parents are Prestly and Darkey - Wife's parents
    are William and Becky Hill - Occupation of husband is Farmer.

Thornton, Lucy (cold.) George Jones (3) -   (1867)
    For further information see - Jones, George.

Thornton, Lucy A. and Mortimer D. Williams (1) -   December 26, 1822

Thornton, Maria E. (cold.) Charles H. McCard (3) -   October 23, 1879
    For further information see - McCard, Charles H.

Thornton, Mary (cold.) Dennis Gore (3) -   September 21, 1890
    For further information see - Gore, Dennis.

Thornton, Mayberry G. (cold.) Susan Throgmorton (3) -   August 27, 1874
    Place of marriage, near Summit Point - Age of husband, 29 - Age of
    wife, 25 - Both are Single - Both were born in Jefferson County,
    West Virginia - Both reside in Jefferson County, West Virginia.

Thornton, Rebecca (cold.) James F. Patterson (3) -   March 15, 1888
    For further information see - Patterson, James F.

Thornton, Richard (cold.) Rose Whiting (3) -   December 25, 1888
    Place of marriage, Summit Point - Age of husband, 23 - Age of wife,
    21 - Both are Single - Both were born in Jefferson County, West
    Virginia - Both reside in Jefferson County, West Virginia.

573

Thornton, Samuel (cold.) Lizzie Johnson (3) - February 1, 1888
Place of marriage, Charlestown - Age of husband, 47 - Age of wife,
23 - Husband is a Widower - Wife is Single - Husband was born in
Berkeley County, West Virginia - Wife was born in Jefferson County -
Both reside in Jefferson County, West Virginia.

Thornton, Wesley (cold.) Rebeca Weaver (3) - April 29, 1888
Place of marriage, Middleway - Age of husband, 56 - Age of wife,
50 - Both are Single - Both were born in Jefferson County - Both
reside in Jefferson County, West Virginia.

Thornton, William Carter (cold.) Mary Whiting (3) - November 15, 1877
Place of marriage, near Charlestown - Age of husband, 22 - Age of
wife, 22 - Both are Single - Both were born in Jefferson County,
West Virginia - Both reside in Jefferson County, West Virginia.

Thrift, William and Mary Wilson (3) - August 18, 1868
Place of marriage, Jefferson County - Age of husband, 50 - Age of
wife, 40 - Husband is Single - Wife is a Widow - Husband was born in
Maryland - Wife was born in Virginia - Both reside in Jefferson
County - Wife's parents are Samuel - Occupation of husband is Cooper.

Throckmorton, B. and George Whiting (3) - January 24, 1872
For further information see - Whiting, George.

Throckmorton, J. W. (cold.) Sarah E. Morris (3) - May 15, 1888
Place of marriage, Halltown - Age of husband, 30 - Age of wife, 21 -
Both are Single - Both were born in Jefferson County, West
Virginia - Both reside in Jefferson County, West Virginia.

Throgmorton, Susan (cold.) Mayberry G. Thornton (3) - August 27, 1874
For further information see - Thornton, Mayberry G.

Throp, Samuel and Casandry Nicholds (1) - 1822

Thropp, Sarah and James Overton (1) - December 27, 1831

Thurman, Kate and George H. Hageley (3) - December 15, 1870
For further information see - Hageley, George H.

Tidvall, William and Mary Swartzwilder (3) - September 25, 1883
Place of marriage, near Shepherdstown - Both were born in Frederick
County, Virginia - Husband resides in Texas - Wife resides in
Jefferson County, West Virginia.

Tierney, James and Mary Elizabeth Cretan (2) - (L) December 20, 1851

Tilghman, Elizabeth and Leonard Thomas (1) - December 8, 1825

Tilghman, Henry and Elizabeth Thomas (1) - November 17, 1825

Timberlake, Alcinda and Harfield Timberlake, Jr. (1) - June 18, 1822

Timberlake, Ambrose C. and Eliza Lee Griggs (2) - (L) October 5, 1858

Timberlake, Ann and Brockenbrough McCormick (1) - April 8, 1830

Timberlake, David W. and Mary C. Timberlake (3) -   December 25, 1879
    Place of marriage, near Middleway - Age of husband, 48 - Age of
    wife, 39 - Husband is a Widower - Wife is Single - Husband was born
    in Frederick County, Virginia - Wife was born in Jefferson County,
    West Virginia - Husband resides in Berkeley County, West Virginia -
    Wife resides in Jefferson County, West Virginia.

Timberlake, Elizabeth L. and Thomas Maslin, Jr. (3) -   December 15, 1875
    For further information see - Maslin, Thomas, Jr.

Timberlake, Harfield, Jr. and Alcinda Timberlake (1) -   June 18, 1822

Timberlake, James H. and Martha V. Crane (3) -   June 14, 1876
    Place of marriage, Charlestown - Age of husband, 31 - Age of wife,
    25 - Both are Single - Both were born in Jefferson County, West
    Virginia - Both reside in Jefferson County, West Virginia.

Timberlake, Lizzie D. and Henry C. Page (3) -   September 5, 1883
    For further information see - Page, Henry C.

Timberlake, Mrs. Martha V. and Henderson M. Bell (3) -   October 19, 1886
    For further information see - Bell, Henderson M.

Timberlake, Mary C. and David W. Timberlake (3) -   December 25, 1879
    For further information see - Timberlake, David W.

Timberlake, Mildred C. and William Waters (2) -   (L) April 2, 1860

Timberlake, Nellie and Edmund Herbs (3) -   November 29, 1866
    For further information see - Herbs, Edmund.

Timberlake, Sarah and Edward Carter (1) -   1825

Timberlake, Thomas W. and Fanie J. Greggs (3) -   (September 1865)

Timbers, Oliver and Rachel Freeman (3) -   December 23, 1871
    Place of marriage, Jefferson County - Age of husband, 27 - Age of
    wife, 22 - Both are Single - Husband was born in Rappahannock
    County - Wife was born in Jefferson County - Both reside in
    Jefferson County - Husband's parents are Thornton and Betsy - Wife's
    parents are George and Amanda - Occupation of husband is Farmer.

Times, Henry (cold.) Mary McDaniel (3) -   November 22, 1882
    Place of marriage, Charlestown - Age of husband, 23 - Age of wife,
    17 - Both are Single - Husband was born in Fauquier County,
    Virginia - Wife was born in Jefferson County, West Virginia - Both
    reside in Jefferson County, West Virginia. (Consent of bride's
    mother in writing.)

Tinsinan, A. M. and Sarah E. Nichols (2) -   (L) December 16, 1854

Tise, John F. and Ellen Fox (3) -   January 21, 1880
    Place of marriage, Shepherdstown - Age of husband, 38 - Age of wife,
    23 - Husband is Single - Wife is a Widow - Husband was born in
    Washington County, Maryland - Wife was born in Jefferson County,
    West Virginia - Husband resides in Washington County, Maryland -
    Wife resides in Jefferson County, West Virginia.

Tochman, Major Gaspar and Miss Apollonia Jagielle (2) -   (L) August 4, 1851

Todd, E. C. (bride) and I. F. Snook (3) - November 14, 1887
    For further information see - Snook, I. F.

Todd, Grafton and Nancy Jackson (3) - November 26, 1872
    Place of marriage, Charlestown - Age of husband, 39 - Age of wife,
    36 - Both are Single - Husband's parents are Upton and Dinah.

Tolbert, Bettie (colored persons) Peter Gordon (3) - August 3, 1865
    For further information see - Gordon, Peter.

Tolbert, D. Lee (cold.) Georgie Taylor (3) - September 11, 1879
    Place of marriage, Charlestown - Age of husband, 24 - Age of wife,
    19 - Both are Single - Both were born in Jefferson County, West
    Virginia - Both reside in Jefferson County, West Virginia.
    (Consent of bride's father in person.)

Tolbert, Edmund and Amanda Warick (3) - December 1866
    Age of husband, 21 - Age of wife, 20 - Both are Single - Both were
    born in Jefferson County, West Virginia - Both reside in Jefferson
    County, West Virginia - Husband's parents are John and Rosetta
    Tolbert - Wife's parents are Robert and Emily Warick - Occupation of
    husband is Laborer.

Toles, James H. (cold.) Annie Morris (3) - December 6, 1887
    Place of marriage, near Shepherdstown - Age of husband, 22 - Age of
    wife, 20 - Both are Single - Husband was born in State of Virginia -
    Wife was born in Jefferson County, West Virginia - Both reside in
    Jefferson County.

Toliver, Madison (cold.) Hetty Ross (3) - August 29, 1873
    Place of marriage, Shepherdstown - Age of husband, 22 - Age of wife,
    21 - Both are Single - Husband was born in Rockingham County,
    Virginia - Wife was born in Jefferson County, West Virginia -
    Husband resides at Martinsburg, Berkeley County, West Virginia -
    Wife resides at Shepherdstown, Jefferson County, West Virginia.

Tolley, Mary and Charles Allwen (3) - November 11, 1871
    For further information see - Allwen, Charles.

Tomar, Polly and Henry Wilt (1) - November 4, 1816

Tomblinson, Margaret and Ephraim Shirley (1) - August 18, 1807

Tomlinson, Benjamin and Elizabeth Emma Gibbons (1) - March 1, 1832

Tomlinson, Maria and Rezin Shugert (2) - (L) November 12, 1863
    For further information see - Shugert, Rezin.

Tomlinson, Mary G. and Luke C. Strider (3) - February 11, 1880
    For further information see - Strider, Luke C.

Tomlinson, Sarah E. and George H. Turner (2) - (L) April 27, 1857

Tompkins, Catharine and Henry Kline (1) - September 7, 1832

Tonge, James and Hannah Watson (2) -   (L) September 2, 1863
Time of marriage, September 3, 1863 - Place of marriage, on
Shenandoah River - Names, James Tonge and Hannah Watson - Age of
husband, 29 years - Age of wife, 21 years - Both are Single - Both
were born in Lancashire, England - Both reside in Jefferson County,
Virginia - Names of husband's parents are John and Ann Tonge -
Names of wife's parents are James and Eliza Watson - Occupation of
husband is Manufacturer - License issued September 2, 1863 -
Thomas A. Moore, Clerk.

Torner, Benjamin and Susannah Near (1) -   October 11, 1821

Toup, Henry and Sarah C. Benner (3) -   December 20, 1866
Place of marriage, near Summit Point, Jefferson County - Age of
husband, 23 - Age of wife, 21 - Both are Single - Husband was born
at Martinsburg, Berkeley County, West Virginia - Wife was born in
Frederick County, Virginia - Husband resides at Martinsburg,
Berkeley County, West Virginia - Wife resides in Jefferson County,
West Virginia - Husband's parents are George and Elizabeth Toup -
Wife's parents are Benjamin and Rachel Benner - Occupation of
husband is Railroad Hand.

Towner, Ann and John Kahler (1) -   September 16, 1819

Towner, Ellen Lee and Samuel V. Link (2) -   (L) December 3, 1859

Towner, Thomas H. and Laura E. Parran (2) -   (L) April 26, 1859

Tracey, Catherine and David Tracey (1) -   December 28, 1815

Tracey, David and Catherine Tracey (1) -   December 28, 1815

Tracey, Rebecca and E. Carey (3) -   September 5, 1869
For further information see - Carey, E.

Tracey, Sarah and John Pyle (1) -   May 19, 1822

Trammel, Jacob S. and Elizabeth V. Marshall (3) -   May 28, 1866
Place of marriage, John Marshall's near Charlestown - Age of husband,
21 - Age of wife, 22 - Both are Single - Husband was born in
Berkeley County, Virginia - Wife was born in Jefferson County,
Virginia - Husband resides at Baltimore, Maryland - Wife resides in
Jefferson County, West Virginia - Husband's parents are Philip and
Sarah Trammel - Wife's parents are John and Sarah M. Marshall -
Occupation of husband is Merchant.

Trapnell, Joseph and Rebecca H. White (3) -   November 20, 1866
Place of marriage, Charlestown, Jefferson County, West Virginia -
Age of husband, 24 - Age of wife, 21 - Both are Single - Husband was
born at Annapolis, Maryland - Wife was born at Charlestown,
Jefferson County, West Virginia - Both reside at Charlestown -
Jefferson County, West Virginia - Husband's parents are Joseph and
Emily G. Trapnell - Wife's parents are Nathan S. and Frederica
White - Occupation of husband is Attorney.

Travener, Howard and Addie Littleton (3) -   December 23, 1870
Place of marriage, Jefferson County - Age of husband, 23 - Age of
wife, 22 - Both were born in Virginia - Both reside in Jefferson
County.

Travers, Lucy (cold.) James Cowan (3) -   August 2, 1883
    For further information see - Cowan, James.

Travers, Mary S. (colored) Albert Harris (3) -   January 1, 1870
    For further information see - Harris, Albert.

Travers, Sallie R. and William W. Coe (3) -   January 7, 1880
    For further information see - Coe, William W.

Travers, Walter (cold.) Hannah F. Simmons (3) -   November 17, 1881
    Place of marriage, Charlestown - Age of husband, 22 - Age of wife,
    24 - Both are Single - Both were born in Jefferson County, West
    Virginia - Both reside in Jefferson County, West Virginia.

Travers, William H. and Elizabeth P. Hunter (2) -   (L) August 16, 1853

Travis, Annie and Samuel House (3) -   August 28, 1881
    For further information see - House, Samuel.

Traynor, Elizabeth and John William Crow (3) -   March 31, 1869
    For further information see - Crow, John William.

Traynor, Fannie and Thomas Clegget (3) -   October 3, 1871
    For further information see - Clegget, Thomas.

Traynor, Frances V. and T. W. Leggett (3) -   October 3, 1871
    For further information see - Leggett, T. W.

Traynor, Mary E. and Henry F. Needy (2) -   (L) November 23, 1857

Traynor, Rachel and John Wright (3) -   May 23, 1872
    For further information see - Wright, John.

Tredrea, Thomas and Caroline King (3) -   September 29, 1875
    Place of marriage, Charlestown - Age of husband, 39 - Age of wife,
    35 - Both are Single - Husband was born in England - Wife was born
    in Virginia - Both reside in Jefferson County, West Virginia.

Tree, Jacob and Emily C. Bescue (3) -   March 4, 1884
    Place of marriage, near Kabletown - Age of husband, 37 - Age of
    wife, 34 - Both are Single - Husband was born in Switzerland - Wife
    was born in Loudoun County, Virginia - Husband resides in Loudoun
    County, Virginia - Wife resides in Jefferson County, West Virginia.

Trenary, Bertie and J. C. Marcus (3) -   January 27, 1885
    For further information see - Marcus, J. C.

Trenary, Singleton and Catharine Lucinda Ainsworth (2) -   (L) May 28, 1860

Trent, Edward and Sarah J. Jackson (3) -   October 23, 1872
    Place of marriage, Jefferson County - Age of husband, 21 - Age of
    wife, 16 - Both are Single - Husband was born in Augusta County,
    Virginia - Wife was born in Jefferson County, Virginia - Both reside
    in Jefferson County - Husband's parents are William and Mary -
    Wife's parents are William and Mary - Occupation of husband is
    Farming.

Trent, Robert (cold.) Martha Redman (3) -   December 25, 1873
    Place of marriage, Jefferson County - Age of husband, 22 - Age of
    wife, 21 - Both are Single - Husband was born at Richmond - Wife was
    born in Jefferson County, West Virginia - Both reside in Jefferson
    County, West Virginia.

Tribut, Zebede and Mary Magdalen Nicolds (1) -.   October 21, 1819

Trigg, Jeremiah and Catherine Wilson (1) -   November 10, 1821

Triggs, Citha Jane and George W. Athey (2) -   (L) (1862)
    For further information see - Athey, George W.

Triggs, Dennis and Nancy Willson (2) -   (L) August 9, 1852

Triggs, Eliza and John Wilson (2) -   (L) January 12, 1858

Triggs, Eliza and James N. Carper (3) -   March 25, 1886
    For further information see - Carper, James N.

Triggs, Mary Catharine and George W. Nicely (2) -   (L) April 5, 1856

Trimer, Nancy and Fenton Clarke (3) -   February 16, 1867
    For further information see - Clarke, Fenton.

Trinafer, Maria (cold.) John Lewis (3) -   September 16, 1875
    For further information see - Lewis, John.

Triplett, James W. and Margaret Jane Nichols (2) -.   (L) March 18, 1858

Trishnan, Sarah E. and William M. Weller (2) -   (L) February 27, 1860

Trivitt, Sarah E. and James L. Eversole (1) -   September 28, 1848

Troy, Lawrence and Mary S. Melvin (widow) (2) -   (L) March 15, 1858

Trump, Fannie M. and J. E. Seibert (3) -   December 24, 1888
    For further information see - Seibert, J. E.

Trundle, George T. and Georgia A. L. Moler (3) -   May 28, 1872
    Place of marriage, Jefferson County - Age of husband, 25 - Age of
    wife, 20 - Both are Single - Husband was born in Maryland - Wife was
    born in Virginia - Husband resides in Maryland - Wife resides in
    West Virginia - Husband's parents are John A. and Elizabeth - Wife's
    parents are Philip and Sarah - Occupation of husband is Farmer.
    (Consent of father in person.)

Trussell, Bayliss and Nettie J. Conley (3) -   March 30, 1875
    Place of marriage, Shepherdstown - Age of husband, 62 - Age of wife,
    31 - Husband is a Widower - Wife is Single - Husband was born in
    Clarke County, Virginia - Wife was born in Jefferson County, West
    Virginia - Both reside in Jefferson County, West Virginia.

Trussell, C. W. and Betty L. Starry (3) -   December 21, 1871
    Place of marriage, Jefferson County - Age of husband, 36 - Age of
    wife, 25 - Husband is a Widower - Wife is Single - Husband was born
    in Loudoun County - Wife was born in Jefferson County - Both reside
    In Jefferson County - Husband's parents are Moses and Delila - Wife's
    parents are Jacob and Lauretta L. - Occupation of husband is
    Merchant.   (Voucher C. N. Starry.)

Trussell, Charles A. and Mary A. Fleming (3) -   January 10, 1877
    Place of marriage, near Charlestown - Age of husband, 23 - Age of
    wife, 22 - Both are Single - Husband was born in Jefferson County,
    West Virginia - Wife was born in Clarke County, Virginia - Both
    reside in Jefferson County, West Virginia.

Trussell, Edna Jane and Milton B. Miller (2) -   (L) November 15, 1864
    For further information see - Miller, Milton B.

Trussell, Fannie D. and George J. Hill (3) -   November 28, 1888
    For further information see - Hill, George J.

Trussell, Fannie M. and William A. Sites (3) -   August 18, 1874
    For further information see - Sites, William A.

Trussell, James M. and Anna M. Strider (3) -   February 8, 1876
    Place of marriage, near Unionville - Age of husband, 23 - Age of
    wife, 21 - Both are Single - Both were born in Jefferson County,
    West Virginia - Both reside in Jefferson County, West Virginia.

Trussell, John N. and Mattie M. Colbert (3) -   February 28, 1877
    Place of marriage, near Halltown - Age of husband, 28 - Age of wife,
    29 - Both are Single - Husband was born in Clarke County, Virginia -
    Wife was born in Jefferson County, West Virginia - Both reside in
    Jefferson County, West Virginia.

Trussell, John P. and Mary E. Beltz (1) -   April 12, 1849

Trussell, John T. and Annie E. D. Anderson (3) -   January 13, 1875
    Place of marriage, near Charlestown - Age of husband, 24 - Age of
    wife, 23 - Both are Single - Husband was born in Frederick County,
    Virginia - Wife was born in Jefferson County, West Virginia - Both
    reside in Jefferson County, West Virginia.

Trussell, Jonah T. and Lydia R. Watson (3) -   January 2, 1866
    Place of marriage, near Leetown - Age of husband, 28 - Age of wife,
    22 - Both are Single - Husband was born in Loudoun County, Virginia -
    Wife was born in Jefferson County, West Virginia - Both reside in
    Jefferson County, West Virginia - Husband's parents are Moses and
    Delila Trussell - Wife's parents are James and Elizabeth Watson -
    Occupation of husband is Farmer.

Trussell, Joseph W. and Mollie E. Dovenberger (3) -   January 27, 1875
    Place of marriage, Jefferson County - Age of husband, 23 - Age of
    wife, 20 - Both are Single - Both were born in Jefferson County,
    West Virginia - Both reside in Jefferson County, West Virginia.
    (Consent of bride's father in person.)

Trussell, Julia Ann and Volney P. Hill (3) -   June 4, 1873
    For further information see - Hill, Volney P.

Trussell, Martha A. and George H. Hagley (3) -   November 19, 1874
    For further information see - Hagley, George H.

Trussell, Mary Elizabeth and John W. Gibson (2) -   (L) January 11, 1865
    For further information see - Gibson, John W.

Trussell, Mary V. and James A. Melvin (3) -   December 12, 1871
    For further information see - Melvin, James A.

Trussell, Nimrod and Katie H. Shugert (3) -   October 6, 1880
　　Place of marriage, Charlestown - Age of husband, 24 - Age of wife,
　　22 - Both are Single - Husband was born in Frederick County,
　　Virginia - Wife was born in Jefferson County, West Virginia - Both
　　reside in Jefferson County, West Virginia.

Trussell, Richard F. and Maggie E. Ridenour (3) -   January 31, 1877
　　Place of marriage, Harpers Ferry - Age of husband, 29 - Age of wife,
　　20 - Both are Single - Both were born in Jefferson County, West
　　Virginia - Both reside in Jefferson County, West Virginia.
　　(Consent of bride's father in writing.)

Trussell, Sarah Virginia and William Wilt (3) -   November 26, 1872
　　For further information see - Wilt, William.

Trussell, Straith and Lula B. Rowland (3) -   December 31, 1889
　　Place of marriage, Charlestown - Age of husband, 24 - Age of wife,
　　18 - Both are Single - Husband was born in Jefferson County, West
　　Virginia - Wife was born in Clarke County, Virginia - Both reside in
　　Jefferson County, West Virginia. (Consent of bride's father in
　　person.)

Trussell, Thomas C. and Frances M. Gardner (2) -   (L) January 26, 1857

Tucker, Beverly D. and Anna Maria Washington (3) -   July 22, 1873
　　Place of marriage, Charles Town - Age of husband, 26 - Age of wife,
　　21 - Both are Single - Husband was born in Jefferson County, West
　　Virginia - Wife was born in Fairfax County, Virginia - Husband
　　resides at Baltimore, Maryland - Wife resides in Jefferson County,
　　West Virginia.

Tucker, Emily Beverly and Forrest W. Brown (3) -   June 11, 1885
　　For further information see - Brown, Forrest W.

Tucker, Emma (cold.) Frederick McDaniel (3) -   May 28, 1885
　　For further information see - McDaniel, Frederick.

Tucker, Fanny (cold.) George Key (3) -   May 23, 1883
　　For further information see - Key, George.

Tucker, Mary L. and John A. Rodrick (3) -   August 3, 1879
　　For further information see - Rodrick, John A.

Tucker, Sally and Louis Wilson (3) -   June 13, 1867
　　For further information see - Wilson, Louis.

Tucker, Samuel (cold.) Nancy Taylor (3) -   August 5, 1875
　　Place of marriage, Charlestown - Age of husband, 21 - Age of wife,
　　21 - Both are Single - Both were born in Jefferson County, West
　　Virginia - Both reside in Jefferson County, West Virginia.

Tucker, William H. (cold.) Jennie Botts (3) -   December 26, 1888
　　Place of marriage, Charlestown - Age of husband, 27 - Age of wife,
　　27 - Both are Single - Husband was born in Jefferson County, West
　　Virginia - Wife was born in Page County, Virginia - Both reside in
　　Jefferson County, West Virginia.

Tumblin, Mary and Jacob Spotts (2) -   (L) March 21, 1859

Turflinger, Thomas and Susan Francis (1) -   October 9, 1806

Turk, Emma J. F. and Lawrence L. Kirwan (2) -   (L) September 4, 1860

Turk, Sarah E. and George M. Schuster (3) -   February 5, 1874
For further information see - Schuster, George M.

Turk, William H. and Martha S. Lemon (2) -   (L) September 12, 1856

Turley, John H. (cold.) Sarah B. Hook (3) -   March 24, 1875
Place of marriage, Shepherdstown - Age of husband, 22 - Age of wife, 22 - Both are Single - Husband was born at Washington, D. C. - Wife was born in Jefferson County, West Virginia - Both reside in Jefferson County, West Virginia.

Turner, A. P. and James S. Smith (3) -   May 12, 1868
For further information see - Smith, James S.

Turner, Adeline (cold.) Jesse Peterson (3) -   March 9, 1873
For further information see - Peterson, Jesse.

Turner, Anna Alice and Edwin K. Weis (3) -   January 29, 1879
For further information see - Weis, Edwin K.

Turner, Anthony (cold.) Lee Ann Willis (3) -   December 29, 1880
Place of marriage, Kearneysville - Age of husband, 22 - Age of wife, 18 - Both are Single - Both were born in Jefferson County, West Virginia - Both reside in Jefferson County, West Virginia. (Consent of bride's father in writing.)

Turner, C. M. (cold.) Martha Brunswick (3) -   December 24, 1888
Place of marriage, Middleway - Age of husband, 40 - Age of wife, 28 - Both are Single - Both were born in Jefferson County, West Virginia - Both reside in Jefferson County, West Virginia.

Turner, Daniel (cold.) Eliza Herod (3) -   November 3, 1874
Place of marriage, Harpers Ferry - Age of husband, 23 - Age of wife, 22 - Both are Single - Husband was born in Washington County, Maryland - Wife was born in Essex County, Virginia - Husband resides in Washington County, Maryland - Wife resides in Jefferson County, West Virginia.

Turner, Donly and Mary Ellen Gatrell (2) -   (L) April 17, 1858

Turner, Eliza (cold.) George W. Jones (3) -   October 17, 1885
For further information see - Jones, George W.

Turner, Elizabeth and John Perrell (1) - .   December 26, 1805

Turner, Emma (cold.) Peter Rideout (3) -   July 20, 1876
For further information see - Rideout, Peter.

Turner, Evelina (cold.) Sam Jones (3) -   November 10, 1881
For further information see - Jones, Sam.

Turner, George H. and Sarah E. Tomlinson (2) -   (L) April 27, 1857

Turner, Harry M. and Rose Snyder (3) -   November 25, 1880
Place of marriage, Shepherdstown - Age of husband, 24 - Age of wife, 24 - Both are Single - Both were born in Jefferson County, West Virginia - Both reside in Jefferson County, West Virginia.

Turner, Helen V. and Francis Morter (3) -   .   . July 10, 1884
   For further information see - Morter, Francis.

Turner, Jacob and Agnes Bowls (3) -   (L) October 13, 1866
   Time of marriage, November 25, 1866 - Place of marriage,
   Martinsburg - Age of husband, 26 - Age of wife, 19 - Both are
   Single - Husband was born in Jefferson County, West Virginia - Wife
   was born in Berkeley County, West Virginia - Both reside in Jefferson
   County, West Virginia - Husband's parents are Walker and Arazine
   Turner - Occupation of husband is Laborer.

Turner, Jacob (cold.) Mary Jones (3) -   . April 26, 1883
   Place of marriage, Charlestown - Age of husband, 39 - Age of wife,
   23 - Husband is a Widower - Wife is Single - Both were born in
   Jefferson County, West Virginia - Both reside in Jefferson County,
   West Virginia.

Turner, James B. and Mary Morningstar (3) -   May 14, 1871
   Place of marriage, Jefferson County - Age of husband, 22 - Age of
   wife, 25 - Both are Single - Husband was born in Maryland - Wife
   was born in Jefferson County - Both reside in Jefferson County -
   Husband's parents are John and Sallie - Wife's parents are Jacob
   and Sallie - Occupation of husband is Farmer.

Turner, Jane C. and Charles C. Byrd (1) -   October 3, 1823

Turner, Jane E. and Charles Huyett (3) -   October 28, 1868
   For further information see - Huyett, Charles.

Turner, John and Sarah Gill (1) -   February 19, 1818

Turner, John B. and Helen T. Johnston (2) -   (L) April 25, 1857

Turner, John R. and Celia Ann Swope (3) -   June 2, 1873
   Place of marriage, Harpers Ferry - Age of husband, 24 - Age of wife,
   23 - Both are Single - Husband was born in Warren County, Virginia -
   Wife was born in Frederick County, Maryland - Husband resides in
   Frederick County, Maryland - Wife resides in Jefferson County, West
   Virginia - Husband's parents are James and Sarah Turner. -
   Occupation of husband is Laborer.

Turner, John W. and Kate Jenkins (3) -   November 15, 1888
   Place of marriage, Charlestown - Age of husband, 22 - Age of wife,
   22 - Both are Single - Husband was born in Jefferson County, West
   Virginia - Wife was born at Frederick, Maryland - Both reside in
   Jefferson County, West Virginia.

Turner, Joseph A. and Martha Pritchard (3) -   October 12, 1875
   Place of marriage, near Porter's Factory - Age of husband, 24 - Age
   of wife, 20 - Both are Single - Husband was born in State of
   Maryland - Wife was born in Clarke County, Virginia - Both reside in
   Jefferson County, West Virginia. (Consent of bride's father in
   person.)

Turner, Joseph D. and Emma C. Williams (3) -   March 22, 1876
   Place of marriage, Shepherdstown - Age of husband, 23 - Age of wife,
   21 - Both are Single - Both were born in Washington County,
   Maryland - Both reside in Jefferson County, West Virginia.

Turner, Lizzie and George Nathan Brown (3) - May 9, 1872
   For further information see - Brown, George Nathan.

Turner, Mary A. (cold.) Henry Moore (3) - August 8, 1883
   For further information see - Moore, Henry.

Turner, Mary C. and J. A. R. Matheny (3) - February 28, 1878
   For further information see - Matheny, J. A. R.

Turner, Mary L. and Abraham Miller (3) - July 29, 1874
   For further information see - Miller, Abraham.

Turner, May V. and John E. Schley (1) - October 24, 1844

Turner, Milly (cold.) Beverly Brooks (3) - July 6, 1882
   For further information see - Brooks, Beverly.

Turner, Moses and Eveline Strothers (3) - June 14, 1868
   Place of marriage, Jefferson County - Age of husband, 22 - Age of
   wife, 25 - Husband is Single - Wife is a Widow - Both were born in
   Jefferson County, West Virginia - Husband resides in West Virginia -
   Wife resides in Jefferson County - Occupation of husband is Farmer.

Turner, Nannie (cold.) William F. Payne (3) - December 27, 1888
   For further information see - Payne, William F.

Turner, S. A. and Joshua Greenfellow (3) - January 30, 1868
   For further information see - Greenfellow, Joshua.

Turner, Thomas and Hanah Carson (1) - May 7, 1818

Turner, Thomas and Annie P. Snyder (3) - February 27, 1873
   Place of marriage, Bride's Father's - Age of husband, 42 - Age of
   wife, 20 - Both are Single - Both were born in Jefferson County,
   West Virginia - Both reside in Jefferson County, West Virginia -
   Husband's parents are Thomas and Nancy - Wife's parents are
   Jeremiah N. and Jane - Occupation of husband is Farmer. (Father's
   consent in writing, witness sworn.) (Jeremiah N. Snyder gives
   his daughter Annie Phineas Snyder to Thomas Turner in marriage.
   Witness Elisha S. Snyder.)

Turner, W. S. and A. A. Johnson (bride) (3) - October 31, 1872
   Place of marriage, Jefferson County - Age of husband, 20 - Age of
   wife, 20 - Both are Single - Husband was born in Berkeley - Wife was
   born in Jefferson - Both reside in Jefferson County, West Virginia -
   Husband's parents are Thomas and Sarah A. - Wife's parents are
   George W. and Mary E. - Occupation of husband is Farmer.
   (G. W. Johnson and Thomas Turner.)

Turner, William A. H. and L. Winie McNanly (3) - April 26, 1890
   Place of marriage, Charlestown - Age of husband, 31 - Age of wife,
   21 - Both are Single - Husband was born in Jefferson County, West
   Virginia - Wife was born at Baltimore, Maryland - Husband resides in
   Berkeley County, West Virginia - Wife resides in Jefferson County,
   West Virginia.

Tutwiler, Ann E. and Joseph C. Rawlins (1) - September 16, 1841

Tutwiler, Carrie V. and Edward S. Souders (3) - March 2, 1890
   For further information see - Souders, Edward S.

Tutwiler, Ida Jane and H. J. Taff (2) -   (L) July 1, 1858

Tutwiler, Jacob C. and Elizabeth Virginia McGinnis (2) -   (L) August 5, 1858

Twiggs, Rachel Ann and Gerard D. Rutherford (2) -   (L) August 8, 1864
   For further information see - Rutherford, Gerard D.

Twinman, Reubin (colored) Susan Hite (3) -   June 4, 1870
   Place of marriage, Jefferson County - Age of husband, 21 - Age of
   wife, 16 - Husband was born in Virginia - Wife was born in Jefferson
   County - Both reside in Jefferson County. (Step Father consents.)

Twyman, George (cold.) Fanny Ridout (3) -   July 3, 1888
   Place of marriage, Bolivar - Age of husband, 22 - Age of wife, 23 -
   Both are Single - Husband was born in Jefferson County, West
   Virginia - Wife was born in Frederick County, Maryland - Both reside
   in Jefferson County, West Virginia.

Twyman, James (cold.) Annie Clinton (3) -   December 30, 1875
   Place of marriage, Bolivar - Age of husband, 23 - Age of wife, 18 -
   Both are Single - Both were born in Jefferson County, West
   Virginia - Both reside in Jefferson County, West Virginia.
   (Consent of bride's mother certified to be Joseph Page brother-in-law
   of bride.)

Twyman, Mary Jane (cold.) George Harris (3) -   July 3, 1890
   For further information see - Harris, George.

Twyman, Nelson (cold.) Rosa Mackey (3) -   December 27, 1876
   Place of marriage, near Duffields - Age of husband, 22 - Age of
   wife, 24 - Husband is Single - Wife is a Widow - Both were born in
   Jefferson County, West Virginia - Both reside in Jefferson County,
   West Virginia.

Twyman, Rachael (cold.) Ed. Johnson (3) -   March 15, 1888
   For further information see - Johnson, Ed.

Tyler, Lucy (cold.) Thomas Wallace (3) -   December 6, 1883
   For further information see - Wallace, Thomas.

Tylman, Ann M. and John Henry Cookus (2) -   (L) September 21, 1853

Tylman, Ann M. and John Henry Cookus (1) -   September 28, 1853

Tyson, Dorsey and Margaret Morgan (3) -   October 16, 1878
   Place of marriage, near Shepherdstown - Age of husband, 25 - Age of
   wife, 21 - Both are Single - Husband was born at Frederick City,
   Maryland - Wife was born in Jefferson County, West Virginia -
   Husband resides at Frederick City, Maryland - Wife resides in
   Jefferson County, West Virginia.

Ullum, Mary S. and William Dovenbarger (2) -   (L) January 1, 1861

Underdonk, David H. and Mary E. Farnsworth (3) -   February 7, 1877
　　Place of marriage, near Middleway - Age of husband, 22 - Age of wife,
　　21 - Both are Single - Husband was born in Berkeley County, West
　　Virginia - Wife was born in Jefferson County, West Virginia -
　　Husband resides in Berkeley County, West Virginia - Wife resides in
　　Jefferson County, West Virginia.

Underdonk, Jacob and Margaret A. Bast (3) -   December 10, 1883
　　Place of marriage, Charlestown - Age of husband, 26 - Age of wife,
　　24 - Both are Single - Both were born in Jefferson County, West
　　Virginia - Both reside in Jefferson County, West Virginia.

Underdonk, Jacob V. and Sarah A. Robinson (2) -   (L) February 17, 1855

Underdonk, Mary Ellen and Edward T. Manuel (3) -   March 28, 1871
　　For further information see - Manuel, Edward T.

Underdonk, Sadie M. and Charles W. Show (3) -   September 3, 1885
　　For further information see - Show, Charles W.

Underdonk, Sarah E. and Daniel W. Hannah (3) -   March 29, 1866
　　For further information see - Hannah, Daniel W.

Underdunk, Ann M. and James F. Randal (2) -   (L) January 17, 1859

Undernunk, Rachael and Rezin Guillam (1) -   December 27, 1806

Underwood, James and Sarah Cameron (2) -   (L) January 1, 1859

Unseld, Benjamin C. and Sallie H. Rickard (3) -   September 6, 1887
　　Place of marriage, Shepherdstown - Age of husband, 43 - Age of wife,
　　31 - Both are Single - Husband was born in Jefferson County, West
　　Virginia - Wife was born in Jefferson County - Husband resides at
　　New York City - Wife resides in Jefferson County, West Virginia.

Unseld, Bettie C. and George McCan (3) -   January 4, 1870
　　For further information see - McCan, George.

Unseld, Charles F. and Agatha R. Merritt (3) -   October 11, 1881
　　Place of marriage, Harpers Ferry - Age of husband, 29 - Age of wife,
　　21 - Both are Single - Husband was born at Harpers, Ferry - Wife was
　　born in Maryland - Husband resides in Maryland - Wife resides in
　　Jefferson County, West Virginia.

Unseld, John G. and Emma J. Ronemous (3) -   February 3, 1881
　　Place of marriage, Shepherdstown - Age of husband, 43 - Age of wife,
　　28 - Both are Single - Both were born in Jefferson County, West
　　Virginia - Both reside in Jefferson County, West Virginia.

Unseld, Mrs. Susan and John M. Fall (1) -   January 29, 1850

Unseld, Taylor and Fanny Voorhees (3) -   February 13, 1877
　　Place of marriage, near Shepherdstown - Age of husband, 28 - Age of
　　wife, 22 - Both are Single - Husband was born in Jefferson County,
　　West Virginia - Wife was born in Jefferson County, West Virginia -
　　Both reside in Jefferson County, West Virginia.

Upright, Lewis and Caroline C. Bridener (3) -   February 10, 1869
    Place of marriage, Jefferson County - Age of husband, 28 - Age of
    wife, 22 - Both are Single - Both were born in Jefferson County -
    Both reside in Jefferson County - Husband's parents are Charles and
    Sophia - Wife's parents are John C. and Hannah - Occupation of
    husband is Butcher.

Urton, Mary Catherine and George W. Marlow (3) -   June 24, 1875
    For further information see - Marlow, George W.

Ury, William H. and Sally E. Bender (3) -   May 16, 1878
    Place of marriage, Harpers Ferry - Age of husband, 41 - Age of wife,
    22 - Husband is a Widower - Wife is Single - Both were born in State
    of Maryland - Husband resides in Maryland - Wife resides in Jefferson
    County, West Virginia.

Utart, Frank and Eveline Dittinger (2) -   (L) January 31, 1860

Utt, Rebecca and Jacob Nicholls (1) -   January 5, 1821

Utt, Susan and Ignatius Perrell (1) -   1812

Utter, Mary Alice and James H. Smallwood (3) -   February 25, 1869
    For further information see - Smallwood, James H.

Valentine, Annie and James V. Shriner (3) - December 31, 1878
   For further information see - Shriner, James V.

VanAlstyne, Lester and Sallie E. Cook (3) - November 12, 1884
   Place of marriage, Shepherdstown - Age of husband, 33 - Age of wife,
   25 - Both are Single - Husband was born in State of New York - Wife
   was born in State of Maryland - Both reside in Jefferson County,
   West Virginia.

VanCamp, Amosa and Maria L. Bestor (1) - August 8, 1836

Vanderbilt, Cornelius and Jane Wilkens (1) - March 31, 1819

VanDevinter, William H. and Elizabeth V. McDonald (3) - August 27, 1866
   Place of marriage, Shepherdstown, Jefferson County - Age of husband,
   31 - Age of wife, 27 - Both are Single - Husband was born in Bucks
   County, Pennsylvania - Wife was born at Eastport, State of Maine -
   Husband resides in Mercer County, Pennsylvania - Wife resides at
   Shepherdstown, Jefferson County, West Virginia - Husband's parents
   are Isaiah and Rachel VanDevinter - Wife's parents are William T.
   and Mary McDonald - Occupation of husband is Farmer.

VanDoren, Nannie H. and F. E. Armstrong (2) - . (L) July 21, 1857

Vanhorn, George W. and Ann Sheetz (1) - September 23, 1830

VanHorn, Maud E. and J. M. Bauserman (3) - October 2, 1890
   For further information see - Bauserman, J. M.

Vanhorn, Simeon H. and Sarah A. K. Fossett (2) - (L) February 3, 1859

VanHorn, Thacker and Katie Roberts (3) - March 23, 1880
   Place of marriage, Middleway - Age of husband, 55 - Age of wife,
   26 - Both are Single - Both were born in Jefferson County, West
   Virginia - Both reside in Jefferson County, West Virginia.

VanLear, May P. and Charles C. Furr (3) - July 4, 1889
   For further information see - Furr, Charles C.

Vanmeter, Thomas B. and Mollie A. Buckles (3) - March 16, 1869
   Place of marriage, Jefferson County - Age of husband, 29 - Age of
   wife, 24 - Both are Single - Husband was born in Berkeley County -
   Wife was born in Jefferson County - Husband resides in Berkeley
   County - Wife resides in Jefferson County - Husband's parents are
   Thomas and Mary - Wife's parents are William and Nancy - Occupation
   of husband is Farmer.

Vanmetre, America V. and C. W. H. Cooper (3) - October 22, 1866
   For further information see - Cooper, C. W. H.

Vanmetre, Caroline B. and William M. Johnson (3) - November 26, 1878
   For further information see - Johnson, William M.

Vanmetre, Elizabeth J. and James A. Engle (3) - October 31, 1876
   For further information see - Engle, James A.

Vanmetre, Isabella J. and William R. Stewart (1) - April 5, 1849

Vanmetre, Isabella and William N. Thompson (1) - January 13, 1830

Vanmetre, John J. and America Virginia Roper (2) -.   (L) September 9, 1858

Vanmetre, Rebecca and John Shell (1) -   January 31, 1819

Vanmetre, Ruth and Jacob Stipp (1) -   April 23, 1835

Vanmetre, William H. and Nettie B. Moler (3) -   October 22, 1885
Place of marriage, near Unionville - Age of husband, 22. - Age of wife, 23 - Both are Single - Husband was born in Berkeley County - Wife was born in Jefferson County, West Virginia. - Both reside in Jefferson County.

Vansant, Mary E. and George C. Eakle (2) -   (L) September 24, 1851

Vansant, Mary E. and George C. Eakle (1) -   September 25, 1851

Vansant, Thomas M. and Mary E. Sappington (1) -   March 13, 1844

VanSwearingen, Hannah and Rev. H. Mathews (2) -   (L) June 18, 1855

VanSwearingen, Mary Elvira and John Quigley (1) -   October 20, 1827

Vanvacter, Harriet and William H. Farr (1) -   January 31, 1833

Vanvacter, Joseph and Mary E. Hammond (1) -   May 24, 1832

Vanvacter, Rachel and William H. Griggs (1) -   May 26, 1831

VanVactor, Ann Catharine and John Osburn, Jr. (1) -   November 6, 1827

Vanvactor, Anna M. and Henry D. Rust (2) -   (L) September 20, 1860

Vanvactor, Harriet S. and William M. Myers (2) -   (L) June 15, 1864
For further information see - Myers, William M.

Vanvactor, Joseph H. and Sallie E. Boyers (3) -   December 30, 1872
Place of marriage, Jefferson County, West Virginia - Age of husband, 26 - Age of wife, 23 - Both are Single - Husband was born in Jefferson County, West Virginia - Wife was born in Maryland - Both reside in Jefferson County, West Virginia. - Husband's parents are Joseph and Mary E.

Vanvactor, R. O. and M. F. Hill (bride) (3) -   August 3, 1884
Place of marriage, Shannondale Furnace - Age of husband, 28 - Age of wife, 18 - Both are Single - Both were born in Jefferson County, West Virginia - Both reside in Jefferson County, West Virginia. (Consent of bride's father in person.)

VanWyck, John C. and Rosalie T. Berry (2) -   (L) April 5, 1858

Varner, Henry and Elizabeth Compton (1) -   July 31, 1827

Vaughn, Sarah E. and Alonz B. Brown (3) -   March 16, 1871
For further information see - Brown, Alonz B.

Veney, B. F. (cold.) Sarah Harris (3) -   July 29, 1887
Place of marriage, Harpers Ferry - Age of husband, 27 - Age of wife, 21 - Both are Single - Both were born in Augusta County, Virginia - Both reside in Jefferson County, West Virginia.

Veney, Nannie E. (cold.) James Hamilton (3) - May 6, 1885
    For further information see - Hamilton, James.

Verdier
Verdier, Adam and Elizabeth Mercer (1) - September 2, 1802

Verner, Abigal and William Brooks (1) - March 28, 1820

Vestal, George and Anne Andson (1) - November 20, 1828

Vestal, Jane and James McKinney (1) - November 18, 1823

Vester, Annie (cold.) James Davis (3) - June 13, 1886
    For further information see - Davis, James.

Vian, Price W. and Emma J. Lewelynn (3) - July 23, 1872
    Place of marriage, Jefferson County - Age of husband, 22 - Age of
    wife, 21 - Both are Single - Both were born in Virginia - Both
    reside in West Virginia - Husband's parents are John and May -
    Wife's parents are William and Clara - Occupation of husband is
    Farmer. (Sworn to by H. P. Jackson.)

Viands, Angelthta and Hezekiah Wiley (3) - July 17, 1889
    For further information see.- Wiley, Hezekiah.

Viands, George W. and Frances Ellen Gray (3) - May 2, 1876
    Place of marriage, near Shanan Dale Furnace - Age of husband, 21 -
    Age of wife, 22 - Both are Single - Both were born in Jefferson
    County, West Virginia - Both reside in Jefferson County, West
    Virginia.

Vickers, Ebenezer and Helen V. Beall (2) - (L) November 7, 1857

Vincenhellar, Robert and Prudence Yontz (1) - March 31, 1814

Vincent, Matilda and James Shirley, Sr. (1) - December 24, 1821

Vinconhall, Robert and Catherine Feyman (1) - July 15, 1823

Vinds, Louisa and Thomas W. Robey (3) - February 25, 1869
    For further information see - Robey, Thomas W.

Vinsonheller, Laura Lavinia and Jacob F. Saylor (2) - (L) October 2, 1850

Vinsonheller, Laura Lavinia and Jacob F. Saylor (1) - October 2, 1850

Vint, Bettie and Adam Ginter (3) - February 5, 1878
    For further information see - Ginter, Adam.

Virts, James M. and Mary Elizabeth Lay (3) - March 20, 1873
    Place of marriage, Harpers Ferry - Age of husband, 24 - Age of wife,
    22 - Both are Single - Both were born in Loudoun County, Virginia -
    Husband resides in Loudoun County, Virginia - Wife resides in
    Jefferson County, West Virginia - Husband's parents are Joseph F.
    and Eliza E. - Wife's parents are Edward and Susan - Occupation of
    husband is Farmer and Rail Road Hand.

VonBlucher, Emily and Thomas Hicks (3) - November 12, 1885
    For further information see - Hicks, Thomas.

Voorhees, Fanny and Taylor Unseld (3) -   February 13, 1877
    For further information see - Unseld, Taylor.

Voorhees, J. F. and M. Howard (bride) (3) -   (1867)
    Age of husband, 27 - Age of wife, 20 - Both are Single - Both were
    born in Jefferson County - Both reside in Jefferson - Wife's parents
    are Grafton and Mary S.

Voorhees, Virginia and Franklin P. Hill (3) -   January 22, 1889
    For further information see - Hill, Franklin P.

Vorens, Maggie L. and James L. Wiley (3) -   September 16, 1885
    For further information see - Wiley, James L.

Vores, Mary and Conrad Hartness (1) -   November 22, 1825

Vorhees, Jacob and Margaret Wageley (1) -   March 31, 1843

Vornes, Philip and Lula T. Freeman (3) -   May 7, 1885
    Place of marriage, Charlestown -. Age of husband, 28 - Age of wife,
    18 - Both are Single - Husband was born in Berkeley County, West
    Virginia - Wife was born in Jefferson County, West Virginia - Both
    reside in Jefferson County, West Virginia. (Consent of bride's
    father in writing.)

Vorous, Annie E. and Charles J. Custer (3) -   October 25, 1881
    For further information see - Custer, Charles J.

Vorous, Elmira J. and George R. Merchant (3) -   October 22, 1889
    For further information see - Merchant, George R.

591

Wachter, Elijah R. and Virginia I. Loman (3) - February 19, 1867
   Place of marriage, Rock Spring, West Virginia - Age of husband, 22 -
   Age of wife, 18 - Both are Single - Husband was born in Frederick
   County, Maryland - Wife was born in Jefferson County, West
   Virginia - Husband resides at Frederick City, Maryland - Wife resides
   in Jefferson County, West Virginia - Husband's parents are Daniel
   and Catharine Wachter - Wife's parents are John B. and Sarah Loman -
   Occupation of husband is Carpenter. (Father's permission, present.)

Waddell, Elizabeth and Phillip D. Copeland (3) - January 24, 1867
   For further information see - Copeland, Phillip D.

Wade, Ann and William Coss (1) - April 16, 1803

Wade, Clara (cold.) Charles William Holmes (3) - February 17, 1881
   For further information see - Holmes, Charles William.

Wade, Elizabeth A. D. and James A. Duncan (3) - July 3, 1873
   For further information see - Duncan, James A.

Wade, Margaret and Philip Wiltshire (2) - (L) February 25, 1851

Wade, Margaret and Philip Wiltshire (1) - February 25, 1851

Wade, Mary and James Hannah (1) - April 27, 1836

Wade, Pheobe Ann and John W. Sheetz (2) - (L) March 20, 1854

Wageley, Benjamin F. and Mary Elizabeth Custer (3) - December 3, 1878
   Place of marriage, Mount Zion Church - Age of husband, 22 - Age of
   wife, 18 - Both are Single - Both were born in Jefferson County,
   West Virginia - Both reside in Jefferson County, West Virginia.
   (Consent of bride's father in person.)

Wageley, Catherine N. and James W. Chapman (2) - (L) April 1, 1856

Wageley, Cora and George W. Packett (3) - November 27, 1884
   For further information see - Packett, George W.

Wageley, David A. and Mary E. Rowland (2) - (L) April 25, 1856

Wageley, Fannie E. and William E. McKown (3) - January 15, 1872
   For further information see - McKown, William E.

Wageley, Ida and Charles S. Lewis (3) - November 17, 1880
   For further information see - Lewis, Charles S.

Wageley, James F. and Anna L. Grantham (3) - January 22, 1878
   Place of marriage, Middleway - Age of husband, 26 - Age of wife,
   22 - Both are Single - Both were born in Jefferson County, West
   Virginia - Both reside in Jefferson County, West Virginia.

Wageley, James W. and Mary Ellen Roberts (1) - January 21, 1847

Wageley, James W. and Ann West (3) - November 21, 1865
   (Miss Vic Gilbert, Mechanics Town, Frederick County, Maryland.)

Wageley, John H. and Sarah Elizabeth Roberts (3) -   December 22, 1880
   Place of marriage, near Berkeley Line - Age of husband, 26 - Age of
   wife, 17 - Both are Single - Husband was born in Jefferson County,
   West Virginia - Wife was born in Frederick County, Virginia - Both
   reside in Jefferson County, West Virginia. (Consent of bride's
   father in person.)

Wageley, Laura A. and James H. Willis (3) -   December 3, 1878
   For further information see - Willis, James H.

Wageley, Louisa L. and Theodore F. Yeamans (3) -   January 4, 1866
   For further information see - Yeamans, Theodore F.

Wageley, Margaret and Jacob Vorhees (1) -   March 31, 1843

Wageley, Mary E. and Conrad A. Johnson (3) -   August 31, 1871
   For further information see - Johnson, Conrad A.

Wagely, Joseph and Sarah Riley (3) -   November 21, 1872
   Place of marriage, Jefferson County - Age of husband, 27-- Age of
   wife, 23 - Both are Single - Husband's parents are Dave and Marg -
   Wife's parents are Lusta and Sidney.

Wager, Caroline E. and John W. Arvin (2) -   (L) April 29, 1856

Wager, Catharine M. and Thomas A. Nicholson (2) -   (L) November 28, 1860

Wager, Edward L. and Anne E. Hurst (2) -   (L) July 5, 1851

Wager, Edward L. and Anne E. Hurst (1) -   July 7, 1851

Wager, Elizabeth and Joseph Hooffman (1) -   June 27, 1812

Wager, Ellen A. and Walter Taylor (3) -   July 29, 1868
   For further information see - Taylor, Walter.

Wager, Hannah and Roger Humphreys (1) -   June 25, 1807

Wager, Mary and Frederick Selig (1) -   January 1, 1807

Wager, Sarah Ann St.Clair and N. H. Swayne (1) -   September 5, 1832

Waggoner, Robert J. and Catherine E. Buckles (1) -   March 31, 1841

Wagley, John and Elizabeth Showman (1) -   March 18, 1819

Wagner, Charles W. and Jenett B. Yates (3) -   November 1, 1870
   Place of marriage, Jefferson County - Age of husband, 29 - Age of
   wife, 27 - Husband was born at Baltimore - Wife was born in
   Jefferson County - Husband resides at Baltimore - Wife resides in
   Jefferson County.

Wagner, Edmund and Zuriah Beall (1) -   July 8, 1810

Waite, Harrison and Mary Miller (1) -   September 2, 1817

593

Wakeman, G. H. and M. J. Anderson (bride) (3) -   March 29, 1882
    Place of marriage, Charlestown - Age of husband, 25 - Age of wife,
    28 - Both are Single - Husband was born in State of Virginia - Wife
    was born in Rappahannock, Virginia - Husband resides in Warren
    County, Virginia - Wife resides in Jefferson County, West Virginia.

Walch, Patrick and Mary O'Brien (2) -   (L) February 27, 1854

Waldeck, Joseph and Rosa Shell (3) -   May 27, 1886
    Place of marriage, Charlestown - Age of husband, 24 - Age of wife,
    23 - Both are Single - Both were born in Jefferson County, West
    Virginia - Both reside in Jefferson County, West Virginia.

Walen, Samuel and Fannie Gray (3) -   December 1866
    Age of husband, 22 - Age of wife, 23 - Both are Single - Husband was
    born at Staunton, Virginia - Wife was born in Jefferson County, West
    Virginia - Both reside in Jefferson County, West Virginia -
    Husband's parents are Samuel and Mariah Walen - Wife's parents are
    David and Bettie Gray - Occupation of husband is Laborer.

Walker, Annie (cold.) Henry Stanton (3) -   November 6, 1884
    For further information see.- Stanton, Henry.

Walker, Eliza (cold.) William Clay Douglas (3) -   October 30, 1884
    For further information see - Douglas, William Clay.

Walker, Elizabeth and Benjamin D. Green (1) -   June 16, 1834

Walker, Ida and Moses Wood (3) -   July 23, 1890
    For further information see - Wood, Moses.

Walker, Jacob (cold.) Mary Dodd (3) -   October 10, 1876
    Place of marriage, near Shepherdstown - Age of husband, 50 - Age of
    wife, 45 - Husband is a Widower - Wife is Single - Husband was born
    in North Carolina - Wife was born in Jefferson County, West
    Virginia - Both reside in Jefferson County, West Virginia.

Walker, James and Mary E. Sigler (2) -   (L) October 9, 1850

Walker, James and Mary E. Sigler (1) -   October 11, 1850

Walker, James William (cold.) Rosa Smith (3) -   December 31, 1890
    Place of marriage, Kabletown - Age of husband, 21 - Age of wife,
    18 - Both are Single - Husband was born in Warren County, Virginia -
    Wife was born in Jefferson County, West Virginia - Both reside in
    Jefferson County, West Virginia.

Walker, Jennie (cold.) George Powell (3) -   November 20, 1884
    For further information see - Powell, George.

Walker, John (cold.) Ella Zeon Morris (3) -   July 15, 1880
    Place of marriage, Middleway District - Age of husband, 22 - Age of
    wife, 21 - Both are Single - Husband was born in Frederick County,
    Virginia - Wife was born in Jefferson County, West Virginia - Both
    reside in Jefferson County, West Virginia.

Walker, Joseph and Lizzie Johnson (3) -   October 24, 1872
   Place of marriage, Jefferson County - Age of husband, 23 - Age of
   wife, 17 - Both are Single - Husband was born in Jefferson County -
   Wife was born in Jefferson County, Virginia - Both reside in
   Jefferson County - Husband's parents are Joseph and Nancy - Wife's
   parents are Wilfred and Hannah - Occupation of husband is Laborer.
   (Consent of mother.)

Walker, Joseph (cold.) Alice Jenkins (3) -   September 4, 1884
   Place of marriage, Charlestown - Age of husband, 60 - Age of wife,
   37 - Husband is a Widower - Wife is a Widow - Husband was born in
   State of Maryland - Wife was born in Jefferson County - Both reside
   in Jefferson County.

Walker, Lina P. and John R. Shell (3) -   November 3, 1875
   For further information see - Shell, John R.

Walker, Martha Ellen (cold.) John Herbert (3) -   August 23, 1877
   For further information see - Herbert, John.

Walker, Mary J. and O. A. Jones (3) -   November 26, 1867
   For further information see - Jones, O. A.

Walker, Mary J. (cold.) John Richardson (3) -   October 17, 1889
   For further information see - Richardson, John.

Walker, Mordecai H. and Lettie Fraley (2) -   (L) November 24, 1855

Walker, Rebecca (cold.) Benjamin W. Branson (3) -   October 13, 1890
   For further information see.- Branson, Benjamin W.

Walker, Richard (cold.) Eliza Burwell (3) -   December 29, 1881
   Place of marriage, Charlestown - Age of husband, 24 - Age of wife,
   21 - Both are Single - Both were born in Jefferson County, West
   Virginia - Both reside in Jefferson County, West Virginia.
   (Consent of bride's mother in writing.)

Walker, Sarah E. and Adrian W. Lemen (3) -   September 21, 1870
   For further information see - Lemen, Adrian W.

Walker, Simon (cold.) Bettie E. Fountain (3) -   May 25, 1866
   Place of marriage, Smithfield, Jefferson County - Age of husband,
   21 - Age of wife, 17 - Both are Single - Husband was born in South
   Carolina - Wife was born at Smithfield, Jefferson County, Virginia -
   Both reside at Smithfield, Jefferson County, West Virginia -
   Husband's parents are Henry and Lettie Walker - Wife's parents are
   Joseph and Maria Thornton - Occupation of husband is Laborer.

Walker, Simon (cold.) Sally Jefferson (3) -   January 22, 1874
   Place of marriage, Middleway - Age of husband, 28 - Age of wife,
   31 - Husband is a Widower - Wife is Single - Husband was born in
   Chester County, South Carolina - Wife was born in Jefferson County,
   West Virginia - Both reside in Jefferson County, West Virginia.

Walker, Simon P. (cold.) Mary Arnesty (3) -   December 23, 1880
   Place of marriage, Charlestown - Age of husband, 34 - Age of wife,
   24 - Husband is a Widower - Wife is Single - Husband was born in
   South Carolina - Wife was born in Frederick County, Virginia - Both
   reside in Jefferson County, West Virginia.

Walker, Virginia (cold.) Thomas Jones (3) -   May 10, 1877
     For further information see - Jones, Thomas.

Wall, Charles F. and S. Gertrude Easterday (3) -   December 23, 1884
     Place of marriage, Charlestown - Age of husband, 22 - Age of wife, 20 - Both are Single - Husband was born at Danville, Illinois - Wife was born in Jefferson County, West Virginia - Both reside in Jefferson County, West Virginia. (Consent of bride's father in writing.)

Wallace, Sarah B. and Samuel Cash (3) -   January 3, 1870
     For further information see - Cash, Samuel.

Wallace, Thomas (cold.) Lucy Tyler (3) -   December 6, 1883
     Place of marriage, Shepherdstown - Age of husband, 24 - Age of wife, 21 - Husband is a Widower - Wife is Single - Both were born in Rappahannock County, Virginia - Both reside in Jefferson County, West Virginia.

Wallace, Thomas K. and Helen V. Stone (2) -   (L) July 19, 1858

Wallace, William and Jennie A. Hurst (2) -   (L) October 11, 1859

Walling, Emma and John S. Markell (1) -   November 19, 1844

Wallingsford, Eveline and Daniel Chapman (1) -   April 11, 1822

Walman, Mary and Thomas Loudon (1) -   September 14, 1815

Walper, Elizabeth and Josiah T. Kerney (1) -   February 3, 1825

Walpert, John and Mary Reynolds (1) -   November 11, 1810

Walpert, Mary and Nicholas Roush (1) -   August 21, 1806

Walpert, Sally and Jacob Mayer (1) -   November 22, 1811

Walraven, John W. and Pleasant C. Backhouse (2) -   (L) October 18, 1856

Walraven, Sarah Elizabeth and Thomas Potts (2) -   (L) February 18, 1856

Walsh, James and Elizabeth Slaven (3) -   May 24, 1873
     Place of marriage, Harpers Ferry - Age of husband, 23 - Age of wife, 22 - Both are Single - Husband was born in Ireland - Wife was born in Jefferson County, West Virginia - Husband resides in Ohio - Wife resides in Jefferson County, West Virginia - Husband's parents are Michael and Catherine - Wife's parents are Christopher and Mary - Occupation of husband is Carpenter.

Walsh, John and Kate L. Tearney (3) -   February 9, 1871
     Place of marriage, Harpers Ferry - Age of husband, 34 - Age of wife, 23 - Both are Single - Husband was born in Ireland - Wife was born in Jefferson County - Husband resides at Cumberland, Maryland - Wife resides in Jefferson County - Husband's parents are John and Sarah - Wife's parents are Edward and Jane - Occupation of husband is Merchant.

Walsh, Kate and John Byrne (3) -   January 19, 1874
     For further information see - Byrne, John.

Walsh, Thomas and Ann Halpin (2) - (L) May 6, 1858
   (T. Boesley says they are both 21.)

Walter, Henry and Sarah M. Feltner (3) - September 19, 1865
   Place of marriage, At residence of William Loyd in Jefferson
   County - Age of husband, 21 years - Age of wife, 22 years - Both are
   Single - Husband was born in Preston County, West Virginia - Wife
   was born in Clarke County, Virginia - Husband resides in Preston
   County, West Virginia - Wife resides in Jefferson County, West
   Virginia - Husband's parents are John and Elizabeth Walter - Wife's
   parents are Martin and Mary Feltner - Occupation of husband is Farmer.

Walters, A. E. and James Purcell (3) - April 5, 1874
   For further information see - Purcell, James.

Walters, Amelia Lucretia and John Philip Entler (2) - (L) May 23, 1861
   For further information see - Entler, John Philip.

Walters, Ann and Henry Lee (1) - April 12, 1827

Walters, Edward and Mary C. Kane (3) - April 19, 1882
   Place of marriage, Harpers Ferry - Age of husband, 27 - Age of wife,
   21 - Both are Single - Both were born in Jefferson County - Both
   reside in Jefferson County.

Walters, Fannie and John W. Williams (3) - February 26, 1867
   For further information see - Williams, John W.

Walters, Georgiana and C. C. Manuel (3) - January 4, 1873
   For further information see - Manuel, C. C.

Walters, Ira and Katie Morris (3) - September 29, 1889
   Place of marriage, Shepherdstown - Age of husband, 21 - Age of wife,
   21 - Both are Single - Husband was born in Frederick County,
   Maryland - Wife was born at Baltimore, Maryland - Both reside in
   Jefferson County, West Virginia.

Walters, Isaac N. and Ann Rebecca Hawn (2) - (L) April 17, 1856

Walters, J. E. and Eliza Harris (2) - (L) April 22, 1863
   Time of marriage, April 22, 1863 - Place of marriage, Shepherdstown -
   Names, J. E. Walters and Eliza Harris - Age of husband, 60 years
   next October - Age of wife, 19 years - Husband is a Widower - Wife
   is Single - Both were born in Jefferson County - Both reside in
   Jefferson County - Names of husband's parents are Isaac and Susan
   Walters - Names of wife's parents are George and ? Harris -
   Occupation of husband is Marketman and Pedler - License issued,
   April 22, 1863 - Thomas A. Moore, Clerk.

Walters, J. H. and Mary E. Proby (3) - February 22, 1890
   Place of marriage, Harpers Ferry - Age of husband, 33 - Age of wife,
   22 - Both are Single - Husband was born in Page County, Virginia -
   Wife was born in Jefferson County, West Virginia - Husband resides
   in Page County, Virginia - Wife resides in Jefferson County, West
   Virginia.

Walters, John William and Catharine Overton (2) - (L) December 23, 1851

Walters, Rebecca and Henry D. Rust (3) - October 23, 1872
   For further information see - Rust, Henry D.

Walters, Robert (cold.) Margaret Lee (3) -   January 13, 1890
    Place of marriage, Harpers Ferry - Age of husband, 45 - Age of wife,
    40 - Both are Single - Both were born in Shenandoah County,
    Virginia - Both reside in Jefferson County, West Virginia.

Walters, S. Kate and D. Arthur Philips (3) -   June 7, 1876
    For further information see - Philips, D. Arthur.

Walters, Sarah I. and Charles A. Allen (3) -   December 17, 1866
    For further information see - Allen, Charles A.

Walton, James and Elizabeth Lindsay (1) -   November 19, 1812

Walton, Lillie M. and R. W. Morrow (3) -   January 27, 1886
    For further information see - Morrow, R. W.

Walton, Samuel and Margaret C. Miller (3) -   February 27, 1879
    Place of marriage, Charlestown - Age of husband, 33 - Age of wife,
    29 - Both are Single - Husband was born in Pennsylvania - Wife was
    born at Cumberland, Maryland - Both reside in Jefferson County,
    West Virginia.

Wamix, Thomas and Roxillanna Barrow (3) -   February 1, 1866
    Place of marriage, Stover Mills, Jefferson County - Age of husband,
    24 - Age of wife, 25 - Both are Single - Husband was born in Warren
    County, Virginia - Wife was born in Frederick County, Virginia -
    Husband resides in Clarke County, Virginia - Wife resides in
    Jefferson County, West Virginia - Husband's parents are Jesse and
    Lucy Wamix - Wife's parents are William and Edith Barrow - Occupation
    of husband is Laborer.

Waple, H. S. and Rosa E. Langdon (3) -   June 1, 1881
    Place of marriage, Kabletown - Age of husband, 25 - Age of wife,
    22 - Both are Single - Husband was born in Pennsylvania - Wife was
    born in Jefferson County, West Virginia - Husband resides at
    Washington City - Wife resides in Jefferson County, West Virginia.

Ward, Catharine and Oliver J. Garrett (2) -   (L) February 9, 1853

Ward, Elizabeth Rebecca and John Foreman (3) -   March 18, 1877
    For further information see - Foreman, John.

Ward, J. M. and Sarah A. Earle (3) -   April 5, 1875
    Place of marriage, Harpers Ferry - Age of husband, 30 - Age of wife,
    26 - Husband is Single - Wife is a Widow - Husband was born in
    Berkeley County, West Virginia - Wife was born in Jefferson County,
    West Virginia - Both reside in Jefferson County, West Virginia.

Ward, Margaret R. and John L. Bonham (2) -   (L) May 18, 1857

Ware, Benjamin F. and Josephine Coleman (3) -   February 25, 1886
    Place of marriage, near Middleway - Age of husband, 29 - Age of
    wife, 23 - Both are Single - Husband was born in Jefferson County -
    Wife was born in Jefferson County, West Virginia - Both reside in
    Jefferson County, West Virginia.

Ware, Catharine and George Comer (3) -   February 22, 1877
    For further information see - Comer, George.

Ware, Christana and Jonathan (J. W.) Johnson (2) -   (L) May 14, 1855

Ware, Eliza P. and Joseph E. Anderson (2) -   (L) April 6, 1852

Ware, Eliza P. and Joseph E. Anderson (1) -   April 8, 1852

Ware, Eugenia W. and A. S. Crim (3) -   December 20, 1876
For further information see - Crim, A. S.

Ware, George and Kitty Kraps (1) -   December 4, 1817

Ware, George R. and S. Ann Benner (3) -   November 29, 1870
Place of marriage, Jefferson County - Age of husband, 23 - Age of wife, 20 - Both were born in Virginia - Both reside in Jefferson County. (Father in person consents.)

Ware, James W. and Margaret McCarroll (1) -   April 1850

Ware, John W. and Elizabeth McEndrie (1) -   December 26, 1816

Ware, Olive C. and Joseph M. Gruber (3) -   February 3, 1887
For further information see - Gruber, Joseph M.

Warfield, Elizabeth and Charles W. Kidwell (1) -   December 28, 1848

Warfield, Ella J. and Silas E. Griffith (3) -   December 24, 1889
For further information see - Griffith, Silas E.

Warfield, James (col.) M. E. Robinson (3) -   November 28, 1867
Place of marriage, Jefferson County - Age of husband, 24 - Age of wife, 17 - Both are Single - Both were born in Jefferson - Both reside in Jefferson - Husband's parents are Henry and Maria - Wife's parents are Harrison and Mary - Occupation of husband is Laborer. (Parents consent.)

Warfield, Mary B. and W. S. Magruder (3) -   October 2, 1877
For further information see - Magruder, W. S.

Warfield, Nathaniel and Mary Margaret Ellen Mitchell (3) -   October 28, 1875
Place of marriage, near Shepherdstown - Age of husband, 22 - Age of wife, 19 - Both are Single - Husband was born in State of Maryland - Wife was born in Jefferson County, West Virginia - Both reside in Jefferson County, West Virginia. (Consent of bride's father in person.)

Warick, Amanda and Edmund Tolbert (3) -   December 1866
For further information see - Tolbert, Edmund.

Warick, Thompson (cold.) Mary Stephenson (3) -   August 12, 1880
Place of marriage, Charlestown - Age of husband, 35 - Age of wife, 24 - Both are Single - Husband was born in Loudoun County, Virginia - Wife was born in Jefferson County, West Virginia - Both reside in Jefferson County, West Virginia.

Warner, Amanda and G. B. Nunburger (3) -   August 1, 1882
For further information see - Nunburger, G. B.

Warner, Aron (cold.) Sabina Carey (3) -   September 20, 1880
Place of marriage, near Charlestown - Age of husband, 26 - Age of wife, 21 - Both are Single - Both were born in Loudoun County, Virginia - Both reside in Jefferson County, West Virginia.

Warner, Christiana and Larkin Cockrill (1) - May 27, 1806

Warner, Cora L. (cold.) Thomas H. Nelson (3) - December 26, 1888
    For further information see - Nelson, Thomas H.

Warner, George and Catherine Laurence (1) - November 6, 1813

Warner, H. E. (bride) and T. F. Ray (3) - September 28, 1867
    For further information see - Ray, T. F.

Warner, Wilmena T. and S. P. Humrickhouse (3) - February 17, 1870
    For further information see - Humrickhouse, S. P.

Warrick, Lucas (colored) Lizzie Thompson (3) - (1870)
    Age of husband, 22 - Age of wife, 19 - Husband was born in
    Virginia - Wife was born in Washington - Both reside in Jefferson
    County. (Consent of parents.)

Warson, Darkey (free mixtures) David M. Richcreek (1) - June 25, 1826

Warters, William and Elizabeth Ott (1) - May 16, 1822

Warwick, Rodney (free cold.) Eliza Gibson (2) - (L) April 6, 1863
    Time of marriage, April 9, 1863 - Place of marriage, Charlestown -
    Names, Rodney Warwick and Eliza Gibson (free cold.) - Age of
    husband, 29 years - Age of wife, 30 years - Both are Single - Both
    were born in Jefferson County - Both reside in Jefferson County -
    Occupation of husband is Farm Hand - License issued April 6, 1863 -
    Thomas A. Moore, Clerk.

Washburn, P. B.
    For further information see - Dearing, Notley W.

Washburn, Paul and Delilah Doleman (1) - 1825

Washburn, Paul and Sarah Ann Avis (1) - 1827

Washburn, Mrs. Sarah Ann (widow of P. B. Washburn) and Notley W. Dearing (1) -
    October 4, 1835

Washington, Albert (cold.) Annie Saunders (3) - November 13, 1889
    Place of marriage, Charlestown - Age of husband, 41 - Age of wife,
    21 - Both are Single - Husband was born in Culpepper County,
    Virginia - Wife was born in Jefferson County, West Virginia - Both
    reside in Jefferson County, West Virginia.

Washington, Amanda (cold.) John Frame (3) - October 3, 1867
    For further information see - Frame, John.

Washington, Anna M. (cold.) S. G. Griffin (3) - September 3, 1873
    For further information see - Griffin, S. G.

Washington, Anna Maria and Beverly D. Tucker (3) - July 22, 1873
    For further information see - Tucker, Beverly D.

Washington, Annie (cold.) Benjamin Drew (3) - December 18, 1873
    For further information see - Drew, Benjamin.

Washington, Augusta and William Hillary (3) - May 7, 1867
    For further information see - Hillary, William.

Washington, B. C. and Emma E. Willis (3) -   November 14, 1878
   Place of marriage, Charlestown - Age of husband, 39 - Age of wife,
   35 - Husband is a Widower - Wife is Single - Both were born in
   Jefferson County, West. Virginia - Both reside in Jefferson County,
   West Virginia.

Washington, Caroline (cold.) Robert Green (3) -   December 26, 1883
   For further information see - Green, Robert.

Washington, Caroline (cold.) Joseph Mitchell (3) -   May 12, 1887
   For further information see - Mitchell, Joseph.

Washington, Cecelia P. and Edwin B. Burwell (1) -   March 15, 1822

Washington, Charles and Mary Ross (3) -   June 8, 1867
   Place of marriage, Albert Hoof's Residence - Age of husband, 33 - Age
   of wife, 40 - Husband is Single - Wife is a Widow - Husband was born
   at Shepherdstown - Wife was born in Clarke County, Virginia -
   Husband resides at Rippon, West Virginia - Wife resides in Jefferson
   County, West Virginia - Wife's parents are Randolf - Occupation of
   husband is Farmer.

Washington, Cora (cold.) Charles Colston (3) -   September 22, 1885
   For further information see - Colston, Charles.

Washington, David, Jr. (cold.) Lucinda Carter (3) -   July 26, 1883
   Place of marriage, Kearneysville - Age of husband, 24 - Age of wife,
   18 - Both are Single - Both were born in Jefferson County, West
   Virginia - Both reside in Jefferson County, West Virginia.
   (Consent of bride's father in writing.)

Washington, David D. (cold.) Lydia A. Parter (3) -   May 22, 1884
   Place of marriage, Summit Point - Age of husband, 25 - Age of wife,
   22 - Both are Single - Both were born in Jefferson County, West
   Virginia - Both reside in Jefferson County, West Virginia.

Washington, Dora (cold.) James Thomas (3) -   October 25, 1888
   For further information see - Thomas, James.

Washington, E. C. and George H. Flagg (3) -   January 23, 1868
   For further information see - Flagg, George H.

Washington, Edward and Lucy Galloway (3) -   March 23, 1871
   Place of marriage, Jefferson County - Age of husband, 23 - Age of
   wife, 18 - Both are Single - Both were born in Jefferson County -
   Both reside in Jefferson County - Husband's parents are George and
   Sarah - Wife's parents are Benjamin and Carlota - Occupation of
   husband is Plasterer.   (Father consents.)

Washington, Eleanor L. and Julian Howard (3) -.   May 5, 1880
   For further information see - Howard, Julian.

Washington, Flora (cold.) Stephen Jones (3) -   February 23, 1888
   For further information see - Jones, Stephen.

Washington, George and Ann Jones (3) -   September 28, 1871
   Place of marriage, Jefferson County - Age of husband, 53 - Age of
   wife, 45 - Both are Single - Both were born in Jefferson County -
   Both reside in Jefferson - Husband's parents are Nelson and Rachel -
   Wife's parents are Joshua and Nancy - Occupation of husband is Laborer.

Washington, George (cold.) Margaret Dixon (3) -   December 10, 1874
   Place of marriage, Charles Town - Age of husband, 32 - Age of wife,
   24 - Husband is a Widower - Wife is Single - Both were born in
   Jefferson County, West Virginia - Both reside in Jefferson County,
   West Virginia.

Washington, George (cold.) Georgiana Bowman (3) -   December 30, 1879
   Place of marriage, near Charlestown - Age of husband, 47 - Age of
   wife, 21 - Husband is a Widower - Wife is Single - Husband was born
   in Edgecombe County, North Carolina - Wife was born in Jefferson
   County, West Virginia - Both reside in Jefferson County, West
   Virginia.

Washington, George and Emma Serena Porterfield (3) -   February 16, 1886
   Place of marriage, Charlestown - Age of husband, 28 - Age of wife,
   23 - Both are Single - Husband was born in Fairfax County,
   Virginia - Wife was born in Jefferson County, West Virginia - Both
   reside in Jefferson County, West Virginia.

Washington, George Anna and John W. Smith (2) -   (L) November 18, 1851

Washington, George W. (cold.) Kate Patterson (3) -   December 13, 1883
   Place of marriage, Charlestown - Age of husband, 23 - Age of wife,
   23 - Both are Single - Both were born in Jefferson County, West
   Virginia - Both reside in Jefferson County, West Virginia.

Washington, Hannah and John H. Fox (3) -   November 1866
   For further information see - Fox, John H.

Washington, Hatty (cold.) William Goens (3) -   May 26, 1886
   For further information see - Goens, William.

Washington, Henry (cold.) Bettie Lee (3) -   April 3, 1884
   Place of marriage, Duffields - Age of husband, 29 - Age of wife,
   35 - Husband is Single - Wife is a Widow by divorce - Both were born
   in Jefferson County, West Virginia - Both reside in Jefferson
   County, West Virginia.

Washington, James (colored) Hannah Short (3) -   January 24, 1867
   Place of marriage, Duffields - Age of husband, 23 - Age of wife,
   20 - Both are Single - Both were born at Duffields, Jefferson
   County - Both reside at Duffields, Jefferson County - Husband's
   parents are S. and Adeline Washington - Wife's parents are Jesse
   and Margaret Short - Occupation of husband is Farmer.

Washington, James (cold.) Annie Woods (3) -   March 6, 1890
   Place of marriage, Shepherdstown - Age of husband, 25 - Age of wife,
   23 - Both are Single - Both were born in Jefferson County, West
   Virginia - Both reside in Jefferson County, West Virginia.

Washington, Jennie C. and Nathaniel H. Willis (3) -   January 13, 1869
   For further information see - Willis, Nathaniel H.

Washington, John A. and Jane K. Ambler (3) -   November 26, 1890
   Place of marriage, Charlestown - Age of husband, 43 - Age of wife,
   28 - Both are Single - Both were born in Jefferson County, West
   Virginia - Both reside in Jefferson County, West Virginia.

Washington, John Griffin (free cold.) Julia Blue (2) -   (L) July 1, 1863
   Time of marriage, July 2, 1863 - Place of marriage, Charlestown -
   Names, John Griffin Washington and Julia Blue (free cold.) - Age of
   husband, 29 years - Age of wife, 28 years - Both are Single - Both
   were born in Jefferson County - Both reside in Jefferson County -
   Husband's parents are James and Hannah - Wife's parents are Tony and
   Caroline Blue - Occupation of husband is Farmhand - License issued,
   July 1, 1863 - Thomas A. Moore, Clerk.

Washington, John H. and Louisa Jackson (3) -   July 29, 1869
   Age of husband, 23 - Age of wife, 23 - Husband was born in Jefferson
   County - Wife was born in West Virginia - Husband resides in
   Jefferson County - Wife resides in West Virginia.

Washington, Kate (cold.) S. C. Petterson (3) -   November 21, 1867
   For further information see - Petterson, S. C.

Washington, Katy T. (cold.) Charles Lucas (3) -   March 4, 1884
   For further information see - Lucas, Charles.

Washington, Laurence and Ellen R. Hopewell (3) -   August 14, 1867
   Place of marriage, Shepherdstown - Age of husband, 26 - Age of wife,
   17 - Both are Single - Both were born in Jefferson County, West
   Virginia - Both reside in Jefferson County, West Virginia - Husband's
   parents are Peyton and Revata - Wife's parents are Thomas and Jane -
   Occupation of husband is Laborer. (Father present and gives consent.)

Washington, Lawrence and Fanny Lackland (3) -   June 14, 1876
   Place of marriage, Charles Town - Age of husband, 21 - Age of wife,
   22 - Both are Single - Husband was born at Mount Vernon, Fairfax
   County, Virginia - Wife was born in Jefferson County, West Virginia -
   Husband resides in Fauquier County, Virginia - Wife resides in
   Jefferson County, West Virginia.

Washington, Lawrence (cold.) Annie Talbott (3) -   March 12, 1883
   Place of marriage, Bolivar - Age of husband, 24 - Age of wife, 22 -
   Both are Single - Husband was born in Jefferson County, West
   Virginia - Wife was born in Page County, Virginia - Both reside in
   Jefferson County, West Virginia.

Washington, Louisa Fontaine and Roger Preston Chew (3) -   August 15, 1871
   For further information see - Chew, Roger Preston.

Washington, Lucy (cold.) John H. Fox (3) -   January 7, 1877
   For further information see - Fox, John H.

Washington, Lucy (cold.) John H. Hunter (3) -   February 25, 1880
   For further information see - Hunter, John H.

Washington, Margaret (black) John Strother (3) -   (1870)
   For further information see - Strother, John.

Washington, Mary and David Johnson (3) -   June 8, 1867
   For further information see - Johnson, David.

Washington, Mary (cold.) Edmund Dangerfield (3) -   February 4, 1886
   For further information see - Dangerfield, Edmund.

Washington, Mildred B. and Solomon S. Bedinger (2) -   (L) February 8, 1854

Washington, Millie and Solomon Coleston (3) -   October 13, 1866
   For further information see - Coleston, Solomon.

Washington, Pagton (cold.) Sarah Wood (3) -   November 28, 1874
   Place of marriage, Shepherdstown - Age of husband, 60 - Age of wife,
   40 - Husband is a Widower - Wife is a Widow - Both were born in
   Jefferson County, West Virginia - Both reside in Jefferson County,
   West Virginia.

Washington, Perrin and Farinda Fairfax (1) -   February 5, 1822

Washington, Robert (cold.) Margaret Somers (3) -   May 5, 1874
   Place of marriage, County - Age of husband, 23 - Age of wife, 22 -
   Both are Single - Both were born in Jefferson County, West
   Virginia - Both reside in Jefferson County, West Virginia.

Washington, Rose (cold.) Samuel Mitchell (3) -   November 25, 1889
   For further information see - Mitchell, Samuel.

Washington, Sally (cold.) William F. Freeman (3) -   December 25, 1873
   For further information see - Freeman, William F.

Washington, Samuel A. and Annie R. Harris (3) -   May 29, 1890
   Place of marriage, Duffields - Age of husband, 22 - Age of wife,
   18 - Both are Single - Both were born in Jefferson County, West
   Virginia - Both reside in Jefferson County, West Virginia.

Washington, Sarah and Robert Mackey (3) -   February 2, 1871
   For further information see - Mackey, Robert.

Washington, Thomas (cold.) Evaline Williams (3) -   October 30, 1876
   Place of marriage, Harpers Ferry - Age of husband, 23 - Age of wife,
   18 - Both are Single - Both were born in Clarke County, Virginia -
   Both reside in Jefferson County, West Virginia.

Washington, Thomas G. (cold.) Martha Brown (3) -   May 2, 1889
   Place of marriage, Charlestown - Age of husband, 24 - Age of wife,
   26 - Husband is Single - Wife is a Widow - Husband was born in
   Jefferson County, West Virginia - Wife was born in Maryland - Both
   reside in Jefferson County, West Virginia.

Washington, Virginia (cold.) George H. Robinson (3) -   December 18, 1873
   For further information see - Robinson, George H.

Washington, W. (cold.) Mary Drew (3) -   March 26, 1868
   Place of marriage, Jefferson County - Age of husband, 26 - Age of
   wife, 19 - Both are Single - Both were born in Jefferson County -
   Both reside in Jefferson County - Occupation of husband, Farmer.

Water, John A. and Annie Leaning (nee Shults) (3) -   November 19, 1878
   Place of marriage, Harpers Ferry - Age of husband, 27 - Age of wife,
   26 - Husband is Single - Wife is a Widow - Husband was born in
   Jefferson County, West Virginia - Wife was born in Germany - Both
   reside in Jefferson County, West Virginia.

Waters, Adeline and Isaac Riley (2) -   (L) September 21, 1850

Waters, Adeline and Isaac Riley (1) -   September 30, 1850

Waters, Annie E. and Samuel D. Barnhart (3) -   January 19, 1881
   For further information see - Barnhart, Samuel D.

Waters, Arthur (cold.) Elizabeth Cole (3) -   September 18, 1884
   Place of marriage, Shepherdstown - Age of husband, 24 - Age of wife,
   22 - Both are Single - Husband was born in Loudoun County, Virginia -
   Wife was born in Jefferson County, West Virginia - Both reside in
   Jefferson County.

Waters, Catharine and John Mills (3) -   (1867)
   For further information see - Mills, John.

Waters, Henry and Jane Foreman (3) -   February 24, 1870
   Place of marriage, Jefferson County - Age of husband, 50 - Age of
   wife, 45 - Husband was born in Loudoun County, Virginia - Wife was
   born in Jefferson - Husband resides in Virginia - Wife resides in
   Jefferson County.

Waters, J. D. and Anna Strickler (3) -   April 22, 1888
   Place of marriage, Charlestown - Age of husband, 21 - Age of wife,
   23 - Both are Single - Husband was born in Canada - Wife was born in
   Frederick County, Virginia - Both reside in Jefferson County, West
   Virginia.

Waters, Jacob and Fanny Gardner (3) -   September 24, 1877
   Place of marriage, Harpers Ferry - Age of husband, 26 - Age of wife,
   25 - Both are Single - Husband was born in Maryland - Wife was born
   in Virginia - Husband resides in Maryland - Wife resides in
   Jefferson County, West Virginia.

Waters, Joseph W. and S. A. Entler (3) -   May 5, 1868
   Place of marriage, Jefferson County - Age of husband, 33 - Age of
   wife, 26 - Both are Single - Both were born in Jefferson County -
   Both reside in Jefferson County - Husband's parents are Jonathan E.
   and Elizabeth - Wife's parents are Philip and Eliza - Occupation of
   husband is Carpenter.

Waters, Laura C. and Thomas C. Greenwood (3) -   September 3, 1884
   For further information see - Greenwood, Thomas C.

Waters, Mary and C. J. Siford (3) -   September 10, 1884
   For further information see - Siford, C. J.

Waters, Richard A. and Elizabeth O'Kelly (1) -   November 7, 1821

Waters, Tighlman and Ellen M. Briscoe (2) -   (L) July 31, 1854

Waters, William and Frances C. Hite (1) -   December 22, 1825

Waters, William and Mildred C. Timberlake (2) -   (L) April 2, 1860

Watkins, Anna Bell and Richard McSherry (3) -   February 27, 1878
   For further information see - McSherry, Richard.

Watkins, John J. and Jane Wilson (3) -   June 12, 1867
   Place of marriage, Jefferson County, West Virginia - Age of husband,
   60 - Age of wife, 35 - Husband is a Widower - Wife is Single - Both
   were born in Jefferson County, West Virginia - Both reside in
   Jefferson County, West Virginia - Occupation of husband is
   Shoemaker.   (William Hank.)

Watkins, Mary E. and John Pope (3) - February 3, 1874
    For further information see - Pope, John.

Watson, Abigail and George W. Canpher (3) - October 5, 1886
    For further information see - Canpher, George W.

Watson, Alexander and Sally McCarty (1) - July 5, 1821

Watson, Charles S. and Milly C. Crim (3) - November 18, 1874
    Place of marriage, Leetown - Age of husband, 29 - Age of wife, 24 -
    Both are Single - Both were born in Jefferson County, West Virginia -
    Both reside in Jefferson County, West Virginia.

Watson, E. C. and M. C. Allen (bride) (3) - February 12, 1868
    Place of marriage, Jefferson County - Age of husband, 27 - Age of
    wife, 25 - Both are Single - Husband was born in Jefferson - Wife
    was born in Loudoun - Both reside in Jefferson - Husband's parents
    are James and Elizabeth - Wife's parents are Edward and Mary -
    Occupation of husband is Farmer.

Watson, Elizabeth L. and George McCarty (1) - September 10, 1834

Watson, Emma E. and Ed. D. Nicely (3) - September 19, 1889
    For further information see - Nicely, Ed. D.

Watson, Floyd L. and Joanna Watson (3) - March 17, 1885
    Place of marriage, Wadesville, Clarke County, Virginia - Age of
    husband, 26 - Age of wife, 26 - Both are Single - Both were born
    in Jefferson County, West Virginia - Both reside in Jefferson
    County, West Virginia.

Watson, Frances V. and Christian Y. Rosenberger (3) - December 21, 1865
    For further information see - Rosenberger, Christian Y.

Watson, George T. and Susan M. Peterman (2) - (L) October 1, 1857

Watson, Hannah and James Tonge (2) - (L) September 2, 1863
    For further information see - Tonge, James.

Watson, Ida M. and Joseph M. Shaull (3) - November 21, 1888
    For further information see - Shaull, Joseph M.

Watson, J. J. and Mrs. E. V. Rutherford (3) - March 26, 1885
    Place of marriage, near Kearneysville - Age of husband, 48 - Age of
    wife, 36 - Husband is Single - Wife is a Widow - Both were born in
    Jefferson County, West Virginia - Both reside in Jefferson County,
    West Virginia.

Watson, J. T. and Annie R. Rosenberger (3) - June 8, 1865
    Place of marriage, Shepherdstown - Age of husband, 28 years - Age of
    wife, 22 years - Both are Single - Husband was born in Jefferson
    County, Virginia - Wife was born in Shenandoah County, Virginia -
    Husband resides in Jefferson County, Virginia - Wife resides in
    Shenandoah County, Virginia - Husband's parents are Ephraim and
    Salina Watson - Occupation of husband is Farmer.

Watson, James and Elizabeth Shaull (1) - August 5, 1834

Watson, James A. and Maggie J. Swigart (3) - (1872)
   Place of marriage, Jefferson County, West Virginia - Age of husband,
   23 - Age of wife, 22 - Both are Single - Both were born in Jefferson
   County, West Virginia - Both reside in Jefferson County, West
   Virginia - Husband's parents are James and Annie - Wife's parents
   are Jacob and Ruey Ann - Occupation of husband is Manufacturer.

Watson, James A. and Mary E. Swigart (3) - September 5, 1875
   Place of marriage, Bolivar - Age of husband, 26 - Age of wife, 25 -
   Husband is a Widower - Wife is Single - Both were born in Jefferson
   County, West Virginia - Both reside in Jefferson County, West
   Virginia.

Watson, James E. and Elizabeth Roberts (3) - September 14, 1869
   Place of marriage, Jefferson County - Age of husband, 29 - Age of
   wife, 23 - Husband was born in Jefferson County - Wife was born in
   Berkeley County - Both reside in Jefferson County.

Watson, Joanna and Floyd L. Watson (3) - March 17, 1885
   For further information see - Watson, Floyd L.

Watson, John B. and Mary C. Smith (2) - (L) November 12, 1860

Watson, John Y. and Elizabeth Hunter (3) - September 6, 1870
   Place of marriage, Jefferson County - Age of husband, 32 - Age of
   wife, 28 - Husband was born in Clarke County, Virginia - Wife was
   born in Berkeley County, Virginia - Both reside in Jefferson County.

Watson, Jonah and Mary Mahony (1) - August 30, 1832

Watson, L. Elizabeth and Charles D. Ogden (3) - January 22, 1874
   For further information see - Ogden, Charles D.

Watson, Lena Belle and Zephaniah Bane (3) - December 20, 1888
   For further information see - Bane, Zephaniah.

Watson, Lloyd and Lydia E. Hyatt (3) - November 12, 1879
   Place of marriage, Leetown - Age of husband, 24 - Age of wife, 22 -
   Both are Single - Husband was born in Jefferson County, West
   Virginia - Wife was born in Frederick County, Virginia - Both reside
   in Jefferson County, West Virginia.

Watson, Lydia R. and Jonah T. Trussell (3) - January 2, 1866
   For further information see - Trussell, Jonah T.

Watson, Mary M. and Harry S. Nicely (3) - September 10, 1874
   For further information see - Nicely, Harry S.

Watson, Robert and Lizzie Stuart (3) - December 8, 1881
   Place of marriage, Bolivar - Age of husband, 23 - Age of wife, 19 -
   Both are Single - Husband was born at Baltimore - Wife was born in
   Oceana County, Michigan - Both reside in Jefferson County, West
   Virginia. (Consent of bride's father in writing.)

Watson, Samuel and Cornelia A. Orem (3) - December 19, 1867
   Place of marriage, Jefferson County - Age of husband, 28 - Age of
   wife, 26 - Both are Single - Husband was born in England - Wife was
   born in Jefferson County - Both reside in Jefferson - Wife's parents
   are Armstead and May - Occupation of husband is Manufacturer.

Watson, Sarah and Bartholomew Shaull (1) -   1824/1825

Watson, Snowden H. and Ann C. Homer (3) -   November 23, 1875
   Place of marriage, Leetown - Age of husband, 26 - Age of wife, 25 -
   Both are Single - Husband was born in Jefferson County, West
   Virginia - Wife was born in State of Pennsylvania - Both reside in
   Jefferson County, West Virginia.

Watson, Squire and Victoria Lee (3) -   August 5, 1877
   Place of marriage, Harpers Ferry - Age of husband, 33 - Age of wife,
   21 - Husband is a Widower - Wife is Single - Husband was born in
   England - Wife was born in Virginia - Both reside in Jefferson
   County, West Virginia.

Watson, T. E. (bride) and J. J. Ogden (3) -   November 7, 1872
   For further information see - Ogden, J. J.

Watson, Thomas and Elizabeth Showers (1) -   August 14, 1825

Watson, Thomas and Frances Shaul (1) -   May 3, 1832

Watson, Thomas and Henretta Swimley (3) -   October 6, 1870
   Place of marriage, Jefferson County - Age of husband, 22 - Age of
   wife, 22 - Both were born in Jefferson County - Both reside in
   Jefferson County. (Ages sworn to by Joseph F. Hess.)

Watson, Thomas and Henerita Swimley (3) -   October 6, 1870
   Place of marriage, Jefferson County - Age of husband, 22 - Age of
   wife, 22 - Both were born in Virginia - Both reside in Jefferson
   County. (This record is crossed out in the original.)

Watson, Watts and Mrs. Sarah Strider (widow) (2) -   (L) January 6, 1857

Watson, William and Mary Jane Orem (2) -   (L) September 13, 1864
   Time of marriage, September 15, 1864 - Place of marriage, at
   Armstead Orem's - Names of parties, William Watson and Mary Jane
   Orem - Age of husband, 21 years last - Age of wife, 18 years last
   January - Both are Single - Place of husband's birth was England -
   Place of wife's birth was Jefferson County, Virginia - Both reside
   in Jefferson County - Names of husband's parents are James and Eliza
   Watson - Names of wife's parents are Armstead A. and Mary Orem -
   Occupation of husband is Manufacturer - License issued, September
   13, 1864 - I certify that Armstead Orem, the father of Miss Mary
   Jane Orem has given his consent for the marriage of William Watson
   and his daughter Mary Jane - James Tonge.

Watson, William S. and Katy Pool (3) -   July 4, 1884
   Place of marriage, Harpers Ferry - Age of husband, 26 - Age of wife,
   21 - Both are Single - Both were born in Jefferson County, West
   Virginia - Both reside in Jefferson County, West Virginia.

Watt, Annie E. and Jerome M. Pierce (3) -   August 25, 1878
   For further information see - Pierce, Jerome M.

Watts, John M. and Lizzie Boswell (3) -   December 26, 1889
   Place of marriage, Shepherdstown - Age of husband, 22 - Age of wife,
   23 - Both are Single - Husband was born in Augusta County, Virginia -
   Wife was born at Shepherdstown, West Virginia - Husband resides in
   Augusta County, Virginia - Wife resides in Jefferson County, West
   Virginia.

Watts, Susan M. and Andrew Sumers (1) - October 28, 1827

Waugh, Henrietta Maria and William Grantham (1) - January 15, 1824

Way, Ann and William McClellan (1) - October 4, 1834

Way, E. G. (bride) and W. B. Clemmer (3) - November 10, 1868
For further information see - Clemmer, W. B.

Way, Rebecca and Samuel K. Lindsay (1) - October 9, 1847

Wealth, Julia Ann and James T. Manuel (3) - July 11, 1869
For further information see - Manuel, James T.

Weaver, Brown (cold.) Carry Allen (3) - December 30, 1884
Place of marriage, Middleway - Age of husband, 22 - Age of wife,
21 - Both are Single - Husband was born in Jefferson County, West
Virginia - Wife was born in Frederick County, Virginia - Both reside
in Jefferson County, West Virginia.

Weaver, Charles and Sarah White (3) - December 27, 1869
Age of husband, 23 - Age of wife, 24 - Both were born in Jefferson
County - Both reside in Jefferson County. (The original of this
record is marked through.)

Weaver, Charles and Mary Virginia Jones (3) - July 8, 1871
Place of marriage, Jefferson County - Age of husband, 22 - Age of
wife, 24 - Both are Single - Husband was born in Jefferson County -
Wife was born in Berkeley County - Both reside in Jefferson
County - Husband's parents are Charles and Rebecca - Wife's parents
are Simon and Lydia - Occupation of husband is Farmer.

Weaver, Charles (black) Sarah White (3) - December 24, 1870
Age of husband, 23 - Age of wife, 24 - Both born in Virginia - Both
reside in Jefferson County.

Weaver, Charles (cold.) Josephine Carter (3) - December 30, 1879
Place of marriage, Middleway - Age of husband, 25 - Age of wife,
23 - Both are Single - Both were born in Jefferson County - Both
reside in Jefferson County.

Weaver, Charles M. and Lillie M. Miller (3) - March 20, 1884
Place of marriage, Charlestown - Age of husband, 27 - Age of wife,
21 - Both are Single - Husband was born in Frederick, Maryland -
Wife was born in Berkeley County - Both reside in Jefferson County,
West Virginia.

Weaver, James L. (cold.) Sarah L. Brunswick (3) - September 4, 1888
Place of marriage, Harpers Ferry - Age of husband, 21 - Age of wife,
21 - Both are Single - Both were born in Jefferson County, West
Virginia - Both reside in Jefferson County, West Virginia.

Weaver, John (cold.) Emma Wood (3) - June 7, 1888
Place of marriage, Middleway - Age of husband, 22 - Age of wife,
22 - Both are Single - Both were born in Jefferson County, West
Virginia - Both reside in Jefferson County, West Virginia.

Weaver, Lyddy (cold.) James Carter (3) - February 22, 1890
For further information see - Carter, James.

Weaver, Rebeca (cold.) Wesley Thornton (3) -   April 29, 1888
    For further information see - Thornton, Wesley.

Webb, Alice and William E. Manuel (3) -   July 24, 1883
    For further information see - Manuel, William E.

Webb, Charles Franklin (cold.) Easter Jones (3) -   September 13, 1883
    Place of marriage, Charlestown - Age of husband, 24 - Age of wife, 24 - Both are Single - Both were born in Jefferson County, West Virginia - Both reside in Jefferson County, West Virginia.

Webb, Cressey and Edmond Barber (1) -   February 4, 1819

Webb, Elisha and Elizabeth Hartness (1) -   November 6, 1817

Webb, Emma J. and Lewis W. Angell (3) -   December 22, 1886
    For further information see - Angell, Lewis W.

Webb, James (free coloured) Matilda Bowman (2) -   (L) December 26, 1854

Webb, James L. and Rhenbecker Montgomery (3) -   August 1889
    Place of marriage, Harpers Ferry - Age of husband, 22 - Age of wife, 17 - Both are Single - Husband was born in Loudoun County, Virginia - Wife was born at Petersburg, Maryland - Both reside in Jefferson County, West Virginia. (Consent of bride's mother in writing.)

Webb, Joseph E. and Louisa R. Heafer (3) -   April 1889
    Place of marriage, Harpers Ferry - Age of husband, 22 - Age of wife, 19 - Both are Single - Wife was born in Jefferson County, West Virginia - Both reside in Jefferson County, West Virginia. (Consent of bride's father in writing.)

Webb, Joseph R. and Elizabeth Thompson (2) -   (L) May 24, 1858

Webb, Mary E. and William I. Avis (3) -   January 19, 1882
    For further information see - Avis, William I.

Webb, Samuel and Mary Bull (1) -   January 5, 1806

Webber, John B. and Elizabeth Shutt (1) -   December 21, 1805

Weber, Annie C. and James Cullman (3) -   January 10, 1889
    For further information see - Cullman, James.

Weber, Leonard and Mary Dittmyer (3) -   February 21, 1867
    Place of marriage, Harpers Ferry, West Virginia - Age of husband, 24 - Age of wife, 21 - Both are Single - Husband was born in Germany - Wife was born at Bolivar, West Virginia - Both reside at Bolivar, West Virginia - Husband's parents are George and Catharina Weber - Wife's parents are John and E. Dittmyer.- Occupation of husband is Laborer.

Webster, Annie R. and W. P. Steadman (3) -.   March 24, 1870
    For further information see - Steadman, W. P.

Webster, Caroline and Oliver H. B. Sappington (1) -   March 30, 1848

Webster, John Wesley and Jennie Alexander (3) - January 24, 1884
　　Place of marriage, Shepherdstown - Age of husband, 22 - Age of wife,
　　24 - Both are Single - Both were born in State of Maryland - Both
　　reside in Jefferson County, West Virginia.

Webster, Richard (cold.) Lucy Jones (3) - December 27, 1881
　　Place of marriage, near Ripon - Age of husband, 22 - Age of wife,
　　21 - Both are Single - Husband was born in Madison County,
　　Virginia - Wife was born in Clarke County, Virginia - Both reside in
　　Jefferson County, West Virginia.

Webster, Thomas D. and Caroline Starry (3) - October 25, 1877
　　Place of marriage, Charlestown - Age of husband, 33 - Age of wife,
　　23 - Both are Single - Both were born in Jefferson County, West
　　Virginia - Both reside in Jefferson County, West Virginia.

Weddell, Virginia and J. H. Easterday (2) - (L) November 3, 1856

Weeks, Anna (cold.) John James Wood (3) - November 16, 1876
　　For further information see - Wood, John James.

Weinbrenner, Denis and Susan R. Sappington (3) - (1869)
　　Age of husband, 51 - Age of wife, 40 - Husband was born in Maryland -
　　Wife was born in Berkeley County - Husband resides in Berkeley
　　County - Wife resides in Jefferson County.

Weirick, William F. and Eliza A. Hudson (2) - (L) November 26, 1851

Weis, Bertha E. and George R. Yontz (3) - April 13, 1882
　　For further information see - Yontz, George R.

Weis, Edwin K. and Anna Alice Turner (3) - January 29, 1879
　　Place of marriage, Shepherdstown - Age of husband, 29 - Age of wife,
　　26 - Husband is Single - Wife is a Widow - Both were born in
　　Jefferson County, West Virginia - Both reside in Jefferson County,
　　West Virginia.

Weis, Mary Elizabeth and Charles Henry Wright (3) - December 12, 1877
　　For further information see - Wright, Charles Henry.

Weis, William F. and Eliza J. Carper (3) - December 5, 1882
　　Place of marriage, Charlestown - Age of husband, 25 - Age of wife,
　　21 - Both are Single - Husband was born in Washington County,
　　Maryland - Wife was born in Jefferson County, West Virginia - Both
　　reside in Jefferson County, West Virginia.

Weisinger, Susan and John H. Keadle (1) - December 25, 1832

Welch, Margaret C. and George B. Stephenson (2) - (L) June 4, 1858

Welch, Thomas and Fannie A. Covert (3) - February 10, 1887
　　Place of marriage, Charlestown - Age of husband, 22 - Age of wife,
　　18 - Both are Single - Both were born in Warren County, Virginia -
　　Both reside in Jefferson County. (Consent of bride's father in
　　person.)

Welcome, John (free mixtures) Bearsheba Lucas (1) - November 23, 1826

Welcome, John (colored) Ellen Thornton (3) - April 28, 1870
   Place of marriage, Jefferson County - Age of husband, 60 - Age of
   wife, 59 - Both were born in Virginia - Both reside in Jefferson
   County.

Welcome, John W. (cold.) Mary Anderson (3) - April 15, 1880
   Place of marriage, Harpers Ferry - Age of husband, 31 - Age of wife,
   25 - Husband is a Widower - Wife is Single - Husband was born in
   Jefferson County, West Virginia - Wife was born in State of
   Virginia - Both reside in Jefferson County, West Virginia.

Weller, John F. and Harriet Benner (3) - November 24, 1874
   Place of marriage, County - Age of husband, 21 - Age of wife, 18 -
   Both are Single - Husband was born in Jefferson County, West
   Virginia - Wife was born in Pennsylvania - Both reside in Jefferson
   County, West Virginia. (Consent of bride's father in person.)

Weller, John L. and Maria E. Metcalf (2) - (L) December 22, 1852

Weller, Joseph A. and Mary E. Randall (2) - (L) November 12, 1855

Weller, Josiah P. and Deliah J. Keyser (2) - (L) December 6, 1858

Weller, Michael S. and Mary W. Gallaher (3) - December 24, 1868
   Place of marriage, Jefferson County - Age of husband, 20 - Age of
   wife, 22 - Both are Single - Husband was born in Maryland - Wife was
   born in Jefferson, Virginia - Both reside in Jefferson County -
   Husband's parents are John and Alice - Wife's parents are John W.
   and Mary.

Weller, William M. and Sarah E. Trishnan (2) - (L) February 27, 1860

Wells, Charlotte (cold.) Benjamin Jackson (3) - September 13, 1888
   For further information see - Jackson, Benjamin.

Wells, D. R. and Emma Price (3) - May 15, 1885
   Place of marriage, Charlestown - Age of husband, 28 - Age of wife,
   22 - Both are Single - Husband was born in State of Pennsylvania -
   Wife was born in Page County, Virginia - Husband resides at
   Hagerstown, Maryland - Wife resides in Jefferson County, West
   Virginia at present.

Wells, George (cold.) Susan Jordan (3) - September 29, 1880
   Place of marriage, Summit Point - Age of husband, 23 - Age of wife,
   21 - Both are Single - Both were born in Jefferson County, West
   Virginia - Both reside in Jefferson County, West Virginia.

Wells, George (cold.) Julia Taylor (3) - September 5, 1883
   Place of marriage, near Ripon - Age of husband, 24 - Age of wife,
   26 - Both are Single - Both were born in Jefferson County, West
   Virginia - Both reside in Jefferson County, West Virginia.

Wells, Girtie (cold.) Barger Johnson (3) - December 23, 1880
   For further information see - Johnson, Barger.

Wells, Samuel and Elizabeth Matheny (1) - February 4, 1821

Wells, T. T. D. (colored) Louisa Richardson (3) -   September 29, 1870
    Place of marriage, Jefferson County - Age of husband, 22 - Age of
    wife, 22 - Husband was born in Berkeley County - Wife was born in
    Jefferson County - Both reside in Jefferson County.

Wells, William (cold.) Hannah McChann (3) -   June 2, 1879
    Place of marriage, Shepherdstown - Age of husband, 29 - Age of wife,
    22 - Both are Single - Both were born at Shepherdstown, West
    Virginia - Both reside in Jefferson County, West Virginia.

Welsh, Ann and Dennis W. Ceanon (2) -   (L) February 11, 1854

Welsh, Ann Elizabeth and James W. Myers (1) -   October 25, 1847

Welsh, Benjamin and Eleanor __?__ (1) -   February 8, 1825

Welsh, Elizabeth and James Hunt (2) -   (L) November 15, 1852

Welsh, Ellen R. and Henry H. Moore (2) -   (L) December 12, 1856

Welsh, Emily A. and John R. Rodrick (3) -   June 11, 1873
    For further information see - Rodrick, John R.

Welsh, George W. and Maria W. Harley (2) -   (L) April 8, 1859

Welsh, George W. and Annie F. Myers (3) -   June 26, 1867
    Place of marriage, Charlestown - Age of husband, 38 - Age of wife,
    27 - Husband is a Widower - Wife is Single - Both were born in
    Jefferson County, Virginia - Both reside in Jefferson County, West
    Virginia - Husband's parents are B. F. and Emily Welsh - Wife's
    parents are Nathaniel and Margaret - Occupation of husband is
    Carpenter.

Welsh, James and Maggie Bowler (3) -   January 8, 1889
    Place of marriage, Harpers Ferry - Age of husband, 34 - Age of wife,
    28 - Both are Single - Husband was born in Pennsylvania - Wife was
    born in Ireland - Husband resides in Pennsylvania - Wife resides in
    Jefferson County, West Virginia.

Welsh, Margaret Catherine and Charles C. Conklyn (2) -   (L) December 17, 1860

Welsh, Maria and Ben Lock (1) -   February 3, 1842

Welsh, Michael and Mollie Howard (3) -   March 3, 1870
    Place of marriage, Jefferson County - Age of husband, 25 - Age of
    wife, 21 - Husband was born in Loudoun County, Virginia - Wife was
    born in Maryland - Both reside in Jefferson County. (Sworn to by
    Thomas Hepley.)

Welsh, Molly and Monroe Nicewarner (3) -   October 3, 1877
    For further information see - Nicewarner, Monroe.

Welsh, R. W. and S. J. Anderson (bride) (3) -   December 17, 1867
    Place of marriage, Jefferson County - Age of husband, 31 - Age of
    wife, 22 - Both are Single - Both were born in Jefferson County -
    Both reside in Jefferson - Husband's parents are Benjamin B. and
    Elenor - Wife's parents are H. A. and Mary - Occupation of husband
    is Carpenter.

Welshance, Elizabeth and Jacob Staley (1) -   April 8, 1821

Welshans, Emma M. and George W. Port (3) - January 1, 1879
   For further information see - Port, George W.

Welshans, Harriet and John Miller (2) - (L) February 14, 1855

Welshans, S. M. (bride) and S. H. Davis (3) - January 20, 1869
   For further information see - Davis, S. H.

Welshimer, Elizabeth and Thomas James (1) - March 22, 1810

Welshimer, Margaret and Daniel Entler (1) - January 20, 1809

Welty, George C. and Mary C. Avey (3) - July 18, 1876
   Place of marriage, Bolivar - Age of husband, 38 - Age of wife, 20 - Both are Single - Husband was born in Maryland - Wife wasborn in Jefferson County, West Virginia - Both reside in Jefferson County, West Virginia. (Consent of bride's father in writing.)

Weltzheimer, Adam and Elizabeth T. Cooper (1) - November 15, 1825

Weltzheimer, Adam and Elizabeth Smallwood (1) - April 5, 1827

Weltzheimer, Kate and J. Francis Wheatley (2) - (L) June 25, 1855

Wenis, Margaret and James Abel. (2) - (L) August 28, 1852

Wentsell, W. W. and E. J. Chambers (bride) (3) - December 12, 1871
   Place of marriage, Jefferson County - Age of husband, 24 - Age of wife, 19 - Both are Single - Both were born in Jefferson County. - Husband resides in Jefferson - Wife resides in Jefferson County - Husband's parents are W. H. Wentsell and M. C. Wentsell - Wife's parents are Singleton and Mary M. - Occupation of husband is Painter. (Singleton and Mary Chambers.)

Wentzel, Mary Y. and William S. Winters (3) - July 27, 1868
   For further information see - Winters, William S.

Wentzell, Ann Rebecca and Charles Griffiths (1) - December 25, 1836

Wentzell, Charles B. and Annie L. Daniels (3) - January 5, 1873
   Place of marriage, Harpers Ferry - Age of husband, 22 - Age of wife, 19 - Both are Single - Husband was born at Harpers Ferry - Wife was born at Philadelphia - Husband resides in Fauquier County, Virginia - Wife resides at Harpers Ferry - Husband's parents are W. H. and M. C. Wentzell - Wife's parents are, mother Jane, father not known - Occupation of husband is Merchant. (Mother's consent in writing.)

Wentzell, J. B. and Clara V. Rau (3) - November 28, 1878
   Place of marriage, Bolivar - Age of husband, 26 - Age of wife, 18 - Both are Single - Both were born in Jefferson County, West Virginia - Both reside in Jefferson County, West Virginia. (Consent of bride's father in person.)

Wentzell, Joseph and Mary Stipes (2) - (L) January 18, 1855

Wentzell, Susanna and John W. Buckly (1) - July 5, 1851

Wernway, Julia A. and Rudolph S. Littlejohn (1) - October 21, 1845

Wernway, William B. and Ann E. Yantis (2) - (L) April 29, 1858

Werrick, Lucretia and Isaac Miller (3) - June 15, 1869
    For further information see - Miller, Isaac.

Werthime, Michael Leopold and Louisa Pfister (2) - (L) August 5, 1857

Weskell, Phil and Anna Harrison (3) - (1872)
    Place of marriage, Jefferson County - Age of husband, 57 - Age of wife, 34 - Husband is a Widower - Wife is Single - Both were born in Virginia - Both reside in West Virginia - Occupation of husband is Farmer.

West, Agness and Conrad Demend (1) - September 21, 1815

West, Andrew J. and Ann Eliza Campbell (2) - (L) January 9, 1856

West, Ann and William Boggess (1) - October 1, 1835

West, Ann and James W. Wageley (3) - November 21, 1865
    (Miss Vic Gilbert, Mechanics Town, Frederick County, Maryland.)

West, Ann M. and R. V. McDonald (3) - November 24, 1881
    For further information see - McDonald, R. V.

West, Annie and Thomas Davis (3) - December 23, 1868
    For further information see - Davis, Thomas.

West, Corban and Mary Ann Abigail Buckles (1) - March 31, 1825

West, E. J. and John Benner (3) - April 4, 1872
    For further information see - Benner, John.

West, George W. and Fanny Clipp (3) - January 27, 1886
    Place of marriage, Charlestown - Age of husband, 24 - Age of wife, 23 - Both are Single - Husband was born in Jefferson County, West Virginia - Wife was born in Jefferson County - Both reside in Jefferson County, West Virginia.

West, John E. and Eliza Burnet (2) - (L) January 2, 1864
    Time of marriage, January 3, 1864 - Place of marriage, Charlestown, Jefferson County, Virginia - Names, John E. West and Eliza Burnet - Age of husband, 27 years - Age of wife, 22 years - Both are Single - Place of husband's birth was Montgomery County, Maryland - Place of wife's birth was Jefferson County, Virginia - Both reside in Jefferson County, Virginia - Husband's parents are Tilghman and Mary West - Wife's parents are Robert and Sarah Burnet - Occupation of husband is Farmer - License issued January 2, 1864 - Thomas A. Moore, Clerk.

West, Lucinda and Jefferson Smith (1) - February 18, 1834

West, Martha and William Willis (2) - (L) February 2, 1852

West, Nancy J. and Israel V. Boyd (3) - December 17, 1874
    For further information see - Boyd, Israel V.

West, Ruth and Jeremiah Anderson (1) - March 29, 1835

615

West, Theodore Clark and Maude Swartzwelder (3) - November 19, 1885
    Place of marriage, Shepherdstown - Age of husband, 26 - Age of wife, 22 - Both are Single - Husband was born at Waco, Texas - Wife was born at Maysville, Kentucky - Both reside at Waco, Texas.

West, Thomas and Caroline Howell (2) - (L) April 5, 1852

West, Thomas and Caroline Howell (1) - April 6, 1852

West, Thomas J. and Mary Eliza Campbell (3) - January 2, 1879
    Place of marriage, near Ripon - Age of husband, 23 - Age of wife, 22 - Both are Single - Husband was born in Jefferson County, West Virginia - Wife was born in Clarke County, Virginia - Both reside in Jefferson County, West Virginia.

Whalan, Alice and Henry Edward Rust (3) - June 14, 1871
    For further information see - Rust, Henry Edward.

Whalen, Betty (cold.) Ben Slaughter (3) - April 1, 1877
    For further information see - Slaughter, Ben.

Whalen, E. A. (bride) and P. W. Riley (3) - May 21, 1872
    For further information see - Riley, P. W.

Whalen, Frances (cold.) Alfred Irvin (3) - October 4, 1876
    For further information see - Irvin, Alfred.

Whalen, John P. and Isadore V. Anderson (3) - August 7, 1873
    Place of marriage, Bolivar - Age of husband, 21 - Age of wife, 22 - Both are Single - Husband was born at Ellicote City - Wife was born in Jefferson County, West Virginia - Husband resides at Baltimore City - Wife resides in Jefferson County, West Virginia.

Whalin, Helen (cold.) Ed. P. Talbott (3) - April 6, 1876
    For further information see - Talbott, Ed. P.

Wheatley, J. Francis and Kate Weltzheimer (2) - (L) June 25, 1855

Wheatley, Mary and William Sagle (1) - July 12, 1832

Wheatly, William and Mary Sagle (1) - September 30, 1821

Wheeler, Isaiah (cold.) E. Morris (3) - November 17, 1867
    Place of marriage, Jefferson County - Age of husband, 46 - Age of wife, 26 - Husband is a Widower - Wife is a Widow - Husband was born in Jefferson County, Virginia - Wife was born in Maryland - Both reside in Jefferson County - Occupation of husband is Laborer.

Wheeler, J. Ann (colored) Benjamin Hendon (3) - March 10, 1870
    For further information see - Hendon, Benjamin.

Wheeler, Jacob (cold.) Rosa Bowman (3) - August 15, 1876
    Place of marriage, Kearneysville - Age of husband, 21 - Age of wife, 18 - Both are Single - Husband was born in Berkeley County - Wife was born in Jefferson County, West Virginia - Both reside in Jefferson County, West Virginia. (John Wheeler certifies to consent of bride's father.)

Wheeler, James and Lucy Clinton (3) - October 22, 1871
    Place of marriage, Jefferson County - Age of husband, 58 - Age of
    wife, 46 - Husband is Single - Wife is a Widow - Both were born in
    Virginia - Both reside in Jefferson - Husband's parents are Benjamin
    and Larina - Wife's parents are Harrison and Allie - Occupation of
    husband is Contractor.

Whip, Adam and Matilda Reed (1) - February 28, 1832

Whip, Mary Ann and George Seanafer (1) - December 5, 1816

Whiston, Mary Ann and Benjamin Engle (1) - November 14, 1833

White, Alexander and Harriet Foreman (2) - (L) December 10, 1853

White, Alice (cold.) Charles H. Reeler (3) - March 5, 1884
    For further information see - Reeler, Charles H.

White, Elizabeth M. and George Foreman (2) - (L) December 1, 1853
    (Consent of Miss White's mother proved by the oath of Alexander
    White the brother of the intended bride.)

White, George and Bettie C. Pope (3) - August 16, 1882
    Place of marriage, near Summit Point - Age of husband, 25 - Age of
    wife, 17 - Both are Single - Husband was born in Jefferson County,
    West Virginia - Wife was born in Warren County, Virginia - Both
    reside in Jefferson County, West Virginia. (Consent of bride's
    father in person.)

White, George T. and Anne E. Staley (3) - November 15, 1888
    Place of marriage, Shepherdstown - Age of husband, 32 - Age of wife,
    24 - Both are Single - Husband was born at Richmond, Virginia - Wife
    was born in Jefferson County, West Virginia - Husband resides in
    Berkeley County, West Virginia - Wife resides in Jefferson County,
    West Virginia.

White, Humphrey K. and Elizabeth Steadman (1) - September 25, 1822

White, James (cold.) Emily Crawford (3) - August 23, 1876
    Place of marriage, Shepherdstown - Age of husband, 28 - Age of wife,
    22 - Husband is a Widower - Wife is Single - Both were born in
    Jefferson County, West Virginia - Both reside in Jefferson County,
    West Virginia.

White, James and Sarah Harden (3) - April 6, 1871
    Place of marriage, Jefferson County - Age of husband, 23 - Age of
    wife, 25 - Both are Single - Husband was born in Jefferson County -
    Wife was born in Virginia - Both reside in Jefferson County -
    Husband's parents are Solomon and Dorotha - Wife's parents are
    Daniel and Rebecca - Occupation of husband is Farmer.

White, John K. and Ellen M. Jewett (1) - November 19, 1839

White, Joseph T. and Ann F. Duke (3) - November 27, 1877
    Place of marriage, near Halltown - Age of husband, 23 - Age of wife,
    25 - Both are Single - Husband was born in Maryland - Wife was born
    in Clarke County, Virginia - Husband resides in Montgomery County,
    Maryland - Wife resides in Jefferson County, West Virginia.

White, Joseph T. and Laura A. McGarry (3) -　　　　　December 3, 1889
　　Place of marriage, Bride's Residence - Age of husband, 35 - Age of
　　wife, 29 - Husband is a Widower - Wife is Single - Husband was born
　　in Montgomery County, Maryland - Wife was born in Jefferson County,
　　West Virginia - Husband resides in Montgomery County, Maryland -
　　Wife resides in Jefferson County, West Virginia.

White, Lucy V. and J. R. Williams (3) -　　　　　March 25, 1885
　　For further information see - Williams, J. R.

White, Martha Jane and Elias E. Grove (3) -　　　　　August 10, 1882
　　For further information see - Grove, Elias E.

White, Rebecca H. and Joseph Trapnell (3) -　　　　　November 20, 1866
　　For further information see - Trapnell, Joseph.

White, Robert (colored) Eliza Carter (3) -　　　　　October 12, 1870
　　Place of marriage, Jefferson County - Age of husband, 40 - Age of
　　wife, 40 - Both were born in Jefferson County - Both reside in
　　Jefferson County.

White, Rosanna and David C. Adams (3) -　　　　　January 31, 1877
　　For further information see - Adams, David C.

White, S. F. and F. S. Macoughtry (bride) (3) -　　　　　June 25, 1867
　　Place of marriage, Smithfield - Age of husband, 30 - Age of wife,
　　23 - Both are Single - Husband was born in Carrol County, Maryland -
　　Wife was born in Jefferson County - Both reside at Smithfield, West
　　Virginia - Husband's parents are John and Mary - Wife's parents are
　　William O. and Elizabeth - Occupation of husband is Merchant.

White, Sarah and Charles Weaver (3) -　　　　　December 27, 1869
　　For further information see - Weaver, Charles.

White, Sarah (black) Charles Weaver (3) -　　　　　December 24, 1870
　　For further information see - Weaver, Charles.

White, Virginia (cold.) John A. Arter (3) -　　　　　January 13, 1881
　　For further information see - Arter, John A.

Whitehouse, Alsey and Jacob Hill (1) -　　　　　1824

Whitehouse, Nancy and David Dillow (1) -　　　　　November 22, 1827

Whiting, Abraham and Elisa Furlong (3) -　　　　　November 19, 1868
　　Place of marriage, Jefferson County - Age of husband, 40 - Age of
　　wife, 30 - Husband is a Widower - Wife is a Widow - Both were born
　　in Jefferson County - Both reside in Jefferson County - Husband's
　　parents are George and Sally - Wife's parents are Anthony and
　　Milly - Occupation of husband is Laborer.

Whiting, Chlora (cold.) William Williams (3) -　　　　　March 25, 1886
　　For further information see - Williams, William.

Whiting, David (cold.) Lucy Bowman (3) -　　　　　May 29, 1878
　　Place of marriage, Charlestown - Age of husband, 22 - Age of wife,
　　21 - Both are Single - Husband was born in Jefferson County, West
　　Virginia - Wife was born in Maryland - Both reside in Jefferson
　　County, West Virginia.

Whiting, George and B. Throckmorton (3) - January 24, 1872
Place of marriage, Jefferson County, West Virginia - Age of husband, 28 - Age of wife, 26 - Both are Single - Husband was born in Clarke County, Virginia - Wife was born in Jefferson County, Virginia - Husband resides in Clarke County, Virginia - Wife resides in Jefferson County, West Virginia - Husband's parents are F. H. and Rebecca - Wife's parents are Warner and Susan - Occupation of husband is Farmer.

Whiting, James (cold.) Jane Hill (3) - July 24, 1873
Place of marriage, Charles Town - Age of husband, 21 - Age of wife, 21 - Both are Single - Both were born in Jefferson County, West Virginia - Both reside in Jefferson County, West Virginia.

Whiting, James (cold.) Eliza Harious (3) - December 25, 1877
Place of marriage, near Duffields - Age of husband, 28 - Age of wife, 23 - Both are Single - Both were born in Jefferson County, West Virginia - Both reside in Jefferson County, West Virginia.

Whiting, James (cold.) Jennie Powell (3) - June 1, 1882
Place of marriage, Charlestown - Age of husband, 29 - Age of wife, 16 - Husband is a Widower - Wife is Single - Both were born in Jefferson County, West Virginia - Husband resides in Jefferson County, West Virginia - Wife resides in Jefferson County. (Consent of bride's father certified by her brother-in-law.)

Whiting, Martha (cold.) Horace Lowry (3) - September 9, 1874
For further information see - Lowry, Horace.

Whiting, Mary (cold.) William Carter Thornton (3) - November 15, 1877
For further information see - Thornton, William Carter.

Whiting, Rose (cold.) Richard Thornton (3) - December 25, 1888
For further information see - Thornton, Richard.

Whiting, Samuel (cold.) Mary Jenkins (3) - December 1, 1881
Place of marriage, Duffields - Age of husband, 21 - Age of wife, 18 - Both are Single - Both were born in Jefferson County, West Virginia - Both reside in Jefferson County, West Virginia. (Consent of bride's mother in writing.)

Whiting, Sarah M. (cold.) George W. Robinson (3) - April 24, 1882
For further information see - Robinson, George W.

Whitington, Corleccus and Ellen Hodges (3) - February 18, 1868
Place of marriage, Jefferson County - Age of husband, 28 - Age of wife, 21 - Both are Single - Both were born in Jefferson - Both reside in Jefferson - Husband's parents are Joseph and Jane - Wife's parents are John and Mary E. - Occupation of husband is Farmer.

Whitington, John N. and Celestine Gallaher (3) - November 27, 1867
Place of marriage, Jefferson County - Age of husband, 26 - Age of wife, 19 - Both are Single - Husband was born in Fairfax County - Wife was born in Jefferson County - Both reside in Jefferson County - Husband's parents are William and Sarah - Wife's parents are John and Mary - Occupation of husband is Painter.

Whitington, Vance R. and Ann C. Hodge (3) -   April 23, 1867
    Place of marriage, Summit Point - Age of husband, 26 - Age of wife,
    25 - Both are Single - Both were born in Jefferson County, West
    Virginia - Both reside at Summit Point, West Virginia - Husband's
    parents are Benjamin and Elizabeth Whitington - Wife's parents are
    John and Margaret Hodge - Occupation of husband is Farmer.
    (William W. Wilson sworn to the age of young lady.)

Whitlock, James Henry and Mary Jane Lee (3) -   May 6, 1871
    Place of marriage, Jefferson County - Age of husband, 30 - Age of
    wife, 26 - Both are Single - Husband was born in Virginia - Wife was
    born in Jefferson County - Both reside in Jefferson County -
    Husband's parents are Frank and Sallie - Wife's parents are Frank
    and Lavina - Occupation of husband is Farmer.

Whitmer, William H. and Annie C. Wilt (3) -   February 26, 1879
    Place of marriage, Charlestown - Age of husband, 25 - Age of wife,
    24 next May - Both are Single - Husband was born in Loudoun County,
    Virginia - Wife was born in Jefferson County, West Virginia - Both
    reside in Jefferson County, West Virginia.

Whitmore, George and Lydia Ann Blue (3) -   July 30, 1866
    Place of marriage, Charlestown, Jefferson County - Age of husband,
    35 - Age of wife, 20 - Both are Single - Husband was born in Augusta
    County, Virginia - Wife was born in Jefferson County, West
    Virginia - Both reside at Charlestown, Jefferson County, West
    Virginia - Husband's parents are Aaron and Lila Whitmore - Wife's
    parents are Jeremiah and Louisa Blue - Occupation of husband is
    Laborer.

Whitmore, George H. and Florence Hoffmaster (3) -   November 16, 1876
    Place of marriage, near Charlestown - Age of husband, 25 - Age of
    wife, 20 - Both are Single - Husband was born in Loudoun County -
    Wife was born in Jefferson County, West Virginia - Both reside in
    Jefferson County, West Virginia. (Consent of bride's father in
    person.)

Whitmore, Martha E. and Harry B. Middlekauff (3) -   January 8, 1890
    For further information see.- Middlekauff, Harry B.

Whitmore, Mary Alice and W. B. Alder (3) -   June 30, 1886
    For further information see - Alder, W. B.

Whitmore, Virginia A. and T. W. Rhineman (3) -   December 21, 1886
    For further information see - Rhineman, T. W.

Whitnall, Charles E. and Octavia Elizabeth Lay (3) -   December 19, 1885
    Place of marriage, Halltown - Age of husband, 21 - Age of wife, 17 -
    Both are Single - Husband was born in England - Wife was born in
    Frederick County, Virginia - Both reside in Jefferson County, West
    Virginia. (Consent of bride's father in person.)

Whitson, Anna P. and William F. Manuel (2) -   (L) December 13, 1855

Whittington, Annie B. and John William Wyndham (3) -   February 17, 1880
    For further information see - Wyndham, John William.

Whittington, Barbara and John Shewbridge (2) -   (L) February 9, 1852
    (Thomas Hicks sworn.)

Whittington, Barbara and John Shoebridge (1) - . . February 17, 1852

Whittington, Catharine and Morris Conrad (2) - . (L) December 5, 1854

Whittington, Catharine R. and Samuel W. Barrett (2) - (L) December 24, 1858

Whittington, Charles L. and Alice O. Avey (3) - . March 7, 1872
  Place of marriage, Jefferson County, West Virginia - Age of husband,
  26 - Age of wife, 19 - Both are Single - Husband was born in
  Frederick County - Wife was born in Maryland - Husband resides in
  Jefferson County - Wife resides in Jefferson County, West Virginia -
  Husband's parents are Fran and Mary - Wife's parents are John and
  Mary - Occupation of husband is Farmer. (Father.)

Whittington, David L. and Caroline Virginia Manuel (3) - December 28, 1875
  Place of marriage, near Summit Point - Age of husband, 26 - Age of
  wife, 23 - Both are Single - Husband was born in Jefferson County,
  West Virginia - Wife was born in Rappahannock County, Virginia -
  Both reside in Jefferson County, West Virginia.

Whittington, Ed. L. and Jennie V. Amey (3) - December 16, 1885
  Place of marriage, Kearneysville - Age of husband, 25 - Age of wife,
  21 - Husband is a Widower - Wife is Single - Husband was born in
  Jefferson County, West Virginia - Wife was born in Berkeley County -
  Both reside in Jefferson County, West Virginia.

Whittington, Elizabeth and George Strain (1) - . April 19, 1827

Whittington, Fanny and James W. Gore (3) - January 26, 1876
  For further information see - Gore, James W.

Whittington, George W. and Lottie C. Burnett (3) - August 26, 1890
  Place of marriage, Charlestown - Age of husband, 21 - Age of wife,
  21 - Both are Single - Husband was born in Warren County, Virginia -
  Wife was born in Jefferson County, West Virginia - Both reside in
  Jefferson County, West Virginia.

Whittington, Henrietta and Lewis Wood (3) - . . March 23, 1881
  For further information see - Wood, Lewis.

Whittington, Ida May and W. T. Whittington (3) - . September 23, 1890
  For further information see.- Whittington, W. T.

Whittington, J. B. and Emma Jane Fletcher (3) - . . December 27, 1881
  Place of marriage, Charlestown - Age of husband, 22 - Age of wife,
  25 - Both are Single - Husband was born in Jefferson County, West
  Virginia - Wife was born in Orange County, Virginia - Both reside in
  Jefferson County, West Virginia.

Whittington, James and Emma Thomas (3) - October 26, 1876
  Place of marriage, Duffields - Age of husband, 21 - Age of wife,
  21 - Both are Single - Husband was born in Jefferson County, West
  Virginia - Wife was born in Loudoun County, Virginia - Both reside
  in Jefferson County, West Virginia.

Whittington, James C. and Ruth Anna Jane Morningstar (2) -(L) December 6, 1856

Whittington, James E. and Ann Elizabeth Morris (3) -   December 20, 1888
    Place of marriage, Charlestown - Age of husband, 26 - Age of wife,
    17 - Both are Single - Both were born in Loudoun County, Virginia -
    Both reside in Jefferson County, West Virginia. (Consent of bride's
    father in person.)

Whittington, James K. and Mary Schoppart (2) -   (L) February 13, 1865
    Time of marriage, February 14, 1865 - Place of marriage,
    Charlestown - Names, James K. Whittington and Mary Schoppart - Age
    of husband, 23 years last April - Age of wife, 22 years last April -
    Both are Single - Husband was born in Loudoun County, Virginia -
    Wife was born in Berkeley County, Virginia - Both reside in
    Jefferson County, Virginia - Husband's parents are Joseph and Jane
    Whittington - Wife's parents are Samuel C. and __?__ Schoppart -
    Occupation of husband is Farmer - License issued February 13, 1865 -
    T. A. Moore, Clerk.

Whittington, John Newton and Sarah Jane Krout (2) -   (L) February 9, 1853

Whittington, John N. and Sarah Jane Krout (1) -   February 10, 1853

Whittington, John R. and Margaret A. O'Farrell (3) -   September 10, 1874
    Place of marriage, Kearneysville - Age of husband, 26 - Age of wife,
    22 - Both are Single - Husband was born in Frederick County,
    Virginia - Wife was born in Georgia - Both reside in Jefferson
    County, West Virginia.

Whittington, John W. and Mary Jane Virginia Johnson (2) -(L) February 16, 1854

Whittington, John W. and Matilda C. Golliday (3) -   June 12, 1877
    Place of marriage, Charlestown - Age of husband, 28 - Age of wife,
    35 - Both are Single - Husband was born in Jefferson County, West
    Virginia - Wife was born in Shenandoah County, Virginia - Both
    reside in Jefferson County, West Virginia.

Whittington, Joseph J. and Margaret A. Campbell (2) -   (L) July 10, 1852

Whittington, Joseph S. and Eliza Davis (3) -   January 14, 1868
    Place of marriage, Jefferson County - Age of husband, 22 - Age of
    wife, 17 - Both are Single - Husband was born in Jefferson County -
    Wife was born in Berkeley County - Husband resides in Jefferson -
    Wife resides in Berkeley - Husband's parents are Joseph and Mary -
    Wife's parents are Mary - Occupation of husband is Farmer.
    (Parents willing.)

Whittington, Margaret Elizabeth and Randolph Campbell (3) - February 20, 1884
    For further information see - Campbell, Randolph.

Whittington, Martha Ann and James W. Collins (2) -   (L) December 26, 1856

Whittington, Martha C. and William H. Griffith (3) -   March 6, 1878
    For further information see - Griffith, William H.

Whittington, Mary and Strother Chapman (1) -   November 15, 1832

Whittington, Mary and T. M. Baker (3) -   October 29, 1890
    For further information see - Baker, T. M.

Whittington, Mary Jane and Bushrod Smallwood (2) -   (L) April 1, 1859

Whittington, Mary Jane and Barthelomew Morrison (2) - . (L) August 3, 1859

Whittington, Maurice N. and Lizzie M. Smith (3) - July 16, 1890
Place of marriage, Charlestown - Age of husband, 27 - Age of wife,
18 - Both are Single - Both were born in Jefferson County, West
Virginia - Both reside in Jefferson County, West Virginia.
(Consent of bride's father in person.)

Whittington, Richard and Barbary Smith (1) - . 1821

Whittington, Sarah and Jacob Mack Winkler (3) - April 30, 1879
For further information see - Winkler, Jacob Mack.

Whittington, W. T. and Mary Selina Morris (3) - December 2, 1885
Place of marriage, Charlestown - Age of husband, 26 - Age of wife,
18 - Both are Single - Both were born in Clarke County, Virginia -
Husband resides in Fauquier County, Virginia - Wife resides in
Jefferson County, West Virginia.

Whittington, W. T. and Ida May Whittington (3) - September 23, 1890
Place of marriage, Charlestown - Age of husband, 30 - Age of wife,
19 - Husband is a Widower - Wife is Single - Husband was born in
Clarke County, Virginia - Wife was born in Jefferson County, West
Virginia - Husband resides at Roanoke, Virginia - Wife resides in
Jefferson County, West Virginia.

Whover, Sally and Zachariah Williams (1) - February 24, 1807

Wickham, Marain T. and Ma. Breedin (1) - December 19, 1805

Wiggenton, Elizabeth B. and John Seibert (3) - November 24, 1868
For further information see - Seibert, John.

Wiggington, John and Sarah Harden (1) - 1816

Wiggington, John and Eliza V. Engram (2) - (L) August 2, 1855

Wigginton, James D. and M. F. Barns (3) - March 31, 1875
Place of marriage, Middleway - Age of husband, 34 - Age of wife,
27 - Both are Single - Husband was born in Berkeley County, West
Virginia - Wife was born in Jefferson County, West Virginia - Both
reside in Jefferson County, West Virginia.

Wigginton, Joshua F. and Ann Stephens (2) - (L) October 16, 1856

Wigginton, Martha Ann and N. O. Allison (2) - (L) September 18, 1858

Wigginton, Mary Elizabeth and Thomas J. McKennan (2) - (L) May 23, 1855

Wightman, Sadie and Levi G. Cummins (3) - October 23, 1889
For further information see - Cummins, Levi G.

Wilborn, Charlotte Anna and James A. Neff (2) - (L) February 15, 1859

Wilborn, Jane Catharine and Alexander Boley (2) - (L) January 28, 1854

Wilcher, John and Camilla Simpson (1) - January 13, 1825

Wilders, Thomas and Hester Long (1) - December 19, 1824

Wiley, Hezekiah and Angelthta Viands (3) -   July 17, 1889
    Place of marriage, Charlestown - Age of husband, 25 - Age of wife,
    25 - Both are Single - Both were born in Jefferson County, West
    Virginia - Both reside in Jefferson County, West Virginia.

Wiley, James William and Amanda Mobley (3) -   October 28, 1875
    Place of marriage, Mountain - Age of husband, 21 - Age of wife, 22 -
    Both are Single - Husband was born in Clarke County, Virginia - Wife
    was born in Jefferson County, West Virginia - Both reside in
    Jefferson County, West Virginia.

Wiley, James L. and Maggie L. Vorens (3) -   September 16, 1885
    Place of marriage, Charlestown - Age of husband, 26 - Age of wife,
    24 - Both are Single - Both were born in Clarke County, Virginia -
    Both reside in Clarke County, Virginia.

Wiley, John and Rose A. Dillow (3) -   July 13, 1882
    Place of marriage, County - Age of husband, 21 - Age of wife, 22 -
    Both are Single - Husband was born in Clarke County, Virginia -
    Wife was born in Jefferson County, West Virginia - Husband resides
    in Jefferson County, West Virginia - Wife resides in Jefferson County.

Wiley, John and Harriet Painter (3) -   September 3, 1885
    Place of marriage, Charlestown - Age of husband, 30 - Age of wife,
    25 - Husband is Single - Wife is a Widow of Thomas J. Dillow by
    divorce - Both were born in Jefferson County, West Virginia - Both
    reside in Jefferson County, West Virginia.

Wiley, Joseph and Sarah Shepherd (1) -   February 18, 1809

Wiley, Sarah E. and John H. Dillow (3) -   December 15, 1881
    For further information see - Dillow, John H.

Wilhelm, William H. and Fanny Grant (3) -   December 30, 1878
    Place of marriage, Shepherdstown - Age of husband, 23 - Age of wife,
    23 - Both are Single - Husband was born in Berkeley County, West
    Virginia - Wife was born in Jefferson County, West Virginia - Both
    reside in Jefferson County, West Virginia.

Wilkens, Jane and Cornelius Vanderbilt (1) -   March 31, 1819

Wilkenson, Grace and C. Coale (3) -   (1869)
    For further information see - Coale, C.

Wilkeson, Bettie and John W. Norris (3) -   December 24, 1868
    For further information see - Norris, John W.

Wilkins, James B. and Mary Ann Adams (1) -   May 7, 1829

Wilkinson, Charles (cold.) Annie Johnson (3) -   March 5, 1874
    Place of marriage, Shepherdstown - Age of husband, 23 - Age of wife,
    25 - Both are Single - Husband was born in Jefferson County, West
    Virginia - Wife was born in Louisiana - Both reside in Jefferson
    County, West Virginia.

Wilkinson, Sallie (cold.) Henry Hopewell (3) -   July 21, 1877
    For further information see - Hopewell, Henry.

Wilkison, Mary (cold.) Charles Shorts (3) -   December 26, 1887
    For further information see - Shorts, Charles.

Will, George and Margaret Smittotz (1) -   April 22, 1849

Williams, Adam (cold.) Fanny Stripling (3) -   December 17, 1879
   Place of marriage, Shepherdstown - Age of husband, 25 - Age of wife,
   21 - Both are Single - Husband was born in Wythe County, Virginia -
   Wife was born in Jefferson County, West Virginia - Both reside in
   Jefferson County, West Virginia.

Williams, Alice (cold.) Harry Powell (3) -   July 21, 1877
   For further information see - Powell, Harry.

Williams, Annie and Isaac Martin (3) -   October 22, 1885
   For further information see - Martin, Isaac.

Williams, Anthony (cold.) Sally Jenkins (3) -   December 21, 1876
   Place of marriage, Shepherdstown - Age of husband, 22 - Age of wife,
   22 - Both are Single - Both were born in Jefferson County, West
   Virginia - Both reside in Jefferson County, West Virginia.

Williams, Ashby and Ann E. Crim (3) -   June 5, 1888
   Place of marriage, Charlestown - Age of husband, 25 - Age of wife,
   21 - Both are Single - Husband was born in Hardy County, West
   Virginia - Wife was born in Jefferson County, West Virginia - Both
   reside in Jefferson County, West Virginia.

Williams, Charles (cold.) Sarah Hicks (3) -   December 20, 1885
   Place of marriage, near Bloomery Mills - Age of husband, 22 - Age of
   wife, 18 - Both are Single - Both were born in Jefferson County, West
   Virginia - Both reside in Jefferson County, West Virginia.
   (Consent of bride's father in writing.)

Williams, Cora Bell (cold.) J. W. Nelson (3) -   November 20, 1888
   For further information see - Nelson, J. W.

Williams, E. J. and S. R. Young (bride) (3) -   December 17, 1879
   Place of marriage, Charlestown - Age of husband, 35 - Age of wife,
   35 - Both are Single - Both were born in Jefferson County, West
   Virginia - Both reside in Jefferson County, West Virginia.

Williams, Edward (cold.) Alice Johnson (3) -   October 4, 1883
   Place of marriage, Charlestown - Age of husband, 24 - Age of wife,
   24 - Both are Single - Husband was born in Clarke County, Virginia -
   Wife was born in Page County, Virginia - Both reside in Jefferson
   County, West Virginia.

Williams, Emily (cold.) David Jackson (3) -   November 20, 1882
   For further information see - Jackson, David.

Williams, Emma C. and Joseph D. Turner (3) -   March 22, 1876
   For further information see - Turner, Joseph D.

Williams, Euphemia and Andrew Hays (1) -   January 8, 1834

Williams, Evaline (cold.) Thomas Washington (3) -   October 30, 1876
   For further information see - Washington, Thomas.

Williams, Fanny (cold.) William Henry Bargason (3) -   May 20, 1886
   For further information see - Bargason, William Henry.

Williams, Frank and Annie Lee Kenney (3) - December 11, 1889
    Place of marriage, Harpers Ferry - Age of husband, 36 - Age of wife,
    25 - Both are Single - Both were born in Loudoun County, Virginia -
    Both reside in Jefferson County, West Virginia.

Williams, George Henry (cold.) Mary Reed (3) - July 15, 1874
    Place of marriage, near Charlestown - Age of husband, 25 - Age of
    wife, 19 - Both are Single - Husband was born in Rappahannock
    County, Virginia - Wife was born in Jefferson County, West
    Virginia - Both reside in Jefferson County, West Virginia.
    (Father's consent in writing.)

Williams, Geraldine (cold.) Frank Ashby (3) - October 2, 1890
    For further information see - Ashby, Frank.

Williams, Harriet A. and Lemuel B. Grandstaff (3) - February 8, 1887
    For further information see - Grandstaff, Lemuel B.

Williams, Harry (cold.) Lucy Daugherty (3) - July 13, 1876
    Place of marriage, Summit Point - Age of husband, 25 - Age of wife,
    22 - Both are Single - Both were born in Jefferson County, West
    Virginia - Both reside in Jefferson County, West Virginia.

Williams, Henry and Emily Patterson (3) - December 25, 1866
    Place of marriage, Charlestown - Age of husband, 30 - Age of wife,
    27 - Husband is Single - Wife is a Widow - Husband was born in
    Rappahannock County, Virginia - Wife was born in Jefferson County,
    West Virginia - Both reside in Jefferson County, West Virginia -
    Husband's parents are Henry and Gracy Williams - Wife's parents are
    Osborn and Charity Gibson - Occupation of husband is Blacksmith.

Williams, Isaac and Mary Clemmons (1) - December 24, 1818

Williams, J. R. and Lucy V. White (3) - March 25, 1885
    Place of marriage, Charlestown - Age of husband, 25 - Age of wife,
    17 - Both are Single - Husband was born in Hardy County, West
    Virginia - Wife was born in Jefferson County, West Virginia - Both
    reside in Jefferson County, West Virginia. (Consent of bride's
    mother in writing.)

Williams, Jacob and Barbara J. Hill (3) - September 15, 1870
    Place of marriage, Jefferson County - Age of husband, 26 - Age of
    wife, 28 - Both were born in Virginia - Husband resides in West
    Virginia - Wife resides in Jefferson County.

Williams, James (free cold.) Mary Blue (2) - (L) December 25, 1856

Williams, James (cold.) Rose Spenser (3) - December 12, 1878
    Place of marriage, Rippon - Age of husband, 22 - Age of wife, 19 -
    Both are Single - Husband was born at Front Royal, Virginia - Wife
    was born in Page County, Virginia - Both reside in Jefferson County,
    West Virginia. (Consent of bride's father in writing.)

Williams, James (cold.) Louisa Guy (3) - March 20, 1888
    Place of marriage, near Charlestown - Age of husband, 30 - Age of
    wife, 32 - Husband is Single - Wife is a Widow - Husband was born
    in Jefferson County, West Virginia - Wife was born in Hanover
    County, Virginia - Both reside in Jefferson County, West Virginia.

Williams, Jenine (colored) Robert Berry (3) -   September 22, 1870
    For further information see - Berry, Robert.

Williams, John W. and Fannie Walters (3) -   February 26, 1867
    Place of marriage, School House - Age of husband, 22 - Age of wife,
    22 - Both are Single - Husband was born in Rockbridge County,
    Virginia - Wife was born in Jefferson County, West Virginia - Both
    reside in Jefferson County, West Virginia - Husband's parents are
    J. W. and Lucinda Williams - Occupation of husband is Farmer.
    (William Hunter swore to the young lady over 21.)

Williams, Laurence (cold.) Fanny Lee (3) -   September 2, 1875
    Place of marriage, Charlestown - Age of husband, 23 - Age of wife,
    21 - Both are Single - Husband was born in Orange County, Virginia -
    Wife was born in Jefferson County, West Virginia - Both reside in
    Jefferson County, West Virginia.

Williams, Lee (cold.) Maria Williams (3) -   September 22, 1867
    Place of marriage, Jefferson - Age of husband, 23 - Age of wife,
    32 - Both are Single - Both were born in Jefferson County - Both
    reside in Jefferson County - Husband's parents are Frank and Violet -
    Occupation of husband is Laborer.

Williams, Lee (cold.) Tina Roberts (3) -   June 25, 1888
    Place of marriage, Charlestown - Age of husband, 25 - Age of wife,
    28 - Both are Single - Husband was born in Page County, Virginia -
    Wife was born in Jefferson County, West Virginia - Husband resides
    in Page County, Virginia - Wife resides in Jefferson County, West
    Virginia.

Williams, Lelia and Charles Hall (3) -   December 26, 1871
    For further information see - Hall, Charles.

Williams, Lucy L. and John W. Smith (3) -   September 25, 1890
    For further information see - Smith, John W.

Williams, M. Salina and Claude Baxley (3) -   September 5, 1867
    For further information see - Baxley, Claude.

Williams, Margaret and William McClure (1) -   1819

Williams, Margaret Ellen (cold.) Robert R. McDaniel (3) -   September 15, 1886
    For further information see - McDaniel, Robert R.

Williams, Maria (cold.) Lee Williams (3) -   September 22, 1867
    For further information see - Williams, Lee.

Williams, Martha and Harrison McDaniel (3) -   May 21, 1866
    For further information see - McDaniel, Harrison.

Williams, Mary Catherine (cold.) Arthur Green (3) -   May 16, 1878
    For further information see - Green, Arthur.

Williams, Mary E. (cold.) Charles Creamer (3) -   September 25, 1884
    For further information see - Creamer, Charles.

Williams, Mary W. (cold.) James H. Thompson (3) -   August 19, 1890
    For further information see - Thompson, James H.

Williams, Mortimer D. and Lucy A. Thornton (1) -   December 26, 1822

Williams, Nelly (cold.) Henry Robinson (3) - October 15, 1879
   For further information see - Robinson, Henry.

Williams, Newton (cold.) Sally Ranson (3) - September 28, 1867
   Place of marriage, Jefferson - Age of husband, 34 - Age of wife,
   16 - Husband is a Widower - Wife is Single - Husband was born in
   Jefferson County - Wife was born in Loudoun County, Virginia - Both
   reside in Jefferson County - Husband's parents are Frank and Viley -
   Wife's parents are George and Margaret - Occupation of husband is
   Laborer. (Cold. Father consents.)

Williams, Oscar (cold.) Lucy Thomas (3) - December 12, 1878
   Place of marriage, near Charlestown - Age of husband, 23 - Age of
   wife, 25 - Husband is Single - Wife is a Widow - Husband was born at
   Harrisonburg, Virginia - Wife was born in Rockingham County,
   Virginia - Both reside in Jefferson County, West Virginia.

Williams, Philip and Patsy Stewart (3) - June 10, 1867
   Age of husband, 24 - Age of wife, 25 - Both are Single - Both were
   born in Jefferson County, West Virginia - Both reside in Jefferson
   County, West Virginia - Husband's parents are Harriet - Wife's
   parents are Daniel and Maria Stewart - Occupation of husband is
   Farmer.

Williams, Philip (cold.) Alice Murray (3) - July 19, 1877
   Place of marriage, Summit Point - Age of husband, 27 - Age of wife,
   22 - Husband is a Widower - Wife is Single - Both were born in
   Jefferson County, West Virginia - Both reside in Jefferson County,
   West Virginia.

Williams, Prudence Rebecca and Joseph H. Renner (2) -   (L) August 23, 1861
   For further information see - Renner, Joseph H.

Williams, R. W. and Carrie Lee Fletcher (3) - December 14, 1886
   Place of marriage, Duffields - Age of husband, 22 - Age of wife,
   19 - Both are Single - Husband was born in Loudoun County,
   Virginia - Wife was born in Frederick County, Virginia - Both reside
   in Jefferson County, West Virginia. (Consent of bride's mother in
   person.)

Williams, Rachel Ann and Asa W. Renner (2) -   (L) April 26, 1858

Williams, Richard and Virginia Chapline (1) -   June 1849

Williams, Robert (cold.) Lettie McCard (3) - May 6, 1880
   Place of marriage, Charlestown - Age of husband, 23 - Age of wife,
   25 - Both are Single - Husband was born in Clarke County, Virginia -
   Wife was born in Jefferson County, West Virginia - Husband resides
   in Clarke County, Virginia - Wife resides in Jefferson County, West
   Virginia.

Williams, Robert (cold.) Emily Massey (3) - May 14, 1888
   Place of marriage, Kearneysville - Age of husband, 24 - Age of wife,
   25 - Husband is Single - Wife is a Widow - Husband was born in
   Loudoun County, Virginia - Wife was born in Fauquier County,
   Virginia - Both reside in Jefferson County, West Virginia.

Williams, Thomas (cold.) Isabel Carter (3) - July 3, 1878
Place of marriage, Jefferson County - Age of husband, 25 - Age of
wife, 23 - Both are Single - Husband was born in Clarke County,
Virginia - Wife was born in Virginia - Both reside in Jefferson
County, West Virginia.

Williams, Thomas D. and Ann Margaret Staub (2) - (L) August 1, 1863
Time of marriage, August 6, 1863 - Place of marriage, near
Shenandoah River - Names, Thomas D. Williams and Ann Margaret Staub -
Age of husband, 24 years - Age of wife, 21 years last March -. Both
are Single - Husband was born in Ohio - Wife was born in Maryland -
Both reside in Jefferson County - Names of husband's parents are
Unknown - Names of wife's parents are Jesse and Stacy Ann -
Occupation of husband is Laborer - License issued on application of
bride's brother August 1, 1863 - T. A. Moore, Clerk.

Williams, Thomas P. and Isabella Keyes (1) - March 13, 1821

Williams, Tiny (cold.) James Henry Furr (3) - April 29, 1886
For further information see - Furr, James Henry.

Williams, William and Elizabeth Kesler (2) - (L) July 22, 1852

Williams, William and Elizabeth Kessler (1) - July 29, 1852

Williams, William (cold.) Chlora Whiting (3) - March 25, 1886
Place of marriage, Charlestown - Age of husband, 22 - Age of wife,
30 - Both are Single - Husband was born in Clarke County, Virginia -
Wife was born in Jefferson County, West Virginia - Both reside in
Jefferson County, West Virginia.

Williams, Zachariah and Sally Whover (1) - February 24, 1807

Williamson, L. F. and Eliza Hamtrauck (3) - January 1869
Place of marriage, Jefferson County - Age of husband, 47 - Age of
wife, 28 - Both are Single - Husband was born in Baltimore County,
Maryland - Wife was born in Jefferson County, Virginia - Husband
resides in Baltimore County, Maryland - Wife resides in Jefferson
County - Husband's parents are David and Maria - Wife's parents are
J. F. and Eliza - Occupation of husband is Farmer.

Williamson, Polly and Thomas Lemon (1) - 1806

Willingham, Berta Augustine and Charles N. Snyder (3) - December 20, 1888
For further information see - Snyder, Charles N.

Willingham, D. W. and Mildred Marshall Owens (3) - February 24, 1876
Place of marriage, near Summit Point - Age of husband, 27 - Age of
wife, 20 - Both are Single - Husband was born in Clarke County,
Virginia - Wife was born in Fauquier County, Virginia - Husband
resides in Clarke County, Virginia - Wife resides in Jefferson
County, West Virginia. (Consent of bride's father certified by
W. A. Owens brother of bride.)

Willingham, George F. and Cora V. Crim (3) - September 14, 1885
Place of marriage, Charlestown - Age of husband, 23 - Age of wife,
21 - Both are Single - Husband was born in Clarke County, Virginia -
Wife was born in Jefferson County, West Virginia - Husband resides
in Clarke County, Virginia - Wife resides in Jefferson County, West
Virginia.

Willingham, George H. and Margaret C. Brown (3) -   June 21, 1866
    Place of marriage, M. Parsonage, Shepherdstown - Age of husband,
    24 - Age of wife, 23 - Both are Single - Husband was born in Clarke
    County, Virginia - Wife was born in Jefferson County, Virginia - Both
    reside in Jefferson County, West Virginia - Husband's parents are
    John and Nancie Willingham - Wife's parents are John W. and
    Catharine Brown - Occupation of husband is Farmer.

Willingham, George W. and Mary Ann Edwards (2) -   (L) December 13, 1858

Willingham, James H. and Mary E. Simpson (3) -   May 26, 1887
    Place of marriage, Unionville - Age of husband, 22 - Age of wife,
    18 - Both are Single - Both were born in Jefferson County, West
    Virginia - Both reside in Jefferson County, West Virginia.
    (Consent of bride's mother in writing,)

Willingham, John N. and Hannah F. Conner (3) -   September 14, 1869
    Place of marriage, Jefferson County - Age of husband, 26 - Age of
    wife, 24 - Husband was born in Clarke County, Virginia - Wife was
    born in Jefferson County - Both reside in Jefferson County.

Willingham, Joseph F. and Maggie Clipp (3) -   September 17, 1885
    Place of marriage, Charlestown - Age of husband, 22 - Age of wife,
    24 - Both are Single - Both were born in Jefferson County - Both
    reside in Jefferson County.

Willingham, Mollie A. and Ed. H. Wintermoyer (3) -   June 10, 1886
    For further information see - Wintermoyer, Ed. H.

Willis, Annie M. and R. J. Ambler (2) -   (L) August 12, 1857

Willis, Betsy (cold.) Lawrence Parker (3) -   September 4, 1890
    For further information see - Parker, Lawrence.

Willis, C. Peachy and John T. Shanks (2) -   (L) May 27, 1857

Willis, Edward J. and Mary M. Rogers (3) -   March 15, 1876
    Place of marriage, Charles Town - Age of husband, 55 - Age of wife,
    36 - Husband is a Widower - Wife is Single - Husband was born in
    Culpeper County, Virginia - Wife was born in Loudoun County,
    Virginia - Husband resides at Clarksburg, Harrison County, West
    Virginia - Wife resides in Jefferson County, West Virginia.

Willis, Elizabeth E. and Arthur Brown (1) -   June 1, 1826

Willis, Emily (cold.) John Herbert (3) -   October 23, 1884
    For further information see - Herbert, John.

Willis, Emma E. and B. C. Washington (3) -   November 14, 1878
    For further information see - Washington, B. C.

Willis, Frances B. and William B. Willis (1) -   April 1, 1829

Willis, Frank (cold.) Burniss Jones (3) -   April 19, 1883
    Place of marriage, Charlestown - Age of husband, 26 - Age of wife,
    20 - Both are Single - Husband was born in Hardy County, West
    Virginia - Wife was born in Jefferson County, West Virginia - Both
    reside in Jefferson County, West Virginia.   (Consent of bride's
    father certified by her brother.)

Willis, James H. and Laura A. Wageley (3) - December 3, 1878
   Place of marriage, Mount Zion Church - Age of husband, 25 - Age of
   wife, 18 - Both are Single - Both were born in Jefferson County,
   West Virginia - Both reside in Jefferson County, West Virginia.
   (Consent of bride's father in person.)

Willis, John T. and Sarah E. Kimble (3) - January 19, 1871
   Age of husband, 22 - Age of wife, 24 - Both are Single - Husband was
   born in Jefferson County - Wife was born in Berkeley - Both reside
   in Jefferson County - Husband's parents are William and Martha -
   Wife's parents are Pendleton and Sarah - Occupation of husband is
   Farmer. (Vouched for by C. Aglionby.)

Willis, Lee Ann (cold.) Anthony Turner (3) - December 29, 1880
   For further information see - Turner, Anthony.

Willis, Louisa (cold.) Peter Brooks (3) - May 16, 1883
   For further information see - Brooks, Peter.

Willis, Martha Ellen and Thomas Lackland (2) - (L) August 22, 1851

Willis, Martha Ellen and Thomas Lackland (1) - August 26, 1851

Willis, Nathaniel H. and Jennie C. Washington (3) - January 13, 1869
   Place of marriage, Jefferson County - Age of husband, 26 - Age of
   wife, 22 - Both are Single - Husband was born in Jefferson County -
   Wife was born in Fairfax County - Both reside in Jefferson County -
   Husband's parents are Thomas H. and Eliza F. - Wife's parents are
   John A. and Nellie - Occupation of husband is Farmer.

Willis, William and Martha West (2) - (L) February 2, 1852

Willis, William B. and Frances B. Willis (1) - April 1, 1829

Willis, William Beale and Mary Monroe Manning (2) - (L) October 25, 1864
   Time of marriage - Place of marriage, Buena Vista the residence of
   bride's father - Names, William Beale Willis and Mary Monroe Manning -
   Age of husband, 26 years - Age of wife, 23 years - Both are Single -
   Both were born in Jefferson County, Virginia - Husband's residence
   in Howard County, Maryland - Wife's residence in Jefferson County,
   Virginia - Names of husband's parents are William B. and Fanny B.
   Willis - Names of wife's parents are N. W. Manning and Patsy C.
   Manning - Occupation of husband is Farmer - License issued by R. T.
   Brown, Deputy Clerk, October 25, 1864.

Willson, Eliza F. and Silas H. Courtney (1) - December 28, 1826

Willson, Kitty and Paliteah Thompson (1) - 1820

Willson, Louisa and Francis M. Hawkens (1) - 1825

Willson, Nancy and Dennis Triggs (2) - (L) August 9, 1852

Wilson, Adam and Elizabeth Grove (2) - (L) August 2, 1851

Wilson, Alfred B. and Lucy J. Houke (3) -   December 7, 1871
　　Place of marriage, Jefferson County - Age of husband, 22 - Age of
　　wife, 19 - Both are Single - Husband was born at Washington, D. C. -
　　Wife was born in Jefferson County, West Virginia - Husband resides
　　at Wheeling - Wife resides in Jefferson County - Husband's parents
　　are William L. and Henrietta - Wife's parents are Henry and Julia -
　　Occupation of husband is School Teacher. (Henry Houke.)

Wilson, Arthur E. and Annie T. Moler (2) -   (L) December 15, 1856

Wilson, Catherine and Jeremiah Trigg (1) -   November 10, 1821

Wilson, Cecilia and Jacob Keyes (2) -   (L) January 26, 1855

Wilson, David C. and Elizabeth Shirley (1) -   September 15, 1828

Wilson, David F. and Sally McHenry Ashby (3) -   April 18, 1881
　　Place of marriage, Charlestown -- Age of husband, 23 next August -
　　Age of wife, 18 next July - Both are Single - Both were born in
　　Jefferson County, West Virginia - Both reside in Jefferson County,
　　West Virginia. (Consent of bride's father in person.)

Wilson, Emma J. (cold.) James Green (3) -   March 26, 1883
　　For further information see - Green, James.

Wilson, Enos (cold.) Hatty Adams. (3) -   December 16, 1875
　　Place of marriage, Harpers Ferry - Age of husband, 27 - Age of wife,
　　25 - Both are Single - Husband was born in Jefferson County, West
　　Virginia - Wife was born in Frederick County, Virginia - Both reside
　　in Jefferson County, West Virginia.

Wilson, Florence C. and William C. Sanner (3) -   August 18, 1885
　　For further information see - Sanner, William C.

Wilson, George N. and Emma E. Peacher (3) -   September 24, 1885
　　Place of marriage, Shepherdstown - Age of husband, 27 - Age of wife,
　　22 - Both are Single - Husband was born in Connecticut - Wife was
　　born in Jefferson County - Both reside in Jefferson County.

Wilson, Georigna and Daniel H. Luck (3) -   December 28, 1869
　　For further information see - Luck, Daniel H.

Wilson, Hannah and Henry Turner Ensworth (2) -   (L) September 17, 1863
　　For further information see - Ensworth, Henry Turner.

Wilson, Isaac (cold.) Hester Crawford (3) -   February 2, 1878
　　Place of marriage, Shepherdstown - Age of husband, 23 - Age of wife,
　　21 - Both are Single - Husband was born in Clarke County, Virginia -
　　Wife was born in Jefferson County, West Virginia - Both reside in
　　Jefferson County, West Virginia.

Wilson, Jane and John J. Watkins (3) -   June 12, 1867
　　For further information see - Watkins, John J.

Wilson, John and Kitty Moore .(1) -   October 14, 1813

Wilson, John and Eliza Triggs (2) -   (L) January 12, 1858

Wilson, Kiger and Mary McBride (2) -   (L) October 14, 1857

Wilson, Lance L. and Elizabeth Frances McBride (2). -   (L) December 23, 1858

Wilson, Louis and Sally Tucker (3) -   June 13, 1867
    Age of husband, 24 - Age of wife, 24 - Both are Single - Both were
    born in Jefferson County, West Virginia - Both reside in Jefferson
    County, West Virginia - Husband's parents are George and Mary
    Wilson - Wife's parents are Richard and Rachel Tucker - Occupation
    of husband is Farmer.

Wilson, Lucy (cold.) Edgenier Brown (3) -   September 4, 1886
    For further information see - Brown, Edgenier.

Wilson, Lucy Ann (cold.) John W. Burk (3) -   October 24, 1888
    For further information see - Burk, John W.

Wilson, Lydia A. and William H. Bodine (3) -   November 25, 1880
    For further information see - Bodine, William H.

Wilson, M. E. (bride) and E. F. Kirby (3) -   (1872)
    For further information see - Kirby, E. F.

Wilson, Maggie and W. H. Lamon (3) -   April 26, 1887
    For further information see - Lamon, W. H.

Wilson, Margaret (cold.) James Sims (3) -   August 13, 1878
    For further information see - Sims, James.

Wilson, Margarett and William Snodgrass (1) -   March 21, 1822

Wilson, Maria and Emanuel Myers (3) -   August 11, 1869
    For further information see - Myers, Emanuel.

Wilson, Maria Louisa and Martin H. Miller (2) -   (L) January 9, 1865
    For further information see - Miller, Martin H.

Wilson, Mary and John Wilt (2) -   (L) May 6, 1857

Wilson, Mary and William Thrift (3) -   August 18, 1868
    For further information see - Thrift, William.

Wilson, Mary Ellen Jane and Jacob J. Foreman (2) -   (L) February 16, 1855

Wilson, Nancy and Robert Florence (1) -   January 1, 1818

Wilson, Rachel (cold.) James William Porter (3) -   October 7, 1875
    For further information see - Porter, James William.

Wilson, Richard (cold.) Lydia Jane McDaniel (3) -   August 1, 1878
    Place of marriage, Charlestown - Age of husband, 34 - Age of wife,
    19 - Husband is a Widower - Wife is Single - Both were born in
    Jefferson County, West Virginia - Both reside in Jefferson County,
    West Virginia.

Wilson, Sarah (cold.) Fairfax Harris (3) -   October 25, 1879
    For further information see - Harris, Fairfax.

Wilson, Sidney (cold.) Susan Swann (3) -   October 30, 1873
   Place of marriage, Charlestown - Age of husband, 28 - Age of wife,
   22 - Both are Single - Husband was born in Ann Arundel County,
   Maryland - Wife was born in Jefferson County, West Virginia - Both
   reside in Jefferson County, West Virginia.

Wilson, Sidney (cold.) Ann Herbert (3) -   December 18, 1889
   Place of marriage, Charlestown - Age of husband, 40 - Age of wife,
   40 - Husband is Divorced - Wife is a Widow - Both were born in
   Jefferson County, West Virginia - Both reside in Jefferson County,
   West Virginia.

Wilson, Susan and John O'Neal (1) -   May 28, 1812

Wilson, Susanah and William Dobsin (1) -   August 5, 1819

Wilson, Thomas (cold.) Milly Jenkins (3) -   April 20, 1876
   Place of marriage, Shepherdstown - Age of husband, 23 - Age of wife,
   21 - Both are Single - Both were born in Jefferson County, West
   Virginia - Both reside in Jefferson County, West Virginia.

Wilson, William and Selona Tapp (3) -   November 28, 1867
   Place of marriage, Jefferson County - Age of husband, 24 - Age of
   wife, 18 - Both are Single - Husband was born in Jefferson - Wife
   was born in Frederick - Both reside in Jefferson - Wife's parents
   are James - Occupation of husband is Farmer. (Father consents.)

Wilt, Alice M. and George W. Shull (3) -   May 15, 1879
   For further information see - Shull, George W.

Wilt, Amanda Isabella and Zach T. Fleming (3) -   December 19, 1876
   For further information see - Fleming, Zach T.

Wilt, Mrs. Ann (widow of George W. Wilt) and Lee H. Dillow (2) -
   (L) May 22, 1852

Wilt, Mrs. Ann (widow) and Lee H. Dillow (1) -   May 24, 1852

Wilt, Annie C. and William H. Whitmer (3) -   February 26, 1879
   For further information see - Whitmer, William H.

Wilt, Catharine and Christopher Knox (2) -   (L) December 25, 1850

Wilt, George and Mary E. Grove (3) -   December 23, 1877
   Place of marriage, Harpers Ferry - Age of husband, 23 - Age of wife,
   21 - Both are Single - Both were born in Jefferson County, West
   Virginia - Both reside in Jefferson County, West Virginia.

Wilt, George W. and Margaret A. McSherry (3) -   January 23, 1868
   Place of marriage, Jefferson County - Age of husband, 23 - Age of
   wife, 20 - Both are Single - Both were born in Jefferson County -
   Both reside in Jefferson - Husband's parents are George W. - Wife's
   parents are Dennis and Kitty - Occupation of husband is Distiller.

Wilt, Henry and Polly Tomar (1) -   November 4, 1816

Wilt, Henry and L. C. Shannon (3) - February 26, 1868
Age of husband, 52 - Age of wife, 37 - Husband is a Widower - Wife
is Single - Husband was born in Jefferson - Wife was born in Loudoun
County, Virginia - Both reside in Jefferson - Occupation of husband
is Farmer.

Wilt, Jacob and Vanetta Yontz (2) - (L) (1862)
Time of marriage, May 28, 1862 - Place of marriage, Shepherdstown -
Names of parties, Jacob Wilt and Vanetta Yontz - Age of husband,
Twenty One years - Age of wife, Nineteen years - Both are Single -
Place of husband's birth was at Hagerstown, Maryland - Place of
wife's birth was at Shepherdstown - Place of husband's residence is
at Martinsburg, Berkeley County, Virginia - Place of wife's
residence is at Shepherdstown, Jefferson County, Virginia - Names
of husband's parents are Adam Christian and Catharine Elizabeth -
Names of wife's parents are Jacob and Emily Ann Yontz - Occupation
of husband is Confectioner - Consent of bride's father given in
writing.

Wilt, Jacob S. and Malinda Davis (3) - December 27, 1869
Place of marriage, Jefferson County - Age of husband, 22 - Age of
wife, 20 - Husband was born in Jefferson County - Wife was born in
Maryland - Both reside in Jefferson County. (Parents dead. No
guardian. Endorsed by Assessor of Jefferson County.)

Wilt, John and Margaret Lay (1) - April 15, 1827

Wilt, John and Mary Wilson (2) - (L) May 6, 1857

Wilt, John H. and Jane Barrett (3) - April 19, 1882
Place of marriage, County - Age of husband, 35 - Age of wife, 35 -
Both are Single - Husband was born in Jefferson County - Wife was
born in Berkeley County - Both reside in Jefferson County.

Wilt, John Henry and Nance Sophrania Pearl (3) - July 23, 1885
Place of marriage, Blue Ridge Mountain - Age of husband, 39 - Age of
wife, 14 - Husband is a Widower - Wife is Single - Both were born in
Jefferson County, West Virginia - Both reside in Jefferson County,
West Virginia. (Mother's consent.)

Wilt, Levi and Mary Buzzard (3) - November 17, 1881
Place of marriage, Bolivar - Age of husband, 25 - Age of wife, 19 -
Both are Single - Both were born in Jefferson County, West Virginia -
Both reside in Jefferson County, West Virginia. (Consent of bride's
father in writing.)

Wilt, Lewis and Georgia Fleming (3) - September 2, 1873
Place of marriage, Charles Town - Age of husband, 26 - Age of wife,
22 - Both are Single - Husband was born in Jefferson County, West
Virginia - Wife was born in Clarke County, Virginia - Both reside
in Jefferson County, West Virginia.

Wilt, Margaret E. and James M. Wright (3) - October 12, 1887
For further information see - Wright, James M.

Wilt, Martha J. and Jere O. Clipp (3) - March 7, 1882
For further information see - Clipp, Jere O.

Wilt, Mary Ellen and James Henry Hawk (3) - December 25, 1884
For further information see - Hawk, James Henry.

635

Wilt, Michael and Elizabeth Hammon (1) - August 2, 1827

Wilt, Pleasant R. and O. W. Shull (3) - October 5, 1882
For further information see - Shull, O. W.

Wilt, Thomas and Catherine Ayer (1) - December 29, 1825

Wilt, Thomas and Elizabeth McSherry (3) - March 25, 1875
Place of marriage, Charlestown - Age of husband, 25 - Age of wife, 19 - Both are Single - Both were born in Jefferson County, West Virginia - Both reside in Jefferson County, West Virginia. (Consent of bride's mother in writing.)

Wilt, William and Sarah Virginia Trussell (3) - November 26, 1872
Place of marriage, Jefferson County, West Virginia - Age of husband, 26 - Age of wife, 21 - Both are Single - Both were born in Jefferson County, West Virginia - Husband resides in Clarke County, Virginia - Wife resides in Jefferson County - Husband's parents are H. W. and S. A. Wilt - Wife's parents are B. T. and A. T. Trussell - Occupation of husband is Farmer. (B. T. Trussell.)

Wiltsher, Elizabeth and Leroy Gary (1) - January 11, 1846

Wiltsher, William and Elizabeth Eversole (1) - November 5, 1845

Wiltshire, Anna M. and Eugene Baker (2) - (L) April 1, 1859

Wiltshire, Benjamin and Margaret Feaman (1) - November 9, 1826

Wiltshire, Betsey and Samuel Engle (1) - April 13, 1805

Wiltshire, Davenport and Sarah Jane Burr (2) - (L) March 19, 1855

Wiltshire, John W. and Sarah Jane Pearl (2) - (L) June 13, 1860

Wiltshire, Julia and George William Ott (3) - November 4, 1886
For further information see - Ott, George William.

Wiltshire, Lucy D. and E. E. Dunaway (3) - December 18, 1883
For further information see - Dunaway, E. E.

Wiltshire, Mary Louisa and Robert Milton Moore (3) - April 26, 1883
For further information see - Moore, Robert Milton.

Wiltshire, Philip and Margaret Wade (2) - (L) February 25, 1851

Wiltshire, Philip and Margaret Wade (1) - February 25, 1851

Wiltshire, William H. and Mary E. Rodrick (3) - December 15, 1881
Place of marriage, Harpers Ferry - Age of husband, 54 - Age of wife, 25 - Husband is a Widower - Wife is Single - Both were born in Jefferson County, West Virginia - Both reside in Jefferson County, West Virginia.

Wiltshire, Willie E. and John William Burr (2) - (L) February 22, 1855

Wimmer, Elizabeth and Charles Barrett (1) - July 4, 1822

Windel, Nathaniel and Mary Baker (3) - September 15, 1875
    Place of marriage, Harpers Ferry - Age of husband, 28 - Age of wife, 29 - Both are Single - Husband was born in State of Indiana - Wife was born in Shenandoah County, Virginia - Both reside in Jefferson County, West Virginia.

Winebrenner, Alice and R. M. Baroff (3) - December 19, 1872
    For further information see - Baroff, R. M.

Winebrenner, Annie E. and William R. Grove (3) - April 14, 1872
    For further information see - Grove, William R.

Winebrenner, George W. and Annie E. Bowers (3) - December 23, 1879
    Place of marriage, near Shepherdstown - Age of husband, 29 - Age of wife, 15 - Both are Single - Both were born in Jefferson County, West Virginia - Both reside in Jefferson County, West Virginia. (Consent of bride's father in person.)

Winebrenner, John W. and Margaret Show (1) - February 19, 1846

Winebrenner, Margaret and Lewis J. Garrison (2) - (L) June 24, 1858

Wingas, Virginia F. and E. F. Potts (2) - (L) February 18, 1861

Wingate, Arthur S. and Martha Cordell (1) - February 16, 1836

Wingate, Ellie May and James W. Kelly (3) - February 19, 1882
    For further information see - Kelly, James W.

Wingate, Martha J. (widow) and David Hitaffer (2) - (L) December 27, 1852

Wingate, Mary E. and Thomas E. Arvin (3) - February 9, 1882
    For further information see - Arvin, Thomas E.

Winkler, J. M. and Mary E. Manuel (3) - December 30, 1873
    Place of marriage, Charlestown - Age of husband, 28 - Age of wife, 33 - Both are Single - Husband was born in Jefferson County, West Virginia - Wife was born in Prince William County, Virginia - Both reside in Jefferson County, West Virginia.

Winkler, Jacob Mack and Sarah Whittington (3) - April 30, 1879
    Place of marriage, Charlestown - Age of husband, 35 - Age of wife, 24 - Husband is a Widower - Wife is Single - Both were born in Jefferson County, West Virginia - Both reside in Jefferson County, West Virginia.

Winkoop, Mary Ellen and William Mack (2) - (L) July 18, 1853

Winn, Patrick and Anne Hogan (2) - (L) April 24, 1851

Winston, Julia (cold.) Richard Burke (3) - December 25, 1890
    For further information see - Burke, Richard.

Winston, Thomas and Annie Gallaher (3) - September 28, 1887
    Place of marriage, Harpers Ferry - Age of husband, 31 - Age of wife, 28 - Both are Single - Husband was born in Ireland - Wife was born in Jefferson County, West Virginia - Both reside in Jefferson County, West Virginia.

Wintermoyer, Drusilla and George Harris (1) - February 11, 1847

Wintermoyer, Ed. H. and Mollie A. Willingham (3). -   June 10, 1886
  Place of marriage, Charlestown - Age of husband, 22 - Age of wife,
  18 - Both are Single - Husband was born in Jefferson County, West
  Virginia - Wife was born in Jefferson County - Both reside in
  Jefferson County, West Virginia. (Consent of bride's mother in
  writing.)

Wintermoyer, Eliza and Henry Clanly (2) -   (L) January 22, 1863
  For further information see - Clanly, Henry.

Wintermoyer, Ellen and Caleb Campbell (3) -   July 9, 1883
  For further information see - Campbell, Caleb.

Wintermoyer, Hallie and Joseph S. Tennant (3) -   February 19, 1885
  For further information see - Tennant, Joseph S.

Wintermoyer, Henry and Harriet B. Evans (1) -   October 19, 1848

Wintermoyer, J. and Susan McBee (3) -   (1868)
  Place of marriage, Jefferson County - Age of husband, 36 - Age of
  wife, 30 - Husband is a Widower - Wife is Single - Husband was born
  in Jefferson County - Wife was born in Berkeley County - Both reside
  in Jefferson County - Occupation of husband is Butcher.

Wintermoyer, James P. and Fanny H. Bender (3) -   November 14, 1878
  Place of marriage, Shepherdstown - Age of husband, 26 - Age of wife,
  21 - Both are Single - Husband was born in Jefferson County, West
  Virginia - Wife was born in State of Maryland - Both reside in
  Jefferson County, West Virginia.

Wintermoyer, John and Elizabeth Burns (2) -   (L) July 28, 1851

Wintermoyer, John and Elizabeth McGaha (3) -   June 20, 1870
  Place of marriage, Jefferson County - Age of husband, 45 - Age of
  wife, 50 - Both were born in Jefferson County, Virginia - Both
  reside in Jefferson County.

Wintermoyer, Mary Ellen and James McAlister (2) -   (L) June 21, 1851

Wintermoyer, Mary Ellen and Samuel Jones (3) -   May 12, 1869
  For further information see - Jones, Samuel.

Wintermoyer, May Alperetta and W. Hoke Crowl (3) -   January 21, 1886
  For further information see - Crowl, W. Hoke.

Wintermoyer, Thomas M. and Ann E. Shirley (3) -   October 19, 1869
  Place of marriage, Jefferson County - Age of husband, 34 - Age of
  wife, 26 - Both were born in Jefferson County - Both reside in
  Jefferson County.

Winters, Annie (free colored) Samuel Shorts (2) -   (L) May 11, 1863
  For further information see - Shorts, Samuel.

Winters, Josephine V. and Rev. James C. Stewart (3) -   (1869)
  For further information see - Stewart, Rev. James C.

Winters, Mary Ellen (free cold.) Henry Crane (2) -   (L) July 13, 1860

Winters, William S. and Mary Y. Wentzel (3) - . July 27, 1868
   Age of husband, 26 - Age of wife, 19 - Both are Single - Both were
   born in Jefferson County - Both reside in Jefferson County -
   Husband's parents are William and Maria - Wife's parents are W. H.
   and Mary C. - Occupation of husband is Tobacconist.

Wire, David B. and Mahala Hartness (1) - March 29, 1829

Wise, John and Elizabeth Bishop (1) - June 2, 1823

Wisenall, Elizabeth and George Feaman, Jr. (1) - April 2, 1815

Wisenall, Ellen and Jacob S. Sheetz (2) - (L) April 13, 1857

Wisenall, Margaret and Michael Smith (1) - June 7, 1818

Wisenall, Sarah and John Criswell (1) - April 7, 1850

Witherm, Kate and John Reynolds (2) - (L) June 19, 1854

Witherow, John and Lucy A. Rowland (1) - November 5, 1834

Wolf, Jacob, Jr. and Rachel Ann McGolrick (2) - (L) October 24, 1856

Wolf, Mary A. and William H. Herbert (3) - December 13, 1877
   For further information see - Herbert, William H.

Wolf, Michael and Elizabeth Drenner (2) - (L) February 19, 1851

Wolff, Christian J. and Elizabeth G. Likens (1) - April 21, 1825

Wolff, James H. and Selma A. Hout (3) - February 20, 1873
   Place of marriage, Shepherdstown - Age of husband, 37 - Age of wife,
   26 - Both are Single - Husband was born in Berkeley County, West
   Virginia - Wife was born in Jefferson County, West Virginia -
   Husband resides in Berkeley County, West Virginia - Wife resides in
   Jefferson County, West Virginia - Husband's parents are John W. and
   Maria C. - Wife's parents are David and Ann - Occupation of husband
   is Minister of the Gospel, Southern Methodist.

Wolffe, Susan and Jerimiah Thompson (1) - December 23, 1819

Wolford, Stephen B. and Eliza Grove Hamilton (1) - July 26, 1853

Wolverton, Sarah and Isaac Eversole (1) - January 13, 1811

Wood, Ann Elizabeth and Andrew J. Little (3) - June 6, 1871
   For further information see - Little, Andrew J.

Wood, Ann Elizabeth and Andrew Jackson Little (3) - July 5, 1871
   For further information see - Little, Andrew Jackson.

Wood, Berta A. and E. W. Guilford (3) - October 21, 1890
   For further information see - Guilford, E. W.

Wood, Charles (cold.) Elizabeth Colbert (3) - November 3, 1886
   Place of marriage, Duffields - Age of husband, 25 - Age of wife,
   21 - Both are Single - Both were born in Jefferson County, West
   Virginia - Both reside in Jefferson County, West Virginia.

639

Wood, Emma (cold.) John Weaver (3) -   June 7, 1888
     For further information see - Weaver, John.

Wood, James (cold.) Katie Jemckings (3) -   June 26, 1879
     Place of marriage, Shepherdstown - Age of husband, 23 - Age of wife, 19 - Both are Single - Both were born in Jefferson County, West Virginia - Both reside in Jefferson County, West Virginia. (Consent of bride's mother in writing.)

Wood, Jane and Benjamin Beeler (1) -   December 31, 1807

Wood, John Henry (cold.) Elizabeth Panitt (3) -   December 19, 1883
     Place of marriage, Middleway - Age of husband, 59 - Age of wife, 54 - Husband is a Widower - Wife is a Widow - Both were born in Jefferson County, West Virginia - Both reside in Jefferson County, West Virginia.

Wood, John James (cold.) Anna Weeks (3) -   November 16, 1876
     Place of marriage, Shepherdstown - Age of husband, 22 - Age of wife, 22 - Both are Single - Both were born in Jefferson County, West Virginia - Husband resides in Jefferson County, West Virginia - Wife resides in West Virginia.

Wood, Lewis and Henrietta Whittington (3) -   March 23, 1881
     Place of marriage, Charlestown - Age of husband, 40 - Age of wife, 26 - Both are Single - Husband was born in Clarke County, Virginia - Wife was born in Jefferson County, West Virginia - Both reside in Jefferson County, West Virginia.

Wood, Maggie and William R. Avis (3) -   January 18, 1872
     For further information see - Avis, William R.

Wood, Margaret (cold.) George Clark (3) -   December 16, 1880
     For further information see - Clark, George.

Wood, Maria (free colored) Andrew Gray (1) -   July 27, 1821

Wood, Mary Ann (blks.) __?__ Coleman (1) -   1821

Wood, Moses and Mollie E. Etchison (3) -   November 9, 1869
     Place of marriage, Jefferson County - Age of husband, 38 - Age of wife, 24 - Both were born in Maryland - Husband resides in Maryland - Wife resides in Jefferson County.

Wood, Moses and Ida Walker (3) -   July 23, 1890
     Place of marriage, Charlestown - Age of husband, 28 - Age of wife, 22 - Husband is a Widower - Wife is Single - Husband was born in Page County, Virginia - Wife was born in Jefferson County, West Virginia - Husband resides in Page County, Virginia - Wife resides in Jefferson County, West Virginia.

Wood, Nancy and Joseph Cockrell (1) -   January 4, 1816

Wood, Sally (cold.) Benjamin Sephus (3) -   January 23, 1875
     For further information see - Sephus, Benjamin.

Wood, Samuel T. (cold.) Julia Berry (3) - August 10, 1876
Place of marriage, Summit Point - Age of husband, 27 - Age of wife,
25 - Both are Single - Husband was born in Clarke County, Virginia -
Wife was born in Jefferson County, West Virginia - Both reside in
Jefferson County, West Virginia.

Wood, Sarah (cold.) Pagton Washington (3) - November 28, 1874
For further information see - Washington, Pagton.

Wood, Susan and Thomas Lauglin (1) - November 2, 1820

Wood, Thomas (cold.) Milly Hunter (3) - September 25, 1873
Place of marriage, Smithfield - Age of husband, 22 - Age of wife,
20 - Both are Single - Both were born in Jefferson County, West
Virginia - Both reside in Jefferson County, West Virginia.
(Father's consent in person.)

Wooddy, John J. and Alberta Fydinger (3) - January 24, 1883
Place of marriage, Bride's Residence - Age of husband, 26 - Age of
wife, 22 - Both are Single - Husband was born in Loudoun County,
Virginia - Wife was born in Maryland - Both reside in Jefferson
County, West Virginia.

Wooddy, Maggie A. and John S. Campbell (3) - June 29, 1887
For further information see - Campbell, John S.

Wooddy, Mary E. and Joseph L. Sappington (3) - January 5, 1876
For further information see - Sappington, Joseph L.

Wooddy, Mary M. and James William Garney (3) - September 7, 1876
For further information see - Garney, James William.

Wooddy, Rebecca and John Elliott Hough (3) - July 28, 1880
For further information see - Hough, John Elliott.

Woodford, Catesby and Amelia C. Davenport (3) - May 28, 1890
Place of marriage, Bride's Residence - Age of husband, 40 - Age of
wife, 22 - Both are Single - Husband was born in Bourbon County,
Kentucky - Wife was born in Jefferson County, West Virginia -
Husband resides in Bourbon County, Kentucky - Wife resides in
Jefferson County, West Virginia.

Woodly, Albina and George W. Young (2) - (L) March 24, 1856

Woodly, Caleb and Sarah Miller (1) - September 16, 1819

Woods, Annie (cold.) James Washington (3) - March 6, 1890
For further information see - Washington, James.

Woods, Elizabeth C. and Uriah B. Kerney (1) - November 17, 1836

Woods, John L. (cold.) Luly Busy (3) - November 8, 1887
Place of marriage, Shepherdstown - Age of husband, 27 - Age of wife,
23 - Both are Single - Husband was born in Jefferson County, West
Virginia - Wife was born in Berkeley County, West Virginia - Both
reside in Jefferson County, West Virginia.

Woods, Margaret K. and Samuel H. Allemong (1) - September 17, 1829

Woods, Susan S. and Stephen P. Capehart (2) - (L) November 6, 1855

Woodward, John James and Fannie Mary Miller (3) -   January 17, 1871
    Place of marriage, Jefferson County - Age of husband, 23 - Age of
    wife, 18 - Both are Single - Husband was born in Jefferson County -
    Wife was born in Frederick County - Both reside in Jefferson County -
    Husband's parents are Thomas E. and Mary Ann - Wife's parents are
    J. H. and Sallie E. - Occupation of husband is Farmer. (Father
    consents in person.)

Woodward, Mary E. and Charles W. Conrad (3) -   December 11, 1889
    For further information see - Conrad, Charles W.

Woodward, Mary F. and Richard C. Johnson (3) -   August 10, 1865
    For further information see - Johnson, Richard C.

Woodward, Susan B. and John B. Gruber (1) -   June 23, 1850

Woodward, Thomas E. and Maria L. Anderson (3) -   May 1, 1866
    Place of marriage, Jefferson County, West Virginia - Age of husband,
    46 - Age of wife, 39 - Husband is a Widower - Wife is Single -
    Husband was born in Berkeley County, Virginia - Wife was born in
    Clarke County, Virginia - Husband resides in Jefferson County, West
    Virginia - Wife resides in Clarke County, Virginia - Husband's
    parents are Thomas and Frances Woodward - Wife's parents are Joseph
    Anderson - Occupation of husband is Farmer.

Woody, Robert R. and Delia Ann Reynolds (3) -   September 17, 1872
    Place of marriage, Jefferson County - Age of husband, 22 - Age of
    wife, 21 - Both are Single - Both were born in Jefferson County -
    Husband resides in Jefferson County - Wife resides in Jefferson
    County, West Virginia - Husband's parents are Samuel and Mary E. -
    Wife's parents are John and Elizabeth - Occupation of husband is
    Laborer.

Woolard, Bettie (cold.) Milford Smith (3) -   March 13, 1890
    For further information see - Smith, Milford.

Workman, Barbara and George Norman (1) -   1813

Workman, Margaret and John T. Pierce (1) -   1813

Workman, Susannah and James Allen (1) -   October 5, 1818

Worley, Louisa C. and Thornton C. Dunham (1) -   January 25, 1830

Worthington, Eleanor A. and Joseph C. Bartlett (2) -   (L) May 19, 1860

Worthington, Martha and Thomas H. Hall (1) -   May 15, 1817

Worthington, Mary M. and Nathaniel G. North (1) -   April 30, 1834

Worthington, Ro. and Sarah B. Morrow (1) -   October 24, 1805

Worthington, Sarah B. and Wells J. Hawk (2) -   (L) August 11, 1856

Wortman, Rachael and John Baylis (1) -   1813

Wren, Ann and Anthony Bruce (2) -   (L) November 18, 1854

Wright, Andrew and Ruah Pierce (2) -   (L) April 12, 1852

Wright, Andrew and Lettie Ann Ingram (2) - (L) October 15, 1855

Wright, Ann A. and H. C. Beckham (3) - October 7, 1868
For further information see - Beckham, H. C.

Wright, Charles H. and Mollie E. Taylor (3) - August 18, 1884
Place of marriage, Charlestown - Age of husband, 27 - Age of wife, 20 - Husband is a Widower - Wife is Single - Husband was born in Jefferson County, West Virginia - Wife was born in Jefferson County - Husband resides in Jefferson County - Wife resides in Jefferson County, West Virginia. (Bride's father and mother both dead.)

Wright, Charles Henry and Mary Elizabeth Weis (3) - December 12, 1877
Place of marriage, near Shepherdstown - Age of husband, 25 - Age of wife, 21 - Both are Single - Both were born in Jefferson County, West Virginia - Both reside in Jefferson County, West Virginia.

Wright, Daniel and Margaret Shope (1) - November 23, 1819

Wright, Elizabeth and James Wysong (1) - February 10, 1818

Wright, George W. and Lottie J. Rodrick (3) - April 2, 1883
Place of marriage, Shepherdstown - Age of husband, 33 - Age of wife, 21 - Both are Single - Both were born in Loudoun County, Virginia - Both reside in Jefferson County, West Virginia.

Wright, James M. and Margaret E. Wilt (3) - October 12, 1887
Place of marriage, Harpers Ferry - Age of husband, 21 - Age of wife, 18 - Both are Single - Both were born in Jefferson County, West Virginia - Both reside in Jefferson County, West Virginia. (Consent of bride's mother in writing.)

Wright, John and Elizabeth Snyder (1) - October 20, 1818

Wright, John and Rachel Traynor (3) - May 23, 1872
Place of marriage, Jefferson County - Age of husband, 28 - Age of wife, 24 - Both are Single - Husband's parents are John - Wife's parents are John.

Wright, John Henry and Mary Potts (3) - March 5, 1872
Place of marriage, Jefferson County, West Virginia - Age of husband, 23 - Age of wife, 18 - Both are Single - Husband was born in Jefferson County - Wife was born in Pennsylvania - Husband resides in Jefferson County - Wife resides in Jefferson County, West Virginia - Husband's parents are James and Mary - Wife's parents are John and Mary - Occupation of husband is Miner. (Parents Consent.)

Wright, Joseph Edward and Annie Beall Hoffmaster (3) - February 18, 1887
Place of marriage, Charlestown - Age of husband, 28 - Age of wife, 27 - Both are Single - Both were born in Jefferson County - Both reside in Jefferson County.

Wright, Lawrence and Susan C. Beltz (3) - May 10, 1888
Place of marriage, Harpers Ferry - Age of husband, 45 - Age of wife, 38 - Both are Single - Husband was born in Harford County, Maryland - Wife was born in Jefferson County, West Virginia - Both reside in Jefferson County, West Virginia.

Wright, Margaret Ann and John J. W. Miller (3) - September 16, 1869
For further information see - Miller, John J. W.

Wright, Mary and Joseph Caldwell (1) -   March 24, 1831

Wright, Mary E. and James H. L. Hunter (2) -   (L) May 16, 1855

Wright, Michael and Luvena Beltz (3) -   February 10, 1880
    Place of marriage, Harpers Ferry - Age of husband, 31 - Age of wife,
    27 - Both are Single - Husband was born in Harford County,
    Maryland - Wife was born in Jefferson County, West Virginia - Both
    reside in Jefferson County, West Virginia.

Wright, Samuel and Mary Snyder (1) -   October 30, 1823

Wright, Sarah and John Butts (1) -   March 24, 1831

Wright, Susanah and John Butts (1) -   March 2, 1823

Write, John and Polly Jett (1) -   June 2, 1825

Wyatt, J. G. and K. D. Hurst (bride) (2) -   (L) January 10, 1860

Wyatt, James Ed. and E. W. Aisquith (3) -   November 22, 1881
    Place of marriage, Charlestown - Age of husband, 21 - Age of wife,
    21 - Both are Single - Both were born in Jefferson County, West
    Virginia - Both reside in Jefferson County, West Virginia.

Wycoff, Elizabeth and James Golsbary (1) -   June 15, 1820

Wyet, J. G. and Bettie Moore (3) -   April 22, 1868
    Place of marriage, Jefferson County - Age of husband, 45 - Age of
    wife, 25 - Husband is a Widower - Wife is Single - Husband was born
    in Virginia - Wife was born in Jefferson County - Husband resides in
    North Carolina - Wife resides in Jefferson - Husband's parents are
    William and Margaret - Wife's parents are J. V. and Phebe -
    Occupation of husband is Merchant.

Wykoff, Pheby and Peter Dillow (1) -   March 23, 1820

Wykoff, Sarah and Solomon Ator (1) -   1814

Wyndham, Annie E. and Alfred W. Riley (3) -   April 20, 1875
    For further information see - Riley, Alfred W.

Wyndham, George and Mary F. Sinclair (3) -   December 17, 1878
    Place of marriage, Middleway - Age of husband, 26 - Age of wife,
    24 - Both are Single - Husband was born in Clarke - Wife was born
    in Jefferson County, West Virginia - Both reside in Jefferson
    County, West Virginia.

Wyndham, John William and Annie B. Whittington (3) -   February 17, 1880
    Place of marriage, Charlestown - Age of husband, 29 - Age of wife,
    23 - Both are Single - Husband was born in Clarke County, Virginia -
    Wife was born in Jefferson County, West Virginia - Both reside in
    Jefferson County, West Virginia.

Wynkoop, Mary Ellen and William Mack (1) -   July 18, 1853

Wysong, Amanda and Charles H. McCurdy (2) -   (L) October 31, 1853

Wysong, Charles D. and L. K. Rentch (3) - December 8, 1881
    Place of marriage, Shepherdstown - Age of husband, 32 - Age of wife,
    25 - Both are Single - Both were born in Jefferson County, West
    Virginia - Both reside in Jefferson County, West Virginia.

Wysong, Elizabeth and Nicholas Starry (1) - July 17, 1806

Wysong, Elizabeth and Raleigh Brantner (1) - April 1, 1827

Wysong, Hester and Aquila Davis (1) - December 4, 1816

Wysong, J. W. and Nanie Show (3) - December 24, 1872
    Place of marriage, Jefferson County - Age of husband, 27 - Age of
    wife, 23 - Both are Single - Both were born in Virginia - Both
    reside in West Virginia - Husband's parents are John W. and Phreny -
    Wife's parents are George and Margaret - Occupation of husband is
    Mechanic.

Wysong, Jacob, Jr. and Elizabeth Cookus (1) - March 14, 1813

Wysong, James and Elizabeth Wright (1) - February 10, 1818

Wysong, James and Lucie S. Campbell (2) - (L) October 14, 1856

Wysong, John J. and Elizabeth F. Kearsley (3) - March 26, 1879
    Place of marriage, Charlestown - Age of husband, 22 - Age of wife,
    21 - Both are Single - Both were born in Jefferson County, West
    Virginia - Both reside in Jefferson County, West Virginia.

Wysong, Joseph and Elizabeth Patton (1) - May 24, 1810

Wysong, Mary and Thomas Kennedy (1) - February 23, 1813

Wysong, Mary B. and Jac Line (son of Henry) (1) - April 24, 1823

Wysong, Mary Elizabeth and J. S. Lefevre (3) - June 8, 1881
    For further information see - Lefevre, J. S.

Wysong, Michael and Elizabeth Smallwood (1) - March 15, 1826

Yantis, Ann E. and William B. Wernway (2) -   (L) April 29, 1858

Yantis, Ella N. and George L. Sencindiver (3) -   April 26, 1883
    For further information see - Sencindiver, George L.

Yantis, Gertie W. and J. Calvin Tabler (3) -   February 15, 1888
    For further information see - Tabler, J. Calvin.

Yantis, Maggie and Rev. Luther R. Dyott (3) -   June 7, 1888
    For further information see - Dyott, Rev. Luther R.

Yantis, Shaulter V. and Mary V. Colbert (3) -   January 23, 1883
    Place of marriage, Shepherdstown - Age of husband, 30 - Age of wife, 25 - Both are Single - Both were born in Jefferson County, West Virginia - Both reside in Jefferson County, West Virginia.

Yantz, Martin and Franciscus Folk (1) -   June 10, 1832

Yates, Anne and William T. Leavell (1) -   November 18, 1847

Yates, Francis and Sydney Virginia Rookes (2) -   (L) June 23, 1863
    Time of marriage, June 25, 1863 - Place of marriage, Charlestown - Names, Francis Yates and Sydney Virginia Rookes - Age of husband, 51 years - Age of wife, 38 years - Husband is a Widower - Wife is Single - Husband was born in Jefferson County - Wife was born in Fairfax County - Both reside in Jefferson County - Husband's parents are John and Julia Yates - Wife's parents are - Husband is a Farmer - License issued June 23, 1863 - Thomas A. Moore, Clerk.

Yates, Janet and George B. Beall (1) -   October 1826

Yates, Jenett B. and Charles W. Wagner (3) -   November 1, 1870
    For further information see - Wagner, Charles W.

Yates, John and Sallie Ann Philips (3) -   November 10, 1866
    Place of marriage, Mr. Leavell's Farm - Age of husband, 57 - Age of wife, 21 - Husband is a Widower - Wife is Single - Both were born in Jefferson County, West Virginia - Both reside in Jefferson County, West Virginia - Husband's parents are John and Phoeby - Wife's parents are Alice Philips - Occupation of husband is Laborer.

Yates, John Israel (cold.) Emma Marsh (3) -   October 8, 1885
    Place of marriage, near Ripon - Age of husband, 21 - Age of wife, 18 - Both are Single - Husband was born in Rappahannock County, Virginia - Wife was born in Jefferson County - Both reside in Jefferson County. (Consent of bride's father in person.)

Yates, Lucy C. and Thomas L. Rissler (3) -   December 18, 1877
    For further information see - Rissler, Thomas L.

Yates, Mary and Humphrey Keyes (1) -   September 1826

Yates, O. L. (bride) and W. S. Mason (3) -   October 29, 1868
    For further information see - Mason, W. S.

Yates, William and Ann S. Daugherty (1) -   January 10, 1832

Yauck, Mary B. and David Lewis (1) -   1825

Yeamans, Theodore F. and Louisa L. Wageley (3) - .   January 4, 1866
   Place of marriage, near Leetown - Age of husband, 34 - Age of wife,
   32 - Husband is a Widower - Wife is Single - Husband was born at
   Springfield, Ohio - Wife was born in Jefferson County, West Virginia -
   Husband resides in Berkeley County, West Virginia - Wife resides in
   Jefferson County, West Virginia - Husband's parents are William and
   Catharine Yeaman - Wife's parents are John and Elizabeth Wageley -
   Occupation of husband is Farmer.

Yeamans, William B. and Catherine Lentz Shough (1) -   September 22, 1825

Yerkes, Josiah and Sarah Lupton (1) -   . December 12, 1805

Yesony, Frederick C. and Catharine Reynolds (3) -   November 3, 1868
   Place of marriage, Jefferson County - Age of husband, 35 - Age of
   wife, 33 - Husband is a Widower - Wife is Single - Husband was born
   in Ireland - Wife was born in Jefferson County - Husband resides in
   Jefferson County - Wife resides in West Virginia - Occupation of
   husband is Laborer.

Yontz, Alice V. and George E. Adams (3) -   January 4, 1866
   For further information see - Adams, George E.

Yontz, Ann E. and Charles F. Ferrell (3) -   October 9, 1866
   For further information see - Ferrell, Charles F.

Yontz, Catharine and Jacob Spotts (2) -   (L) (1862)
   For further information see - Spotts, Jacob.

Yontz, Catherine and Ely Conley (1) -   February 22, 1827

Yontz, Elizabeth and James Jones (1) -   May 26, 1853

Yontz, Ellen E. and Jacob B. Crow (2) -   (L) December 18, 1854

Yontz, George R. and Bertha E. Weis (3) -   April 13, 1882
   Place of marriage, Shepherdstown - Age of husband, 33 - Age of wife,
   31 - Both are Single - Husband was born in Jefferson County - Wife
   was born in Jefferson County, West Virginia - Husband resides in
   Jefferson County - Wife resides in Jefferson County, West Virginia.

Yontz, Joseph S. and Isabela Reynolds (3) -   April 18, 1869
   Place of marriage, Jefferson County - Age of husband, 21 - Age of
   wife, 21 - Both are Single - Husband was born in Jefferson County -
   Wife was born in Maryland - Both reside in Jefferson County -
   Occupation of husband is Farmer.

Yontz, Prudence and Robert Vincenhellar (1) -   March 31, 1814

Yontz, Vanetta and Jacob Wilt (2) -   (L) (1862)
   For further information see - Wilt, Jacob.

Yost, Sarah Ann and Elisha Lock (1) -   June 10, 1844

Young, Adam and Mary E. Brua (1) -   April 25, 1833

Young, Adam and Elizabeth H. Huntsberry (3) -   May 21, 1866
   Age of husband, 33 - Age of wife, 23 - Both are Single - Husband was
   born in Frederick County, Maryland - Wife was born in Frederick
   County, Virginia - Both reside in Jefferson County, West Virginia -
   Husband's parents are Peter and Elizabeth Young - Wife's parents are
   Henry P. and Lucy G. Huntsberry - Occupation of husband is
   Manufacturer.

Young, Annie M. and D. M. Sheetz (3) -   January 16, 1868
   For further information see - Sheetz, D. M.

Young, Charles E. and Elizabeth Chambers (1) -   April 25, 1848

Young, Charles Edward and Imogene F. Koonce (3) -   July 6, 1875
   Place of marriage, Harpers Ferry - Age of husband, 26 - Age of wife,
   27 - Both are Single - Husband was born in Jefferson County, West
   Virginia - Wife was born in State of Illinois - Husband resides in
   State of Maryland - Wife resides in Jefferson County, West Virginia.

Young, D. H. and Emma K. Fayman (3) -   September 7, 1881
   Place of marriage, Shepherdstown - Age of husband, 27 - Age of wife,
   18 - Both are Single - Husband was born in Washington County,
   Maryland - Wife was born in Jefferson County, West Virginia - Both
   reside in Jefferson County, West Virginia. (Consent of bride's
   father in Writing.)

Young, Eliza Maria and George W. Boyers (2) -   (L) September 30, 1851

Young, Eliza Maria and George W. Boyers (1) -   September 30, 1851

Young, Elizabeth and Henry Miller (1) -   January 22, 1807

Young, Ezekiel D. and Jeannette Avis (2) -   (L) October 11, 1856

Young, George W. and Albina Woodly (2) -   (L) March 24, 1856

Young, Hannah and Henry Frank (1) -   April 21, 1824

Young, Henrietta and David Kelsey (2) -   (L) December 27, 1850

Young, Henrietta M. and John Z. Glessner (1) -   May 1, 1832

Young, James H. (cold.) Mary Ellen Madison (3) -   November 15, 1890
   Place of marriage, Shepherdstown - Age of husband, 45 - Age of wife,
   35 - Husband is Single - Wife is a Widow - Husband was born in Saint
   Mary County, Maryland - Wife was born in Jefferson County - Both
   reside in Jefferson County, West Virginia.

Young, John and Mary Lott (1) -   September 8, 1808

Young, Lewis F. and Margaret Deen (1) -   December 4, 1817

Young, Louisa and George L. Harris (1) -   May 16, 1816

Young, Margaret and William Burr (1) -   May 18, 1809

Young, Mary and George Little (1) -   April 19, 1810

Young, Mary and Robert Stewart (1) -   March 1826

Young, Mason and Mollie Sheets (3) - August 2, 1870
   Place of marriage, Jefferson County - Age of husband, 26 - Age of
   wife, 21 - Husband was born in Jefferson County - Wife was born in
   Jefferson County, Virginia - Both reside in Jefferson County.
   (Age of Miss Mollie Sheets sworn to by herself and Mason Young and
   endorsement of same by W. H. Hedges.)

Young, Moses (colored) Lydia Moore (3) - 1867
   Age of husband, 26 - Age of wife, 19 - Both are Single - Husband was
   born in Clarke County, Virginia - Wife was born in Jefferson County,
   West Virginia - Both reside in Jefferson County - Husband's parents
   are Moses and Harriet Young - Wife's parents are John and Fannie
   Moore - Occupation of husband is Blacksmith.

Young, Nettie (cold.) Washington Johnson (3) - January 4, 1877
   For further information see - Johnson, Washington.

Young, Robert and Mary Bennett (1) - September 20, 1816

Young, S. R. (bride) and E. J. Williams (3) - December 17, 1879
   For further information see - Williams, E. J.

Young, Samuel and Sarah Ann Gardner (1) - June 25, 1829

Young, Sarah D. A. and Andrew J. Gill (3) - November 16, 1869
   For further information see - Gill, Andrew J.

Young, Susana and James McDonald (1) - January 23, 1806

Young, Thomas B. and Julia Painter (3) - December 20, 1877
   Place of marriage, Charlestown - Age of husband, 38 - Age of wife,
   25 - Both are Single - Both were born in Jefferson County, West
   Virginia - Both reside in Jefferson County, West Virginia.

Young, W. A. and Georgia Dooley (3) - December 19, 1867
   Place of marriage, Jefferson County - Age of husband, 28 - Age of
   wife, 22 - Both are Single - Husband was born in Frederick County,
   Virginia - Wife was born in Jefferson - Husband resides in Frederick,
   Virginia - Wife resides in Jefferson - Husband's parents are Philip
   and Julia - Wife's parents are George and Margaret.

Young, Washington P. and Sarah C. Lock (1) - December 30, 1849

Young, Wied. and Joseph H. Cockrell (3) - November 25, 1868
   For further information see - Cockrell, Joseph H.

Young, William H. and Belle Roderick (3) - November 24, 1874
   Place of marriage, Bolivar - Age of husband, 22 - Both are Single -
   Both were born in Jefferson County, West Virginia - Both reside in
   Jefferson County, West Virginia. (Consent of bride's father in
   writing.)

649

Zeller, Mary Virginia and F. B. Sowders (3) - June 4, 1878
    For further information see - Sowders, F. B.

Zimerman, Aletha and Daniel B. Pearl (3) - October 7, 1869
    For further information see - Pearl, Daniel B.

Zimerman, Henrietta and Thomas H. Russell (1) - November 22, 1846

Zimmerman, Jennie and Aaron Baum (3) - January 6, 1886
    For further information see - Baum, Aaron.

Zimmerman, Michael and Susan Purnell (1) - May 18, 1809

Zoigar, Charlotte and Cary Thompson (1) - July 21, 1822

Zoll, Barbara and John Medder (2) - (L) November 16, 1850

Zoll, Barbara and John Medder (1) - November 18, 1850

Zoll, Mary and Antone Busse (2) - (L) April 30, 1852

Zombro, Ann and J. W. Edwards (3) - February 3, 1874
    For further information see - Edwards, J. W.

Zombro, Benjamin Lee and Rachel Jane Edwards (3) - November 20, 1878
    Place of marriage, Charlestown - Age of husband, 28 - Age of wife, 25 - Both are Single - Both were born in Jefferson County, West Virginia - Both reside in Jefferson County, West Virginia.

Zombro, Daniel and Eliza Foreman (1) - July 31, 1828

Zombro, George P. and Sophia Coleman (1) - May 15, 1832

Zombro, H. N. and Mary Jane Keyes (2) - (L) September 7, 1863
    Time of marriage, September 10, 1863 - Place of marriage, near Porter's Factory - H. N. Zombro and Mary Jane Keyes - Age of husband, 24 years - Age of wife, 22 years - Both are Single - Husband was born in Jefferson County - Wife was born in Maryland - Both reside in Jefferson County - Names of husband's parents are John and Lucinda Zombro - Names of wife's parents are Joseph and Mary Jane Keyes - Occupation of husband is Farmhand - License issued September 7, 1863 - T. A. Moore, Clerk.

Zombro, J. W. and J. Anderson (bride) (3) - January 3, 1872
    Place of marriage, Jefferson County, West Virginia - Age of husband, 35 - Age of wife, 19 - Both are Single - Both were born in Jefferson County - Both reside in Jefferson County - Husband's parents are G. P. Zombro and Sophiah - Wife's parents are Joseph H. and Betty - Occupation of husband is Farmer. (B. R. Whittington.)

Zombro, M. C. and Miss Virginia Talbot (3) - August 22, 1875
    Place of marriage, near Ripon - Age of husband, 37 - Age of wife, 29 - Both are Single - Husband was born in Jefferson County, West Virginia - Wife was born in Warren County, Virginia - Both reside in Jefferson County, West Virginia.

Zombro, Margaret and John Elliott (3) - July 9, 1889
    For further information see - Elliott, John.

Zombro, Sarah and Daniel Foreman (1) - May 28, 1822

Zombro, Virginia and William R. Jenkins (3) - . . .   June 18, 1885
    For further information see - Jenkins, William R.

Zorge, George and Elizabeth Briscoe (1) -   August 26, 1830

Zumbro, Peter and Eve Poltz (1) -   June 25, 1809

www.ingramcontent.com/pod-product-compliance
Ingram Content Group UK Ltd.
Pitfield, Milton Keynes, MK11 3LW, UK
UKHW021301180426
11947UKWH00015B/952